CONSTITUTIONAL
CRIMINAL PROCEDURE

CONSTITUTIONAL CRIMINAL PROCEDURE
An Examination of the Fourth, Fifth, and Sixth Amendments and Related Areas

Second Edition

RONALD J. ALLEN
Professor of Law
Northwestern University

RICHARD B. KUHNS
Professor of Law
Washington University

Little, Brown and Company
Boston   Toronto   London

HAL

Published simultaneously in Canada
by Little, Brown & Company (Canada) Limited

Printed in the United States of America

To my parents,
J. Mattson and Carolyn Latchum Allen

To my son,
Peter Barton Kuhns

SUMMARY OF CONTENTS

CONTENTS

PREFACE

It is our firm belief that the teaching of criminal procedure in law schools has evolved to the point where two mainstream courses are essential. It is our understanding that this evolution has resulted at many schools in a rough division of coverage that has one course whose content is primarily right to counsel, fourth amendment, self-incrimination, and related areas, and a second course whose content is primarily post-arrest and trial and appellate issues. We think this is a felicitous allocation of responsibility, and our effort in this book has been to provide a usable set of materials for a course whose primary focus is on right to counsel, the fourth amendment, and self-incrimination. We have also included chapters covering the derivative issues as well. Thus, following the fourth amendment chapter is one on entrapment, and concluding the book is a chapter on the administration of the exclusionary rules.

The book begins with three interrelated chapters that are designed as an extended introduction to the study of both the criminal justice system and criminal procedure. These chapters will vary in utility depending on an instructor's predilections and the points at which this course is offered in the curriculum. Chapter 1 presents an overview of the criminal process and traces a hypothetical case through it, demonstrating en route the potential each phase of the process possesses to generate serious and complex legal issues. Chapter 2 is a selection of readings from the literature on the criminal process that is designed to acquaint the student with a variety of perspectives on the criminal justice system. Chapter 3 is a brief treatment of the nature of Supreme Court decisionmaking.

There are two overriding themes of this book. The first is the evolving significance of the assistance of counsel, which is treated in Part II. The second theme is an examination of the relationship between the government and the citizen, which is treated in Part III and involves an inquiry into the fourth and fifth amendments. That inquiry has its intellectual roots in the remarkable case of Boyd v. United States, and we examine the rise and fall of *Boyd* in Chapter 6.

It is our belief that the study of constitutional criminal procedure entails inquiry into the fundamental problems of reasoning, decisionmaking, political science, and sociology, among others. Indeed, in large measure we view this undertaking as an inquiry into this nation's ever-changing view of the demands of human autonomy as reflected by the formal relationship between government and citizen at various points in our history. Thus, we have tried to bring intellectual rigor to these materials and not to shy away from addressing intractable problems. Moreover, we have endeavored to give a picture not only of present "law" but also of its etiology. We hope our selection of cases and materials reflects these considerations.

We have also endeavored to keep editing of cases at a minimum, opting at times for textual description over a series of edited excerpts. Editing is unavoidable, however. In all cases and materials reproduced here, we have kept the original footnoting sequence. Wherever our own footnotes might be confused with those of the primary material, our own footnotes are identified by the legend " — Eds." Given our preferences, we were required to concentrate largely on Supreme Court cases, and this book contains Supreme Court cases through January 1991. We do not, however, disparage the importance of the state courts or the lower federal courts. In the teacher's manual that accompanies this book, we have included numerous references to these cases.

Finally, we would like to acknowledge our very many debts to those who have assisted us in the preparation of these materials. Professors Francis A. Allen of the University of Michigan and Donald E. Wilkes of the University of Georgia generously agreed to read and comment on portions of the manuscript. Renée Patton was indefatigable in the many secretarial tasks that manuscript preparation entails. We are also greatly indebted to Bard Ferrall for his excellent research assistance. Finally, we are indebted to the editorial staff of the publisher for having provided invaluable assistance throughout the preparation of the book.

Ronald J. Allen
Chicago, Illinois

Richard B. Kuhns
St. Louis, Missouri

February 1991

ACKNOWLEDGMENTS

Allen, R., Procedural Due Process of Law, Criminal, Encyclopedia of the American Constitution (Supp. 1990). Copyright © 1990 by Macmillan Publishing Co. Reprinted by permission.

Allen, R., The Police and Substantive Rulemaking: Reconciling Principle and Expediency, 125 U. Pa. L. Rev. 62 (1976). Copyright © 1977 by the University of Pennsylvania Law Review. Reprinted by permission of the author and the University of Pennsylvania Law Review.

Allen, R., The Police and Substantive Rulemaking: A Brief Rejoinder, 125 U. Pa. L. Rev. 1172 (1977). Copyright © 1977 by the University of Pennsylvania Law Review. Reprinted by permission of the author and the University of Pennsylvania Law Review.

ABA Special Committee on Criminal Justice in a Free Society, Criminal Justice in Crisis (1988). Copyright © 1988 by the American Bar Association.

Amsterdam, A., The Supreme Court and the Rights of Suspects in Criminal Cases, from The Rights of Americans: What They Are—What They Should Be, N. Dorsen, ed. Copyright © 1970, 1971 by Random House, Inc. Reprinted by permission of the author and Pantheon Books, a division of Random House, Inc.

Amsterdam, A., Perspectives on the Fourth Amendment, 58 Minn. L. Rev. 349 (1974). Copyright © 1974 by the Minnesota Law Review Foundation. Reprinted by permission of the author and the Minnesota Law Review.

Arenella, P., Schmerber and the Privilege against Self-Incrimination: A Reappraisal, 20 Am. Crim. L. Rev. 31 (1982). Copyright © 1982 by the American Bar Association.

Arenella, P., Rethinking the Function of Criminal Procedure: The Warren and Burger Courts' Competing Ideologies, 72 Geo. L.J. 185 (1983). Copyright © 1983 by the Georgetown Law Journal Association and Peter Arenella. Reprinted by permission of the author and the Georgetown Law Journal.

Blumberg, A., The Practice of Law as Confidence Game: Organizational Coop-
tation of a Profession, 1(2) L. & Socy. Rev. 15 (1967). Copyright © 1967
by the Law and Society Association. Reprinted by permission.

Burton, S., Comment on "Empty Ideas": Logical Positivist Analyses of Equality
and Rules, 91(6) Yale L.J. 1136 (1982). Copyright © 1982 by the Yale
Law Journal Co., Inc. Reprinted by permission of the author, the Yale
Law Journal, and Fred B. Rothman & Co.

Damaska, M., Evidentiary Barriers to Conviction and Two Models of Criminal
Procedure: A Comparative Study, 121(3) U. Pa. L. Rev. 506 (1973).
Copyright © 1973 by the University of Pennsylvania. Reprinted by the
permission of the University of Pennsylvania Law Review and Fred B.
Rothman & Co.

Davis, K., Police Rulemaking on Selective Enforcement: A Reply, 125 U. Pa.
L. Rev. 1167 (1977). Copyright © 1977 by the University of Pennsylvania.
Reprinted by permission of the author and the University of Pennsylvania
Law Review.

Dershowitz, A., The Best Defense (1982). Copyright © 1982 by Alan M. Dershowitz. Reprinted by permission of Random House, Inc.

Galloway, R., The Intruding Eye: A Status Report on the Constitutional Ban
Against Paper Searches, 25 How. L.J. 367 (1982). Copyright © 1982 by
the Howard University School of Law. Reprinted by permission of the
author and the Howard Law Journal.

Grano, J., Kirby, Biggers and Ash: Do Any Constitutional Safeguards Remain
against the Danger of Convicting the Innocent?, 72 Mich. L. Rev. 717
(1974). Copyright © 1974 by the Michigan Law Review Association. Reprinted by permission of the author and the Michigan Law Review.

Grano, J., Voluntariness, Free Will, and the Law of Confessions, 65 Va. L.
Rev. 859, 865-868 (1979). Copyright © 1979 by the Virginia Law Review
Association. Reprinted by permission of the author, the Virginia Law Re-
view Association and Fred B. Rothman & Co.

Grossman, S., Suggestive Identifications: The Supreme Court's Due Process
Fails to Meet Its Own Criteria, 11 U. Balt. L. Rev. 1 (1981). Copyright
© 1981 by the University of Baltimore Law Review. Reprinted by permission
of the author and the University of Baltimore Law Review.

Holmes, O., The Common Law (1881). Reprinted by permission of Little,
Brown and Co.

Jonakit, R., Reliable Identification: Could the Supreme Court Tell in Manson
v. Brathwaite?, 52 U. Colo. L. Rev. 511 (1981). Copyright © 1981 by the
University of Colorado Law Review, Inc. Reprinted by permission of the
author and the University of Colorado Law Review.

Kamisar, Y., The Right to Counsel and the Fourteenth Amendment: A Dialogue on "The Most Persuasive Rights" of an Accused, 30(1) U. Chi. L. Rev. 1 (1962).

Kauper, P., Judicial Examination of the Accused—A Remedy for the Third Degree, 30 Mich. L. Rev. 1224 (1932). Copyright © 1932 by the Michigan Law Review Association. Reprinted by permission.

Kuhns, R., The Concept of Personal Aggrievement in Fourth Amendment Standing Cases, 65 Iowa L. Rev. 493 (1980). Copyright © 1980 by the University of Iowa (Iowa Law Review). Reprinted by permission of the author and the University of Iowa Law Review.

Lowenthal, G., Joint Representation in Criminal Cases: A Critical Appraisal, 64 Va. L. Rev. 939, 941-942 (1978). Copyright © 1978 by the Virginia Law Review Association. Reprinted by permission of the author, the Virginia Law Review Association, and Fred B. Rothman & Co.

Mileski, M., Courtroom Encounters: An Observation Study of a Lower Criminal Court, 5 L. & Socy. Rev. 473 (1971). Copyright © 1971 by the Law and Society Association. Reprinted by permission.

Note, Did Your Eyes Deceive You? Expert Psychological Testimony on the Unreliability of Eyewitness Identification, 29 Stan. L. Rev. 969 (1977). Copyright © 1977 by the Board of Trustees of the Leland Stanford Junior University. Reprinted by permission of the Stanford Law Review.

Note, Formalism, Legal Realism, and Constitutionally Protected Privacy Under the Fourth and Fifth Amendments, 90 Harv. L. Rev. 969 (1977). Copyright © 1977 by the Harvard Law Review Association. Reprinted by permission.

Note, The Life and Times of Boyd v. United States (1886-1976), 76 Mich. L. Rev. 184 (1977). Copyright © 1978 by the Michigan Law Review Association. Reprinted by permission.

Packer, H., The Courts, the Police, and the Rest of Us, 57 J. Crim. L., Criminology & Police Sci. 238 (1966). Copyright © 1966 by the Northwestern University School of Law. Reprinted by the special permission of the Journal of Criminal Law and Criminology.

Schwarzer, W., Dealing with Incompetent Counsel—The Trial Judges' Role, 93 Harv. L. Rev. 633 (1980). Copyright © 1980 by the Harvard Law Review Association. Reprinted by permission of the author and the Harvard Law Review Association.

Skolnick, J., & D. Bayley, Community Policing: Issues and Practices around the World (1988).

Tague, P., Multiple Representation and Conflicts of Interest in Criminal Cases, 67 Geo. L.J. 1075 (1979). Copyright © 1979 by the Georgetown Law

Journal Association. Reprinted by permission of the author and the George-town Law Journal Association.

Westen, P., The Empty Idea of Equality, 95(3) Harv. L. Rev. 537 (1982). Copyright © 1982 by the Harvard Law Review Association. Reprinted by permission of the author and the Harvard Law Review Association.

Wice, P., Chaos in the Courthouse: The Inner Workings of the Urban Criminal Courts (1985). Copyright © 1985 by Praeger Publishers. Reprinted by permission of Praeger Publishers.

Wilson, J., Varieties of Police Behavior: The Management of Law and Order in Eight Communities (1973). Copyright © 1968 by the President and Fellows of Harvard College. Reprinted by permission of the publisher, Harvard University Press.

CONSTITUTIONAL
CRIMINAL PROCEDURE

PART ONE

THE CRIMINAL PROCESS

CHAPTER 1

INTRODUCTION TO THE CRIMINAL JUSTICE "SYSTEM"

A. INTRODUCTION

The system of criminal justice America uses to deal with those crimes it cannot prevent and those criminals it cannot deter is not a monolithic, or even a consistent, system. It was not designed or built in one piece at one time. Its philosophic core is that a person may be punished by the Government if, and only if, it has been proved by an impartial and deliberate process that he has violated a specific law. Around that core layer upon layer of institutions and procedures, some carefully constructed and some improvised, some inspired by principle and some by expediency, have accumulated. Parts of the system—magistrates' courts, trial by jury, bail—are of great antiquity. Other parts—juvenile courts, probation and parole, professional policemen—are relatively new. The entire system represents an adaptation of the English common law to America's peculiar structure of government, which allows each local community to construct institutions that fill its special needs. Every village, town, county, city, and State has its own criminal justice system, and there is a Federal one as well. All of them operate somewhat alike. No two of them operate precisely alike.

President's Commission on Law Enforcement and
Administration of Justice, The Challenge of Crime
in a Free Society 7 (1967).

3

Some of the differences in operation are a result of different formal mechanisms. For example, in the federal and approximately two-fifths of the state systems, a defendant cannot be prosecuted for a serious crime unless a grand jury—a group usually composed of 17 to 21 citizens selected from the voter registration lists—has reviewed the evidence and decided to return an indictment;[1] in other jurisdictions there is no right to a grand jury indictment.[2] In some jurisdictions the authority to decide whether to proceed with a criminal prosecution rests with the local prosecutor; in others the ultimate authority, although rarely exercised, rests with the attorney general. See F. Miller, The Decision to Charge a Suspect with a Crime 322-327 (1969). In some jurisdictions the prosecutor's consent is usually required for the issuance of an arrest warrant; in others it is not. See W. LaFave, Arrest: The Decision to Take a Suspect into Custody 54-55 (1965). In some jurisdictions, judicial approval is required for the dismissal of a serious charge; in others the prosecutor has unilateral discretion to dismiss. See F. Miller, supra, at 309-310.

Other, less formal differences contribute even more to variations in the operation of the criminal justice process. For example, the institutional components that constitute the criminal justice system—the police agencies, the public prosecutors, the courts, the correctional departments—each have independent functions, but the operation of each is in part dependent on the operation of the others. They interrelate differently from community to community, and how they interrelate will have an impact on how the entire system operates. Thus, for the most part the prosecutors, the courts, and the correctional officials can deal only with those individuals whom the police arrest. A police officer's decision whether to arrest may in turn be influenced by how the officer believes the other institutional components of the system will respond to a situation. If an officer believes that an individual will be dealt with too leniently, the officer may arrest the individual and not press charges or perhaps not even make the arrest. W. LaFave, supra, at 126; see also id. at 509-524.

Allocation of resources also affects the manner in which the system operates. Limited prosecutorial or judicial resources, for example, will

1. An individual, of course, may waive the right to a grand jury indictment.
2. The Bill of Rights—the first 10 amendments to the federal Constitution—protects citizens against certain actions by the *federal* government. Among these protections are a number of rights applicable to criminal defendants, including the fifth amendment right not to be prosecuted for a serious crime in the absence of a grand jury indictment. Over the years the Supreme Court has "incorporated" most of these rights into the due process clause of the fourteenth amendment, which restricts the actions of state governments. See Chapter 3 infra. The federal right to a grand jury indictment is one of the few rights that has not been so incorporated. Thus, states are free to adopt or reject the use of grand juries to screen criminal charges.

force prosecutors to be more selective in choosing cases with which to proceed. Even allocation of resources within a single component of the criminal justice system has an impact on its operation. For example, at some point fairly early in the process, a member of the prosecutor's staff will review a case to determine whether it is appropriate to proceed with prosecution and, if so, on what charges. Usually the first opportunity to make this decision will be soon after an arrest, and the decision will be based on information contained in a police report. If the information in the report is complete enough to permit an informed decision about prosecution, and if the prosecutor is willing to assign experienced assistants to perform this screening function, cases inappropriate for prosecution can be eliminated from the system early without incurring the cost of proceeding with preliminary hearings or presentation of evidence to the grand jury. On the other hand, if experienced prosecutors are not used for this task or if the quality of initial information from the police is not high, there may be little serious screening of cases by the prosecutor until some later stage in the proceeding.

Even within a single jurisdiction, the order in which the various steps of the criminal justice process occur will depend on how the potential defendant first becomes involved in the system. Typically, for a serious crime there will be an arrest followed by a decision to prosecute. In some situations, however, the decision to prosecute may have been made secretly by the grand jury and prosecutor prior to any attempt to arrest the defendant.[3]

Despite the variations in the operation of the criminal justice process, there are substantial similarities among the federal and various state criminal justice systems.[4] Each share the following characteristics:

1. The initial enforcement responsibility rests with police agencies that have vast discretion in deciding whether to involve individuals in the criminal justice process.
2. The decision whether formally to charge an individual with a crime is the responsibility of a public prosecutor.

---

3. The grand jury, in addition to performing a screening function, may also act as an investigatory body. Information about an individual's criminal activity may come to light from such an investigation rather than from a citizen complaint or police investigation. On the basis of such information the grand jury may return an indictment prior to the defendant's arrest. Indeed, the arrest may be intentionally delayed for some period of time after the indictment is returned so that the grand jury can complete its investigation without alerting a defendant's confederates.

4. The similarities are greater with respect to prosecutions for serious criminal violations. Variations in both the formal judicial structure and in the degree of informality with which cases are resolved increase when one focuses on relatively minor crimes.

3. There is some mechanism for screening serious criminal charges to determine whether there is a factual basis for the charge.

4. A criminal defendant is entitled to the assistance of counsel and, if indigent, to have one appointed at public expense if incarceration will result from conviction.

5. A defendant may make various pretrial motions challenging the prosecutor's evidence and the fairness of the criminal process.

6. A defendant is entitled to a trial before an impartial judge, to confront and cross-examine opposing witnesses, to present witnesses, to a trial by jury unless the charge is only a "petty offense"[5] and to an acquittal unless the prosecutor proves each element of the offense beyond a reasonable doubt.[6]

7. A guilty defendant has the right to address the court prior to sentencing.

8. A convicted defendant usually has the right to some form of appellate review.[7]

The chart on page 7 provides a general overview of the role of the criminal justice process in dealing with crime in the United States.[8]

B. PRETRIAL PROCESS

The following hypothetical case illustrates how the criminal justice process might operate prior to trial in an ordinary felony prosecution. The

5. See Duncan v. Louisiana, page 79 infra.

6. Just as a defendant may waive the right to a grand jury indictment, see note 1 supra, a defendant can waive these various trial rights and plead guilty. This is in fact what the majority of defendants do. In most jurisdictions anywhere from 70-90 percent of the cases that are not dismissed are resolved by guilty pleas.

7. In many, but not all, jurisdictions the decision to plead guilty is viewed as a waiver of most of the contentions that a defendant might have raised at trial. For example, if a defendant prior to trial moved to exclude a confession on the ground that it was involuntary and if the confession were admitted at the trial, the defendant on appeal, could challenge the admissibility of the confession. If the defendant decided to plead guilty after receiving an unfavorable ruling on the pretrial motion to suppress, however, the defendant would not be permitted in many jurisdictions to raise the involuntariness issue on appeal. The defendant, of course, could attack the guilty plea itself as involuntary or claim ineffective assistance of counsel. See generally Lefkowitz v. Newsome, 420 U.S. 283 (1975) (describing New York procedure that permits defendant to raise constitutional claims following guilty plea and holding that existence of such procedure precludes state from relying on guilty plea to foreclose consideration of same constitutional issues in federal habeas corpus proceeding).

8. This chart is taken from President's Commission on Law Enforcement and Administration of Justice, The Challenge of Crime in a Free Society 8-9 (1967).

A general view of The Criminal Justice System

This chart seeks to present a simple yet comprehensive view of the movement of cases through the criminal justice system. The differing weights of line indicate the relative volumes of cases disposed of at various points in the system, but this is only suggestive since no nationwide data of this sort exists. Procedures in individual jurisdictions may vary from the pattern shown here.

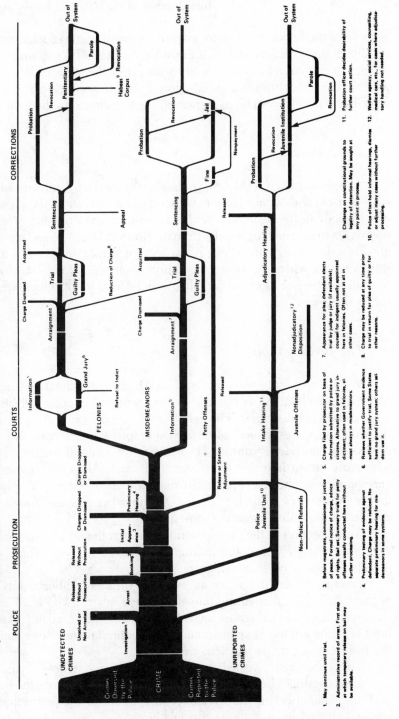

1. May continue until trial.

2. Administrative record of arrest. First step at which temporary release on bail may be available.

3. Before magistrate, commissioner, or justice of peace. Formal notice of charge, advice of rights. Bail set. Summary trials for petty offenders usually conducted here without further processing.

4. Preliminary testing of evidence against defendant. Charge may be reduced. No separate preliminary hearing for misdemeanors in some systems.

5. Charge filed by prosecutor on basis of information submitted by police or citizens. Alternative to grand jury indictment; often used in felonies, almost always in misdemeanors.

6. Reviews whether Government evidence sufficient to justify trial. Some States have no grand jury system; others seldom use it.

7. Appearance for plea; defendant elects trial by judge or jury (if available); counsel for indigent usually appointed here in felonies. Often not at all in other cases.

8. Charge may be reduced at any time prior to trial in return for plea of guilty or for other reasons.

9. Challenge on constitutional grounds to legality of detention. May be sought at any point in process.

10. Police often hold informal hearings, dismiss or adjust many cases without further processing.

11. Probation officer decides desirability of further court action.

12. Welfare agency, social services, counselling, medical care, etc., for cases where adjudicatory handling not needed.

7

purpose of the hypothetical is to provide a general frame of reference for consideration of the materials in the ensuing chapters. There is no attempt to deal in a comprehensive manner with all of the ways in which the process may differ from one jurisdiction or case to another. Some of the more likely possible variations, however, are mentioned in the footnotes.

The Crime

At approximately 1:00 A.M. on a late August day, Alma Crenshaw, a 68-year-old widow, awoke from a sound sleep and sensed the presence of somebody in her bedroom. Without stirring she opened her eyes and observed a man removing jewelry from the dresser. When he had removed all of the jewels, the man left. Alma remained motionless until a few minutes later when she heard the sound of an automobile starting in front of her house. After the car left, Alma hurried to the telephone and called the police.

The Investigation

Within an hour, the police were at Alma's house interviewing her about the incident. Alma related her harrowing experience and offered a description of the burglar. The light from the moon was shining through the window, she explained, and she had a "pretty good" opportunity to observe the intruder's features. He was a white male of medium build with curly brown hair and a moustache. In fact, Alma said, he looked very much like the television repairman who had come to her house earlier in the week to fix her TV set. Without her glasses, though, she couldn't be sure that it was the same person.

An inspection of the premises indicated that the burglar had gained entry by cutting a screen and raising an unlocked window. There were no other clues or physical evidence.

Later in the day the police interviewed Alma's neighbors. Only one of them had noticed anything unusual. James Adams, who lived across the street, remembered seeing an unfamiliar dark green sedan parked in front of Alma's house at approximately midnight. The last three digits of the license number, he recalled, were 999.

Two officers also visited the Acme TV Service, whose repairman had come to Alma's house earlier in the week. Donna Mason, the owner of Acme, after checking the service records, informed the police that the service call had been made by Roger Garrison, a new and so far very conscientious employee. She didn't know very much about his background, but she did give the police his address and loaned them a photograph, which he had submitted with his job application.

One of the officers returned to Alma with the photograph, and she identified Garrison as the burglar. In the meantime, another officer checked with the Department of Motor Vehicles and learned that Roger Garrison was the registered owner of a green Ford Torino with the license number DXC 899.

The Arrest Warrant

To make a valid arrest, the police must have "probable cause" to believe that the arrestee committed the crime for which he is arrested.

> Probable cause exists where "the facts and circumstances within their [the arresting officers'] knowledge and of which they had reasonably trustworthy information [are] sufficient in themselves to warrant a man of reasonable caution in the belief that" an offense has been or is being committed [by the person to be arrested]. [Brinegar v. United States, 338 U.S. 160, 175-176 (1949) (quoting Carroll v. United States, 267 U.S. 132 (1925)).]

The officer in charge of the investigation believed that the information the police had obtained was sufficient to constitute probable cause, and he decided to seek an arrest warrant.[9] He filled out a form requesting the issuance of a warrant for the arrest of Roger Garrison and attached it to the *complaint*,[10] a sworn statement that set forth the information that implicated Roger Garrison in the Alma Crenshaw burglary and theft. The officer presented the documents to the local prosecutor who autho-

---

9. A police officer may arrest a suspect without a warrant if the officer observes the suspect committing a misdemeanor or if the officer has probable cause to believe that the suspect committed a felony. A felony is generally defined as a crime punishable by imprisonment for more than one year in the state penitentiary. Since nighttime burglary and grand theft are both punishable by more than a year's imprisonment, the police were not required to seek an arrest warrant.

In fact, the vast majority of arrests are made without warrants. In some instances, however, the police may prefer to utilize the warrant process. This might occur, for example, if they believe the authority of the warrant will reduce the likelihood of resistance from the arrestee or if the police are not themselves sure whether they have probable cause. See generally W. LaFave, supra, at 36-52.

10. The complaint is the name usually given to the initial charging document that is filed with a court. It is a sworn statement of the facts constituting the offense, and it may be filed by either a police officer or a private citizen.

If an arrest is made without a warrant, the complaint will be filed after the suspect is arrested and before the initial court appearance. In some jurisdictions, a magistrate presented with a complaint following an arrest without a warrant will affirm the officer's probable cause judgement by issuing an after-the-fact arrest warrant.

rized him to proceed.[11] The officer then presented these documents to a local magistrate, who had the statutory authority to issue arrest and search warrants.[12] The magistrate reviewed the information in the complaint, agreed that there was probable cause to arrest Garrison, and issued the arrest warrant.

The Arrest

That afternoon at approximately four o'clock[13] two uniformed police officers, armed with the warrant, approached Garrison's house. Just outside the front door they met Garrison, who was leaving with an attache case. They showed him the warrant and announced that he was under arrest. One officer immediately searched Garrison while the other opened the attache case. The attache case contained two diamond rings and a gold watch, which the police confiscated. They later determined that the watch and one ring belonged to George Jensen, whose home had been burglarized several weeks earlier. The other ring belonged to Alma Crenshaw.

Garrison was handcuffed and placed in the police car. On the way to the stationhouse, one of the officers remarked, "It's a good thing Mrs. Crenshaw is still alive; otherwise, this would be a case of murder."

"What do you mean 'still alive'?" asked Garrison. "I never touched the old lady; she was asleep."

"You'll see soon enough," the officer responded.

The Booking

Upon arrival at the police station, Garrison went through the *booking process*. Booking involves making a record of an arrestee's name and

---

11. At some point or points in the process, the prosecutor will review a case to determine whether there is a sufficient basis for pursuing a prosecution. In cases in which an arrest warrant is sought, the prosecutor will frequently have reviewed the case and determined that arrest is appropriate. See W. LaFave, supra, at 30-33.

12. The purpose of the warrant process—whether it is for an arrest warrant or a search warrant—is to provide a neutral, detached evaluation of probable cause. To ensure that this purpose can be served, individuals with authority to issue the warrant must be presented with sufficient factual allegations in a sworn statement to permit them to make the probable cause assessments. Moreover, they must be "neutral." They cannot, for example, be members of the police department or prosecutor's staff. Usually they are judicial officers with jurisdiction to try relatively minor crimes. In some jurisdictions, however, clerks of court have authority to issue warrants.

13. In approximately one-half of the states, a warrant can be executed only in the "daylight hours" or during the daytime unless there is some special showing of need for nighttime execution.

address and the offense charged, and noting the time at which the arrestee arrived at the police station. In addition, on occasion the arrestee will be photographed and fingerprinted. Usually the arrestee will be notified of the charge and given the opportunity to make a telephone call.

If the offense is a relatively minor one, the arrestee may be able to post bail with the police and obtain immediate release. An individual like Garrison, who is arrested on a felony charge, is likely to remain in police custody at least until his initial appearance before a judicial officer.[14] This is what happened to Garrison. The police searched him once again, took and inventoried all of his personal belongings, and placed him in a cell.

The Lineup

Occasionally as part of or immediately following the booking process the police will engage in further investigatory activity. For example, they may ask a suspect to provide a handwriting exemplar or to waive the right to remain silent and submit to interrogation. In Garrison's case, the police put the suspect in a hastily assembled lineup with four other individuals and took a photograph of the lineup. The following day the police showed the photograph to Alma Crenshaw, who after some hesitation tentatively identified Garrison as the burglar.

The Initial Appearance[15]

An individual who has been arrested must be brought before a judicial officer[16] without unnecessary delay.[17] Usually this means within

14. Sometimes the judicial officer who issues an arrest warrant will indicate the amount of bail on the back of the warrant. If the arrestee is able to meet the bail requirement, release will be immediate.

15. This stage of the process is sometimes referred to as an initial presentment or an arraignment on the warrant.

16. The judicial officer is usually a magistrate or a judge of a court with limited criminal jurisdiction. Usually the jurisdiction will extend to the trial of misdemeanors and the preliminary screening of felony cases. See the text following note 22 infra.

17. Prior to the initial appearance, if not prior to the arrest, the police will file a complaint setting forth the criminal acts that the arrestee has allegedly committed. If the prosecutor has not reviewed the case prior to the arrest, see note 11, supra, the prosecutor may well review it to determine what, if any, charges should be alleged in the complaint.

In the case of a misdemeanor charge, the complaint will constitute the formal charging document. In the case of a felony charge, the complaint will eventually be supplanted by an indictment or information unless the charge is dismissed or reduced to a misdemeanor.

several hours of the arrest for an individual who remains in police custody following the arrest. [18] If an individual is arrested in the evening, however, the initial appearance may not take place until the next morning; and if a person is arrested on the eve of a weekend or holiday, the initial appearance will probably not take place until the morning of the next working day. Since Garrison was arrested in the evening, he remained incarcerated overnight and appeared before a magistrate the following morning.

The initial appearance, which may take no more than a few minutes, serves several purposes. First, the magistrate will ascertain that the person before the court is indeed the individual referred to in the complaint or warrant. Second, the magistrate will inform the person of the charges and usually says a few words about the defendant's rights and the ensuing steps in the process. Third, the person will be informed of the right to counsel, including the right to appointed counsel for indigents. If the person claims to be indigent, the magistrate, after asking several questions to verify the claim, may appoint an attorney at the initial appearance. Finally, the magistrate will set the amount of "bail" or other conditions of release that, if they can be satisfied, will permit the person to remain free prior to the trial. [19]

Because Garrison could not afford to hire his own lawyer, the magistrate appointed the public defender to represent him. The magistrate then set Garrison's bail at $5,000. [20] The attorney from the public defender's office, who met Garrison for the first time at the initial appearance, made a brief but unsuccessful argument for the reduction of bail.

The Return to Custody

Because Garrison was unable to satisfy the bail condition, he was remanded to the custody of the police. He was placed in a cell with another burglary suspect, and the two of them began to compare their sad fates. In the course of the conversation Garrison admitted that he had recently committed five other burglaries in addition to those at the Alma Crenshaw and George Jensen residences. The conversation was recorded on an electronic listening device that the police had planted in the cell.

18. For individuals who are released immediately after their arrests, the initial appearance may not take place for several days.

19. If the charge is a misdemeanor, over which the initial appearance court is likely to have continuing jurisdiction, the defendant may be asked to enter a plea at this time.

20. If he were financially able to do so, Garrison could pay a bondsman $500 (10 percent) to secure a $5,000 bond.

Pretrial Release

Garrison's lawyer was prepared to go back to court the following day to argue that this client's bail should be reduced.[21] That became unnecessary, however. Donna Mason, Garrison's employer, paid a bailbondsman the $500 that was necessary to secure a $5,000 bond. Garrison was released from custody.

The Prosecutorial Decision to Proceed

The next formal stage in the processing of a felony case is the presentation of evidence to a magistrate in a preliminary examination or to a grand jury for the purpose of determining whether there is a sufficient factual basis for proceeding with the prosecution. Regardless of whether the forum is the preliminary hearing or the grand jury, the prosecutor will be presenting the evidence. Usually, at least by this time, the prosecutor will have made an independent review of the evidence and will have decided to proceed only with those cases that the prosecutor believes are appropriate for felony prosecution. In Garrison's case, the prosecutor had decided that it was appropriate to proceed with burglary and grand theft charges for both the Crenshaw and Jensen incidents.

The Preliminary Hearing

At Garrison's initial appearance, the magistrate scheduled the preliminary hearing for the following week. The purpose of this hearing is to determine whether there is probable cause to proceed with a felony prosecution. A magistrate, of course, had already made a probable cause determination with respect to the Crenshaw burglary for the purpose of issuing the arrest warrant. Additional investigation between the time of arrest and the preliminary hearing, however, might reveal that the defendant should be prosecuted for additional or different crimes from those for which a defendant was initially arrested. In Garrison's case, for ex-

---

21. The purpose of bail is to ensure that the defendant will appear for trial, and the bail decision is always open to reconsideration. By the following day the public defender would have had an opportunity to speak with Garrison and ascertain what community ties he had. The lawyer could then urge that factors such as Garrison's present job and his apparent reliability minimize the risk that he would flee the jurisdiction, and that the bail should be reduced to something he could reasonably afford.

In some communities a member of the public defender's office or a specially funded "bail project" will attempt to gather and verify this type of information about arrestees prior to their initial appearance.

ample, the prosecutor was prepared to present evidence regarding the Jensen as well as the Crenshaw break-in. Moreover, the purpose and consequences of the two probable cause determinations are different. The arrest simply begins the process toward possible prosecution and conviction. If the arrestee is able to make bail, the initial incarceration will be brief; and after reviewing the evidence the prosecutor may decide not to proceed with the case. By contrast, the prosecutor in all likelihood has made a firm decision to prosecute an individual prior to the preliminary hearing, and the hearing is designed to ensure that there is an adequate factual basis for this decision. Finally, the manner in which the two probable cause decisions are made is quite different. The warrant process is an ex parte proceeding, in which the magistrate simply reviews allegations presented by the police. The preliminary hearing, on the other hand, is an adversary-type proceeding. Although the rules of evidence are not likely to be applied with the same rigor as during a trial, the prosecutor's witnesses will be subject to cross-examination by the defendant, and the defendant may present witnesses.[22]

The preliminary hearing usually takes place in a court of limited jurisdiction. Typically, such a court has the power to try misdemeanors but not felonies. Thus, a finding of probable cause to believe that the defendant committed a felony requires the court to *bind over* or transfer the case to the component of the criminal justice system that will be dealing with it next. After finding probable cause to believe that Garrison committed burglary and grand theft against both Mrs. Crenshaw and Mr. Jensen, the court bound the case over to the general jurisdiction court.

Grand Jury Review

Depending on the jurisdiction, the evidence against Garrison may be subjected to a second or a substitute screening process to determine whether there is probable cause to proceed. In some states, a suspect has the right to have the evidence reviewed by a grand jury; in other states, the grand jury process may be available for the prosecutor to use if the prosecutor chooses to do so. If the grand jury, by a vote of a majority of its members, determines that there is probable cause, the foreman of the grand jury will sign an indictment listing the crime or crimes with which the defendant is charged. The indictment will include a statement of

---

22. Perry Mason to the contrary notwithstanding, the defendant is unlikely to call witnesses. At best, defense witnesses would contradict prosecution witnesses in some critical respect, and the judge probably would not view mere contradiction as undermining probable cause.

when the crime was committed and a brief description of the defendant's conduct.

In most jurisdictions that utilize the grand jury to screen cases for probable cause, the issuance of an indictment prior to the date set for a preliminary hearing will result in the cancellation of the scheduled hearing. In these jurisdictions, prosecutors are often anxious to present cases to the grand jury in order to avoid preliminary hearings. Unlike the adversarial preliminary hearing, the grand jury screening process is ex parte. The prosecutor presents evidence to the grand jury, and while the grand jurors are free to ask questions of witnesses and to call additional witnesses on their own, the defendant has no right to be present during the proceedings, and the defendant has no right to present evidence.

Since the prosecutor did not take Garrison's case to the grand jury prior to the preliminary hearing, it is unlikely that the prosecutor would want at this point to devote resources to a second probable cause screening. The case would probably be presented to a grand jury only if Garrison had a state constitutional or statutory right to a grand jury indictment and if he refused to waive the right. To continue our story, let us assume that if the case was presented to the grand jury, its probable cause determination was the same as that reached at the preliminary hearing.

Filing the Formal Charge

The formal commencement of prosecution in the general jurisdiction court comes with the filing of either an indictment or a *prosecutor's information*. If the case has gone to the grand jury, the prosecutor will sign and file the grand jury's indictment to begin the prosecution. If the case has not gone to the grand jury and the defendant has no right to an indictment, the prosecutor will simply file an information charging the defendant with the crimes for which probable cause was found to exist at the preliminary hearing. Like the indictment, the information will briefly describe the acts constituting the crime(s) and allege when they were committed.[23]

In Garrison's case, the prosecutor filed a single information—or indictment if the case went to the grand jury—listing four separate offenses or counts:

---

23. There is no requirement that the charges in the indictment or information be the same as those that initially led to the defendant's arrest. Moreover, in jurisdictions that utilize grand juries, the grand jury may return an indictment for charges that were dismissed for want of probable cause at a preliminary hearing. In most jurisdictions, though, felonies charged in an information must be supported by a probable cause finding at a preliminary hearing unless the defendant has waived the right to the hearing.

1. Burglary of the Crenshaw residence
2. Grand theft of property from the Crenshaw residence
3. Burglary of the Jensen residence
4. Grand theft of property from the Jensen residence

The Arraignment

The process of formally notifying the defendant of the charges and seeking a plea to those charges is referred to as the arraignment. Following the filing of the information (or indictment), Garrison was summoned before the trial court to go through this process. The charges were read to him and he was asked to plead either guilty or not guilty. Garrison pled not guilty to all of the charges.[24]

Pretrial Motions

At this point in the process, Garrison has the opportunity to file pretrial motions on a variety of grounds. For example, he may move to dismiss the indictment or information on the ground that it does not properly charge a punishable offense; if he was indicted, he may move to dismiss the indictment on the ground that the grand jury was improperly constituted or that there were improprieties in the manner in which the grand jury indicted him; he may make various motions for the suppression of evidence and for the discovery of evidence in the hands of the prosecution. In addition, during this period of time before trial, he may be required to reveal some information about his defense. A number of jurisdictions, for example, require a defendant who plans to rely on an alibi defense to give advance notice of that fact to the prosecutor.

The preceding account of Garrison's involvement with the criminal justice process suggests the following possible issues for resolution by pretrial motion:

1. Whether the contents of the attache case and testimony about its contents are inadmissible because the evidence was discovered as a result of a violation of Garrison's fourth amendment rights;

---

24. The vast majority of cases—both felony and misdemeanor—result in guilty pleas. If Garrison were willing to plead guilty to all of the charges, or if he and the prosecutor could work out an agreement whereby Garrison would plead guilty to some of the charges in return for dismissal of the others or a recommendation for a lenient sentence, he would probably enter his guilty plea at this time. No such agreement existed, however.

2. Whether Garrison's statement in the police car is inadmissible because it was obtained in violation of his fourth, fifth, or sixth amendment rights;

3. Whether testimony about Alma Crenshaw's identification of the photograph obtained from Garrison's employer is inadmissible because the identification procedure violated Garrison's right to due process of law;

4. Whether testimony about Alma Crenshaw's identification of Garrison in the lineup photograph is inadmissible because the identification procedure violated Garrison's right to due process or his sixth amendment right to counsel;

5. Whether Alma's in-court identification of Garrison at the trial should be prohibited because it is fatally tainted by the previous unconstitutional identifications;

6. Whether Garrison's statements that were overheard as a result of the electronic monitoring device are inadmissible because the statements were obtained in violation of Garrison's fourth, fifth, or sixth amendment rights;

7. Whether Garrison should be entitled to a severance of the Crenshaw charges from the Jensen charges so that each incident will be the subject of a separate trial.

The various motions can usually be presented orally as well as in writing. To ensure serious consideration of the motions, however, they should probably be presented in writing with an accompanying supporting brief and, when appropriate, affidavits setting forth essential factual matters. Whether there will be oral arguments on the motions or presentation of witnesses is within the discretion of the trial judge. If, however, there are factual disputes underlying a suppression of evidence claim, both parties will probably be permitted to call witnesses.[25]

Resolution of the pretrial motions may also bring a resolution to the case. For example, if the defendant prevails on a motion to suppress critical evidence, the prosecutor may have no choice except to dismiss the case. Alternatively, once the defendant has lost such a motion and with it the hope of a dismissal, the defendant may be willing to plead guilty.

---

25. Various aspects of the suppression process are considered in more detail in Chapter 10, infra.

C. TRIAL AND BEYOND

NATIONAL ADVISORY COMMISSION ON CRIMINAL JUSTICE STANDARDS AND GOALS, COURTS
13-15 (1973)

TRIAL

Unless the defendant enters a guilty plea, the full adversary process is put into motion. The prosecution now must establish to a jury or a judge the guilt of the defendant beyond a reasonable doubt. If the defendant elects to have the case tried by a jury, much effort is expended on the selection of a jury. Prospective jurors are questioned to ascertain whether they might be biased and what their views on numerous matters might be. Both sides have the right to have a potential juror rejected on the ground that he may be biased. In addition, both have the right to reject a limited number of potential jurors without having to state any reason. When the jury has been selected and convened, both sides may make opening statements explaining what they intend to prove or disprove.

The prosecution presents its evidence first, and the defendant has the option of making no case and relying upon the prosecution's inability to establish guilt beyond a reasonable doubt. He also has the option of presenting evidence tending to disprove the prosecution's case or tending to prove additional facts constituting a defense under applicable law. Throughout, however, the burden remains upon the prosecution. Procedurally, this is effectuated by defense motions to dismiss, which often are made after the prosecution's case has been presented and after all of the evidence is in. These motions in effect assert that the prosecution's case is so weak that no reasonable jury could conclude beyond a reasonable doubt that the defendant was guilty. If the judge grants the motion, he is in effect determining that no jury could reasonably return a verdict of guilty. This not only results in a dismissal of the prosecution but also prevents the prosecution from bringing another charge for the same crime.

After the evidence is in and defense motions are disposed of, the jury is instructed on the applicable law. Often both defense and prosecution lawyers submit instructions which they ask the court to read to the jury, and the court chooses from those and others it composes itself. It is in the formulation of these instructions that many issues regarding the definition of the applicable law arise and must be resolved. After— or sometimes before—the instructions are read, both sides present formal arguments to the jury. The jury then retires for its deliberations.

Generally, the jury may return only one of two verdicts: guilty or not guilty. A verdict of not guilty may be misleading; it may mean not that the jury believed that the defendant was not guilty but rather that the jury determined that the prosecution had not established guilt by the criterion—beyond a reasonable doubt—the law imposes. If the insanity defense has been raised, the jury may be told it should specify if insanity is the reason for acquittal; otherwise, there is no need for explanation. If a guilty verdict is returned, the court formally enters a judgment of conviction unless there is a legally sufficient reason for not doing so.

The defendant may attack his conviction, usually by making a motion to set aside the verdict and order a new trial. In his attack, he may argue that evidence was improperly admitted during the trial, that the evidence was so weak that no reasonable jury could have found that it established guilt beyond a reasonable doubt, or that there is newly discovered evidence which, had it been available at the time of trial, would have changed the result. If the court grants a motion raising one of these arguments, the effect generally is not to acquit the defendant but merely to require the holding of a new trial.

SENTENCING

Sentencing then follows. (If the court has accepted a plea of guilty, this step follows acceptance of the plea.) In an increasing number of jurisdictions, an investigation called the presentence report is conducted by professional probation officers. This involves investigation of the offense, the offender and his background, and any other matters of potential value to the sentencing judge. Following submission of the report to the court, the defendant is given the opportunity to comment upon the appropriateness of sentencing. In some jurisdictions, this has developed into a more extensive court hearing on sentencing issues, with the defendant given the opportunity to present evidence as well as argument for leniency. Sentencing itself generally is the responsibility of the judge, although in some jurisdictions juries retain that authority.

APPEAL

Following the conclusion of the proceeding in the trial court, the matter shifts to the appellate courts. In some jurisdictions, a defendant who is convicted of a minor offense in a lower court has the right to a new trial (trial de novo) in a higher court. But in most situations—and in all cases involving serious offenses—the right to appeal is limited to the right to have an appellate court examine the record of the trial proceedings for error. If error is found, the appellate court either may take definitive action—such as ordering that the prosecution be dismissed—or it may set aside the conviction and remand the case for a new trial. The latter gives the prosecution the opportunity to obtain a valid conviction. Generally, a time limit is placed upon the period during which an appeal may be taken.

COLLATERAL ATTACK

Even if no appeal is taken or the conviction is upheld, the courts' participation in the criminal justice process is not necessarily ended. To some extent, a convicted defendant who has either exhausted his appeal rights or declined to exercise them within the appropriate time limits can seek further relief by means of collateral attack upon the conviction. This method involves a procedure collateral to the standard process of conviction and appeal.

Traditionally this relief was sought by applying for a writ of habeas corpus on the ground that the conviction under which the applicant was held was invalid. Many jurisdictions have found this vehicle too cumbersome for modern problems and have developed special procedures for collateral attacks. Despite variations in terminology and procedural technicalities, however, opportunities remain for an accused convicted in Federal court to seek such collateral relief from his conviction in Federal courts and for those convicted in State courts to seek similar relief in State and, to a somewhat more limited extent, in Federal courts.

The matter has become an increasingly significant point of State-Federal friction as issues of Federal constitutional law have become more important parts of criminal litigation. Defendants convicted in State courts apparently have thought that Federal courts offered a more sympathetic forum for assertions that Federal constitutional rights were violated during a State criminal prosecution. State judges and prosecutors have indicated resentment with the actions of Federal courts in reversing State convictions for reasons State courts either considered of no legal merit or refused to consider for what they felt were valid reasons.

In any case, because collateral attack upon a conviction remains available until (and even after) the defendant has gone through the correctional process, the courts' role in the criminal justice process extends from the earliest points of criminal investigation to the final portions of the correctional process. . . .

CHAPTER 2

PERSPECTIVES ON THE CRIMINAL JUSTICE SYSTEM

Perceptions of the criminal justice system are as varied as the system itself. Commentators, by virtue of their individual training and experience with the system, inevitably make their observations and evaluations from different perspectives. Moreover, commentators will have, if not different values, at least different priorities that they would like to see reflected in the criminal justice system. The materials in this chapter, without attempting to be comprehensive, offer some important perceptions and insights about the criminal justice system. You, of course, should approach these materials with the same questioning mind and skepticism that you bring to bear on the study of cases.

A. SOME PERSPECTIVES ON THE SYSTEM AS A WHOLE

AMERICAN BAR ASSOCIATION SPECIAL COMMITTEE ON CRIMINAL JUSTICE IN A FREE SOCIETY, CRIMINAL JUSTICE IN CRISIS
4-5 (1988)

With the exception of the crime of murder, only a small fraction of the serious criminal acts committed in the United States ever enter the criminal justice system, for reasons totally unrelated to constitutional restric-

21

tions. The overwhelming majority of these crimes, which keep Americans in fear, are untouched by the work of police, prosecutors, judges, and prison officials.

The Committee compiled, as best it could, the available data published by the Justice Department through the middle of 1988. This compilation reveals that of the approximately 34 million serious crimes committed against persons or property in the United States in 1986, approximately 31 million never were exposed to arrest, because either they were not reported to the police or if reported, they were not solved by arrests. Further, of the crimes that result in felony arrests, roughly one half will likely result in felony prosecutions and convictions, and of those convictions, only about one half will likely result in prison sentences.[7]

7. These numbers are derived from data provided in three government studies, the National Crime Survey (NCS) as reported in Bureau of Justice Statistics, U.S. Dep't of Just., BJS Data Report, 1987, at 8 (1988); Uniform Crime Reports (UCR) as reported in Federal Bureau of Investigation, U.S. Dep't of Just., Crime in the United States, 1986, at 41, 154 (1987); and B. Boland, W. Logan, R. Sones & W. Martin, The Prosecution of Felony Arrests, 1982, at 2 (Bureau of Justice Statistics, U.S. Dep't of Just., 1987). There is no one United States government sponsored survey that tracks all crime and the response to it, although a developing survey (Offender-Based Transaction Statistics) comprehensively tracks felony arrests in 11 states and may someday provide this information. The Committee used a number of different surveys to create a rough idea of the relationship between crime committed and the criminal justice system. One survey tracks victimizations, another tracks reported crime and police clearance rates, and a third far smaller survey tracks what happens after arrest in 37 jurisdictions. The figures reported here take the liberty of combining these three studies to give the reader a sense of the relationship between crime and criminal justice in the United States. This relationship is inexact because each of these studies has its own methodology and tracks different crimes.

The NCS measures the incidence of rape, robbery, assault, personal larceny, household burglary and larceny, and motor vehicle theft. It estimates that in 1986 there were 34.1 million victimizations. BJS Data Report, 1987, at 8. Fewer than two-fifths of NCS crimes are reported to the police. *Id.* at 32. From 1973-1985 only about one-third of the crimes tracked by NCS were reported to the police. Bureau of Justice Statistics, U.S. Dep't of Just., Report to the Nation on Crime and Justice 34 (2nd ed. 1988).

NCS does not trace what happens after arrest. That information is tracked by the UCR, which collects statistics for eight index offenses as reported to the police. These crimes, [murder and nonnegligent manslaughter, forcible rape, robbery, aggravated assault, burglary, larceny/theft, motor vehicle theft, and arson,] . . . are *not* the same as those tracked by NCS. Of the more than 13.2 million UCR index offenses known to the police in 1986, only one in five was "cleared" by an arrest. . . . Crime in the United States, 1986, at 41, 154. . . .

Neither NCS nor UCR track what happens after arrest. The information concerning what happens after arrest is based upon a study of 1982 felony arrests in 37 urban jurisdictions. For each 100 adult felony arrests, 49 will not be prosecuted as felonies, either because they were rejected by the prosecutor at screening, referred to a diversion program or other courts for prosecution or dismissed at some form of preliminary hearing. Of the 51 cases that proceed further, 47 result in convictions by guilty plea. Only four of the 100 cases are tried, and three of these result in convictions. For the 50 convictions obtained, 13 are sentenced to more than one year in prison, 13 are sentenced to less

Thus, out of 34 million victimizations occurring in America, only several hundred thousand resulted in felony convictions and were punished by imprisonment. And, despite the fact that a tiny fraction of all felonies committed will result in prison sentences being imposed, the prisons of America are crowded, operating at between 6% and 21% above capacity.

The Committee believes that it is urgent that these facts be known and fully understood by the public, legislators, and federal and state government policy-makers. They create, in large part, some of the real problems police, prosecutors, and judges face in their efforts to perform their criminal justice duties successfully. . . . [T]hese officials consistently told the Committee that they are regularly frustrated in their work because of the public's perception that if they did their jobs competently, they should be able to protect the public from crime completely. They reported that even if they were given sufficient resources, they could only effectively prosecute and punish a small percentage of the crime against which the public demands protection.

Their principal complaint, however, was that they were not given the resources to do what they could do well. Less than 3% of all government spending in the United States went to support all civil and criminal justice system activities in fiscal 1985. This compares with 20.8% for social insurance payments, 18.3% for national defense and international relations, and 10.9% for interest on debt. Less than 1% of all government spending went into operation of the Nation's correctional system (including jails, prisons, probation, and parole.)[1]

PACKER, THE COURTS, THE POLICE, AND THE REST OF US
57 J. Crim. L., Criminology & Police Sci. 238, 239 (1966)

[T]he kind of criminal process that we have is profoundly affected by a series of competing value choices which, consciously or unconsciously, serve to resolve tensions that arise in the system. These values represent polar extremes which, in real life, are subject to almost infinite modulation and compromise. But the extremes can be identified. The choice, basically, is between what I have termed the Crime Control and the Due

---

than one year in prison, and 24 are sentenced to probation or other conditions. The Prosecution of Felony Arrests, at 2.

1. For a discussion of the role of law enforcement in crime reduction, see Frase, Defining the Limits of Crime Control and Due Process, 73 Calif. L. Rev. 212 (1985) (review of and commentary on H. Zeisel, The Limits of Law Enforcement (1982).)— EDS.

Process models. The Crime Control model sees the efficient, expeditious and reliable screening and disposition of persons suspected of crime as the central value to be served by the criminal process. The Due Process model sees that function as limited by and subordinate to the maintenance of the dignity and autonomy of the individual. The Crime Control model is administrative and managerial; the Due Process model is adversary and judicial. The Crime Control model may be analogized to an assembly line, the Due Process model to an obstacle course.[2]

What we have at work today is a situation in which the criminal process as it actually operates in the large majority of cases probably approximates fairly closely the dictates of the Crime Control model. The real-world criminal process tends to be far more administrative and managerial than it does adversary and judicial. Yet, the officially prescribed norms for the criminal process, as laid down primarily by the Supreme Court, are rapidly providing a view that looks more and more like the Due Process model. This development . . . has been in the direction of "judicializing" each stage of the criminal process, of enhancing the capacity of the accused to challenge the operation of the process, and of equalizing the capacity of all persons to avail themselves of the opportunity for challenge so created. . . .

ARENELLA, RETHINKING THE FUNCTIONS OF CRIMINAL PROCEDURE: THE WARREN AND BURGER COURTS' COMPETING IDEOLOGIES
72 Geo. L.J. 185, 197-202 (1983)

THE FUNCTIONS OF AMERICAN CRIMINAL PROCEDURE

A. DETERMINING SUBSTANTIVE GUILT—HISTORICAL FACT RECONSTRUCTION AND MORAL EVALUATION

Criminal procedure must provide a process that promotes the goals of the substantive criminal law. Accordingly, an analysis of criminal procedure's functions is inextricably interwoven with one's vision of these substantive goals. Most commentators assume that the primary goal of any criminal process is to discover the "truth." But what "truth" are we trying to discover? To many, the concept of truth-discovery implies that

2. The *Crime Control* and *Due Process* concepts admittedly reflect different value choices, and the concepts provide a helpful way to articulate and focus on these value choices. But do they represent two different "models" of the criminal justice system? For a negative answer to this question, see Griffiths, Ideology in Criminal Procedure, or a Third "Model" of the Criminal Process, 79 Yale L.J. 359 (1970).—EDS.

guilt is an empirical fact ready to be discovered and verified. Debate then focuses on what processes best promote the detection and reliable determination of historical facts.

Equating the substantive criminal law's concept of guilt with historical fact would be defensible if crimes were defined solely in terms of the defendant's acts. But the criminal law usually refuses to predicate criminal liability on acts alone. Such a restrictive definition of substantive guilt would erode one of the major distinctions between criminal and civil liability: Only the former imposes a special moral stigma of community condemnation. Criminalizing acts alone would also greatly enhance the state's power to intervene in the lives of its citizens. Accordingly, the substantive criminal law's definition of guilt protects individual autonomy and preserves the moral force of the criminal sanction by requiring some showing of the defendant's moral culpability.

Our substantive criminal law requires a moral evaluation of the actor's conduct by including some mental element (e.g., purpose, knowledge, recklessness, or negligence) in its definition of most offenses and by its recognition of affirmative defenses that either justify the defendant's conduct or excuse it. Since substantive guilt includes both facts and value judgments about the actor's moral culpability, criminal procedure must provide a procedural mechanism that reliably reconstructs historical facts and morally evaluates their significance. The combination of these two procedural functions—reliable historical fact reconstruction and moral evaluation—cannot be equated with "truth-discovery."

Admittedly, in many criminal prosecutions, guilt or innocence will depend solely on a contested issue of historical fact. When a defendant presents an alibi defense or claims a mistaken eyewitness identification, she is disputing the "truth" of the state's factual claim that she committed the proscribed conduct. But, even in these cases, criminal procedure reconstructs facts in a manner that expresses an error-deflection preference. At least in theory, our system prefers erroneous acquittals over erroneous convictions. Consequently, it requires compelling proof that the defendant engaged in the proscribed conduct to provide maximum protection of the substantively innocent. Recognizing the fallibility of any human process used to reconstruct facts, criminal procedure deliberately places the risk of factual error on the state to protect the integrity and moral force of a guilty verdict.

Thus, when commentators describe the primary function of criminal procedure as "truth-discovery," they provide an oversimplified and misleading account of how our system is designed to determine guilt. The "truth-discovery" label ignores the moral content and force of substantive guilt and the resulting need for a process that evaluates the moral quality of the defendant's actions.

B. PROMOTING THE AIMS OF PUNISHMENT

Once guilt is reliably established, criminal procedure must provide a process that determines the appropriate disposition for the guilty offender. In theory, the substantive criminal law has already decided the most important aspects of this question. The legislature determines the kind and potential degree of punishment involved for each offense and the identity of the sentencing authority. The legislature's sentencing system should reflect its underlying view of the purposes served by the criminal sanction—retribution, specific and general deterrence, incapacitation, or rehabilitation. For example, if the legislature views rehabilitation and/or incapacitation of the dangerous offender as the most important aims of the criminal sanction, it will probably choose a relatively indeterminate sentencing structure that gives a parole board most of the real sentencing power. If the legislature views retribution and general deterrence as the paramount goals, it is likely to adopt a more determinate sentencing scheme that limits the judge's sentencing discretion.

The criminal process should be structured to promote the legislature's sentencing system and goals. First, the procedural mechanism used to determine substantive guilt should provide the sentencing authority with some of the information it needs to make an appropriate sentencing decision. Second, the guilt-determining process should minimize the effect of the parties' tactical choices upon appropriate sentencing decisions. Finally, criminal procedure should protect the substantive criminal law's proportionality principle—that the defendant's degree of punishment not exceed his "just deserts"—by providing some check against legislative abuse of its sentencing powers.

Up to this point, we have examined the substantive criminal law objectives that criminal procedure should promote. However, the functions of American criminal procedure extend beyond vindication of substantive criminal law goals.

C. AMERICAN CRIMINAL PROCEDURE'S INDEPENDENT FUNCTIONS

1. ALLOCATION OF POWER TO RESOLVE DISPUTE

Our accusatorial system structures criminal proceedings as an adversarial contest between the state and the accused in which the parties themselves control, for the most part, the course of the dispute. To provide a workable dispute-resolution mechanism, American criminal procedure must allocate power in a manner that implements the system's judgments about which state officials, institutions, and community representatives are best suited to investigate, apprehend, charge, adjudicate, and sentence. These institutional competency judgments will reflect in part political norms (e.g., separation of powers, federalism) about the appropriate structure and distribution of government authority. These judgments will also be influenced by the need to allocate scarce resources efficiently. Some officials must distribute the scarce resources society gives to the criminal justice system in a manner that promotes procedure's goals with minimal allocative inefficiency. All of these factors will affect how American criminal procedure allocates power and protects its distribution by preventing one actor from encroaching on the powers of another.

2. LEGITIMATION

Regardless of how a criminal justice system characterizes the nature of the dispute between the state and the individual, it cannot resolve the controversy without exercising coercive power over individuals. Since the state monopolizes the use of physical violence, it must validate its monopoly by providing impersonal criteria for resolving conflicts with its citizens. Some of these impersonal criteria flow from the substantive criminal law's definition of guilt. Criminal procedure can also attempt to justify the state's use of coercion[90] by articulating fair process norms that place some substantive and procedural limits on the state's exercise of power.

Some of these fair process norms (e.g., compelling proof of guilt, timely and final resolution of the dispute, independent adjudication, assistance of counsel) are valued in part because of their instrumental effect on the system's outcome. These process norms contribute to good results—the reliable conviction of the guilty and the exoneration of the innocent—by providing a means for realizing the commands of the substantive criminal law. But, "in legal ordering man does not live by results alone."[91] Criminal procedure also articulates fair process norms that have value independent of their "result-efficacy."[92] Most of these fair process

90. I am not suggesting that the only way or even the most effective way the state can ethically validate its use of coercion in the criminal process is by articulating fair process norms. The dominant political ideology of the state may itself serve this legitimation function. American criminal procedure's preoccupation with abuse of power issues reflects a basic theme in liberal political theory that views government authority with suspicion. In contrast, socialist political theory assumes that the interests of the state and the individual are in harmony and that state officials will exercise their power to promote society's general welfare. Consequently, one would expect that socialist criminal procedure would not need to rely primarily on fair process norms to ethically validate the state's use of coercion.

91. Summers, Evaluating and Improving Legal Processes—A Plea for Process Values, 60 Cornell L. Rev. 1, 51 (1974).

92. Id. at 2.

norms operate as substantive and procedural restraints on state power to ensure that the individual suspect is treated with dignity and respect. The content of these dignitary norms should reflect society's normative aspirations, embodied in its positive laws, customs, religions, and ideologies about the proper relationship between the individual and the state. Some of these fair process norms (e.g., grand jury review of the prosecutor's charging decision) also promote political values like community participation that affect criminal procedure's institutional competency judgments. Finally, some of these norms also reflect procedural values (e.g., procedural regularity, rationality and intelligibility) that underlie society's conception of the rule of law. . . .

One can take American criminal procedure's protection of fair process norms at face value as an ethical prerequisite of a just legal system that places some substantive and procedural restraints on the state's exercise of power. Or, one can explain this legitimation function from an instrumentalist perspective. To perform its dispute-resolution function effectively, American criminal procedure must provide a mechanism that settles the conflict in a manner that induces community respect for the fairness of its processes as well as the reliability of its outcomes. From this instrumentalist perspective, the most important consideration is how the process appears to the community. Given this definition of legitimation, criminal procedure need not in fact consistently respect these fair process norms, but it must create the appearance of doing so. Regardless of one's explanation for why American criminal procedure performs this legitimation function, its presence suggests that the fairness of the state-individual interaction in the criminal process cannot be defined solely in terms of procedures that contribute to good substantive criminal law results. Simply put, American constitutional criminal procedure values and protects fair process norms even when they impair procedure's guilt-determination function.

ALAN DERSHOWITZ, THE BEST DEFENSE
xxi-xxii (1982)

In the process of litigating . . . cases, writing this book and teaching my classes, I have discerned a series of "rules" that seem—in practice—to govern the justice game in America today. Most of the participants in the criminal justice system understand them. Although these rules never appear in print, they seem to control the realities of the process. Like all rules, they are necessarily stated in oversimplified terms. But they tell an important part of how the system operates in practice. Here are some of the key rules of the justice game:

Rule I: Almost all criminal defendants are, in fact, guilty.

Rule II: All criminal defense lawyers, prosecutors and judges understand and believe Rule I.

Rule III: It is easier to convict guilty defendants by violating the Constitution than by complying with it, and in some cases it is impossible to convict guilty defendants without violating the Constitution.

Rule IV: Almost all police lie about whether they violated the Constitution in order to convict guilty defendants.

Rule V: All prosecutors, judges, and defense attorneys are aware of Rule IV.

Rule VI: Many prosecutors implicitly encourage police to lie about whether they violated the Constitution in order to convict guilty defendants.

Rule VII: All judges are aware of Rule VI.

Rule VIII: Most trial judges pretend to believe police officers who they know are lying.

Rule IX: All appellate judges are aware of Rule VIII, yet many pretend to believe the trial judges who pretend to believe the lying police officers.

Rule X: Most judges disbelieve defendants about whether their constitutional rights have been violated, even if they are telling the truth.

Rule XI: Most judges and prosecutors would not knowingly convict a defendant who they believe to be innocent of the crime charged (or a closely related crime).

Rule XII: Rule XI does not apply to members of organized crime, drug dealers, career criminals, or potential informers.

Rule XIII: Nobody really wants justice.

B. THE POLICE

HERBERT PACKER, THE LIMITS OF THE CRIMINAL SANCTION
283-284 (1968)

The aggressively interventionist character of much of our criminal law thrusts the police into the role of snoopers and harassers. There is simply no way for the police to provide so much as a semblance of enforcement of laws against prostitution, sexual deviance, gambling, narcotics, and the like without widespread and visible intrusion into what people regard as their private lives. . . .

There are three generic types of police investigatory conduct that are so at odds with values of privacy and human dignity that we should resort to them only under the most exigent circumstances. They are physical intrusion, electronic surveillance, and the use of decoys. Although there arguably are circumstances under which each of the three can justifiably be employed, it is safe to say that any use of the criminal sanction that requires consistent use to be made of any of them should be suspect.

NORVAL MORRIS & GORDON HAWKINS, THE HONEST POLITICIAN'S GUIDE TO CRIME CONTROL
88-89 (1970)

[I]n this country we have one of the most moralistic criminal law systems that the world has yet produced. It is enforceable only in a sporadic, uneven, and discriminatory fashion. We have the most severe drug laws and the largest number of addicts. We have highly restrictive sex laws in a society that can hardly be regarded as dedicated either to monogamy or the missionary position in copulation, and in which sexual stimuli are ubiquitous. In relation to these laws the police have ritual, sacerdotal functions to perform, like a secular priesthood. And they have also to handle our drunks and alcoholics, our snarled and feverish traffic, our vagrants, our treed cats, our parading dignitaries, some of our gamblers, our burgeoning riots, and in the remainder of their time to protect us from serious crime.

. . . [T]he community and the politicians are . . . irresponsibly ambivalent in what they expect of the police in the violent, mobile, anonymous, race-conscious, crowded swirl of urban existence. In many of our cities we pay the police less than the garbage collectors, overload them with a morally pretentious law, and require them to demonstrate wisdom and skill higher than that expected of any of the established professions. The policeman is required to be an expert on the law, a psychologist, a strategist, on occasion a midwife, a protector of public safety, a ruthless prosecutor of crime, and at the same time a guardian of civil liberty.

JEROME H. SKOLNICK & DAVID H. BAYLEY, COMMUNITY POLICING: ISSUES AND PRACTICES AROUND THE WORLD
49-52 (1988)

One way of comprehending a police department is through a table of organization. Such tables do offer useful, indeed indispensable, information. . . . But however indispensable they might be, tables of organization are limited in the information they offer—they don't tell us anything about the human side of the landscape they describe. The most significant features of police departments—their attitudes, internal divisions, belief systems, traditions, values—cannot be captured by the labelled boxes of a table of organization. . . .

How police officers learn to see the world around them and their role in it has come to be acknowledged by all scholars of police as an indispensable key to understanding the behavior and attitudes of police. "It is a commonplace of the now voluminous sociological literature on police operations and discretion," writes Robert Reiner, "that the rank-and-file officer is the primary determinant of policing where it really counts—on the street."[1] Moreover, . . . there are identifiable commonalities in police culture. . . .

[There is] the perception of *danger*, which, although real, is typically magnified. Police officers are sometimes shot at and killed, of course. But the first line of defense against anticipated danger is *suspicion*, the development of a cognitive map of the social world to protect against signs of trouble, offense, and potential threat.

The combination of danger and suspicion leads to a third feature of police culture, namely solidarity or *brotherhood*. Most police tend to socialize with other police. . . . There are any number of reasons for police solidarity. One is that police do not work normal hours. As emergency service workers, they often find themselves in the position of having to work nights, weekends, and other odd hours. Police work time is one of the major stresses of police work. When one's days off are Wednesday and Thursday, one becomes a deviant in the social world and is drawn to socialize with others who are similarly situated.

Another reason is that cops don't feel they fit into many worlds they might occupy. Every cop has a story about how they were stared at or otherwise adversely noted at a party or social occasion. This has been a special problem for young police in the 1970's and 1980's, when many of their peers might light up a joint and pass it around at a festive occasion.

1. Robert Reiner, The Politics of the Police (Sussex, England: Wheatsheaf Books, 1985), p.85.

When faced with this dilemma, young police will find new friends—
among police.

A third reason is the policeman's felt need for support from other
police. Police are in fact in dangerous or potentially dangerous situations.
When cops, looking for drug dealers, walk through a pool hall occupied
by unfriendly young men, they depend on their partners for cover and
assistance. But, as Mark Baker comments:

> The real reason most police officers socialize exclusively with other police
> officers is that they just don't trust the people they police—which is every-
> body who is not a cop. They know the public generally resents their
> authority and is fickle in its support of police policy and individual police
> officers. Older officers teach younger ones that it is best to avoid civilians.
> Civilians will try to "hurt" the cop in the end, they say.[2]

. . .

Students of the police have frequently noted the *machismo* qualities
in the world of policing.[3] Those who are attracted to the occupation are
often very young, in chronological age and in maturity of temperament
and judgment. . . . Recruits typically have athletic backgrounds, are
sports minded, and are trained in self-defense. It is not uncommon for
trainees to bulk the upper body—like football players, through weight
lifting—so as to offer a more formidable appearance as a potential adversary in street encounters. They are also trained to handle a variety of
offensive weapons, including deadly weapons. They are taught how to
disable and kill people with their bare hands. No matter how many
warnings may be offered by superiors about limitations on the use of
force, its possible use is a central feature of the police role, and of the
policemen's perceptions of themselves.

The training and permission in the use of force combined with the
youth of police can well inhibit the capacity of a police officer to em-
pathize with the situation of those being policed in ethnically diverse and
low-income neighborhoods. . . . Senior officers are . . . less likely to
be macho. . . .

When scholars write about the culture of policing, they usually have
in mind the street-wise cop who follows a blue code of solidarity with
fellow officers. Street-wise officers are likely to be cynical, tough, skeptical
of innovation within management. By contrast, management cops tend
to project a vision of policing that is more acceptable to the general
public. This concept of two contrasting cultures of policing grew out of
research conducted in New York City by Ianni and Ianni (1983), who

  2. Mark Baker, Cops: Their Lives in Their Own Words (New York: Fawcett, 1985),
p.211.
  3. See Robert Reiner, The Politics of the Police, p.99.

developed a distinction between "street cops" and "management cops."

The "street-wise" cop is apt to approve of cutting corners, of throwing weight around on the street, of expressing the qualities of in-group solidarity referred to above. Management cops tend to be more legalistic, rule oriented, rational. . . . [S]ome street cops are hard-boiled cynics who deride innovations in policing as needless and unworkable incursions into the true and eternal role of the cop—the one they were socialized into as recruits by a sometimes venerated field training officer. These "street-wise" police, instead of gradually developing a broader perspective, taking advanced degrees in management, law, or criminal justice and so forth, reinforce their post-recruit identity. Unfortunately, this reinforcement sometimes develops into a lifelong occupational vision rooted in an abiding, even growing, bitterness that seems impervious to any sort of hope for change or new ideas.

The cynicism typifying these officers may of course also be present at higher levels of management—after all, . . . all American police begin their career as street cops, and the learning that takes place on the street is never outgrown by many. . . . The innovative management cop employs prior street experience to overcome the resistance of the street cop. By contrast, the self-conception of the traditional street cop remains firmly rooted in his earliest training experiences.

Elizabeth Ruess-Ianni summarizes the difference between the two cultures as follows, based on her study of the New York City Police Department:

> In a sense, the management cop culture represents those police who have decided that the old way of running a police department is finished (for a variety of external reasons, such as social pressures, economic realities of the city, increased visibility, minority recruitment, and growth in size that cannot be managed easily in the informal fashion of the old days) and they are "going to get in on the ground floor of something new." They do not, like the street cops, regard community relations, for example, as "Mickey Mouse bullshit," but as something that must be done for politically expedient reasons if not for social ones.[4]

JAMES Q. WILSON, VARIETIES OF POLICE BEHAVIOR
16-19, 21-24, 30-31, 36-37 (1973)

The patrolman's role is defined more by his responsibility for *maintaining order* than by his responsibility for enforcing the law . . . for several

---

4. Elizabeth Ruess-Ianni, The Two Cultures of Policing: Street Cops and Management Cops (Brunswick, N.J.: Transaction Books, New Brunswick, 1983), p. 121.

reasons. First, in at least the larger or more socially heterogeneous cities, the patrolman encounters far more problems of order maintenance than opportunities for law enforcement, except with respect to traffic laws. . . .

Second, the maintenance of order exposes the patrolman to physical danger, and his reaction in turn may expose the disputants to danger. Statistically, the risk of injury or death to the patrolman may not be great in order maintenance situations but it exists and, worse, it is unpredictable, occurring, as almost every officer interviewed testified, "when you least expect it." . . .

But most important, the order maintenance function necessarily involves the exercising of substantial discretion[3] over matters of the greatest importance (public and private morality, honor and dishonor, life and death) in a situation that is, by definition, one of conflict and in an environment that is apprehensive and perhaps hostile.

Discretion exists both because many of the relevant laws are necessarily ambiguous and because, under the laws of many states governing arrests for certain forms of disorder, the "victim" must cooperate with the patrolman if the law is to be invoked at all. . . . Laws regarding disorderly conduct and the like assert, usually by implication, that there is a *condition* ("public order") that can be diminished by various actions. The difficulty, of course, is that public order is nowhere defined and can never be defined unambiguously. . . .

Certain forms of disorderly or disputatious behavior can be given a relatively unambiguous legal definition—assault or battery, for example. Striking or wounding another person is legally definable because we can agree on what an unstruck or unwounded person looks like. But here another difficulty arises—the need for victim cooperation. Most crimes the patrolman is concerned with are misdemeanors. . . . [U]nder the law of many states, an officer can make an arrest for a misdemeanor only when the act has been committed in his presence or upon the properly sworn complaint of a citizen in whose presence it was committed.

But it is the exception, not the rule, for the "victim" to cooperate in this way. . . . Even though he or she may not want to swear out a complaint, especially if this requires going downtown the next morning, the victim usually wants the police to "do something." A typical case, one which I witnessed many times, involves a wife with a black eye telling the patrolman she wants her husband, who she alleges hit her, "thrown out of the house." The officer knows he has no authority to throw husbands out of their homes and he tells her so. She is dissatisfied. He suggests she file a complaint, but she does not want her husband arrested.

---

3. Earlier Wilson observed, "[T]he police department has the special property (shared with few other organizations) that within it discretion increases as one moves *down* the hierarchy." Varieties of Police Behavior, page 7.—EDS.

She may promise to make a complaint the next morning, but the patrolman knows from experience that she will probably change her mind
later. If the officer does nothing about the quarrel, he is "uncooperative";
if he steps in, he is in danger of exceeding his authority. Some patrolmen
develop ways of mollifying everyone, others get out as quickly as they
can, but all dislike such situations and find them awkward and risky.

The difficulty of maintaining order is further exacerbated by the fact
that the patrolman's discretion is exercised in an emotional, apprehensive,
and perhaps hostile environment. . . .

In sum, the order-maintenance function of the patrolman defines
his role and that role, which is unlike that of any other occupation, can
be described as one in which *sub-professionals, working alone, exercise
wide discretion in matters of utmost importance (life and death, honor
and dishonor) in an environment that is apprehensive and perhaps hostile.*
The agents of various other governmental organizations may display one
or two of these characteristics, but none or almost none display all in
combination. The doctor has wide discretion over matters of life and
death, but he is a professional working in a supportive environment. The
teacher works alone and has considerable discretion, but he may be a
professional and in any case education, though important, is not a matter
of life or death. A welfare worker, though working alone among apprehensive clients, has relatively little discretion—the laws define rather
precisely what payments he can authorize to a client and supervisors
review his written reports and proposed family budgets.

. . . To the patrolman, the law is one resource among many that
he may use to deal with disorder, but it is not the only one or even the
most important; beyond that, the law is a constraint that tells him what
he must *not* do but is peculiarly unhelpful in telling him what he *should*
do. Thus, he approaches incidents that threaten order *not in terms of
enforcing the law but in terms of "handling the situation."* The officer
is expected, by colleagues as well as superiors, to "handle his beat." This
means keeping things under control so that there are no complaints that
he is doing nothing or that he is doing too much. To handle his beat,
the law provides one resource, the possibility of arrest, and a set of
constraints, *but it does not supply to the patrolman a set of legal rules to
be applied.* A phrase heard by interviewers countless times is "You can't
go by what the book says." . . .

JUSTICE AS A CONSTRAINT

Because of their function, patrolmen face in a special way the problem
of justice. Justice—by which I mean, provisionally, fairness, or treating

equals equally—is a constraint on the conduct of any organization, especially any public bureaucracy. . . .

The implicit conception of justice the patrolman brings to his task is quite different from that assumed to operate in "the administration of criminal justice" or "law enforcement." Treating equals equally in a courtroom means to assume that all who enter there are equal before the law. Because such persons are by then meek in demeanor and correct in speech, the assumption seems plausible. The patrolman, however, sees these people when they are dirty, angry, rowdy, obscene, dazed, savage, or bloodied. To him, they are not in these circumstances "equal," they are *different*. What they deserve depends on what they *are*. "Decent people" and "bums" are not equal; "studs" and "working stiffs" are not equal; victims and suspects are not equal, except in some ultimate and, at the moment, irrelevant sense. To be just to these people means to give each what he deserves and to judge what he deserves by how he acts and talks. This is close to the ancient conception of "distributive" justice, which holds that things and honors should be divided among persons according to merit or so that inequality in person is reflected by a proportional inequality in treatment. . . .

A "wise guy" deserves less than a "good guy," a man who does not accept police authority, and thus legal authority, deserves less than a man who does. The courts, however, view such situations, not in terms of distributive justice, but in terms of assigning guilt and correcting, by appropriate penalties, a specific and individual departure from a condition of initial equality. Again, the judge and the patrolman see things differently and consequently view each other with chronic suspicion and sometimes active dislike.

The problem is, of course, exacerbated when the participants in an incident are of radically different subcultures—white officers and Negro citizens, for example. The officer, less familiar with what is "normal" behavior, may make imputations of virtue and just deserts along racial lines, overlooking important (and, among white persons, obvious) individual differences. And the citizens may believe the patrolman *is* making such arbitrary imputations, whether or not he is, and by acting on that belief, resist or challenge his authority in such a way as to intensify the conflict between them.

ALLEN, THE POLICE AND SUBSTANTIVE RULEMAKING: RECONCILING PRINCIPLE AND EXPEDIENCY

125 U. Pa. L. Rev. 62, 62-67, 69-71, 73-75, 81-82, 85-86, 94-95, 97-98 (1976)

Until recently the police were often regarded as impartial, unbiased, nondiscriminating enforcers of the criminal law, possessing and exercising no discretion in the decision to invoke the criminal process when a violation of the criminal law is brought to their attention. This conception, known as the "myth of full enforcement," was thought to represent the appropriate role of police in our society: "The police, in our legal tradition, are essentially ministerial officers. To them have been delegated relatively few grants of discretionary power. . . ."[2] Accordingly, it has long been assumed that the "police will arrest all who violate the criminal law."[3]

This charming folklore of the policeman as an impartial ministerial officer who enforces the letter of the law against all known violators did not prove to be an accurate reflection of reality, and there has been a growing realization that the cop on the beat often exercises discretion in his decision to invoke or not to invoke the criminal process. As a result of this realization that the police are not simply ministerial officers, we have been forced to face some very hard questions that have been ignored until recently. The most obvious of these questions is the propriety, both as a legal and as a policy matter, of the police exercising discretion in enforcing the criminal law. As might be expected, there is no consensus on the answer. Some think that the myth of full enforcement should reflect reality, even though it presently does not, and that the appropriate role of the police is to enforce to the best of their abilities whatever statutes are enacted by the legislature. Others believe that the exercise of discretion not to invoke the criminal process is inevitable and "that idealism or naivete or both must be present in king-size doses in order to sustain the position that the legislature can or should play an exclusive role in the molding of criminal law policy."[9]

This dispute over the appropriate relationship of the police to the legislature is largely a function of a perceived divergence of theory and practice in the administration of criminal law. Those who feel that the

---

2. Parratt, How Effective Is a Police Department?, 199 Annals 153 (1938).
3. Remington & Rosenblum, The Criminal Law and the Legislative Process, 1960 U. Ill. L.F. 481, 496. Professors Remington and Rosenblum do not accept the myth. In fact, their article is one of the earlier pieces arguing its inaccuracy.
9. Remington & Rosenblum, supra note 3, at 482 n.2.

police should not exercise discretion believe that the rule of law mandates that conclusion regardless of actual police practice on the streets. Others, however, are more impressed by the apparent inevitability of police discretion and believe that theory ought to be conformed to reality. The latter individuals are concerned with controlling discretion "so as to avoid the unequal, the arbitrary, the discriminatory and the oppressive."[13] As one observer noted, the relevant inquiry "is to try to find or invent better ways to control police discretion in determining whether and when to enforce particular law."[14]

An unmistakable trend has developed in these attempts "to devise procedures which will result in police officers employing norms acceptable to society, rather than their personal norms, in their exercise of discretion";[15] criminal law theorists have become increasingly enchanted with the use of administrative rulemaking to limit and guide the exercise of discretion. The genesis of this development is largely attributable to The President's Commission on Law Enforcement and Administration of Justice, which gave national exposure to the idea of administrative rulemaking as a method of controlling police discretion. Since then the idea of administrative rulemaking has been heralded by numerous commentators as a cure for myriad ills. Some argue that rulemaking offers a viable alternative to the exclusionary rule as a means of protecting procedural rights of the populace. Others suggest that rulemaking may be useful in developing guidelines to facilitate police work in sensitive areas such as the use of firearms, the appropriate police posture during times of civil unrest, and appropriate responses to domestic disturbances. Still others believe that rulemaking should be used to deal with the most intractable problem of all—selective enforcement of the substantive criminal law—and suggest that the police should cut back, and in essence amend, overly broad and consequently unenforceable statutes to manageable size through the administrative rulemaking process. . . .

I. SUBSTANTIVE RULEMAKING BY THE POLICE . . .

A. FULL ENFORCEMENT LEGISLATION

Wayne LaFave has observed that "[a]lmost every state has some legislation relevant to police discretion,"[46] and, although he is correct in

13. Breitel, [Controls in Criminal Law Enforcement, 27 U. Chi. L. Rev. 427 (1960)].
14. K. Davis, Preface to Police Discretion (1975) at iii. . . .
15. Goldstein, [Police Policy Formulation: A Proposal for Improving Police Performance, 65 Mich. L. Rev. 1123 (1967)].
46. W. LaFave, [Arrest: The Decision to Take a Suspect into Custody 76 (1965)].

his further observation that "there is a distinct lack of originality"[47] in these statutes, an examination of them makes one point abundantly clear—these statutes consistently purport to deny police the discretion not to invoke the criminal law. . . .

[Notwithstanding the fact] . . . that police discretion has not received "express recognition," it may still be argued that these statutes should not be interpreted literally. . . . As Kenneth Culp Davis concluded after reviewing the full enforcement statutes: . . .

> . . . Legislators know that their criminal legislation often overshoots. Their draftsmen know that if they make too much criminal, the law enforcement people—police, prosecutors, and judges—will cut it back to make it sensible. Their intent often is clear that the police should not interpret criminal legislation literally and then enforce it fully. . . . [A]ll informed persons are in agreement that full enforcement is impossible with the present appropriation and the present system of operation. So the legislative voice in the appropriation speaks with irresistible power; the police clearly lack the resources for full enforcement.[58] . . .

Davis apparently believes that since the full enforcement statutes cannot be taken as unqualified commands to enforce every criminal prohibition against all offenders, the police are free to pick and choose the statutes to be enforced, and he thinks the picking and choosing should be done by way of administrative rulemaking. Davis reaches this result by equating the admitted inability to enforce fully our criminal laws with the legality of a consistent practice of nonenforcement. Since such a practice is legal, he reasons, a rule authorizing or describing it must also be legal. Were the inability to enforce fully all the laws and a consistent, legal practice of nonenforcement equivalents, the rest of his argument would be unassailable; there seems little reason not to allow a consistent, legal practice to be codified by rule. Davis' major premise, however, is invalid. The mere inability to enforce fully all laws says little about what the police are authorized to do in response to the inability. Thus, even if the police are unable to enforce "all the criminal laws," that alone does not necessarily justify the deliberate nonenforcement of any particular statute, nor does it necessarily accord the police the power to nullify penal provisions by administrative rulemaking. Similarly, "legislative acquiescence" does not further Davis' argument, even if its existence is conceded. Acquiescence in selective enforcement only proves that legislatures realize the impossibility of full enforcement. That falls far short of legitimating the power Davis wishes the police to exercise. . . .

47. Id.
58. Police Discretion, supra note 14, at 80-81.

C. SEPARATION OF POWERS APPLIED: DESUETUDE AND DELEGATION

"Desuetude" is the ancient doctrine that long and continuous failure to enforce a statute, coupled with open and widespread violation of it by the populace, is tantamount to repeal of the statute: . . .

Although there is some dispute over how well desuetude has fared elsewhere, courts in the United States have consistently rejected it. . . .

Consider what the rejection of desuetude as a principle of our law suggests about the power of the police to provide by rule for the nonenforcement of a criminal statute. As I have already shown, such a rule would, in effect, amend or repeal the relevant statute. If a law cannot be "rendered ineffective . . . by failure of those entrusted with its administration to enforce it"[107] over a long and continuous period of time, and in the face of known widespread violations, what power is there for "those entrusted with its administration" to render that law ineffective by rule simply because in their judgment it is not a wise enactment? The analogy is a powerful one, and compels the conclusion that the police may *not* "legally provide for nonenforcement of a criminal statute or ordinance."[109]

This conclusion is supported further by the role that the principle of delegation of powers plays in the criminal law. . . .

The delegation of rulemaking authority to an agency . . . will often be upheld where the subject matter requires a technical expertise. Delegation will also be upheld where another special attribute, the ability to spend vast amounts of time on relatively inconsequential matters, is required. Thus the mundane affairs of running sewers and airports can be delegated to an agency; legislative time is better spent on other matters. . . .

Neither of these characteristics is involved in the aspects of the criminalization process with which Davis and other substantive rulemaking advocates are concerned. A legislature does not need experts to tell whether to criminalize possession of marijuana or to prohibit drinking in the park. In fact, there is no better body than the legislature, assuming it is representative of the populace, to do this task of criminalizing. Furthermore, these decisions to criminalize conduct are not trivial matters. Thus the two justifications for delegation of rulemaking power to agencies—the need for technical expertise and the repetitive, relatively trivial nature of the subject matter—are not applicable to those portions of the substantive criminal law Davis' police rulemaking is designed to affect. . . .

107. J. Sutherland, [IA Statutes and Statutory Constructions, §23.25, at 267].
109. Police Discretion, supra note 14, at 90. Of course, Davis was making the opposite point.

Davis' belief to the contrary rests largely on his assumption that the police are closely analogous to administrative agencies and should be dealt with accordingly. The crucial error permeating this view is a failure to perceive, or at least to acknowledge, the different roles of the typical administrative agency and the police. Administrative agencies are regulatory bodies created to supervise relationships within their jurisdictions. The police, on the other hand, are not instructed to regulate; their purpose is to enforce prohibitions articulated by the legislature. We do not say to the police: "Here is the problem. Deal with it." We say: "Here is a detailed code. Enforce it." In short, the police perform a very different function from that of a regulatory agency.

The confusions that emanate from this beguiling analogy are evident in the following passage from another of substantive rulemaking's proponents:

> Certainly there is no reason to expect that legislatures can be more effective with respect to the work of police than they were with respect to the task of the economic regulatory agency. The "administrative process" and administrative flexibility, expertise, and, most important, administrative responsibility are as necessary and as appropriate with respect to the regulation of deviant social behavior as they are with respect to other governmental regulatory activity. This seems perfectly obvious. [157]

I suppose it is "perfectly obvious" that if the role of the police is "the regulation of deviant social behavior," then "there is no reason to expect" miracles from the legislature. The purpose of the police, however, is not *regulation* of deviant behavior; it is *enforcement* of legislative proscriptions. When the proper role of the police is kept in mind, the role of the legislature can be viewed in its proper perspective. It then becomes very reasonable indeed to expect, and even demand, that the legislature fulfill its responsibilities.

In any case, whether for policy reasons or because of the constitutional doctrines discussed in this Article, no state legislature has ever delegated to the police the power to promulgate rules affecting the scope of the substantive criminal law. To the contrary, many states have full enforcement statutes that explicitly deny the police the discretion not to enforce criminal laws. Thus, even if I am incorrect that no delegations to the police in this area would be upheld by the courts, it is still clear that the police have no present authority to engage in substantive rulemaking. Indeed, if the delegation cases in this area tell us anything, it is that the police have no authority to engage in substantive rulemaking

---

157. [The President's Commission on Law Enforcement and Administration of Justice, Task Force Report: The Police 18 (1967).]

without explicit legislative authorization accompanied by precise standards. This requirement of precise and explicit legislative standards demonstrates that, contrary to Davis' position, neither legislative acquiescence in selective enforcement nor legislative appropriations that are insufficient for full enforcement provide adequate authorization for the police to engage in substantive rulemaking, even if there were no full enforcement statutes. . . .

DAVIS, POLICE RULEMAKING ON SELECTIVE ENFORCEMENT: A REPLY
125 U. Pa. L. Rev. 1167, 1168-1170 (1977)

My view is the rather obvious one, which [Professor Allen] rejects, that because "full enforcement is impossible," some law must be wholly or partially unenforced even if the result is what he considers to be repeal or amendment of enacted law.

Because "full enforcement is impossible" and "departmental priorities" are necessary, I think any solution probably has to involve a choice between two main courses of action (or some mixture of the two): (1) the present system of allowing selective enforcement policies to be made primarily by patrolmen, with some significant but unsystematic instructions from top officers, or (2) something along the line of my proposal that top officers should make the main selective enforcement policies through systematic studies and rulemaking proceedings. Professor Allen strongly opposes the second course. . . .

In advancing his thesis that police rules on selective enforcement are "inconsistent with our theory of government," Professor Allen apparently does not realize that the police have always had such rules. Selective enforcement in the Anglo-American system goes all the way back to the early English constables. American police organizations have always had some rules about selective enforcement. No court has ever held such rules invalid, and no court is likely to do so.

A rookie patrolman asks his sergeant: "When I'm hurrying to my beat and I find someone smoking in the elevator, do I have to arrest him?" The sergeant says: "Hell no." Thus is created a rule on selective enforcement.

While the men stand at attention on Monday morning, the chief expresses his anger about what one of the neophytes has done: "When you're after a robber, for God's sake don't stop to make an arrest for spitting on the sidewalk or drinking in the park." That is a rule on selective enforcement.

A patrolman brings in a sixteen-year-old for smoking marijuana.

After the booking, the watch commander says to the patrolman: "Why did you waste your time on that? Don't you know the state's attorney's office won't prosecute?" The result is a rule on selective enforcement for that patrolman, and he will spread the word to his colleagues.

No patrolman would arrest a twelve-year-old who gets a new bicycle and innocently rides it on the sidewalk. Even if the unspoken rule that the boy first should be warned is inconsistent with what the legislative body has said and, in Professor Allen's view, is an "amendment" of the ordinance and therefore a violation of the theory of separation of powers, we may all be thankful that the common sense of the patrolman supersedes that kind of legal thinking.

The reader can make his own guess as to whether any department in the country is likely to be without a rule on selective enforcement along the following line: "When you can arrest only one of two offenders, ordinarily you should choose the one who has committed the more serious offense." Such a rule is a rule on selective enforcement. It need not be made explicit. Any intelligent officer, without instruction, is likely under his own power to arrive at some such rule. . . .

ALLEN, THE POLICE AND SUBSTANTIVE RULEMAKING: A BRIEF REJOINDER
125 U. Pa. L. Rev. 1172, 1174-1179 (1977)

Professor Davis' belief that substantive rulemaking is permissible rests largely on his unwillingness to discriminate among the various reasons for nonenforcement by the police. He is correct in observing that "nonenforcement" in certain circumstances is "legal." No one, for example, would hold the police responsible for not enforcing a particular statute in a situation in which an offense never became known to the police and would not have become known to them on the basis of the most diligent inquiry. This kind of "legal" nonenforcement, however, simply does not accord the police the power to decide not to enforce particular statutes that they think are unwise or unjust. Nor does the fact that allocation decisions must be made, or that a patrolman might have to decide which of two offenders to arrest, or that individual officers are violating the full enforcement mandate, require the conclusion that the police may institutionally decide not to enforce selected penal prohibitions. In essence, Professor Davis' argument amounts to no more than the assertion that because nonenforcement is "legal" in certain circumstances, it is legal in all circumstances (barring constitutional limitation). Obviously, the legality of nonenforcement is more complex than that.

Apart from refusing to discriminate among the sources of nonenforcement, Professor Davis attempts to buttress his position by invoking some appealing hypotheticals. . . .

Professor Davis' hypotheticals are designed to show the absurdity of advocating enforcement according to the letter of the law of the statutes the legislature enacts. They are designed to make the reader think: "Does Allen really wish to see 'innocent twelve-year-olds' thrown in the slammer for riding bicycles on sidewalks, and does he really think that the police should squander precious resources, and perhaps assign undercover agents, to enforce the smoking ban in elevators?" Of course I do not think such things, and I would often applaud the refusal of a police officer to enforce the law in appealing circumstances; but the fact that a police officer, Professor Davis and I may happen to agree that a particular law ought not to be enforced in a particular instance hardly forces the conclusion that substantive rulemaking with respect to that statute is permissible, or that a police officer should be excused from enforcing a statute because he, Professor Davis, and I agree that the law makes no sense at all. More importantly, our happy concurrence does not support the conclusion that empowering the police to enact substantive rules mandating nonenforcement would be wise.

In the final analysis, these hypotheticals do not support substantive rulemaking because they merely demonstrate the absurdity of certain statutes as written, rather than the absurdity of mandating enforcement of those statutes. Professor Davis appears to take the position that if the legislature refuses to repeal a silly law on the books, then the police through substantive rulemaking should nullify the enactment. What this view fails to consider, as I pointed out in my Article, is the possible costs of granting the police this power, and I will not repeat my arguments here. I will summarize them, however, in my own hypothetical that presents many of the issues that Professor Davis has not considered.

Consider a police chief of a small town—a hardened veteran who has "come up the ranks" and who has just been informed by Professor Davis that he can choose not to enforce those statutes that he thinks are unwise or unjust. What if he happens to believe that enforcing the "no riding on sidewalks" ban is not nearly as troublesome as enforcing the rape law? What if he also thinks that, as a rule, only those women who "ask for it" are raped, and that enforcing the stiff rape law against men whose only crime, in our hypothetical police chief's view, is that of obliging these immoral women is a tremendous waste of valuable resources—resources that could better be used to stop twelve-year-olds from harassing elderly ladies with their kamikaze activities on bicycles? Can the chief "lawfully" decide not to enforce the rape law? If he can lawfully decide not to enforce the cohabitation law and certain drug laws, as Professor Davis intimates, why not the rape law, or, for that matter, the bribery law, the extortion law, or the robbery law? Where, in short, is the line to be drawn in this process of independent evaluation by the police of the wisdom of legislative actions? It is not enough to point to what he and I might think are silly or overly broad statutes. Others may disagree with our assessment, which is precisely why we have legislative bodies. And even if there is general agreement regarding what "silly laws" should not be on the books, Professor Davis fails to indicate how substantive rulemaking would be limited to such laws and why, if there is such universal agreement, the legislative process is an inadequate mechanism for reform. . . .

So far, I have elaborated only specific problems that I have with Professor Davis' proposal, and I think a few words concerning my own views on the control of police discretion are in order. It seems to me that we should give the cop on the beat as much guidance as we can on how to spend his time in order to maximize his effectiveness, and we should also give him guidance on which course of action he should choose if faced with alternative possibilities. We should make crystal clear, however, that we expect him to enforce the law as provided by the legislature, and that he will be sanctioned if discovered not doing so. . . . Even if discretionary decisionmaking is inevitable, our efforts to eliminate such behavior should at least serve to restrict it.

More should be done, however, than merely exhorting police officers to do their duty and threatening them with sanctions if they swerve from the tight and narrow. I will not address revising the substantive criminal law to eliminate overly broad provisions and sumptuary prohibitions, which is theoretically the most promising means of reducing police discretion, because there seems to be agreement that the chance of major legislative effort in those directions is small. Even without major substantive revision, though, there is much the legislature can do to reduce the incidence of lawless discretionary action by the police. One of the most significant sources of lawless police decisions not to invoke the criminal process surely must be the lack of a set of flexible responses to the widely varying situations the police often face. To use one of Professor Davis' hypotheticals, if an officer is forced to choose between arresting an "innocent" twelve-year-old for riding his bicycle on the sidewalk or letting him go free, what is he going to do? The answer is obvious, assuming that the chief of police and the mayor are nowhere in sight. Yet why should the officer be forced to choose between an asinine but legal alternative and a more reasonable but unlawful response? Instead of placing the officer in this dilemma, the legislature should explicitly provide him with the power to explain to the child his mistake, coupled with a warning that if the behavior does not cease, the child's parents, and, if necessary, the juvenile authorities, will be contacted. . . .

For a different view of the significance of full-enforcement statutes and a superb discussion of police discretion generally, see G. Williams, The Law and Politics of Police Discretion (1984).

C. THE LAWYERS AND THE TRIAL COURTS

PAUL B. WICE, CHAOS IN THE COURTHOUSE: THE INNER WORKINGS OF THE URBAN CRIMINAL COURTS
21-24, 63-65 (1985)

The first problem faced by all cities visited[4] was inadequate staffing. Although particular agencies or institutions within each city's criminal justice system may have differing levels of understaffing, all were handicapped in some degree by personnel shortages. . . . These shortages were documented by federal commission studies in 1967 and 1973.[2] . . .

. . . The judges appeared to be most understaffed at the earlier stages of the adjudicative process—initial appearance, preliminary hearing and arraignment. The arraignment court may also be responsible for deciding pretrial motions, scheduling trials, and conducting pre-sentencing hearings in addition to accepting guilty pleas. By the trial stage, the staffing shortages had generally abated to a tolerable level in most cities. . . .

Closely related to the staffing problems, is the serious backlog of cases. . . .

The most common method criminal courts utilize in dealing with their caseload and delay problems is the practice of plea bargaining. Despite the negative connotations of this term, it describes a negotiating process which has been taking place within our nation's court systems . . . for many decades. A *plea bargain* is simply an agreement between the defendant (with the advice of his attorney) and the prosecutor, that in exchange for a plea of guilty, he will receive favorable consideration

---

4. This book is based on the study of criminal courts in fifteen major jurisdictions over a twelve year period. Chaos in the Courthouse, at 1.—Eds.

2. President's Commission on Law Enforcement and the Administration of Justice, Task Force Report: The Courts. (Washington, D.C.: Government Printing Office, 1967). National Advisory Commission on Criminal Justice Goals and Standards, Courts. (Washington, D.C.: Government Printing Office, 1973).

by the court. This consideration usually takes the form of being charged
with a less serious crime, which will usually result in a lighter sentence
or receiving the minimum punishment allowable for the originally-charged
offense. The rationale behind this exchange of favors is that the defendant
is given the lesser sentence because of his cooperation with the court in
choosing not to go to trial and thereby saving the city a great deal of time
and expense. . . . .

. . . . Various studies have indicated that approximately 75 percent
of all defendants indicted for felonies plead guilty.[5] . . .

Since nearly two thirds of all defendants accused of committing a
felony are indigent, the state is constitutionally obligated to provide the
overwhelming majority of defendants with assistance of counsel. In nearly
every city visited, the local courts decided to establish a public defender
program in order to meet this mandate. . . .

The two alternatives to the public defender plan, for indigent defendants, are either to rely entirely upon an assigned counsel system—
privately-appointed members of the bar who are typically paid on a per
hour basis—or a mixed system in which the courts have decided to limit
the percentage of cases which the local public defender can handle, and
reserve the sizable remainder for private attorneys through an assigned
counsel system. Large cities rarely find the assigned counsel system cost-
effective (although it is most popular in small cities and rural areas). . . .

In most cities, the defendant first notifies the judge of his indigent
status and desire to have a court-appointed lawyer at his initial appearance. . . . The judge rarely inquires into the financial capabilities of
the defendant. . . . Most judges seem to feel that if a defendant is
willing to settle for a public defender, then he is not likely to be in
possession of the funds necessary to hire a private attorney. Rarely is a
representative from the public defender's office present at this initial
appearance, except in an administrative capacity to commence the pa-
perwork. . . .

Two of the major frustrations facing the indigent defendant who is
being represented by a public defender are apparent very early in the
process. The first, and for many defendants, the most disheartening, is
the absence of choice of attorney. . . .

The second frustration, exacerbating the already noted absence of
choice, is the assembly-line system of defense in which the indigent
defendant may be assisted by a different attorney at nearly every stage of
the proceedings up to the arraignment. This means that the indigent will
briefly meet with three or four different public defenders for a few minutes

5. Pasqual DeVito. An Experiment in the Use of Court Statistics, Judicature. 56
(August/September, 1972), p. 56.

before each of his pretrial proceedings. It is also likely that interviews and meetings outside of court may be with an assortment of different public defenders. . . .

For many defendants, the assembly-line style of operation is another indication that the public defender's office is simply an uncaring bureaucracy which is both financially and emotionally subservient to the criminal court judiciary. . . .

Although I am sure that their clientele would vociferously disagree, I do not believe that the quality of public defender services has suffered. After conducting national studies of both public defender programs and private criminal lawyers, I am in agreement with the findings of nearly all of the empirical research which concluded that the ultimate case dispositions are not significantly affected by the type of defense.[31] I still concur with the personal conclusions reached in 1978 that

> although the middle 50 percent of public defenders and private attorneys were operating at similar levels of ability and achieving nearly identical results, there were marked differences at the extremes. Thus it was generally agreed by the criminal lawyers that the top 25 percent of private attorneys were clearly superior to the best public defenders, while the bottom 25 of the public defenders were believed to be significantly better than the bottom group of private attorneys. [Paul Wice, Criminal Lawyers: An Endangered Species. Beverly Hills, Sage Publications, 1978, p. 201.]

. . . [T]he public defender office may even offer some distinct advantages unavailable to certain private practitioners. Most public defenders have access to their own law libraries, as well as limited use of investigators. Additionally, the public defender is clearly a criminal law specialist. Finally, because of his continual involvement with the prosecutors and judiciary, the public defender can frequently develop a positive working relationship in which the exchange of favors, so necessary to greasing the squeaky wheel of justice, can directly benefit the indigent defendant.

BRUCE JACKSON, LAW AND DISORDER: CRIMINAL JUSTICE IN AMERICA
81 (1984)

Private counsel retained by wealthy clients may assume their clients are innocent, civil rights lawyers representing defendants in politically mo-

31. Jean Taylor et al. An Analysis of Defense Counsel in the Processing of Felony Defendants in San Diego, Denver Law Journal (1972), p. 233.

tivated cases may assume their clients are innocent, but most public defender and court-appointed attorneys—and they handle the greatest bulk of the criminal cases—assume their clients are guilty. "If he's not guilty of this one, he's guilty of one just like it," one public defense lawyer said to me. "He knows it and I know it. Why go up there and argue? Almost everybody in these tanks is guilty of something. Everybody knows that. My job is to see that these people get out of here with as little jail time as possible. You don't win anything in this job because none of these clients are winners." The only time a defendant without funds gets extensive trial and appeal representation is when his case has political aspects and it is picked up by an organization willing to fund it or by an attorney who is not concerned with money. There are not many such organizations and there are not many such attorneys.

Most criminal justice lawyers work as partners with the court and the prosecutors, not as unequivocal representatives of the defendants. The defendants come and go, but the attorney's relationships with the other officers of the court continue for years.

BLUMBERG, THE PRACTICE OF LAW AS CONFIDENCE GAME: ORGANIZATIONAL COOPTATION OF A PROFESSION
1 Law & Socy. Rev. 15, 18-26, 29-31 (No. 2 1967)

The overwhelming majority of convictions in criminal cases (usually over 90 percent) are not the product of a combative, trial-by-jury process at all, but instead merely involve the sentencing of the individual after a negotiated, bargained-for plea of guilty has been entered. . . .

Organizational goals and discipline impose a set of demands and conditions of practice on the respective professions in the criminal court, to which they respond by abandoning their ideological and professional commitments to the accused client, in the service of these higher claims of the court organization. All court personnel, including the accused's own lawyer, tend to be coopted to become agent-mediators who help the accused redefine his situation and restructure his perceptions concomitant with a plea of guilty.

Of all the occupational roles in the court the only private individual who is officially recognized as having a special status and concomitant obligations is the lawyer. His legal status is that of "an officer of the court" and he is held to a standard of ethical performance and duty to his client as well as to the court. This obligation is thought to be far higher than that expected of ordinary individuals occupying the various occupational statuses in the court community. However, lawyers, whether privately retained or of the legal-aid, public defender variety, have close and continuing relations with the prosecuting office and the court itself through discreet relations with the judges via their law secretaries or "confidential" assistants. Indeed, lines of communication, influence and contact with those offices, as well as with the Office of the Clerk of the court, Probation Division, and with the press, are essential to present and prospective requirements of criminal law practice. Similarly, the subtle involvement of the press and other mass media in the court's organizational network is not readily discernible to the casual observer. Accused persons come and go in the court system schema, but the structure and its occupational incumbents remain to carry on their respective career, occupational and organizational enterprises. The individual stridencies, tensions, and conflicts a given accused person's case may present to all the participants are overcome, because the formal and informal relations of all the groups in the court setting require it. The probability of continued future relations and interaction must be preserved at all costs.

This is particularly true of the "lawyer regulars" i.e., those defense lawyers, who by virtue of their continuous appearances in behalf of defendants, tend to represent the bulk of a criminal court's non-indigent case workload, and those lawyers who are not "regulars," who appear almost casually in behalf of an occasional client. Some of the "lawyer regulars" are highly visible as one moves about the major urban centers of the nation, their offices line the back streets of the courthouses, at times sharing space with bondsmen. Their political "visibility" in terms of local club house ties, reaching into the judge's chambers and prosecutor's office, are also deemed essential to successful practitioners. . . .

. . . The accused's lawyer has far greater professional, economic, intellectual and other ties to the various elements of the court system than he does to his own client. In short, the court is a closed community.

This is more than just the case of the usual "secrets" of bureaucracy which are fanatically defended from an outside view. Even all elements of the press are zealously determined to report on that which will not offend the board of judges, the prosecutor, probation, legal-aid, or other officials, in return for privileges and courtesies granted in the past and to be granted in the future. Rather than any view of the matter in terms of some variation of a "conspiracy" hypothesis, the simple explanation is one of an ongoing system handling delicate tensions, managing the trauma produced by law enforcement and administration, and requiring almost pathological distrust of "outsiders" bordering on group paranoia.

The hostile attitude toward "outsiders" is in large measure engendered by a defensiveness itself produced by the inherent deficiencies of assembly line justice, so characteristic of our major criminal courts.

Intolerably large caseloads of defendants which must be disposed of in an organizational context of limited resources and personnel, potentially subject the participants in the court community to harsh scrutiny from appellate courts, and other public and private sources of condemnation. As a consequence, an almost irreconcilable conflict is posed in terms of intense pressures to process large numbers of cases on the one hand, and the stringent ideological and legal requirements of "due process of law," on the other hand. A rather tenuous resolution of the dilemma has emerged in the shape of a large variety of bureaucratically ordained and controlled "work crimes," short cuts, deviations, and outright rule violations adopted as court practice in order to meet production norms. Fearfully anticipating criticism on ethical as well as legal grounds, all the significant participants in the court's social structure are bound into an organized system of complicity. This consists of a work arrangement in which the patterned, covert, informal breaches, and evasions of "due process" are institutionalized, but are, nevertheless, denied to exist.

These institutionalized evasions will be found to occur to some degree, in all criminal courts. Their nature, scope and complexity are largely determined by the size of the court, and the character of the community in which it is located, e.g., whether it is a large, urban institution, or a relatively small rural county court. In addition, idiosyncratic, local conditions may contribute to a unique flavor in the character and quality of the criminal law's administration in a particular community. However, in most instances a variety of stratagems are employed—some subtle, some crude, in effectively disposing of what are often too large caseloads. A wide variety of coercive devices are employed against an accused-client, couched in a depersonalized, instrumental, bureaucratic version of due process of law, and which are in reality a perfunctory obeisance to the ideology of due process. These include some very explicit pressures which are exerted in some measure by all court personnel, including judges, to plead guilty and avoid trial. In many instances the sanction of a potentially harsh sentence is utilized as the visible alternative to pleading guilty, in the case of recalcitrants. Probation and psychiatric reports are "tailored" to organizational needs, or are at least responsive to the court organization's requirements for the refurbishment of a defendant's social biography, consonant with his new status. A resourceful judge can, through his subtle domination of the proceedings, impose his will on the final outcome of a trial. Stenographers and clerks, in their function as record keepers, are on occasion pressed into service in support of a judicial need to "rewrite" the record of a courtroom event. Bail practices are usually employed for purposes other than simply assuring a defendant's presence on the date of a hearing in connection with his case. Too often, the discretionary power as to bail is part of the arsenal of weapons available to collapse the resistance of an accused person. The foregoing is a most cursory examination of some of the more prominent "short cuts" available to any court organization. . . .

The real key to understanding the role of defense counsel in a criminal case is to be found in the area of the fixing of the fee to be charged and its collection. The problem of fixing and collecting the fee tends to influence to a significant degree the criminal court process itself, and not just the relationship of the lawyer and his client. In essence, a lawyer-client "confidence game" is played. . . . Legal service lends itself particularly well to confidence games. . . .

. . . [M]uch legal activity, whether it is at the lowest or highest "white shoe" law firm levels, is of the brokerage, agent, sales representative, lobbyist type of activity, in which the lawyer acts for someone else in pursuing the latter's interests and designs. The service is intangible. . . .

. . . Defense lawyers condition even the most obtuse clients to recognize that there is a firm interconnection between fee payment and the zealous exercise of professional expertise, secret knowledge, and organizational "connections" in their behalf. Lawyers, therefore, seek to keep their clients in a proper state of tension, and to arouse in them the precise edge of anxiety which is calculated to encourage prompt fee payment. Consequently, the client attitude in the relationship between defense counsel and an accused is in many instances a precarious admixture of hostility, mistrust, dependence, and sycophancy. By keeping his client's anxieties aroused to the proper pitch, and establishing a seemingly causal relationship between a requested fee and the accused's ultimate extrication from his onerous difficulties, the lawyer will have established the necessary preliminary groundwork to assure a minimum of haggling over the fee and its eventual payment.

In varying degrees, as a consequence, all law practice involves a manipulation of the client and a stage management of the lawyer-client relationship so that at least an *appearance* of help and service will be forthcoming. This is accomplished in a variety of ways, often exercised in combination with each other. At the outset, the lawyer-professional employs with suitable variation a measure of sales-puff which may range from an air of unbounding selfconfidence, adequacy, and dominion over events, to that of complete arrogance. This will be supplemented by the affectation of a studied, faultless mode of personal attire. In the larger firms, furnishings and office trappings will serve as the backdrop to help in impression management and client intimidation. In all firms, solo or large scale, an access to secret knowledge, and to the seats of power and influence is inferred, or presumed to a varying degree as the basic vendible commodity of the practitioners. . . .

The fee is often collected in stages, each installment usually payable prior to a necessary court appearance required during the course of an accused's career journey. At each stage, in his interviews and communications with the accused, or in addition, with members of his family, if they are helping with the fee payment, the lawyer employs an air of professional confidence and "inside-dopesterism" in order to assuage anxieties on all sides. He makes the necessary bland assurances, and in effect manipulates his client, who is usually willing to do and say the things, true or not, which will help his attorney extricate him. Since the dimensions of what he is essentially selling, organizational influence and expertise, are not technically and precisely measurable, the lawyer can make extravagant claims of influence and secret knowledge with impunity. Thus, lawyers frequently claim to have inside knowledge in connection with information in the hands of the D.A., police, probation officials or to have access to these functionaries. Factually, they often do, and need only to exaggerate the nature of their relationships with them to obtain the desired effective impression upon the client. But, as in the genuine confidence game, the victim who has participated is loathe to do anything which will upset the lesser plea which his lawyer has "conned" him into accepting.

In effect, in his role as double agent, the criminal lawyer performs an extremely vital and delicate mission for the court organization and the accused. Both principals are anxious to terminate the litigation with a minimum of expense and damage to each other. There is no other personage or role incumbent in the total court structure more strategically located, who by training and in terms of his own requirements, is more ideally suited to do so than the lawyer. In recognition of this, judges will cooperate with attorneys in many important ways. For example, they will adjourn the case of an accused in jail awaiting plea or sentence if the attorney requests such action. While explicitly this may be done for some innocuous and seemingly valid reason, the tacit purpose is that pressure is being applied by the attorney for the collection of his fee, which he knows will probably not be forthcoming if the case is concluded. Judges are aware of this tactic on the part of lawyers, who, by requesting an adjournment, keep an accused incarcerated a while longer as a not too subtle method of dunning a client for payment. However, the judges will go along with this, on the ground that important ends are being served. Often, the only end served is to protect a lawyer's fee.

The judge will help an accused's lawyer in still another way. He will lend the official aura of his office and courtroom so that a lawyer can stage manage an impression of an "all out" performance for the accused in justification of his fee. The judge and other court personnel will serve as a backdrop for a scene charged with dramatic fire, in which the accused's lawyer makes a stirring appeal in his behalf. With a show of restrained passion, the lawyer will intone the virtues of the accused and recite the social deprivations which have reduced him to his present state. The speech varies somewhat, depending on whether the accused has been convicted after trial or has pleaded guilty. In the main, however, the incongruity, superficiality, and ritualistic character of the total performance is underscored by a visibly impassive, almost bored reaction on the part of the judge and other members of the court retinue.

Afterward, there is a hearty exchange of pleasantries between the lawyer and district attorney, wholly out of context in terms of the supposed adversary nature of the preceding events. The fiery passion in defense of his client is gone, and the lawyers for both sides resume their offstage relations, chatting amiably and perhaps including the judge in their restrained banter. No other aspect of their visible conduct so effectively serves to put even a casual observer on notice, that these individuals have claims upon each other. These seemingly innocuous actions are indicative of continuing organizational and informal relations, which, in their intricacy and depth, range far beyond any priorities or claims a particular defendant may have. . . .

MILESKI, COURTROOM ENCOUNTERS: AN OBSERVATION STUDY OF A LOWER CRIMINAL COURT
5 Law & Socy. Rev. 473, 479-480, 489-490, 496-498, 508-509, 523, 530-531 (1971)

COMPOSITIONAL FEATURES OF ENCOUNTERS

Many American courts have a workload problem. Court systems have what their participants, spokesmen, and critics consider too much to do. . . .

One obvious way the court can allay pressures from heavy caseloads is to handle the accused rapidly. In this court 72% of the cases are handled in one minute or less. . . . It is noteworthy that routine police encounters with citizens in the field last on the average far longer than court encounters. The climax of many an alleged offender's contact with the criminal justice machinery is dwarfed by his police contact on the one side and the time he is incarcerated on the other. . . .

Lawyers no doubt receive positive or negative reinforcement for their own behavior in the judicial bureaucracy. One attorney, to give a minor example, noted that whenever he obtained an "unreasonable" acquittal, the prosecutor penalized him by not calling his cases until the end of the day's session. This "penalty" would last about a week after the dis-approved disposition. Not only the lawyer but also his client, then, must sometimes sit all day in court for reasons irrelevant to the substance of the cases at hand. Ordinarily, clients with attorneys have their cases scheduled for very early or very late in the day's session. The court thus allows the attorneys to salvage most of each day for out-of-court matters. Defendants without attorneys are told the day, but not the time, of their court appearances. This favor may add to the court's leverage in coaxing attorneys toward routine cooperation.

Perhaps the obvious or only available way in which the system can reward or penalize an attorney is to reward or penalize his client, which in turn affects the lawyer's reputation. For instance, an attorney who appeared in this court claimed that one of his clients was given a sentence which was considerably more severe than that usually given for similar offenses. He attributed the severe sentence to his own numerous requests for "probable cause hearings" for other defendants. These hearings con-sume valuable court time. . . .

THE DISPOSITION . . .

Both deterrence and police practice feed back upon the court. To the extent that the court deters both those it finds guilty and other potential offenders, it lessens its own workload. Complicating the courts' deterrent role, however, is the relation between the court and the police. It is the police relation to appellate courts that is emphasized in discussions of the criminal justice system. Surprisingly, students of the criminal process have slighted the routine, day-to-day relations of trial courts and the police. . . . The practices of trial courts surely are highly associated with police behavior. Faced with a lenient court, police officers sometimes take the law into their own hands, becoming self-appointed judges and applying informal sanctions from time to time. . . . Or, police them-selves may not sanction suspects at all when they have reason to believe that the judge will not uphold their sanction with one of his own. A consistently harsh court might give rise to more professional police be-havior. Trial court practice feeds back on police practice; together both have implications for deterrence. The manner and degree to which the specific deterrence function is served by the court can only stem from the cases that the court obtains for processing, which depend primarily upon police arrest practices. But the court's handling of these cases in turn affects police arrest practice to some degree. The impact of any control system is always limited by the nature of the cases it comes to process. . . .

There is a sufficient number of intoxication cases . . . to investigate the relation between situational excuses by defendants, and dispositions. . . . In only 14% of the intoxication cases did the offender present an excuse. Yet, virtually all of them had earlier pleaded guilty to their charges. The data show that penalties of self-excusers are considerably more severe than those of other defendants. While over half the latter receive suspended sentences, merely 18% of the former are freed on suspended sentences. . . . Furthermore, 54% of the self-excusers are incarcerated, whereas only 15% of the other defendants are incarcerated.

Numerous explanations of this pattern could be suggested. Perhaps defendants who somehow realize that their chances for suspended sentences are slight tend to excuse themselves from punishment. On the other hand, an underlying factor may again relate to considerations of bureaucratic efficiency. The court is a system whose currency of operation is information. Citizen witnesses, police reports and testimony, prosecutorial investigations, the defendants, and sometimes attorneys together provide information through which the judge sifts to determine guilt or to set penalties. Information allows the court to work, but *extra* information drives the court toward *extra* work. If the court disproportionately uses the sanction of jail as a defense against the injection of extra information during the courtroom encounter, then defendants might come to offer it less often. Were the court to bend immediately to the excuses of the defendants, defendants might in a short time learn always to excuse themselves. Alternatively, were the court to probe further into the defendants' excuses to find whether they could be considered justified, much time would be lost. To respond more often with jail sentences to defendants who excuse themselves is at least a relatively rational way to respond not necessarily from an ideological standpoint but from the standpoint of the court as a bureaucracy. Even if such does not *account* for the pattern, it speaks to part of the consequences of the pattern. . . .

. . . On occasion, defendants also receive what could be called situational sanctions during their courtroom encounters with the judge. The judge's manner toward them may be harsh or severe rather than goodnatured or distant and bureaucratic. Besides the relative subtlety of a harsh manner, the judge at times openly reprimands defendants in the courtroom. The judge traditionally has been a moral agent not only in his actions but also in his style.

Only a small portion of defendants are singled out to be situationally sanctioned during courtroom encounters, and the selection does not directly follow the seriousness of the charge. The courtroom is removed from the immediacy of the criminal event. Thus, it is removed from the tension, disgust, outrage, or defensiveness that might attach to the witnessing of violative behavior and its consequences in the field. The courtroom is usually the stage for the comparatively dull aftermath of the passion, disruption, fun, or danger of deviance. . . .

The situational sanctioning that the judge does engage in is woven in unexpected patterns. First, it is suggested that persons who violate the informal rules of the court, regardless of their violations of legal rules, are particularly susceptible to situational condemnation. Indeed, when the disruption is sufficiently severe, the court can invoke the legal rule against contempt of court. The court protects itself as it protects the larger society, responding to its own victimization at the same time as it responds to the victimization of others.

Second, situational sanctioning relates to the seriousness of the charge and to the seriousness of the material penalty. It seems, overall, to be more common with minor than with serious charges. Thus it is possible that situational sanctioning works in such a way as to compensate for the lesser degree of condemnation that a minor charge itself carries. Furthermore, situational sanctioning is more common, in all but petty misdemeanor cases, when the penalty is slight. Indeed, when a defendant is not punished severely, his encounter with the judge more often outwardly appears as a degradation ceremony. With opprobrious words the judge might buoy the legitimacy of processing minor offenders and offenders he does not severely punish. In a greater majority of felony cases and in a greater majority of cases where the penalty is relatively stiff, by contrast, the judge can remain uninvolved without jeopardizing the manifest condemnation of the offender. . . .

D. THE SUPREME COURT

AMSTERDAM, THE SUPREME COURT AND THE RIGHTS OF SUSPECTS IN CRIMINAL CASES
45 N.Y.U.L. Rev. 785, 785-794 (1970)

The impression is widespread that decisions of the Supreme Court of the United States during the past decade have vastly enlarged the rights of criminal suspects and defendants. That impression is not wholly unfounded, but the broad form in which it is generally entertained ignores very significant limitations upon what the Supreme Court can do, and what it has in fact done, to create and enforce such rights. . . .

According to Par Lagerkvist,[1] the role of the Pythia or priestess of

1. P. Lagerkvist, The Sibyl (N. Walford transl. 1958).

the Oracle at Delphi was of incomparable grandeur and futility. This young maiden was periodically lashed to a tripod above a noisome abyss, where her god dwelt and from which nauseating odors rose and assaulted her. There, the god entered her body and soul, so that she thrashed madly and uttered inspired, incomprehensible cries. The cries were interpreted by the corps of professional priests of the Oracle, and their interpretations were, of course, for mere mortals the words of the god. The Pythia experienced incalculable ecstasy and degradation; she was viewed with utmost reverence and abhorrence; to her every utterance, enormous importance attached; but, from the practical point of view, what she said did not matter much.

On its tripod atop the system of American criminal justice, the Supreme Court of the United States performs in remarkably Pythian fashion. Occasional ill-smelling cases are wafted up to it by the fortuities of litigation, evoking its inspired and spasmodic reaction. Neither the records nor the issues presented by these cases give the Court a comprehensive view—or even a reliably representative view—of the doings in the dark pit in which criminal suspects, police and the functionaries of the criminal courts wrestle with each other in the sightless ooze. It is not surprising, then, that in these cases the Court should be incapable of announcing judgments which respond coherently to the real problems of the pit. No matter. The significance of the Court's pronouncements— their power to shake the assembled faithful with awful tremors of exultation and loathing—does not depend upon their correspondence with reality. Once uttered, these pronouncements will be interpreted by arrays of lower appellate courts, trial judges, magistrates, commissioners and police officials. *Their* interpretation of the Pythia, for all practical purposes, will become the word of god.

To some extent this Pythian metaphor describes the Supreme Court's functioning in all the fields of law with which the Court deals. But the metaphor has special cogency with regard to the field of criminal procedure and particularly procedure that regulates the rights of suspects in their dealings with police prior to the time of the suspect's first court appearance. Let me explain why this is so and some of the implications of that fact.

First, the Supreme Court, like any other court, lacks the sort of supervisory power over the practices of the police that is possessed by the chief of police or the district attorney. The Court can only review those practices, and thus can only define the rights of suspects subject to those practices, when the practices become an issue in a lawsuit. There are several ways in which police practices may become the subject of a lawsuit. An individual who thinks that he has been mistreated by the police may file a civil action for damages or, in limited circumstances, for an injunction, complaining of false arrest or false imprisonment or assault or the violation of his constitutional rights. But such lawsuits are very rare, and until recently were so rare as to be insignificant, because the obstacles to their maintenance are formidable. Most persons mistreated by the police are marginal types who are quite happy, once out of police clutches, to let well enough alone. Few have the knowledge or resources to obtain the services of a lawyer. Many lawyers who might otherwise be available to them cannot afford to tangle with the police because these lawyers depend upon the good will of the police in other cases (e.g., to protect a divorce client who is being badgered by her estranged husband or to reduce charges against a criminal client) or upon police testimony in other cases (e.g., motor vehicle accident cases) or upon more dubious police services (e.g., referrals).

Juries are not sympathetic to suits against the police; policemen are seldom sufficiently solvent to make verdicts against them worth the trouble to obtain; even fairly solid citizens who sue policemen may have to fear reprisals in the form of traffic tickets, refusals to give needed aid and similar harassments. As a result, civil suits seldom bring police practices under judicial scrutiny. And for reasons too obvious to detail, criminal charges against policemen for mistreatment of citizens are even rarer than civil suits.

So, to date the Supreme Court has had occasion to review the conduct of police almost exclusively in criminal cases where the defendant is the asserted victim of police misconduct. The way in which the issue of police misconduct is presented in such cases almost invariably involves the application of the "exclusionary rule"—that is, an evidentiary rule which disallows the admission against a criminal defendant, at his trial, of certain kinds of evidence obtained in violation of his rights. This exclusionary rule, whose scope and utility in enforcing various constitutional guarantees has been considerably expanded by the Supreme Court in the past decade, is today the principal instrument of judicial control of the police and the principal vehicle for announcement by the courts of the rights of suspects in their dealings with the police.

This last point, in itself, has important implications. Certain police practices (for example, the "booking" and "mugging" of suspects and the assorted minor or major indignities that attend station-house detention of suspects, ranging from the taking of a suspect's belt and shoelaces to vicious beatings) will virtually never become the subjects of judicial scrutiny because they virtually never produce evidence against the suspect. Since there can arise no exclusionary rule challenges to these practices, there have been no significant judicial decisions concerning them; and since (as I shall develop shortly) judicial decisions are almost the only source of legal rights of suspects, suspects do not now have legal rights against or in connection with such practices.

Other police practices (for example, refusing arrested suspects the right to use the telephone or detaining them in pig-sty cells) may or may not come under judicial consideration, depending upon whether they do or do not produce evidentiary consequences such as confessions. For several reasons, judicial control of the latter practices and judicial definition of a suspect's rights in connection with those practices must remain an imprecise, haphazard business. Under the exclusionary rule, judicial attention is focused upon an evidentiary product of the practices rather than upon the practices themselves. For example, a confession will ordinarily be the product of several such practices and of other adventitious circumstances such as the suspect's age and psychological makeup, the nature of police interrogation, etc. Consequently, a judicial ruling admitting or excluding it will seldom give occasion for a clear-cut pronouncement concerning the legality of any one of the underlying practices. Moreover, because these practices themselves are not the focus of the litigation, they will usually be imperfectly explained and explored in the record made before the courts. Courts which pass judgment on them may do so half-sightedly; or, realizing this danger, the courts may strive to avoid passing judgment upon practices that they know they do not understand. The result, once again, is that courts are unable to speak clearly concerning any particular or specific rights of a criminal suspect. Still less are they able to develop systematically any comprehensive canon or register of suspects' rights in the context of the entire range of police practices that affect the suspect.

Second, the Supreme Court of the United States is uniquely unable to take a comprehensive view of the subject of suspects' rights. In part its inability is simply a function of the Court's workload. Saddled with a back-breaking docket and properly occupied with other matters of grave national importance, the Court can only hear three or four cases a year involving the treatment of criminal suspects by the police.

Workload is not the Court's only problem. I have said earlier that fortuities determine which criminal cases reach the Supreme Court. Because police practices are ordinarily challengeable only through the exclusionary rule and because the exclusionary rule ordinarily comes into play only at trial following a plea of not guilty, police treatment of a suspect is effectively insulated against Supreme Court review in that large percentage of criminal convictions (as many as 90 percent in some jurisdictions) that rest upon a guilty plea.

Guilty pleas may be entered for many reasons in cases that involve serious questions of violations of a suspect's rights in the precourt phases. The arguable violations may have had no evidentiary consequences. The prosecution may have sufficient evidence for conviction apart from that obtained through the arguable violations. The defendant may be detained pending trial in default of bail on a charge for which a probationary or "time-served" sentence is likely, so that he will be imprisoned longer awaiting trial on a plea of not guilty than he would as a result of a quick guilty plea. The prosecutor may offer an attractive plea bargain, or the known sentencing practices of the trial judge may promise similar consideration for a guilty plea. Obviously, these factors that determine the entry of a guilty plea do not systematically send to trial a selection of cases which present the courts with any comprehensive set of issues relative to suspects' rights.

Additional selective factors prevent many of the cases that are tried from being appealed or from being carried all the way to the Supreme Court. Factual findings by the trial judge concerning contested police conduct frequently obscure or entirely obstruct the presentation to appellate courts of issues relating to that conduct. A convicted defendant cannot challenge on appeal any treatment by the police that the trial court, crediting incredible police denials, finds did not occur. (For example, suspects invariably "trip" and strike their heads while entering their cells; they are never shoved against the bars by police.) Also, the trial court may admit the police conduct but credit incredible explanations of it. (For example, the humiliating anal examinations to which some suspects are subjected in police stations are justified as "weapons searches" on police testimony that such suspects are known to conceal razor blades between their buttocks.) Finally, the trial court may admit and resolve against the defendant an issue relating to the legality of police conduct, then sentence him so lightly that an appeal is not worthwhile. (Some trial judges will impose light sentences in cases in which they have made dubious evidentiary rulings, thereby "buying off" appeals.) In any event the presentation of a convicted defendant's appeal—still more, the taking of his case to the Supreme Court—depends upon the energy, dedication and painstaking care of his lawyer, commodities understandably scarce on the part of overworked public defenders or private lawyers conscripted without compensation to represent the indigents who constitute the bulk of convicted persons.

For these reasons, the Supreme Court simply never gets to see many of the police practices that raise the most pervasive and significant issues of suspects' rights. The cases which do come to the Court are selected by a process that can only be described as capricious insofar as it may be relied upon to present the Court any opportunity for systematic development of a body of legal rights of individuals in the police, or precourt, phases of criminal proceedings. Therefore, the Court's ability to serve as architect of such a body of rights is woefully slight.

Third, the Court is further disabled by the fact that almost the only law relating to police practices or to suspects' rights is the law that the Court itself makes by its judicial decisions. Statutes and administrative regulations governing these matters are virtually nonexistent. The ubiquitous lack of legislative and executive attention to the problems of police treatment of suspects both forces the Court into the role of lawmaker in this area and makes it virtually impossible for the Court effectively to play that role.

This point has been largely ignored by the Court's conservative critics. The judicial "activism" that they deplore, usually citing the Court's "handcuffing" of the police, has been the almost inevitable consequence of the failure of other agencies of law to assume responsibility for regulating police practices. In most areas of constitutional law the Supreme Court of the United States plays a backstopping role, reviewing the ultimate permissibility of dispositions and policies guided in the first instance by legislative enactments, administrative rules or local common-law traditions. In the area of controls upon the police, a vast abnegation of responsibility at the level of each of these ordinary sources of legal rulemaking has forced the Court to construct *all* the law regulating the everyday functioning of the police. Of course, the Court has responded by being "activist"; it has had to. Its decisions have seemed wildly "liberal" because the only other body of principles operating in the field, against which the Court's principles may be measured, are the principles under which individual policemen act in the absence of any legal restraint.

This same subconstitutional lawlessness which forces the Court to act also prevents it from acting informedly. When the Court reviews the operation of legislation or of administrative regulations or of common-law rules governing, for example, criminal trial procedure, its consideration of the constitutional issues raised is informed and greatly assisted by the very fact that it *is* legislation or a regulation or a rule of some sort that is in question. Because the rule is articulated in more or less general terms, its contour is more or less visible; its relations and interactions with the rules are more or less perceptible, and some of the judgments and policies that underlie or oppose its acceptance are more or less intelligible. However, when the Court reviews conduct, such as police conduct, that is essentially rule-less, it is seriously impeded in understanding the nature, purposes and effects of what it is reviewing. Its view of the questioned conduct is limited to the appearance of the conduct on a particular trial record or records—records which may not even isolate or focus precisely upon that conduct. The Court cannot know whether the conduct before it is typical or atypical, unconnected or connected with a set of other practices or—if there is some connection—what is the comprehensive shape of the set of practices involved, what are their relations, their justifications, their consequences.

Operating thus darkly, the Court is obviously deprived of the ability to make any coherent response to, or to develop any organized regulation of, police conduct. Nor can the Court predict or understand the implications of any rule of constitutional law that it may itself project into this well of shadows. If the Court announces a decision striking down or modifying, for example, some rule of criminal trial practice, it can reasonably foresee how a trial will be conducted following its decision since the decision will operate within a system governed by other visible and predictable rules. But if the Court strikes down a police practice, announces a "right" of a criminal suspect in his dealings with the police, God only knows what the result will be.[5] Out there in the formless void, some adjustment will undoubtedly be made to accommodate the new "right," but what the product of this whole exercise will be remains unfathomable. So, again, the Court is effectively disarmed.

Fourth, when and if the Supreme Court ventures to announce some constitutional right of a suspect, that "right" filters down to the level of flesh and blood suspects only through the refracting layers of lower courts, trial judges, magistrates and police officials. All pronouncements of the Supreme Court undergo this filtering process, but in few other areas of law are the filters as opaque as in the area of suspects' rights.

Let there be no mistake about it. To a mind-staggering extent—to an extent that conservatives and liberals alike who are not criminal trial lawyers simply cannot conceive—the entire system of criminal justice below the level of the Supreme Court of the United States is solidly massed against the criminal suspect. Only a few appellate judges can throw off the fetters of their middle-class backgrounds—the dimly remembered, friendly face of the school crossing guard, their fear of a crowd of "toughs," their attitudes engendered as lawyers before their elevation to the bench by years of service as prosecutors or as private lawyers for honest, respectable business clients—and identify with the criminal suspect instead of with the policeman or with the putative victim of the suspect's theft, mugging, rape or murder. Trial judges still more, and magistrates beyond belief, are functionally and psychologically allied

---

5. One possible result is that prosecutors may offer greater concessions to defendants during plea bargaining. If a bargain is too good to refuse, the defendant may forego the opportunity to challenge a police practice or assert a constitutional right. To the extent that this occurs, "what the due process revolution will have gained is simply shorter sentences." D. Oaks & W. Lehman, A Criminal Justice System and the Indigent 80 (1968).—Eds.

with the police, their co-workers in the unending and scarifying work of bringing criminals to book.

These trial judges and magistrates are the human beings that must find the "facts" when cases involving suspects' rights go into court (that is, when police treatment of a suspect is not conclusively masked behind a guilty plea or ignored by a defense lawyer too overworked or undercompensated to develop the issues adequately). Their factual findings resolve the inevitable conflict between the testimony of the police and the testimony of the suspect—usually a down-and-outer or a bad type, and often a man with a record. The result is about what one would expect. Even when the cases go to court, a suspect's rights as announced by the Supreme Court are something he has, not something he gets.

But, of course, for the reasons mentioned previously, most cases do not go to court. In these cases, the "rights" of the suspect are defined by how the police are willing to treat him. With regard to matters of treatment that have no evidentiary consequences and hence will not be judicially reviewable in exclusionary rule proceedings, the police have no particular reason to obey the law, even if the Supreme Court has had occasion to announce it. With regard to police practices that may have evidentiary consequences, the police are motivated to obey the law only to the extent that (1) they are more concerned with securing a conviction than with some other police purpose which is served by disobeying the law (in this connection, it is worth noting that police departments almost invariably measure their own efficiency in terms of "clearances by arrest," not by conviction), and (2) they think that they can secure the evidence necessary for conviction within the law.

Police work is hard work; it is righteous work; it is combative work, and competitive. Policemen are undereducated, they are scandalously underpaid, and their personal advancement lies in producing results according to the standards of the police ethic. When they go to the commander's office or to court, their conformity to this ethic is almost always vindicated. Neither their superiors nor the judges whom they know nor the public find it necessary to impede the performance of their duties with fettering rules respecting rights of suspects. If the Supreme Court finds this necessary, it must be that the Court is out of step. So its decisions—which are difficult to understand anyway—cannot really be taken seriously.

This concludes my observations concerning the Supreme Court's power to guarantee rights of criminal suspects in any other than an unworldly sense. The idealist would conclude from what I have said that the priests surrounding the Pythia are unfaithful to their priesthood. The cynic would conclude that the whole damned system is corrupt. I forgo such judgments and conclude only that Supreme Court power to enlarge the rights of suspects is very, very limited. . . .

. . . I do not mean to suggest that Supreme Court decisions respecting suspects' and defendants' rights are unimportant. Like the Pythia's cries, they have vast mystical significance. They state our aspirations. They give a few good priests something to work with. They give some of the faithful the courage to carry on and reason to improve the priesthood instead of tearing down the temple.

Also, they have *some* practical significance. With the Pythia shrieking underground, the priests may pervert the word of god, but they cannot ignore it entirely, nor entirely silence those who offer interpretations of it different from their own. Indeed, fear lest these alternative explanations gain popular support may cause the priests to bend a little in their direction.

So it is worth the effort to examine what the Supreme Court has pronounced concerning suspects' and defendants' rights. . . .[6]

6. For more on the relationship between Supreme Court decisionmaking and the operation of the criminal justice system, see Weisberg, Forward: Criminal Procedure Doctrine: Some Versions of the Skeptical, 76 J. Crim. L. & Crim. 832 (1985). For differing perspectives on the role of the Burger Court in adjudicating the rights of criminal defendants, compare Whitebread, The Burger Court's Counter-Revolution in Criminal Procedure: The Recent Criminal Decisions of the United States Supreme Court, 24 Washburn L.J. 471 (1985), with Israel, Criminal Procedure, the Burger Court, and the Legacy of the Warren Court, 75 Mich. L. Rev. 1319 (1977). See also O'Neill, The Good, The Bad, and the Burger Court: Victim's Rights and a New Model of Criminal Review, 75 J. Crim. L. & Criminology 363 (1984). —EDS.

CHAPTER 3

THE PROCESS OF CONSTITUTIONAL DECISIONMAKING

A. CONSTITUTIONAL DECISIONMAKING

In the process of evaluating the criminal justice system by reference to, and attempting to infuse it with, constitutional values, the courts have had to wrestle with two fundamental, a priori questions. The first is how to determine the meaning and scope of the relevant constitutional provisions, and the second is determining the extent of constitutional authority over the states. The first question centers primarily on determining the appropriate method of applying the illusory specificity of the provisions in the Bill of Rights, and to a lesser extent in the body of the Constitution itself, to the infinite variety of factual nuances that percolate through the criminal justice system, while the second question focuses essentially the same inquiry on the even more ambiguous language of the fourteenth amendment due process and equal protection clauses.

How, then, are these questions to be answered? What are their referents? Unfortunately, the Constitution does not, as it could not, contain a provision detailing how the document is to be interpreted. Thus, the courts have had to make that determination themselves, and the dominant philosophy of interpretation has changed over time. Indeed, the process of changing views continues apace. Consider the implications of the following three cases, paying more attention to the *methods* of analysis than the results.

HURTADO v. PEOPLE OF CALIFORNIA
In Error to the Supreme Court of California
110 U.S. 516 232 (1884)

MR. JUSTICE MATTHEWS delivered the opinion of the court.

[The California constitution provided for the initiation of criminal proceedings by information. The defendant, who was convicted of first degree murder, contended that charging him by information rather than by grand jury indictment was a violation of fourteenth amendment due process.]

The Constitution of the United States was ordained, it is true, by descendants of Englishmen, who inherited the traditions of English law and history; but it was made for an undefined and expanding future, and for a people gathered and to be gathered from many nations and of many tongues. And while we take just pride in the principles and institutions of the common law, we are not to forget that in lands where other systems of jurisprudence prevail, the ideas and processes of civil justice are also not unknown. Due process of law, in spite of the absolutism of Continental governments, is not alien to that code which survived the Roman Empire as the foundation of modern civilization in Europe, and which has given us that fundamental maxim of distributive justice—suum cuique tribuere. There is nothing in Magna Charta, rightly construed as a broad charter of public right and law, which ought to exclude the best ideas of all systems and of every age; and as it was the characteristic principle of the common law to draw its inspiration from every fountain of justice, we are not to assume that the sources of its supply have been exhausted. On the contrary, we should expect that the new and various experiences of our own situation and system will mould and shape it into new and not less useful forms.

The concessions of Magna Charta were wrung from the King as guaranties against the oppressions and usurpations of his prerogative. It did not enter into the minds of the barons to provide security against their own body or in favor of the Commons by limiting the power of Parliament; so that bills of attainder, ex post facto laws, laws declaring forfeitures of estates, and other arbitrary acts of legislation which occur so frequently in English history, were never regarded as inconsistent with the law of the land; for notwithstanding what was attributed to Lord Coke in Bonham's Case, 8 Rep. 115, 118a, the omnipotence of Parliament over the common law was absolute, even against common right and reason. The actual and practical security for English liberty against legislative tyranny was the power of a free public opinion represented by the Commons.

In this country written constitutions were deemed essential to protect the rights and liberties of the people against the encroachments of power delegated to their governments, and the provisions of Magna Charta were incorporated into Bills of Rights. They were limitations upon all the powers of government, legislative as well as executive and judicial.

It necessarily happened, therefore, that as these broad and general maxims of liberty and justice held in our system a different place and performed a different function from their position and office in English constitutional history and law, they would receive and justify a corresponding and more comprehensive interpretation. Applied in England only as guards against executive usurpation and tyranny, here they have become bulwarks also against arbitrary legislation; but, in that application, as it would be incongruous to measure and restrict them by the ancient customary English law, they must be held to guarantee not particular forms of procedure, but the very substance of individual rights to life, liberty, and property.

Restraints that could be fastened upon executive authority with precision and detail, might prove obstructive and injurious when imposed on the just and necessary discretion of legislative power; and, while in every instance, laws that violated express and specific injunctions and prohibitions, might, without embarrassment, be judicially declared to be void, yet, any general principle or maxim, founded on the essential nature of law, as a just and reasonable expression of the public will and of government, as instituted by popular consent and for the general good, can only be applied to cases coming clearly within the scope of its spirit and purpose, and not to legislative provisions merely establishing forms and modes of attainment. Such regulations, to adopt a sentence of Burke's, "may alter the mode and application but have no power over the substance of original justice." Tract on the Property Laws, 6 Burke's Works, ed. Little & Brown, 323. . . .

We are to construe this phrase in the Fourteenth Amendment by the usus loquendi of the Constitution itself. The same words are contained in the Fifth Amendment. That article makes specific and express provision for perpetuating the institution of the grand jury, so far as relates to prosecutions for the more aggravated crimes under the laws of the United States. . . .

According to a recognized canon of interpretation, especially applicable to formal and solemn instruments of constitutional law, we are forbidden to assume, without clear reason to the contrary, that any part of this most important amendment is superfluous. The natural and obvious inference is, that in the sense of the Constitution, "due process of law" was not meant or intended to include, ex vi termini, the institution and procedure of a grand jury in any case. The conclusion is equally irresistible, that when the same phrase was employed in the Fourteenth Amendment to restrain the action of the States, it was used in the same sense and with no greater extent; and that if in the adoption of that amendment it had been part of its purpose to perpetuate the institution of the grand jury in all the States, it would have embodied, as did the Fifth Amendment, express declarations to that effect. Due process of law in the latter refers to that law of the land which derives its authority from the legislative powers conferred upon Congress by the Constitution of the United States, exercised within the limits therein prescribed, and interpreted according to the principles of the common law. In the Fourteenth Amendment, by parity of reason, it refers to that law of the land in each State, which derives its authority from the inherent and reserved powers of the State, exerted within the limits of those fundamental principles of liberty and justice which lie at the base of all our civil and political institutions, and the greatest security for which resides in the right of the people to make their own laws, and alter them at their pleasure. . . .

But it is not to be supposed that these legislative powers are absolute and despotic, and that the amendment prescribing due process of law is too vague and indefinite to operate as a practical restraint. It is not every act, legislative in form, that is law. Law is something more than mere will exerted as an act of power. It must be not a special rule for a particular person or a particular case, but, in the language of Mr. Webster, in his familiar definition, "the general law, a law which hears before it condemns, which proceeds upon inquiry, and renders judgment only after trial," so "that every citizen shall hold his life, liberty, property and immunities under the protection of the general rules which govern society," and thus excluding, as not due process of law, acts of attainder, bills of pains and penalties, acts of confiscation, acts reversing judgments, and acts directly transferring one man's estate to another, legislative judgments and decrees, and other similar special, partial and arbitrary exertions of power under the forms of legislation. Arbitrary power, enforcing its edicts to the injury of the persons and property of its subjects, is not law, whether manifested as the decree of a personal monarch or of an impersonal multitude. And the limitations imposed by our constitutional law upon the action of the governments, both State and national, are essential to the preservation of public and private rights, notwithstanding the representative character of our political institutions. The enforcement of these limitations by judicial process is the device of self-governing communities to protect the rights of individuals and minorities, as well against the power of numbers, as against the violence of public agents transcending the limits of lawful authority, even when acting in the name and wielding the force of the government. . . .

It follows that any legal proceeding enforced by public authority, whether sanctioned by age and custom, or newly devised in the discretion of the legislative power, in furtherance of the general public good, which regards and preserves these principles of liberty and justice, must be held to be due process of law. . . .

Tried by these principles, we are unable to say that the substitution for a presentment or indictment by a grand jury of the proceeding by information, after examination and commitment by a magistrate, certifying to the probable guilt of the defendant, with the right on his part to the aid of counsel, and to the cross-examination of the witnesses produced for the prosecution, is not due process of law. It is, as we have seen, an ancient proceeding at common law, which might include every case of an offense of less grade than a felony, except misprision of treason; and in every circumstance of its administration, as authorized by the statute of California, it carefully considers and guards the substantial interest of the prisoner. It is merely a preliminary proceeding, and can result in no final judgment, except as the consequence of a regular judicial trial, conducted precisely as in cases of indictments. . . .

For these reasons, finding no error therein, the judgment of the Supreme Court of California is affirmed.

MR. JUSTICE HARLAN, dissenting. . . .

"Due process of law," within the meaning of the national Constitution, does not import one thing with reference to the powers of the States, and another with reference to the powers of the general government. If particular proceedings conducted under the authority of the general government, and involving life, are prohibited, because not constituting that due process of law required by the Fifth Amendment of the Constitution of the United States, similar proceedings, conducted under the authority of a State, must be deemed illegal as not being due process of law within the meaning of the Fourteenth Amendment. What, then, is the meaning of the words "due process of law" in the latter amendment? . . .

My brethren concede that there are principles of liberty and justice, lying at the foundation of our civil and political institutions, which no State can violate consistently with that due process of law required by the Fourteenth Amendment in proceedings involving life, liberty, or property. Some of these principles are enumerated in the opinion of the court. But, for reasons which do not impress my mind as satisfactory, they exclude from that enumeration the exemption from prosecution, by information, for a public offence involving life. By what authority is that exclusion made? Is it justified by the settled usages and modes of procedure existing under the common and statute law of England at the emigration of our ancestors, or at the foundation of our government? Does not the fact that people of the original States required an amendment of the national Constitution, securing exemption from prosecution, for a capital offence, except upon the indictment or presentment of a grand jury, prove that, in their judgement, such an exemption was essential to protection against accusation and unfounded prosecution, and, therefore, was a fundamental principle in liberty and justice? By the side of that exemption, in the same amendment, is the declaration that no person shall be put twice in jeopardy for the same offence, nor compelled to criminate himself, nor shall private property be taken for public use without just compensation. Are not these principles fundamental in every free government established to maintain liberty and justice? If it be supposed that immunity from prosecution for a capital offence, except upon the presentment or indictment of a grand jury, was regarded at the common law any less secured by the law of the land, or any less valuable, or any less essential to due process of law, than the personal rights and immunities just enumerated, I take leave to say that no such distinction is authorized by any adjudged case, determined in England, or in this country prior to the adoption of our Constitution, or by an elementary writer upon the principles established by Magna Charta and the statutes subsequently enacted in explanation or enlargement of its provisions.

But it is said that the framers of the Constitution did not suppose that due process of law necessarily required for a capital offence the institution and procedure of a grand jury, else they would not in the same amendment prohibiting the deprivation of life, liberty, or property, without due process of law, have made specific and express provision for a grand jury where the crime is capital or otherwise infamous; therefore, it is argued, the requirement by the Fourteenth Amendment of due process of law in all proceedings involving life, liberty, and property, without specific reference to grand juries in any case whatever, was not intended as a restriction upon the power which it is claimed the States previously had, so far as the express restrictions of the national Constitution are concerned, to dispense altogether with grand juries.

This line of argument, it seems to me, would lead to results which are inconsistent with the vital principles of republican government. If the presence in the Fifth Amendment of a specific provision for grand juries in capital cases, alongside the provision for due process of law in proceedings involving life, liberty, or property, is held to prove that "due process of law" did not, in the judgment of the framers of the Constitution, necessarily require a grand jury in capital cases, inexorable logic would require it to be, likewise, held that the right not to be put twice in jeopardy of life and limb for the same offence, nor compelled in a criminal case to testify against one's self—rights and immunities also specifically recognized in the Fifth Amendment—were not protected by that due process of law required by the settled usages and proceedings existing under the common and statute law of England at the settlement of this country. More than that, other amendments of the Constitution proposed at the same time, expressly recognized the right of persons to just compensation for private property taken for public use; their right, when accused of crime, to be informed of the nature and cause of the accusation against them, and to a speedy and public trial, by an impartial jury of the State and district wherein the crime was committed; to be confronted by the witnesses against them; and to have compulsory process for obtaining witnesses in their favor. Will it be claimed that these rights were not secured by the "law of the land" or by "due process of law," as declared and established at the foundation of our government? Are they to be excluded from the enumeration of the fundamental principles of liberty and justice, and, therefore, not embraced by "due process of law"? If the argument of my brethren be sound, those rights—although universally recognized at the establishment of our institutions as secured by that due process of law which for centuries had been the foundation of Anglo-Saxon liberty—were not deemed by our fathers as essential in the due process of law prescribed by our Constitution; because—such seems to be the argument—had they been regarded as involved in due process of law they would not have been specifically and expressly provided for, but left to the protection given by the general clause forbidding the deprivation of life, liberty, or property without due process of law. Further, the reasoning of the opinion indubitably leads to the conclusion that but for the specific provisions made in the Constitution for the security of the personal rights enumerated, the general inhibition against deprivation of life, liberty, and property without due process of law would not have prevented Congress from enacting a statute in derogation of each of them. . . .

It is said by the court that the Constitution of the United States was made for an undefined and expanding future, and that its requirement of due process of law in proceedings involving life, liberty and property, must be so interpreted as not to deny to the law the capacity of progress and improvement; that the greatest security for the fundamental principles of justice resides in the right of the people to make their own laws and alter them at pleasure. It is difficult, however, to perceive anything in the system of prosecuting human beings for their lives, by information, which suggests that the State which adopts it has entered upon an era of progress and improvement in the law of criminal procedure. . . . Under the local statutes in question, even the district attorney of the county is deprived of any discretion in the premises; for, if in the judgment of the magistrate before whom the accused is brought—and, generally, he is

only a justice of the peace—a public offence has been committed, it
becomes the duty of the district attorney to proceed against him by information for the offence indicated by the committing magistrate. Thus,
in California, nothing stands between the citizen and prosecution for his
life, except the judgment of a justice of the peace. . . . Anglo-Saxon
liberty would, perhaps, have perished long before the adoption of our
Constitution, had it been in the power of government to put the subject
on trial for his life whenever a justice of the peace, holding his office at
the will of the crown, should certify that he had committed a capital
crime. That such officers are, in some of the States, elected by the people,
does not add to the protection of the citizen; for, one of the peculiar
benefits of the grand jury system, as it exists in this country and England,
is that it is composed, as a general rule, of a body of private persons,
who do not hold office at the will of the government, or at the will of
voters. In many if not in all of the States civil officers are disqualified to
sit on grand juries. In the secrecy of the investigations by grand juries,
the weak and helpless—proscribed, perhaps, because of their race, or
pursued by an unreasoning public clamor—have found, and will continue to find, security against official oppression, the cruelty of mobs,
the machinations of falsehood, and the malevolence of private persons
who would use the machinery of the law to bring ruin upon their personal
enemies. . . .

    To these considerations may be added others of very great signifi-
cance. When the Fourteenth Amendment was adopted, all the States of
the Union, some in terms, all substantially, declared, in their constitutions, that no person shall be deprived of life, liberty, or property, otherwise than "by the judgment of his peers, or the law of the land," or
"without due process of law." When that Amendment was adopted, the
constitution of each State, with few exceptions, contained, and still contains, a Bill of Rights, enumerating the rights of life, liberty, and property
which cannot be impaired or destroyed by the legislative department. In
some of them, as in those of Pennsylvania, Kentucky, Ohio, Alabama,
Illinois, Arkansas, Florida, Mississippi, Missouri and North Carolina,
the rights so enumerated were declared to be embraced by "the general, great and essential principles of liberty and free government"; in
others, as in those of Connecticut, in 1818, and Kansas, in 1857, to be
embraced by "the great and essential principles of free government."
Now, it is a fact of momentous interest in this discussion, that, when
the Fourteenth Amendment was submitted and adopted, the Bill of Rights
and the constitutions of twenty-seven States expressly forbade criminal
prosecutions, by information, for capital cases; while, in the remaining
ten States, they were impliedly forbidden by a general clause declaring
that no person should be deprived of life otherwise than by "the judgment

of his peers or the law of the land," or "without due process of law." It may be safely affirmed that, when that Amendment was adopted, a criminal prosecution, by information, for a crime involving life, was not permitted in any one of the States composing the Union. So that the court, in this case, while conceding that the requirement of due process of law protects the fundamental principles of liberty and justice, adjudges, in effect, that an immunity or right, recognized at the common law to be essential to personal security, jealously guarded by our national Constitution against violation by any tribunal or body exercising authority under the general government, and expressly or impliedly recognized, *when the Fourteenth Amendment was adopted*, in the Bill of Rights or Constitution of every State in the Union, is, yet, not a fundamental principle in governments established, as those of the States of the Union are, to secure to the citizen liberty and justice, and, therefore, is not involved in that due process of law required in proceedings conducted under the sanction of a State. My sense of duty constrains me to dissent from this interpretation of the supreme law of the land.

   MR. JUSTICE FIELD did not take part in the decision of this case.

PALKO v. CONNECTICUT
Appeal from the Supreme Court of Errors of Connecticut
302 U.S. 319 (1937)

MR. JUSTICE CARDOZO delivered the opinion of the Court.
   A statute of Connecticut permitting appeals in criminal cases to be taken by the state is challenged by appellant as an infringement of the Fourteenth Amendment of the Constitution of the United States. Whether the challenge should be upheld is now to be determined.
   Appellant was indicted in Fairfield County, Connecticut, for the crime of murder in the first degree. A jury found him guilty of murder in the second degree, and he was sentenced to confinement in the state prison for life. Thereafter the State of Connecticut, with the permission of the judge presiding at the trial, gave notice of appeal to the Supreme Court of Errors. . . . Upon such appeal, the Supreme Court of Errors reversed the judgment and ordered a new trial. . . . It found that there had been error of law to the prejudice of the state (1) in excluding testimony as to a confession by defendant; (2) in excluding testimony upon cross-examination of defendant to impeach his credibility, and (3) in the instructions to the jury as to the difference between first and second degree murder.
   Pursuant to the mandate of the Supreme Court of Errors, defendant was brought to trial again. Before a jury was impaneled and also at later

stages of the case he made the objection that the effect of the new trial was to place him twice in jeopardy for the same offense, and in so doing to violate the Fourteenth Amendment of the Constitution of the United States. Upon the overruling of the objection the trial proceeded. The jury returned a verdict of murder in the first degree, and the court sentenced the defendant to the punishment of death. The Supreme Court of Errors affirmed the judgment of conviction. . . . The case is here upon appeal. . . .

1. The execution of the sentence will not deprive appellant of his life without the process of law assured to him by the Fourteenth Amendment of the Federal Constitution.

The argument for appellant is that whatever is forbidden by the Fifth Amendment is forbidden by the Fourteenth also. The Fifth Amendment, which is not directed to the states, but solely to the federal government, creates immunity from double jeopardy. No person shall be "subject for the same offense to be twice put in jeopardy of life or limb." The Fourteenth Amendment ordains, "nor shall any State deprive any person of life, liberty, or property, without due process of law." To retry a defendant, though under one indictment and only one, subjects him, it is said, to double jeopardy in violation of the Fifth Amendment, if the prosecution is one on behalf of the United States. From this the consequence is said to follow that there is a denial of life or liberty without due process of law, if the prosecution is one on behalf of the People of a State. . . .

We have said that in appellant's view the Fourteenth Amendment is to be taken as embodying the prohibitions of the Fifth. His thesis is even broader. Whatever would be a violation of the original bill of rights (Amendments I to VIII) if done by the federal government is now equally unlawful by force of the Fourteenth Amendment if done by a state. There is no such general rule.

The Fifth Amendment provides, among other things, that no person shall be held to answer for a capital or otherwise infamous crime unless on presentment or indictment of a grand jury. This court has held that, in prosecutions by a state, presentment or indictment by a grand jury may give way to informations at the instance of a public officer. Hurtado v. California, 110 U.S. 516. . . . The Fifth Amendment provides also that no person shall be compelled in any criminal case to be a witness against himself. This court has said that, in prosecutions by a state, the exemption will fail if the state elects to end it. Twining v. New Jersey, 211 U.S. 78, 106, 111, 112. . . . The Sixth Amendment calls for a jury trial in criminal cases and the Seventh for a jury trial in civil cases at common law where the value in controversy shall exceed twenty dollars. This court has ruled that consistently with those amendments trial by jury may be modified by a state or abolished altogether. Walker v. Sauvinet, 92 U.S. 90. . . .

On the other hand, the due process clause of the Fourteenth Amendment may make it unlawful for a state to abridge by its statutes the freedom of speech which the First Amendment safeguards against encroachment by the Congress, De Jonge v. Oregon, 299 U.S. 353, 364; Herndon v. Lowry, 301 U.S. 242, 259; or the like freedom of the press, Grosjean v. American Press Co., 297 U.S. 233; Near v. Minnesota ex rel. Olson, 283 U.S. 697, 707; or the free exercise of religion, Hamilton v. Regents, 293 U.S. 245, 262, cf. Grosjean v. American Press Co., supra; Pierce v. Society of Sisters, 268 U.S. 510; or the right of peaceable assembly, without which speech would be unduly trammeled, De Jonge v. Oregon, supra; Herndon v. Lowry, supra; or the right of one accused of crime to the benefit of counsel, Powell v. Alabama, 287 U.S. 45. In these and other situations immunities that are valid as against the federal government by force of the specific pledges of particular amendments have been found to be implicit in the concept of ordered liberty, and thus, through the Fourteenth Amendment, become valid as against the states.

The line of division may seem to be wavering and broken if there is a hasty catalogue of the cases on the one side and the other. Reflection and analysis will induce a different view. There emerges the perception of a rationalizing principle which gives to discrete instances a proper order and coherence. The right to trial by jury and the immunity from prosecution except as the result of an indictment may have value and importance. Even so, they are not of the very essence of a scheme of ordered liberty. To abolish them is not to violate a "principle of justice so rooted in the traditions and conscience of our people as to be ranked as fundamental." Snyder v. Massachusetts, [291 U.S. 97 (1934)], p.105; Brown v. Mississippi, [297 U.S. 278 (1936)], p.285; Hebert v. Louisiana, 272 U.S. 312, 316. Few would be so narrow or provincial as to maintain that a fair and enlightened system of justice would be impossible without them. What is true of jury trials and indictments is true also, as the cases show, of the immunity from compulsory self-incrimination. Twining v. New Jersey, supra. This too might be lost, and justice still be done. Indeed, today as in the past there are students of our penal system who look upon the immunity as a mischief rather than a benefit, and who would limit its scope, or destroy it altogether. No doubt there would remain the need to give protection against torture, physical or mental. Brown v. Mississippi, supra. Justice, however, would not perish if the accused were subject to a duty to respond to orderly inquiry. The exclusion of these immunities and privileges from the privileges and immunities protected against the action of the states has not been arbitrary or casual.

It has been dictated by a study and appreciation of the meaning, the essential implications, of liberty itself.

We reach a different plane of social and moral values when we pass to the privileges and immunities that have been taken over from the earlier articles of the federal bill of rights and brought within the Fourteenth Amendment by a process of absorption. These in their origin were effective against the federal government alone. If the Fourteenth Amendment has absorbed them, the process of absorption has had its source in the belief that neither liberty nor justice would exist if they were sacrificed. Twining v. New Jersey, supra, p.99.[4] This is true, for illustration, of freedom of thought, and speech. Of that freedom one may say that it is the matrix, the indispensable condition, of nearly every other form of freedom. With rare aberrations a pervasive recognition of that truth can be traced in our history, political and legal. So it has come about that the domain of liberty, withdrawn by the Fourteenth Amendment from encroachment by the states, has been enlarged by latterday judgments to include liberty of the mind as well as liberty of action.[5] The extension became, indeed, a logical imperative when once it was recognized, as long ago it was, that liberty is something more than exemption from physical restraint, and that even in the field of substantive rights and duties the legislative judgment, if oppressive and arbitrary, may be overridden by the courts. . . . Fundamental too in the concept of due process, and so in that of liberty, is the thought that condemnation shall be rendered only after trial. Scott v. McNeal, 154 U.S. 34; Blackmer v. United States, 284 U.S. 421. The hearing, moreover, must be a real one, not a sham or a pretense. Moore v. Dempsey, 261 U.S. 86; Mooney v. Holohan, 294 U.S. 103. For that reason, ignorant defendants in a capital case were held to have been condemned unlawfully when in truth, though not in form, they were refused the aid of counsel. Powell v. Alabama, supra, pp. 67, 68. The decision did not turn upon the fact that the benefit of counsel would have been guaranteed to the defendants by the provisions of the Sixth Amendment if they had been prosecuted in a federal court. The decision turned upon the fact that in the particular situation laid before us in the evidence the benefit of counsel was essential to the substance of a hearing.

Our survey of the cases serves, we think, to justify the statement

4. ". . . it is possible that some of the personal rights safeguarded by the first eight Amendments against National action may also be safeguarded against state action, because a denial of them would be a denial of due process of law. Chicago, Burlington & Quincy Railroad v. Chicago, 166 U.S. 226. If this is so, it is not because those rights are enumerated in the first eight Amendments, but because they are of such a nature that they are included in the conception of due process of law."

5. The cases are brought together in Warren, The New Liberty under the 14th Amendment, 39 Harv. L. Rev. 431.

that the dividing line between them, if not unfaltering throughout its course, has been true for the most part to a unifying principle. On which side of the line the case made out by the appellant has appropriate location must be the next inquiry and the final one. Is that kind of double jeopardy to which the statute has subjected him a hardship so acute and shocking that our polity will not endure it? Does it violate those "fundamental principles of liberty and justice which lie at the base of all our civil and political institutions"? Hebert v. Louisiana, supra. The answer surely must be "no." What the answer would have to be if the state were permitted after a trial free from error to try the accused over again or to bring another case against him, we have no occasion to consider. We deal with the statute before us and no other. The state is not attempting to wear the accused out by a multitude of cases with accumulated trials. It asks no more than this, that the case against him shall go on until there shall be a trial free from the corrosion of substantial legal error. . . . This is not cruelty at all, nor even vexation in any immoderate degree. If the trial had been infected with error adverse to the accused, there might have been review at his instance, and as often as necessary to purge the vicious taint. A reciprocal privilege, subject at all times to the discretion of the presiding judge, . . . has now been granted to the state. There is here no seismic innovation. The edifice of justice stands, its symmetry, to many, greater than before. . . .

The judgment is Affirmed.

Mr. Justice Butler dissents.

DUNCAN v. LOUISIANA
Appeal from the Supreme Court of Louisiana
391 U.S. 145 (1968)

Mr. Justice White delivered the opinion of the Court.

Appellant, Gary Duncan, was convicted of simple battery in the Twenty-fifth Judicial District Court of Louisiana. Under Louisiana law simple battery is a misdemeanor, punishable by a maximum of two years' imprisonment and a $300 fine. Appellant sought trial by jury, but because the Louisiana Constitution grants jury trials only in cases in which capital punishment or imprisonment at hard labor may be imposed, the trial judge denied the request. Appellant was convicted and sentenced to serve 60 days in the parish prison and pay a fine of $150. Appellant sought review in the Supreme Court of Louisiana, asserting that the denial of jury trial violated rights guaranteed to him by the United States Constitution. The Supreme Court, finding "[n]o error of law in the ruling complained of," denied appellant a writ of certiorari. Pursuant to 28

U.S.C. §1257(2) appellant sought review in this Court, alleging that the Sixth and Fourteenth Amendments to the United States Constitution secure the right to jury trial in state criminal prosecutions where a sentence as long as two years may be imposed. . . .

I

The Fourteenth Amendment denies the States the power to "deprive any person of life, liberty, or property, without due process of law." In resolving conflicting claims concerning the meaning of this spacious language, the Court has looked increasingly to the Bill of Rights for guidance; many of the rights guaranteed by the first eight Amendments to the Constitution have been held to be protected against state action by the Due Process Clause of the Fourteenth Amendment. That clause now protects the right to compensation for property taken by the State;[4] the rights of speech, press, and religion covered by the First Amendment;[5] the Fourth Amendment rights to be free from unreasonable searches and seizures and to have excluded from criminal trials any evidence illegally seized;[6] the right guaranteed by the Fifth Amendment to be free of compelled self-incrimination;[7] and the Sixth Amendment rights to counsel,[8] to a speedy[9] and public[10] trial, to confrontation of opposing witnesses,[11] and to compulsory process for obtaining witnesses.[12]

The test for determining whether a right extended by the Fifth and Sixth Amendments with respect to federal criminal proceedings is also protected against state action by the Fourteenth Amendment has been phrased in a variety of ways in the opinions of this Court. The question has been asked whether a right is among those " 'fundamental principles of liberty and justice which lie at the base of all our civil and political institutions,' " Powell v. Alabama, 287 U.S. 45, 67 (1932);[13] whether it is "basic in our system of jurisprudence," In re Oliver, 333 U.S. 257, 273 (1948); and whether it is "a fundamental right, essential to a fair trial," Gideon v. Wainright, 372 U.S. 335, 343-344 (1963); Malloy v. Hogan, 378 U.S. 1, 6 (1964): Pointer v. Texas, 380 U.S. 400, 403

4. Chicago, B. & Q.R. Co. v. Chicago, 166 U.S. 226 (1897).
5. See, e.g., Fiske v. Kansas, 274 U.S. 380 (1927).
6. See Mapp v. Ohio, 367 U.S. 643 (1961).
7. Malloy v. Hogan, 378 U.S. 1 (1964).
8. Gideon v. Wainwright, 372 U.S. 335 (1963).
9. Klopfer v. North Carolina, 386 U.S. 213 (1967).
10. In re Oliver, 333 U.S. 257 (1948).
11. Pointer v. Texas, 380 U.S. 400 (1965).
12. Washington v. Texas, 388 U.S. 14 (1967).
13. Quoting from Hebert v. Louisiana, 272 U.S. 312, 316 (1926).

(1965). The claim before us is that the right to trial by jury guaranteed by the Sixth Amendment meets these tests. The position of Louisiana, on the other hand, is that the Constitution imposes upon the States no duty to give a jury trial in any criminal case, regardless of the seriousness of the crime or the size of the punishment which may be imposed. Because we believe that trial by jury in criminal cases is fundamental to the American scheme of justice, we hold that the Fourteenth Amendment guarantees a right of jury trial in all criminal cases which—were they to be tried in a federal court—would come within the Sixth Amendment's guarantee.[14] Since we consider the appeal before us to be such a case, we hold that the Constitution was violated when appellant's demand for jury trial was refused. . . .

[The Court proceeded to review the history of trial by jury.]

The guarantees of jury trial in the Federal and State Constitutions

14. In one sense recent cases applying provisions of the first eight Amendments to the States represent a new approach to the "incorporation" debate. Earlier the Court can be seen as having asked, when inquiring into whether some particular procedural safeguard was required of a State, if a civilized system could be imagined that would not accord the particular protection. . . . The recent cases, on the other hand, have proceeded upon the valid assumption that state criminal processes are not imaginary and theoretical schemes but actual systems bearing virtually every characteristic of the common-law system that has been developing contemporaneously in England and in this country. The question thus is whether given this kind of system a particular procedure is fundamental— whether, that is, a procedure is necessary to an Anglo-American regime of ordered liberty. It is this sort of inquiry that can justify the conclusions that state courts must exclude evidence seized in violation of the Fourth Amendment, Mapp v. Ohio, 367 U.S. 643 (1961): that state prosecutors may not comment on a defendant's failure to testify, Griffin v. California, 380 U.S. 609 (1965); and that criminal punishment may not be imposed for the status of narcotics addiction, Robinson v. California, 370 U.S. 660 (1962). Of immediate relevance for this case are the Court's holdings that the States must comply with certain provisions of the Sixth Amendment, specifically that the States may not refuse a speedy trial, confrontation of witnesses, and the assistance, at state expense if necessary, of counsel. See cases cited in nn. 8-12, supra. Of each of these determinations that a constitutional provision originally written to bind the Federal Government should bind the States as well it might be said that the limitation in question is not necessarily fundamental to fairness in every criminal system that might be imagined but is funda- mental in the context of the criminal processes maintained by the American States.

When the inquiry is approached in this way the question whether the States can impose criminal punishment without granting a jury trial appears quite different from the way it appeared in the older cases opining that States might abolish jury trial. See, e.g., Maxwell v. Dow, 176 U.S. 581 (1900). A criminal process which was fair and equitable but used no juries is easy to imagine. It would make use of alternative guarantees and protections which would serve the purposes that the jury serves in the English and American systems. Yet no American State has undertaken to construct such a system. Instead, every American State, including Louisiana, uses the jury extensively, and imposes very serious punishments only after a trial at which the defendant has a right to a jury's verdict. In every State, including Louisiana, the structure and style of the criminal process—the supporting framework and the subsidiary procedures—are of the sort that naturally complement jury trial, and have developed in connection with and in reliance upon jury trial.

reflect a profound judgment about the way in which law should be enforced and justice administered. A right to jury trial is granted to criminal defendants in order to prevent oppression by the Government.[23] Those who wrote our constitutions knew from history and experience that it was necessary to protect against unfounded criminal charges brought to eliminate enemies and against judges too responsive to the voice of higher authority. The framers of the constitutions strove to create an independent judiciary but insisted upon further protection against arbitrary action. Providing an accused with the right to be tried by a jury of his peers gave him an inestimable safeguard against the corrupt or overzealous prosecutor and against the compliant, biased, or eccentric judge. If the defendant preferred the common-sense judgment of a jury to the more tutored but perhaps less sympathetic reaction of the single judge, he was to have it. Beyond this, the jury trial provisions in the Federal and State Constitutions reflect a fundamental decision about the exercise of official power—a reluctance to entrust plenary powers over the life and liberty of the citizen to one judge or to a group of judges. Fear of unchecked power, so typical of our State and Federal Governments in other respects, found expression in the criminal law in this insistence upon community participation in the determination of guilt or innocence. The deep commitment of the Nation to the right of jury trial in serious criminal cases as a defense against arbitrary law enforcement qualifies for protection under the Due Process Clause of the Fourteenth Amendment, and must therefore be respected by the States.

Of course jury trial has "its weakness and the potential for misuse," Singer v. United States, 380 U.S. 24, 35 (1965). We are aware of the long debate, especially in this century, among those who write about the administration of justice, as to the wisdom of permitting untrained laymen to determine the facts in civil and criminal proceedings. Although the debate has been intense, with powerful voices on either side, most of the controversy has centered on the jury in civil cases. Indeed, some of the severest critics of civil juries acknowledge that the arguments for criminal juries are much stronger. In addition, at the heart of the dispute have been express or implicit assertions that juries are incapable of adequately understanding evidence or determining issues of fact, and that they are unpredictable, quixotic, and little better than a roll of dice. Yet,

23. "The [jury trial] clause was clearly intended to protect the accused from oppression by the Government. . . ." Singer v. United States, 380 U.S. 24, 31 (1965).

"The first object of any tyrant in Whitehall would be to make Parliament utterly subservient to his will; and the next to overthrow or diminish trial by jury, for no tyrant could afford to leave a subject's freedom in the hands of twelve of his countrymen. So that trial by jury is more than an instrument of justice and more than one wheel of the constitution; it is the lamp that shows that freedom lives." P. Devlin, Trial by Jury 164 (1956).

the most recent and exhaustive study of the jury in criminal cases concluded that juries do understand the evidence and come to sound conclusions in most of the cases presented to them and that when juries differ with the result at which the judge would have arrived, it is usually because they are serving some of the very purposes for which they were created and for which they are now employed.[26] . . .

II

Louisiana's final contention is that even if it must grant jury trials in serious criminal cases, the conviction before us is valid and constitutional because here the petitioner was tried for simple battery and was sentenced to only 60 days in the parish prison. We are not persuaded. It is doubtless true that there is a category of petty crimes or offenses which is not subject to the Sixth Amendment jury trial provision and should not be subject to the Fourteenth Amendment jury trial requirement here applied to the States. Crimes carrying possible penalties up to six months do not require a jury trial if they otherwise qualify as petty offenses, Cheff v. Schnackenberg, 384 U.S. 373 (1966). But the penalty authorized for a particular crime is of major relevance in determining whether it is serious or not and may in itself, if severe enough, subject the trial to the mandates of the Sixth Amendment. . . . . In the case before us the Legislature of Louisiana has made simple battery a criminal offense punishable by imprisonment for up to two years and a fine. The question, then, is whether a crime carrying such a penalty is an offense which Louisiana may insist on trying without a jury. . . . .

In determining whether the length of the authorized prison term or the seriousness of other punishment is enough in itself to require a jury trial, we are counseled by [the decisions of this Court] to refer to objective criteria, chiefly the existing laws and practices in the Nation. In the federal system, petty offenses are defined as those punishable by no more than six months in prison and a $500 fine. In 49 of the 50 States crimes subject to trial without a jury, which occasionally include simple battery, are punishable by no more than one year in jail. Moreover, in the late 18th century in America crimes triable without a jury were for the most part punishable by no more than a six-month prison term, although there appear to have been exceptions to this rule. We need not, however, settle in this case the exact location of the line between petty offenses and serious crimes. It is sufficient for our purposes to hold that a crime punishable by two years in prison is, based on past and contemporary

---

26. Kalven & Zeisel, [The American Jury].

standards in this country, a serious crime and not a petty offense. Consequently, appellant was entitled to a jury trial and it was error to deny it.

The judgment below is reversed and the case is remanded for proceedings not inconsistent with this opinion. . . .

MR. JUSTICE BLACK, with whom MR. JUSTICE DOUGLAS joins, concurring.

The Court today holds that the right to trial by jury guaranteed defendants in criminal cases in federal courts by Art. II of the United States Constitution and by the Sixth Amendment is also guaranteed by the Fourteenth Amendment to defendants tried in state courts. With this holding I agree for reasons given by the Court. I also agree because [it is my view] . . . that the Fourteenth Amendment made all of the provisions of the Bill of Rights applicable to the States.

While I do not wish at this time to discuss at length my disagreement with Brother Harlan's forthright [dissent], . . . I do want to point out what appears to me to be the basic difference between us. His view . . . is that "due process is an evolving concept" and therefore that it entails a "gradual process of judicial inclusion and exclusion" to ascertain those "immutable principles of free government which no member of the Union may disregard." Thus the Due Process Clause is treated as prescribing no specific and clearly ascertainable constitutional command that judges must obey in interpreting the Constitution, but rather as leaving judges free to decide at any particular time whether a particular rule or judicial formulation embodies an "immutable princip[e] of free government" or is "implicit in the concept of ordered liberty," or whether certain conduct "shocks the judge's conscience" or runs counter to some other similar, undefined and undefinable standard. Thus due process, according to my Brother Harlan, is to be a phrase with no permanent meaning, but one which is found to shift from time to time in accordance with judges' predilections and understandings of what is best for the country. If due process means this, the Fourteenth Amendment, in my opinion, might as well have been written that "no person shall be deprived of life, liberty or property except by laws that the judges of the United States Supreme Court shall find to be consistent with the immutable principles of free government." It is impossible for me to believe that such unconfined power is given to judges in our Constitution that is a written one in order to limit governmental power.

Another tenet of . . . my Brother Harlan is that "due process of law requires only fundamental fairness." But the "fundamental fairness" test is one on a par with that of shocking the conscience of the Court. Each of such tests depends entirely on the particular judge's idea of ethics and morals instead of requiring him to depend on the boundaries fixed by the written words of the Constitution. Nothing in the history of the phrase "due process of law" suggests that constitutional controls are to depend on any particular judge's sense of values. . . . There is not one word of legal history that justifies making the term "due process of law" mean a guarantee of a trial free from laws and conduct which the courts deem at the time to be "arbitrary," "unreasonable," "unfair," or "contrary to civilized standards." The due process of law standard for a trial is one in accordance with the Bill of Rights and laws passed pursuant to constitutional power, guaranteeing to all alike a trial under the general law of the land.

Finally I want to add that I am not bothered by the argument that applying the Bill of Rights to the States, "according to the same standards that protect those personal rights against federal encroachment,"[5] interferes with our concept of federalism in that it may prevent States from trying novel social and economic experiments. I have never believed that under the guise of federalism the States should be able to experiment with the protections afforded our citizens through the Bill of Rights. As Justice Goldberg said so wisely in his concurring opinion in Pointer v. Texas, 380 U.S. 400:

> to deny to the States the power to impair a fundamental constitutional right is not to increase federal power, but, rather, to limit the power of both federal and state governments in favor of safeguarding the fundamental rights and liberties of the individual. In my view this promotes rather than undermines the basic policy of avoiding excess concentration of power in government, federal or state, which underlies our concepts of federalism. [380 U.S., at 414.]

It seems to me totally inconsistent to advocate, on the one hand, the power of this Court to strike down any state law or practice which it finds "unreasonable" or "unfair" and, on the other hand, urge that the States be given maximum power to develop their own laws and procedures. Yet the due process approach of my Brothers Harlan and Fortas . . . does just that since in effect it restricts the States to practices which a majority of this Court is willing to approve on a case-by-case basis. No one is more concerned than I that the States be allowed to use the full scope of their powers as their citizens see fit. And that is why I have continually fought against the expansion of this Court's authority over the States through the use of a broad, general interpretation of due process that permits judges to strike down state laws they do not like.

5. See Malloy v. Hogan, 378 U.S. 1, 10; Pointer v. Texas, 380 U.S. 400, 406; Miranda v. Arizona, 384 U.S. 436, 464.

In closing I want to emphasize that I believe as strongly as ever that the Fourteenth Amendment was intended to make the Bill of Rights applicable to the States. I have been willing to support the selective incorporation doctrine, however, as an alternative, although perhaps less historically supportable than complete incorporation. The selective incorporation process, if used properly, does limit the Supreme Court in the Fourteenth Amendment field to specific Bill of Rights' protections only and keeps judges from roaming at will in their own notions of what policies outside the Bill of Rights are desirable and what are not. And, most importantly for me, the selective incorporation process has the virtue of having already worked to make most of the Bill of Rights' protections applicable to the States.

MR. JUSTICE HARLAN, whom MR. JUSTICE STEWART joins, dissenting.

Every American jurisdiction provides for trial by jury in criminal cases. The question before us is not whether jury trial is an ancient institution, which it is; nor whether it plays a significant role in the administration of criminal justice, which it does; nor whether it will endure, which it shall. The question in this case is whether the State of Louisiana, which provides trial by jury for all felonies, is prohibited by the Constitution from trying charges of simple battery to the court alone. In my view, the answer to that question, mandated alike by our constitutional history and by the longer history of trial by jury, is clearly "no."

The States have always borne primary responsibility for operating the machinery of criminal justice within their borders, and adapting it to their particular circumstances. In exercising this responsibility, each State is compelled to conform its procedures to the requirements of the Federal Constitution. The Due Process Clause of the Fourteenth Amendment requires that those procedures be fundamentally fair in all respects. It does not, in my view, impose or encourage nationwide uniformity for its own sake; it does not command adherence to forms that happen to be old; and it does not impose on the States the rules that may be in force in the federal courts except where such rules are also found to be essential to basic fairness.

The Court's approach to this case is an uneasy and illogical compromise among the views of various Justices on how the Due Process Clause should be interpreted. The Court does not say that those who framed the Fourteenth Amendment intended to make the Sixth Amendment applicable to the States. And the Court concedes that it finds nothing unfair about the procedure by which the present appellant was tried. Nevertheless, the Court reverses his conviction: it holds, for some reason not apparent to me, that the Due Process Clause incorporates the particular clause of the Sixth Amendment that requires trial by jury in federal criminal cases—including, as I read its opinion, the sometimes trivial accompanying baggage of judicial interpretation in federal contexts. . . . With all respect, the Court's approach and its reading of history are altogether topsy-turvy.

I

I believe I am correct in saying that every member of the Court for at least the last 135 years has agreed that our Founders did not consider the requirements of the Bill of Rights so fundamental that they should operate directly against the States.[2] They were wont to believe rather that the security of liberty in America rested primarily upon the dispersion of governmental power across a federal system.[3] The Bill of Rights was considered unnecessary by some[4] but insisted upon by others in order to curb the possibility of abuse of power by the strong central government they were creating.[5]

The Civil War Amendments dramatically altered the relation of the Federal Government to the States. The first section of the Fourteenth Amendment imposes highly significant restrictions on state action. But the restrictions are couched in very broad and general terms: citizenship; privileges and immunities; due process of law; equal protection of the laws. Consequently for 100 years this Court has been engaged in the difficult process Professor Jaffe has well called "the search for intermediate premises."[6] The question has been, Where does the Court properly look to find the specific rules that define and give content to such terms as "life, liberty, or property" and "due process of law"?

A few members of the Court have taken the position that the intention of those who drafted the first section of the Fourteenth Amendment was simply, and exclusively to make the provisions of the first eight Amendments applicable to state action.[7] This view has never been ac-

2. Barron v. Baltimore, 7 Pet. 243 (1833), held that the first eight Amendments restricted only federal action.
3. The locus classicus for this viewpoint is The Federalist No. 51 (Madison).
4. The Bill of Rights was opposed by Hamilton and other proponents of a strong central government. See The Federalist No. 84; see generally C. Rossiter, 1787: The Grand Convention 284, 302-303.
5. In Barron v. Baltimore, supra, at 250, Chief Justice Marshall said, "These amendments demanded security against the apprehended encroachments of the general government—not against those of the local governments."
6. Jaffe, Was Brandeis an Activist? The Search for Intermediate Premises, 80 Harv. L. Rev. 986 (1967).
7. See Adamson v. California, 332 U.S. 46, 71 (dissenting opinion of Black, J.); O'Neil v. Vermont, 144 U.S. 323, 366, 370 (dissenting opinion of Harlan, J.) (1892); H. Black, "Due Process of Law," in A Constitutional Faith 23 (1968).

cepted by this Court. In my view . . . the first section of the Fourteenth Amendment was meant neither to incorporate, nor to be limited to, the specific guarantees of the first eight Amendments. The overwhelming historical evidence marshalled by Professor Fairman demonstrates, to me conclusively, that the Congressmen and state legislators who wrote, debated, and ratified the Fourteenth Amendment did not think they were "incorporating" the Bill of Rights[9] and the very breadth and generality of the Amendment's provisions suggest that its authors did not suppose that the Nation would always be limited to mid-19th century conceptions of "liberty" and "due process of law" but that the increasing experience and evolving conscience of the American people would add new "intermediate premises." In short, neither history, nor sense, supports using the Fourteenth Amendment to put the States in a constitutional straitjacket with respect to their own development in the administration of criminal or civil law. . . .

Apart from the approach taken by the absolute incorporationists, I can see only one method of analysis that has any internal logic. That is to start with the words "liberty" and "due process of law" and attempt to define them in a way that accords with American traditions and our system of government. This approach, involving a much more discriminating process of adjudication than does "incorporation," is, albeit difficult, the one that was followed throughout the 19th and most of the present century. It entails a "gradual process of judicial inclusion and exclusion,"[10] seeking, with due recognition of constitutional tolerance for state experimentation and disparity, to ascertain those "immutable principles . . . of free government which no member of the Union may disregard."[11] Due process was not restricted to rules fixed in the past, for that "would be to deny every quality of the law but its age, and to render it incapable of progress or improvement."[12] Nor did it impose nationwide uniformity in details, for

> [t]he Fourteenth Amendment does not profess to secure to all persons in the United States the benefit of the same laws and the same remedies. Great diversities in these respects may exist in two States separated only by an imaginary line. On one side of this line there may be a right of trial by jury, and on the other side no such right. Each State prescribes its own modes of judicial proceeding.[13]

9. Fairman, Does the Fourteenth Amendment Incorporate the Bill of Rights? The Original Understanding, 2 Stan. L. Rev. 5 (1949). . . .
10. Davidson v. New Orleans, 96 U.S. 97, 104.
11. Holden v. Hardy, 169 U.S. 366, 389.
12. Hurtado v. California, 110 U.S. 516, 529.
13. Missouri v. Lewis, 101 U.S. 22, 31.

Through this gradual process, this Court sought to define "liberty" by isolating freedoms that Americans of the past and of the present considered more important than any suggested countervailing public objective. The Court also, by interpretation of the phrase "due process of law," enforced the Constitution's guarantee that no State may imprison an individual except by fair and impartial procedures.

The relationship of the Bill of Rights to this "gradual process" seems to me to be twofold. In the first place it has long been clear that the Due Process Clause imposes some restrictions on state action that parallel Bill of Rights restrictions on federal action. Second, and more important than this accidental overlap, is the fact that the Bill of Rights is evidence, at various points, of the content Americans find in the term "liberty" and of American standards of fundamental fairness. . . .

Today's Court still remains unwilling to accept the total incorporationists' view of the history of the Fourteenth Amendment. This, if accepted, would afford a cogent reason for applying the Sixth Amendment to the States. The Court is also, apparently, unwilling to face the task of determining whether denial of trial by jury in the situation before us, or in other situations, is fundamentally unfair. Consequently, the Court has compromised on the ease of the incorporationist position, without its internal logic. It has simply assumed that the question before us is whether the Jury Trial Clause of the Sixth Amendment should be incorporated into the Fourteenth, jot-for-jot and case-for-case, or ignored. Then the Court merely declares that the clause in question is "in" rather than "out."

The Court has justified neither its starting place nor its conclusion. If the problem is to discover and articulate the rules of fundamental fairness in criminal proceedings, there is no reason to assume that the whole body of rules developed in this Court constituting Sixth Amendment jury trial must be regarded as a unit. The requirement of trial by jury in federal criminal cases has given rise to numerous subsidiary questions respecting the exact scope and content of the right. It surely cannot be that every answer the Court has given, or will give, to such a question is attributable to the Founders; or even that every rule announced carries equal conviction of this Court; still less can it be that every such subprinciple is equally fundamental to ordered liberty. . . .

Even if I could agree that the question before us is whether Sixth Amendment jury trial is totally "in" or totally "out," I can find in the Court's opinion no real reasons for concluding that it should be "in." The basis for differentiating among clauses in the Bill of Rights cannot be that only some clauses are in the Bill of Rights, or that only some are old and much praised, or that only some have played an important role in the development of federal law. These things are true of all. The Court says that some clauses are more "fundamental" than others, but it turns out to be using this word in a sense that would have astonished Mr. Justice Cardozo and which, in addition, is of no help. The word does not mean "analytically critical to procedural fairness" for no real analysis of the role of the jury in making procedures fair is even attempted. Instead, the word turns out to mean "old," "much praised," and "found in the Bill of Rights." The definition of "fundamental" thus turns out to be circular.

II

Since, as I see it, the Court has not even come to grips with the issues in this case, it is necessary to start from the beginning. When a criminal defendant contends that his state conviction lacked "due process of law," the question before this Court, in my view, is whether he was denied any element of fundamental procedural fairness. Believing, as I do, that due process is an evolving concept and that old principles are subject to re-evaluation in light of later experience, I think it appropriate to deal on its merits with the question whether Louisiana denied appellant due process of law when it tried him for simple assault without a jury.

The obvious starting place is the fact that this Court has, in the past, *held* that trial by jury is not a requisite of criminal due process. . . .

Although it is of course open to this Court to reexamine these decisions, I can see no reason why they should now be overturned. It can hardly be said that time has altered the question, or brought significant new evidence to bear upon it. The virtues and defects of the jury system have been hotly debated for a long time, and are hotly debated today, without significant change in the lines of argument. . . .

The jury is of course not without virtues. It affords ordinary citizens a valuable opportunity to participate in a process of government, an experience fostering, one hopes, a respect for law. It eases the burden on judges by enabling them to share a part of their sometimes awesome responsibility. A jury may, at times, afford a higher justice by refusing to enforce harsh laws (although it necessarily does so haphazardly, raising the questions whether arbitrary enforcement of harsh laws is better than total enforcement, and whether the jury system is to be defended on the ground that jurors sometimes disobey their oaths). And the jury may, or may not, contribute desirably to the willingness of the general public to accept criminal judgments as just.

It can hardly be gainsaid, however, that the principal original virtue of the jury trial—the limitations a jury imposes on a tyrannous judiciary— has largely disappeared. We no longer live in a medieval or colonial

society. Judges enforce laws enacted by democratic decision, not by regal
fiat. They are elected by the people or appointed by the people's elected
officials, and are responsible not to a distant monarch alone but to reviewing courts, including this one. . . .

Indeed, even if I were persuaded that trial by jury is a fundamental
right in some criminal cases, I could see nothing fundamental in the
rule, not yet formulated by the Court, that places the prosecution of
appellant for simple battery within the category of "jury crimes" rather
than "petty crimes." . . .

The point is not that many offenses that English-speaking communities have, at one time or another, regarded as triable without a jury
are more serious, and carry more serious penalties, than the one involved
here. The point is rather that until today few people would have thought
the exact location of the line mattered very much. There is no obvious
reason why a jury trial is a requisite of fundamental fairness when the
charge is robbery, and not a requisite of fairness when the same defendant,
for the same actions, is charged with assault and petty theft. The reason
for the historic exception for relatively minor crimes is the obvious one:
the burden of jury trial was thought to outweigh its marginal advantages.
Exactly why the States should not be allowed to make continuing adjustments, based on the state of their criminal dockets and the difficulty
of summoning jurors, simply escapes me.

In sum, there is a wide range of views on the desirability of trial by
jury, and on the ways to make it most effective when it is used; there is
also considerable variation from State to State in local conditions such
as the size of the criminal caseload, the ease or difficulty of summoning
jurors, and other trial conditions bearing on fairness. We have before us,
therefore, an almost perfect example of a situation in which the celebrated
dictum of Mr. Justice Brandeis should be invoked. It is, he said, "one
of the happy incidents of the federal system that a single courageous State
may, if its citizens choose, serve as a laboratory. . . ." New State Ice
Co. v. Liebmann, 285 U.S. 262, 280, 311 (dissenting opinion). This
Court, other courts, and the political process are available to correct any
experiments in criminal procedure that prove fundamentally unfair to
defendants. That is not what is being done today: instead, and quite
without reason, the Court has chosen to impose upon every State one
means of trying criminal cases; it is a good means, but it is not the only
fair means, and it is not demonstrably better than the alternatives States
might devise.

I would affirm the judgment of the Supreme Court of Louisiana.

MR. JUSTICE FORTAS, concurring.
I join the judgments and opinions of the Court in these cases because

I agree that the Due Process Clause of the Fourteenth Amendment requires that the States accord the right to jury trial in prosecutions for offenses that are not petty. A powerful reason for reaching this conclusion is that the Sixth Amendment to the Constitution guarantees the right to jury trial in federal prosecutions for such offenses. It is, of course, logical and reasonable that in seeking, from time to time, the content of "due process of law," we should look to and be guided by the great Bill of Rights in our Constitution. Considerations of the practice of the forum States, of the States generally, and of the history and office of jury trials are also relevant to our task. I believe, as my Brother White's opinion for the Court in Duncan v. Louisiana persuasively argues, that the right to jury trial in major prosecutions, state as well as federal, is so fundamental to the protection of justice and liberty that "due process of law" cannot be accorded without it. . . .

But although I agree with the decision of the Court, I cannot agree with the implication, . . . that the tail must go with the hide: that when we hold, influenced by the Sixth Amendment, that "due process" requires that the States accord the right of jury trial for all but petty offenses, we automatically import all of the ancillary rules which have been or may hereafter be developed incidental to the right to jury trial in the federal courts. I see no reason whatever, for example, to assume that our decision today should require us to impose federal requirements such as unanimous verdicts or a jury of 12 upon the States. We may well conclude that these and other features of federal jury practice are by no means fundamental—that they are not essential to due process of law—and that they are not obligatory on the States.

I would make these points clear today. Neither logic nor history nor the intent of the draftsmen of the Fourteenth Amendment can possibly be said to require that the Sixth Amendment or its jury trial provision be applied to the States together with the total gloss that this Court's decisions have supplied. The draftsmen of the Fourteenth Amendment intended what they said, not more or less: that no State shall deprive any person of life, liberty, or property without due process of law. It is ultimately the duty of this Court to interpret, to ascribe specific meaning to this phrase. There is no reason whatever for us to conclude that, in so doing, we are bound slavishly to follow not only the Sixth Amendment but all of its bag and baggage, however securely or insecurely affixed they may be by law and precedent to federal proceedings. To take this course, in my judgment, would be not only unnecessary but mischievous because it would inflict a serious blow upon the principle of federalism. The Due Process Clause commands us to apply its great standard to state court proceedings to assure basic fairness. It does not command us rigidly and arbitrarily to impose the exact pattern of federal proceedings upon the 50

States. On the contrary, the Constitution's command, in my view, is that in our insistence upon state observance of due process, we should, so far as possible, allow the greatest latitude for state differences. It requires, within the limits of the lofty basic standards that it prescribes for the States as well as the Federal Government, maximum opportunity for diversity and minimal imposition of uniformity of method and detail upon the States. Our Constitution sets up a federal union, not a monolith. . . .

NOTES AND QUESTIONS

1. In comparing *Hurtado, Palko,* and *Duncan,* reflect on the concerns that appear to influence the various opinions. To what extent, for example, do the cases reflect changing views concerning the relationship between institutions of government or between citizens and government? Do the cases appear to reflect differing views of the role of the Supreme Court? Of the role or nature of human autonomy?

2. *Palko* was subsequently overruled on selective incorporationist grounds in Benton v. Maryland, 395 U.S. 784 (1969). In fact, the Supreme Court has now explicitly "incorporated" into the due process clause of the fourteenth amendment each of the provisions of the Bill of Rights relevant to criminal trials except the right to a grand jury indictment and the bail provision of the eighth amendment. The problems are not at an end, however. As the Court has proceeded to incorporate various provisions of the Bill of Rights, it has done so by applying the applicable federal standard. Yet there are significant differences between state and federal systems that make it difficult for the states (usually because of inordinate expense) to apply the federal standard. This has resulted in pressure on the Supreme Court to water down the applicable standard, and the results of that pressure can easily be seen in the jury trial cases following *Duncan.* Although the tradition in the federal system has always been that jury trials require a unanimous verdict of a 12-person jury, in Apodaca v. Oregon, 406 U.S. 404 (1972), and Johnson v. Louisiana, 406 U.S. 356 (1972), the Court held that unanimity was *not* required by the sixth amendment, and in Williams v. Florida, 399 U.S. 78 (1970), the Court held that juries of less than 12 were permissible under the sixth amendment.[1] Thus, Justice Black's concern that the Court not

1. The Court drew the line at six, however, in Ballew v. Georgia, 435 U.S. 223 (1978); held that a six person jury must be unanimous, Burch v. Louisiana, 441 U.S. 130 (1979); and held that the sixth amendment right to jury trial applies whenever the authorized penalty exceeds six months, Baldwin v. New York, 399 U.S. 117 (1970). In Blanton v. City of North Las Vegas, 109 S. Ct. 1289 (1989), the Court held that under

impose a watered down constitutional standard on the states probably has resulted in watering down the standard generally, as it applies to *both* the states and the federal government. See in particular, Justice Harlan's separate opinion in *Williams* for a discussion.

Apodaca and *Johnson* are curious for another reason. Eight members of the Court agreed that, whatever it means, the sixth amendment is to be applied to the states and the federal government; but they split 4-4 on the meaning of the sixth amendment. Justice Powell, echoing the position of Justice Harlan, concluded that due process does not require that the sixth amendment be incorporated in its entirety and that unanimity was not the essence of fairness. Thus, there was an 8-1 decision "totally" incorporating the sixth amendment, and a 5-4 decision that the sixth amendment requires unanimity but that the states may dispense with it. Justice Powell's view may now be shared by Chief Justice Burger and Justice Rehnquist, who joined with Justice Powell in dissent on these grounds in Crist v. Bretz, 437 U.S. 28 (1978).

3. One of the factors motivating the nonincorporationists is Justice Brandeis's view, quoted in Justice Harlan's dissent in *Duncan*, to the effect that the states may act as laboratories. Does that view entail the possibility of concluding that an experiment has failed? Consider the following passage from Packer, The Courts, the Police, and the Rest of Us, 57 J. Crim. L., Criminology & Police Sci. 238, 239-240 (1966).

> Typically, the Court's intervention in any given phase of the criminal process has started with a highly particularistic decision dealing on a narrow basis with the facts of a particularly flagrant or shocking case brought before it. That was true of the first right to counsel case, Powell v. Alabama,[14] and it was true also of the first confession case, Brown v. Mississippi.[15] The confession cases are particularly instructive on this issue. For approximately twenty years following Brown v. Mississippi, a number of confession cases came before the court. As the standards it sought to lay down emerged, they placed great emphasis on the "special circumstances" of the cases. A given confession was deemed involuntary because of the defendant's personal characteristics—illiterate, of low intelligence, immature, a member of a disadvantaged minority group—or because of coercive forces at work in the interrogation process, or because of some combination of these factors. In those decisions, the Court tried, among other things, to influence police behavior by dealing, in its traditional way, with the facts of the specific case before it. But the gap between aspiration and reality proved too great to bridge in the Court's traditional

---

the sixth amendment a jury was not required for the trial of a DUI charge, even though there was a mandatory jail term upon conviction of at least two days.

14. 287 U.S. 45 (1932).
15. 297 U.S. 278 (1936).

way. And so, the movement has been to ever increasing generality of statement: from *this* confession was coerced for the following particularistic reasons unique to this case, to *all* confessions are bad when they are obtained from an arrestee who has not been promptly brought before a magistrate, as in the famous *Mallory* rule announced for the federal criminal courts in 1957. . . .

The great criminal procedure decisions of the last few years can all be regarded as exemplifying this movement toward increasingly generalized statement, sparked by the court's despair over the prospect of significantly affecting police practices through its more traditional activity. The court has sensed a law-making vacuum into which, rightly or wrongly, it has seen itself as having to rush. Mapp v. Ohio, in extending the exclusionary rule, on unreasonable searches and seizures to the state courts, was explicitly based on the proposition that no other presently available means of control held out any hope for deterring police disregard for the dictates of the Fourth Amendment (which had been held applicable to the states in Wolf v. Colorado,[16] in 1949). Gideon v. Wainwright substituted a blanket rule on right to counsel explicitly because the earlier case-by-case approach of Betts v. Brady[17] had failed to bring about universal compliance with what the court perceived as needed reform in the provision of counsel to indigent defendants.

Moves of this sort by the Supreme Court are, in my view, moves of desperation. Nobody else is exerting control over the law enforcement process, so the justices think that they must. But they can do so, in state cases at any rate, only in the discharge of their duty to construe the Constitution in cases that come before them. And so, the rules of the criminal process, which ought to be the subject of flexible inquiry and adjustment by law-making bodies having the institutional capacity to deal with them, are evolved through a process that its warmest defenders recognize as to some extent awkward and inept: the rules become "constitutionalized." The Bill of Rights becomes, as Judge Henry Friendly's gibe has it, a code of criminal procedure.[18] . . .

4. Reconsider footnote 14 in *Duncan*, supra. What is the sense and significance of that footnote? What difference does it make to ask if something is "fair" as compared to asking whether something is "fair" in the context of "an Anglo-American regime of ordered liberty"? Is the language in *Duncan* simply rhetoric designed to make the Court's apparent departure from *Palko* more palatable? Is an implicit comparison being drawn between adversarial and nonadversarial systems? If so, how useful or cogent is that comparison? Consider the following from Da-

16. 338 U.S. 25 (1949).
17. 316 U.S. 455 (1942).
18. See Friendly, The Bill of Rights as a Code of Criminal Procedure, 53 Cal. L. Rev. 929 (1965).

maska, Evidentiary Barriers to Conviction and Two Models of Criminal Procedure: A Comparative Study, 121 U. Pa. L. Rev. 506, 563-565 (1973).

[L]et me quickly outline the sequence of procedural ideas inherent in the adversary model. The fundamental matrix is based upon the view that proceedings should be structured as a dispute between two sides in a position of theoretical equality before a court which must decide on the outcome of the contest. The procedural aim is to settle the conflict stemming from the allegation of commission of crime. Since the proceeding is essentially a contest, devices such as pleadings and stipulations are not only acceptable but, indeed, essential because they establish the existence of a contest and delineate its borders. The protagonists of the model have definite, independent, and conflicting functions: the prosecutor's role is to obtain a conviction; the defendant's role is to block this effort. In his charge the prosecutor determines which factual propositions he will attempt to prove and must marshal evidence in support of his factual contentions. Not only does he have the burden of persuasion with respect to the latter, but also the burden of presenting evidence in court. In doing so he is expected to be partisan. The defendant decides which facts favorable to his theses he will attempt to prove, and must adduce evidence in support of all his factual contentions. He cannot be examined by the court, for reasons which will appear shortly, nor can he be questioned by the prosecution. For if only one side to a contest were to use the other as an evidentiary source, such practice would destroy the balance of advantages and the position of theoretical equality between the contestants. Furthermore, such practice would fly in the face of the idea of rival use of informational sources: the informational source and its partisan user would merge in the person of the defendant. The role of the adjudicator becomes that of an umpire who sees to it that the parties abide by the rules regulating their contest. Even here his basic attitude is one of passivity: he is to rule on the propriety of conduct only upon the objection of the side adversely affected. When the contest is over the adjudicator must, of course, decide on the outcome.[133] An important outgrowth of the fundamental matrix is a great number of technical rules regarding proper conduct of the protagonists. Proceedings tend to become "over-lawyered."

Many features of actual criminal procedures in common law countries are not essential characteristics of this model. Judgment by one's peers, ambushes as a result of lack of discovery, publicity, emphasis on oral testimony—these and many other features are not indispensable to the adversary model. Yet, . . . the ideological assumptions underlying the model make many of these non-essential features a matter of natural

133. The adjudicator's passivity explains why it is that under the "pure" model the judge cannot interrogate the defendant. In locating actual American practices on the spectrum between the present model and its rival, the passivity of the *jury* in factfinding should not be overlooked.

choice. Borrowing a scholastic term, they are *naturalia* rather than *essentialia* of the adversary style.

Non-adversary proceedings emerge from the following central structural idea. Rather than being conceived of as a dispute, they are considered an official and thorough inquiry, triggered by the initial probability that a crime has been committed. The procedural aim is to establish whether this is in fact the case, and whether the imposition of criminal sanctions is justified. Of course, the matrix of an official investigation is incompatible with formal pleadings and stipulations: the court-controlled pursuit of facts cannot be limited by mutual consent of the participants."[134] "Parties" in the sense of independent actors are not needed, and proceedings may, for instance, be a mere "affaire a deux." Factfinding is "unilateral" and detached. All reliable sources of information may in principle be used, and the defendant may be subjected to interrogation. Obviously, then, this much simpler structure of proceedings leads to fewer technicalities. The non-adversary model is, thus, "under-lawyered."[135]

Many historically-determined features of continental procedures are not essential to the model. It is, moreover, theoretically possible that the presentation of evidence could outwardly proceed in an adversary fashion, as long as the adjudicators were at least subsidiarily authorized to raise new issues, examine proof sua sponte, and hear evidence themselves whenever necessary to advance the official inquiry. But, once again, the ideological assumptions behind the model make many features of real-life continental proceedings a matter of natural choice.

So much for the two analytical models devoid of ideological underpinnings. Turning now to the opposition of the two ideologies underlying the rival procedural models, we find little more in Western European writing than passing remarks and sporadic embryonic ideas in need of elaboration. Little effort seems to have been spent on the study of how broad ideological orientations determine the choice of procedural arrangements. However, where the issue of rival ideologies has squarely been faced, collectivistic values and benevolent paternalism were isolated as preconceptions of the non-adversary model, while traditional Lockean liberal values, with distrust of the state and freedom from its restraint, were found to be in the ideological matrix of the adversary model. . . .

5. Bear in mind that the federal constitutional decisions only determine the minimum requirements of the criminal system. Congress and state legislatures are free to go beyond that minimum by statute, and state constitutional provisions may be interpreted by state courts to impose greater restraints on state power than that imposed by current federal

---

134. Thus, even if the defendant declares that he is guilty, the inquiry must proceed in the ordinary fashion.

135. Not only is the technical scaffolding of procedure simpler; as indicated, legal counsel are not indispensable for the model to function. If they do appear, however, the more active the court, the less important their role.

constitutional doctrine. Although state courts have long recognized and implemented their independent right to determine the meaning of state constitutional provisions, there has been an upsurge of such activity in recent years. For discussions, see Brennan, State Courts and the Protection of Individual Rights, 90 Harv. L. Rev. 489 (1977); Developments: The Interpretation of State Constitutional Rights, 95 Harv. L. Rev. 1324 (1982); Howard, State Courts and Constitutional Rights in the Day of the Burger Court, 62 Va. L. Rev. 873 (1976); Wilkes, The New Federalism in Criminal Procedure: State Court Evasion of the Burger Court, 62 Ky. L.J. 421 (1974). However, there has also been a recent trend to amend state constitutions to curtail the rights of the accused. Wilkes, First Things Last: Amendomania and State Bills of Rights, 54 Miss. L.J. 223 (1984).

B. RETROACTIVITY

Each constitutional decision generates the related question of the scope of its application. Is it to be applied, apart from the parties before the Court, only to trials that begin after the date of the decision? To cases still on direct review? To all cases, even those that are otherwise "final"? Only to state practices that occur after the date of the decision? Purely "prospectively" so as not to benefit even the parties before the court? The problem of the retroactivity of constitutional decisionmaking became particularly acute in the late fifties and sixties as the Supreme Court wrought fundamental changes in criminal procedure. The greater the retroactive effect of the Court's decisions, the greater the disruption of the penal process of the states. Perhaps in an effort to ameliorate the political impact of its criminal procedure cases, the Court did not impose each new rule completely retroactively. However, no consistent practice developed, and the Court employed in one context or another each of the possibilities mentioned above. The "law" of retroactivity, in short, appears to be largely ad hoc, as the Supreme Court's recent struggles with the doctrine amply demonstrate:

UNITED STATES v. JOHNSON
Certiorari to the Ninth Circuit Court of Appeals
457 U.S. 537 (1982)

JUSTICE BLACKMUN delivered the opinion of the Court.
    In Payton v. New York, 445 U.S. 573 (1980), this Court held that

the Fourth Amendment prohibits the police from making a warrantless and nonconsensual entry into a suspect's home to make a routine felony arrest. The question before us in the present case is whether the rule announced in *Payton* applies to an arrest that took place before *Payton* was decided. . . .

II

"[T]he federal constitution has no voice upon the subject" of retrospectivity. Great Northern R. Co. v. Sunburst Oil & Refining Co., 287 U.S. 358, 364 (1932). Before 1965, when this Court decided Linkletter v. Walker, 381 U.S. 618, "both the common law and our own decisions recognized a general rule of retrospective effect for the constitutional decisions of this Court . . . subject to [certain] limited exceptions." Robinson v. Neil, 409 U.S. 505, 507 (1973). . . .

In *Linkletter*, however, the Court concluded "that the Constitution neither prohibits nor requires [that] retrospective effect" be given to any "new" constitutional rule. 381 U.S., at 629. Since *Linkletter*, the Court's announcement of a constitutional rule in the realm of criminal procedure has frequently been followed by a separate decision explaining whether, and to what extent, that rule applies to past, pending, and future cases. See generally Beytagh, Ten Years of Non-Retroactivity: A Critique and a Proposal, 61 Va. L. Rev. 1557 (1975).

Linkletter itself addressed the question whether the Fourth Amendment exclusionary rule of Mapp v. Ohio, 367 U.S. 643 (1961), should apply to state convictions that had become final before *Mapp* was decided.[8] At the outset, the *Linkletter* Court noted that cases still pending on direct review when *Mapp* was handed down had already received the benefit of *Mapp*'s rule. . . . This limited retrospective application of *Mapp* was consistent with the common-law rule, recognized in both civil and criminal litigation, "that a change in law will be given effect while a case is on direct review." 381 U.S., at 627, citing United States v. Schooner Peggy, 1 Cranch 103 (1801).

To determine whether a particular ruling should also extend to cases that were already final, *Linkletter* directed courts to "weigh the merits and demerits in each case by looking to the prior history of the rule in question, its purpose and effect, and whether retrospective operation will

---

8. "By final we mean where the judgment of conviction was rendered, the availability of appeal exhausted, and the time for petition for certiorari had elapsed [or a petition for certiorari finally denied, all] before our decision in Mapp v. Ohio." Linkletter v. Walker, 381 U.S., at 622, n.5. See also Tehan v. United States ex rel. Shott, 382 U.S. 406, 409, n.3 (1966).

further or retard its operation." 381 U.S., at 629. Employing that test, the Court concluded that the *Mapp* rule should not apply to convictions that had become final before *Mapp* was decided. . . . Thus, after *Link-letter* . . . it appeared that all newly-declared constitutional rules of criminal procedure would apply retrospectively at least to judgments of conviction not yet final when the rule was established.

In Johnson v. New Jersey, 384 U.S. 719 (1966), and Stovall v. Denno, 388 U.S. 293 (1967), however, the Court departed from that basic principle. Those cases held that, in the interest of justice, the Court may balance three factors to determine whether a "new" constitutional rule should be retrospectively or prospectively applied: "(a) the purpose to be served by the new standards, (b) the extent of the reliance by law enforcement authorities on the old standards, and (c) the effect on the administration of justice of a retroactive application of the new standards." Id., at 297. . . . Because the outcome of that balancing process might call for different degrees of retroactivity in different cases, the Court concluded that "no distinction is justified between convictions now final . . . and convictions at various stages of trial and direct review." Stovall v. Denno, 388 U.S., at 300. . . .

Because the balance of the three *Stovall* factors inevitably has shifted from case to case, it is hardly surprising that, for some, "[t]he subsequent course of *Linkletter* became almost as difficult to follow as the tracks made by a beast of prey in search of its intended victim." Mackey v. United States, 401 U.S. 667, 676 (1971) (separate opinion of Harlan, J.). At one extreme, the Court has regularly given complete retroactive effect to new constitutional rules whose major purpose "is to overcome an aspect of the criminal trial that substantially impairs its truth-finding function and so raises serious questions about the accuracy of guilty verdicts in past trials." Williams v. United States, 401 U.S. 646, 653 (1971) (plurality opinion). . . .

At the other extreme, the Court has applied some standards only to future cases, denying the benefit of the new rule even to the parties before the Court. See, e.g., Morrissey v. Brewer, 408 U.S. 471, 490 (1972) (establishing basic requirements applicable only to "future revocations of parole"). . . . As an intermediate position, the Court has applied a change in the law to all future litigants, but retroactively only to the parties at bar. See, e.g., Stovall v. Denno, 388 U.S., at 301. . . .

In a consistent stream of separate opinions since *Linkletter*, Members of this Court have argued against selective awards of retroactivity. Those opinions uniformly have asserted that, at a minimum, all defendants whose cases were still pending on direct appeal at the time of the law-changing decision should be entitled to invoke the new rule. In Desist v. United States, 394 U.S. 244, 256 (1969) (dissenting opinion), and

Mackey v. United States, 401 U.S. 667, 675 (1971) (separate opinion) Justice Harlan presented a comprehensive analysis in support of that principle. In his view, failure to apply a newly-declared constitutional rule at least to cases pending on direct review at the time of the decision violated three norms of constitutional adjudication.

First, Justice Harlan argued, the Court's "ambulatory retroactivity doctrine," id., at 681, conflicts with the norm of principled decision-making. "Some members of the Court, and I have come to regret that I was among them, initially grasped this doctrine as a way of limiting the reach of decisions that seemed to them fundamentally unsound. Others rationalized this resort to prospectivity as a 'technique' that provided an 'impetus . . . for the implementation of long overdue reforms, which otherwise could not be practicably effected.' " Id., at 676, citing Jenkins v. Delaware, 395 U.S. 213, 218 (1969). "The upshot of this confluence of viewpoints," 401 U.S., at 676, was that the coalitions favoring nonretroactivity had realigned from case to case, inevitably generating a welter of "incompatible rules and inconsistent principles," Desist v. United States, 394 U.S., at 258. . . .

Second, Justice Harlan found it difficult to accept the notion that the Court, as a judicial body, could apply a 'new' constitutional rule entirely prospectively, while making an exception only for the particular litigant whose case was chosen as the vehicle for establishing that rule." Desist v. United States, 394 U.S., at 258 (dissenting opinion). A legislature makes its new rules "wholly or partially retroactive or only prospective as it deems wise." Mackey v. United States, 401 U.S., at 677 (Harlan, J., dissenting). This Court, however,

> announce[s] new constitutional rules . . . only as a correlative of our dual duty to decide those cases over which we have jurisdiction and to apply the Federal Constitution as one source of the matrix of governing legal rules. . . . Simply fishing one case from the stream of appellate review, using it as a vehicle for pronouncing new constitutional standards, and then permitting a stream of similar cases subsequently to flow by unaffected by that new rule constitute an indefensible departure from this model of judicial review." Id., at 678-679.

Third, Justice Harlan asserted that the Court's selective application of new constitutional rules departed from the principle of treating similarly situated defendants similarly:

> [W]hen another similarly situated defendant comes before us, we must grant the same relief or give a principled reason for acting differently. We depart from this basic judicial tradition when we simply pick and choose from among similarly situated defendants those who alone will receive the

benefit of a "new" rule of constitutional law. [Desist v. United States, 394 U.S., at 258-259 (dissenting opinion).]

Justice Harlan suggested one simple rule to satisfy all three of his concerns. "I have concluded that *Linkletter* was right in insisting that all 'new' rules of constitutional law must, at a minimum, be applied to all those cases which are still subject to direct review by this Court at the time the 'new' decision is handed down." Id., at 258. "[A] proper perception of our duties as a court of law, charged with applying the Constitution to resolve every legal dispute within our jurisdiction on direct review, mandates that we apply the law as it is at the time, not as it once was." Mackey v. United States, 401 U.S., at 681 (separate opinion).

We now agree with Justice Harlan that " '[r]etroactivity' must be rethought," Desist v. United States, 394 U.S., at 258 (dissenting opinion). We therefore examine the circumstances of this case to determine whether it presents a retroactivity question clearly controlled by past precedents, and if not, whether application of the Harlan approach would resolve the retroactivity issue presented in a principled and equitable manner.

III

A

At the outset, we must first ask whether respondent's case presents a retrospectivity problem clearly controlled by existing precedent. Re-examination of the post-*Linkletter* decisions convinces us that in three narrow categories of cases, the answer to the retroactivity question has been effectively determined, not by application of the *Stovall* factors, but rather, through application of a threshold test.

First, when a decision of this Court merely has applied settled precedents to new and different factual situations, no real question has arisen as to whether the later decision should apply retrospectively. In such cases, it has been a foregone conclusion that the rule of the later case applies in earlier cases, because the later decision has not in fact altered that rule in any material way. . . . Conversely, where the Court has expressly declared a rule of criminal procedure to be "a clear break with the past," Desist v. United States, 394 U.S., at 248, it almost invariably has gone on to find such a newly-minted principle nonretroactive. Once the Court has found that the new rule was unanticipated, the second and third *Stovall* factors—reliance by law enforcement authorities on the old standards and effect on the administration of justice of a retroactive application of the new rule—has virtually compelled a finding of non-retroactivity. . . .

Third, the Court has recognized full retroactivity as a necessary adjunct to a ruling that a trial court lacked authority to convict or punish a criminal defendant in the first place. The Court has invalidated inconsistent prior judgments where its reading of a particular constitutional guarantee immunizes a defendant's conduct from punishment, see, e.g., United States v. United States Coin & Currency, 401 U.S. 715, 724 (1971) (penalty against assertion of Fifth Amendment privilege against self-incrimination), or serves "to prevent [his] trial from taking place at all, rather than to prescribe procedural rules that govern the conduct of [that] trial," Robinson v. Neil, 409 U.S., at 509 (double jeopardy). In such cases, the Court has relied less on the technique of retroactive application than on the notion that the prior inconsistent judgments or sentences were void ab initio. . . .

Respondent's case neatly fits none of these three categories. First, Payton v. New York did not simply apply settled precedent to a new set of facts. In *Payton*, the Court acknowledged that the "important constitutional question presented" there had been "expressly left open in a number of our prior opinions." . . .

By the same token, however, *Payton* also did not announce an entirely new and unanticipated principle of law. In general, the Court has not subsequently read a decision to work a "sharp break in the web of the law," Milton v. Wainwright, 407 U.S. 371, 381, n.2 (1972) (Stewart, J., dissenting), unless that ruling caused "such an abrupt and fundamental shift in doctrine as to constitute an entirely new rule which in effect replaced an older one," Hanover Shoe, Inc. v. United Shoe Machinery Corp., 392 U.S. 481, 498 (1968). Such a break has been recognized only when a decision explicitly overrules a past precedent of this Court, . . . or disapproves a practice this Court arguably has sanctioned in prior cases, . . . or overturns a longstanding and widespread practice to which this Court has not spoken, but which a near-unanimous body of lower court authority has expressly approved. . . .

Payton did none of these. *Payton* expressly overruled no clear past precedent of this Court on which litigants may have relied. Nor did *Payton* disapprove an established practice that the Court had previously sanctioned. To the extent that the Court earlier had spoken to the conduct engaged in by the police officers in *Payton*, it had deemed it of doubtful constitutionality. The Court's own analysis in *Payton* makes it clear that its ruling rested on both long-recognized principles of Fourth Amendment law and the weight of historical authority as it had appeared to the Framers of the Fourth Amendment. Finally, *Payton* overturned no long-standing practice approved by near-unanimous body of lower court authority. *Payton* therefore does not fall into that narrow class of decisions whose nonretroactivity is effectively preordained because they unmistakably sig-

nal "a clear break with the past," Desist v. United States, 394 U.S., at
248.

It is equally plain that *Payton* does not fall into the third category
of cases that do not pose difficult retroactivity questions. *Payton* did not
hold that the trial court lacked authority to convict or sentence Theodore
Payton, nor did *Payton's* reading of the Fourth Amendment immunize
Payton's conduct from punishment. The holding in *Payton* did not prevent the defendant's trial from taking place; rather, it reversed the New
York Court of Appeals' judgment and remanded for a new trial to be
conducted without unconstitutionally-obtained evidence.

B

Having determined that the retroactivity question here is not clearly
controlled by our prior precedents, we next must ask whether that question
would be fairly resolved by applying the rule in *Payton* to all cases still
pending on direct appeal at the time when *Payton* was decided. Answering
that question affirmatively would satisfy each of the three concerns stated
in Justice Harlan's opinions in *Desist* and *Mackey*.

First, retroactive application of *Payton* to all previously nonfinal
convictions would provide a principle of decisionmaking consonant with
our original understanding of retroactivity in *Linkletter*. . . . Moreover,
such a principle would be one capable of general applicability, satisfying
Justice Harlan's central concern:

> Refusal to apply new constitutional rules to all cases arising on direct
> review . . . tends to cut this Court loose from the force of precedent,
> allowing us to restructure artificially those expectations legitimately created
> by extant law and thereby mitigate the practical force of stare decisis . . .
> a force which ought properly to bear on the judicial resolution of any legal
> problem. [Mackey v. United States, 401 U.S., at 680-681 (separate opin-
> ion).]

Second, application of *Payton* to cases pending on direct review
would comport with our judicial responsibilities "to do justice to each
litigant on the merits of his own case," Desist v. United States, 394 U.S.,
at 259 (Harlan, J., dissenting), and "to resolve all cases before us on
direct review in light of our best understanding of governing constitutional
principles." Mackey v. United States, 401 U.S., at 679 (separate opinion
of Harlan, J.). The Court of Appeals held that the circumstances of
respondent's arrest violated *Payton*, and the Government does not dispute
that contention. See n.6, supra. It would be ironic indeed were we now
to reverse a judgment applying *Payton's* rule, when in *Payton* itself, we

reversed a directly contrary judgment of the New York Court of Appeals. . . .

Third, application of the Harlan approach to respondent's case would further the goal of treating similarly situated defendants similarly. The Government contends that respondent may not invoke *Payton* because he was arrested before *Payton* was decided. Yet it goes without saying that Theodore Payton also was arrested before *Payton* was decided, and he received the benefit of the rule in his case. Furthermore, at least one other defendant whose conviction was not final when *Payton* issued benefited from *Payton's* rule, although he, too, was arrested before *Payton* was decided.[16] An approach that resolved all nonfinal convictions under the same rule of law would lessen the possibility that this Court might mete out different constitutional protection to defendants simultaneously subjected to identical police conduct.

V

To the extent necessary to decide today's case, we embrace Justice Harlan's views in *Desist* and *Mackey*. We therefore hold that, subject to the exceptions stated below, a decision of this Court construing the Fourth Amendment is to be applied retroactively to all convictions that were not yet final at the time the decision was rendered.

By so holding, however, we leave undisturbed our precedents in other areas. First, our decision today does not affect those cases that would be clearly controlled by our existing retroactivity precedents. Second, because respondent's case arises on direct review, we need not address the retroactive reach of our Fourth Amendment decisions to those cases that still may raise Fourth Amendment issues on collateral attack. . . . Third, we express no view on the retroactive application of decisions construing any constitutional provision other than the Fourth Amendment.[21] . . .

16. The New York Court of Appeals affirmed Payton's conviction along with that of Obie Riddick. See Payton v. New York, 445 U.S., at 578-579. This Court noted probable jurisdiction in Riddick's appeal, consolidated it with Payton's, then reversed both convictions. Id., at 603.

21. The logic of our ruling, however, is not inconsistent with our precedents giving complete retroactive effect to constitutional rules whose purpose is to overcome an aspect of the criminal trial that substantially impairs its truth-finding function. See, e.g., Hankerson v. North Carolina, 432 U.S. 233 (1977); Ivan V. v. City of New York, 407 U.S. 203 (1972). Depending on the constitutional provision involved, additional factors may warrant giving a particular ruling retroactive effect beyond those cases pending on direct review. See Hankerson v. North Carolina, 432 U.S., at 248, n.2 (Powell, J., concurring in the judgment).

Curiously, the dissent faults us not only for limiting our ruling to the only context

Respondent's case was pending on direct appeal when Payton v. New York was decided. Because the Court of Appeals correctly held that the rule in *Payton* should apply to respondent's case, its judgment is affirmed.

It is so ordered.

JUSTICE BRENNAN, concurring.

I join the Court's opinion on my understanding that the decision leaves undisturbed our retroactivity precedents as applied to convictions final at the time of decision. See, e.g., Stovall v. Denno, 388 U.S. 293 (1967).

JUSTICE WHITE, with whom THE CHIEF JUSTICE, JUSTICE REHN-QUIST and JUSTICE O'CONNOR join, dissenting.

In my view, this case is controlled by United States v. Peltier, 422 U.S. 531 (1975). *Peltier* established two propositions. First, retroactive application of a new constitutional doctrine is appropriate when that doctrine's major purpose is "to overcome an aspect of the criminal trial that substantially impairs its truth-finding function and so raises serious questions about the accuracy of guilty verdicts in past trials." Id., at 535, quoting Williams v. United States, 401 U.S. 646, 653 (1971). Second, new extensions of the exclusionary rule do not serve this purpose and, therefore, will not generally be applied retroactively. There was surely nothing extraordinary about our ruling in Payton v. New York, 445 U.S. 573 (1980), that would justify an exception to this general rule.

Peltier was only the latest of a number of cases involving the question of whether rulings extending the reach of the exclusionary rule should be given retroactive effect. We noted there, that "in every case in which the Court has addressed the retroactivity problem in the context of the exclusionary rule . . . the Court has concluded that any new constitutional principle would be accorded only prospective application." 422 U.S., at 535. We suggested that there were two reasons for this consistent

---

properly presented by this case—the Fourth Amendment—but also for preserving, rather than overruling, clearly controlling retroactivity precedents. The dissent then recasts those precedents in its own simplistic way, arguing that rules related to truth-finding automatically receive full retroactive effect, while implying that all other rules—including Fourth Amendment rules—should receive none.

There are, however, two problems with this. First, the Court's decisions regularly giving complete retroactive effect to truth-finding rules have in no way required that newly-declared Fourth Amendment rulings be denied all retroactive effect. For the reasons already stated, retroactive application of Fourth Amendment rules at least to cases pending on direct review furthers the policies underlying the exclusionary rule. Second, and more important, the Fourth Amendment "rule" urged by the dissent is far from a "perfectly good" one. As we already have shown, that "rule" condones obviously inequitable treatment of similarly situated litigants and judicial injustice to individual litigants.

pattern of decisions and that these two reasons were directly related to the justifications for the exclusionary rule.

That rule has traditionally been understood to serve two purposes: first, it preserves "judicial integrity;" second, it acts as a deterrent to unconstitutional police conduct. Neither of these purposes, however, is furthered by retroactive application of new extensions of the rule. First, "if law enforcement officers reasonably believed in good faith that evidence they had seized was admissible at trial, the 'imperative of judicial integrity' is not offended by the introduction into evidence of that material." Id., at 537. Second, a deterrence purpose can only be served when the evidence to be suppressed is derived from a search which the law enforcement officers knew or should have known was unconstitutional under the Fourth Amendment. Id., at 542.

In focusing on the purpose of the exclusionary rule in order to decide the question of retroactivity, the Court was following settled principles. In Linkletter v. Walker, 381 U.S. 618 (1965), which the majority agrees is the first of the modern retroactivity cases, the Court set forth a three-pronged model for analysis of the retroactivity question presented there. . . . This three-prong analysis was consistently applied in the cases which followed . . . Stovall v. Denno, 388 U.S. 293, 297 (1967). Indeed, in *Stovall*, the Court specifically announced that these three considerations—purpose of the new rule, reliance on the old rule, and effect on the administration of justice—were generally to guide resolution of all retroactivity problems relating to constitutional rules of criminal procedure. In each of these cases, the purpose of the new rule was the first consideration. That this was not accidental was made absolutely clear in Desist v. United States, 394 U.S. 244, 249 (1969): "Foremost among these factors is the purpose to be served by the new constitutional rule."[*] And as we went on to say there, "[t]his criterion strongly supports prospectivity for a decision amplifying the evidentiary exclusionary rule." Ibid. . . .

All of these principles are well settled and require reversal of the judgment of the Court of Appeals. The majority, in an intricate and confusing opinion disagrees. Two reasons for its disagreement seem to be presented. First, the majority discerns no consistent reading of our precedents that would control this case. . . . Given the clarity with which we have previously set out the applicable principles and the consistent application of those principles in cases involving extensions of the exclusionary rule, this is surely a strange conclusion. Eschewing the

[*]See also 394 U.S. at 251. "It is to be noted also that we have relied heavily on the factors of the extent of reliance and consequent burden on the administration of justice only when the purpose of the rule in question did not clearly favor either retroactivity or prospectivity."

straight-forward reading of the cases set forth above, which looks primarily to the substantive purpose of the relevant rule of law, the majority replaces it with an exceedingly formal set of three categories. . . . Because these categories turn out to be dicta only, they merit little comment. Suffice it to say that their inadequacy is obvious from even a moment's reflection: That category to which the majority agrees "the Court has regularly given complete retroactive effect" is nowhere included in this formal scheme—cases announcing new constitutional rules whose major purpose "is to overcome an aspect of the criminal trial that substantially impairs its truth-finding function and so raises serious questions about the accuracy of guilty verdicts in past trials." . . . It is little wonder that the majority finds this case difficult, when it has failed to learn the most obvious lessons of the previous cases.

Second, the majority seems to think that the problems of principle that Justice Harlan struggled with in his dissent in Desist v. United States, supra, are unanswerable under any rule that fails to give the benefits of a new constitutional ruling to all criminal defendants whose cases are pending on appeal at the time of the announcement. . . . The majority's approach, however, does not resolve these theoretical problems; it simply draws what is necessarily an arbitrary line in a somewhat different place than the Court had previously settled upon. Anything less than full retroactivity will necessarily appear unjust in some instances; it will provide different treatment to similarly situated individuals. The majority recognizes that the vagaries of the appellate process will cause this same problem to reappear under its proposed rule. . . . We had previously held that the best way to deal with this problem of inherent arbitrariness was to abide by the substantive principles outlined in *Stovall*. The majority makes no better suggestion today and is fooling itself if it believes that its proposal is a reasoned response to this problem of arbitrariness, rather than an exercise in line-drawing.

The insubstantiality of the majority's analysis and proposal is well illustrated by its conclusion. Despite the appearance of having resolved the difficult problem of the apparent injustice of any rule of partial retroactivity, the Court announces at the end that its decision today applies only to decisions "construing the Fourth Amendment" and asserts that it is not disturbing any of our retroactivity precedents. . . . That is, it returns from its abstract procedural approach to the substantive rule of law at issue. There are two problems with this, however. First, there is no connection between the analysis and the conclusion. Second, and more important, we already had a perfectly good rule for resolving retroactivity problems involving the Fourth Amendment.

Accordingly, I dissent.

———————————

When the Court returned to retroactivity following the *Johnson* case, perhaps not surprisingly the Court did not follow the apparent dictates of *Johnson*. In Solem v. Stumes, 465 U.S. 638 (1984), the Court held that Edwards v. Arizona, 451 U.S. 447 (1981), was not to be applied retroactively (*Edwards* is discussed in Chapter 9). The Court reached this conclusion by applying the three step process of Linkletter v. Walker, 381 U.S. 618 (1965), which was discussed but not followed in *Johnson*. The Court in *Solem* read *Johnson* as being limited to fourth amendment issues. 465 U.S. 643 n.3. The better lesson of *Solem* seems to be that retroactivity decisions are virtually unpredictable. The Court recently attempted to explain its apparently erratic course from *Johnson* to *Solem*. How well did it do so?

SHEA v. LOUISIANA
Certiorari to the Supreme Court of Louisiana
470 U.S. 51 (1985)

MR. JUSTICE BLACKMUN delivered the opinion of the Court.

[The defendant was interrogated in violation of the dictates of Edwards v. Arizona (discussed in Chapter 9), although *Edwards* had not yet been decided at the time of the interrogation. *Edwards* was decided while defendant's appeal was pending in the Louisiana Supreme Court, and the question the Court faced was whether *Edwards* applied to such a case. To answer that question, the Court analyzed the relationship between *Johnson* and *Stumes* on the question of retroactivity.]

The primary difference between *Johnson*, on the one hand, and *Stumes*, on the other, is the difference between a pending and undecided direct review of a judgment of conviction and a federal collateral attack upon a state conviction which has become final.[4] We must acknowledge,

---

4. In Solem v. Stumes, the Court observed:

"At a minimum, nonretroactivity means that a decision is not to be applied in collateral review of final convictions. For purposes of this case, that is all we need decide about *Edwards*." 465 U.S., at 650.

Of course, under the rationale of our decision today, the question is whether the conviction became final before *Edwards* was decided. As we hold, if a case was pending on direct review at the time *Edwards* was decided, the appellate court must give retroactive effect to *Edwards*, subject, of course, to established principles of waiver, harmless error, and the like. If it does not, then a court conducting collateral review of such a conviction should rectify the error and apply *Edwards* retroactively. This is consistent with Justice Harlan's view that cases on collateral review ordinarily should be considered in light of the law as it stood when the conviction became final. Thus, the result of our decisions

of course, that *Johnson* does not directly control the disposition of the present case. In *Johnson*, the Court specifically declined to address the implications of its holding for a case in a constitutional area other than the Fourth Amendment, or for a case in which a Fourth Amendment issue is raised on collateral attack.[5] We now conclude, however, that there is no reason to reach in this case a result that is different from the one reached in *Johnson*. There is nothing about a Fourth Amendment rule that suggests that in this context it should be given greater retroactive effect than a Fifth Amendment rule. Indeed, a Fifth Amendment violation may be more likely to affect the truth-finding process than a Fourth Amendment violation. And Justice Harlan's reasoning that principled decisionmaking and fairness to similarly situated petitioners requires application of a new rule to all cases pending on direct review is applicable with equal force to the situation presently before us. We hold that our analysis in *Johnson* is relevant for petitioner's direct-review Fifth Amendment claim under *Edwards*. He is entitled to the benefit of the ruling in that case. . . .

. . . [A]rguments that have been made in support of the judgment below are not persuasive. First, it is said that drawing a distinction between a case pending on direct review and a case on collateral attack produces inequities and injustices that are not any different from those that *Johnson* purported to cure. The argument is that the litigant whose *Edwards* claim will not be considered because it is presented on collateral review will be just as unfairly treated as the direct-review litigant whose claim would be bypassed were *Edwards* not the law. The distinction, however, properly rests on considerations of finality in the judicial process. The one litigant already has taken his case through the primary system. The other has not. For the latter, the curtain of finality has not been drawn. Somewhere, the closing must come. . . .

Next, it is said that the application of *Edwards* to cases pending on direct review will result in the nullification of many convictions and will relegate prosecutors to the difficult position of having to retry cases concerning events that took place years ago. We think this concern is overstated. We are given no empirical evidence in its support and Louisiana

concerning the retroactive applicability of the ruling in Edwards v. Arizona is fully congruent with both aspects of the approach to retroactivity propounded by Justice Harlan. . . .

5. The Court in *Johnson* also declined to address situations clearly controlled by existing retroactivity precedents, such as where the new rule of law is so clear a break with the past that it has been considered nonretroactive almost automatically. Whatever the merits of a different retroactivity rule for cases of that kind may be, we have no need to be concerned with the question here. In Solem v. Stumes the Court recognized that *Edwards* was "not the kind of clear break with the past that is automatically nonretroactive." — U.S., at —, 104 S. Ct., at 1343.

states that any such evidence is unavailable. We note, furthermore, that several courts have applied *Edwards* to cases pending on direct review without expressing concern about lapse of time or retroactivity and without creating any apparent administrative difficulty. . . . And if a case is unduly slow in winding its way through a State's judicial system, that could be as much the State's fault as the defendant's, and should not serve to penalize the defendant.

In addition, it is said that in every case, *Edwards* alone excepted, reliance on existing law justifies the nonapplication of *Edwards*. But, as we have pointed out, there is no difference between the petitioner in *Edwards* and the petitioner in the present case. If the *Edwards* principle is not to be applied retroactively, the only way to dispense equal justice to Edwards and to Shea would be a rule that confined the *Edwards* principle to prospective application unavailable even to *Edwards* himself.

Finally, it is said that the *Edwards* rule is only prophylactic in character and is not one designed to enhance accuracy in criminal jurisprudence. . . . The argument, we feel, is fully answered by the decision in United States v. Johnson, and by what we have said above in this opinion.

The judgment of the Supreme Court of Louisiana is reversed, and the case is remanded to that court for further proceedings not inconsistent with this opinion.

JUSTICE WHITE, with whom THE CHIEF JUSTICE, JUSTICE REHNQUIST, and JUSTICE O'CONNOR join, dissenting.

Last Term, in Solem v. Stumes, we held that the rule announced by the Court in Edwards v. Arizona, 451 U.S. 477 (1981), should not be applied retroactively in collateral attacks on criminal convictions. We concluded that the prophylactic purpose of the *Edwards* rule, the justifiable failure of police and prosecutors to foresee the Court's decision in *Edwards*, and the substantial disruption of the criminal justice system that retroactive application of *Edwards* would entail all indicated the wisdom of holding *Edwards* nonretroactive. Today, however, the majority concludes that notwithstanding the substantial reasons for restricting the application of *Edwards* to cases involving interrogations that postdate the Court's opinion in *Edwards*, the *Edwards* rule must be applied retroactively to all cases in which the process of direct appeal had not yet been completed when *Edwards* was decided. In so holding, the majority apparently adopts a rule long advocated by a shifting minority of Justices and endorsed in limited circumstances by the majority in United States v. Johnson, 457 U.S. 537 (1982): namely, the rule that any new constitutional decision—except, perhaps, one that constitutes a "clear break with the past"—must be applied to all cases pending on direct appeal at the time it is handed down.

Two concerns purportedly underlie the majority's decision. The first is that retroactivity is somehow an essential attribute of judicial decision-making, and that when the Court announces a new rule and declines to give it retroactive effect, it has abandoned the judicial role and assumed the function of a legislature—or, to use the term justice Harlan employed in describing the problem, a "super-legislature." Desist v. United States, 394 U.S. 244, 259 (1969) (Harlan, J., dissenting). The second (and not completely unrelated) concern is fairness. It is the business of a court, the majority reasons, to treat like cases alike; accordingly, it is unfair for one litigant to receive the benefit of a new decision when another, identically situated, is denied the same benefit. The majority's concerns are no doubt laudable, but I cannot escape the conclusion that the rule they have spawned makes no sense.

As a means of avoiding what has come to be known as the super-legislature problem, the rule announced by the majority is wholly inadequate. True, the Court is not and cannot be a legislature, super or otherwise. But I should think that concerns about the supposed usurpation of legislative authority by this Court generally go more to the substance of the Court's decisions than to whether or not they are retroactive. Surely those who believe that the Court has overstepped the bounds of its legitimate authority in announcing a new rule of constitutional law will find little solace in a decision holding the new rule retroactive. If a decision is in some sense illegitimate, making it retroactive is a useless gesture that will fool no one. If, on the other hand, the decision is a salutary one, but one whose purposes are ill-served by retroactive application, retroactivity may be worse than useless, imposing costs on the criminal justice system that will likely be uncompensated for by any perceptible gains in "judicial legitimacy."

The futility of this latest attempt to use retroactivity doctrine to avoid the super-legislature difficulty is highlighted by the majority's unwillingness to commit itself to the logic of its position. For even as it maintains that retroactivity is essential to the judicial function, today's majority, like the majority in *Johnson*, supra, continues to hold out the possibility that a "really" new rule—one that marks a clear break with the past—may not have to be applied retroactively even to cases pending on direct review at the time the new decision is handed down. . . . Of course, if the majority were truly concerned with the super-legislature problem, it would be "clear break" decisions that would trouble it the most. Indeed, one might expect that a Court as disturbed about the problem as the majority purports to be would swear off such decisions altogether, not reserve the power both to issue them and to decline to apply them retroactively. In leaving open the possibility of an exception for "clear break" decisions, the majority demonstrates the emptiness of its proposed solution to the super-legislature problem.

The claim that the majority's rule serves the interest of fairness is equally hollow. Although the majority finds it intolerable to apply a new rule to one case on direct appeal but not to another, it is perfectly willing to tolerate disparate treatment of defendants seeking direct review of their convictions and prisoners attacking their convictions in collateral proceedings. As I have stated before, see *Johnson*, supra, at 566-568 (White, J., dissenting), it seems to me that the attempt to distinguish between direct and collateral challenges for purposes of retroactivity is misguided. Under the majority's rule, otherwise identically situated defendants may be subject to different constitutional rules, depending on just how long ago now-unconstitutional conduct occurred and how quickly cases proceed through the criminal justice system. The disparity is no different in kind from that which occurs when the benefit of a new constitutional rule is retroactively afforded to the defendant in whose case it is announced but to no others; the Court's new approach equalizes nothing except the numbers of defendants within the disparately treated classes.

The majority recognizes that the distinction between direct review and habeas is problematic, but justifies its differential treatment by appealing to the need to draw "the curtain of finality". . . on those who were unfortunate enough to have exhausted their last direct appeal at the time *Edwards* was decided. Yet the majority offers no reasons for its conclusion that finality should be the decisive factor. When a conviction is overturned on direct appeal on the basis of an *Edwards* violation, the remedy offered the defendant is a new trial at which any inculpatory statements obtained in violation of *Edwards* will be excluded. It is not clear to me why the majority finds such a burdensome remedy more acceptable when it is imposed on the state on direct review than when it is the result of a collateral attack. The disruption attendant upon the remedy does not vary depending on whether it is imposed on direct review or habeas;[1] accordingly, if the remedy must be granted to defendants on

---

1. The distinction between direct review and collateral attack may bear some relationship to the recency of the crime; thus, to the extent that the difficulties presented by a new trial may be more severe when the underlying offense is more remote in time, it may be that new trials would tend to be somewhat more burdensome in habeas cases than in cases involving reversals on direct appeal. However, this relationship is by no means direct, for the speed with which cases progress through the criminal justice system may vary widely. Thus, if the Court is truly concerned with treating like cases alike, it could accomplish its purpose far more precisely by applying new constitutional rules only to conduct of appropriately recent vintage. I assume, however, that no one would argue for an explicit "five-year rule," for example.

The notion that a new trial is a significantly less burdensome remedy when it is

direct appeal, there is no strong reason to deny it to prisoners attacking their convictions collaterally. Conversely, if it serves no worthwhile purpose to grant the remedy to a defendant whose conviction was final before *Edwards*, it is hard to see why the remedy should be available on direct review.

The underlying flaw of the majority's opinion is its failure to articulate the premises on which the retroactivity doctrine it announces actually rests. In recognizing that a decision marking a clear break from the past may not be retroactive and in holding that the concern of finality trumps considerations of fairness that might otherwise dictate retroactivity in collateral proceedings, the majority implicitly recognizes that there is in fact more at issue in decisions involving retroactivity than treating like cases alike. In short, the majority recognizes that there are *reasons* why certain decisions ought not be retroactive. But the rules the majority announces fail to reflect any thoughtful inquiry into what those reasons might be. By contrast, the principles of retroactivity set forth in Linkletter v. Walker, 381 U.S. 618 (1965), and most recently applied in Solem v. Stumes, supra, provide a rational framework for thinking about the question whether retroactive application of any particular decision makes sense—that is, whether the benefits of retroactivity outweigh its costs. Because the Court has already determined that the relevant considerations set forth in *Linkletter* (the purpose of the new rule, the extent of law enforcement officials' justifiable reliance on the prior rule, and the effects on the criminal justice system of retroactivity) dictate nonretroactive application of the rule in *Edwards*, I cannot join in the majority's conclusion that that rule should be applied retroactively to cases pending on direct review at the time of our decision in *Edwards*. More importantly, I cannot concur in the approach to retroactivity adopted by today's majority an approach that, if our precedents regarding the nonretroactivity of decisions marking a clear break with the past remain undisturbed, merely adds a confusing and unjustifiable addendum to our retroactivity jurisprudence.[2]

---

imposed on direct review than when it is ordered on habeas is also called into serious question by the facts of this particular case. The remedy the Court grants the petitioner is a new trial that will be held almost six years after the commission of the offense with which he is charged. I have no doubt that there are many prisoners whose convictions were final at the time *Edwards* was decided who could be given a new trial as conveniently as petitioner.

Of course, it will be less burdensome in the aggregate to apply *Edwards* only to cases pending when *Edwards* was decided than to give it full retroactive effect; by the same token, it would be less burdensome to apply *Edwards* retroactively to all cases involving defendants whose last names begin with the letter "S" than to make the decision fully retroactive. The majority obviously would not countenance the latter course, but its failure to identify any truly relevant distinction between cases on direct appeal and cases raising collateral challenges makes the rule it announces equally indefensible.

2. After today, a decision that is foreshadowed—not new at all—is applicable both

I respectfully dissent.

[JUSTICE REHNQUIST's dissenting opinion is omitted.]

Demonstrating a seemingly infinite capacity to write opinions on retroactivity, the Supreme Court has returned to the issue numerous times since *Shea*. In Allen v. Hardy, 476 U.S. 1157 (1986), in a per curiam opinion, the Court held that Batson v. Kentucky, 476 U.S. 79 (1986) (holding that a defendant could establish a prima facie case of racial discrimination based on the prosecution's use of peremptory challenges to strike prospective jurors based on their race) was not to be applied retroactively to cases on federal habeas review. Subsequently, in Griffith v. Kentucky, 479 U.S. 314 (1987), the Court, per Justice Blackmun, held that *Batson* was to be applied to all cases pending on direct review or not yet final at the time of the decision. In doing so, the Court rejected the "clear break with prior precedent" exception, holding that *Batson* was to be applied to cases still on direct review notwithstanding that the case was a clear break with precedent. In dissent, the Chief Justice expressed a willingness to embrace both aspects of Justice Harlan's views, discussed in United States v. Johnson, page 98 supra, but dissented because the majority had only embraced the part of his views dealing with retroactivity as applied to cases on direct review and declined to state clearly that new constitutional cases were not to apply to cases on habeas corpus. Justice White, joined by Justice O'Connor and the Chief Justice, reiterated his dissent in *Johnson*.

In Teague v. Lane, 109 S. Ct. 1060 (1989), the Court continued its practice of providing splintered opinions on retroactivity issues. A majority reaffirmed Allen v. Hardy, supra, while a plurality of four (O'Connor, Rehnquist, Scalia, and Kennedy) wrote an opinion to the effect that a court faced with a new constitutional claim may consider first whether the benefits of the claim would be extended to the litigant before the court should the new claim be found valid. If the court concludes that the benefits would not be extended to the litigant, even if the claim were found to be valid, the court need not proceed to determine the merits of the claim.

Although predictions about the Court's treatment of retroactivity are

---

on direct review and in collateral proceedings. A decision that makes law that is somewhat new is to apply to all cases on direct review but will generally not be a basis for collateral relief. Really new decisions breaking with the past, however, will likely apply neither in collateral proceedings nor to cases on direct review other than that in which the decision is announced. The majority thus recognizes for purposes of retroactivity doctrine three categories of decisions: not new, newish, and brand new. I had hoped that after plenary review, we could do better than that.

obviously problematic, *Griffith* and *Teague* suggest that a majority of the Court may be willing to embrace Harlan's views. Recent cases bear out this prediction. In Butler v. McKeller, 110 S. Ct. 1212 (1990), and Saffle v. Parks, 110 S. Ct. 1257 (1990), the Court held that habeas petitioners would not benefit from the Court's announcement of new rules. One commentator has suggested that the concern of the Court that has resulted in its wandering approach to the law of retroactivity is the Court's desire to insulate convictions that have become final from reversal on habeas corpus. Haddad, The Finality Distinction in Supreme Court Retroactivity Analysis: An Inadequate Surrogate for Modification of the Scope of Federal Habeas Corpus, 79 Nw. U.L. Rev. 1062 (1984-85). As the title of Professor Haddad's article suggests, he argues that, if the concern is with preserving final convictions, the Court should narrow the scope of habeas corpus along the lines of Stone v. Powell, 428 U.S. 465 (1976), discussed at pages 888-890 infra, rather than attempt to accomplish the purpose indirectly through retroactivity decisions.

C. REFLECTIONS ON THE CONCEPT OF "DUE PROCESS OF LAW"

ALLEN, PROCEDURAL DUE PROCESS OF LAW, CRIMINAL
Encyclopedia of the American Constitution (Supp. 1990)

Integral to the law's aspirations is the set of variables differentiating law and politics: reason and passion; rationality and bias; free inquiry and ideology; fairness and self-interest. At the heart of the law's aspirations is the ardent hope that these variables permit distinctions between that which will endure and that which will pass, for it is the relative mix of the enduring and the ephemeral that determines whether a nation is one of disinterested laws or of very interested individuals. Thus it is that the Supreme Court strives to justify its decisions through well reasoned opinions. The task of the Court is to surmount the seductive allure of politics and rest judgment on principle.

But is this task possible? The difficulties are legion. Disagreements abound concerning the correct interpretative methodology, the data relevant to the various interpretive approaches, and indeed over such fundamental matters as the proper role of the judiciary in a democratic scheme. These disagreements are compounded because the Supreme Court does not speak with a monolithic voice but instead is spoken for by each of the justices in a setting where the implications of Arrow's Theorem are not just theoretically interesting but practically observable. And, superimposed over all these difficulties, is the fact that the Supreme Court is essentially a reactive institution, constantly responding to the problems generated for it by social factors beyond its control. No matter how fervently the Court wishes to promulgate a consistent and principled jurisprudence, the diversity and unpredictability of the grist for the Court's mill make the task formidable.

The task is more formidable the more open ended the interpretive problem, and among the most open ended of the Supreme Court's tasks is the interpretation of the twin due process of law clauses in the Fifth and Fourteenth Amendments. The language of these clauses is not confining, their historical purposes are unclear, and to the extent there is agreement concerning those purposes, their implications for contemporary issues are not obvious. The Fifth Amendment, for example, was adopted as part of a set of guarantees that the newly created central government would respect its proper sphere, and the Fourteenth Amendment was adopted to recognize and reflect the changes wrought in the country by the Civil War. Neither was adopted with the contemporary set of issues in mind to which these clauses have been asserted, by litigants and judges, to be relevant.

For all these reasons, the Supreme Court's interpretation of the due process clauses consistently is as much a reflection of the times as the product of timeless interpretive methodologies. The first century of the national existence was a time of territorial expansion and the creation and consolidation of governmental institutions in which criminal due process adjudication played virtually no role, and there were virtually no criminal due process cases. The second century brought an increasing emphasis on the role of individual rights, which culminated in the remarkable creativity of the Supreme Court's procedural revolution in the mid-1960s. The question now is what will the third century bring.

Certain matters are already obvious. The procedural revolution is over and the resulting legal landscape is stable. Whatever its theoretical attraction, the theory of total incorporation has essentially won, even though ironically a majority of the Court has never adopted the theory. Each of the criminal provisions of the Bill of Rights has been found to be binding on the states through the due process clause of the Fourteenth Amendment, excepting only the relatively insignificant requirement of an indictment by grand jury. Furthermore, notwithstanding the dramatic reorientation of the Supreme Court due to recent appointments, the Court has not overruled a single major criminal procedure case finding a Bill of Rights provision incorporated in the Fourteenth Amendment, and there is little evidence of any substantial interest on the Court to revisit the general question of the incorporation of the provisions of the Bill of Rights into the Fourteenth Amendment due process clause. The incorporationist controversy is so definitively over that the opinions of the Court addressing questions of state criminal procedure discuss directly the applicable Bill of Rights provision with at most a cursory reference to the due process clause of the Fourteenth Amendment. The casualness with which the distinction is drawn between Fourteenth Amendment due process and the specific provisions of the Bill of Rights is exemplified by the opinion for a unanimous Court in Crane v. Kentucky, 476 U.S. 683 (1986). In holding that due process was violated by the exclusion of testimony concerning the circumstances of a defendant's confession, the Court said that "Whether rooted directly in the Due Process Clause of the Fourteenth Amendment or in the Compulsory Process or Confrontation clauses of the Sixth Amendment, the Constitution guarantees criminal defendants 'a meaningful opportunity to present a complete defense.'"

Justices also appear to have little interest in giving either due process clause much independent significance. In those few instances in recent years in which the Court has discussed either clause directly rather than as a surrogate for some other constitutional provision, it typically has done so to deny that due process has any meaning independent of the specific provisions of the Bill of rights. In Moran v. Burbine, 475 U.S. 412 (1986), the Court held that the failure of the police to inform a criminal suspect subjected to custodial interrogation of the efforts of an attorney to reach him did not violate the due process clause. Due process also does not require appointed counsel for collateral review of a conviction, Pennsylvania v. Finley, 481 U.S. 551 (1987), not even for collateral review of capital convictions. Murray v. Giarratano, 109 S. Ct. 2765 (1989). Similarly, in Strickland v. Wahington, 466 U.S. 668 (1984), the Court commented that although "the Constitution guarantees a fair trial through the Due Process Clauses, it defines the basic elements of a fair trial largely through the several provisions of the Sixth Amendment." The Court applied this approach in Caplin & Drysdale, Chartered v. United States, 109 S. Ct. 2646 (1989), to find that the Fifth Amendment due process clause adds little or nothing to the Sixth Amendment right to counsel clause, and in United States v. Salerno, 481 U.S. 739 (1987), to reach a similar conclusion concerning the relationship between Fifth Amendment due process and the requirement of bail in the Eighth Amendment.

The most significant exception to the general lack of independent significance of the due process clauses is in jury neutrality cases. The Court has not retreated from its stance in Ham v. South Carolina, 409 U.S. 524 (1973), that due process requires trial judges to interrogate potential jurors on racial prejudice in cases where a realistic prospect of racial animus exists. In Turner v. Murray, 476 U.S. 28 (1986), the Court found due process to require "that a capital defendant accused of an interracial crime is entitled to have prospective jurors informed of the race of the victim and questioned on the issue of racial bias."

The failure of the court to overrule prior criminal procedure decisions and to give independent force to the due process clauses does not mean that the creative energies of the Supreme Court are quiescent. Rather, they are finding outlets in different directions. Through the mid-1960s, the Court's agenda was to tame the unruly manner in which the criminal process operated, particularly in the states. Employing the due process clause of the Fourteenth Amendment as its primary weapon, the Court succeeded in subjecting state criminal process to the formal limits on governmental power in the Bill of Rights, and succeeded in breaking down resistance to its innovations in the lower state and federal courts. One measure of this is the increasingly common phenomenon of state supreme courts imposing greater constraints on state officials than the federal constitution requires.

Because its previous messages have been largely absorbed by the lower courts, and perhaps in response to the increasingly conservative politics in the country, the Court has refocused the target of procedural criminal due process analysis from the specific provisions of the Bill of Rights to the question of the appropriate remedy. There are three interrelated variables driving the refocusing: 1. A concern that exclusion of evidence premised upon the policy of deterring undesirable state action have a reasonable chance of advancing that goal; 2. A belief that finality is an important value in adjudication; and 3. An emphasis on accuracy in outcome.

The primary remedies that the Court employed to effect its revisions of criminal process were the exclusionary rule and the threat of reversing convictions. Cases such as Gideon v. Wainwright, 372 U.S. 335 (1963), Mapp v. Ohio, 367 U.S. 643 (1961), and Miranda v. Arizona, 384 U.S. 436 (1966), fit a general pattern of announcements of new rules to be enforced by the threat of excluding evidence seized in violation of those rules or the reversal of convictions if the rules are not followed. The theory was that law enforcement officials would not jeopardize convictions by ignoring the new rules, and thus the threats of exclusion and reversal would deter unwanted behavior.

The present Court perceives two difficulties with this theory. First, as the new rules became accepted, and thus became the norm, the power of exclusion or the threat of reversal to affect law enforcement behavior diminished. It is one thing to exclude evidence or reverse a conviction because the police broke into a person's house, in the process apparently lying about whether they possessed a warrant, as occurred in *Mapp*, but it is another do so where the police made every effort to comply with the Supreme Court's pronouncements, as the Court refused to do in United States v. Leon, 468 U.S. 897 (1984). Second, the nature of Supreme Court innovation is that it begins with the core problem an area poses, which is followed by expansion of innovations into peripheral areas. As the cases press the logic of the original innovations further, the relationship between the cases and the policies underlying the original innovations becomes increasingly attenuated. It is one thing to sanction state officials for extensively interrogating an individual without warning him of his rights or allowing him to consult counsel, as occurred in *Miranda*, but it is another to do so because the state official gave a set of *Miranda* warnings differing somewhat from the language specifically approved in *Miranda*, as the Court refused to do in California v. Prysock, 453 U.S. 355 (1981).

The Supreme Court has fashioned a number of principles to limit the exclusionary rule to situations where there is a reasonable prospect that deterrence will operate. Chief among them is the good faith exception to the exclusionary rule fashioned in *Leon*. Exclusion of evidence is not likely to deter behavior if the law enforcement personnel have a good faith belief in the correctness of their conduct. Similarly, the Court has refused to extend the exclusionary rule into peripheral areas where deterrence is unlikely to result, such as the grand jury setting, United States v. Calandra, 414 U.S. 338 (1974), and civil matters such as forfeiture proceedings, United States v. Janis, 428 U.S. 433 (1976), or deportation proceedings, I.N.S. v. Lopez-Mendoza, 468 U.S. 1032 (1984).

The Court has also limited who may litigate the legality of state action to restrict exclusion of evidence to cases where a deterrent effect is likely. Because law enforcement officials will not typically know in advance who the culprit is, or who will be permitted to litigate the legality of their behavior, they will not jeopardize an investigation through illegal action so long as someone affected by their behavior may be in a position to complain. Thus, in Rakas v. Illinois, 439 U.S. 128 (1978), the Court held that the passengers of a car could not contest the legality of the search of the car, which included a search of the glove compartment that had been used with the owner's apparent knowledge. In Rawlings v. Kentucky, 448 U.S. 98 (1980), the Court held that the defendant could not contest the validity of the search of an acquaintance's purse where, again, the defendant had placed items with the knowledge of the purse's owner.

Intimately related to the Court's concern about the deterrent efficacy of its remedies is its growing emphasis on finality. As the time increases between alleged state misbehavior and judicial intervention, the likelihood of reversals affecting behavior decreases. In addition, permitting the relitigation of issues is an intelligent tactic if the work product of the lower courts is not trusted, as was the case three decades ago, but as greater confidence in that work product is achieved, departures from finality are less desirable. A system that allows multiple attacks on the legitimacy of its work product undermines itself in various ways. Allowing repetitive relitigation of issues increases the probability of aberrational results simply because a litigant will eventually come before a court that for whatever reason—randomness, bias, or simple lack of attention—will act aberrationally. Reversals in such cases are not likely to advance deterrence of undesirable behavior, or any other significant value. Allowing relitigation may also detract from the primary values of the penal system by encouraging individuals to deny responsibility for their acts. Regardless whether confession is good for the soul, it is less likely to occur while avenues of appeal remain open.

Finality has been advanced in various ways. In particular, the scope of habeas corpus has been reduced. In Stone v. Powell, 428 U.S. 465 (1976), the Court held that fourth amendment issues could not be relitigated on habeas corpus if the defendant had been provided an adequate opportunity to litigate the issue at trial. In Teague v. Lane, 109 S. Ct. 1060 (1989), the Court held that the retroactivity of new constitutional rulings is limited to cases still pending on direct appeal at the time the new decision is handed down. In a series of cases, the Court has also developed a strict waiver rule to the effect that failure to raise an issue at trial or on appeal precludes litigating it on habeas corpus unless failure to raise it amounted to ineffective assistance of counsel or unless a miscarriage of justice would result.

The third variable informing the Court's recent due process jurisprudence is a heightened concern for accuracy in adjudication. As the Court has become convinced that little remains of the disrespect for individual rights that it believed previously characterized the criminal process, it has become increasingly concerned with encouraging accurate outcomes. On the one hand, this has resulted in a further tightening of the avenues on appeal for a convicted defendant. In a series of cases beginning with Chapman v. California, 386 U.S. 18 (1967), the Court has held that harmless error—error that does not cast doubt on the outcome of the trial—does not justify reversing a conviction. In Nix v. Williams, 467 U.S. 431 (1984), the Court held that a conviction would not be reversed as a result of the admission of evidence illegally seized that would have been inevitably discovered by legitimate means. On the other hand, the Court has extended rights integral to the accuracy of convictions. For example, the Court has continued in its broad reading of the right to counsel, holding in Evitts v. Lucey, 469 U.S. 387 (1985), that an individual is guaranteed effective assistance of counsel on a first appeal as a matter of right, even though a state is not required to provide for an appeal, and in Ake v. Oklahoma, 470 U.S. 68 (1985), that a state must guarantee defendants access to a competent psychiatrist to assist in evaluation, preparation, and presentation of the defense.

The present state of due process adjudication is accurately captured by the recent holding in James v. Illinois, 110 S. Ct. 648 (1990). In James, the Court held that the principle first fashioned in Walder v. United States, 347 U.S. 62 (1954), that illegally obtained evidence can be used to impeach defendants' testimony so that exclusionary rules do not encourage perjury, did not extend to defense witnesses other than the defendant. Allowing the state to impeach witnesses other than the defendant would increase significantly the value of illegally obtained evidence, thus substantially impairing the efficacy of the exclusionary rule. Increasing the incentive of law enforcement officials to obtain evidence illegally would, in turn, put core constitutional values at risk. As significant as finality and accuracy are, they remain less significant than the core values of the various provisions of the Bill of Rights.

The implication of cases like *James* is that criminal due process has evolved from a club to beat recalcitrant officials into line with the Court's innovations into a more subtle tool used to adjust the margins of the various doctrines. This use of procedural due process will surely continue for the foreseeable future. The next stage in the development of due process is presently unknowable, but its origins are predictable. The nation is in the midst of a subtle devolution of political authority from the central government to the states. Due process jurisprudence has mirrored this trend, as the Court has shown an increasing reluctance to intervene in the criminal process. As state officials in particular become aware of their increasing autonomy, they will take advantage of it to rework state criminal process. As innovations are implemented over the next decades, they will be subjected to constitutional challenges, and out of that process will come the next stage in the continuing evolution of the meaning of the due process clauses for criminal procedure.

PART TWO

THE RIGHT TO COUNSEL—THE LINCHPIN OF CONSTITUTIONAL PROTECTION

CHAPTER 4

THE RIGHT TO COUNSEL
AND OTHER ASSISTANCE

A. THE CONSTITUTIONAL REQUIREMENTS

1. The Right to the Assistance of Counsel at Trial

*In all criminal prosecutions, the accused shall enjoy the right
. . . to have the Assistance of Counsel for his defence.*

U.S. Const., Amend. VI

*It never has been doubted by this court, or any other so far
as we know, that notice and hearing are preliminary steps
essential to the passing of an enforceable judgment, and that
they, together with a legally competent tribunal having jurisdiction of the case, constitute basic elements of the constitutional requirement of due process of law. . . .*

*What, then, does a hearing include? Historically and
in practice, in our own country at least, it has always included the right to the aid of counsel when desired and
provided by the party asserting the right. The right to be
heard would be, in many cases, of little avail if it did not
comprehend the right to be heard by counsel. Even the intelligent and educated layman has small and sometimes no
skill in the science of law. If charged with crime, he is in-*

capable, generally, of determining for himself whether the indictment is good or bad. He is unfamiliar with the rules of evidence. Left without the aid of counsel he may be put on trial without a proper charge, and convicted upon incompetent evidence, or evidence irrelevant to the issue or otherwise inadmissible. He lacks both the skill and knowledge adequately to prepare his defense, even though he have a perfect one. He requires the guiding hand of counsel at every step in the proceedings against him. Without it, though he be not guilty, he faces the danger of conviction because he does not know how to establish his innocence. If that be true of men of intelligence, how much more true is it of the ignorant and illiterate, or those of feeble intellect. If in any case, civil or criminal, a state or federal court were arbitrarily to refuse to hear a party by counsel, employed by and appearing for him, it reasonably may not be doubted that such a refusal would be a denial of a hearing, and, therefore, of due process in the constitutional sense.

Justice Sutherland, for the Court,
in Powell v. Alabama, 287 U.S. 45,
68-69 (1932)

The meaning and scope of the sixth amendment right to counsel in criminal proceedings has been contested, for the most part, in the context of the right of an indigent to have counsel appointed and financed by the state. As the preceding quote from *Powell* indicates, the right to be heard by retained counsel has never been seriously questioned in the United States. Quite early in our history, we rejected the English common law that denied accused felons the right to the assistance of retained counsel. For a discussion of the history of the right to counsel, see Note, An Historical Argument for the Right to Counsel During Police Interrogation, 73 Yale L.J. 1000, 1018-1034 (1964).

However, we proved to be much less solicitous of the plight of the indigent. In capital cases, federal law required the appointment of counsel, 1 Stat. 118 (1790), and a number of states followed a similar path. Nonetheless, it was not until *Powell* that the Supreme Court held that in capital cases fourteenth amendment due process is violated by state action that in effect denied a defendant access to effective assistance of counsel. Moreover, *Powell* appeared to be limited to those cases in which the defendant is "incapable adequately of making his own defense because of ignorance, feeble mindedness, illiteracy, or the like." *Powell*, supra, 287 U.S. at 71. The Court did hold, however, that the state's "duty is not discharged by an assignment [of counsel] at such a time or under

such circumstances as to preclude the giving of effective aid in the preparation and trial of the case." Id.

Powell, in essence, created a *special circumstances rule*—effective
assistance, or an adequate opportunity to obtain it, must be provided in
capital cases if defendants are unable to represent themselves adequately.
This special circumstances rule was transmuted into a "flat" requirement
of counsel in capital cases at least by 1961 in Hamilton v. Alabama, 368
U.S. 52 (1961), in large measure due to the awesome finality of capital
punishment. See Kamisar, Betts v. Brady Twenty Years Later: The Right
to Counsel and Due Process Values, 61 Mich. L. Rev. 219, 255 (1962).
But see id. at 255-260 (arguing that sentence is immaterial to need for
counsel).

In noncapital cases a special circumstances rule also developed that
required the appointment of counsel only when the absence of counsel
would result in a "trial . . . offensive to the common and fundamental
ideas of fairness and right." Betts v. Brady, 316 U.S. 455, 473 (1942).
In *Betts*, the Court, over a sharp and prescient dissent by Justice Black,
held that due process does not demand the appointment of counsel for
indigent defendants in every state case because "the furnishing of counsel
in all cases whatever" is *not* "dictated by natural, inherent and fundamental principles of justice." Id. at 464.

Four years prior to *Betts*, the Supreme Court held that the sixth
amendment required the appointment of counsel in noncapital federal
criminal prosecutions. In doing so, the Court commented:

> The Sixth Amendment stands as a constant admonition that if the con-
> stitutional safeguards it provides be lost, justice will not "still be done." It
> embodies a realistic recognition of the obvious truth that the average
> defendant does not have the professional legal skill to protect himself when
> brought before a tribunal with power to take his life or liberty, wherein
> the prosecution is presented by experienced and learned counsel. That
> which is simple, orderly and necessary to the lawyer, to the untrained
> layman may appear intricate, complex and mysterious. [Johnson v. Zerbst,
> 304 U.S. 458, 462-463 (1938).]

But if "justice cannot be done" in all federal prosecutions and state
capital cases without the assistance of counsel, and if, in state noncapital
cases, the right to counsel "when desired and provided by the party
asserting the right" is something that the party "requires . . . at every
step," in order to minimize the chance of an erroneous conviction,[1] how

---

1. Indeed, the Supreme Court had gone so far as to say that a defendant's right to
be heard by retained counsel was "unqualified." Chandler v. Fretag, 348 U.S. 3, 9

could the *Betts* "special circumstances rule" be maintained? How could it be that justice *could* be done in a state but not in a federal prosecution when an indigent is tried without counsel? And how does the absence of wealth minimize the need for counsel's guiding hand whether in a capital or noncapital case? Prior to *Gideon*, in short, had not the Court *already concluded*, even if it had still to be articulated, that the absence of counsel was itself a "special circumstance"?[2]

GIDEON v. WAINWRIGHT
Certiorari to the Supreme Court of Florida
372 U.S. 335 (1963)

MR. JUSTICE BLACK delivered the opinion of the Court.

Petitioner was charged in a Florida state court with having broken and entered a poolroom with intent to commit a misdemeanor. This offense is a felony under Florida law. Appearing in court without funds and without a lawyer, petitioner asked the court to appoint counsel for him, whereupon the following colloquy took place:

> *The Court:*　Mr. Gideon, I am sorry, but I cannot appoint Counsel to represent you in this case. Under the laws of the State of Florida, the only time the Court can appoint Counsel to represent a Defendant is when that person is charged with a capital offense. I am sorry, but I will have to deny your request to appoint Counsel to defend you in this case.
> *The Defendant:*　The United States Supreme Court says I am entitled to be represented by Counsel.

Put to trial before a jury, Gideon conducted his defense about as well as could be expected from a layman. He made an opening statement to the jury, cross-examined the State's witnesses, presented witnesses in his own defense, declined to testify himself, and made a short argument "emphasizing his innocence to the charge contained in the Information filed in this case." The jury returned a verdict of guilty, and petitioner was sentenced to serve five years in the state prison. . . . Since 1942, when

---

(1954). The reason for this conclusion surely was the Court's recognition of the significance of counsel. 348 U.S. at 9-10. But the very same "significance" that results in a conclusion of an unqualified right to be heard by retained counsel obviously highlights the untenable plight of the indigent unable to obtain counsel. This, too, appears to have contributed to the Court's willingness to reconsider *Betts*.

2. From 1950 until *Gideon*, the Supreme Court found a "special circumstance" requiring the appointment of counsel in every case that it heard that raised the issue. By 1962, the standard had apparently become "potential prejudice," a standard that will virtually always be met. Chewning v. Cunningham, 368 U.S. 443 (1962).

Betts v. Brady, 316 U.S. 455, was decided by a divided Court, the problem
of a defendant's federal constitutional right to counsel in a state court
has been a continuing source of controversy and litigation in both state
and federal courts. To give this problem another review here, we granted
certiorari. Since Gideon was proceeding in forma pauperis, we appointed
counsel to represent him and requested both sides to discuss in their briefs
and oral arguments the following: "Should this Court's holding in Betts
v. Brady . . . be reconsidered?" . . .

I

The facts upon which Betts claimed that he had been unconstitutionally
denied the right to have counsel appointed to assist him are strikingly
like the facts upon which Gideon here bases his federal constitutional
claim. Betts was indicted for robbery in a Maryland state court. On
arraignment, he told the trial judge of his lack of funds to hire a lawyer
and asked the court to appoint one for him. Betts was advised that it was
not the practice in that county to appoint counsel for indigent defendants
except in murder and rape cases. He then pleaded not guilty, had witnesses
summoned, cross-examined the State's witnesses, examined his own, and
chose not to testify himself. He was found guilty by the judge, sitting
without a jury, and sentenced to eight years in prison. Like Gideon, Betts
sought release by habeas corpus, alleging that he had been denied the
right to assistance of counsel in violation of the Fourteenth Amendment.
Betts was denied any relief, and on review this Court affirmed. It was
held that a refusal to appoint counsel for an indigent defendant charged
with a felony did not necessarily violate the Due Process Clause of the
Fourteenth Amendment, which for reasons given the Court deemed to
be the only applicable federal constitutional provision. The Court said:

> Asserted denial [of due process] is to be tested by an appraisal of the totality
> of facts in a given case. That which may, in one setting, constitute a denial
> of fundamental fairness, shocking to the universal sense of justice, may,
> in other circumstances, and in the light of other considerations fall short
> of such denial. [316 U.S. at 462.]

Treating due process as "a concept less rigid and more fluid than those
envisaged in other specific and particular provisions of the Bill of Rights,"
the Court held that refusal to appoint counsel under the particular facts
and circumstances in the Betts case was not so "offensive to the common
and fundamental ideas of fairness" as to amount to a denial of due process.
Since the facts and circumstances of the two cases are so nearly indistin-

guishable, we think the Betts v. Brady holding if left standing would require us to reject Gideon's claim that the Constitution guarantees him the assistance of counsel. Upon full reconsideration we conclude that Betts v. Brady should be overruled.

II

The Sixth Amendment provides, "In all criminal prosecutions, the accused shall enjoy the right . . . to have the Assistance of Counsel for his defence." We have construed this to mean that in federal courts counsel must be provided for defendants unable to employ counsel unless the right is competently and intelligently waived.[3] Betts argued that this right is extended to indigent defendants in state courts by the Fourteenth Amendment. In response the Court stated that, while the Sixth Amendment laid down "no rule for the conduct of the States, the question recurs whether the constraint laid by the Amendment upon the national courts expresses a rule so fundamental and essential to a fair trial, and so, to due process of law, that it is made obligatory upon the States by the Fourteenth Amendment." 316 U.S., at 465. In order to decide whether the Sixth Amendment's guarantee of counsel is of this fundamental nature, the court in *Betts* set out and considered "[r]elevant data on the subject . . . afforded by constitutional and statutory provisions subsisting in the colonies and the States prior to the inclusion of the Bill of Rights in the national Constitution, and in the constitutional, legislative, and judicial history of the States to the present date." 316 U.S., at 465. On the basis of his historical data the Court concluded that "appointment of counsel is not a fundamental right, essential to a fair trial." 316 U.S., at 471. It was for this reason the *Betts* Court refused to accept the contention that the Sixth Amendment's guarantee of counsel for indigent federal defendants was extended to or, in the words of that Court, "made obligatory upon the States by the Fourteenth Amendment." Plainly, had the Court concluded that appointment of counsel for an indigent criminal defendant was "a fundamental right, essential to a fair trial," it would have held that the Fourteenth Amendment requires appointment of counsel in a state court, just as the Sixth Amendment requires in a federal court.

We think the Court in *Betts* had ample precedent for acknowledging that those guarantees of the Bill of Rights which are fundamental safeguards of liberty immune from federal abridgment are equally protected against state invasion by the Due Process Clause of the Fourteenth Amendment. This same principle was recognized, explained, and applied

3. Johnson v. Zerbst, 304 U.S. 458 (1938).

in Powell v. Alabama, 287 U.S. 45 (1932), a case upholding the right of counsel, where the Court held that despite sweeping language to the contrary in Hurtado v. California, 110 U.S. 516 (1884), the Fourteenth Amendment "embraced" those " 'fundamental principles of liberty and justice which lie at the base of all our civil and political institutions,' " even though they had been "specifically dealt with in another part of the federal Constitution." 287 U.S., at 67. In many cases other than *Powell* and *Betts*, this Court has looked to the fundamental nature of original Bill of Rights guarantees to decide whether the Fourteenth Amendment makes them obligatory on the States. Explicitly recognized to be of this "fundamental nature" and therefore made immune from state invasion by the Fourteenth, or some part of it, are the First Amendment's freedoms of speech, press, religion, assembly, association, and petition for redress of grievances. For the same reason, though not always in precisely the same terminology, the Court has made obligatory on the States the Fifth Amendment's command that private property shall not be taken for public use without just compensation, the Fourth Amendment's prohibition of unreasonable searches and seizures, and the Eighth's ban on cruel and unusual punishment. On the other hand, this Court in Palko v. Connecticut, 302 U.S. 319 (1937), refused to hold that the Fourteenth Amendment made the double jeopardy provision of the Fifth Amendment obligatory on the States. In so refusing, however, the Court, speaking through Mr. Justice Cardozo, was careful to emphasize that "immunities that are valid as against the federal government by force of the specific pledges of particular amendments have been found to be implicit in the concept of ordered liberty, and thus, through the Fourteenth Amendment, become valid as against the states" and that guarantees "in their origin . . . effective against the federal government alone" had by prior cases "been taken over from the earlier articles of the federal bill of rights and brought within the Fourteenth Amendment by a process of absorption." 302 U.S., at 324-325, 326.

We accept Betts v. Brady's assumption, based as it was on our prior cases, that a provision of the Bill of Rights which is "fundamental and essential to a fair trial" is made obligatory upon the States by the Fourteenth Amendment. We think the Court in *Betts* was wrong, however, in concluding that the Sixth Amendment's guarantee of counsel is not one of these fundamental rights. Ten years before Betts v. Brady, this Court, after full consideration of all the historical data examined in *Betts*, had unequivocally declared that "the right to the aid of counsel is of this fundamental character." Powell v. Alabama, 287 U.S. 25, 68 (1932). . . . And again in 1938 this Court said:

> [The assistance of counsel] is one of the safeguards of the Sixth Amendment deemed necessary to insure fundamental human rights of life and lib-

erty. . . . The Sixth Amendment stands as a constant admonition that if
the constitutional safeguards it provides be lost, justice will not "still be
done." [Johnson v. Zerbst, 304 U.S. 458, 462 (1938).] . . .

   In light of these and many other prior decisions of this Court, it is
not surprising that the *Betts* Court, when faced with the contention that
"one charged with crime, who is unable to obtain counsel, must be
furnished counsel by the State," conceded that "[e]xpressions in the opinions of this court lend color to the argument. . . ." 316 U.S., at 462-
463. The fact is that in deciding as it did—that "appointment of counsel
is not a fundamental right, essential to a fair trial"—the Court in Betts
v. Brady made an abrupt break with its own well-considered precedents.
In returning to these old precedents, sounder we believe than the new,
we but restore constitutional principles established to achieve a fair system
of justice. Not only these precedents but also reason and reflection require
us to recognize that in our adversary system of criminal justice, any
person haled into court, who is too poor to hire a lawyer, cannot be
assured a fair trial unless counsel is provided for him. This seems to us
to be an obvious truth. Governments, both state and federal, quite properly spend vast sums of money to establish machinery to try defendants
accused of crime. Lawyers to prosecute are everywhere deemed essential
to protect the public's interest in an orderly society. Similarly, there are
few defendants charged with crime, few indeed, who fail to hire the best
lawyers they can get to prepare and present their defenses. That government hires lawyers to prosecute and defendants who have the money hire
lawyers to defend are the strongest indications of the widespread belief
that lawyers in criminal courts are necessities, not luxuries. The right of
one charged with crime to counsel may not be deemed fundamental and
essential to fair trials in some countries, but it is in ours. From the very
beginning, our state and national constitutions and laws have laid great
emphasis on procedural and substantive safeguards designed to assure fair
trials before impartial tribunals in which every defendant stands equal
before the law. This noble idea cannot be realized if the poor man charged
with crime has to face his accusers without a lawyer to assist him. . . .
The Court in Betts v. Brady departed from the sound wisdom upon which
the Court's holding in Powell v. Alabama rested. Florida, supported by
two other States, has asked that Betts v. Brady be left intact. Twenty-two
states, as friends of the Court, argue that *Betts* was "an anachronism
when handed down" and that it should now be overruled. We agree.
   Reversed.

MR. JUSTICE DOUGLAS, concurring.
While I join the opinion of the Court, a brief historical resume of

the relation between the Bill of Rights and the first section of the Four-teenth Amendment seems pertinent. Since the adoption of that Amend-ment, ten Justices have felt that it protects from infringement by the States the privileges, protections, and safeguards granted by the Bill of Rights. . . . Unfortunately it has never commanded a Court. Yet, hap-pily, all constitutional questions are always open. And what we do today does not foreclose the matter.

My Brother Harlan is of the view that a guarantee of the Bill of Rights that is made applicable to the States by reason of the Fourteenth Amendment is a lesser version of that same guarantee as applied to the Federal Government. Mr. Justice Jackson shared that view. But that view has not prevailed[4] and rights protected against state invasion by the Due Process Clause of the Fourteenth Amendment are not watered-down versions of what the Bill of Rights guarantees.

MR. JUSTICE CLARK, concurring in the result.

That the Sixth Amendment requires appointment of counsel in "all criminal prosecutions" is clear, both from the language of the Amend-ment and from this Court's interpretation. . . . It is equally clear from the above cases, all decided after *Betts* . . . that the Fourteenth Amend-ment requires such appointment in all prosecutions for capital crimes. The Court's decision today, then, does no more than erase a distinction which has no basis in logic and an increasingly eroded basis in authority. In Kinsella v. United States ex rel. Singleton, 361 U.S. 234 (1960), we specifically rejected any constitutional distinction between capital and noncapital offenses as regards congressional power to provide for court-martial trials of civilian dependents of armed forces personnel. Having previously held that civilian dependents could not constitutionally be deprived of the protections of Article III and the Fifth and Sixth Amend-ments in capital cases, Reid v. Covert, 354 U.S. 1 (1957), we held that the same result must follow in noncapital cases. . . .

I must conclude here, as in *Kinsella*, supra, that the Constitution makes no distinction between capital and noncapital cases. The Four-teenth Amendment requires due process of law for the deprival of "liberty" just as for deprival of "life," and there cannot constitutionally be a dif-ference in the quality of the process based merely upon a supposed difference in the sanction involved. How can the Fourteenth Amendment tolerate a procedure which it condemns in capital cases on the ground that deprival of liberty may be less onerous than deprival of life—a value judgment not universally accepted—or that only the latter deprival is

4. The cases are collected by Mr. Justice Black in Speiser v. Randall, 357 U.S. 513, 530. And see Eaton v. Price, 364 U.S. 263, 274-276.

irrevocable? I can find no acceptable rationalization for such a result, and I therefore concur in the judgment of the Court.

MR. JUSTICE HARLAN, concurring.

I agree that Betts v. Brady should be overruled, but consider it entitled to a more respectful burial than has been accorded, at least on the part of those of us who were not on the Court when that case was decided.

I cannot subscribe to the view that Betts v. Brady represented "an abrupt break with its own well-considered precedents." . . . . In 1932, in Powell v. Alabama, . . . a capital case, this Court declared that under the particular facts there presented—"the ignorance and illiteracy of the defendants, their youth, the circumstances of public hostility . . . and above all that they stood in deadly peril of their lives" (287 U.S., at 71)—the state court had a duty to assign counsel for the trial as a necessary requisite of due process of law. It is evident that these limiting facts were not added to the opinion as an afterthought; they were repeatedly emphasized, see 287 U.S., at 52, 57-58, 71, and were clearly regarded as important to the result.

Thus when this Court, a decade later, decided Betts v. Brady, it did no more than to admit of the possible existence of special circumstances in noncapital as well as capital trials, while at the same time insisting that such circumstances be shown in order to establish a denial of due process. The right to appointed counsel had been recognized as being considerably broader in federal prosecutions, see Johnson v. Zerbst, 304 U.S. 458, but to have imposed these requirements on the States would indeed have been "an abrupt break" with the almost immediate past. The declaration that the right to appointed counsel in state prosecutions, as established in Powell v. Alabama, was not limited to capital cases was in truth not a departure from, but an extension of, existing precedent.

The principles declared in *Powell* and in *Betts*, however, have had a troubled journey throughout the years that have followed first the one case and then the other. Even by the time of the *Betts* decision, dictum in at least one of the Court's opinions had indicated that there was an absolute right to the services of counsel in the trial of state capital cases.[1] Such dicta continued to appear in subsequent decisions,[2] and any lingering doubts were finally eliminated by the holding of Hamilton v. Alabama, 368 U.S. 52.

In noncapital cases, the "special circumstances" rule has continued to exist in form while its substance has been substantially and steadily eroded. In the first decade after *Betts*, there were cases in which the

1. Avery v. Alabama, 308 U.S. 444, 445.
2. E.g., Bute v. Illinois, 333 U.S. 640, 674; Uveges v. Pennsylvania, 335 U.S. 437, 441.

Court found special circumstances to be lacking, but usually by a sharply divided vote. However, no such decision has been cited to us, and I have found none, after Quicksall v. Michigan, 339 U.S. 660, decided in 1950. At the same time, there have been not a few cases in which special circumstances were found in little or nothing more than the "complexity" of the legal questions presented, although those questions were often of only routine difficulty. The Court has come to recognize, in other words, that the mere existence of a serious criminal charge constituted in itself special circumstances requiring the services of counsel at trial. In truth the Betts v. Brady rule is no longer a reality.

This evolution, however, appears not to have been fully recognized by many state courts, in this instance charged with the front-line responsibility for the enforcement of constitutional rights. To continue a rule which is honored by this Court only with lip service is not a healthy thing and in the long run will do disservice to the federal system.

The special circumstances rule has been formally abandoned in capital cases, and the time has now come when it should be similarly abandoned in noncapital cases, at least as to offenses which, as the one involved here, carry the possibility of a substantial prison sentence. (Whether the rule should extend to *all* criminal cases need not now be decided.) This indeed does no more than to make explicit something that has long since been foreshadowed in our decisions.

In agreeing with the Court that the right to counsel in a case such as this should now be expressly recognized as a fundamental right embraced in the Fourteenth Amendment, I wish to make a further observation. When we hold a right or immunity, valid against the Federal Government, to be "implicit in the concept of ordered liberty" and thus valid against the States, I do not read our past decisions to suggest that by so holding, we automatically carry over an entire body of federal law and apply it in full sweep to the States. Any such concept would disregard the frequently wide disparity between the legitimate interests of the States and of the Federal Government, the divergent problems that they face, and the significantly different consequences of their actions.

. . . In what is done today I do not understand the Court to depart from the principles laid down in Palko v. Connecticut, 302 U.S. 319, or to embrace the concept that the Fourteenth Amendment "incorporates" the Sixth Amendment as such.

On these premises I join in the judgment of the Court.

NOTES AND QUESTIONS

1. In one sense the result in *Gideon* appears to have been inevitable. Even if there are cases that could be tried fairly without defense counsel,

one cannot determine from the record in uncounseled cases which ones would have benefited from counsel. Records that look good on appeal might have looked quite different had counsel been present. Indeed, *Betts* is such a case. Each of the courts that reviewed the record in *Betts* concluded that Betts had not been prejudiced by the absence of counsel. In an insightful analysis of the factual setting of *Betts*, Professor Kamisar has demonstrated quite forcefully that a competent lawyer may very well have had an impact on the outcome of the trial. Kamisar, The Right to Counsel and the Fourteenth Amendment: A Dialogue on "The Most Pervasive Right" of an Accused, 30 U. Chi. L. Rev. 1, 42-56 (1962). Consider just one of the many points Professor Kamisar makes. One of the witnesses at trial, Bollinger, identified at the jailhouse, in addition to the defendant, a coat, dark glasses, and handkerchief allegedly worn by Betts during the robbery in question. *But:*

> *What* coat? *Whose* dark glasses and handkerchief? . . .
>
> Is it possible that the coat Bollinger "identified" at the jail was simply one the police procured from somebody other than Betts—pursuant to Bollinger's own description of the dark gray, bagged-pocketed coat the man wore who robbed him?
>
> Even if a coat were offered in evidence, "objects or things offered in evidence do not generally identify themselves." The object must be shown to have some connection with Betts. Not only was this not done; no coat was ever offered in evidence. . . .
>
> As for the other items, there was testimony by the state that "smoked glasses were put on Betts' eyes and a handkerchief around his neck like the man was supposed to have had that did the holding up." But once again, no handkerchief or glasses were offered in evidence. Presumably, Betts owned a handkerchief or two, but once again, the state failed to establish that he even owned a pair of dark glasses. One alibi witness who was asked about this on cross simply did "not know," and the matter was dropped.
>
> Why did the state fail to offer any of these items in evidence? Why was one of Betts' own witnesses cross-examined, albeit casually, about the defendant's ownership of a dark gray overcoat and smoked glasses? If the state had possessed these items, why would it have asked such questions? Although the matter is not free from doubt—because neither trial judge nor prosecutor seemed to care much and Betts evidently failed to realize how this would weaken the state's case—it is difficult to avoid the conclusion that the following "bootstraps" operation occurred: Bollinger described to the police the various items the robber was supposed to have worn; the police simply went out, begged or borrowed the requisite coat, glasses and handkerchief, and slapped them on Betts; Bollinger then made his identification, based largely on the coat, glasses and handkerchief the police had put on Betts.

2. Even if it is true that defense counsel normally is of value, does it follow that the result in *Gideon* is constitutionally mandated? There is no requirement that the state provide everything that is useful or of value to defendants. Thus, there must be some other criteria that determine what the state must provide. To what extent, for example, should constitutional analysis be informed by general practice in the states? By the "intent of the Framers" of the relevant constitutional provisions? By the cost to government of a decision one way or the other? By what is "fair" or "just"? If notions of fairness or justice are to play a role, how does one determine what those words mean?

3. Regardless of the scope of words such as "fairness" or "justice," there probably would be general agreement that any practice that generated a relatively high risk of erroneous convictions is "unfair," as the absence of counsel most likely does. Why was that not emphasized more in *Gideon*? Justice Black's opinion for the Court in *Gideon* primarily asserted that *Betts* was an abrupt change from its precedents and thus was wrong, although the excerpt from *Powell* at the beginning of this section was quoted but not developed. Is that adequate? If a court decides to overrule a case, how can it go about it? How *should* it go about it, or does it matter? For an interesting discussion, see Israel, Gideon v. Wainwright: The "Art" of Overruling, 1963 Sup. Ct. Rev. 211. Does the method employed in the majority opinion explain, at least in part, why the concurrences were written to what was a unanimous judgment?

4. What was the judgment in *Gideon*, apart from the overruling of *Betts*? What, for example, is the scope of the right to counsel imposed on the states by *Gideon*? Consider the following case.

ARGERSINGER v. HAMLIN
Certiorari to the Supreme Court of Florida
407 U.S. 25 (1972)

MR. JUSTICE DOUGLAS delivered the opinion of the Court.

Petitioner, an indigent, was charged in Florida with carrying a concealed weapon, an offense punishable by imprisonment up to six months, a $1,000 fine, or both. The trial was to a judge, and petitioner was unrepresented by counsel. He was sentenced to serve 90 days in jail, and brought this habeas corpus action in the Florida Supreme Court, alleging that, being deprived of his right to counsel, he was unable as an indigent layman properly to raise and present to the trial court good and sufficient defenses to the charge for which he stands convicted. The Florida Supreme Court by a four-to-three decision, in ruling on the right to counsel, followed the line we marked out in Duncan v. Louisiana, 391 U.S. 145,

159, as respects the right to trial by jury and held that the right to court-appointed counsel extends only to trials "for non-petty offenses punishable by more than six months imprisonment." We reverse.

The Sixth Amendment . . . provides specified standards for "all criminal prosecutions."

One is the requirement of a "public trial." In re Oliver [333 U.S. 257 (1948)] held that the right to a "public trial" was applicable to a state proceeding even though only a 60-day sentence was involved. 333 U.S., at 272.

Another guarantee is the right to be informed of the nature and cause of the accusation. Still another, the right of confrontation. Pointer v. Texas [380 U.S. 400 (1965)]. And another, compulsory process for obtaining witnesses in one's favor. Washington v. Texas [388 U.S. 14 (1967)]. We have never limited these rights to felonies or to lesser but serious offenses. . . .

The right to trial by jury, also guaranteed by the Sixth Amendment by reason of the Fourteenth, was limited by Duncan v. Louisiana, supra, to trials where the potential punishment was imprisonment for six months or more. But . . . the right to trial by jury has a different genealogy and is brigaded with a system of trial to a judge alone. As stated in *Duncan*:

> Providing an accused with the right to be tried by a jury of his peers gave him an inestimable safeguard against the corrupt or overzealous prosecutor and against the compliant, biased, or eccentric judge. If the defendant preferred the common-sense judgment of a jury to the more tutored but perhaps less sympathetic reaction of the single judge, he was to have it. Beyond this, the jury trial provisions in the Federal and State Constitutions reflect a fundamental decision about the exercise of official power—a reluctance to entrust plenary powers over the life and liberty of the citizen to one judge or to a group of judges. Fear of unchecked power, so typical of our State and Federal Governments in other respects, found expression in the criminal law in this insistence upon community participation in the determination of guilt or innocence. The deep commitment of the Nation to the right of jury trial in serious criminal cases as a defense against arbitrary law enforcement qualifies for protection under the Due Process Clause of the Fourteenth Amendment, and must therefore be respected by the States. [391 U.S., at 156.]

While there is historical support for limiting the "deep commitment" to trial by jury to "serious criminal cases,"[2] there is no such support for a similar limitation on the right to assistance of counsel:

2. See Frankfurter & Corcoran, Petty Offenses and the Constitutional Guaranty of Trial by Jury, 39 Harv. L. Rev. 917, 980-982 (1926). . . .

> Originally, in England, a person charged with treason or felony was denied the aid of counsel, except in respect of legal questions which the accused himself might suggest. At the same time parties in civil cases and persons accused of misdemeanors were entitled to the full assistance of counsel. . . . [It] appears that in at least twelve of the thirteen colonies the rule of the English common law, in the respect now under consideration, had been definitively rejected and the right to counsel fully recognized in all criminal prosecutions, save that in one or two instances the right was limited to capital offenses or to the more serious crimes. . . . [Powell v. Alabama, 287 U.S. 45, 60 and 64-65.]

The Sixth Amendment thus extended the right to counsel beyond its common-law dimensions. But there is nothing in the language of the Amendment, its history, or in the decisions of this Court, to indicate that it was intended to embody a retraction of the right in petty offenses wherein the common law previously did require that counsel be provided. . . .

We reject, therefore, the premise that since prosecutions for crimes punishable by imprisonment for less than six months may be tried without a jury, they may also be tried without a lawyer. . . .

The requirement of counsel may well be necessary for a fair trial even in a petty-offense prosecution. We are by no means convinced that legal and constitutional questions involved in a case that actually leads to imprisonment even for a brief period are any less complex than when a person can be sent off for six months or more. . . .

Beyond the problem of trials and appeals is that of the guilty plea, a problem which looms large in misdemeanor as well as in felony cases. Counsel is needed so that the accused may know precisely what he is doing, so that he is fully aware of the prospect of going to jail or prison, and so that he is treated fairly by the prosecution.

In addition, the volume of misdemeanor cases, far greater in number than felony prosecutions, may create an obsession for speedy dispositions, regardless of the fairness of the result. . . .

There is evidence of the prejudice which results to misdemeanor defendants from this "assembly-line justice." One study concluded that "[m]isdemeanants represented by attorneys are five times as likely to emerge from police court with all charges dismissed as are defendants who face similar charges without counsel." American Civil Liberties Union, Legal Counsel for Misdemeanants, Preliminary Report 1 (1970).

We must conclude, therefore, that the problems associated with misdemeanor and petty offenses often require the presence of counsel to insure the accused a fair trial. Mr. Justice Powell suggests that these problems are raised even in situations where there is no prospect of imprisonment. . . . We need not consider the requirements of the Sixth

Amendment as regards the right to counsel where loss of liberty is not involved, however, for here petitioner was in fact sentenced to jail. . . .

We hold, therefore, that absent a knowing and intelligent waiver, no person may be imprisoned for any offense, whether classified as petty, misdemeanor, or felony, unless he was represented by counsel at his trial.[7] . . .

Under the rule we announce today, every judge will know when the trial of a misdemeanor starts that no imprisonment may be imposed, even though local law permits it, unless the accused is represented by counsel. He will have a measure of the seriousness and gravity of the offense and therefore know when to name a lawyer to represent the accused before the trial starts.

The run of misdemeanors will not be affected by today's ruling. But in those that end up in the actual deprivation of a person's liberty, the accused will receive the benefit of "the guiding hand of counsel" so necessary when one's liberty is in jeopardy.

Reversed.

MR. JUSTICE BRENNAN, with whom MR. JUSTICE DOUGLAS and MR. JUSTICE STEWART join, concurring.

I join the opinion of the Court and add only an observation upon its discussion of legal resources, ante, at n.7. Law students as well as practicing attorneys may provide an important source of legal representation for the indigent. . . . Given the huge increase in law school enrollments over the past few years, see Ruud, That Burgeoning Law School Enrollment, 58 A.B.A.J. 146 (1972), I think it plain that law students can be expected to make a significant contribution, quantitatively and qualitatively, to the representation of the poor in many cases, including cases reached by today's decision.

MR. CHIEF JUSTICE BURGER, concurring in the result. . . .

Trial judges sitting in petty and misdemeanor cases—and prosecutors—should recognize exactly what will be required by today's decision. Because no individual can be imprisoned unless he is represented

---

7. We do not share Mr. Justice Powell's doubt that the Nation's legal resources are sufficient to implement the rule we announce today. It has been estimated that between 1,575 and 2,300 full-time counsel would be required to represent *all* indigent misdemeanants, excluding traffic offenders. Note, Dollars and Sense of an Expanded Right to Counsel, 55 Iowa L. Rev. 1249, 1260-1261 (1970). These figures are relatively insignificant when compared to the estimated 355,200 attorneys in the United States (Statistical Abstract of the United States 153 (1971)), a number which is projected to double by the year 1985. See Ruud, That Burgeoning Law School Enrollment, 58 A.B.A.J. 146, 147. Indeed, there are 18,000 new admissions to the bar each year—3,500 more lawyers than are required to fill the "estimated 14,500 average annual openings." Id., at 148.

by counsel, the trial judge and the prosecutor will have to engage in a predictive evaluation of each case to determine whether there is a significant likelihood that, if the defendant is convicted, the trial judge will sentence him to a jail term. The judge can preserve the option of a jail sentence only by offering counsel to any defendant unable to retain counsel on his own. This need to predict will place a new loan on courts already overburdened and already compelled to deal with far more cases in one day than is reasonable and proper. Yet the prediction is not one beyond the capacity of an experienced judge, aided as he should be by the prosecuting officer. As to jury cases, the latter should be prepared to inform the judge as to any prior record of the accused, the general nature of the case against the accused, including any use of violence, the severity of harm to the victim, the impact on the community, and the other factors relevant to the sentencing process. Since the judge ought to have some degree of such information after judgment of guilt is determined, ways can be found in the more serious misdemeanor cases when jury trial is not waived to make it available to the judge before trial.* This will not mean a full "presence" report on every defendant in every case before the jury passes on guilt, but a prosecutor should know before trial whether he intends to urge a jail sentence, and if he does he should be prepared to aid the court with the factual and legal basis for his view on that score. . . .

The step we take today should cause no surprise to the legal profession. More than five years ago the profession, speaking through the American Bar Association in a Report on Standards Relating to Providing Defense Services, determined that society's goal should be "that the system for providing counsel and facilities for the defense be as good as the system which society provides for the prosecution." American Bar Association Project on Standards for Criminal Justice, Providing Defense Services 1 (Approved Draft 1968). The ABA was not addressing itself, as we must in this case, to the constitutional requirement but only to the board policy issue. . . . After considering the same general factors involved in the issue we decide today, the ABA Report specifically concluded that:

> Counsel should be provided in all criminal proceedings for offenses punishable by loss of liberty, except those types of offenses for which such punishment is not likely to be imposed, regardless of their denomination as felonies, misdemeanors or otherwise. [Id., 4.1, pp. 37-38.] . . .

---

*In a nonjury case the prior record of the accused should not be made known to the trier of fact except by way of traditional impeachment.

The right to counsel has historically been an evolving concept. The constitutional requirements with respect to the issue have dated in recent times from Powell v. Alabama, 287 U.S. 45 (1932), to Gideon v. Wainwright, 372 U.S. 335 (1963). Part of this evolution has been expressed in the policy prescriptions of the legal profession itself, and the contributions of the organized bar and individual lawyers—such as those appointed to represent the indigent defendants in the *Powell* and *Gideon* cases—have been notable. The holding of the Court today may well add large new burdens on a profession already overtaxed, but the dynamics of the profession have a way of rising to the burdens placed on it.

MR. JUSTICE POWELL, with whom MR. JUSTICE REHNQUIST joins, concurring in the result. . . .
    I am unable to agree with the Supreme Court of Florida that an indigent defendant, charged with a petty offense, may in every case be afforded a fair trial without the assistance of counsel. Nor can I agree with the new rule of due process, today enunciated by the Court, that "absent a knowing and intelligent waiver, no person may be imprisoned . . . unless he was represented by counsel at his trial." . . . It seems to me that the line should not be drawn with such rigidity.
    There is a middle course, between the extremes of Florida's six-month rule and the Court's rule, which comports with the requirements of the Fourteenth Amendment. I would adhere to the principle of due process that requires fundamental fairness in criminal trials, a principle which I believe encompasses the right to counsel in petty cases whenever the assistance of counsel is necessary to assure a fair trial.

I

I am in accord with the Court that an indigent accused's need for the assistance of counsel does not mysteriously evaporate when he is charged with an offense punishable by six months or less. . . . Many petty offenses will also present complex legal and factual issues that may not be fairly tried if the defendant is not assisted by counsel. Even in relatively simple cases, some defendants, because of ignorance or some other handicap, will be incapable of defending themselves. The consequences of a misdemeanor conviction, whether they be a brief period served under the sometimes deplorable conditions found in local jails or the effect of a criminal record on employability, are frequently of sufficient magnitude not to be casually dismissed by the label "petty."
    Serious consequences also may result from convictions not punishable by imprisonment. Stigma may attach to a drunken-driving conviction

or a hit-and-run escapade. Losing one's driver's license is more serious for some individuals than a brief stay in jail. . . . When the deprivation of property rights and interests is of sufficient consequences,[11] denying the assistance of counsel to indigents who are incapable of defending themselves is a denial of due process.

This is not to say that due process requires the appointment of counsel in all petty cases, or that assessment of the possible consequences of conviction is the sole test for the need for assistance of counsel. The flat six-month rule of the Florida court and the equally inflexible rule of the majority opinion apply to all cases within their defined areas regardless of circumstances. It is precisely because of this mechanistic application that I find these alternatives unsatisfactory. Due process, perhaps the most fundamental concept in our law, embodies principles of fairness rather than immutable line drawing as to every aspect of a criminal trial. While counsel is often essential to a fair trial, this is by no means a universal fact. Some petty offense cases are complex; others are exceedingly simple. As a justification for furnishing counsel to indigents accused of felonies, the Court noted, "That government hires lawyers to prosecute and defendants who have the money hire lawyers to defend are the strongest indications of the widespread belief that lawyers in criminal courts are necessities, not luxuries."[12] Yet government often does not hire lawyers to prosecute petty offenses; instead the arresting police officer presents the case. Nor does every defendant who can afford to do so hire lawyers to defend petty charges. Where the possibility of a jail sentence is remote and the probable fine seems small, or where the evidence of guilt is overwhelming, the costs of assistance of counsel may exceed the benefits.[13] It is anomalous that the Court's opinion today will extend the right of appointed counsel to indigent defendants in cases where the right to counsel would rarely be exercised by nonindigent defendants. . . .

A survey of state courts in which misdemeanors are tried showed

11. A wide range of civil disabilities may result from misdemeanor convictions, such as forfeiture of public office (State ex rel. Stinger v. Kruger, 280 Mo. 293, 217 S.W. 310 (1919)); disqualification for a licensed profession (Cal. Bus. & Prof. Code §3094 (1962) (optometrists); N.C. Gen. Stat. §93A-4(b) (1965) (real estate brokers)), and loss of pension rights (Fla. Stat. Ann. §185.18(3) (1966) (police disability pension denied when injury is result of participation in fights, riots, civil insurrections, or while committing crime); Ind. Ann. Stat. §28-4616 (1948) (teacher convicted of misdemeanor resulting in imprisonment); Pa. Stat. Ann., Tit. 53 §39323 (Supp. 1972-1973) and §65599 (1957) (conviction of crime or misdemeanor)). See generally Project, The Collateral Consequences of a Criminal Conviction, 23 Vand. L. Rev. 929 (1970).

12. Gideon v. Wainwright, 372 U.S., at 344.

13. In petty offenses, there is much less plea negotiation than in serious offenses. See Report by the President's Commission of Law Enforcement and Administration of Justice, The Challenge of Crime in a Free Society (hereinafter Challenge) 134 (1967). Thus, in cases where the evidence of guilt is overwhelming, the assistance of counsel is less essential to obtain a lighter sentence.

that procedures were often informal, presided over by lay judges. Jury trials were rare, prosecution was not vigorous. It is as inaccurate to say that no defendant can obtain a fair trial without the assistance of counsel in such courts as it is to say that no defendant needs the assistance of counsel if the offense charged is only a petty one.[15]

Despite its overbreadth, the easiest solution would be a prophylactic rule that would require the appointment of counsel to indigents in all criminal cases. The simplicity of such a rule is appealing because it could be applied automatically in every case, but the price of pursuing this easy course could be high indeed in terms of its adverse impact on the administration of the criminal justice systems of 50 states. . . .

The Fifth and Fourteenth Amendments guarantee that property, as well as life and liberty, may not be taken from a person without affording him due process of law. The majority opinion suggests no constitutional basis for distinguishing between deprivations of liberty and property. In fact, the majority suggests no reason at all for drawing this distinction. The logic it advances for extending the right to counsel to all cases in which the penalty of any imprisonment is imposed applies equally well to cases in which other penalties may be imposed. Nor does the majority deny that some "nonjail" penalties are more serious than brief jail sentences.

Thus, although the new rule is extended today only to the imprisonment category of cases, the Court's opinion foreshadows the adoption of a broad prophylactic rule applicable to all petty offenses. No one can foresee the consequences of such a drastic enlargement of the constitutional right to free counsel. But even today's decision could have seriously adverse impact upon the day-to-day functioning of the criminal justice system. We should be slow to fashion a new constitutional rule with consequences of such unknown dimensions, especially since it is supported neither by history nor precedent.

II

The majority opinion concludes that, absent a valid waiver, a person may not be imprisoned even for lesser offenses unless he was represented

---

15. Neither the Report by the President's Commission on Law Enforcement and Administration of Justice nor the American Bar Association went the route the Court takes today. The President's Commission recommended that counsel be provided for criminal defendants who face "a significant penalty" and at least to those who are in danger of "substantial loss of liberty." Challenge, supra, n.13, at 150. The American Bar Association standard would not extend the right to counsel to cases where "loss of liberty" is not "likely to be imposed." American Bar Association Project on Standards for Criminal Justice, Providing Defense Services 37-40 (Approved Draft 1968). Neither supports a new, inflexible constitutional rule.

by counsel at the trial. In simplest terms this means that under no circumstances, in any court in the land, may anyone be imprisoned—
however briefly—unless he was represented by, or waived his right to,
counsel. The opinion is disquietingly barren of details as to how this rule
will be implemented.

There are thousands of statutes and ordinances which authorize
imprisonment for six months or less, usually as an alternative to a fine.
These offenses include some of the most trivial of misdemeanors, ranging
from spitting on the sidewalk to certain traffic offenses. They also include
a variety of more serious misdemeanors. This broad spectrum of petty-
offense cases daily floods the lower criminal courts. The rule laid down
today will confront the judges of each of these courts with an awkward
dilemma. If counsel is not appointed or knowingly waived, no sentence
of imprisonment for any duration may be imposed. The judge will therefore be forced to decide in advance of trial—and without hearing the
evidence—whether he will forgo entirely his judicial discretion to impose
some sentence of imprisonment and abandon his responsibility to consider
the full range of punishments established by the legislature. His alternatives, assuming the availability of counsel, will be to appoint counsel
and retain the discretion vested in him by law, or to abandon this discretion in advance and proceed without counsel. . . .

III

I would hold that the right to counsel in petty-offense cases is not absolute
but is one to be determined by the trial courts exercising a judicial
discretion on a case-by-case basis. The determination should be made
before the accused formally pleads; many petty cases are resolved by guilty
pleas in which the assistance of counsel may be required. If the trial court
should conclude that the assistance of counsel is not required in any
case, it should state its reasons so that the issue could be preserved for
review. The trial court would then become obligated to scrutinize carefully the subsequent proceedings for the protection of the defendant. If
an unrepresented defendant sought to enter a plea of guilty, the Court
should examine the case against him to insure that there is admissible
evidence tending to support the elements of the offense. If a case went
to trial without defense counsel, the court should intervene, when necessary, to insure that the defendant adequately brings out the facts in his
favor and to prevent legal issues from being overlooked. Formal trial rules
should not be applied strictly against unrepresented defendants. Finally,
appellate courts should carefully scrutinize all decisons not to appoint
counsel and the proceedings which follow.

It is impossible, as well as unwise, to create a precise and detailed set of guidelines for judges to follow in determining whether the appointment of counsel is necessary to assure a fair trial. Certainly three general factors should be weighed. First, the court should consider the complexity of the offense charged. . . .

Second, the court should consider the probable sentence that will follow if a conviction is obtained. The more serious the likely consequences, the greater is the probability that a lawyer should be appointed. . . .

Third, the court should consider the individual factors peculiar to each case. These, of course, would be the most difficult to anticipate. One relevant factor would be the competency of the individual defendant to present his own case. The attitude of the community toward a particular defendant or particular incident would be another consideration. But there might be other reasons why a defendant would have a peculiar need for a lawyer which would compel the appointment of counsel in a case where the court would normally think this unnecessary. Obviously, the sensitivity and diligence of individual judges would be crucial to the operation of a rule of fundamental fairness requiring the consideration of the varying factors in each case.

Such a rule is similar in certain respects to the special-circumstances rule applied to felony cases in Betts v. Brady, 316 U.S. 455 (1942), and Bute v. Illinois, 333 U.S. 640 (1948), which this Court overruled in *Gideon*.[33] One of the reasons for seeking a more definitive standard in felony cases was the failure of many state courts to live up to their responsibilities in determining on a case-by-case basis whether counsel should be appointed. . . .

. . . But this Court should not assume that the past insensitivity of some state courts to the right of defendants will continue. Certainly if the Court follows the course of reading rigid rules into the Constitution, so that the state courts will be unable to exercise judicial discretion within the limits of fundamental fairness, there is little reason to think that insensitivity will abate. . . .

As the proceedings in the courts below were not in accord with the views expressed above, I concur in the result of the decision in this case.

NOTES AND QUESTIONS

1. After *Argersinger*, what procedures should a trial judge follow before deciding whether to appoint counsel? Should the judge request

33. I do not disagree with the overruling of *Betts*; I am in complete accord with *Gideon*. *Betts*, like *Gideon*, concerned the right to counsel in a felony case. See n.1, supra. Neither case controls today's result.

something on the order of a presentence investigation? Without such information, how can an intelligent decision be reached concerning the appropriate sanctions? Should the judge also take into account the likelihood of conviction? How can that be done *before* trial, and at what cost? The financial burden can perhaps be minimized by simply asking the prosecutor to relate the basis of the charge, but should the trial judge be exposed to a one-sided summary of the case prior to trial? Does the answer to that depend in part on whether there is a jury?

2. The Supreme Court in *Argersinger* rejected as too constrictive the analogy to the jury trial right that the Florida Supreme Court embraced, which permits jury trials as a right for all offenses punishable by more than six months imprisonment. But while the Court gave with the left hand, did it take away with the right? In those jurisdictions that extend the right to a jury to petty offenses (those punishable by six months or less), does the invocation of that right carry with it a constitutional right to counsel? Chief Justice Burger apparently thinks not. The problem extends beyond petty cases. Consider the plight of an individual charged with either a petty or a more serious misdemeanor, conviction for which will cause unpleasant collateral consequences to the defendant, loss of a driver's license for example. If, after hearing a summary of the case and perhaps the defendant's record, the trial judge decides not to appoint counsel, the defendant must choose between self-representation before a jury or permitting the judge, who has already heard a one-sided presentation of the case, to sit as a fact finder. Do you see a way to avoid this dilemma?

3. Reconsider Justice Powell's concurrence. Why does he wish to resurrect the *Betts* special circumstance rule? Are you convinced or unpersuaded? Which is likely to be more difficult, to determine whether imprisonment may be the preferred sanction if the defendant is guilty or to determine, without the aid of defense counsel, whether a case is sufficiently complex as to require the assistance of counsel? Note further that Justice Powell asserts that "Due Process . . . . embodies principles of fairness rather than immutable line drawing." How helpful is that? How do you determine what is "fair" without "drawing a line" between that and what is "unfair"?

4. Does *Argersinger* supplement, or modify, *Gideon?* Does counsel need to be appointed in a felony case where the judge determines before trial not to sentence the defendant to a term of imprisonment? If so, why? What is the significance of labeling one offense a felony and another a misdemeanor? How do aggravated misdemeanors fit into the taxonomy? See, e.g., Iowa Criminal Code §903.1 (aggravated misdemeanor punishable by two-year imprisonment). Consider the following case.

SCOTT v. ILLINOIS
Certiorari to the Supreme Court of Illinois
440 U.S. 367 (1979)

MR. JUSTICE REHNQUIST delivered the opinion of the Court.

We granted certiorari in this case to resolve a conflict among state and lower federal courts regarding the proper application of our decision in Argersinger v. Hamlin. . . . Scott was convicted of theft and fined $50 after a bench trial in the Circuit Court of Cook County, Ill. . . . The applicable Illinois statute set the maximum penalty for such an offense at a $500 fine or one year in jail, or both. The petitioner argues that a line of this Court's cases culminating in Argersinger v. Hamlin, . . . requires state provision of counsel whenever imprisonment is an authorized penalty.

The Supreme Court of Illinois rejected this contention, . . . stat[ing] that it was not inclined to extend Argersinger to the case where a defendant is charged with a statutory offense for which imprisonment upon conviction is authorized but not actually imposed upon the defendant. . . . We agree with the Supreme Court of Illinois that the Federal Constitution does not require a state trial court to appoint counsel for a criminal defendant such as petitioner, and we therefore affirm its judgment. . . .

The number of separate opinions in [this court's right to counsel and jury trial cases] suggests that constitutional line drawing becomes more difficult as the reach of the Constitution is extended further, and as efforts are made to transpose lines from one area of Sixth Amendment jurisprudence to another. The process of incorporation creates special difficulties, for the state and federal contexts are often different and application of the same principle may have ramifications distinct in degree and kind. The range of human conduct regulated by state criminal laws is much broader than that of the federal criminal laws, particularly on the "petty" offense part of the spectrum. As a matter of constitutional adjudication, we are, therefore, less willing to extrapolate an already extended line when, although the general nature of the principle sought to be applied is clear, its precise limits and their ramifications become less so. We have now in our decided cases departed from the literal meaning of the Sixth Amendment. And we cannot fall back on the common law as it existed prior to the enactment of that Amendment, since it perversely gave less in the way of right to counsel to accused felons than to those accused of misdemeanors. . . .

In Argersinger the Court rejected arguments that social cost or a lack of available lawyers militated against its holding, in some part because it thought these arguments were factually incorrect. 407 U.S., at 37 n.7.

But they were rejected in much larger part because of the Court's conclusion that incarceration was so severe a sanction that it should not be imposed as a result of a criminal trial unless an indigent defendant had been offered appointed counsel to assist in his defense, regardless of the cost to the States implicit in such a rule. . . .

Although the intentions of the *Argersinger* Court are not unmistakably clear from its opinion, we conclude today that *Argersinger* did indeed delimit the constitutional right to appointed counsel in state criminal proceedings. Even were the matter res nova, we believe that the central premise of *Argersinger*—that actual imprisonment is a penalty different in kind from fines or the mere threat of imprisonment—is eminently sound and warrants adoption of actual imprisonment as the line defining the constitutional right to appointment of counsel. *Argersinger* has proved workable, whereas any extension would create confusion and impose unpredictable, but necessarily substantial, costs on 50 quite diverse States.[5] We therefore hold that the Sixth and Fourteenth Amendments to the United States Constitution require only that no indigent criminal defendant be sentenced to a term of imprisonment unless the State has afforded him the right to assistance of appointed counsel in his defense. The judgement of the Supreme Court of Illinois is accordingly affirmed.

MR. JUSTICE POWELL, concurring.

For the reasons stated in my opinion in Argersinger v. Hamlin, 407 U.S. 25, 44 (1972), I do not think the rule adopted by the Court in that case is required by the Constitution. Moreover, the drawing of a line based on whether there is imprisonment (even for overnight) can have the practical effect of precluding provision of counsel in other types of cases in which conviction can have more serious consequences. The *Argersinger* rule also tends to impair the proper functioning of the criminal justice system in that trial judges, in advance of hearing any evidence and before knowing anything about the case except the charge, all too often will be compelled to forgo the legislatively granted option to impose a sentence of imprisonment upon conviction. Preserving this option by providing counsel often will be impossible or impracticable—particularly in congested urban courts where scores of cases are heard in a single sitting, and in small and rural communities where lawyers may not be available.

5. Unfortunately, extensive empirical work has not been done. That which exists suggests that the requirements of *Argersinger* have not proved to be unduly burdensome. See, e.g., Ingraham, The Impact of *Argersinger*—One Year Later, 8 Law & Soc. Rev. 615 (1974). That some jurisdictions have had difficulty implementing *Argersinger* is certainly not an argument for extending it. S. Kramz, C. Smith, D. Rossman, P. Froyd & J. Hoffman, Right to Counsel in Criminal Cases 1-18 (1976).

Despite my continuing reservations about the *Argersinger* rule, it was approved by the Court in the 1972 opinion and four Justices have reaffirmed it today. It is important that this Court provide clear guidance to the hundreds of courts across the country that confront this problem daily. Accordingly, and mindful of stare decisis, I join the opinion of the Court. I do so, however, with the hope that in due time a majority will recognize that a more flexible rule is consistent with due process and will better serve the cause of justice.

MR. JUSTICE BRENNAN, with whom MR. JUSTICE MARSHALL and MR. JUSTICE STEVENS join, dissenting. . . .

This case presents the question whether the right to counsel extends to a person accused of an offense that, although punishable by incarceration, is actually punished only by a fine. . . .

The Court, in an opinion that at best ignores the basic principles of prior decisions, affirms Scott's conviction without counsel because he was sentenced only to pay a fine. In my view, the plain wording of the Sixth Amendment and the Court's precedents compel the conclusion that Scott's uncounseled conviction violated the Sixth and Fourteenth Amendments and should be reversed.

I

The Court's opinion intimates that the Court's precedents ordaining the right to appointed counsel for indigent accuseds in state criminal proceedings fail to provide a principled basis for deciding this case. That is demonstrably not so. The principles developed in the relevant precedents are clear and sound. The Court simply chooses to ignore them. . . .

II

In my view petitioner could prevail in this case without extending the right to counsel beyond what was assumed to exist in *Argersinger*. Neither party in that case questioned the existence of the right to counsel in trials involving "non-petty" offenses punishable by more than six months in jail. The question the Court addressed was whether the right applied to some "petty" offenses to which the right to jury trial did not extend. The Court's reasoning in applying the right to counsel in the case before it— that the right to counsel is more fundamental to a fair proceeding than the right to jury trial and that the historical limitations on the jury trial right are irrelevant to the right to counsel—certainly cannot support a

standard for the right to counsel that is more restrictive than the standard
for granting a right to jury trial. . . . *Argersinger* thus established a "two
dimensional" test for the right to counsel: the right attaches to any "non-
petty" offense punishable by more than six months in jail and in addition
to any offense where actual incarceration is likely regardless of the maximum authorized penalty. See Duke, The Right to Appointed Counsel:
Argersinger and Beyond, 12 Am. Crim. L. Rev. 601 (1975).

The offense of "theft" with which Scott was charged is certainly not
a "petty" one. It is punishable by a sentence of up to one year in jail.
Unlike many traffic or other "regulatory" offenses, it carries the moral
stigma associated with common-law crimes traditionally recognized as
indicative of moral depravity. The State indicated at oral argument that
the services of a professional prosecutor were considered essential to the
prosecution of this offense. . . . Likewise, nonindigent defendants
charged with this offense would be well advised to hire the "best lawyers
they can get." Scott's right to the assistance of appointed counsel is thus
plainly mandated by the logic of the Court's prior cases, including *Argersinger* itself.

III

But rather than decide consonant with the assumption in regard to non-
petty offenses that was both implicit and explicit in *Argersinger*, the Court
today retreats to the indefensible position that the *Argersinger* "actual
imprisonment" standard is the *only* test for determining the boundary of
the Sixth Amendment right to appointed counsel in state misdemeanor
cases, thus necessarily deciding that in many cases (such as this one) a
defendant will have no right to appointed counsel even when he has a
constitutional right to a jury trial. This is simply an intolerable result.
Not only is the "actual imprisonment" standard unprecedented as the
exclusive test, but also the problems inherent in its application demonstrate the superiority of an "authorized imprisonment" standard that would
require the appointment of counsel for indigents accused of any offense
for which imprisonment for any time is authorized.

First, the "authorized imprisonment" standard more faithfully implements the principles of the Sixth Amendment identified in *Gideon*.
The procedural rules established by state statutes are geared to the nature
of the potential penalty for an offense, not to the actual penalty imposed
in particular cases. The authorized penalty is also a better predictor of
the stigma and other collateral consequences that attach to conviction of
an offense. With the exception of *Argersinger*, authorized penalties have
been used consistently by this Court as the true measures of the seriousness

of offenses. . . . . Imprisonment is a sanction particularly associated with criminal offenses; trials of offenses punishable by imprisonment accordingly possess the characteristics found by *Gideon* to require the appointment of counsel. By contrast, the "actual imprisonment" standard, as the Court's opinion in this case demonstrates, denies the right to counsel in criminal prosecutions to accuseds who suffer the severe consequences of prosecution other than imprisonment.

Second, the "authorized imprisonment" test presents no problems of administration. It avoids the necessity for time-consuming consideration of the likely sentence in each individual case before trial and the attendant problems of inaccurate predictions, unequal treatment, and apparent and actual bias. . . .

Finally, the "authorized imprisonment" test ensures that courts will not abrogate legislative judgments concerning the appropriate range of penalties to be considered for each offense. . . .

The apparent reason for the Court's adoption of the "actual imprisonment" standard for all misdemeanors is concern for the economic burden that an "authorized imprisonment" standard might place on the States. But, with all respect, that concern is both irrelevant and speculative.

This Court's role in enforcing constitutional guarantees for criminal defendants cannot be made dependent on the budgetary decisions of state governments. . . .

In any event, the extent of the alleged burden on the States is, as the Court admits, speculative. Although more persons are charged with misdemeanors punishable by incarceration than are charged with felonies, a smaller percentage of persons charged with misdemeanors qualify as indigent, and misdemeanor cases as a rule require far less attorney time.

Furthermore, public defender systems have proved economically feasible, and the establishment of such systems to replace appointment of private attorneys can keep costs at acceptable levels even when the number of cases requiring appointment of counsel increases dramatically. The public defender system alternative also answers the argument that an "authorized imprisonment" standard would clog the courts with inexperienced appointed counsel.

Perhaps the strongest refutation of the respondent's alarmist prophecies that an "authorized imprisonment" standard would wreak havoc on the States is that the standard has not produced that result in the substantial number of States that already provide counsel in all cases where imprisonment is authorized—States that include a large majority of the country's population and a great diversity of urban and rural environments. Moreover, of those States that do not yet provide counsel in all cases where any imprisonment is authorized, many provide counsel when periods of imprisonment longer than 30 days, 3 months, or 6 months are authorized. In fact, Scott would be entitled to appointed counsel under the current laws of at least 33 States. . . .

MR. JUSTICE BLACKMUN, dissenting.

For substantially the reasons stated by MR. JUSTICE BRENNAN in Parts I and II of his dissenting opinion, I would hold that the right to counsel secured by the Sixth and Fourteenth Amendments extends at least as far as the right to jury trial secured by those Amendments. Accordingly, I would hold that an indigent defendant in a state criminal case must be afforded appointed counsel whenever the defendant is prosecuted for a nonpetty criminal offense, that is, one punishable by more than six months' imprisonment, or whenever the defendant is convicted of an offense and is actually subjected to a term of imprisonment. . . .

NOTES AND QUESTIONS

1. Does *Scott* dramatically change the prior understanding of the scope of the sixth amendment? *Argersinger* referred explicitly to "the trial of a misdemeanor," thus apparently leaving intact the general understanding that *Gideon* requires the appointment of counsel for indigents in all felony cases, but does that understanding survive *Scott*? If the only constitutional criterion is actual imprisonment, then it should apply equally to misdemeanors and felonies. Also, reconsider Note 2, page 147 supra. Is it now clear that the right to counsel and the right to trial by jury are entirely independent and that invocation of a right to a jury trial is not a "special circumstance" that initiates a right to counsel? And is it also now clear that there is no longer any form of a "special circumstances" rule?

2. Or is there a better way to read *Scott*? If you read *Scott* broadly, it fundamentally reworks the meaning of the sixth amendment, but can it also be read more narrowly, as essentially refining *Argersinger's* treatment of less serious criminal cases? Read more narrowly, would the aftermath of *Scott* contain a series of principles, any one of which would be adequate to require counsel in any particular case? What are those principles?

3. How do you know whether to read *Scott* broadly or narrowly? Is the Court's opinion enlightening? Of what significance, for example, is the Court's reluctance "to extrapolate an already extended line"? Its reference to "social costs or a lack of available lawyers"? For an excellent discussion of these and related issues, see Herman & Thompson, Scott

v. Illinois and the Right to Counsel: A Decision in Search of a Doctrine?, 17 Am. Crim. L. Rev. 71 (1979).

4. Is the alignment of the justices another indicator of how *Scott* should be read? Of what significance is Justice Powell's concurrence?

5. How cogent is the majority's emphasis on imprisonment as the controlling factor? Criminal conviction apparently has a stigmatizing effect on the defendant, and there are other, more tangible collateral consequences that can follow from conviction, such as the loss of various kinds of licenses or of the right to vote. Did the Court adequately address these kinds of consequences? Indeed, did the Court address these at all? How should they be addressed?

6. As by now is obvious, the Court's right to counsel cases have not always been models of conceptual clarity. The conceptual inadequacies, and the disagreement among the justices concerning the meaning of the various decisions, is most evident in Baldasar v. Illinois, 446 U.S. 222 (1980). In *Baldasar*, the Court reviewed the constitutionality of a statute that converted a second conviction for misdemeanor theft (property worth less than $150) into a felony with enhanced punishment. Baldasar was convicted of the first offense without counsel, and the question before the Court was whether the uncounselled conviction could trigger the enhancement provisions after the second, counselled conviction. The Court, per curiam, said no "[f]or reasons stated in the concurring opinions." Justice Stewart, joined by Justices Brennan and Stevens, was content to assert that *Scott* was violated because Baldasar "was sentenced to an increased term of imprisonment *only* because he had been convicted in a previous prosecution in which he had *not* had the assistance of appointed counsel in his defense." Id. at 224. Justice Stewart did not address the problem posed by the fact that, under *Scott*, Baldasar's first conviction was certainly valid for other purposes.

Justice Marshall, joined by Justices Brennan and Stevens, addressed the issue avoided by Justice Stewart by noting that "petitioner's prior conviction was not valid for all purposes. Specifically, under the rule of *Scott* and *Argersinger*, it was invalid for the purpose of depriving petitioner of his liberty." Moreover, Justice Marshall stated:

> That petitioner has been deprived of his liberty "as a result of [the first] criminal trial" could not be clearer. If it had not been for the prior conviction, petitioner could not have been sentenced to more than one year for the present offense. Solely because of the previous conviction the second offense was transformed from a misdemeanor into a felony, with all the serious collateral consequences that a felony conviction entails, and he received a sentence that may result in imprisonment for two years in excess of that 1-year maximum. [Id. at 226-227.]

This was constitutionally suspect because of the "underlying rationale of *Argersinger*, that without counsel defendant's . . . . conviction is not sufficiently reliable to support the severe sanction of imprisonment." Id. at 226-227. Justice Blackmun simply reiterated his dissent in *Scott* to the effect that the Court should make the right to counsel and the right to jury trial coextensive and be done with it.

Justice Powell, joined by the Chief Justice and Justices White and Rehnquist, dissented:

> The question presented today is different from that decided in *Scott*. This case concerns the enhanced sentence imposed on petitioner Baldasar for a subsequent conviction for misdemeanor theft. Petitioner, who was represented by counsel at the second trial, concedes that he could have been sentenced to one year in jail for the second offense. He challenges only the addition of two years to his sentence, an enhancement that was based on his record as a recidivist. The Court holds that, even though the first conviction was valid, the State cannot rely upon it for enhancement purposes following a subsequent valid conviction. This holding undermines the rationale of *Scott* and *Argersinger* and leaves no coherent rationale in its place. A constitutionally valid conviction is now constitutionally invalid if relied upon as the predicate for enhancing the sentence of a recidivist. In my view, this result is logically indefensible. More seriously, the courts that try misdemeanor cases daily no longer have clear guidance from this Court. No court can predict with confidence whether a misdemeanor defendant is likely to become a recidivist. The option of not imposing a jail sentence on an uncounselled misdemeanant, expressly preserved by *Argersinger* and *Scott*, no longer exists unless the court is willing prospectively to preclude enhancement of future convictions. I dissent both because I believe that *Scott* dictates a contrary result, and because the courts of our Nation are entitled, at a minimum, to a clear rule on this important question. [Id. at 230-231.]

Although *Baldasar* only challenged the potential two extra years, does the Court's decision present other kinds of problems? For example, could Baldasar have been sentenced to one year or less after the second conviction, if the judge relied in part on the first conviction as demonstrating that a harsher sentence was now justified? Consider a statute that permits a sentence of either a fine or imprisonment of up to two years. May a trial judge constitutionally follow a policy of not appointing counsel for first offenses (and not sentencing anyone to jail) but routinely appointing counsel for second offenses *and* jailing convicted defendants for, say, 18 months? How does such a practice differ in any significant way from *Baldasar*? If it is *not* allowable, does a first conviction without counsel paradoxically guarantee that a second conviction, even with counsel, *cannot* result in imprisonment (at least if the second offense is not more heinous than the first)? What, in short, is going on here?

For a discussion of these issues, see Rudstein, The Collateral Use of Uncounseled Misdemeanor Convictions After *Scott* and *Baldasar*, 34 U. Fla. L. Rev. 517 (1982).

7. In elaborating on *Gideon*, the Supreme Court has held that the right to counsel applies at every critical stage of a criminal prosecution, Coleman v. Alabama, 399 U.S. 1 (1970), which raises two issues—what is a "criminal prosecution" and which of its stages are "critical." It now seems fairly well settled that a "criminal prosecution" begins for purposes of right to counsel when adversary judicial proceedings have been initiated, and that it continues throughout the sentencing process. Thus, the criminal prosecution begins as early as the initial appearance or any formal charging process such as the filing of an indictment or information, Brewer v. Williams, 430 U.S. 387 (1977), and it continues until the final determination by the trial judge of the sentence to be imposed. Mempa v. Rhay, 389 U.S. 128 (1967) (right to counsel applicable at probation revocation hearing at which judge imposed sentence).

What makes a stage "critical" is somewhat more problematic. The word apparently refers to any formal interaction between the defendant and the state that could adversely affect the defendant's ability effectively to exercise a legal right. Thus, preliminary hearings, *Coleman*, supra, initial appearances, *Brewer*, supra, and arraignments, Hamilton v. Alabama, 368 U.S. 52 (1961), are *critical* stages of a criminal prosecution, but ex parte proceedings that will not adversely affect a defendant's legal rights, such as photographic identification procedures (discussed in Chapter 5 infra), or warrant procedures (discussed in Chapter 7 infra), are not. Moreover, the concept of a "critical stage" also extends to any *informal* meeting between the defendant and a representative of the state that is designed or is likely to elicit incriminating information from the defendant (discussed in Chapter 9 infra).[3] It does not extend, however, so far as to require the appointment of counsel to inmates placed in administrative segregation, as a result of crimes committed while incarcerated, prior to the initiation of adversary judicial proceedings against the inmates. United States v. Gouveia, 467 U.S. 180 (1984).

The sixth amendment has been held to be not applicable past the point of sentencing. In Morrissey v. Brewer, 408 U.S. 471 (1972), the Court held that parole revocation is not a part of a criminal prosecution but that due process nonetheless mandates certain procedural protections.

---

3. If an interrogation of a suspect occurs prior to the initiation of adversarial proceedings, the accused's protections rest on the fifth amendment right to be free from compelled self-incrimination. See Chapter 9 infra.

In Gagnon v. Scarpelli, 411 U.S. 778 (1973), the Court held that one of those protections is right to counsel at parole or probation revocation proceedings where, unlike *Mempa*, sentence was not imposed at the hearing and where there are "special circumstances." The special circumstances calling for counsel exist whenever

> "the probationer or parolee makes a request for counsel, based on a timely and colorable claim (i) that he has not committed the alleged violation of the conditions upon which he is at liberty; or (ii) that, even if the violation is a matter of public record and is uncontested, there are substantial reasons which justified or mitigated the violation and make revocation inappropriate, and that the reasons are complex or otherwise difficult to develop or present. [Id. at 790.]

For a prescient criticism of this approach, see Kadish, The Advocate and the Expert-Counsel in the Peno-Correctional Process, 45 Minn. L. Rev. 803 (1961).[4] Curiously enough, the Court in *Gagnon* made a point of emphasizing that it was *not* deciding anything about the scope of the right to be heard by retained counsel in revocation proceedings. 411 at 783 n.6.[5] In addition to its "special circumstances" holding in *Gagnon*, the Court has read the fourteenth amendment to impose constraints on the states in other areas where the sixth amendment is not formally applicable. Some of these constraints are considered in the following section.

2. Further Emanations of the Right to Counsel— Counsel on Appeal and Other Forms of Assistance

Seven years prior to *Gideon*, page 128 supra, in Griffin v. Illinois, 351 U.S. 12 (1956), the Court rendered a decision with enormous implications that nonetheless remained dormant for the most part until the day *Gideon* was decided. It was not *Gideon* that resurrected *Griffin*,

4. The Court has also determined that a prisoner has a right to be heard in prison disciplinary hearings that could adversely affect his liberty interests, but not necessarily with the assistance of counsel. Wolff v. McDonnell, 418 U.S. 539 (1974).

5. The Court has protected the access of prisoners to the courts, however. In Johnson v. Avery, 393 U.S. 483 (1969), the Court held that prisoners without counsel could not be denied the aid of literate prisoners in filing habeas corpus motions. The Court based its holding primarily on its belief that some prisoners would be effectively denied access to the courts if they were unable at least to secure the aid of other, literate prisoners in filing these motions. Similarly, in Bounds v. Smith, 430 U.S. 817 (1977), the Court held a state had to provide prisoners either with adequate law libraries or with adequate legal assistance to facilitate prisoners' requests for post-conviction relief. See Potuto, The Right of Prisoner Access: Does *Bounds* Have Bounds?, 53 Ind. L.J. 207 (1977-1978).

however; rather, it was *Gideon's* companion case, Douglas v. California, 372 U.S. 353 (1963). In *Griffin*, the Court struck down an Illinois statute that denied free transcripts of trial proceedings to indigents in circumstances where a transcript was necessary for an appeal under Illinois law. A four-person plurality, with Justice Frankfurter concurring, concluded that the Constitution prohibits a state from structuring an appellate process that had the effect of denying an effective review to indigents while permitting it to those with financial means.

If all *Griffin* stood for is that a state may not deny access to an important process on the basis of wealth, it still would have been an important decision interpreting the due process requirement of fairness in the criminal process, but not a particularly startling one. The plurality, however, did not stop at the point of access as a requirement of fairness. Instead, the plurality suggested that the real issue in *Griffin* was not access but any discrimination between the rich and the poor. Indeed, the opinion went so far as to say: "There can be no equal justice when the kind of trial a man gets depends on the amount of money he has." Were that to be taken literally, fundamental changes in the criminal process would have to be brought about, for a defendant of means is better off in myriad ways than a person without substantial funds.

Douglas v. California gave the appearance of beginning to take literally the dicta of *Griffin*. Petitioners in *Douglas* were convicted and appealed as of right to the Court of Appeals. On appeal, petitioners requested, and were denied, the assistance of appellate counsel. However, the denial came only after the Court of Appeals, following the applicable California rule of criminal procedure, made an independent investigation of the record to determine whether the assistance of counsel would be helpful to the petitioner or the court. Thus, petitioners were not denied access to the appellate process; they were only denied state-financed assistance after a determination was made that such assistance would be futile. Nonetheless, the Court found the California procedure unconstitutional, in large part on the basis of *Griffin*. Consequently, *Griffin*, as modified by *Douglas*, no longer appeared to be limitable to questions of access if indeed it ever was.

What was unclear, however, was what the limits of *Douglas* are. Read broadly, it would seem to require the extirpation of all differences resulting from the financial condition of defendants. However, it is difficult to tell from the opinions in *Douglas* how broadly to read it, because the underlying rationale of the decision is not adequately specified. As in *Griffin*, the decision could have been based either upon some notion of fairness that was now seen to extend beyond questions of access or, by contrast, upon the requirement of equal treatment. The greater the reliance on equal treatment as the operative principle, however, the more difficult it becomes to draw limits on the reach of *Douglas*. And indeed in the years following *Douglas*, the Court appeared to interpret *Douglas* as providing an equality principle that was extended in a series of cases, and each succeeding case heightened the perceived tension between the equality principle and the other possible explanation for *Douglas*—fundamental fairness. This process culminated in Ross v. Moffitt.

ROSS v. MOFFITT
Certiorari to the United States Court of Appeals for the Fourth Circuit
417 U.S. 600 (1974)

MR. JUSTICE REHNQUIST delivered the opinion of the Court.

We are asked in this case to decide whether Douglas v. California, . . . which requires appointment of counsel for indigent state defendants on their first appeal as of right, should be extended to require counsel for discretionary state appeals and for applications for review in this Court. The Court of Appeals for the Fourth Circuit held that such appointment was required by the Due Process and Equal Protection Clauses of the Fourteenth Amendment. . . .

II

This Court, in the past 20 years, has given extensive consideration to the rights of indigent persons on appeal. In Griffin v. Illinois, 351 U.S. 12 (1956), the first of the pertinent cases, the Court had before it an Illinois rule allowing a convicted criminal defendant to present claims of trial error to the Supreme Court of Illinois only if he procured a transcript of the testimony adduced at his trial. No exception was made for the indigent defendant, and thus one who was unable to pay the cost of obtaining such a transcript was precluded from obtaining appellate review of asserted trial error. . . . The Court in *Griffin* held that this discrimination violated the Fourteenth Amendment.

Succeeding cases invalidated similar financial barriers to the appellate process, at the same time reaffirming the traditional principle that a State is not obliged to provide any appeal at all for criminal defendants. McKane v. Durston, 153 U.S. 684 (1894). The cases encompassed a variety of circumstances but all had a common theme. For example, Lane v. Brown, 372 U.S. 477 (1963), involved an Indiana provision declaring that only a public defender could obtain a free transcript of a hearing on a coram nobis application. If the public defender declined to request one, the indigent prisoner seeking to appeal had no recourse. In

Draper v. Washington, 372 U.S. 487 (1963), the State permitted an indigent to obtain a free transcript of the trial at which he was convicted only if he satisfied the trial judge that his contentions on appeal would not be frivolous. The appealing defendant was in effect bound by the trial court's conclusions in seeking to review the determination of frivolousness, since no transcript or its equivalent was made available to him. In Smith v. Bennett, 365 U.S. 708 (1961), Iowa had required a filing fee in order to process a state habeas corpus application by a convicted defendant, and in Burns v. Ohio, 360 U.S. 252 (1959), the State of Ohio required a $20 filing fee in order to move the Supreme Court of Ohio for leave to appeal from a judgment of the Ohio Court of Appeals affirming a criminal conviction. Each of these state-imposed financial barriers to the adjudication of a criminal defendant's appeal was held to violate the Fourteenth Amendment.

The decisions discussed above stand for the proposition that a State cannot arbitrarily cut off appeal rights for indigents while leaving open avenues of appeal for more affluent persons. In Douglas v. California, 372 U.S. 353 (1963), however, a case decided the same day as *Lane*, supra, and *Draper*, supra, the Court departed somewhat from the limited doctrine of the transcript and fee cases and undertook an examination of whether an indigent's access to the appellate system was adequate. The Court in *Douglas* concluded that a State does not fulfill its responsibility toward indigent defendants merely by waiving its own requirements that a convicted defendant procure a transcript or pay a fee in order to appeal, and held that the State must go further and provide counsel for the indigent on his first appeal as of right. It is this decision we are asked to extend today.

Petitioners in *Douglas*, each of whom had been convicted by a jury on 13 felony counts, took appeals as of right to the California District Court of Appeal. No filing fee was exacted of them, no transcript was required in order to present their arguments to the Court of Appeal, and the appellate process was therefore open to them. Petitioners, however, claimed that they not only had the right to make use of the appellate process, but were also entitled to court-appointed and state-compensated counsel because they were indigent. The California appellate court examined the trial record on its own initiative, following the then-existing rule in California, and concluded that " 'no good whatever could be served by appointment of counsel.' " 372 U.S., at 355. It therefore denied petitioners' request for the appointment of counsel.

This Court held unconstitutional California's requirement that counsel on appeal would be appointed for an indigent only if the appellate court determined that such appointment would be helpful to the defendant or to the court itself. The Court noted that under this system an indigent's case was initially reviewed on the merits without the benefit of any organization or argument by counsel. By contrast, persons of greater means were not faced with the preliminary "ex parte examination of the record," id., at 356, but had their arguments presented to the court in fully briefed form. The Court noted, however, that its decision extended only to initial appeals as of right, and went on to say:

> "We need not now decide whether California would have to provide counsel for an indigent seeking a discretionary hearing from the California Supreme Court after the District Court of Appeal has sustained his conviction . . . or whether counsel must be appointed for an indigent seeking review of an appellate affirmance of his conviction in this Court by appeal as of right or by petition for a writ of certiorari which lies within the Court's discretion. But it is appropriate to observe that a State can, consistently with the Fourteenth Amendment, provide for differences so long as the result does not amount to a denial of due process or an "invidious discrimination." Williamson v. Lee Optical Co., 348 U.S. 483, 489; Griffin v. Illinois, supra, p.18. Absolute equality is not required; lines can be and are drawn and we often sustain them." Id., at 356-357.

The precise rationale for the *Griffin* and *Douglas* lines of cases has never been explicitly stated, some support being derived from the Equal Protection Clause of the Fourteenth Amendment, and some from the Due Process Clause of that Amendment.[8] Neither Clause by itself provides an entirely satisfactory basis for the result reached, each depending on a different inquiry which emphasizes different factors. "Due process" emphasizes fairness between the State and the individual dealing with the State, regardless of how other individuals in the same situation may be treated. "Equal protection," on the other hand, emphasizes disparity in treatment by a State between classes of individuals whose situations are arguably indistinguishable. We will address these issues separately in the succeeding sections.

---

8. The Court of Appeals in this case, for example, examined both possible rationales, stating: "If the holding [in *Douglas*] be grounded on the equal protection clause, inequality in the circumstances of these cases is as obvious as it was in the circumstances of *Douglas*. If the holding *Douglas* were grounded on the due process clause, and Mr. Justice Harlan in dissent thought the discourse should have been in those terms, due process encompasses elements of equality. There simply cannot be due process of the law to a litigant deprived of all professional assistance when other litigants, similarly situated, are able to obtain professional assistance and to be benefited by it. The same concepts of fairness and equality, which require counsel in a first appeal of right, require counsel in other and subsequent discretionary appeals." 483 F.2d, at 655.

III

Recognition of the due process rationale in *Douglas* is found both in the Court's opinion and in the dissenting opinion of Mr. Justice Harlan. The Court in *Douglas* stated that "[w]hen an indigent is forced to run this [gauntlet] of a preliminary showing of merit, the right to appeal does not comport with fair procedure." 372 U.S., at 357. Mr. Justice Harlan thought that the due process issue in *Douglas* was the only one worthy of extended consideration, remarking: "The real question in this case, I submit, and the only one that permits of satisfactory analysis, is whether or not the state rule, as applied in this case, is consistent with the requirements of fair procedure guaranteed by the Due Process Clause." Id., at 363.

We do not believe that the Due Process Clause requires North Carolina to provide respondent with counsel on his discretionary appeal to the State Supreme Court. At the trial stage of a criminal proceeding, the right of an indigent defendant to counsel is fundamental and binding upon the States by virtue of the Sixth and Fourteenth Amendments. Gideon v. Wainwright, 372 U.S. 335 (1963). But there are significant differences between the trial and appellate stages of a criminal proceeding. The purpose of the trial stage from the State's point of view is to convert a criminal defendant from a person presumed innocent to one found guilty beyond a reasonable doubt. To accomplish this purpose, the State employs a prosecuting attorney who presents evidence to the court, challenges any witnesses offered by the defendant, argues rulings of the court, and makes direct arguments to the court and jury seeking to persuade them of the defendant's guilt. Under these circumstances "reason and reflection require us to recognize that in our adversary system of criminal justice, any person haled into court, who is too poor to hire a lawyer, cannot be assured a fair trial unless counsel is provided for him." Id., at 344.

By contrast, it is ordinarily the defendant, rather than the State, who initiates the appellate process, seeking not to fend off the efforts of the State's prosecutor but rather to overturn a finding of guilt made by a judge or jury below. The defendant needs an attorney on appeal not as a shield to protect him against being "haled into court" by the State and stripped of his presumption of innocence, but rather as a sword to upset the prior determination of guilt. This difference is significant for, while no one would agree that the State may simply dispense with the trial stage of proceedings without a criminal defendant's consent, it is clear that the State need not provide any appeal at all. McKane v. Durston, 153 U.S. 684 (1894). The fact that an appeal *has* been provided does not automatically mean that a State then acts unfairly by refusing to provide counsel to indigent defendants at every stage of the way. Douglas v. California, supra. Unfairness results only if indigents are singled out by the State and denied meaningful access to the appellate system because of their poverty. That question is more profitably considered under an equal protection analysis.

IV

Language invoking equal protection notions is prominent both in *Douglas* and in other cases treating the rights of indigents on appeal. The Court in *Douglas*, for example, stated: "[W]here the merits of *the one and only appeal* an indigent has as of right are decided without benefit of counsel, we think an unconstitutional line has been drawn between rich and poor." 372 U.S., at 357. (Emphasis in original.) . . .

. . . Despite the tendency of all rights "to declare themselves absolute to their logical extreme,"[9] there are obviously limits beyond which the equal protection analysis may not be pressed without doing violence to principles recognized in other decisions of this Court. The Fourteenth Amendment "does require absolute equality or precisely equal advantages," San Antonio Independent School District v. Rodriguez, 411 U.S. 1, 24 (1973), nor does it require the Sate to "equalize economic conditions." Griffin v. Illinois, 351 U.S., at 23 (Frankfurter, J., concurring). It does require that the state appellate system be "free of unreasoned distinctions," Rinaldi v. Yeager, 384 U.S. 305, 310 (1966), and that indigents have an adequate opportunity to present their claims fairly within the adversary system. Griffin v. Illinois, supra; Draper v. Washington, 372 U.S. 487 (1963). The State cannot adopt procedures which leave an indigent defendant "entirely cut off from any appeal at all," by virtue of his indigency, Lane v. Brown, 372 U.S., at 481, or extend to such indigent defendants merely a "meaningless ritual" while others in better economic circumstances have a "meaningful appeal." Douglas v. California, supra, at 358. The question is not one of absolutes, but one of degrees. In this case we do not believe that the Equal Protection Clause, when interpreted in the context of these cases, requires North Carolina to provide free counsel for indigent defendants seeking to take discretionary appeals to the North Carolina Supreme Court, or to file petitions for certiorari in this Court.

9. Hudson County Water Co. v. McCarter, 209 U.S. 349, 355 (1908).

A

The North Carolina appellate system, as are the appellate systems of almost half the States, is multitiered, providing for both an intermediate Court of Appeals and a Supreme Court. . . . In criminal cases, an appeal as of right lies directly to the Supreme Court in all cases which involve a sentence of death or life imprisonment, while an appeal of right in all other criminal cases lies to the Court of Appeals. . . .

The statute governing discretionary appeals to the Supreme Court is N.C. Gen. Stat. §7A-31 (1969). This statute provides, in relevant part, that "[i]n any cause in which appeal has been taken to the Court of Appeals . . . the Supreme Court may in its discretion, on motion of any party to the cause or on its own motion, certify the cause for review by the Supreme Court, either before or after it has been determined by the Court of Appeals." The statute further provides that "[i]f the cause is certified for transfer to the Supreme Court after its determination by the Court of Appeals, the Supreme Court reviews the decision of the Court of Appeals." . . .

Appointment of counsel for indigents in North Carolina is governed by N.C. Gen. Stat. §7A-450 et seq. (1969 and Supp. 1973). These provisions . . . have generally been construed to limit the right to appointed counsel in criminal cases to direct appeals taken as of right. Thus North Carolina has followed the mandate of Douglas v. California, supra, and authorized appointment of counsel for a convicted defendant appealing to the intermediate Court of Appeals, but has not gone beyond *Douglas* to provide for appointment of counsel for a defendant who seeks either discretionary review in the Supreme Court of North Carolina or a writ of certiorari here.

B

The facts show that respondent . . . received the benefit of counsel in examining the record of his trial and in preparing an appellate brief on his behalf for the state Court of Appeals. Thus, prior to his seeking discretionary review in the State Supreme Court, his claims had "once been presented by a lawyer and passed upon by an appellate court." Douglas v. California, 372 U.S. at 356. We do not believe that it can be said, therefore, that a defendant in respondent's circumstances is denied meaningful access to the North Carolina Supreme Court simply because the State does not appoint counsel to aid him in seeking review in that court. At that stage he will have, at the very least, a transcript or other record of trial proceedings, a brief on his behalf in the Court of

Appeals setting forth his claims of error, and in many cases an opinion by the Court of Appeals disposing of his case. These materials, supplemented by whatever submission respondent may make pro se, would appear to provide the Supreme Court of North Carolina with an adequate basis for its decision to grant or deny review.

We are fortified in this conclusion by our understanding of the function served by discretionary review in the North Carolina Supreme Court. The critical issue in that court, as we perceive it, is not whether there has been "a correct adjudication of guilt" in every individual case, see Griffin v. Illinois, 351 U.S., at 18, but rather whether "the subject matter of the appeal has significant public interest," whether "the cause involves legal principles of major significance to the jurisprudence of the State," or whether the decision below is in probable conflict with a decision of the Supreme Court. The Supreme Court may deny certiorari even though it believes that the decision of the Court of Appeals was incorrect, see Peaseley v. Virginia Iron, Coal & Coke Co., 282 N.C. 585, 194 S.E.2d 133 (1973), since a decision which appears incorrect may nevertheless fail to satisfy any of the criteria discussed above. Once a defendant's claims of error are organized and presented in a lawyerlike fashion to the Court of Appeals, the justices of the Supreme Court of North Carolina who make the decision to grant or deny discretionary review should be able to ascertain whether his case satisfies the standards established by the legislature for such review.

This is not to say, of course, that a skilled lawyer, particularly one trained in the somewhat arcane art of preparing petitions for discretionary review, would not prove helpful to any litigant able to employ him. An indigent defendant seeking review in the Supreme Court of North Carolina is therefore somewhat handicapped in comparison with a wealthy defendant who has counsel assisting him in every conceivable manner at every stage in the proceeding. But both the opportunity to have counsel prepare an initial brief in the Court of Appeals and the nature of discretionary review in the Supreme Court of North Carolina make this relative handicap far less than the handicap borne by the indigent defendant denied counsel on his initial appeal as of right in *Douglas*. And the fact that a particular service might be of benefit to an indigent defendant does not mean that the service is constitutionally required. The duty of the State under our cases is not to duplicate the legal arsenal that may be privately retained by a criminal defendant in a continuing effort to reverse his conviction, but only to assure the indigent defendant an adequate opportunity to present his claims fairly in the context of the State's appellate process. We think respondent was given that opportunity under the existing North Carolina system.

V

Much of the discussion in the preceding section is equally relevant to the question of whether a State must provide counsel for a defendant seeking review of his conviction in this Court. North Carolina will have provided counsel for a convicted defendant's only appeal as of right, and the brief prepared by that counsel together with one and perhaps two North Carolina appellate opinions will be available to this Court in order that it may decide whether or not to grant certiorari. This Court's review, much like that of the Supreme Court of North Carolina, is discretionary and depends on numerous factors other than the perceived correctness of the judgment we are asked to review.

There is also a significant difference between the source of the right to seek discretionary review in the Supreme Court of North Carolina and the source of the right to seek discretionary review in this Court. The former is conferred by the statutes of the State of North Carolina, but the latter is granted by statute enacted by Congress. Thus the argument relied upon in the *Griffin* and *Douglas* cases, that the State having once created a right of appeal must give all persons an equal opportunity to enjoy the right, is by its terms inapplicable. The right to seek certiorari in this Court is not granted by any State, and exists by virtue of federal statute with or without the consent of the State whose judgment is sought to be reviewed.

The suggestion that a State is responsible for providing counsel to one petitioning this Court simply because it initiated the prosecution which led to the judgment sought to be reviewed is unsupported by either reason or authority. It would be quite as logical under the rationale of *Douglas* and *Griffin,* and indeed perhaps more so, to require that the Federal Government or this Court furnish and compensate counsel for petitioners who seek certiorari here to review state judgments of conviction. Yet this Court has followed a consistent policy of denying applications for appointment of counsel by persons seeking to file jurisdictional statements or petitions for certiorari in this Court. See, e.g., Drumm v. California, 373 U.S. 947 (1963). . . . In the light of these authorities, it would be odd, indeed, to read the Fourteenth Amendment to impose such a requirement on the States, and we decline to do so.

VI

We do not mean by this opinion to in any way discourage those States which have, as a matter of legislative choice, made counsel available to convicted defendants at all stages of judicial review. Some States which might well choose to do so as a matter of legislative policy may conceivably find that other claims for public funds within or without the criminal justice system preclude the implementation of such a policy at the present time. North Carolina, for example, while it does not provide counsel to indigent defendants seeking discretionary review on appeal, does provide counsel for indigent prisoners in several situations where such appointments are not required by any constitutional decision of this Court. Our reading of the Fourteenth Amendment leaves these choices to the State, and respondent was denied no right secured by the Federal Constitution when North Carolina refused to provide counsel to aid him in obtaining discretionary appellate review.

The judgment of the Court of Appeals' holding to the contrary is reversed.

MR. JUSTICE DOUGLAS, with whom MR. JUSTICE BRENNAN and MR. JUSTICE MARSHALL concur, dissenting.

I would affirm the judgment below because I am in agreement with the opinion of Chief Judge Haynsworth for a unanimous panel in the Court of Appeals. 483 F.2d 650. . . .

Chief Judge Haynsworth could find "no logical basis for differentiation between appeals of right and permissive review procedures in the context of the Constitution and the right to counsel." 483 F.2d, at 653. More familiar with the functioning of the North Carolina criminal justice system than are we, he concluded that "in the context of constitutional questions arising in criminal prosecutions, permissive review in the state's highest court may be predictably the most meaningful review the conviction will receive." Ibid. The North Carolina Court of Appeals, for example, will be constrained in diverging from an earlier opinion of the State Supreme Court, even if subsequent developments have rendered the earlier Supreme Court decision suspect. "[T]he state's highest court remains the ultimate arbiter of the rights of its citizens." Ibid.

Chief Judge Haynsworth also correctly observed that the indigent defendant proceeding without counsel is at a substantial disadvantage relative to wealthy defendants represented by counsel when he is forced to fend for himself in seeking discretionary review from the State Supreme Court or from this Court. It may well not be enough to allege error in the courts below in layman's terms; a more sophisticated approach may be demanded. . . . Furthermore, the lawyer who handled the first appeal in a case would be familiar with the facts and legal issues involved in the case. It would be a relatively easy matter for the attorney to apply his expertise in filing a petition for discretionary review to a higher court, or to advise his client that such a petition would have no chance of succeeding.

Douglas v. California was grounded on concepts of fairness and equality. The right to seek discretionary review is a substantial one, and one where a lawyer can be of significant assistance to an indigent defendant. It was correctly perceived below that the "same concepts of fairness and equality, which require counsel in a first appeal of right, require counsel in other and subsequent discretionary appeals." Id., at 655.

NOTES AND QUESTIONS

1. How convincing is the Court's argument in *Ross* that a lawyer will generally not materially advance a defendant's interests during a discretionary appeal process, especially given the nature of discretionary reviews? Does that view adequately reflect the realities of criminal litigation? Reconsider Justice Douglas's dissent, supra. Even if discretionary reviewing courts sit to hear cases of "significant public interest," cases "in probable conflict" with applicable precedent, or cases involving "legal principles of major significance to the jurisprudence" of the jurisdictions, why should a person of means have a better chance of having his case heard than an indigent? What, in short, should be the limits of the state's responsibility to offset the constraints of poverty? Consider the following:

> One of the prime objectives of the civilized administration of justice is to render the poverty of the litigant an irrelevancy. While this is true of the entire range of judicial administration, the interests involved make the attainment of this objective peculiarly urgent in the administration of criminal justice. The interests sought to be protected by the enforcement of criminal statutes involve no less than the order and internal security of the community. At the same time, the administration of criminal justice raises fundamental problems as to the relations of the individual to the state; for it is in the criminal law that the most stringent sanctions at the disposal of government are sought to be imposed on the individual. Here government proposes to deprive the individual of his property, his liberty, and even, on occasion his life. . . .
>
> It should be understood that governmental obligation to deal effectively with problems of poverty in the administration of criminal justice does not rest or depend upon some hypothetical obligation of government to indulge in acts of public charity. It does not presuppose a general commitment on the part of the federal government to relieve impoverished persons of the consequences of limited means, whenever or however manifested. It does not even presuppose that government is always required to take into account the means of the citizen when dealing directly with its citizens. Few would maintain that in disposing of surplus property, for

example, government is required to set prices at such levels that all citizens are rendered equally able to buy.

The obligation of government in the criminal cases rests on wholly different considerations and reflects principles of much more limited application. The essential point is that the problems of poverty with which this Report is concerned arise in a process *initiated* by government for the achievement of basic governmental purposes. It is, moreover, a process that has as one of its consequences the imposition of severe disabilities on the persons proceeded against. Duties arise from action. When a course of conduct, however legitimate, entails the possibility of serious injury to persons, a duty on the actor to avoid the reasonably avoidable injuries is ordinarily recognized. When government chooses to exert its powers in the criminal area, its obligation is surely no less than that of taking reasonable measures to eliminate those factors that are irrelevant to just administration of the law but which, nevertheless, may occasionally affect determinations of the accused's liability or penalty. While government may not be required to relieve the accused of his poverty, it may properly be required to minimize the influence of poverty on its administration of justice.

The Committee, therefore, conceives the obligation of government less as an undertaking to eliminate "discrimination" against a class of accused persons and more as a broad commitment by government to rid its processes of all influences that tend to defeat the ends a system of justice is intended to serve. Such a concept of "equal justice" does not confuse equality of treatment with identity of treatment. We assume that government must be conceded flexibility in devising its measures and that reasonable classifications are permitted. The crucial question is, has government done all that can reasonably be required of it to eliminate those factors that inhibit the proper and effective assertion of grounds relevant to the criminal liability of the accused or to the imposition of sanctions and disabilities on the accused at all stages of the criminal process?

. . . It is not only the interests of accused persons that require attention be given to the problems of poverty in criminal-law administration. Other and broader social interests are involved. We believe that the problems considered in this Report concern no less than the proper functioning of the rule of law in the criminal area and that, therefore, the interests and welfare of all citizens are in issue. . . .

The essence of the adversary system is challenge. The survival of our system of criminal justice and the values which it advances depends upon a constant, searching, and creative questioning of official decisions and assertions of authority at all stages of the process. The proper performance of the defense function is thus as vital to the health of the system as the performance of the prosecuting and adjudicatory functions. It follows that insofar as the financial status of the accused impedes vigorous and proper challenges, it constitutes a threat to the viability of the adversary system. We believe that the system is imperiled by the large numbers of accused persons unable to employ counsel or to meet even modest bail requirements and by the large, but indeterminate, numbers of persons, able to pay some part of the costs of defense, but unable to finance a full and proper defense. Persons suffering such disabilities are incapable of providing the challenges that are indispensable to satisfactory operation of the system. The loss to the interests of accused individuals, occasioned by these failures, are great and apparent. It is also clear that a situation in which persons are required to contest a serious accusation but are denied access to the tools of contest is offensive to fairness and equity. Beyond these considerations, however, is the fact that the conditions produced by the financial incapacity of the accused are detrimental to the proper functioning of the system of justice and that the loss in vitality of the adversary system, thereby occasioned, significantly endangers the basic interests of a free community. [Report of the Attorney General's Committee on Poverty and Administration of Criminal Justice 8-11 (1963).]

2. Assuming that the Court is correct that it is helpful to distinguish "fairness" from "equality," what does "fairness" seem to mean to the Court in the context of *Ross?* What are the word's parameters and, more important, how were they arrived at? Can the Court be serious, for example, when it says "unfairness results only if indigents are singled out by the State and denied meaningful access to the appellate system because of their poverty"? Why should access be the sole criterion of fairness? What role should other values play, such as reliability in fact-finding or concern for basic notions of human dignity? Indeed, if access is the primary criterion, does *Ross* substantially undercut *Douglas?* If not, what does the word *access* mean, and why is not that meaning as applicable to the petitioner in *Ross* as it was to those in *Douglas?* Are any of these questions answered by the following case?

EVITTS v. LUCEY

Certiorari to the United States Court of Appeals for the Sixth Circuit
469 U.S. 387 (1985)

JUSTICE BRENNAN delivered the opinion of the Court.

Douglas v. California held that the Fourteenth Amendment guarantees a criminal defendant the right to counsel on his first appeal as of right. In this case, we must decide whether the Due Process Clause of the Fourteenth Amendment guarantees the criminal defendant the effective assistance of counsel on such an appeal.

I

On March 21, 1976, a Kentucky jury found respondent guilty of trafficking in controlled substances. His retained counsel filed a timely notice
of appeal to the Court of Appeals of Kentucky, the state intermediate
appellate court. Kentucky Rule of Appellate Procedure 1.095(a)(1) required appellants to serve on the appellate court the record on appeal
and a "statement of appeal" that was to contain the names of appellants
and appellees, counsel, and the trial judge, the date of judgment, the
date of notice of appeal, and additional information. . . . Respondent's
counsel failed to file a statement of appeal when he filed his brief and
the record on appeal on September 12, 1977.

When the Commonwealth filed its brief, it included a motion to
dismiss the appeal for failure to file a Statement of Appeal. The Court
of Appeals granted this motion because "appellant has failed to supply
the information required by RAP 1.095(a)(1)." Respondent moved for
reconsideration, arguing that all of the information necessary for a statement of appeal was in fact included in his brief, albeit in a somewhat
different format. At the same time, respondent tendered a statement of
appeal that formally complied with the Commonwealth Rules. The Court
of Appeals summarily denied the motion for reconsideration. Petitioner
sought discretionary review in the Supreme Court of Kentucky, but the
judgment of the Court of Appeals was affirmed in a one-sentence order.
In a final effort to gain state appellate review of his conviction, respondent
moved the trial court to vacate the judgment or to grant a belated appeal.
The trial court denied the motion.

Respondent then sought federal habeas corpus relief in the United
States District Court for the Eastern District of Kentucky. He challenged
the constitutionality of the Commonwealth's dismissal of his appeal because of his lawyer's failure to file the statement of appeal, on the ground
that the dismissal deprived him of his right to effective assistance of
counsel on appeal guaranteed by the Fourteenth Amendment. The District Court granted respondent a conditional writ of habeas corpus ordering his release unless the Commonwealth either reinstated his appeal
or retried him.[3] Petitioner appealed to the Court of Appeals for the Sixth
Circuit, which reached no decision on the merits but instead remanded
the case to the District Court for determination whether respondent had
a claim under the Equal Protection Clause.

On remand, counsel for both parties stipulated that there was no

_____

3. The District Court also referred petitioner's counsel to the Board of Governors
of the Kentucky State Bar Association for disciplinary proceedings for "attacking his own
work product." Petitioner is not represented by the same counsel before this Court.

equal protection issue in the case, the only issue being whether the Commonwealth's action in dismissing respondent's appeal violated the Due Process Clause. The District Court thereupon reissued the conditional writ of habeas corpus. On January 12, 1984, the Court of Appeals for the Sixth Circuit affirmed the judgment of the District Court.

II

Respondent has for the past seven years unsuccessfully pursued every avenue open to him in an effort to obtain a decision on the merits of his appeal and to prove that his conviction was unlawful. The Kentucky appellate courts' refusal to hear him on the merits of his claim does not stem from any view of those merits, and respondent does not argue in this Court that the Commonwealth was constitutionally required to render judgment on the appeal in his favor. Rather the issue we must decide is whether the Commonwealth's dismissal of the appeal, despite the ineffective assistance of respondent's counsel on appeal, violates the Due Process Clause of the Fourteenth Amendment.

Respondent's claim arises at the intersection of two lines of cases. In one line, we have held that the Fourteenth Amendment guarantees a criminal appellant pursuing a first appeal as of right certain minimum safeguards necessary to make that appeal "adequate and effective," see Griffin v. Illinois, 351 U.S. 12, 20 (1956); among those safeguards is the right to counsel, see Douglas v. California. In the second line, we have held that the trial-level right to counsel, created by the Sixth Amendment and applied to the States through the Fourteenth Amendment, see Gideon v. Wainwright, comprehends the right to effect assistance of counsel. See Cuyler v. Sullivan, 446 U.S. 335, 344 (1980). The question presented in this case is whether the appellate-level right to counsel also comprehends the right to effective assistance of counsel.

A

Almost a century ago, the Court held that the Constitution does not require States to grant appeals as of right to criminal defendants seeking to review alleged trial court errors. McKane v. Durston, 153 U.S. 684 (1894). Nonetheless, if a State has created appellate courts as "an integral part of the . . . system for finally adjudicating the guilt or innocence of a defendant," Griffin v. Illinois, 351 U.S., at 18, the procedures used in deciding appeals must comport with the demands of the Due Process and Equal Protection Clauses of the Constitution. In Griffin itself, a transcript of the trial court proceedings was a prerequisite to a decision on the merits of an appeal. We held that the State must provide such a transcript to indigent criminal appellants who could not afford to buy one if that was the only way to assure an "adequate and effective" appeal.

Just as a transcript may by rule of custom be a prerequisite to appellate review, the services of a lawyer will for virtually every layman be necessary to present an appeal in a form suitable for appellate consideration on the merits. Therefore, Douglas v. California, supra, recognized that the principles of *Griffin* required a State that afforded a right of appeal to make that appeal more than a "meaningless ritual" by supplying an indigent appellant in a criminal case with an attorney. This right to counsel is limited to the first appeal as of right, see Ross v. Moffitt, 417 U.S. 600 (1974), and the attorney need not advance *every* argument, regardless of merit, urged by the appellant, see Jones v. Barnes, 463 U.S. 745 (1983). But the attorney must be available to assist in preparing and submitting a brief to the appellate court, Swenson v. Bosler, 386 U.S. 258 (1967) (per curiam), and must play the role of an active advocate, rather than a mere friend of the court assisting in a detached evaluation of the appellant's claim. See Anders v. California, 386 U.S. 738 (1967); see also Entsminger v. Iowa, 386 U.S. 748 (1967).[6] . . .

C

The two lines of cases mentioned—the cases recognizing the right to counsel on a first appeal as of right and the cases recognizing that the right to counsel at trial includes a right to effective assistance of counsel—are dispositive of respondent's claim. In bringing an appeal as of right from his conviction, a criminal defendant is attempting to demonstrate that the conviction, and the consequent drastic loss of liberty, is unlawful. To prosecute the appeal, a criminal appellant must face an adversary proceeding that—like a trial—is governed by intricate rules that to a layperson would be hopelessly forbidding. An unrepresented appellant—

---

6. Our cases dealing with the right to counsel—whether at trial or on appeal—have often focused on the defendant's need for an attorney to meet the adversary presentation of the prosecutor. See, e.g., Douglas v. California, 372 U.S. 353, 358 (1963) (noting the benefit of "counsel's examination into the record, research of the law, and marshalling of arguments on [client's] behalf"). Such cases emphasize the defendant's need for counsel in order to obtain a *favorable* decision. The facts of this case emphasize a different, albeit related, aspect of counsel's role, that of expert professional whose assistance is necessary in a legal system governed by complex rules and procedures for the defendant to obtain a decision at all—much less a favorable decision—on the merits of the case. In a situation like that here, counsel's failure was particularly egregious in that it essentially waived respondent's opportunity to make a case on the merits; in this sense, it is difficult to distinguish respondent's situation from that of someone who had no counsel at all. Cf. Anders v. California, 386 U.S. 738 (1967); Entsminger v. Iowa, 386 U.S. 748 (1967).

like an unrepresented defendant at trial—is unable to protect the vital interests at stake. To be sure, respondent did have nominal representation when he brought this appeal. But nominal representation on an appeal as of right—like nominal representation at trial—does not suffice to render the proceedings constitutionally adequate; a party whose counsel is unable to provide effective representation is in no better position than one who has no counsel at all.

A first appeal as of right therefore is not adjudicated in accord with due process of law if the appellant does not have the effective assistance of an attorney.[7] This result is hardly novel. The petitioners in both Anders v. California, 386 U.S. 738 (1967), and Entsminger v. Iowa, 386 U.S. 748 (1967), claimed that, although represented in name by counsel, they had not received the type of assistance constitutionally required to render the appellate proceedings fair. In both cases, we agreed with the petitioners, holding that counsel's failure in *Anders* to submit a brief on appeal and counsel's waiver in *Entsminger* of the petitioner's right to a full transcript tendered the subsequent judgments against the petitioners unconstitutional.[8] In short, the promise of *Douglas* that a criminal defendant has a right to counsel on appeal—like the promise of *Gideon* that a criminal defendant has a right to counsel at trial—would be a futile gesture unless it comprehended the right to the effective assistance of counsel.

Recognition of the right to effective assistance of counsel on appeal requires that we affirm the Sixth Circuit's decision in this case. Petitioners object that this holding will disable state courts from enforcing a wide range of vital procedural rules governing appeals. Counsel may, according to petitioners, disobey such rules with impunity if the state courts are precluded from enforcing them by dismissing the appeal.

Petitioner's concerns are exaggerated. The lower federal courts— and many state courts—overwhelmingly have recognized a right to effective assistance of counsel on appeal. These decisions do not seem to have had dire consequences for the States' ability to conduct appeals in

7. As Ross v. Moffitt, 417 U.S. 600 (1974), held, the considerations governing a discretionary appeal are somewhat different. Of course, the right to effective assistance of counsel is dependent on the right to counsel itself. See Wainwright v. Tona, 455 U.S. 586, 587-588 (1982) (per curiam) ("Since respondent had no constitutional right to counsel, he could not be deprived of the effective assistance of counsel by his retained counsel's failure to file the application timely") (footnote omitted).

8. Moreover, Jones v. Barnes, 463 U.S. 745 (1983), adjudicated a similar claim "of ineffective assistance by appellate counsel." Id., at 749. In *Jones*, the appellate attorney had failed to raise every issue requested by the criminal defendant. This Court rejected the claim, not because there was no right to effective assistance of appellate counsel, but because counsel's conduct in fact served the goal of "vigorous and effective advocacy." Id., at 754. The Court's reasoning would have been entirely superfluous if there were no right to effective assistance of counsel in the first place.

accordance with reasonable procedural rules. Nor for that matter has the longstanding recognition of a right to effective assistance of counsel at trial—including the recognition in Cuyler v. Sullivan, 446 U.S. 335 (1980), that this right extended to retained as well as appointed counsel— rendered ineffectual the perhaps more complex procedural rules governing the conduct of trials.

To the extent that a State believes its procedural rules are in jeopardy, numerous courses remain open. For example, a State may certainly enforce a vital procedural rule by imposing sanctions against the attorney, rather than against the client. Such a course may well be more effective than the alternative of refusing to decide the merits of an appeal and will reduce the possibility that a defendant who was powerless to obey the rules will serve a term of years in jail on an unlawful conviction. If instead a State chooses to dismiss an appeal when an incompetent attorney has violated local rules, it may do so if such action does not intrude upon the client's due process rights. For instance the Commonwealth of Kentucky itself in other contexts has permitted a postconviction attack on the trial judgment as "the appropriate remedy for frustrated right of appeal," Hammershoy v. Commonwealth, 398 S.W.2d 883 (Ky. 1966); this is but one of several solutions that state and federal courts have permitted in similar cases. A system of appeal as of right is established precisely to assure that only those who are validly convicted have their freedom drastically curtailed. A State may not extinguish this right because another right of the appellant—the right to effective assistance of counsel—has been violated.

III

Petitioners urge that our reasoning rests on faulty premises. First, petitioners argue that because the Commonwealth need not establish a system of appeals as of right in the first instance, it is immune from all constitutional scrutiny when it chooses to have such a system. Second, petitioners deny that respondent had the right to counsel on his appeal to the Kentucky Court of Appeals because such an appeal was a "conditional appeal," rather than an appeal as of right. Third, petitioners argue that, even if the Commonwealth's actions here are subject to constitutional scrutiny and even if the appeal sought here was an appeal as of right, the Due Process Clause—upon which respondent's claimed right to effective assistance of counsel is based—has no bearing on the Commonwealth's actions in this case. We take up each of these three arguments in turn.

A

In support of their first argument, petitioners initially rely on McKane v. Durston, 153 U.S. 684 (1894), which held that a State need not provide a system of appellate review as of right at all. Petitioners derive from this proposition the much broader principle that "whatever a state does or does not do on appeal—whether or not to have an appeal and if so, how to operate it—is of no due process concern to the Constitution. . . ." Brief for Petitioners 23. It would follow that the Commonwealth's action in cutting off respondent's appeal because of his attorney's incompetence would be permissible under the Due Process Clause.

The right to appeal would be unique among state actions if it could be withdrawn without consideration of applicable due process norms. For instance, although a State may choose whether it will institute any given welfare program, it must operate whatever programs it does establish subject to the protections of the Due Process Clause. See Goldberg v. Kelly, 397 U.S. 254, 262 (1970). Similarly, a State has great discretion in setting policies governing parole decisions, but it must nonetheless make those decisions in accord with the Due Process Clause. See Morrissey v. Brewer, 408 U.S. 471, 481-484. In short, when a State opts to act in a field where its action has significant discretionary elements, it must nonetheless act in accord with the dictates of the Constitution— and, in particular, in accord with the Due Process Clause.

B

Petitioners' second argument relies on the holding of Ross v. Moffitt, *supra*, that a criminal defendant has a right to counsel only on appeals as of right, not on discretionary state appeals. According to petitioners, the Kentucky courts permit criminal appeals only on condition that the appellant follow the local rules and statutes governing such appeals. Therefore, the system does not establish an appeal as of right, but only a "conditional appeal" subject to dismissal if the state rules are violated. Petitioners conclude that if respondent has no appeal as of right, he has no right to counsel—or to effective assistance of counsel—on his "conditional appeal."

Under any reasonable interpretation of the line drawn in *Ross* between discretionary appeals and appeals as of right, a criminal defendant's appeal of a conviction to the Kentucky Court of Appeals is an appeal as of right. Section 115 of the Kentucky Constitution provides that "[i]n all cases, civil and criminal, there shall be allowed as a matter of right at least one appeal to another court." Unlike the appellant in the discretionary appeal in *Ross*, a criminal appellant in the Kentucky Court of

Appeals typically has not had the benefit of a previously prepared trial transcript, a brief on the merits of the appeal, or a previous written opinion. In addition, petitioners fail to point to any source of Kentucky law indicating that a decision on the merits in an appeal like that of respondent—unlike the discretionary appeal in *Ross*—is contingent on a discretionary finding by the Court of Appeals that the case involves significant public or jurisprudential issues; the purpose of a first appeal in the Kentucky court system appears to be precisely to determine whether the individual defendant has been lawfully convicted. In short, a criminal defendant bringing an appeal to the Kentucky Court of Appeals has not previously had "an adequate opportunity to present his claims fairly in the context of the State's appellate process." It follows that for purposes of analysis under the Due Process Clause, respondent's appeal was an appeal as of right, thus triggering the right to counsel recognized in *Douglas*.

C

Finally, petitioners argue that even if the Due Process Clause does apply to the manner in which a State conducts its system of appeals and even if the appeal denied to respondent was an appeal as of right, the Due Process Clause nonetheless is not offended by the Commonwealth's refusal to decide respondent's appeal on the merits, because that Clause has no role to play in granting a criminal appellant the right to counsel— or *a fortiori* to the effective assistance of counsel—on appeal. Although it may seem that *Douglas* and its progeny defeat this argument, petitioners attempt to distinguish these cases by exploiting a seeming ambiguity in our previous decisions.

According to the petitioners, the constitutional requirements recognized in *Griffin, Douglas,* and the cases that followed had their source in the Equal Protection Clause, and not the Due Process Clause, of the Fourteenth Amendment. In support of this contention, petitioners point out that all of the cases in the *Griffin* line have involved claims by indigent defendants that they have the same right to a decision on the merits of their appeal as do wealthier defendants who are able to afford lawyers, transcripts, or the other prerequisites of a fair adjudication on the merits. As such, petitioners claim, the cases all should be understood as equal protection cases challenging the constitutional validity of the distinction made between rich and poor criminal defendants. Petitioners conclude that if the Due Process Clause permits criminal appeals as of right to be forfeited because the appellant has no transcript or no attorney, it surely permits such appeals to be forfeited when the appellant has an attorney who is unable to assist in prosecuting the appeal.

Petitioners' argument rests on a misunderstanding of the diverse sources of our holdings in this area. In Ross v. Moffitt, we held that "[t]he precise rationale for the *Griffin* and *Douglas* lines of cases has never been explicitly stated, some support being derived from the Equal Protection Clause of the Fourteenth Amendment, and some from the Due Process Clause of that Amendment." This rather clear statement in *Ross* that the Due Process Clause played a significant role in prior decisions is well supported by the cases themselves.

In *Griffin*, for instance, the State had in effect dismissed petitioner's appeal because he could not afford a transcript. In establishing a system of appeal as of right, the State had implicitly determined that it was unwilling to curtail drastically a defendant's liberty unless a second judicial decisionmaker, the appellate court, was convinced that the conviction was in accord with law. But having decided that this determination was so important—having made the appeal the final step in the adjudication of guilt or innocence of the individual—the State could not in effect make it available only to the wealthy. Such a disposition violated equal protection principles because it distinguished between poor and rich with respect to such a vital right. But it also violated due process principles because it decided the appeal in a way that was arbitrary with respect to the issues involved. In *Griffin*, we noted that a court dispensing "justice" at the trial level by charging the defendant for the privilege of pleading not guilty "would make the constitutional promise of a fair trial a worthless thing." Deciding an appeal on the same basis would have the same obvious—and constitutionally fatal—defect.

Our decisions in *Anders*, Entsminger v. Iowa, and Jones v. Barnes, are all inconsistent with petitioners' interpretation. As noted above, all of these cases dealt with the responsibilities of an attorney representing an indigent criminal defendant on appeal. Although the Court reached a different result in *Jones* from that reached in *Anders* and *Entsminger*, all of these cases rest on the premise that a State must supply indigent criminal appellants with attorneys who can provide specified types of assistance—that is, that such appellants have a right to effective assistance of counsel. Petitioners claim that all such rights enjoyed by criminal appellants have their source in the Equal Protection Clause, and that such rights are all measured by the rights of nonindigent appellants. But if petitioners' argument in the instant case is correct, nonindigent appellants themselves have no right to effective assistance of counsel. It would follow that indigent appellants also have no right to effective assistance of counsel, and all three of these cases erred in reaching the contrary conclusion.

The lesson of our cases, as we pointed out in *Ross*, is that each Clause triggers a distinct inquiry: " 'Due Process' emphasizes fairness between the State and the individual dealing with the State, regardless of how other individuals in the same situation may be treated. 'Equal Protection,' on the other hand, emphasizes disparity in treatment by a State between classes of individuals whose situations are arguably indistinguishable."[12] In cases like *Griffin* and *Douglas*, due process concerns were involved because the States involved had set up a system of appeals as of right but had refused to offer each defendant a fair opportunity to obtain an adjudication on the merits of his appeal. Equal protection concerns were involved because the State treated a class of defendants— indigent ones—differently for purposes of offering them a meaningful appeal. Both of these concerns were implicated in the *Griffin* and *Douglas* cases and both Clauses supported the decisions reached by this Court.

Affirmed.

CHIEF JUSTICE BURGER, dissenting.

Few things have so plagued the administration of criminal justice, or contributed more to lowered public confidence in the courts, than the interminable appeals, the retrials, and the lack of finality. Today, the Court, as Justice Rehnquist cogently points out, adds another barrier to finality and one that offers no real contribution to fairer justice. I join Justice Rehnquist in dissenting.

JUSTICE REHNQUIST, with whom THE CHIEF JUSTICE joins, dissenting.

In this case the Court creates virtually out of whole cloth a Fourteenth Amendment due process right to effective assistance of counsel on the appeal of a criminal conviction. The materials with which it works—previous cases requiring that indigents be afforded the same basic tools as those who are not indigent in appealing their criminal convictions, and our cases interpreting the Sixth Amendment's guarantee of the "assistance of counsel" at a criminal *trial*—simply are not equal to the task they are called upon to perform.

The Court relies heavily on the statement in Ross v. Moffitt, 417 U.S. 600, 608-609 (1974), that "[t]he precise rationale for the *Griffin* and *Douglas* lines of cases has never been explicitly stated, some support being derived from the Equal Protection Clause . . . and some from the Due Process Clause." But today's Court ignores the conclusion of the six justices who joined in *Ross*:

12. See also Bearden v. Georgia, 461 U.S. 660 (1983). We went on in *Ross* to analyze the issue presented there—the right to counsel on discretionary appeals—primarily in terms of the Equal Protection Clause. See 417 U.S., at 611. However, neither *Ross* nor any of the other cases in the *Griffin* line ever rejected the proposition that the Due Process Clause exerted a significant influence on our analysis in this area.

> Unfairness results only if indigents are singled out by the State and denied meaningful access to the appellate system because of their poverty. That question is more profitably considered under an equal protection analysis. [417 U.S., at 611.]

As further precedential support for a right to due process on appeal, the Court cites passing dictum in Bearden v. Georgia, 461 U.S. 660 (1983), but that case has nothing to do with appellate review. In fact, this Court's precedents have not imposed any procedural requirements on state appeals other than to bar procedures that operate to accord indigents a narrower scope of appellate review than nonindigents.

At one place in Douglas v. California, 372 U.S. 353, 357 (1963), the Court stated that the additional obstacles placed in the path of an indigent seeking to appeal a conviction did not "comport with fair procedure," but it explained this unfairness entirely in terms of inequality:

> There is lacking that equality demanded by the Fourteenth Amendment where the rich man, who appeals as of right, enjoys the benefit of counsel's examination into the record, research of the law, and marshalling of arguments on his behalf, while the indigent, already burdened by a preliminary determination that his case is without merit, is forced to shift for himself. [Id., at 357-358.]

Even the plurality in Griffin v. Illinois, 351 U.S. 12, 18-19 (1956), simply held that the Due Process Clauses protect indigents from "invidious discriminations" on appeal and that such persons "must be afforded as adequate appellate review as defendants who have money enough to buy transcripts." Moreover, Justice Frankfurter, whose concurrence was necessary to the decision, viewed the decision as a matter of equal protection. Id., at 21-22.

In similar vein, a fair reading of our other cases dealing with appellate review cited by the Court reveals uniform reliance on equal protection concepts and not due process. Contrary to the Court characterization, Anders v. California, Entsminger v. Iowa, and Jones v. Barnes, do not create for indigents a right to effective assistance of counsel on appeal and thus per force confer such a right on nonindigents; these cases simply require appointed appellate counsel to represent their clients with the same vigor as retained counsel ordinarily represent their paying clients.

Neither the language of the Constitution nor this Court's precedents establish a right to effective assistance of counsel on appeal. The Sixth Amendment provides that: "In all criminal *prosecutions*, the accused shall enjoy the right . . . to have the Assistance of Counsel for his *defense*" (emphasis added). As the Court observes, this language has been inter-

preted to confer a right to *effective* assistance of counsel, and its guarantee
has been extended to state criminal prosecutions by incorporation into
the Due Process Clause of the Fourteenth Amendment. But the words
"prosecutions" and "defense" plainly indicate that the Sixth Amendment
right to counsel applies only to trial level proceedings. At this stage, the
accused needs an attorney "as a shield to protect him against being 'haled
into court' by the State and stripped of his presumption of innocence."
Ross v. Moffitt, 417 U.S., at 610-611.

An appeal by a convicted criminal is an entirely different matter.
He has been found guilty beyond a reasonable doubt and, if sentenced
to a term of imprisonment, is subject to immediate deprivation of his
liberty without any constitutional requirement of further proceedings. He
seeks "to upset the prior determination of guilt" and universally is permitted to retain an attorney to serve "as a sword" in that endeavor. Id.,
at 611. There is no question that an attorney is of substantial, if not
critical, assistance on appeal, and those who can afford an attorney are
well advised to retain one and commonly do so. Accordingly, as a matter
of equal protection, we held in Douglas v. California, supra, that the
States must provide an attorney to those who cannot afford one so that
they stand on equal footing with nonindigents in seeking to upset their
convictions. The Court, however, extends that right beyond its supporting
rationale.

There is no constitutional requirement that a State provide an appeal
at all. "It is wholly within the discretion of the State to allow or not to
allow such a review." McKane v. Durston, 153 U.S. 684, 687 (1894).
If a State decides to confer a right of appeal, it is free to do so "upon
such terms as in its wisdom may be deemed proper." Id., at 687-688.
This decision was not a constitutional aberration. There was no right of
appeal from federal convictions until 1889 when Congress granted a right
of direct review in the Supreme Court in capital cases. In 1891 Congress
extended this right to include "otherwise infamous" crimes. Similarly,
there was no right of appeal from criminal convictions in England until
1907. In both countries, the concept of due process in criminal proceedings is addressed almost entirely to the fairness of the trial.

Citing Wainwright v. Torna, the Court candidly acknowledges that
"[o]f course, the right to effective assistance of counsel is dependent on
the right to counsel itself." Ante, at n.7. Proper analysis of our precedents
would indicate that apart from the Equal Protection Clause, which respondent has not invoked in this case, there cannot be a constitutional
right to *counsel* on appeal, and that, therefore, even under the logic of
the Court there cannot be derived a constitutional right to *effective assistance of counsel* on appeal.

The Court cites by analogy Goldberg v. Kelly, for the proposition that a State that confers a right to appeal, though not required to confer such a right, must establish appellate procedures that satisfy the Due Process Clause. *Goldberg* and the other so-called "entitlement" cases are totally inapposite. They turn on the fact that the State has created a form of "property," and the Due Process Clause by its express terms applies to deprivations of "property." True, the Due Process Clause also expressly applies to deprivations of "liberty," which is the basis for incorporating the Sixth Amendment right to counsel into the Fourteenth Amendment. But petitioner's "liberty" was deprived by his lawful state criminal conviction, not his unsuccessful attempt to upset that conviction by appellate attack. The statement in Griffin v. Illinois that Illinois has created appellate courts as "an integral part of the Illinois trial system for finally adjudicating the guilt or innocence of a defendant" is only a characterization of the Illinois court system by a plurality of the Court and is inconsistent with the general view of state appellate review expressed more recently by six Members of the Court in Ross v. Moffitt, supra, at 610-611.

The consequences of the Court's decision seem undesirable. Challenges to trial counsel's performance have become routine in federal habeas petitions. Now lawfully convicted criminals who have no meritorious bases for attacking the conduct of their trials will be able to tie up the courts with habeas petitions alleging defective performance by appellate counsel. The result is akin to the effect created when a mirror is held facing another mirror, the image repeating itself to infinity.

Today's decision also undermines the ability of both the state and the federal courts to enforce procedural rules on appeal. Presumably, rules which are common to almost every appellate system in our country providing for dismissal of an appeal for failure to comply with reasonable time limits, see, e.g., Fed. Rule App. Proc. 31(c), can no longer be enforced against a criminal defendant on appeal. The Court's understandable sympathy with a criminal defendant who has been badly served by the lawyer whom he hired to represent him in appealing his conviction has [led] it to treat the Due Process Clause of the Fourteenth Amendment as a general dispensing authority, by the use of which the Court may indiscriminately free litigants from the consequences of their attorneys' neglect or malpractice. In most other areas of life and law we are bound, often to our prejudice, by the acts and omissions of our agents, and I do not believe that the Fourteenth Amendment prohibits the States from carrying over that generally recognized principle to the prosecution of appeals from a judgment of conviction.

Much of the debate in these cases centers on the distinction between fairness and equality. How do these two concepts differ? Consider the following exchange.

WESTEN, THE EMPTY IDEA OF EQUALITY, 95 HARV. L. REV. 537, 539-540, 543-545, 545-550 (1982): Equality is commonly perceived to differ from rights and liberties. . . .

I believe that this contrasting of rights and equality is fundamentally misconceived. It is based on a misunderstanding, both in law and in morals, about the role of equality in ethical discourse. To avoid possible misunderstanding, let me emphasize what I mean by equality and rights. By "equality" I mean the proposition in law and morals that "people who are alike should be treated alike" and its correlative, that "people who are unalike should be treated unalike." Equality thus includes all statements to the effect that the reason one person should be treated in a certain way is that he is "like" or "equal to" or "similar to" or "identical to" or "the same as" another who receives such treatment. "Rights," by contrast, means all claims that can justly be made by or on behalf of an individual or group of individuals to some condition or power—except claims that "people who are alike be treated alike." . . .

The proposition that "likes should be treated alike" is said to be a universal moral truth—a truth that can "be intuitively known with perfect clearness and certainty." Why? What is the connection between the fact that people are alike and the normative conclusion that they ought to be treated alike? How can one move from an "is" to an "ought"?

The answer can be found in the component parts of the equality formula. The formula "people who are alike should be treated alike" involves two components: (1) a determination that two people are alike; and (2) a moral judgment that they ought to be treated alike. The determinative component is the first. Once one determines that two people are alike for purposes of the equality principle, one knows how they ought to be treated. To understand why this is so—that is, to understand how (1) works—one must understand what kind of determination (1) is. One must know precisely what it means to say for purposes of equality that two persons are alike.

First, "people who are alike" might mean people who are alike in every respect. The trouble is that no two people are alike in every respect. The only things that are completely alike in every respect are immaterial symbols and forms, such as ideal numbers and geometric figures, which are not themselves the subject of morals.

Second, "people who are alike" may mean people, who, though

not alike in every respect, are alike in some respects. Unfortunately, while the previous definition excludes every person in the world, the present definition includes every person and thing because all people and things are alike in some respect; and one is left with the morally absurd proposition that "all people and things should be treated alike."

Third, "people who are alike" may refer to people who are *morally* alike in a certain respect. The latter interpretation successfully avoids the philosophical hurdle of deriving an "ought" from an "is." It starts with a normative determination that two people are alike in a morally significant respect and moves to a normative conclusion that the two should be treated alike. Instead of deriving an "ought" from an "is," it derives an "ought" from an "ought." However, categories of morally alike objects do not exist in nature; moral alikeness is established only when people define categories. To say that people are morally alike is therefore to articulate a moral standard of treatment—a standard or rule specifying certain treatment for certain people—by reference to which they are, and thus are to be treated, alike. . . . Just as no categories of "like" people exist in nature, neither do categories of "like" treatment exist; treatments can be alike only in reference to some moral rule. Thus, to say that people who are morally alike in a certain respect "should be treated alike" means that they should be treated in accord with the moral rule by which they are determined to be alike. Hence "likes should be treated alike" means that people for whom a certain treatment is prescribed by a standard should all be given the treatment prescribed by the standard. Or, more simply, people who by a rule should be treated alike should by the rule be treated alike.

So there it is: equality is entirely "[c]ircular." It tells us to treat like people alike; but when we ask who "like people" are, we are told they are "people who should be treated alike." Equality is an empty vessel with no substantive moral content of its own. Without moral standards, equality remains meaningless, a formula that can have nothing to say about how we should act. With such standards, equality becomes superfluous, a formula that can do nothing but repeat what we already know. As Bernard Williams observed, "when the statement of equality ceases to claim more than is warranted, it rather rapidly reaches the point where it claims less than is interesting." . . . Relationships of equality (and inequality) are derivative, secondary relationships; they are logically posterior, not anterior, to rights. To say that two persons are the same in a certain respect is to presuppose a rule—a prescribed standard for treating them—that both fully satisfy. Before such a rule is established, no standard of comparison exists. After such a rule is established, equality between them is a "logical consequence" of the established rule. They are then "equal" in respect of the rule because that is what equal means:

"Equally" means " 'according to one and the same rule.' " They are also then entitled to equal treatment under the rule because that is what possessing a rule means: "To conform to a rule is (tautologically) to apply it to the cases to which it applies." To say that two people are "equal" and entitled to be treated "equally" is to say that they both fully satisfy the criteria of a governing rule of treatment. It says nothing at all about the content or wisdom of the governing rule. . . .

It might be thought that, while relationships of equality logically follow substantive definitions of right, equality may also precede definitions of right. Thus, it might be thought that a substantive right of persons to be treated with human respect is itself a product of an antecedent judgment that all persons are equal. That is not so. To see why, consider how one would go about deciding whether monstrously deformed neonates or human embryos or stroke victims in irreversible comas should be treated as "persons" for purposes of the right to respect. In trying to make the decision, one gets nowhere by intoning that all persons are equal, because the very question is whether the three candidates are indeed "persons" within the meaning of the rule. Nor does it do any good to say that likes should be treated alike, because the very question is whether the three candidates are indeed alike for purposes of human respect. Rather, one must first identify the trait that entitles anyone to be treated with respect and then ascertain empirically whether the trait appears in one or more of the three candidates.[40] If the candidates possess the relevant trait, they become "persons" within the meaning of the rule and hence entitled to respect. If they lack the relevant trait, they are not "persons," not equal to persons, and not to be treated like persons for purposes of the rule.

BURTON, COMMENT ON "EMPTY IDEAS": LOGICAL POSITIVIST ANALYSES OF EQUALITY AND RULES, 91 YALE L.J. 1136-1141, 1144-1147 (1982):

In a recent article in the Harvard Law Review, Professor Peter Westen directs his considerable capacity for logical analysis at the idea of equality. Professor Westen asserts and defends

---

40. The issue of the empirical basis for moral traits has caused some confusion. Some commentators, believing that relationships of equality must be grounded in some verifiable traits, tend to conclude that equality is entirely empirical. . . . Others, believing that an "ought" cannot be inferred from an "is," tend to conclude that moral notions of equality have no empirical basis.

. . . In fact, both contending camps are correct. Statements of moral and legal equality do have an empirical base, because otherwise one would have no way of distinguishing those creatures who are equal from those who are not. . . . Yet at the same time, statements of moral or legal equality also presuppose a normative element. . . . in short, statements of equality presuppose the presence of empirical traits that we decide ought to carry certain moral consequences.

"two propositions: (1) that statements of equality logically entail (and necessarily collapse into) simpler statements of rights; and (2) that the additional step of transforming simple statements of rights into statements of equality not only involves unnecessary work but also engenders profound conceptual confusion." Therefore, he says, equality is an "empty idea" that "should be banished from moral and legal discourse as an explanatory norm."

Many, no doubt, will wish to defend equality as a concept with independent content, at least in some situations. This Comment takes a different tack. "Statements of rights" (rules) are the heroes of Professor Westen's story, though they are spared the scrutiny lavished on equality. He seems to regard rules as suitable norms for explanatory moral and legal discourse—norms that in themselves are independent of equality, imbued with content, and comparatively simple to apply without confusion.[4] Using methods of logical analysis similar to those Westen used to criticize equality, this Comment will demonstrate that rules collapse into equality and also are empty, in the sense that Westen regards equality as empty. By the logical positivist method of analysis, both equality and rules must be banished from explanatory legal and moral discourse, a move that would render such discourse impossible. The alternative is to reject that method of analysis because it proves too much, and to retain both equality and rules as instruments of thought and argument. . . .

Now the assumption seems to be that "the terms of the rule *dictate* that it be applied," and that they do so by an intellectual process that does not depend of necessity on considerations of equality, or on other norms that are vulnerable to the criticisms made of equality.[13] Though

---

4. . . . Professor Westen might regard substantive rights as empty ideas analytically, but useful ones nonetheless. Cf. Westen at 579 n.147 ("Some formal concepts [such as rights] are quite handy, even indispensible [*sic*].") He argues that equality as a form of analysis is not useful, id. at 577-92, largely because "people do not realize that [equality] is derivative [from substantive rights], and not realizing it, they allow equality to distort the substance of their decisionmaking." Id. at 592. It would seem to be at least equally so that "people" often do not realize that statements of substantive rights themselves are empty of content in the same sense, and allow the so-called plain meanings of such statements to distort their decisionmaking. Westen offers no empirical grounds for concluding that equality causes more confusion than rules. Cf. infra note 14 (such grounds might support Westen's position if rights did not collapse into equality); note 50 (like equality, rules hide their incompleteness).

13. To summarize, the principal criticisms were (1) that statements of equality have no substantive content *of their own*, but depend on norms outside equality *itself*, id. at 553, 566, 571-72, 574, 577-78, 580-81; (2) that equality is a wholly normative concept, lacking the identification of empirical traits, the presence of which would entitle a person to the treatment claimed, id. at 544-47, 549; and (3) that application of the equality norm requires logically illicit moves between "is" and "ought," id. at 544-45. To justify banishing equality while retaining rules requires at least that rules be different from and better than equality by the same criteria.

Professor Westen did not undertake to analyze the logic of rules in his paper, such an analysis is necessary to the soundness of his thesis, which appeals to the meaningfulness and analytical simplicity of rules as contrasted with equality. We would have two choices if the idea of substantive rights, determined by the language of rules, were as empty as, and collapsed into, the idea of equality. We could conclude that rules also should be "banished from moral and legal discourse as an explanatory norm," or that neither concept should be banished because the method of analysis yielding such an absurd result is inappropriate. . . .

It is simply wrong, however, to suggest that substantive rights can be determined in any case without reference to a person's normative relationship to other rightsholders, at least if the statement is meant to convey what is involved in legal reasoning. Let us consider the right of free speech. The general terms of the First Amendment appear on their face to be simple to apply: "Congress shall make no law . . . abridging the freedom of speech. . . ." We will apply this general proscription to two particular cases, which will serve as illustrations throughout the remainder of this Part.

Imagine that a state has made it a crime to hang the Governor in effigy, and that a state has made it a crime to hang any person, including the Governor. It will be seen that the Supreme Court could not reach conclusions as to the validity of these laws without considering the normative relationship of (1) hanging the Governor or (2) hanging the Governor in effigy to other activities that enjoy (or do not enjoy) First Amendment protection. The Court must determine whether hanging the Governor in effigy or in the flesh is in some important aspect "like" such other activities—for example, (3) making a public speech criticizing the Governor or (4) hanging one's spouse. Because "the terms of the rule" do not "dictate" which aspect of each activity is *important*, arguments based on the rule collapse into arguments by analogy, which themselves are claims to equal treatment under the law. . . .

. . . In the analysis of reasoning, analogies necessarily appeal to the principle that "like cases should be treated alike"—the equality principle—and are vulnerable to the criticisms Westen makes of equality, to the same extent. . . .

To separate rules from equality completely, one who would adopt Professor Westen's position seems forced to regard legal reasoning as fundamentally deductive, rather than purposive, inductive, or analogical in character. Only a logical positivist model of legal reasoning can purport to explain rules and rights independently of equality or other similarly vulnerable norms. Thus, in the hypothetical free speech cases, a statement of the state's general duty of behavior (the rule) would stand as the major premise of a syllogism. A statement of the state's treatment of the person (the facts) would stand as the minor premise. Whether the state acted in accord with its duty would depend on whether the rule logically entailed the facts.

That this is Professor Westen's view of all defensible legal reasoning seems a fair interpretation of his expressions in this work, despite the facial implausibility of such a mechanical model. To repeat, he says that "[t]o decide whether a person's speech rights are violated, one *juxtaposes* the state's general duty of behavior against the state's particular treatment of the person to determine whether the state treats the person in *accord* with its prescribed duty." He emphasizes that equality between two persons "is a 'logical consequence' of the established rule." Thus, "[r]elationships of equality are derivative, secondary relationships; they are logically posterior, not anterior, to rights." . . .

I suggest that the two Governor-hanging cases are clear because we engage in analogical reasoning. We posit a clear case of protected speech (a lecture criticizing the Governor's policies) and a clear case of murder (killing one's spouse). In the light of the values underlying the First Amendment, we regard hanging the Governor in effigy as more like the first case, and hanging the Governor as more like the second. And we regard all four cases as easy ones. Of course, no two of the four cases are alike in all respects, and all four cases are alike in some respects. We make a normative judgment as to what respects are the important ones.

That judgment, however, is not a logical consequence of the terms of the First Amendment, which cannot be applied in a particular case without recourse to such analogies. For example, all four cases are "expression" in some respect, while none of the four cases is "expression" in all respects; and all are "anti-social behaviors" in some but not all respects. To apply the rule, we must make judgments about which respects are important in each case. The judgment of importance in applying a rule, like the judgment of similarity in using an analogy, depends on unspecified values outside the rule itself, and involves us in analytical problems of moving from "ought" to "is" when we apply the rule. Professor Westen therefore errs in stating that the conclusions are the "logical consequences" of the rule—not normative judgments but logically deduced from a "given." Where are the "given" rules that distinguish the Governor-hanging cases?

To test the point further, let us posit some rules (really meta-rules) that stand on a different logical plane and tell us how to apply the enacted rules: (1) the First Amendment shall not invalidate state statutes if the statutes are necessary to protect a compelling state interest; and (2) a constitutional provision shall be construed according to the intention of the framers or according to its purpose. It should be observed that both of the meta-rules are judge-made and consequently partake of the problems of common-law rules, making the process of applying enacted rules wholly dependent on analogical reasoning in the same manner. But let us pass over that problem and inquire whether these rules can be applied without engaging in reasoning by analogy—without using the equality principle to determine substantive rights.

The logic of the so-called "compelling state interest" test is fairly transparent. To say that the First Amendment invalidates a state statute unless the statute is necessary to protect a compelling state interest is logically reducible to saying something like: freedom of expression is more important than a state statute unless the state statute is more important than freedom of expression. Again, what do we mean by "important"? Surely nothing follows as a "logical consequence" in any real-world case from "important" as the key term in the major premise of a syllogism. Neither "compelling state interest" nor "importance" are things that exist in nature (observables), nor can they be reduced analytically to necessary and sufficient conditions that are observable without deriving an "is" from an "ought." They are normative concepts. As such, they beg the question whether application of a state murder statute to one who hung the Governor, or a state statute against hanging the Governor in effigy, should be invalidated by the First Amendment: it should if it should. One might offer another rule to tell us, as a "logical consequence," what a compelling state interest is—a meta-meta-rule—but it should be apparent that this tack leads to an infinite regress of no small significance.

The logic of construing a constitutional provision according to the intention of the framers or according to its purpose could lead us into a similar regress. Neither "intention" nor "purpose" are observables, if we state them in the abstract. We can say that the framers intended the First Amendment to protect "expression" or "political expression," though they said "speech" or that this was the purpose of the text. The problems of knowing such things, with the assurance necessary to exclude de novo normative judgments, are well-known. And even if we knew that the framers had such an intention or purpose, we still do not know that hanging the Governor in effigy and in the flesh are not both "expression," or neither "expression," or one "expression" and the other not, or the other "expression" and the one not, so far as the logical consequences of the meta-rule take us. Again, we need a meta-meta-rule and are off into the darkness of a regress.

Alternatively, the purpose or intention (of "freedom of speech" or of "compelling state interest") can be stated in the particular. To do so, however, is to state a case, be it hypothetical or historical. To say merely that the evil before the minds of the framers was, for example, suppression of the political opposition is again abstract, a negative version of the statement analyzed in the preceding paragraph. We must have a *case*, such as what happened to Zenger, or what Zenger did. As "general propositions do not decide concrete cases," however, "[c]oncrete decisions do not make law." What Zenger did can be described in narrow terms and limited to the press, or in broad terms and expanded to cover all thought and action. Another meta-meta-rule seems necessary to tell us what the rule of the *Zenger* case is, unless we break the regress by shifting from deduction to analogy. Then, we might say, hanging the Governor in effigy is like what Zenger did but hanging the Governor is not, and all might agree.

Of course, shifting from deduction to analogy (equality) does not solve our problems as analysts of legal reasoning. The problem identified by Professor Westen and others—identifying normative grounds for purposes of determining whether cases are alike or unalike—is no small problem. It is not solved, however, by shifting from equality to rules, which also depend on unspecified values outside the rules themselves. Thus, if rules are given the same kind of intensive logical analysis that Westen gives to equality, they too stand empty and collapse into equality. This logical analysis of rules and equality drives us back and forth between the two in a regress, as when we stand between the barber's mirrors. . . .

NOTES AND QUESTIONS

1. Professor Westen has responded to Professor Burton, On "Confusing Ideas": Reply, 91 Yale L.J. 1153 (1982), and indeed a rather rich literature is developing as a result of Professor Westen's initial effort. See, e.g., Chemerinsky, In Defense of Equality: A Reply to Professor Westen, 81 Mich. L. Rev. 575 (1983); D'Amato, Comment: Is Equality a Totally Empty Idea?, 81 Mich. L. Rev. 600 (1983); Greenawalt, How Empty Is the Idea of Equality?, 83 Colum. L. Rev. 1167 (1983); Karst, Why Equality Matters, 17 Ga. L. Rev. 245 (1983). For Professor Westen's responses, see Westen, To Lure the Tarantula from Its Hole: A Response, 83 Colum. L. Rev. 1186 (1983); Westen, The Meaning of Equality in Law, Science, Math, and Morals: A Reply, 81 Mich. L. Rev. 604 (1983).

2. Can *Ross* be reconciled with Mayer v. City of Chicago, 404 U.S. 189 (1971)? In *Mayer*, the Court held that a state must provide an indigent defendant, free of charge, with a record of sufficient completeness to permit proper consideration of his claims on appeal, even though such a record is *not*, unlike in *Griffin*, a condition precedent for an appeal.

One interesting aspect of *Mayer* was the state's argument that *Griffin* should not be extended to cases where the relevant sentence is a fine rather than punishment. The Court, per Justice Brennan, responded:

The city of Chicago urges another distinction to set this case apart from *Griffin* and its progeny. The city notes that the defendants in all the transcript cases previously decided by this Court were sentenced to some term of confinement. Where the accused, as here, is not subject to imprisonment, but only a fine, the city suggests that his interest in a transcript is outweighed by the State's fiscal and other interests in not burdening the appellate process. This argument misconceives the principle of *Griffin*. . . . *Griffin* does not represent a balance between the needs of the accused and the interests of society; its principle is a flat prohibition against pricing indigent defendants out of as effective an appeal as would be available to others able to pay their own way. The invidiousness of the discrimination that exists when criminal procedures are made available only to those who can pay is not erased by any differences in the sentences that may be imposed. The State's fiscal interest is, therefore, irrelevant.

We add that even approaching the problem in the terms the city suggests hardly yields the answer the city tenders. The practical effects of conviction of even petty offenses of the kind involved here are not to be minimized. A fine may bear as heavily on an indigent accused as forced confinement. The collateral consequences of conviction may be even more serious, as when (as was apparently a possibility in this case) the impecunious medical student finds himself barred from the practice of medicine because of a conviction he is unable to appeal for lack of funds. Moreover, the State's long-term interest would not appear to lie in making access to appellate processes from even its most inferior courts depend upon the defendant's ability to pay. It has been aptly said: "[F]ew citizens even have contact with the higher courts. In the main, it is the police and the lower court Bench and Bar that convey the essence of our democracy to the people.

"Justice, if it can be measured, must be measured by the experience the average citizen has with the police and the lower courts."[7] Arbitrary denial of appellate review of proceedings of the State's lowest trial courts may save the State some dollars and cents, but only at the substantial risk of generating frustration and hostility toward its courts among the most numerous consumers of justice. . . . [Id. at 196-199.]

3. Compare *Mayer* to *Scott*, page 148 supra. *Griffin* and its progeny reflect the basic need for legal assistance. Why, then, should a defendant be better off on appeal than at trial? Or does that misconstrue the basic thrust of *Griffin?* Are its referents outside the policies that inform the sixth amendment right to counsel? If so, where are they?

In considering that question, consider also United States v. MacCollom, 426 U.S. 317 (1976). In *MacCollom*, the Court sustained the constitutionality of 28 U.S.C. §753(f), which provides for a free

7. Murphy, The Role of the Police in Our Modern Society, 26 The Record of the Association of the Bar of the City of New York 292, 293 (1971).

transcript for indigent prisoners asserting a claim under 28 U.S.C. §2255 (the statutory counterpart to habeas corpus for federal prisoners) only if the trial judge certifies that the asserted claim is not frivolous and that the transcript is necessary. Had the defendant directly appealed his conviction, a free transcript would have been provided by direction of law; but the defendant did not appeal the conviction. In disposing of the defendant's claim, the Court, per Justice Rehnquist, argued:

> Respondent chose to forgo his opportunity for direct appeal with its attendant unconditional free transcript. This choice affects his later equal protection claim as well as his due process claim. Equal protection does not require the Government to furnish to the indigent a delayed duplicate of a right of appeal with attendant free transcript which it offered in the first instance, even though a criminal defendant of means might well decide to purchase such a transcript in pursuit of relief under §2255. The basic question is one of adequacy of respondent's access to procedures for review of his conviction, Ross v. Moffitt, supra, and it must be decided in the light of avenues which respondent chose not to follow as well as those he now seeks to widen. We think it enough at the collateral-relief stage that Congress has provided that the transcript be paid for by public funds if one demonstrates to a district judge that his §2255 claim is not frivolous, and that the transcript is needed to decide the issue presented. [426 U.S. at 325-326.]

Justice Brennan, joined by Justice Marshall, was unconvinced:

> . . . the plurality's opinion today that respondent may be required to show more than indigency before being entitled to his trial transcript for purposes of collateral review is a plain departure from *Griffin* and its progeny.
> The denial in this case is particularly egregious, for one of respondent's claims on the merits is that he was denied effective assistance of counsel. Substantiation of such a claim is virtually impossible without the aid of a trial transcript. Yet the plurality denigrates respondent's claim as a "naked allegation." . . . Essentially, therefore, he is denied a transcript for making an unsubstantiated allegation, an allegation that obviously he cannot establish without a transcript.
> It bears emphasis that where, as here, denial of equal protection is the issue, it matters not, under our cases, that the indigent had a fair opportunity to present a defense and have his conviction reviewed on direct appeal. The unfairness born of discrimination denying equal protection is as offensive to the Constitution as any unfairness resulting from procedural deficiencies in the criminal system. Thus, I cannot accept the plurality's argument that respondent could constitutionally be denied a free transcript because "[r]espondent in this case had an opportunity for direct appeal,

and had he chosen to pursue it he would have been furnished a free transcript of the trial proceedings." . . . The Constitution demands that respondent, despite his indigency, be afforded the same opportunity for collateral review of his conviction as the nonindigent. "If [the Government] has a general policy of allowing [collateral relief], it cannot make lack of means an effective bar to the exercise of this opportunity. The [Government] cannot keep the word of promise to the ear of those illegally convicted and break it to their hope." Griffin v. Illinois, 351 U.S., at 24 (Frankfurter, J., concurring in judgment).

The plurality's reliance, . . . upon Ross v. Moffitt, 417 U.S. 600, 616 (1974), for the proposition that "[i]n the context of a criminal proceeding [equal protection] require[s] only 'an adequate opportunity to present [one's] claims fairly' " is patently misplaced. This quotation from Ross, read in context, speaks not merely to equality of opportunity in the overall criminal process, but also to equality of opportunity at any stage of the process where the validity of the defendant's restraint or conviction is the primary consideration.

I reject as wholly fallacious the argument that adequacy of opportunity to present claims at trial and on direct appeal so far diminishes the importance of collateral review, that discrimination between indigent and nonindigent in post-conviction proceedings is constitutionally tolerable. That argument is implicitly if not explicitly rejected in the unbroken line of our decisions that make no distinction, for purposes of equal protection analysis, between collateral proceedings and trials and direct appeals. Any distinction must necessarily be constitutionally intolerable where the stakes are no less than the constitutionality of a criminal conviction. Any distinction would also be plainly inconsistent with the explicit recognition given habeas corpus in Art. I, §9, cl. 2, of the Constitution. . . . Today's decision empties of all promise the Court's assurance only six years ago that decisions applying *Griffin* "have pointedly demonstrated that the passage of time has heightened rather than weakened the attempts [by this Court] to mitigate the disparate treatment of indigents in the criminal process." Williams v. Illinois, 309 U.S. 235, 241 (1970). I dissent. [426 U.S. at 332-334.]

Consider also the per curiam decision of Wainwright v. Torna, 455 U.S. 586 (1982), which is discussed in the *Evitts* case:

Respondent is in custody pursuant to several felony convictions. The Florida Supreme Court dismissed an application for a writ of certiorari, on the ground that the application was not filed timely. . . . A petition for rehearing and clarification was later denied. . . .

Respondent thereafter filed a petition for habeas corpus in the United States District Court for the Southern District of Florida, contending that he had been denied his right to the effective assistance of counsel by the failure of his retained counsel to file the application for certiorari timely.

The District Court denied the petition, on the ground that the failure to file a timely application for certiorari did not render counsel's actions "so grossly deficient as to render the proceedings fundamentally unfair." . . . In reaching this conclusion, the District Court noted that review by the Florida Supreme Court was discretionary; "[f]ailure of counsel to timely petition for certiorari to the Supreme Court, therefore, only prevented [respondent] from applying for further discretionary review." The Court of Appeals reversed. 649 F.2d 290 (C.A.5 1981).[2]

In Ross v. Moffitt, . . . this Court held that a criminal defendant does not have a constitutional right to counsel to pursue discretionary state appeals or applications for review in this Court. Respondent does not contest the finding of the District Court that he had no absolute right to appeal his convictions to the Florida Supreme Court. Since respondent had no constitutional right to counsel, he could not be deprived of the effective assistance of counsel by his retained counsel's failure to file the application timely.[4] The District Court was correct in dismissing the petition.

The motion of respondent for leave to proceed in forma pauperis is granted. The petition for writ of certiorari is granted and the judgment of the Court of Appeals is therefore reversed.

It is so ordered.

JUSTICE BRENNAN would set the case for oral argument

JUSTICE MARSHALL, dissenting. . . .

Respondent's counsel promised him that he would seek review in the Florida Supreme Court. Respondent reasonably relied on that promise. Counsel nonetheless failed to file a timely application.* As a result, re-

2. Citing its decision in Pressley v. Wainwright, the court first noted that "the failure of court-appointed counsel to file a timely notice of certiorari in the Florida Supreme Court has been held to constitute ineffective assistance." 649 F.2d, at 291. On the basis of the recent decision in Cuyler v. Sullivan, the court then stated that "there is no distinction between court-appointed and privately retained counsel in the evaluation of a claim of ineffective assistance." 649 F.2d, at 292. Finally, the court quoted its recent decision in Perez v. Wainwright, for the proposition that "when a lawyer . . . does not perform his promise to his client that an appeal will be taken, fairness requires that the deceived defendant be granted an out-of-time appeal." 649 F.2d, at 292. On the basis of these statements, the court reversed "the district court's denial of the writ of habeas corpus," ibid., and remanded the case to the District Court for further proceedings consistent with its opinion.

4. Respondent was not denied due process of law by the fact that counsel deprived him of his right to petition the Florida Supreme Court for review. Such deprivation— if even implicating a due process interest—was caused by his counsel, and not by the State. Certainly, the actions of the Florida Supreme Court in dismissing an application for review that was not filed timely did not deprive respondent of due process of law.

*Notice of the intent to apply for discretionary review was due in the office of the Clerk for the District Court of Appeals, Third District of Florida, on July 17, 1978. It was filed one day late, on July 18, 1978. According to respondent, a secretary in his attorney's office attempted to deliver the required papers on July 14, 1978. She became lost while traveling to the Clerk's office, and did not arrive until after it had closed.

spondent was deprived of his right to seek discretionary review by the State's highest court. . . . I would hold that when a defendant can show that he reasonably relied on his attorney's promise to seek discretionary review, due process requires the State to consider his application, even when the application is untimely. To deny the right to seek discretionary review simply because of counsel's error is fundamentally unfair. Requiring the state courts to consider untimely applications when a defendant can show that he reasonably relied on his counsel will not impose a heavy burden.

4. May indigency affect the nature of the sanction imposed on conviction? In at least some circumstances, the answer is no. In Williams v. Illinois, 399 U.S. 235 (1970), the Court held a statute unconstitutional that permitted the maximum jail sentence to be increased if the defendant fails to pay the fine that was also imposed, where the reason for the failure to pay is the defendant's indigency. Subsequently, in Tate v. Short, 401 U.S. 395 (1971), the Court struck down a statute that permitted a sentence of a fine to be converted into a jail sentence where the defendant is unable to pay the fine. Consider the following passage from the Tate opinion:

Our opinion in Williams stated the premise of this conclusion in saying that "the Equal Protection Clause of the Fourteenth Amendment requires that the statutory ceiling placed on imprisonment for any substantive offense be the same for all defendants irrespective of their economic status." 399 U.S., at 244. Since Texas has legislated a "fines only" policy for traffic offenses, that statutory ceiling cannot, consistently with the Equal Protection clause, limit the punishment to payment of the fine if one is able to pay it, yet convert the fine into a prison term for an indigent defendant without the means to pay his fine. Imprisonment in such a case is not imposed to further any penal objective of the State. It is imposed to augment the state's revenues but obviously does not serve that purpose; the defendant cannot pay because he is indigent and his imprisonment, rather than aiding collection of the revenue, saddles the State with the cost of feeding and housing him for the period of his imprisonment.

There are, however, other alternatives to which the State may constitutionally resort to serve its concededly valid interest in enforcing payment of fines. We repeat our observation in Williams in that regard, 399 U.S., at 244-245 (footnotes omitted):

"The State is not powerless to enforce judgments against those financially unable to pay a fine; indeed, a different result would amount to inverse discrimination since it would enable an indigent to avoid both the

---

Because she did not realize that she could have placed the papers in a night depository box, she took them home and placed them in the mail. R. 29. To deny respondent the right to seek discretionary review, where he reasonably relied on his counsel's promise to apply for such review, and where counsel failed to comply with this promise only because of circumstances beyond his control, would be doubly unfair.

fine and imprisonment for nonpayment whereas other defendants must always suffer one or the other conviction.

"It is unnecessary for us to canvass the numerous alternatives to which the State by legislative enactment—or judges within the scope of their authority—may resort in order to avoid imprisoning an indigent beyond the statutory maximum for involuntary nonpayment of a fine or court costs. Appellant has suggested several plans, some of which are already utilized in some States, while others resemble those proposed by various studies. The State is free to choose from among the variety of solutions already proposed and, of course, it may devise new ones."[5]

We emphasize that our holding today does not suggest any constitutional infirmity in imprisonment of a defendant with the means to pay a fine who refuses or neglects to do so. Nor is our decision to be understood as precluding imprisonment as an enforcement method when alternative means are unsuccessful despite the defendant's reasonable efforts to satisfy the fines by those means; the determination of the constitutionality of imprisonment in that circumstance must await the presentation of a concrete case. . . . [401 U.S. at 395-401.]

In light of *Tate* and *Williams*, under what circumstances may a state take the financial condition of the defendant into account in sentencing? Consider Justice Harlan, concurring in *Williams*:

[A] conceivable justification [for the statute] is that the jail alternative serves a penological purpose that cannot be served by collection of a fine over time. It is clear that having declared itself satisfied by a fine, the alternative

5. Several States have a procedure for paying fines in installments. E.g., Cal. Penal Code §1205 (1970) (misdemeanors); Del. Code Ann., Tit. 11, §4332(c) (Supp. 1968); Md. Ann. Code, Art. 38, §4(a)(2) (Supp. 1970); Mass. Gen. Laws Ann., c.279, §1A (1959); N.Y. Code Crim. Proc. §470-d(1)(b) (Supp. 1970); Pa. Stat. Ann., Tit. 19, §953 (1964); Wash. Rev. Code §9.92.070.
    This procedure has been widely endorsed as effective not only to collect the fine but also to save the expense of maintaining a prisoner and avoid the necessity of supporting his family under the state welfare program while he is confined. See, e.g., Final Report of the National Commission on Reform of Federal Criminal Laws, Proposed New Federal Criminal Code §3302(2) (1971); American Bar Association, Project on Standards for Criminal Justice, Sentencing Alternatives and Procedures §2.7(b), pp. 119-122 (Approved Draft 1968); President's Commission on Law Enforcement and Administration of Justice, Task Force Report: The Courts 18 (1967); ALI, Model Penal Code §302.1(1) (Proposed Official Draft 1962). See also Comment, Equal Protection and the Use of Fines as Penalties for Criminal Offenses, 1966 U. Ill. L.F. 460; Note, The Equal Protection Clause and Imprisonment of the Indigent for Nonpayment of Fines, 64 Mich. L. Rev. 938 (1966); Note, Imprisonment for Nonpayment of Fines and Costs: A New Look at the Law and the Constitution, 22 Vand. L. Rev. 611 (1969); Note, Fines and Fining— An Evaluation, 101 U. Pa. L. Rev. 1013 (1953); J. Sellin, Recent Penal Legislation in Sweden 14 (1947); Cordes, Fines and Their Enforcement, 2 J. Crim. Sci. 46 (1950); S. Rubin, H. Weihofen, G. Edwards, & S. Rosenzweig, The Law of Criminal Correction 253 and n.154 (1963); E. Sutherland & D. Cressey, Principles of Criminology 276 (6th ed. 1960). See also Williams v. Illinois, 399 U.S., at 244-245, n.21.

of jail to a fine serves neither a rehabilitative nor a retributive interest. The question is, then, whether the requirement of a lump-sum payment can be sustained as a rational legislative determination that deterrence is effective only when a fine is exacted at once after sentence and by lump sum, rather than over a term. This is a highly doubtful proposition, since, apart from the mere fact of conviction and the humiliation associated with it and the token of punishment evidenced by the forfeiture, the deterrent effect of a fine is apt to derive more from its pinch on the purse than the time of payment.

That the Illinois statute represents a considered judgment, evincing the belief that jail is a rational and necessary trade-off to punish the individual who possesses no accumulated assets seems most unlikely, since the substitute sentence provision, phrased in terms of a judgment collection statute, does not impose a discretionary jail term as an alternative sentence, but rather equates days in jail with a fixed sum. Thus, given that the only conceivable justification for this statute that would satisfy due process— that a lump-sum fine is a better deterrent than one payable over a period of time—is the one that is least likely to represent a considered legislative judgment, I would hold this statute invalid.

The conclusion I reach is only that when a State declares its penal interest may be satisfied by a fine or a forfeiture in combination with a jail term the administrative inconvenience in a judgment collection procedure does not, as a matter of due process, justify sending to jail, or extending the jail term of, individuals who possess no accumulated assets.* I would reserve the question as to whether a considered legislative judgment that a lump-sum fine is the only effective kind of forfeiture for deterrence and that the alternative must be jail, would be constitutional. It follows, a fortiori, that no conclusion reached herein casts any doubt on the conventional "$30 or 30 days" if the legislature decides that should be the *penalty* for the crime. Note, Discriminations Against the Poor and the Fourteenth Amendment, 81 Harv. L. Rev. 435 (1967). Such a statute evinces the perfectly rational determination that some individuals will be adequately punished by a money fine, and others, indifferent to money— whether by virtue of indigency or other reasons—can be punished only by a jail term. Still more patently nothing said herein precludes the State from punishing ultimately by jail individuals who fail to pay fines or imprisoning immediately individuals who, in the judgment of a court, will not undertake to pay their fines. [399 U.S. at 264-265.]

May a state sentence a defendant to compulsory, and useful, labor to "work-off" a fine? Consider the following case.

---

*In this regard, unlike the Court, I see no distinction between circumstances where the State through its judicial agent determines that effective punishment requires less than the maximum prison term plus a fine, or a fine alone, and the circumstances of this case.

BEARDEN v. GEORGIA
Certiorari to the Georgia Court of Appeals
461 U.S. 660 (1983)

JUSTICE O'CONNOR delivered the opinion of the Court.

The question in this case is whether the Fourteenth Amendment prohibits a State from revoking an indigent defendant's probation for failure to pay a fine and restitution. Its resolution involves a delicate balance between the acceptability, and indeed wisdom, of considering all relevant factors when determining an appropriate sentence for an individual and the impermissibility of imprisoning a defendant solely because of his lack of financial resources. We conclude that the trial court erred in automatically revoking probation because petitioner could not pay his fine, without determining that petitioner had not made sufficient bona fide efforts to pay or that adequate alternative forms of punishment did not exist. We therefore reverse the judgment of the Georgia Court of Appeals upholding the revocation of probation, and remand for a new sentencing determination.

I

In September 1980, petitioner was indicted for the felonies of burglary and theft by receiving stolen property. He pleaded guilty, and was sentenced on October 8, 1980. Pursuant to the Georgia First Offender's Act, the trial court did not enter a judgment of guilt, but deferred further proceedings and sentenced petitioner to three years on probation for the burglary charge and a concurrent one year on probation for the theft charge. As a condition for probation, the trial court ordered petitioner to pay a $500 fine and $250 in restitution. Petitioner was to pay $100 that day, $100 the next day, and the $550 balance within four months.

Petitioner borrowed money from his parents and paid the first $200. About a month later, however, petitioner was laid off from his job. Petitioner, who has only a ninth grade education and cannot read, tried repeatedly to find other work but was unable to do so. The record indicates that petitioner had no income or assets during this period.

Shortly before the balance of the fine and restitution came due in February 1981, petitioner notified the probation officer he was going to be late with his payment because he could not find a job. In May 1981, the State filed a petition in the trial court to revoke petitioner's probation because he had not paid the balance. After an evidentiary hearing, the trial court revoked probation for failure to pay the balance of the fine and restitution, entered a conviction and sentenced petitioner to serve the remaining portion of the probationary period in prison. The Georgia Court of Appeals, relying on earlier Georgia Supreme Court cases, rejected petitioner's claim that imprisoning him for inability to pay the fine violated the Equal Protection Clause of the Fourteenth Amendment. The Georgia Supreme Court denied review. Since other courts have held that revoking the probation of indigents for failure to pay fines does violate the Equal Protection Clause,[6] we granted certiorari to resolve this important issue in the administration of criminal justice.

II

This Court has long been sensitive to the treatment of indigents in our criminal justice system. . . .

Due process and equal protection principles converge in the Court's analysis in these cases. . . . Most decisions in this area have rested on an equal protection framework, although Justice Harlan in particular has insisted that a due process approach more accurately captures the competing concerns. . . . As we recognized in Ross v. Moffitt, we generally analyze the fairness of relations between the criminal defendant and the State under the Due Process Clause, while we approach the question whether the State has invidiously denied one class of defendants a substantial benefit available to another class of defendants under the Equal Protection Clause.

The question presented here is whether a sentencing court can revoke a defendant's probation for failure to pay the imposed fine and restitution, absent evidence and findings that the defendant was somehow responsible for the failure or that alternative forms of punishment were inadequate. The parties, following the framework of *Williams* and *Tate*, have argued the question primarily in terms of equal protection, and debate vigorously whether strict scrutiny or rational basis is the appropriate standard of review. There is no doubt that the State has treated the petitioner differently from a person who did not fail to pay the imposed fine and therefore did not violate probation. To determine whether this differential treatment violates the Equal Protection Clause, one must determine whether, and under what circumstances, a defendant's indigent status may be considered in the decision whether to revoke probation. This is substantially similar to asking directly the due process question of whether

6. See, e.g., Frazier v. Jordan, 457 F.2d 726 (C.A.5 1972); In re Antazo, 3 Cal. 3d 100, 89 Cal. Rptr. 255, 473 P.2d 999 (1970); State v. Tackett, 52 Haw. 601, 483 P.2d 191 (1971); State v. De Bonis, 58 N.J. 182, 276 A.2d 137 (1971); State ex rel. Pedersen v. Blessinger, 56 Wis. 2d 286, 201 N.W.2d 778 (1972).

and when it is fundamentally unfair or arbitrary for the State to revoke probation when an indigent is unable to pay the fine.[7] Whether analyzed in terms of equal protection or due process,[8] the issue cannot be resolved by resort to easy slogans or pigeon-hole analysis, but rather requires a careful inquiry into such factors as "the nature of the individual interest affected, the extent to which it is affected, the rationality of the connection between legislative means and purpose, [and] the existence of alternative means for effectuating the purpose. . . ." Williams v. Illinois, supra, 399 U.S., at 260 (Harlan, J., concurring).

In analyzing this issue, of course, we do not write on a clean slate, for both *Williams* and *Tate* analyzed similar situations. The reach and limits of their holdings are vital to a proper resolution of the issue here. . . .

The rule of *Williams* and *Tate*, . . . is that the State cannot "impos[e] a fine as a sentence and then automatically conver[t] it into a jail term solely because the defendant is indigent and cannot forthwith pay the fine in full." *Tate*, supra, at 398. In other words, if the State determines a fine or restitution to be the appropriate and adequate penalty for the crime, it may not therefore imprison a person solely because he lacked the resources to pay it. Both *Williams* and *Tate* carefully distinguished this substantive limitation on the imprisonment of indigents from the situation where a defendant was at fault in failing to pay the fine. As the

7. We have previously applied considerations of procedural and substantive fairness to probation and parole revocation proceedings. In Morrissey v. Brewer, 408 U.S. 471 (1972), where we established certain procedural requirements for parole revocation hearings, we recognized that society has an "interest in treating the parolee with basic fairness." Id., at 484. We addressed the issue of fundamental fairness more directly in Gagnon v. Scarpelli, 411 U.S. 778 (1972), where we held that in certain cases "fundamental fairness—the touchstone of due process—will require that the State provide at its expense counsel for indigent probationers or parolees." Id., 411 U.S., at 790. Fundamental fairness, we determined, presumptively requires counsel when the probationer claims that "there are substantial reasons which justified or mitigated the violation and make revocation inappropriate." Ibid. In Douglas v. Buder, 412 U.S. 430 (1973), we found a substantive violation of due process when a state court had revoked probation with no evidence that the probationer had violated probation. Today we address whether a court can revoke probation for failure to pay a fine and restitution when there is no evidence that the petitioner was at fault in his failure to pay or that alternate means of punishment were inadequate.

8. A due process approach has the advantage in this context of directly confronting the intertwined question of the role that a defendant's financial background can play in determining an appropriate sentence. When the court is initially considering what sentence to impose, a defendant's level of financial resources is a point on a spectrum rather than a classification. Since indigency in this context is a relative term rather than a classification, fitting "the problem of this case into an equal protection framework is a task too Procrustean to be rationally accomplished," North Carolina v. Pearce, 395 U.S. 711, 723 (1969). The more appropriate question is whether consideration of a defendant's financial background in setting or resetting a sentence is so arbitrary or unfair as to be a denial of due process.

Court made clear in *Williams*, "nothing in our decision today precludes imprisonment for willful refusal to pay a fine or court costs." 399 U.S., at 242, n.19. Likewise in *Tate*, the Court "emphasize[d] that our holding today does not suggest any constitutional infirmity in imprisonment of a defendant with the means to pay a fine who refuses or neglects to do so." 401 U.S., at 400.

This distinction, based on the reasons for non-payment, is of critical importance here. If the probationer has willfully refused to pay the fine or restitution when he has the means to pay, the State is perfectly justified in using imprisonment as a sanction to enforce collection. Similarly, a probationer's failure to make sufficient bona fide efforts to seek employment or borrow money in order to pay the fine or restitution may reflect an insufficient concern for paying the debt he owes to society for his crime. In such a situation, the State is likewise justified in revoking probation and using imprisonment as an appropriate penalty for the offense. But if the probationer has made all reasonable efforts to pay the fine or restitution, and yet cannot do so through no fault of his own,[9] it is fundamentally unfair to revoke probation automatically without considering whether adequate alternative methods of punishing the defendant are available. This lack of fault provides a "substantial reaso[n] which justifie[s] or mitigate[s] the violation and make[s] revocation inappropriate." Gagnon v. Scarpelli, supra, 411 U.S. at 790.

The State, of course, has a fundamental interest in appropriately punishing persons—rich and poor—who violate its criminal laws. A defendant's poverty in no way immunizes him from punishment. Thus, when determining initially whether the State's penological interests require imposition of a term of imprisonment, the sentencing court can consider the entire background of the defendant, including his employment history and financial resources. See Williams v. New York, 337 U.S. 247, 250, and n. 15 (1949). As we said in Williams v. Illinois, "[a]fter having taken into consideration the wide range of factors underlying the exercise of his sentencing function, nothing we now hold precludes a judge from imposing on an indigent, as on any defendant, the maximum penalty prescribed by law." 399 U.S., at 243.

---

9. We do not suggest that, in other contexts, the probationer's lack of fault in violating a term of probation would necessarily prevent a court from revoking probation. For instance, it may indeed be reckless for a court to permit a person convicted of driving while intoxicated to remain on probation once it becomes evident that efforts at controlling his chronic drunken driving have failed. Cf. Powell v. Texas, 392 U.S. 514 (1968); Robinson v. California, 370 U.S. 660 (1962). Ultimately, it must be remembered that the sentence was not imposed for a circumstance beyond the probationer's control "but because he had committed a crime." *Williams*, supra, 399 U.S., at 242. In contrast to a condition like chronic drunken driving, however, the condition at issue here—indigency—is itself no threat to the safety or welfare of society.

The decision to place the defendant on probation, however, reflects a determination by the sentencing court that the State's penological interests do not require imprisonment. . . . A probationer's failure to make reasonable efforts to repay his debt to society may indicate that this original determination needs reevaluation, and imprisonment may now be required to satisfy the State's interests. But a probationer who has made sufficient bona fide efforts to pay his fine and restitution, and who has complied with the other conditions of probation, has demonstrated a willingness to pay his debt to society and an ability to conform his conduct to social norms. The State nevertheless asserts three reasons why imprisonment is required to further its penal goals.

First, the State argues that revoking probation furthers its interest in ensuring that restitution be paid to the victims of crime. A rule that imprisonment may befall the probationer who fails to make sufficient bona fide efforts to pay restitution may indeed spur probationers to try hard to pay, thereby increasing the number of probationers who make restitution. Such a goal is fully served, however, by revoking probation only for persons who have not made sufficient bona fide efforts to pay. Revoking the probation of someone who through no fault of his own is unable to make restitution will not make restitution suddenly forthcoming. Indeed, such a policy may have the perverse effect of inducing the probationer to use illegal means to acquire funds to pay in order to avoid revocation.

Second, the State asserts that its interest in rehabilitating the probationer and protecting society requires it to remove him from the temptation of committing other crimes. This is no more than a naked assertion that a probationer's poverty by itself indicates he may commit crimes in the future and thus that society needs for him to be incapacitated. We have already indicated that a sentencing court can consider a defendant's employment history and financial resources in setting an initial punishment. Such considerations are a necessary part of evaluating the entire background of the defendant in order to tailor an appropriate sentence for the defendant and crime. But it must be remembered that the State is seeking here to use as the *sole* justification for imprisonment the poverty of a probationer who, by assumption, has demonstrated sufficient bona fide efforts to find a job and pay the fine and whom the State initially thought it unnecessary to imprison. Given the significant interest of the individual in remaining on probation . . . the State cannot justify incarcerating a probationer who has demonstrated sufficient bona fide efforts to repay his debt to society, solely by lumping him together with other poor persons and thereby classifying him as dangerous. This would be little more than punishing a person for his poverty.

Third, and most plausibly, the State argues that its interests in punishing the lawbreaker and deterring others from criminal behavior require it to revoke probation for failure to pay a fine or restitution. The State clearly has an interest in punishment and deterrence, but this interest can often be served fully by alternative means. As we said in *Williams*, 399 U.S., at 244, and reiterated in *Tate*, 401 U.S., at 399, "[t]he State is not powerless to enforce judgments against those financially unable to pay a fine." For example, the sentencing court could extend the time for making payments, or reduce the fine, or direct that the probationer perform some form of labor or public service in lieu of the fine. Justice Harlan appropriately observed in his concurring opinion in *Williams* that "the deterrent effect of a fine is apt to derive more from its pinch on the purse than the time of payment." Ibid., 399 U.S., at 265. Indeed, given the general flexibility of tailoring fines to the resources of a defendant, or even permitting the defendant to do specified work to satisfy the fine, see *Williams*, supra, at 244, n.21, a sentencing court can often establish a reduced fine or alternate public service in lieu of a fine that adequately serves the State's goals of punishment and deterrence, given the defendant's diminished financial resources. Only if the sentencing court determines that alternatives to imprisonment are not adequate in a particular situation to meet the State's interest in punishment and deterrence may the State imprison a probationer who has made sufficient bona fide efforts to pay.

We hold, therefore, that in revocation proceedings for failure to pay a fine or restitution, a sentencing court must inquire into the reasons for the failure to pay. If the probationer willfully refused to pay or failed to make sufficient bona fide efforts legally to acquire the resources to pay, the court may revoke probation and sentence the defendant to imprisonment within the authorized range of its sentencing authority. If the probationer could not pay despite sufficient bona fide efforts to acquire the resources to do so, the court must consider alternate measures of punishment other than imprisonment. Only if alternate measures are not adequate to meet the State's interests in punishment and deterrence may the court imprison a probationer who has made sufficient bona fide efforts to pay. To do otherwise would deprive the probationer of his conditional freedom simply because, through no fault of his own, he cannot pay the fine. Such a deprivation would be contrary to the fundamental fairness required by the Fourteenth Amendment. . . .[12]

12. As our holding makes clear, we agree with Justice White that poverty does not insulate a criminal defendant from punishment or necessarily prevent revocation of his probation for inability to pay a fine. We reject as impractical, however, the approach suggested by Justice White. He would require a "good-faith effort" by the sentencing court to impose a term of imprisonment "roughly equivalent" to the fine and restitution that the defendant failed to pay. Even putting to one side the question of judicial "good

The judgment is reversed, and the case remanded for further proceedings not inconsistent with this opinion.

It is so ordered.

JUSTICE WHITE, with whom THE CHIEF JUSTICE, JUSTICE POWELL, and JUSTICE REHNQUIST join, concurring in the judgment.

We deal here with the recurring situation where a person is convicted under a statute that authorizes fines or imprisonment or both, as well as probation. The defendant is then fined and placed on probation, one of the conditions of which is that he pay the fine and make restitution. In such a situation, the Court takes as a given that the state has decided that imprisonment is inappropriate because it is unnecessary to achieve its penal objectives. But that is true only if the defendant pays the fine and makes restitution and thereby suffers the financial penalty that such payment entails. Had the sentencing judge been quite sure that the defendant could not pay the fine, I cannot believe that the court would not have imposed some jail time or that either the Due Process or Equal Protection Clause of the Constitution would prevent such imposition.

Poverty does not insulate those who break the law from punishment. When probation is revoked for failure to pay a fine, I find nothing in the Constitution to prevent the trial court from revoking probation and imposing a term of imprisonment if revocation does not automatically result in the imposition of a long jail term and if the sentencing court makes a good-faith effort to impose a jail sentence that in terms of the state's sentencing objectives will be roughly equivalent to the fine and restitution that the defendant failed to pay. See Wood v. Georgia, 450 U.S. 261, 284-287 (White, J., dissenting).

The Court holds, however, that if a probationer cannot pay the fine for reasons not of his own fault, the sentencing court must at least consider alternative measures of punishment other than imprisonment, and may imprison the probationer only if the alternative measures are deemed inadequate to meet the State's interests in punishment and deterrence. . . . There is no support in our cases or, in my view, the Constitution, for this novel requirement.

---

faith," we perceive no meaningful standard by which a sentencing or reviewing court could assess whether a prison sentence has an equivalent sting to the original fine. Under our holding the sentencing court must focus on criteria typically considered daily by sentencing courts throughout the land in probation revocation hearings: whether the defendant has demonstrated sufficient efforts to comply with the terms of probation and whether nonimprisonment alternatives are adequate to satisfy the State's interests in punishment and deterrence. Nor is our requirement that the sentencing court consider alternative forms of punishment a "novel" requirement. In both *Williams* and *Tate*, the Court emphasized the availability of alternate forms of punishment in holding that indigents could not be subjected automatically to imprisonment.

The Court suggests, ... that if the sentencing court rejects non-prison alternatives as "inadequate," it is "impractical" to impose a prison term roughly equivalent to the fine in terms of achieving punishment goals. Hence, I take it, that had the trial court in this case rejected nonprison alternatives, the sentence it imposed would be constitutionally impregnable. Indeed, there would be no bounds on the length of the imprisonment that could be imposed, other than those imposed by the Eighth Amendment. But Williams v. Illinois, 399 U.S. 235 (1970) and Tate v. Short, 401 U.S. 395 (1971), stand for the proposition that such "automatic" conversion of a fine into a jail term is forbidden by the Equal Protection Clause, and by so holding, the Court in those cases was surely of the view that there is a way of converting a fine into a jail term that is not "automatic." In building a superstructure of procedural steps that sentencing courts must follow, the Court seems to forget its own concern about imprisoning an indigent person for failure to pay a fine.

In this case, in view of the long prison term imposed, the state court obviously did not find that the sentence was "a rational and necessary trade-off to punish the individual who possessed no accumulated assets," Williams v. Illinois, supra, 399 U.S., at 265 (Harlan, J., concurring). Accordingly, I concur in the judgment.

NOTES AND QUESTIONS

1. The interacting problems of equality and fairness dealt with by the Supreme Court in the cases in this section continue to trouble the lower courts. For example:

a. If there is a constitutional right to have a transcript of a hearing in certain situations, does it follow that there is a right to have a court reporter present? Does it matter that a wealthy defendant could obtain the services of a reporter? In the context of a preliminary hearing, one court has answered both questions in the negative. Phegley v. Greer, 497 F. Supp. 519 (C.D. Ill. 1980). The *Phegley* opinion discusses the split in authority on this issue.

b. Does an indigent without counsel have a right of access to preexisting records, at government expense, where a person with counsel could obtain access through the services of counsel? Yes, said the Seventh Circuit in Rush v. United States, 559 F.2d 455 (1977). No, said the Eighth Circuit in United States v. Losing, 601 F.2d 351 (1979), specifically rejecting *Rush*.

c. Consider Cleaver v. BordenKircher, 634 F.2d 1010 (6th Cir. 1980), cert. denied, 451 U.S. 1008 (1981), where the court of appeals held that an indigent state prisoner, whose appointed counsel on appeal

was so overworked as to be unable to service the appeal within the time
limit set by the Kentucky Supreme Court, was denied equal protection
and deprived of his right to effective assistance of counsel. A public
defender was appointed as counsel on appeal. The public defender got
repeated extensions to allow for filing of the record on appeal. Then he
got a 40-day limit on filing of the brief. When those 40 days were up,
he got an additional 30-day extension. When he requested another extension, the Kentucky Supreme Court denied the extension and dismissed
the appeal. The public defender went back to the trial court and got an
order reinstating the appeal, which the Kentucky Supreme Court overturned saying the trial court had no authority to reinstate the appeal. A
writ of habeas corpus was then granted by the district court and affirmed
by the court of appeals. The denial of equal protection arose from the
fact that Cleaver was effectively denied counsel while others in Kentucky
who could pay would have been able to perfect their appeals. According
to the court, the petitioner was deprived of the right to appeal (granted
by Kentucky's Constitution) solely because his indigency status made the
overburdened public defender his only source of legal representation.
The court went on to say, however, that "in the event the largely equal
protection rationale employed . . . is found inadequate to sustain this
writ, alternatively, we endorse the opinion authored by the district judge
[employing a due process analysis based on denial of counsel]." Id. at
1012. What do you think of the Court's craftsmanship? What do you
think of the result?

    2. Notwithstanding the stirring rhetoric of the Supreme Court cases
interpreting the sixth amendment, providing effective counsel for indigents has proven difficult. Predictably, the primary problem has been
expense. State legislatures have been unwilling to allocate substantial
resources to pay for counsel for the indigent. For a discussion of the
problem in New York City, see M. McConville & C. Mirsky, Criminal
Defense of the Poor in New York City (1989). In Jewell v. Maynard,
383 S.E.2d 536 (W. Va. 1989), the Supreme Court of Appeals of West
Virginia ordered substantial changes in the system for providing counsel.
The state provided compensation of $20 per hour for out-of-court work,
and $25 per hour for in-court work, with a $1,000 maximum. The result
of the low fees was that few lawyers were willing to take appointments,
thus overburdening those that were.

    In addition to low fees, lawyers accepting appointment in criminal
cases often are doubly burdened by onerous reporting requirements, which
increases the disincentives to take indigent cases. For an example of
obviously unnecessary red tape, compounded by shocking insensitivity
to the justifiable frustration of lawyers working under such constraints,
see In re Snyder, 472 U.S. 634 (1985).

3. Statutes in various jurisdictions provide for the furnishing of aid to indigents, other than counsel and transcripts, that may assist in the preparation for trial or be useful at trial itself, e.g., investigative aids or expert evaluation and testimony. In federal litigation, the relevant statute is 18 U.S.C. §3006A.

In Ake v. Oklahoma, 470 U.S. 68 (1985), the Court held that when an indigent defendant "demonstrates to the trial judge that his sanity at the time of the offense is to be a significant factor at trial, the State must, at a minimum, assure the defendant access to a competent psychiatrist who will conduct an appropriate examination and assist in evaluation, preparation, and presentation of the defense." 470 U.S. at 83. In emphasizing that a defendant must have access to the "basic tools of an adequate defense," id. at 77, the Court further held that a defendant must have access to psychiatric expertise if his future dangerousness is relevant as an aggravating factor in a capital sentencing proceeding.

4. The Supreme Court has extended, in certain respects, the analysis developed in the Griffin/Douglas line of cases to civil suits. The Court, for example, struck down a state filing fee that restricted access to indigents to a divorce proceeding in Boddie v. Connecticut, 401 U.S. 371 (1971). In Little v. Streater, 452 U.S. 1 (1981), the Court held that appellant, the putative father in a paternity suit, was denied due process where the state refused to fund potentially dispository blood grouping tests that appellant could not afford. However, on the same day Little was decided, the Court held in Lassiter v. Department of Social Services of Durham County, 452 U.S. 18 (1981), that failure to appoint counsel for indigent parents in a state-initiated proceeding to terminate parental status did not violate due process. For a discussion, see The Supreme Court, 1980 Term: Indigents' Rights to State Funding in Civil Actions, 95 Harv. L. Rev. 132 (1981). For a discussion of the general problem of providing indigents access to legal services, see Note, Court Appointment of Attorneys in Civil Cases: The Constitutionality of Uncompensated Legal Assistance, 81 Colum. L. Rev. 366 (1981). The Court has upheld certain limitations on retained counsel. In Walters v. National Association of Radiation Survivors, 473 U.S. 305 (1985), the Court upheld a federal statute that limits to $10 the fee that may be paid counsel representing a veteran seeking benefits from the Veterans Administration, remarking in passing: "Simple factual questions are capable of resolution in a non-adversarial context, and it is less than crystal clear why lawyers must be available to identify possible errors in medical judgment." Id. at 330. Citing Walters, the Court in Washington v. Harper, 110 S. Ct. 1028 (1990), found no violation of due process in a state statute permitting the decision to give state prisoners anti-psychotic drugs to be made by medical personnel and without judicial involvement or counsel for the prisoner.

Recently, the Supreme Court held that 28 U.S.C. §1915(d), which authorizes a federal district court to "request" counsel to represent an indigent person in a civil action, does not authorize a court to require an attorney to accept such an assignment. However, the Court did not discuss whether federal district courts possess an inherent power to require such representation; the Court limited its discussion to the question of statutory interpretation. Mallard v. U.S. District Court for the Southern District of Iowa, 109 S. Ct. 1814 (1989).

B. EFFECTIVE ASSISTANCE OF COUNSEL

1. Developing Standards

The mere appointment of counsel does not satisfy the constitutional guarantee of right to counsel. Indeed, the trial court in Powell v. Alabama appointed counsel but in such a way as to preclude the giving of effective aid in the preparation and trial of the case. The concern for effectiveness has been a consistent thread running through the Supreme Court's cases, as evidenced by the rhetoric in McMann v. Richardson, 397 U.S. 759 (1970) ("if the right to counsel guaranteed by the Constitution is to serve its purpose, defendants cannot be left to the mercies of incompetent counsel," 397 U.S. at 771).

In order to ensure the conditions under which effective assistance is likely to be obtained, the Supreme Court has rendered a series of decisions prohibiting certain forms of interference with the attorney-client relationship. An attorney may not be prohibited from conferring with the client during an overnight recess that falls between direct and cross examination. Geders v. United States, 425 U.S. 80 (1976). A lawyer may not be denied the right to give a closing summation in a nonjury trial. Herring v. New York, 422 U.S. 853 (1975). The state may not prohibit the attorney from eliciting the client's testimony on direct examination, Ferguson v. Georgia, 365 U.S. 570 (1961), nor may the state restrict the attorney's choice as to when to put the defendant on the stand, Brooks v. Tennessee, 406 U.S. 605 (1972). There are limits on the Court's solicitude for criminal defendants, however. In Perry v. Leeke, 488 U.S. 272 (1989), the Court held that the trial court did not err by ordering the defendant not to consult with his lawyer during a 15-minute recess that followed immediately his direct examination and preceded cross-examination.

Until quite recently the Supreme Court had not elaborated on the

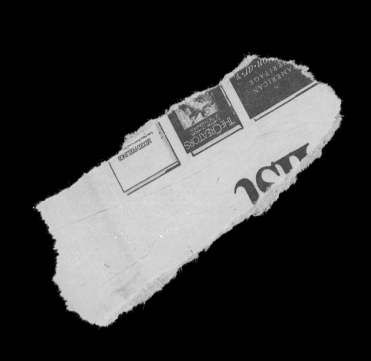

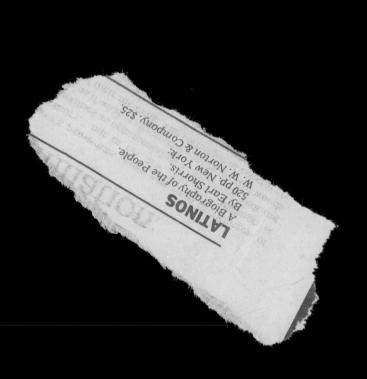

LATINOS

A Biography of the People.
By Earl Shorris.
520 pp. New York:
W. W. Norton & Company. $25

meaning of "effectiveness" outside of these, and similar, relatively narrow areas. Moreover, the primary problem of effective assistance resides not in these narrow areas but in counsel's general performance at trial. In the absence of guidance from the Supreme Court, the lower courts almost uniformly adopted the "mockery of justice" standard to test claims of ineffectiveness under which ineffectiveness was found only in such shocking circumstances as to reduce the trial to a farce or charade. Even inebriated counsel often was insufficient cause to find lack of effectiveness. See generally Finer, Ineffective Assistance of Counsel, 58 Cornell L. Rev. 1077 (1973).

Although the courts' apparent lack of concern for the level of performance may seem peculiar today, there are some justifications for it. The higher the level of scrutiny, the greater is the impetus on the part of the trial judge to intervene in derogation of basic premises of the adversary system. Moreover, intervention may occur at a point of what appears to be problematic action by counsel but in fact is an integral part of a trial strategy known only to counsel. Also, the more active trial judges become, the more they are implicitly or explicitly critical of the bar that practices before them; and the more active appellate courts become, the more critical they become of the trial judges. For a discussion of these and related problems, see Waltz, Inadequacy of Trial Defense Representation as a Ground for Post-Conviction Relief in Criminal Cases, 59 Nw. U.L. Rev. 289 (1964).

The last 15 years have seen considerable change in the standards governing ineffective assistance. A large proportion of the states, and most of the federal circuits, have replaced the previous standard with one that requires counsel to possess and exercise the legal competence customarily found in the jurisdiction. For an early and influential example, see Moore v. United States, 432 F.2d 730 (3d Cir. 1970). This process has been stimulated by two developments in addition to the simple recognition that the previous standards were a bit disgraceful. The first development was the Supreme Court's legitimation of plea bargaining in 1970. See McMann v. Richardson, supra. The significance of the legitimation of plea bargaining was that if pleas were now to receive greater protection against challenge, then the legal advice received by an accused assumes greater importance. Moreover, one of the challenges to a guilty plea that could not be deemed waived by it is the very advice that led to the plea in the first instance, which has the effect of focusing greater attention on the competency of counsel throughout the plea negotiations. See Cover & Aleinikoff, Dialectical Federalism: Habeas Corpus and the Court, 86 Yale L.J. 1035, 1060-1067 (1977).

The other development that has stimulated a greater concern for the competency of counsel has been the Supreme Court's tightening of habeas corpus. See, e.g., Stone v. Powell, 428 U.S. 465 (1976) (defendant may not relitigate fourth amendment issue on habeas if state provided an adequate opportunity to litigate the issue at trial). For discussions, see Halpern, Federal Habeas Corpus and the *Mapp* Exclusionary Rule After Stone v. Powell, 82 Colum. L. Rev. 1 (1982); Olsen, Judicial Proposals to Limit the Jurisdictional Scope of Federal Post-Conviction Habeas Corpus Consideration of the Claims of State Prisoners, 32 Buffalo L. Rev. 301 (1982). As more avenues are narrowed to petitioners on habeas, the greater the incentive to relitigate those closed avenues under the rubric of right to counsel.

Although there has been a dramatic shift in the articulated standards used to determine effectiveness, the question remains whether the shift has been more than rhetorical. Judge Bazelon of the U.S. Court of Appeals for the D.C. Circuit thinks not. In the first place, as he rightly points out, to say that something must be within the *normal* or *customary* range says nothing about what is normal or customary, Bazelon, The Realities of *Gideon* and *Argersinger*, 64 Geo. L.J. 811 (1976), and, he asserts, the courts have not addressed these problems. Bazelon, The Defective Assistance of Counsel, 42 U. Cin. L. Rev. 1 (1973). How should a court address such problems?

STRICKLAND v. WASHINGTON
Certiorari to the United States Court of Appeals for the Eleventh Circuit
466 U.S. 668 (1984)

JUSTICE O'CONNOR delivered the opinion of the Court.

This case requires us to consider the proper standards for judging a criminal defendant's contention that the Constitution requires a conviction or death sentence to be set aside because counsel's assistance at the trial or sentencing was ineffective.

I

A

During a ten-day period in September 1976, respondent planned and committed three groups of crimes, which included three brutal stabbing murders, torture, kidnapping, severe assaults, attempted murders, attempted extortion, and theft. After his two accomplices were arrested, respondent surrendered to police and voluntarily gave a lengthy statement confessing to the third of the criminal episodes. The State of Florida indicted respondent for kidnapping and murder and appointed an experienced criminal lawyer to represent him.

Counsel actively pursued pretrial motions and discovery. He cut his efforts short, however, and he experienced a sense of hopelessness about the case, when he learned that, against his specific advice, respondent had also confessed to the first two murders. By the date set for trial, respondent was subject to indictment for three counts of first degree murder and multiple counts of robbery, kidnapping for ransom, breaking and entering and assault, attempted murder, and conspiracy to commit robbery. Respondent waived his right to a jury trial, again acting against counsel's advice, and pleaded guilty to all charges, including the three capital murder charges.

In the plea colloquy, respondent told the trial judge that, although he had committed a string of burglaries, he had no significant prior criminal record and that at the time of his criminal spree he was under extreme stress caused by his inability to support his family. . . . He also stated, however, that he accepted responsibility for the crimes. . . . The trial judge told respondent that he had "a great deal of respect for people who are willing to step forward and admit their responsibility" but that he was making no statement at all about his likely sentencing decision. . . .

Counsel advised respondent to invoke his right under Florida law to an advisory jury at his capital sentencing hearing. Respondent rejected the advice and waived the right. He chose instead to be sentenced by the trial judge without a jury recommendation.

In preparing for the sentencing hearing, counsel spoke with respondent about his background. He also spoke on the telephone with respondent's wife and mother, though he did not follow up on the one unsuccessful effort to meet with them. He did not otherwise seek out character witnesses for respondent. . . . Nor did he request a psychiatric examination, since his conversations with his client gave no indication that respondent had psychological problems. . . .

Counsel decided not to present and hence not to look further for evidence concerning respondent's character and emotional state. That decision reflected trial counsel's sense of hopelessness about overcoming the evidentiary effect of respondent's confessions to the gruesome crimes. . . . It also reflected the judgment that it was advisable to rely on the plea colloquy for evidence about respondent's background and about his claim of emotional stress: the plea colloquy communicated sufficient information about these subjects, and by [forgoing] the opportunity to present new evidence on these subjects, counsel prevented the State from cross-examining respondent on his claim and from putting on psychiatric evidence of its own. . . .

Counsel also excluded from the sentencing hearing other evidence he thought was potentially damaging. He successfully moved to exclude respondent's "rap sheet." . . . Because he judged that a presentence report might prove more detrimental than helpful, as it would have included respondent's criminal history and thereby undermined the claim of no significant history of criminal activity, he did not request that one be prepared. . . .

At the sentencing hearing, counsel's strategy was based primarily on the trial judge's remarks at the plea colloquy as well as on his reputation as a sentencing judge who thought it important for a convicted defendant to own up to his crime. Counsel argued that respondent's remorse and acceptance of responsibility justified sparing him from the death penalty. . . . Counsel also argued that respondent had no history of criminal activity and that respondent committed the crimes under extreme mental or emotional disturbance, thus coming within the statutory list of mitigating circumstances. He further argued that respondent should be spared death because he had surrendered, confessed, and offered to testify against a co-defendant and because respondent was fundamentally a good person who had briefly gone badly wrong in extremely stressful circumstances. The State put on evidence and witnesses largely for the purpose of describing the details of the crimes. Counsel did not cross-examine the medical experts who testified about the manner of death of respondent's victims. . . .

. . . The trial judge found numerous aggravating circumstances and no (or a single comparatively insignificant) mitigating circumstance. With respect to each of the three convictions for capital murder, the trial judge concluded: "A careful consideration of all matters presented to the court impels the conclusion that there are insufficient mitigating circumstances . . . to outweigh the aggravating circumstances." He therefore sentenced respondent to death on each of the three counts of murder and to prison terms for the other crimes. The Florida Supreme Court upheld the convictions and sentences on direct appeal.

B

Respondent subsequently sought collateral relief in state court on numerous grounds, among them that counsel had rendered ineffective assistance at the sentencing proceeding. Respondent challenged counsel's assistance in six respects. He asserted that counsel was ineffective because he failed to move for a continuance to prepare for sentencing, to request a psychiatric report, to investigate and present character witnesses, to seek a presentence investigation report, to present meaningful arguments to the sentencing judge, and to investigate the medical examiner's reports or cross-examine the medical experts. In support of the claim, respondent submitted fourteen affidavits from friends, neighbors, and relatives stating that they would have testified if asked to do so. He also submitted one psychiatric report and one psychological report stating that respondent, though not under the influence of extreme mental or emotional disturbance, was "chronically frustrated and depressed because of his economic dilemma" at the time of his crimes. . . .

The trial court denied relief without an evidentiary hearing, finding that the record evidence conclusively showed that the ineffectiveness claim was meritless. . . . Four of the assertedly prejudicial errors required little discussion. *First*, there were no grounds to request a continuance, so there was no error in not requesting one when respondent pleaded guilty. . . . *Second*, failure to request a presentence investigation was not a serious error because the trial judge had discretion not to grant such a request and because any presentence investigation would have resulted in admission of respondent's rap sheet and thus undermined his assertion of no significant history of criminal activity. . . . *Third*, the argument and memorandum given to the sentencing judge were "admirable" in light of the overwhelming aggravating circumstances and absence of mitigating circumstances. . . . *Fourth*, there was no error in failure to examine the medical examiner's reports or to cross-examine the medical witnesses testifying on the manner of death of respondent's victims, since respondent admitted that the victims died in the ways shown by unchallenged medical evidence. . . .

The trial court dealt at greater length with the two other bases for the ineffectiveness claim. The court pointed out that a psychiatric examination of respondent was conducted by state order soon after respondent's initial arraignment. That report states that there was no indication of major mental illness at the time of the crimes. Moreover, both the reports submitted in the collateral proceeding state that, although respondent was "chronically frustrated and depressed because of his economic dilemma," he was not under the influence of extreme mental or emotional disturbance. All three reports thus directly undermine the contention made at the sentencing hearing that respondent was suffering from extreme mental or emotional disturbance during his crime spree. Accordingly, counsel could reasonably decide not to seek psychiatric reports; indeed, by relying solely on the plea colloquy to support the emotional disturbance contention, counsel denied the State an opportunity to rebut his claim with psychiatric testimony. In any event, the aggravating circumstances were so overwhelming that no substantial prejudice resulted from the absence at sentencing of the psychiatric evidence offered in the collateral attack.

The court rejected the challenge to counsel's failure to develop and to present character evidence for much the same reasons. The affidavits submitted in the collateral proceeding showed nothing more than that certain persons would have testified that respondent was basically a good person who was worried about his family's financial problems. Respondent himself had already testified along those lines at the plea colloquy. Moreover, respondent's admission of a course of stealing rebutted many of the factual allegations in the affidavits. For those reasons, and because the sentencing judge had stated that the death sentence would be appropriate even if respondent had no significant prior criminal history, no substantial prejudice resulted from the absence at sentencing of the character evidence offered in the collateral attack.

Applying the standard for ineffectiveness claims articulated by the Florida Supreme Court in Knight v. State, the trial court concluded that respondent had not shown that counsel's assistance reflected any substantial and serious deficiency measurably below that of competent counsel that was likely to have affected the outcome of the sentencing proceeding. The court specifically found that, "as a matter of law, the record affirmatively demonstrates beyond any doubt that even if [counsel] had done each of the . . . things [that respondent alleged counsel had failed to do] at the time of sentencing, there is not even the remotest chance that the outcome would have been any different. The plain fact is that the aggravating circumstances proved in this case were completely *overwhelming*. . . ." . . .

The Florida Supreme Court affirmed the denial of relief. . . .

C

Respondent next filed a petition for a writ of habeas corpus in the United States District Court for the Southern District of Florida.

The District Court held an evidentiary hearing to inquire into trial counsel's efforts to investigate and to present mitigating circumstances. Respondent offered the affidavits and reports he had submitted in the state collateral proceedings; he also called his trial counsel to testify. The State of Florida, over respondent's objection, called the trial judge to testify. [The court denied the petition for a writ of habeas corpus.]

On appeal, a panel of the United States Court of Appeals for the Fifth Circuit affirmed in part, vacated in part, and remanded with instructions to apply to the particular facts the framework for analyzing ineffectiveness claims that it developed in its opinion. The panel decision was itself vacated when Unit B of the former Fifth Circuit, now the Eleventh Circuit, decided to rehear the case en banc. The full Court of Appeals developed its own framework for analyzing ineffective assistance claims and reversed the judgment of the District Court and remanded the case for new fact-finding under the newly announced standards. . . .

Turning to the merits, the Court of Appeals stated that the Sixth Amendment right to assistance of counsel accorded criminal defendants a right to "counsel reasonably likely to render and rendering reasonably effective assistance given the totality of the circumstances." The court remarked in passing that no special standard applies in capital cases such as the one before it: the punishment that a defendant faces is merely one of the circumstances to be considered in determining whether counsel was reasonably effective. The court then addressed respondent's contention that his trial counsel's assistance was not reasonably effective because counsel breached his duty to investigate nonstatutory mitigating circumstances.

The court agreed that the Sixth Amendment imposes on counsel a duty to investigate, because reasonably effective assistance must be based on professional decisions and informed legal choices can be made only after investigation of options. The court observed that counsel's investigatory decisions must be assessed in light of the information known at the time of the decisions, not in hindsight, and that "[t]he amount of pretrial investigation that is reasonable defies precise measurement." Nevertheless, putting guilty-plea cases to one side, the court attempted to classify cases presenting issues concerning the scope of the duty to investigate before proceeding to trial.

If there is only one plausible line of defense, the court concluded, counsel must conduct a "reasonably substantial investigation" into that line of defense, since there can be no strategic choice that renders such an investigation unnecessary. The same duty exists if counsel relies at trial on only one line of defense, although others are available. In either case, the investigation need not be exhaustive. It must include "an independent examination of the facts, circumstances, pleadings and laws involved." The scope of the duty, however, depends on such facts as the strength of the government's case and the likelihood that pursuing certain leads may prove more harmful than helpful.

If there is more than one plausible line of defense, the court held, counsel should ideally investigate each line substantially before making a strategic choice about which lines to rely on at trial. If counsel conducts such substantial investigations, the strategic choices made as a result "will seldom if ever" be found wanting. Because advocacy is an art and not a science, and because the adversary system requires deference to counsel's informed decisions, strategic choices must be respected in these circumstances if they are based on professional judgment.

If counsel does not conduct a substantial investigation into each of several plausible lines of defense, assistance may nonetheless be effective.

Counsel may not exclude certain lines of defense for other than strategic reasons. Limitations of time and money, however, may force early strategic choices, often based solely on conversations with the defendant and a review of the prosecution's evidence. Those strategic choices about which lines of defense to pursue are owed deference commensurate with the reasonableness of the professional judgments on which they are based. Thus, "when counsel's assumptions are reasonable given the totality of the circumstances and when counsel's strategy represents a reasonable choice based upon those assumptions, counsel need not investigate lines of defense that he has chosen not to employ at trial." Among the factors relevant to deciding whether particular strategic choices are reasonable are the experience of the attorney, the inconsistency of unpursued and pursued lines of defense, and the potential for prejudice from taking an unpursued line of defense.

Having outlined the standards for judging whether defense counsel fulfilled the duty to investigate, the Court of Appeals turned its attention to the question of the prejudice to the defense that must be shown before counsel's errors justify reversal of the judgment. The court observed that only in cases of outright denial of counsel, of affirmative government interference in the representation process, or of inherently prejudicial conflicts of interest had this Court said that no special showing of prejudice need be made. For cases of deficient performance by counsel, where the government is not directly responsible for the deficiencies and where evidence of deficiency may be more accessible to the defendant than to the prosecution, the defendant must show that counsel's error "resulted in actual and substantial disadvantage to the course of his defense." This standard, the Court of Appeals reasoned, is compatible with the "cause and prejudice" standard for overcoming procedural defaults in federal collateral proceedings and discourages insubstantial claims by requiring more than a showing, which could virtually always be made, of some conceivable adverse effect on the defense from counsel's errors. The specified showing of prejudice would result in reversal of the judgment, the court concluded, unless the prosecution showed that the constitutionally deficient performance was, in light of all the evidence, harmless beyond a reasonable doubt.

The Court of Appeals thus laid down the tests to be applied in the Eleventh Circuit in challenges to convictions on the ground of ineffectiveness of counsel. . . . Summarily rejecting respondent's claims other than ineffectiveness of counsel, the court accordingly reversed the judgment of the District Court and remanded the case. On remand, the court finally ruled, the state trial judge's testimony, though admissible "to the extent that it contains personal knowledge of historical facts or expert opinion," was not to be considered admitted into evidence to explain the judge's mental processes in reaching his sentencing decision. . . .

D

Petitioners, who are officials of the State of Florida, filed a petition for a writ of certiorari seeking review of the decision of the Court of Appeals. The petition presents a type of Sixth Amendment claim that this Court has not previously considered in any generality. . . . With the exception of Cuyler v. Sullivan which involved a claim that counsel's assistance was rendered ineffective by a conflict of interest, the Court has never directly and fully addressed a claim of "actual ineffectiveness" of counsel's assistance in a case going to trial. . . .

In assessing attorney performance, all the Federal Courts of Appeals and all but a few state courts have now adopted the "reasonably effective assistance" standard in one formulation or another. . . . Yet this Court has not had occasion squarely to decide whether this is the proper standard. With respect to the prejudice that a defendant must show from deficient attorney performance, the lower courts have adopted tests that purport to differ in more than formulation. . . . In particular, the Court of Appeals in this case expressly rejected the prejudice standard articulated by Judge Leventhal in his plurality opinion in United States v. Decoster and adopted by the State of Florida in Knight v. State, a standard that requires a showing that specified deficient conduct of counsel was likely to have affected the outcome of the proceeding.

For these reasons, we granted certiorari to consider the standards by which to judge a contention that the Constitution requires that a criminal judgment be overturned because of the actual ineffective assistance of counsel.

II . . .

Because of the vital importance of counsel's assistance, this Court has held that, with certain exceptions, a person accused of a federal or state crime has the right to have counsel appointed if retained counsel cannot be obtained. That a person who happens to be a lawyer is present at trial alongside the accused, however, is not enough to satisfy the constitutional command. The Sixth Amendment recognizes the right to the assistance of counsel because it envisions counsel's playing a role that is critical to the ability of the adversarial system to produce just results. An accused is entitled to be assisted by an attorney, whether retained or appointed, who plays the role necessary to ensure that the trial is fair. For that reason, the Court has recognized that "the right to counsel is the right to the effective assistance of counsel." McMann v. Richardson, 397 U.S. 759, 771, n.14 (1970). . . .

In giving meaning to the requirement [of effective assistance of counsel,] we must take its purpose—to ensure a fair trial—as the guide. The benchmark for judging any claim of ineffectiveness must be whether counsel's conduct so undermined the proper functioning of the adversarial process that the trial cannot be relied on as having produced a just result.

The same principle applies to a capital sentencing proceeding such as that provided by Florida law. We need not consider the role of counsel in an ordinary sentencing, which may involve informal proceedings and standardless discretion in the sentencer, and hence may require a different approach to the definition of constitutionally effective assistance. A capital sentencing proceeding like the one involved in this case, however, is sufficiently like a trial in its adversarial format and in the existence of standards for decision . . . that counsel's role in the proceeding is comparable to counsel's role at trial—to ensure that the adversarial testing process works to produce a just result under the standards governing decision. For purposes of describing counsel's duties, therefore, Florida's capital sentencing proceeding need not be distinguished from an ordinary trial.

III

A convicted defendant's claim that counsel's assistance was so defective as to require reversal of a conviction or death sentence has two components. First, the defendant must show that counsel's performance was deficient. This requires showing that counsel made errors so serious that counsel was not functioning as the "counsel" guaranteed the defendant by the Sixth Amendment. Second, the defendant must show that the deficient performance prejudiced the defense. This requires showing that counsel's errors were so serious as to deprive the defendant of a fair trial, a trial whose result is reliable. Unless a defendant makes both showings, it cannot be said that the conviction or death sentence resulted from a breakdown in the adversary process that renders the result unreliable.

A

As all the Federal Courts of Appeals have now held, the proper standard for attorney performance is that of reasonably effective assistance. . . . When a convicted defendant complains of the ineffectiveness

of counsel's assistance, the defendant must show that counsel's representation fell below an objective standard of reasonableness.

More specific guidelines are not appropriate. The Sixth Amendment
refers simply to "counsel," not specifying particular requirements of effective assistance. It relies instead on the legal profession's maintenance
of standards sufficient to justify the law's presumption that counsel will
fulfill the role in the adversary process that the Amendment envisions. . . . The proper measure of attorney performance remains simply
reasonableness under prevailing professional norms.

Representation of a criminal defendant entails certain basic duties.
Counsel's function is to assist the defendant, and hence counsel owes
the client a duty of loyalty, a duty to avoid conflicts of interest. . . .
From counsel's function as assistant to the defendant derive the overarching duty to advocate the defendant's cause and the more particular
duties to consult with the defendant on important decisions and to keep
the defendant informed of important developments in the course of
the prosecution. Counsel also has a duty to bring to bear such skill
and knowledge as will render the trial a reliable adversarial testing process . . . .

These basic duties neither exhaustively define the obligations of
counsel nor form a checklist for judicial evaluation of attorney performance. In any case presenting an ineffectiveness claim, the performance
inquiry must be whether counsel's assistance was reasonable considering
all the circumstances. Prevailing norms of practice as reflected in American Bar Association standards and the like, e.g., ABA Standards for
Criminal Justice 4-1.1 to 4-8.6 (2d ed. 1980) ("The Defense Function"),
are guides to determining what is reasonable, but they are only guides.
No particular set of detailed rules for counsel's conduct can satisfactorily
take account of the variety of circumstances faced by defense counsel or
the range of legitimate decisions regarding how best to represent a criminal
defendant. Any such set of rules would interfere with the constitutionally
protected independence of counsel and restrict the wide latitude counsel
must have in making tactical decisions. . . . Indeed, the existence of
detailed guidelines for representation could distract counsel from the
overriding mission of vigorous advocacy of the defendant's cause. Moreover, the purpose of the effective assistance guarantee of the Sixth Amendment is not to improve the quality of legal representation, although that
is a goal of considerable importance to the legal system. The purpose is
simply to ensure that criminal defendants receive a fair trial.

Judicial scrutiny of counsel's performance must be highly deferential. It is all too tempting for a defendant to second-guess counsel's assistance after conviction or adverse sentence, and it is all too easy for a
court, examining counsel's defense after it has proved unsuccessful, to

conclude that a particular act or omission of counsel was unreasonable. . . . A fair assessment of attorney performance requires that every effort be made to eliminate the distorting effects of hindsight, to reconstruct the circumstances of counsel's challenged conduct, and to evaluate the conduct from counsel's perspective at the time. Because of the difficulties inherent in making the evaluation, a court must indulge a strong presumption that counsel's conduct falls within the wide range of reasonable professional assistance. . . . There are countless ways to provide effective assistance in any given case. Even the best criminal defense attorneys would not defend a particular client in the same way. See Goodpaster, The Trial for Life: Effective Assistance of Counsel in Death Penalty Cases, 58 N.Y.U.L. Rev. 299, 343 (1983).

The availability of intrusive post-trial inquiry into attorney performance or of detailed guidelines for its evaluation would encourage the proliferation of ineffectiveness challenges. Criminal trials resolved unfavorably to the defendant would increasingly come to be followed by a second trial, this one of counsel's unsuccessful defense. Counsel's performance and even willingness to serve could be adversely affected. Intensive scrutiny of counsel and rigid requirements for acceptable assistance could dampen the ardor and impair the independence of defense counsel, discourage the acceptance of assigned cases, and undermine the trust between attorney and client.

Thus, a court deciding an actual ineffectiveness claim must judge the reasonableness of counsel's challenged conduct on the facts of the particular case, viewed as of the time of counsel's conduct. A convicted defendant making a claim of ineffective assistance must identify the acts or omissions of counsel that are alleged not to have been the result of reasonable professional judgment. The court must then determine whether, in light of all the circumstances, the identified acts or omissions were outside the wide range of professionally competent assistance. In making that determination, the court should keep in mind that counsel's function, as elaborated in prevailing professional norms, is to make the adversarial testing process work in the particular case. At the same time, the court should recognize that counsel is strongly presumed to have rendered adequate assistance and made all significant decisions in the exercise of reasonable professional judgment.

These standards require no special amplification in order to define counsel's duty to investigate, the duty at issue in this case. As the Court of Appeals concluded, strategic choices made after thorough investigation of law and facts relevant to plausible options are virtually unchallengeable; and strategic choices made after less than complete investigation are reasonable precisely to the extent that reasonable professional judgments support the limitations on investigation. In other words, counsel has a duty to make reasonable investigations or to make a reasonable decision that makes particular investigations unnecessary. In any ineffectiveness case, a particular decision not to investigate must be directly assessed for reasonableness in all the circumstances, applying a heavy measure of deference to counsel's judgments.

The reasonableness of counsel's actions may be determined or substantially influenced by the defendant's own statements or actions. Counsel's actions are usually based, quite properly, on informed strategic choices made by the defendant and on information supplied by the defendant. In particular, what investigation decisions are reasonable depends critically on such information. For example, when the facts that support a certain potential line of defense are generally known to counsel because of what the defendant has said, the need for further investigation may be considerably diminished or eliminated altogether. And when a defendant has given counsel reason to believe that pursuing certain investigations would be fruitless or even harmful, counsel's failure to pursue those investigations may not later be challenged as unreasonable. In short, inquiry into counsel's conversations with the defendant may be critical to a proper assessment of counsel's investigation decisions, just as it may be critical to a proper assessment of counsel's other litigation decisions. . . .

B

An error by counsel, even if professionally unreasonable, does not warrant setting aside the judgment of a criminal proceeding if the error had no effect on the judgment. . . . The purpose of the Sixth Amendment guarantee of counsel is to ensure that a defendant has the assistance necessary to justify reliance on the outcome of the proceeding. Accordingly, any deficiencies in counsel's performance must be prejudicial to the defense in order to constitute ineffective assistance under the Constitution.

In certain Sixth Amendment contexts, prejudice is presumed. Actual or constructive denial of the assistance of counsel altogether is legally presumed to result in prejudice. So are various kinds of state interference with counsel's assistance. . . . Prejudice in these circumstances is so likely that case by case inquiry into prejudice is not worth the cost. Moreover, such circumstances involve impairments of the Sixth Amendment right that are easy to identify and, for that reason and because the prosecution is directly responsible, easy for the government to prevent.

One type of actual ineffectiveness claim warrants a similar, though more limited, presumption of prejudice. In Cuyler v. Sullivan, 446 U.S., at 345-350, the Court held that prejudice is presumed when counsel is burdened by an actual conflict of interest. In those circumstances, counsel breaches the duty of loyalty, perhaps the most basic of counsel's duties. Moreover, it is difficult to measure the precise effect on the defense or representation corrupted by conflicting interests. Given the obligation of counsel to avoid conflicts of interest and the ability of trial courts to make early inquiry in certain situations likely to give rise to conflicts, see e.g., Fed. R. Crim. Proc. 44(c), it is reasonable for the criminal justice system to maintain a fairly rigid rule of presumed prejudice for conflicts of interest. Even so, the rule is not quite the per se rule of prejudice that exists for the Sixth Amendment claims mentioned above. Prejudice is presumed only if the defendant demonstrates that counsel "actively represented conflicting interests" and "that an actual conflict of interest adversely affected his lawyer's performance." Cuyler v. Sullivan, supra, 446 U.S., at 350, 348 (footnote omitted).

Conflict of interest claims aside, actual ineffectiveness claims alleging a deficiency in attorney performance are subject to a general requirement that the defendant affirmatively prove prejudice. The government is not responsible for, and hence not able to prevent, attorney errors that will result in reversal of a conviction or sentence. Attorney errors come in an infinite variety and are as likely to be utterly harmless in a particular case as they are to be prejudicial. They cannot be classified according to likelihood of causing prejudice. Nor can they be defined with sufficient precision to inform defense attorneys correctly just what conduct to avoid. Representation is an art, and an act or omission that is unprofessional in one case may be sound or even brilliant in another. Even if a defendant shows that particular errors of counsel were unreasonable, therefore, the defendant must show that they actually had an adverse effect on the defense.

It is not enough for the defendant to show that the errors had some conceivable effect on the outcome of the proceeding. Virtually every act or omission of counsel would meet that test, . . . and not every error that conceivably could have influenced the outcome undermines the reliability of the result of the proceeding. Respondent suggests requiring a showing that the errors "impaired the presentation of the defense." That standard, however, provides no workable principle. Since any error, if it is indeed an error, "impairs" the presentation of the defense, the proposed standard is inadequate because it provides no way of deciding what impairments are sufficiently serious to warrant setting aside the outcome of the proceeding.

On the other hand, we believe that a defendant need not show that counsel's deficient conduct more likely than not altered the outcome in the case. This outcome-determinative standard has several strengths. It defines the relevant inquiry in a way familiar to courts, though the inquiry, as is inevitable, is anything but precise. The standard also reflects the profound importance of finality in criminal proceedings. Moreover, it comports with the widely used standard for assessing motions for new trial based on newly discovered evidence. . . . Nevertheless, the standard is not quite appropriate.

Even when the specified attorney error results in the omission of certain evidence, the newly discovered evidence standard is not an apt source from which to draw a prejudice standard for ineffectiveness claims. The high standard for newly discovered evidence claims presupposes that all the essential elements of a presumptively accurate and fair proceeding were present in the proceeding whose result is challenged. . . . An ineffective assistance claim asserts the absence of one of the crucial assurances that the result of the proceeding is reliable, so finality concerns are somewhat weaker and the appropriate standard of prejudice should be somewhat lower. The result of a proceeding can be rendered unreliable, and hence the proceeding itself unfair, even if the errors of counsel cannot be shown by a preponderance of the evidence to have determined the outcome.

Accordingly, the appropriate test for prejudice finds its roots in the test for materiality of exculpatory information not disclosed to the defense by the prosecution, United States v. Agurs, 427 U.S., at 104, 112-113, and in the test for materiality of testimony made unavailable to the defense by Government deportation of a witness, United States v. Valenzuela-Bernal, 458 U.S., at 872-874. The defendant must show that there is a reasonable probability that, but for counsel's unprofessional errors, the result of the proceeding would have been different. A reasonable probability is a probability sufficient to undermine confidence in the outcome.

In making the determination whether the specified errors resulted in the required prejudice, a court should presume, absent challenge to the judgment on grounds of evidentiary insufficiency, that the judge or jury acted according to law. An assessment of the likelihood of a result more favorable to the defendant must exclude the possibility of arbitrariness, whimsy, caprice, "nullification," and the like. A defendant has no entitlement to the luck of a lawless decisionmaker, even if a lawless decision cannot be reviewed. The assessment of prejudice should proceed on the assumption that the decisionmaker is reasonably, conscientiously, and impartially applying the standards that govern the decision. It should not depend on the idiosyncracies of the particular decisionmaker, such as unusual propensities toward harshness or leniency. Although these factors may actually have entered into counsel's selection of strategies and, to that limited extent, may thus affect the performance inquiry, they are irrelevant to the prejudice inquiry. Thus, evidence about the actual process of decision, if not part of the record of the proceeding under review, and evidence about, for example, a particular judge's sentencing practices, should not be considered in the prejudice determination.

The governing legal standard plays a critical role in defining the question to be asked in assessing the prejudice from counsel's errors. When a defendant challenges a conviction, the question is whether there is a reasonable probability that, absent the errors, the fact-finder would have had a reasonable doubt respecting guilt. When a defendant challenges a death sentence such as the one at issue in this case, the question is whether there is a reasonable probability that, absent the errors, the sentencer—including an appellate court, to the extent it independently reweighs the evidence—would have concluded that the balance of aggravating and mitigating circumstances did not warrant death.

In making this determination, a court hearing an ineffectiveness claim must consider the totality of the evidence before the judge or jury. Some of the factual findings will have been unaffected by the errors, and factual findings that were affected will have been affected in different ways. Some errors will have had a pervasive effect on the inferences to be drawn from the evidence, altering the entire evidentiary picture, and some will have had an isolated, trivial effect. Moreover, a verdict or conclusion only weakly supported by the record is more likely to have been affected by the errors than one with overwhelming record support. Taking the unaffected findings as a given, and taking due account of the effect of the errors on the remaining findings, a court making the prejudice inquiry must ask if the defendant has met the burden of showing that the decision reached would reasonably likely have been different absent the errors.

IV

A number of practical considerations are important for the application of the standards we have outlined. Most important, in adjudicating a claim of actual ineffectiveness of counsel, a court should keep in mind that the principles we have stated do not establish mechanical rules. Although those principles should guide the process of decision, the ultimate focus of inquiry must be on the fundamental fairness of the proceeding whose result is being challenged. In every case the court should be concerned with whether, despite the strong presumption of reliability, the result of the particular proceeding is unreliable because of a breakdown in the adversarial process that our system counts on to produce just results.

To the extent that this has already been the guiding inquiry in the lower courts, the standards articulated today do not require reconsideration of ineffectiveness claims rejected under different standards. Cf.

Trapnell v. United States, 725 F.2d, at 153 (in several years of applying
"farce and mockery" standard along with "reasonable competence" standard, court "never found that the result of a case hinged on the choice
of a particular standard"). In particular, the minor differences in the
lower courts' precise formulations of the performance standard are insignificant: the different formulations are mere variations of the overarching
reasonableness standard. With regard to the prejudice inquiry, only the
strict outcome-determinative test, among the standards articulated in the
lower courts, imposes a heavier burden on defendants than the tests laid
down today. The difference, however, should alter the merit of an ineffectiveness claim only in the rarest case.

Although we have discussed the performance component of an ineffectiveness claim prior to the prejudice component, there is no reason
for a court deciding an ineffective assistance claim to approach the inquiry
in the same order or even to address both components of the inquiry if
the defendant makes an insufficient showing on one. In particular, a
court need not determine whether counsel's performance was deficient
before examining the prejudice suffered by the defendant as a result of
the alleged deficiencies. The object of an ineffectiveness claim is not to
grade counsel's performance. If it is easier to dispose of an ineffectiveness
claim on the ground of lack of sufficient prejudice, which we expect will
often be so, that course should be followed. Courts should strive to ensure
that ineffectiveness claims not become so burdensome to defense counsel
that the entire criminal justice system suffers as a result.

The principles governing ineffectiveness claims should apply in federal collateral proceedings as they do on direct appeal or in motions for
a new trial. As indicated by the "cause and prejudice" test for overcoming
procedural waivers of claims of error, the presumption that a criminal
judgment is final is at its strongest in collateral attacks on that judgment. . . . An ineffectiveness claim, however, as our articulation of the
standards that govern decision of such claims makes clear, is an attack
on the fundamental fairness of the proceeding whose result is challenged.
Since fundamental fairness is the central concern of the writ of habeas
corpus, . . . no special standards ought to apply to ineffectiveness claims
made in habeas proceedings.

Finally, in a federal habeas challenge to a state criminal judgment,
a state court conclusion that counsel rendered effective assistance is not
a finding of fact binding on the federal court to the extent stated by 28
U.S.C. §2254(d). Ineffectiveness is not a question of "basic, primary, or
historical fac[t]." Rather, like the question whether multiple representation in a particular case gave rise to a conflict of interest, it is a mixed
question of law and fact. . . . Although state court findings of fact made
in the course of deciding an ineffectiveness claim are subject to the

deference requirement of §2254(d), and although District Court findings are subject to the clearly erroneous standard of Fed. R. Civ. Proc. 52(a), both the performance and prejudice components of the ineffectiveness inquiry are mixed questions of law and fact.

V

Having articulated general standards for judging ineffectiveness claims, we think it useful to apply those standards to the facts of this case in order to illustrate the meaning of the general principles. The record makes it possible to do so. There are no conflicts between the state and federal courts over findings of fact, and the principles we have articulated are sufficiently close to the principles applied both in the Florida courts and in the District Court that it is clear that the fact-finding was not affected by erroneous legal principles. . . .

Application of the governing principles is not difficult in this case. The facts as described above, . . . make clear that the conduct of respondent's counsel at and before respondent's sentencing proceeding cannot be found unreasonable. They also make clear that, even assuming the challenged conduct of counsel was unreasonable, respondent suffered insufficient prejudice to warrant setting aside his death sentence.

With respect to the performance component, the record shows that respondent's counsel made a strategic choice to argue for the extreme emotional distress mitigating circumstance and to rely as fully as possible on respondent's acceptance of responsibility for his crimes. Although counsel understandably felt hopeless about respondent's prospects, . . . nothing in the record indicates, as one possible reading of the District Court's opinion suggests . . . that counsel's sense of hopelessness distorted his professional judgment. Counsel's strategy choice was well within the range of professionally reasonable judgments, and the decision not to seek more character or psychological evidence than was already in hand was likewise reasonable.

The trial judge's views on the importance of owning up to one's crimes were well known to counsel. The aggravating circumstances were utterly overwhelming. Trial counsel could reasonably surmise from his conversations with respondent that character and psychological evidence would be of little help. Respondent had already been able to mention at the plea colloquy the substance of what there was to know about his financial and emotional troubles. Restricting testimony on respondent's character to what had come in at the plea colloquy ensured that contrary character and psychological evidence and respondent's criminal history, which counsel had successfully moved to exclude, would not come in. On these facts, there can be little question, even without application of the presumption of adequate performance, that trial counsel's defense, though unsuccessful, was the result of reasonable professional judgment.

With respect to the prejudice component, the lack of merit of respondent's claim is even more stark. The evidence that respondent says his trial counsel should have offered at the sentencing hearing would barely have altered the sentencing profile presented to the sentencing judge. As the state courts and District Court found, at most this evidence shows that numerous people who knew respondent thought he was generally a good person and that a psychiatrist and a psychologist believed he was under considerable emotional stress that did not rise to the level of extreme disturbance. Given the overwhelming aggravating factors, there is no reasonable probability that the omitted evidence would have changed the conclusion that the aggravating circumstances outweighed the mitigating circumstances and, hence, the sentence imposed. Indeed, admission of the evidence respondent now offers might even have been harmful to his case: his "rap sheet" would probably have been admitted into evidence, and the psychological reports would have directly contradicted respondent's claim that the mitigating circumstance of extreme emotional disturbance applied to his case.

Our conclusions on both the prejudice and performance components of the ineffectiveness inquiry do not depend on the trial judge's testimony at the District Court hearing. We therefore need not consider the general admissibility of that testimony, although, as noted . . . , that testimony is irrelevant to the prejudice inquiry. Moreover, the prejudice question is resolvable, and hence the ineffectiveness claim can be rejected, without regard to the evidence presented at the District Court hearing. The state courts properly concluded that the ineffectiveness claim was meritless without holding an evidentiary hearing.

Failure to make the required showing of either deficient performance or sufficient prejudice defeats the ineffectiveness claim. Here there is a double failure. More generally, respondent has made no showing that the justice of his sentence was rendered unreliable by a breakdown in the adversary process caused by deficiencies in counsel's assistance. Respondent's sentencing proceeding was not fundamentally unfair.

We conclude, therefore, that the District Court properly declined to issue a writ of habeas corpus. The judgment of the Court of Appeals is accordingly reversed.

[JUSTICE BRENNAN's opinion concurring in the opinion of the Court, but dissenting from its judgment (due to the death penalty aspects) is omitted.]

JUSTICE MARSHALL, dissenting.

The Sixth and Fourteenth Amendments guarantee a person accused of a crime the right to the aid of a lawyer in preparing and presenting his defense. It has long been settled that "the right to counsel is the right to the effective assistance of counsel." McMann v. Richardson, 397 U.S. 759, 771, n.14 (1970). The state and lower federal courts have developed standards for distinguishing effective from inadequate assistance. Today, for the first time, this Court attempts to synthesize and clarify those standards. For the most part, the majority's efforts are unhelpful. Neither of its two principal holdings seems to me likely to improve the adjudication of Sixth Amendment claims. And, in its zeal to survey comprehensively this field of doctrine, the majority makes many other generalizations and suggestions that I find unacceptable. Most importantly, the majority fails to take adequate account of the fact that the locus of this case is a capital sentencing proceeding. Accordingly, I join neither the Court's opinion nor its judgment.

I

The opinion of the Court revolves around two holdings. First, the majority ties the constitutional minima of attorney performance to a simple "standard of reasonableness." . . . Second, the majority holds that only an error of counsel that has sufficient impact on a trial to "undermine confidence in the outcome" is grounds for overturning a conviction. . . . I disagree with both of these rulings.

A

My objection to the performance standard adopted by the Court is that it is so malleable that, in practice, it will either have no grip at all or will yield excessive variation in the manner in which the Sixth Amendment is interpreted and applied by different courts. To tell lawyers and the lower courts that counsel for a criminal defendant must behave "reasonably" and must act like "a reasonably competent attorney," . . . is to tell them almost nothing. In essence, the majority has instructed judges called upon to assess claims of ineffective assistance of counsel to advert to their own intuitions regarding what constitutes "professional" representation, and has discouraged them from trying to develop more detailed standards governing the performance of defense counsel. In my view, the Court has thereby not only abdicated its own responsibility to interpret the Constitution, but also impaired the ability of the lower courts to exercise theirs.

The debilitating ambiguity of an "objective standard of reasonableness" in this context is illustrated by the majority's failure to address important issues concerning the quality of representation mandated by the Constitution. It is an unfortunate but undeniable fact that a person of means, by selecting a lawyer and paying him enough to ensure he prepares thoroughly, usually can obtain better representation than that available to an indigent defendant, who must rely on appointed counsel, who, in turn, has limited time and resources to devote to a given case. Is a "reasonably competent attorney" a reasonably competent adequately paid retained lawyer or a reasonably competent appointed attorney? It is also a fact that the quality of representation available to ordinary defendants in different parts of the country varies significantly. Should the standard of performance mandated by the Sixth Amendment vary by locale? The majority offers no clues as to the proper responses to these questions.

The majority defends its refusal to adopt more specific standards primarily on the ground that "[n]o particular set of detailed rules for counsel's conduct can satisfactorily take account of the variety of circumstances faced by defense counsel or the range of legitimate decisions regarding how best to represent a criminal defendant." . . . I agree that counsel must be afforded "wide latitude" when making "tactical decisions" regarding trial strategy, . . . but many aspects of the job of a criminal defense attorney are more amenable to judicial oversight. For example, much of the work involved in preparing for a trial, applying for bail, conferring with one's client, making timely objections to significant, arguably erroneous rulings of the trial judge, and filing a notice of appeal if there are colorable grounds therefor could profitably be made the subject of uniform standards.

The opinion of the Court of Appeals in this case represents one sound attempt to develop particularized standards designed to ensure that all defendants receive effective legal assistance. . . . By refusing to address the merits of these proposals, and indeed suggesting that no such effort is worthwhile, the opinion of the Court, I fear, will stunt the development of constitutional doctrine in this area.

B

I object to the prejudice standard adopted by the Court for two independent reasons. *First,* it is often very difficult to tell whether a defendant convicted after a trial in which he was ineffectively represented would have fared better if his lawyer had been competent. Seemingly impregnable cases can sometimes be dismantled by good defense counsel. On the basis of a cold record, it may be impossible for a reviewing court confidently to ascertain how the government's evidence and arguments would have stood up against rebuttal and cross-examination by a shrewd, well prepared lawyer. The difficulties of estimating prejudice after the fact are exacerbated by the possibility that evidence of injury to the defendant may be missing from the record precisely because of the incompetence of defense counsel. In view of all these impediments to a fair evaluation of the probability that the outcome of a trial was affected by ineffectiveness of counsel, it seems to me senseless to impose on a defendant whose lawyer has been shown to have been incompetent the burden of demonstrating prejudice.

Second and more fundamentally, the assumption on which the Court's holding rests is that the only purpose of the constitutional guarantee of effective assistance of counsel is to reduce the chance that innocent persons will be convicted. In my view, the guarantee also functions to ensure that convictions are obtained only through fundamentally fair procedures. The majority contends that the Sixth Amendment is not violated when a manifestly guilty defendant is convicted after a trial in which he was represented by a manifestly ineffective attorney. I cannot agree. Every defendant is entitled to a trial in which his interests are vigorously and conscientiously advocated by an able lawyer. A proceeding in which the defendant does not receive meaningful assistance in meeting the forces of the state does not, in my opinion, constitute due process.

In Chapman v. California, 386 U.S. 18, 23 (1967), we acknowledged that certain constitutional rights are "so basic to a fair trial that their infraction can never be treated as harmless error." Among these rights is "the right to the assistance of counsel at trial." Id., at 23, n.8; see Gideon v. Wainwright, 372 U.S. 335 (1963). In my view, the right to *effective* assistance of counsel is entailed by the right to counsel, and abridgment of the former is equivalent to abridgment of the latter. I would thus hold that a showing that the performance of a defendant's lawyer departed from constitutionally prescribed standards requires a new trial regardless of whether the defendant suffered demonstrable prejudice thereby.

II

Even if I were inclined to join the majority's two central holdings, I could not abide the manner in which the majority elaborates upon its rulings. Particularly regrettable are the majority's discussion of the "presumption" of reasonableness to be accorded lawyers' decisions and its attempt to prejudge the merits of claims previously rejected by lower courts using different legal standards.

A

In defining the standard of attorney performance required by the Constitution, the majority appropriately notes that many problems confronting criminal defense attorneys admit of "a range of legitimate" responses. . . . And the majority properly cautions courts, when reviewing a lawyer's selection amongst a set of options, to avoid the hubris of hindsight. . . . The majority goes on, however, to suggest that reviewing courts should "indulge a strong presumption that counsel's conduct" was constitutionally acceptable, . . . and should "appl[y] a heavy measure of deference to counsel's judgments." . . .

I am not sure what these phrases mean, and I doubt that they will be self-explanatory to lower courts. If they denote nothing more than that a defendant claiming he was denied effective assistance of counsel has the burden of proof, I would agree. . . . But the adjectives "strong" and "heavy" might be read as imposing upon defendants an unusually weighty burden of persuasion. If that is the majority's intent, I must respectfully dissent. The range of acceptable behavior defined by "prevailing professional norms," . . . seems to me sufficiently broad to allow defense counsel the flexibility they need in responding to novel problems of trial strategy. To afford attorneys more latitude, by "strongly presuming" that their behavior will fall within the zone of reasonableness, is covertly to legitimate convictions and sentences obtained on the basis of incompetent conduct by defense counsel.

The only justification the majority itself provides for its proposed presumption is that undue receptivity to claims of ineffective assistance of counsel would encourage too many defendants to raise such claims and thereby would clog the courts with frivolous suits and "dampen the ardor" of defense counsel. . . . I have more confidence than the majority in the ability of state and federal courts expeditiously to dispose of meritless arguments and to ensure that responsible, innovative lawyering is not inhibited. In my view, little will be gained and much may be lost by instructing the lower courts to proceed on the assumption that a defendant's challenge to his lawyer's performance will be insubstantial.

B

For many years the lower courts have been debating the meaning of "effective" assistance of counsel. Different courts have developed different standards. On the issue of the level of performance required by the Constitution, some courts have adopted the forgiving "farce-and-mockery" standard, while others have adopted various versions of the "reasonable competence" standard. On the issue of the level of prejudice necessary to compel a new trial, the courts have taken a wide variety of positions, ranging from the stringent "outcome-determinative" test, to the rule that a showing of incompetence on the part of defense counsel automatically requires reversal of the conviction regardless of the injury to the defendant.

The Court today substantially resolves these disputes. The majority holds that the Constitution is violated when defense counsel's representation falls below the level expected of reasonably competent defense counsel, . . . and so affects the trial that there is a "reasonable probability" that, absent counsel's error, the outcome would have been different. . . .

Curiously, though, the Court discounts the significance of its rulings, suggesting that its choice of standards matters little and that few if any cases would have been decided differently if the lower courts had always applied the tests announced today. . . . Surely the judges in the state and lower federal courts will be surprised to learn that the distinctions they have so fiercely debated for many years are in fact unimportant.

The majority's comments on this point seem to be prompted principally by a reluctance to acknowledge that today's decision will require a reassessment of many previously rejected ineffective-assistance-of-counsel claims. The majority's unhappiness on this score is understandable, but its efforts to mitigate the perceived problem will be ineffectual. Nothing the majority says can relieve lower courts that hitherto have been using standards more tolerant of ineffectual advocacy of their obligation to scrutinize all claims, old as well as new, under the principles laid down today.

III

The majority suggests that, "[f]or purposes of describing counsel's duties," a capital sentencing proceeding "need not be distinguished from an ordinary trial." I cannot agree.

The Court has repeatedly acknowledged that the Constitution requires stricter adherence to procedural safeguards in a capital case than in other cases.

> [T]he penalty of death is qualitatively different from a sentence of imprisonment, however long. Death, in its finality, differs more from life imprisonment than a 100-year prison term differs from one of only a year or two. Because of that qualitative difference, there is a corresponding difference in the need for reliability in the determination that death is the

appropriate punishment in a specific case. Woodson v. North Carolina, 428 U.S. 280, 305 (1976) (plurality opinion) (footnote omitted).

The performance of defense counsel is a crucial component of the system of protections designed to ensure that capital punishment is administered with some degree of rationality. "Reliability" in the imposition of the death sentence can be approximated only if the sentencer is fully informed of "all possible relevant information about the individual defendant whose fate it must determine." Jurek v. Texas, 428 U.S. 262, 276 (1976) (plurality opinion). The job of amassing that information and presenting it in an organized and persuasive manner to the sentencer is entrusted principally to the defendant's lawyer. The importance to the process of counsel's efforts, combined with the severity and irrevocability of the sanction at stake, require that the standards for determining what constitutes "effective assistance" be applied especially stringently in capital sentencing proceedings.

It matters little whether strict scrutiny of a claim that ineffectiveness of counsel resulted in a death sentence is achieved through modification of the Sixth Amendment standards or through especially careful application of those standards. Justice Brennan suggests that the necessary adjustment of the level of performance required of counsel in capital sentencing proceedings can be effected simply by construing the phrase, "reasonableness under prevailing professional norms," in a manner that takes into account the nature of the impending penalty. . . . Though I would prefer a more specific iteration of counsel's duties in this special context, I can accept that proposal. However, when instructing lower courts regarding the probability of impact upon the outcome that requires a resentencing, I think the Court would do best explicitly to modify the legal standard itself. In my view, a person on death row, whose counsel's performance fell below constitutionally acceptable levels, should not be compelled to demonstrate a "reasonable probability" that he would have been given a life sentence if his lawyer had been competent . . . ; if the defendant can establish a significant chance that the outcome would have been different, he surely should be entitled to a redetermination of his fate. . . .

IV

The views expressed in the preceding section oblige me to dissent from the majority's disposition of the case before us. It is undisputed that respondent's trial counsel made virtually no investigation of the possibility of obtaining testimony from respondent's relatives, friends, or former employers pertaining to respondent's character or background. Had counsel done so, he would have found several persons willing and able to testify that, in their experience, respondent was a responsible, nonviolent man, devoted to his family, and active in the affairs of his church. . . . Respondent contends that his lawyer could have and should have used that testimony to "humanize" respondent, to counteract the impression conveyed by the trial that he was little more than a cold-blooded killer. Had this evidence been admitted, respondent argues, his chances of obtaining a life sentence would have been significantly better.

Measured against the standards outlined above, respondent's contentions are substantial. Experienced members of the death-penalty bar have long recognized the crucial importance of adducing evidence at a sentencing proceeding that establishes the defendant's social and familial connections. . . . The State makes a colorable—though in my view not compelling—argument that defense counsel in this case might have made a reasonable "strategic" decision not to present such evidence at the sentencing hearing on the assumption that an unadorned acknowledgement of respondent's responsibility for his crimes would be more likely to appeal to the trial judge, who was reputed to respect persons who accepted responsibility for their actions. But however justifiable such a choice might have been after counsel had fairly assessed the potential strength of the mitigating evidence available to him, counsel's failure to make any significant effort to find out what evidence might be garnered from respondent's relatives and acquaintances surely cannot be described as "reasonable." Counsel's failure to investigate is particularly suspicious in light of his candid admission that respondent's confessions and conduct in the course of the trial gave him a feeling of "hopelessness" regarding the possibility of saving respondent's life. . . .

That the aggravating circumstances implicated by respondent's criminal conduct were substantial, . . . does not vitiate respondent's constitutional claim; judges and juries in cases involving behavior at least as egregious have shown mercy, particularly when afforded an opportunity to see other facets of the defendant's personality and life. Nor is respondent's contention defeated by the possibility that the material his counsel turned up might not have been sufficient to establish a *statutory* mitigating circumstance under Florida law; Florida sentencing judges and the Florida Supreme Court sometimes refuse to impose death sentences in cases "in which, even though *statutory* mitigating circumstances do not outweigh statutory aggravating circumstances, the addition of nonstatutory mitigating circumstances tips the scales in favor of life imprisonment." Barclay v. Florida, 463 U.S. 939, 964 (Stevens, J., concurring in the judgment) (emphasis in original).

If counsel had investigated the availability of mitigating evidence, he might well have decided to present some such material at the hearing. If he had done so, there is a significant chance that respondent would have been given a life sentence. In my view, those possibilities, conjoined with the unreasonableness of counsel's failure to investigate, are more than sufficient to establish a violation of the Sixth Amendment and to entitle respondent to a new sentencing proceeding.

I respectfully dissent.

Compare *Strickland* with the D.C. Circuit's earlier effort to address the same issues. That effort produced three decisions. In the *first decision*, a panel noted that the defendant's right to counsel may have been violated, and it remanded the case to the district court for further findings. United States v. DeCoster, 487 F.2d 1197 (D.C. Cir. 1973). The district court affirmed the conviction, and the panel subsequently reversed. The circuit, en banc, then reversed the panel, reinstating the conviction.

The *second decision* of the panel is appended to the en banc decision at 624 F.2d 300 (D.C. Cir. 1976). The en banc opinion is the third decision and is at 624 F.2d 196 (D.C. Cir. 1976), and the defendant's name is now spelled Decoster.

Unfortunately, the various opinions generated by the *Decoster* litigation are as confusing as the case history. In brief, the case centered on whether Decoster's conviction for armed robbery was obtained in violation of his right to effective assistance of counsel. Decoster was identified at various stages of the proceedings as the assailant by the victim and two police officers. The defendant denied the allegation at trial, but he also wrote a letter to his counsel in which he virtually confessed to the offense and, in any event, substantially contradicted his trial testimony. Although it is not free from doubt, this letter appears to have been written prior to trial. The defendant subsequently sent a similar letter to the trial judge.

Prior to trial, according to the court of appeals, defense counsel did not rigorously investigate the matter and did not, for example, interview all the possible witnesses. The district court found that defense counsel's efforts did not deprive the defendant of effective assistance, or if they did, that no prejudice was shown. In reversing the district court, the panel held that in cases of a failure to investigate, as occurred here according to the panel, the correct standard is to presume that the failure to investigate impaired the defense and to require the government to prove harmless error beyond reasonable doubt. Moreover, the panel did so even though in cases such as these "it is impossible to know precisely how the defendant was affected by counsel's failures; consequently, it will be most difficult for a defendant to prove prejudice or for the Government to negate it." In short, the panel reversed the conviction of an almost certainly guilty individual because of the failure of defense counsel to engage in "investigations" that apparently could only have produced a concocted defense.

The court of appeals en banc reversed the panel, but in a decision that reflected a badly split court. The en banc court did appear to accept the panel's conclusion that the standard for effective assistance of counsel was henceforth no longer to be the "mockery of justice" standard but instead one of "incompetency that falls measurably below the perfor- mance ordinarily expected of fallible lawyers." The court was split as to how to apply the new standard, however. The opinion announcing the decision of the court stated that "the accused must bear the initial burden of demonstrating a likelihood that counsel's inadequacy affected the out- come of the trial. Once the appellant has made this initial showing, the burden passes to the government, and the conviction cannot survive unless the government demonstrates that it is not tainted by the deficiency, and that in fact no prejudice resulted."

The concurring opinion, by contrast, stated that "a defendant who alleges that his counsel was ineffective must show that substantial prej- udice to his defense resulted from the alleged violation of duty owed him by counsel." The concurring judges asserted that such a showing amounted to a "prima facie" case, which the government could then "rebut" by "disproving" the prima facie case.

Judge Bazelon, the author of the panel opinion, dissented and was joined by Judge Wright. The dissent eloquently presents the fundamental dilemma that Judge Bazelon perceives to be presented by the right to effective assistance of counsel, and in addition it raises a number of im- portant concerns.

UNITED STATES v. DECOSTER
Appeal to the D.C. Circuit
624 F.2d 196 (1976)

[BAZELON, J., with whom J. SKELLY WRIGHT, joins dissenting.]

Willie Decoster was denied the effective assistance of counsel guar- anteed by the Sixth Amendment because he could not afford to hire a competent and conscientious attorney. His plight is an indictment of our system of criminal justice, which promises "Equal Justice Under Law," but delivers only "Justice for Those Who Can Afford It." Though pur- porting to address the problem of ineffective assistance, the majority's decision ignores the sordid reality that the kind of slovenly, indifferent representation provided Willie Decoster is uniquely the fate allotted to the poor. Underlying the majority's antiseptic verbal formulations is a disturbing tolerance for a criminal justice system that consistently provides less protection and less dignity for the indigent. I cannot accept a system that conditions a defendant's right to a fair trial on his ability to pay for it. . . .

The analysis of this case should be guided by the principles established in *DeCoster I.* [62]. . .

The heart of this approach lies in defining ineffective assistance in terms of the *quality of counsel's performance*, rather than looking to the effect of counsel's actions on the outcome of the case. If the Sixth Amendment is to serve a central role in eliminating second-class justice for the poor, then it must proscribe second-class performances by counsel, whatever the consequences in a particular case. Moreover, by focusing on the quality of representation and providing incentives in all cases for counsel to meet or exceed minimum standards, this approach reduces the likelihood that any particular defendant will be prejudiced by counsel's shortcomings. In this way, courts can safeguard the defendant's rights to a constitutionally adequate trial without engaging in the inherently difficult task of speculating about the precise effect of each error or omission by an attorney. Although the question of prejudice remains part of the court's inquiry, it is distinct from the determination of whether the defendant has received effective assistance. Rather, prejudice is considered only in order to spare defendants, prosecutors and the courts alike a truly futile repetition of the pretrial and trial process. . . .

In *DeCoster I* this court . . . did not attempt to prescribe categorical standards of attorney performance. Instead, we took pains to note that the articulated duties were "meant as a starting point for the court to develop, on a case by case basis, clearer guidelines for courts and for lawyers as to the meaning of effective assistance." We recognized, however, that there were certain tasks, such as the ones we enumerated in our decision, that can never be ignored: conferring with the client without delay and as often as necessary; fully discussing potential strategies and tactical choices; advising the client of his rights and taking all actions necessary to preserve them; and conducting appropriate factual and legal investigations. I submit that no one can dispute that a reasonably competent lawyer, absent good cause, would or should do less. Counsel should proceed in the representation of his client under the guidance of these minimal duties, departing only when the particular needs of his client compel a different course of action.

Prominent among the duties of defense counsel is the obligation to

---

62. . . . . Although the division of this court in today's decision places our previous ruling in *DeCoster I* in question, a majority of the court today explicitly reaffirms the standard adopted in that opinion: a defendant is entitled to the reasonably competent assistance of an attorney acting as his diligent conscientious advocate. . . .

"conduct appropriate investigations, both factual and legal, to determine what matter of defense can be developed." As the Commentary of the ABA Standards stresses, "[I]nvestigation and preparation are the keys to effective representation. [It] is impossible to overemphasize the importance of appropriate investigation to the effective and fair administration of criminal justice." . . .

At a minimum, the duty to investigate requires counsel (or his investigator) to contact persons whom he has or should have reason to believe were witnesses to the events in question, to seek witnesses in places where he has or should have reason to believe the events occurred, and to conduct these interviews and investigations as promptly as possible, before memories fade or witnesses disappear.

In the present case, Decoster's attorney did none of these things. Although the failure to interview a particular witness, by itself, may not rise to the level of inadequate assistance, defense counsel's investigation and preparation for this case was so perfunctory that it clearly violated his duties to his client. The prosecution called three witnesses at trial—Roger Crump and Officers Box and Ehler. Despite the cardinal rule that proper investigation begins with interviews of those witnesses whom the government intends to call, particularly the arresting and investigating officers, defense counsel made no attempt to interview any of these witnesses at any time prior to trial. Nor did he request or obtain a transcript of the preliminary hearing where these witnesses testified. Defense counsel did not even contact and interview Decoster's codefendants, Eley and Taylor, before trial. Nor did he seek or talk to any witnesses at the hotel or bar. In fact, defense counsel made absolutely no effort to discover, contact, or interview *a single witness* prior to trial. Apparently, he was willing to go to trial without having made any real effort to determine what could be elicited by way of defense or to evaluate the strengths and weaknesses of his client's case. . . .

Perhaps counsel concluded from this limited information that his client had no alibi defense and was guilty, and that therefore counsel was excused from conducting any investigation. But the suggestion that a client whose lawyer believes him to be guilty deserves less pretrial investigation is simply wrong. An attorney's duty to investigate is not relieved by his own perception of his client's guilt or innocence. I can think of nothing more destructive of the adversary system than to excuse inadequate investigation on the grounds that defense counsel—the accused's only ally in the entire proceedings—disbelieved his client and therefore thought that further inquiry would prove fruitless. The Constitution entitles a criminal defendant to a trial in court by a jury of his peers—not to a trial by his court-appointed defense counsel.[105] . . .

105. The dangers that can result from excusing counsel's inadequate representation

It is true that appellant complicated defense counsel's task when, sometime before trial, he sent counsel a letter suggesting a new version of what happened on the day of his arrest. Again, however, this has no bearing on counsel's failure to investigate. By his own account, counsel did not learn of the self-defense theory until the day before or the day of the trial. Appellant's conflicting stories, therefore, obviously cannot excuse counsel's inaction during the previous seventeen months. If anything, appellant's differing accounts should have emphasized the need for an independent investigation to determine which, if either, version

---

on the ground that his client's "guilt is obvious" are vividly illustrated by a series of events occurring shortly after appellant's trial involving the same attorney whose performance is challenged in the present case. In December 1971, Decoster's lawyer was appointed to represent another indigent defendant, Samuel A. Saunders, who was accused of purse snatching. The victim, an elderly woman who owned a restaurant near Saunders' residence, saw Saunders some five and a half weeks after the robbery, called the police, and had him arrested. Although the Bail Agency recommended release with third-party custody, bond was set for Saunders at $5,000. Decoster's lawyer filed no motion for bond reduction or review; as a result, Saunders remained incarcerated through the trial and appellate stages.

Saunders, who spent over 9 years in an institution for the mentally retarded and is half-blind, maintained that he was innocent and that he had been working on the day of the robbery. Decoster's lawyer evidently did not believe him; as in the present case, the lawyer apparently conducted no investigation whatsoever. At trial, Saunders' entire defense consisted of his own testimony. Counsel offered no opening statement. On direct examination, he elicited a statement from Saunders that he had not stolen the purse. Decoster's lawyer made no attempt to develop the defense beyond this single denial. On cross-examination, counsel sat silently as Saunders became increasingly confused about whether each question of the U.S. Attorney referred to the day of the robbery or the day of his arrest. Nor did counsel attempt to clarify matters on redirect, despite the prosecutor's use of this confusion to imply that Saunders was lying. The most critical dereliction, however, was the lawyer's failure to pursue either in redirect examination or through post-trial investigation, Saunders' assertion during cross-examination that he had been working on the D.C. Employment Service on the day of the robbery and that "they will verify that date."

Not surprisingly, Saunders was convicted and sentenced to 2-6 years. Fortunately, this court appointed a conscientious attorney to represent Saunders on appeal. This lawyer, after reading the transcript of the trial, was disturbed by Saunders' protestations of innocence, and she had her secretary call the U.S. Employment Service. The labor office checked their records for the date of the robbery and found indisputable documentary proof that Saunders had been working on a Washington Star delivery truck on that day and was nowhere near the scene of the crime. The district court granted a motion for a new trial based on the newly-discovered evidence and the charges against Saunders were dismissed. In the meantime, Saunders had spent a year in jail for a crime he had not committed.

Saunders, of course, could demonstrate prejudice, even under the majority's proposed analyses. But there are undoubtedly countless other indigent defendants, like Decoster himself, who are represented with the same callous indifference by court-appointed trial counsel, and who are not fortunate enough to have indisputable evidence, preserved in documentary form, attesting to the prejudice they have suffered. Even if many of these defendants are "probably guilty," they deserve the effective services of a lawyer who is a "conscientious advocate in their behalf." And we can achieve this end only by assuring that counsel fulfills the minimum obligations of a competent attorney without regard to his—or our—subjective beliefs about the defendant's guilt.

was accurate and could be presented as a defense. Yet, even after receiving appellant's letter, counsel was ready to go to trial without having attempted to contact the codefendants to learn their version of the events on the night of the robbery.

In the end, the majority's conclusion that appellant was not denied the effective assistance of counsel rests on their perception that the record contains overwhelming evidence of appellant's guilt. "[U]ltimately, there was a total failure of appellant to show that it was likely that counsel's deficiencies had any effect on the outcome of the trial." The logic of their position seems to be as follows: If the accused was probably guilty, then nothing helpful could have been found even through a properly conducted investigation. Thus, any violation of that duty—no matter how egregious—was inconsequential and hence excusable.

Even on its own terms, such reasoning is faulty. It assumes that the value of investigation is measured only by information it yields that will exonerate the defendant. Yet, even if an investigation produces not a scintilla of evidence favorable to the defense—an unlikely hypothesis— appellant still will benefit from a full investigation. One of the essential responsibilities of the defense attorney is to conduct an independent examination of the law and facts so that he can offer his professional evaluation of the strength of the defendant's case. If this full investigation reveals that a plea of guilty is in the defendant's best interests, then the attorney should advise his client and explore the possibility of initiating plea discussions with the prosecutor. It is no secret that in the majority of criminal prosecutions the accused is in fact guilty, notwithstanding any initial protestations of innocence. It is also no secret that the vast majority of criminal prosecutions culminating in conviction are settled through plea bargaining. . . .

More importantly, the majority's position confuses the defendant's burden of showing that counsel's violation was "substantial" with the government's burden of proving that the violation was not "prejudicial." The former entails a forward-looking inquiry into whether defense counsel acted in the manner of a diligent and competent attorney; it asks whether, at the time the events occurred, defense counsel's violations of the duties owed to his client were justifiable. In contrast, the inquiry into "prejudice" requires an after-the-fact determination of whether a violation that was admittedly "substantial," nevertheless did not produce adverse conse- quences for the defendant.

All that the accused must show to establish a Sixth Amendment violation is that counsel's acts or omissions were substantial enough to have deprived him of the effective assistance of counsel in his defense. He need not prove that counsel's violations were ultimately harmful in affecting the outcome of his trial. Quite simply, the inquiry into the

adequacy of counsel is distinct *from the inquiry into guilt or innocence.*
The Constitution entitles every defendant to counsel who is "an active
advocate in behalf of his client."[122] Where such advocacy is absent, the
accused has been denied effective assistance, regardless of his guilt or
innocence. The majority opinions nevertheless force the appellant to
shoulder the burden of proving that counsel's acts or omissions actually
or likely affected the outcome of the trial. To thus condition the right to
effective assistance of counsel on the defendant's ability to demonstrate
his innocence is to assure that only the constitutional rights of the innocent will be vindicated. Our system of criminal justice does not rest
on such a foundation. . . .

Having determined in this case that counsel's violation of his duty
to his client was substantial, and that appellant consequently was denied
the effective assistance of counsel, we now must consider whether this
violation of the Sixth Amendment mandates reversing appellant's conviction. . . .

On the record before us in the present case, I would conclude that
the government has failed to discharge its burden of proving that no
adverse consequences resulted from counsel's gross violations of his duties
to his client. Several important questions on the matter of prejudice
remain unanswered, and in the absence of any evidence on these critical
issues, I am unable to find that counsel's violations were "so unimportant
and insignificant" that reversing appellant's conviction would be a futile
exercise. No inquiry was made, for example, on the relationship between
counsel's failure to investigate and Decoster's decision to go to trial rather
than to seek and possibly accept a plea bargain comparable to that of his
codefendants. Nor was there exploration of whether counsel's failure to
offer any allocution at the sentencing hearing had any bearing on the
trial judge's decision to sentence Decoster to a prison term of 2-8 years
while his codefendants received only probation. . . .

Because, as this case demonstrates, ineffective representation is often
rooted in inadequate preparation, a first step that a trial judge can take
is to refuse to allow a trial to begin until he is assured that defense counsel
had conducted the necessary factual and legal investigation. The simple
question, "Is the defense ready?" may be insufficient to provide that
assurance. Instead, we should consider formalizing the procedure by
which the trial judge is informed about the extent of counsel's preparation.
Before the trial begins—or before a guilty plea is accepted—defense
counsel could submit an investigative checklist certifying that he has
conducted a complete investigation and reviewing the steps he has taken
in pretrial preparation, including what records were obtained, which

122. Anders v. California, 386 U.S. 738, 744 (1967).

witnesses were interviewed, when the defendant was consulted, and what motions were filed. Although a worksheet alone cannot assure that adequate preparation is undertaken, it may reveal gross violations of counsel's obligations; at a minimum, it should heighten defense counsel's sensitivity to the need for adequate investigation and should provide a record of counsel's asserted actions for appeal.

The trial judge's obligation does not end, however, with a determination that counsel is prepared for trial. Whenever during the course of the trial it appears that defense counsel is not properly fulfilling his obligations, the judge must take appropriate action to prevent the deprivation of the defendant's constitutional rights. "It is the judge, not counsel, who has the ultimate responsibility for the conduct of a fair and lawful trial."

My colleagues fear that judicial "inquiry and standards [may] tear the fabric of our adversary system." *But for so very many indigent defendants, the adversary system is already in shreds.* Indeed, until judges are willing to take the steps necessary to guarantee the indigent defendant "the reasonably competent assistance of an attorney acting as his diligent conscientious advocate," we will have an adversary system in name only. . . .

NOTES AND QUESTIONS

1. The full opinions in *Decoster* are too lengthy to reproduce here, but they should be consulted by those wishing to pursue these matters further. They are a goldmine of perspectives on the implications of the right to effective assistance of counsel.

2. One dominant point of disagreement between the majority opinions and the dissents appears to be the role of the defendant's probable guilt on the outcome and another whether the purported error likely would have affected the outcome. What do you think of the dissenters argument that these factors are largely irrelevant? Note that Judge Bazelon in *Decoster I* asserted that a violation of a duty must be "substantial," but how does one determine that without reference to the likely impact on outcome, and how, in turn, can that be determined without evaluating the strength of the prosecution's case?

Assuming that counsel was inadequate in *Decoster* or *Strickland*, who ought to be sanctioned and how can that be accomplished? Under what circumstances would it make sense to reverse a conviction due to ineffectiveness? Further, under what circumstances would it make sense to have an automatic reversal rule as compared to one that must be applied to the facts of each case? In a companion case to *Strickland*,

United States v. Cronic, 466 U.S. 648 (1984), the Court held that the *Strickland* criteria were to apply except where "counsel failed to function in any meaningful sense as the government's adversary," which is the only time a presumption of prejudice is warranted.

In Hill v. Lockhart, 477 U.S. 52 (1985), the defendant alleged that his guilty plea was involuntary as a result of ineffective assistance of counsel because he received erroneous information about his parole eligibility from his counsel. Counsel advised defendant that he would have to serve one-third of his time before he would be eligible for parole, whereas in fact he had to serve one-half of his time as a result of a previous conviction, of which counsel was apparently not informed by defendant. In applying *Strickland* to this case, the Court stated:

> We hold, therefore, that the two-part Strickland v. Washington test applies to challenges to guilty pleas based on ineffective assistance of counsel. In the context of guilty pleas, the first half of the Strickland v. Washington test is nothing more than a restatement of the standard of attorney competence already set forth in Tollett v. Henderson and McMann v. Richardson. The second, or "prejudice," requirement, on the other hand, focuses on whether counsel's constitutionally ineffective performance affected the outcome of the plea process. In other words, in order to satisfy the "prejudice" requirement, the defendant must show that there is a reasonable probability that, but for counsel's errors, he would not have pleaded guilty and would have insisted on going to trial.
>
> In many guilty plea cases, the "prejudice" inquiry will closely resemble the inquiry engaged in by courts reviewing ineffective assistance challenges to convictions obtained through a trial. For example, where the alleged error of counsel is a failure to investigate or discover potentially exculpatory evidence, the determination whether the error "prejudiced" the defendant by causing him to plead guilty rather than go to trial will depend on the likelihood that discovery of the evidence would have led counsel to change his recommendation as to the plea. This assessment, in turn, will depend in large part on a prediction whether the evidence likely would have changed the outcome of a trial. Similarly, where the alleged error of counsel is a failure to advise the defendant of a potential affirmative defense to the crime charged, the resolution of the "prejudice" inquiry will depend largely on whether the affirmative defense likely would have succeeded at trial. As we explained in Strickland v. Washington, these predictions of the outcome at a possible trial, where necessary, should be made objectively, without regard for the "idiosyncrasies of the particular decisionmaker." 466 U.S., at 695.
>
> In the present case the claimed error of counsel is erroneous advice as to eligibility for parole under the sentence agreed to in the plea bargain. We find it unnecessary to determine whether there may be circumstances under which erroneous advice by counsel as to parole eligibility may be

deemed constitutionally ineffective assistance of counsel, because in the present case we conclude that petitioner's allegations are insufficient to satisfy the Strickland v. Washington requirement of "prejudice." Petitioner did not allege in his habeas petition that, had counsel correctly informed him about his parole eligibility date, he would have pleaded not guilty and insisted on going to trial. He alleged no special circumstances that might support the conclusion that he placed particular emphasis on his parole eligibility in deciding whether or not to plead guilty. Indeed, petitioner's mistaken belief that he would become eligible for parole after serving one-third of his sentence would seem to have affected not only his calculation of the time he likely would serve if sentenced pursuant to the proposed plea agreement, but also his calculation of the time he likely would serve if he went to trial and were convicted.

Because petitioner in this case failed to allege the kind of "prejudice" necessary to satisfy the second half of the Strickland v. Washington test, the District Court did not err in declining to hold a hearing on petitioner's ineffective assistance of counsel claim. The judgment of the Court of Appeals is therefore affirmed.

In Kimmelman v. Morrison, 477 U.S. 365 (1986), the Court held that a habeas petitioner may raise an ineffective assistance of counsel claim founded primarily on the failure of counsel adequately to contest a fourth amendment issue, notwithstanding Stone v. Powell, discussed at page 888 infra, which forbids the raising of fourth amendment issues on habeas if the forum state provided an adequate opportunity to litigate the fourth amendment issue.

3. Regardless of when or whether reversal is an appropriate remedy for ineffectiveness, what is wrong with articulating a basic checklist of obligations for counsel and enforcing it in an appropriate fashion? The first suggestion of that idea was Grano, The Right to Counsel: Collateral Issues Affecting Due Process, 54 Minn. L. Rev. 1175, 1248 (1970). Judge Bazelon developed Grano's suggestion in his article, The Realities of *Gideon* and *Argersinger*, 64 Geo. L.J. 811 (1976). Consider his proposed list, id. at 837-838:

PRELIMINARY HEARING _____

Date

_____

Comments

_____

_____

_____

_____

_____

Official Records	*Obtained**
1. Complaint	_____
2. Bail Agency form	_____
3. Narcotics Treatment Ad. report	_____
4. Arrest warrant (affidavit)	_____
5. Search warrant (affidavit)	_____
6. Defendant's record	_____
7. PD 251	_____
8. PD 252, 253, 254	_____
9. PD 163	_____
10. Other _____	_____

Statements	*Obtained**
1. Written	_____
2. Oral	_____
3. Co-defendant	_____

Scientific Exams	AUSA *Requested*	*Obtained**
1. Mental	_____	_____
2. Fingerprints	_____	_____
3. Blood	_____	_____
4. Semen	_____	_____
5. Hair	_____	_____
6. Fiber	_____	_____
7. Pathologist	_____	_____
8. Ballistics	_____	_____
9. Chemist report	_____	_____
10. Handwriting	_____	_____
11. Other _____	_____	_____

Police Officer Witnesses	*Name & Precinct*	*Interview Obtained**
1. Arresting Officer	_____	_____
2. Mobile Crime Lab	_____	_____
3. Invest. Officer	_____	_____
4. Line-Up Officer	_____	_____
5. Search Officer	_____	_____
6. Confession Officer	_____	_____

	Name & Address	*Interview Obtained**
Other Witnesses		
1. Victim	_____	_____
2. Eyewitnesses	_____	_____
3. Other	_____	_____

Motions to be Filed (check) Comments

____1.   Suppression of Tangible Objects _____

____2.   Suppression of Statements _____

____3.   Identification _____

____4.   Severance _____

____5.   Notice of Alibi _____

____6.   Notice of Insanity Defense _____

____7.   Mental Competency Exam _____

____8.   Bond Review _____

____9.   Other _____

Defendant's Version of Events _____

_____

_____

_____

I hereby certify that the case referred to in the above work-sheet has been completely investigated and information contained therein and attached thereto is accurate to the best of my knowledge.

Date _____   *Attorney's Signature* _____

*Attached is a copy of all statements, oral or written, obtained by counsel, all documents, reports, interviews, and other materials received in the preparation of this case. A completed time sheet is also to be maintained for purposes of administrative records.

4.   Reconsider footnote 105 of Judge Bazelon's *Decoster* dissent. Did he, perhaps, simply choose a less than ideal case to make his point about the level of assistance generally obtaining in the case of indigents? In one

part of his opinion that was not reproduced, Judge Bazelon makes an argument that pretrial investigation would have at least put counsel in a position to offer effective advice concerning plea bargaining. His point is advanced considerably by the fact that Decoster's accomplices both pled guilty to lesser offenses than the offense of which Decoster was found guilty. If that is the problem, what should, or could, the remedy be?

5. One of the concerns of the Court in *Strickland* and the plurality opinions in *Decoster* was the consequences of requiring trial court supervision of trial counsel. U.S. District Judge William W. Schwarzer has written on that problem in Dealing with Incompetent Counsel—The Trial Judge's Role, 93 Harv. L. Rev. 633, 637, 638, 642-656, 659-666 (1980):

Intervention does present certain undeniable difficulties. It requires the judge to depart from his traditional neutral rule. Moreover, inquiry into counsel's litigation strategy could jeopardize the confidential relationship between counsel and client and impair the adversary process. Indeed, the mere threat of intervention may have a chilling effect on the freedom of counsel to act in the manner which he thinks will best serve his client, whether the court approves or not. But the interest in preserving the adversary process militates more strongly in favor of intervention than against it. We long ago came to accept that process as more than a game and the judge's role in it as more than that of a moderator charged with seeing that the rules of the game are observed. Inasmuch as the administration of justice is the judge's ultimate responsibility, he cannot be indifferent to events which diminish the quality of justice in his court. The propriety of sua sponte intervention is unquestioned when counsel's conduct disrupts the proceeding. Its propriety should be equally clear when counsel is manifestly incompetent. For the effect of incompetence on the administration of justice, even if less dramatic, is likely to be just as destructive.

When incompetence is so serious as to lead to reversals on appeal or to subsequent malpractice actions, the administration of justice is destabilized. Reversals and damage awards stemming from a lawyer's failure to perform adequately impair the orderliness, predictability, and fairness of the judicial process and undermine public confidence. Even where lawyers' incompetence is not so serious as to justify reversal, the administration of justice suffers if one side is not adequately represented and inadvertent defaults occur. . . .

Reservations about having trial judges openly monitor the performance of counsel, and intervene when necessary, are likely to persist. They are founded on the traditional conception of the judge's role, buttressed by the belief that criminal defendants may be better protected against the shortcomings of counsel by subsequent judicial review, since appellate judges unaffected by the adversarial battle can evaluate counsel's performance more objectively. They are also supported by an assumption that malpractice actions provide an adequate relief to clients in both criminal and civil cases. It is therefore appropriate to examine the adequacy of these alternatives to intervention. . . .

Although appellate review, founded on the reviewing court's general supervisory power over the lower courts, is broad in theory, it suffers from structural . . . limitations which reduce its effectiveness as a remedy for the violation of the right to effective counsel. The structural limitations arise because an appellate court is bound by the record of the trial court; it lacks the benefit of observing counsel in action. As a result, most of the trial lawyer's preparation and performance will be difficult to evaluate. The lifeless and fragmentary appellate record will provide few insights into, and a poor perspective of counsel's knowledge of the law, capacity to analyze and plan, and ability to conduct effective direct and cross-examination of witnesses. This problem will be magnified to the extent that the lawyer was incompetent. In such a case, the record is likely to be particularly deficient. . . .

Even if a standard for adjudicating claims of counsel incompetence could be defined, courts might be loath to reverse judgments on this ground, believing that such an action would serve little useful purpose. Appellate decisions normally establish guidelines for trial court conduct; reversals serve as a deterrent against future departures from these guidelines by the lower court. Since trial judges customarily are thought to have little control over inadequate performance by counsel, appellate courts might decide that reversal would fail to serve that purpose. . . .

Nevertheless, a different rule would reduce the administration of justice to chaos. Judgments after trial would be robbed of finality if almost any tactical decision were subject to reexamination and any significant omission of counsel a ground for a new trial. Counsel would have little incentive to employ effective trial advocacy at the first trial since errors and defaults would provide the basis for a new trial. As a consequence, the trial courts, deprived of effective advocacy, would bear a greater burden and face increasing numbers of retrials. Finally, more defendants would go free because witnesses would become unavailable and memories would fade by the time the appeal is concluded. . . .

Similarly, actions for damages based on legal malpractice are unlikely to provide effective relief to clients in . . . criminal . . . litigation. Even if the client is knowledgeable and sophisticated enough to recognize that his lawyer has failed him and that a legal malpractice action is available, and even if he has the initiative, endurance, and resources to maintain such an action, the obstacles to success are formidable. It is true that the elements of a legal malpractice claim are no different than those for other professional malpractice actions. However, establishing these elements poses a series of problems unique to legal malpractice suits.

To prove a breach of duty by his former lawyer, the client must retry the underlying litigation. This "suit within a suit" brings with it many of the difficulties and diseconomies of other kinds of after-the-fact scrutiny. . . .

Often the hardest problem is establishing that the client was damaged by counsel's incompetence. In civil cases it is well-settled that the client must prove that a more favorable outcome would have resulted but for his attorney's incompetence, proof that will often be speculative at best. The outcome of any action is subject to so many uncertainties that the causal role of counsel may defy proof. . . .

The trial judge therefore has a responsibility, grounded on and tempered by the adversary process and constitutional principles and reinforced by the absence of adequate alternatives, to ensure a fair trial by maintaining minimum standards of performance by counsel. But the judge must wield the correlative power with caution lest its exercise defeat its purpose: fairness in the administration of justice.

Assessment of an attorney's performance involves comparison with other performances ranging over a broad spectrum of skill, experience and diligence. It is influenced by the observer's perspective and his knowledge of the facts and circumstances of the case. Without that knowledge, not usually fully accessible to the trial judge, litigation strategy is difficult to evaluate. Evaluation, moreover, must eschew the trial judge's idealized conception of how he would have tried the case in favor of what could reasonably be expected. The trial judge's discretion, consequently, must be guided by an awareness that the assertion of judicial power can have serious consequences for the independence of counsel, the integrity of the attorney-client relationship, and the proper functioning of the adversary process. . . .

6. One response to the increasing concern with the level of performance by trial counsel has been calls for specialization, certification, and continuing education. See Burger, The Special Skills of Advocacy: Are Specialized Training and Certification of Advocates Essential to Our System of Justice?, 42 Fordham L. Rev. 227 (1973).

7. In Cuyler v. Sullivan, 446 U.S. 335 (1980), the Court held that ineffective assistance by retained counsel violated the constitutional right to counsel, thus disposing of the issue whether there is "state action" in such circumstances. Nonetheless, whatever the "state action" is in criminal cases generally, it is inadequate to permit an indigent to sue appointed counsel under 42 U.S.C. §1983 for damages resulting from allegedly ineffective assistance in derogation of defendant's right to counsel. In Polk County v. Dodson, 454 U.S. 312 (1981), the Court held that an attorney engaged in representing a client does not act "under color of state law." Therefore, §1983 is not applicable. Cuyler is considered further at page 272, infra.

8. One of the problems throughout the Decoster litigation was the specter of an implicit suggestion that the lawyer was under a duty to

concoct a fraudulent defense. What is the lawyer's responsibility when dealing with possibly perjurious testimony? Consider the following case.

NIX v. WHITESIDE
Certiorari to the United States Court of Appeals for the Eighth Circuit
475 U.S. 157 (1986)

CHIEF JUSTICE BURGER delivered the opinion of the Court.

We granted certiorari to decide whether the Sixth Amendment right of a criminal defendant to assistance of counsel is violated when an attorney refuses to cooperate with the defendant in presenting perjured testimony at his trial.[1]

I

A

Whiteside was convicted of second degree murder by a jury verdict which was affirmed by the Iowa courts. The killing took place on February 8, 1977 in Cedar Rapids, Iowa. Whiteside and two others went to one Calvin Love's apartment late that night, seeking marihuana. Love was in bed when Whiteside and his companions arrived; an argument between Whiteside and Love over the marihuana ensued. At one point, Love directed his girlfriend to get his "piece," and at another point got up, then returned to his bed. According to Whiteside's testimony, Love then started to reach under his pillow and moved toward Whiteside. Whiteside stabbed Love in the chest, inflicting a fatal wound.

Whiteside was charged with murder, and when counsel was appointed he objected to the lawyer initially appointed, claiming that he felt uncomfortable with a lawyer who had formerly been a prosecutor. Gary L. Robinson was then appointed and immediately began investigation. Whiteside gave him a statement that he had stabbed Love as the

1. Although courts universally condemn an attorney's assisting in presenting perjury, Courts of Appeals have taken varying approaches on how to deal with a client's insistence on presenting perjured testimony. The Seventh Circuit, for example, has held that an attorney's refusal to call the defendant as a witness did not render the conviction constitutionally infirm where the refusal to call the defendant was based on the attorney's belief that the defendant would commit perjury. United States v. Curtis, 742 F.2d 1070 (C.A.7 1984). The Third Circuit found a violation of the Sixth Amendment where the attorney could not state any basis for her belief that defendant's proposed alibi testimony was perjured. United States ex rel. Wilcox v. Johnson, 555 F.2d 115 (C.A.3 1977). See also Lowery v. Cardwell, 575 F.2d 727 (C.A.9 1978) (withdrawal request in the middle of a bench trial, immediately following defendant's testimony).

latter "was pulling a pistol from underneath the pillow on the bed." Upon questioning by Robinson, however, Whiteside indicated that he had not actually seen a gun, but that he was convinced that Love had a gun. No pistol was found on the premises; shortly after the police search following the stabbing, which had revealed no weapon, the victim's family had removed all of the victim's possessions from the apartment. Robinson interviewed Whiteside's companions who were present during the stabbing and none had seen a gun during the incident. Robinson advised Whiteside that the existence of a gun was not necessary to establish the claim of self defense, and that only a reasonable belief that the victim had a gun nearby was necessary even though no gun was actually present.

Until shortly before trial, Whiteside consistently stated to Robinson that he had not actually seen a gun, but that he was convinced that Love had a gun in his hand. About a week before trial, during preparation for direct examination, Whiteside for the first time told Robinson and his associate Donna Paulsen that he had seen something "metallic" in Love's hand. When asked about this, Whiteside responded that "in Howard Cook's case there was a gun. If I don't say I saw a gun I'm dead." Robinson told Whiteside that such testimony would be perjury and repeated that it was not necessary to prove that a gun was available but only that Whiteside reasonably believed that he was in danger. On Whiteside's insisting that he would testify that he saw "something metallic" Robinson told him, according to Robinson's testimony,

> we could not allow him to [testify falsely] because that would be perjury, and as officers of the court we would be suborning perjury if we allowed him to do it; . . . I advised him that if he did do that it would be my duty to advise the Court of what he was doing and that I felt he was committing perjury; also, that I probably would be allowed to attempt to impeach that particular testimony.

Robinson also indicated he would seek to withdraw from the representation if Whiteside insisted on committing perjury.[2]

Whiteside testified in his own defense at trial and stated that he "knew" that Love had a gun and that he believed Love was reaching for a gun and he had acted swiftly in self defense. On cross examination,

2. Whiteside's version of the events at this pretrial meeting is considerably more cryptic:

> Q.   And as you went over the questions, did the two of you come into conflict with regard to whether or not there was a weapon?
> A.   I couldn't—I couldn't say a conflict. But I got the impression at one time that maybe if I didn't go along with—with what was happening, that it was no gun being involved, maybe that he will pull out of my trial.

he admitted that he had not actually seen a gun in Love's hand. Robinson presented evidence that Love had been seen with a sawed-off shotgun on other occasions, that the police search of the apartment may have been careless, and that the victim's family had removed everything from the apartment shortly after the crime. Robinson presented this evidence to show a basis for Whiteside's asserted fear that Love had a gun.

The jury returned a verdict of second-degree murder and Whiteside moved for a new trial, claiming that he had been deprived of a fair trial by Robinson's admonitions not to state that he saw a gun or "something metallic." The trial court held a hearing, heard testimony by Whiteside and Robinson, and denied the motion. The trial court made specific findings that the facts were as related by Robinson.

The Supreme Court of Iowa affirmed respondent's conviction. That court held that the right to have counsel present all appropriate defenses does not extend to using perjury, and that an attorney's duty to a client does not extend to assisting a client in committing perjury. Relying on DR 7-102(A)(4) of the Iowa Code of Professional Responsibility for Lawyers, which expressly prohibits an attorney from using perjured testimony, and Iowa Code §721.2 (now Iowa Code §720.3 (1985)), which criminalizes subornation of perjury, the Iowa court concluded that not only were Robinson's actions permissible, but were required. The court commended "both Mr. Robinson and Ms. Paulsen for the high ethical manner in which this matter was handled."

B

Whiteside then petitioned for a writ of habeas corpus in the United States District Court for the Southern District of Iowa. In that petition Whiteside alleged that he had been denied effective assistance of counsel and of his right to present a defense by Robinson's refusal to allow him to testify as he had proposed. The District Court denied the writ. Accepting the State trial court's factual finding that Whiteside's intended testimony would have been perjurious, it concluded that there could be no grounds for habeas relief since there is no constitutional right to present a perjured defense.

The United States Court of Appeals for the Eighth Circuit reversed and directed that the writ of habeas corpus be granted. We granted certiorari, and we reverse.

II

A

The right of an accused to testify in his defense is of relatively recent origin. Until the latter part of the preceding century, criminal defendants in this country, as at common law, were considered to be disqualified from giving sworn testimony at their own trial by reason of their interest as a party to the case. Iowa was among the states that adhered to this rule of disqualification. State v. Laffer, 38 Iowa 422 (1874).

By the end of the nineteenth century, however, the disqualification was finally abolished by statute in most states and in the federal courts. Act of Mar. 16, 1878, ch. 37, 20 Stat. 30-31; see Thayer, A Chapter of Legal History in Massachusetts, 9 Harv. L. Rev. 1, 12 (1895). Although this Court has never explicitly held that a criminal defendant has a due process right to testify in his own behalf, cases in several Circuits have so held and the right has long been assumed. We have also suggested that such a right exists as a corollary to the Fifth Amendment privilege against compelled testimony, see Harris v. New York, supra, 401 U.S., at 225.

B

In Strickland v. Washington, we held that to obtain relief by way of federal habeas corpus on a claim of a deprivation of effective assistance of counsel under the Sixth Amendment, the movant must establish both serious attorney error and prejudice. To show such error, it must be established that the assistance rendered by counsel was constitutionally deficient in that "counsel made errors so serious that counsel was not functioning as 'counsel' guaranteed the defendant by the Sixth Amendment." To show prejudice, it must be established that the claimed lapses in counsel's performance rendered the trial unfair so as to "undermine confidence in the outcome" of the trial.

In *Strickland*, we acknowledged that the Sixth Amendment does not require any particular response by counsel to a problem that may arise. Rather, the Sixth Amendment inquiry is into whether the attorney's conduct was "reasonably effective." To counteract the natural tendency to fault an unsuccessful defense, a court reviewing a claim of ineffective assistance must "indulge a strong presumption that counsel's conduct falls within the wide range of reasonable professional assistance." In giving shape to the perimeters of this range of reasonable professional assistance, *Strickland* mandates that "prevailing norms of practice as reflected in American Bar Association Standards and the like . . . are guides to determining what is reasonable, but they are only guides."

Under the *Strickland* standard, breach of an ethical standard does not necessarily make out a denial of the Sixth Amendment guarantee of assistance of counsel. When examining attorney conduct, a court must be careful not to narrow the wide range of conduct acceptable under the Sixth Amendment so restrictively as to constitutionalize particular standards of professional conduct and thereby intrude into the State's proper authority to define and apply the standards of professional conduct applicable to those it admits to practice in its courts. In some future case challenging attorney conduct in the course of a state court trial, we may need to define with greater precision the weight to be given to recognized canons of ethics, the standards established by the State in statutes or professional codes, and the Sixth Amendment, in defining the proper scope and limits on that conduct. Here we need not face that question, since virtually all of the sources speak with one voice.

C

We turn next to the question presented: the definition of the range of "reasonable professional" responses to a criminal defendant client who informs counsel that he will perjure himself on the stand. We must determine whether, in this setting, Robinson's conduct fell within the wide range of professional responses to threatened client perjury acceptable under the Sixth Amendment.

In *Strickland*, we recognized counsel's duty of loyalty and his "overarching duty to advocate the defendant's cause." Ibid. Plainly, that duty is limited to legitimate, lawful conduct compatible with the very nature of a trial as a search for truth. Although counsel must take all reasonable lawful means to attain the objectives of the client, counsel is precluded from taking steps or in any way assisting the client in presenting false evidence or otherwise violating the law. This principle has consistently been recognized in most unequivocal terms by expositors of the norms of professional conduct since the first Canons of Professional Ethics were adopted by the American Bar Association in 1908. The 1908 Canon 32 provided that

> No client, corporate or individual, however powerful, nor any cause, civil or political, however important, is entitled to receive nor should any lawyer render any service or advice involving disloyalty to the law whose ministers we are, or disrespect of the judicial office, which we are bound to uphold, or corruption of any person or persons exercising a public office or private trust, or deception or betrayal of the public. . . . He must . . . observe and advise his clients to observe the statute law.

Of course, this Canon did no more than articulate centuries of accepted standards of conduct. Similarly, Canon 37, adopted in 1928, explicitly acknowledges as an exception to the attorney's duty of confidentiality a client's announced intention to commit a crime. "The announced intention of a client to commit a crime is not included within the confidences which [the attorney] is bound to respect."

These principles have been carried through to contemporary codifications of an attorney's professional responsibility. Disciplinary Rule 7-102 of the Model Code of Professional Responsibility (1980), entitled "Representing a Client Within the Bounds of the Law," provides that

> (A) In his representation of a client, a lawyer shall not: . . .
>   (4) Knowingly use perjured testimony or false evidence. . . .
>   (7) Counsel or assist his client in conduct that the lawyer knows to be illegal or fraudulent.

This provision has been adopted by Iowa, and is binding on all lawyers who appear in its courts. See Iowa Code of Professional Responsibility for Lawyers (1985). The more recent Model Rules of Professional Conduct (1983) similarly admonish attorneys to obey all laws in the course of representing a client:

> RULE 1.2 Scope of Representation . . .
>   (d) A lawyer shall not counsel a client to engage, or assist a client, in conduct that the lawyer knows is criminal or fraudulent. . . .

Both the Model Code of Professional Conduct and the Model Rules of Professional Conduct also adopt the specific exception from the attorney-client privilege for disclosure of perjury that his client intends to commit or has committed. DR 4-101(C)(3) (intention of client to commit a crime); Rule 3.3 (lawyer has duty to disclose a falsity of evidence even if disclosure compromises client confidences). Indeed, both the Model Code and the Model Rules do not merely *authorize* disclosure by counsel of client perjury; they *require* such disclosure. See Rule 3.3(a)(4); DR 7-102(B)(1); Committee on Professional Ethics and Conduct of Iowa State Bar Association v. Crary, 245 N.W.2d 298 (Iowa 1976).

These standards confirm that the legal profession has accepted that an attorney's ethical duty to advance the interests of his client is limited by an equally solemn duty to comply with the law and standards of professional conduct; it specifically ensures that the client may not use false evidence. This special duty of an attorney to prevent and disclose frauds upon the court derives from the recognition that perjury is as much a crime as tampering with witnesses or jurors by way of promises and threats, and undermines the administration of justice.

The offense of perjury was a crime recognized at common law, and has been made a felony in most states by statute, including Iowa. An attorney who aids false testimony by questioning a witness when perjurious responses can be anticipated, risks prosecution for subornation of perjury under Iowa Code §720.3 (1985).

It is universally agreed that at a minimum the attorney's first duty when confronted with a proposal for perjurious testimony is to attempt to dissuade the client from the unlawful course of conduct. Model Rules of Professional Conduct, Rule 3.3, Comment; Wolfram, Client Perjury, 50 S. Cal. L. Rev. 809, 846 (1977). A statement directly in point is found in the Commentary to the Model Rules of Professional Conduct under the heading "False Evidence":

> When false evidence is offered by the client, however, a conflict may arise between the lawyer's duty to keep the client's revelations confidential and the duty of candor to the court. Upon ascertaining that material evidence is false, the lawyer *should seek to persuade the client that the evidence should not be offered* or, if it has been offered, that its false character should immediately be disclosed. [Model Rules of Professional Conduct, Rule 3.3, Comment (1983) (emphasis added).]

The Commentary thus also suggests that an attorney's revelation of his client's perjury to the court is a professionally responsible and acceptable response to the conduct of a client who has actually given perjured testimony. Similarly, the Model Rules and the commentary, as well as the Code of Professional Responsibility adopted in Iowa expressly permit withdrawal from representation as an appropriate response of an attorney when the client threatens to commit perjury. Model Rules of Professional Conduct, Rule 1.16(a)(1), Rule 1.6, Comment (1983); Code of Professional Responsibility, DR 2-110(B), (C) (1980). Withdrawal of counsel when this situation arises at trial gives rise to many difficult questions including possible mistrial and claims of double jeopardy.[6]

---

6. In the evolution of the contemporary standards promulgated by the American Bar Association, an early draft reflects a compromise suggesting that when the disclosure of intended perjury is made during the course of trial, when withdrawal of counsel would raise difficult questions of a mistrial holding, counsel had the option to let the defendant take the stand but decline to affirmatively assist the presentation of perjury by traditional direct examination. Instead, counsel would stand mute while the defendant undertook to present the false version in narrative form in his own words unaided by any direct examination. This conduct was thought to be a signal at least to the presiding judge that the attorney considered the testimony to be false and was seeking to disassociate himself from that course. Additionally, counsel would not be permitted to discuss the known

The essence of the brief amicus of the American Bar Association reviewing practices long accepted by ethical lawyers, is that under no circumstance may a lawyer either advocate or passively tolerate a client's giving false testimony. This, of course, is consistent with the governance of trial conduct in what we have long called "a search for truth." The suggestion sometimes made that "a lawyer must believe his client not judge him" in no sense means a lawyer can honorably be a party to or in any way give aid to presenting known perjury.

D

Considering Robinson's representation of respondent in light of these accepted norms of professional conduct, we discern no failure to adhere to reasonable professional standards that would in any sense make out a deprivation of the Sixth Amendment right to counsel. Whether Robinson's conduct is seen as a successful attempt to dissuade his client from committing the crime of perjury, or whether seen as a "threat" to withdraw from representation and disclose the illegal scheme, Robinson's representation of Whiteside falls well within accepted standards of professional conduct and the range of reasonable professional conduct acceptable under *Strickland*.

The Court of Appeals assumed for the purpose of the decision that Whiteside would have given false testimony had counsel not intervened; its opinion states,

> [W]e presume that appellant would have testified falsely. . . . Counsel's actions prevented [Whiteside] from testifying falsely. We hold that counsel's action deprived appellant of due process and effective assistance of counsel. . . .
>
> Counsel's actions also impermissibly compromised appellant's right to testify in his own defense by conditioning continued representation by counsel and confidentiality upon appellant's restricted testimony. [Whiteside v. Scurr, 750 F.2d 713, 714-15 (C.A.8 1984).]

While purporting to follow the Iowa's highest court "on all questions of state law," the Court of Appeals reached its conclusions on the basis of federal constitutional due process and right to counsel.

---

false testimony in closing arguments. See ABA Standards for Criminal Justice, 4-7.7 (2d ed. 1980). Most courts treating the subject rejected this approach and insisted on a more rigorous standard, see, e.g., United States v. Curtis, 742 F.2d 1070 (C.A.7 1984). . . .
The Eighth Circuit in this case and the Ninth Circuit have expressed approval of the "free narrative" standards. Whiteside v. Scurr, 744 F.2d 1323, 1331 (C.A.8 1984); Lowery v. Cardwell, 575 F.2d 727 (C.A.9 1978).
    The Rule finally promulgated in the current Model Rules of Professional Conduct rejects any participation or passive role whatever by counsel in allowing perjury to be presented without challenge.

The Court of Appeals' holding that Robinson's "action deprived [Whiteside] of due process and effective assistance of counsel" is not supported by the record since Robinson's action, at most, deprived Whiteside of his contemplated perjury. Nothing counsel did in any way undermined Whiteside's claim that he believed the victim was reaching for a gun. Similarly, the record gives no support for holding that Robinson's action "also impermissibly compromised [Whiteside's] right to testify in his own defense by conditioning continued representation . . . and confidentiality upon [Whiteside's] *restricted* testimony." The record in fact shows the contrary: (a) that Whiteside did testify, and (b) he was "restricted" or restrained only from testifying falsely and was aided by Robinson in developing the basis for the fear that Love was reaching for a gun. Robinson divulged no client communications until he was compelled to do so in response to Whiteside's post-trial challenge to the quality of his performance. We see this as a case in which the attorney successfully dissuaded the client from committing the crime of perjury.

Paradoxically, even while accepting the conclusion of the Iowa trial court that Whiteside's proposed testimony would have been a criminal act, the Court of Appeals held that Robinson's efforts to persuade Whiteside not to commit that crime were improper, *first*, as forcing an impermissible choice between the right to counsel and the right to testify; and *second*, as compromising client confidences because of Robinson's threat to disclose the contemplated perjury.[7]

Whatever the scope of a constitutional right to testify, it is elementary that such a right does not extend to testifying *falsely*. In Harris v. New York, we assumed the right of an accused to testify "in his own defense, or to refuse to do so" and went on to hold that "that privilege cannot be construed to include the right to commit perjury. Having voluntarily taken the stand, petitioner was under an obligation to speak truthfully. . . ." 401 U.S., at 225. In *Harris* we held the defendant could be impeached by prior contrary statements which had been ruled inadmissible under Miranda v. Arizona. *Harris* and other cases make it crystal clear that there is no right whatever—constitutional or otherwise—for a defendant to use false evidence.

The paucity of authority on the subject of any such "right" may be

---

7. The Court of Appeals also determined that Robinson's efforts to persuade Whiteside to testify truthfully constituted an impermissible threat to testify against his own client. We find no support for a threat to testify against Whiteside while he was acting as counsel. The record reflects testimony by Robinson that he had admonished Whiteside that if he withdrew he "probably would be allowed to attempt to impeach that particular testimony," if Whiteside testified falsely. The trial court accepted this version of the conversation as true.

explained by the fact that such a notion has never been responsibly advanced; the right to counsel includes no right to have a lawyer who will cooperate with planned perjury. A lawyer who would so cooperate would be at risk of prosecution for suborning perjury, and disciplinary proceedings, including suspension or disbarment.

Robinson's admonitions to his client can in no sense be said to have forced respondent into an *impermissible* choice between his right to counsel and his right to testify as he proposed for there was no *permissible* choice to testify falsely. For defense counsel to take steps to persuade a criminal defendant to testify truthfully, or to withdraw, deprives the defendant of neither his right to counsel nor the right to testify truthfully. In United States v. Havens, supra, we made clear that "when defendants testify, they must testify truthfully or suffer the consequences." Id., at 626. When an accused proposes to resort to perjury or to produce false evidence, one consequence is the risk of withdrawal of counsel.

On this record, the accused enjoyed continued representation within the bounds of reasonable professional conduct and did in fact exercise his right to testify; at most he was denied the right to have the assistance of counsel in the presentation of false testimony. Similarly, we can discern no breach of professional duty in Robinson's admonition to respondent that he would disclose respondent's perjury to the court. The crime of perjury in this setting is indistinguishable in substance from the crime of threatening or tampering with a witness or a juror. A defendant who informed his counsel that he was arranging to bribe or threaten witnesses or members of the jury would have no "right" to insist on counsel's assistance or silence. Counsel would not be limited to advising against that conduct. An attorney's duty of confidentiality, which totally covers the client's admission of guilt, does not extend to a client's announced plans to engage in future criminal conduct. See Clark v. United States, 289 U.S. 1, 15 (1933). In short, the responsibility of an ethical lawyer, as an officer of the court and a key component of a system of justice, dedicated to a search for truth, is essentially the same whether the client announces an intention to bribe or threaten witnesses or jurors or to commit or procure perjury. No system of justice worthy of the name can tolerate a lesser standard.

The rule adopted by the Court of Appeals, which seemingly would require an attorney to remain silent while his client committed perjury, is wholly incompatible with the established standards of ethical conduct and the laws of Iowa and contrary to professional standards promulgated by that State. The position advocated by petitioner, on the contrary, is wholly consistent with the Iowa standards of professional conduct and law, with the overwhelming majority of courts, and with codes of professional ethics. Since there has been no breach of any recognized professional duty, it follows that there can be no deprivation of the right to assistance of counsel under the *Strickland* standard.

E

We hold that, as a matter of law, counsel's conduct complained of here cannot establish the prejudice required for relief under the second strand of the *Strickland* inquiry. Although a defendant need not establish that the attorney's deficient performance more likely than not altered the outcome in order to establish prejudice under *Strickland*, a defendant must show "that there is a reasonable probability that, but for counsel's unprofessional errors, the result of the proceeding would have been different." 466 U.S., at 694. According to *Strickland*, "[a] reasonable probability is a probability sufficient to undermine confidence in the outcome." Ibid. The *Strickland* Court noted that the "benchmark" of an ineffective assistance claim is the fairness of the adversary proceeding, and that in judging prejudice and the likelihood of a different outcome, "[a] defendant has no entitlement to the luck of a lawless decisionmaker." Id., at 695.

Whether he was persuaded or compelled to desist from perjury, Whiteside has no valid claim that confidence in the result of his trial has been diminished by his desisting from the contemplated perjury. Even if we were to assume that the jury might have believed his perjury, it does not follow that Whiteside was prejudiced.

In his attempt to evade the prejudice requirement of *Strickland*, Whiteside relies on cases involving conflicting loyalties of counsel. In Cuyler v. Sullivan, 446 U.S. 335 (1980), we held that a defendant could obtain relief without pointing to a specific prejudicial default on the part of his counsel, provided it is established that the attorney was "actively represent[ing] conflicting interests." Id., at 350.

Here, there was indeed a "conflict," but of a quite different kind; it was one imposed on the attorney by the client's proposal to commit the crime of fabricating testimony without which, as he put it, "I'm dead." This is not remotely the kind of conflict of interests dealt with in Cuyler v. Sullivan. Even in that case we did not suggest that all multiple representations necessarily resulted in an active conflict rendering the representation constitutionally infirm. If a "conflict" between a client's proposal and counsel's ethical obligation gives rise to a presumption that counsel's assistance was prejudicially ineffective, every guilty criminal's conviction would be suspect if the defendant had sought to obtain an acquittal by illegal means. Can anyone doubt what practices and problems would be spawned by such a rule and what volumes of litigation it would generate?

Whiteside's attorney treated Whiteside's proposed perjury in accord with professional standards, and since Whiteside's truthful testimony could not have prejudiced the result of his trial, the Court of Appeals was in error to direct the issuance of a writ of habeas corpus and must be reversed.

JUSTICE BRENNAN, concurring in the judgment.

This Court has no constitutional authority to establish rules of ethical conduct for lawyers practicing in the state courts. Nor does the Court enjoy any statutory grant of jurisdiction over legal ethics.

Accordingly, it is not surprising that the Court emphasizes that it "must be careful not to narrow the wide range of professional conduct acceptable under the Sixth Amendment so restrictively as to constitutionalize particular standards of professional conduct and thereby intrude into the State's proper authority to define and apply the standards of professional conduct applicable to those it admits to practice in its courts." I read this as saying in another way that the Court *cannot* tell the states or the lawyers in the states how to behave in their courts, unless and until federal rights are violated.

Unfortunately, the Court seems unable to resist the temptation of sharing with the legal community its vision of ethical conduct. But let there be no mistake: the Court's essay regarding what constitutes the correct response to a criminal client's suggestion that he will perjure himself is pure discourse without force of law. As Justice Blackmun observes, *that* issue is a thorny one, but it is not an issue presented by this case. Lawyers, judges, bar associations, students and others should understand that the problem has not now been "decided."

I join Justice Blackmun's concurrence because I agree that respondent has failed to prove the kind of prejudice necessary to make out a claim under Strickland v. Washington.

JUSTICE BLACKMUN, with whom JUSTICE BRENNAN, JUSTICE MARSHALL, and JUSTICE STEVENS join, concurring in the judgment.

How a defense attorney ought to act when faced with a client who intends to commit perjury at trial has long been a controversial issue.[1]

1. See, e.g., Callan and David, Professional Responsibility and the Duty of Confidentiality: Disclosure of Client Misconduct in an Adversary System, 29 Rutgers L. Rev. 332 (1976); Rieger, Client Perjury: A Proposed Resolution of the Constitutional and Ethical Issues, 70 Minn. L. Rev. 121 (1985); compare, e.g., Freedman, Professional Responsibility of the Criminal Defense Lawyer; The Three Hardest Questions, 64 Mich. L. Rev. 1469 (1966), and ABA Standards for Criminal Justice, Proposed Standard 4-7.7 (2d ed. 1980) (approved by the Standing Committee on Association Standards for Criminal

But I do not believe that a federal habeas corpus case challenging a state criminal conviction is an appropriate vehicle for attempting to resolve this thorny problem. When a defendant argues that he was denied effective assistance of counsel because his lawyer dissuaded him from committing perjury, the only question properly presented to this Court is whether the lawyer's actions deprived the defendant of the fair trial which the Sixth Amendment is meant to guarantee. Since I believe that the respondent in this case suffered no injury justifying federal habeas relief, I concur in the Court's judgment. . . .

II

A

The District Court found that the trial judge's statement that "I find the facts to be as testified to by Ms. Paulsen and Mr. Robinson" was a factual finding that Whiteside "would have perjured himself if he had testified at trial that he actually saw a gun in his victim's hand." This factual finding by the state court is entitled to a presumption of correctness under 28 U.S.C. §2254(d), which Whiteside has not overcome.

Respondent has never attempted to rebut the presumption by claiming that the fact-finding procedure employed by Iowa in considering new trial motions in any sense deprived him of a full and fair hearing or failed to provide a sufficient basis for denying his motion.[3] Although respondent's argument to this Court in large part assumes that the precluded testimony would have been false, he contends, first, that the record does not fairly support the conclusion that he intended to perjure himself because he claimed in his first written statement that Love had been pulling a pistol from under a pillow at the time of the stabbing, and, second, that whether Robinson had sufficient knowledge to conclude he

---

Justice, but not yet submitted to the House of Delegates), with Noonan, The Purposes of Advocacy and the Limits of Confidentiality, 64 Mich. L. Rev. 1485 (1966), and ABA Model Rules of Professional Conduct, Rule 3.3 and comment, at 66-67 (1983).

3. Whiteside's motion for a new trial rested on his recantation of his testimony at trial. As a matter of Iowa law, when a trial judge is faced with a motion for a new trial based on a witness' recantation of his trial testimony, the judge must decide whether the recantation is believable:

"The trial court is not required to believe the recantation, but must make its decision on the basis of the whole trial and the matters presented on the hearing on the motion. Premised thereon, if it believes the [post conviction] statements . . . are false, and is not reasonably well satisfied that the testimony given by the witness on the trial was false, it should deny the motion, and it is not at liberty to shift upon the shoulders of another jury the responsibility to seek out the truth of that matter." State v. Compiano, 261 Iowa 509, 517, 154 N.W.2d 845, 849 (1967).

was going to commit perjury was a mixed question of law and fact to which the presumption of correctness does not apply.

Neither contention overcomes the presumption of correctness due the state court's finding. First, the trial judge's implicit decision not to credit the written statement is fairly supported by Robinson's testimony that the written statement had not been prepared by Whiteside alone and that, from the time of their initial meeting until the week before trial, Whiteside never again claimed to have seen a gun. Second, the finding properly accorded a presumption of correctness by the courts below was that Whiteside's "proposed testimony would [have been] deliberately untruthful." The lower courts did not purport to presume the correctness of the Iowa Supreme Court's holding concerning the mixed question respondent identifies—whether Robinson's response to Whiteside's proposed testimony deprived Whiteside of effective representation.

B

The Court approaches this case as if the performance and prejudice standard requires us in every case to determine "the perimeters of [the] range of reasonable professional assistance," but Strickland v. Washington explicitly contemplates a different course:

> Although we have discussed the performance component of an ineffectiveness claim prior to the prejudice component, there is no reason for a court deciding an ineffective assistance claim to approach the inquiry in the same order or even to address both components of the inquiry if the defendant makes an insufficient showing on one. In particular, a court need not determine whether counsel's performance was deficient before examining the prejudice suffered by the defendant as a result of the alleged deficiencies. . . . If it is easier to dispose of an ineffectiveness claim on the ground of lack of sufficient prejudice, which we expect will often be so, that course should be followed.

In this case, respondent has failed to show any legally cognizable prejudice. Nor, as is discussed below, is this a case in which prejudice should be presumed.

The touchstone of a claim of prejudice is an allegation that counsel's behavior did something "to deprive the defendant of a fair trial, a trial whose result is reliable." Strickland v. Washington, 466 U.S., at 687. The only effect Robinson's threat had on Whiteside's trial is that Whiteside did not testify, falsely, that he saw a gun in Love's hand.[4] Thus, this

---

4. This is not to say that a lawyer's threat to reveal his client's confidences may never have other effects on a defendant's trial. Cf. United States ex rel. Wilcox v. Johnson, 555 F.2d 115 (C.A.3 1977) (finding a violation of Sixth Amendment when an attorney's threat to reveal client's purported perjury caused defendant not to take the stand at all).

Court must ask whether its confidence in the outcome of Whiteside's trial is in any way undermined by the knowledge that he refrained from presenting false testimony.

This Court long ago noted: "All perjured relevant testimony is at war with justice, since it may produce a judgment not resting on truth. Therefore it cannot be denied that it tends to defeat the sole ultimate objective of a trial." In re Michael, 326 U.S. 224, 227 (1945). When the Court has been faced with a claim by a defendant concerning prosecutorial use of such evidence, it has "consistently held that a conviction obtained by the knowing use of perjured testimony is fundamentally unfair, and must be set aside if there is any reasonable likelihood that the false testimony could have affected the judgment of the jury" (footnote omitted). United States v. Agurs, 427 U.S. 97, 103 (1976). Similarly, the Court has viewed a defendant's use of such testimony as so antithetical to our system of justice that it has permitted the prosecution to introduce otherwise inadmissible evidence to combat it. The proposition that presenting false evidence could contribute to (or that withholding such evidence could detract from) the reliability of a criminal trial is simply untenable.

It is no doubt true that juries sometimes have acquitted defendants who should have been convicted, and sometimes have based their decisions to acquit on the testimony of defendants who lied on the witness stand. It is also true that the Double Jeopardy Clause bars the reprosecution of such acquitted defendants, although on occasion they can be prosecuted for perjury. But the privilege every criminal defendant has to testify in his own defense "cannot be construed to include the right to commit perjury." Harris v. New York, 401 U.S., at 225.[5] To the extent that Whiteside's claim rests on the assertion that he would have been acquitted had he been able to testify falsely, Whiteside claims a right the law simply does not recognize. Since Whiteside was deprived of neither

5. Whiteside was not deprived of the right to testify in his own defense, since no suggestion has been made that Whiteside's testimony was restricted in any way beyond the fact that he did not claim, falsely, to have seen a gun in Love's hand.

I must confess that I am somewhat puzzled by the Court's implicit suggestion that whether a defendant has a constitutional right to testify in his own defense remains an open question. It is true that in Ferguson v. Georgia, 365 U.S. 570 (1961), the Court expressly declined to address the question of a defendant's constitutional right to testify, but that was because the case did not properly raise the issue. Since then, the Court repeatedly has referred to the existence of such a right. See, e.g., Jones v. Barnes, 463 U.S. 745, (1983) (the defendant has the "ultimate authority to make certain fundamental decisions regarding the case, [such as] . . . whether to . . . testify in his or her own behalf"); Brooks v. Tennessee, 406 U.S. 605, 612 (1972) ("Whether the defendant is to testify is an important tactical decision as well as a matter of constitutional right."); Harris v. New York, supra. I cannot imagine that if we were presented with a state statute that prohibited a defendant from testifying at his own trial, we would not rule that it violates both the Sixth and Fourteenth Amendments, as well as, perhaps, the Fifth.

a fair trial nor any of the specific constitutional rights designed to guarantee a fair trial, he has suffered no prejudice.

The Court of Appeals erred in concluding that prejudice should have been presumed. Strickland v. Washington found such a presumption appropriate in a case where an attorney labored under "an actual conflict of interest [that] adversely affected his . . . performance." In this case, however, no actual conflict existed. I have already discussed why Whiteside had no right to Robinson's help in presenting perjured testimony. Moreover, Whiteside has identified no right to insist that Robinson keep confidential a plan to commit perjury. See Committee on Professional Ethics and Conduct of the Iowa State Bar Association v. Crary, 245 N.W.2d 298, 306 (Iowa 1976). The prior cases where this Court has reversed convictions involved conflicts that infringed a defendant's legitimate interest in vigorous protection of his constitutional rights. Here, Whiteside had no legitimate interest that conflicted with Robinson's obligations not to suborn perjury and to adhere to the Iowa Code of Professional Responsibility.

In addition, the lawyer's interest in not presenting perjured testimony was entirely consistent with Whiteside's best interest. If Whiteside had lied on the stand, he would have risked a future perjury prosecution. Moreover, his testimony would have been contradicted by the testimony of other eyewitnesses and by the fact that no gun was ever found. In light of that impeachment, the jury might have concluded that Whiteside lied as well about his lack of premeditation and thus might have convicted him of first-degree murder. And if the judge believed that Whiteside had lied, he could have taken Whiteside's perjury into account in setting the sentence. United States v. Grayson, 438 U.S. 41, 52-54 (1978).[6] In the face of these dangers, an attorney could reasonably conclude that dissuading his client from committing perjury was in the client's best interest and comported with standards of professional responsibility.[7] In short, Whiteside failed to show the kind of conflict that poses a danger to the values of zealous and loyal representation embodied in the Sixth Amendment. A presumption of prejudice is therefore unwarranted.

---

6. In fact, the State apparently asked the trial court to impose a sentence of 75 years, see Tr. 4 (Aug. 26 1977), but the judge sentenced Whiteside to 40 years' imprisonment instead.

7. This is not to say that an attorney's ethical obligations will never conflict with a defendant's right to effective assistance. For example, an attorney who has previously represented one of the State's witnesses has a continuing obligation to that former client not to reveal confidential information received during the course of the prior representation. That continuing duty could conflict with his obligation to his present client, the defendant, to cross-examine the State's witnesses zealously. See Lowenthal, Successive Representation by Criminal Lawyers, 93 Yale L.J. 1 (1983).

C

In light of respondent's failure to show any cognizable prejudice, I see no need to "grade counsel's performance." The only federal issue in this case is whether Robinson's behavior deprived Whiteside of the effective assistance of counsel; it is not whether Robinson's behavior conformed to any particular code of legal ethics.

Whether an attorney's response to what he sees as a client's plan to commit perjury violates a defendant's Sixth Amendment rights may depend on many factors: how certain the attorney is that the proposed testimony is false, the stage of the proceedings at which the attorney discovers the plan, or the ways in which the attorney may be able to dissuade his client, to name just three. The complex interaction of factors, which is likely to vary from case to case, makes inappropriate a blanket rule that defense attorneys must reveal, or threaten to reveal, a client's anticipated perjury to the court. Except in the rarest of cases, attorneys who adopt "the role of the judge or jury to determine the facts," United States ex rel. Wilcox v. Johnson, 555 F.2d 115, 122 (CA3 1977), pose a danger of depriving their clients of the zealous and loyal advocacy required by the Sixth Amendment.[8]

I therefore am troubled by the Court's implicit adoption of a set of standards of professional responsibility for attorneys in state criminal proceedings. The States, of course, do have a compelling interest in the integrity of their criminal trials that can justify regulating the length to which an attorney may go in seeking his client's acquittal. But the American Bar Association's implicit suggestion in its brief amicus curiae that the Court find that the Association's Model Rules of Professional Conduct should govern an attorney's responsibilities is addressed to the wrong audience. It is for the States to decide how attorneys should conduct themselves in state criminal proceedings, and this Court's responsibility extends only to ensuring that the restrictions a State enacts do not infringe a defendant's federal constitutional rights. Thus, I would follow the suggestion made in the joint brief amici curiae filed by 37 States at the

---

8. A comparison of this case with *Wilcox* is illustrative. Here, Robinson testified in detail to the factors that led him to conclude that respondent's assertion he had seen a gun was false. See, e.g., Tr. 38-39, 43, 59 (July 29, 1977). The Iowa Supreme Court found "good cause" and "strong support" for Robinson's conclusion. State v. Whiteside, 272 N.W.2d, at 471. Moreover, Robinson gave credence to those parts of Whiteside's account which, although he found them implausible and unsubstantiated, were not clearly false. See Tr. 52-53 (July 29, 1977). By contrast, in *Wilcox*, where defense counsel actually informed the judge that she believed her client intended to lie and where her threat to withdraw in the middle of the trial led the defendant not to take the stand at all, the Court of Appeals found "no evidence on the record of this case indicating that Mr. Wilcox intended to perjure himself," and characterized counsel's beliefs as "private conjectures about the guilt or innocence of [her] client." 522 F.2d, at 122.

certiorari stage that we allow the States to maintain their "differing approaches" to a complex ethical question. Brief for the State of Indiana, et al., as Amici Curiae 5. The signal merit of asking first whether a defendant has shown any adverse prejudicial effect before inquiring into his attorney's performance is that it avoids unnecessary federal interference in a State's regulation of its bar. Because I conclude that the respondent in this case failed to show such an effect, I join the Court's judgment that he is not entitled to federal habeas relief.

[JUSTICE STEVENS' concurring opinion is omitted.]

NOTES AND QUESTIONS

1. The classic contributions to the debate over defense counsel's obligations are Freedman, Professional Responsibility of the Criminal Defense Lawyer: The Three Hardest Questions, 64 Mich. L. Rev. 1469, and Noonan, The Purposes of Advocacy and the Limits of Confidentiality, 64 Mich. L. Rev. 1485 (1966). This debate will not be still by either the Supreme Court's decision in Nix nor the ABA's promulgating the Model Rules of Professional Conduct. For a sample of the robust debate, see M. Frankel, Partisan Justice (1980); Alschuler, The Preservation of a Client's Confidences: One Value Among Many or a Categorical Imperative?, 52 U. Colo. L. Rev. 349 (1981); and Pizzi, Judge Frankel and the Adversary System, 52 U. Colo. L. Rev. 357 (1981).

2. Both federal and state governments have become increasingly aggressive toward defense counsel. For example, defense counsel are more frequently being subpoenaed to provide information potentially relevant to criminal investigations. For an exhaustive discussion, see Suni, Subpoenas to Criminal Defense Lawyers: A Proposal for Limits, 65 Or. L. Rev. 215 (1986). In some cases, Justice Department attorneys have encouraged defense counsel to provide damaging information about clients, although efforts have been taken to reduce the likelihood of violations of the attorney-client privilege. For an example, see United States v. Ofshe, 817 F.2d 1508 (11th Cir. 1987). The Symposium, Limitations on the Effectiveness of Criminal Defense Counsel, 136 U. Pa. L. Rev. 1779 (1988), contains a discussion of the Ofshe case by Professor Uviller, as well as many other interesting contributions.

2. Multiple Representation

A special problem of effective assistance arises in cases where a lawyer represents more than one client in either joint or separate proceedings.

The difficulty results from the potential conflict of interest among the defendants. In separate trials of accomplices, for example, a lawyer will have to choose whether to call certain potentially exculpating witnesses at the first trial. If the lawyer chooses not to call the witnesses, the defense in the present case will be impaired in order to protect the defense in the later trial. If, on the other hand, the witnesses are called, the defense at the first trial will be bolstered at the cost to the defense at the second trial of exposing to the prosecution the contents of the defendant's case. Moreover, it is the lawyer, who owes the duty of essentially undivided allegiance to the client, who will have to make the choices. Obviously, the necessity of making such choices compromises the faithful discharge of the duty and may impact adversely on the client's interests.

The problems are exacerbated in joint proceedings. Consider the following passage from Lowenthal, Joint Representation in Criminal Cases: A Critical Appraisal, 64 Va. L. Rev. 939, 941-942 (1978):

> An attorney appeared in a municipal court for the purpose of requesting a reduction of bail for four defendants jointly charged with possession of a large cache of drugs seized from a communal house. Referring to the first of his clients, the lawyer stated: "This defendant should be released on his own recognizance, Your Honor, because he has no rap sheet. Obviously he is not a hardened criminal and should not be locked up with others who are." When the second defendant's case was called, counsel argued: "No drugs were found in this defendant's bedroom, Your Honor. His chance for an acquittal is great and consequently it is highly likely that he will show up for trial." On behalf of the third defendant, the lawyer began to argue that his client had lived in the area all of his life. The judge interrupted the lawyer, asking him if any drugs had been seized from the bedroom of defendant number three. The lawyer responded. "No comment, Your Honor." The judge countered with the remark: "I suppose that this client also has a prior record, making him a hardened criminal," evoking the response that although the defendant had a prior record, he certainly was not a hardened criminal. The fourth defendant then interrupted the proceedings by eagerly requesting to be represented by the public defender.[11] . . .
>
> The episode related above illustrates a circumstance of the criminal process that is essential to an understanding of joint representation in practice. Decisionmakers exercise considerable discretion in evaluating and

11. This incident occurred in March 1972, before Judge Jacqueline Taber in Department Six of the Oakland-Piedmont Municipal Court, Oakland, California, when I was an Assistant Public Defender for Alameda County, California. See Letter from Judge Jacqueline Taber to Gary T. Lowenthal (Oct. 23, 1978) (copy on file with the Virginia Law Review Association). It is the most vivid of many such incidents that prompted me to write this article.

comparing defendants at every stage of a criminal case. The government, for example, has substantial leeway in determining which charges, if any, to file against an accused; a judge or magistrate may consider a broad range of factors when predicting whether a defendant will appear in court if released on bail; the prosecutor's discretion in plea bargaining is almost unlimited in most jurisdictions; a trier of fact is free to ignore the evidence in acquitting the defendant; and a judge or jury is expected to differentiate among convicted offenders to arrive at an appropriate sentence for each. At each step in the process, a defendant's appearance, attitude, and background, as well as the extent of his culpability, will influence decisionmakers. As a result, a lawyer's effectiveness in representing a client will depend in virtually every case on how well he can manipulate these factors to the advantage of the client. Thus the lawyer must differentiate his client from others charged with the same or similar conduct and emphasize those attributes of his client that will have a favorable effect on the prosecutor, judge, or jury.

As Professor Lowenthal proceeds to point out in great detail, the ability of the lawyer to distinguish one client from another is greatly compromised in cases of joint representation. See also Geer, Representation of Multiple Criminal Defendants: Conflicts of Interest and the Professional Responsibilities of the Defense Attorney, 62 Minn. L. Rev. 119 (1978). Yet joint representation may offer advantages at times. As Justice Frankfurter noted: "Joint representation is a means of insuring against reciprocal recrimination. A common defense often gives strength against a common attack." Glasser v. United States, 315 U.S. 60, 92 (1942) (Frankfurter, J., dissenting). The question thus arises whether there are circumstances that render joint representation so defective as to violate the right to counsel, and at least where joint representation is forced on defendants, the answer is yes.

The seminal decision is Glasser v. United States, supra, which is concisely summarized in the second major Supreme Court opinion analyzing these problems, Holloway v. Arkansas, 435 U.S. 475 (1978):

> More than 35 years ago, in Glasser v. United States, 315 U.S. 60 (1942), this Court held that by requiring an attorney to represent two codefendants whose interests were in conflict the District Court had denied one of the defendants his Sixth Amendment right to the effective assistance of counsel. In that case the Government tried five codefendants in a joint trial for conspiracy to defraud the United States. Two of the defendants, Glasser and Kretske, were represented initially by separate counsel. On the second day of trial, however, Kretske became dissatisfied with his attorney and dismissed him. The District Judge thereupon asked Glasser's attorney, Stewart, if he would also represent Kretske. Stewart responded by noting a possible conflict of interests: His representation of both Glasser and

Kretske might lead the jury to link the two men together. Glasser also made known that he objected to the proposal. The District Court nevertheless appointed Stewart, who continued as Glasser's retained counsel, to represent Kretske. Both men were convicted.

Glasser contended in this Court that Stewart's representation at trial was ineffective because of a conflict between the interests of his two clients. This Court held that "the 'assistance of counsel' guaranteed by the Sixth Amendment contemplates that such assistance be untrammeled and unimpaired by a court order requiring that one lawyer should simultaneously represent conflicting interests." Id., at 70. The record disclosed that Stewart failed to cross-examine a Government witness whose testimony linked Glasser with the conspiracy and failed to object to the admission of arguably inadmissible evidence. This failure was viewed by the Court as a result of Stewart's desire to protect Kretske's interests, and was thus "indicative of Stewart's struggle to serve two masters. . . ." Id., at 75. After identifying this conflict of interests, the Court declined to inquire whether the prejudice flowing from it was harmless and instead ordered Glasser's conviction reversed.

In *Holloway*, the Court reversed a conviction on the basis of *Glasser* in circumstances that effectively highlight the difficulties of joint representation as well as the apparent shocking insensitivity to fundamental fairness that some observers feel still characterizes too many of our trial courts. In *Holloway*, a single public defender was appointed to represent three co-defendants. Counsel moved the court to appoint separate counsel because of a possibility of conflict of interest. He later renewed his motion "on the grounds that one or two of the defendants may testify and, if they do, then I will not be able to cross-examine them because I have received confidential information from them." To which, the trial court responded: "I don't know why you wouldn't," and denied the motion. 435 U.S. at 478. Now, consider the following dialogue:

> On the second day of trial, after the prosecution had rested its case, Hall [trial counsel] advised the court that, against his recommendation, all three defendants had decided to testify. He then stated:
>
>> Now, since I have been appointed, I had previously filed a motion asking the Court to appoint a separate attorney for each defendant because of a possible conflict of interest. This conflict will probably be now coming up since each one of them wants to testify.
>>
>> *The Court:* That's all right; let them testify. There is no conflict of interest. Every time I try more than one person in this court each one blames it on the other one.
>> *Mr. Hall:* I have talked to each one of these defendants, and I have talked to them individually, not collectively.
>> *The Court:* Now talk to them collectively.

The court then indicated satisfaction that each petitioner understood the nature and consequences of his right to testify on his own behalf, whereupon Hall observed:

> I am in a position now where I am more or less muzzled as to any cross-examination.
>
> *The Court:*   You have no right to cross-examine your own witness.
>
> *Mr. Hall:*   Or to examine them.
>
> *The Court:*   You have a right to examine them, but have no right to cross-examine them. The prosecuting attorney does that.
>
> *Mr. Hall:*   If one [defendant] takes the stand, somebody needs to protect the other two's interest while that one is testifying, and I can't do that since I have talked to each one individually.
>
> *The Court:*   Well, you have talked to them, I assume, individually and collectively, too. They all say they want to testify. I think it's perfectly alright [*sic*] for them to testify if they want to, or not. It's their business. . . . Each defendant said he wants to testify, and there will be no cross-examination of these witnesses, just a direct examination by you.
>
> *Mr. Hall:*   Your Honor, I can't even put them on direct examination because if I ask them—
>
> *The Court:*   (Interposing) You can just put them on the stand and tell the Court that you have advised them of their rights and they want to testify; then you tell the man to go ahead and relate what he wants to. That's all you need to do.

Holloway took the stand on his own behalf, testifying that during the time described as the time of the robbery he was at his brother's home. His brother had previously given similar testimony. When Welch, a co-defendant, took the witness stand, the record shows Hall advised him, as he had Holloway, that "I cannot ask you any questions that might tend to incriminate any one of the three of you. . . . Now, the only thing I can say is tell these ladies and gentlemen of the jury what you know about this case." Welch responded that he did not "have any kind of speech ready for the jury or anything. I thought I was going to be questioned." When Welch denied, from the witness stand, that he was at the restaurant the night of the robbery, Holloway interrupted, asking:

> Your Honor, are we allowed to make an objection?
>
> *The Court:*   No, sir. Your counsel will take care of any objections.
>
> *Mr. Hall:*   Your Honor, that is what I am trying to say. I can't cross-examine them.
>
> *The Court:*   You proceed like I tell you to, Mr. Hall. You have no right to cross-examine your own witness anyhow. [Id. at 478-480.]

Because of the actions of the trial court in *Holloway*, the Supreme Court reversed, but its opinion is unenlightening in several crucial respects, as is summarized by Professor Tague in Multiple Representation and Conflicts of Interest in Criminal Cases, 67 Geo. L.J. 1075, 1086-1087 (1979):

> The decisions in both *Glasser* and *Holloway*, however, begged the crucial issue of identifying what acts or omissions by a trial judge "force" counsel on an unwilling defendant. Although the remarkable insensitivity of the Arkansas trial judge made the Court's decision to reverse understandable, the Court left the role of counsel and of the trial court undefined. What must counsel do to trigger the trial court's obligation to inquire? Is it enough if counsel identifies the nature of the conflict in generic terms, as Hall had done, or must counsel identify the relevant disciplinary rules or facts that create the conflict? With respect to counsel's obligation to identify the conflict, for example, the Court said that Hall could have explained the conflict more clearly, but did not indicate what other information would have proven helpful or how far Hall could have gone without violating the attorney-client privilege. Further, must the trial court accept counsel's claim that a conflict exists or may it probe to satisfy itself that a conflict does exist? If the trial court may inquire, may it question the defendants as well as counsel? On these points, the Court vacillated. Although it approved accepting counsel's claim and appointing separate counsel without inquiry, it did not "preclude" inquiry into the sufficiency of counsel's representations. If the court can inquire, what does it do if met with counsel's refusal to amplify his claim on the ground of privilege? Similarly, the Court did not address whether the trial court could evaluate the conflict, as stated by counsel or as inferred by the court, to determine if it was de minimis on the facts of the given case and therefore did not require separate counsel.

How many of those questions did the Court answer two years later? Read the following case.

CUYLER v. SULLIVAN

Certiorari to the United States Court of Appeals for the Third Circuit
446 U.S. 335 (1980)

MR. JUSTICE POWELL delivered the opinion of the Court.

I

Respondent John Sullivan was indicted with Gregory Carchidi and Anthony DiPasquale for the first-degree murders of John Gorey and Rita Janda. The victims, a labor official and his companion, were shot to death in Gorey's second-story office at the Philadelphia headquarters of Teamsters' Local 107. Francis McGrath, a janitor, saw the three defendants in the building just before the shooting. They appeared to be awaiting someone, and they encouraged McGrath to do his work on another day. McGrath ignored their suggestions. Shortly afterward, Gorey arrived and went to his office. McGrath then heard what sounded like firecrackers exploding in rapid succession. Carchidi, who was in the room where McGrath was working, abruptly directed McGrath to leave the building and to say nothing. McGrath hastily complied. When he returned to the building about 15 minutes later, the defendants were gone. The victims' bodies were discovered the next morning.

Two privately retained lawyers, G. Fred DiBona and A. Charles Peruto, represented all three defendants throughout the state proceedings that followed the indictment. Sullivan had different counsel at the medical examiner's inquest, but he thereafter accepted representation from the two lawyers retained by his codefendants because he could not afford to pay his own lawyer.[1] At no time did Sullivan or his lawyers object to the multiple representation. Sullivan was the first defendant to come to trial. The evidence against him was entirely circumstantial, consisting primarily of McGrath's testimony. At the close of the Commonwealth's case, the defense rested without presenting any evidence. The jury found Sullivan guilty and fixed his penalty at life imprisonment. . . . Sullivan's codefendants, Carchidi and DiPasquale, were acquitted at separate trials.

Sullivan then petitioned for collateral relief. . . . He alleged, among other claims, that he had been denied effective assistance of counsel because his defense lawyers represented conflicting interests. In five days of hearings, the Court of Common Pleas heard evidence from Sullivan, Carchidi, Sullivan's lawyers, and the judge who presided at Sullivan's trial.

DiBona and Peruto had different recollections of their roles at the trials of the three defendants. DiBona testified that he and Peruto had been "associate counsel" at each trial. . . . Peruto recalled that he had been chief counsel for Carchidi and DiPasquale, but that he merely had assisted DiBona in Sullivan's trial. DiBona and Peruto also gave conflicting accounts of the decision to rest Sullivan's defense. DiBona said he had encouraged Sullivan to testify even though the Commonwealth had presented a very weak case. Peruto remembered that he had not "want[ed] the defense to go on because I thought we would only be exposing the [defense] witnesses for the other two trials that were coming

---

1. DiBona and Peruto were paid in part with funds raised by friends of the three defendants. The record does not disclose the source of the balance of their fee, but no part of the money came from either Sullivan or his family. See United States ex rel. Sullivan v. Cuyler, 593 F.2d 512, 518, and n.7 (C.A.3 1979).

up." . . . Sullivan testified that he had deferred to his lawyers' decision not to present evidence for the defense. But other testimony suggested that Sullivan preferred not to take the stand because cross-examination might have disclosed an extramarital affair. Finally, Carchidi claimed he would have appeared at Sullivan's trial to rebut McGrath's testimony about Carchidi's statement at the time of the murders.

The Court of Common Pleas . . . did not pass directly on the claim that defense counsel had a conflict of interest, but it found that counsel fully advised Sullivan about his decision not to testify. . . . All other claims for collateral relief were rejected or reserved for consideration in the new appeal.

The Pennsylvania Supreme Court affirmed both Sullivan's original conviction and the denial of collateral relief. . . .

Having exhausted his state remedies, Sullivan sought habeas corpus relief in the United States District Court for the Eastern District of Pennsylvania. The petition was referred to a Magistrate, who found that Sullivan's defense counsel had represented conflicting interests. The District Court, however, accepted the Pennsylvania Supreme Court's conclusion that there had been no multiple representation. The court also found that, assuming there had been multiple representation, the evidence adduced in the state postconviction proceeding revealed no conflict of interest. . . .

The Court of Appeals for the Third Circuit reversed. . . . We granted certiorari to consider recurring issues left unresolved by Holloway v. Arkansas. We now vacate and remand. . . .

IV

We come . . . to Sullivan's claim that he was denied the effective assistance of counsel guaranteed by the Sixth Amendment because his lawyers had a conflict of interest. The claim raises two issues expressly reserved in Holloway v. Arkansas, 435 U.S., at 483-484. The first is whether a state trial judge must inquire into the propriety of multiple representation even though no party lodges an objection. The second is whether the mere possibility of a conflict of interest warrants the conclusion that the defendant was deprived of his right to counsel.

A

In *Holloway*, a single public defender represented three defendants at the same trial. The trial court refused to consider the appointment of separate counsel despite the defense lawyer's timely and repeated assertions that the interests of his clients conflicted. This Court recognized that a lawyer forced to represent codefendants whose interests conflict cannot provide the adequate legal assistance required by the Sixth Amendment. Given the trial court's failure to respond to timely objections, however, the Court did not consider whether the alleged conflict actually existed. It simply held that the trial court's error unconstitutionally endangered the right to counsel.

Holloway requires state trial courts to investigate timely objections to multiple representation. But nothing in our precedents suggests that the Sixth Amendment requires state courts themselves to initiate inquiries into the propriety of multiple representation in every case.[10] Defense counsel have an ethical obligation to avoid conflicting representations and to advise the court promptly when a conflict of interest arises during the course of trial.[11] Absent special circumstances, therefore, trial courts

---

10. In certain cases, proposed Federal Rule of Criminal Procedure 44(c) provides that the federal district courts "shall promptly inquire with respect to . . . joint representation and shall personally advise each defendant of his right to the effective assistance of counsel, including separate representation." See also ABA Project on Standards for Criminal Justice, Function of the Trial Judge §3.4(b) (App. Draft 1972).

Several Courts of Appeals already invoke their supervisory power to require similar inquiries. As our promulgation of Rule 44(c) suggests, we view such an exercise of the supervisory power as a desirable practice. See generally Schwarzer, Dealing with Incompetent Counsel—The Trial Judge's Role, 93 Harv. L. Rev. 633, 653-654 (1980).

Although some Circuits have said explicitly that the Sixth Amendment does not require an inquiry into the possibility of conflicts, a recent opinion in the Second Circuit held otherwise, Colon v. Fogg, 603 F.2d 403, 407 (1979).

11. ABA Code of Professional Responsibility, D.R. 5-105, E.C. 5-15 (1976); ABA Project on Standards for Criminal Justice, Defense Function §3.5 (b) (App. Draft 1971).

Seventy percent of the public defender offices responding to a recent survey reported a strong policy against undertaking multiple representation in criminal cases. Forty-nine percent of the offices responding never undertake such representation. Lowenthal, Joint Representation in Criminal Cases: A Critical Appraisal, 64 Va. L. Rev. 939, 950, and n.40 (1978). The private bar may be less alert to the importance of avoiding multiple representation in criminal cases. See Geer, Representation of Multiple Criminal Defendants: Conflicts of Interest and the Professional Responsibilities of the Defense Attorney, 62 Minn. L. Rev. 119, 152-157 (1978); Lowenthal, supra, at 961-963. [Also, see A.B.A. Model Rule of Professional Conduct:

RULE 1.7. Conflict of Interest: General Rule

(a) A lawyer shall not represent a client if the representation of that client will be directly adverse to another client, unless:

(1) the lawyer reasonably believes the representation will not adversely affect the relationship with the other client; and

(2) each client consents after consultation.

(b) A lawyer shall not represent a client if the representation of that client may be materially limited by the lawyer's responsibilities to another client or to a third person, or by the lawyer's own interests, unless:

(1) the lawyer reasonably believes the representation will not be adversely affected; and

(2) the client consents after consultation. When representation of multiple

may assume either that multiple representation entails no conflict or that the lawyer and his clients knowingly accept such risk of conflict as may exist. Indeed, as the Court noted in *Holloway*, trial courts necessarily rely in large measure upon the good faith and good judgment of defense counsel. "An 'attorney representing two defendants in a criminal matter is in the best position professionally and ethically to determine when a conflict of interest exists or will probably develop in the course of a trial.' "

Nothing in the circumstances of this case indicates that the trial court had a duty to inquire whether there was a conflict of interest. The provision of separate trials for Sullivan and his codefendants significantly reduced the potential for a divergence in their interests. No participant in Sullivan's trial ever objected to the multiple representation. DiBona's opening argument for Sullivan outlined a defense compatible with the view that none of the defendants was connected with the murders. . . . The opening argument also suggested that counsel was not afraid to call witnesses whose testimony might be needed at the trials of Sullivan's codefendants. . . . Finally, as the Court of Appeals noted, counsel's critical decision to rest Sullivan's defense was on its face a reasonable tactical response to the weakness of the circumstantial evidence presented by the prosecutor. On these facts, we conclude that the Sixth Amendment imposed upon the trial court no affirmative duty to inquire into the propriety of multiple representation.

B

Holloway reaffirmed that multiple representation does not violate the Sixth Amendment unless it gives rise to a conflict of interest. Since a possible conflict inheres in almost every instance of multiple representation, a defendant who objects to multiple representation must have the opportunity to show that potential conflicts impermissibly imperil his right to a fair trial. But unless the trial court fails to afford such an opportunity, a reviewing court cannot presume that the possibility for conflict has resulted in ineffective assistance of counsel. Such a presumption would preclude multiple representation even in cases where "[a] common defense . . . gives strength against a common attack."

In order to establish a violation of the Sixth Amendment, a defendant who raised no objection at trial must demonstrate that an actual conflict of interest adversely affected his lawyer's performance. In Glasser v. United States, for example, the record showed that defense counsel failed to

---

clients in a single matter is undertaken, the consultation shall include explanation of the implications of the common representation and the advantages and risks involved.
— EDS.]

cross-examine a prosecution witness whose testimony linked Glasser with the crime, and failed to resist the presentation of arguably inadmissible evidence. The Court found that both omissions resulted from counsel's desire to diminish the jury's perception of a codefendant's guilt. Indeed, the evidence of counsel's "struggle to serve two masters [could not] seriously be doubted." Since this actual conflict of interest impaired Glasser's defense, the Court reversed his conviction.

Dukes v. Warden, 406 U.S. 250 (1972), presented a contrasting situation. Dukes pleaded guilty on the advice of two lawyers, one of whom also represented Dukes' codefendants on an unrelated charge. Dukes later learned that this lawyer had sought leniency for the codefendants by arguing that their cooperation with the police induced Dukes to plead guilty. Dukes argued in this Court that his lawyer's conflict of interest had infected his plea. We found "nothing in the record . . . which would indicate that the alleged conflict resulted in ineffective assistance of counsel and did in fact render the plea in question involuntary and unintelligent." Since Dukes did not identify an actual lapse in representation, we affirmed the denial of habeas corpus relief.

Glasser established that unconstitutional multiple representation is never harmless error. Once the Court concluded that Glasser's lawyer had an actual conflict of interest, it refused "to indulge in nice calculations as to the amount of prejudice" attributable to the conflict. The conflict itself demonstrated a denial of the "right to have the effective assistance of counsel." 315 U.S., at 76. Thus, a defendant who shows that a conflict of interest actually affected the adequacy of his representation need not demonstrate prejudice in order to obtain relief. But until a defendant shows that his counsel actively represented conflicting interests, he has not established the constitutional predicate for his claim of ineffective assistance. . . .

C

The Court of Appeals granted Sullivan relief because he had shown that the multiple representation in this case involved a possible conflict of interest. We hold that the possibility of conflict is insufficient to impugn a criminal conviction. In order to demonstrate a violation of his Sixth Amendment rights, a defendant must establish that an actual conflict of interest adversely affected his lawyer's performance. Sullivan believes he should prevail even under this standard. He emphasizes Peruto's admission that the decision to rest Sullivan's defense reflected a reluctance to expose witnesses who later might have testified for the other defendants. The petitioner, on the other hand, points to DiBona's contrary testimony and to evidence that Sullivan himself wished to avoid taking the stand.

Since the Court of Appeals did not weigh these conflicting contentions under the proper legal standard, its judgment is vacated and the case is remanded for further proceedings consistent with this opinion.

So ordered.

MR. JUSTICE BRENNAN, concurring in Part III of the opinion of the Court and in the result. . . .

It is no imposition on a trial court to require it to find out whether attorneys are representing "two or more defendants [who] have been jointly charged . . . or have been joined for trial . . . ," to use the language of proposed Federal Rule of Criminal Procedure 44(c). It is probable as a practical matter that virtually all instances of joint representation will appear from the face of the charging papers and the appearances filed by attorneys. The American Bar Association's standards under the ABA Project on Standards for Criminal Justice, Function of the Trial Judge §3.4(b) (App. Draft 1972), are framed on the premise that judges will be readily able to ascertain instances of joint representation.

"[A] possible conflict inheres in almost every instance of multiple representation." . . . Therefore, upon discovery of joint representation, the duty of the trial court is to ensure that the defendants have not unwittingly given up their constitutional right to effective counsel. This is necessary since it is usually the case that defendants will not know what their rights are or how to raise them. This is surely true of the defendant who may not be receiving the effective assistance of counsel as a result of conflicting duties owed to other defendants. Therefore, the trial court cannot safely assume that silence indicates a knowledgeable choice to proceed jointly. The court must at least affirmatively advise the defendants that joint representation creates potential hazards which the defendants should consider before proceeding with the representation.

Had the trial record in the present case shown that respondent made a knowing and intelligent choice of joint representation, I could accept the Court's standard for a postconviction determination as to whether respondent in fact was denied effective assistance. Where it is clear that a defendant has voluntarily chosen to proceed with joint representation, it is fair, if he later alleges ineffective assistance growing out of a conflict, to require that he demonstrate "that a conflict of interest actually affected the adequacy of his representation." . . . Here, however, where there is no evidence that the court advised respondent about the potential for conflict or that respondent made a knowing and intelligent choice to forgo his right to separate counsel, I believe that respondent, who has shown a significant possibility of conflict,[3] is entitled to a presumption that his representation in fact suffered. Therefore, I would remand the case to allow the petitioners an opportunity to rebut this presumption by demonstrating that respondent's representation was not actually affected by the possibility of conflict.

MR. JUSTICE MARSHALL, concurring in part and dissenting in part. . . .

I believe . . . that the potential for conflict of interest in representing multiple defendants is "so grave," see ABA Project on Standards for Criminal Justice, Defense Function, Standard 4-3.5(b) (App. Draft, 2d ed. 1979), that whenever two or more defendants are represented by the same attorney the trial judge must make a preliminary determination that the joint representation is the product of the defendants' informed choice. I therefore agree with Mr. Justice Brennan that the trial court has a duty to inquire whether there is multiple representation, to warn defendants of the possible risks of such representation, and to ascertain that the representation is the result of the defendants' informed choice.

I dissent from the Court's formulation of the proper standard for determining whether multiple representation has violated the defendant's right to the effective assistance of counsel. The Court holds that in the absence of an objection at trial, the defendant must show "that an actual conflict of interest adversely affected his lawyer's performance." . . . If the Court's holding would require a defendant to demonstrate that his attorney's trial performance differed from what it would have been if the defendant had been the attorney's only client, I believe it is inconsistent with our previous cases. Such a test is not only unduly harsh, but incurably speculative as well. The appropriate question under the Sixth Amendment is whether an actual, relevant conflict of interests existed

---

3. The Court of Appeals held that respondent successfully carried the burden of demonstrating "a possibility of prejudice or conflict of interest and that independent counsel might well have chosen a different trial strategy." United States ex. rel. Sullivan v. Cuyler, 593 F.2d 512, 521 (1979). The court based its holding, in part, on the testimony of one of respondent's two trial attorneys. He testified that they chose not to present a defense in respondent's case partly because they did not want to expose their defense before the upcoming trials of respondent's codefendants. Also, they did not want to risk having any evidence come out which, while exculpating respondent, might inculpate one of the codefendants. Ibid. The court credited this testimony. Id., at 522.

The facts of this case demonstrate that, contrary to the view of the Court, the provision of separate trials does not always reduce the potential for conflict. Here, in fact, "the potential for a divergence in [the codefendant's] interest," arose, in part, precisely because there were separate trials.

during the proceedings. If it did, the conviction must be reversed. Since such a conflict was present in this case, I would affirm the judgment of the Court of Appeals.[2]

Our cases make clear that every defendant has a constitutional right to "the assistance of an attorney unhindered by a conflict of interests." Holloway v. Arkansas, 435 U.S. 475, 483, n.5 (1978). "[T]he 'assistance of counsel' guaranteed by the Sixth Amendment contemplates that such assistance be untrammeled and unimpaired by a court order requiring that one lawyer shall simultaneously represent conflicting interests." Glasser v. United States, 315 U.S. 60, 70 (1942). If "[t]he possibility of the inconsistent interests of [the clients] was brought home to the court" by means of an objection at trial, id., at 71, the court may not require joint representation. But if no objection was made at trial, the appropriate inquiry is whether a conflict actually existed during the course of the representation.

Because it is the simultaneous representation of conflicting interests against which the Sixth Amendment protects a defendant, he need go no further than to show the existence of an actual conflict. An actual conflict of interests negates the unimpaired loyalty a defendant is constitutionally entitled to expect and receive from his attorney.

Moreover, a showing that an actual conflict adversely affected counsel's performance is not only unnecessary, it is often an impossible task. As the Court emphasized in *Holloway*:

> [I]n a case of joint representation of conflicting interests the evil—it bears repeating—is in what the advocate finds himself compelled to *refrain* from doing. . . . It may be possible in some cases to identify from the record the prejudice resulting from an attorney's failure to undertake certain trial tasks, but even with a record of the sentencing hearing available it would be difficult to judge intelligently the impact of a conflict on the attorney's representation of a client. And to assess the impact of a conflict of interests on the attorney's options, tactics, and decisions in plea negotiations would be virtually impossible. 435 U.S., at 490-491.

Accordingly, in *Holloway* we emphatically rejected the suggestion that a defendant must show prejudice in order to be entitled to relief. For the same reasons, it would usually be futile to attempt to determine how

2. The Court of Appeals cast its decision in terms of a "potential for conflict of interest," United States ex rel. Sullivan v. Cuyler, 593 F.2d 512, 522 (1979), and made no explicit statement that an actual conflict of interest existed. The court's analysis was premised, however, on its conclusion that "[w]e have no basis on which to reject Peruto's sworn admission that he injected improper considerations in the attorney-client relationship." Ibid. This statement clearly demonstrates that the court found an actual, relevant conflict of interests.

counsel's conduct would have been different if he had not been under conflicting duties. . . .

NOTES AND QUESTIONS

1. After *Cuyler*, what are the consequences of making, as compared to *not* making, a pretrial objection to joint representation?

2. What does it mean that "a defendant who shows that a conflict of interest actually affected the adequacy of his representation need not demonstrate prejudice in order to obtain relief"?

3. What result under *Cuyler* if a defendant, in full knowledge of a potential conflict, waives the right not to have separate counsel, and subsequently the potential conflict is actualized? In this regard, consider Rule 44(c) of the Federal Rules of Criminal Procedure, which is cited in note 17 of *Cuyler* and which has now gone into effect:

> Whenever two or more defendants have been jointly charged pursuant to rule 8(b) or have been joined for trial pursuant to Rule 13, and are represented by the same retained or assigned counsel or by retained or assigned counsel who are associated in the practice of law, the court shall promptly inquire with respect to such joint representation and shall personally advise each defendant of his right to the effective assistance of counsel, including separate representation. Unless it appears that there is good cause to believe no conflict of interest is likely to arise, the court shall take such measures as may be appropriate to protect each defendant's right to counsel.

In an insightful analysis of Rule 44(c) prior to its effective date, Professor Tague commented:

> If the rule values the assistance of conflict-free representation above the right to choose one's attorney, it has three distressing omissions. First, the rule orders the "court" to make an inquiry about possible conflicts whenever defendants "are charged pursuant to Rule 8(b) or have been joined for trial pursuant to Rule 13." Does the rule apply only after the defendants have been indicted or an information has been filed in district court? Is there then no obligation to inquire at any earlier stage, such as at the presentment or the preliminary hearing? The rule's reference to the "court" as the inquiring entity supports this apparent restriction. Rule 44(a) distinguishes between the "court" and the magistrate who usually appoints counsel at the presentment and presides at the preliminary hearing. A magistrate could appoint a single attorney whose representation would continue at least until arraignment on the indictment. Indeed, the Advisory Committee implies that separate counsel need not be initially appointed for each defendant. This limitation is unfortunate. The rule recognizes the im-

portance of the inquiry even if the defendants decide to plead guilty before trial. Many defendants seek to plead guilty before they are indicted, because the defendants frequently obtain a more favorable plea bargain if they plead early in the process. A guilty plea might bury a glaring conflict that infected the plea bargaining for the codefendants.

Second, the rule does not appear to cover cases like Dukes v. Warden, in which a defendant, charged alone in one proceeding, is a codefendant in a second proceeding and one attorney represents defendants in both proceedings. The rule's reference to rules 8(b) and 13 suggests that the court is not under any obligation even if it knows of the separate indictments. The rule also would appear to apply if the codefendants are severed under rule 14.

Third, the rule fails to provide adequate guidelines for review of a postconviction attack based on conflict. The Committee indicates that although a trial court's failure to make a rule 44(c) inquiry will not necessarily result in reversal, an appellate court is more likely to find that a conflict existed in this instance. Further, because conflicts that were not apparent initially may surface later in the proceeding, even an adequate initial inquiry does not preclude reversal on conflict grounds. If the trial court makes an inadequate inquiry or none at all, the appellate court would still face the problem of defining and allocating the burden of proving the existence of a conflict. The proposed rule thus fails to solve one of the major problems of multiple representation. [Tague, Multiple Representation and Conflicts of Interest in Criminal Cases, 67 Geo. L.J. 1075, 1094-1095 (1979).]

These limitations led Professor Tague to conclude that the rule should be further amended to require the appointment of separate counsel for all indigents and to require that nonindigents at least discuss the matter with separate counsel. Second, if defendants insist on joint representation, they should have to establish an intelligent waiver. Other commentators have concluded that there should be a flat prohibition on joint representation. Lowenthal, Joint Representation in Criminal Cases: A Critical Appraisal, 64 Va. L. Rev. 939, 986 (1978). How would you work out these conflicting concerns of autonomy and procedural fairness? In this regard, see United States v. Dolan, 570 F.2d 1177 (3d Cir. 1978), which is one of the few decisions allowing counsel to be disqualified on grounds of conflict over the client's objection. The general view seems to be that a client may waive the right to conflict-free representation. See, e.g., United States v. Curcio, 680 F.2d 881 (2d Cir. 1982). However, in Wheat v. United States, 486 U.S. 153 (1988), the Court held that trial courts did not have to accept defendants' waivers of conflict-free representation, notwithstanding the presumption in favor of counsel of choice. In part the Court was motivated by the fact that the courts of appeals have indicated a willingness to entertain ineffective assistance of counsel claims by defendants who have specifically waived the right to conflict-free representation.

4. If there is a claim of conflict of interest, should the defense be forced to divulge the confidential information upon which the claim is premised? See United States v. Young, 644 F.2d 1008 (4th Cir. 1981). Should counsel be allowed to withdraw where it appears that a former client would testify against the present client? See United States v. Morando, 628 F.2d 535 (9th Cir. 1980).

5. In Burger v. Kemp, 483 U.S. 776 (9187), the Court held that an actual conflict of interest was not present where defense counsel's law partner represented a separately tried participant in the same crime and where counsel prepared appellate briefs for both defendants, even though counsel did not argue that his client was less culpable than the individual represented by his law partner.

C. SOME IMPLICATIONS OF THE RIGHT TO COUNSEL

1. The Right to Control the Lawyering Process

As the Court has continued to expand the implications of the right to counsel, it has also made clear that the right to counsel is not an exception to the normal rule that a right carries by implication the correlative right of waiver. In order for a waiver of counsel to be effective, however, the waiver must be "an intentional relinquishment or abandonment of a known right or privilege," Johnson v. Zerbst, 304 U.S. 458, 464 (1938), a standard from which the Court has not deviated. But it also has not deviated from the position that an effective waiver of counsel can occur. Consider the implications of the following case.

FARETTA v. CALIFORNIA
Certiorari to the Court of Appeal of California, Second Appellate District
422 U.S. 806 (1975)

MR. JUSTICE STEWART delivered the opinion of the Court.

The question before us now is whether a defendant in a state criminal trial has a constitutional right to proceed *without* counsel when he voluntarily and intelligently elects to do so. Stated another way, the question is whether a State may constitutionally hale a person into its criminal

courts and there force a lawyer upon him, even when he insists that he
wants to conduct his own defense. It is not an easy question, but we have
concluded that a State may not constitutionally do so.

I

Anthony Faretta was charged with grand theft in an information filed in
the Superior Court of Los Angeles County, Cal. At the arraignment, the
Superior Court Judge assigned to preside at the trial appointed the public
defender to represent Faretta. Well before the date of trial, however,
Faretta requested that he be permitted to represent himself. Questioning
by the judge revealed that Faretta had once represented himself in a
criminal prosecution, that he had a high school education, and that he
did not want to be represented by the public defender because he believed
that the office was "very loaded down with . . . a heavy case load." The
judge responded that he believed Faretta was "making a mistake" and
emphasized that in further proceedings Faretta would receive no special
favors. Nevertheless, after establishing that Faretta wanted to represent
himself and did not want a lawyer, the judge, in a "preliminary ruling,"
accepted Faretta's waiver of the assistance of counsel. The judge indicated, however, that he might reverse this ruling if it later appeared that
Faretta was unable adequately to represent himself.
    Several weeks thereafter, but still prior to trial, the judge sua sponte
held a hearing to inquire into Faretta's ability to conduct his own defense,
and questioned him specifically about both the hearsay rule and the state
law governing the challenge of potential jurors. After consideration of
Faretta's answers, and observation of his demeanor, the judge ruled that
Faretta had not made an intelligent and knowing waiver of his right to
the assistance of counsel, and also ruled that Faretta had no constitutional
right to conduct his own defense. The judge, accordingly, reversed his
earlier ruling permitting self-representation and again appointed the public defender to represent Faretta. Faretta's subsequent request for leave
to act as cocounsel was rejected, as were his efforts to make certain motions
in his own behalf.[5] Throughout the subsequent trial, the judge required
that Faretta's defense be conducted only through the appointed lawyer
from the public defender's office. At the conclusion of the trial, the jury
found Faretta guilty as charged, and the judge sentenced him to prison.
    The California Court of Appeal, relying upon a then-recent Cali-

---

5. Faretta also urged without success that he was entitled to counsel of his choice,
and three times moved for the appointment of a lawyer other than the public defender.
These motions, too, were denied.

fornia Supreme Court decision that had expressly decided the issue, affirmed the trial judge's ruling that Faretta had no federal or state constitutional right to represent himself.[7] Accordingly, the appellate court affirmed Faretta's conviction. A petition for rehearing was denied without opinion, and the California Supreme Court denied review. We granted certiorari.

II

In the federal courts, the right of self-representation has been protected by statute since the beginnings of our Nation. Section 35 of the Judiciary Act of 1789, 1 Stat. 73, 92, enacted by the First Congress and signed by President Washington one day before the Sixth Amendment was proposed, provided that "in all the courts of the United States, the parties may plead and manage their own causes personally or by the assistance of . . . counsel." The right is currently codified in 28 U.S.C. §1654.

With few exceptions, each of the several States also accords a defendant the right to represent himself in any criminal case. The Constitutions of 36 States explicitly confer that right. Moreover, many state courts have expressed the view that the right is also supported by the Constitution of the United States.

This Court has more than once indicated the same view. In Adams v. United States ex rel. McCann, 317 U.S. 269, 279, the Court recognized that the Sixth Amendment right to the assistance of counsel implicitly embodies a "correlative right to dispense with a lawyer's help." The defendant in that case, indicted for federal mail fraud violations, insisted on conducting his own defense without benefit of counsel. He also requested a bench trial and signed a waiver of his right to trial by jury. The prosecution consented to the waiver of a jury, and the waiver was accepted by the court. The defendant was convicted, but the Court of Appeals reversed the conviction on the ground that a person accused of a felony could not competently waive his right to trial by jury except upon the advice of a lawyer. This Court reversed and reinstated the conviction, holding that "an accused, in the exercise of a free and intelligent choice, and with the considered approval of the court, may waive trial by jury, and so likewise may he competently and intelligently waive his Constitutional right to assistance of counsel." Id., at 275.

The Adams case does not, of course, necessarily resolve the issue

7. The Court of Appeal also held that the trial court had not "abused its discretion in concluding that Faretta had not made a knowing and intelligent waiver of his right to be represented by counsel," since "Faretta did not appear aware of the possible consequences of waiving the opportunity for skilled and experienced representation at trial."

before us. It held only that "the Constitution does not force a lawyer upon a defendant." Id., at 279.[12] Whether the Constitution forbids a State from forcing a lawyer upon a defendant is a different question. But the Court in *Adams* did recognize, albeit in dictum, an affirmative right of self-representation:

> The right to assistance of counsel and the *correlative right to dispense with a lawyer's help* are not legal formalisms. They rest on considerations that go to the substance of an accused's position before the law. . . .
>   . . . What were contrived as protections for the accused should not be turned into fetters. . . . To deny an accused a choice of procedure in circumstances in which he, though a layman, is as capable as any lawyer of making an intelligent choice, is to impair the worth of great Constitutional safeguards by treating them as empty verbalisms.
>   . . . When the administration of the criminal law . . . is hedged about as it is by the Constitutional safeguards for the protection of an accused, to deny him in the exercise of his free choice the right to dispense with some of these safeguards . . . is to imprison a man in his privileges and call it the Constitution.

In other settings as well, the Court has indicated that a defendant has a constitutionally protected right to represent himself in a criminal trial. For example, in Snyder v. Massachusetts, 291 U.S. 97, the Court held that the Confrontation Clause of the Sixth Amendment gives the accused a right to be present at all stages of the proceedings where fundamental fairness might be thwarted by his absence. This right to "presence" was based upon the premise that the "defense may be made easier if the accused is permitted to be present at the examination of jurors or the summing up of counsel, *for it will be in his power,* if present, to give advice or suggestion or *even to supersede his lawyers altogether and conduct the trial himself.*" Id., at 106 (emphasis added). And in Price v. Johnston, 334 U.S. 266, the Court, in holding that a convicted person had no absolute right to argue his own appeal, said this holding was in "sharp contrast" to his "recognized privilege of conducting his own defense at the trial."

The United States Courts of Appeals have repeatedly held that the right of self-representation is protected by the Bill of Rights. . . .

12. The holding of *Adams* was reaffirmed in a different context in Carter v. Illinois, 329 U.S. 173, 174-175, where the Court again adverted to the right of self-representation: "Neither the historic conception of Due Process nor the vitality it derives from progressive standards of justice denies a person *the right to defend himself* or to confess guilt. Under appropriate circumstances the Constitution requires that counsel be tendered; it does not require that under all circumstances counsel be forced upon a defendant." (Emphasis added.) See also Moore v. Michigan, 355 U.S. 155, 161.

This Court's past recognition of the right of self-representation, the federal-court authority holding the right to be of constitutional dimension, and the state constitutions pointing to the right's fundamental nature form a consensus not easily ignored. "[T]he mere fact that a path is a beaten one," Mr. Justice Jackson once observed, "is a persuasive reason for following it."[13] We confront here a nearly universal conviction, on the part of our people as well as our courts, that forcing a lawyer upon an unwilling defendant is contrary to his basic right to defend himself if he truly wants to do so.

III

This consensus is soundly premised. The right of self-representation finds support in the structure of the Sixth Amendment, as well as in the English and colonial jurisprudence from which the Amendment emerged.

A . . .

The Sixth Amendment does not provide merely that a defense shall be made for the accused; it grants to the accused personally the right to make his defense. It is the accused, not counsel, who must be "informed of the nature and cause of the accusation," who must be "confronted with the witnesses against him," and who must be accorded "compulsory process for obtaining witnesses in his favor." Although not stated in the Amendment in so many words, the right to self-representation—to make one's own defense personally—is thus necessarily implied by the structure of the Amendment.[15] The right to defend is given directly to the accused; for it is he who suffers the consequences if the defense fails.

13. Jackson, Full Faith and Credit—The Lawyer's Clause of the Constitution, 45 Col. L. Rev. 1, 26 (1945).
15. This Court has often recognized the constitutional stature of rights that, though not literally expressed in the document, are essential to due process of law in a fair adversary process. It is now accepted, for example, that an accused has a right to be present at all stages of the trial where his absence might frustrate the fairness of the proceedings, Snyder v. Massachusetts, 291 U. S. 97; to testify on his own behalf, see Harris v. New York, 401 U.S. 222, 225; Brooks v. Tennessee, 406 U.S. 605, 612; cf. Ferguson v. Georgia, 365 U.S. 570; and to be convicted only if his guilt is proved beyond a reasonable doubt, In re Winship, 397 U.S. 358; Mullaney v. Wilbur, 421 U.S. 684.
The inference of rights is not, of course, a mechanical exercise. In Singer v. United States, 380 U.S. 24, the Court held that an accused has no right to a bench trial, despite his capacity to waive his right to a jury trial. In so holding, the Court stated that "[t]he ability to waive a constitutional right does not ordinarily carry with it the right to insist upon the opposite of that right." Id., at 34-35. But that statement was made only *after* the Court had concluded that the Constitution does not affirmatively protect any right to be tried by a judge. Recognizing that an implied right must arise independently from

The counsel provision supplements this design. It speaks of the "assistance" of counsel, and an assistant, however expert, is still an assistant. The language and spirit of the Sixth Amendment contemplate that counsel, like the other defense tools guaranteed by the Amendment, shall be an aid to a wiling defendant—not an organ of the State interposed between an unwilling defendant and his right to defend himself personally. To thrust counsel upon the accused, against his considered wish, thus violates the logic of the Amendment. In such a case, counsel is not an assistant, but a master;[16] and the right to make a defense is stripped of the personal character upon which the Amendment insists. It is true that when a defendant chooses to have a lawyer manage and present his case, law and tradition may allocate to the counsel the power to make binding decisions of trial strategy in many areas. Cf. Henry v. Mississippi, 379 U.S. 443, 451; Brookhart v. Janis, 384 U.S. 1, 7-8; Fay v. Noia, 372 U.S. 391, 439. This allocation can only be justified, however, by the defendant's consent, at the outset, to accept counsel as his representative. An unwanted counsel "represents" the defendant only through a tenuous and unacceptable legal fiction. Unless the accused has acquiesced in such representation, the defense presented is not the defense guaranteed him by the Constitution, for, in a very real sense, it is not *his* defense.

B

The Sixth Amendment, when naturally read, thus implies a right of self-representation. This reading is reinforced by the Amendment's roots in English legal history. [The Court proceeded to an examination of English legal history, concluding that the "common law rule has evidently always been that 'no person charged with a criminal offense can have counsel forced upon him against his will.' "]

---

the design and history of the constitutional text, the Court searched for, but could not find, any "indication that the colonists considered the ability to waive a jury trial to be equal importance to the right to demand one." Id., at 26. Instead, the Court could locate only "isolated instances" of a right to trial by judge, and concluded that these were "clear departures from the common law." Ibid.

We follow the approach of *Singer* here. Our concern is with an *independent* right of self-representation. We do not suggest that this right arises mechanically from a defendant's power to waive the right to the assistance of counsel. See supra, at 814-815. On the contrary, the right must be independently found in the structure and history of the constitutional text.

16. Such a result would sever the concept of counsel from its historic roots. The first lawyers were personal friends of the litigant, brought into court by him so that he might "take 'counsel' with them" before pleading. 1 F. Pollock & F. Maitland, The History of English Law 211 (2d ed. 1909). Similarly, the first "attorneys" were personal agents, often lacking any professional training, who were appointed by those litigants who had secured royal permission to carry on their affairs through a representative, rather than personally. Id., at 212-213.

C

In the American Colonies the insistence upon a right of self-representation was, if anything, more fervent than in England. . . . [After a lengthy examination of the colonial experience, the Court concluded that] there is no evidence that the colonists and the Framers ever doubted the right of self-representation, or imagined that this right might be considered inferior to the right of assistance of counsel. To the contrary, the colonists and the Framers, as well as their English ancestors, always conceived of the right to counsel as an "assistance" for the accused, to be used at his option, in defending himself. The Framers selected in the Sixth Amendment a form of words that necessarily implies the right of self-representation. That conclusion is supported by centuries of consistent history.

IV

There can be no blinking the fact that the right of an accused to conduct his own defense seems to cut against the grain of this Court's decisions holding that the Constitution requires that no accused can be convicted and imprisoned unless he has been accorded the right to the assistance of counsel. . . . For it is surely true that the basic thesis of those decisions is that the help of a lawyer is essential to assure the defendant a fair trial. And a strong argument can surely be made that the whole thrust of those decisions must inevitably lead to the conclusion that a State may constitutionally impose a lawyer upon even an unwilling defendant.

But it is one thing to hold that every defendant, rich or poor, has the right to the assistance of counsel, and quite another to say that a State may compel a defendant to accept a lawyer he does not want. The value of state-appointed counsel was not unappreciated by the Founders, yet the notion of compulsory counsel was utterly foreign to them. And whatever else may be said of those who wrote the Bill of Rights, surely there can be no doubt that they understood the inestimable worth of free choice.

It is undeniable that in most criminal prosecutions defendants could better defend with counsel's guidance than by their own unskilled efforts. But where the defendant will not voluntarily accept representation by counsel, the potential advantage of a lawyer's training and experience can be realized, if at all, only imperfectly. To force a lawyer on a defendant can only lead him to believe that the law contrives against him. Moreover, it is not inconceivable that in some rare instances, the defendant might in fact present his case more effectively by conducting his own defense. Personal liberties are not rooted in the law of averages. The right to defend is personal. The defendant, and not his lawyer or the State, will bear the personal consequences of a conviction. It is the defendant, therefore, who must be free personally to decide whether in his particular case counsel is to his advantage. And although he may conduct his own defense ultimately to his own detriment, his choice must be honored out of "that respect for the individual which is the lifeblood of the law." Illinois v. Allen, 397 U.S. 337, 350-351 (Brennan, J., concurring).[46]

V

When an accused manages his own defense, he relinquishes, as a purely factual matter, many of the traditional benefits associated with the right to counsel. For this reason, in order to represent himself, the accused must "knowingly and intelligently" forego those relinquished benefits. Johnson v. Zerbst, 304 U.S., at 464-465. Cf. Von Moltke v. Gillies, 332 U.S. 708, 723-724 (plurality opinion of Black, J.). Although a defendant need not himself have the skill and experience of a lawyer in order competently and intelligently to choose self-representation, he should be made aware of the dangers and disadvantages of self-representation, so that the record will establish that "he knows what he is doing and his choice is made with eyes open." Adams v. United States ex rel. McCann, 317 U.S., at 279.

Here, weeks before trial, Faretta clearly and unequivocally declared to the trial judge that he wanted to represent himself and did not want counsel. The record affirmatively shows that Faretta was literate, competent, and understanding, and that he was voluntarily exercising his informed free will. The trial judge had warned Faretta that he thought

---

46. We are told that many criminal defendants representing themselves may use the courtroom for deliberate disruption of their trials. But the right of self-representation has been recognized from our beginnings by federal law and by most of the States, and no such result has thereby occurred. Moreover, the trial judge may terminate self-representation by a defendant who deliberately engages in serious and obstructionist misconduct. See Illinois v. Allen, 397 U.S. 337. Of course, a State may—even over objection by the accused—appoint a "standby counsel" to aid the accused if and when the accused requests help, and to be available to represent the accused in the event that termination of the defendant's self-representation is necessary. See United States v. Dougherty, 154 U.S. App. D.C. 76, 87-89, 473 F.2d 1113, 1124-1126.

The right of self-representation is not a license to abuse the dignity of the courtroom. Neither is it a license not to comply with relevant rules of procedural and substantive law. Thus, whatever else may or may not be open to him on appeal, a defendant who elects to represent himself cannot thereafter complain that the quality of his own defense amounted to a denial of "effective assistance of counsel."

it was a mistake not to accept the assistance of counsel, and that Faretta would be required to follow all the "ground rules" of trial procedure. We need make no assessment of how well or poorly Faretta had mastered the intricacies of the hearsay rule and the California code provisions that govern challenges of potential jurors on voir dire. For his technical legal knowledge, as such, was not relevant to an assessment of his knowing exercise of the right to defend himself.

In forcing Faretta, under these circumstances, to accept against his will a state-appointed public defender, the California courts deprived him of his constitutional right to conduct his own defense. Accordingly, the judgment before us is vacated, and the case is remanded for further proceedings not inconsistent with this opinion.

It is so ordered.

MR. CHIEF JUSTICE BURGER, with whom MR. JUSTICE BLACKMUN and MR. JUSTICE REHNQUIST join, dissenting.

This case . . . is another example of the judicial tendency to constitutionalize what is thought "good." That effort fails on its own terms here, because there is nothing desirable or useful in permitting every accused person, even the most uneducated and inexperienced, to insist upon conducting his own defense to criminal charges. Moreover, there is no constitutional basis for the Court's holding, and it can only add to the problems of an already malfunctioning criminal justice system. I therefore dissent.

I

The most striking feature of the Court's opinion is that it devotes so little discussion to the matter which it concedes is the core of the decision, that is, discerning an independent basis in the Constitution for the supposed right to represent oneself in a criminal trial.[2] . . . Its ultimate assertion that such a right is tucked between the lines of the Sixth Amendment is contradicted by the Amendment's language and its consistent judicial interpretation.

As the Court seems to recognize . . . the conclusion that the rights guaranteed by the Sixth Amendment are "personal" to an accused reflects nothing more than the obvious fact that it is he who is on trial and therefore has need of a defense. But neither that nearly trivial proposition nor the language of the Amendment, which speaks in uniformly man-

2. The Court deliberately, and in my view properly, declines to characterize this case as one in which the defendant was denied a fair trial. . . .

datory terms, leads to the further conclusion that the right to counsel is merely supplementary and may be dispensed with at the whim of the accused. Rather, this Court's decisions have consistently included the right to counsel as an integral part of the bundle making up the larger right to a defense as we know it." . . .

The reason for this hardly requires explanation. The fact of the matter is that in all but an extraordinarily small number of cases an accused will lose whatever defense he may have if he undertakes to conduct the trial himself. . . . Obviously, [the necessity of counsel to guarantee a fair trial does] not vary depending upon whether the accused actively desires to be represented by counsel or wishes to proceed pro se. Nor is it accurate to suggest, as the Court seems to later in its opinion, that the quality of his representation at trial is a matter with which only the accused is legitimately concerned. . . . Although we have adopted an adversary system of criminal justice, . . . the prosecution is more than an ordinary litigant, and the trial judge is not simply an automaton who insures that technical rules are adhered to. Both are charged with the duty of insuring that justice, in the broadest sense of that term, is achieved in every criminal trial. . . . That goal is ill-served, and the integrity of and public confidence in the system are undermined, when an easy conviction is obtained due to the defendant's ill-advised decision to waive counsel. The damage thus inflicted is not mitigated by the lame explanation that the defendant simply availed himself of the "freedom" "to go to jail under his own banner. . . ." United States ex rel. Maldonado v. Denno, 348 F. 2d 12, 15 (C.A.2 1965). The system of criminal justice should not be available as an instrument of self-destruction.

In short, both the "spirit and the logic" of the Sixth Amendment are that every person accused of crime shall receive the fullest possible defense; in the vast majority of cases this command can be honored only by means of the expressly guaranteed right to counsel, and the trial judge is in the best position to determine whether the accused is capable of conducting his defense. True freedom of choice and society's interest in seeing that justice is achieved can be vindicated only if the trial court retains discretion to reject any attempted waiver of counsel and insist that the accused be tried according to the Constitution. This discretion is as critical an element of basic fairness as a trial judge's discretion to decline to accept a plea of guilty. See Santobello v. New York, 404 U.S. 257, 262 (1971).

II

The Court's attempt to support its result by collecting dicta from prior decisions is no more persuasive than its analysis of the Sixth Amendment. Considered in context, the cases upon which the Court relies to "beat its path" either lead it nowhere or point in precisely the opposite direction.

In Adams v. United States ex rel. McCann, 317 U.S. 269 (1942), and Carter v. Illinois, 329 U.S. 173 (1946), the defendants had competently waived counsel but later sought to renounce actions taken by them while proceeding pro se. In both cases this Court upheld the convictions, holding that neither an uncounseled waiver of jury trial nor an uncounseled guilty plea is inherently defective under the Constitution. The language which the Court so carefully excises from those opinions relates, not to an affirmative right of self-representation, but to the consequences of waiver.[4] In Adams, for example, Mr. Justice Frankfurter was careful to point out that his reference to a defendant's "correlative right to dispense with a lawyer's help" meant only that "[h]e may waive his Constitutional right to assistance of counsel." But, as the Court recognizes, the power to *waive* a constitutional right does not carry with it the right to insist upon its opposite.

Similarly, in Carter the Court's opinion observed that the Constitution "does not require that *under all circumstances* counsel be forced upon a defendant," citing Adams, 329 U.S., at 174-175 (emphasis added). I, for one, find this statement impossible to square with the Court's present holding that an accused is absolutely entitled to *dispense* with a lawyer's help under all conditions. Thus, although Adams and Carter support the Court's conclusion that a defendant who represents himself may not thereafter disaffirm his deliberate trial decisions, . . . they provide it no comfort regarding the primary issue in this case.[5] . . .

In short, what the Court represents as a well-traveled road is in reality a constitutional trail which it is blazing for the first time today, one that has not even been hinted at in our previous decisions. Far from an interpretation of the Sixth Amendment, it is a perversion of the provision to which we gave full meaning in Gideon v. Wainwright and Argersinger v. Hamlin.

4. Indeed, the portion of the Court's quotation which warns against turning constitutional protections into "fetters" refers to the right to trial by jury, not the right to counsel. See Adams v. United States ex rel. McCann, 317 U.S. 269, 279 (1942). This Court has, of course, squarely held that there is no constitutional right to dispense with a jury. Singer v. United States, 380 U.S. 24 (1965).

5. No more relevant is Snyder v. Massachusetts, 291 U.S. 97 (1934). The reference in that case to an accused's "power . . . to supersede his lawyers" simply helped explain why his defense might "be made easier" if he were "permitted to be present at the examination of jurors or the summing up of counsel. . . ." Id., at 106. . . .

III

Like Mr. Justice Blackmun, I hesitate to participate in the Court's attempt to use history to take it where legal analysis cannot. Piecing together shreds of English legal history and early state constitutional and statutory provisions, without a full elaboration of the context in which they occurred or any evidence that they were relied upon by the drafters of our Federal Constitution, creates more questions than it answers and hardly provides the firm foundation upon which the creation of new constitutional rights should rest. We are well reminded that this Court once employed an exhaustive analysis of English and colonial practices regarding the right to counsel to justify the conclusion that it was fundamental to a fair trial and, less than 10 years later, used essentially the same material to conclude that it was not. Compare Powell v. Alabama, 287 U.S., at 60-65, with Betts v. Brady, 316 U.S. 455, 465-471 (1942).

As if to illustrate this point, the single historical fact cited by the Court which would appear truly relevant to ascertaining the meaning of the Sixth Amendment proves too much. As the Court points out, . . . §35 of the Judiciary Act of 1789 provided a statutory right to self-representation in federal criminal trials. The text of the Sixth Amendment, which expressly provides only for a right to counsel, was proposed the day after the Judiciary Act was signed. It can hardly be suggested that the Members of the Congress of 1789, then few in number, were unfamiliar with the Amendment's carefully structured language, which had been under discussion since the 1787 Constitutional Convention. And it would be most remarkable to suggest, had the right to conduct one's own defense been considered so critical as to require constitutional protection, that it would have been left to implication. Rather, under traditional canons of construction, *inclusion* of the right in the Judiciary Act and its *omission* from the constitutional amendment drafted at the same time by many of the same men, supports the conclusion that the omission was intentional.

There is no way to reconcile the idea that the Sixth Amendment impliedly guaranteed the right of an accused to conduct his own defense with the contemporaneous action of the Congress in passing a statute explicitly giving that right. If the Sixth Amendment created a right to self-representation it was unnecessary for Congress to enact any statute on the subject at all. In this case, therefore, history ought to lead judges to conclude that the Constitution leaves to the judgment of legislatures, and the flexible process of statutory amendment, the question whether criminal defendants should be permitted to conduct their trials pro se.

. . . And the fact that we have not hinted at a contrary view for 185 years is surely entitled to some weight in the scales.[6] . . .

6. The fact that Congress has retained a statutory right to self-representation suggests

IV

Society has the right to expect that, when courts find new rights implied in the Constitution, their potential effect upon the resources of our criminal justice system will be considered. However, such considerations are conspicuously absent from the Court's opinion in this case.

It hardly needs repeating that courts at all levels are already handicapped by the unsupplied demand for competent advocates, with the result that it often takes far longer to complete a given case than experienced counsel would require. If we were to assume that there will be widespread exercise of the newly discovered constitutional right to self-representation, it would almost certainly follow that there will be added congestion in the courts and that the quality of justice will suffer. Moreover, the Court blandly assumes that once an accused has elected to defend himself he will be bound by his choice and not be heard to complain of it later. . . . This assumption ignores the role of appellate review, for the reported cases are replete with instances of a convicted defendant being relieved of a deliberate decision even when made *with the advice of counsel.* See Silber v. United States, 370 U.S. 717 (1962). It is totally unrealistic, therefore, to suggest that an accused will always be held to the consequences of a decision to conduct his own defense. Unless, as may be the case, most persons accused of crime have more wit than to insist upon the dubious benefit that the Court confers today, we can expect that many expensive and good-faith prosecutions will be nullified on appeal for reasons that trial courts are now deprived of the power to prevent.[7]

MR. JUSTICE BLACKMUN, with whom THE CHIEF JUSTICE and MR. JUSTICE REHNQUIST join, dissenting.

Today the Court holds that the Sixth Amendment guarantees to every defendant in a state criminal trial the right to proceed without counsel whenever he elects to do so. I find no textual support for this conclusion in the language of the Sixth Amendment. I find the historical evidence relied upon by the Court to be unpersuasive, especially in light of the recent history of criminal procedure. Finally, I fear that the right to self-representation constitutionalized today frequently will cause pro-

---

that it has also assumed that the Sixth Amendment does not guarantee such a right. See 28 U.S.C. §1654.

7. Some of the damage we can anticipate from a defendant's ill-advised insistence on conducting his own defense may be mitigated by appointing a qualified lawyer to sit in the case as the traditional "friend of the court." The Court does not foreclose this option. . . .

cedural confusion without advancing any significant strategic interest of the defendant. I therefore dissent.

I

The starting point, of course, is the language of the Sixth Amendment. . . .

It is self-evident that the Amendment makes no direct reference to self-representation. Indeed, the Court concedes that the right to self-representation is "not stated in the Amendment in so many words." . . .

Where then in the Sixth Amendment does one find this right to self-representation? According to the Court, it is "necessarily implied by the structure of the Amendment." . . . The Court's chain of inferences is delicate and deserves scrutiny. The Court starts with the proposition that the Sixth Amendment is "a compact statement of the rights necessary to a full defense." . . . From this proposition the Court concludes that the Sixth Amendment "constitutionalizes the right in an adversary criminal trial to make a defense as we know it." . . . Up to this point, at least as a general proposition, the Court's reasoning is unexceptionable. The Court, however, then concludes that because the specific rights in the Sixth Amendment are personal to the accused, the accused must have a right to exercise those rights personally. Stated somewhat more succinctly, the Court reasons that because the accused has a personal right to "a defense as we know it," he necessarily has a right to make that defense personally. I disagree. Although I believe the specific guarantees of the Sixth Amendment are personal to the accused, I do not agree that the Sixth Amendment guarantees any particular procedural method of asserting those rights. If an accused has enjoyed a speedy trial by an impartial jury in which he was informed of the nature of the accusation, confronted with the witnesses against him, afforded the power of compulsory process, and represented effectively by competent counsel, I do not see that the Sixth Amendment requires more.

The Court suggests that thrusting counsel upon the accused against his considered wish violates the logic of the Sixth Amendment because counsel is to be an assistant, not a master. . . . [However] [t]his is not a case where defense counsel, against the wishes of the defendant or with inadequate consultation, had adopted a trial strategy that significantly affects one of the accused's constitutional rights. For such overbearing conduct by counsel, there is a remedy. Brookhart v. Janis, 384 U.S. 1 (1966); Fay v. Noia, 372 U.S. 391, 439 (1963). Nor is this a case where distrust, animosity, or other personal differences between the accused and his would-be counsel have rendered effective representation unlikely or impossible. See Brown v. Craven, 424 F.2d 1166, 1169-1170 (C.A.9 1970). See also Anders v. California, 386 U.S. 738 (1967). Nor is this even a case where a defendant has been forced, against his wishes to expend his personal resources to pay for counsel for his defense. See generally Fuller v. Oregon, 417 U.S. 40 (1974); James v. Strange, 407 U.S. 128 (1972). Instead, the Court holds that any defendant in any criminal proceeding may insist on representing himself regardless of how complex the trial is likely to be and regardless of how frivolous the defendant's motivations may be. I cannot agree that there is anything in the Due Process Clause or the Sixth Amendment that requires the States to subordinate the solemn business of conducting a criminal prosecution to the whimsical—albeit voluntary—caprice of every accused who wishes to use his trial as a vehicle for personal or political self-gratification.

The Court seems to suggest that so long as the accused is willing to pay the consequences of his folly, there is no reason for not allowing a defendant the right to self-representation. . . . That view ignores the established principle that the interest of the State in a criminal prosecution "is not that it shall win a case, but that justice shall be done." Berger v. United States, 295 U.S. 78, 88 (1935). See also Singer v. United States, 380 U.S., at 37. For my part, I do not believe that any amount of pro se pleading can cure the injury to society of an unjust result, but I do believe that a just result should prove to be an effective balm for almost any frustrated pro se defendant. . . .

III

In conclusion, I note briefly the procedural problems that, I suspect, today's decision will visit upon trial courts in the future. Although the Court indicates that a pro se defendant necessarily waives any claim he might otherwise make of ineffective assistance of counsel, . . . the opinion leaves open a host of other procedural questions. Must every defendant be advised of his right to proceed pro se? If so, when must that notice be given? Since the right to assistance of counsel and the right to self-representation are mutually exclusive, how is the waiver of each right to be measured? If a defendant has elected to exercise his right to proceed pro se, does he still have a constitutional right to assistance of standby counsel? How soon in the criminal proceeding must a defendant decide between proceeding by counsel or pro se? Must he be allowed to switch in midtrial? May a violation of the right to self-presentation ever be harmless error? Must the trial court treat the pro se defendant differently than it would professional counsel? I assume that many of these questions will be answered with finality in due course. Many of them, however, such as the standards of waiver and the treatment of the pro se defendant, will haunt the trial of every defendant who elects to exercise his right to self-representation. The procedural problems spawned by an absolute right to self-representation will far outweigh whatever tactical advantage the defendant may feel he has gained by electing to represent himself.

If there is any truth to the old proverb that "one who is his own lawyer has a fool for a client," the Court by its opinion today now bestows a *constitutional* right on one to make a fool of himself.

Are the difficulties predicted by the dissenters in *Faretta* reflected in the Court's most recent consideration of the area?

McKASKLE v. WIGGINS
Certiorari to the Fifth Circuit Court of Appeals
465 U.S. 168 (1984)

JUSTICE O'CONNOR delivered the opinion of the Court.

In Faretta v. California, 422 U.S. 806 (1975), this Court recognized a defendant's Sixth Amendment right to conduct his own defense. The Court also held that a trial court may appoint "standby counsel" to assist the pro se defendant in his defense. Today we must decide what role standby counsel who is present at trial over the defendant's objection may play consistent with the protection of the defendant's *Faretta* rights.

I

Carl Edwin Wiggins was convicted of robbery and sentenced to life imprisonment as a recidivist. His conviction was set aside because of a defective indictment. When Wiggins was retried he was again convicted and sentenced to life imprisonment. Standby counsel were appointed to assist Wiggins at both trials. Wiggins now challenges counsel's participation in his second trial.

Prior to the first trial, a hearing was held on Wiggins' motion to proceed pro se. The court granted the motion, but simultaneously appointed two attorneys to act as standby counsel. Wiggins initially objected to their presence. Shortly thereafter, however, counsel asked Wiggins how they should conduct themselves at trial, and Wiggins expressly requested that they bring appropriate objections directly to the attention of the court, without first consulting him. After the trial, newly appointed counsel discovered that the original indictment was defective, and a new trial was granted.

On April 16, 1973, about two months before the second trial began, Wiggins filed a request for appointed counsel, stating that he wished to rescind his earlier waiver of counsel. The next day Wiggins filled out and signed a form captioned "Petition for Appointment of Counsel and Order Thereon." The trial court appointed Benjamin Samples. About a month later Wiggins filed an additional request for counsel. Five days later Wiggins filled out another appointment of counsel form, and the trial court appointed R. Norvell Graham.

Wiggins' wishes respecting appointed counsel remained volatile as his second trial approached. When pretrial proceedings began on June 4, 1973, Wiggins announced that he would be defending himself pro se; he then firmly requested that counsel not be allowed to interfere with Wiggins' presentations to the court. Wiggins reaffirmed his desire to proceed pro se on the following morning, June 5, and objected even to the court's insistence that counsel remain available for consultation. The trial began later that day, and shortly thereafter Wiggins interrupted his cross-examination of a witness to consult with Graham off the record. Still later, Wiggins expressly agreed to allow Graham to conduct voir dire of another witness.

Wiggins started the next day of trial, June 6, with a request that the trial not proceed in Samples' absence from the courtroom. Later that morning Wiggins requested that counsel not be allowed to assist or interrupt, but a short while after Wiggins interrupted his own cross-examination of a witness to confer with Samples off the record. When the trial reconvened in the afternoon, Wiggins agreed to proceed in Samples' absence. After Samples returned, however, Wiggins again interrupted his own cross-examination of a witness to confer with him. Later Wiggins insisted that counsel should not initiate private consultations with Wiggins. Before the end of the day Wiggins once again found occasion to interrupt his own examination of a witness to confer with Samples.

On the following day, June 7, Wiggins agreed that Graham would make Wiggins' opening statement to the jury. On June 8, Wiggins was once again willing to have the trial proceed in the absence of one of his standby counsel. Following his conviction, Wiggins moved for a new trial. At the July 31 hearing on Wiggins' motion, Wiggins denounced the services standby counsel had provided. He insisted that they had unfairly interfered with his presentation of his defense.

After exhausting direct appellate and state habeas review Wiggins filed a petition for federal habeas corpus relief. He argued that standby counsel's conduct deprived him of his right to present his own defense, as guaranteed by *Faretta*. The District Court denied the habeas petition, but the Court of Appeals for the Fifth Circuit reversed. Wiggins v. Estelle, 681 F.2d 266, rehearing denied, 691 F.2d 213 (C.A.5 1982). The Court of Appeals held that Wiggins' Sixth Amendment right of self-representation was violated by the unsolicited participation of overzealous standby counsel:

> [T]he rule that we establish today is that court-appointed standby counsel is 'to be seen, but not heard.' By this we mean that he is not to compete with the defendant or supersede his defense. Rather, his presence is there for advisory purposes only, to be used or not used as the defendant sees fit.

We do not accept the Court of Appeals' rule, and reverse its judgment.

II . . .

B

. . . A defendant's right to self-representation plainly encompasses certain specific rights to have his voice heard. The pro se defendant must be allowed to control the organization and content of his own defense, to make motions, to argue points of law, to participate in voir dire, to question witnesses, and to address the court and the jury at appropriate points in the trial. The record reveals that Wiggins was in fact accorded all of these rights.

III

Wiggins claims, and the Court of Appeals agreed, that the pro se defendant may insist on presenting his own case wholly free from interruption or other uninvited involvement by standby counsel. Wiggins relies primarily on *Faretta's* sole reference to standby counsel:

> Of course, a State may—even over objection by the accused—appoint a 'standby counsel' to aid the accused if and when the accused requests help, and to be available to represent the accused in the event that termination of the defendant's self-representation is necessary.

Wiggins contends that the "if and when" language defines the limits on standby counsel's role. He argues that the *Faretta* right will be eviscerated if counsel is allowed to argue with the defendant, make motions to the court contrary to the defendant's wishes, and take other steps not specifically approved by the defendant.

In our view, both *Faretta's* logic and its citation of the *Dougherty* case indicate that no absolute bar on standby counsel's unsolicited participation is appropriate or was intended. The right to appear pro se exists to affirm the dignity and autonomy of the accused and to allow the presentation of what may, at least occasionally, be the accused's best possible defense. Both of these objectives can be achieved without categorically silencing standby counsel.

In determining whether a defendant's *Faretta* rights have been respected, the primary focus must be on whether the defendant had a fair chance to present his case in his own way. *Faretta* itself dealt with the defendant's affirmative right to participate, not with the limits on standby counsel's additional involvement. The specific rights to make his voice heard that Wiggins was plainly accorded, form the core of a defendant's right of self-representation.

We recognize, nonetheless, that the right to speak for oneself entails more than the opportunity to add one's voice to a cacophony of others. As Wiggins contends, the objectives underlying the right to proceed pro se may be undermined by unsolicited and excessively intrusive participation by standby counsel. In proceedings before a jury the defendant may legitimately be concerned that multiple voices "for the defense" will confuse the message the defendant wishes to convey, thus defeating *Faretta's* objectives.[7] Accordingly, the *Faretta* right must impose some limits on the extent of standby counsel's unsolicited participation.[8]

First, the pro se defendant is entitled to preserve actual control over

---

7. A pro se defendant must generally accept any unsolicited help or hindrance that may come from the judge who chooses to call and question witnesses, from the prosecutor who faithfully exercises his duty to present evidence favorable to the defense, from the plural voices speaking "for the defense" in a trial of more than one defendant, or from an amicus counsel appointed to assist the court, see Brown v. United States, 105 U.S. App. D.C. 77, 83, 264 F.2d 363, 369 (C.A.D.C. 1959) (Judge Burger, concurring in part).

8. Since the right of self-representation is a right that when exercised usually increases the likelihood of a trial outcome unfavorable to the defendant, its denial is not amenable to "harmless error" analysis. The right is either respected or denied; its deprivation cannot be harmless.

As a corollary, however, a defendant who exercises his right to appear pro se "cannot thereafter complain that the quality of his own defense amounted to a denial of 'effective assistance of counsel.' " *Faretta*, 422 U.S., at 834 n.46. Moreover, the defendant's right to proceed pro se exists in the larger context of the criminal trial designed to determine whether or not a defendant is guilty of the offense with which he is charged. The trial judge may be required to make numerous rulings reconciling the participation of standby counsel with a pro se defendant's objection to that participation; nothing in the nature of the *Faretta* right suggests that the usual deference to "judgment calls" on these issues by the trial judge should not obtain here as elsewhere.

the case he chooses to present to the jury. This is the core of the *Faretta* right. If standby counsel's participation over the defendant's objection effectively allows counsel to make or substantially interfere with any significant tactical decisions, or to control the questioning of witnesses, or to speak *instead* of the defendant on any matter of importance, the *Faretta* right is eroded.

Second, participation by standby counsel without the defendant's consent should not be allowed to destroy the jury's perception that the defendant is representing himself. The defendant's appearance in the status of one conducting his own defense is important in a criminal trial, since the right to appear pro se exists to affirm the accused's individual dignity and autonomy. In related contexts the courts have recognized that a defendant has a right to be present at all important stages of trial, Snyder v. Massachusetts, that he may not normally be forced to appear in court in shackles or prison garb, Estelle v. Williams, and that he has a right to present testimony in his own behalf, see Harris v. New York; Brooks v. Tennessee. Appearing before the jury in the status of one who is defending himself may be equally important to the pro se defendant. From the jury's perspective, the message conveyed by the defense may depend as much on the messenger as on the message itself. From the defendant's own point of view, the right to appear pro se can lose much of its importance if only the lawyers in the courtroom know that the right is being exercised.

IV

Participation by standby counsel outside the presence of the jury engages only the first of these two limitations. A trial judge, who in any event receives a defendant's original *Faretta* request and supervises the protection of the right throughout the trial, must be considered capable of differentiating the claims presented by a pro se defendant from those presented by standby counsel. . . . Accordingly, the appearance of a pro se defendant's self-representation will not be unacceptably undermined by counsel's participation outside the presence of the jury.

Thus, *Faretta* rights are adequately vindicated in proceedings outside the presence of the jury if the pro se defendant is allowed to address the court freely on his own behalf and if disagreements between counsel and the pro se defendant are resolved in the defendant's favor whenever the matter is one that would normally be left to the discretion of counsel. . . . [W]e are satisfied that counsel's participation outside the presence of the jury fully satisfied the first standard we have outlined. Wiggins was given ample opportunity to present his own position to the court on every matter discussed. He was given time to think matters over, to explain his problems and concerns informally, and to speak to the judge off the record. Standby counsel participated actively, but for the most part in an orderly manner. The one instance of overbearing conduct by counsel was a direct result of Wiggins' own indecision as to who would question the witness on voir dire. Wiggins was given abundant opportunity to argue his contentions to the court.

Equally important, all conflicts between Wiggins and counsel were resolved in Wiggins' favor. The trial judge repeatedly explained to all concerned that Wiggins' strategic choices, not counsel's, would prevail. . . . Not every motion made by Wiggins was granted, but in no instance was counsel's position adopted over Wiggins' on a matter that would normally be left to the defense's discretion.

V

Participation by standby counsel in the presence of the jury is more problematic. It is here that the defendant may legitimately claim that excessive involvement by counsel will destroy the appearance that the defendant is acting pro se. This, in turn, may erode the dignitary values that the right to self-representation is intended to promote and may undercut the defendant's presentation to the jury of his own most effective defense. Nonetheless, we believe that a categorical bar on participation by standby counsel in the presence of the jury is unnecessary.

A

In measuring standby counsel's involvement against the standards we have described, it is important not to lose sight of the defendant's own conduct. A defendant can waive his *Faretta* rights. Participation by counsel with a pro se defendant's express approval is, of course, constitutionally unobjectionable. A defendant's invitation to counsel to participate in the trial obliterates any claim that the participation in question deprived the defendant of control over his own defense. Such participation also diminishes any general claim that counsel unreasonably interfered with the defendant's right to appear in the status of one defending himself.

Although this is self-evident, it is also easily overlooked. A defendant like Wiggins, who vehemently objects at the beginning of trial to standby counsel's very presence in the courtroom, may express quite different views as the trial progresses. Even when he insists that he is not waiving his *Faretta* rights, a pro se defendant's solicitation of or acquiescence in certain types of participation by counsel substantially undermines later protestations that counsel interfered unacceptably.

The record in this case reveals that Wiggins' pro se efforts were undermined primarily by his own, frequent changes of mind regarding counsel's role. Early in the trial Wiggins insisted he wished to proceed entirely without assistance, but shortly thereafter he expressly agreed that counsel should question a witness on voir dire. Wiggins objected vehemently to some of counsel's motions, but warmly embraced others. Initially Wiggins objected to standby counsel's presence; later he refused to allow the trial to proceed in their absence; in the end he agreed that counsel would make a closing statement for the defense. The only two long appearances by counsel at Wiggins' trial, one before the jury and one outside its presence, were both initiated with Wiggins' express approval. In these circumstances it is very difficult to determine how much of counsel's participation was in fact contrary to Wiggins' desires of the moment.

Faretta does not require a trial judge to permit "hybrid" representation of the type Wiggins was actually allowed. But if a defendant is given the opportunity and elects to have counsel appear before the court or jury, his complaints concerning counsel's subsequent unsolicited participation lose much of their force. A defendant does not have a constitutional right to choreograph special appearances by counsel. Once a pro se defendant invites or agrees to any substantial participation by counsel, subsequent appearances by counsel must be presumed to be with the defendant's acquiescence, at least until the defendant expressly and unambiguously renews his request that standby counsel be silenced.

B

Faretta rights are also not infringed when standby counsel assists the pro se defendant in overcoming routine procedural or evidentiary obstacles to the completion of some specific task, such as introducing evidence or objecting to testimony, that the defendant has clearly shown he wishes to complete. Nor are they infringed when counsel merely helps to ensure the defendant's compliance with basic rules of courtroom protocol and procedure. In neither case is there any significant interference with the defendant's actual control over the presentation of his defense. The likelihood that the defendant's appearance in the status of one defending himself will be eroded is also slight, and in any event it is tolerable. A defendant does not have a constitutional right to receive personal instruction from the trial judge on courtroom procedure. Nor does the Constitution require judges to take over chores for a pro se defendant that would normally be attended to by trained counsel as a matter of course. . . .

Accordingly, we make explicit today what is already implicit in *Faretta:* A defendant's Sixth Amendment rights are not violated when a trial judge appoints standby counsel—even over the defendant's objection—to relieve the judge of the need to explain and enforce basic rules of courtroom protocol or to assist the defendant in overcoming routine obstacles that stand in the way of the defendant's achievement of his own clearly indicated goals. Participation by counsel to steer a defendant through the basic procedures of trial is permissible even in the unlikely event that it somewhat undermines the pro se defendant's appearance of control over his own defense. . . .

C

Putting aside participation that was either approved by Wiggins or attendant to routine clerical or procedural matters, counsel's unsolicited comments in front of the jury were infrequent and for the most part innocuous. On two occasions Graham interrupted a witness's answer to a question put by Wiggins. The first interruption was trivial. When the second was made the jury was briefly excused and subsequently given a cautionary instruction as requested by Graham. Wiggins made no objection. Standby counsel also moved for a mistrial three times in the presence of the jury. Each motion was in response to allegedly prejudicial questions or comments by the prosecutor. Wiggins did not comment on the first motion, but he opposed the following two. All three motions were immediately denied by the trial court. Regrettably, counsel used profanity to express his exasperation on the second occasion.[15] Finally, counsel played an active role at the punishment phase of the trial. The record supplies no explanation for the sudden change in this regard. Wiggins made no objection to counsel's participation in this phase of the trial. We can only surmise that by then Wiggins had concluded that appearing pro se was not in his best interests.

15.

> *Mr. Graham:*   Objection, Your Honor. The district attorney is testifying.
> *The Court:*   Don't lead.
> *Mr. Graham:*   I ask the Court to instruct the jury to disregard the remarks of counsel as not being testimony in the case.
> *The Court:*   The Court will instruct the jury to disregard the last statement made by Mr. Rodriguez.
> *Mr. Graham:*   Notwithstanding the Court's instruction, I am sure it is so prejudicial as to require a mistrial.
> *Defendant:*   No, Your Honor. I object to a mistrial. I object to counsel—
> *The Court:*   I denied the motion for mistrial. Overruled.
> *Mr. Graham:*   Jesus Christ. . . .

The statements made by counsel during the guilt phase of the trial, in the presence of the jury and without Wiggins' express consent, occupy only a small portion of the transcript. Most were of an unobjectionable, mechanical sort. While standby counsel's participation at Wiggins' trial should not serve as a model for future trials, we believe that counsel's involvement fell short of infringing on Wiggins' *Faretta* rights. Wiggins unquestionably maintained actual control over the presentation of his own defense at all times.

We are also persuaded that Wiggins was allowed to appear before the jury in the status of one defending himself. At the outset the trial judge carefully explained to the jury that Wiggins would be appearing pro se. Wiggins, not counsel, examined prospective jurors on voir dire, cross-examined the prosecution's witnesses, examined his own witnesses, and made an opening statement for the defense. Wiggins objected to the prosecutor's case at least as often as did counsel. If Wiggins' closing statement to the jury had to compete with one made by counsel, it was only because Wiggins agreed in advance to that arrangement.

By contrast, counsel's interruptions of Wiggins or witnesses being questioned by Wiggins in the presence of the jury were few and perfunctory. Most of counsel's uninvited comments were directed at the prosecutor. Such interruptions present little threat to a defendant's *Faretta* rights, at least when the defendant's view regarding those objections has not been clearly articulated. On the rare occasions that disagreements between counsel and Wiggins were aired in the presence of the jury the trial judge consistently ruled in Wiggins' favor. This was a pattern more likely to reinforce than to detract from the appearance that Wiggins was controlling his own defense. The intrusions by counsel at Wiggins' trial were simply not substantial or frequent enough to have seriously undermined Wiggins' appearance before the jury in the status of one representing himself.

VI

Faretta affirmed the defendant's constitutional right to appear on stage at his trial. We recognize that a pro se defendant may wish to dance a solo, not a pas de deux. Standby counsel must generally respect that preference. But counsel need not be excluded altogether, especially when the participation is outside the presence of the jury or is with the defendant's express or tacit consent. The defendant in this case was allowed to make his own appearances as he saw fit. In our judgment counsel's unsolicited involvement was held within reasonable limits.

The judgment of the Court of Appeals is therefore reversed.

JUSTICE BLACKMUN concurs in the result.

JUSTICE WHITE, with whom JUSTICE BRENNAN and JUSTICE MAR-SHALL join, dissenting. . . .

. . . The Court concludes, on the basis of its examination of the record, that Wiggins was afforded "a fair chance to present his case in his own way," and that "counsel's unsolicited involvement was held within reasonable limits." It arrives at this conclusion by applying a two-part test that, in my judgment, provides little or no guidance for counsel and trial judges, imposes difficult, if not impossible, burdens on appellate courts, and undoubtedly will lead to the swift erosion of defendants' constitutional right to proceed pro se.

Under the Court's new test, it is necessary to determine whether the pro se defendant retained "actual control over the case he [chose] to present to the jury," and whether standby counsel's participation "destroy[ed] the jury's perception that the defendant [was] representing himself." Although this test purports to protect all of the values underlying our holding in *Faretta*, it is unclear whether it can achieve this result.

As long as the pro se defendant is allowed his say, the first prong of the Court's test accords standby counsel at a bench trial or any proceeding outside the presence of a jury virtually untrammeled discretion to present any factual or legal argument to which the defendant does not object. The limits placed on counsel's participation in this context by the "actual control" test are more apparent than real. First, counsel may not "make or substantially interfere with any significant tactical decisions." Unless counsel directly overrides a defendant's strategy in the presence of the judge, however, it is apparent that courts will be almost wholly incapable of assessing the subtle and not-so-subtle effects of counsel's participation of the defense. Second, the Court suggests that conflicts between the pro se defendant and standby counsel on "matter[s] that would normally be left to the defense's discretion," id., at 953, will be resolved in the defendant's favor. But many disagreements will not produce direct conflicts requiring a trial court to choose one position over another. Under the Court's opinion, the burden apparently will fall on the pro se defendant to comprehend counsel's submissions and to create conflicts for the trial court to resolve. If applied this way, the Court's test surely will prove incapable of safeguarding the interest in individual autonomy from which the *Faretta* right derives.

Although the Court is more solicitous of a pro se defendant's interests when standby counsel intervenes before a jury, the test's second prong suffers from similar shortcomings. To the extent that trial and appellate courts can discern the point at which counsel's unsolicited participation substantially undermines a pro se defendant's appearance before the jury, a matter about which I harbor substantial doubts, their decisions will, to a certain extent, "affirm the accused's individual dignity and autonomy." But they will do so incompletely, for in focusing on how the jury views the defendant, the majority opinion ignores *Faretta's* emphasis on the defendant's own perception of the criminal justice system, Faretta v. California, supra, 422 U.S., at 834, and implies that the Court actually adheres to the result-oriented harmless error standard it purports to reject.

As a guide for standby counsel and lower courts, moreover, the Court's two-part test is clearly deficient. Instead of encouraging counsel to accept a limited role, the Court plainly invites them to participate despite their clients' contrary instructions until the clients renew their objections and trial courts draw the line. Trial courts required to rule on pro se defendants' objections to counsel's intervention also are left at sea. They clearly must prevent standby counsel from overtly muzzling their pro se clients and resolve certain conflicts in defendants' favor. But the Court's opinion places few, if any, other clear limits on counsel's un-invited participation; instead it requires trial courts to make numerous subjective judgments concerning the effect of counsel's actions on defendants' *Faretta* rights. Because trial courts generally will consider only isolated actions of standby counsel expressly challenged by pro se defendants, only appellate courts may be in a position to form impressions on the basis of the entire trial. These courts, however, also will suffer from the lack of clear standards and from their inability or unwillingness to make the factual inquiries necessitated by the Court's two-part test.

In short, I believe that the Court's test is unworkable and insufficiently protective of the fundamental interests we recognized in *Faretta*. . . .

NOTES AND QUESTIONS

1. Who wins the historical argument in *Faretta* centering on the intent of the framers of the sixth amendment? Which way does the statutory history cut?

2. What does it mean that a waiver of counsel must be "knowing and intelligent"? Is that phrase internally inconsistent? If not, what are its referents? The Court asserts that "technical knowledge" is not even relevant to the inquiry and implies that on being convicted a technically incompetent individual may not assert ineffectiveness as a grounds for relief. How realistic is that? How would you react as a judge to a case where an untrained person unknowingly forwent a potentially dispositive defense? See United States v. Weninger, 624 F.2d 163 (10th Cir. 1980),

disallowing a defense of ineffectiveness from a defendant who proceeded pro se at trial.

3. Is there, or ought there to be, a requirement of competency to waive separate from the issues of competency to proceed to trial and an intelligent waiver? The New York Court of Appeals answered the question negatively in the aptly named case of People v. Reason, 37 N.Y.2d 351 (1975). According to the court, "it would be difficult to say that a standard which was designed to determine whether a defendant was capable of defending himself, is inadequate when he chooses to conduct his own defense." Id. at 354. The court consequently affirmed defendant's convictions of murder and attempted murder. Bearing in mind the limits of anecdotal data, consider the decision in *Reason* in light of the following excerpts from Mr. Reason's opening and closing to the jury:

> *The Court:*   The order of business before the Court now, Mr. Reason, is your opening statement. Will you proceed and make it properly?
>
> *The Defendant:*   I will try to prove the existence of the dead, reincarnation of the realm of Todis, . . . Hays, . . . Hell, the underworld and the hushed truth of society based upon the entities of which our way of life is based. Fighting among themselves even for possession of the living and the dead and the association of whatever rationality or religion.
>
>   I will prove an angel, demon, a devil and a soul. Paradoxically I will introduce proof of police corruption, political control of government, criminal affairs according to certain arbitrations, abiding the way of life for a particular entity of homage of their dues for the bargaining of their souls. . . .
>
>   I will prove or I will disprove Christ as our God, saints, the devil and let these entities of the power to take human life and due—there is many deeply religious people that say it was the will of God who in many instances—it isn't always the will of God, but the will of other entities or as we read at the bottom of insurance contracts except by acts of God, sometimes by those acts of men too, by means of what may be considered a spiritual sort seemingly to have been of natural causes and often some that would have died by the cause of another is used as an instrument to die; that the other would be subject to the instrument of society such as fate, destiny, pre-destiny. But history is an accepted fact as disorderly as it may be which I will also attempt to prove, and historically men have proved, prayed to something of a greater competency, to Jehovah, Brahma, Ghatama, God and others. They believe, practice and perform rituals of sorcery, Budabo, witchcraft, Christianity, black magic, occult, Bubanza, . . . soothsayers, fortune tellers and priests. . . .
>
>   I will introduce the defendant's bad character to show his good intention or expose his entire criminal record, acts of his criminal

importance, accomplishments, activities and disciplinary reports be considered. . . .

[In closing, the defendant argued in part:]

The issue of the dead belonged to God. It's in the bible. Each of the dead belong to God. God seeks the past. Life gives birth to time, time is passed, just passed, time passed, just passed. Anticipate time. Time is past. Hour has already been. I wrote right here, I would like to repeat that and I would, I would like to repeat that.

A long time ago, anticipating this, I would like to repeat that.

The issue of the dead belong of God. God seeks what is passed. Life gives birth to time. Time is past. We set time ahead of us confusing time and motion with duration. We are towards a delusion, perhaps, create illusion of a present that don't really exist; create instantaneous occurring successions on the same pattern offset by the evolving sun as time though it made difference to the sun how fast— (Unintelligible).

Now, look at that, you people. I wrote it for you people. Memorized the whole thing if I had the time. This is not only pedantics, I quote Corinthian, Chapter 13, 8th Verse.

4. If a defendant's right to proceed pro se is violated, what should be the remedy?

5. Should a waiver of counsel ever be allowed without appointing counsel to discuss the matter with the defendant?

6. Should a defendant be permitted to act as co-counsel with appointed or retained counsel? What may be gained or lost by that? For a discussion of a case of joint representation, see A. Davis, If They Come in the Morning (1971). The general trend is to disallow "hybrid representation." Wright v. Estelle, 572 F.2d 1071 (5th Cir. 1978); United States v. Olson, 576 F.2d 1267 (8th Cir. 1978); Burney v. State, 244 Ga. 33, 257 S.E.2d 543 (1979).

7. If an individual has the right to proceed pro se as an implication of basic demands of human dignity, should the person also have the right, if indigent, to choose who shall be appointed counsel if the person wishes to have counsel appointed? The general view is that there is no such right, the leading case being Drumgo v. Superior Court, 8 Cal. 3d 930, 506 P.2d 1007, 106 Cal. Rptr. 631 (1973). Five years after *Drumgo*, the California Supreme Court held that failure to respect an indigent's choice of counsel may amount to an abuse of discretion by the trial court where there are objective circumstances making defendant's request reasonable. Harris v. Superior Court, 19 Cal. 3d 786, 567 P.2d 750, 140 Cal. Rptr. 318 (1977). The objective circumstances found persuasive in *Harris* were that the counsel defendants desired to be appointed represented defendants in related matters and were intimately acquainted with

the factual and legal matters likely to be relevant to the present litigation. Moreover, counsel appointed by the trial court were essentially ignorant of the case. For a discussion of the general problem, see Tague, An Indigent's Right to the Attorney of His Choice, 27 Stan. L. Rev. 73 (1974). The problem of the right to choose one's own counsel may have been resolved by Morris v. Slappy, 461 U.S. 1 (1983). In *Morris*, the Court held that the sixth amendment did not guarantee a "meaningful relationship" between attorney and client. Therefore, it was not error to refuse to grant a continuance to allow one public defender, whom the defendant desired as counsel, rather than another to try the case. The primary issue, according to the Court, was whether the attorney who actually tried the case did so competently.

8. May counsel "waive" the honor of representing an indigent defendant? The problem arises primarily after conviction where counsel is of the view that an appeal would be fruitless. In Anders v. California, 386 U.S. 738 (1967), the Court held that an attorney who wishes to withdraw from a case after conviction on the grounds that an appeal would be wholly frivolous may request permission to do so but must file a brief referring to anything in the record that might support an appeal. The relevant court is then to decide whether to permit withdrawal. Requiring counsel to write a brief in support of what counsel believes to be a wholly frivolous appeal may seem curious, but there are cases where such briefs have led to reversals. Carrington, Meador & Rosenberg, Justice on Appeal 77 (1976). In McCoy v. Court of Appeals of Wisconsin, District 1, 486 U.S. 429 (1988), the Court upheld a Wisconsin statute that required counsel writing *Anders* briefs to include a discussion of why the issues raised in the brief lacked merit. In Pennsylvania v. Finley, 481 U.S. 551 (1987), the Supreme Court concluded that an indigent does not have either an equal protection or a due process right to appointed counsel in post-conviction proceedings and thus has no right to insist that the *Anders* procedures for withdrawal of appointed counsel be followed when the state nonetheless had provided counsel. The Court rejected the argument that Evitts v. Lucey, page 170 supra, mandated that whenever a state supplies counsel, due process is implicated in such a manner that demands the *Anders* procedures. The Court reaffirmed *Anders* in Penson v. Ohio, 488 U.S. 75 (1988), holding that it was error to fail to appoint counsel to brief and argue any claim that a court of appeals finds to be colorable, even if problematic. The Court also held that Washington v. Strickland does not apply in this context, for otherwise *Anders* would be virtually overruled.

Is *Finley* inconsistent with Bounds v. Smith, discussed at page 157, note 5 supra, in the context of death penalty litigation? Recall that in *Bounds* the Court held that a state had to provide prisoners either with adequate law libraries or adequate legal assistance to facilitate prisoners' requests for post-conviction relief. Given the complexity of death penalty litigation and the stringent time constraints under which it is done, does a person on death row have a sixth amendment right to counsel since without counsel a prisoner on death row is effectively barred from competently litigating any claims for error that may be present in the case? No, said the Court in Murray v. Giarratano, 109 S. Ct. 2765 (1989). A four-member plurality (the Chief Justice, White, O'Connor, and Scalia) held that *Bounds* was limited to an adequate law library (or legal assistance instead of a law library). Justice Kennedy concurred on the ground that:

> The requirement of access can be satisfied in various ways. . . . While Virginia has not adopted procedures for securing representation that are as far reaching as those available in other States, no prisoner on death row in Virginia has been unable to obtain counsel to represent him in post-conviction proceedings, and Virginia's prison system is staffed with institutional lawyers to assist in preparing petitions for post-conviction relief. I am not prepared to say that this scheme violates the Constitution.

Also consider the implications of the following case where the Court rejected the assertion that "defense counsel has a constitutional duty to raise every nonfrivolous issue requested by the defendant."

JONES v. BARNES, 463 U.S. 745 (1983): CHIEF JUSTICE BURGER delivered the opinion of the court. . . .

Experienced advocates since time beyond memory have emphasized the importance of winnowing out weaker arguments on appeal and focusing on one central issue if possible, or at most on a few key issues. Justice Jackson, after observing appellate advocates for many years, stated:

> One of the first tests of a discriminating advocate is to select the question, or questions, that he will present orally. Legal contentions, like the currency, depreciate through over-issue. The mind of an appellate judge is habitually receptive to the suggestion that a lower court committed an error. But receptiveness declines as the number of assigned errors increases. Multiplicity hints at lack of confidence in any one. . . . [E]xperience on the bench convinces me that multiplying assignments of error will dilute and weaken a good case and will not save a bad one. [Jackson, Advocacy Before the Supreme Court, 25 Temple L.Q. 115, 119 (1951).]

Justice Jackson's observation echoes the advice of countless advocates before him and since. An authoritative work on appellate practice observes:

Most cases present only one, two, or three significant questions. . . .
Usually, . . . if you cannot win on a few major points, the others are not
likely to help, and to attempt to deal with a great many in the limited
number of pages allowed for briefs will mean that none may receive
adequate attention. The effect of adding weak arguments will be to dilute
the force of the stronger ones." [R. Stern, Appellate Practice in the United
States 266 (1981).]

There can hardly be any question about the importance of having
the appellate advocate examine the record with a view to selecting the
most promising issues for review. This has assumed a greater importance
in an era when oral argument is strictly limited in most courts—often
to as little as 15 minutes—and when page limits on briefs are widely
imposed. See, e.g., Fed. Rules App. Proc. 28(g); McKinney's 1982 New
York Rules of Court §§670.17(g)(2), 670.22. Even in a court that imposes
no time or page limits, however, the new per se rule laid down by the
Court of Appeals is contrary to all experience and logic. A brief that raises
every colorable issue runs the risk of burying good arguments—those
that, in the words of the great advocate John W. Davis, "go for the
jugular," Davis, The Argument of an Appeal, 26 A.B.A.J. 895, 897
(1940)—in a verbal mound made up of strong and weak contentions.
See generally, e.g., Godbold, Twenty Pages and Twenty Minutes—
Effective Advocacy on Appeal, 30 Sw. L.J. 801 (1976).[6]
This Court's decision in *Anders*, far from giving support to the new
per se rule announced by the Court of Appeals [that all nonfrivolous
issues raised by the client must be argued by the attorney], is to the
contrary. *Anders* recognized that the role of the advocate "requires that
he support his client's appeal to the best of his ability." 386 U.S., at 744.

---

6. The ABA Model Rules of Professional Conduct provide: "A lawyer shall abide
by a client's decisions concerning the objectives of representation . . . and shall consult
with the client as to the means by which they are to be pursued. . . . In a criminal
case, the lawyer shall abide by the client's decision, . . . *as to a plea to be entered,
whether to waive jury trial and whether the client will testify.*" Model Rules of Professional
Conduct, Proposed Rule 1.2(a) (Final Draft 1982) (emphasis added). With the exception
of these specified fundamental decisions, an attorney's duty is to take professional responsibility for the conduct of the case, after consulting with his client.
Respondent points to the ABA Standards for Criminal Appeals, which appear to
indicate that counsel should accede to a client's insistence on pressing a particular contention on appeal, see ABA Standards for Criminal Justice 21-3.2, at 21-42 (2d ed. 1980).
The ABA Defense Function Standards provide, however, that, with the exceptions specified above, strategic and tactical decisions are the exclusive province of the defense
counsel, after consultation with the client. See ABA Standards for Criminal Justice
4-5.2 (2d ed. 1980). See also ABA Project on Standards for Criminal Justice, The
Prosecution Function and The Defense Function §5.2 (Tent. Draft 1970). In any event,
the fact that the ABA may have chosen to recognize a given practice as desirable or
appropriate does not mean that that practice is required by the Constitution.

Here the appointed counsel did just that. For judges to second-guess reasonable professional judgments and impose on appointed counsel a duty to raise every "colorable" claim suggested by a client would disserve the very goal of vigorous and effective advocacy that underlies *Anders*. Nothing in the Constitution or our interpretation of that document requires such a standard.[7]

JUSTICE BRENNAN, with whom JUSTICE MARSHALL joins, dissenting.

The Sixth Amendment provides that "[i]n all criminal prosecutions, the accused shall enjoy the right . . . to have the *Assistance* of Counsel for his defense" (emphasis added). I find myself in fundamental disagreement with the Court over what a right to "the assistance of counsel" means. The import of words like "assistance" and "counsel" seems inconsistent with a regime under which counsel appointed by the State to represent a criminal defendant can refuse to raise issues with arguable merit on appeal when his client, after hearing his assessment of the case and his advice, has directed him to raise them. I would remand for a determination whether respondent did in fact insist that his lawyer brief the issues that the Court of Appeals found were not frivolous. . . .

. . . The Court argues that good appellate advocacy demands selectivity among arguments. That is certainly true—the Court's advice is good. It ought to be taken to heart by every lawyer called upon to argue an appeal in this or any other court, and by his client. It should take little or no persuasion to get a wise client to understand that, if staying out of prison is what he values most, he should encourage his lawyer to raise only his two or three best arguments on appeal, and he should defer to his lawyer's advice as to which are the best arguments. The Constitution, however, does not require clients to be wise, and other policies should be weighed in the balance as well.

It is no secret that indigent clients often mistrust the lawyers appointed to represent them. See generally Burt, Conflict and Trust Between Attorney and Client, 69 Geo. L.J. 1015 (1981); Skolnick, Social Control in the Adversary System, 11 J. Conflict Res. 52 (1967). There are many reasons for this, some perhaps unavoidable even under perfect conditions—differences in education, disposition, and socioeconomic class—and some that should (but may not always) be zealously avoided.

---

7. The only question presented by this case is whether a criminal defendant has a constitutional right to have appellate counsel raise every nonfrivolous issue that the defendant requests. The availability of federal habeas corpus to review claims that counsel declined to raise is not before us, and we have no occasion to decide whether counsel's refusal to raise requested claims would constitute "cause" for a petitioner's default within the meaning of Wainwright v. Sykes, 433 U.S. 72 (1977). See also Engle v. Isaac, 456 U.S. 107, 128 (1982).

A lawyer and his client do not always have the same interests. Even with paying clients, a lawyer may have a strong interest in having judges and prosecutors think well of him, and, if he is working for a flat fee—a common arrangement for criminal defense attorneys—or if his fees for court appointments are lower than he would receive for other work, he has an obvious financial incentive to conclude cases on his criminal docket swiftly. Good lawyers undoubtedly recognize these temptations and resist them, and they endeavor to convince their clients that they will. It would be naive, however, to suggest that they always succeed in either task. A constitutional rule that encourages lawyers to disregard their clients' wishes without compelling need can only exacerbate the clients' suspicion of their lawyers. As in *Faretta*, to force a lawyer's *decisions* on a defendant "can only lead him to believe that the law conspires against him." See 422 U.S., at 834. In the end, what the Court hopes to gain in effectiveness of appellate representation by the rule it imposes today may well be lost to decreased effectiveness in other areas of representation.

The Court's opinion also seems to overstate somewhat the lawyer's role in an appeal. While excellent presentation of issues, especially at the briefing stage, certainly serves the client's best interests, I do not share the Court's implicit pessimism about appellate judges' ability to recognize a meritorious argument, even if it is made less elegantly or in fewer pages than the lawyer would have liked, and even if less meritorious arguments accompany it. If the quality of justice in this country really depended on nice gradations in lawyers' rhetorical skills, we could no longer call it "justice." Especially at the appellate level, I believe that for the most part good claims will be vindicated and bad claims rejected, with truly skillful advocacy making a difference only in a handful of cases. In most of such cases—in most cases generally—clients ultimately will do the wise thing and take their lawyers' advice. I am not willing to risk deepening the mistrust between clients and lawyers in all cases to ensure optimal presentation for that fraction-of-a-handful in which presentation might really affect the result reached by the Court of Appeals.

Finally, today's ruling denigrates the values of individual autonomy and dignity central to many constitutional rights, especially those Fifth and Sixth Amendment rights that come into play in the criminal process. Certainly a person's life changes when he is charged with a crime and brought to trial. He must, if he harbors any hope of success, defend himself on terms—often technical and hard to understand—that are the State's, not his own. As a practical matter, the assistance of counsel is necessary to that defense. . . . Yet, until his conviction becomes final and he has had an opportunity to appeal, any restrictions on individual autonomy and dignity should be limited to the minimum necessary to vindicate the State's interest in a speedy, effective prosecution. The role of the defense lawyer should be above all to function as the instrument and defender of the client's autonomy and dignity in all phases of the criminal process. . . .

2. The Implications of Forfeiture Statutes

CAPLIN & DRYSDALE, CHARTERED v. UNITED STATES
—U.S.—, 109 S. Ct. 2646 (1989)

JUSTICE WHITE delivered the opinion of the Court.

We are called on to determine whether the federal drug forfeiture statute includes an exemption for assets that a defendant wishes to use to pay an attorney who conducted his defense in the criminal case where forfeiture was sought. Because we determine that no such exemption exists, we must decide whether that statute, so interpreted, is consistent with the Fifth and Sixth Amendments. We hold that it is.

I

In January 1985, Christopher Reckmeyer was charged in a multicount indictment with running a massive drug importation and distribution scheme. The scheme was alleged to be a continuing criminal enterprise (CCE), in violated of 21 U.S.C. §848 (1982 ed., Supp. V). Relying on a portion of the CCE statute that authorizes forfeiture to the government of "property constituting, or derived from . . . proceeds . . . obtained" from drug-law violations,[1] the indictment sought forfeiture of specified assets in Reckmeyer's possession. At this time, the District Court entered a restraining order forbidding Reckmeyer to transfer any of the listed assets that were potentially forfeitable.

Sometime earlier, Reckmeyer had retained petitioner, a law firm, to represent him in the ongoing grand jury investigation which resulted

---

1. The forfeiture statute provides, in relevant part, that any person convicted of a particular class of criminal offenses: "shall forfeit to the United States, irrespective of any provision of State law— "(1) any property constituting, or derived from, any proceeds the person obtained, directly or indirectly, as the result of such violation. . . .

"The court, in imposing sentence on such person, shall order, in addition to any other sentence imposed . . . that the person forfeit to the United States all property described in this subsection." 21 U.S.C. §853 (1982 ed., Supp. V). There is no question here that the offenses respondent was accused of in the indictment fell within the class of crimes triggering this forfeiture provision.

in the January 1985 indictments. Notwithstanding the restraining order, Reckmeyer paid the firm $25,000 for preindictment legal services a few days after the indictment was handed down; this sum was placed by petitioner in an escrow account. Petitioner continued to represent Reckmeyer following the indictment.

On March 7, 1985, Reckmeyer moved to modify the District Court's earlier restraining order to permit him to use some of the restrained assets to pay petitioner's fees; Reckmeyer also sought to exempt from any post-conviction forfeiture order the assets that he intended to use to pay petitioner. However, one week later, before the District Court could conduct a hearing on this motion, Reckmeyer entered a plea agreement with the Government. Under the agreement, Reckmeyer pleaded guilty to the drug-related CCE charge, and agreed to forfeit all of the specified assets listed in the indictment. The day after the Reckmeyer's plea was entered, the District Court denied his earlier motion to modify the restraining order, concluding that the plea and forfeiture agreement rendered irrelevant any further consideration of the propriety of the court's pretrial restraints. Subsequently, an order forfeiting virtually all of the assets in Reckmeyer's possession was entered by the District Court in conjunction with his sentencing.

After this order was entered, petitioner filed a petition under 21 U.S.C. §853(n) (1982 ed., Supp. V), which permits third parties with an interest in forfeited property to ask the sentencing court for an adjudication of their rights to that property; specifically, §853(n)(6)(B) gives a third party who entered into a bona fide transaction with a defendant a right to make claims against forfeited property, if that third party was "at the time of [the transaction] reasonably without cause to believe that the [defendant's assets were] subject to forfeiture." Petitioner claimed an interest in $170,000 of Reckmeyer's assets, for services it had provided Reckmeyer in conducting his defense; petitioner also sought the $25,000 being held in the escrow account, as payment for preindictment legal services. Petitioner argued alternatively that assets used to pay an attorney were exempt from forfeiture under §853, and if not, the failure of the statute to provide such an exemption rendered it unconstitutional. The District Court granted petitioner's claim for a share of the forfeited assets.

A panel of the Fourth Circuit affirmed, finding that—while §853 contained no statutory provision authorizing the payment of attorneys' fees out of forfeited assets—the statute's failure to do so impermissibly infringed a defendant's Sixth Amendment right to the counsel of his choice. The Court of Appeals agreed to hear the case en banc, and reversed. All the judges of the Fourth Circuit agreed that the language of the CCE statute acknowledged no exception to its forfeiture requirement that would recognize petitioner's claim to the forfeited assets. A majority found this statutory scheme constitutional; four dissenting judges, however, agreed with the panel's view that the statute so-construed violated the Sixth Amendment.

Petitioner sought review of the statutory and constitutional issues raised by the Court of Appeals' holding. We granted certiorari, and now affirm.

II

Petitioner's first submission is that the statutory provision that authorizes pretrial restraining orders on potentially forfeitable assets in a defendant's possession grants district courts equitable discretion to determine when such orders should be imposed. This discretion should be exercised under "traditional equitable standards," petitioner urges, including a "weigh[ing] of the equities and competing hardships on the parties"; under this approach, a court "must invariably strike the balance so as to allow a defendant [to pay] . . . for bona fide attorneys fees," petitioner argues. Petitioner further submits that once a district court so exercises its discretion, and fails to freeze assets that a defendant then uses to pay an attorney, the statute's provision for recapture of forfeitable assets transferred to third parties, may not operate on such sums.

Petitioner's argument, as it acknowledges, is based on the view of the statute expounded by Judge Winter of the Second Circuit in his concurring opinion in that Court of Appeals' en banc decision, United States v. Monsanto, 852 F.2d 1400, 1405-1411 (1988). We reject this interpretation of the statute today in our decision in United States v. Monsanto [109 S. Ct. 2657(1989)], which reverses the Second Circuit's holding in that case. As we explain in our *Monsanto* decision, whatever discretion §853(e) provides district court judges to refuse to enter pretrial restraining orders, it does not extend as far as petitioner urges—nor does the exercise of that discretion "immunize" nonrestrained assets from subsequent forfeiture under §853(c), if they are transferred to an attorney to pay legal fees. Thus, for the reasons provided in our opinion in *Monsanto*, we reject petitioner's statutory claim.

III

We therefore address petitioner's constitutional challenges to the forfeiture law. Petitioner contends that the statute infringes on criminal defendants' Sixth Amendment right to counsel of choice, and upsets the "balance of power" between the government and the accused in a manner contrary to the Due Process Clause of the Fifth Amendment. We consider these contentions in turn.

A

Petitioner's first claim is that the forfeiture law makes impossible, or at least impermissibly burdens, a defendant's right "to select and be represented by one's preferred attorney." Wheat v. United States, 486 U.S. 153, 159 (1988). Petitioner does not, nor could it defensibly do so, assert that impecunious defendants have a Sixth Amendment right to choose their counsel. The amendment guarantees defendants in criminal cases the right to adequate representation, but those who do not have the means to hire their own lawyers have no cognizable complaint so long as they are adequately represented by attorneys appointed by the courts. "[A] defendant may not insist on representation by an attorney he cannot afford." Wheat, supra, at 159. Petitioner does not dispute these propositions. Nor does the Government deny that the Sixth Amendment guarantees a defendant the right to be represented by an otherwise qualified attorney whom that defendant can afford to hire, or who is willing to represent the defendant even though he is without funds. Applying these principles to the statute in question here, we observe that nothing in §853 prevents a defendant from hiring the attorney of his choice, or disqualifies any attorney from serving as a defendant's counsel. Thus, unlike Wheat, this case does not involve a situation where the Government has asked a court to prevent a defendant's chosen counsel from representing the accused. Instead, petitioner urges that a violation of the Sixth Amendment arises here because of the forfeiture, at the instance of the Government, of assets that defendants intend to use to pay their attorneys.

Even in this sense, of course, the burden the forfeiture law imposes on a criminal defendant is limited. The forfeiture statute does not prevent a defendant who has nonforfeitable assets from retaining any attorney of his choosing. Nor is it necessarily the case that a defendant who possesses nothing but assets the Government seeks to have forfeited will be prevented from retaining counsel of choice. Defendants like Reckmeyer may be able to find lawyers willing to represent them, hoping that their fees will be paid in the event of acquittal, or via some other means that a defendant might come by in the future. The burden placed on defendants by the forfeiture law is therefore a limited one.

Nonetheless, there will be cases where a defendant will be unable to retain the attorney of his choice, when that defendant would have been able to hire that lawyer if he had access to forfeitable assets, and if there was no risk that fees paid by the defendant to his counsel would later be recouped under §853(c).[4] It is in these cases, petitioner argues, that the Sixth Amendment puts limits on the forfeiture statute.

This submission is untenable. Whatever the full extent of the Sixth Amendment's protection of one's right to retain counsel of his choosing, that protection does not go beyond "the individual's right to spend his own money to obtain the advice and assistance of . . . counsel." A defendant has no Sixth Amendment right to spend another person's money for services rendered by an attorney, even if those funds are the only way that that defendant will be able to retain the attorney of his choice. A robbery suspect, for example, has no Sixth Amendment right to use funds he has stolen from a bank to retain an attorney to defend him if he is apprehended. The money, though in his possession is not rightfully his; the government does not violate the Sixth Amendment if it seizes the robbery proceeds, and refuses to permit the defendant to use them to pay for his defense. . . .

Petitioner seeks to distinguish such cases for Sixth Amendment purposes by arguing that the bank's claim to robbery proceeds rests on "pre-existing property rights," while the Government's claim to forfeitable assets rests on a "penal statute" which embodies the "fictive property-law concept of . . . relation-back" and is merely "a mechanism for preventing fraudulent conveyances of the defendant's assets, not . . . a device for determining true title to property." Brief for Petitioner 40-41. In light of this, petitioner contends, the burden placed on defendant's Sixth Amendment rights by the forfeiture statute outweighs the Government's interest in forfeiture.

The premises of petitioner's constitutional analysis are unsound in several respects. First, the property rights given the Government by virtue of the forfeiture statute are more substantial than petitioner acknowledges. In §853(c), the so-called "relation-back" provision, Congress dictated that "[a]ll right, title and interest in property" obtained by criminals via the illicit means described in the statute "vests in the United States upon the commission of the act giving rise to forfeiture." As Congress observed when the provision was adopted, this approach, known as the "taint theory," is one that "has long been recognized in forfeiture cases," including the decision in United States v. Stowell, 133 U.S. 1 (1890). In

---

4. That section of the statute, which includes the so-called "relation back" provision, states: "All right, title, and interest in property described in [§853] vests in the United States upon the commission of the act giving rise to forfeiture under this section. Any such property that is subsequently transferred to a person other than the defendant may be the subject of a special verdict of forfeiture and thereafter shall be forfeited to the United States, unless the transferee [establishes his entitlement to such property pursuant to §853(n)]." 21 U.S.C. §853(c) (1982 ed., Supp. V).

Stowell, the Court explained the operation of a similar forfeiture provision (for violations of the Internal Revenue Code) as follows:

> As soon [as the possessor of the forfeitable asset committed the violation] of the internal revenue laws, the forfeiture under those laws took effect, and (though needing judicial condemnation to perfect it) operated from that time as a statutory conveyance to the United States of all the right, title, and interest then remaining in the [possessor]; and was as valid and effectual, against all the world, as a recorded deed. The right so vested in the United States could not be defeated or impaired by any subsequent dealings of the . . . [possessor]." *Stowell*, supra, at 19.

In sum, §853(c) reflects the application of the long-recognized and lawful practice of vesting title to any forfeitable assets, in the United States, at the time of the criminal act giving rise to forfeiture. Concluding that Reckmeyer cannot give good title to such property to petitioner because he did not hold good title is neither extraordinary or novel. Nor does petitioner claim, as a general proposition that the relation-back provision is unconstitutional, or that Congress cannot, as a general matter, vest title to assets derived from the crime in the Government, as of the date of the criminal act in question. Petitioner's claim is that whatever part of the assets that is necessary to pay attorney's fees cannot be subjected to forfeiture. But given the Government's title to Reckmeyer's assets upon conviction, to hold that the Sixth Amendment creates some right in Reckmeyer to alienate such assets, or creates a right on petitioner's part to receive these assets, would be peculiar.

There is no constitutional principle that gives one person the right to give another's property to a third party, even where the person seeking to complete the exchange wishes to do so in order to exercise a constitutionally protected right. While petitioner and its supporting amici attempt to distinguish between the expenditure of forfeitable assets to exercise one's Sixth Amendment rights, and expenditures in the pursuit of other constitutionally protected freedoms, there is no such distinction between, or hierarchy among, constitutional rights. If defendants have a right to spend forfeitable assets on attorney's fees, why not on exercises of the right to speak, practice one's religion, or travel? The full exercise of these rights, too, depends in part on one's financial wherewithal; and forfeiture, or even the threat of forfeiture, may similarly prevent a defendant from enjoying these rights as fully as he might otherwise. Nonetheless, we are not about to recognize an antiforfeiture exception for the exercise of each such right; nor does one exist for the exercise of Sixth Amendment rights, either.

Petitioner's "balancing analysis" to the contrary rests substantially on the view that the Government has only a modest interest in forfeitable assets that may be used to retain an attorney. Petitioner takes the position that, in large part, once assets have been paid over from client to attorney, the principal ends of forfeiture have been achieved: dispossessing a drug dealer or racketeer of the proceeds of his wrongdoing. We think that this view misses the mark for three reasons.

First, the Government has a pecuniary interest in forfeiture that goes beyond merely separating a criminal from his ill-gotten gains; that legitimate interest extends to recovering *all* forfeitable assets, for such assets are deposited in a Fund that supports law-enforcement efforts in a variety of important and useful ways. The sums of money that can be raised for law-enforcement activities this way are substantial,[6] and the Government's interest in using the profits of crime to fund these activities should not be discounted.

Second, the statute permits "rightful owners" of forfeited assets to make claims for forfeited assets before they are retained by the government. The Government's interest in winning undiminished forfeiture thus includes the objective of returning property, in full, to those wrongfully deprived or defrauded of it. Where the Government pursues this restitutionary end, the government's interest in forfeiture is virtually indistinguishable from its interest in returning to a bank the proceeds of a bank robbery; and a forfeiture-defendant's claim of right to use such assets to hire an attorney, instead of having them returned to their rightful owners, is not more persuasive than a bank robber's similar claim.

Finally, as we have recognized previously, a major purpose motivating congressional adoption and continued refinement of the RICO and CCE forfeiture provisions has been the desire to lessen the economic power of organized crime and drug enterprises. This includes the use of such economic power to retain private counsel. As the Court of Appeals put it: "Congress has already underscored the compelling public interest in stripping criminals such as Reckmeyer of their undeserved economic power, and part of that undeserved power may be the ability to command high-priced legal talent." The notion that the government has a legitimate interest in depriving criminals of economic power, even in so far as that power is used to retain counsel of choice, may be somewhat unsettling. But when a defendant claims that he has suffered some substantial impairment of his Sixth Amendment rights by virtue of the seizure or forfeiture of assets in his possession, such a complaint is no more than the reflection of "the harsh reality that the quality of a criminal defendant's

---

6. For example, just one of the assets which Reckmeyer agreed to forfeit, a parcel of land known as "Shelburne Glebe," see App. 57 (forfeiture order), was recently sold by federal authorities for $5.8 million. Washington Post, May 10, 1989, p. D1, cols. 1-4. The proceeds of the sale will fund federal, state, and local law enforcement activities.

representation frequently may turn on his ability to retain the best counsel money can buy." Again, the Court of Appeals put it aptly: "The modern day Jean Valijean must be satisfied with appointed counsel. Yet the drug merchant claims that his possession of huge sums of money . . . entitles him to something more. We reject this contention, and any notion of a constitutional right to use the proceeds of crime to finance an expensive defense."[7]

It is our view that there is a strong governmental interest in obtaining full recovery of all forfeitable assets, an interest that overrides any Sixth Amendment interest in permitting criminals to use assets adjudged forfeitable to pay for their defense. Otherwise, there would be an interference with a defendant's Sixth Amendment rights whenever the government freezes or takes some property in a defendant's possession before, during or after a criminal trial. So-called "jeopardy assessments"—IRS seizures of assets to secure potential tax liabilities, see 26 U.S.C. §6861—may impair a defendant's ability to retain counsel in a way similar to that complained of here. Yet these assessments have been upheld against constitutional attack. . . . Moreover, petitioner's claim to a share of the forfeited assets postconviction would suggest that the government could never impose a burden on assets within a defendant's control that could be used to pay a lawyer.[9] Criminal defendants, however, are not exempted from federal, state, and local taxation simply because these financial levies may deprive them of resources that could be used to hire an attorney.

We therefore reject petitioner's claim of a Sixth Amendment right of criminal defendants to use assets that are the government's—assets

7. We also reject the contention, advanced by amici, see, e.g., Brief for Amicus Curiae of the American Bar Association as Amicur Curiae 20-22, and accepted by some courts considering claims like petitioner's, see, e.g., United States v. Rogers, 602 F. Supp. 1332, 1349-1350 (Col. 1985), that a type of "per se" ineffective assistance of counsel results—due to the particular complexity of RICO or drug-enterprise cases—when a defendant is not permitted to use assets in his possession to retain counsel of choice, and instead must rely on appointed counsel. If such an argument were accepted, it would bar the trial of indigents charged with such offenses, because those persons would have to rely on appointed counsel—which this view considers per se ineffective.

If appointed counsel is ineffective in a particular case, a defendant has resort to the remedies discussed in Strickland v. Washington, 466 U.S. 668 (1984). But we cannot say that the Sixth Amendment's guarantee of effective assistance of counsel is a guarantee of a privately-retained counsel in every complex case, irrespective of a defendant's ability to pay.

9. A myriad of other law-enforcement mechanisims operate in a manner similar to IRS jeopardy assessments, and might also be subjected to Sixth Amendment invalidation if petitioner's claim were accepted. See Brickey, Attorneys' Fee Forfeitures, 36 Emory L.J. 761, 770-772 (1987).

adjudged forfeitable, as Reckmeyer's were—to pay attorneys' fees, merely because those assets are in their possession.[10]

B

Petitioner's second constitutional claim is that the forfeiture statute is invalid under the Due Process Clause of the Fifth Amendment because it permits the Government to upset the "balance of forces between the accused and his accuser." We are not sure that this contention adds anything to petitioner's Sixth Amendment claim, because, while "[t]he Constitution guarantees a fair trial through the Due Process Clauses . . . it defines the basic elements of a fair trial largely through the several provisions of the Sixth Amendment." We have concluded above that the

---

10. Petitioner advances three additional reasons for invalidating the forfeiture statute, all of which concern possible ethical conflicts created for lawyers defending persons facing forfeiture of assets in their possession.

Petitioner first notes the statute's exemption from forfeiture of property transferred to a bona fide purchaser who was "reasonably without cause to believe that the property was subject to forfeiture." 21 U.S.C. §853(n)(6)(B). This provision, it is said, might give an attorney an incentive not to investigate a defendant's case as fully as possible, so that the lawyer can invoke it to protect from forfeiture any fees he has received. Yet given the requirement that any assets which the Government wishes to have forfeited must be specified in the indictment, see Fed. Rule Crim. Proc. 7(c)(2), the only way a lawyer could be a beneficiary of §853(n)(6)(B) would be to fail to read the indictment of his client. In this light, the prospect that a lawyer might find himself in conflict with his client, by seeking to take advantage of §853(n)(6)(B), amounts to very little. Petitioner itself concedes that such a conflict will, as a practical matter, never arise: a defendant's "lawyer . . . could not demonstrate that he was 'reasonably without cause to believe that the property was subject to forfeiture,'" petitioner concludes at one point. Brief for Petitioner 31.

The second possible conflict arises in plea bargaining: petitioner posits that a lawyer may advise a client to accept an agreement entailing a more harsh prison sentence but no forfeiture—even where contrary to the client's interests—in an effort to preserve the lawyer's fee. Following such a strategy, however, would surely constitute ineffective assistance of counsel. We see no reason why our cases such as Strickland v. Washington are inadequate to deal with any such ineffectiveness where it arises. In any event, there is no claim that such conduct occurred here, nor could there be, as Reckmeyer's plea agreement included forfeiture of virtually every asset in his possession.

Finally, petitioner argues that the forfeiture statute, in operation, will create a system akin to "contingency fees" for defense lawyers: only a defense lawyer who wins acquittal for his client will be able to collect his fees, and contingent fees in criminal cases are generally considered unethical. See ABA Model Rules of Professional Conduct, Rule 1.5(d)(2) (1983); ABA Model Code of Professional Responsibility DR 2-106(C) (1979). But there is no indication here that petitioner, or any other firm, has actually sought to charge a defendant on a contingency basis; rather the claim is that a law firm's prospect of collecting its fee may turn on the outcome at trial. This, however, may often be the case in criminal defense work. Nor is it clear why permitting contingent fees in criminal cases—if that is what the forfeiture statute does—violates a criminal defendant's Sixth Amendment rights. The fact that a federal statutory scheme authorizing contingency fees—again, if that is what Congress has created in §853 (a premise we doubt)—is at odds with model disciplinary rules or state disciplinary codes hardly renders the federal statute invalid.

Sixth Amendment is not offended by the forfeiture provisions at issue here. Even if, however, the Fifth Amendment provides some added protection not encompassed in the Sixth Amendment's more specific provisions, we find petitioner's claim based on the Fifth Amendment unavailing.

Forfeiture provisions are powerful weapons in the war on crime; like any such weapons, their impact can be devastating when used unjustly. But due process claims alleging such abuses are cognizable only in specific cases of prosecutorial misconduct (and petitioner has made no such allegation here) or when directed to a rule that is inherently unconstitutional. "The fact that the . . . Act might operate unconstitutionally under some conceivable set of circumstances is insufficient to render it . . . invalid," United States v. Salerno, 481 U.S. 739, 745 (1987). Petitioner's claim—that the power available to prosecutors under the statute could be abused—proves too much, for many tools available to prosecutors can be misused in a way that violates the rights of innocent persons. As the Court of Appeals put it, in rejecting this claim when advanced below: "Every criminal law carries with it the potential for abuse, but a potential for abuse does not require a finding of facial invalidity."

We rejected a claim similar to petitioner's last Term, in Wheat v. United States, 486 U.S. 153 (1988). In *Wheat*, the petitioner argued that permitting a court to disqualify a defendant's chosen counsel because of conflicts of interest—over that defendant's objection to the disqualification—would encourage the government to "manufacture" such conflicts to deprive a defendant of his chosen attorney. While acknowledging that this was possible, we declined to fashion the per se constitutional rule petitioner sought in *Wheat*, instead observing that "trial courts are undoubtedly aware of [the] possibility" of abuse, and would have to "take it into consideration," when dealing with disqualification motions.

A similar approach should be taken here. The Constitution does not forbid the imposition of an otherwise permissible criminal sanction, such as forfeiture, merely because in some cases prosecutors may abuse the processes available to them, e.g., by attempting to impose them on persons who should not be subjected to that punishment. Cases involving particular abuses can be dealt with individually by the lower courts, when (and if) any such cases arise.

IV

For the reasons given above, we find that petitioner's statutory and constitutional challenges to the forfeiture imposed here are without merit. The judgment of the Court of Appeals is therefore affirmed.

JUSTICE BLACKMUN, with whom JUSTICE BRENNAN, JUSTICE MAR-
SHALL, and JUSTICE STEVENS join, dissenting.

Those jurists who have held forth against the result the majority
reaches in these cases have been guided by one core insight; that it is
unseemly and unjust for the Government to beggar those it prosecutes
in order to disable their defense at trial. The majority trivializes "the
burden the forfeiture law imposes on a criminal defendant." Instead, it
should heed the warnings of our district court judges, whose day-to-day
exposure to the criminal-trial process enables them to understand, perhaps
far better than we, the devastating consequences of attorney's fee forfeiture
for the integrity of our adversarial system of justice.

The criminal forfeiture statute we consider today could have been
interpreted to avoid depriving defendants of the ability to retain private
counsel—and should have been so interpreted, given the grave "constitutional and ethical problems" raised by the forfeiture of funds used to
pay legitimate counsel fees.

II

The majority has decided otherwise, however, and for that reason is
compelled to reach the constitutional issue it could have avoided. But
the majority pauses hardly long enough to acknowledge "the Sixth
Amendment's protection of one's right to retain counsel of his choosing,"
let alone to explore its "full extent." Instead, it moves rapidly from the
observation that "a defendant may not insist on representation by an
attorney he cannot afford," Wheat v. United States, 486 U.S. 153, 161
(1988), to the conclusion that the Government is free to deem the defendant indigent by declaring his assets "tainted" by criminal activity the
Government has yet to prove. That the majority implicitly finds the Sixth
Amendment right to counsel of choice so insubstantial that it can be
outweighed by a legal fiction demonstrates, still once again, its "apparent
unawareness of the function of the independent lawyer as a guardian of
our freedom."

A

Over 50 years ago, this Court observed: "It is hardly necessary to
say that the right to counsel being conceded, a defendant should be
afforded a fair opportunity to secure counsel of his own choice." Powell
v. Alabama, 287 U. S. 45, 53 (1932). For years, that proposition was
settled; the controversial question was whether the defendant's right to
use his own funds to retain his chosen counsel was the outer limit of the
right protected by the Sixth Amendment. The Court's subsequent de-

cisions have made clear that an indigent defendant has the right to appointed counsel, and that the Sixth Amendment guarantees at least minimally effective assistance of counsel. But while court appointment of effective counsel plays a crucial role in safeguarding the fairness of criminal trials, it has never defined the outer limits of the Sixth Amendment's demands. The majority's decision in this case reveals that it has lost track of the distinct role of the right to counsel of choice in protecting the integrity of the judicial process, a role that makes "the right to be represented by privately retained counsel . . . the primary, preferred component of the basic right" protected by the Sixth Amendment.

The right to retain private counsel serves to foster the trust between attorney and client that is necessary for the attorney to be a truly effective advocate. Not only are decisions crucial to the defendant's liberty placed in counsel's hands, but the defendant's perception of the fairness of the process, and his willingness to acquiesce in its results, depend upon his confidence in his counsel's dedication, loyalty, and ability. When the Government insists upon the right to choose the defendant's counsel for him, that relationship of trust is undermined: counsel is too readily perceived as the Government's agent rather than his own. Indeed, when the Court in *Faretta* held that the Sixth Amendment prohibits a court from imposing appointed counsel on a defendant who prefers to represent himself, its decision was predicated on the insight that "[t]o force a lawyer on a defendant can only lead him to believe that the law contrives against him."

The right to retain private counsel also serves to assure some modicum of equality between the Government and those it chooses to prosecute. The Government can be expected to "spend vast sums of money . . . to try defendants accused of crime," Gideon v. Wainwright, 372 U.S., at 344, and of course will devote greater resources to complex cases in which the punitive stakes are high. Precisely for this reason, "there are few defendants charged with crime, few indeed, who fail to hire the best lawyers they can get to prepare and present their defenses." Ibid. But when the Government provides for appointed counsel, there is no guarantee that levels of compensation and staffing will be even average. Where cases are complex, trials long, and stakes high, that problem is exacerbated. Over the long haul, the result of lowered compensation levels will be that talented attorneys will "decline to enter criminal practice. . . . This exodus of talented attorneys could devastate the criminal defense bar." Winick, Forfeiture of Attorneys' Fees under RICO and CCE and the Right to Counsel of Choice: the Constitutional Dilemma and How to Avoid It, 43 U. Miami L. Rev. 765, 781 (1989). Without the defendant's right to retain private counsel, the Government too readily could defeat its adversaries simply by outspending them.

The right to privately chosen and compensated counsel also serves broader institutional interests. The "virtual socialization of criminal defense work in this country" that would be the result of a widespread abandonment of the right to retain chosen counsel, too readily would standardize the provision of criminal-defense services and diminish defense counsel's independence. There is a place in our system of criminal justice for the maverick and the risk-taker, for approaches that might not fit into the structured environment of a public defender's office, or that might displease a judge whose preference for nonconfrontational styles of advocacy might influence the judge's appointment decisions. There is also a place for the employment of "specialized defense counsel" for techical and complex cases. The choice of counsel is the primary means for the defendant to establish the kind of defense he will put forward. Only a healthy, independent defense bar can be expected to meet the demands of the varied circumstances faced by criminal defendants. . . .

In sum, our chosen system of criminal justice is built upon a truly equal and adversarial presentation of the case, and upon the trust that can exist only when counsel is independent of the Government. Without the right, reasonably exercised, to counsel of choice, the effectiveness of that system is imperilled.

B

Had it been Congress' express aim to undermine the adversary system as we know it, it could hardly have found a better engine of destruction than attorney's-fee forfeiture. The main effect of forfeitures under the Act, of course, will be to deny the defendant the right to retain counsel, and therefore the right to have his defense designed and presented by an attorney he has chosen and trusts.[14] If the Government restrains the defendant's assets before trial, private counsel will be unwilling to continue or to take on the defense. Even if no restraining order is entered, the possibility of forfeiture after conviction will itself substantially diminish the likelihood that private counsel will agree to take the case. The "message [to private counsel] is 'Do not represent this defendant or you will lose your fee.' That being the kind of message lawyers are likely to take seriously, the defendant will find it difficult or impossible to secure

14. There is reason to fear that, in addition to depriving a defendant of counsel of choice, there will be circumstances in which the threat of forfeiture will deprive the defendant of any counsel. If the Government chooses not to restrain transfers by employing §853(e)(1), it is likely that the defendant will not qualify as "indigent" under the Criminal Justice Act. Potential private counsel will be aware of the threat of forfeiture, and, as a result, will likely refuse to take the case. Although it is to be hoped that a solution will be developed for a defendant who "falls between the cracks" in this manner, there is no guarantee that accommodation will be made in an orderly fashion, and that trial preparation will not be substantially delayed because of the difficulties in securing counsel.

representation.' " United States v. Badalamenti, 614 F. Supp., at 196.

The resulting relationship between the defendant and his court-appointed counsel will likely begin in distrust, and be exacerbated to the extent that the defendant perceives his new-found "indigency" as a form of punishment imposed by the Government in order to weaken his defense. If the defendant had been represented by private counsel earlier in the proceedings, the defendant's sense that the Government has stripped him of his defense will be sharpened by the concreteness of his loss. Appointed counsel may be inexperienced and undercompensated and, for that reason, may not have adequate opportunity or resources to deal with the special problems presented by what is likely to be a complex trial. The already scarce resources of a public defender's office will be stretched to the limit. Facing a lengthy trial against a better-armed adversary, the temptation to recommend a guilty plea will be great. The result, if the defendant is convicted, will be a sense, often well grounded, that justice was not done.

Even if the defendant finds a private attorney who is "so foolish, ignorant, beholden or idealistic as to take the business," the attorney-client relationship will be undermined by the forfeiture statute. Perhaps the attorney will be willing to violate ethical norms by working on a contingent fee basis in a criminal case. But if he is not—and we should question the integrity of any criminal-defense attorney who would violate the ethical norms of the profession by doing so—the attorney's own interests will dictate that he remain ignorant of the source of the assets from which he is paid. Under §853(c), a third-party transferee may keep assets if "the transferee establishes . . . that he is a bona fide purchaser for value of such property who at the time of purchase was reasonably without cause to believe that the property was subject to forfeiture under this section." The less an attorney knows, the greater the likelihood that he can claim to have been an "innocent" third party. The attorney's interest in knowing nothing is directly adverse to his client's interest in full disclosure. The result of the conflict may be a less vigorous investigation of the defendant's circumstances, leading in turn to a failure to recognize or pursue avenues of inquiry necessary to the defense. Other conflicts of interest are also likely to develop. The attorney who fears for his fee will be tempted to make the Government's waiver of fee-forfeiture the sine qua non for any plea agreement, a position which conflicts with his client's best interests.

Perhaps most troubling is the fact that forfeiture statutes place the Government in the position to exercise an intolerable degree of power over any private attorney who takes on the task of representing a defendant in a forfeiture case. The decision whether to seek a restraining order rests with the prosecution, as does the decision whether to waive forfeiture upon a plea of guilty or a conviction at trial. The Government will be ever tempted to use the forfeiture weapon against a defense attorney who is particularly talented or aggressive on the client's behalf—the attorney who is better than what, in the Government's view, the defendant deserves. The spectre of the Government's selectively excluding only the most talented defense counsel is a serious threat to the equality of forces necessary for the adversarial system to perform at its best. An attorney whose fees are potentially subject to forfeiture will be forced to operate in an environment in which the Government is not only the defendant's adversary, but also his own.

The long-term effects of the fee-forfeiture practice will be to decimate the private criminal-defense bar. As the use of the forfeiture mechanism expands to new categories of federal crimes and spreads to the States, only one class of defendants will be free routinely to retain private counsel: the affluent defendant accused of a crime that generates no economic gain. As the number of private clients diminishes, only the most idealistic and the least skilled of young lawyers will be attracted to the field, while the remainder seek greener pastures elsewhere.

In short, attorney's-fee forfeiture substantially undermines every interest served by the Sixth Amendment right to chosen counsel, on the individual and institutional levels, over the short term and the long haul. . . .

III

In my view, the Act as interpreted by the majority is inconsistent with the intent of Congress, and seriously undermines the basic fairness of our criminal-justice system. That a majority of this Court has upheld the constitutionality of the Act as so interpreted will not deter Congress, I hope, from amending the Act to make clear that Congress did not intend this result. This Court has the power to declare the Act constitutional, but it cannot thereby make it wise.

CHAPTER 5

THE SIXTH AMENDMENT AND DUE PROCESS APPLIED—THE PROBLEM OF EYEWITNESS IDENTIFICATION

Eyewitness testimony is often crucial to the outcome of criminal litigation, and eyewitness identifications of criminal offenders is an especially troublesome component of that type of evidence. Although there is some disagreement concerning the impact of eyewitness identification testimony, especially when the witness was previously unacquainted with the accused and the chance to observe facial features was not optimal, it is generally agreed that in many situations eyewitness identification testimony is quite influential with triers of fact.[1]

1. The standard cite to a work demonstrating the impact of eyewitness testimony is Loftus, Reconstructing Memory: The Incredible Eyewitness, Psychology Today, Dec. 1974, at 116. Dr. Loftus reports the results of a study where 150 students were given a description of a crime and summaries of evidence and argument. Some students were told that there were no eyewitnesses, others that there was one who was credible, and still others that there was one that had been "discredited" by the defense attorney having "claimed the witness had not been wearing his glasses on the day of the robbery," id. at 117-118, which would have prevented the witness from seeing what happened. Eighty-two percent of the jurors who had not heard about an eyewitness voted to acquit; 72 percent who thought there was a credible witness voted to convict; and "[m]ost important, 68 percent of the jurors who had heard about the discredited witness still voted for conviction, in spite of the defense attorney's remarks." Id. at 118. From this it was concluded that "people are convinced by a witness who declares with conviction, 'That's the man.' "

The conclusion may be true, but this experiment, as reported, certainly does not demonstrate it. In addition to suffering from all the problems of simulation, the "evidence" given the subjects is not presented. If it created even a marginally close question, one would expect an eyewitness to tip the scale. Also, in the third set of students, the witness was not "discredited." Rather, the defense counsel, who clearly is biased, simply asserted the witness was not to be believed. Without knowing more, it's no surprise that such "discrediting" was apparently discredited.

At any rate, we wish to emphasize that we are not suggesting that any of the accepted

Moreover, there appears to be further, but less solidly based, agreement that, in the words of the Supreme Court in United States v. Wade, page 339 infra, "The vagaries of eyewitness identification are well-known; the annals of criminal law are rife with instances of mistaken identification." Unfortunately, the strength of the rhetoric is not matched by supporting data. To be sure, there are numerous works, cited in the cases that follow, that collect incidents of apparently wrongful convictions in some of which erroneous eyewitness testimony seems to have contributed significantly to the outcome. Nonetheless, we do not know to what extent the collected examples are aberrational and to what extent they reflect a profound problem in the administration of justice. Mistakes are unavoidable, and thus we need to know the incidence of error, not just the fact of its occurrence that the present data demonstrate.

Nevertheless, our understanding of psychological reality has progressed to the point where we can safely say that various identification techniques present differing potentials for error due to the variable of suggestiveness. A witness who identifies a suspect in a lineup situation that does not suggest to the witness whom to choose seems to be much more trustworthy than a witness who is brought down to the stationhouse and views a suspect alone in a room to see if the police "have caught the right man." In the case of the lineup, the witness's identification is his own without much input from the police; in the case of the showup, the police implicitly have informed the witness that they think they have the offender, thus putting pressure on the witness to conform to the expectations of the police.

Consider the following excerpt summarizing the relevant psychological data.

---

views about eyewitness testimony is wrong. Rather, it is just that as of now they are not well enough established, and we are in very bad need of rigorous efforts to study the phenomenon.

For a somewhat differing account of the same experiment, as well as a discussion of similar experiments, see E. Loftus, Eyewitness Testimony 8-19 (1979). Both the view that jurors are likely to misevaluate the reliability of eyewitness testimony and that, assuming jurors do misevaluate such evidence, expert witnesses would be a helpful antidote have been seriously questioned on empirical and pragmatic grounds. See McCloskey & Egeth, Eyewitness Identification: What Can a Psychologist Tell a Jury?, 38 Am. Psy. 550 (1983).

NOTE, DID YOUR EYES DECEIVE YOU? EXPERT PSYCHOLOGICAL TESTIMONY ON THE UNRELIABILITY OF EYEWITNESS IDENTIFICATION
29 Stan. L. Rev. 969, 975-988 (1977)

The need for scientific study in this area was occasioned by the earlier "sensationalist"[14] thinking in the field, which assumed that the human brain operates more or less as a mechanical recording device: A person sees everything and records this information on a memory "tape." When necessary to describe a past event, the person simply selects the appropriate memory tape and plays it back, producing a faithful recounting of the original perception.

Over the past half-century, however, psychological research emphatically has demonstrated the invalidity of this conception and has revealed that the "videotape recorder" analogy is misleading in three respects discussed briefly here and analyzed more fully in the remainder of this section. First, perception is not a mere passive recording of an event but instead is a constructive process by which people consciously and unconsciously use decisional strategies to attend selectively to only a minimal number of environmental stimuli. Second, over time, the representation of an event stored in memory undergoes constant change; some details are added or altered unconsciously to conform the original memory representation to new information about the event, while others simply are forgotten. Finally, the manner in which information is retrieved from memory almost always distorts the remembered image; most often, very powerful—yet imperceptibly subtle—suggestions shape the resulting recollection.

1. PERCEPTION OF THE ORIGINAL EVENT

Perceptual selectivity. The inherent limitations of the human brain are the major source of inaccuracy in perception. People can perceive only a limited number of the simultaneous stimuli in the environment at any time; the number of these that can be encoded in memory is even smaller. In order to cope with these innate limitations, an observer develops unconscious strategies to aid in the selectivity of perceptual processes and

---

14. Sensationalism is a psychological theory positing that all knowledge has a sensory base and that all ideas are identified in a one-to-one correspondence with elementary unstructured sensations. See J. Anderson & G. Bower, Human Associative Memory 9-12 (1973). . . .

ultimately to concentrate attention on the most necessary and useful details. In short, a human must "learn" how to perceive efficiently. . . .

The major difficulty that selective perceptual processes cause is the failure to observe the details of an event, especially those that are at first unimportant but later assume great significance. The ability to perceive and recall such details plays a crucial role in eyewitness identifications, yet numerous studies have confirmed that even trained observers find it difficult to describe such obvious physical characteristics as height, weight and age. . . .

Time perception. Humans also find it especially difficult to perceive time accurately, that is, to estimate either the duration of an event or the interval between successive events. Studies have shown that people tend to judge time by the amount of activity occurring; during sudden, actionpacked events such as crimes, people almost always overestimate the length of time involved because the flurry of activity leads them to conclude that a significant amount of time has passed. Time is also perceived to pass more slowly when the observer is caught in an anxiety-producing situation; the desire to "escape" makes it seem as if the unpleasant event is lasting longer than it actually is. Thus, the witness or victim who . . . may claim to have observed her attacker 1 or 2 minutes, in reality probably saw him for only 10 or 15 seconds.

Poor observation conditions. In addition to perceptual inaccuracies caused by the brain's inherent limitations, many identification errors are due to the circumstances of the observation. A major variable influencing perception is the duration of the observation period. Crimes in which the primary evidence is an eyewitness identification characteristically are brief, fast-moving events; the victim and witnesses consequently will have difficulty getting a sufficiently good "look" to allow them to process enough visual features of the event and the offender to make a reliable subsequent recognition. This durational constraint has particularly deleterious effects when the crime occurs suddenly, and the witness is thus unprepared to focus perceptual attention on the important features of the event.

Furthermore, visual efficiency drops markedly when the observation occurs under poor or rapidly changing lighting conditions or over great distances, reducing the absolute amount of visual information impinging on the retina, or in conjunction with distracting noises or other activity, forcing the already limited attentional capacities to be spread even thinner. Each of these conditions frequently accompanies the observation of crimes and may reduce the reliability of a witness' identification.

Stressful situation. Another important environmental factor limiting the accuracy of perception is the stressful situation facing the victim. Although judges and juries often may be convinced by the victim's assertion that "I was so frightened that his face is etched in my memory forever," psychological research demonstrates that perceptual abilities actually *decrease* significantly when the observer is in a fearful or anxiety-provoking situation.

Studies have shown that an increase in anxiety generally produces a cluster of certain physiological responses. The frightened victim or eyewitness may report increases in heart rate, rapid breathing and excessive perspiration, but usually does not notice that the anxiety also has caused fixation of the eyes. Yet, because visual information is processed by contrasting successive retinal images, this fixation reduces visual acuity, particularly for details on the periphery of the environment. . . .

Expectancy. Although many of the organic and environmental limitations on perceptual abilities come quickly to mind, other social psychological factors operate more subtly, if quite powerfully, to distort perception. In order to compensate for the perceptual selectivity made necessary by the brain's limitations, observers make extensive use of expectancy, not only in developing strategies for determining what to look at, but also in interpreting what they see. Because the human mind can process only a small portion of what is visible at any given time, it develops the ability to form conclusions about what has been perceived based on limited amounts of sensory information. It accomplishes this task by integrating fragmentary visual information into existing conceptual schemata based upon a fund of general knowledge acquired over time. In essence, witnesses unconsciously reconstruct what *has* occurred from what they assume *must have* occurred. Consequently, they exhibit a pronounced tendency to perceive the expected. . . .

Personal needs and biases. In addition to expectancies caused by prior experience and information about the world, the personal needs and motives of the observer also distort perception. In short, witnesses tend to see what they *want* to see. Thus, the need and desire to produce a complete description of an assailant may foster perception that is more the product of an unconscious imagination than a keen eye.

Personal biases and latent prejudices also shape expectancies, often distorting perceptions to fit the various stereotypes that all humans possess. Social psychology experiments indicate that people tend to correlate physical characteristics with personality traits, and that perceptual distortion increases when the viewer regards objects unfavorably. These findings imply that a victim may unwittingly distort her perception of an assailant to include physical features that the victim associates with the personality traits typified by the criminal's behavior.

Cross-racial identifications. Finally, considerable evidence indicates that people are poorer at identifying members of another race than of their own. Some studies have found that, in the United States at least, whites have greater difficulty recognizing black faces than vice versa. Moreover, counterintuitively, the ability to perceive the physical characteristics of a person from another racial group apparently does not improve significantly upon increased contact with other members of that race. Because many crimes are cross-racial, these factors may play an important part in reducing the accuracy of eyewitness perception.

2. ENCODING AND STORAGE IN MEMORY

Memory decay over time. Even if someone accurately perceived an event, its representation in the observer's memory would not remain entirely intact for very long. People forget both quickly and easily. The phenomenon of forgetting what once has been perceived and encoded in memory, known as "retroactive inhibition," is one of the earliest and most consistent findings of cognitive psychology. Simply put, the more time that has elapsed since the perception of some event—and, therefore, the more intervening occurrences that must be stored in memory—the poorer a person's memory is of that event. Particularly with visual images, memory begins to decay within minutes of the event, so that considerable memory loss probably occurs during the many days—and often months—that typically elapse between the offense and an eyewitness identification of the suspect in a criminal case.

Filling gaps in memory. Many psychologists once thought that automatic decay of the memory trace caused all distortions of memory. More recently, however, they have discovered that memory, like perception, is an active, constructive process that often introduces inaccuracies by adding details not present in the initial representation or in the event itself. The mind combines all the information acquired about a particular event into a single storage "bin," making it difficult to distinguish what the witness saw originally from what she learned later. Because all of the research on human memory indicates that the actual memorial representation must decay in accuracy over time, any reported increases in the completeness of a description come only at the risk of a reduction in the description's correctness. If a witness' description of a suspect becomes more detailed as the investigation proceeds from the police report through the preliminary hearing to trial, the witness in this situation probably unconsciously has changed the image in memory to include details subsequently acquired from, for example, newspaper reports of the event or a mug shot of the defendant.

Moreover, because of a psychological need to reduce uncertainty and eliminate inconsistencies, witnesses have a tendency not only to fill any gaps in memory by adding extraneous details but also to change mental representations unconsciously so that they "all make sense." This mental process of adding and changing little details is an efficient strategy in everyday life, where the total sum of information contained in memory usually matters more than the specific circumstances surrounding its acquisition. In the context of an eyewitness identification of a criminal defendant, such unconscious modifications of memory can have tragic consequences.

False feelings of confidence. Psychological research also indicates that a witness' feeling of confidence in the details of a memory concerning a particular event generally does not measure validly the accuracy of that recollection. In fact, a negative correlation sometimes exists between accuracy and confidence. Surprisingly, witnesses—particularly victims— often become more confident of the correctness of their identification as time progresses. For example, a victim who originally voiced grave doubts as to any ability to identify the assailant and who showed some hesitancy in making a pretrial identification commonly may exude and express absolute certainty in testifying on the witness stand that the defendant committed the crime.

3. RETRIEVAL OF INFORMATION FROM MEMORY

Inadequacy of verbal descriptions. The final source of errors in identification, and the one discussed most thoroughly in the legal literature, is the process by which information is retrieved from memory for purposes of making an identification. Because few eyewitnesses have the artistic ability to draw an accurate representation of the criminal—the closest analogy to free recall—the criminal justice system must rely upon the eyewitness' vocabulary. Initially, therefore, the recall process suffers from the inadequacy of the verbal form to convey fully the physiognomical details of the witness' memory of the offender. Moreover, numerous studies have shown that even the most free and accurate form of verbal recall—a narrative description unprompted by questions—results in exceedingly incomplete information retrieval. On the other hand, as the questions become more structured in order to achieve completeness, the resulting responses become more inaccurate, because witnesses may feel compelled to answer questions completely in spite of incomplete knowledge. Faced with this inverse relationship between accuracy and completeness of a description, law enforcement officials generally opt for the latter at the expense of the former.

Suggestion in the composition of an identification test. . . . The lineup is a multiple-choice recognition test. Moreover, witnesses very likely will perceive it as a multiple-choice test that lacks a "none of the above" alternative because, despite contrary admonitions, there is always the implicit suggestion that the lineup includes the criminal. Thus, the witness often may treat the task as one of identifying the individual who best matches the witness' recollection of the culprit, even if that match is not perfect, rather than as one of identifying the true criminal.

The reliability of an identification made at a lineup, therefore, depends upon the similarity between the "target" item, the suspect, and the "distractor" items, the other members of the lineup. If, for example, the witness described the assailant as "tall," and only one of the participants in the lineup could be considered tall, then the choice of that one individual has little meaning for the purpose of identifying the true criminal. In addition to the tendency of the defendant in a lineup to be dangerously dissimilar in overall physical characteristics to the other participants, he may also have one distinctive feature, which generally suffices to bias the witness toward identifying him. Some of the more common factors potentially exerting suggestive influences include any unusual physical characteristics such as scars or tattoos, differences in the clothing worn by the participants and their demeanor and facial expressions.

The common practice of securing identifications by first using a photo array and subsequently conducting a corporeal lineup further tends to reduce reliability. From the standpoint of memory recall, the crucial identification is that made from the photo array, because a witness most likely will not identify anyone at a later corporeal lineup other than the individual chosen from the photo array. Obtaining identifications by using photographs is particularly dangerous, however, for they exclude a multitude of characteristics typically relied upon in recognizing people, such as views of the whole body or from varying angles, or any individual mannerisms or gestures, and therefore cause a greater number of mistaken identifications.

Suggestion in the administration of an identification test. In addition to the possibility that the police will make and reinforce suggestions as to the "proper" choice by the manner in which they construct the lineup or photo array, police officers while conducting the identification procedure often themselves provide more or less unwitting clues. An officer who is cognizant of the identity of the prime suspect subtly may influence the witness' choice simply by changes in voice intonation, increased attention to the response, the hint of a smile, or by more obvious gestures such as nodding agreement or asking the witness to take another, more careful, look if the "correct" identification has not been made. It is very difficult, if not impossible, to avoid unknowingly giving such clues; even trained psychologists who design their investigations to avoid these effects occasionally pass on their own expectations to the participants in their experiments.

Social psychological influences. Various social psychological factors also increase the danger of suggestibility in a lineup confrontation. Witnesses, like other people, are motivated by a desire to be correct and to avoid looking foolish. By arranging a lineup, the police have evidenced their belief that they have caught the criminal; witnesses, realizing this, probably will feel foolish if they cannot identify anyone and therefore may choose someone despite residual uncertainty. Moreover, the need to reduce psychological discomfort often motivates the victim of a crime to find a likely target for feelings of hostility. . . .

See also Johnson, Cross-Racial Identification Errors in Criminal Cases, 69 Cornell L. Rev. 934 (1984); Levine & Tapp, The Psychology of Criminal Identification: The Gap from *Wade* to *Kirby*, 121 U. Pa. L. Rev. 1079 (1973).

The Supreme Court has responded to the concerns raised by identification techniques by developing two different approaches, one focusing on the sixth amendment right to counsel and the other on fourteenth amendment due process.

A. THE RIGHT TO COUNSEL AT LINEUPS, SHOWUPS, AND PHOTOGRAPHIC ARRAYS

UNITED STATES v. WADE
Certiorari to the United States Court of Appeals for the Fifth Circuit
388 U.S. 218 (1967)

MR. JUSTICE BRENNAN delivered the opinion of the Court.

The question here is whether courtroom identifications of an accused at trial are to be excluded from evidence because the accused was exhibited to the witnesses before trial at a post-indictment lineup conducted for identification purposes without notice to and in the absence of the accused's appointed counsel.

The federally insured bank in Eustace, Texas, was robbed on September 21, 1964. A man with a small strip of tape on each side of his face entered the bank, pointed a pistol at the female cashier and the vice president, the only persons in the bank at the time, and forced them to fill a pillowcase with the bank's money. The man then drove away with an accomplice who had been waiting in a stolen car outside the bank. On March 23, 1965, an indictment was returned against respondent, Wade, and two others for conspiring to rob the bank, and against Wade and the accomplice for the robbery itself. Wade was arrested on April 2, and counsel was appointed to represent him on April 26. Fifteen days later an FBI agent, without notice to Wade's lawyer, arranged to have the two bank employees observe a lineup made up of Wade and five or six other prisoners and conducted in a courtroom of the local county courthouse. Each person in the line wore strips of tape such as allegedly worn by the robber and upon direction each said something like "put the money in the bag," the words allegedly uttered by the robber. Both bank employees identified Wade in the lineup as the bank robber.

At trial, the two employees, when asked on direct examination if the robber was in the courtroom, pointed to Wade. The prior lineup identification was then elicited from both employees on cross-examination. At the close of testimony, Wade's counsel moved for a judgment of acquittal or, alternatively, to strike the bank officials' courtroom identifications on the ground that conduct of the lineup, without notice to and in the absence of his appointed counsel, violated his Fifth Amendment privilege against self-incrimination and his Sixth Amendment right to the assistance of counsel. The motion was denied, and Wade was convicted. The Court of Appeals for the Fifth Circuit reversed the conviction and ordered a new trial at which the in-court identification evidence was to be excluded, holding that, though the lineup did not violate Wade's Fifth Amendment rights, "the lineup, held as it was, in the absence of counsel, already chosen to represent appellant, was a violation of his Sixth Amendment rights. . . ." We granted certiorari, and set the case for oral argument with Gilbert v. California, . . . Stovall v. Denno, . . . which present similar questions. We reverse the judgment of the Court of Appeals and remand to that court with direction to enter a new judgment vacating the conviction and remanding the case to the District Court for further proceedings consistent with this opinion.

I

[The Court proceeded to dispose of defendant's fifth amendment claim. For a discussion, see Chapter 6, infra.] . . .

II

The fact that the lineup involved no violation of Wade's privilege against self-incrimination does not, however, dispose of his contention that the courtroom identifications should have been excluded because the lineup was conducted without notice to and in the absence of his counsel. . . . [I]n this case it is urged that the assistance of counsel at the lineup was indispensable to protect Wade's most basic right as a criminal defendant—

his right to a fair trial at which the witnesses against him might be meaningfully cross-examined.

The Framers of the Bill of Rights envisaged a broader role for counsel than under the practice then prevailing in England of merely advising his client in "matters of law," and eschewing any responsibility for "matters of fact." This background is reflected in the scope given by our decisions to the Sixth Amendment's guarantee to an accused of the assistance of counsel for his defense. When the Bill of Rights was adopted, there were no organized police forces as we know them today. The accused confronted the prosecutor and the witnesses against him, and the evidence was marshalled, largely at the trial itself. In contrast, today's law enforcement machinery involves critical confrontations of the accused by the prosecution at pretrial proceedings where the results might well settle the accused's fate and reduce the trial itself to a mere formality. In recognition of these realities of modern criminal prosecution, our cases have construed the Sixth Amendment guarantee to apply to "critical" stages of the proceedings. The guarantee reads: "In all criminal prosecutions, the accused shall enjoy the right . . . to have the Assistance of Counsel *for his defence.*" (Emphasis supplied.) The plain wording of this guarantee thus encompasses counsel's assistance whenever necessary to assure a meaningful "defence." . . .

In sum, the principle of Powell v. Alabama and succeeding cases requires that we scrutinize *any* pretrial confrontation of the accused to determine whether the presence of his counsel is necessary to preserve the defendant's basic right to a fair trial as affected by his right meaningfully to cross-examine the witnesses against him and to have effective assistance of counsel at the trial itself. It calls upon us to analyze whether potential substantial prejudice to defendant's rights inheres in the particular confrontation and the ability of counsel to help avoid that prejudice.

III

The Government characterizes the lineup as a mere preparatory step in the gathering of the prosecution's evidence, not different—for Sixth Amendment purposes—from various other preparatory steps, such as systematized or scientific analyzing of the accused's fingerprints, blood sample, clothing, hair, and the like. We think there are differences which preclude such stages being characterized as critical stages at which the accused has the right to the presence of his counsel. Knowledge of the techniques of science and technology is sufficiently available, and the variables in techniques few enough, that the accused has the opportunity for a meaningful confrontation of the Government's case at trial through the ordinary processes of cross-examination of the Government's expert witnesses and the presentation of the evidence of his own experts. The denial of a right to have his counsel present at such analyses does not therefore violate the Sixth Amendment; they are not critical stages since there is minimal risk that his counsel's absence at such stages might derogate from his right to a fair trial.

IV

But the confrontation compelled by the State between the accused and the victim or witnesses to a crime to elicit identification evidence is peculiarly riddled with innumerable dangers and variable factors which might seriously, even crucially, derogate from a fair trial. The vagaries of eyewitness identification are well-known; the annals of criminal law are rife with instances of mistaken identification.[6] . . . A major factor contributing to the high incidence of miscarriage of justice from mistaken identification has been the degree of suggestion inherent in the manner in which the prosecution presents the suspect to witnesses for pretrial identification. A commentator has observed that "[t]he influence of improper suggestion upon identifying witnesses probably accounts for more miscarriages of justice than any other single factor—perhaps it is responsible for more such errors than all other factors combined." Wall, Eye-Witness Identification in Criminal Cases 26. Suggestion can be created intentionally or unintentionally in many subtle ways.[7] And the dangers for the suspect are particularly grave when the witness' opportunity for observation was insubstantial, and thus his susceptibility to suggestion the greatest.

Moreover, "[i]t is a matter of common experience that, once a witness has picked out the accused at the line-up, he is not likely to go back on his word later on, so that in practice the issue of identity may (in the absence of other relevant evidence) for all practical purposes be determined there and then, before the trial."[8]

The pretrial confrontation for purpose of identification may take the form of a lineup, also known as an "identification parade" or "showup," as in the present case, or presentation of the suspect alone to the witness,

---

6. Borchard, Convicting the Innocent; Frank & Frank, Not Guilty; Wall, Eye-Witness Identification in Criminal Cases. . . .

7. See Wall, supra, n.6, at 26-65; Murray, The Criminal Lineup at Home and Abroad, 1966 Utah L. Rev. 610; Napley, Problems of Effecting the Presentation of the Case for a Defendant, 66 Col. L. Rev. 94, 98-99 (1966). . . .

8. Williams & Hammelmann, Identification Parades, Part I, [1963] Crim. L. Rev. 479, 482.

as in Stovall v. Denno. It is obvious that risks of suggestion attend either form of confrontation and increase the dangers inhering in eyewitness identification. But as is the case with secret interrogations, there is serious difficulty in depicting what transpires at lineups and other forms of identification confrontations. . . . [T]he defense can seldom reconstruct the manner and mode of lineup identification for judge or jury at trial. Those participating in a lineup with the accused may often be police officers; in any event, the participants' names are rarely recorded or divulged at trial. The impediments to an objective observation are increased when the victim is the witness. Lineups are prevalent in rape and robbery prosecutions and present a particular hazard that a victim's understandable outrage may excite vengeful or spiteful motives. In any event, neither witnesses nor lineup participants are apt to be alert for conditions prejudicial to the suspect. And if they were, it would likely be of scant benefit to the suspect since neither witnesses nor lineup participants are likely to be schooled in the detection of suggestive influences.[13] Improper influences may go undetected by a suspect, guilty or not, who experiences the emotional tension which we might expect in one being confronted with potential accusers. Even when he does observe abuse, if he has a criminal record he may be reluctant to take the stand and open up the admission of prior convictions. Moreover, any protestations by the suspect of the fairness of the lineup made at trial are likely to be in vain; the jury's choice is between the accused's unsupported version and that of the police officers present. In short, the accused's inability to reconstruct at trial any unfairness that occurred at the lineup may deprive him of his only opportunity meaningfully to attack the credibility of the witness' courtroom identification.

What facts have been disclosed in specific cases about the conduct of pretrial confrontations for identification illustrate both the potential for substantial prejudice to the accused at that stage and the need for its revelation at trial. A commentator provides some striking examples:

> In a Canadian case . . . the defendant had been picked out of a line-up of six men, of which he was the only Oriental. In other cases, a black-haired suspect was placed among a group of light-haired persons, tall suspects have been made to stand with short non-suspects, and, in a case where the perpetrator of the crime was known to be a youth, a suspect

13. An additional impediment to the detection of such influences by participants, including the suspect, is the physical conditions often surrounding the conduct of the lineup. In many, lights shine on the stage in such a way that the suspect cannot see the witness. See Gilbert v. United States, 366 F.2d 923 (C.A. 9th Cir. 1966). In some a one-way mirror is used and what is said on the witness' side cannot be heard. . . .

under twenty was placed in a line-up with five other persons, all of whom were forty or over.[17]

Similarly state reports, in the course of describing prior identifications admitted as evidence of guilt, reveal numerous instances of suggestive procedures, for example, that all in the lineup but the suspect were known to the identifying witness, that the other participants in a lineup were grossly dissimilar in appearance to the suspect, that only the suspect was required to wear distinctive clothing which the culprit allegedly wore, that the witness is told by the police that they have caught the culprit after which the defendant is brought before the witness alone or is viewed in jail, that the suspect is pointed out before or during a lineup, and that the participants in the lineup are asked to try on an article of clothing which fits only the suspect.

The potential for improper influence is illustrated by the circumstances, insofar as they appear, surrounding the prior identifications in the three cases we decide today. In the present case, the testimony of the identifying witnesses elicited on cross-examination revealed that those witnesses were taken to the courthouse and seated in the courtroom to await assembly of the lineup. The courtroom faced on a hallway observable to the witness through an open door. The cashier testified that she saw Wade "standing in the hall" within sight of an FBI agent. Five or six other prisoners later appeared in the hall. The vice president testified that he saw a person in the hall in the custody of the agent who "resembled the person that we identified as the one that had entered the bank."

The lineup in *Gilbert*, . . . was conducted in an auditorium in which some 100 witnesses to several alleged state and federal robberies charged to Gilbert made wholesale identifications of Gilbert as the robber in each other's presence, a procedure said to be fraught with dangers of suggestion. And the vice of suggestion created by the identification in *Stovall*, . . . was the presentation to the witness of the suspect alone handcuffed to police officers. It is hard to imagine a situation more clearly conveying the suggestion to the witness that the one presented is believed guilty by the police. See Frankfurter, The Case of Sacco and Vanzetti 31-32.

The few cases that have surfaced therefore reveal the existence of a process attended with hazards of serious unfairness to the criminal accused and strongly suggest the plight of the more numerous defendants who are unable to ferret out suggestive influences in the secrecy of the con-

17. Wall, Eye-Witness Identification in Criminal Cases 53. For other such examples see Houts, From Evidence to Proof 25; Frankfurter, The Case of Sacco and Vanzetti 12-14, 30-32; 3 Wigmore, Evidence §786a, at 164, n.2 (3d ed. 1940); Paul, Identification of Accused Persons, 12 Austl. L.J. 42, 44 (1938); Rolph, Personal Identity 34-43.

frontation. We do not assume that these risks are the result of police procedures intentionally designed to prejudice an accused. Rather we assume they derive from the dangers inherent in eyewitness identification and the suggestibility inherent in the context of the pretrial identification. Williams & Hammelmann, in one of the most comprehensive studies of such forms of identification, said,

> [T]he fact that the police themselves have, in a given case, little or no doubt that the man put up for identification has committed the offense, and that their chief pre-occupation is with the problem of getting sufficient proof, because he has not "come clean," involves a danger that this persuasion may communicate itself even in a doubtful case to the witness in some way. . . . Identification Parades, Part I, 1963 Crim. L. Rev. 479, 483.

Insofar as the accused's conviction may rest on a courtroom identification in fact the fruit of a suspect pretrial identification which the accused is helpless to subject to effective scrutiny at trial, the accused is deprived of that right of cross-examination which is an essential safeguard to his right to confront the witnesses against him. And even though cross-examination is a precious safeguard to a fair trial, it cannot be viewed as an absolute assurance of accuracy and reliability. Thus in the present context, where so many variables and pitfalls exist, the first line of defense must be the prevention of unfairness and the lessening of the hazards of eyewitness identification at the lineup itself. The trial which might determine the accused's fate may well not be that in the courtroom but that at the pretrial confrontation, with the State aligned against the accused, the witness the sole jury, and the accused unprotected against the overreaching, intentional or unintentional, and with little or no effective appeal from the judgment there rendered by the witness—"that's the man."

Since it appears that there is grave potential for prejudice, intentional or not, in the pretrial lineup, which may not be capable of reconstruction at trial, and since presence of counsel can often avert prejudice and assure a meaningful confrontation at trial,[26] there can be little doubt that for

---

26. One commentator proposes a model statute providing not only for counsel, but other safeguards as well:

> Most, if not all, of the attacks on the lineup process could be averted by a uniform statute modeled upon the best features of the civilian codes. Any proposed statute should provide for the right to counsel during any lineup or during any confrontation. Provision should be made that any person, whether a victim or a witness, must give a description of the suspect before he views any arrested person. A written record of this description should be required, and the witness should be made to sign it. This written record would be available for inspection by defense

Wade the post-indictment lineup was a critical stage of the prosecution at which he was "as much entitled to such aid [of counsel] . . . as at the trial itself." Powell v. Alabama, 287 U.S. 45, 57. Thus both Wade and his counsel should have been notified of the impending lineup, and counsel's presence should have been a requisite to conduct of the lineup, absent an "intelligent waiver." . . .

No substantial countervailing policy considerations have been advanced against the requirement of the presence of counsel. Concern is expressed that the requirement will forestall prompt identifications and result in obstruction of the confrontations. As for the first, we note that in the two cases in which the right to counsel is today held to apply, counsel had already been appointed and no argument is made in either case that notice to counsel would have prejudicially delayed the confrontations. Moreover, we leave open the question whether the presence of substitute counsel might not suffice where notification and presence of the suspect's own counsel would result in prejudicial delay. And to refuse to recognize the right to counsel for fear that counsel will obstruct the course of justice is contrary to the basic assumptions upon which this Court has operated in Sixth Amendment cases. . . . In our view counsel can hardly impede legitimate law enforcement; on the contrary, for the reasons expressed, law enforcement may be assisted by preventing the infiltration of taint in the prosecution's identification evidence. That result

---

counsel for copying before the trial and for use at the trial in testing the accuracy of the identification made during the lineup and during the trial.

This ideal statute would require at least six persons in addition to the accused in a lineup, and these persons would have to be of approximately the same height, weight, coloration of hair and skin, and bodily types as the suspect. In addition, all of these men should, as nearly as possible, be dressed alike. If distinctive garb was used during the crime, the suspect should not be forced to wear similar clothing in the lineup unless all of the other persons are similarly garbed. A complete written report of the names, addresses, descriptive details of the other persons in the lineup, and of everything which transpired during the identification would be mandatory. This report would include everything stated by the identifying witness during this step, including any reasons given by him as to what features, etc., have sparked his recognition.

This statute should permit voice identification tests by having each person in the lineup repeat identical innocuous phrases, and it would be impermissible to force the use of words allegedly used during a criminal act.

The statute would enjoin the police from suggesting to any viewer that one or more persons in the lineup had been arrested as a suspect. If more than one witness is to make an identification, each witness should be required to do so separately and should be forbidden to speak to another witness until all of them have completed the process.

The statute could require the use of movie cameras and tape recorders to record the lineup process in those states which are financially able to afford these devices. Finally, the statute should provide that any evidence obtained as the result of a violation of this statute would be inadmissible.

Murray, The Criminal Lineup at Home and Abroad, 1966 Utah L. Rev. 610, 627-628.

cannot help the guilty avoid conviction but can only help assure that the right man has been brought to justice.

Legislative or other regulations, such as those of local police departments, which eliminate the risks of abuse and unintentional suggestion at lineup proceedings and the impediments to meaningful confrontation at trial may also remove the basis for regarding the stage as "critical." But neither Congress nor the federal authorities have seen fit to provide a solution. What we hold today "in no way creates a constitutional straitjacket which will handicap sound efforts at reform, nor is it intended to have this effect." Miranda v. Arizona, [384 U.S. 436] at 467.

V

We come now to the question whether the denial of Wade's motion to strike the courtroom identification by the bank witnesses at trial because of the absence of his counsel at the lineup required, as the Court of Appeals held, the grant of a new trial at which such evidence is to be excluded. We do not think this disposition can be justified without first giving the Government the opportunity to establish by clear and convincing evidence that the in-court identifications were based upon observations of the suspect other than the lineup identification.

. . . Where, as here, the admissibility of evidence of the lineup identification itself is not involved, a per se rule of exclusion of courtroom identification would be unjustified.[32] . . . A rule limited solely to the exclusion of testimony concerning identification at the lineup itself, without regard to admissibility of the courtroom identification, would render the right to counsel an empty one. The lineup is most often used, as in the present case, to crystallize the witnesses' identification of the defendant for future reference. We have already noted that the lineup identification will have that effect. The State may then rest upon the witnesses' unequivocal courtroom identification, and not mention the pretrial identification as part of the State's case at trial. Counsel is then in the predicament in which Wade's counsel found himself—realizing that possible unfairness at the lineup may be the sole means of attack upon the unequivocal courtroom identification, and having to probe in the dark in an attempt to discover and reveal unfairness, while bolstering the government witness' courtroom identification by bringing out and dwelling upon his prior identification. Since counsel's presence at the lineup would equip him to attack not only the lineup identification but the courtroom identifi-

32. We reach a contrary conclusion in Gilbert v. California, supra, as to the admissibility of the witness' testimony that he also identified the accused at the lineup.

cation as well, limiting the impact of violation of the right to counsel to exclusion of evidence only of identification at the lineup itself disregards a critical element of that right.

We think it follows that the proper test to be applied in these situations is that quoted in Wong Sun v. United States, 371 U.S. 471, 488, " '[W]hether, granting establishment of the primary illegality, the evidence to which instant objection is made has been come at by exploitation of that illegality or instead by means sufficiently distinguishable to be purged of the primary taint.' Maguire, Evidence of Guilt 221 (1959)."

. . . Application of this test in the present context requires consideration of various factors; for example, the prior opportunity to observe the alleged criminal act, the existence of any discrepancy between any prelineup description and the defendant's actual description, any identification prior to lineup of another person, the identification by picture of the defendant prior to the lineup, failure to identify the defendant on a prior occasion, and the lapse of time between the alleged act and the lineup identification. It is also relevant to consider those facts which, despite the absence of counsel, are disclosed concerning the conduct of the lineup.[33] On the record now before us we cannot make the determination whether the in-court identifications had an independent origin. This was not an issue at trial, although there is some evidence relevant to a determination. That inquiry is most properly made in the District Court. We therefore think the appropriate procedure to be followed is to vacate the conviction pending a hearing to determine whether the in-court identifications had an independent source, or whether, in any event, the introduction of the evidence was harmless error, Chapman v. California, 386 U.S. 18, and for the District Court to reinstate the conviction or order a new trial, as may be proper. . . .

The judgment of the Court of Appeals is vacated and the case is remanded to that court with direction to enter a new judgment vacating the conviction and remanding the case to the District Court for further proceedings consistent with this opinion.

It is so ordered.

THE CHIEF JUSTICE joins the opinion of the Court except for Part I. . . .

MR. JUSTICE DOUGLAS joins the opinion of the Court except for Part I. . . .

33. Thus it is not the case that "[i]t matters not how well the witness knows the suspect, whether the witness is the suspect's mother, brother, or long-time associate, and no matter how long or well the witness observed the perpetrator at the scene of the crime." Such factors will have an important bearing upon the true basis of the witness' in-court identification. . . .

MR. JUSTICE BLACK, dissenting in part. . . .

I would reverse Wade's conviction without further ado had the prosecution at trial made use of his lineup identification either in place of courtroom identification or to bolster in a harmful manner crucial courtroom identification. But the prosecution here did neither of these things. After prosecution witnesses under oath identified Wade in the courtroom, it was the defense, and not the prosecution, which brought out the prior lineup identification. While stating that "a per se rule of exclusion of courtroom identification would be unjustified," the Court, nevertheless, remands this case for "a hearing to determine whether the in-court identifications had an independent source," or were the tainted fruits of the invalidly conducted lineup. From this holding I dissent.

In the first place, even if this Court has power to establish such a rule of evidence, I think the rule fashioned by the Court is unsound. The "tainted fruit" determination required by the Court involves more than considerable difficulty. I think it is practically impossible. How is a witness capable of probing the recesses of his mind to draw a sharp line between a courtroom identification due exclusively to an earlier lineup and a courtroom identification due to memory not based on the lineup? What kind of "clear and convincing evidence" can the prosecution offer to prove upon what particular events memories resulting in an in-court identification rest? How long will trials be delayed while judges turn psychologists to probe the subconscious minds of witnesses? All these questions are posed but not answered by the Court's opinion. In my view, the Fifth and Sixth Amendments are satisfied if the prosecution is precluded from using lineup identification as either an alternative to or corroboration of courtroom identification. If the prosecution does neither and its witnesses under oath identify the defendant in the courtroom, then I can find no justification for stopping the trial in midstream to hold a lengthy "tainted fruit" hearing. The fact of and circumstances surrounding a prior lineup identification might be used by the defense to impeach the credibility of the in-court identifications, but not to exclude them completely.

But more important, there is no constitutional provision upon which I can rely that directly or by implication gives this Court power to establish what amounts to a constitutional rule of evidence to govern, not only the Federal Government, but the States in their trial of state crimes under state laws in state courts. . . . The Constitution deliberately reposed in the States very broad power to create and to try crimes according to their own rules and policies. Before being deprived of this power, the least that they can ask is that we should be able to point to a federal constitutional provision that either by express language or by necessary implication grants us the power to fashion this novel rule of evidence to govern their criminal trials. . . . I would affirm Wade's conviction.

MR. JUSTICE WHITE, whom MR. JUSTICE HARLAN and MR. JUSTICE STEWART join, dissenting in part and concurring in part.

The Court has again propounded a broad constitutional rule barring use of a wide spectrum of relevant and probative evidence, solely because a step in its ascertainment or discovery occurs outside the presence of defense counsel. . . .

The Court's opinion is far-reaching. It proceeds first by creating a new per se rule of constitutional law: a criminal suspect cannot be subjected to a pretrial identification process in the absence of his counsel without violating the Sixth Amendment. If he is, the State may not buttress a later courtroom identification of the witness by any reference to the previous identification. Furthermore, the courtroom identification is not admissible at all unless the State can establish by clear and convincing proof that the testimony is not the fruit of the earlier identification made in the absence of defendant's counsel—admittedly a heavy burden for the State and probably an impossible one. To all intents and purposes, courtroom identifications are barred if pretrial identifications have occurred without counsel being present.

The rule applies to any lineup, to any other techniques employed to produce an identification and a fortiori to a face-to-face encounter between the witness and the suspect alone, regardless of when the identification occurs, in time or place, and whether before or after indictment or information. It matters not how well the witness knows the suspect, whether the witness is the suspect's mother, brother, or long-time associate, and no matter how long or well the witness observed the perpetrator at the scene of the crime. The kidnap victim who has lived for days with his abductor is in the same category as the witness who has had only a fleeting glimpse of the criminal. Neither may identify the suspect without defendant's counsel being present. The same strictures apply regardless of the number of other witnesses who positively identify the defendant and regardless of the corroborative evidence showing that it was the defendant who had committed the crime.

The premise for the Court's rule is not the general unreliability of eyewitness identifications nor the difficulties inherent in observation, recall, and recognition. The Court assumes a narrower evil as the basis for its rule—improper police suggestion which contributes to erroneous identifications. The Court apparently believes that improper police procedures are so widespread that a broad prophylactic rule must be laid down, requiring the presence of counsel at all pretrial identifications, in order to detect recurring instances of police misconduct.[1] I do not share this pervasive distrust of all official investigations. None of the materials the Court relies upon supports it. Certainly, I would bow to solid fact, but the Court quite obviously does not have before it any reliable, comprehensive survey of current police practices on which to base its new rule. Until it does, the Court should avoid excluding relevant evidence from state criminal trials. . . .

The Court goes beyond assuming that a great majority of the country's police departments are following improper practices at pretrial identifications. To find the lineup a "critical" stage of the proceeding and to exclude identifications made in the absence of counsel, the Court must also assume that police "suggestion," if it occurs at all, leads to erroneous rather than accurate identifications and that reprehensible police conduct will have an unavoidable and largely undiscoverable impact on the trial. This in turn assumes that there is now no adequate source from which defense counsel can learn about the circumstances of the pretrial identification in order to place before the jury all of the considerations which should enter into an appraisal of courtroom identification evidence. But these are treacherous and unsupported assumptions,[3] resting as they do on the notion that the defendant will not be aware, that the police and the witnesses will forget or prevaricate, that defense counsel will be unable to bring out the truth and that nether jury, judge, nor appellate court is a sufficient safeguard against unacceptable police conduct occurring at a pretrial identification procedure. I am unable to share the Court's view of the willingness of the police and the ordinary citizen-witness to dissemble, either with respect to the identification of the defendant or with respect to the circumstances surrounding a pretrial identification.

There are several striking aspects to the Court's holding. First, the rule does not bar courtroom identifications where there have been no previous identifications in the presence of the police, although when

1. Yet in Stovall v. Denno, . . . the Court recognizes that improper police conduct in the identification process has not been so widespread as to justify full retroactivity for its new rule.

3. The instant case and its companions, Gilbert v. California, . . . and Stovall v. Denno, . . . certainly lend no support to the Court's assumptions. The police conduct deemed improper by the Court in the three cases seems to have come to light at trial in the ordinary course of events. One can ask what more counsel would have learned at the pretrial identifications that would have been relevant for truth determination at trial. When the Court premises its constitutional rule on police conduct so subtle as to defy description and subsequent disclosure it deals in pure speculation. If police conduct is intentionally veiled, the police will know about it, and I am unwilling to speculate that defense counsel at trial will be unable to reconstruct the known circumstances of the pretrial identification. And if the "unknown" influence on identifications is "innocent," the Court's general premise evaporates and the problem is simply that of the inherent shortcomings of eyewitness testimony.

identified in the courtroom, the defendant is known to be in custody and charged with the commission of a crime. Second, the Court seems to say that if suitable legislative standards were adopted for the conduct of pretrial identifications, thereby lessening the hazards in such confrontations, it would not insist on the presence of counsel. But if this is true, why does not the Court simply fashion what it deems to be constitutionally acceptable procedures for the authorities to follow? Certainly the Court is correct in suggesting that the new rule will be wholly inapplicable where police departments themselves have established suitable safeguards.

Third, courtroom identification may be barred, absent counsel at a prior identification, regardless of the extent of counsel's information concerning the circumstances of the previous confrontation between witness and defendant—apparently even if there were recordings or sound movies of the events as they occurred. But if the rule is premised on the defendant's right to have his counsel know, there seems little basis for not accepting other means to inform. A disinterested observer, recordings, photographs—any one of them would seem adequate to furnish the basis for a meaningful cross-examination of the eyewitness who identifies the defendant in the courtroom.

I share the Court's view that the criminal trial, at the very least, should aim at truthful factfinding, including accurate eyewitness identifications. I doubt, however, on the basis of our present information, that the tragic mistakes which have occurred in criminal trials are as much the product of improper police conduct as they are the consequence of the difficulties inherent in eyewitness testimony and in resolving evidentiary conflicts by court or jury. I doubt that the Court's new rule will obviate these difficulties, or that the situation will be measurably improved by inserting defense counsel into the investigative processes of police departments everywhere.

But, it may be asked, what possible state interest militates against requiring the presence of defense counsel at lineups? After all, the argument goes, he *may* do some good, he *may* upgrade the quality of identification evidence in state courts and he can scarcely do any harm. Even if true, this is a feeble foundation for fastening an ironclad constitutional rule upon state criminal procedures. Absent some reliably established constitutional violation, the processes by which the States enforce their criminal laws are their own prerogative. The States *do* have an interest in conducting their own affairs, an interest which cannot be displaced simply by saying that there are no valid arguments with respect to the merits of a federal rule emanating from this Court.

Beyond this, however, requiring counsel at pretrial identifications as an invariable rule trenches on other valid state interests. One of them is its concern with the prompt and efficient enforcement of its criminal laws. Identifications frequently take place after arrest but before an indictment is returned or an information is filed. The police may have arrested a suspect on probable cause but may still have the wrong man. Both the suspect and the State have every interest in a prompt identification at that stage, the suspect in order to secure his immediate release and the State because prompt and early identification enhances *accurate* identification and because it must know whether it is on the right investigative track. Unavoidably, however, the absolute rule requiring the presence of counsel will cause significant delay and it may very well result in no pretrial identification at all. Counsel must be appointed and a time arranged convenient for him and the witnesses. Meanwhile, it may be necessary to file charges against the suspect who may then be released on bail, in the federal system very often on his own recognizance, with neither the State nor the defendant having the benefit of a properly conducted identification procedure.

Nor do I think the witnesses themselves can be ignored. They will now be required to be present at the convenience of counsel rather than their own. Many may be much less willing to participate if the identification stage is transformed into an adversary proceeding not under the control of a judge. Others may fear for their own safety if their identity is known at an early date, especially when there is no way of knowing until the lineup occurs whether or not the police really have the right man.

Finally, I think the Court's new rule is vulnerable in terms of its own unimpeachable purpose of increasing the reliability of identification testimony.

Law enforcement officers have the obligation to convict the guilty and to make sure they do not convict the innocent. They must be dedicated to making the criminal trial a procedure for the ascertainment of the true facts surrounding the commission of the crime. To this extent, our so-called adversary system is not adversary at all; nor should it be. But defense counsel has no comparable obligation to ascertain or present the truth. Our system assigns him a different mission. He must be and is interested in preventing the conviction of the innocent, but, absent a voluntary plea of guilty, we also insist that he defend his client whether he is innocent or guilty. The State has the obligation to present the evidence. Defense counsel need present nothing, even if he knows what the truth is. He need not furnish any witnesses to the police, or reveal any confidences of his client, or furnish any other information to help the prosecution's case. If he can confuse a witness, even a truthful one, or make him appear at a disadvantage, unsure or indecisive, that will be his normal course.[6] Our interest in not convicting the innocent permits counsel to put the State to its proof, to put the State's case in the worst possible light, regardless of what he thinks or knows to be the truth. Undoubtedly there are some limits which defense counsel must observe but more often than not, defense counsel will cross-examine a prosecution witness, and impeach him if he can, even if he thinks the witness is telling the truth, just as he will attempt to destroy a witness who he thinks is lying. In this respect, as part of our modified adversary system and as part of the duty imposed on the most honorable defense counsel, we countenance or require conduct which in many instances has little, if any, relation to the search for truth.

I would not extend this system, at least as it presently operates, to police investigations and would not require counsel's presence at pretrial identification procedures. Counsel's interest is in not having his client placed at the scene of the crime, regardless of his whereabouts. Some counsel may advise their clients to refuse to make any movements or to speak any words in a lineup or even to appear in one. To that extent the

---

6. One point of view about the role of the courtroom lawyer appears in Frank, Courts on Trial 82-83.

> What is the role of the lawyers in bringing the evidence before the trial court? As you may learn by reading any one of a dozen or more handbooks on how to try a law-suit, an experienced lawyer uses all sorts of strategems to minimize the effect on the judge or jury of testimony disadvantageous to his client, even when the lawyer has no doubt of the accuracy and honesty of that testimony. . . . If such a witness happens to be timid, frightened by the unfamiliarity of court-room ways, the lawyer, in his cross-examination, plays on that weakness, in order to confuse the witness and make it appear that he is concealing significant facts. Longenecker, in his book Hints on the Trial of a Law Suit (a book endorsed by the great Wigmore), in writing of the "truthful, honest, over-cautious" witness, tells how "a skillful advocate by a rapid cross-examination may ruin the testimony of such a witness." The author does not even hint any disapproval of that accomplishment. Longenecker's and other similar books recommend that a lawyer try to prod an irritable but honest "adverse" witness into displaying his undesirable characteristics in their most unpleasant form, in order to discredit him with the judge or jury. "You may," writes Harris, "sometimes destroy the effect of an adverse witness by making him appear more hostile than he really is. You may make him exaggerate or unsay something and say it again." Taft says that a clever cross-examiner, dealing with an honest but egotistic witness, will "deftly tempt the witness to indulge in his propensity for exaggeration, so as to make him 'hang himself.' " "And thus," adds Taft, "it may happen that not only is the value of his testimony lost, but the side which produces him suffers for seeking aid from such a source"—although, I would add, that may be the only source of evidence of a fact on which the decision will turn.
>
> "An intimidating manner in putting questions," writes Wigmore, "may so coerce or disconcert the witness that his answers do not represent his actual knowledge on the subject. So also, questions which in form or subject cause embarrassment, shame or anger in the witness may unfairly lead him to such demeanor or utterances that the impression produced by his statements does not do justice to its real testimonial value."

impact on truthful factfinding is quite obvious. Others will not only observe what occurs and develop possibilities for later cross-examination then, menacing truthful fact-finding as thoroughly as the Court fears the police now do. Certainly there is an implicit invitation to counsel to suggest rules for the lineup and to manage and produce it as best he can. I therefore doubt that the Court's new rule, at least absent some clearly defined limits on counsel's role, will measurably contribute to more reliable pretrial identifications. My fears are that it will have precisely the opposite result. It may well produce fewer convictions, but that is hardly a proper measure of its long-run acceptability. In my view, the State is entitled to investigate and develop its case outside the presence of defense counsel. This includes the right to have private conversations with identification witnesses, just as defense counsel may have his own consultations with these and other witnesses without having the prosecutor present.

Whether today's judgment would be an acceptable exercise of supervisory power over federal courts is another question. But as a constitutional matter, the judgment in this case is erroneous and although I concur in Parts I and III of the Court's opinion I respectfully register this dissent.

MR. JUSTICE FORTAS, THE CHIEF JUSTICE and MR. JUSTICE DOUGLAS [dissented on the fifth amendment issue. See Chapter 6, infra.] . . .

NOTES AND QUESTIONS

1. In the companion case of Gilbert v. California, the Court held that a per se exclusionary rule was applicable to out of court identification made in violation of the suspect's right to counsel. In the other companion case, Stovall v. Denno, the Court held that Wade was to be applied only to lineups or showups occurring after the decision in Wade but that prior lineups could be tested by a due process standard. For a treatment of that development, see Part B infra.

2. What is the role of counsel at a lineup? Is counsel simply a passive observer or an active participant? What are the implications of those differing roles? Consider, for example, whether a suspect could have ineffective assistance at a lineup. May counsel attend subsequent witness interviews? Consider the following case.

UNITED STATES v. BIEREY, 588 F.2d 620 (8th Cir. 1978): VAN SICKLE, J. Robert Bierey was indicted, tried by a jury, and convicted on two counts of armed bank robbery in violation of Title 18, United States Code, Section 2113(a) and (d). He was sentenced to a term of twenty years imprisonment on each count, with the sentences to run concurrently. On appeal, Bierey contends that the district court erred (1) by not suppressing the out-of-court and subsequent trial identifications and (2) by not granting his motion for judgment of acquittal. We reject the appellant's contentions and affirm the judgment of conviction.

On January 19, 1978, Bierey participated in a lineup during which he was identified by witnesses from both of the robberies. Bierey contends that the lineup was had without a valid court order and against his will, that he was deprived of effective assistance of counsel during the lineup, and that the lineup was impermissibly suggestive. Because of these factors, Bierey contends that the identifications should have been suppressed. We disagree.

Bierey contends the lineup was conducted without a lawful order. On the day of the lineup, Bierey's attorney was presented with an unsigned copy of an order authorizing the lineup. The order signed by the judge bears the date January 20, 1978, one day after the lineup took place. Thus, Bierey contends the court order was not in existence at the time that the lineup was held. The order that bore the judge's signature, however, was file stamped by the clerk's office on January 19, 1978, the day of the lineup. It is clear to us that the trial court merely made a clerical error in dating the order and that on the date of the lineup there was a valid court order. See Rule 36 of the Federal Rules of Criminal Procedure.

Bierey further contends that he was deprived of effective assistance of counsel during the lineup. Bierey's attorney made several requests of the government prior to the lineup: (1) that he be permitted to interview the witnesses and review their statements concerning the description of the robbers prior to the lineup; (2) that each witness view the lineup separately; and (3) that he be present when the witness actually made an identification. Each of these requests were denied.

The lineup was conducted in an auditorium at the St. Louis Police Department. Bierey was displayed as part of a five man lineup viewed simultaneously by four government eyewitnesses, Reiff, Atkins, Eatherton, and Giacoletto, who had been employed by the victim banks at the time of the robberies. The witnesses were positioned ten to fifteen feet away from each other and each was accompanied by a Federal Bureau of Investigation agent. The witnesses were instructed not to say anything or point during the lineup. Bierey's attorney was present at this lineup but he was not allowed to be present during or immediately after the lineup when the FBI agents discussed with the witnesses any identification they might have made. Three of the government eyewitnesses identified Bierey at this lineup and testified to this effect during the trial. The witnesses also identified Bierey at the trial.

Bierey contends that this identification evidence should have been excluded . . . in that the lineup procedure denied Bierey effective assistance of counsel at a critical stage in the government's criminal prosecution against him. . . .

Although the lineup in the present case was attended by Bierey's attorney, Bierey contends that the attorney's role during the lineup was so severely restricted by the government that the attorney could not effectively carry out the purpose for which *Wade* and *Gilbert* require an attorney's presence. . . .

In this case, Bierey's attorney asked to be provided with the witnesses' statements concerning the description of the robber prior to the lineup and also that each witness view the lineup separately. He was rejected as to both requests. We do not agree that the rejection of these requests amounted to a denial of effective assistance of counsel at a critical stage.

Title 18, United States Code, Section 3500(a) provides that no statement made by a government witness shall be subject to discovery until the witness has testified on direct examination in the trial of the case. Section 3500(b) provides that after a government witness testifies on direct examination, the court shall, on motion of the defendant, order the government to produce any statement by the witness which relates to the subject matter about which the witness has testified. Thus, before cross examination, Bierey's attorney could have requested and received any statements that the witness may have made concerning the description of the robber. During the cross examination, the attorney would have his opportunity to meaningfully attack the credibility of the witness' courtroom identification and there would be no denial of Bierey's sixth amendment right to counsel. . . .

The five individuals in the lineup were all white males. The evidence indicates that an attempt was made to gather individuals that resembled Bierey. All four government eyewitnesses were separated in the same room and each was accompanied by an FBI agent. Bierey's attorney was present and observed the complete procedure. We feel that the attorney's noticeable presence at the lineup, although it was conducted with four witnesses simultaneously, satisfied the constitutional requirement of *Wade* and *Gilbert*. As Justice Stewart, concurring in United States v. Ash, stated:

> . . . counsel was required at a lineup, primarily as an observer, to ensure that defense counsel could effectively confront the prosecution's evidence at trial. Attuned to the possibilities of suggestive influences, a lawyer could see any unfairness at a lineup, question the witnesses about it at trial, and effectively reconstruct what had gone on for the benefit of the jury or trial judge. [413 U.S. at 324.]

In this case, Bierey's counsel was given sufficient opportunity to observe the lineup to ensure a meaningful confrontation and thus effective assistance of counsel at trial.

Bierey further contends that the exclusion of his attorney from the interviews of the FBI agents with the witnesses immediately after the lineup amounted to a denial of his right to effective assistance of counsel. Virtually all the courts which have had occasion to consider this problem have refused to extend *Wade* beyond the actual confrontation between the accused and the witnesses to a crime. . . .

Cunningham is one of the leading cases on this subject. In that case, counsel was present at the lineup but, because of some argument between counsel for the government and counsel for the defendant, the latter was ejected. It was while counsel for the defendant was absent that the in-court identification witness identified the defendant from the lineup. The defendant asserted that the interrogation of the identifying witness in the absence of counsel was constitutionally invalid, thus, raising the same issue as does Bierey. In rejecting that claim, the Court stated as follows:

> Here, the lineup was terminated and witnesses were being interrogated outside of the presence of suspects. Confrontation had occurred and was terminated. By the rationale of *Wade* and *Gilbert*, counsel was no longer required unless we were prepared to hold that defense counsel must be present whenever the government interrogates a witness whose testimony may be used as part of the government's case at trial.
>
> The interrogation of witnesses in the investigation of crime or in the preparation for trial is not limited by the rules of evidence or the order of proof, and conscious or unconscious attempts to lead witnesses may occur. We do not think that these dangers are any greater in the case of identification witnesses than witnesses who possess other types of knowledge with regard to the commission of a crime. It is not claimed that to date the Supreme Court has required the presence of counsel during the interrogation of all witnesses, and we will not so require with regard to the interrogation of identification witnesses once the actual confrontation has been completed. [423 F.2d 1269, at 1274.]

Thus, if the requirement of counsel applies solely to the period of confrontation between the accused and the witnesses, then the subsequent interrogation of the witnesses by the prosecution as to whether they identified the accused or not at the lineup does not present that serious potential for prejudice that occurs in the confrontation between an eyewitness and a suspect where counsel is required. . . .

———————————

3. How can a lawyer possibly determine if there is suggestiveness if the lawyer is excluded from the post-lineup interview? Is there any reason not to give the lawyer the witnesses' pre-lineup statements? Does it matter that the statements will be turned over if the witness testifies at trial?

4. Do you need to consider the purpose for counsel's presence in order to determine the appropriate role? What is the purpose of the right to counsel in *Wade?* Does it have obvious or implicit limits? The Supreme Court apparently thought so in Kirby v. Illinois.

KIRBY v. ILLINOIS

Certiorari to the Appellate Court of Illinois, First District
406 U.S. 682 (1972)

MR. JUSTICE STEWART announced the judgment of the Court and an opinion in which THE CHIEF JUSTICE, MR. JUSTICE BLACKMUN, and MR. JUSTICE REHNQUIST join. . . .

On February 21, 1968, a man named Willie Shard reported to the Chicago police that the previous day two men had robbed him on a Chicago street of a wallet containing, among other things, traveler's checks and a Social Security card. On February 22, two police officers stopped the petitioner and a companion, Ralph Bean, on West Madison Street in Chicago.[1] When asked for identification, the petitioner produced a wallet that contained three traveler's checks and a Social Security card, all bearing the name of Willie Shard. Papers with Shard's name on them were also found in Bean's possession. When asked to explain his possession of Shard's property, the petitioner first said that the traveler's checks were "play money," and then told the officers that he had won them in a crap game. The officers then arrested the petitioner and Bean and took them to a police station.

Only after arriving at the police station, and checking the records there, did the arresting officers learn of the Shard robbery. A police car was then dispatched to Shard's place of employment, where it picked up Shard and brought him to the police station. Immediately upon entering the room in the police station where the petitioner and Bean were seated at a table, Shard positively identified them as the men who had robbed

---

1. The officers stopped the petitioner and his companion because they thought the petitioner was a man named Hampton, who was "wanted" in connection with an unrelated criminal offense. The legitimacy of this stop and the subsequent arrest is not before us.

him two days earlier. No lawyer was present in the room, and neither the petitioner nor Bean had asked for legal assistance, or been advised of any right to the presence of counsel.

More than six weeks later, the petitioner and Bean were indicted for the robbery of Willie Shard. Upon arraignment, counsel was appointed to represent them, and they pleaded not guilty. A pretrial motion to suppress Shard's identification testimony was denied, and at the trial Shard testified as a witness for the prosecution. In his testimony he described his identification of the two men at the police station on February 22,[2] and identified them again in the courtroom as the men who had robbed him on February 20. He was cross-examined at length regarding the circumstances of his identification of the two defendants. . . . The jury found both defendants guilty, and the petitioner's conviction was affirmed on appeal. . . . The Illinois appellate court held that the admission of Shard's testimony was not error . . . , holding that the *Wade-Gilbert* per se exclusionary rule is not applicable to pre-indictment confrontations. We granted certiorari, limited to this question.

I . . .

In a line of constitutional cases in this Court stemming back to the Court's landmark opinion in Powell v. Alabama, it has been firmly established that a person's Sixth and Fourteenth Amendment right to counsel attaches only at or after the time that adversary judicial proceedings have been initiated against him. . . .

   2.

Q: All right. Now, Willie, calling your attention to February 22, 1968, did you receive a call from the police asking you to come down to the station?
A: Yes, I did. . . .
Q: When you went down there, what if anything, happened, Willie?
A: Well, I seen the two men was down there who robbed me. . . .
Q: Who took you to the police station?
A: The policeman picked me up. . . .
Mr. Pomaro: When you went to the police station did you see the two defendants?
A: Yes, I did.
Q: Do you see them in Court today?
A: Yes, sir.
Q: Point them out, please?
A: Yes, that one there and the other one. (Indicating.)
Mr. Pomaro: Indicating for the record the defendants Bean and Kirby.
Q: And you positively identified them at the police station, is that correct?
A: Yes.
Q: Did any police officers make any suggestions to you whatsoever?
The Witness: No, they didn't.

This is not to say that a defendant in a criminal case has a constitutional right to counsel only at the trial itself. The *Powell* case makes clear that the right attaches at the time of arraignment, and the Court has recently held that it exists also at the time of a preliminary hearing. Coleman v. Alabama. . . . But the point is that, while members of the Court have differed as to existence of the right to counsel in the contexts of some of the above cases, *all* of those cases have involved points of time at or after the initiation of adversary judicial criminal proceedings—whether by way of formal charge, preliminary hearing, indictment, information, or arraignment. . . .

The initiation of judicial criminal proceedings is far from a mere formalism. It is the starting point of our whole system of adversary criminal justice. For it is only then that the government has committed itself to prosecute, and only then that the adverse positions of government and defendant have solidified. It is then that a defendant finds himself faced with the prosecutorial forces of organized society, and immersed in the intricacies of substantive and procedural criminal law. It is this point, therefore, that marks the commencement of the "criminal prosecutions" to which alone the explicit guarantees of the Sixth Amendment are applicable. . . .

In this case we are asked to import into a routine police investigation an absolute constitutional guarantee historically and rationally applicable only after the onset of formal prosecutorial proceedings. We decline to do so. Less than a year after *Wade* and *Gilbert* were decided, the Court explained the rule of those decisions as follows: "The rationale of those cases was that an accused is entitled to counsel at any 'critical stage of the *prosecution*,' and that a post-indictment lineup is such a 'critical stage.' " We decline to depart from that rationale today by imposing a per se exclusionary rule upon testimony concerning an identification that took place long before the commencement of any prosecution whatever.

II

What has been said is not to suggest that there may not be occasions during the course of a criminal investigation when the police do abuse identification procedures. Such abuses are not beyond the reach of the Constitution. As the Court pointed out in *Wade* itself, it is always necessary to "scrutinize *any* pretrial confrontation. . . . " The Due Process Clause of the Fifth and Fourteenth Amendments forbids a lineup that is unnecessarily suggestive and conducive to irreparable mistaken identification. When a person has not been formally charged with a criminal offense, *Stovall* strikes the appropriate constitutional balance between the right of a suspect to be protected from prejudicial procedures and the interest of society in the prompt and purposeful investigation of an unsolved crime.

The judgment is affirmed.

MR. CHIEF JUSTICE BURGER, concurring.

I agree that the right to counsel attaches as soon as criminal charges are formally made against an accused and he becomes the subject of a "criminal prosecution." Therefore, I join in the plurality opinion and in the judgment.

MR. JUSTICE POWELL, concurring in the result.

As I would not extend the *Wade-Gilbert* per se exclusionary rule, I concur in the result reached by the Court.

MR. JUSTICE BRENNAN, with whom MR. JUSTICE DOUGLAS and MR. JUSTICE MARSHALL join, dissenting.

After petitioner and Ralph Bean were arrested, police officers brought Willie Shard, the robbery victim, to a room in a police station where petitioner and Bean were seated at a table with two other police officers. Shard testified at trial that the officers who brought him to the room asked him if petitioner and Bean were the robbers and that he indicated they were. The prosecutor asked him, "And you positively identified them at the police station, it that correct?" Shard answered, "Yes." Consequently, the question in this case is whether, under Gilbert v. California, it was constitutional error to admit Shard's testimony that he identified petitioner at the pretrial stationhouse showup when that showup was conducted by the police without advising petitioner that he might have counsel present. *Gilbert* held, in the context of a post-indictment lineup, that "[o]nly a per se exclusionary rule as to such testimony can be an effective sanction to assure that law enforcement authorities will respect the accused's constitutional right to the presence of his counsel at the critical lineup." I would apply *Gilbert* and the principles of its companion case, United States v. Wade, and reverse.

In *Wade*, . . . the Court addressed the argument "that the assistance of counsel at the lineup was indispensable to protect Wade's most basic right as a criminal defendant—his right to a fair trial at which the witnesses against him might be meaningfully cross-examined." . . . The Court began by emphasizing that the Sixth Amendment guarantee "encompasses counsel's assistance whenever necessary to assure a meaningful 'defence.' " . . .

It was that constitutional principle that the Court applied in *Wade* to pretrial confrontations for identification purposes. The Court first met the Government's contention that a confrontation for identification is "a mere preparatory step in the gathering of the prosecution's evidence," much like the scientific examination of fingerprints and blood samples. The Court responded that in the latter instances "the accused has the opportunity for a meaningful confrontation of the Government's case at trial through the ordinary processes of cross-examination of the Government's expert witnesses and the presentation of the evidence of his own experts." The accused thus has no right to have counsel present at such examinations: "they are not critical stages since there is minimal risk that his counsel's absence at such stages might derogate from his right to a fair trial." . . .

In contrast, the Court said, "the confrontation compelled by the State between the accused and the victim or witnesses to a crime to elicit identification evidence is peculiarly riddled with innumerable dangers and variable factors which might seriously, even crucially, derogate from a fair trial." Most importantly, "the accused's inability effectively to re-construct at trial any unfairness that occurred at the lineup may deprive him of his only opportunity meaningfully to attack the credibility of the witness' courtroom identification." . . . The Court then applied that conclusion to the specific facts of the case. "Since it appears that there is grave potential for prejudice, intentional or not, in the pretrial lineup, which may not be capable of reconstruction at trial, and since presence of counsel itself can often avert prejudice and assure a meaningful con-frontation at trial, there can be little doubt that for Wade the post-indictment lineup was a critical stage of the prosecution at which he was 'as much entitled to such aid [of counsel] . . . as at the trial it-self.' " . . .

While it should go without saying, it appears necessary, in view of the plurality opinion today, to re-emphasize that *Wade* did not require the presence of counsel at pretrial confrontations for identification pur-poses simply on the basis of an abstract consideration of the words "crim-inal prosecutions" in the Sixth Amendment. Counsel is required at those confrontations because "the dangers inherent in eyewitness identification and the suggestibility inherent in the context of the pretrial identification," . . . .[4] mean that protection must be afforded to the "most basic right [of]

4. The plurality refers to "occasions during the course of a criminal investigation when the police do abuse identification procedures" and assert that "[s]uch abuses are not beyond the reach of the Constitution." . . . The constitutional principles established in *Wade* explicitly pointed out:

"The few cases that have surfaced therefore reveal the existence of a process attended with hazards of serious unfairness to the criminal accused and strongly suggest the plight of the more numerous defendants who are unable to ferret out suggestive influences in the secrecy of the confrontation. We do not assume that these risks are the result of

a criminal defendant—his right to a fair trial at which the witness against him might be meaningfully cross-examined." . . . Indeed, the Court expressly stated that "[l]egislative or other regulations, such as those of local police departments, which eliminate the risks of abuse and unintentional suggestion at lineup proceedings and the impediments to meaningful confrontation at trial may also remove the basis for regarding the stage as 'critical.' ". . . Hence, "the initiation of adversary judicial criminal proceedings," . . . is completely irrelevant to whether counsel is necessary at a pretrial confrontation for identification in order to safeguard the accused's constitutional rights to confrontation and the effective assistance of counsel at his trial.

In view of Wade, it is plain, and the plurality today does not attempt to dispute it, that there inhere in a confrontation for identification conducted after arrest the identical hazards to a fair trial that inhere in such a confrontation conducted "after the onset of formal prosecutorial proceedings." The plurality apparently considers an arrest, which for present purposes we must assume to be based upon probable cause, to be nothing more than a part of "a routine police investigation," . . . and thus not "the starting point of our whole system of adversary criminal justice," . . . An arrest, according to the plurality, does not face the accused "with the prosecutorial forces of organized society," nor immerse him "in the intricacies of substantive and procedural criminal law." Those consequences ensue, says the plurality, only with "[t]he initiation of judicial criminal proceedings," "[f]or it is only then that the government has committed itself to prosecute, and only then that the adverse positions of government and defendant have solidified."[7] . . . If these propositions do not amount to "mere formalism," . . . it is difficult to know how to characterize them.[8] An arrest evidences the belief of the police that the

---

police procedures intentionally designed to prejudice an accused. Rather we assume they derive from the dangers inherent in eyewitness identification and the suggestibility inherent in the context of the pretrial identification." 388 U.S., at 234-235.

7. The plurality concludes that "[i]t is this point, therefore, that marks the commencement of the 'criminal prosecutions' to which alone the explicit guarantees of the Sixth Amendment are applicable." . . . This Court has taken the contrary position with respect to the speedy-trial guarantee of the Sixth Amendment: "Invocation of the speedy trial provision thus need not await indictment, information, or other formal charge. But we decline to extend the reach of the amendment to the period prior to arrest." "In the case before us, neither appellee was arrested, charged, or otherwise subjected to formal restraint prior to indictment. It was this event, therefore, which transformed the appellees into 'accused' defendants who are subject to the speedy trial protections of the Sixth Amendment." United States v. Marion, 404 U.S. 307, 321, 325 (1971).

8. As the California Supreme Court pointed out, with an eye toward the real world, "the establishment of the date of formal accusation as the time wherein the right to counsel at lineup attaches could only lead to a situation wherein substantially all lineups would be conducted prior to indictment or information." People v. Fowler, 1 Cal. 3d 335, 344, 461 P.2d 643, 650 (1969).

perpetrator of a crime has been caught. A post-arrest confrontation for identification is not "a mere preparatory step in the gathering of the prosecution's evidence." . . . A primary, and frequently sole, purpose of the confrontation for identification at that stage is to accumulate proof to buttress the conclusion of the police that they have the offender in hand. The plurality offers no reason, and I can think of none, for concluding that a post-arrest confrontation for identification, unlike a post-charge confrontation, is not among those "critical confrontations of the accused by the prosecution at pretrial proceedings where the results might well settle the accused's fate and reduce the trial itself to a mere formality." . . .

The highly suggestive form of confrontation employed in this case underscores the point. This showup was particularly fraught with the peril of mistaken identification. In the setting of a police station squad room where all present except petitioner and Bean were police officers, the danger was quite real that Shard's understandable resentment might lead him too readily to agree with the police that the pair under arrest, and the only persons exhibited to him, were indeed the robbers. "It is hard to imagine a situation more clearly conveying the suggestion to the witness that the one presented is believed guilty by the police." [Wade, 388 U.S. at 234.] The State had no case without Shard's identification testimony, and safeguards against that consequence were therefore of critical importance. Shard's testimony itself demonstrates the necessity for such safeguards. On direct examination, Shard identified petitioner and Bean not as the alleged robbers on trial in the courtroom, but as the pair he saw at the police station. His testimony thus lends strong support to the observation, quoted by the Court in Wade, 388 U.S., at 229, that "[i]t is a matter of common experience that, once a witness has picked out the accused at the line-up, he is not likely to go back on his word later on, so that in practice the issue of identity may (in the absence of other relevant evidence) for all practical purposes be determined there and then, before the trial." Williams & Hammelmann, Identification Parades, Part I, [1963] Crim. L. Rev. 479, 482.

The plurality today "decline[s] to depart from [the] rationale" of Wade and Gilbert. . . . The plurality discovers that "rationale" not by consulting those decisions themselves, which would seem to be the appropriate court, but by reading one sentence in Simmons v. United States where no right-to-counsel claim was either asserted or considered.[2] The

2. Simmons involved an allegedly overly suggestive photographic array that occurred prior to indictment. The Court held that Wade was not applicable, that the due process test developed in Stovall was, but that due process was not violated in Simmons. For a discussion of the due process test, see page 393 infra. For a discussion of photographic arrays, see page 372 infra. —EDS.

"rationale" the plurality discovers is, apparently, that a post-indictment confrontation for identification is part of the prosecution. The plurality might have discovered a different "rationale" by reading one sentence in Foster v. California, a case decided after Simmons, where the Court explained that in Wade and Gilbert "this Court held that because of the possibility of unfairness to the accused in the way a lineup is conducted, a lineup is a 'critical stage' in the prosecution, at which the accused must be given the opportunity to be represented by counsel."[3] In Foster, more-over, although the Court mentioned that the lineups took place after the accused's arrest, it did not say whether they were also after the information was filed against him.[10] Instead, the Court simply pointed out that under Stovall v. Denno, Wade and Gilbert were "applicable only to lineups conducted after those cases were decided." . . .

The plurality might also have discovered a different "rationale" for Wade and Gilbert had it examined Stovall v. Denno, . . . decided the same day. In Stovall, the confrontation for identification took place one day after the accused's arrest. Although the accused was first brought to an arraignment, it "was postponed until [he] could retain counsel." Hence, in the plurality's terms today, the confrontation was held "before the commencement of any prosecution." . . . Yet in that circumstance the Court in Stovall stated that the accused raised "the same alleged consti-tutional errors in the admission of allegedly tainted identification evidence that were before us" in Wade and Gilbert. The Court therefore found

3. Foster is the only case in which the Supreme Court has found a due process violation. See note 1, page 355 supra, and n. 8, page 396 infra. The facts in Foster, as summarized by the Court are:

> Except for the robbers themselves, the only witness to the crime was Joseph David, the late-night manager of the Western Union office. After Foster had been arrested, David was called to the police station to view a lineup. There were three men in the lineup. One was petitioner. He is a tall man—close to six feet in height. The other two men were short—five feet, five or six inches. Petitioner wore a leather jacket which David said was similar to the one he had seen un-derneath the coveralls worn by the robber. After seeing this lineup, David could not positively identify petitioner as the robber. He "thought" he was the man, but he was not sure. David then asked to speak to petitioner, and petitioner was brought into an office and sat across from David at a table. Except for prosecuting officials there was no one else in the room. Even after this one-to-one confrontation David still was uncertain whether petitioner was one of the robbers: "truthfully—I was not sure," he testified at trial. A week or 10 days later, the police arranged for David to view a second lineup. There were five men in that lineup. Petitioner was the only person in the second lineup who had appeared in the first lineup. This time David was "convinced" petitioner was the man.

394 U.S. at 440-441.—Eds.

10. In fact, the lineups in Foster took place before the information was filed. The crime occurred on January 25, 1966. After the accused was arrested, he was exhibited to the witness in two lineups, both conducted within two weeks of January 25. The information was not filed until March 17.

that the case "provide[d] a vehicle for deciding the extent to which the rules announced in *Wade* and *Gilbert*—requiring the exclusion of identification evidence which is tainted by exhibiting the accused to identifying witnesses before trial in the absence of his counsel—are to be applied retroactively." Indeed, the Court's explicit holding was "that *Wade* and *Gilbert* affect only those cases and all future cases which involve confrontations for identification purposes conducted in the absence of counsel after this date. The rulings of *Wade* and *Gilbert* are therefore inapplicable in the present case." Hence, the accused in *Stovall* did not receive the benefit of the new exclusionary rules because they were not applied retroactively; he was not denied their benefit because his confrontation took place before he had "been formally charged with a criminal offense." . . . Moreover, in the course of its retroactivity discussion, the Court repeated the phrase "pretrial confrontations for identification" or its equivalent no less than 10 times. Not once did the Court so much as hint that *Wade* and *Gilbert* applied only to confrontations after the accused "had been indicted or otherwise formally charged with [a] criminal offense." . . . In fact, at one point the Court summarized *Wade* as holding "that the confrontation [for identification] is a 'critical stage,' and that counsel is required at *all* confrontations."

Wade and *Gilbert*, of course, happened to involve post-indictment confrontations. Yet even a cursory perusal of the opinions in those cases reveals that nothing at all turned upon that particular circumstance.[13] In short, it is fair to conclude that rather than "declin[ing] to depart from [the] rationale" of *Wade* and *Gilbert*, . . . the plurality today, albeit purporting to be engaged in "principled constitutional adjudication," . . . refuses even to recognize that "rationale." For my part, I do not agree that we "extend" *Wade* and *Gilbert*, . . . by holding that the principles of those cases apply to confrontations for identification conducted after arrest. Because Shard testified at trial about his identification of petitioner at the police station showup, the exclusionary rule of *Gilbert*, requires reversal.

MR. JUSTICE WHITE, dissenting.

United States v. Wade, and Gilbert v. California, govern this case and compel reversal of the judgment below.

---

13. The *Wade* dissenters found no such limitation: "The rule applies to any lineup, to any other techniques employed to produce an identification and a fortiori to a face-to-face encounter between the witness and the suspect alone, regardless of when the identification occurs, in time or place, and whether before or after indictment or information." United States v. Wade, 388 U.S., at 251 (White, J., joined by Harlan and Stewart, JJ., dissenting in part and concurring in part).

NOTES AND QUESTIONS

1. What is the Court's holding in *Kirby?* Can you determine that without attempting to decipher Justice Powell's concurring sentence? What might it mean?

2. Taking the opinions at face value, who wins in *Kirby*, the plurality or the dissent? Taking the plurality opinion alone, how does its result fare when evaluated by its reasoning? Do you think there was a "hidden agenda" in *Kirby?* What might it have been?

3. Does a defendant have a right to a pretrial lineup? Most courts have held that it is a matter left to the trial judge's discretion, see, e.g., People v. Baines, 30 Cal. 3d 143, 635 P.2d 455, 177 Cal. Rptr. 861 (1981), but consider the implications of Moore v. Illinois, 434 U.S. 220 (1977), in which the defendant was identified by the complaining witness at a preliminary hearing at which he was not represented by counsel. The defendant was convicted and appealed on the grounds that his identification at the preliminary hearing violated *Wade.* The Court of Appeals was unpersuaded, but the Supreme Court reversed:

> The Court of Appeals . . . read *Kirby* as holding that evidence of a corporeal identification conducted in the absence of defense counsel must be excluded only if the identification is made after the defendant is *indicted.* . . . Such a reading cannot be squared with *Kirby* itself, which held that an accused's rights under *Wade* and *Gilbert* attach to identifications conducted "at or after the initiation of adversary judicial criminal proceedings," including proceedings instituted "by way of formal charge [or] preliminary hearing." 406 U.S., at 689. The prosecution in this case was commenced under Illinois law when the victim's complaint was filed in court. The purpose of the preliminary hearing was to determine whether there was probable cause to bind petitioner over to the grand jury and to set bail. Petitioner had the right to oppose the prosecution at that hearing by moving to dismiss the charges and to suppress the evidence against him. He faced counsel for the State, who elicited the victim's identification, summarized the State's other evidence against petitioner, and urged that the State be given more time to marshal its evidence. It is plain that "the government ha[d] committed itself to prosecute," and that petitioner found "himself faced with the prosecutorial forces of organized society, and immersed in the intricacies of substantive and procedural criminal law." *Kirby.* The State candidly concedes that this preliminary hearing marked the "initiation of adversary judicial criminal proceedings" against petitioner, . . . and it hardly could contend otherwise. The Court of Appeals therefore erred in holding that petitioner's rights under *Wade* and *Gilbert* had not yet attached at the time of the preliminary hearing.
>
> The Court of Appeals also suggested that *Wade* and *Gilbert* did not apply here because the "in-court identification could hardly be considered

a line-up." . . . The meaning of this statement is not entirely clear. If the court meant that a one-on-one identification procedure, as distinguished from a lineup, is not subject to the counsel requirement, it was mistaken. Although *Wade* and *Gilbert* both involved lineups, *Wade* clearly contemplated that counsel would be required in both situations: "The pretrial confrontation for purpose of identification may take the form of a lineup . . . or presentation of the suspect alone to the witness. . . . It is obvious that risks of suggestion attend either form of confrontation. . . ." Indeed, a one-on-one confrontation generally is thought to present greater risks of mistaken identification than a lineup. E.g., P. Wall, Eye-Witness Identification in Criminal Cases 27-40 (1965); Williams & Hammelmann, Identification Parades—I, Crim. L. Rev. 479, 480-481 (1963). There is no reason, then, to hold that a one-on-one identification procedure is not subject to the same requirements as a lineup.

If the court believed that petitioner did not have a right to counsel at this identification procedure because it was conducted in the course of a judicial proceeding, we do not agree. The reasons supporting *Wade's* holding that a corporeal identification is a critical stage of a criminal prosecution for Sixth Amendment purposes apply with equal force to this identification. It is difficult to imagine a more suggestive manner in which to present a suspect to a witness for their critical first confrontation than was employed in this case. The victim, who had seen her assailant for only 10 to 15 seconds, was asked to make her identification after she was told that she was going to view a suspect, after she was told his name and heard it called as he was led before the bench, and after she heard the prosecutor recite the evidence believed to implicate petitioner. Had petitioner been represented by counsel, some or all of this suggestiveness could have been avoided.[5] . . .

Could an attorney in *Moore* have required that the complaining witness first view the accused in a lineup?

4. Can the police arrange a noncustodial, surreptitious viewing of the accused? Does it matter when it would occur—pre- or post-indictment?

5. A number of police departments responded to *Wade* by promulgating rules to govern lineups that were designed to ensure counsel's

---

5. For example, counsel could have requested that the hearing be postponed until a lineup could be arranged at which the victim would view petitioner in a less suggestive setting. Short of that, counsel could have asked that the victim be excused from the courtroom while the charges were read and the evidence against petitioner was recited, and that petitioner be seated with other people in the audience when the victim attempted an identification. Counsel might have sought to cross-examine the victim to test her identification before it hardened. Because it is in the prosecution's interest as well as the accused's that witnesses' identifications remain untainted, we cannot assume that such requests would have been in vain. Such requests ordinarily are addressed to the sound discretion of the court; we express no opinion as to whether the preliminary hearing court would have been required to grant any such requests.

presence. For a discussion, see Read, Lawyers at Lineups: Constitutional Necessity or Avoidable Extravagance?, 17 U.C.L.A. L. Rev. 339 (1969). As the title implies, Professor Read is unsure of the wisdom of *Wade's* primary thrust. Although he agrees that the presence of counsel is likely to enhance the fairness of lineups, he is unconvinced that the incremental gain is worth the effort, and he is convinced that other forms of regulation would better ameliorate the Supreme Court's concerns. Recognizing that the Court in *Wade* implied that regulation designed to offset the potential for prejudice at lineups and to preserve a defendant's right to confrontation at trial could supplant the requirement of counsel emanating from *Wade*, Professor Read proposed the following Model Regulation, id. at 388-393:

Proposed Regulation of Eyewitness Identification Procedures

(1) *Restrictions on Identification*

(a) Restrictions on Police. No law enforcement officer shall conduct a lineup or otherwise attempt, by having a witness view or hear the voice of an arrested person, to secure the identification of an arrested person as a person involved in a crime unless such identification procedure is authorized by this regulation. . . .

(b) Restrictions on Witnesses. No witness at trial shall hereafter be permitted to identify a criminal defendant as the person involved in a crime unless the prosecution has first shown, to the Court's satisfaction, and in the absence of the jury:

(1) That the witness was sufficiently acquainted with the defendant before the alleged offense to make recognition then likely; or

(2) That the witness' recognition of the defendant arose from an independent origin or source under circumstances other than that the police or other authorities were attempting to elicit identification; or

(3) That all pertinent provisions of this regulation were followed by police in conducting eyewitness confrontation or lineup identification procedures. . . .

(2) *Required Procedures*

A lineup or identification procedure is authorized only if there has been compliance with the following rules:

(a) No person participating in any police lineup or other identification procedure and no person present at such lineup or identification procedure shall do any act or say any thing which shall directly, indirectly, or impliedly suggest to or influence any identifying witness to make or not to make a particular identification, or which suggests to or influences any identifying witness to believe or suspect that any member or members of the group standing [in] the lineup has been arrested for the offense in question or for any offense.

(b) The officer conducting any police lineup or identification proceeding shall take all steps necessary to guarantee that any identification or failure to identify shall be the product of the free choice of the identifying witness based on the independent recollection or recognition of such witness. . . .

(c) All police lineups or identification proceedings shall be composed of a minimum of five persons, in addition to the suspect, and these additional five or more persons shall be of the same general age, sex, race and general physical characteristics as the suspect and be required to wear clothing similar to that worn by the suspect. . . .

(d) All body movements, gestures or verbal statements that may be necessary shall be done one time only by each person participating in the lineup and shall be repeated only at the express request of the identifying witness. . . .

(e) The suspect may select his own position in any police lineup or identification procedure and may change his position after each identifying witness has completed his viewing. . . .

(f) Under no circumstances shall any identifying witness be allowed to see a suspect or any member of the lineup in custody or otherwise prior to the lineup or identification procedure and no interrogation of the suspect or any member of the lineup group shall occur in the presence of an identifying witness. . . .

(g) Two (2) or more identifying witnesses shall not view the same lineup or identification procedure in each other's presence nor shall they be permitted to communicate with each other before completion of all attempted identifications by all witnesses. . . .

(h) Prior to viewing the lineup, an identifying witness shall be required to give a description of the person or persons responsible for the crime in question and such description shall be written and signed or otherwise verified and a copy of such description and all other descriptions that may have been given to the police prior to the lineup shall be made available to defense counsel. . . .

(i) Any identifying witness may remain unseen or masked when viewing the lineup or identification procedure. . . .

(j) The officer conducting any police lineup or identification proceeding shall record the names and addresses of persons participating in the lineup or identification, including the suspect or defendant, the others standing in the lineup group with the suspect or defendant, the police officers present, any person representing the suspect, and any independent observers; provided however, that names of identifying witnesses shall not be required to be disclosed; a copy of said list of names and addresses so recorded shall be furnished to defense counsel.

(k) A full record of all statements made by the identifying witness regarding the identification shall be made by voice recording, or, if no such recording equipment is available, a complete transcript of all statements made by the identifying witness regarding the identification shall be made; a copy of such voice recording or transcript shall be made available to defense counsel.

(l) A visual recording of the conduct of the lineup or identification procedure shall be made by videotape or other appropriate moving picture-type process, or, if no such videotape or moving picture type equipment is available, a minimum of one good quality color photograph of the entire group included in the lineup which was viewed by the identifying witness shall be taken and a copy of such photograph shall be made available to defense counsel. . . .

(3) *Urgent Necessity*

In cases of urgent necessity, as where a witness is dying at the scene of the crime, an identification confrontation shall be lawful with only such compliance with subsections a, b, j, k, and l of section 2, above, as may be reasonable under the circumstances. . . .

6. When faced with the issue, the lower courts almost always find that an in-court identification is based on an independent source and not impermissibly tainted by a prior unconstitutional out-of-court identification. One notable exception is Dickerson v. Fogg, 692 F.2d 238 (2d Cir. 1982).

7. How do the principles of *Wade* and *Kirby* apply to photographic arrays? Consider United States v. Ash.

UNITED STATES v. ASH
Certiorari to the United States Court of Appeals for the District of Columbia Circuit
413 U.S. 300 (1973)

MR. JUSTICE BLACKMUN delivered the opinion of the Court.

In this case the Court is called upon to decide whether the Sixth Amendment grants an accused the right to have counsel present whenever the Government conducts a post-indictment photographic display, containing a picture of the accused, for the purpose of allowing a witness to attempt an identification of the offender. The United States Court of Appeals for the District of Columbia Circuit, sitting en banc, held, by a 5-to-4 vote, that the accused possesses this right to counsel. The court's holding is inconsistent with decisions of the courts of appeals of nine other circuits. We granted certiorari to resolve the conflict and to decide this important constitutional question. We reverse and remand.

I

On the morning of August 26, 1965, a man with a stocking mask entered a bank in Washington, D.C., and began waving a pistol. He ordered an employee to hang up the telephone and instructed all others present not to move. Seconds later a second man, also wearing a stocking mask, entered the bank, scooped up money from tellers' drawers into a bag, and left. The gunman followed, and both men escaped through an alley. The robbery lasted three or four minutes.

A Government informer, Clarence McFarland, told authorities that he had discussed the robbery with Charles J. Ash, Jr., the respondent here. Acting on this information, an FBI agent, in February 1966, showed five black-and-white mug shots of Negro males of generally the same age, height, and weight, one of which was of Ash, to four witnesses. All four made uncertain identifications of Ash's picture. At this time Ash was not in custody and had not been charged. On April 1, 1966, an indictment was returned charging Ash and a co-defendant, John L. Bailey, in five counts related to this bank robbery.

Trial was finally set for May 1968, almost three years after the crime. In preparing for trial, the prosecutor decided to use a photographic display to determine whether the witnesses he planned to call would be able to make in-court identifications. Shortly before the trial, an FBI agent and the prosecutor showed five color photographs to the four witnesses who previously had tentatively identified the black-and-white photograph of Ash. Three of the witnesses selected the picture of Ash, but one was unable to make any selection. None of the witnesses selected the picture of Bailey which was in the group. This post-indictment identification provides the basis for respondent Ash's claim that he was denied the right to counsel at a "critical stage" of the prosecution.

No motion for severance was made, and Ash and Bailey were tried jointly. The trial judge held a hearing on the suggestive nature of the pretrial photographic displays. The judge did not make a clear ruling on suggestive nature, but held that the Government had demonstrated by "clear and convincing" evidence that in-court identifications would be "based on observation of the suspect other than the intervening observation." . . .

At trial, the three witnesses who had been inside the bank identified Ash as the gunman, but they were unwilling to state that they were certain of their identifications. None of these made an in-court identification of Bailey. The fourth witness, who had been in a car outside the bank and who had seen the fleeing robbers after they had removed their masks, made positive in-court identifications of both Ash and Bailey. Bailey's counsel then sought to impeach this in-court identification by calling the FBI agent who had shown the color photographs to the witnesses immediately before trial. Bailey's counsel demonstrated that the witness who had identified Bailey in court had failed to identify a color photograph of Bailey. During the course of the examination, Bailey's counsel also, before the jury, brought out the fact that this witness had selected another man as one of the robbers. At this point the prosecutor became concerned that the jury might believe that the witness had selected a third person when, in fact, the witness had selected a photograph of Ash. After a conference at the bench, the trial judge ruled that all five color photographs would be admitted into evidence. The Court of Appeals held that this constituted the introduction of a post-indictment identification at the prosecutor's request and over the objection of defense counsel.

McFarland testified as a Government witness. He said he had discussed plans for the robbery with Ash before the event and, later, had discussed the results of the robbery with Ash in the presence of Bailey. McFarland was shown to possess an extensive criminal record and a history as an informer.

The jury convicted Ash on all counts. It was unable to reach a verdict on the charges against Bailey, and his motion for acquittal was granted. Ash received concurrent sentences on the several counts, the two longest being 80 months to 12 years.

The five-member majority of the Court of Appeals held that Ash's right to counsel, guaranteed by the Sixth Amendment, was violated when his attorney was not given the opportunity to be present at the photographic displays conducted in May 1968 before the trial. . . .

II . . .

[After discussing the history of the right to counsel, the Court proceeded to summarize its import.]

This historical background suggests that the core purpose of the counsel guarantee was to assure "Assistance" at trial, when the accused was confronted with both the intricacies of the law and the advocacy of the public prosecutor. Later developments have led this Court to recognize that "Assistance" would be less than meaningful if it were limited to the formal trial itself.

This extension of the right to counsel to events before trial has resulted from changing patterns of criminal procedure and investigation that have tended to generate pretrial events that might appropriately be considered to be parts of the trial itself. At these newly emerging and significant events, the accused was confronted, just as at trial, by the procedural system, or by his expert adversary, or by both. . . .

Throughout this expansion of the counsel guarantee to trial-like confrontations, the function of the lawyer has remained essentially the same as his function at trial. In all cases considered by the Court, counsel has continued to act as a spokesman for, or advisor to, the accused. The accused's right to the "Assistance of Counsel" has meant just that, namely, the right of the accused to have counsel acting as his assistant. . . .

The function of counsel in rendering "Assistance" continued at the lineup under consideration in *Wade* and its companion cases. Although the accused was not confronted there with legal questions, the lineup offered opportunities for prosecuting authorities to take advantage of the accused. Counsel was seen by the Court as being more sensitive to, and aware of, suggestive influences than the accused himself, and as better able to reconstruct the events at trial. Counsel present at lineup would be able to remove disabilities of the accused in precisely the same fashion that counsel compensated for the disabilities of the layman at trial. Thus, the Court mentioned that the accused's memory might be dimmed by "emotional tension," that the accused's credibility at trial would be diminished by his status as defendant, and that the accused might be unable to present his version effectively without giving up his privilege against compulsory self-incrimination. United States v. Wade. It was in order to compensate for these deficiencies that the Court found the need for the assistance of counsel.

This review of the history and expansion of the Sixth Amendment counsel guarantee demonstrates that the test utilized by the Court has called for examination of the event in order to determine whether the accused required aid in coping with legal problems or assistance in meeting his adversary. Against the background of this traditional test, we now consider the opinion of the Court of Appeals.

III

Although the Court of Appeals' majority recognized the argument that "a major purpose behind the right to counsel is to protect the defendant from errors that he himself might make if he appeared in court alone," the court concluded that "other forms of prejudice," mentioned and recognized in *Wade*, could also give rise to a right to counsel. . . . These forms of prejudice were felt by the court to flow from the possibilities for mistaken identification inherent in the photographic display.[8]

---

8. "[T]he dangers of mistaken identification from uncounseled lineup identifications

We conclude that the dangers of mistaken identification, mentioned in *Wade*, were removed from context by the Court of Appeals and were incorrectly utilized as a sufficient basis for requiring counsel. Although *Wade* did discuss possibilities for suggestion and the difficulty for reconstructing suggestivity, this discussion occurred only after the Court had concluded that the lineup constituted a trial-like confrontation, requiring the "Assistance of Counsel" to preserve the adversary process by compensating for advantages of the prosecuting authorities.

The above discussion of *Wade* has shown that the traditional Sixth Amendment test easily allowed extension of counsel to a lineup. The similarity to trial was apparent, and counsel was needed to render "Assistance" in counterbalancing any "overreaching" by the prosecution.

After the Court in *Wade* held that a lineup constituted a trial-like confrontation requiring counsel, a more difficult issue remained in the case for consideration. The same changes in law enforcement that led to lineups and pretrial hearings also generated other events at which the accused was confronted by the prosecution. The Government had argued in *Wade* that if counsel was required at a lineup, the same forceful considerations would mandate counsel at other preparatory steps in the "gathering of the prosecution's evidence," such as, for particular example, the taking of fingerprints or blood samples. . . .

The Court concluded that there were differences. Rather than distinguishing these situations from the lineup in terms of the need for counsel to assure an equal confrontation at the time, the Court recognized that there were times when the subsequent trial would cure a one-sided confrontation between prosecuting authorities and the uncounseled defendant. In other words, such stages were not "critical." Referring to fingerprints, hair, clothing, and other blood samples, the Court explained:

> Knowledge of the techniques of science and technology is sufficiently available, and the variables in techniques few enough, that the accused

---

set forth in *Wade* are applicable in large measure to photographic as well as corporeal identifications. These include, notably, the possibilities of suggestive influence or mistake—particularly where witnesses had little or no opportunity for detailed observation during the crime; the difficulty of reconstructing suggestivity—even greater when the defendant is not even present; the tendency of a witness's identification, once given under these circumstances, to be frozen. While these difficulties may be somewhat mitigated by preserving the photograph shown, it may also be said that a photograph can preserve the record of a lineup; yet this does not justify a lineup without counsel. The same may be said of the opportunity to examine the participants as to what went on in the course of the identification, whether at lineup or on photograph. Sometimes this may suffice to bring out all pertinent facts, even at a lineup, but this would not suffice under *Wade* to offset the constitutional infringement wrought by proceeding without counsel. The presence of counsel avoids possibilities of suggestiveness in the manner of presentation that are otherwise ineradicable." 149 U.S. App. D.C., at 9-10, 461 F.2d, at 100-101.

has the opportunity for a meaningful confrontation of the Government's case at trial through the ordinary processes of cross-examination of the Government's expert witnesses and the presentation of the evidence of his own experts.

The structure of Wade, viewed in light of the careful limitation of the Court's language to "confrontations," makes it clear that lack of scientific precision and inability to reconstruct an event are not the tests for requiring counsel in the first instance. These are, instead, the tests to determine whether confrontation with counsel at trial can serve as a substitute for counsel at the pretrial confrontation. If accurate reconstruction is possible, the risks inherent in any confrontation still remain, but the opportunity to cure defects at trial causes the confrontation to cease to be "critical." The opinion of the Court even indicated that changes in procedure might cause a lineup to cease to be a "critical" confrontation:

> Legislative or other regulations, such as those of local police departments, which eliminate the risks of abuse and unintentional suggestion at lineup proceedings and the impediments to meaningful confrontation at trial may also remove the basis for regarding the stage as critical.

The Court of Appeals considered its analysis complete after it decided that a photographic display lacks scientific precision and ease of accurate reconstruction at trial. That analysis, under Wade, however, merely carries one to the point where one must establish that the trial itself can provide no substitute for counsel if a pretrial confrontation is conducted in the absence of counsel. Judge Friendly, writing for the Second Circuit in United States v. Bennett, recognized that the "criticality" test of Wade, if applied outside the confrontation context, would result in drastic expansion of the right to counsel:

> None of the classical analyses of the assistance to be given by counsel, Justice Sutherland's in Powell v. Alabama . . . and Justice Black's in Johnson v. Zerbst . . . and Gideon v. Wainwright . . . suggests that counsel must be present when the prosecution is interrogating witnesses in the defendant's absence even when, as here, the defendant is under arrest; counsel is rather to be provided to prevent the defendant himself from falling into traps devised by a lawyer on the other side and to see to it that all available defenses are proffered. Many other aspects of the prosecution's interviews with a victim or a witness to a crime afford just as much opportunity for undue suggestion as the display of photographs; so, too, do the defense's interviews, notably with alibi witnesses.

We now undertake the threshhold analysis that must be addressed.

IV

A substantial departure from the historical test would be necessary if the Sixth Amendment were interpreted to give Ash a right to counsel at the photographic identification in this case. Since the accused himself is not present at the time of the photographic display, and asserts no right to be present, Brief for Respondent 40, no possibility arises that the accused might be misled by his lack of familiarity with the law or overpowered by his professional adversary. Similarly, the counsel guarantee would not be used to produce equality in a trial-like adversary confrontation. Rather, the guarantee was used by the Court of Appeals to produce confrontation at an event that previously was not analogous to an adversary trial.

Even if we were willing to view the counsel guarantee in broad terms as a generalized protection of the adversary process, we would be unwilling to go so far as to extend the right to a portion of the prosecutor's trial-preparation interviews with witnesses. Although photography is relatively new, the interviewing of witnesses before trial is a procedure that predates the Sixth Amendment. In England in the 16th and 17th centuries counsel regularly interviewed witnesses before trial. 9 W. Holdsworth, History of English Law 226-228 (1926). The traditional counterbalance in the American adversary system for these interviews arises from the equal ability of defense counsel to seek and interview witnesses himself.

That adversary mechanism remains as effective for a photographic display as for other parts of pretrial interviews.[10] No greater limitations are placed on defense counsel in constructing displays, seeking witnesses, and conducting photographic identifications than those applicable to the prosecution.[11] Selection of the picture of a person other than the accused, or the inability of a witness to make any selection, will be useful to the defense in precisely the same manner that the selection of a picture of the defendant would be useful to the prosecution.[12] In this very case, for

10. Duplication by defense counsel is a safeguard that normally is not available when a formal confrontation occurs. Defense counsel has no statutory authority to conduct a preliminary hearing, for example, and defense counsel will generally be prevented by practical considerations from conducting his own lineup. Even in some confrontations, however, the possibility of duplication may be important. The Court noted this in holding that the taking of handwriting exemplars did not constitute a "critical stage": "If, for some reason, an unrepresentative exemplar is taken, this can be brought out and corrected through the adversary process at trial since the accused can make an unlimited number of additional exemplars for analysis and comparison by government and defense hand-writing experts." Gilbert v. California.

11. We do not suggest, of course, that defense counsel has any greater freedom than the prosecution to abuse the photographic identification. Evidence of photographic identifications conducted by the defense may be excluded as unreliable under the same standards that would be applied to unreliable identifications conducted by the Government.

12. The Court of Appeals deemed it significant that a photographic identification

example, the initial tender of the photographic display was by Bailey's counsel, who sought to demonstrate that the witness had failed to make a photographic identification. Although we do not suggest that equality of access to photographs removes all potential for abuse,[13] it does remove any inequality in the adversary process itself and thereby fully satisfies the historical spirit of the Sixth Amendment's counsel guarantee.

The argument has been advanced that requiring counsel might compel the police to observe more scientific procedures or might encourage them to utilize corporeal rather than photographic displays. This Court has recognized that improved procedures can minimize the dangers of suggestion. Simmons v. United States. Commentators have also proposed more accurate techniques.[15]

Pretrial photographic identifications, however, are hardly unique in offering possibilities for the actions of the prosecutor unfairly to prejudice the accused. Evidence favorable to the accused may be withheld; testimony of witnesses may be manipulated; the results of laboratory tests may be contrived. In many ways the prosecutor, by accident or by design, may improperly subvert the trial. The primary safeguard against abuses of this kind is the ethical responsibility of the prosecutor,[16] who, as so often has been said, may "strike hard blows" but not "foul ones." If that safeguard fails, review remains available under due process standards. . . .

We are not persuaded that the risks inherent in the use of photographic displays are so pernicious that an extraordinary system of safeguards is required.

We hold, then, that the Sixth Amendment does not grant the right

---

is admissible as substantive evidence, whereas other parts of interviews may be introduced only for impeachment. . . . In this case defense counsel for Bailey introduced the inability to identify, and that was received into evidence. Thus defense counsel still received benefits equivalent to those available to the prosecution. Although defense counsel may be concerned that repeated photographic displays containing the accused's picture as the only common characteristic will tend to promote identification of the accused, the defense has other balancing devices available to it, such as the use of a sufficiently large number of photographs to counteract this possibility.

13. Although the reliability of in-court identifications and the effectiveness of impeachment may be improved by equality of access, we do not suggest that the prosecution's photographic identification would be more easily reconstructed at trial simply because defense counsel could conduct his own photographic display. But, as we have explained, . . . the possibility of perfect reconstruction is relevant to the evaluation of substitutes for counsel, not to the initial designation of an event as a "critical stage."

15. E.g., P. Wall, Eye-Witness Identification in Criminal Cases 77-85 (1965); Sobel, supra, n.14, at 309-310; Comment, 56 Iowa L. Rev. 408, 420-421 (1970).

16. Throughout a criminal prosecution the prosecutor's ethical responsibility extends, of course, to supervision of any continuing investigation of the case. By prescribing procedures to be used by his agents and by screening the evidence before trial with a view to eliminating unreliable identifications, the prosecutor is able to minimize abuse in photographic displays even if they are conducted in his absence.

to counsel at photographic displays conducted by the Government for the purpose of allowing a witness to attempt an identification of the offender. This holding requires reversal of the judgment of the Court of Appeals. Although respondent Ash has urged us to examine this photographic display under the due process standard enunciated in Simmons v. United States, the Court of Appeals, expressing the view that additional findings would be necessary, refused to decide the issue. . . . We decline to consider this question on this record in the first instance. It remains open, of course, on the Court of Appeals' remand to the District Court.

Reversed and remanded.

MR. JUSTICE STEWART, concurring in the judgment. . . .

In United States v. Wade, supra, the Court determined that a pretrial proceeding is a "critical stage" if "the presence of . . . counsel is necessary to preserve the defendant's . . . right meaningfully to cross-examine the witnesses against him and to have effective assistance of counsel at the trial itself." Pretrial proceedings are "critical," then, if the presence of counsel is essential "to protect the fairness of the trial itself."

The Court held in Wade that a post-indictment, pretrial lineup at which the accused was exhibited to identifying witnesses was such a critical stage, because of the substantial possibility that the accused's right to a fair trial would otherwise be irretrievably lost. The hazard of unfair suggestive influence at a lineup, which, because of the nature of the proceeding, could seldom be reconstructed at trial, left little doubt, the Court thought, "that for Wade the post-indictment lineup was a critical stage of the prosecution at which he was 'as much entitled to such aid [of counsel] . . . as at the trial itself.' "

The Court stressed in Wade that the danger of mistaken identification at trial was appreciably heightened by the "degree of suggestion inherent in the manner in which the prosecution presents the suspect to witnesses for pretrial identification." Id., at 228. There are numerous and subtle possibilities for such improper suggestion in the dynamic context of a lineup. Judge Wilkey, dissenting in the present case, accurately described a lineup as:

> a little drama, stretching over an appreciable span of time. The accused is there in the flesh, three-dimensional and always full-length. Further, he isn't merely there, he acts. He walks on stage, he blinks in the glare of lights, he turns and twists, often muttering asides to those sharing the spotlight. He can be required to utter significant words, to turn a profile or back, to walk back and forth, to doff one costume and don another. All the while the potentially identifying witness is watching, a prosecuting attorney and a police detective at his elbow, ready to record the witness' every word and reaction.

With no attorney for the accused present at this "little drama," defense counsel at trial could seldom convincingly discredit a witness' courtroom identification by showing it to be based on an impermissibly suggestive lineup. In addition to the problems posed by the fluid nature of a lineup, the Court in *Wade* pointed out that neither the witnesses nor the lineup participants were likely to be alert for suggestive influences or schooled in their detection. "In short, the accused's inability effectively to reconstruct at trial any unfairness that occurred at the lineup may deprive him of his only opportunity meaningfully to attack the credibility of the witness' courtroom identification."

The Court held, therefore, that counsel was required at a lineup, primarily as an observer, to ensure that defense counsel could effectively confront the prosecution's evidence at trial. Attuned to the possibilities of suggestive influences, a lawyer could see any unfairness at a lineup, question the witnesses about it at trial, and effectively reconstruct what had gone on for the benefit of the jury or trial judge.*

A photographic identification is quite different from a lineup, for there are substantially fewer possibilities of impermissible suggestion when photographs are used, and those unfair influences can be readily reconstructed at trial. It is true that the defendant's photograph may be markedly different from the others displayed, but this unfairness can be demonstrated at trial from an actual comparison of the photographs used or from the witness' description of the display. Similarly, it is possible that the photographs could be arranged in a suggestive manner, or that by comment or gesture the prosecuting authorities might single out the defendant's picture. But these are the kinds of overt influence that a witness can easily recount and that would serve to impeach the identification testimony. In short, there are few possibilities for unfair suggestiveness—and those rather blatant and easily reconstructed. Accordingly, an accused would not be foreclosed from an effective cross-examination of an identification witness simply because his counsel was not present at the photographic display. For this reason, a photographic display cannot fairly be considered a "critical stage" of the prosecution. . . .

Preparing witnesses for trial by checking their identification testimony against a photographic display is little different, in my view, from the prosecutor's other interviews with the victim or other witnesses before trial. . . . While these procedures can be improperly conducted, the

---

*I do not read *Wade* as requiring counsel because a lineup is a "trial-type" situation, nor do I understand that the Court required the presence of an attorney because of the advice or assistance he could give to his client at the lineup itself. Rather, I had thought the reasoning of *Wade* was that the right to counsel is essentially a protection for the defendant at trial, and that counsel is necessary at a lineup in order to ensure a meaningful confrontation and the effective assistance of counsel at trial.

possibility of irretrievable prejudice is remote, since any unfairness that does occur can usually be flushed out at trial through cross-examination of the prosecution witnesses. The presence of defense counsel at such pretrial preparatory sessions is neither appropriate nor necessary under our adversary system of justice "to preserve the defendant's basic right to a fair trial as affected by his right meaningfully to cross-examine the witnesses against him and to have effective assistance of counsel at the trial itself." United States v. Wade, supra, at 227.

MR. JUSTICE BRENNAN, with whom MR. JUSTICE DOUGLAS and MR. JUSTICE MARSHALL join, dissenting.

The court holds today that a pretrial display of photographs to the witnesses of a crime for the purpose of identifying the accused, unlike a lineup, does not constitute a "critical stage" of the prosecution at which the accused is constitutionally entitled to the presence of counsel. In my view, today's decision is wholly unsupportable in terms of such considerations as logic, consistency, and, indeed, fairness. As a result, I must reluctantly conclude that today's decision marks simply another[1] step towards the complete evisceration of the fundamental constitutional principles established by this Court, only six years ago, in . . . *Gilbert* . . . and *Stovall*. . . . I dissent. . . .

III

As the Court of Appeals recognized, "the dangers of mistaken identification . . . set forth in *Wade* are applicable in large measure to photographic as well as corporeal identifications." To the extent that misidentification may be attributable to a witness' faulty memory or perception, or inadequate opportunity for detailed observation during the crime, the risks are obviously as great at a photographic display as at a lineup. But "[b]ecause of the inherent limitations of photography, which presents its subject in two dimensions rather than the three dimensions of reality, . . . a photographic identification, even when properly obtained, is clearly inferior to a properly obtained corporeal identification." P. Wall, Eye-Witness Identification in Criminal Cases 70 (1965). Indeed, noting "the hazards of initial identification by photograph," we have expressly recognized that "a corporeal identification . . . is normally more accurate" than a photographic identification. Simmons v. United

1. See Kirby v. Illinois, 406 U.S. 682 (1972).

States.[9] Thus, in this sense at least, the dangers of misidentification are even greater at a photographic display than at a lineup.

Moreover, as in the lineup situation, the possibilities for impermissible suggestion in the context of a photographic display are manifold. Such suggestion, intentional, or unintentional, may derive from three possible sources. First, the photographs themselves might tend to suggest which of the pictures is that of the suspect. For example, differences in age, pose, or other physical characteristics of the persons represented, and variations in the mounting, background, lighting, or markings of the photographs all might have the effect of singling out the accused.

Second, impermissible suggestion may inhere in the manner in which the photographs are displayed to the witness. The danger of misidentification is, of course, "increased if the police display to the witness . . . the pictures of several persons among which the photograph of a single such individual recurs or is in some way emphasized." And, if the photographs are arranged in an asymmetrical pattern, or if they are displayed in a time sequence that tends to emphasize a particular photograph, "any identification of the photograph which stands out from the rest is no more reliable than an identification of a single photograph, exhibited alone." P. Wall, supra, at 81.

Third, gestures or comments of the prosecutor at the time of the display may lead an otherwise uncertain witness to select the "correct" photograph. For example, the prosecutor might "indicate to the witness that [he has] other evidence that one of the persons pictured committed the crime,"[11] and might even point to a particular photograph and ask whether the person pictured "looks familiar." More subtly, the prosecutor's inflection, facial expressions, physical motions, and myriad other almost imperceptible means of communication might tend, intentionally or unintentionally, to compromise the witness' objectivity. Thus, as is the case with lineups, "[i]mproper photographic identification procedures, . . . by exerting a suggestive influence upon the witnesses, can often lead to an erroneous identification. . . ." P. Wall, supra, at 89.[12]

9. See also Sobel, Assailing the Impermissible Suggestion: Evolving Limitations on the Abuse of Pre-Trial Criminal Identification Methods, 38 Brooklyn L. Rev. 261, 264, 296 (1971); Williams, Identification Parades, [1955] Crim. L. Rev. 525, 531; Comment, Photographic Identification: The Hidden Persuader, 56 Iowa L. Rev. 408, 419 (1970); Note, Pretrial Photographic Identification—A "Critical Stage" of Criminal Proceedings?, 21 Syracuse L. Rev. 1235, 1241 (1970). Indeed, recognizing the superiority of corporeal to photographic identifications, English courts have long held that once the accused is in custody, pre-lineup photographic identification is "indefensible" and grounds for quashing the conviction. See also P. Wall, Eye-Witness Identification in Criminal Cases 71 (1965).

11. Simmons v. United States, supra, at 383.

12. The Court maintains that "the ethical responsibility of the prosecutor" is in itself a sufficient "safeguard" against impermissible suggestion at a photographic dis-

And "[r]egardless of how the initial misidentification comes about, the witness thereafter is apt to retain in his memory the image of the photograph rather than of the person actually seen. . . ." Simmons v. United States. As a result, " 'the issue of identity may (in the absence of other relevant evidence) for all practical purposes be determined there and then, before the trial.' " United States v. Wade. . . .

Moreover, as with lineups, the defense can "seldom reconstruct" at trial the mode and manner of photographic identification. It is true, of course, that the photographs used at the pretrial display might be preserved for examination at trial. But "it may also be said that a photograph can preserve the record of a lineup; yet this does not justify a lineup without counsel. Indeed, in reality, preservation of the photographs affords little protection to the unrepresented accused. For, although retention of the photographs may mitigate the dangers of misidentification due to the suggestiveness of the photographs themselves, it cannot in any sense reveal to defense counsel the more subtle, and therefore more dangerous, suggestiveness that might derive from the manner in which the photographs were displayed or any accompanying comments or gestures. Moreover, the accused cannot rely upon the witnesses themselves to expose these latter sources of suggestion, for the witnesses are not "apt to be alert for conditions prejudicial to the suspect. And if they were, it would likely be of scant benefit to the suspect" since the witnesses are hardly "likely to be schooled in the detection of suggestive influences." Id., at 230

Finally, and *unlike* the lineup situation, the accused himself is not even present at the photographic identification, thereby reducing the likelihood that irregularities in the procedures will ever come to light. Indeed, in *Wade*, the Government itself observed:[14]

> When the defendant is present—as he is during a lineup—he may per-
> sonally observe the circumstances, report them to his attorney, and (if he

---

play. . . . The same argument might, of course, be made with respect to lineups. Moreover, it is clear that the "prosecutor" is not always present at such pretrial displays. Indeed, in this very case, one of the four eyewitnesses was shown the color photographs on the morning of trial by an agent of the FBI, *not* in the presence of the "prosecutor." And even though "the ethical responsibility of the prosecutor" might be an adequate "safeguard" against *intentional* suggestion, it can hardly be doubted that a "prosecutor" is, after all, only human. His behavior may be fraught with wholly *unintentional* and indeed unconscious nuances that might effectively suggest the "proper" response. See P. Wall, supra, n.9, at 26-65; Napley, Problems of Effecting the Presentation of the Case for a Defendant, 66 Col. L. Rev. 94, 98-99 (1966); Williams & Hammelmann, Identification Parades—I, [1963] Crim. L. Rev. 479, 483. And, of course, as *Wade* itself makes clear, unlike other forms of unintentional prosecutorial "manipulation," even unintentional suggestiveness at an identification procedure involves serious risks of "freezing" the witness' mistaken identification and creates almost insurmountable obstacles to reconstruction at trial.

14. Brief for United States 24-25 in United States v. Wade, No. 334, O.T. 1966.

chooses to take the stand) testify about them at trial. . . . [I]n the absence of an accused, on the other hand, there is no one present to verify the fairness of the interview or to report any irregularities. If the prosecution were tempted to engage in "sloppy or biased or fraudulent" conduct . . . , it would be far more likely to do so when the accused is absent than when he himself is being "used."

Thus, the difficulties of reconstructing at trial an uncounseled photographic display are at least equal to, and possibly greater than, those involved in reconstructing an uncounseled lineup.[15] And, as the Government argued in Wade, in terms of the need for counsel, "[t]here is no meaningful difference between a witness' pretrial identification from photographs and a similar identification made at a lineup." For, in both situations "the accused's inability effectively to reconstruct at trial any unfairness that occurred at the [pretrial identification] may deprive him of his only opportunity meaningfully to attack the credibility of the witness' courtroom identification." United States v. Wade, supra, at 231-232. As a result, both photographic and corporeal identifications create grave dangers that an innocent defendant might be convicted simply because of his inability to expose a tainted identification. This being so, considerations of logic, consistency, and, indeed, fairness compel the conclusion that a pretrial photographic identification, like a pretrial corporeal identification, is a "critical stage of the prosecution at which [the

---

15. The Court's assertion, . . . that these difficulties of reconstruction are somehow minimized because the defense can "duplicate" a photographic identification reflects a complete misunderstanding of the issues in this case. Aside from the fact that lineups can also be "duplicated," the Court's assertion is wholly inconsistent with the underlying premises of both Wade and Gilbert. For, unlike the Court today, the Court in both of those decisions recognized a critical difference between "systematized or scientific analyzing of the accused's fingerprints, blood sample, clothing, hair, and the like," on the one hand, and eyewitness identification, on the other. In essence, the Court noted in Wade and Gilbert that, in the former situations, the accused can preserve his right to a fair trial simply by "duplicating" the tests of the Government, thereby enabling him to expose any errors in the Government's analysis. Such "duplication" is possible, however, only because the accused's tests can be made independently of those of the Government—that is, any errors in the Government's analyses cannot affect the reliability of the accused's tests. That simply is not the case, however, with respect to eyewitness identifications, whether corporeal or photographic. Due to the "freezing effect" recognized in Wade, once suggestion has tainted the identification, its mark is virtually indelible. For once a witness has made a mistaken identification, " 'he is not likely to go back on his word later on.' " United States v. Wade. As a result, any effort of the accused to "duplicate" the initial photographic display will almost necessarily lead to a reaffirmation of the initial misidentification.

The Court's related assertion, that "equality of access" to the results of a Government conducted photographic display "remove[s] any inequality in the adversary process," . . . is similarly flawed. For due to the possibilities for suggestion, intentional or unintentional, the so-called "equality of access" is, in reality, skewed sharply in favor of the prosecution.

accused is] 'as much entitled to such aid [of counsel] . . . as at the trial itself.' " Id., at 237, quoting Powell v. Alabama, 287 U.S., at 57.

IV

Ironically, the Court does not seriously challenge the proposition that presence of counsel at a pretrial photographic display is essential to preserve the accused's right to a fair trial on the issue of identification. Rather, in what I can only characterize a triumph of form over substance, the Court seeks to justify its result by engrafting a wholly unprecedented—and wholly unsupportable—limitation on the Sixth Amendment right of "the accused . . . to have the Assistance of Counsel for his defence." Although apparently conceding that the right to counsel attaches, not only at the trial itself, but at all "critical stages" of the prosecution, . . . the Court holds today that, in order to be deemed "critical," the particular "stage of the prosecution" under consideration must, at the very least, involve the physical "presence of the accused," at a "trial-like confrontation" with the Government, at which the accused requires the "guiding hand of counsel." According to the Court a pretrial photographic identification does not, of course, meet these criteria.

In support of this rather crabbed view of the Sixth Amendment, the Court . . . [relies on decisions, such as Coleman v. Alabama and Hamilton v. Alabama that] guaranteed the assistance of counsel in pretrial proceedings at least arguably involving the physical "presence of the accused," at a "trial-like confrontation" with the Government, at which the accused required the "guiding hand of counsel." Moreover, as the Court points out, these decisions are consistent with the view that the Sixth Amendment "embodies a realistic recognition of the obvious truth that the average defendant does not have the professional legal skill to protect himself when brought before a tribunal with power to take his life or liberty, wherein the prosecution is presented by experienced and learned counsel." Johnson v. Zerbst. But, contrary to the Court's assumption, this is merely one *facet* of the Sixth Amendment guarantee, and the decisions relied upon by the Court represent, not the boundaries of the right to counsel, but mere applications of a far broader and more reasoned understanding of the Sixth Amendment than that espoused today.

The fundamental premise underlying *all* of this Court's decisions holding the right to counsel applicable at "critical" pretrial proceedings, is that a "stage" of the prosecution must be deemed "critical" for the purposes of the Sixth Amendment if it is one at which the presence of counsel is necessary "to protect the fairness of *the trial itself*." Thus, in

Hamilton v. Alabama, supra, for example, we made clear that an arraignment under Alabama law is a "critical stage" of the prosecution, not only because the accused at such an arraignment requires "the guiding hand of counsel," but, more broadly, because "[w]hat happens there may affect the whole trial." Indeed, to exclude counsel from a pretrial proceeding at which his presence might be necessary to assure the fairness of the subsequent trial would, in practical effect, render the Sixth Amendment guarantee virtually meaningless, for it would "deny a defendant 'effective representation by counsel at the only stage when legal aid and advice would help him.' " Massiah v. United States.

This established conception of the Sixth Amendment guarantee is, of course, in no sense dependent upon the physical "presence of the accused," at a "trial-like confrontation" with the Government, at which the accused requires the "guiding hand of counsel." On the contrary, in Powell v. Alabama, the seminal decision in this area, we explicitly held the right to counsel applicable at a stage of the pretrial proceedings involving *none* of the three criteria set forth by the Court today. In *Powell*, the defendants in a state felony prosecution were not appointed counsel until the very eve of trial. This Court held, in no uncertain terms, that such an appointment could not satisfy the demands of the Sixth Amendment, for " '[i]t is vain . . . to guarantee [the accused] counsel without giving the latter any opportunity to acquaint himself with the facts or law of the case.' " In other words, *Powell* made clear that, in order to preserve the accused's right to a fair trial and to "effective and substantial" assistance of counsel at that trial, the Sixth Amendment guarantee necessarily encompasses a reasonable period of time before trial during which counsel might prepare the defense. Yet it can hardly be said that this preparatory period of research and investigation involves the physical "presence of the accused," at a "trial-like confrontation" with the Government, at which the accused requires the "guiding hand of counsel."

Moreover, despite the Court's efforts to rewrite *Wade* so as to suggest a precedential basis for its own analysis, the rationale of *Wade* lends no support whatever to today's decision. [Justice Brennan reviewed the opinion in *Wade*.] . . .

Thus, contrary to the suggestion of the Court, the conclusion in *Wade* that a pretrial lineup is a "critical stage" of the prosecution did not in any sense turn on the fact that a lineup involves the physical "presence of the accused" at a "trial-like confrontation" with the Government. And that conclusion most certainly did not turn on the notion that presence of counsel was necessary so that counsel could offer legal advice or "guidance" to the accused at the lineup. On the contrary, *Wade* envisioned counsel's function at the lineup to be primarily that of a trained observer, able to detect the existence of any suggestive influences and

capable of understanding the legal implications of the events that tran-
spire. Having witnessed the proceedings, counsel would then be in a
position effectively to reconstruct at trial any unfairness that occurred at
the lineup, thereby preserving the accused's fundamental right to a fair
trial on the issue of identification.

There is something ironic about the Court's conclusion today that
a pretrial lineup identification is a "critical stage" of the prosecution
because counsel's presence can help to compensate for the accused's
deficiencies as an observer, but that a pretrial photographic identification
is not a "critical stage" of the prosecution because the accused is not able
to observe at all. In my view, there simply is no meaningful difference,
in terms of the need for attendance of counsel, between corporeal and
photographic identifications. And applying established and well-reasoned
Sixth Amendment principles, I can only conclude that a pretrial photographic display, like a pretrial lineup, is a "critical stage" of the prosecution at which the accused is constitutionally entitled to the presence
of counsel.

NOTES AND QUESTIONS

1. According to the *Ash* opinion, why was there a right to counsel
in *Wade* but not in *Ash*? At page 377 supra, the Court says: "If accurate
reconstruction is possible, the risks inherent in any confrontation still
remain, but the opportunity to cure defects at trial causes the confrontation to cease to be 'critical.' " Does that mean that the inability to
reconstruct photographic arrays undermines confrontation, thus making
the event "critical"? If so, what does the following passage from the case,
note 13, page 379 supra, mean: ". . . as we have explained [referring
to the first quoted passage] the possibility of perfect reconstruction is
relevant to the evaluation of substitutes for counsel, not to the initial
designation of an event as a 'critical stage' "? What, then, *is* relevant to
the designation of an critical stage in *Ash*? How does that compare to
Wade? In this regard, reconsider Justice Stewart's conclusion, and compare it to his opinion in *Kirby*. Why is the formal invocation of criminal
proceedings dispository in *Kirby* but not *Ash*? Why is confrontation important in *Ash* but not in *Kirby*? Consider Grano, *Kirby, Biggers*, and
Ash: Do Any Constitutional Safeguards Remain Against the Danger of
Convicting the Innocent?, 72 Mich. L. Rev., 717, 763-764, 766-767
(1974):

> In *Ash's* favor, the Court did correctly note the defendant's presence at all
> stages where the right to counsel had previously been extended. Beyond

that, not much can be said in support of Ash's analysis—or, more accurately, lack of analysis. The crucial question, not really addressed by Ash, is why the defendant's presence should matter. To say that the framers intended the sixth amendment to guarantee counsel's assistance at trial does not provide a satisfactory answer. The Court arguably moved beyond the framers' literal intent by recognizing the sixth amendment as a source of appointed counsel for indigents and, as Ash acknowledged, by extending the sixth amendment into pretrial stages. Ash itself recognized that the evolution of criminal procedure from its embryonic, eighteenth-century prototype made doctrinal modifications necessary to prevent the sixth amendment from becoming an empty formalism, a result certainly not intended by the framers. Rather than ignoring original purposes, the Court demonstrated its commitment to the spirit of the sixth amendment by applying the right to counsel to pretrial stages that could "well settle the accused's fate and reduce the trial itself to a mere formality."[291] Having already charted a path to preserve the sixth amendment's effectiveness from the force of modern developments, it is anomalous now to rely on historical facts that bear little relation to the core purposes of the right to counsel. In Wade's view, the plain wording of the sixth amendment encompassed counsel's assistance "*whenever* necessary to assure a meaningful 'defense' "[292] or a fair trial. With the issue so stated, the accused's presence should be no more crucial than the "at trial" limitation of an earlier day. This should be especially so with respect to police photographic procedures, which developed long after the sixth amendment's adoption. . . . If the sixth amendment can ever apply without a confrontation between the defendant and the state, then Ash is dead wrong: Such a confrontation simply cannot constitute a necessary antecedent for right-to-counsel analysis. Of course, Ash's proponents may argue that the confrontation characteristic depends on the nature of the particular procedure, not on the defendant's presence, but this gambit would also result in their checkmate. If the nature of the proceeding is determinative, Ash erred in chastising the lower court for asserting the need for counsel in photographic displays. Once the defendant's presence is disregarded, the right to counsel should follow a fortiori from Wade, unless photographic displays are inherently different from lineups. . . .

2. How can Justice Stewart's concurrence in Ash be reconciled with his opinion in Kirby?

3. How responsive is Ash to the real problem of photographic identification? The Supreme Court did not purport to determine the extent to which due process analysis is relevant to photographic arrays, an issue apparently settled by Manson v. Brathwaite, section B infra. Inappropriate suggestiveness is the central problem, however. Consider the following

291. United States v. Wade, 388 U.S. 218, 224 (1967).
292. 388 U.S. at 225 (emphasis added).

from Jonakait, Reliable Identification: Could the Supreme Court Tell in
Manson v. Brathwaite?, 52 U. Colo. L. Rev. 511, 523-525 (1981):

> Untrustworthy identifications will be admitted if the courts do not understand
> what criteria truly indicate reliability. Untrustworthy identifications will
> also be admitted if courts cannot discern suggestive identification proce-
> dures. Scientific studies indicate that two prevalent identification proce-
> dures, looking at mugshots and lineups, are often suggestive.[47] One of the

47. Suggestiveness, of course, not only affects identifications; it can affect many
areas of litigation. For example, the suggestiveness of questioning by police officers
investigating a crime or lawyers preparing a witness for trial can alter a witness's memory
of an event. Thus, in one set of experiments, subjects were shown a film of a moving
automobile. Some were then asked, "How fast was the white sports car going while
traveling along the country road?" Others were asked, "How fast was the white sports car
going when it passed the barn while traveling along the country road?" No barn was
visible in the film. A week later, all the subjects were asked whether they remembered
seeing a barn in the movie. Of those given the misinformation, 17% remembered the
nonexistent structure, while only 3% who had been asked the neutral question said they
saw it. E. Loftus, [Eyewitness Testimony (1979)] at 60.

Questioning does not have to be this blatant to produce a similar effect. One set of
subjects who had viewed a film of a car accident was asked to estimate the speed of the
cars when they "smashed." The other set was asked to give the speed when they "hit."
Later, all subjects were tested on their memory of seeing broken glass in the collision.
Nearly 33% of those whose question included the word "smashed" reported broken glass;
only 14% of the other set did. No broken glass was evident in the film.

Limitations on these distortions have been discovered. For instance, the memory
can be affected mainly about peripheral items, not central items. Furthermore, once a
witness resists blatantly false information, his resistance to other misleading suggestions
also increases. The timing of the suggestive questioning also affects the distortion. The
greater the lapse of time between the perception and the suggestion, the greater the
likelihood of memory alteration. If the suggestion occurs shortly after the perception,
both the memory of the event and the suggestion will fade. Loftus summarizes: "Longer
retention intervals lead to worse performance, consistent information improves performance, and misleading information that is given immediately after an event has less of
an impact on the memory than misleading information that is delayed until just prior
to the test. Apparently, giving the event information a chance to fade in memory makes
it easier to introduce misleading information." In practical terms, then, the greatest danger
is not with the police investigating immediately after a crime, but with attorneys preparing
witnesses for trial.

The mere wording of a question designed to elicit recall, however, can affect the
recollection given. For instance, one half of a group of subjects was asked how "tall" a
person was and gave an average answer of seventy-nine inches. The other half was asked
how "short." The average answer to that question was "sixty-nine inches." Similarly,
how "long" was a movie brought the reply, "130 minutes;" how short, "100 minutes."
Of course, leading questions are controlled in court, but not before. The time before
trial is the crucial period. Once an answer is stamped upon one's memory, subsequent
attempts to recall the memory may not elicit the original memory, but only the response
to an earlier question.

These studies, of course, only begin to provide the information needed to make
litigation more just. Current data merely indicate some factors tending to cause inaccurate
memories; it does not reveal whether a memory has been distorted in particular instances.
See A.D. Yarmey, [The Psychology of Eyewitness Identification (1979)] at 73. The studies
do, however, provide guidance to those desirous of the fullest, most reliable recollections.

reasons for their suggestiveness relates to the psychological phenomenon of unconscious transference: a face seen in one situation is mistakenly remembered to have been seen in another. In one study, two or three days after a staged crime, witnesses looked at mugshots. Some of the pictures were of "criminals" from the event, while others were of people the witnesses had never before seen. Four or five days after the photos were inspected, a corporeal lineup was held. "18 percent of the persons in the lineup who had never been seen before were mistakenly identified. However, if a person's mugshot had been seen in the interim, this percentage rose to 29 percent."[48]

It frequently happens in criminal cases that a few days after a crime the witnesses thumb through pictures and are later asked to make identifications from a lineup. Unconscious transference might cause an innocent person to be positively identified in a lineup simply because his picture was in police files. Several things can be done to protect against this effect. For instance, if a suspect is identified at a lineup and his picture was viewed earlier by the witness who did not identify that picture as depicting the criminal, the identification procedure should be regarded as suggestive. No determination about this unconscious transference can be made, however, if there is no way to ascertain what pictures the witness saw. Often the witness looks through large books or file drawers of photos, and the police usually have no records of what is in those books or drawers. By the time an identification is challenged in court, no one can discover whether the witness saw a picture of the defendant before the lineup identification. The starting point, then, should be to require police to keep accurate records of the mugshots shown to witnesses.

Some of the suggestiveness of showing pictures can be lessened by the use of control people. After a description is obtained from a witness, pictures of people who fit the description but who could not have committed the crime—police officers, for example—should be inserted with the other pictures to be viewed. At a subsequent lineup, the control people as well as the suspects should be present in the lineup. This would not eliminate false identifications, but it might lessen the chance of unconscious transference.

Another difficulty identification procedures pose is known as the "Rosenthal Effect"; this is summarized in Grossman, Suggestive Identifications: The Supreme Court's Due Process Test Fails to Meet Its Own Criteria, 11 U. Balt. L. Rev. 53, 103 n.276:

Even trained researchers are often unaware of the information they unconsciously communicate. Professor Robert Rosenthal informed his class that they were about to do research designed to test the ability of genetically

---

Loftus suggests that the investigator interested in getting the most complete and accurate story should first solicit a free narrative and then follow up with questions to fill in the gaps.
48. E. Loftus, supra . . . at 151.

bred intelligent rats to solve a maze when compared to genetically bred dull rats. The students assigned to work with the bright rats reported their ability to learn the maze in significantly less time than it took the dull rats. The fact that in reality all of the rats were chosen totally at random led Rosenthal to conclude that the expectations of the testers were passed unconsciously and obviously non-verbally to the rats. Fanselow, How to Bias an Eyewitness, Soc. Act. & L., May 1975, at 3, 3.

Professor Grossman also gives an example of the Rosenthal effect being perceived in lineup situations, id. at 84:

Regardless of whether the identification proceeding is a lineup or photographic array, or a one-on-one confrontation, police comments indicating that one of the persons being viewed is a suspect will greatly increase the probability of obtaining an identification. The effect of informing a witness that a suspect is included in a lineup was demonstrated in a 1975 experiment. In that experiment, one half of those who observed a staged criminal incident were told that a suspect would be present in the lineup they were about to view; the other half were informed only that one might be present. Although the culprit was not in fact included in the lineup, twenty-eight percent of those told he would be present selected someone in the lineup as the criminal, while only four percent of the second group made inaccurate identifications.

4. The tendency in the courts is not to exclude identifications made from quite suggestive photo identification processes. State v. Mark, 286 N.W.2d 396 (Iowa 1978), is fairly typical. In *Mark*, the police showed a single photograph of a suspected murderer to eight witnesses who identified the defendant. Seven of the eight subsequently picked Mark out of a lineup. The Iowa Supreme Court admitted testimony concerning both out-of-court identifications and allowed in-court identifications as well.

Compare United States v. Cueto, 611 F.2d 1056 (5th Cir. 1980), to *Mark*. In *Cueto* the single passenger of a car tried to rob the teller of a drive-up bank by placing a canvas bag containing a false bomb in the teller's drawer, threatening to detonate it if the teller did not cooperate. The teller fell to the floor and set off an alarm; the robber drove away. The FBI, investigating this as one of a series of similar robberies involving two robbers, showed a single photograph of each suspect to the witness, who identified the photograph of the defendant but incorrectly identified the other photograph as well. At trial the witness testified that he had identified a photograph but did not indicate who the photograph depicted. The FBI agent testified that the witness correctly identified the photograph of the defendant and incorrectly identified the other photograph. The Court of Appeals held that the showing of two single photographs was impermissibly suggestive and that the witness's testimony should have been barred because there were no other factors presented indicating the testimony was reliable.

B. THE DUE PROCESS APPROACH

Apparently a defendant may contest any identification procedure on due process grounds. The Court's development of the governing standards is charted and discussed in Manson v. Brathwaite.

MANSON v. BRATHWAITE
Certiorari to the United States Court of Appeals for the Second Circuit
432 U.S. 98 (1977)

MR. JUSTICE BLACKMUN delivered the opinion of the Court.

This case presents the issue as to whether the Due Process Clause of the Fourteenth Amendment compels the exclusion, in a state criminal trial, apart from any consideration of reliability, of pretrial identification evidence obtained by a police procedure that was both suggestive and unnecessary. This Court's decisions in Stovall v. Denno and Neil v. Biggers are particularly implicated.

I

Jimmy D. Glover, a full-time trooper of the Connecticut State Police, in 1970 was assigned to the Narcotics Division in an undercover capacity. On May 5 of that year, about 7:45 P.M., e.d.t., and while there was still daylight, Glover and Henry Alton Brown, an informant, went to an apartment building at 201 Westland, in Hartford, for the purpose of purchasing narcotics from "Dickie Boy" Cicero, a known narcotics dealer. Cicero, it was thought, lived on the third floor of that apartment building. . . . Glover and Brown entered the building, observed by backup Officers D'Onofrio and Gaffey, and proceeded by stairs to the third floor. Glover knocked at the door of one of the two apartments served by the stairway. The area was illuminated by natural light from a window in the third floor hallway. . . . The door was opened 12 to 18 inches in response to the knock. Glover observed a man standing at the door and, behind him, a woman. Brown identified himself. Glover then asked for "two things" of narcotics. . . . The man at the door held out his hand, and Glover gave him two $10 bills. The door closed. Soon the man returned and handed Glover two glassine bags. While the door was open, Glover stood within two feet of the person from whom he made the purchase and observed his face. Five to seven minutes elapsed from the time the door first opened until it closed the second time. . . .

Glover and Brown then left the building. This was about eight minutes after their arrival. Glover drove to headquarters where he described the seller to D'Onofrio and Gaffey. Glover at that time did not know the identity of the seller. . . . He described him as being "a colored man, approximately five feet eleven inches tall, dark complexion, black hair, short Afro style, and having high cheekbones, and of heavy build. He was wearing at the time blue pants and a plaid shirt." . . . D'Onofrio, suspecting from this description that respondent might be the seller, obtained a photograph of respondent from the Records Division of the Hartford Police Department. He left it at Glover's office. D'Onofrio was not acquainted with respondent personally, but did know him by sight and had seen him "[s]everal times" prior to May 5. . . . Glover, when alone, viewed the photograph for the first time upon his return to headquarters on May 7; he identified the person shown as the one from whom he had purchased the narcotics. . . .

Respondent was charged, in a two-count information, with possession and sale of heroin. At his trial in January 1971, the photograph from which Glover had identified respondent was received in evidence without objection on the part of the defense. . . . Glover also testified that, although he had not seen respondent in the eight months that had elapsed since the sale, "there [was] no doubt whatsoever" in his mind that the person shown on the photograph was respondent. . . . Glover also made a positive in-court identification without objection. . . .

No explanation was offered by the prosecution for the failure to utilize a photographic array or to conduct a lineup. . . .

The jury found respondent guilty on both counts of the information. . . .

Fourteen months later, respondent filed a petition for habeas corpus in the United States District Court for the District of Connecticut. He alleged that the admission of the identification testimony at his state trial deprived him of due process of law to which he was entitled under the Fourteenth Amendment. The District Court, by an unreported written opinion based on the court's review of the state trial transcript, dismissed respondent's petition. On appeal, the United States Court of Appeals for the Second Circuit reversed, with instructions to issue the writ unless the State gave notice of a desire to retry respondent and the new trial occurred within a reasonable time to be fixed by the District Judge. . . .

In brief summary, the court felt that evidence as to the photograph should have been excluded, regardless of reliability, because the examination of the single photograph was unnecessary and suggestive. And, in the court's view, the evidence was unreliable in any event. We granted certiorari. . . .

II

Stovall v. Denno, supra, decided in 1967, concerned a petitioner who had been convicted in a New York court of murder. He was arrested the day following the crime and was taken by the police to a hospital where the victim's wife, also wounded in the assault, was a patient. After observing Stovall and hearing him speak, she identified him as the murderer. She later made an in-court identification. On federal habeas, Stovall claimed the identification testimony violated his Fifth, Sixth, and Fourteenth Amendment rights. The District Court dismissed the petition, and the Court of Appeals, en banc, affirmed. This Court also affirmed. On the identification issue, the Court reviewed the practice of showing a suspect singly for purposes of identification, and the claim that this was so unnecessarily suggestive and conducive to irreparable mistaken identification that it constituted a denial of due process of law. The Court noted that the practice "has been widely condemned," 388 U.S., at 302, but it concluded that "a claimed violation of due process of law in the conduct of a confrontation depends on the totality of the circumstances surrounding it." Ibid. In that case, showing Stovall to the victim's spouse "was imperative.". . .

Neil v. Biggers, supra, decided in 1972, concerned a respondent who had been convicted in a Tennessee court of rape, on evidence consisting in part of the victim's visual and voice identification of Biggers at a station-house showup seven months after the crime. The victim had been in her assailant's presence for some time and had directly observed him indoors and under a full moon outdoors. She testified that she had "no doubt" that Biggers was her assailant. She previously had given the police a description of the assailant. She had made no identification of others presented at previous showups, lineups, or through photographs. On federal habeas, the District Court held that the confrontation was so suggestive as to violate due process. The Court of Appeals affirmed. This Court reversed on that issue, and held that the evidence properly had been allowed to go to the jury. The Court reviewed Stovall and certain later cases where it had considered the scope of due process protection against the admission of evidence derived from suggestive identification procedures, namely, Simmons v. United States; Foster v. California; and

Coleman v. Alabama.[8] The Court concluded that general guidelines emerged from these cases "as to the relationship between suggestiveness and misidentification." The "admission of evidence of a showup without more does not violate due process." The Court expressed concern about the lapse of seven months between the crime and the confrontation and observed that this "would be a seriously negative factor in most cases." The "central question," however, was "whether under the 'totality of the circumstances' the identification was reliable even though the confrontation procedure was suggestive." Applying that test, the Court found "no substantial likelihood of misidentification. The evidence was properly allowed to go to the jury."

Biggers well might be seen to provide an unambiguous answer to the question before us: The admission of testimony concerning a suggestive and unnecessary identification procedure does not violate due process so long as the identification possesses sufficient aspects of reliability.[9] In

8. Simmons involved photographs, mostly group ones, shown to bankteller victims who made in-court identifications. The Court discussed the "chance of misidentification," 390 U.S., at 383; declined to prohibit the procedure "either in the exercise of our supervisory power or, still less, as a matter of constitutional requirement," id., at 384; and held that each case must be considered on its facts and that a conviction would be set aside only if the identification procedure "was so impermissibly suggestive as to give rise to a very substantial likelihood of irreparable misidentification." Id. The out-of-court identification was not offered. Mr. Justice Black would have denied Simmons' due process claim as frivolous. Id., at 395-396.

Foster concerned repeated confrontations between a suspect and the manager of an office that had been robbed. At a second lineup, but not at the first and not at a personal one-to-one confrontation, the manager identified the suspect. At trial he testified as to this and made an in-court identification. The Court reaffirmed the Stovall standard and then concluded that the repeated confrontations were so suggestive as to violate due process. The case was remanded for the state courts to consider the question of harmless error.

In Coleman a plurality of the Court was of the view that the trial court did not err when it found that the victim's in-court identifications did not stem from a lineup procedure so impermissibly suggestive as to give rise to a substantial likelihood of misidentification. 399 U.S., at 5-6.

9. Mr. Justice Marshall argues in dissent that our cases have "established two different due process tests for two very different situations." . . . Pretrial identifications are to be covered by Stovall, which is said to require exclusion of evidence concerning unnecessarily suggestive pretrial identifications without regard to reliability. In-court identifications, on the other hand, are to be governed by Simmons and admissibility turns on reliability. The Court's cases are sorted into one category or the other. Biggers, which clearly adopts the reliability of the identification as the guiding factor in the admissibility of both pretrial and in-court identifications, is condemned for mixing the two lines and for adopting a uniform rule.

Although it must be acknowledged that our cases are not uniform in their emphasis, they hardly suggest the formal structure the dissent would impose on them. If our cases truly established two different rules, one might expect at some point at least passing reference to the fact. There is none. And if Biggers departed so grievously from the past cases, it is surprising that there was not at least some mention of the point in Mr. Justice Brennan's dissent. In fact, the cases are not so readily sorted as the dissent suggests.

one passage, however, the Court observed that the challenged procedure occurred pre-*Stovall* and that a strict rule would make little sense with regard to a confrontation that preceded the Court's first indication that a suggestive procedure might lead to the exclusion of evidence. One perhaps might argue that, by implication, the Court suggested that a different rule could apply post-*Stovall*. The question before us, then, is simply whether the *Biggers* analysis applies to post-*Stovall* confrontations as well to those pre-*Stovall*. . . .

IV

Petitioner at the outset acknowledges that "the procedure in the instant case was suggestive [because only one photograph was used] and unnecessary" [because there was no emergency or exigent circumstance]. The respondent, in agreement with the Court of Appeals, proposes a per se rule of exclusion that he claims is dictated by the demands of the Fourteenth Amendment's guarantee of due process. He rightly observes that this is the first case in which this Court has had occasion to rule upon strictly post-*Stovall* out-of-court identification evidence of the challenged kind.

Since the decision in *Biggers*, the Courts of Appeals appear to have developed at least two approaches to such evidence. See Pulaski, *Neil v. Biggers*: The Supreme Court Dismantles the *Wade* Trilogy's Due Process Protection, 26 Stan. L. Rev. 1097, 1111-1114 (1974). The first, or per se approach, employed by the Second Circuit in the present case, focuses on the procedures employed and requires exclusion of the out-of-court identification evidence, without regard to reliability, whenever it has been obtained through unnecessarily suggested confrontation procedures.[10] The justifications advanced are the elimination of evidence of uncertain reliability, deterrence of the police and prosecutors, and the stated "fair assurance against the awful risks of misidentification."

The second, or more lenient, approach is one that continues to rely

---

Although *Foster* involved both in-court and out-of-court identifications, the Court seemed to apply only a single standard for both. And although *Coleman* involved only an in-court identification, the plurality cited *Stovall* for the guiding rule that the claim was to be assessed on the "totality of the surrounding circumstances." 399 U.S., at 4. Thus, *Biggers* is not properly seen as a departure from the past cases, but as a synthesis of them.

10. Although the per se approach demands the exclusion of testimony concerning unnecessarily suggestive identifications, it does permit the admission of testimony concerning a subsequent identification, including an in-court identification, if the subsequent identification is determined to be reliable. 527 F. 2d, at 367. The totality approach, in contrast, is simpler: if the challenged identification is reliable, then testimony as to it and any identification in its wake is admissible.

on the totality of the circumstances. It permits the admission of the confrontation evidence if, despite the suggestive aspect, the out-of-court identification possesses certain features of reliability. Its adherents feel that the per se approach is not mandated by the Due Process Clause of the Fourteenth Amendment. This second approach, in contrast to the other, is ad hoc and serves to limit the societal costs imposed by a sanction that excludes relevant evidence from consideration and evaluation by the trier of fact.

The respondent here stresses . . . the need for deterrence of improper identification practice, a factor he regards as preeminent. Photographic identification, it is said, continues to be needlessly employed. He notes that the legislative regulation "the Court had hoped [United States v.] Wade would engender" has not been forthcoming. He argues that a totality rule cannot be expected to have a significant deterrent impact; only a strict rule of exclusion will have direct and immediate impact on law enforcement agents. Identification evidence is so convincing to the jury that sweeping exclusionary rules are required. Fairness of the trial is threatened by suggestive confrontation evidence, and thus, it is said, an exclusionary rule has an established constitutional predicate.

There are, of course, several interests to be considered and taken into account. The driving force behind . . . Wade, . . . Gilbert . . . and Stovall, all decided on the same day, was the Court's concern with the problems of eyewitness identification. Usually the witness must testify about an encounter with a total stranger under circumstances of emergency or emotional stress. The witness' recollection of the stranger can be distorted easily by the circumstances or by later actions of the police. Thus, Wade and its companion cases reflect the concern that the jury not hear eyewitness testimony unless that evidence has aspects of reliability. It must be observed that both approaches before us are responsive to this concern. The per se rule, however, goes too far since its application automatically and peremptorily, and without consideration of alleviating factors, keeps evidence from the jury that is reliable and relevant.

The second factor is deterrence. Although the per se approach has the more significant deterrent effect, the totality approach also has an influence on police behavior. The police will guard against unnecessarily suggestive procedures under the totality rule, as well as the per se one, for fear that their actions will lead to the exclusion of identifications as unreliable.

The third factor is the effect on the administration of justice. Here the per se approach suffers serious drawbacks. Since it denies the trier reliable evidence, it may result, on occasion, in the guilty going free. Also, because of its rigidity, the per se approach may make error by the trial judge more likely than the totality approach. And in those cases in which the admission of identification evidence is error under the per se approach but not under the totality approach—cases in which the identification is reliable despite an unnecessarily suggestive identification procedure—reversal is a Draconian sanction. Certainly, inflexible rules of exclusion that may frustrate rather than promote justice have not been viewed recently by this Court with unlimited enthusiasm. . . .

It is true, as has been noted, that the Court in *Biggers* referred to the pre-*Stovall* character of the confrontation in that case. But that observation was only one factor in the judgmental process. It does not translate into a holding that post-*Stovall* confrontation evidence automatically is to be excluded.

The standard, after all, is that of fairness as required by the Due Process Clause of the Fourteenth Amendment. . . . *Stovall*, with its reference to "the totality of the circumstances," and *Biggers*, with its continuing stress on the same totality, did not, singly or together, establish a strict exclusionary rule or new standard of due process. Judge Leventhal, although speaking pre-*Biggers* and of a pre-*Wade* situation, correctly has described *Stovall* as protecting an *evidentiary* interest and, at the same time, as recognizing the limited extent of that interest in our adversary system.[14]

We therefore conclude that reliability is the linchpin in determining the admissibility of identification testimony for both pre- and post-*Stovall* confrontations. The factors to be considered are set out in *Biggers*. These include the opportunity of the witness to view the criminal at the time of the crime, the witness' degree of attention, the accuracy of his prior description of the criminal, the level of certainty demonstrated at the confrontation, and the time between the crime and the confrontation. Against these factors is to be weighed the corrupting effect of the suggestive identification itself.

---

14. "In essence what the *Stovall* due process right protects is an evidentiary interest. . . .

"It is part of our adversary system that we accept at trial much evidence that has strong elements of untrustworthiness—an obvious example being the testimony of witnesses with a bias. While identification testimony is significant evidence, such testimony is still only evidence, and unlike the presence of counsel, is not a factor that goes to the very heart—the 'integrity'—of the adversary process.

"Counsel can both cross-examine the identification witnesses and argue in summation as to factors causing doubts as to the accuracy of the identification—including reference to both any suggestibility in the identification procedure and any countervailing testimony such as alibi." Clemons v. United States, 133 U.S. App. D.C. 27, 48, 408 F.2d 1230, 1251 (1968) (concurring opinion) (footnote omitted), cert. denied, 394 U.S. 964 (1969).

V

We turn, then, to the facts of this case and apply the analysis:

1. *The opportunity to view.* Glover testified that for two to three minutes he stood at the apartment door, within two feet of the respondent. The door opened twice, and each time the man stood at the door. The moments passed, the conversation took place, and payment was made. Glover looked directly at his vendor. It was near sunset, to be sure, but the sun had not yet set, so it was not dark or even dusk or twilight. Natural light from outside entered the hallway through a window. There was natural light, as well, from inside the apartment.

2. *The degree of attention.* Glover was not a casual or passing observer, as is so often the case with eyewitness identification. Trooper Glover was a trained police officer on duty—and specialized and dangerous duty—when he called at the third floor of 201 Westland in Hartford on May 5, 1970. . . .

3. *The accuracy of the description.* Glover's description was given to D'Onofrio within minutes after the transaction. It included the vendor's race, his height, his build, the color and style of his hair, and the high cheekbone facial feature. It also included clothing the vendor wore. . . .

4. *The witness' level of certainty.* There is no dispute that the photograph in question was that of respondent. Glover, in response to a question whether the photograph was that of the person from whom he made the purchase, testified: "There is no question whatsoever." . . . This positive assurance was repeated. . . .

5. *The time between the crime and the confrontation.* Glover's description of his vendor was given to D'Onofrio within minutes of the crime. The photographic identification took place only two days later. We do not have here the passage of weeks or months between the crime and the viewing of the photograph.

These indicators of Glover's ability to make an accurate identification are hardly outweighed by the corrupting effect of the challenged identification itself. Although identifications arising from single-photograph displays may be viewed in general with suspicion, see Simmons v. United States, we find in the instant case little pressure on the witness to acquiesce in the suggestion that such a display entails. D'Onofrio had left the photograph at Glover's office and was not present when Glover first viewed it two days after the event. There thus was little urgency and Glover could view the photograph at his leisure. And since Glover examined the photograph alone, there was no coercive pressure to make an identification arising from the presence of another. The identification was made in circumstances allowing care and reflection. . . .

Surely, we cannot say that under all the circumstances of this case there is "a very substantial likelihood of irreparable misidentification." . . . Short of that point, such evidence is for the jury to weigh. We are content to rely upon the good sense and judgment of American juries, for evidence with some element of untrustworthiness is customary grist for the jury mill. Juries are not so susceptible that they cannot measure intelligently the weight of identification testimony that has some questionable feature.

Of course, it would have been better had D'Onofrio presented Glover with a photographic array including "so far as practicable . . . a reasonable number of persons similar to any person then suspected whose likeness is included in the array." Model Code [of Pre-Arraignment Procedure] §160.2(2). The use of that procedure would have enhanced the force of the identification at trial and would have avoided the risk that the evidence would be excluded as unreliable. But we are not disposed to view D'Onofrio's failure as one of constitutional dimension to be enforced by a rigorous and unbending exclusionary rule. The defect, if there be one, goes to weight and not to substance.

We conclude that the criteria laid down in *Biggers* are to be applied in determining the admissibility of evidence offered by the prosecution concerning a post-*Stovall* identification, and that those criteria are satisfactorily met and complied with here.

The judgment of the Court of Appeals is reversed. It is so ordered.

MR. JUSTICE STEVENS, concurring.

While I join the Court's opinion, I would emphasize two points.

First, as I indicated in my opinion in United States ex rel. Kirby v. Sturges, the arguments in favor of fashioning new rules to minimize the danger of convicting the innocent on the basis of unreliable eyewitness testimony carry substantial force. Nevertheless, for the reasons stated in that opinion, as well as those stated by the Court today, I am persuaded that this rulemaking function can be performed "more effectively by the legislative process than by a somewhat clumsy judicial fiat," id., at 408, and that the Federal Constitution does not foreclose experimentation by the States in the development of such rules. . . .

MR. JUSTICE MARSHALL, with whom MR. JUSTICE BRENNAN joins, dissenting.

Today's decision can come as no surprise to those who have been watching the Court dismantle the protections against mistaken eyewitness testimony erected a decade ago in United States v. Wade; Gilbert v. California; and Stovall v. Denno. But it is still distressing to see the Court virtually ignore the teaching of experience embodied in those decisions and blindly uphold the conviction of a defendant who may well be innocent.

I

The magnitude of the Court's error can be seen by analyzing the cases in the *Wade* trilogy and the decisions following it. The foundation of the *Wade* trilogy was the Court's recognition of the "high incidence of miscarriage of justice" resulting from the admission of mistaken eyewitness identification evidence at criminal trials. Relying on numerous studies made over many years by such scholars as Professor Wigmore and Mr. Justice Frankfurter, the Court concluded that "[t]he vagaries of eyewitness identification are well-known; the annals of criminal law are rife with instances of mistaken identification." It is, of course, impossible to control one source of such errors—the faulty perceptions and unreliable memories of witnesses—except through vigorously contested trials conducted by diligent counsel and judges. The Court in the *Wade* cases acted, however, to minimize the more preventable threat posed to accurate identification by "the degree of suggestion inherent in the manner in which the prosecution presents the suspect to witnesses for pretrial identification." Ibid. . . .

Stovall v. Denno, while holding that the *Wade* prophylactic rules were not retroactive, was decided at the same time and reflects the same concerns about the reliability of identification testimony. *Stovall* recognized that, regardless of Sixth Amendment principles, "the conduct of a confrontation" may be "so unnecessarily suggestive and conducive to irreparable mistaken identification" as to deny due process of law. The pretrial confrontation in *Stovall* was plainly suggestive, and evidence of it was introduced at trial along with the witness' in-court identification. The Court ruled that there had been no violation of due process, however, because the unusual necessity for the procedure outweighed the danger of suggestion.

Stovall thus established a due process right of criminal suspects to be free from confrontations that, under all the circumstances, are unnecessarily suggestive. The right was enforceable by exclusion at trial of evidence of the constitutionally invalid identification. Comparison with *Wade* and *Gilbert* confirms this interpretation. Where their Sixth Amendment holding did not apply, *Stovall* found an analogous Fourteenth Amendment right to a lineup conducted in a fundamentally fair manner. This interpretation is reinforced by the Court's statement that "a claimed violation of due process of law *in the conduct of a confrontation* depends on the totality of the circumstances surrounding it." Significantly, several years later, *Stovall* was viewed in precisely the same way, even as the Court limited *Wade* and *Gilbert* to post-indictment confrontations: "The Due Process Clause . . . *forbids a lineup* that is unnecessarily suggestive and conducive to irreparable mistaken identification. Stovall v. Denno; Foster v. California." Kirby v. Illinois.

The development of due process protections against mistaken identification evidence, begun in *Stovall*, was continued in Simmons v. United States. There, the Court developed a different rule to deal with the admission of in-court identification testimony that the accused claimed had been fatally tainted by a previous suggestive confrontation. In *Simmons*, the exclusionary effect of *Stovall* had already been accomplished, since the prosecution made no use of the suggestive confrontation. *Simmons*, therefore, did not deal with the constitutionality of the pretrial identification procedure. The only question was the impact of the Due Process Clause on an in-court identification that was not itself unnecessarily suggestive. *Simmons* held that due process was violated by the later identification if the pretrial procedure had been "so impermissibly suggestive as to give rise to a very substantial likelihood of irreparable misidentification." This test focused, not on the necessity for the challenged pretrial procedure, but on the degree of suggestiveness that it entailed. In applying this test, the Court understandably considered the circumstances surrounding the witnesses' initial opportunity to view the crime. Finding that any suggestion in the pretrial confrontation had not affected the fairness of the in-court identification, *Simmons* rejected petitioner's due process attack on his conviction.

Again, comparison with the *Wade* cases is instructive. The inquiry mandated by *Simmons* is similar to the independent source test used in *Wade* where an in-court identification is sought following an uncounseled lineup. In both cases, the issue is whether the witness is identifying the defendant solely on the basis of his memory of events at the time of the crime, or whether he is merely remembering the person he picked out in a pretrial procedure. Accordingly, in both situations, the relevant inquiry includes factors bearing on the accuracy of the witness' identification, including his opportunity to view the crime.

Thus, *Stovall* and *Simmons* established two different due process tests for two very different situations. Where the prosecution sought to use evidence of a questionable pretrial identification, *Stovall* required its exclusion, because due process had been violated by the confrontation, unless the necessity for the unduly suggestive procedure outweighed its potential for generating an irreparably mistaken identification. The *Simmons* test, on the other hand, was directed to ascertaining due process violations in the introduction of in-court identification testimony that the defendant claimed was tainted by pretrial procedures. In the latter situation, a court could consider the reliability of the identification under all the circumstances.

This distinction between *Stovall* and *Simmons* was preserved in two succeeding cases. Foster v. California, like *Stovall*, involved both unduly suggestive pretrial procedures, evidence of which was introduced at trial, and a tainted in-court identification. Accordingly, *Foster* applied the *Stovall* test, and held that the police "procedure so undermined the reliability of the eyewitness identification as to violate due process." In contrast, in Coleman v. Alabama, where the witness' pretrial identification was not used to bolster his in-court identification, the plurality opinion applied the test enunciated in *Simmons*. It concluded that an in-court identification did not violate due process because it did not stem from an allegedly suggestive lineup.

The Court inexplicably seemed to erase the distinction between *Stovall* and *Simmons* situations in Neil v. Biggers. In *Biggers* there was a pretrial confrontation that was clearly both suggestive and unnecessary.[6] Evidence of this, together with an in-court identification, was admitted at trial. *Biggers* was, in short, a case plainly cast in the *Stovall* mold. Yet the Court, without explanation or apparent recognition of the distinction, applied the *Simmons* test. The Court stated: "[T]he primary evil to be avoided is 'a very substantial likelihood of irreparable misidentification.' Simmons v. United States. . . . It is the likelihood of misidentification which violates a defendant's right to due process. . . ." While this statement accurately describes the lesson of *Simmons*, it plainly ignores the teaching of *Stovall* and *Foster* that an unnecessarily suggestive pretrial confrontation itself violates due process.

But the Court did not simply disregard the due process analysis of *Stovall*. It went on to take the *Simmons* standard for assessing the constitutionality of an in-court identification—" 'a very substantial likelihood of irreparable misidentification' "—and transform it into the "standard for the admissibility of testimony concerning [an] out-of-court identification." It did so by deleting the word "irreparable" from the *Simmons* formulation. This metamorphosis could be accomplished, however, only by ignoring the fact that *Stovall*, fortified only months earlier by Kirby v. Illinois, see supra, at 121, had established a test for precisely the same situation that focused on the need for the suggestive procedure. It is not surprising that commentators almost unanimously mourned the demise of *Stovall* in the *Biggers* decision.[7]

6. "The showup itself consisted of two detectives walking respondent past the victim." 409 U.S., at 195. The police also ordered respondent to repeat the words used by the criminal. Inadequate efforts were made to secure participants for a lineup, and there was no pressing need to use a showup.

7. See, e.g., N. Sobel, supra, n.1, §§37, 38 (Supp. 1977); Grano, *Kirby, Biggers, and Ash*: Do Any Constitutional Safeguards Remain Against the Danger of Convicting

II

Apparently, the Court does not consider *Biggers* controlling in this case. I entirely agree, since I believe that *Biggers* was wrongly decided. The Court, however, concludes that *Biggers* is distinguishable because it, like the identification decisions that preceded it, involved a pre-*Stovall* confrontation, and because a paragraph in *Biggers* itself, 409 U.S., at 198-199, seems to distinguish between pre- and post-*Stovall* confrontations. Accordingly, in determining the admissibility of the post-*Stovall* identification in this case, the Court considers two alternatives, a per se exclusionary rule and a totality-of-the-circumstances approach. . . . The Court weighs three factors in deciding that the totality approach, which is essentially the test used in *Biggers*, should be applied. . . . In my view, the Court wrongly evaluates the impact of these factors.

First, the Court acknowledges that one of the factors, deterrence of police use of unnecessarily suggestive identification procedures, favors the per se rule. Indeed, it does so heavily, for such a rule would make it unquestionably clear to the police they must never use a suggestive procedure when a fairer alternative is available. I have no doubt that conduct would quickly conform to the rule.

Second, the Court gives passing consideration to the dangers of eyewitness identification recognized in the *Wade* trilogy. It concludes, however, that the grave risk of error does not justify adoption of the per se approach because that would too often result in exclusion of relevant evidence. In my view, this conclusion totally ignores the lessons of *Wade*. The dangers of mistaken identification are, as *Stovall* held, simply too great to permit unnecessarily suggestive identifications. Neither *Biggers* nor the Court's opinion today points to any contrary empirical evidence. Studies since *Wade* have only reinforced the validity of its assessment of the dangers of identification testimony.[8] While the Court is "content to

---

the Innocent? 72 Mich. L. Rev. 717 (1974); M. Hartman & N. Goldberg, The Death of the Warren Court, The Doctrine of Suggestive Identification, 32 NLADA Briefcase 78 (1974); Pulaski, *Neil v. Biggers*: The Supreme Court Dismantles the *Wade* Trilogy's Due Process Protection, 26 Stan. L. Rev. 1097 (1974); Recent Developments, Identification: Unnecessary Suggestiveness May Not Violate Due Process, 73 Colum. L. Rev. 1168 (1973).

8. See, e.g., People v. Anderson, 389 Mich. 155, 172-180, 192-220, 205 N.W. 2d 461, 468-472, 479-494 (1973); Levine & Tapp, The Psychology of Criminal Identification: The Gap from *Wade* to *Kirby*, 121 U. Pa. L. Rev. 1079 (1973); O'Connor, "That's the Man": A Sobering Study of Eyewitness Identification and the Polygraph, 49 St. John's L. Rev. 1 (1974); McGowan, supra, n.4, at 238-239; Grano, supra, n.7, at 723-724, 768-770; Recent Developments, supra, n. 7, at 1169 n. 11.

Moreover, as the exhaustive opinion of the Michigan Supreme Court in People v. Anderson, supra, noted:

"For a number of obvious reasons, however, including the fact that there is no on-going systematic study of the problem, the reported cases of misidentification are in every likelihood only the top of the iceberg. The writer of this opinion, for example, was able

rely on the good sense and judgment of American juries," . . . the impetus for *Stovall* and *Wade* was repeated miscarriages of justice resulting from juries' willingness to credit inaccurate eyewitness testimony.

Finally, the Court errs in its assessment of the relative impact of the two approaches on the administration of justice. The Court relies most heavily on this factor, finding that "reversal is a Draconian sanction" in cases where the identification is reliable despite an unnecessarily suggestive procedure used to obtain it. Relying on little more than a strong distaste for "inflexible rules of exclusion," the Court rejects the per se test. . . . In so doing, the Court disregards two significant distinctions between the per se rule advocated in this case and the exclusionary remedies for certain other constitutional violations.

First, the per se rule here is not "inflexible." Where evidence is suppressed, for example, as the fruit of an unlawful search, it may well be forever lost to the prosecution. Identification evidence, however, can by its very nature be readily and effectively reproduced. The in-court identification, permitted under *Wade* and *Simmons* if it has a source independent of an uncounseled or suggestive procedure, is one example. Similarly, when a prosecuting attorney learns that there has been a suggestive confrontation, he can easily arrange another lineup conducted under scrupulously fair conditions. Since the same factors are evaluated in applying both the Court's totality test and the *Wade-Simmons* independent-source inquiry, any identification which is "reliable" under the Court's test will support admission of evidence concerning such a fairly conducted lineup. The evidence of an additional, properly conducted confrontation will be more persuasive to a jury, thereby increasing the chance of a justified conviction where a reliable identification was tainted by a suggestive confrontation. At the same time, however, the effect of an unnecessarily suggestive identification—which has no value whatsoever in the law enforcement process—will be completely eliminated.

Second, other exclusionary rules have been criticized for preventing jury consideration of relevant and usually reliable evidence in order to serve interests unrelated to guilt or innocence, such as discouraging illegal searches or denial of counsel. Suggestively obtained eyewitness testimony is excluded, in contrast, precisely because of its unreliability and concomitant irrelevance. Its exclusion both protects the integrity of the truth-seeking function of the trial and discourages police use of needlessly inaccurate and ineffective investigatory methods. . . .

For these reasons, I conclude that adoption of the per se rule would enhance, rather than detract from, the effective administration of justice.

---

to turn up three very recent unreported cases right here in Michigan in the course of a few hours' inquiry." 389 Mich., at 179-180, 205 N.W.2d, at 472.

In my view, the Court's totality test will allow seriously unreliable and misleading evidence to be put before juries. Equally important, it will allow dangerous criminals to remain on the streets while citizens assume that police action has given them protection. According to my calculus, all three of the factors upon which the Court relies point to acceptance of the per se approach. . . .

III

Despite my strong disagreement with the Court over the proper standards to be applied in this case, I am pleased that its application of the totality test does recognize the continuing vitality of *Stovall*. In assessing the reliability of the identification, the Court mandates weighing "the corrupting effect of the suggestive identification itself" against the "indicators of [a witness'] ability to make an accurate identification." . . . The Court holds, as Neil v. Biggers failed to, that a due process identification inquiry must take account of the suggestiveness of a confrontation and the likelihood that it led to misidentification, as recognized in *Stovall* and *Wade*. Thus, even if a witness did have an otherwise adequate opportunity to view a criminal, the later use of a highly suggestive identification procedure can render his testimony inadmissible. Indeed, it is my view that, assuming applicability of the totality test enunciated by the Court, the facts of the present case require that result.

I consider first the opportunity that Officer Glover had to view the suspect. Careful review of the record shows that he could see the heroin seller only for the time it took to speak three sentences of four or five short words, to hand over some money, . . . and later after the door reopened, to receive the drugs in return. . . . The entire face-to-face transaction could have taken as little as 15 or 20 seconds. But during this time, Glover's attention was not focused exclusively on the seller's face. He observed that the door was opened 12 to 18 inches, . . . that there was a window in the room behind the door, . . . and, most importantly, that there was a woman standing behind the man. . . . Glover was, of course, also concentrating on the details of the transaction—he must have looked away from the seller's face to hand him the money and receive the drugs. The observation during the conversation thus may have been as brief as 5 or 10 seconds.

As the Court notes, Glover was a police officer trained in and attentive to the need for making accurate identifications. Nevertheless, both common sense and scholarly study indicate that while a trained observer such as a police officer "is somewhat less likely to make an erroneous identification than the average untrained observer, the mere fact that he has been so trained is no guarantee that he is correct in a specific case. His identification testimony should be scrutinized just as carefully as that of the normal witness." Wall, . . . [Eye-witness Identification in Criminal Cases (1965)] at 14; see also Levine & Tapp, supra, n.8, at 1088. Moreover, "identifications made by policemen in highly competitive activities, such as undercover narcotic agents . . . , should be scrutinized with special care." Wall, supra, . . . at 14. Yet it is just such a searching inquiry that the Court fails to make here.

Another factor on which the Court relies—the witness' degree of certainty in making the identification—is worthless as an indicator that he is correct. Even if Glover had been unsure initially about his identification of respondent's picture, by the time he was called at trial to present a key piece of evidence for the State that paid his salary, it is impossible to imagine his responding negatively to such questions as "is there any doubt in your mind whatsoever" that the identification was correct. . . .

Next, the Court finds that because the identification procedure took place two days after the crime, its reliability is enhanced. While such temporal proximity makes the identification more reliable than one occurring months later, the fact is that the greatest memory loss occurs within hours after an event. After that, the dropoff continues much more slowly.[11] Thus, the reliability of an identification is increased only if it was made within several hours of the crime. If the time gap is any greater, reliability necessarily decreases.

Finally, the Court makes much of the fact that Glover gave a description of the seller to D'Onofrio shortly after the incident. . . . [T]he description given by Glover was actually no more than a general summary of the seller's appearance. . . . We may discount entirely the seller's clothing, for that was of no significance later in the proceeding. Indeed, to the extent that Glover noticed clothes, his attention was diverted from the seller's face. Otherwise, Glover merely described vaguely the seller's height, skin color, hairstyle, and build. He did say that the seller had "high cheekbones," but there is no other mention of facial features, nor even an estimate of age. Conspicuously absent is any indication that the seller was a native of the West Indies, certainly something which a

_____

11. See, e.g., Levine & Tapp, supra, n.8, at 1100-1101; Note, Pretrial Identification Procedures—Wade to Gilbert to Stovall: Lower Courts Bobble the Ball, 55 Minn. L. Rev. 779, 789 (1971); People v. Anderson, supra, at 214-215, 205 N.W.2d, at 491. Reviewing a number of its cases, the Court of Appeals for the District of Columbia Circuit concluded several years ago that while showups occurring up to perhaps 30 minutes after a crime are generally permissible, one taking place four hours later, far removed from the crime scene, was not. McRae v. United States, 137 U.S. App. D.C. 80, 87, 420 F.2d 1283, 1290 (1969).

member of the black community could immediately recognize from both appearance and accent.[12]

From all of this, I must conclude that the evidence of Glover's ability to make an accurate identification is far weaker than the Court finds it. In contrast, the procedure used to identify respondent was both extraordinarily suggestive and strongly conducive to error. In dismissing "the corrupting effect of the suggestive identification" procedure here, . . . the Court virtually grants the police license to convict the innocent. By displaying a single photograph of respondent to the witness Glover under the circumstances in this record almost everything that could have been done wrong was done wrong.

In the first place, there was no need to use a photograph at all. Because photos are static, two-dimensional, and often outdated, they are "clearly inferior in reliability" to corporeal procedures. Wall, supra, . . . at 70. . . . While the use of photographs is justifiable and often essential where the police have no knowledge of an offender's identity, the poor reliability of photos makes their use inexcusable where any other means of identification is available. Here, since Detective D'Onofrio believed that he knew the seller's identity, . . . further investigation without resort to a photographic showup was easily possible. With little inconvenience, a corporeal lineup including Brathwaite might have been arranged.[13] Properly conducted, such a procedure would have gone far to remove any doubt about the fairness and accuracy of the identification.

Worse still than the failure to use an easily available corporeal identification was the display to Glover of only a single picture, rather than a photo array. With good reason, such single-suspect procedures have "been widely condemned." They give no assurance that the witness can identify the criminal from among a number of persons of similar appearance, surely the strongest evidence that there was no misidentification. In Simmons v. United States, our first decision involving photographic identification, we recognized the danger that a witness seeing a suggestively displayed picture will "retain in his memory the image of the photograph rather than of the person actually seen.". . . As *Simmons* warned, the danger of error is at its greatest when "the police display to the witness only the picture of a single individual . . . [and] is also

---

12. Brathwaite had come to the United States from his native Barbados as an adult. . . . It is also noteworthy that the informant who witnessed the transaction and was described by Glover as "trustworthy," . . . disagreed with Glover's recollection of the event. The informant testified that it was a woman in the apartment who took the money from Glover and gave him the drugs in return. . . .

13. Indeed, the police carefully staged Brathwaite's arrest in the same apartment that was used for the sale, . . . indicating that they were fully capable of keeping track of his whereabouts and using this information in their investigation.

heightened if the police indicate to the witness that they have other evidence that . . . the perso[n] pictured committed the crime."

The use of a single picture (or the display of a single live suspect, for that matter) is a grave error, of course, because it dramatically suggests to the witness that the person shown must be the culprit. Why else would the police choose the person? And it is deeply ingrained in human nature to agree with the expressed opinions of others—particularly others who should be more knowledgeable—when making a difficult decision. In this case, moreover, the pressure was not limited to that inherent in the display of a single photograph. Glover, the identifying witness, was a state police officer on special assignment. He knew that D'Onofrio, an experienced Hartford narcotics detective, presumably familiar with local drug operations, believed respondent to be the seller. There was at work, then, both loyalty to another police officer and deference to a better-informed colleague.[16] Finally, of course, there was Glover's knowledge that without an identification and arrest, government funds used to buy heroin had been wasted.

The Court discounts this overwhelming evidence of suggestiveness, however. It reasons that because D'Onofrio was not present when Glover viewed the photograph, there was "little pressure on the witness to acquiesce in the suggestion." . . . . That conclusion blinks psychological reality. There is no doubt in my mind that even in D'Onofrio's absence, a clear and powerful message was telegraphed to Glover as he looked at respondent's photograph. He was emphatically told that "*this* is the man," and he responded by identifying respondent then and at trial "whether or not he was in fact 'the man.' "[18]

---

16. In fact, the trial record indicates that D'Onofrio was remarkably ill-informed, although it does not appear that Glover knew this at the time of the identification. While the Court is impressed by D'Onofrio's immediate response to Glover's description, . . . that cannot alter the fact that the detective, who had not witnessed the transaction, acted on a wild guess that respondent was the seller. D'Onofrio's hunch rested solely on Glover's vague description, yet D'Onofrio had seen respondent only "[s]everal times, mostly in his vehicle."

. . . There was no evidence that respondent was even a suspected narcotics dealer, and D'Onofrio thought that the drugs had been purchased at a different apartment from the one Glover actually went to. . . . The identification of respondent provides a perfect example of the investigator and the witness bolstering each other's inadequate knowledge to produce a seemingly accurate but actually worthless identification. See Sobel, supra, n.1, §3.02, at 12.

18. This discussion does not imply any lack of respect for the honesty and dedication of the police. We all share the frailties of human nature that create the problem. Justice Frank O'Connor of the New York Supreme Court decried the dangers of eyewitness testimony in a recent article that began with this caveat:

> From the vantage point of ten years as District Attorney of Queens County (1956-66) and six years on the trial bench (1969 to [1974]), the writer holds in high regard the professional competence and personal integrity of most policemen.

I must conclude that this record presents compelling evidence that there was "a very substantial likelihood of misidentification" of respondent Brathwaite. The suggestive display of respondent's photograph to the witness Glover likely erased any independent memory that Glover had retained of the seller from his barely adequate opportunity to observe the criminal.

IV

Since I agree with the distinguished panel of the Court of Appeals that the legal standard of *Stovall* should govern this case, but that even if it does not, the facts here reveal a substantial likelihood of misidentification in violation of respondent's right to due process of law, I would affirm the grant of habeas corpus relief. Accordingly, I dissent from the Court's reinstatement of respondent's conviction.

NOTES AND QUESTIONS

1. The Court's treatment of the facts in *Manson* is criticized in Jonakait, Reliable Identification: Could the Supreme Court Tell in Manson v. Brathwaite?, 52 U. Colo. L. Rev. 511, 517-522 (1981):

> The Supreme Court analyzed the reliability of the identification in light of several criteria. The first of these was whether there was adequate opportunity to view the criminal. The Court stressed that there was sufficient light to see and that Glover had two to three minutes to observe the seller at a distance of only a few feet. Psychologists confirm that the less time one looks, the less accurately one perceives. Subjects can, for example, remember faces better after viewing them for thirty-two seconds than after seeing them for ten. Therefore, in this respect, the Court's assessment of the importance of length of observation happened to coincide with psychological evidence.
>
> Had the Court been familiar with perception studies, however, it would have made another inquiry. The majority stressed that the undercover officer had observed the drug dealer for two to three minutes. The Court did not state how this duration was established, but it apparently

---

Laudable instances of police efforts to clear a doubtful suspect are legion. Deliberate, willful efforts to frame or railroad an innocent man are totally unknown, at least to me. Yet, once the best-intentioned officer becomes honestly convinced that he has the right man, human nature being what it is, corners may be cut, some of the niceties forgotten, and serious error committed.

O'Connor, supra, n.8, at 1 n.1.

came from the witness himself. The Court needed to deal also with the witness's ability to perceive time. While many people would consider estimates of time to be in the same category as estimations of height, weight, distance, and speed, time estimates are in fact different. While estimates of height and weight might be high or low, estimates of distance long or short, and estimates of speed fast or slow, estimates of the duration of an event are invariably incorrect in one direction: people believe events last longer than they do. The duration of an observation cannot be judged by the observer's estimate. He will state that it lasted longer than it did, and if a court relies on such an estimate, the court will give the observer more credence than he deserves. In this case, "two to three minutes" was probably longer than the actual observation.

The Court did analyze the degree of Glover's attention to the man at the door. The Court noted that Glover was black and therefore concluded that Glover was unlikely to perceive only the general features of the black seller. If the Court was accepting in an offhand manner the proposition that it is harder to recognize the face of a person belonging to another race than one's own, the Court's conclusion is borne out by experimental data. The Court went on to stress, however, that Glover "was a trained police officer on duty . . . [and], that as a specially trained, assigned, and experienced officer, he could be expected to pay scrupulous attention to detail, for he knew that subsequently he would have to find and arrest his vendor." The Court, therefore, assumed that the perceptions of a trained police officer are more reliable than the perceptions of those not so trained. Unfortunately, this assumption is unwarranted. Studies do not support the idea that police make more reliable witnesses than civilians or that their training in any way improves their ability to make identifications. Thus, in one major study, both police and civilians were shown a film of a street scene. Police "saw" many more crimes that had in fact not occurred than the civilians, while the police were no more accurate than the civilians in correctly reporting the true crimes.

In another study, identification tests were given to subjects who had undergone a program specifically designed to increase the ability to identify faces. The results showed "absolutely no evidence for any effect of the training course on the ability of subjects to remember photographed faces. . . ."[27]

Finally, in mentioning the assignments of the trained undercover officer, the Court characterized them as "specialized and dangerous. . . ." The Court did not explicitly attach any significance to this description. Perhaps the Court implicitly reasoned that since the officer was on a dangerous mission, he must have been especially alert; therefore, his observations were reliable. If, however, Glover's job was very dangerous, he performed his duties under great stress. While the Supreme Court might think that danger heightens awareness, psychologists have known for some time that stress does not aid perception and learning, but inhibits

27. E. Loftus, [Eyewitness Testimony (1979)] at 168.

them. Thus, the Court may have incorrectly assessed the effect of the dangerousness of Glover's duties on the reliability of his observations.

As a third indication of reliability, the Court believed that the specificity of the undercover officer's initial description supported the reliability of his subsequent identification: "Glover's description was given . . . within minutes after the transaction. It included the vendor's race, his height, his build, the color and style of his hair, and the high cheekbone facial feature. It also included clothing the vendor wore. No claim has been made that Brathwaite did not possess the physical characteristics so described."

It would seem logical that one who is able to give a highly detailed and accurate description of another would be more likely to recognize the other person than somebody who cannot give such a description. Unfortunately, this common-sense conclusion has no scientific support, and indeed may be false. A. Daniel Yarmey states that not many studies have been done in this area, but the results of those that have been done are consistent: "[A]lthough faces easily evoke verbal labels as word associates, ease of labeling was not related to accuracy of facial recognition."[32] In fact, an early study found that "subjects who were most accurate in the recognition test were the poorest in verbally recalling details of the faces."[33] However, the Supreme Court, ignorant of these studies, erroneously concluded that a description indicated the reliability of a subsequent identification. The majority in Manson v. Brathwaite also found the certainty with which Glover made his identification to be an indication of reliability. In response to a question whether the photograph was that of the seller, Glover said, "There is no question whatsoever." Once again, the evidence does not support the Court's assumption. Although studies have found some relationship between confidence of a response and its accuracy, this correlation does not hold true for identifications. Yarmey summarizes: "The expressed confidence of an eyewitness does not mean that his or her identification is necessarily accurate. In fact, research indicates no relationship."[36]

Finally, the Court considered the time lapse prior to the identification and concluded that the forty-eight hours between the sale and Glover's viewing of the photograph supported reliability. It is commonly believed that as time goes on, one is able to remember less and less about an event. While science generally confirms this notion, it has been shown that forgetting does not always correlate directly with the passage of time. Instead, the "forgetting curve" shows that most of the memory loss occurs shortly after the learning and then tapers off. The rapidity of memory loss can be startling. In one test, subjects achieved ninety percent accuracy in

---

32. A. D. Yarmey, [The Psychology of Eyewitness Testimony (1979)] at 138.

33. A. D. Yarmey, supra . . . at 114. Yarmey flatly concludes, "[O]bservers' ability to verbally describe faces is not predictive of their ability to recognize these faces." A. D. Yarmey, supra . . . at 139.

36. A. D. Yarmey, supra . . . at 180; see also id. at 150-51.

describing an event immediately after its conclusion, while two days later, recall was just slightly better than mere guessing. Of course, not everything is forgotten that quickly. In fact this pattern of forgetting might be subject to an exception of crucial significance to criminal law: it may not pertain to the recall of faces. Evidence exists for the proposition that recall of faces may improve with time. For instance, in one study, the recollection of pictures improved over time, while over that same span the recall of words dropped. In another experiment, subjects were shown candid photos and then later shown front bust views for identification. Accuracy remained constant in tests conducted four minutes after the viewing and one week after the viewing. Once again, however, the Manson v. Brathwaite Court was ignorant of this important evidence. Thus, in concluding that the identification resulting from the suggestive procedures was reliable, the Court stressed that the disputed showing of the picture came only two days after the crime, not weeks or months later. As discussed above, there is evidence indicating that recall may be lost within a period as short as forty-eight hours. On the other hand, the Supreme Court could have bolstered its conclusion by citing the studies showing no loss of memory over time for visual images. The Court chose neither of these approaches but instead relied on its own intuitive conclusions. . . .

2. How should the identification issue be decided in the following situations?

[a.] The victim . . . was robbed by a man holding a rifle and wearing a bandana across his face. The description of the assailant given to the police by the victim was of a "teenager, 5'6"-5'10" tall, very heavyset, having dark hair and dark eyes, and who spoke with a soft, or low, stuttering voice." One or two days after the crime, the victim was shown a "mug shot" photograph of the defendant with a card over the nose and mouth of the face in the picture and informed "that the subject of the photograph had previously been imprisoned on burglary charges, had a speech impediment and was a good suspect." The victim indicated that there was physical similarity between the defendant and the perpetrator, but without an opportunity to hear the defendant's voice, he could not be certain that the two were the same man. Later that same week, the victim was brought to the sheriff's office and told he would be hearing, from behind a partition, the voice of the man whose picture he had previously seen. Upon hearing the defendant's voice and observing the defendant after he emerged from behind the partition, the victim made an identification.

[b.] [F]orty-five minutes after they had been the victims of a robbery, two people were taken by the police to an area outside a motel where two suspects had been apprehended. Informed by the officer that "they thought they had the guys," the complainants viewed the two defendants who were standing together, handcuffed, illuminated by the headlights of a police car.

[c.] On the same day in which she was sexually attacked in her dormitory, a woman was shown photographs of several possible assailants. Although the defendant's photograph was among them, the victim passed by it without making any sign of recognition. The investigating police officer then singled out the picture of the defendant so the victim could see that the photograph contained information concerning the defendant's prior rape conviction. In addition, the officer informed the victim that the man in this photograph was a suspect and had been seen in the area shortly after the attack. Upon taking another look at the photograph, the victim said that the defendant was not her assailant. Four days later, the victim was again unable to identify the defendant from among 171 prints but, later that same day, selected the defendant from a group of 546 slides. Three months after the photographic arrays, the victim viewed a lineup from which she chose the defendant as her attacker.

These quoted fact patterns are from cases discussed in Grossman, Suggestive Identifications: The Supreme Court's Due Process Test Fails to Meet Its Own Criteria, 11 U. Balt. L. Rev. 53, 61, 83, 91-92 (1981).

3. For an example of the subtleties that may affect the identification process, including an example of the Rosenthal effect, discussed at page 391 supra, and a court attempting to struggle with them, consider the sorry story of the Reaves Brothers. The first opinion concerns Steven Reaves, and the second Rodger Reaves. Reaves v. State, 649 P.2d 777 (Okla. Crim. App. 1982):

The appellant was charged with Burglary in the Second Degree in Tulsa County District Court. The appellant waived a jury trial. The trial court found the appellant guilty and sentenced him to five (5) years imprisonment.

The sole issue is whether the pretrial identification procedures were impermissively suggestive as to taint the in-court identification in violation of the appellant's due process rights.

Reaves asserts that the photographic identification procedure was impermissively suggestive for several reasons. He contends: (1) that a comment by the police officer after the victim had only tentatively identified his picture was unnecessarily suggestive, (2) that the repeated showing of the pictures was prejudicial, and (3) that the other persons depicted in the photographic display did not even remotely possess the same physical characteristics as the appellant.

On December 22, 1979, Alvin Rhodes returned to his apartment and noticed his door was ajar. As he attempted to push the door open someone from inside his apartment grabbed him. A struggle ensued and Rhodes was hit in the head with a pry bar. Rhodes managed to gain possession of the pry bar and swung at his assailant, but missed. At this time, a second assailant emerged from the apartment. This second assailant was later identified as Rodger Reaves. He pointed a gun at Rhodes and ordered him to drop the pry bar. Rodger Reaves allegedly handed the pistol to his accomplice who ordered Rhodes inside the apartment. Once inside, Rhodes grabbed the pistol, but was unable to overpower his assailants. During the scuffle that ensued, Rhodes was severely beaten up by the two assailants.

At gunpoint, Rhodes, who was at this time in a semi-conscious state, was ordered into the bathroom where he was robbed of his wallet. The assailants then fled and Rhodes managed to contact the police. He was later taken to the hospital where he stayed for approximately ten days recovering from severe body and facial injuries.

On December 26, 1979, while the victim was in the hospital, Detective Campbell showed Rhodes a photographic display consisting of nine photographs. Rhodes carefully looked through the photographs several times. He tentatively picked out two photographs of his alleged assailants, Rodger Reaves and his brother, Steven Reaves. He informed the detective that he was not positive they were his assailants. Detective Campbell determined this initial identification by Rhodes of the suspects was insufficient to make an arrest.

After the victim had tentatively identified his assailants, Detective Campbell informed him that the two guys were brothers. Campbell also informed Rhodes that "one of the dudes was bad." Rhodes then asked Campbell whether they were capable of murdering someone. Campbell responded that they were.

When Rhodes was released from the hospital, Detective Campbell went to his apartment and showed him the two pictures he had tentatively identified in the hospital. This time Rhodes positively identified Rodger Reaves and Steve Reaves. Rhodes stated that he was sure they were the two assailants. Rhodes was shown the original stack of nine photographs a third time while in the presence of the assistant district attorney. Placed in this stack of photographs was an additional picture of Rodger Reaves. This second picture was a more recent photograph of Reaves, depicting him as having gained weight. Once again, immediately prior to the preliminary hearing, Rhodes was shown the two photographs of Rodger Reaves. . . . Under the totality of the circumstances, in this case, we hold that the pretrial identifications procedures were impermissively suggestive. First, we find that the nine picture photographic display was suggestive. It is difficult to find anyone in the photographs with the same general physical characteristics as the accused. The accused is four to six inches shorter than any of the other persons in the photo display. Only one person other than the accused has a mustache. Seven of the photographs depict persons with medium length and long hair. The accused is shown as having short hair and is the only person with his arm in a sling. Also, he looks markedly older than most of the other persons shown in the photo display. Lastly, only one person is shown as having long sideburns similar to the accused.

We further find unnecessarily suggestive the fact that Detective Campbell told the victim that the persons he had tentatively identified were "bad." Campbell stated that the initial identification was too weak to even arrest the suspects. Additionally, we conclude that the repeated showing of the photographs of the accused was very suggestive, especially the single photograph displays. Therefore, we find that the pretrial photographic identification procedure was impermissively suggestive. We now turn to the second inquiry. Did the victim's identification of the appellant possess sufficient independent indicia of reliability, despite the suggestive aspects of pretrial identification procedures? . . .

The record does not establish sufficient aspect of reliability. The victim stated that he returned home between 9:45 P.M. and 10:00 P.M. The light outside the appellant's apartment was burned out. Additionally, it was dark inside the victim's apartment. It was very difficult for the victim to get a clear view of the accused.

It appears that most of the victim's attention was directed toward the first assailant who hit him with the pry bar and wrestled him for the gun. The victim did not observe his second assailant for any great length of time. Additionally, shortly after the incident the victim informed the police that he did not get a very good look at the accused. Further, Rhodes lost his eye glasses prior to becoming aware that a second assailant was inside his apartment. Rhodes was unable to give the police any description of the second assailant. Officer Turner testified that the victim stated to him that he was not sure if he could identify the second assailant.

Based upon these factors and the unnecessarily suggestive pretrial identification procedure, we find that the in-court identification of this appellant was violative of due process principles. The judgment and sentence is reversed and remanded.

Now, compare Reaves v. State, 649 P.2d 780 (Okla. Crim. App. 1982):

The appellant was convicted of Burglary in the Second Degree in Tulsa County District Court. After waiving a trial by jury, the trial judge found Reaves guilty and sentenced him to ten (10) years' imprisonment. . . .

The appellant contends that the pre-trial identification procedures were unduly suggestive so as to render the in-court identification unreliable and violative of due process. We addressed the identification procedures utilized in this case in the companion case, Reaves v. State, 649 P.2d 777 [(1982)]. That case dealt with the identification procedures in regard to Rodger Reaves, the appellant's brother and alleged accomplice in the burglary. . . .

With regard to the appellant, Steven Reaves, we find that the photographic display was not violative of due process. The individuals pictured in the photo display possessed the same general characteristics of the appellant. The trial judge properly conducted an in-camera hearing as to the propriety of the identification procedures. The trial judge concluded that the identification procedures were not so impermissively suggestive as to give rise to a very substantial likelihood of misidentification. On review, we cannot hold that his ruling was erroneous with regard to Steven Reaves. Under the totality of the circumstances, we find that the identification procedure did not create a substantial risk of misidentification. The police comment at the hospital was made after the victim had already identified his assailants. The comment was not intended to pressure the victim into identifying anyone. Further we find that the procedure allowing the victim to view the photographs on three occasions did not create a substantial likelihood of misidentification. Although we do not condone the third viewing of the photographs by the victim, we find that it was not so unduly suggestive as to violate due process. We also hold that the victim's in-court identification possessed independent aspects of reliability. Neil v. Biggers, 409 U.S. 188 (1972). Even if the pretrial identification procedures are impermissively suggestive, it does not require exclusion of an in-court identification provided the in-court identification is reliable. Manson v. Brathwaite, 432 U.S. 98 at 114. . . .

In this case, the victim had ample opportunity to view Steven Reaves, even though it was fairly dark at his apartment. Rhodes struggled with his assailant at very close range. Outside the apartment, Rhodes wrestled Richard Reaves for possession of a pry bar. Inside the apartment Rhodes attempted to disarm Richard Reaves of the pistol he had aimed at his head. Further, he had an excellent opportunity to view Steven Reaves in his lighted bathroom when he robbed him of his wallet.

Rhodes apparently directed most of his attention toward the appellant. The struggle for the pry bar and the pistol ensured that the victim's attention was directed toward the appellant. His attention on the assailant was clearly more than a casual observer. The victim was fighting with his assailant for his life.

The victim also gave the police a fairly good description of the assailant later identified as the appellant, Steven Reaves. He accurately described the appellant as a white male, blond hair, five foot-seven to five foot-eight, and light complexion. He also described the coat worn by the assailant during the burglary.

Although the victim could not positively identify the appellant at the hospital, he did tentatively identify both assailants. Later, he positively identified the appellant. Lastly, time lapse between the crime and the identification was reasonably short. He identified the appellant about five days after the incident. A sooner identification was impossible because Rhodes' eyes were swollen shut during the first few days he was in the hospital. The second and positive identification of the appellant was merely eleven or twelve days after the burglary.

Considering the totality of the circumstances, we find that the photographic identification was not impermissively suggestive. In addition, we find that the in-court identification possessed sufficient aspects of reliability. . . .

4. The commentary on the Supreme Court's identification decisions consistently criticizes the Court for being overly sanguine about the ability of jurors to assess the limitations of eyewitness testimony. One developing strategy to assist the jury in this regard is to employ experts—usually psychologists—to testify to the limits of human perception, memory, etc. as well as to the potential for suggestiveness such encounters possess. The courts have not been very receptive to such evidence, although a few courts have admitted it. For a discussion of the cases, and an argument for admission, see Grossman, Suggestive Identifications: The Supreme Court's Due Process Test Fails to Meet Its Own Criteria, 11 U. Balt. L. Rev. 53 (1981). One case has held that exclusion of expert testimony on the limits of eyewitness identifications was an abuse of discretion. State v. Chapple, 135 Ariz. 281, 660 P.2d 1208 (1983). *Chapple* was subsequently limited to its facts. State v. Poland, 144 Ariz. 388, 698 P.2d 183 (1985).

5. Another possible response to the problem of identifications is to provide for special jury instructions. See State v. Green, 86 N.J. 281, 430 A.2d 914 (1981), reversing for the failure of the trial court to give such instructions. Compare Illinois Pattern Jury Instruction (Criminal) 3.15, which recommends leaving the matter to the argument of counsel. In Grano, *Kirby, Biggers*, and *Ash*: Do Any Constitutional Safeguards Remain Against the Danger of Convicting the Innocent?, 72 Mich. L. Rev. 717, 796-797 (1974), Professor Grano suggests the following:

> Because of the scientifically proven dangers of mistaken identification, the law has established certain rules for the conduct of identification procedures. One of the most significant dangers is that the identification procedure will itself mislead the witness into identifying the wrong person. For example, when the police present only one person to the witness, they magnify the risk of mistake. The witness, though perfectly honest, is likely to be misled into believing that the police must have captured the right person if they are presenting him . . . for identification. A much safer procedure is to conduct a lineup, where the witness is tested by being forced to pick the defendant from a group of men. Because lineups are much more reliable, . . . the police [should not] conduct . . . one-man showups when a lineup can be held. In this case, the police, without justifiable excuse, [did so]. In doing this, they unnecessarily increased the risk of mistaken identification. In evaluating the identification evidence in this case, you should consider this . . . and the unnecessary risk it caused.

6. In this area, as in others, state courts of last resort are extending procedural protections to defendants as a matter of state law that exceed

the federal constitutional requirements. See, e.g., People v. Adams, 440 N.Y.S.2d 902 (Ct. Ap. 1981), forbidding the admission of testimony concerning an unnecessarily suggestive identification, but also applying harmless error analysis; People v. Bustamonte, 634 P.2d 927, 177 Cal. Rptr. 576 (1981), extending right to counsel to pre-indictment lineups.

7. Does *Manson* keep out only what normal evidentiary rules would exclude as irrelevant in any event? Conversely, does *Manson* constitutionalize the relevancy rule? Why should unreliable identification evidence be treated differently from any other unreliable, inculpating evidence?

PART THREE

THE RIGHT TO BE LET ALONE—AN EXAMINATION OF THE FOURTH AND FIFTH AMENDMENTS AND RELATED AREAS

CHAPTER 6

THE RISE AND FALL OF
BOYD v. UNITED STATES

. . . *Boyd v. United States [is] a case that will be remembered as long as civil liberty lives in the United States.*

Justice Brandeis, dissenting, in
Olmstead v. United States,
277 U.S. 438, at 474 (1928).

. . . Boyd *is dead.*

Note, The Life and Times of
Boyd v. United States (1886-1976),
76 Mich. L. Rev. 184, 212 (1977)
(hereinafter cited as Note).

It is a trivial exercise in two different senses to learn what the law "is." Because of the nature of common law and legislative processes, law is in a constant state of change; thus, to "know" the law is to know only what was, not what is. Secondly, legal principles are conclusions or labels applied to a synthesis of competing interests, considerations and developments that change over time. To understand the principles, one must understand their etiologies and implications, not just their logical relationships. As Oliver Wendell Holmes put it in The Common Law (1881):

It is something to show that the consistency of a system requires a particular result, but it is not all. The life of the law has not been logic: it has been experience. The felt necessities of the time, the prevalent moral and political theories, intuitions of public policy, avowed or unconscious, even the prejudices which judges share with their fellow-men, have had a good

423

deal more to do than the syllogism in determining the rules by which men should be governed. The law embodies the story of a nation's development through many centuries, and it cannot be dealt with as if it contained only the axioms and corollaries of a book of mathematics. In order to know what it is, we must know what it has been, and what it tends to become. We must alternately consult history and existing theories of legislation. But the most difficult labor will be to understand the combination of the two into new products at every stage. The substance of the law at any given time pretty nearly corresponds, so far as it goes, with what is then understood to be convenient; but its form and machinery, and the degree to which it is able to work out desired results, depend very much upon its past. . . .

. . . In [using history to explicate legal principles, however,] there are two errors equally to be avoided both by writer and reader. One is that of supposing, because an idea seems very familiar and natural to us, that it has always been so. Many things which we take for granted have had to be laboriously fought out or thought out in past times. The other mistake is the opposite one of asking too much of history. We start with man full grown. It may be assumed that the earliest barbarian whose practices are to be considered, had a good many of the same feelings and passions as ourselves. [Id. at 1-2.]

The necessity of understanding the source of contemporary developments in order to understand, and more importantly to evaluate, the developments themselves is nowhere more evident than in the areas of the fourth and fifth amendments. A starting point is the following case.

BOYD v. UNITED STATES

Error to the Circuit Court of the United States for the Southern District of New York
116 U.S. 616 (1886)

MR. JUSTICE BRADLEY delivered the opinion of the court.

This was an information filed by the District Attorney of the United States in the District Court for the Southern District of New York, in July, 1884, in a cause of seizure and forfeiture of property, against thirty-five cases of plate glass, seized by the collector as forfeited to the United States, under §12 of the "Act to amend the customs revenue laws, and to repeal moieties," passed June 22, 1874, 18 Stat. 186.

It is declared by that section that any owner, importer, consignee, &c., who shall, with intent to defraud the revenue, make, or attempt to make, any entry of imported merchandise, by means of any fraudulent or false invoice, affidavit, letter or paper, or by means of any false statement, written or verbal, or who shall be guilty of any wilful act or omission by means whereof the United States shall be deprived of the lawful duties, or any portion thereof, accruing upon the merchandise, or any portion thereof, embraced or referred to in such invoice, affidavit, letter, paper, or statement, or affected by such act or omission, shall for each offence be fined in any sum not exceeding $5000 nor less than $50, or be imprisoned for any time not exceeding two years, or both; and, in addition to such fine, such merchandise shall be forfeited.

The charge was that the goods in question were imported into the United States to the port of New York, subject to the payment of duties; and that the owners or agents of said merchandise, or other person unknown, committed the alleged fraud, which was described in the words of the statute. The plaintiffs in error entered a claim for the goods, and pleaded that they did not become forfeited in manner and form as alleged. On the trial of the cause it became important to show the quantity and value of the glass contained in twenty-nine cases previously imported. To do this the district attorney offered in evidence an order made by the District Judge under §5 of the same act of June 22, 1874, directing notice under seal of the court to be given to the claimants, requiring them to produce the invoice of the twenty-nine cases. The claimants, in obedience to the notice, but objecting to its validity and to the constitutionality of the law, produced the invoice; and when it was offered in evidence by the district attorney they objected to its reception on the ground that, in a suit for forfeiture, no evidence can be compelled from the claimants themselves, and also that the statute, so far as it compels production of evidence to be used against the claimants is unconstitutional and void.

The evidence being received, and the trial closed, the jury found a verdict for the United States, condemning the thirty-five cases of glass which were seized, and judgment of forfeiture was given. This judgment was affirmed by the Circuit Court, and the decision of that court is now here for review. . . .

The 5th section of the act of June 22, 1874, under which this order was made, is in the following words, to wit:

> In all suits and proceedings other than criminal arising under any of the revenue laws of the United States, the attorney representing the government, whenever in his belief any business book, invoice, or paper belonging to, or under the control of, the defendant or claimant, will tend to prove any allegation made by the United States, may make a written motion, particularly describing such book, invoice, or paper, and setting forth the allegation which he expects to prove; and thereupon the court in which suit or proceeding is pending may, at its discretion, issue a notice to the defendant or claimant to produce such book, invoice, or paper in court, at a day and hour to be specified in said notice, which, together with a copy of said motion, shall be served formally on the defendant or claimant

by the United States marshal by delivering to him a certified copy thereof, or otherwise serving the same as original notices of suit in the same court are served; and if the defendant or claimant shall fail or refuse to produce such book, invoice, or paper in obedience to such notice, the allegations stated in the said motion shall be taken as confessed, unless his failure or refusal to produce the same shall be explained to the satisfaction of the court. And if produced the said attorney shall be permitted, under the direction of the court, to make examination (at which examination the defendant, or claimant, or his agent, may be present) of such entries in said book, invoice, or paper as relate to or tend to prove the allegation aforesaid, and may offer the same in evidence on behalf of the United States. But the owner of said books and papers, his agent or attorney, shall have, subject to the order of the court, the custody of them, except pending their examination in court as aforesaid.

This section was passed in lieu of the 2d section of the act of March 2, 1867, . . . which section of said last-mentioned statute authorized the district judge, on complaint and affidavit that any fraud on the revenue had been committed by any person interested or engaged in the importation of merchandise, to issue his warrant to the marshal to enter any premises where any invoices, books, or papers were deposited relating to such merchandise, and take possession of such books and papers and produce them before said judge, to be subject to his order, and allowed to be examined by the collector, and to be retained as long as the judge should deem necessary.

The section last recited was passed in lieu of the 7th section of the act of March 3, 1863, . . . 12 Stat. 737. The 7th section of this act was in substance the same as the 2d section of the act of 1867, except that the warrant was to be directed to the collector instead of the marshal. It was the first legislation of the kind that ever appeared on the statute book of the United States, and, as seen from its date, was adopted at a period of great national excitement, when the powers of the government were subjected to a severe strain to protect the national existence.

The clauses of the Constitution, to which it is contended that these laws are repugnant, are the Fourth and Fifth Amendments. The Fourth declares, "The right of the people to be secure in their persons, houses, papers, and effects, against unreasonable searches and seizures, shall not be violated, and no warrants shall issue, but upon probable cause, supported by oath or affirmation, and particularly describing the place to be searched, and the persons or things to be seized." The Fifth Article, amongst other things, declares that no person "shall be compelled in any criminal case to be a witness against himself."

But, in regard to the Fourth Amendment, it is contended that, whatever might have been alleged against the constitutionality of the acts of 1863 and 1867, that of 1874, under which the order in the present case was made, is free from constitutional objection, because it does not authorize the search and seizure of books and papers, but only requires the defendant or claimant to produce them. That is so; but it declares that if he does not produce them, the allegations which it is affirmed they will prove shall be taken as confessed. This is tantamount to compelling their production; for the prosecuting attorney will always be sure to state the evidence expected to be derived from them as strongly as the case will admit of. It is true that certain aggravating incidents of actual search and seizure, such as forcible entry into a man's house and searching amongst his papers, are wanting, and to this extent the proceeding under the act of 1874 is a mitigation of that which was authorized by the former acts; but it accomplishes the substantial object of those acts in forcing from a party evidence against himself. It is our opinion, therefore, that a compulsory production of a man's private papers to establish a criminal charge against him, or to forfeit his property, is within the scope of the Fourth Amendment to the Constitution, in all cases in which a search and seizure would be; because it is a material ingredient, and effects the sole object and purpose of search and seizure.

The principal question, however, remains to be considered. Is a search and seizure, or, what is equivalent thereto, a compulsory production of a man's private papers, to be used in evidence against him in a proceeding to forfeit his property for alleged fraud against the revenue laws—is such a proceeding for such a purpose an "*unreasonable* search and seizure" within the meaning of the Fourth Amendment of the Constitution? or, is it a legitimate proceeding? It is contended by the counsel for the government, that it is a legitimate proceeding, sanctioned by long usage, and the authority of judicial decision. No doubt long usage, acquiesced in by the courts, goes a long way to prove that there is some plausible ground or reason for it in the law, or in the historical facts which have imposed a particular construction of the law favorable to such usage. . . . But we do not find any long usage, or any contemporary construction of the Constitution, which would justify any of the acts of Congress now under consideration. As before stated, the act of 1863 was the first act in this country, and, we might say, either in this country or in England, so far as we have been able to ascertain, which authorized the search and seizure of a man's private papers, or the compulsory production of them, for the purpose of using them in evidence against him in a criminal case, or in a proceeding to enforce the forfeiture of his property. Even the act under which the obnoxious writs of assistance were issued did not go as far as this, but only authorized the examination of ships and vessels, and persons found therein, for the purpose of finding goods prohibited to be imported or exported, or on which the duties were not paid, and to enter into and search any suspected vaults, cellars, or warehouses for such goods. The search for and seizure of stolen or forfeited goods, or goods liable to duties and concealed to avoid the payment thereof, are totally different things from a search for and seizure of a man's private books and papers for the purpose of obtaining information therein contained, or of using them as evidence against him. The two things differ toto coelo. In the one case, the government is entitled to the possession of the property; in the other it is not. The seizure of stolen goods is authorized by the common law; and the seizure of goods forfeited for a breach of the revenue laws, or concealed to avoid the duties payable on them, has been authorized by English statutes for at least two centuries past; and the like seizures have been authorized by our own revenue acts from the commencement of the government. The first statute passed by Congress to regulate the collection of duties, the act of July 31, 1789, 1 Stat. 29, 43, contains provisions to this effect. As this act was passed by the same Congress which proposed for adoption the original amendments to the Constitution, it is clear that the members of that body did not regard searches and seizures of this kind as "unreasonable," and they are not embraced within the prohibition of the amendment. So, also, the supervision authorized to be exercised by officers of the revenue over the manufacture or custody of excisable articles, and the entries thereof in books required by law to be kept for their inspection, are necessarily excepted out of the category of unreasonable searches and seizures. So, also, the laws which provide for the search and seizure of articles and things which it is unlawful for a person to have in his possession for the purpose of issue or disposition, such as counterfeit coin, lottery tickets, implements of gambling, &c., are not within this category. Many other things of this character might be enumerated. The entry upon premises, made by a sheriff or other officer of the law, for the purpose of seizing goods and chattels by virtue of a judicial writ, such as an attachment, a sequestration, or an execution, is not within the prohibition of the Fourth or Fifth Amendment, or any other clause of the Constitution; nor is the examination of a defendant under oath after an ineffectual execution, for the purpose of discovering secreted property or credits, to be applied to the payment of a judgment against him, obnoxious to those amendments.

But, when examined with care, it is manifest that there is a total unlikeness of these official acts and proceedings to that which is now under consideration. In the case of stolen goods, the owner from whom they were stolen is entitled to their possession; and in the case of excisable or dutiable articles, the government has an interest in them for the payment of the duties thereon, and until such duties are paid has a right to keep them under observation, or to pursue and drag them from concealment; and in the case of goods seized on attachment or execution, the creditor is entitled to their seizure in satisfaction of his debt; and the examination of a defendant under oath to obtain a discovery of concealed property or credits is a proceeding merely civil to effect the ends of justice, and is no more than what the court of chancery would direct on a bill for discovery. Whereas, by the proceeding now under consideration, the court attempts to extort from the party his private books and papers to make him liable for a penalty or to forfeit his property.

In order to ascertain the nature of the proceedings intended by the Fourth Amendment to the Constitution under the terms "unreasonable searches and seizures," it is only necessary to recall the contemporary or then recent history of the controversies on the subject, both in this country and in England. The practice had obtained in the colonies of issuing writs of assistance to the revenue officers, empowering them, in their discretion, to search suspected places for smuggled goods, which James Otis pronounced "the worst instrument of arbitrary power, the most destructive of English liberty, and the fundamental principles of law, that ever was found in an English law book;" since they placed "liberty of every man in the hands of every petty officer."* This was in February, 1761, in Boston, and the famous debate in which it occurred was perhaps the most prominent event which inaugurated the resistance of the colonies to the oppressions of the mother country. "Then and there," said John Adams, "then and there was the first scene of the first act of opposition to the arbitrary claims of Great Britain. Then and there the child Independence was born."

These things, and the events which took place in England immediately following the argument about writs of assistance in Boston, were fresh in the memories of those who achieved our independence and established our form of government. . . . Prominent and principal among these was the practice of issuing general warrants by the Secretary of State, for searching private houses for the discovery and seizure of books and papers that might be used to convict their owner of the charge of libel. . . . The case . . . which will always be celebrated as being the occasion of Lord Camden's memorable discussion of the subject, was that of Entick v. Carrington and Three Other King's Messengers, reported at length in 19 Howell's State Trials, 1029.¹ The action was trespass for

---

*Note by the Court.—Cooley's Constitutional Limitations, 301-303, (5th ed. 368, 369). A very full and interesting account of this discussion will be found in the works of John Adams, vol. 2, Appendix A, pp. 523-525; vol. 10, pp. 183, 233, 244, 256, &c., and in Quincy's Reports, pp. 469-482: and see Paxton's Case, do. 51-57, which was argued in November of the same year (1761). An elaborate history of the writs of assistance is given in the Appendix to Quincy's Reports, above referred to, written by Horace Gray, Jr., Esq., now a member of this court.

1. For a discussion of *Entick* and its background, see Galloway, The Intruding Eye:

entering the plaintiff's dwelling-house in November, 1762, and breaking open his desks, boxes, &c., and searching and examining his papers. The jury rendered a special verdict, and the case was twice solemnly argued at the bar. Lord Camden pronounced the judgment of the court in Michaelmas Term, 1765, and the law as expounded by him has been regarded as settled from that time to this, and his great judgment on that occasion is considered as one of the landmarks of English liberty. It was welcomed and applauded by the lovers of liberty in the colonies as well as in the mother country. It is regarded as one of the permanent monuments of the British Constitution, and is quoted as such by the English authorities on that subject down to the present time.

As every American statesmen, during our revolutionary and formative period as a nation, was undoubtedly familiar with this monument of English freedom, and considered it as the true and ultimate expression of constitutional law, it may be confidently asserted that its propositions were in the minds of those who framed the Fourth Amendment to the Constitution, and were considered as sufficiently explanatory of what was meant by unreasonable searches and seizures. We think, therefore, it is pertinent to the present subject of discussion to quote somewhat largely from this celebrated judgment.

After describing the power claimed by the Secretary of State for issuing general search warrants, and the manner in which they were executed, Lord Camden says:

> Such is the power, and, therefore, one would naturally expect that the law to warrant it should be clear in proportion as the power is exorbitant. If it is law, it will be found in our books; if it is not to be found there, it is not law.
>
> The great end for which men entered into society was to secure their property. That right is preserved sacred and incommunicable in all instances where it has not been taken away or abridged by some public law for the good of the whole. The cases where this right of property is set aside by positive law are various. Distresses, executions, forfeitures, taxes, &c., are all of this description, wherein every man by common consent gives up that right for the sake of justice and the general good. By the laws of England, every invasion of private property, be it ever so minute, is a trespass. No man can set his foot upon my ground without my license, but he is liable to an action though the damage be nothing; which is proved by every declaration in trespass where the defendant is called upon to answer for bruising the grass and even treading upon the soil. If he admits the fact, he is bound to show, by way of justification, that some positive law has justified or excused him. The justification is submitted to the

A Status Report on the Constitutional Ban Against Paper Searches, 25 Howard L.J. 367 (1982). —Eds.

judges, who are to look into the books, and see if such a justification can be maintained by the text of the statute law, or by the principles of the common law. If no such excuse can be found or produced, the silence of the books is an authority, against the defendant, and the plaintiff must have judgment. According to this reasoning, it is now incumbent upon the defendants to show the law by which this seizure is warranted. If that cannot be done, it is a trespass.

Papers are the owner's goods and chattels; they are his dearest property; and are so far from enduring a seizure, that they will hardly bear an inspection; and though the eye cannot by the laws of England be guilty of a trespass, yet where private papers are removed and carried away the secret nature of those goods will be an aggravation of the trespass, and demand more considerable damages in that respect. Where is the written law that gives any magistrate such a power? I can safely answer, there is none; and, therefore, it is too much for us, without such authority, to pronounce a practice legal which would be subversive of all the comforts of society.

But though it cannot be maintained by any direct law, yet it bears a resemblance, as was urged, to the known case of search and seizure for stolen goods. I answer that the difference is apparent. In the one, I am permitted to seize my own goods, which are placed in the hands of a public officer, till the felon's conviction shall entitle me to restitution. In the other, the party's own property is seized before and without conviction, and he has no power to reclaim his goods, even after his innocence is declared by acquittal. . . .

Then, after showing that these general warrants for search and seizure of papers originated with the Star Chamber, and never had any advocates in Westminster Hall except Chief Justice Scroggs and his associates, Lord Camden proceeds to add:

Lastly, it is urged as an argument of utility, that such a search is a means of detecting offenders by discovering evidence. I wish some cases had been shown, where the law forceth evidence out of the owner's custody by process. There is no process against papers in civil causes. It has been often tried, but never prevailed. Nay, where the adversary has by force or fraud got possession of your own proper evidence, there is no way to get it back but by action. In the criminal law such a proceeding was never heard of; and yet there are some crimes, such, for instance, as murder, rape, robbery, and house-breaking, to say nothing of forgery and perjury, that are more atrocious than libelling. But our law has provided no paper-search in these cases to help forward the conviction. Whether this proceedeth from the gentleness of the law towards criminals, or from a consideration that such a power would be more pernicious to the innocent than useful to the public, I will not say. It is very certain that the law obligeth no man to accuse himself; because the necessary means of compelling self-accusation, falling upon the innocent as well as the guilty, would be both cruel and unjust; and it would seem, that search for evidence is disallowed upon the same principle. Then, too, the innocent would be confounded with the guilty.

After a few further observations, his Lordship concluded thus: "I have now taken notice of everything that has been urged upon the present point; and upon the whole we are all of opinion, that the warrant to seize and carry away the party's papers in the case of a seditious libel, is illegal and void."*

The principles laid down in this opinion affect the very essence of constitutional liberty and security. They reach farther than the concrete form of the case then before the court, with its adventitious circumstances; they apply to all invasions on the part of the government and its employees of the sanctity of a man's home and the privacies of life. It is not the breaking of his doors, and the rummaging of his drawers, that constitutes the essence of the offence; but it is the invasion of his indefeasible right of personal security, personal liberty and private property, where that right has never been forfeited by his conviction of some public offence, — it is the invasion of this sacred right which underlies and constitutes the essence of Lord Camden's judgment. Breaking into a house and opening boxes and drawers are circumstances of aggravation; but any forcible and compulsory extortion of a man's own testimony or of his private papers to be used as evidence to convict him of crime or to forfeit his goods, is within the condemnation of that judgment. In this regard the Fourth and Fifth Amendments run almost into each other.

Can we doubt that when the Fourth and Fifth Amendments to the Constitution of the United States were penned and adopted, the language of Lord Camden was relied on as expressing the true doctrine on the subject of searches and seizures, and as furnishing the true criteria of the reasonable and "unreasonable" character of such seizures? Could the men who proposed those amendments, in the light of Lord Camden's opinion, have put their hands to a law like those of March 3, 1863, and March 2, 1867, before recited? If they could not, would they have approved the 5th section of the act of June 22, 1874, which was adopted as a substitute for the previous laws? It seems to us that the question cannot admit of a doubt. They never would have approved of them. The struggles against arbitrary power in which they had been engaged for more than twenty years, would have been too deeply engraved in their memories

---

*Note by the Court.—See further as to searches and seizures, Story on the Constitution, §§1901, 1902, and notes; Cooley's Constitutional Limitations, 299, (5th ed. 365); Sedgwick on Stat. and Const. Law, 2d Ed. 498; Wharton Com. on Amer. Law, §560; Robinson v. Richardson, 13 Gray, 454.

to have allowed them to approve of such insidious disguises of the old grievance which they had so deeply abhorred. . . .

Reverting then to the peculiar phraseology of this act, and to the information in the present case, which is founded on it, we have to deal with an act which expressly excludes criminal proceedings from its operation (though embracing civil suits for penalties and forfeitures), and with an information not technically a criminal proceeding, and neither, therefore, within the literal terms of the Fifth Amendment to the Constitution any more than it is within the literal terms of the Fourth. Does this relieve the proceedings or the law from being obnoxious to the prohibitions of either? We think not; we think they are within the spirit of both.

We have already noticed the intimate relation between the two amendments. They throw great light on each other. For the "unreasonable searches and seizures" condemned in the Fourth Amendment are almost always made for the purpose of compelling a man to give evidence against himself, which in criminal cases is condemned in the Fifth Amendment; and compelling a man "in a criminal case to be a witness against himself," which is condemned in the Fifth Amendment, throws light on the question as to what is an "unreasonable search and seizure" within the meaning of the Fourth Amendment. And we have been unable to perceive that the seizure of a man's private books and papers to be used in evidence against him is substantially different from compelling him to be a witness against himself. We think it is within the clear intent and meaning of those terms. We are also clearly of opinion that proceedings instituted for the purpose of declaring the forfeiture of a man's property by reason of offences committed by him, though they may be civil in form, are in their nature criminal. In this very case, the ground of forfeiture as declared in the 12th section of the act of 1874, on which the information is based, consists of certain acts of fraud committed against the public revenue in relation to imported merchandise, which are made criminal by the statute; and it is declared, that the offender shall be fined not exceeding $5000 nor less than $50, or be imprisoned not exceeding two years, or both; and in addition to such fine such merchandise shall be forfeited. These are the penalties affixed to the criminal acts; the forfeiture sought by this suit being one of them. If an indictment had been presented against the claimants, upon conviction the forfeiture of the goods could have been included in the judgment. If the government prosecutor elects to waive an indictment, and to file a civil information against the claimants—that is, civil in form—can he by this device take from the proceeding its criminal aspect and deprive the claimants of their immunities as citizens, and extort from them a production of their private papers, or, as an alternative, a confession of

guilt? This cannot be. The information, though technically a civil proceeding, is in substance and effect a criminal one. . . . As, therefore,
suits for penalties and forfeitures incurred by the commission of offences
against the law, are of this quasi-criminal nature, we think that they are
within the reason of criminal proceedings for all the purposes of the
Fourth Amendment of the Constitution, and of that portion of the Fifth
Amendment which declares that no person shall be compelled in any
criminal case to be a witness against himself; and we are further of opinion
that a compulsory production of the private books and papers of the owner
of goods sought to be forfeited in such a suit is compelling him to be a
witness against himself, within the meaning of the Fifth Amendment to
the Constitution, and is the equivalent of a search and seizure—and an
unreasonable search and seizure—within the meaning of the Fourth
Amendment. Though the proceeding in question is divested of many of
the aggravating incidents of actual search and seizure, yet, as before said,
it contains their substance and essence, and effects their substantial purpose. It may be that it is the obnoxious thing in its mildest and least
repulsive form; but illegitimate and unconstitutional practices get their
first footing in that way, namely, by silent approaches and slight deviations
from legal modes of procedure. This can only be obviated by adhering
to the rule that constitutional provisions for the security of person and
property should be liberally construed. A close and literal construction
deprives them of half their efficacy, and leads to gradual depreciation of
the right, as if it consisted more in sound than in substance. It is the
duty of courts to be watchful for the constitutional rights of the citizen,
and against any stealthy encroachments thereon. Their motto should be
obsta principiis. We have no doubt that the legislative body is actuated
by the same motives; but the vast accumulation of public business brought
before it sometimes prevents it on a first presentation, from noticing
objections which become developed by time and the practical application
of the objectionable law. . . .

   We think that the notice to produce the invoice in this case, the
order by virtue of which it was issued, and the law which authorized
the order, were unconstitutional and void, and that the inspection by the
district attorney of said invoice, when produced in obedience to said
notice, and its admission in evidence by the court, were erroneous and
unconstitutional proceedings. We are of opinion, therefore, that

   The judgment of the Circuit Court should be reversed, and the
cause remanded, with directions to award a new trial.

   MR. JUSTICE MILLER, with whom was THE CHIEF JUSTICE, concurring.

   I concur in the judgment of the court, reversing that of the Circuit

Court, and in so much of the opinion of this court as holds the 5th section of the act of 1874 void as applicable to the present case.

I am of opinion that this is a criminal case within the meaning of that clause of the Fifth Amendment to the Constitution of the United States which declares that no person "shall be compelled in any criminal case to be a witness against himself."

And I am quite satisfied that the effect of the act of Congress is to compel the party on whom the order of the court is served to be a witness against himself. The order of the court under the statute is in effect a subpoena duces tecum, and, though the penalty for the witness's failure to appear in court with the criminating papers is not fine and imprisonment, it is one which may be made more severe, namely, to have charges against him of a criminal nature, taken for confessed, and made the foundation of the judgment of the court. That this is within the protection which the Constitution intended against compelling a person to be a witness against himself, is, I think, quite clear.

But this being so, there is no reason why this court should assume that the action of the court below, in requiring a party to produce certain papers as evidence on the trial, authorizes an unreasonable search or seizure of the house, papers, or effects of that party.

There is in fact no search and no seizure authorized by the statute. No order can be made by the court under it which requires or permits anything more than service of notice on a party to the suit. . . .

Nothing in the nature of a search is here hinted at. Nor is there any seizure, because the party is not required at any time to part with the custody of the papers. They are to be produced in court, and, when produced, the United States attorney is permitted, under the direction of the court, to make examination in presence of the claimant, and may offer in evidence such entries in the books, invoices, or papers as relate to the issue. The act is careful to say that "the owner of said books and papers, his agent or attorney, shall have, subject to the order of the court, the custody of them, except pending their examination in court as aforesaid." . . .

The things . . . forbidden [by the Fourth Amendment] are two—search and seizure. And not all searches nor all seizures are forbidden, but only those that are unreasonable. Reasonable searches, therefore, may be allowed, and if the thing sought be found, it may be seized.

But what search does this statute authorize? If the mere service of a notice to produce a paper to be used as evidence, which the party can obey or not as he chooses is a search, then a change has taken place in the meaning of words, which has not come within my reading, and which I think was unknown at the time the Constitution was made. The searches meant by the Constitution were such as led to seizure when the search was successful. But the statute in this case uses language carefully framed to forbid any seizure under it, as I have already pointed out.

While the framers of the Constitution had their attention drawn, no doubt, to the abuses of this power of searching private houses and seizing private papers, as practiced in England, it is obvious that they only intended to restrain the abuse, while they did not abolish the power. Hence it is only *unreasonable* searches and seizures that are forbidden, and the means of securing this protection was by abolishing searches under warrants, which were called general warrants, because they authorized searches in any place, for any thing.

This was forbidden, while searches founded on affidavits, and made under warrants which described the thing to be searched for, the person and place to be searched, are still permitted.

I cannot conceive how a statute aptly framed to require the production of evidence in a suit by mere service of notice on the party, who has that evidence in his possession, can be held to authorize an unreasonable search or seizure, when no seizure is authorized or permitted by the statute.

I am requested to say that THE CHIEF JUSTICE concurs in this opinion.

NOTES AND QUESTIONS

1. To what extent does the decision in *Boyd* rest on concerns of privacy, desire to protect a person's papers, or an expansive view of the incriminating pressures that are inappropriate for a government to bring to bear on an individual? To what extent do these concerns interrelate? Does it matter which concern *Boyd* primarily is based on? Can you tell from the opinions in *Boyd* how these questions might be answered?

Thirty-five years after *Boyd*, the Court in Gouled v. United States, 255 U.S. 298 (1921), returned to these issues. *Gouled* applied *Boyd* to a search and seizure pursuant to a warrant that produced documents of the defendant, later used at trial over objection. In finding the fourth amendment violated by the search and seizure, and the use of the evidence at trial in violation of the fifth, the Court said:

> Although search warrants have thus been used in many cases ever since the adoption of the Constitution, and although their use has been extended from time to time to meet new cases within the old rules, nevertheless it is clear that, at common law and as the result of . . . *Boyd* . . . they may not be used as a means of gaining access to a man's house or office and papers solely for the purpose of making search to secure evidence to

be used against him in a criminal or penal proceeding, but that they may be resorted to only when a primary right to such search and seizure may be found in the interest which the public or the complainant may have in the property to be seized, or in the right to the possession of it, or when a valid exercise of the police power renders possession of the property by the accused unlawful and provides that it may be taken. *Boyd Case*, pp. 623, 624.

There is no special sanctity in papers, as distinguished from other forms of property, to render them immune from search and seizure, if only they fall within the scope of the principles of the cases in which other property may be seized, and if they be adequately described in the affidavit and warrant. . . .

Is the Court's last sentence about the lack of "special sanctity in papers" significant? Consider the following passage:

> This passing remark, which was not without support in *Boyd*, reflected the common-sense judgment that, if the government's appropriation of an individual's documents as mere evidence is wrongful because it makes him "the unwilling source" of incrimination evidence, the same must be true of the seizure of any of his other possessions. Its effect, however, was to transform the paper-search rule of *Boyd* into a broader rule under which the search for or seizure of any item as "mere evidence" was proscribed. In this roundabout way, the fourth amendment in fact became the protector of privacy. [Note, page 423 supra, at 190.]

2. What is the significance of property for the "intimate relation-ship" of the fourth and fifth amendments that is so important to *Boyd*? Consider the following passage:

> Justice Bradley offered no positive definition of "the indefeasible right of personal security, personal liberty and private property" that he considered to be at the core of the intimate relation between the two amendments. It is clear, however, that confidentiality was not the interest that the Court sought to protect. Whether the Boyds had kept the invoice a secret to the world or whether they had made its contents a matter of public knowledge was irrelevant; either way, the government's action was illegal. But, perhaps because the opinion was couched in such sweeping language, the positive nature of the fundamental right was unclear.
>
> Later courts[20] interpreted *Boyd* as identifying the privilege against self-

20. See, e.g., Olmstead v. United States, 277 U.S. 438 (1928), . . . Brown v. Walker, 161 U.S. 591 (1896).

In holding that an individual who has been granted immunity may be compelled to testify against himself, the majority in *Brown* must have concluded that *Boyd* had been solely concerned with protecting the individual from compelled self-incrimination. The four dissenting justices, on the other hand, cited *Boyd* in support of the proposition that, because the Constitution grants the individual an *absolute* right to remain silent, testimony compelled under a grant of immunity is subject to constitutional attack.

incrimination as the concept at the heart of the intimate relation. Viewing an individual's papers as an extension of his "self," adherents of this view treated the unreasonable search clause of the fourth amendment as an extension of the fifth amendment. On this theory, the amendments, taken together, define the ultimate scope of each person's right not to be compelled to serve as the source of evidence against himself.

But this guarantee that a person's papers are free from official inspection was absolute only in theory. The *Boyd* majority had to reconcile its doctrine with traditional practices. Historically, the government had been allowed to require recordkeeping with regard to certain goods, such as those subject to duties, in which it had some property interest, and those records had always been deemed seizable. The Court in *Boyd* incorporated this tradition into its constitutional theory by proclaiming the seizure of documents to be inherently unconstitutional only when they were taken as mere evidence and by granting that, on the basis of its property interest in such goods, the government had a superior right to the corresponding records. Because any such record did not truly belong to the accused, it could not be viewed as an extension of his "self"; thus, its use against him did not constitute a compelled self-incrimination. This accommodation to tradition did not seem to compromise the general paper-search rule significantly. The rule attached to all documents in an individual's possession to which he had a superior claim of right. Consequently, although it was not viewed as having been designed to protect property rights per se, the scope of the privilege embodied in the unreasonable search clause came to be defined in terms of the law of property. In that respect, the doctrine contained the seeds of its own destruction. [Note, page 423 supra, at 188-189.]

3. The initial stage of the assault on *Boyd* is accurately summarized by Note, page 423 supra, at 191-195:

Over the years, the Court grew increasingly dissatisfied with interpreting the unreasonable search clause in terms of property interests. This dissatisfaction had several possible sources. Traditional views of the sanctity of property were quickly giving way to the demand for increasing governmental control over its ownership, use, and disposition. The view that a fundamental right to privacy exists, espoused in the famous article by Brandeis and Warren,[35] was gaining acceptance. This concept was defined in terms of a basic right "to be left alone,"[36] rather than in terms of the technicalities of English property law. Finally, perhaps the Court simply was not content with the results that would have been entailed by strict

35. Warren & Brandeis, The Right to Privacy, 4 Harv. L. Rev. 193 (1890).
36. Olmstead v. United States, 277 U.S. 438, 478 (1928) (Brandeis, J., dissenting).

adherence to the mere evidence rule as it had been propounded in Boyd and expanded by *Gouled*.

Where strict adherence would not interfere with governmental regulation of economic activity, the rule was duly applied. . . .

Where the mere evidence rule interfered with governmental regulation of economic activity, however, it was modified or "refined." In a group of cases involving subpoenas directed to business organizations, the Court refused to include such associations within the class of entities protected by the fifth amendment privilege. In Hale v. Henkel,[38] the Court held that the privilege does not apply to corporations. Thus, an agent cannot refuse to answer questions or to comply with a subpoena duces tecum[39] on the ground that the corporation might be incriminated. Moreover, because the documents are in the custody of and are being subpoenaed from the corporate entity rather than from the agent, the agent cannot refuse to comply on the ground that compliance might incriminate him.[40]

. . . Of the decisions that considered Boyd during this period of retreat, perhaps Shapiro v. United States[43] had the greatest impact on the individual's ability to shield the details of his life from the government. In that case the Court enunciated the "required records" doctrine, under which no person can invoke the fourth or fifth amendment to justify refusal to comply with a facially valid subpoena compelling the production of records that the person is legally required to keep. This decision represented a complete rejection of the fundamental limitations that the Court in Boyd had placed on the government's power to compel the production of records kept pursuant to its command. The Court in effect recognized the power of the legislature to acquire any and all information it wants from an individual.[44]

The Court also narrowed the scope of the protection provided by the

38. 201 U.S. 43 (1906).
39. The order involved in the Boyd case differed from a subpoena duces tecum only in the penalty imposed for noncompliance. Hale held that the paper-search rule enunciated in Boyd applied as well to subpoenas duces tecum.
40. In Wilson v. United States, 221 U.S. 361 (1911), the writ was directed to the corporation. In Dreier v. United States, 221 U.S. 394 (1911), it was directed to the agent. In both cases the Court held that the self-incrimination clause did not allow the agent to refuse to comply with the subpoena. It was later held, however, that the custodian of an organization's "missing" documents can refuse to answer questions about their whereabouts when to do so would incriminate him. Curcio v. United States, 354 U.S. 118, 125 (1957).
43. 335 U.S. 1 (1948).
44. Congress eventually exercised this authority to require the keeping of records to aid its fight against crime, as well as its regulation of economic activity. On the basis of this "required records" doctrine, the Court has sanctioned congressional enactments that have intruded substantially upon personal privacy. See United States v. Miller, 425 U.S. 435, 447 (1976) (Brennan, J., dissenting); California Bankers Assn. v. Shultz, 416 U.S. 21, 93 (1974) (Marshall, J., dissenting). But see Grosso v. United States, 390 U.S. 62 (1968); Marchetti v. United States, 390 U.S. 39 (1968).

mere evidence rule in Marron v. United States.[45] In that case the Court
distinguished between property that is merely evidence of a crime and
property used in the commission of a crime.[46] Whereas *Gouled* had allowed
the seizure of an instrumentality of a crime only insofar as it was contraband, *Marron* allowed the seizure of *any* such instrumentality. Because
even papers can be characterized as instrumentalities of crime,[47] *Marron*
represented a serious threat to the zone of protection established by *Boyd*
and broadened by *Gouled*.[48] . . .

To the extent that the decisions following *Boyd* and *Gouled* reduced
the obstacles to governmental seizure of an individual's property, they also
narrowed his effective zone of privacy. A conflict arose within the Court
over this development. Although the dispute concerned the fundamental
nature of the rights protected by the fourth and fifth amendments, it took
the form of a debate over the "real" meaning of *Boyd*. One the one hand,
proponents of the traditional interpretation of *Boyd* believed that the core
of the "intimate relation" between the amendments was the privilege against
self-incrimination. Since the key question to these Justices was whether
the evidence belonged to the defendant, they found the government's
increasing power to intrude into the life of the individual to be constitutionally permissible so long as the exercise of that power was consistent
with the rules of property law. On the other hand, advocates of a revisionist
interpretation of *Boyd* argued that the true concern of the framers of the
fourth and fifth amendments was the protection of a fundamental right of
privacy. . . .

This revisionist interpretation of the "intimate relation" first appeared
as a fully articulated doctrine in Justice Brandeis' dissent in Olmstead v.
United States.[52] That case concerned the applicability of the fourth amendment to warrantless wiretapping by government agents. The majority,
which was as eager to facilitate the government's efforts to combat crime
as it had been a year earlier in *Marron*, analyzed the issue in terms of the
privilege against self-incrimination,[53] whose parameters were determined
by property law. Finding that speech is not property within the context of
the fourth amendment, they concluded that wiretapping infringed upon
an interest protected by the fourth amendment, and thereby the fifth, only
if it involved trespassing upon the accused's tangible property. Justice

45. 275 U.S. 192 (1927).
46. The Court in *Marron* did not attempt to explain its holding in terms of a superior
title theory. A possible rationale for the decision is that, by using an object to commit a
crime, the criminal has forfeited it to the state.
47. In *Marron*, the Court treated records maintained in an establishment where
liquor was sold as instrumentalities. *Gouled* had also recognized that papers might be
used as instrumentalities of crime. See 255 U.S. at 309.
48. For a discussion of the ingenuity of prosecutors in characterizing different types
of property as instrumentalities, see Comment, The Search and Seizure of Private Papers:
Fourth and Fifth Amendment Considerations, 6 Loy. L.A. L. Rev. 274, 282-83 (1973).
52. 277 U.S. 438 (1928).
53. See 277 U.S. at 462-63.

Brandeis' dissent, however, argued that the majority opinion was based on the false premise that the fourth amendment had been designed either to perpetuate antiquated notions of English property law or to bolster the privilege against self-incrimination.[54] In Justice Brandeis' view, at the heart of *Entick, Boyd,* and *Gouled* was the premise that the amendment had been designed to protect a fundamental "right to be left alone":[55] "Every unjustifiable intrusion by the Government upon the private life of the individual, whatever the means employed, must be deemed a violation of the Fourth Amendment. And the use, as evidence in a criminal proceeding, of facts ascertained by such intrusion must be deemed a violation of the Fifth."[56] Although Justice Brandeis had lost the battle in *Olmstead,* by the second half of the twentieth century he had won the war. The theory that his dissenting opinion espoused eventually became the official position of the Court.[57] Moreover, during this period it became clear that the mere evidence rule had outlived its usefulness. The criteria for determining whether an object was immune from seizure had become so structured that the rule no longer served as a bulwark for the privilege against self-incrimination. Furthermore, the rule was at odds with public opinion, as it frustrated the popular demand for law and order that was increasing along with the crime rate. Although Justice Brandeis had identified the right of privacy as the basic interest to be protected, he had indicated neither the manner in which this protection would be ensured nor the extent to which the law derived from *Boyd* would have to be repudiated. The Court undertook this task in three cases decided three decades after *Olmstead:* Schmerber v. California,[58] Warden v. Hayden,[59] and [Katz v. United States][60] . . .

SCHMERBER v. CALIFORNIA

Certiorari to the Appellate Department of the Superior Court of California, County of Los Angeles
384 U.S. 757 (1966)

MR. JUSTICE BRENNAN delivered the opinion of the Court.
Petitioner was convicted in Los Angeles Municipal Court of the

---

54. Justice Brandeis advocated a privacy rationale for the fifth amendment, also. See text at note 56 infra.
55. 277 U.S. at 478.
56. 277 U.S. at 478-79.
57. Regarding the fourth amendment, see, e.g., Wolf v. Colorado, 338 U.S. 25, 27 (1949) ("The security of one's privacy against arbitrary intrusion by the police . . . is at the core of the Fourth Amendment."). Regarding the fifth amendment, see, e.g., Griswold v. Connecticut, 381 U.S. 479, 484 (1965) ("The Fifth Amendment in its Self-Incrimination Clause enables the citizen to create a zone of privacy which government may not force him to surrender to his detriment.").
58. 384 U.S. 757 (1966).
59. 387 U.S. 294 (1967).
60. [Katz is reproduced and considered in detail in Chapter 7.]

criminal offense of driving an automobile while under the influence of intoxicating liquor. He had been arrested at a hospital while receiving treatment for injuries suffered in an accident involving the automobile that he had apparently been driving. At the direction of a police officer, a blood sample was then withdrawn from petitioner's body by a physician at the hospital. The chemical analysis of this sample revealed a percent by weight of alcohol in his blood at the time of the offense which indicated intoxication, and the report of this analysis was admitted in evidence at the trial. Petitioner objected to receipt of this evidence of the analysis on the ground that the blood had been drawn despite his refusal, on the advice of his counsel, to consent to the test. He contended that in that circumstance the withdrawal of the blood and the admission of the analysis in evidence denied him due process of law under the Fourteenth Amendment, as well as specific guarantees of the Bill of Rights secured against the States by that Amendment: his privilege against self-incrimination under the Fifth Amendment; his right to counsel under the Sixth Amendment; and his right not to be subjected to unreasonable searches and seizures in violation of the Fourth Amendment. The Appellate Department of the California Superior Court rejected these contentions and affirmed the conviction. . . .

II. The Privilege Against Self-Incrimination Claim

. . . We . . . must now decide whether the withdrawal of the blood and admission in evidence of the analysis involved in this case violated petitioner's privilege. We hold that the privilege protects an accused only from being compelled to testify against himself, or otherwise provide the State with evidence of a testimonial or communicative nature,[5] and that the withdrawal of blood and use of the analysis in question in this case did not involve compulsion to these ends.

It could not be denied that in requiring petitioner to submit to the withdrawal and chemical analysis of his blood the State compelled him to submit to an attempt to discover evidence that might be used to

5. A dissent suggests that the report of the blood test was "testimonial" or "communicative," because the test was performed in order to obtain the testimony of others, communicating to the jury facts about petitioner's condition. Of course, all evidence received in court is "testimonial" or "communicative" if these words are thus used. But the Fifth Amendment relates only to acts on the part of the person to whom the privilege applies, and we use these words subject to the same limitations. A nod or head-shake is as much a "testimonial" or "communicative" act in this sense as are spoken words. But the terms as we use them do not apply to evidence of acts noncommunicative in nature as to the person asserting the privilege, even though, as here, such acts are compelled to obtain the testimony of others.

prosecute him for a criminal offense. He submitted only after the police officer rejected his objection and directed the physician to proceed. The officer's direction to the physician to administer the test over petitioner's objection constituted compulsion for the purposes of the privilege. The critical question, then, is whether petitioner was thus compelled "to be a witness against himself."[6]

If the scope of the privilege coincided with the complex of values it helps to protect, we might be obliged to conclude that the privilege was violated. In Miranda v. Arizona, [discussed in Chapter 9 infra] the Court said of the interests protected by the privilege:

> All these policies point to one overriding thought: the constitutional foundation underlying the privilege is the respect a government—state or federal—must accord to the dignity and integrity of its citizens. To maintain a "fair state-individual balance," to require the government "to shoulder the entire load," . . . to respect the inviolabilty of the human personality, our accusatory system of criminal justice demands that the government seeking to punish an individual produce the evidence against him by its own independent labors, rather than by the cruel, simple expedient of compelling it from his own mouth.

The withdrawal of blood necessarily involves puncturing the skin for extraction, and the percent by weight of alcohol in that blood, as established by chemical analysis, is evidence of criminal guilt. Compelled submission fails on one view to respect the "inviolability of the human personality." Moreover, since it enables the State to rely on evidence forced from the accused, the compulsion violates at least one meaning of the requirement that the State procure the evidence against an accused "by its own independent labors."

As the passage in *Miranda* implicitly recognizes, however, the privilege has never been given the full scope which the values it helps to protect suggest. History and a long line of authorities in lower courts have consistently limited its protection to situations in which the State seeks to submerge those values by obtaining the evidence against an accused through "the cruel, simple expedient of compelling it from his own

6. Many state constitutions, including those of most of the original Colonies, phrase the privilege in terms of compelling a person to give "evidence" against himself. But our decision cannot turn on the Fifth Amendment's use of the word "witness." "[A]s the manifest purpose of the constitutional provisions, both of the States and of the United States, is to prohibit the compelling of testimony of a self-incriminating kind from a party or a witness, the liberal construction which must be placed upon constitutional provisions for the protection of personal rights would seem to require that the constitutional guaranties, however differently worded, should have as far as possible the same interpretation. . . ." Counselman v. Hitchcock, 142 U.S. 547, 584-585. 8 Wigmore, Evidence §2252 (McNaughton rev. 1961).

mouth. . . . In sum, the privilege is fulfilled only when the person is guaranteed the right 'to remain silent unless he chooses to speak in the unfettered exercise of his own will.' " Ibid. The leading case in this Court is Holt v. United States. There the question was whether evidence was admissible that the accused, prior to trial and over his protest, put on a blouse that fitted him. It was contended that compelling the accused to submit to the demand that he model the blouse violated the privilege. Mr. Justice Holmes, speaking for the Court, rejected the argument as "based upon an extravagant extension of the Fifth Amendment," and went on to say:

> [T]he prohibition of compelling a man in a criminal court to be witness against himself is a prohibition of the use of physical or moral compulsion to extort communications from him, not an exclusion of his body as evidence when it may be material. The objection in principle would forbid a jury to look at a prisoner and compare his features with a photograph in proof.

It is clear that the protection of the privilege reaches an accused's communications, whatever form they might take, and the compulsion of responses which are also communications, for example, compliance with a subpoena to produce one's papers. Boyd v. United States, 116 U.S. 616. On the other hand, both federal and state courts have usually held that it offers no protection against compulsion to submit to finger-printing, photographing, or measurements, to write or speak for identi-fication, to appear in court, to stand, to assume a stance, to walk, or to make a particular gesture. The distinction which has emerged, often expressed in different ways, is that the privilege is a bar against compelling "communications" or "testimony," but that compulsion which makes a suspect or accused the source of "real or physical evidence" does not violate it.

Although we agree that this distinction is a helpful framework for analysis, we are not to be understood to agree with past applications in all instances. There will be many cases in which such a distinction is not readily drawn. Some tests seemingly directed to obtain "physical evidence," for example, lie detector tests measuring changes in body function during interrogation, may actually be directed to eliciting re-sponses which are essentially testimonial. To compel a person to submit to testing in which an effort will be made to determine his guilt or innocence on the basis of physiological responses, whether willed or not, is to evoke the spirit and history of the Fifth Amendment. Such situations call to mind the principle that the protection of the privilege "is as broad as the mischief against which it seeks to guard."

In the present case, however, no such problem of application is presented. Not even a shadow of testimonial compulsion upon or enforced communication by the accused was involved either in the extraction or in the chemical analysis. Petitioner's testimonial capacities were in no way implicated; indeed, his participation, except as a donor, was irrelevant to the results of the test, which depend on chemical analysis and on that alone.[9] Since the blood test evidence, although an incriminating product of compulsion, was neither petitioner's testimony nor evidence relating to some communicative act or writing by the petitioner, it was not inadmissible on privilege grounds.

III. THE RIGHT TO COUNSEL CLAIM

This conclusion also answers petitioner's claim that, in compelling him to submit to the test in face of the fact that his objection was made on the advice of counsel, he was denied his Sixth Amendment right to the assistance of counsel. Since petitioner was not entitled to assert the privilege, he has no greater right because counsel erroneously advised him that he could assert it. His claim is strictly limited to the failure of the police to respect his wish, reinforced by counsel's advice, to be left inviolate. No issue of counsel's ability to assist petitioner in respect of any rights he did possess is presented. The limited claim thus made must be rejected.

IV. THE SEARCH AND SEIZURE CLAIM . . .

The overriding function of the Fourth Amendment is to protect personal privacy and dignity against unwarranted intrusion by the State. . . .

The values protected by the Fourth Amendment thus substantially overlap those the Fifth Amendment helps to protect. History and precedent have required that we today reject the claim that the Self-Incrim-

9. This conclusion would not necessarily govern had the State tried to show that the accused had incriminated himself when told that he would have to be tested. Such incriminating evidence may be an unavoidable by-product of the compulsion to take the test, especially for an individual who fears the extraction or opposes it on religious grounds. If it wishes to compel persons to submit to such attempts to discover evidence, the State may have to forgo the advantage of any *testimonial* products of administering the test— products which would fall within the privilege. Indeed, there may be circumstances in which the pain, danger, or severity of an operation would almost inevitably cause a person to prefer confession to undergoing the "search," and nothing we say today should be taken as establishing the permissibility of compulsion in that case. But no such situation is presented in this case. . . .

ination Clause of the Fifth Amendment requires the human body in all circumstances to be held inviolate against state expeditions seeking evidence of crime. But if compulsory administration of a blood test does not implicate the Fifth Amendment, it plainly involves the broadly conceived reach of a search and seizure under the Fourth Amendment. That Amendment expressly provides that "[t]he right of the people to be secure in their *persons*, houses, papers, and effects, against unreasonable searches and seizures, shall not be violated. . . ." (Emphasis added.) It could not reasonably be argued, and indeed respondent does not argue, that the administration of the blood test in this case was free of the constraints of the Fourth Amendment. Such testing procedures plainly constitute searches of "persons," within the meaning of that Amendment.

Because we are dealing with intrusions into the human body rather than with state interferences with property relationships or private papers—"houses, papers, and effects"—we write on a clean slate. Limitations on the kinds of property which may be seized under warrant,[10] as distinct from the procedures for search and the permissible scope of search,[11] are not instructive in this context. We begin with the assumption that once the privilege against self-incrimination has been found not to bar compelled intrusions into the body for blood to be analyzed for alcohol content, the Fourth Amendment's proper function is to constrain, not against all intrusions as such, but against intrusions which are not justified in the circumstances, or which are made in an improper manner. In other words, the questions we must decide in this case are whether the police were justified in requiring petitioner to submit to the blood test, and whether the means and procedures employed in taking his blood respected relevant Fourth Amendment standards of reasonableness.

In this case, as will often be true when charges of driving under the influence of alcohol are pressed, these questions arise in the context of an arrest made by an officer without a warrant. Here, there was plainly probable cause for the officer to arrest petitioner and charge him with driving an automobile while under the influence of intoxicating liquor. The police officer who arrived at the scene shortly after the accident smelled liquor on petitioner's breath, and testified that petitioner's eyes were "bloodshot, watery, sort of a glassy appearance." The officer saw petitioner again at the hospital, within two hours of the accident. There he noticed similar symptoms of drunkenness. He thereupon informed

10. See, e.g., Gouled v. United States, 255 U.S. 298; Boyd v. United States, 116 U.S. 616; contra, People v. Thayer, 63 Cal. 2d 635, 408 P.2d 108 (1965); State v. Bisaccia, 45 N.J. 504, 213 A.2d 185 (1965); Note, Evidentiary Searches: The Rule and the Reason, 54 Geo. L.J. 593 (1966).
11. See, e.g., Silverman v. United States, 365 U.S. 505; Abel v. United States, 362 U.S. 217, 235; United States v. Rabinowitz, 339 U.S. 56.

petitioner "that he was under arrest and that he was entitled to the services of an attorney, and that he could remain silent, and that anything that he told me would be used against him in evidence." . . .

Although the facts which established probable cause to arrest in this case also suggested the required relevance and likely success of a test of petitioner's blood for alcohol, the question remains whether the arresting officer was permitted to draw these inferences himself, or was required instead to procure a warrant before proceeding with the test. Search warrants are ordinarily required for searches of dwellings, and, absent an emergency, no less could be required where intrusions into the human body are concerned. . . . The importance of informed, detached and deliberate determinations of the issue whether or not to invade another's body in search of evidence of guilt is indisputable and great.

The officer in the present case, however, might reasonably have believed that he was confronted with an emergency, in which the delay necessary to obtain a warrant, under the circumstances, threatened "the destruction of evidence," Preston v. United States, 376 U.S. 364, 367. We are told that the percentage of alcohol in the blood begins to diminish shortly after drinking stops, as the body functions to eliminate it from the system. Particularly in a case such as this, where time had to be taken to bring the accused to a hospital and to investigate the scene of the accident, there was no time to seek out a magistrate and secure a warrant. Given these special facts, we conclude that the attempt to secure evidence of blood-alcohol content in this case was an appropriate incident to petitioner's arrest.

Similarly, we are satisfied that the test chosen to measure petitioner's blood-alcohol level was a reasonable one. Extraction of blood samples for testing is a highly effective means of determining the degree to which a person is under the influence of alcohol. . . .

Finally, the record shows that the test was performed in a reasonable manner. Petitioner's blood was taken by a physician in a hospital environment according to accepted medical practices. We are thus not presented with the serious questions which would arise if a search involving use of a medical technique, even of the most rudimentary sort, were made by other than medical personnel or in other than a medical environment—for example, if it were administered by police in the privacy of the stationhouse. To tolerate searches under these conditions might be to invite an unjustified element of personal risk of infection and pain.

We thus conclude that the present record shows no violation of petitioner's right under the Fourth and Fourteenth Amendments to be free of unreasonable searches and seizures. It bears repeating, however, that we reach this judgment only on the facts of the present record. The integrity of an individual's person is a cherished value of our society.

That we today hold that the Constitution does not forbid the States minor intrusions into an individuals' body under stringently limited conditions in no way indicates that it permits more substantial intrusions, or intrusions under other conditions.

Affirmed. . . .

MR. CHIEF JUSTICE WARREN, dissenting.

While there are other important constitutional issues in this case, I believe it is sufficient for me to reiterate my dissenting opinion in Breithaupt v. Abram, 352 U.S. 432, 440, [which upheld a conviction based in part on an analysis of blood extracted from an unconscious suspect] as the basis on which to reverse this conviction.

MR. JUSTICE BLACK with whom MR. JUSTICE DOUGLAS joins, dissenting.

I would reverse petitioner's conviction. . . . I disagree with the Court's holding that California did not violate petitioner's constitutional right against self-incrimination when it compelled him, against his will, to allow a doctor to puncture his blood vessels in order to extract a sample of blood and analyze it for alcoholic content, and then used that analysis as evidence to convict petitioner of a crime.

The Court admits that "the State compelled [petitioner] to submit to an attempt to discover evidence [in his blood] that might be [and was] used to prosecute him for a criminal offense." To reach the conclusion that compelling a person to give his blood to help the State convict him is not equivalent to compelling him to be a witness against himself strikes me as quite an extraordinary feat. The Court, however, overcomes what had seemed to me to be an insuperable obstacle to its conclusion by holding that

> . . . the privilege protects an accused only from being compelled to testify against himself, or otherwise provide the State with evidence of a testimonial or communicative nature, and that the withdrawal of blood and use of the analysis in question in this case did not involve compulsion to these ends.

I cannot agree that this distinction and reasoning of the Court justify denying petitioner his Bill of Rights' guarantee that he must not be compelled to be a witness against himself.

In the first place it seems to me that the compulsory extraction of petitioner's blood for analysis so that the person who analyzed it could give evidence to convict him had both a "testimonial" and a "communicative nature." The sole purpose of this project which proved to be successful was to obtain "testimony" from some person to prove that petitioner had alcohol in his blood at the time he was arrested. And the purpose of the project was certainly "communicative" in that the analysis of the blood was to supply information to enable a witness to communicate to the court and jury that petitioner was more or less drunk.

I think it unfortunate that the Court rests so heavily for its very restrictive reading of the Fifth Amendments privilege against self-incrimination on the words "testimonial" and "communicative." These words are not models of clarity and precision as the Court's rather labored explication shows. Nor can the Court, so far as I know, find precedent in the former opinions of this Court for using these particular words to limit the scope of the Fifth Amendment's protection. . . .

It concedes, as it must so long as Boyd v. United States stands, that the Fifth Amendment bars a State from compelling a person to produce papers he has that might tend to incriminate him. It is a strange hierarchy of values that allows the State to extract a human being's blood to convict him of a crime because of the blood's content but proscribes compelled production of his lifeless papers. Certainly there could be few papers that would have any more "testimonial" value to convict a man of drunken driving than would an analysis of the alcoholic content of a human being's blood introduced in evidence at a trial for driving while under the influence of alcohol. In such a situation blood, of course, is not oral testimony given by an accused but it can certainly "communicate" to a court and jury the fact of guilt.

The Court itself . . . expresses its own doubts, if not fears, of its own shadowy distinction between compelling "physical evidence" like blood which it holds does not amount to compelled self-incrimination, and "eliciting responses which are essentially testimonial." And in explanation of its fears the Court goes on to warn that

> To compel a person to submit to testing [by lie detectors for example] in which an effort will be made to determine his guilt or innocence on the basis of physiological responses, whether willed or not, is to evoke the spirit and history of the Fifth Amendment. Such situations call to mind the principle that the protection of the privilege "is as broad as the mischief against which it seeks to guard." Counselman v. Hitchcock, 142 U.S. 547, 562.

A basic error in the Court's holding and opinion is its failure to give the Fifth Amendment's protection against compulsory self-incrimination the broad and liberal construction that *Counselman* and other opinions of this Court have declared it ought to have.

The liberal construction given the Bill of Rights' guarantee in Boyd

v. United States, supra, . . . makes that one among the greatest constitutional decisions of this Court. . . . The Court today departs from
the teachings of *Boyd.* Petitioner Schmerber has undoubtedly been compelled to give his blood "to furnish evidence against himself," yet the
Court holds that this is not forbidden by the Fifth Amendment. With
all deferences I must say that the Court here gives the Bill of Rights'
safeguard against compulsory self-incrimination a construction that would
generally be considered too narrow and technical even in the interpretation of an ordinary commercial contract. . . . How can it reasonably
be doubted that the blood test evidence was not in all respects the actual
equivalent of "testimony" taken from petitioner when the result of the
test was offered as testimony, was considered by the jury as testimony,
and the jury's verdict of guilt rests in part on that testimony? The refined,
subtle reasoning and balancing process used here to narrow the scope of
the Bill of Rights' safeguard against self-incrimination provides a handy
instrument for further narrowing of that constitutional protection, as well
as others, in the future. Believing with the Framers that these constitutional safeguards broadly construed by independent tribunals of justice
provide our best hope for keeping our people free from governmental
oppression, I deeply regret the Court's holding. . . .

MR. JUSTICE DOUGLAS, dissenting.
I adhere to the views of The Chief Justice in his dissent in Breithaupt
v. Abram, 352 U.S. 432, 440, and to the views I stated in my dissent
in that case (id., 442) and add only a word. We are dealing with the
right of privacy which, since the *Breithaupt* case, we have held to be
within the penumbra of some specific guarantees of the Bill of Rights.
Griswold v. Connecticut, 381 U.S. 479. Thus, the Fifth Amendment
marks "a zone of privacy" which the Government may not force a person
to surrender. Id., 484. Likewise the Fourth Amendment recognizes that
right when it guarantees the right of the people to be secure "in their
persons." Ibid. No clearer invasion of this right of privacy can be imagined
than forcible bloodletting of the kind involved here.

MR. JUSTICE FORTAS, dissenting.
I would reverse. In my view, petitioner's privilege against self-
incrimination applies. I would add that, under the Due Process Clause,
the State, in its role as prosecutor, has no right to extract blood from an
accused or anyone else, over his protest. As prosecutor, the State has no
right to commit any kind of violence upon the person, or to utilize the
results of such a tort, and the extraction of blood, over protest, is an act
of violence. Cf. Chief Justice Warren's dissenting opinion in Breithaupt
v. Abram, 352 U.S. 432, 440.

WARDEN, MARYLAND PENITENTIARY v. HAYDEN

Certiorari to the United States Court of Appeals for the Fourth Circuit
387 U.S. 294 (1967)

MR. JUSTICE BRENNAN delivered the opinion of the Court.

We review in this case the validity of the proposition that there is under the Fourth Amendment a "distinction between merely evidentiary materials, on the one hand, which may not be seized either under the authority of a search warrant or during the course of a search incident to arrest, and on the other hand, those objects which may validly be seized including the instrumentalities and means by which a crime is committed, the fruits of crime such as stolen property, weapons by which escape of the person arrested might be effected, and property the possession of which is a crime."[1]

A Maryland court sitting without a jury convicted respondent of armed robbery. Items of his clothing, a cap, jacket, and trousers, among other things, were seized during a search of his home, and were admitted in evidence without objection. After unsuccessful state court proceedings, he sought and was denied federal habeas corpus relief in the District Court for Maryland. A divided panel of the Court of Appeals for the Fourth Circuit reversed. The Court of Appeals believed that Harris v. United States, 331 U.S. 145, 154, sustained the validity of the search, but held that respondent was correct in his contention that the clothing seized was improperly admitted in evidence because the items had "evidential value only" and therefore were not lawfully subject to seizure. We granted certiorari. We reverse. . . .

[The Court disposed of the validity of the search. For a discussion, see page 609 infra.]

We come, then, to the question whether, even though the search was lawful, the Court of Appeals was correct in holding that the seizure and introduction of the items of clothing violated the Fourth Amendment because they are "mere evidence." The distinction made by some of our cases between seizure of items of evidential value only and seizure of instrumentalities, fruits, or contraband has been criticized by courts and commentators. The Court of Appeals, however, felt "obligated to adhere to it." We today reject the distinction as based on premises no longer accepted as rules governing the application of the Fourth Amendment.[8] . . .

---

1. Harris v. United States, 331 U.S. 145, 154; see also Gouled v. United States, 255 U.S. 298; United States v. Lefkowitz, 285 U.S. 452, 465-466; United States v. Rabinowitz, 339 U.S. 56, 64, n.6; Abel v. United States, 362 U.S. 217, 234-235.

8. This Court has approved the seizure and introduction of items having only

Nothing in the language of the Fourth Amendment supports the distinction between "mere evidence" and instrumentalities, fruits of crime, or contraband. On its face, the provision assures the "right of the people to be secure in their persons, houses, papers, and effects . . . ," without regard to the use to which any of these things are applied. This "right of the people" is certainly unrelated to the "mere evidence" limitation. Privacy is disturbed no more by a search directed to a purely evidentiary object than it is by a search directed to an instrumentality, fruit, or contraband. A magistrate can intervene in both situations, and the requirements of probable cause and specificity can be preserved intact. Moreover, nothing in the nature of the property seized as evidence renders it more private than property seized, for example, as an instrumentality; quite the opposite may be true. Indeed, the distinction is wholly irrational, since, depending on the circumstances, the same "papers and effects" may be "mere evidence" in one case and "instrumentality" in another.

In Gouled v. United States, the Court said that search warrants "may not be used as a means of gaining access to a man's house or office and papers solely for the purpose of making search to secure evidence to be used against him in a criminal or penal proceeding. . . ." The Court derived from Boyd v. United States, supra, the proposition that warrants "may be resorted to only when a primary right to such search and seizure may be found in the interest which the public or the complainant may have in the property to be seized, or in the right to the possession of it, or when a valid exercise of the police power renders possession of the property by the accused unlawful and provides that it may be taken," 255 U.S., at 309; that is, when the property is an instrumentality or fruit of crime, or contraband. Since it was "impossible to say, on the record . . . that the Government had any interest" in the papers involved "other than as evidence against the accused . . . ," "to permit them to be used in evidence would be, in effect, as ruled in the *Boyd Case,* to compel the defendant to become a witness against himself." Id., at 311.

The items of clothing involved in this case are not "testimonial" or "communicative" in nature, and their introduction therefore did not compel respondent to become a witness against himself in violation of the Fifth Amendment. This case thus does not require that we consider whether there are items of evidential value whose very nature precludes them from being the object of a reasonable search and seizure.

The Fourth Amendment ruling in *Gouled* was based upon the dual, related premises that historically the right to search for and seize property depended upon the assertion by the Government of a valid claim of

---

evidential value without, however, considering the validity of the distinction rejected today. See Schmerber v. California, 384 U.S. 757; Cooper v. California, 386 U.S. 58.

superior interest, and that it was not enough that the purpose of the search and seizure was to obtain evidence to use in apprehending and convicting criminals. . . .

The premise that property interests control the right of the Government to search and seize has been discredited. Searches and seizures may be "unreasonable" within the Fourth Amendment even though the Government asserts a superior property interest at common law. We have recognized that the principal object of the Fourth Amendment is the protection of privacy rather than property, and have increasingly discarded fictional and procedural barriers rested on property concepts. . . . And with particular relevance here, we have given recognition to the interest in privacy despite the complete absence of a property claim by suppressing the very items which at common law could be seized with impunity: stolen goods, Henry v. United States, 361 U.S. 98; instrumentalities, Beck v. Ohio, 379 U.S. 89; McDonald v. United States, supra; and contraband, Trupiano v. United States, 334 U.S. 699; Aguilar v. Texas, 378 U.S. 108.

The premise in *Gouled* that government may not seize evidence simply for the purpose of proving crime has likewise been discredited. The requirement that the Government assert in addition some property interest in material it seizes has long been a fiction,[11] obscuring the reality that government has an interest in solving crime. *Schmerber* settled the proposition that it is reasonable, within the terms of the Fourth Amendment, to conduct otherwise permissible searches for the purpose of obtaining evidence which would aid in apprehending and convicting criminals. The requirements of the Fourth Amendment can secure the same protection of privacy whether the search is for "mere evidence" or for fruits, instrumentalities or contraband. . . .

The rationale most frequently suggested for the rule preventing the seizure of evidence is that "limitations upon the fruit to be gathered tend

11. At common law the Government did assert a superior property interest when it searched lawfully for stolen property, since the procedure then followed made it necessary that the true owner swear that his goods had been taken. But no such procedure need be followed today; the Government may demonstrate probable cause and lawfully search for stolen property even though the true owner is unknown or unavailable to request and authorize the Government to assert his interest. As to instrumentalities, the Court in *Gouled* allowed their seizure, not because the Government had some property interest in them (under the ancient, fictitious forfeiture theory), but because they could be used to perpetrate further crime. 255 U.S., at 309. The same holds true, of course, for "mere evidence"; the prevention of crime is served at least as much by allowing the Government to identify and capture the criminal, as it is by allowing the seizure of his instrumentalities. Finally, contraband is indeed property in which the Government holds a superior interest, but only because the Government decides to vest such an interest in itself. And while there may be limits to what may be declared contraband, the concept is hardly more than a form through which the Government seeks to prevent and deter crime.

to limit the quest itself." But privacy "would be just as well served by a restriction on search to the even-numbered days of the month. . . . And it would have the extra advantage of avoiding hair-splitting questions. . . ." Kaplan, [Search and Seizure: A No-Man's Land in the Criminal Law, 49 Calif. L. Rev. 474,] at 479. The "mere evidence" limitation has spawned exceptions so numerous and confusion so great, in fact, that it is questionable whether it affords meaningful protection. But if its rejection does enlarge the area of permissible searches, the intrusions are nevertheless made after fulfilling the probable cause and particularity requirements of the Fourth Amendment and after the intervention of "a neutral and detached magistrate. . . ." The Fourth Amendment allows intrusions upon privacy under these circumstances, and there is no viable reason to distinguish intrusions to secure "mere evidence" from intrusions to secure fruits, instrumentalities, or contraband.

The judgment of the Court of Appeals is reversed.

MR. JUSTICE BLACK concurs in the result.

MR. JUSTICE FORTAS, with whom THE CHIEF JUSTICE joins, concurring.

While I agree that the Fourth Amendment should not be held to require exclusion from evidence of the clothing as well as the weapons and ammunition found by the officers during the search, I cannot join in the majority's broad—and in my judgment, totally unnecessary—repudiation of the so-called "mere evidence" rule.

Our Constitution envisions that searches will ordinarily follow procurement by police of a valid search warrant. Such warrants are to issue only on probable cause, and must describe with particularity the persons or things to be seized. There are exceptions to this rule. Searches may be made incident to a lawful arrest, and—as today's decision indicates—in the course of "hot pursuit." But searches under each of these exceptions have, until today, been confined to those essential to fulfill the purpose of the exception: that is, we have refused to permit use of articles the seizure of which could not be strictly tied to and justified by the exigencies which excused the warrantless search. The use in evidence of weapons seized in a "hot pursuit" search or search incident to arrest satisfies this criterion because of the need to protect the arresting officers from weapons to which the suspect might resort. The search for and seizure of fruits are, of course, justifiable on independent grounds: The fruits are an object of the pursuit or arrest of the suspect, and should be restored to their true owner. The seizure of contraband has been justified on the ground that the suspect has not even a bare possessory right to contraband. . . .

In the present case, the articles of clothing admitted into evidence are not within any of the traditional categories which describe what materials may be seized, either with or without a warrant. The restrictiveness of these categories has been subjected to telling criticism, and although I believe that we should approach expansion of these categories with the diffidence which their imposing provenance commands, I agree that the use of identifying clothing worn in the commission of a crime and seized during "hot pursuit" is within the spirit and intendment of the "hot pursuit" exception to the search-warrant requirement. That is because the clothing is pertinent to identification of the person hotly pursued as being, in fact, the person whose pursuit was justified by connection with the crime. I would frankly place the ruling on that basis. I would not drive an enormous and dangerous hole in the Fourth Amendment to accommodate a specific and, I think, reasonable exception.

As my Brother Douglas notes, post, opposition to general searches is a fundamental of our heritage and of the history of Anglo-Saxon legal principles. Such searches, pursuant to "writs of assistance," were one of the matters over which the American Revolution was fought. The very purpose of the Fourth Amendment was to outlaw such searches, which the Court today sanctions. I fear that in gratuitously striking down the "mere evidence" rule, which distinguished members of this Court have acknowledged as essential to enforce the Fourth Amendment's prohibition against general searches, the Court today needlessly destroys, root and branch, a basic part of liberty's heritage.

MR. JUSTICE DOUGLAS, dissenting.
We start with the Fourth Amendment. . . .
This constitutional guarantee, . . . has been thought, until today, to have two faces of privacy:

(1) One creates a zone of privacy that may not be invaded by the police through raids, by the legislators through laws, or by magistrates through the issuance of warrants.
(2) A second creates a zone of privacy that may be invaded either by the police in hot pursuit or by a search incident to arrest or by a warrant issued by a magistrate on a showing of probable cause. . . .

This is borne out by what happened in the Congress. In the House the original draft read as follows:

The right of the people to be secured in their persons, houses, papers, and effects, shall not be violated by warrants issuing without probable cause, supported by oath or affirmation, and not particularly describing the place to be searched and the persons or things to be seized. 1 Annals of Cong. 754.

That was amended to read "The right of the people to be secure in their persons, houses, papers, and effects, against unreasonable seizures and searches," etc. Ibid. Mr. Benson, Chairman of a Committee of Three to arrange the amendments, objected to the words "by warrants issuing" and proposed to alter the amendment so as to read "and no warrant shall issue." Ibid. But Benson's amendment was defeated. Ibid. And if the story had ended there, it would be clear that the Fourth Amendment touched only the form of the warrants and the manner of their issuance. But when the Benson Committee later reported the Fourth Amendment to the House, it was in the form he had earlier proposed and was then accepted. 1 Annals of Cong. 779. The Senate agreed. Senate Journal August 25, 1789.

Thus it is clear that the Fourth Amendment has two faces of privacy, a conclusion emphasized by Lasson, The History and Development of the Fourth Amendment to the United States Constitution 103 (1937):

> As reported by the Committee of Eleven and corrected by Gerry, the Amendment was a one-barrelled affair, directed apparently only to the essentials of a valid warrant. The general principle of freedom from unreasonable search and seizure seems to have been stated only by way of premise, and the positive inhibition upon action by the Federal Government limited consequently to the issuance of warrants without probable cause, etc. That Benson interpreted it in this light is shown by his argument that although the clause was good as far as it went, *it was not sufficient*, and by the change which he advocated to obviate this objection. The provision as he proposed it contained *two* clauses. The general right of security from unreasonable search and seizure was given a sanction of its own and the amendment thus intentionally given a broader scope. That the prohibition against 'unreasonable searches' was intended, accordingly, to cover something other than the form of the warrant is a question no longer left to implication to be derived from the phraseology of the Amendment. . . .

. . . Our question is whether the Government, though armed with a proper search warrant or though making a search incident to an arrest, may seize, and use at the trial, testimonial evidence, whether it would otherwise be barred by the Fifth Amendment or would be free from such strictures. The teaching of *Boyd* is that such evidence, though seized pursuant to a lawful search, is inadmissible. . . .

We have, to be sure, breached that barrier, Schmerber v. California, 384 U.S. 757, being a conspicuous example. But I dissented then and renew my opposing view at this time. That which is taken from a person without his consent and used as testimonial evidence violates the Fifth Amendment.

That was the holding in *Gouled;* and that was the line of authority followed by Judge Simon Sobeloff, writing for the Court of Appeals for reversal in this case. 363 F.2d 647. As he said, even if we assume that the search was lawful, the articles of clothing seized were of evidential value only and under *Gouled* could not be used at the trial against petitioner. As he said, the Fourth Amendment guarantees the right of the people to be secure "in their persons, houses, papers, and effects, against unreasonable searches and seizures." Articles of clothing are covered as well as papers. Articles of clothing may be of evidential value as much as documents or papers.

Judge Learned Hand stated a part of the philosophy of the Fourth Amendment in United States v. Poller, 43 F.2d 911, 914:

> [I]t is only fair to observe that the real evil aimed at by the Fourth Amendment is the search itself, that invasion of a man's privacy which consists in rummaging about among his effects to secure evidence against him. If the search is permitted at all, perhaps it does not make so much difference what is taken away, since the officers will ordinarily not be interested in what does not incriminate, and there can be no sound policy in protecting what does. Nevertheless, limitations upon the fruit to be gathered tend to limit the quest itself. . . .

The right of privacy protected by the Fourth Amendment relates in part of course to the precincts of the home or the office. But it does not make them sanctuaries where the law can never reach. . . . A policeman in "hot pursuit" or an officer with a search warrant can enter any house, any room, any building, any office. The privacy of those *places* is of course protected against invasion except in limited situations. The full privacy protected by the Fourth Amendment is, however, reached when we come to books, pamphlets, papers, letters, documents, and other personal effects. Unless they are contraband or instruments of the crime, they may not be reached by any warrant nor may they be lawfully seized by the police who are in "hot pursuit." By reason of the Fourth Amendment the police may not rummage around among these personal effects, no matter how formally perfect their authority may appear to be. They may not seize them. If they do, those articles may not be used in evidence. Any invasion whatsoever of those personal effects is "unreasonable" within the meaning of the Fourth Amendment. That is the teaching of Entick v. Carrington, Boyd v. United States, and Gouled v. United States. . . .

The constitutional philosophy is, I think, clear. The personal effects and possessions of the individual (all contraband and the like excepted) are sacrosanct from prying eyes, from the long arm of the law, from any rummaging by police. Privacy involves the choice of the individual to disclose or to reveal what he believes, what he thinks, what he possesses. The article may be a nondescript work of art, a manuscript of a book, a personal account book, a diary, invoices, personal clothing, jewelry, or whatnot. Those who wrote the Bill of Rights believed that every individual needs both to communicate with others and to keep his affairs to himself. That dual aspect of privacy means that the individual should have the freedom to select for himself the time and circumstances when he will share his secrets with others and decide the extent of that sharing. This is his prerogative not the States'. The Framers, who were as knowledgeable as we, knew what police surveillance meant and how the practice of rummaging through one's personal effects could destroy freedom. . . .

NOTES AND QUESTIONS

1. What is left of the theoretical underpinnings of *Boyd* and *Gouled* after *Schmerber* and *Hayden?* Is it conceivable that the "paper search" component of *Boyd* survived these cases? Is the seizure of spoken words in any crucial respect different from the seizure of private papers? Is it true that the "mere evidence" rule is insupportable? Consider the following passage from Galloway, The Intruding Eye: A Status Report on the Constitutional Ban Against Paper Searches, 25 Howard L.J. 367, 382-385 (1982).

> It is important to recognize that the mere evidence rule was based on rational policy considerations. From the start, one primary purpose was to protect the citizen's privacy. *Entick* repeatedly excoriated the violation of privacy involved in examining a person's secret papers. *Boyd* stressed that the principles of *Entick* were designed to protect the "privacies of life." In Zurcher v. United States,[67] Justice Stevens stated, "[t]he practical effect of the rule prohibiting the issuance of warrants to search for mere evidence was to narrowly limit . . . the character of the privacy interests that might be affected by an unannounced police search."[68] In short, although the *scope* of the mere evidence rule was defined in terms drawn from property law, a major *purpose* of the rule was to protect personal privacy by limiting the government's authority to search.
>
> Moreover, the mere evidence rule was a rational method for protecting privacy. When searches and seizures are limited to contraband, fruits and

67. 436 U.S. 547 (1978).
68. Id. at 579 (Stevens, J., dissenting).

instrumentalities, the only persons who may be searched, in most instances, are criminals. Normally, only the criminals themselves possess contraband, fruits or instrumentalities. In contrast, innocent people (so-called "third parties") frequently possess evidence that may tie some *other* person to a crime. Thus, the mere evidence rule ensures that the government will not be able to invade the privacy of innocent third parties.[69] Moreover, evidence searches often result in much more serious invasions of personal privacy. Rarely will a person's private papers contain contraband, fruits or instrumentalities. Yet searches for evidence of crime lead easily and directly into private paper where descriptions of prior acts and statements may be recorded side by side with the most intimate details of private life and thought. A search for a stolen television, for example, will normally be far less intrusive than a search for written statements concerning the suspect's whereabouts on the night the television was stolen. For reasons such as these, Learned Hand described the policy underlying the mere evidence rule as follows: "Limitations upon the fruit to be gathered tend to limit the quest itself."[70] . . .

The reasons given for the repudiation of the mere evidence rule are unconvincing. The absence of explicit reference to the mere evidence rule in the fourth amendment means little in light of the Court's insistence that *Entick* was in the forefront of the framers' minds when they banned unreasonable searches.[78] The Court's assurances notwithstanding, evidence searches tend to disturb privacy *much more deeply* than searches for contraband, fruits and instrumentalies. One need only consider, for example,

69. See, e.g., Zurcher v. Stanford Daily, 436 U.S. 547, 579 (1978) (Stevens, J., dissenting):

> The practical effect of the rule prohibiting the issuance of warrants to search for mere evidence was to narrowly limit not only the category of objects, but also the category of persons and the character of the privacy interests that might be affected by an unannounced police search.
>
> Just as the witnesses who participate in an investigation or a trial far outnumber the defendants, the persons who possess evidence that may help to identify an offender, or explain an aspect of a criminal transaction, far outnumber those who have custody of weapons or plunder. Countless law-abiding citizens—doctors, lawyers, merchants, customers, bystanders—may have documents in their possession that relate to an on-going criminal investigation. The consequences of subjecting this large category of persons to unannounced police searches are extremely serious.

For these reasons, Justice Stevens concluded that evidence searches involve a "vastly expanded 'degree of intrusion' " in comparison with searches for fruits, instrumentalities and contraband. Id. at 578.

70. United States v. Poller, 43 F.2d 911, 914 (2d Cir. 1930).

78. See, e.g., Boyd v. United States, 116 U.S. 616, 626-27 (1886), which stated: "As every American statesm[a]n, during our revolutionary and formative period as a nation, was undoubtedly familiar with [Entick v. Carrington] . . . , and considered it as the true and ultimate expression of constitutional law, it may be confidently asserted that its propositions were in the minds of those who framed the Fourth Amendment to the Constitution, and were considered as sufficiently explanatory of what was meant by unreasonable searches and seizures."

that neither extended electronic surveillance, one of the most insidious invasions of privacy, nor the reading of most private papers would be possible if the mere evidence rule had been retained. The mere evidence rule was definitely not an irrational restriction like "a restriction on search to even-numbered days." The mere evidence rule was a rational limitation which operated to restrict searches of innocent third parties and to ban the most intrusive invasions of private papers and conversations.

Moreover, although it must be admitted that the mere evidence rule did spawn confusion and criticism, this should not justify discarding the rule without providing an effective alternative method, hopefully simpler and less confusing, for protecting the privacy interests the rule was intended to protect. Finally, the criticism directed at the discredited property concepts does not undercut the rule itself, but only the method used to define the scope of the rule. Perhaps the exceptions were based on archaic property concepts, but the rule itself was not. The mere evidence rule was based on a valid and very much alive—even urgent—concern to protect individual privacy. Indeed, a strong case can be made that this is one of the most important policy issues facing modern society.[2] . . .

Boyd continues to generate favorable commentary. See, e.g., Schnapper, Unreasonable Searches and Seizures of Papers, 71 Va. L. Rev. 869 (1985). But see Alito, Documents and the Privilege Against Self-Incrimination, 48 U. Pitt. L. Rev. 27 (1986).

2. The Court continued its reconstruction of *Boyd* in Fisher v. United States, 425 U.S. 391 (1976), and Andresen v. Maryland, 427 U.S. 463 (1976). In *Fisher*, the Court upheld a summons that directed the defendants' attorneys to produce documents prepared by defendants' accountants and turned over to the attorneys for purposes of obtaining legal advice. After determining that the materials would be privileged in the hands of the attorney, as a result of the attorney-client privilege, only if the fifth amendment protected the materials when they were in the

---

2. Also consider the following passage from McKenna, The Constitutional Protection of Private Papers: The Role of a Hierarchical Fourth Amendment, 53 Ind. L.J. 55, 69 (1977-1978).

> In addition to the nature of the papers themselves, a second reason for according them strict protection concerns the nature of the search for private papers. The fundamental evil at which the fourth amendment was directed was the sweeping, exploratory search conducted pursuant to a general warrant. A search involving private papers, it has been noted, invariably partakes of a similar generality, for "even a search for a specific, identified paper may involve the same rude intrusion [of an exploratory search] if the quest for it leads to an examination of all of a man's private papers." Thus, both their contents and the inherently intrusive nature of a search for them militates toward the position that private papers are deserving of the fullest possible fourth amendment protection.

—Eds.

possession of the client, the Court proceeded to discuss its understanding of the fourth and the fifth amendments:

> It is true that the Court has often stated that one of the several purposes served by the constitutional privilege against compelled testimonial self-incrimination is that of protecting personal privacy. . . . But the Court has never suggested that every invasion of privacy violates the privilege. Within the limits imposed by the language of the Fifth Amendment, which we necessarily observe, the privilege truly serves privacy interests; but the Court has never on any ground, personal privacy included, applied the Fifth Amendment to prevent the otherwise proper acquisition or use of evidence which, in the Court's view, did not involve compelled testimonial self-incrimination of some sort. [5]
>
> The proposition that the Fifth Amendment protects private information obtained without compelling self-incriminating testimony is contrary to the clear statements of this Court that under appropriate safeguards private incriminating statements of an accused may be overheard and used in evidence, if they are not compelled at the time they were uttered, . . . Berger v. New York; . . . and that disclosure of private information may be compelled if immunity removes the risk of incrimination. If the Fifth Amendment protected generally against the obtaining of private information from a man's mouth or pen or house, its protections would presumably not be lifted by probable cause and a warrant or by immunity. The privacy invasion is not mitigated by immunity; and the Fifth Amendment's strictures, unlike the Fourth's, are not removed by showing reasonableness. The Framers addressed the subject of personal privacy directly in the Fourth Amendment. They struck a balance so that when the State's reason to believe incriminating evidence will be found becomes sufficiently great, the invasion of privacy becomes justified and a warrant to search and seize will issue. They did not seek in still another Amendment—the Fifth—to achieve a general protection of privacy but to deal with the more specific issue of compelled self-incrimination.
>
> We cannot cut the Fifth Amendment completely loose from the moorings of its language, and make it serve as a general protector of privacy—a word not mentioned in its text and a concept directly addressed in the Fourth Amendment. We adhere to the view that the Fifth Amendment protects against "compelled self-incrimination, not [the disclosure

---

5. There is a line of cases in which the Court stated that the Fifth Amendment was offended by the use in evidence of documents or property seized in violation of the Fourth Amendment. Gouled v. United States, 255 U.S. 298, 306 (1921); Agnello v. United States, 269 U.S. 20, 33-34 (1925); United States v. Lefkowitz, 285 U.S. 452, 466-467 (1932); Mapp v. Ohio, 367 U.S. 643, 661 (1961) (Black, J., concurring). But the Court purported to find elements of compulsion in such situations. "In either case he is the unwilling source of the evidence, and the Fifth Amendment forbids that he shall be compelled to be a witness against himself in a criminal case." Gouled v. United States, supra, at 306. In any event the predicate for those cases, lacking here, was a violation of the Fourth Amendment. Cf. Burdeau v. McDowell, 256 U.S. 465, 475-476 (1921).

of] private information." United States v. Nobles, 422 U.S. 225, 233 n.7 (1975).

Insofar as private information not obtained through compelled self-incriminating testimony is legally protected, its protection stems from other sources[6]—the Fourth Amendment's protection against seizures without warrant or probable cause and against subpoenas which suffer from "too much indefiniteness or breadth in the things required to be 'particularly described,' " Oklahoma Press Pub. Co. v. Walling, 327 U.S. 186, 208 (1946); or evidentiary privileges such as the attorney-client privilege.[7] [425 U.S. at 399-401.]

In light of its general understanding of the amendments, the only fifth amendment problem the Court could see with a summons to produce documents prepared by someone else (here the accountants) had to do with the testimonial components of production itself.

A subpoena served on a taxpayer requiring him to produce an accountant's workpapers in his possession without doubt involves substantial compulsion. But it does not compel oral testimony; nor would it ordinarily compel the taxpayer to restate, repeat, or affirm the truth of the contents of the documents sought. Therefore, the Fifth Amendment would not be violated by the fact alone that the papers on their face might incriminate the taxpayer, for the privilege protects a person only against being incriminated by his own compelled testimonial communications. Schmerber v. California, supra. . . . The accountant's workpapers are not the taxpayer's. They were not prepared by the taxpayer, and they contain no testimonial declarations by him. Furthermore, as far as this record demonstrates, the preparation of all of the papers sought in these cases was wholly voluntary, and they cannot be said to contain compelled testimonial evidence, either of the taxpayers or of anyone else.[11] The taxpayer cannot avoid compliance

6. In Couch v. United States, 409 U.S. 322 (1973), on which taxpayers rely for their claim that the Fifth Amendment protects their "legitimate expectation of privacy," the Court differentiated between the things protected by the Fourth and Fifth Amendments. "We hold today that no Fourth or Fifth Amendment claim can prevail where, as in this case, there exists no legitimate expectation of privacy and no semblance of governmental compulsion against the person of the accused." Id.; at 336.

7. The taxpayers and their attorneys have not raised arguments of a Fourth Amendment nature before this Court and could not be successful if they had. The summonses are narrowly drawn and seek only documents of unquestionable relevance to the tax investigation. Special problems of privacy which might be presented by subpoena of a personal diary, United States v. Bennett, 409 F.2d 888, 897 (C.A.2 1969) (Friendly, J.), are not involved here.

First Amendment values are also plainly not implicated in these cases.

11. The fact that the documents may have been written by the person asserting the privilege is insufficient to trigger the privilege, Wilson v. United States, 221 U.S. 361, 378 (1911). And, unless the Government has compelled the subpoenaed person to write the document, cf. Marchetti v. United States, 390 U.S. 39 (1968); Grosso v. United States, 390 U.S. 62 (1968), the fact that it was written by him is not controlling with

with the subpoena merely by asserting that the item of evidence which he is required to produce contains incriminating writing, whether his own or that of someone else.

The act of producing evidence in response to a subpoena nevertheless has communicative aspects of its own, wholly aside from the contents of the papers produced. Compliance with the subpoena tacitly concedes the existence of the papers demanded and their possession or control by the taxpayer. It also would indicate the taxpayer's belief that the papers are those described in the subpoena. Curcio v. United States, 354 U.S. 118, 125 (1957). The elements of compulsion are clearly present, but the more difficult issues are whether the tacit averments of the taxpayer are both "testimonial" and "incriminating" for purposes of applying the Fifth Amendment. These questions perhaps do not lend themselves to categorical answers; their resolution may instead depend on the facts and circumstances of particular cases or classes thereof. In light of the records now before us, we are confident that however incriminating the contents of the accountant's workpapers might be, the act of producing them—the only thing which the taxpayer is compelled to do—would not itself involve testimonial self-incrimination.

It is doubtful that implicitly admitting the existence and possession of the papers rises to the level of testimony within the protection of the Fifth Amendment. The papers belong to the accountant, were prepared by him, and are the kind usually prepared by an accountant working on the tax returns of his client. Surely the Government is in no way relying on the "truthtelling" of the taxpayer to prove the existence of or his access to the documents. 8 Wigmore §2264, p.380. The existence and location of the papers are a foregone conclusion and the taxpayer adds little or nothing to the sum total of the Government's information by conceding that he in fact has the papers. Under these circumstances by enforcement of the summons "no constitutional rights are touched. The question is not of testimony but of surrender." In re Harris, 221 U.S. 274, 279 (1911). . . .

As for the possibility that responding to the subpoena would authenticate[12] the workpapers, production would express nothing more

---

respect to the Fifth Amendment issue. Conversations may be seized and introduced in evidence under proper safeguards, . . . Berger v. New York, 388 U.S. 41 (1967); . . . if not compelled. In the case of a documentary subpoena the only thing compelled is the act of producing the document and the compelled act is the same as the one performed when a chattel or document not authored by the producer is demanded. McCormick §128, p. 269.

12. The "implicit authentication" rationale appears to be the prevailing justification for the Fifth Amendment's application to documentary subpoenas. Schmerber v. California, 384 U. S., at 763-764 ("the privilege reaches . . . the compulsion of responses which are also communications, for example, compliance with a subpoena to produce one's papers. Boyd v. United States, 116 U.S. 616"); Couch v. United States, 409 U.S., at 344, 346 (Marshall, J., dissenting)(the person complying with the subpoena "implicitly testifies that the evidence he brings forth is in fact the evidence demanded"); United States v. Beattie, 522 F.2d 267, 270 (C.A.2 1975)(Friendly, J.)("[a] subpoena demanding

than the taxpayer's belief that the papers are those described in the subpoena. The taxpayer would be no more competent to authenticate the
accountant's workpapers or reports[13] by producing them than he would be
to authenticate them if testifying orally. The taxpayer did not prepare the
papers and could not vouch for their accuracy. The documents would not
be admissible in evidence against the taxpayer without authenticating testimony. Without more, responding to the subpoena in the circumstances
before us would not appear to represent a substantial threat of self-incrimination. Moreover, in [a series of cases] the custodian of corporate, union,
or partnership books or those of a bankrupt business was ordered to respond
to a subpoena for the business' books even though doing so involved a
"representation that documents produced are those demanded by the subpoena," Curcio v. United States, 354 U.S., at 125. [425 U.S. at 409-
413.]

Justice Brennan concurred, but made the point that the fifth amendment in his view would protect against the production of private papers
that were unrelated to the defendant's business activities. Justice Marshall
also concurred, primarily on the ground that *Fisher* would not modify
the scope of the protections previously afforded by the Court's decisions:

> I am hopeful that the Court's new theory, properly understood and applied,
> will provide substantially the same protection as our prior focus on the
> contents of the documents. The Court recognizes, as others have argued,
> that the act of production can verify the authenticity of the documents
> produced. But the promise of the Court's theory lies in its innovative
> discernment that production may also verify the documents' very existence
> and present possession by the producer. This expanded recognition of the
> kinds of testimony inherent in production not only rationalizes the cases,
> but seems to me to afford almost complete protection against compulsory
> production of our most private papers.

---

that an accused produce his own records is . . . the equivalent of requiring him to take
the stand and admit their genuineness"); 8 Wigmore §2264, p. 380 (the testimonial
component involved in compliance with an order for production of documents or chattels
"is the witness' assurance, compelled as an incident of the process, that the articles
produced are the ones demanded"); McCormick §126, p. 268 ("[t]his rule [applying the
Fifth Amendment privilege to documentary subpoenas] is defended on the theory that
one who produces documents (or other matter) described in the subpoena duces tecum
represents, by his production, that the documents produced are in fact the documents
described in the subpoena"); People v. Defore, 242 N.Y. 13, 27, 150 N.E. 585, 590
(1926) (Cardozo, J.) ("A defendant is 'protected from producing his documents in response
to a subpoena duces tecum, for his production of them in court would be his voucher
of their genuineness.' There would then be 'testimonial compulsion' ").

13. In seeking the accountant's "retained copies" of correspondence with the taxpayer in No. 74-611, we assume that the summons sought only "copies" of original
letters sent from the accountant to the taxpayer—the truth of the contents of which could
be testified to only by the accountant.

Thus, the Court's rationale provides a persuasive basis for distinguishing between the corporate document cases and those involving the papers of private citizens. Since the existence of corporate record books is seldom in doubt, the verification of their existence, inherent in their production, may fairly be termed not testimonial at all. On the other hand, there is little reason to assume the present existence and possession of most private papers, and certainly not those Mr. Justice Brennan places at the top of his list of documents that the privilege should protect. . . . Indeed, there would appear to be a precise inverse relationship between the private nature of the document and the permissibility of assuming its existence. Therefore, under the Court's theory, the admission through production that one's diary, letters, prior tax returns, personally maintained financial records, or cancelled checks exist would ordinarily provide substantial testimony. The incriminating nature of such an admission is clear, for while it may not be criminal to keep a diary, or write letters or checks, the admission that one does and that those documents are still available may quickly— or simultaneously—lead to incriminating evidence. If there is a "real danger" of such a result, that is enough under our cases to make such testimony subject to the claim of privilege. Thus, in practice, the Court's approach should still focus upon the private nature of the papers subpoenaed and protect those about which *Boyd* and its progeny were most concerned.

The Court's theory will also limit the prosecution's ability to use documents secured through a grant of immunity. If authentication that the document produced is the document demanded were the only testimony inherent in production, immunity would be a useful tool for obtaining written evidence. So long as a document obtained under an immunity grant could be authenticated through other sources, as would often be possible, reliance on the immunized testimony—the authentication—and its fruits would not be necessary, and the document could be introduced. The Court's recognition that the act of production also involves testimony about the existence and possession of the subpoenaed documents mandates a different result. Under the Court's theory, if the document is to be obtained the immunity grant must extend to the testimony that the document is presently in existence. Such a grant will effectively shield the contents of the document, for the contents are a direct fruit of the immunized testimony—that the document exists—and cannot usually be obtained without reliance on that testimony.[2] Accordingly, the Court's theory offers substantially the same protection against procurement of documents under grant of immunity that our prior cases afford.

2. Similarly, the Court's theory affords protection to one who possesses documents that he cannot authenticate. If authentication were the only relevant testimony inherent in the act of production, such a person would be forced to relinquish his documents, for he provides no authentication testimony of relevance by producing them in response to a subpoena. See United States v. Beattie, 522 F.2d 267 (C.A.2 1975). Under the Court's theory, however, if the existence of these documents were in question, the custodian would still be able to assert a claim of privilege against their production.

In short, while the Court sacrifices our pragmatic, if somewhat ad hoc, content analysis for what might seem an unduly technical focus on the act of production itself, I am far less pessimistic than Mr. Justice Brennan that this new approach signals the end of Fifth Amendment protection for documents we have long held to be privileged. I am not ready to embrace the approach myself, but I am confident in the ability of the trial judges who must apply this difficult test in the first instance to act with sensitivity to our traditional concerns in this uncertain area. . . .
[425 U.S. at 432-434.]

In *Andresen*, the Court dealt with the issue left open in *Fisher*— the production of a person's private papers—but approached it from a different perspective. Defendant was convicted on various counts of fraud. At trial, the government relied on personal business papers of the defendant that were seized under the authority of a search warrant. Some of the documents seized included handwritten memoranda by the defendant. According to the Court, this raised "the issue whether the introduction into evidence of a person's business records, seized during a search of his offices, violates the Fifth Amendment's command."

There is no question that the records seized from petitioner's offices and introduced against him were incriminating. Moreover, it is undisputed that some of these business records contain statements made by petitioner. . . . The question, therefore, is whether the seizure of these business records, and their admission into evidence at his trial, compelled petitioner to testify against himself in violation of the Fifth Amendment. This question may be said to have been reserved in Warden v. Hayden. . . .
Petitioner contends that "the Fifth Amendment prohibition against compulsory self-incrimination applies as well to personal business papers seized from his offices as it does to the same papers being required to be produced under a subpoena." Brief for Petitioner 9. He bases his argument, naturally, on dicta in a number of cases which imply, or state, that the search for and seizure of a person's private papers violate the privilege against self-incrimination. Thus, in Boyd v. United States, the Court said: "[W]e have been unable to perceive that the seizure of a man's private books and papers to be used in evidence against him is substantially different from compelling him to be a witness against himself." And in Hale v. Henkel, it was observed that "the substance of the offense is the compulsory production of private papers, whether under a search warrant or a subpoena duces tecum, against which the person . . . is entitled to protection."
We do not agree, however, that these broad statements compel suppression of this petitioner's business records as a violation of the Fifth Amendment. In the very recent case of Fisher v. United States, the Court held that an attorney's production, pursuant to a lawful summons, of his

client's tax records in his hands did not violate the Fifth Amendment privilege of the taxpayer "because enforcement against a taxpayer's lawyer would not 'compel' the taxpayer to do anything—and certainly would not compel him to be a 'witness' against himself." We recognized that the continued validity of the broad statements contained in some of the Court's earlier cases had been discredited by later opinions. In those earlier cases, the legal predicate for the inadmissibility of the evidence seized was a violation of the Fourth Amendment; the unlawfulness of the search and seizure was thought to supply the compulsion of the accused necessary to invoke the Fifth Amendment.[6] Compulsion of the accused was also absent in Couch v. United States, 409 U.S. 322 (1973), where the Court held that a summons served on a taxpayer's accountant requiring him to produce the taxpayer's personal business records in his possession did not violate the taxpayer's Fifth Amendment rights.[7]

Similarly, in this case, petitioner was not asked to say or to do anything. The records seized contained statements that petitioner had voluntarily committed to writing. The search for and seizure of these records were conducted by law enforcement personnel. Finally, when these records were introduced at trial, they were authenticated by a handwriting expert, not by petitioner. Any compulsion of petitioner to speak, other than the inherent psychological pressure to respond at trial to unfavorable evidence, was not present.

This case thus falls within the principle stated by Mr. Justice Holmes: "A party is privileged from producing the evidence but not from its production." Johnson v. United States, 228 U.S. 457, 458 (1913). This principle recognizes that the protection afforded by the Self-Incrimination Clause of the Fifth Amendment "adheres basically to the person, not to information that may incriminate him." Couch v. United States, 409 U.S., at 328. Thus, although the Fifth Amendment may protect an in-

6. In Boyd v. United States, 116 U.S. 616 (1886), for example, it was held that the Government could not, consistently with the Fourth Amendment, obtain "mere evidence" from the accused; accordingly, a subpoena seeking "mere evidence" constituted compulsion of the accused against which he could invoke the Fifth Amendment. The "mere evidence" rule was overturned in Warden v. Hayden, 387 U.S. 294, 301-302 (1967).

The "convergence theory" of the Fourth and Fifth Amendments is also illustrated by Agnello v. United States, 269 U.S. 20 (1925), where the seizure of contraband pursuant to a search not incident to arrest and otherwise unlawful in violation of the Fourth Amendment was held to permit the accused to invoke the Fifth Amendment when the Government sought to introduce this evidence in a criminal proceeding against him.

7. Petitioner relies on the statement in Couch that "possession bears the closest relationship to personal compulsion forbidden by the Fifth Amendment," 409 U.S., at 331, in support of his argument that possession of incriminating evidence itself supplies the predicate for invocation of the privilege. Couch, of course, was concerned with the production of documents pursuant to a summons directed to the accountant where there might have been a possibility of compulsory self-incrimination by the principal's implicit or explicit "testimony" that the documents were those identified in the summons. The risk of authentication is not present where the documents are seized pursuant to a search warrant.

dividual from complying with a subpoena for the production of his personal records in his possession because the very act of production may constitute a compulsory authentication of incriminating information, see Fisher v. United States, supra, a seizure of the same materials by law enforcement officers differs in a crucial respect—the individual against whom the search is directed is not required to aid in the discovery, production, or authentication of incriminating evidence. . . . .

We find a useful analogy to the Fifth Amendment question in those cases that deal with the "seizure" of oral communications. As the Court has explained, "[t]he constitutional privilege against self-incrimination . . . is designed to prevent the use of legal process to force from the lips of the accused individual the evidence necessary to convict him or to force him to produce and authenticate any personal documents or effects that might incriminate him." Bellis v. United States, 417 U.S., at 88. The significant aspect of this principle was apparent and applied in Hoffa v. United States, where the Court rejected the contention that an informant's "seizure" of the accused's conversation with him, and his subsequent testimony at trial concerning that conversation, violated the Fifth Amendment. The rationale was that, although the accused's statements may have been elicited by the informant for the purpose of gathering evidence against him, they were made voluntarily. We see no reasoned distinction to be made between the compulsion upon the accused in that case and the compulsion in this one. In each, the communication, whether oral or written, was made voluntarily. The fact that seizure was contemporaneous with the communication in *Hoffa* but subsequent to the communication here does not affect the question whether the accused was compelled to speak.

Finally we do not believe that permitting the introduction into evidence of a person's business records seized during an otherwise lawful search would offend or undermine any of the policies undergirding the privilege.[8]

In this case, petitioner, at the time he recorded his communication, at the time of the search, and at the time the records were admitted at trial, was not subjected to "the cruel trilemma of self-accusation, perjury or contempt." Indeed, he was never required to say or to do anything under penalty of sanction. Similarly, permitting the admission of the

---

8. "The privilege against self-incrimination . . . reflects many of our fundamental values and most noble aspirations: our unwillingness to subject those suspected of crime to the cruel trilemma of self-accusation, perjury or contempt; our preference for an accusatorial rather than an inquisitorial system of criminal justice; our fear that self-incriminating statements will be elicited by inhumane treatment and abuses; our sense of fair play which dictates 'a fair state-individual balance by requiring the government to leave the individual alone until good cause is shown for disturbing him and by requiring the government in its contest with the individual to shoulder the entire load' . . . ; our respect for the inviolability of the human personality and of the right of each individual 'to a private enclave where he may lead a private life' . . . ; our distrust of self-deprecatory statements; and our realization that the privilege, while sometimes 'a shelter to the guilty,' is often 'a protection to the innocent.' "

records in question does not convert our accusatorial system of justice into an inquisitorial system. "The requirement of specific charges, their proof beyond a reasonable doubt, the protection of the accused from confessions extorted through whatever form of police pressures, the right to a prompt hearing before a magistrate, the right to assistance of counsel, to be supplied by government when circumstances make it necessary, the duty to advise an accused of his constitutional rights—these are all characteristics of the accusatorial system and manifestations of its demands." Watts v. Indiana, 338 U.S. 49, 54 (1949). None of these attributes is endangered by the introduction of business records "independently secured through skillful investigation." Ibid. Further, the search for and seizure of business records pose no danger greater than that inherent in every search that evidence will be "elicited by inhumane treatment and abuses." 378 U. S., at 55. In this case, the statements seized were voluntarily committed to paper before the police arrived to search for them, and petitioner was not treated discourteously during the search. Also, the "good cause" to "disturb," ibid., petitioner was independently determined by the judge who issued the warrants; and the State bore the burden of executing them. Finally, there is no chance, in this case, of petitioner's statements being self-deprecatory and untrustworthy because they were extracted from him— they were already in existence and had been made voluntarily.

We recognize, of course, that the Fifth Amendment protects privacy to some extent. However, "the Court has never suggested that every invasion of privacy violates the privilege." Fisher v. United States, 425 U.S., at 399. Indeed, we recently held that unless incriminating testimony is "compelled," any invasion of privacy is outside the scope of the Fifth Amendment's protection, saying that "the Fifth Amendment protects against 'compelled self-incrimination, not [the disclosure of] private information.' " Id., at 401. Here, as we have already noted, petitioner was not compelled to testify in any manner.

Accordingly, we hold that the search of an individual's office for business records, their seizure, and subsequent introduction into evidence do not offend the Fifth Amendment's proscription that "[n]o person . . . shall be compelled in any criminal case to be a witness against himself." [427 U.S. at 471-477.]

3. What does *Fisher* protect? Frankly, the answer to that question is not altogether clear. Some of its opacity is eliminated by recognizing that, generally speaking, production of any tangible item may communicate two different types of information. The item may speak for itself, as writings do, and as other kinds of items may (a gun which can be tested by ballistics experts, for example). This is precisely the kind of information that the Court found not to be protected by the fifth amendment because its creation was not compelled. The second type of information communicated by the act of production has to do with the object itself rather than its contents. By producing an object, one admits that

it exists, its genuineness, and that one believes it to be the item requested by the government. By admitting such matters, the person producing the object would provide the government sufficient information to authenticate it under normal evidentiary rules. Unlike the contents, this information is compelled and thus is protected by the fifth amendment.

The difficulty is that the two aspects of information discussed above are paradigm cases, but in the real world they exist as variables. Sometimes the government knows what is in a writing and who possesses it, and sometimes the government possesses virtually no information on either score. How the "act of production" rationale is supposed to apply in the complex manifestations of these two variables that are generated in real life is unclear.

Fisher may seem to be indifferent to whether the government knows the contents of a writing. After all, that is just what the Court said is not protected by the fifth amendment. Nonetheless, there is an intimate connection between knowing the contents and knowing of the existence of a document, a matter that the Court found to be protected. Indeed, in one sense only if the government already knows of the contents of a document can it know of the existence of the document. If the government does not know the contents of a document, producing it admits that it exists and contains whatever it contains, information that the government would not previously have possessed. And of course, if the government already knew what the document contains, in many cases the government would not need it. There is thus often tension between the government's claim that it knows of the existence of a document and that it needs it. How the "act of production" rationale resolves this tension is not clear.

4. Not surprisingly, the lower courts have disagreed on the meaning of *Fisher*. As pointed out in Note, The Rights of Criminal Defendants and the Subpoena Duces Tecum: The Aftermath of *Fisher v. United States*, 95 Harv. L. Rev. 683 (1982), the lower courts have been especially inconsistent over the implication of the idea of implicit authentication, and at least three different views have emerged:

> 1. *The Testimonial Contents Approach.*—Several courts have suggested that implicit authentication occurs only when the content of the evidence is testimonial. For example, courts have distinguished documents containing handwritten remarks from mere records, because remarks are considered more "testimonial." This approach can only be explained as a means of preventing the exposure of personal statements to government scrutiny. Although such a concern is presumably based on the desire to protect privacy, under *Fisher* mere privacy concerns are unprotected by the fifth amendment. The contours of implicit au-

thentication must thus be shaped solely by the need to prevent compulsion. The remarks that documents contain are irrelevant if the government has not compelled the creation of the remarks themselves. The doctrine of implicit authentication is therefore not useful for courts attempting to protect a broader privacy interest of defendants.

2. *The Circumstances-of-Production Approach.*—Other courts attempting to give content to implicit authentication have looked to the circumstances existing when the subpoena was issued. In general, these courts have considered one of two factors: the extent of the government's knowledge of the location or existence of evidence, or the degree to which the defendant would have to cooperate with the government's demand. . . .

3. *The First Circuit Approach.*—A third group of courts starts with the generally accepted proposition that defendants cannot be compelled to authenticate evidence at trial. In their view, the doctrine of implicit authentication is derived from this proposition. The impermissible aspect of compelled production of evidence is not the fact that the defendant gives something to the government, but that when he does so he necessarily assents to the government's characterization of the evidence in the subpoena. Thus, if the evidence may be authenticated in some other way, its admissibility does not hinge on the information conveyed by the defendant's act of production. This view is consistent with *Fisher's* observation that implicit authentication did not apply to the case because, according to the rules of evidence, Fisher was the wrong person to authenticate them. The presence or absence of a third party who can authenticate the documents thus determines the admissibility of the evidence. [Id. at 686-689.]

5. After *Fisher* and *Andresen*, may the state obtain, in any fashion, a diary that it has probable cause to believe would incriminate the diary's owner and possessor? Should it be able to do so? Consider the following passage from Note, Formalism, Legal Realism, and Constitutionally Protected Privacy Under the Fourth and Fifth Amendments, 90 Harv. L. Rev. 945, 985-988 (1977):

While the premises of formalist jurisprudence were both overinclusive and underinclusive in equating personality with property, the legal realist assumption that all individual claims to right are relative to other societal interests is too extreme. Both positions are inadequate insofar as they neglect the dual nature of human experience: one is apart from as well as a part of society. The conclusion that the fourth and fifth amendments should protect absolutely a core of one's expressions and effects is impelled by the moral and symbolic need to recognize and defend the private aspect of personality.

Belief in the uniqueness of each individual is one of the fundamental moral tenets of Western society. Such uniqueness inheres in being human and is not an entitlement to be granted or withheld by the state. In fact, one of the primary purposes of law is to ensure respect for this belief by preserving each person's right to a private life free from unwanted intrusion and disclosure. Justice Brandeis saw this as the purpose underlying the fourth amendment:

> The makers of our Constitution undertook to secure conditions favorable to the pursuit of happiness. They recognized the significance of man's spiritual nature, of his feelings and of his intellect. . . . They sought to protect Americans in their beliefs, their thoughts, their emotions and their sensations. They conferred, as against the Government, the right to be let alone. . . .[247]

A record of one's private beliefs and emotions tells a good deal about the person. Similarly, when one intimately and privately shares such thoughts and feelings with others he reveals much of the inner person he is.[248] Such experiences may include the exchange of letters, tapes, or phone conversations as well as actual gathering and conversation. Just as recognition of the relationship between private reflection, socialization, and personality has led the Court to block legislative attempts to control intimate private conduct,[249] interference with the private life by search or subpoena should be proscribed under the fourth and fifth amendments rather than tolerated as a necessary incident of criminal law enforcement. The privacy value should not suffer abridgement simply because there is reason to believe a person is involved in criminal activity.

The conclusion of the Court last Term that there is no absolute protection for a broad range of personal privacy under either the fourth or fifth amendments has a certain initial plausibility in an age when even the "absolutely" worded first amendment is not so construed. The nature of the values involved, however, justifies absolute protection under the fourth and fifth amendments even if not under the first. There is room in particular first amendment cases for the accommodation of the conflicting societal and personal interests likely to arise from the individual's aggressive public activity by limiting expression so long as the aggregate amount and quality of expression is not reduced enough to impair the process of self-government. By comparison, the primary value underlying the constitutional right to privacy is the preservation of an inviolate enclave for one's private personality. Accommodation by limitation of the right in any particular case is not an incremental adjustment in a societal policy, but a direct violation of the principle to be protected.

247. Olmstead v. United States, 277 U.S. 438, 478 (1928) (Brandeis, J., dissenting).
248. Fried, Privacy, 77 Yale L.J. 475, 477-78 (1968). See also Griswold v. Connecticut, 381 U.S. 479, 486 (1965).
249. Roe v. Wade, 410 U.S. 113 (1973) (abortion); Eisenstadt v. Baird, 405 U.S. 438 (1972) (contraceptives for unmarried persons); Stanley v. Georgia, 394 U.S. 557 (1969) (private possession of obscene material); Griswold v. Connecticut, 381 U.S. 479 (1965) (right of marital privacy).

The need to protect the principle of privacy also follows from the manner in which American political theory legitimizes government action. It is an axiom of that theory that the power of the majority may not be used to deprive the minority of human dignity and equality under the law. The right to privacy deserves primary recognition in such a scheme because of its close connection with the uniqueness of the person and human dignity. To reject the right is to deny these values and thus implicitly to deny the political importance of those singled out by the majority's enactment and enforcement of the criminal law. Moreover, it is the duty of the courts to undertake this "primary responsibility and duty of giving force and effect to constitutional liberties." Unless the fourth and fifth amendments can be read as putting a premium on the value of personal privacy in the face of government encroachment, it is difficult to imagine what these amendments can mean.

Recognition of the right to privacy, and the accompanying willingness to pay the price in marginal social efficiency necessary to make that recognition meaningful, enhance the efficacy of Justice Brandeis' argument that the law may exert a profound long term influence on the perceptions and actions of many members of the society. By granting comprehensive protection to the right of personal privacy courts encourage people to place respect for human personality over the impulse to prejudge and to punish fellow citizens. Consistent and sincere articulation and defense of the values at stake may manifest itself eventually in the behavior of the police.

Once the right to personal privacy and the value of self-realization and private socialization informing it are acknowledged and accorded their appropriate preferred position in the constitutional hierarchy, the meaning of the cryptic observation in *Boyd* that the fourth and fifth amendments "run almost into each other"[258] becomes clear. The amendments must be interpreted in "sufficiently varied ways to accommodate to the various contexts in which these crucial rights may be challenged."[259]

For the reasons already discussed, the fourth and fifth amendments should protect absolutely a core of personal communications, papers, and effects from nonwilled government procurement and disclosure. In determining the scope of this privilege the Court should secure a significant range of human experience intimately related to the private aspect of personality and impose limitations on the protection afforded in a principled manner consistent with the values underlying the right. . . .

The Note also proposes that the "paper search" rule of *Boyd* can be seen to survive *Fisher* as a function of the first amendment. If that point is recognized, the author suggests, the present state of the law provides reasonable protection for the central concerns expressed in *Boyd*.

258. 116 U.S. at 630.
259. McKay, The Preference for Freedom, 34 N.Y.U. L. Rev. 1182, 1222 (1959) (first amendment context).

Properly read, Fisher v. United States stands for the proposition that no defendant may be compelled to authenticate evidence. Although this holding narrows the application of the self-incrimination clause, it adequately protects the rights of criminal defendants if the prohibitions of other amendments and evidentiary rules are properly applied. The implicit authentication doctrine of the fifth amendment prevents defendants from being forced to verify the case against them. The protection of the fourth amendment applicable to subpoenas duces tecum prohibits authorities from wholesale rummaging through a citizen's papers. Finally, the first amendment can prevent the government from probing into a defendant's most personal papers. Specific amendments answer specific concerns. Drawing on all of them, courts can forge a broad constitutional protection for all citizens' rights. [Id. at 702.]

The author of the Note quoted at the beginning of the chapter, page 423 supra, although not considering the first amendment issue, views the state of the law considerably less sanguinely.

> In light of *Andresen* and *Fisher*, *Boyd* is dead. No zone of privacy now exists that the government cannot enter to take an individual's property for the purpose of obtaining incriminating information. In most cases, the zone can be entered by the issuance of a subpoena; in the rest, it can be breached by a search warrant. . . . The words of the Constitution can legitimately be understood in many ways. Precedent and history can be used to support divergent readings. Ultimately, the difference between the various interpretations given to the Constitution can be traced to disagreements on policy.
>
> So it is with *Boyd*. That case reflected the belief of a majority of the Justices then constituting the Supreme Court that the individual's interest in the rights that the privilege against self-incrimination was designed to safeguard was more important than the government's interest in convicting criminals. The Court protected those rights as completely as possible, though it could have read the Constitution as compelling less. At least seven members of that Court shared the views expressed in the *Boyd* opinion:
>
>> Though the proceeding in question is divested of many of the aggravating effects of actual search and seizure, yet, as before said, it contains their substance and essence, and effects their essential purpose. It may be that it is the obnoxious thing in its mildest and least repulsive form, but illegitimate and unconstitutional practices get their first footing in that way, namely, by silent approaches and slight deviations from legal modes of procedure. This can only be obviated by adhering to the rule that constitutional provisions for the security of person and property should be liberally construed. A close and literal construction of them deprives them of half their efficacy, and leads to gradual depreciation of the right, as if it consisted more in sound than in substance. It is the duty of courts to be watchful for the constitutional

rights of the citizen, and guard against any stealthy encroachments thereon. Their motto should be obsta principiis.[138]

The Burger Court has rejected *Boyd* because it no longer considers those values to be paramount; it is more impressed by the government's interest in combatting crime. In *Couch*, Justice Powell captured the spirit of the current Court: "It is important, in applying constitutional principles, to interpret them in light of the fundamental interests of personal liberty they were meant to serve. Respect for these principles is eroded when they leap their proper bounds to interfere with the legitimate interest of society in enforcement of its laws and collection of the revenues."[139] Accordingly, *Boyd* is dead. But the Court refuses to take the final step of overruling it.

Justice Brandeis once called *Boyd* "a case that will be remembered as long as civil liberty lives in the United States."[140] At least it deserves a decent burial. [Id. at 211-212.]

To which view do you subscribe, and why? The possible demise of *Boyd* has not been universally decried. See Gerstein, The Demise of *Boyd*: Self-Incrimination and Private Papers in the Burger Court, 27 U.C.L.A.L. Rev. 343 (1979), arguing that *Boyd* obscured the rationale of the fifth amendment's concern for autonomy, and Friendly, The Fifth Amendment Tomorrow: The Case for Constitutional Change, 37 U. Cin. L. Rev. 671 (1968), arguing that *Boyd* should be overruled.

6. In light of *Schmerber* and the other cases we have been considering, the Court has held that individuals can be required to give voice exemplars, United States v. Wade, supra page 339; and handwriting exemplars, Gilbert v. California, page 355 supra. In such cases, an individual is normally subpoenaed to appear. The Court has held that subpoenas do not need to meet the probable cause standard of the fourth amendment. Rather, they must call for relevant material and not be unduly burdensome. For a discussion, see McKenna, The Constitutional Protection of Private Papers: The Role of a Hierarchical Fourth Amendment, 53 Ind. L.J. 55, 84-90 (1977-1978). The author argues that one solution for fears of overly broad subpoenas, as well as for fears concerning the demise of *Boyd*, is to require a higher than normal standard for obtaining private papers. There are, however, due process limits on the extraction of evidence from a suspect's body. In Rochin v. California, 342 U.S. 165 (1952), the Court reversed a conviction for possession of drugs that was based in part on evidentiary use of morphine tablets obtained by forcibly injecting an emetic into the defendant, over his objection, causing him to vomit up the capsules.

138. 116 U.S. at 635.
139. Couch v. United States, 409 U.S. 322, 336 (1973).
140. Olmstead v. United States, 277 U.S. 438, 474 (1928) (Brandeis, J., dissenting).

In Pennsylvania v. Muniz, 110 S. Ct. 2638 (1990), the Court concluded that the incriminating inferences from a suspect's inability to perform sobriety tests were admissible on the *Wade/Gilbert* ground that there was no testimonial compulsion. *Muniz* is reproduced in its entirety in Chapter 9, page 1166, infra.

7. Has the Supreme Court finally buried *Boyd?* Consider the next two cases.

UNITED STATES v. DOE
Certiorari to the United States Court of Appeals for the Third Circuit
465 U.S. 605 (1984)

JUSTICE POWELL delivered the opinion of the Court.

This case presents the issue whether, and to what extent, the Fifth Amendment privilege against compelled self-incrimination applies to the business records of a sole proprietorship.

I

Respondent is the owner of several sole proprietorships. In late 1980, a grand jury, during the course of an investigation of corruption in the awarding of county and municipal contracts, served five subpoenas on respondent. The first two demanded the production of the telephone records of several of respondent's companies and all records pertaining to four bank accounts of respondent and his companies. The subpoenas were limited to the period between January 1, 1977 and the dates of the subpoenas. The third subpoena demanded the production of a list of virtually all the business records of one of respondent's companies for the period between January 1, 1976, and the date of the subpoena. The fourth subpoena sought production of a similar list of business records belonging to another company. The final subpoena demanded production of all bank statements and cancelled checks of two of respondent's companies that had accounts at a bank in the Grand Cayman Islands.

II

Respondent filed a motion in federal district court seeking to quash the subpoenas. The District Court for the District of New Jersey granted his motion except with respect to those documents and records required by law to be kept or disclosed to a public agency.[3] In reaching its decision, the District Court noted that the Government had conceded that the materials sought in the subpoena were or might be incriminating. The court stated that, therefore, "the relevant inquiry is . . . whether the *act* of producing the documents has communicative aspects which warrant Fifth Amendment protection." The court found that the act of production would compel respondent to "admit that the records exist, that they are in his possession, and that they are authentic." While not ruling out the possibility that the Government could devise a way to ensure that the act of turning over the documents would not incriminate respondent, the court held that the Government had not made such a showing.

The Court of Appeals for the Third Circuit affirmed. It first addressed the question whether the Fifth Amendment ever applies to the records of a sole proprietorship. After noting that an individual may not assert the Fifth Amendment privilege on behalf of a corporation, partnership, or other collective entity under the holding of Bellis v. United States, 417 U.S. 85 (1974), the Court of Appeals reasoned that the owner of a sole proprietorship acts in a personal rather than a representative capacity. As a result, the court held that respondent's claim of the privilege was not foreclosed by the reasoning of *Bellis*.

The Court of Appeals next considered whether the documents at issue in this case are privileged. The court noted that this Court held in Fisher v. United States, 425 U.S. 391 (1976), that the contents of business records ordinarily are not privileged because they are created voluntarily and without compulsion. The Court of Appeals nevertheless found that respondent's business records were privileged under either of two analyses. First, the court reasoned that, notwithstanding the holdings in *Bellis* and *Fisher*, the business records of a sole proprietorship are no different from the individual owner's personal records. Noting that Third Circuit cases had held that private papers, although created voluntarily, are protected by the Fifth Amendment, the court accorded the same protection to respondent's business papers. Second, it held that respondent's act of producing the subpoenaed records would have "communicative aspects of its own." The turning over of the subpoenaed documents to the grand jury would admit their existence and authenticity. Accordingly, respondent was entitled to assert his Fifth Amendment privilege rather than produce the subpoenaed documents.

---

3. The District Court mentioned tax returns and W-2 statements as examples of documents falling within this category. Respondent has not challenged this aspect of the District Court's opinion. We therefore understand that this case concerns only business documents and records not required by law to be kept or disclosed to a public agency. We also note that our opinion addresses only the Fifth Amendment implications of the subpoenas. The subpoenas were drawn in the broadest possible terms. It may be that the breadth of the subpoenas is subject to attack on other grounds that are not before us.

The Government contended that the court should enforce the subpoenas because of the Government's offer not to use respondent's act of production against respondent in any way. The Court of Appeals noted that no format request for use immunity under 18 U.S.C. §§6002 and 6003 had been made. In light of this failure, the court held that the District Court did not err in rejecting the Government's attempt to compel delivery of the subpoenaed records.

We granted certiorari to resolve the apparent conflict between the Court of Appeals holding and the reasoning underlying this Court's holding in *Fisher*. We now affirm in part, reverse in part, and remand for further proceedings.

III

A

The Court in *Fisher* expressly declined to reach the question whether the Fifth Amendment privilege protects the contents of an individual's tax records in his possession. The rationale underlying our holding in that case is, however, persuasive here. As we noted in *Fisher*, the Fifth Amendment only protects the person asserting the privilege from *compelled* self-incrimination. Where the preparation of business records is voluntary, no compulsion is present.[8] A subpoena that demands production of documents "does not compel oral testimony; nor would it ordinarily compel the taxpayer to restate, repeat, or affirm the truth of the contents of the documents sought." . . .

This reasoning applies with equal force here. Respondent does not contend that he prepared the documents involuntarily[9] or that the sub-

---

8. Respondent's principal argument is that the Fifth Amendment should be read as creating a "zone of privacy which protects an individual and his personal records from compelled production." This argument derives from language in Boyd v. United States, 116 U.S. 616, 630 (1886). This Court addressed substantially the same argument in *Fisher*: "Within the limits imposed by the language of the Fifth Amendment, which we necessarily observe, the privilege truly serves privacy interests; but the Court has never on any ground, personal privacy included, applied the Fifth Amendment to prevent the otherwise proper acquisition or use of evidence which, in the Court's view, did not involve compelled testimonial self-incrimination of some sort." 425 U.S., at 399. In Andresen v. Maryland, 427 U.S. 463 (1976), the petitioner also relied on Boyd. In rejecting his argument, we observed that "the continued validity of the broad statements contained in some of the Court's earlier cases [has] been discredited by later opinions." Id., at 472. See also United States v. Nobles, 422 U.S. 225, 233, n.7 (1975).

9. The Court of Appeals recognized the absence of compulsion in the compilation of the records sought in this case and those sought in *Fisher*. "To be sure, the documents requested here, like those sought in *Fisher*, were voluntarily prepared, and therefore 'cannot be said to contain compelled testimonial evidence' in and of themselves." 680

poena would force him to restate, repeat, or affirm the truth of their contents. The fact that the records are in respondent's possession is irrelevant to the determination of whether the creation of the records was compelled. We therefore hold that the contents of those records are not privileged.[10]

B

Although the contents of a document may not be privileged, the act of producing the document may be. A government subpoena compels the holder of the document to perform an act that may have testimonial aspects and an incriminating effect. . . . In *Fisher*, the Court explored the effect that the act of production would have on the taxpayer and determined that the act of production would have only minimal testimonial value and would not operate to incriminate the taxpayer. Unlike the Court in *Fisher*, we have the explicit finding of the District Court that the act of producing the documents would involve testimonial self-incrimination.[11] The Court of Appeals agreed.[12] The District Court's

---

F.2d, at 334. The Court of Appeals nevertheless gave our holding in *Fisher* an unduly restrictive reading and found it not to control the outcome in this case.

10. Accord In re Grand Jury Proceedings, 626 F.2d 1051, 1055 (C.A.1 1980) ("The line of cases culminating in *Fisher* have stripped the content of business records of any Fifth Amendment protection"). While not directly on point, Andresen v. Maryland, 427 U.S. 463 (1976), is consistent with our holding. In *Andresen*, investigators from a bi-county fraud unit obtained warrants to search the petitioner's office. During the search, the investigators seized several incriminating business records relating to the petitioner's practice as a sole practitioner of real estate law. The petitioner sought suppression of the documents on Fourth and Fifth Amendment grounds. The petitioner based his Fifth Amendment argument on "dicta in a number of cases which imply, or state, that the search for and seizure of a person's private papers violate the privilege against self-incrimination." Id., at 471. The Court dismissed this argument and found the documents not to be privileged because the petitioner "had voluntarily committed to writing" any incriminating statements contained therein. Id., at 473. Although *Andresen* involved a search warrant rather than a subpoena, the underlying principle is the same in this context. If the party asserting the Fifth Amendment privilege has voluntarily compiled the document, no compulsion is present and the contents of the document are not privileged.

11. The District Court stated: "With few exceptions, enforcement of the subpoenas would compel [respondent] to admit that the records exist, that they are in his possession, and that they are authentic. These communications, if made under compulsion of a court decree, would violate [respondent's] Fifth Amendment rights. . . . The government argues that the existence, possession and authenticity of the documents can be proved without [respondent's] testimonial communication, but it cannot satisfy this court as to how that representation can be implemented to protect the witness in subsequent proceedings." 541 F. Supp., at 3.

12. The Court of Appeals stated:

> In the matter sub judice, however, we find nothing in the record that would indicate that the United States knows, as a certainty, that each of the myriad documents demanded by the five subpoenas in fact is in the appellee's possession

finding essentially rests on its determination of factual issues. See United States v. Nixon, 418 U.S. 683, 702 (1974). Therefore, we will not overturn that finding unless it has no support in the record. Ibid. Traditionally, we also have been reluctant to disturb findings of fact in which two courts below have concurred. Rogers v. Lodge, 458 U.S. 613, 623 (1982). We therefore decline to overturn the finding of the District Court in this regard, where, as here, it has been affirmed by the Court of Appeals.[13]

IV

The Government, as it concedes, could have compelled respondent to produce the documents listed in the subpoena. Sections 6002 and 6003 of Title 18 provide for the granting of use immunity with respect to the potentially incriminating evidence. The Court upheld the constitutionality of the use immunity statute in Kastigar v. United States.

The Government did state several times before the District Court that it would not use respondent's act of production against him in any way. But counsel for the Government never made a statutory request to the District Court to grant respondent use immunity. We are urged to

---

> or subject to his control. The most plausible inference to be drawn from the broad-sweeping subpoenas is that the Government, unable to prove that the subpoenaed documents exist—or that the appellee even is somehow connected to the business entities under investigation—is attempting to compensate for its lack of knowledge by requiring the appellee to become, in effect, the primary informant against himself.

680 F.2d, at 335.

13. The Government concedes that the act of producing the subpoenaed documents might have had some testimonial aspects, but it argues that any incrimination would be so trivial that the Fifth Amendment is not implicated. The Government finds support for this argument in Marchetti v. United States, 390 U.S. 39 (1968). In *Marchetti*, the Court stated that a party who wishes to claim the Fifth Amendment privilege must be "confronted by substantial and 'real,' and not merely trifling or imaginary, hazards of incrimination." Id., at 53; see United States v. Apfelbaum, 445 U.S. 115, 128 (1980). On the basis of the findings made in this case we think it clear that the risk of incrimination was "substantial and real" and not "trifling or imaginary." Respondent did not concede in the District Court that the records listed in the subpoena actually existed or were in his possession. Respondent argued that by producing the records, he would tacitly admit their existence and his possession. Respondent also pointed out that if the Government obtained the documents from another source, it would have to authenticate them before they would be admissible at trial. See Fed. R. Evid. 901. By producing the documents, respondent would relieve the Government of the need for authentication. These allegations were sufficient to establish a valid claim of the privilege against self-incrimination. This is not to say that the Government was foreclosed from rebutting respondent's claim by producing evidence that possession, existence, and authentication were a "foregone conclusion." *Fisher*, 425 U.S. at 411. In this case, however, the Government failed to make such a showing.

adopt a doctrine of constructive use immunity. Under this doctrine, the courts would impose a requirement on the Government not to use the incriminatory aspects of the act of production against the person claiming the privilege even though the statutory procedures have not been followed.

We decline to extend the jurisdiction of courts to include prospective grants of use immunity in the absence of the formal request that the statute requires.[16] As we stated in Pillsbury Co. v. Conboy, 459 U.S. 248 (1983), in passing the use immunity statute, "Congress gave certain officials in the Department of Justice exclusive authority to grant immunities." "Congress foresaw the courts as playing only a minor role in the immunizing process. . . ." The decision to seek use immunity necessarily involves a balancing of the Government's interest in obtaining information against the risk that immunity will frustrate the Government's attempts to prosecute the subject of the investigation. Congress expressly left this decision exclusively to the Justice Department. If, on remand, the appropriate official concludes that it is desirable to compel respondent to produce his business records, the statutory procedure for requesting use immunity will be available.[17]

V

We conclude that the Court of Appeals erred in holding that the contents of the subpoenaed documents were privileged under the Fifth Amendment. The act of producing the documents at issue in this case is privileged and cannot be compelled without a statutory grant of use immunity pursuant to 18 U.S.C. §§6002 and 6003. The judgment of the Court of Appeals is, therefore, affirmed in part, reversed in part, and the case is remanded to the District Court for further proceedings in accordance with this decision.

16. Of course, courts generally suppress compelled, incriminating testimony that results from a violation of a witness's Fifth Amendment rights. See United States v. Mandujano, 425 U.S. 564, 576 (1976); United States v. Blue, 384 U.S. 251, 255 (1966). The difference between that situation and the Government's theory of constructive use immunity is that in the latter it is the grant of judicially enforceable use immunity that compels the witness to testify. In the former situation, exclusion of the witness' testimony is used to deter the government from future violations of witnesses' Fifth Amendment rights.

17. Respondent argues that any grant of use immunity must cover the contents of the documents as well as the act of production. We find this contention unfounded. To satisfy the requirements of the Fifth Amendment, a grant of immunity need be only as broad as the privilege against self-incrimination. As discussed above, the privilege in this case extends only to the act of production. Therefore, any grant of use immunity need only protect respondent from the self-incrimination that might accompany the act of producing his business records.

It is so ordered.

Affirmed in part, reversed in part, and remanded.

JUSTICE O'CONNOR, concurring.

I concur in both the result and reasoning of Justice Powell's opinion for the Court. I write separately, however, just to make explicit what is implicit in the analysis of that opinion: that the Fifth Amendment provides absolutely no protection for the contents of private papers of any kind. The notion that the Fifth Amendment protects the privacy of papers originated in Boyd v. United States, but our decision in Fisher v. United States, sounded the death-knell for *Boyd*. "Several of *Boyd's* express or implicit declarations [had] not stood the test of time[,]" and its privacy of papers concept "had long been a rule searching for a rationale. . . ." Today's decision puts a long-overdue end to that fruitless search.

JUSTICE MARSHALL, with whom JUSTICE BRENNAN joins, concurring in part and dissenting in part. . . . Contrary to what Justice O'Connor contends, I do not view the Court's opinion in this case as having reconsidered whether the Fifth Amendment provides protection for the contents of "private papers of any kind." This case presented nothing remotely close to the question that Justice O'Connor eagerly poses and answers. First, as noted above, the issue whether the Fifth Amendment protects the contents of the documents was obviated by the Court of Appeals' rulings relating to the act of production and statutory use immunity. Second, the documents at stake here are business records which implicate a lesser degree of concern for privacy interests than, for example, personal diaries.

Were it true that the Court's opinion stands for the proposition that "the Fifth Amendment provides absolutely no protection for the contents of private papers of any kind," I would assuredly dissent. I continue to believe that under the Fifth Amendment "there are certain documents no person ought to be compelled to produce at the Government's request." Fisher v. United States, 425 U.S. 391, 431-432 (Justice Marshall, concurring).

[JUSTICE STEVENS' opinion, concurring in part and dissenting in part, is omitted.]

BRASWELL v. UNITED STATES

Certiorari to the United States Court of Appeals for the Fifth Circuit
487 U.S. 99 (1988)

CHIEF JUSTICE REHNQUIST delivered the opinion of the Court. This case presents the question whether the custodian of corporate records may resist a subpoena for such records on the ground that the act of production would incriminate him in violation of the Fifth Amendment. We conclude that he may not.

From 1965 to 1980, petitioner Randy Braswell operated his business—which comprises the sale and purchase of equipment, land, timber, and oil and gas interests—as a sole proprietorship. In 1980, he incorporated Worldwide Machinery Sales, Inc., a Mississippi corporation, and began conducting the business through that entity. In 1981, he formed a second Mississippi corporation, Worldwide Purchasing, Inc., and funded that corporation with the 100 percent interest he held in Worldwide Machinery. Petitioner was and is the sole shareholder of Worldwide Purchasing, Inc.

Both companies are active corporations, maintaining their current status with the State of Mississippi, filing corporate tax returns, and keeping current corporate books and records. In compliance with Mississippi law, both corporations have three directors, petitioner, his wife, and his mother. Although his wife and mother are secretary-treasurer and vice-president of the corporations, respectively, neither has any authority over the business affairs of either corporation.

In August 1986, a federal grand jury issued a subpoena to "Randy Braswell, President Worldwide Machinery, Inc. (and) Worldwide Purchasing, Inc." requiring petitioner to produce the books and records of the two corporations. The subpoena provided that petitioner could deliver the records to the agent serving the subpoena, and did not require petitioner to testify. Petitioner moved to quash the subpoena, arguing that the act of producing the records would incriminate him in violation of his Fifth Amendment privilege against self-incrimination. The District Court denied the motion to quash, ruling that the "collective entity doctrine" prevented petitioner from asserting that his act of producing the corporations' records was protected by the Fifth Amendment. The court rejected petitioner's argument that the collective entity doctrine does not apply when a corporation is so small that it constitutes nothing more than the individual's alter ego.

The United States Court of Appeals for the Fifth Circuit affirmed, citing Bellis v. United States for the proposition that a corporation's records custodian may not claim a Fifth Amendment privilege no matter how small the corporation may be. The Court of Appeals declared that *Bellis* retained vitality following United States v. Doe, and therefore, "Braswell, as custodian of corporate documents, has no act of production privilege under the fifth amendment regarding corporate documents." We granted certiorari to resolve a conflict among the Courts of Appeals. We now affirm.

There is no question but that the contents of the subpoenaed business records are not privileged. See *Doe*, supra; Fisher v. United States. Similarly, petitioner asserts no self-incrimination claim on behalf of the corporations; it is well established that such artificial entities are not protected by the Fifth Amendment. Petitioner instead relies solely upon the argument that his act of producing the documents has independent testimonial significance, which would incriminate him individually, and that the Fifth Amendment prohibits government compulsion of that act. The bases for this argument are extrapolated from the decisions of this Court in *Fisher* and *Doe*. . . .

Had petitioner conducted his business as a sole proprietorship, *Doe* would require that he be provided the opportunity to show that his act of production would entail testimonial self-incrimination. But petitioner has operated his business through the corporate form, and we have long recognized that for purposes of the Fifth Amendment, corporations and other collective entities are treated differently from individuals. This doctrine—known as the collective entity rule—has a lengthy and distinguished pedigree [which the Court proceeded to discuss, citing cases such as Wilson v. United States, United States v. White, and Bellis v. United States]. . . .

The plain mandate of these decisions is that without regard to whether the subpoena is addressed to the corporation, or as here, to the individual in his capacity as a custodian, a corporate custodian such as petitioner may not resist a subpoena for corporate records on Fifth Amendment grounds. Petitioner argues, however, that this rule falls in the wake of Fisher v. United States, and United States v. Doe. In essence, petitioner's argument is as follows: In response to Boyd v. United States, with its privacy rationale shielding personal books and records, the Court developed the collective entity rule, which declares simply that corporate records are not private and therefore are not protected by the Fifth Amendment. The collective entity decisions were concerned with the contents of the documents subpoenaed, however, and not with the act of production. In *Fisher* and *Doe*, the Court moved away from the privacy based collective entity rule, replacing it with a compelled testimony standard under which the contents of business documents are never privileged but the act of producing the documents may be. Under this new regime, the act of production privilege is available without regard to the entity whose records are being sought. . . .

To be sure, the holding in *Fisher*—later reaffirmed in *Doe*—embarked upon a new course of Fifth Amendment analysis. We cannot agree, however, that it rendered the collective entity rule obsolete. The agency rationale undergirding the collective entity decisions, in which custodians asserted that production of entity records would incriminate them personally, survives. . . . [T]he Court has consistently recognized that the custodian of corporate or entity records holds those documents in a representative rather than a personal capacity. Artificial entities such as corporations may act only through their agents, and a custodian's assumption of his representative capacity leads to certain obligations, including the duty to produce corporate records on proper demand by the Government. Under those circumstances, the custodian's act of production is not deemed a personal act, but rather an act of the corporation. Any claim of Fifth Amendment privilege asserted by the agent would be tantamount to a claim of privilege by the corporation—which of course possesses no such privilege. . . .

Indeed, the opinion in *Fisher*—upon which petitioner places primary reliance[5]—indicates that the custodian of corporate records may not interpose a Fifth Amendment objection to the compelled production of corporate records, even though the act of production may prove personally incriminating. The *Fisher* court cited the collective entity decisions with approval and offered those decisions to support the conclusion that the production of the accountant's workpapers would "not . . . involve testimonial self-incrimination." The Court observed:

> This Court has . . . time and again allowed subpoenas against the custodian of corporate documents or those belonging to other collective entities such as unions and partnerships and those of bankrupt businesses over claims that the documents will incriminate the custodian despite the fact that producing the documents tacitly admits their existence and their location in the hands of their possessor.

The Court later noted that

> in *Wilson, Dreier, White, Bellis,* and In re Harris, the custodian of corporate, union, or partnership books or those of a bankrupt business was ordered to respond to a subpoena for the business' books even though doing so involved a "representation that the documents produced are those demanded by the subpoena," Curcio v. United States, 354 U.S., at 125.

In a footnote, the Court explained:

> In these cases compliance with the subpoena is required even though the books have been kept by the person subpoenaed and his producing them

5. Petitioner also offers United States v. Doe, as support for his position, but that decision is plainly inapposite. The *Doe* opinion begins by explaining that the question presented for review is "whether, and to what extent, the Fifth Amendment privilege against compelled self-incrimination applies to the business records of a sole proprietorship." A sole proprietor does not hold records in a representative capacity. Thus, the absence of any discussion of the collective entity rule can in no way be thought a suggestion that the status of the holder of the records is irrelevant.

would itself be sufficient authentication to permit their introduction against him.

The Court thus reaffirmed the obligation of a corporate custodian to comply with a subpoena addressed to him. . . .

Petitioner also attempts to extract support for his contention from *Curcio v. United States*, 354 U.S.118 (1957). But rather than bolstering petitioner's argument, we think *Curcio* substantiates the Government's position. *Curcio* had been served with two subpoenas addressed to him in his capacity as secretary-treasurer of a local union, which was under investigation. One subpoena required that he produce union books, the other that he testify. *Curcio* appeared before the grand jury, stated that the books were not in his possession, and refused to answer any questions as to their whereabouts. *Curcio* was held in contempt for refusing to answer the questions propounded. We reversed the contempt citation, rejecting the Government's argument "that the representative duty which required the production of union records in the *White* case requires the giving of oral testimony by the custodian."

Petitioner asserts that our *Curcio* decision stands for the proposition that although the contents of a collective entity's records are unprivileged, a representative of a collective entity cannot be required to provide testimony about those records. It follows, according to petitioner, that because *Fisher* recognizes that the act of production is potentially testimonial, such an act may not be compelled if it would tend to incriminate the representative personally. We find this reading of *Curcio* flawed. The *Curcio* Court made clear that with respect to a custodian of a collective entity's records, the line drawn was between oral testimony and other forms of incrimination.

> A custodian, by assuming the duties of his office, undertakes the obligation to produce the books of which he is custodian in response to a rightful exercise of the State's visitorial [sic] powers. But he cannot lawfully be compelled, in the absence of a grant of adequate immunity from prosecution, to condemn himself by his own oral testimony.

354 U.S., at 123-124 (emphasis added).[6]

In distinguishing those cases in which a corporate officer was required to produce corporate records and merely identify them by oral

---

6. See also 354 U.S. at 124-125 ("There is no hint in [the collective entity] decisions that a custodian of corporate or association books waives his constitutional privilege as to oral testimony by assuming the duties of his office. By accepting custodianship of records he 'has voluntarily assumed a duty which overrides his claim of privilege' *only* with respect to the production of the records themselves. Wilson v. United States, 221 U.S. 361, 380.") (emphasis in original).

testimony, the Court showed that it understood the testimonial nature of the act of production:

> The custodian's act of producing books or records in response to a subpoena duces tecum is itself a representation that the documents produced are those demanded by the subpoena. Requiring the custodian to identify or authenticate the documents for admission in evidence merely makes explicit what is implicit in the production itself.

Id., at 125. In the face of this recognition, the Court nonetheless noted: "In this case petitioner might have been proceeded against for his failure to produce the records demanded by the subpoena duces tecum."[7] Id. at 127, n.7. As Justice Brennan later observed in his concurrence in *Fisher*: "The Court in *Curcio*, however, apparently did not note any self-incrimination problem [with the testimonial significance of the act of production] because of the undertaking by the custodian with respect to the documents." 425 U.S. at 430, n.9.[8]

We note further that recognizing a Fifth Amendment privilege on behalf of the records custodians of collective entities would have a detrimental impact on the Government's efforts to prosecute "white-collar crime," one of the most serious problems confronting law enforcement authorities. "The greater portion of evidence of wrongdoing by an organization or its representatives is usually found in the official records and documents of that organization. Were the cloak of the privilege to be thrown around these impersonal records and documents, effective enforcement of many federal and state laws would be impossible." *White*, 322 U.S. at 700. If custodians could assert a privilege, authorities would be stymied not only in their enforcement efforts against those individuals but also in their prosecutions or organizations. In *Bellis*, the Court observed:

> In view of the inescapable fact that an artificial entity can only act to produce its records through its individual officers or agents, recognition

---

7. The dissent's suggestion that we have extracted from *Curcio* a distinction between oral testimony and act of production testimony that is nowhere found in the *Curcio* opinion simply ignores this part of *Curcio*. Similarly, the dissent pays mere lip service to the agency rationale supporting an unbroken chain of collective entity decisions. We have consistently held that for Fifth Amendment purposes a corporate custodian acts in a representative capacity when he produces corporate documents under the compulsion of a subpoena. The dissent's failure to recognize this principle and its suggestion that petitioner was not called upon to act in his capacity as an agent of the corporations cannot be squared with our previous decisions.

8. Doubtless, the compelled production of the records at issue in the subsequent *Bellis* decision would have had testimonial implications; the Court nonetheless upheld the contempt order.

of the individual's claim of privilege with respect to the financial records of the organization would substantially undermine the unchallenged rule that the organization itself is not entitled to claim any Fifth Amendment privilege, and largely frustrate legitimate governmental regulation of such organizations.

417 U.S. at 90.

Petitioner suggests, however, that these concerns can be minimized by the simple expedient of either granting the custodian statutory immunity as to the act of production, 18 U.S.C. §§6002-6003, or addressing the subpoena to the corporation and allowing it to choose an agent to produce the records who can do so without incriminating himself. We think neither proposal satisfactorily addresses these concerns. Taking the last first, it is no doubt true that if a subpoena is addressed to a corporation, the corporation "must find some means by which to comply because no Fifth Amendment defense is available to it." In re Sealed Case, 832 F.2d 1268, 1282, n.9 (1987). The means most commonly used to comply is the appointment of an alternate custodian. But petitioner insists he cannot be required to aid the appointed custodian in his search for the demanded records, for any statement to the surrogate would itself be testimonial and incriminating. If this is correct, then petitioner's "solution" is a chimera. In situations such as this—where the corporate custodian is likely the only person with knowledge about the demanded documents—the appointment of a surrogate will simply not ensure that the documents sought will ever reach the grand jury room; the appointed custodian will essentially be sent on an unguided search.

This problem is eliminated if the Government grants the subpoenaed custodian statutory immunity for the testimonial aspects of his act of production. But that "solution" also entails a significant drawback. All of the evidence obtained under a grant of immunity to the custodian may of course be used freely against the corporation, but if the Government has any thought of prosecuting the custodian, a grant of act of production immunity can have serious consequences. Testimony obtained pursuant to a grant of statutory use immunity may be used neither directly nor derivatively. And "[o]ne raising a claim under [the federal immunity] statute need only show that he testified under a grant of immunity in order to shift to the government the heavy burden of proving that all of the evidence it proposes to use was derived from legitimate independent sources." Kastigar v. United States. Even in cases where the Government does not employ the immunized testimony for any purpose—direct or derivative—against the witness, the Government's inability to meet the "heavy burden" it bears may result in the preclusion of crucial evidence that was obtained legitimately.

Although a corporate custodian is not entitled to resist a subpoena on the ground that his act of production will be personally incriminating, we do think certain consequences flow from the fact that the custodian's act of production is one in his representative rather than personal capacity. Because the custodian acts as a representative, the act is deemed one of the corporation and not the individual. Therefore, the Government concedes, as it must, that it may make no evidentiary use of the "individual act" against the individual. For example, in a criminal prosecution against the custodian, the Government may not introduce into evidence before the jury the fact that the subpoena was served upon and the corporation's documents were delivered by one particular individual, the custodian. The Government has the right, however, to use the corporation's act of production against the custodian. The Government may offer testimony—for example, from the process server who delivered the subpoena and from the individual who received the records—establishing that the corporation produced the records subpoenaed. The jury may draw from the corporation's act of production the conclusion that the records in question are authentic corporate records, which the corporation possessed, and which it produced in response to the subpoena. And if the defendant held a prominent position within the corporation that produced the records, the jury may, just as it would had someone else produced the documents, reasonably infer that he had possession of the documents or knowledge of their contents. Because the jury is not told that the defendant produced the records, any nexus between the defendant and the documents results solely from the corporation's act of production and other evidence in the case.[11] . . .

Affirmed.

JUSTICE KENNEDY, with whom JUSTICE BRENNAN, JUSTICE MARSHALL, and JUSTICE SCALIA join, dissenting.

Our long course of decisions concerning artificial entities and the Fifth Amendment served us well. It illuminated two of the critical foundations for the constitutional guarantee against self-incrimination: first, that it is an explicit right of a natural person, protecting the realm of

---

11. We reject the suggestion that the limitation on the evidentiary use of the custodian's act of production is the equivalent of constructive use immunity barred under our decision in *Doe*, 465 U.S., at 616-617. Rather, the limitation is a necessary concomitant of the notion that a corporate custodian acts as an agent and not an individual when be produces corporate records in response to a subpoena addressed to him in his representative capacity.

We leave open the question whether the agency rationale supports compelling a custodian to produce corporate records when the custodian is able to establish, by showing for example that he is the sole employee and officer of the corporation, that the jury would inevitably conclude that he produced the records.

human thought and expression; second, that it is confined to governmental compulsion.

It is regrettable that the very line of cases which at last matured to teach these principles is now invoked to curtail them, for the Court rules that a natural person forfeits the privilege in a criminal investigation directed against him and that the Government may use compulsion to elicit testimonial assertions from a person who faces the threat of criminal proceedings. A case that might have served as the paradigmatic expression of the purposes served by the Fifth Amendment instead is used to obscure them.

The Court today denies an individual his Fifth Amendment privilege against self-incrimination in order to indicate the rule that a collective entity which employs him has no such privilege itself. To reach this ironic conclusion, the majority must blur an analytic clarity in Fifth Amendment doctrine that has taken almost a century to emerge. After holding that corporate employment strips the individual of his privilege, the Court then attempts to restore some measure of protection by its judicial creation of a new zone of immunity in some vaguely defined circumstances. This exercise admits what the Court denied in the first place, namely that compelled compliance with the subpoena implicates the Fifth Amendment self-incrimination privilege.

The majority's apparent reasoning is that collective entities have no privilege and so their employees must have none either. The Court holds that a corporate agent must incriminate himself even when he is named in the subpoena and is a target of the investigation, and even when it is conceded that compliance requires compelled, personal, testimonial, incriminating assertions. I disagree with that conclusion; find no precedent for it; maintain that if there is a likelihood of personal self-incrimination the narrow use immunity permitted by statute can be granted without frustrating the investigation of collective entities; and submit that basic Fifth Amendment principles should not be avoided and manipulated, which is the necessary effect of this decision.

I

There is some common ground in this case. All accept the longstanding rule that labor unions, corporations, partnerships, and other collective entities have no Fifth Amendment self-incrimination privilege; that a natural person cannot assert such a privilege on their behalf; and that the contents of business records prepared without compulsion can be used to incriminate even a natural person without implicating Fifth Amendment concerns. Further, all appear to concede or at least submit the case to us on the assumption that the act of producing the subpoenaed documents will effect personal incrimination of Randy Braswell, the individual to whom the subpoena is directed.

The petitioner's assertion of the Fifth Amendment privilege against the forced production of documents is based not on any contention that their contents will incriminate him but instead upon the unchallenged premise that the act of production will do so. When the case is presented on this assumption, there exists no historical or logical relation between the so-called collective entity rule and the individual's claim of privilege. . . .

A

. . . The majority does not challenge the assumption that compliance with the subpoena here would require acts of testimonial self-incrimination from Braswell; indeed, the Government itself made this assumption in submitting its argument. The question presented, therefore, is whether an individual may be compelled, simply by virtue of his status as a corporate custodian, to perform a testimonial act which will incriminate him personally. The majority relies entirely on the collective entity rule in holding that such compulsion is constitutional.

B

The collective entity rule provides no support for the majority's holding. The rule, as the majority chooses to call it, actually comprises three distinct propositions, none of which is relevant to the claim in this case. First, since Hale v. Henkel, 201 U.S. 43 (1906), it has been understood that a corporation has no Fifth Amendment privilege and cannot resist compelled production of its documents on grounds that it will be incriminated by their release. Second, our subsequent opinions show the collective entity principle is not confined to corporations, and we apply it as well to labor unions, United States v. White, and partnerships, Bellis v. United States. Finally, in Wilson v. United States, we extended the rule beyond the collective entity itself and rejected an assertion of privilege by a corporate custodian who had claimed that the disclosure of the contents of subpoenaed corporate documents would incriminate him. In none of the collective entity cases cited by the majority, and in none that I have found, were we presented with a claim that the custodian would be incriminated by the act of production, in contrast to the contents of the documents.

The distinction is central. Our holding in *Wilson* was premised squarely on the fact that the custodian's claim rested on the potential for incrimination in the documents' contents, and we reasoned that the State's visitatorial powers over corporations included the authority to inspect corporate books. We compared the issue to that presented by cases involving public papers, explaining that "where, by virtue of their character and the rules of law applicable to them, the books and papers are held subject to examination by the demanding authority, the custodian has no privilege to refuse production although their contents tend to criminate him." Our decision in *Wilson* and in later collective entity cases reflected, I believe, the Court's understandable unease with drawing too close a connection between an individual and an artificial entity. On a more practical level, the Court was also unwilling to draw too close a connection between the custodian and the contents of business documents over which he had temporary control but which belonged to his employer, often were prepared by others, and in all events were prepared voluntarily. This last factor became the focus of our analysis in *Fisher*, where we made clear that the applicability of the Fifth Amendment privilege depends on compulsion. *Fisher* put to rest the notion that a privilege may be claimed with respect to the contents of business records that were voluntarily prepared.

The act of producing documents stands on an altogether different footing. While a custodian has no necessary relation to the contents of documents within his control, the act of production is inescapably his own. Production is the precise act compelled by the subpoena, and obedience, in some cases, will require the custodian's own testimonial assertions. That was the basis of our recognition of the privilege in *Doe*. The entity possessing the documents in *Doe* was, as the majority points out, a sole proprietorship, not a corporation, partnership, or labor union. But the potential for self-incrimination inheres in the act demanded of the individual, and as a consequence the nature of the entity is irrelevant to determining whether there is ground for the privilege.

A holding that the privilege against self-incrimination applies in the context of this case is required by the precedents, and not, as the Government and the majority suggest, inconsistent with them. The collective entity rule established in [our cases] remains valid. It also continues to be the rule . . . that custodians of a collective entity are not permitted to claim a personal privilege with respect to the contents of entity records, although that rule now derives not from the unprotected status of collective entities but from the more rational principle, established by *Fisher* and *Doe* and now recognized, that no one may claim a privilege with respect to the contents of business records not created by compulsion.

The question before us is not the existence of the collective entity rule, but whether it contains any principle which overrides the personal Fifth Amendment privilege of someone compelled to give incriminating testimony. Our precedents establish a firm basis for assertion of the privilege. Randy Braswell, like the respondent in *Doe*, is being asked to draw upon his personal knowledge to identify and to deliver documents which are responsive to the Government's subpoena. Once the Government concedes there are testimonial consequences implicit in the act of production, it cannot escape the conclusion that compliance with the subpoena is indisputably Braswell's own act. To suggest otherwise "is to confuse metaphor with reality." Pacific Gas & Electric Co. v. Public Utilities Commn. of California, 475 U.S. 1, 33 (1986) (Rehnquist, J., dissenting).

C

The testimonial act demanded of petitioner in this case must be analyzed under the same principles applicable to other forms of compelled testimony. In Curcio v. United States, 354 U.S. 118 (1957), we reviewed a judgment holding a union custodian in criminal contempt for failing to give oral testimony regarding the location and possession of books and records he had been ordered to produce. *White* had already established that a labor union was as much a collective entity for Fifth Amendment purposes as a corporation, and the Government argued in *Curcio* that the custodian could not claim a personal privilege because he was performing only a "representative duty" on behalf of the collective entity to which he belonged. We rejected that argument and reversed the judgment below. We stated:

> [F]orcing the custodian to testify orally as to the whereabouts of nonproduced records requires him to disclose the contents of his own mind. He might be compelled to convict himself out of his own mouth. That is contrary to the spirit and letter of the Fifth Amendment.

We confront the same Fifth Amendment claim here. The majority is able to distinguish *Curcio* only by giving much apparent weight to the words "out of his own mouth," reading *Curcio* to stand for the proposition that the Constitution treats oral testimony differently than it does other forms of assertion. There is no basis in the text or history of the Fifth Amendment for such a distinction. The self-incrimination clause speaks of compelled "testimony," and has always been understood to apply to testimony in all its forms. Physical acts will constitute testimony if they probe the state of mind, memory, perception, or cognition of the witness. The Court should not retreat from the plain implications of this rule and hold that such testimony may be compelled, even when self-incriminating, simply because it is not spoken.

The distinction established by *Curcio* is not, of course, between oral and other forms of testimony; rather it is between a subpoena which compels a person to "disclose the contents of his own mind," through words or actions, and one which does not. A custodian who is incriminated simply by the contents of the documents he has physically transmitted has not been compelled to disclose his memory or perception or cognition. A custodian who is incriminated by the personal knowledge he communicates in locating and selecting the document demanded in a Government subpoena has been compelled to testify in the most elemental, constitutional sense.

D

Recognition of the privilege here would also avoid adoption of the majority's metaphysical progression, which, I respectfully submit, is flawed. Beginning from ordinary principles of agency, the majority proceeds to the conclusion that when a corporate employee, or an employee of a labor union or partnership, complies with a subpoena for production of documents, his act is necessarily and solely the act of the entity. That premise, of course, is at odds with the principle under which oral testimony in *Curcio* properly was deemed privileged.

Since the custodian in *Curcio* had been asked to provide testimony on the union's behalf and not his own, the Government argued, as it again argues here, that the attempted compulsion was constitutionally permissible because Curcio was performing only a representative duty. We held, however, that testimony of that sort may not be divorced from the person who speaks it. The questions the Government wished to ask would have required Curcio to disclose his own knowledge, and as a matter of law his responses could not be alienated from him and attributed to the labor union. In similar fashion, the act demanded of Braswell requires a personal disclosure of individual knowledge, a fact which cannot be dismissed by labeling him a mere agent.

The heart of the matter, as everyone knows, is that the Government does not see Braswell as a mere agent at all; and the majority's theory is difficult to square with what will often be the Government's actual practice. The subpoena in this case was not directed to Worldwide Machinery Sales, Inc., or Worldwide Purchasing, Inc. It was directed to "Randy Braswell, President, Worldwide Machinery Sales, Inc., World-wide Purchasing, Inc." and informed him that "[y]ou are hereby commanded" to provide the specified documents. The Government explained at oral argument that it often chooses to designate an individual recipient, rather than the corporation generally, when it serves a subpoena because "[we] want the right to make that individual comply with the subpoena." Tr.

of Oral Arg. 43. This is not the language of agency. By issuing a subpoena which the Government insists is "directed to petitioner personally," it has forfeited any claim that it is simply making a demand on a corporation that, in turn, will have to find a physical agent to perform its duty. What the Government seeks instead is the right to choose any corporate agent as a target of its subpoena and compel that individual to disclose certain information by his own actions.

The majority gives the corporate agent fiction a weight it simply cannot bear. In a peculiar attempt to mitigate the force of its own holding, it impinges upon its own analysis by concluding that, while the Government may compel a named individual to produce records, in any later proceeding against the person it cannot divulge that he performed the act. But if that is so, it is because the Fifth Amendment protects the person without regard to his status as a corporate employee; and once this be admitted, the necessary support for the majority's case has collapsed.

Perhaps the Court makes this concession out of some vague sense of fairness, but the source of its authority to do so remains unexplained. It cannot rest on the Fifth Amendment, for the privilege against self-incrimination does not permit balancing the convenience of the Government against the rights of a witness, and the majority has in any case determined that the Fifth Amendment is inapplicable. If Braswell by his actions reveals information about his state of mind that is relevant to a jury in a criminal proceeding, there are no grounds of which I am aware for declaring the information inadmissible, unless it be the Fifth Amendment.

In *Doe* we declined expressly to do what the Court does today. Noting that there might well be testimonial assertions attendant upon the production of documents, we rejected the argument that compelled production necessarily carried with it a grant of constructive immunity. We held that immunity may be granted only by appropriate statutory proceedings. The Government must make a formal request for statutory use immunity under 18 U.S.C. §§6002-6003 if it seeks access to records in exchange for its agreement not to use testimonial acts against the individual. Rather than beginning the practice of establishing new judicially created evidentiary rules, conferring upon individuals some partial use immunity to avoid results the Court finds constitutionally intolerable, I submit our precedents require the Government to use the only mechanism yet sanctioned for compelling testimony that is privileged: a request for immunity as provided by statute.

II

The majority's abiding concern is that if a corporate officer who is the target of a subpoena is allowed to assert the privilege, it will impede the Government's power to investigate corporations, unions, and partnerships, to uncover and prosecute white collar crimes, and otherwise to enforce its visitatorial powers. There are at least two answers to this. The first, and most fundamental, is that the text of the Fifth Amendment does not authorize exceptions premised on such rationales. Second, even if it were proper to invent such exceptions, the dangers prophesied by the majority are overstated.

Recognition of the right to assert a privilege does not mean it will exist in many cases. In many instances, the production of documents may implicate no testimonial assertions at all. In *Fisher*, for example, we held that the specific acts required by the subpoena before us "would not itself involve testimonial self-incrimination" because, in that case, "the existence and location of the papers [were] a foregone conclusion and the taxpayer adds little or nothing to the sum total of the Government's information by conceding that he in fact has the papers." 425 U.S. at 411. Whether a particular act is testimonial and self-incriminating is largely a factual issue to be decided in each case. In the case before us, the Government has made its submission on the assumption that the subpoena would result in incriminating testimony. The existence of a privilege in future cases, however, is not an automatic result.

Further, to the extent testimonial assertions are being compelled, use immunity can be granted without impeding the investigation. Where the privilege is applicable, immunity will be needed for only one individual, and solely with respect to evidence derived from the act of production itself. The Government would not be denied access to the records it seeks, it would be free to use the contents of the records against everyone, and it would be free to use any testimonial act implicit in production against all but the custodian it selects. In appropriate cases the Government will be able to establish authenticity, possession, and control by means other than compelling assertions about them from a suspect.

In one sense the case before us may not be a particularly sympathetic one. Braswell was the sole stockholder of the corporation and ran it himself. Perhaps that is why the Court suggests he waived his Fifth Amendment self-incrimination rights by using the corporate form. One does not always, however, have the choice of his or her employer, much less the choice of the business enterprise through which the employer conducts its business. Though the Court here hints at a waiver, nothing in Fifth Amendment jurisprudence indicates that the acceptance of employment should be deemed a waiver of a specific protection that is as basic a part of our constitutional heritage as is the privilege against self-incrimination.

The law is not captive to its own fictions. Yet, in the matter before us the Court employs the fiction that personal incrimination of the employee is neither sought by the Government nor cognizable by the law. That is a regrettable holding, for the conclusion is factually unsound, unnecessary for legitimate regulation, and a violation of the Self-Incrimination Clause of the Fifth Amendment of the Constitution. For these reasons, I dissent.

NOTES AND QUESTIONS

1. How do *Doe* and *Braswell* differ? What do you think of a jurisprudence that gives details of enterprise law substantial constitutional significance? Perhaps the problem lies in *Fisher*. Is whatever it stands for too complicated to be administered? Professor Heidt thinks perhaps so. Heidt, The Fifth Amendment Privilege and Documents—Cutting *Fisher's* Tangled Line, 49 Mo. L. Rev. 439 (1984). A substantial literature is being produced that examines the relationship between the fifth amendment and demands for the production of documents. See, e.g., Mosteller, Simplifying Subpoena law: Taking the Fifth Amendment Seriously, 73 Va. L. Rev. 1 (1987); Note, Fifth Amendment Privilege for Producing Corporate Documents, 84 Mich. L. Rev. 1544 (1986).

2. Both *Doe* and *Braswell* discuss grants of immunity, which is the subject matter of Chapter 9A infra. Note two aspects of the treatment given to the question of immunity by these cases, however. In *Doe*, the Court refused to adopt a doctrine of constructive use immunity, whereas in *Braswell* constructive immunity was created. Why? Second, reflect on the scope of the constructive immunity. As we will see in Chapter 9, immunity grants normally entail at least use and derivative use immunity, which means that anything derived from the immunized testimony is also immunized. As the dissent in *Braswell* points out, the form of immunity created by the majority is ambiguous. That ambiguity is eliminated if the majority's opinion is read as suggesting that derivative use immunity is not conferred whenever custodians turn over documents. Were it otherwise, the immunity grant would extend to knowledge of the contents of the documents, as that knowledge is obviously obtained derivatively from the act of production.

The difficulties in the majority's reasoning are well demonstrated by n.11, supra page 489. The text accompanying that footnote expresses in great detail the incriminating inferences that fact finders legitimately may draw from the act of production of corporate documents. By contrast, the footnote "leaves open" the legitimacy of one inference from the act of production—that the custodian was the person producing the records. What possibly could be the point of this? If the fact finder may infer from the act of production that the custodian was in possession of the documents (even if arrived at by the somewhat circuitous route suggested by the Court), of what significance is it to forbid an inference of production? Possession will invariably be as if not more incriminating than production.

3. Why can individuals be required to turn over but not to testify about documents? According to the *Fisher* line of cases, the act of production is, or at least can be, testimonial. If any particular act is testimonial, what coherent theory allows that form of testimony to be compelled but provides protection for some other form of testimony? If a rose by any other name would smell as sweet, why isn't testimony protected no matter what the label?

4. Reconsider n.6, page 486 supra. Why doesn't the act of production rationale apply to such matters as voice and handwriting exemplars, as in essence Justice Fortas argued in dissent?

CHAPTER 7

THE FOURTH AMENDMENT

A. THE MEANING OF "SEARCH AND SEIZURE"

AMSTERDAM, PERSPECTIVES ON THE FOURTH AMEND-MENT, 58 MINN. L. REV. 349, 385-386 (1974): The fourth amendment . . . is ordinarily treated as a monolith: wherever it restricts police activities at all, it subjects them to the same extensive restrictions that it imposes upon physical entries into dwellings. To label any police activity a "search" or "seizure" within the ambit of the amendment is to impose those restrictions upon it. On the other hand, if it is not labeled a "search" or "seizure," it is subject to no significant restrictions of any kind. It is only "searches" or "seizures" that the fourth amendment requires to be reasonable: police activities of any other sort may be as unreasonable as the police please to make them.[1]

Obviously, this kind of all-or-nothing approach to the amendment puts extraordinary strains upon the process of drawing its outer bound-

---

1. Deciding that government activity is not a search or seizure is not the only way of insulating the activity from fourth amendment restrictions. In United States v. Verdugo-Urquidez, 110 S. Ct. 1056 (1990), the Supreme Court held that the fourth amendment was not applicable to the search and seizure by United States agents of property owned by a nonresident alien and located in another country. The nonresident alien was not part of "the people" protected by the fourth amendment.—EDS.

ary lines. It is true, as Mr. Justice Holmes said, that "[w]henever the law draws a line there will be cases very near each other on opposite sides."[373] But where the consequences that turn upon the line are enormous, out of all proportion to the differences between the cases lying close on either side, courts are likely to be impelled either to wiggle the line or to keep it fuzzy. . . .

A sliding scale approach would considerably ease the strains that the present monolithic model of the fourth amendment almost everywhere imposes on the process of defining the amendment's outer boundaries.[2] It would obviously be easier and more likely for a court to say that a patrolman's shining of a flashlight into the interior of a parked car was a "search" if that conclusion did not encumber the flashlight with a warrant requirement but simply required, for example, that the patrolman "be able to point to specific and articulable facts"[419] supporting a reasonable inference that something in the car required his attention. It would be easier and more sensible for a court to say that some "constitutionally adequate, reasonable grounds"[421] must exist before a policeman can enter the common hallways of a tenement house and listen at apartment doors, than to say either that this kind of activity is not a search or that it requires a search warrant. As a general matter, courts working with a graduated model of the fourth amendment would and should approach questions of its coverage with the disposition to extend it so as to find in the amendment—as Mr. Justice Brennan once urged in dissent—"nothing less than a comprehensive right of personal liberty in the face of governmental intrusion."[422] The question of what constitutes a covered "search" or "seizure" would and should be viewed with an appreciation that to exclude any particular police activity from coverage is essentially to exclude it from judicial control and from the command of reasonableness, whereas to include it is to do no more than say that it must be conducted in a reasonable manner. With the question put in this fashion the answer should seldom be delivered against coverage.

The problem with the graduated model, of course, is . . . that . . . it converts the fourth amendment into one immense Rorschach blot. The complaint is being voiced now that fourth amendment law is too complicated and confused for policemen to understand or to obey. Yet present law is a positive paragon of simplicity compared to what a graduated fourth amendment would produce. The varieties of police behavior

---

373. United States v. Wurzbach, 280 U.S. 396, 399 (1930).

2. As Professor Amsterdam notes at 390-393, there are a some areas in which the Supreme Court has taken a sliding scale approach. See, e.g., Terry v. Ohio, 392 U.S. 1 (1968).—EDS.

419. Terry v. Ohio, 392 U.S. 1, 21 (1968).

421. Sibron v. New York, 392 U.S. 40, 64 (1968).

422. Lopez v. United States, 373 U.S. 427, 455 (1963) (dissenting opinion).

and of the occasions that call it forth are so innumerable that their reflection in a general sliding scale approach could only produce more slide than scale. We would shortly slide back to the prescription stated in a now overruled 1950 decision of the Court which is generally regarded as the nadir of fourth amendment development: that "[t]he recurring questions of the reasonableness of searches must find resolution in the facts and circumstances of each case."[426] Under that view, "[r]easonableness is in the first instance for the [trial court] . . . to determine."[427] What it means in practice is that appellate courts defer to trial courts and trial courts defer to the police. What other results should we expect? If there are no fairly clear rules telling the policeman what he may and may not do, courts are seldom going to say that what he did was unreasonable. The ultimate conclusion is that "the people would be 'secure in their persons, houses, papers, and effects,' only in the discretion of the police."[429] And as Mr. Justice Jackson reminded us, "the extent of any privilege of search and seizure without warrant which we sustain, the officers interpret and apply themselves and will push to the limit."[430] . . .

So the Court confronts a dilemma. On the one hand, maintenance of the traditional monolithic model of the fourth amendment makes decisions regarding the boundaries of its coverage excruciatingly difficult. Police practices that cry for some form of constitutional control but not the control of a warrant or a probable cause requirement must be dubbed "searches" and over-restricted or dubbed something other than searches and left completely unrestricted. On the other hand, to subject them to fourth amendment control but exempt them from the warrant or probable cause requirements would threaten the integrity of the structure of internal fourth amendment doctrines. . . .

1. Conversations

KATZ v. UNITED STATES
Certiorari to the United States Court of Appeals for the Ninth Circuit
389 U.S. 347 (1967).

MR. JUSTICE STEWART delivered the opinion of the Court.
The petitioner was convicted in the District Court for the Southern

426. United States v. Rabinowitz, 339 U.S. 56, 63 (1950), *overruled* by Chimel v. California, 395 U.S. 752, 768 (1969). Mr. Justice Frankfurter's dissenting opinion in *Rabinowitz* is now treated as the lore of the fourth amendment, e.g., United States v. United States Dist. Court for the E. Dist. of Mich., 407 U.S. 297, 315-16 (1972).
427. 339 U.S. at 63.
429. Beck v. Ohio, 379 U.S. 89, 97 (1964).
430. Brinegar v. United States, 338 U.S. 160, 182 (1949) (dissenting opinion).

District of California under an eight-count indictment charging him with transmitting wagering information by telephone from Los Angeles to Miami and Boston, in violation of a federal statute. At trial the Government was permitted, over the petitioner's objection, to introduce evidence of the petitioner's end of telephone conversations, overheard by FBI agents who had attached an electronic listening and recording device to the outside of the public telephone booth from which he had placed his calls. In affirming his conviction, the Court of Appeals rejected the contention that the recordings had been obtained in violation of the Fourth Amendment, because "[t]here was no physical entrance into the area occupied by [the petitioner]."[2] We granted certiorari in order to consider the constitutional questions thus presented.

The petitioner has phrased those questions as follows:

A. Whether a public telephone booth is a constitutionally protected area so that evidence obtained by attaching an electronic listening recording device to the top of such a booth is obtained in violation of the right to privacy of the user of the booth.
B. Whether physical penetration of a constitutionally protected area is necessary before a search and seizure can be said to be violative of the Fourth Amendment to the United States Constitution.

We decline to adopt this formulation of the issues. In the first place, the correct solution of Fourth Amendment problems is not necessarily promoted by incantation of the phrase "constitutionally protected area." Secondly, the Fourth Amendment cannot be translated into a general constitutional "right to privacy." That Amendment protects individual privacy against certain kinds of governmental intrusion, but its protections go further, and often have nothing to do with privacy at all.[4] Other provisions of the Constitution protect personal privacy from other forms of governmental invasion.[5] But the protection of a person's *general* right

---

2. 369 F.2d 130, 134.

4. "The average man would very likely not have his feelings soothed any more by having his property seized openly than by having it seized privately and by stealth. . . . And a person can be just as much, if not more, irritated, annoyed and injured by an unceremonious public arrest by a policeman as he is by a seizure in the privacy of his office or home." Griswold v. Connecticut, 381 U.S. 479, 509 (dissenting opinion of Mr. Justice Black).

5. The First Amendment, for example, imposes limitations upon governmental abridgment of "freedom to associate and privacy in one's associations." NAACP v. Alabama, 357 U.S. 449, 462. The Third Amendment's prohibition against the unconsented peacetime quartering of soldiers protects another aspect of privacy from governmental intrusion. To some extent, the Fifth Amendment too "reflects the Constitution's concern for . . . 'the right of each individual "to a private enclave where he may lead a private life." ' " Tehan v. Shott, 382 U.S. 406, 416. Virtually every governmental action interferes with personal privacy to some degree. The question in each case is whether that interference violates a command of the United States Constitution.

to privacy—his right to be let alone by other people—is, like the protection of his property and of his very life, left largely to the law of the individual States.

Because of the misleading way the issues have been formulated, the parties have attached great significance to the characterization of the telephone booth from which the petitioner placed his calls. The petitioner has strenuously argued that the booth was a "constitutionally protected area." The Government has maintained with equal vigor that it was not.[8] But this effort to decide whether or not a given "area," viewed in the abstract, is "constitutionally protected" deflects attention from the problem presented by this case.[9] For the Fourth Amendment protects people, not places. What a person knowingly exposes to the public, even in his own home or office, is not a subject of Fourth Amendment protection. . . . But what he seeks to preserve as private, even in an area accessible to the public, may be constitutionally protected. . . .

The Government stresses the fact that the telephone booth from which the petitioner made his calls was constructed partly of glass, so that he was as visible after he entered it as he would have been if he had remained outside. But what he sought to exclude when he entered the booth was not the intruding eye—it was the uninvited ear. He did not shed his right to do so simply because he made his calls from a place where he might be seen. No less than an individual in a business office,[10] in a friend's apartment,[11] or in a taxicab,[12] a person in a telephone booth may rely upon the protection of the Fourth Amendment. One who occupies it, shuts the door behind him, and pays the toll that permits him to place a call is surely entitled to assume that the words he utters into the mouthpiece will not be broadcast to the world. To read the Constitution more narrowly is to ignore the vital role that the public telephone has come to play in private communication.

The Government contends, however, that the activities of its agents

8. In support of their respective claims, the parties have compiled competing lists of "protected areas" for our consideration. It appears to be common ground that a private home is such an area, Weeks v. United States, 232 U.S. 383, but that an open field is not. Hester v. United States, 265 U.S. 57. Defending the inclusion of a telephone booth in his list the petitioner cites United States v. Stone, 232 F. Supp. 396, and United States v. Madison, 32 L.W. 2243 (D.C. Ct. Gen. Sess.). Urging that the telephone booth should be excluded, the Government finds support in United States v. Borgese, 235 F. Supp. 286.

9. It is true that this Court has occasionally described its conclusions in terms of "constitutionally protected areas," see, e.g., Silverman v. United States, 365 U.S. 505, 510, 512; Lopez v. United States, 373 U.S. 427, 438-439; Berger v. New York, 388 U.S. 41, 57, 59, but we have never suggested that this concept can serve as a talismanic solution to every Fourth Amendment problem.

10. Silverthorne Lumber Co. v. United States, 251 U.S. 385.

11. Jones v. United States, 362 U.S. 257.

12. Rios v. United States, 364 U.S. 253.

in this case should not be tested by Fourth Amendment requirements, for the surveillance technique they employed involved no physical penetration of the telephone booth from which the petitioner placed his calls. It is true that the absence of such penetration was at one time thought to foreclose further Fourth Amendment inquiry, Olmstead v. United States, 277 U.S. 438, 457, 464, 466; Goldman v. United States, 316 U.S. 129, 134-136, for that Amendment was thought to limit only searches and seizures of tangible property.[13] But "[t]he premise that property interests control the right of the Government to search and seize has been discredited." Warden v. Hayden, 387 U.S. 294, 304. Thus, although a closely divided Court supposed in *Olmstead* that surveillance without any trespass and without the seizure of any material object fell outside the ambit of the Constitution, we have since departed from the narrow view on which that decision rested. Indeed, we have expressly held that the Fourth Amendment governs not only the seizure of tangible items, but extends as well to the recording of oral statements, overheard without any "technical trespass under . . . local property law." Silverman v. United States, 365 U.S. 505, 511. Once this much is acknowledged, and once it is recognized that the Fourth Amendment protects people— and not simply "areas"—against unreasonable searches and seizures, it becomes clear that the reach of that Amendment cannot turn upon the presence or absence of a physical intrusion into any given enclosure.

We conclude that the underpinnings of *Olmstead* and *Goldman* have been so eroded by our subsequent decisions that the "trespass" doctrine there enunciated can no longer be regarded as controlling. The Government's activities in electronically listening to and recording the petitioner's words violated the privacy upon which he justifiably relied while using the telephone booth and thus constituted a "search and seizure" within the meaning of the Fourth Amendment. The fact that the electronic device employed to achieve that end did not happen to penetrate the wall of the booth can have no constitutional significance.

The question remaining for decision, then, is whether the search and seizure conducted in this case complied with constitutional standards. In that regard, the Government's position is that its agents acted in an entirely defensible manner: They did not begin their electronic surveillance until investigation of the petitioner's activities had established a strong probability that he was using the telephone in question to transmit gambling information to persons in other States, in violation of federal law. Moreover, the surveillance was limited, both in scope and in duration, to the specific purpose of establishing the contents of the peti-

13. See Olmstead v. United States, 277 U.S. 438, 464-466. We do not deal in this case with the law of detention or arrest under the Fourth Amendment.

tioner's unlawful telephonic communications. The agents confined their surveillance to the brief periods during which he used the telephone booth,[14] and they took great care to overhear only the conversations of the petitioner himself.[15]

Accepting this account of the Government's actions as accurate, it is clear that this surveillance was so narrowly circumscribed that a duly authorized magistrate, properly notified of the need for such investigation, specifically informed of the basis on which it was to proceed, and clearly apprised of the precise intrusion it would entail, could constitutionally have authorized, with appropriate safeguards, the very limited search and seizure that the Government asserts in fact took place. Only last Term we sustained the validity of such an authorization, holding that, under sufficiently "precise and discriminate circumstances," a federal court may empower government agents to employ a concealed electronic device "for the narrow and particularized purpose of ascertaining the truth of the . . . allegations" of a "detailed factual affidavit alleging the commission of a specific criminal offense." Osborn v. United States, 385 U.S. 323, 329-330. . . .

The Government urges that, because its agents relied upon the decisions in *Olmstead* and *Goldman*, and because they did no more here than they might properly have done with prior judicial sanction, we should retroactively validate their conduct. That we cannot do. It is apparent that the agents in this case acted with restraint. Yet the inescapable fact is that this restraint was imposed by the agents themselves, not by a judicial officer. They were not required, before commencing the search, to present their estimate of probable cause for detached scrutiny by a neutral magistrate. They were not compelled, during the conduct of the search itself, to observe precise limits established in advance by a specific court order. Nor were they directed, after the search had been completed, to notify the authorizing magistrate in detail of all that had been seized. In the absence of such safeguards, this Court has never sustained a search upon the sole ground that officers reasonably expected to find evidence of a particular crime and voluntarily confined their activities to the least intrusive means consistent with that end. Searches conducted without warrants have been held unlawful "notwithstanding facts unquestionably showing probable cause," Agnello v. United States,

14. Based upon their previous visual observations of the petitioner, the agents correctly predicted that he would use the telephone booth for several minutes at approximately the same time each morning. The petitioner was subjected to electronic surveillance only during this predetermined period. Six recordings, averaging some three minutes each, were obtained and admitted in evidence. They preserved the petitioner's end of conversations concerning the placing of bets and the receipt of wagering information.

15. On the single occasion when the statements of another person were inadvertently intercepted, the agents refrained from listening to them.

269 U.S. 20, 33, for the Constitution requires "that the deliberate, impartial judgment of a judicial officer . . . be interposed between the citizen and the police. . . ." Wong Sun v. United States, 371 U.S. 471, 481-482. "Over and again this Court has emphasized that the mandate of the [Fourth] Amendment requires adherence to judicial processes," United States v. Jeffers, 342 U.S. 48, 51, and that searches conducted outside the judicial process, without prior approval by judge or magistrate, are per se unreasonable under the Fourth Amendment— subject only to a few specifically established and well-delineated exceptions.

It is difficult to imagine how any of those exceptions could ever apply to the sort of search and seizure involved in this case. . . .

The Government does not question these basic principles. Rather, it urges the creation of a new exception to cover this case. It argues that surveillance of a telephone booth should be exempted from the usual requirement of advance authorization by a magistrate upon a showing of probable cause. We cannot agree. Omission of such authorization

> bypasses the safeguards provided by an objective predetermination of probable cause, and substitutes instead the far less reliable procedure of an after-the-event justification for the . . . search, too likely to be subtly influenced by the familiar shortcomings of hindsight judgment. [Beck v. Ohio, 379 U.S. 89, 96.]

And bypassing a neutral predetermination of the *scope* of a search leaves individuals secure from Fourth Amendment violations "only in the discretion of the police." Id., at 97.

These considerations do not vanish when the search in question is transferred from the setting of a home, an office, or a hotel room to that of a telephone booth. Wherever a man may be, he is entitled to know that he will remain free from unreasonable searches and seizures. The government agents here ignored "the procedure of antecedent justification . . . that is central to the Fourth Amendment,"[24] a procedure that we hold to be a constitutional precondition of the kind of electronic surveillance involved in this case. Because the surveillance here failed to meet that condition, and because it led to the petitioner's conviction, the judgment must be reversed.

It is so ordered.

MR. JUSTICE MARSHALL took no part in the consideration or decision of this case.

---

24. See Osborn v. United States, 385 U.S. 323, 330.

[The concurring opinions of JUSTICE DOUGLAS and JUSTICE WHITE are omitted.]

MR. JUSTICE HARLAN, concurring.

I join the opinion of the Court, which I read to hold only (a) that an enclosed telephone booth is an area where, like a home, Weeks v. United States, 232 U.S. 383, and unlike a field, Hester v. United States, 265 U.S. 57, a person has a constitutionally protected reasonable expectation of privacy; (b) that electronic as well as physical intrusion into a place that is in this sense private may constitute a violation of the Fourth Amendment; and (c) that the invasion of a constitutionally protected area by federal authorities is, as the Court has long held, presumptively unreasonable in the absence of a search warrant.

As the Court's opinion states, "the Fourth Amendment protects people, not places." The question, however, is what protection it affords to those people. Generally, as here, the answer to that question requires reference to a "place." My understanding of the rule that has emerged from prior decisions is that there is a twofold requirement, first that a person have exhibited an actual (subjective) expectation of privacy and, second, that the expectation be one that society is prepared to recognize as "reasonable." Thus a man's home is, for most purposes, a place where he expects privacy, but objects, activities, or statements that he exposes to the "plain view" of outsiders are not "protected" because no intention to keep them to himself has been exhibited. On the other hand, conversations in the open would not be protected against being overheard, for the expectation of privacy under the circumstances would be unreasonable. . . .

The critical fact in this case is that "[o]ne who occupies it, [a telephone booth] shuts the door behind him, and pays the toll that permits him to place a call is surely entitled to assume" that his conversation is not being intercepted. . . . The point is not that the booth is "accessible to the public" at other times, . . . but that it is a temporarily private place whose momentary occupants' expectations of freedom from intrusion are recognized as reasonable. . . .

MR. JUSTICE BLACK, dissenting. . . .

My basic objection is twofold: (1) I do not believe that the words of the Amendment will bear the meaning given them by today's decision, and (2) I do not believe that it is the proper role of this Court to rewrite the Amendment in order "to bring it into harmony with the times" and thus reach a result that many people believe to be desirable.

While I realize that an argument based on the meaning of words lacks the scope, and no doubt the appeal, of broad policy discussions and philosophical discourses on such nebulous subjects as privacy, for me the language of the Amendment is the crucial place to look in construing a written document such as our Constitution. . . . The first clause protects persons, houses, papers, and effects, against unreasonable searches and seizures. . . ." These words connote the idea of tangible things with form, and weight, things capable of being searched, seized, or both. The second clause of the Amendment still further establishes its Framers' purpose to limit its protection to tangible things by providing that no warrants shall issue but those "particularly describing the place to be searched, and the persons or things to be seized." A conversation overheard by eavesdropping, whether by plain snooping or wiretapping, is not tangible and, under the normally accepted meanings of the words, can neither be searched nor seized. In addition the language of the second clause indicates that the Amendment refers not only to something tangible so it can be seized but to something already in existence so it can be described. Yet the Court's interpretation would have the Amendment apply to overhearing future conversations which by their very nature are nonexistent until they take place. How can one "describe" a future conversation, and, if one cannot, how can a magistrate issue a warrant to eavesdrop one in the future? It is argued that information showing what is expected to be said is sufficient to limit the boundaries of what later can be admitted into evidence; but does such general information really meet the specific language of the Amendment which says "particularly describing"? Rather than using language in a completely artificial way, I must conclude that the Fourth Amendment simply does not apply to eavesdropping.

Tapping telephone wires, of course, was an unknown possibility at the time the Fourth Amendment was adopted. But eavesdropping (and wiretapping is nothing more than eavesdropping by telephone) was . . . recognized. . . . There can be no doubt that the Framers were aware of this practice, and if they had desired to outlaw or restrict the use of evidence obtained by eavesdropping, I believe that they would have used the appropriate language to do so in the Fourth Amendment. They certainly would not have left such a task to the ingenuity of language-stretching judges. . . .

The first case to reach this Court which actually involved a clear-cut test of the Fourth Amendment's applicability to eavesdropping through a wiretap was, of course, Olmstead, supra. In holding that the interception of private telephone conversations by means of wiretapping was not a violation of the Fourth Amendment, this Court, speaking through Mr. Chief Justice Taft, examined the language of the Amendment and found, just as I do now, that the words could not be stretched to encompass overheard conversations:

The Amendment itself shows that the search is to be of material things—the person, the house, his papers or his effects. The description of the warrant necessary to make the proceeding lawful, is that it must specify the place to be searched and the person or *things* to be seized. . . .

Justice Bradley in the Boyd case [Boyd v. United States, 116 U.S. 616], and Justice Clark[e] in the *Gouled* case [Gouled v. United States, 255 U.S. 298], said that the Fifth Amendment and the Fourth Amendment were to be liberally construed to effect the purpose of the framers of the Constitution in the interest of liberty. But that can not justify enlargement of the language employed beyond the possible practical meaning of houses, persons, papers, and effects, or so to apply the words search and seizure as to forbid hearing or sight. [277 U.S., at 464-465.]

Goldman v. United States, 316 U.S. 129, is an even clearer example of this Court's traditional refusal to consider eavesdropping as being covered by the Fourth Amendment. There federal agents used a detectaphone, which was placed on the wall of an adjoining room, to listen to the conversation of a defendant carried on in his private office and intended to be confined within the four walls of the room. This Court, referring to Olmstead, found no Fourth Amendment violation. . . .

Since I see no way in which the words of the Fourth Amendment can be construed to apply to eavesdropping, that closes the matter for me. In interpreting the Bill of Rights, I willingly go as far as a liberal construction of the language takes me, but I simply cannot in good conscience give a meaning to words which they have never before been thought to have and which they certainly do not have in common ordinary usage. I will not distort the words of the Amendment in order to "keep the Constitution up to date" or "to bring it into harmony with the times." It was never meant that this Court have such power, which in effect would make us a continuously functioning constitutional convention.

With this decision the Court has completed, I hope, its rewriting of the Fourth Amendment, which started only recently when the Court began referring incessantly to the Fourth Amendment not so much as a law against *unreasonable* searches and seizures as one to protect an individual's privacy. By clever word juggling the Court finds it plausible to argue that language aimed specifically at searches and seizures of things that can be searched and seized may, to protect privacy, be applied to eavesdropped evidence of conversations that can neither be searched nor seized. Few things happen to an individual that do not affect his privacy in one way or another. Thus, by arbitrarily substituting the Court's language, designed to protect privacy, for the Constitution's language, designed to protect against unreasonable searches and seizures, the Court has made the Fourth Amendment its vehicle for holding all laws violative of the Constitution which offend the Court's broadest concept of privacy. . . .

The Fourth Amendment protects privacy only to the extent that it prohibits unreasonable searches and seizures of "persons, houses, papers, and effects." No general right is created by the Amendment so as to give this Court the unlimited power to hold unconstitutional everything which affects privacy. Certainly the Framers, well acquainted as they were with the excesses of governmental power, did not intend to grant this Court such omnipotent lawmaking authority as that. The history of governments proves that it is dangerous to freedom to repose such powers in courts.

For these reasons I respectfully dissent.

NOTES AND QUESTIONS

1. Was the electronic eavesdropping in *Katz* a search or a seizure or both? If the answer is unclear, does this fact lend support to Justice Black's position that eavesdropping is not an activity covered by the fourth amendment?

Note that Justice Black's "language of the Amendment" argument has two parts. First, the "normally accepted meanings of the words" refer only to tangible objects; second, one cannot "particularly describ[e]" a future conversation. Does the second point cut against or in favor of extending the fourth amendment to electronic surveillance? Why? With respect to the former point, consider the following passage from Amsterdam, Perspectives on the Fourth Amendment, 58 Minn. L. Rev. 349, 395-396 (1974):

> As applied to law enforcement activities, the terms "searches," "seizures," "persons," "houses," "papers" and "effects" could not be more capacious or less enlightening. The plain meaning of the English language would surely not be affronted if every police activity that involves seeking out crime or evidence of crime were held to be a search.

If reasonable people can disagree over the plain meaning of the words, what justification is there for Justice Black's narrow view of the scope of the fourth amendment?

2. In *Katz* the Court conceded that the government had probable cause to engage in the electronic surveillance. The fourth amendment violation occurred because the police had failed to obtain a warrant. Even if one concedes that, subject to a few narrowly drawn exceptions, warrantless searches should be per se unreasonable, should there not be an exception, as the government argued, for police activity that at the time

was perfectly legal? Indeed, weren't the police in *Katz* doing exactly what we expect them to do—vigorously investigating criminal activity within the bounds of the law as it exists at the time?

3. In a concurring opinion, Justice White expressed the view that *Katz* left "undisturbed" several earlier decisions upholding the warrantless use of undercover agents, some of whom were wired for sound or carried tape recorders. From those cases the following propositions had emerged:

a. *Unbugged agents.* The activity of a government agent in becoming a confidant of a defendant and eliciting statements from him involves "no interest legitimately protected by the Fourth Amendment." Hoffa v. United States, 385 U.S. 293, 302 (1966); *accord,* Lewis v. United States, 385 U.S. 206 (1966).[3]

b. *Agents with recorders.* The fact that an undercover agent whose status is unknown to the defendant surreptitiously records their conversation does not violate the fourth amendment. The defendant has no "constitutional right to rely on possible flaws in the agent's memory." Lopez v. United States, 373 U.S. 427, 439 (1963). (In *Lopez,* the government relied on both the testimony of the informant and the recording. The majority stressed that the recording was used simply to corroborate the agent's testimony, and Chief Justice Warren, in a concurring opinion, suggested that it might be improper to use the recording if the agent were not present and testifying. Is there any constitutional basis for distinguishing between the testimony of the agent and the recording?)

c. *Agents with transmitting devices.* The transmission via microphone secreted on an undercover agent of defendant's conversation with the agent to a nearby police officer does not violate the fourth amendment. On Lee v. United States, 343 U.S. 747 (1952).

---

3. See also Weatherford v. Bursey, 429 U.S. 545 (1977). Bursey and Weatherford, an undercover agent, participated in the vandalizing of a Selective Service office. In order to maintain Weatherford's undercover status, the authorities charged him, as well as Bursey, with the violation of state criminal statutes. Prior to trial Weatherford, at Bursey's invitation, met twice with Bursey and Bursey's attorney. "At no time did Weatherford discuss with or pass on to his superiors or to the prosecut[ors] . . . 'any details or information regarding the . . . criminal action pending against . . . [Bursey].' " Id. at 548. Although Weatherford testified for the prosecution at Bursey's trial, he did not testify about anything he learned at the meetings. Ibid.

Following his conviction, Bursey brought a federal civil rights action against Weatherford, alleging violations of Bursey's rights to counsel and to a fair trial. The Supreme Court rejected Bursey's claim. The Court noted that Weatherford's activity did not violate Bursey's fourth amendment rights, and because none of the information obtained by Weatherford had been communicated to the prosecutors, the Court found no independent sixth amendment or due process violation.

See generally Donovan, Informers Revisited: Government Surveillance of Domestic Political Organizations and the Fourth and First Amendments, 33 Buffalo L. Rev. 333 (1984).

Four years after *Katz*, the full Court addressed the issue raised by
Justice White's concurrence.

UNITED STATES v. WHITE
Certiorari to the United States Court of Appeals for the Seventh Circuit
401 U.S. 745 (1971)

MR. JUSTICE WHITE announced the judgment of the Court in an opinion
in which THE CHIEF JUSTICE, MR. JUSTICE STEWART, and MR. JUSTICE
BLACKMUN join.

In 1966, respondent James A. White was tried and convicted under
two consolidated indictments charging various illegal transactions in narcotics. . . . The issue before us is whether the Fourth Amendment bars
from evidence the testimony of governmental agents who related certain
conversations which had occurred between defendant White and a government informant, Harvey Jackson, and which the agents overheard by
monitoring the frequency of a radio transmitter carried by Jackson and
concealed on his person. On four occasions the conversations took place
in Jackson's home; each of these conversations was overheard by an agent
concealed in a kitchen closet with Jackson's consent and by a second
agent outside the house using a radio receiver. Four other conversations—
one in respondent's home, one in a restaurant, and two in Jackson's car—
were overheard by the use of radio equipment. The prosecution was
unable to locate and produce Jackson at the trial and the trial court
overruled objections to the testimony of the agents who conducted the
electronic surveillance. The jury returned a guilty verdict and defendant
appealed. . . .

Our problem is not what the privacy expectations of particular defendants in particular situations may be or the extent to which they may
in fact have relied on the discretion of their companions. Very probably,
individual defendants neither know nor suspect that their colleagues have
gone or will go to the police or are carrying recorders or transmitters.
Otherwise, conversation would cease and our problem with these encounters would be nonexistent or far different from those now before us.
Our problem, in terms of the principles announced in *Katz*, is what
expectations of privacy are constitutionally "justifiable"—what expectations the Fourth Amendment will protect in the absence of a warrant.
So far, the law permits the frustration of actual expectations of privacy
by permitting authorities to use the testimony of those associates who for
one reason or another have determined to turn to the police, as well as
by authorizing the use of informants in the manner exemplified by *Hoffa*

and *Lewis*.[4] If the law gives no protection to the wrongdoer whose trusted accomplice is or becomes a police agent, neither should it protect him when that same agent has recorded or transmitted the conversations which are later offered in evidence to prove the State's case. See Lopez v. United States, 373 U.S. 427 (1963).

Inescapably, one contemplating illegal activities must realize and risk that his companions may be reporting to the police. If he sufficiently doubts their trustworthiness, the association will very probably end or never materialize. But if he has no doubts, or allays them, or risks what doubt he has, the risk is his. In terms of what his course will be, what he will or will not do or say, we are unpersuaded that he would distinguish between probable informers on the one hand and probable informers with transmitters on the other. Given the possibility or probability that one of his colleagues is cooperating with the police, it is only speculation to assert that the defendant's utterances would be substantially different or his sense of security any less if he also thought it possible that the suspected colleague is wired for sound. At least there is no persuasive evidence that the difference in this respect between the electronically equipped and the unequipped agent is substantial enough to require discrete constitutional recognition, particularly under the Fourth Amendment which is ruled by fluid concepts of "reasonableness."

Nor should we be too ready to erect constitutional barriers to relevant and probative evidence which is also accurate and reliable. An electronic recording will many times produce a more reliable rendition of what a defendant has said than will the unaided memory of a police agent. It may also be that with the recording in existence it is less likely that the informant will change his mind, less chance that threat or injury will suppress unfavorable evidence and less chance that cross-examination will confound the testimony. Considerations like these obviously do not favor the defendant, but we are not prepared to hold that a defendant who has no constitutional right to exclude the informer's unaided testimony nevertheless has a Fourth Amendment privilege against a more accurate version of the events in question.

---

4. Earlier in the opinion Justice White described *Hoffa* and *Lewis*:

Hoffa . . . , which was left undisturbed by *Katz*, held that however strongly a defendant may trust an apparent colleague, his expectations in this respect are not protected by the Fourth Amendment when it turns out that the colleague is a government agent regularly communicating with the authorities. . . . No warrant to "search and seize" is required in such circumstances, nor is it when the Government sends to defendant's home a secret agent who conceals his identity and makes a purchase of narcotics from the accused, *Lewis*. 401 U.S. at 749.— EDS.

It is thus untenable to consider the activities and reports of the police agent himself, though acting without a warrant, to be a "reasonable" investigative effort and lawful under the Fourth Amendment but to view the same agent with a recorder or transmitter as conducting an "unreasonable" and unconstitutional search and seizure. Our opinion is currently shared by Congress and the Executive Branch, Title III, Omnibus Crime Control and Safe Streets Act of 1968, 82 Stat. 212, 18 U.S.C. §2510 et seq. (1964 ed., Supp. V), and the American Bar Association, Project on Standards for Criminal Justice, Electronic Surveillance §4.1 (Approved Draft 1971).[5] It is also the result reached by prior cases in this Court. . . .

The judgment of the Court of Appeals is reversed.

It is so ordered.[6]

MR. JUSTICE BLACK, concurs in the judgment of the Court for the reasons set forth in his dissent in Katz v. United States, 389 U.S. 347, 364 (1967).

[The concurring opinion of JUSTICE BRENNAN is omitted.]

MR. JUSTICE DOUGLAS, dissenting. . . .

The issue in this case is clouded and concealed by the very discussion of it in legalistic terms. What the ancients knew as "eavesdropping," we now call "electronic surveillance"; but to equate the two is to treat man's first gunpowder on the same level as the nuclear bomb. Electronic surveillance is the greatest leveler of human privacy ever known. How most forms of it can be held "reasonable" within the meaning of the Fourth Amendment is a mystery. To be sure, the Constitution and Bill of Rights are not to be read as covering only the technology known in the 18th century. Otherwise its concept of "commerce" would be hopeless when it comes to the management of modern affairs. At the same time the concepts of privacy which the Founders enshrined in the Fourth Amendment vanish completely when we slavishly allow an all-powerful government, proclaiming law and order, efficiency, and other benign purposes, to penetrate all the walls and doors which men need to shield them from the pressures of a turbulent life around them and give them the health and strength to carry on. . . .

Monitoring, if prevalent, certainly kills free discourse and sponta-

5. The ABA has subsequently reaffirmed this position. 1 American Bar Association, Standards for Criminal Justice, Electronic Surveillance §2-4.1 (2d ed. 1980).—EDS.

6. In Desist v. United States, 394 U.S. 244 (1969), the Court held that Katz applied only to electronic surveillance occurring after the date of the Katz decision. Since the activity in White occurred prior to that time, Justice White's plurality opinion relied on Desist as an independent basis for affirming the conviction. Justice Brennan, although he believed that Katz required overruling both On Lee and Lopez, concurred with the four justice plurality on the retroactivity issue.—EDS.

neous utterances. Free discourse—a First Amendment value—may be frivolous or serious, humble or defiant, reactionary or revolutionary, profane or in good taste; but it is not free if there is surveillance. Free discourse liberates the spirit, though it may produce only froth. The individual must keep some facts concerning his thoughts within a small zone of people. At the same time he must be free to pour out his woes or inspirations or dreams to others. He remains the sole judge as to what must be said and what must remain unspoken. This is the essence of the idea of privacy implicit in the First and Fifth Amendments as well as in the Fourth. . . .

MR. JUSTICE HARLAN, dissenting. . . .

The plurality opinion . . . [adopts] the following reasoning: if A can relay verbally what is revealed to him by B (as in *Lewis* and *Hoffa*), or record and later divulge it (as in *Lopez*), what difference does it make if A conspires with another to betray B by contemporaneously transmitting to the other all that is said? The contention is, in essence, an argument that the distinction between third-party monitoring and *other* undercover techniques is one of form and not substance. The force of the contention depends on the evaluation of two separable but intertwined assumptions: first, that there is no greater invasion of privacy in the third-party situation, and, second, that uncontrolled consensual surveillance in an electronic age is a tolerable technique of law enforcement, given the values and goals of our political system.

The first of these assumptions takes as a point of departure the so called "risk analysis" approach of *Lewis*, and *Lopez*, and to a lesser extent *On Lee*, or the expectations approach of *Katz*. . . . While these formulations represent an advance over the unsophisticated trespass analysis of the common law, they too have their limitations and can, ultimately, lead to the substitution of words for analysis. The analysis must, in my view, transcend the search for subjective expectations or legal attribution of assumptions of risk. Our expectations, and the risks we assume, are in large part reflections of laws that translate into rules the customs and values of the past and present.

Since it is the task of the law to form and project, as well as mirror and reflect, we should not, as judges, merely recite the expectations and risks without examining the desirability of saddling them upon society. The critical question, therefore, is whether under our system of government, as reflected in the Constitution, we should impose on our citizens the risks of the electronic listener or observer without at least the protection of a warrant requirement.

This question must, in my view, be answered by assessing the nature of a particular practice and the likely extent of its impact on the individual's sense of security balanced against the utility of the conduct as a technique of law enforcement. For those more extensive intrusions that significantly jeopardize the sense of security which is the paramount concern of Fourth Amendment liberties, I am of the view that more than self-restraint by law enforcement officials is required and at the least warrants should be necessary. . . .

The impact of the practice of third-party bugging, must, I think, be considered such as to undermine that confidence and sense of security in dealing with one another that is characteristic of individual relationships between citizens in a free society. It goes beyond the impact on privacy occasioned by the ordinary type of "informer" investigation upheld in *Lewis* and *Hoffa*. The argument of the plurality opinion, to the effect that it is irrelevant whether secrets are revealed by the mere tattletale or the transistor, ignores the differences occasioned by third-party monitoring and recording which insures full and accurate disclosure of all that is said, free of the possibility of error and oversight that inheres in human reporting.

Authority is hardly required to support the proposition that words would be measured a good deal more carefully and communication inhibited if one suspected his conversations were being transmitted and transcribed. Were third-party bugging a prevalent practice, it might well smother that spontaneity—reflected in frivolous, impetuous, sacrilegious, and defiant discourse—that liberates daily life. Much off-hand exchange is easily forgotten and one may count on the obscurity of his remarks, protected by the very fact of a limited audience, and the likelihood that the listener will either overlook or forget what is said, as well as the listener's inability to reformulate a conversation without having to contend with a documented record.[24] All these values are sacrificed by a rule of

---

24. From the same standpoint it may also be thought that electronic recording by an informer of a face-to-face conversation with a criminal suspect, as in *Lopez*, should be differentiated from third-party monitoring, as in *On Lee* and the case before us, in that the latter assures revelation to the Government by obviating the possibility that the informer may be tempted to renege in his undertaking to pass on to the Government all that he has learned. While the continuing vitality of *Lopez* is not drawn directly into question by this case, candor compels me to acknowledge that the views expressed in this opinion may impinge upon that part of the reasoning in *Lopez* which suggested that a suspect has no right to anticipate unreliable testimony. I am now persuaded that such an approach misconceives the basic issue, focusing, as it does, on the interests of a particular individual rather than evaluating the impact of a practice on the sense of security that is the true concern of the Fourth Amendment's protection of privacy. Distinctions do, however, exist between *Lopez*, where a known Government agent uses a recording device, and this case which involves third-party overhearing. However unlikely that the participant recorder will not play his tapes, the fact of the matter is that in a third-party situation the intrusion is instantaneous. Moreover, differences in the prior relationship between the investigator and the suspect may provide a focus for future distinctions. . . .

law that permits official monitoring of private discourse limited only by the need to locate a willing assistant. . . .

Finally, it is too easy to forget—and, hence, too often forgotten—that the issue here is whether to interpose a search warrant procedure between law enforcement agencies engaging in electronic eavesdropping and the public generally. By casting its "risk analysis" solely in terms of the expectations and risks that "wrongdoers" or "one contemplating illegal activities" ought to bear, the plurality opinion, I think, misses the mark entirely. *On Lee* does not simply mandate that criminals must daily run the risk of unknown eavesdroppers prying into their private affairs; it subjects each and every law-abiding member of society to that risk. The very purpose of interposing the Fourth Amendment warrant requirement is to redistribute the privacy risks throughout society in a way that produces the results the plurality opinion ascribes to the *On Lee* rule. Abolition of *On Lee* would not end electronic eavesdropping. It would prevent public officials from engaging in that practice unless they first had probable cause to suspect an individual of involvement in illegal activities and had tested their version of the facts before a detached judicial officer. . . .

[The dissenting opinion of JUSTICE MARSHALL is omitted.]

NOTES AND QUESTIONS

1. Justice Harlan faults the plurality's analysis for its failure to "transcend the search for subjective expectations or legal attributions of assumptions of risk." Is the criticism well-founded?

Note that Justice White states that the problem is to determine *not* subjective privacy expectations but rather "what expectations of privacy are constitutionally 'justifiable'—what expectations the Fourth Amendment will protect in the absence of a warrant." At the same time, however, his argument that there is no significant difference between the unbugged agents in *Lewis* and *Hoffa* and the transmitting agent here and in *On Lee* appears to rest in part[7] on an assessment of likely subjective expectations:

> Given the possibility or probability that one of his colleagues is cooperating with the police, it is only speculation to assert that the defendant's utter-

---

7. Justice White also suggested that the Court should not "be too ready to erect constitutional barriers to relevant and probative evidence which is also accurate and reliable." Would the requirements of probable cause and a warrant constitute a significant barrier? In any event, is the accuracy and reliability of the evidence a relevant concern? Isn't the very object of the fourth amendment to regulate the manner in which the police can obtain such evidence?

ances would be substantially different or his sense of security any less if he also thought it possible that the suspected colleague is wired for sound. . . .

Is Justice White being inconsistent? Is his argument any different in kind than Justice Harlan's assertions that "communication [would be] inhibited if one suspected his conversations were being transmitted" and that "[prevalent] third-party bugging . . . might well smother that spontaneity . . . that liberates daily life"? Even if the issue is not solely one of subjective expectations or probable human reactions, does it follow that these factors are irrelevant? Is it perhaps appropriate to take them into account when comparing two closely related investigatory devices— such as the use of bugged and unbugged secret agents?

2. Despite Justice Harlan's pejorative reference to "legal attributions of assumptions of risk," he does not question the correctness of *Hoffa* and *Lewis*, the unbugged agent cases. Yet, the basis for those holdings is that persons assume the risk that their supposedly trusted colleagues may be or may become government agents. Why should each of us have to assume these risks? Why is it not "constitutionally justifiable" to expect that the government will not, in the absence of probable cause and a warrant, place a walking, disguised, cajoling, surveillance device in our midst?

3. Even if the use of unbugged agents does not implicate the fourth amendment, should the same be true of transmitting agents? Should there be a constitutional difference between a transmitting device placed on a telephone booth and a transmitting device placed on a person, who can follow the suspect and try to elicit potentially incriminating statements? If so, from which activity should people be more protected?

If one were to agree with Justice Harlan that the use of transmitting agents should be regulated by the fourth amendment, what about the *Lopez*-type agent who carries a tape recorder? Is it sufficient to say, as the *Lopez* Court did, that an individual has no right to rely on an agent's faulty memory? Note that Justice Harlan, the author of the *Lopez* opinion, expressed some second thoughts about this reasoning in his *White* dissent.

4. Part of the difficulty in dealing with a case like *White* stems from the "monolithic" manner in which the fourth amendment tends to be applied. As Professor Amsterdam suggests, see page 499 supra, this type of "all-or-nothing approach" to the question what constitutes a search or seizure may result in divergent classification of some quite similar activity. There is, however, a much more basic difficulty that one must face in *White* or in any other case raising the question whether some type of investigatory activity should be regulated by the fourth amendment: After

Katz, what are the criteria for determining whether the activity is a "search and seizure"?

Prior to *Katz*, this question presented relatively few problems. Courts tended to define the scope of the fourth amendment in terms of property concepts, in part because much early fourth amendment litigation involved demands for the return of items seized. To be sure, the types of property interests protected by the fourth amendment gradually expanded. Moreover, in Jones v. United States, 362 U.S. 257 (1960), the Court stated that "subtle distinctions developed and refined by the common law in evolving the body of private property law . . . [are] often only of gossamer strength [and] ought not to be determinative of [fourth amendment rights]."[8] Id. at 266. Nonetheless, prior to *Katz*, it was commonly understood that a search and seizure occurred only if some government action infringed upon a "constitutionally protected area." And there was substantial consensus about what constituted such an area.

One of the virtues of *Katz*—for all of the justices except Justice Black—was the abandonment of the strictures inherent in the protected area concept. But what did *Katz* leave in its place? What, if anything, is there in *Katz* to guide courts—to say nothing of police officers, who have primary investigatory responsibility—in deciding whether something is a search and seizure? If police officers had employed a lip reader with binoculars to ascertain what Mr. Katz said on the telephone, would this have been a search and seizure? Would it have been a search and seizure if a police officer using binoculars observed Mr. Katz shooting heroin in a glass-enclosed telephone booth?

5. In his *Katz* concurrence, Justice Harlan suggested that individuals could claim the benefits of the fourth amendment only if they had "actual (subjective)" privacy expectations and if those expectations were ones "that society is prepared to recognize as 'reasonable.' " Note, however, that in *White*, Justice Harlan seemed to abandon the notion that a subjective privacy expectation was critical.

To what extent should the protections of the fourth amendment depend on the existence of a subjective privacy expectation? What determines whether a privacy expectation is "reasonable"? Does the fourth amendment protect only "privacy" interests? Only privacy interests that are "expectations"? Consider the following passage from Amsterdam, Perspectives on the Fourth Amendment, 58 Minn. L. Rev. 349, 385-386 (1974):

---

8. Jones, which is discussed at page 849 infra, held, inter alia, that a temporary apartment guest had a protectable fourth amendment interest in the apartment.

[T]he *Katz* decision was written to resist captivation in any formula. An opinion which sets aside prior formulas with the observation that they cannot "serve as a talismanic solution to every Fourth Amendment problem"[348] should hardly be read as intended to replace them with a new talisman.

As a doctrinal matter, it seems clear that the effect of *Katz* is to expand rather than generally to reconstruct the boundaries of fourth amendment protection. *Katz* is important for its rejection of several limitations upon the operation of the amendment, but it offers neither a comprehensive test of fourth amendment coverage nor any positive principles by which questions of coverage can be resolved. The fourth amendment is not limited to protection against physical trespass, although the preconstitutional history of the amendment was concerned with trespasses. "Searches" are not particular methods by which government invades constitutionally protected interests: they are a description of the conclusion that such interests have been invaded. The key to the amendment is the question of what interests it protects. Mr. Katz's conversation in a pay telephone booth was protected because he "justifiably relied" upon its being protected—relied, not in the sense of an expectation, but in the sense of a claim of right. In the end, the basis of the *Katz* decision seems to be that the fourth amendment protects those interests that may justifiably claim fourth amendment protection.

Of course this begs the question. But I think it begs the question no more or less than any other theory of fourth amendment coverage that the Court has used. *Olmstead* said that "the words search and seizure" could not be enlarged so "as to forbid hearing or sight."[351] But why? . . . *Olmstead* tells us that telephone wires are entitled to no more protection than the highways beneath them. But why? . . . *Olmstead's* answers to these questions remain as conclusionary as the contrary answers of *Katz*.

6. What factors should determine whether a police practice constitutes a search or seizure? Consider the following possibilities:

a. The extent to which a particular police practice interferes with the privacy of the persons against whom it is directed—How does one quantify privacy for this purpose? And what assumptions does one make about the nature of the environment of the affected persons? Listening from the sidewalk or peering through a window from the apartment across the street may be much more of an intrusion to a resident of Cabrini Green[9] on a hot summer evening than it is to the owner of an expensive, air-conditioned condominium only a few miles away on Lakeshore Drive.

---

348. [389 U.S.] at 351 n.9.
351. Olmstead v. United States, 277 U.S. 438, 465 (1928).
9. Cabrini Green is the low-income housing project made famous by former Chicago Mayor Jane Byrne when she decided to take up residence there.

See Katz, Patterns of Arrest and the Dangers of Public Visibility, 9 Crim. L. Bull. 311 (1973).

b. The frequency with which the police are likely to engage in the practice.

c. The impact of the practice on society as we know it today.

d. Whether the police, if left unregulated, would be likely to engage in the practice in a discriminatory or arbitrary manner.

e. Whether the type of regulation that would result from the (usually monolithic) application of the fourth amendment would unduly restrict an important investigatory practice.

See generally Note, Protecting Privacy Under the Fourth Amendment, 91 Yale L.J. 313 (1981).

2. Open Fields and Curtilage

OLIVER v. UNITED STATES, 466 U.S. 170, 173, 176-179, 181-186, 188-193, 195 (1984): JUSTICE POWELL delivered the opinion of the Court.

The "open fields" doctrine, first enunciated by this Court in Hester v. United States, 265 U.S. 57 (1924), permits police officers to enter and search a field without a warrant. We granted certiorari in these cases to clarify confusion that has arisen as to the continued vitality of the doctrine. . . .

[Oliver and Thornton were charged with drug offenses for cultivating marijuana. Oliver had a field of marijuana located on his farm over a mile from the house. Thornton had two patches of marijuana growing in the woods some unspecified distance behind his house. Both locations were highly secluded, and both were posted with "No Trespassing" signs. In each case, police officers discovered the marijuana as the result of a warrantless entry onto and inspection of the property. Both defendants prevailed on their suppression motions before the trial courts. In Oliver's case, the Sixth Circuit, sitting en banc, reversed the trial judge; in Thornton's case, the Maine Supreme Judicial Court affirmed the granting of the suppression motion.]

The rule announced in Hester v. United States was founded upon the explicit language of the Fourth Amendment. That Amendment indicates with some precision the places and things encompassed by its protections. As Justice Holmes explained for the Court in his characteristically laconic style: "[T]he special protection accorded by the Fourth Amendment to the people in their 'persons, houses, papers, and effects,' is not extended to the open fields. The distinction between the latter and the house is as old as the common law." Hester v. United States, 265 U.S., at 59.

Nor are the open fields "effects" within the meaning of the Fourth

Amendment. . . . We conclude, as did the Court in deciding Hester v. United States, that the government's intrusion upon the open fields is not one of those "unreasonable searches" proscribed by the text of the Fourth Amendment. . . .

This interpretation of the Fourth Amendment's language is consistent with the understanding of the right to privacy expressed in our Fourth Amendment jurisprudence. Since Katz v. United States, 389 U.S. 347 (1967), the touchstone of Amendment analysis has been the question whether a person has a "constitutionally protected reasonable expectation of privacy." 389 U.S., at 360 (Harlan, J., concurring). . . .

No single factor determines whether an individual legitimately may claim under the Fourth Amendment that a place should be free of government intrusion not authorized by warrant. . . . In assessing the degree to which a search infringes upon individual privacy, the Court has given weight to such factors as the intention of the Framers of the Fourth Amendment, e.g., United States v. Chadwick, 433 U.S. 1, 7-8 (1977), the uses to which the individual has put a location, e.g., Jones v. United States, 362 U.S. 257, 265 (1960), and our societal understanding that certain areas deserve the most scrupulous protection from government invasion, e.g., Payton v. New York, 445 U.S. 573 (1980). . . .

In this light, the rule of Hester v. United States, supra, that we reaffirm today, may be understood as providing that an individual may not legitimately demand privacy for activities conducted out of doors in fields, except in the area immediately surrounding the home. . . .

[O]pen fields do not provide the setting for those intimate activities that the Amendment is intended to shelter from government interference or surveillance. There is no societal interest in protecting the privacy of those activities, such as the cultivation of crops, that occur in open fields. Moreover, as a practical matter these lands usually are accessible to the public and the police in ways that a home, an office or commercial structure would not be. It is not generally true that fences or no trespassing signs effectively bar the public from viewing open fields in rural areas. And both petitioner Oliver and respondent Thornton concede that the public and police lawfully may survey lands from the air.[9] For these reasons, the asserted expectation of privacy in open fields is not an expectation that "society recognizes as reasonable." . . .

Petitioner Oliver and respondent Thornton contend . . . that the circumstances of a search sometimes may indicate that reasonable ex-

---

9. . . . In practical terms, petitioner Oliver's and respondent Thornton's analysis merely would require law enforcement officers, in most situations, to use aerial surveillance to gather the information necessary to obtain a warrant or to justify warrantless entry onto the property. It is not easy to see how such a requirement would advance legitimate privacy interests.

pectations of privacy were violated; and that courts therefore should analyze these circumstances on a case-by-case basis. The language of the
Fourth Amendment itself answers their contention.

Nor would a case-by-case approach provide a workable accommodation between the needs of law enforcement and the interests protected
by the Fourth Amendment. Under this approach, police officers would
have to guess before every search whether landowners had erected fences
sufficiently high, posted a sufficient number of warning signs, or located
contraband in an area sufficiently secluded to establish a right of privacy. . . . The ad hoc approach . . . also creates a danger that constitutional rights will be arbitrarily and inequitably enforced. . . .

In any event, while the factors that petitioner Oliver and respondent
Thornton urge the courts to consider may be relevant to Fourth Amendment analysis in some contexts, these factors cannot be decisive on the
question whether the search of an open field is subject to the Amendment.
Initially, we reject the suggestion that steps taken to protect privacy establish that expectations of privacy in an open field are legitimate. . . .
The test of legitimacy is not whether the individual chooses to conceal
assertedly "private" activity. Rather, the correct inquiry is whether the
government's intrusion infringes upon the personal and societal values
protected by the Fourth Amendment. . . .

Nor is the government's intrusion upon an open field a "search" in
the constitutional sense because that intrusion is a trespass at common
law. The existence of a property right is but one element in determining
whether expectations of privacy are legitimate. . . .

The common law may guide consideration of what areas are protected by the Fourth Amendment search by defining areas whose invasion
by others is wrongful. . . . The law of trespass, however, forbids intrusions upon land that the Fourth Amendment would not proscribe. For
trespass law extends to instances where the exercise of the right to exclude
vindicates no legitimate privacy interest.[15] . . .

15. The law of trespass recognizes the interest in possession and control of one's
property and for that reason permits exclusion of unwanted intruders. But it does not
follow that the right to exclude conferred by trespass law embodies a privacy interest also
protected by the Fourth Amendment. To the contrary, the common law of trespass
furthers a range of interests that have nothing to do with privacy and that would not be
served by applying the strictures of trespass law to public officers. Criminal laws against
trespass are prophylactic: they protect against intruders who poach, steal livestock and
crops or vandalize property. And the civil action of trespass serves the important function
of authorizing an owner to defeat claims of prescription by asserting his own title. See,
e.g., O. W. Holmes, The Common Law, at 98-100, 244-246. In any event, unlicensed
use of property by others is presumptively unjustified, as anyone who wishes to use the
property is free to bargain for the right to do so with the property owner, cf. Posner,
Economic Analysis of Law, at pp. 10-13, 21 (1973). For these reasons, the law of trespass

. . . We . . . affirm Oliver v. United States; Maine v. Thornton is reversed and remanded for further proceedings not inconsistent with this opinion.

It is so ordered.

[The concurring opinion of Justice White is omitted.]

JUSTICE MARSHALL, with whom JUSTICE BRENNAN and JUSTICE STEVENS join, dissenting. . . .

The first ground on which the Court rests its decision is that the Fourth Amendment "indicates with some precision the places and things encompassed by its protections," and that real property is not included in the list of protected spaces and possessions. . . . This line of argument has several flaws. Most obviously, it is inconsistent with the results of many of our previous decisions, none of which the Court purports to overrule. For example, neither a public telephone booth nor a conversation conducted therein can fairly be described as a person, house, paper, or effect; yet we have held that the Fourth Amendment forbids the police without a warrant to eavesdrop on such a conversation. . . .

The Court's inability to reconcile its parsimonious reading of the phrase "persons, houses, papers, and effects" with our prior decisions or even its own holding is a symptom of a more fundamental infirmity in the Court's reasoning. The Fourth Amendment, like the other central provisions of the Bill of Rights that loom large in our modern jurisprudence, was designed, not to prescribe with "precision" permissible and impermissible activities, but to identify a fundamental human liberty that should be shielded forever from government intrusion. . . .

The second ground for the Court's decision is its contention that any interest a landowner might have in the privacy of his woods and fields is not one that "society is prepared to recognize as 'reasonable.' " . . . The mode of analysis that underlies this assertion is certainly more consistent with our prior decisions than that discussed above. But the Court's conclusion cannot withstand scrutiny.

As the Court acknowledges, we have traditionally looked to a variety of factors in determining whether an expectation of privacy asserted in a physical space is "reasonable." . . . Though those factors do not lend themselves to precise taxonomy, they may be roughly grouped into three categories. First, we consider whether the expectation at issue is rooted in entitlements defined by positive law. Second, we consider the nature of the uses to which spaces of the sort in question can be put. Third, we consider whether the person claiming a privacy interest manifested that

---

confers protections from intrusion by others far broader than those required by Fourth Amendment interests.

interest to the public in a way that most people would understand and respect.[8] When the expectations of privacy asserted by petitioner Oliver and respondent Thornton are examined through these lenses, it becomes clear that those expectations are entitled to constitutional protection. . . .

We have frequently acknowledged that privacy interests are not coterminous with property rights. . . . However, because "property rights reflect society's explicit recognition of a person's authority to act as he wishes in certain areas, [they] should be considered in determining whether an individual's expectations of privacy are reasonable." Rakas v. Illinois, 439 U.S. [128, 153 (1978)] (Powell, J., concurring). . . .

It is undisputed that Oliver and Thornton each owned the land into which the police intruded. That fact alone provides considerable support for their assertion of legitimate privacy interests in their woods and fields. But even more telling is the nature of the sanctions that Oliver and Thornton could invoke, under local law, for violation of their property rights. In Kentucky, a knowing entry upon fenced or otherwise enclosed land, or upon unenclosed land conspicuously posted with signs excluding the public, constitutes criminal trespass. The law in Maine is similar. . . .

The uses to which a place is put are highly relevant to the assessment of a privacy interest asserted therein. . . . If, in light of our shared sensibilities, those activities are of a kind in which people should be able to engage without fear of intrusion by private persons or government officials, we extend the protection of the Fourth Amendment to the space in question, even in the absence of an entitlement derived from positive law. . . .[13]

Privately-owned woods and fields that are not exposed to public view

8. . . . The factors relevant to the assessment of the reasonableness of a non-spatial privacy interest may well be different from the three considerations discussed here. See, e.g., Smith v. Maryland, 442 U.S. 735, 747-748 (1979) (Stewart, J., dissenting); id., at 750-752 (Marshall, J., dissenting).

13. In most circumstances, this inquiry requires analysis of the sorts of uses to which a given space is susceptible, not the manner in which the person asserting an expectation of privacy in the space was in fact employing it. . . . We make exceptions to this principle and evaluate uses on a case-by-case basis in only two contexts: when called upon to assess (what formerly was called) the "standing" of a particular person to challenge an intrusion by government officials into an area over which that person lacked primary control, see, e.g., Rakas v. Illinois, 439 U.S., at 148-149; Jones v. United States, 362 U.S. 257, 265-266 (1960), and when it is possible to ascertain how a person is using a particular space without violating the very privacy interest he is asserting, see, e.g., Katz v. United States, 389 U.S., at 352. . . . Neither of these exceptions is applicable here. Thus, the majority's contention that, because the cultivation of marijuana is not an activity that society wishes to protect, Oliver and Thornton had no legitimate privacy interest in their fields, . . . reflects a misunderstanding of the level of generality on which the constitutional analysis must proceed.

regularly are employed in a variety of ways that society acknowledges deserve privacy. Many landowners like to take solitary walks on their property, confident that they will not be confronted in their rambles by strangers or policemen. Others conduct agricultural businesses on their property.[14] Some landowners use their secluded spaces to meet lovers, others to gather together with fellow worshippers, still others to engage in sustained creative endeavor. Private land is sometimes used as a refuge for wildlife, where flora and fauna are protected from human intervention of any kind. Our respect for the freedom of landowners to use their posted "open fields" in ways such as these partially explains the seriousness with which the positive law regards deliberate invasions of such spaces. . . .

Whether a person "took normal precautions to maintain his privacy" in a given space affects whether his interest is one protected by the Fourth Amendment. . . . The reason why such precautions are relevant is that we do not insist that a person who has a right to exclude others exercise that right. . . .

Certain spaces are so presumptively private that signals of this sort are unnecessary; a homeowner need not post a "do not enter" sign on his door in order to deny entrance to uninvited guests. Privacy interests in other spaces are more ambiguous, and the taking of precautions is consequently more important: placing a lock on one's footlocker strengthens one's claim that an examination of its contents is impermissible. . . . Still other spaces are, by positive law and social convention, presumed accessible to members of the public *unless* the owner manifests his intention to exclude them.

Undeveloped land falls into the last-mentioned category. . . .

A clear, easily administrable rule emerges from the analysis set forth above: Private land marked in a fashion sufficient to render entry thereon a criminal trespass under the law of the state in which the land lies is protected by the Fourth Amendment's proscription of unreasonable searches and seizures. . . .

NOTES AND QUESTIONS

1. The Court further considered the meaning of "open fields" in United States v. Dunn, 480 U.S. 294 (1987). Drug Enforcement Administration agents made several warrantless entries onto defendant's ranch. They approached and looked into—but did not enter—two barns that

---

14. We accord constitutional protection to businesses conducted in office buildings. . . . [I]t is not apparent why businesses conducted in fields that are not open to the public are less deserving of the benefit of the Fourth Amendment.

were approximately 50 yards from a fence surrounding the residence. The agents had to cross several barbed wire fences to get to the barns, and they had to pass through a wooden fence that enclosed the front portion of one of the barns. Relying in part on what they observed in the barn, the agents obtained a warrant to search the ranch. They seized amphetamines and chemicals and equipment used in the manufacturing of controlled substances.

The Court concluded that the initial warrantless entries did not violate Dunn's fourth amendment rights because the officers had entered the "open fields," not the "curtilage." According to the Court,

> curtilage questions should be resolved with particular reference to four factors: the proximity of the area claimed to be curtilage to the home, whether the area is included within an enclosure surrounding the home, the nature of the uses to which the area is put and the steps taken by the resident to protect the area from observations by the people passing by. [Id. at 301.]

In explaining the role of these factors in determining what constitutes curtilage, the Court observed,

> We do not suggest that combining these factors produces a finely tuned formula that, when mechanically applied, yields a "correct" answer to all extent-of-the-curtilage questions. Rather, these factors are useful analytical tools only to the degree that, in any given case, they bear upon the centrally relevant consideration—whether the area in question is so intimately tied to the home itself that it should be placed under the home's "umbrella" of Fourth Amendment protection. [Id.]

Justice Brennan, in a dissenting opinion joined by Justice Marshall, noted that the majority of state courts had held that barns are within the curtilage of a farmhouse, and he argued that the application of the Court's factors to Dunn's situation should lead to the conclusion that the barn was part of the curtilage.

The most interesting discussion and disagreement among the Justices related to the third factor—"the nature of the uses to which the area is put." Justice White, in his opinion for the Court, asserted, "It is especially significant the law enforcement officials possessed objective data [as a result of prior aerial photographs and ' "a very strong odor" of phenylacetic acid'] indicating that the barn was not being used for intimate activities of the home." Id. at 302. In a concurring opinion, Justice Scalia observed:

> It does not seem to me "especially significant that the law enforcement officials possessed objective data indicating that the barn was not being

used for intimate activities of the home." . . . What is significant is that
the barn was not to be so used, whether or not law enforcement officials
knew it. The officers' perceptions might be relevant to whether intrusion
upon curtilage was nevertheless reasonable, but they are no more relevant
to whether the barn was curtilage than to whether the house was a house.
[Id. at 305.]

Justice Brennan, in his dissent, argued:

The third factor . . . has been badly misunderstood and misapplied
by the Court. . . .
     In *Oliver*, the Court held that, as a general matter, the open fields "are
unlikely to provide the setting for activities whose privacy is sought to be
protected by the Fourth Amendment." 466 U.S. at 179 n.10. The Court
expressly refused to do a case-by-case analysis to ascertain whether, on occasion, an individual's expectation of privacy in a certain activity in an open
field should be protected. . . . In the instant case, the court is confronted
with the general rule that a barn *is* in domestic use. To be consistent with
Oliver, the Court should refuse to do a case-by-case analysis of the expectation·
of privacy in any particular barn and follow the general rule that a barn is
in domestic use. What should be relevant here, as in *Oliver*, is the typical
use of an area or structure. The Court's willingness to generalize about the
absence of privacy interest in the open fields and unwillingness to generalize
about the existence of a privacy interest in a barn near a residence are
manifestly inconsistent and reflect a hostility to the purpose of the Fourth
Amendment. [480 U.S. at 310 (emphasis in original).]

2. Do you agree with Justice Brennan that the Court's approaches
in *Oliver* and *Dunn* are inconsistent? To the extent that there arguably
is an inconsistency in that the *Dunn* Court seems more willing to engage
in a "case-by-case" analysis, consider whether the inconsistency stems
more from the specificity with which the Court applies the third factor
in *Dunn* or from the focus in *Dunn* on four factors for resolving curtilage
questions. Even if the Court had taken a more generalized view of the
third factor in *Dunn* and had agreed with the dissent with respect to this
factor, there were still three remaining factors that in the majority's view
cut against the defendant.

3. Would a more generalized, *Oliver*-like approach to the question
of curtilage necessarily have benefited the defendant in *Dunn*? Consider
the following excerpt from the Court's opinion:

We decline the Government's invitation to adopt a "bright-line rule"
that "the curtilage should extend no farther than the nearest fence surrounding a fenced house." . . . Fencing configurations are important
factors in defining the curtilage, . . . but . . . the primary focus is whether

the area in question harbors those intimate activities associated with domestic life and the privacies of the home. Application of the Government's "first fence rule" might well lead to diminished Fourth Amendment protection in those cases where a structure lying outside a home's enclosing fence was used for such domestic activities. [Id. at 301 n.4.]

4. In *Dunn* the Court also rejected the defendant's argument that the officers' actions had violated his privacy interest in the barn. Assuming that the defendant had a protectable interest in the barn, the Court reasoned that prior to obtaining a warrant,

> the officers never entered the barn. . . . Once at their vantage point, they merely stood outside the curtilage of the house and in the open fields upon which the barn was constructed, and peered into the barn's open front. And, standing as they were in the open fields, the Constitution did not forbid them to observe the phenylacetone laboratory located in respondent's barn. . . .
> [T]here is no constitutional difference between police observations conducted while in a public place and while standing in the open fields. Similarly, the fact that the objects observed by the officers lay within an area that we have assumed, but not decided, was protected by the Fourth Amendment does not affect our conclusion. . . . [T]he Fourth Amendment "has never been extended to require law enforcement officers to shield their eyes when passing by a home on public thoroughfares." [California v. Ciraolo, 476 U.S. 207, 213 (1986)]. [480 U.S. at 304.]

Justice Brennan dissented from this part of the Court's holding as well. Assuming that the defendant had a legitimate privacy interest in the barn, Justice Brennan analogized the fenced barn to commercial property not generally open to the public. When the owner of commercial property has taken steps to bar the public generally, the owner, in Justice Brennan's view, has created a "business curtilage" or legitimate privacy interest in the area surrounding the property. Id. at 314-319.

3. Aerial Surveillance

FLORIDA v. RILEY
Certiorari to the Florida Supreme Court
488 U.S. 445 (1989)

JUSTICE WHITE announced the judgment of the Court and delivered an opinion, in which THE CHIEF JUSTICE, JUSTICE SCALIA and JUSTICE KENNEDY join.

On certification to it by a lower state court, the Florida Supreme Court addressed the following question: "Whether surveillance of the interior of a partially covered greenhouse in a residential backyard from the vantage point of a helicopter located 400 feet above the greenhouse constitutes a 'search' for which a warrant is required under the Fourth Amendment. . . . The court answered the question in the affirmative, and we granted the State's petition for certiorari. . . .

Respondent Riley lived in a mobile home located on five acres of rural property. A greenhouse was located 10 to 20 feet behind the mobile home. Two sides of the greenhouse were enclosed. The other two sides were not enclosed but the contents of the greenhouse were obscured from view from surrounding property by trees, shrubs and the mobile home. The greenhouse was covered by corrugated roofing panels, some translucent and some opaque. At the time relevant to this case, two of the panels, amounting to approximately 10% of the roof area, were missing. A wire fence surrounded the mobile home and the greenhouse, and the property was posted with a "DO NOT ENTER" sign.

This case originated with an anonymous tip to the Pasco County Sheriff's office that marijuana was being grown on respondent's property. When an investigating officer discovered that he could not see the contents of the greenhouse from the road, he circled twice over respondent's property in a helicopter at the height of 400 feet. With his naked eye, he was able to see through the openings in the roof and one or more of the open sides of the greenhouse and to identify what he thought was marijuana growing in the structure. A warrant was obtained based on these observations, and the ensuing search revealed marijuana growing in the greenhouse. Respondent was charged with possession of marijuana under Florida law. The trial court granted his motion to suppress; the Florida Court of Appeals reversed but certified the case to the Florida Supreme Court, which quashed the decision of the Court of Appeals and reinstated the trial court's suppression order.

We agree with the State's submission that our decision in California v. Ciraolo, 476 U.S. 207 (1986), controls this case. There, acting on a tip, the police inspected the backyard of a particular house while flying in a fixed-wing aircraft at 1,000 feet. With the naked eye the officers saw what they concluded was marijuana growing in the yard. A search warrant was obtained on the strength of this airborne inspection, and marijuana plants were found. . . . We [held] that the inspection was not a search subject to the Fourth Amendment. We recognized that the yard was within the curtilage of the house, that a fence shielded the yard from observation from the street and that the occupant had a subjective expectation of privacy. We held, however, that such an expectation was not reasonable and not one "that society is prepared to honor." Id., at

214. Our reasoning was that the home and its curtilage are not necessarily protected from inspection that involves no physical invasion. " 'What a person knowingly exposes to the public, even in his own home or office, is not a subject of Fourth Amendment protection.' " Id., at 213, quoting Katz v. United States, 389 U.S. 347, 351 (1967). As a general proposition, the police may see what may be seen "from a public vantage point where [they have] a right to be" 476 U.S., at 213. Thus the police, like the public, would have been free to inspect the backyard garden from the street if their view had been unobstructed. They were likewise, free to inspect the yard from the vantage point of an aircraft flying in the navigable airspace as this plane was. "In an age where private and commercial flight in the public airways is routine, it is unreasonable for respondent to expect that his marijuana plants were constitutionally protected from being observed with the naked eye from an altitude of 1,000 feet. The Fourth Amendment simply does not require the police traveling in the public airways at this altitude to obtain a warrant in order to observe what is visible to the naked eye." Id., at 215.

We arrive at the same conclusion in the present case. In this case, as in *Ciraolo*, the property surveyed was within the curtilage of respondent's home. Riley no doubt intended and expected that his greenhouse would not be open to public inspection, and the precautions he took protected against ground-level observation. Because the sides and roof of his greenhouse were left partially open, however, what was growing in the greenhouse was subject to viewing from the air. Under the holding in *Ciraolo*, Riley could not reasonably have expected the contents of his greenhouse to be immune from examination by an officer seated in a fixed-wing aircraft flying in navigable airspace at an altitude of 1,000 feet or, as the Florida Supreme Court seemed to recognize, at an altitude of 500 feet, the lower limit of the navigable airspace for such an aircraft. . . . Here, the inspection was made from a helicopter, but as is the case with fixed-wing planes, "private and commercial flight [by helicopter] in the public airways is routine" in this country, *Ciraolo*, supra, 476 U.S., at 215, and there is no indication that such flights are unheard of in Pasco County, Florida.[2] Riley could not reasonably have expected that his greenhouse was protected from public or official observation from

2. The first use of the helicopter by police was in New York in 1947, and today every State in the country uses helicopters in police work. As of 1980, there were 1,500 of such aircraft used in police work. E. Brown, The Helicopter in Civil Operations 79 (1981). More than 10,000 helicopters, both public and private, are registered in the United States. Federal Aviation Administration, Census of U.S. Civil Aircraft, Calendar Year 1987, p.12, and there are an estimated 31,697 helicopter pilots. Federal Aviation Administration, Statistical Handbook of Aviation, Calendar Year 1986, p.147. 1988 Helicopter Annual 9.

a helicopter had it been flying within the navigable airspace for fixed-wing aircraft.

Nor on the facts before us, does it make a difference for Fourth Amendment purposes that the helicopter was flying at 400 feet when the officer saw what was growing in the greenhouse through the partially open roof and sides of the structure. We would have a different case if flying at that altitude had been contrary to law or regulation. But helicopters are not bound by the lower limits of the navigable airspace allowed to other aircraft. Any member of the public could legally have been flying over Riley's property in a helicopter at the altitude of 400 feet and could have observed Riley's greenhouse. The police officer did no more. This is not to say that an inspection of the curtilage of a house from an aircraft will always pass muster under the Fourth Amendment simply because the plane is within the navigable airspace specified by law. But it is of obvious importance that the helicopter in this case was not violating the law, and there is nothing in the record or before us to suggest that helicopters flying at 400 feet are sufficiently rare in this country to lend substance to respondent's claim that he reasonably anticipated that his greenhouse would not be subject to observation from that altitude. Neither is there any intimation here that the helicopter interfered with respondent's normal use of the greenhouse or of other parts of the curtilage. As far as this record reveals, no intimate details connected with the use of the home or curtilage were observed, and there was no undue noise, no wind, dust, or threat of injury. In these circumstances, there was no violation of the Fourth Amendment.

The judgment of the Florida Supreme Court is accordingly reversed. So ordered.

JUSTICE O'CONNOR, concurring in the judgment.

. . . I write separately . . . to clarify the standard I believe follows from California v. Ciraolo, 476 U.S. 207 (1986). In my view, the plurality's approach rests the scope of Fourth Amendment protection too heavily on compliance with FAA regulations whose purpose is to promote air safety not to protect "[t]he right of the people to be secure in their persons, houses, papers, and effects, against unreasonable searches and seizures." U.S. Const., Amdt. 4. . . .

Ciraolo's expectation of privacy was unreasonable not because the airplane was operating where it had a "right to be," but because public air travel at 1,000 feet is a sufficiently routine part of modern life that it is unreasonable for persons on the ground to expect that their curtilage will not be observed from the air at that altitude. . . .

In determining whether Riley had a reasonable expectation of privacy from aerial observation, the relevant inquiry after Ciraolo is . . . whether the helicopter was in the public airways at an altitude at which members of the public travel with sufficient regularity that Riley's expectation of privacy from aerial observation was not "one that society is prepared to recognize as 'reasonable.' " Katz [v. United States], 389 U.S. [347, 361 (1967)]. Thus, in determining " 'whether the government's intrusion infringes upon the personal and societal values protected by the Fourth Amendment,' " *Ciraolo*, supra, 476 U.S., at 212, (quoting Oliver [v. United States], 466 U.S. [170, 182-183 (1984)]), it is not conclusive to observe, as the plurality does, that "[a]ny member of the public could legally have been flying over Riley's property in a helicopter at the altitude of 400 feet and could have observed Riley's greenhouse." . . . Nor is it conclusive that police helicopters may often fly at 400 feet. If the public rarely, if ever, travels overhead at such altitudes, the observation cannot be said to be from a vantage point generally used by the public and Riley cannot be said to have "knowingly expose[d]" his greenhouse to public view. However, if the public can generally be expected to travel over residential backyards at an altitude of 400 feet, Riley cannot reasonably expect his curtilage to be free from such aerial observation.

In my view, the defendant must bear the burden of proving that his expectation of privacy was a reasonable one, and thus that a "search" within the meaning of the Fourth Amendment even took place. Cf. Jones v. United States, 362 U.S. 257, 261 (1960) ("Ordinarily, then, it is entirely proper to require of one who seeks to challenge the legality of a search as the basis for suppressing relevant evidence that he allege, and if the allegation be disputed that he establish, that he himself was the victim of an invasion of privacy" . . .).

Because there is reason to believe that there is considerable public use of airspace at altitudes of 400 feet and above, and because Riley introduced no evidence to the contrary before the Florida courts, I conclude that Riley's expectation that his curtilage was protected from naked-eye aerial observation from that altitude was not a reasonable one. However, public use of altitudes lower than that—particularly public observations from helicopters circling over the curtilage of a home—may be sufficiently rare that police surveillance from such altitudes would violate reasonable expectations of privacy, despite compliance with FAA air safety regulations.

JUSTICE BRENNAN, with whom JUSTICE MARSHALL and JUSTICE STEVENS, join, dissenting. . . .

I . . .

The plurality undertakes no inquiry into whether low-level helicopter surveillance by the police of activities in an enclosed backyard is consistent

with the "aims of a free and open society." [Amsterdam, Perspectives on
the Fourth Amendment, 58 Minn. L. Rev. 349, 403 (1974)]. . . .

Under the plurality's exceedingly grudging Fourth Amendment theory, the expectation of privacy is defeated if a single member of the public
could conceivably position herself to see into the area in question without
doing anything illegal. It is defeated whatever the difficulty a person would
have in so positioning herself, and however infrequently anyone would
in fact do so. In taking this view the plurality ignores the very essence of
Katz. The reason why there is no reasonable expectation of privacy in
an area that is exposed to the public is that little diminution in "the
amount of privacy and freedom remaining to citizens" will result from
police surveillance of something that any passerby readily sees. . . .

It is a curious notion that the reach of the Fourth Amendment can
be so largely defined by administrative regulations issued for purposes of
flight safety. It is more curious still that the plurality relies to such an
extent on the legality of the officer's act, when we have consistently refused
to equate police violation of the law with infringement of the Fourth
Amendment.[3] But the plurality's willingness to end its inquiry when it
finds that the officer was in a position he had a right to be in is misguided
for an even more fundamental reason. Finding determinative the fact
that the officer was where he had a right to be is, at bottom, an attempt
to analogize surveillance from a helicopter to surveillance by a police
officer standing on a public road and viewing evidence of crime through
an open window or a gap in a fence. In such a situation, the occupant
of the home may be said to lack any reasonable expectation of privacy
in what can be seen from that road—even if, in fact, people rarely pass
that way.

The police officer positioned 400 feet above Riley's backyard was
not, however, standing on a public road. The vantage point he enjoyed
was not one any citizen could readily share. His ability to see over Riley's
fence depended on his use of a very expensive and sophisticated piece of
machinery to which few ordinary citizens have access. In such circumstances it makes no more sense to rely on the legality of the officer's
position in the skies than it would to judge the constitutionality of the
wiretap in *Katz* by the legality of the officer's position outside the telephone booth. . . . The question before us must be not whether the

---

3. In Oliver v. United States, 466 U.S. 170 (1984), for example, we held that police
officers who trespassed upon posted and fenced private land did not violate the Fourth
Amendment, despite the fact that their action was subject to criminal sanctions. We
noted that the interests vindicated by the Fourth Amendment were not identical with
those served by the common law of trespass. See id., at 183-184, and n.15. . . . Katz
v. United States, 389 U.S. 347 (1967), . . . made plain that the question of whether
or not the disputed evidence had been procured by means of a trespass was irrelevant. . . .

police were where they had a right to be, but whether public observation of Riley's curtilage was so commonplace that Riley's expectation of privacy in his backyard could not be considered reasonable. . . . While, as we held in *Ciraolo*, air traffic at elevations of 1000 feet or more may be so common that whatever could be seen with the naked eye from that elevation is unprotected by the Fourth Amendment, it is a large step from there to say that the Amendment offers no protection against low-level helicopter surveillance of enclosed curtilage areas. To take this step is error enough. That the plurality does so with little analysis beyond its determination that the police complied with FAA regulations is particularly unfortunate.

II

Equally disconcerting is the lack of any meaningful limit to the plurality's holding. . . .

Only in its final paragraph does the plurality opinion suggest that there might be some limits to police helicopter surveillance beyond those imposed by FAA regulations. . . .

If . . . the purpose of the restraints imposed by the Fourth Amendment is to "safeguard the privacy and security of individuals," [Camara v. Municipal Court, 387 U.S. 523, 528 (1967),] then it is puzzling why it should be the helicopter's noise, wind, and dust that provides the measure of whether this constitutional safeguard has been infringed. . . .

[T]he logical consequence of the plurality's rule [is] that, so long as the police are where they have a right to be under air traffic regulations, the Fourth Amendment is offended only if the aerial surveillance interferes with the use of the backyard as a garden spot. Nor is there anything in the plurality's opinion to suggest that any different rule would apply were the police looking from their helicopter, not into the open curtilage, but through an open window into a room viewable only from the air.

III

Perhaps the most remarkable passage in the plurality opinion is its suggestion that the case might be a different one had any "intimate details connected with the use of the home or curtilage [been] observed." . . . What, one wonders, is meant by "intimate details"? If the police had observed Riley embracing his wife in the backyard greenhouse, would we then say that his reasonable expectation of privacy had been infringed?

Where in the Fourth Amendment or in our cases is there any warrant for imposing a requirement that the activity observed must be "intimate" in order to be protected by the Constitution?

It is difficult to avoid the conclusion that the plurality has allowed its analysis of Riley's expectation of privacy to be colored by its distaste for the activity in which he was engaged. It is indeed easy to forget, especially in view of current concern over drug trafficking, that the scope of the Fourth Amendment's protection does not turn on whether the activity disclosed by a search is illegal or innocuous. But we dismiss this as a "drug case" only at the peril of our own liberties. Justice Frankfurter once noted that "[i]t is a fair summary of history to say that the safeguards of liberty have frequently been forged in controversies involving not very nice people," United States v. Rabinowitz, 339 U.S. 56 (1950) (dissenting opinion), and nowhere is this observation more apt than in the area of the Fourth Amendment, whose words have necessarily been given meaning largely through decisions suppressing evidence of criminal activity. The principle enunciated in this case determines what limits the Fourth Amendment imposes on aerial surveillance of any person, for any reason. If the Constitution does not protect Riley's marijuana garden against such surveillance, it is hard to see how it will forbid the Government from aerial spying on the activities of a law-abiding citizen on her fully enclosed outdoor patio. As Professor Amsterdam has eloquently written: "The question is not whether you or I must draw the blinds before we commit a crime. It is whether you and I must discipline ourselves to draw the blinds every time we enter a room, under pain of surveillance if we do not." Amsterdam, 58 Minn. L. Rev., at 403.

IV

I find little to disagree with in the concurring opinion of Justice O'Connor, apart from its closing paragraphs. A majority of the Court thus agrees that the fundamental inquiry is not whether the police were where they had a right to be under FAA regulations, but rather whether Riley's expectation of privacy was rendered illusory by the extent of public observation of his backyard from aerial traffic at 400 feet.

What separates me from Justice O'Connor is essentially an empirical matter concerning the extent of public use of the airspace at that altitude, together with the question of how to resolve that issue. I do not think the constitutional claim should fail simply because "there is reason to believe" that there is "considerable" public flying this close to earth or because Riley "introduced no evidence to the contrary before the Florida courts." . . . I think we could take judicial notice that, while there may be an occasional privately owned helicopter that flies over populated areas at an altitude of 400 feet, such flights are a rarity and are almost entirely limited to approaching or leaving airports or to reporting traffic congestion near major roadways. . . .

If, however, we are to resolve the issue by considering whether the appropriate party carried its burden of proof, I again think that Riley must prevail. Because the State has greater access to information concerning customary flight patterns and because the coercive power of the State ought not be brought to bear in cases in which it is unclear whether the prosecution is a product of an unconstitutional, warrantless search, cf. Bumper v. North Carolina, 391 U.S. 543, 548 (1968) (prosecutor has burden of proving consent to search), the burden of proof properly rests with the State and not with the individual defendant. The State quite clearly has not carried this burden.[7]

V

The issue in this case is, ultimately, "how tightly the Fourth Amendment permits people to be driven back into the recesses of their lives by the risk of surveillance," Amsterdam, supra, at 402. . . . The Fourth Amendment demands that we temper our efforts to apprehend criminals with a concern for the impact on our fundamental liberties of the methods we use. I hope it will be a matter of concern to my colleagues that the police surveillance methods they would sanction were among those described forty years ago in George Orwell's dread vision of life in the 1980's:

> The black-mustachio'd face gazed down from every commanding corner. There was one on the house front immediately opposite. BIG BROTHER IS WATCHING YOU, the caption said. . . . In the far distance a helicopter skimmed down between the roofs, hovered for an instant like a bluebottle, and darted away again with a curving flight. It was the Police Patrol, snooping into people's windows. [G. Orwell, Nineteen Eighty-Four 4 (1949).]

Who can read this passage without a shudder, and without the instinctive reaction that it depicts life in some country other than ours? I respectfully dissent.

---

7. The issue in Jones v. United States, 362 U.S. 257, 261 (1960), cited by Justice O'Connor, was whether the defendant had standing to raise a Fourth Amendment challenge. While I would agree that the burden of alleging and proving facts necessary to show standing could ordinarily be placed on the defendant, I fail to see how that determination has any relevance to the question of where the burden should lie on the merits of the Fourth Amendment claim.

JUSTICE BLACKMUN, dissenting.

[I agree with Justices Brennan, Marshall, Stevens and O'Connor that the question whether the aerial surveillance was a "search"] . . . depends upon whether Riley has a "reasonable expectation of privacy" that no such surveillance would occur, and does not depend upon the fact that the helicopter was flying at a lawful altitude under FAA regulations. . . .

[I also agree with Justices Brennan, Marshall, Stevens and O'Connor] . . . that the reasonableness of Riley's expectation depends, in large measure, on the frequency of nonpolice helicopter flights at an altitude of 400 feet. . . .

How is this factual issue to be decided? Justice Brennan suggests that we may resolve it ourselves without any evidence in the record on this point. I am wary of this approach. While I, too, suspect that for most American communities it is a rare event when nonpolice helicopters fly over one's curtilage at an altitude of 400 feet, I am not convinced that we should establish a per se rule for the entire Nation based on judicial suspicion alone. . . .

But we need not abandon our judicial intuition entirely. The opinions of both Justice Brennan and Justice O'Connor, by their use of "cf." citations, implicitly recognize that none of our prior decisions tells us who has the burden of proving whether Riley's expectation of privacy was reasonable. In the absence of precedent on the point, it is appropriate for us to take into account our estimation of the frequency of nonpolice helicopter flights. . . . [B]ecause I believe that private helicopters rarely fly over curtilages at an altitude of 400 feet, I would impose upon the prosecution the burden of proving contrary facts necessary to show that Riley lacked a reasonable expectation of privacy. Indeed, I would establish this burden of proof for any helicopter surveillance case in which the flight occurred below 1000 feet—in other words, for any aerial surveillance case not governed by the Court's decision in California v. Ciraolo, 476 U.S. 207 (1986).

In this case, the prosecution did not meet this burden of proof, as Justice Brennan notes. This failure should compel a finding that a Fourth Amendment search occurred. But because our prior cases gave the parties little guidance on the burden of proof issue, I would remand this case to allow the prosecution an opportunity to meet this burden. . . .

NOTES AND QUESTIONS

1. Dow Chemical Co. v. United States, 476 U.S. 227 (1986), a companion case to California v. Ciraolo, discussed in *Riley*, involved the following facts:

> Dow Chemical Co. operates a 2,000 acre facility manufacturing chemicals at Midland, Michigan. The facility consists of numerous covered buildings, with manufacturing equipment and piping conduits located between the various buildings exposed to visual observation from the air. At all times, Dow has maintained elaborate security around the perimeter of the complex barring ground-level public views of these areas. It also investigates any low-level flights by aircraft over the facility. Dow has not undertaken, however, to conceal all manufacturing equipment within the complex from aerial views. Dow maintains that the cost of covering its exposed equipment would be prohibitive.
>
> In early 1978, enforcement officials of EPA [the Environmental Protection Agency], with Dow's consent, made an on-site inspection of two power plants in this complex. A subsequent EPA request for a second inspection, however, was denied, and EPA did not thereafter seek an administrative search warrant. Instead, EPA employed a commercial aerial photographer, using a standard floor-mounted, precision aerial mapping camera, to take photographs of the facility from altitudes of 12,000, 3,000, and 1,200 feet. At all times the aircraft was lawfully within navigable airspace. . . .
>
> The photographs . . . are essentially like those commonly used in map-making. Any person with an airplane and an aerial camera could readily duplicate them. [476 U.S. at 229, 231.]

As in *Ciraolo* and *Riley*, the Court concluded that the aerial surveillance did not constitute a search or seizure. In reaching this conclusion the Court observed that the area subjected to surveillance was more like an open field than the curtilage of a home and that using devices that somewhat enhance human vision do not necessarily raise constitutional problems.

2. For an excellent critique of *Oliver, Ciraolo,* and *Dow Chemical Co.*, see LaFave, The Forgotten Motto of Obsta Principiis in Fourth Amendment Jurisprudence, 28 Ariz. L. Rev. 291 (1986). See also Cunningham, A Linguistic Analysis of the Meaning of Search in the Fourth Amendment: A Search for Common Sense, 73 Iowa L. Rev. 541 (1988); DiPippa, Searching for the Fourth Amendment, 7 U. Ark. L.J. 587 (1984); Maclin, Construing Fourth Amendment Principles from the Government Perspective: Whose Fourth Amendment Is It Anyway?, 25 Am. Crim. L. Rev. 669 (1988); Saltzburg, Another Victim of Illegal Narcotics:

The Fourth Amendment (as Illustrated by the Open Fields Doctrine), 48 U. Pitt. L. Rev. 1 (1986).

4. The Reach of the Fourth Amendment in Other Contexts

The Supreme Court has elaborated on the meaning of Katz v. United States and the question what constitutes a search or seizure in a variety of contexts. Consider the following:

1. Air Pollution Variance Board v. Western Alfalfa Corp., 416 U.S. 861 (1974) (daylight visual observation of smoke plumes from "open fields" of respondent's property not a search and seizure);[10]
2. United States v. Miller, 425 U.S. 435 (1976) (bank depositor has no legitimate privacy interest in microfilm copies of deposit slips and checks, which copies bank was required by federal statute to maintain);[11]
3. Rakas v. Illinois, 439 U.S. 128 (1978)[12] (automobile passenger has no legitimate privacy interest in unlocked glove compartment or area under front seat);
4. Smith v. Maryland, 442 U.S. 735 (1979) (individual has no legitimate expectation of privacy with respect to numbers dialed on one's telephone; telephone company's installation at its offices pursuant to police request of pen register, a mechanical device that records numbers dialed on a telephone, not a search or seizure);
5. United States v. Knotts, 460 U.S. 276 (1983) (tracing movement of defendant's automobile by monitoring signals from electronic beeper located in automobile revealed nothing that could not have been observed with the naked eye; monitoring did not

10. See also Cardwell v. Lewis, 417 U.S. 583, 591 (1974) (plurality opinion of Blackmun, J., announcing judgment for Court; "with the 'search' limited to the examination of the tire on the wheel and the taking of paint scrapings from the exterior of the vehicle left in the public parking lot, we fail to comprehend what expectation of privacy was infringed").

11. Following Miller, Congress enacted The Right to Financial Privacy Act, 12 U.S.C. §§3401-3422 (1988). Pursuant to that act, customers whose financial records are subpoenaed must be given notice of the subpoena and an opportunity to challenge it, unless the government can establish that giving the notice would jeopardize its investigation.

12. The opinions in Rakas are set forth at page 853 infra.

invade legitimate privacy expectation of defendant and thus was
neither search nor seizure);

6. United States v. Place, 462 U.S. 696 (1983)[13] ("exposure of
   respondent's luggage, which was located in a public place, to
   trained canine . . . did not constitute a search");
7. Illinois v. Andreas, 463 U.S. 765 (1983) (common carrier legally
   inspected package, discovered that package contained narcotics,
   and notified police; police arranged for delivery of package to
   defendant; defendant was arrested shortly after delivery, and
   police reopened package without warrant; held, in absence of
   "substantial likelihood that contents have been changed," reopening package is not a search because defendant has "no
   legitimate expectation of privacy in the contents of a container
   previously opened under lawful authority");
8. United States v. Jacobsen, 466 U.S. 109 (1984)[14] (legally seized
   white powdery substance subjected to a warrantless field test that
   could determine whether the substance was cocaine but could
   not otherwise identify the substance; held, test was not a search
   because it invaded no legitimate privacy interest; destruction of
   small portion of substance during field test was a reasonable
   seizure);[15]
9. United States v. Karo, 468 U.S. 705 (1984) (warrantless "monitoring of beeper in a private residence, a location not open to
   surveillance, violates the Fourth Amendment rights of those
   who have a justifiable interest in the privacy of the residence";
   prior warrantless installation, with owners' consent, of beeper
   in container and tracing transfer of container to defendant's
   residence is not a search or seizure);
10. Hudson v. Palmer, 468 U.S. 517 (1984) (prisoner has no le-
    gitimate privacy expectation in prison cell; fourth amendment
    not applicable within confines of prison cell);
11. Maryland v. Macon, 472 U.S. 463 (1985) (plainclothes detec-
    tive purchased magazines in adult bookstore with marked $50
    bill; after examining magazines and concluding they were ob-
    scene, officer returned to bookstore, arrested salesclerk, and

13. Other aspects of *Place* are considered at page 796 infra.
14. Other aspects of *Jacobsen* are considered at page 841 infra.
15. In *Jacobsen*, the Court observed that the fourth amendment "protects two types
of expectations, one involving 'searches,' the other 'seizures.' A 'search' occurs when an
expectation of privacy that society is prepared to consider reasonable is infringed. A
'seizure' of property occurs when there is some meaningful interference with an individual's possessory interests in that property." 466 U.S. at 113. See Davison, Warrantless
Investigative Seizures of Real and Tangible Personal Property by Law Enforcement Officials, 25 Am. Crim. L. Rev. 577 (1988).

retrieved marked $50 bill; held, purchase of magazines not a seizure even though officer had intent from outset to retrieve $50 bill);

12. New York v. Class, 475 U.S. 106 (1986)[16] (automobile owner has no legitimate privacy interest in vehicle identification number);

13. O'Connor v. Ortega, 480 U.S. 709 (1987)[17] (public employee's legitimate privacy expectation in workplace depends on openness and access of workplace to others).

14. California v. Greenwood, 486 U.S. 35 (1988) (fourth amendment does not prohibit warrantless seizure and search of garbage placed in opaque containers and left for collection on curb in front of home).

For the most part the preceding cases consider whether a particular police activity is a "search" or a "search and seizure." Occasionally the Supreme Court has grappled with the question what is a "seizure." For example, in Tennessee v. Garner, 471 U.S. 1 (1985), the Court held that a police officer's fatal shooting of a fleeing suspect constituted a fourth amendment seizure,[18] and in Brower v. County of Inyo, 489 U.S. 593 (1989), the Court dealt with the question whether police officers had "seized" Brower when the stolen car he was driving crashed into a police roadblock that was set up to stop him.

Brower was a federal civil rights action. Brower was killed in the accident, and his heirs brought a suit claiming that the use of the roadblock constituted a violation of Brower's fourth amendment rights. According to the complaint in *Brower*:

> [R]espondents (1) caused an 18-wheel tractor-trailer to be placed across both lanes of a two-lane highway in the path of Brower's flight, (2) "effectively concealed" this roadblock by placing it behind a curve and leaving it unilluminated, and (3) positioned a police car, with its headlights on, between Brower's oncoming vehicle and the truck, so that Brower would be "blinded" on his approach. [489 U.S. at 594.]

The Ninth Circuit affirmed the district court's dismissal of the plaintiffs' fourth amendment claim on the ground that there had been no "seizure." The Supreme Court reversed. After observing that "[n]o unconstitutional seizure occurs" when a suspect being chased by the police

---

16. Other aspects of *Class* are considered at page 785 infra.
17. Other aspects of *O'Connor* are considered at page 801 infra.
18. See also page 541 n.15 supra (definition of seizure of property); pages 706-711 infra (discussion of what constitutes seizures commonly referred to as "stops").

suddenly loses control of his car and crashes, Justice Scalia's opinion for the Court stated:

> Violation of the Fourth Amendment requires an intentional acquisition of physical control. A seizure occurs even when an unintended person or thing is the object of the detention or taking, . . . but the detention or taking itself must be wilful. . . .
>
> Thus, if a parked and unoccupied police car slips its brake and pins a passenger against a wall, it is likely that a tort has occurred, but not a violation of the Fourth Amendment. And the situation would not change if the passerby happened, by lucky chance, to be a serial murderer for whom there was an outstanding arrest warrant—even if, at the time he was pinned, he was in the process of running away from two pursuing constables. It is clear, in other words, that a Fourth Amendment seizure . . . occur[s] . . . only when there is a governmental termination of freedom of movement *through means intentionally applied*. . . .
>
> [It is not] possible in determining whether there has been a seizure in a case such as this, to distinguish between a roadblock that is designed to give the oncoming driver the option of a voluntary stop (e.g., one at the end of a long straightaway), and a roadblock that is designed precisely to produce a collision (e.g., one located just around a bend). In determining whether the means that terminates the freedom of movement is the very means that the government intended we cannot draw too fine a line, or we will be driven to saying that one is not seized who has been stopped by the accidental discharge of a gun with which he was meant only to be bludgeoned, or by a bullet in the heart that was meant only for the leg. We think it enough for a seizure that a person be stopped by the very instrumentality set in motion or put in place in order to achieve that result. . . .
>
> This is not to say that the precise character of the roadblock is irrelevant. . . . [For §1983 liability,] the seizure must be "unreasonable." Petitioners can claim the right to recover for Brower's death only because the unreasonableness they allege consists precisely of setting up the roadblock in such manner as to be likely to kill him. This should be contrasted with the situation that would obtain if the sole claim of unreasonableness were that there was no probable cause for the stop. In that case, if Brower had had the opportunity to stop voluntarily at the roadblock, but had negligently or intentionally driven into it, then, because of lack of proximate causality, respondents, though responsible for depriving him of his freedom of movement, would not be liable for his death. . . . Thus the circumstances of this road-block, including the allegation that the headlights were used to blind the oncoming driver, may yet determine the outcome of this case. [489 U.S. 596-599 (emphasis original).]

In a concurring opinion joined by Justices Brennan, Marshall, and Blackmun, Justice Stevens observed: "[T]here is no dispute that the roadblock was intended to stop the decedent. Decision in the case before us is thus not advanced by pursuing a hypothetical inquiry concerning whether an unintentional act might also violate the Fourth Amendment." Id. at 601.

B. THE EXCLUSIONARY RULE: A PRELIMINARY INQUIRY

There is an integral relationship between any right and the remedy for its violation. Without an effective remedy, a right may be little more than an empty platitude; and sometimes the potential effectiveness or cost of a particular remedy may influence the manner in which the right is defined. This relationship between right and remedy has been particularly significant in fourth amendment litigation, where the principal remedy for fourth amendment violations has been the exclusion of unconstitutionally obtained evidence. The exclusionary rule has been justified in part on the ground that it is essential to prevent the fourth amendment from becoming " 'a form of words,' valueless and undeserving of mention in a perpetual charter of inestimable human liberties."[19] At the same time, concerns about the effectiveness and the cost of the exclusionary rule have had an impact on the manner in which the Supreme Court has defined the scope of the fourth amendment.[20]

A full appreciation of the costs and benefits of the exclusionary rule requires some understanding of the nature and scope of rights protected by the fourth amendment. Thus, an extended consideration of the exclusionary rule and possible alternative remedies for fourth amendment violations is reserved until the end of this chapter. However, because the exclusionary rule, like any other remedy, inevitably affects the nature of the right which it is designed to protect, it seems appropriate at this early stage in our consideration of the fourth amendment to examine briefly the development of and rationales for the exclusionary rule.

The Supreme Court's initial articulation of the exclusionary remedy came in Weeks v. United States, 232 U.S. 383 (1914). The defendant was charged, inter alia, with using the mails to promote illegal gambling, and the evidence against him included various letters and documents that had been seized from his house during a warrantless search. Prior

19. Mapp v. Ohio, 367 U.S. 643, 655 (1961).
20. See, e.g., Terry v. Ohio, page 684 infra (stop and frisk on less than probable cause upheld in part on ground that exclusionary rule would not be effective deterrent in any event). See also Rakas v. Illinois, page 853 infra.

to trial the defendant moved for a return of the property on the ground that it had been illegally seized. The district court granted defendant's motion, but only with respect to "such property as was not pertinent to the charge against the defendant. . . ." Id. at 388. Thus, the prosecution retained and, over the defendant's objection, introduced into evidence against him some of the papers seized from his home. Weeks was convicted, and the Supreme Court reversed:

> The effect of the Fourth Amendment is to put the courts of the United States and Federal officials, in the exercise of their power and authority, under limitations and restraints as to the exercise of such power and authority, and to forever secure the people, their persons, houses, papers and effects against all unreasonable searches and seizures under the guise of law. This protection reaches all alike, whether accused of crime or not, and the duty of giving to it force and effect is obligatory upon all entrusted under our Federal system with the enforcement of the laws. The tendency of those who execute the criminal laws of the country to obtain conviction by means of unlawful seizures and enforced confessions, the latter often obtained after subjecting accused persons to unwarranted practices destructive of rights secured by the Federal Constitution, should find no sanction in the judgments of the courts which are charged at all times with the support of the Constitution and to which people of all conditions have a right to appeal for the maintenance of such fundamental rights. . . .
>
> . . . If letters and private documents can thus be seized and held and used in evidence against a citizen accused of an offense, the protection of the Fourth Amendment declaring his right to be secure against such searches and seizures is of no value, and, so far as those thus placed are concerned, might as well be stricken from the Constitution. The efforts of the courts and their officials to bring the guilty to punishment, praiseworthy as they are, are not to be aided by the sacrifice of those great principles established by years of endeavor and suffering which have resulted in their embodiment in the fundamental law of the land. The United States Marshal could only have invaded the house of the accused when armed with a warrant issued as required by the Constitution, upon sworn information and describing with reasonable particularity the thing for which the search was to be made. Instead, he acted without sanction of law, doubtless prompted by the desire to bring further proof to the aid of the Government, and under color of his office undertook to make a seizure of private papers in direct violation of the constitutional prohibition against such action. Under such circumstances, without sworn information and particular description, not even an order of court would have justified such procedure, much less was it within the authority of the United States Marshal to thus invade the house and privacy of the accused. In Adams v. New York, 192 U.S. 585, this court said that the Fourth Amendment was intended to secure the citizen in person and property against unlawful invasion of the sanctity of his home by officers of the law acting under legislative or judicial sanction. This protection is equally extended to the

action of the Government and officers of the law acting under it. . . .
To sanction such proceedings would be to affirm by judicial decision a
manifest neglect if not an open defiance of the prohibitions of the Constitution, intended for the protection of the people against such unauthorized action. . . .

We therefore reach the conclusion that the letters in question were
taken from the house of the accused by an official of the United States
acting under color of his office in direct violation of the constitutional
rights of the defendant; that having made a seasonable application for their
return, which was heard and passed upon by the court, there was involved
in the order refusing the application a denial of the constitutional rights
of the accused, and that the court should have restored these letters to the
accused. In holding them and permitting their use upon the trial, we think
prejudicial error was committed. As to the papers and property seized by
the policemen, it does not appear that they acted under any claim of
Federal authority such as would make the Amendment applicable to such
unauthorized seizures. The record shows that what they did by way of
arrest and search and seizure was done before the finding of the indictment
in the Federal court, under what supposed right or authority does not
appear. What remedies the defendant may have against them we need not
inquire, as the Fourth Amendment is not directed to individual misconduct
of such officials. Its limitations reach the Federal Government and its
agencies. . . . [232 U.S. at 391-392, 393-394, 398.]

Because *Weeks* was a *federal* prosecution interpreting the fourth
amendment, its holding was not binding on the states. The question
whether the due process clause of the fourteenth amendment required
states to exclude evidence derived from an unconstitutional search or
seizure did not reach the Supreme Court until 1949.

WOLF v. COLORADO
Certiorari to the Supreme Court of Colorado
338 U.S. 25 (1949)

MR. JUSTICE FRANKFURTER delivered the opinion of the Court.

The precise question for consideration is this: Does a conviction by
a State court for a State offense deny the "due process of law" required
by the Fourteenth Amendment, solely because evidence that was admitted
at the trial was obtained under circumstances which would have rendered
it inadmissible in a prosecution for violation of a federal law in a court
of the United States because there deemed to be an infraction of the
Fourth Amendment as applied in Weeks v. United States, 232 U.S. 383?
The Supreme Court of Colorado has sustained convictions in which such

evidence was admitted, 117 Col. 279, 187 P.2d 926; 117 Col. 321, 187 P.2d 928, and we brought the cases here. . . .

For purposes of ascertaining the restrictions which the Due Process Clause imposed upon the States in the enforcement of their criminal law, we adhere to the views expressed in Palko v. Connecticut, . . . 302 U.S. 319. . . . In rejecting the suggestion that the Due Process Clause incorporated the original Bill of Rights, Mr. Justice Cardozo reaffirmed on behalf of that Court a different but deeper and more pervasive conception of the Due Process Clause. This Clause exacts from the States for the lowliest and the most outcast all that is "implicit in the concept of ordered liberty." 302 U.S. at 325.

Due process of law thus conveys neither formal nor fixed nor narrow requirements. It is the compendious expression for all those rights which the courts must enforce because they are basic to our free society. But basic rights do not become petrified as of any one time. . . . Representing as it does a living principle, due process is not confined within a permanent catalogue of what may at a given time be deemed the limits or the essentials of fundamental rights.

. . . The real clue to the problem confronting the judiciary in the application of the Due Process Clause is not to ask where the line is once and for all to be drawn but to recognize that it is for the Court to draw it by the gradual and empiric process of "inclusion and exclusion." Davidson v. New Orleans, 96 U.S. 97, 104. This was the Court's insight when first called upon to consider the problem; to this insight the Court has on the whole been faithful as case after case has come before it since Davidson v. New Orleans was decided.

The security of one's privacy against arbitrary intrusion by the police—which is at the core of the Fourth Amendment—is basic to a free society. It is therefore implicit in "the concept of ordered liberty" and as such enforceable against the States through the Due Process Clause. The knock at the door, whether by day or by night, as a prelude to a search, without authority of law but solely on the authority of the police, did not need the commentary of recent history to be condemned as inconsistent with the conception of human rights enshrined in the history and the basic constitutional documents of English-speaking peoples.

Accordingly, we have no hesitation in saying that were a State affirmatively to sanction such police incursion into privacy it would run counter to the guaranty of the Fourteenth Amendment. But the ways of enforcing such a basic right raise questions of a different order. How such arbitrary conduct should be checked, what remedies against it should be afforded, the means by which the right should be made effective, are all questions that are not to be so dogmatically answered as to preclude the varying solutions which spring from an allowable range of judgment on issues not susceptible of quantitative solution.

In Weeks v. United States, supra, this Court held that in a federal prosecution the Fourth Amendment barred the use of evidence secured through an illegal search and seizure. This ruling was made for the first time in 1914. It was not derived from the explicit requirements of the Fourth Amendment; it was not based on legislation expressing Congressional policy in the enforcement of the Constitution. The decision was a matter of judicial implication. Since then it has been frequently applied and we stoutly adhere to it. But the immediate question is whether the basic right to protection against arbitrary intrusion by the police demands the exclusion of logically relevant evidence obtained by an unreasonable search and seizure because, in a federal prosecution for a federal crime, it would be excluded. As a matter of inherent reason, one would suppose this to be an issue as to which men with complete devotion to the protection of the right of privacy might give different answers. When we find that in fact most of the English-speaking world does not regard as vital to such protection the exclusion of evidence thus obtained, we must hesitate to treat this remedy as an essential ingredient of the right. The contrariety of views of the States is particularly impressive in view of the careful reconsideration which they have given the problem in the light of the Weeks decision. . . .

> Before the Weeks decision 27 States had passed on the admissibility of evidence obtained by unlawful search and seizure. . . .
> Of these, 26 States opposed the Weeks doctrine. . . .
> Of these, 1 State anticipated the Weeks doctrine. . . .
> Since the Weeks decision 47 States all told have passed on the Weeks doctrine. . . .
> As of today 31 States reject the Weeks doctrine, 16 States are in agreement with it. . . .
> Of 10 jurisdictions within the United Kingdom and the British Commonwealth of Nations which have passed on the question, none has held evidence obtained by illegal search and seizure inadmissible. . . .

The jurisdictions which have rejected the Weeks doctrine have not left the right to privacy without other means of protection.[1] Indeed, the

---

1. The common law provides actions for damages against the searching officer, . . . against one who procures the issuance of a warrant maliciously and without probable cause, . . . against a magistrate who has acted without jurisdiction in issuing a warrant. . . . One may also without liability use force to resist an unlawful search. . . .

Statutory sanctions in the main provide for the punishment of one maliciously procuring a search warrant or willfully exceeding his authority in exercising it. . . . Some statutes more broadly penalize unlawful searches. E.g., 18 U.S.C. (1946 ed.) §53a;

exclusion of evidence is a remedy which directly serves only to protect those upon whose person or premises something incriminating has been found. We cannot, therefore, regard it as a departure from basic standards to remand such persons, together with those who emerge scatheless from a search, to the remedies of private action and such protection as the internal discipline of the police, under the eyes of an alert public opinion, may afford. Granting that in practice the exclusion of evidence may be an effective way of deterring unreasonable searches, it is not for this Court to condemn as falling below the minimal standards assured by the Due Process Clause a State's reliance upon other methods which, if consistently enforced, would be equally effective. Weighty testimony against such an insistence on our own view is furnished by the opinion of Mr. Justice (then Judge) Cardozo in People v. Defore, 242 N.Y. 13, 150 N.E. 585. We cannot brush aside the experience of States which deem the incidence of such conduct by the police too slight to call for a deterrent remedy not by way of disciplinary measures but by overriding the relevant rules of evidence. There are, moreover, reasons for excluding evidence unreasonably obtained by the federal police which are less compelling in the case of police under State or local authority. The public opinion of a community can far more effectively be exerted against oppressive conduct on the part of police directly responsible to the community itself than can local opinion, sporadically aroused, be brought to bear upon remote authority pervasively exerted throughout the country.

We hold, therefore, that in a prosecution in a State court for a State crime the Fourteenth Amendment does not forbid the admission of evidence obtained by an unreasonable search and seizure. And though we have interpreted the Fourth Amendment to forbid the admission of such evidence, a different question would be presented if Congress under its legislative powers were to pass a statute purporting to negate the *Weeks* doctrine. We would then be faced with the problem of the respect to be accorded the legislative judgment on an issue as to which, in default of that judgment, we have been forced to depend upon our own. Problems of a converse character, also not before us, would be presented should Congress under §5 of the Fourteenth Amendment undertake to enforce the rights there guaranteed by attempting to make the Weeks doctrine binding upon the States.

Idaho Code Ann. §§17-1004, 17-1024 (1932); Minn. Stat. §§613.54, 621.17 (1945); Va. Code Ann. §4822d (Michie, 1942); Wash. Rev. Stat. Ann. §§2240-1, 2240-2. Virginia also makes punishable one who issues a general search warrant or a warrant unsupported by affidavit. Va. Code Ann. §4822e (Michie, 1942). A few States have provided statutory civil remedies. See, e.g., Ga. Code Ann. §27-301 (1935); Ill. Rev. Stat., c. 38, §698 (Smith-Hurd, 1935); Miss. Code Ann. §1592 (1942). And in one State, misuse of a search warrant may be an abuse of process punishable as contempt of court. See Mich. Stat. Ann. §27.511 (1938).

Affirmed. . . .

[The concurring opinion of JUSTICE BLACK and the dissenting opinion of JUSTICE DOUGLAS are omitted.]

MR. JUSTICE MURPHY, with whom MR. JUSTICE RUTLEDGE joins, dissenting. . . .

Imagination and zeal may invent a dozen methods to give content to the commands of the Fourth Amendment. But this Court is limited to the remedies currently available. It cannot legislate the ideal system. If we would attempt the enforcement of the search and seizure clause in the ordinary case today, we are limited to three devices: judicial exclusion of the illegally obtained evidence; criminal prosecution of violators; and civil action against violators in the action of trespass.

Alternatives are deceptive. Their very statement conveys the impression that one possibility is as effective as the next. In this case their statement is blinding. For there is but one alternative to the rule of exclusion. That is no sanction at all. . . .

. . . Little need be said concerning the possibilities of criminal prosecution. Self-scrutiny is a lofty ideal, but its exaltation reaches new heights if we expect a District Attorney to prosecute himself or his associates for well-meaning violations of the search and seizure clause during a raid the District Attorney or his associates have ordered. But there is an appealing ring in another alternative. A trespass action for damages is a venerable means of securing reparation for unauthorized invasion of the home. Why not put the old writ to a new use? When the Court cites cases permitting the action, the remedy seems complete.

But what an illusory remedy this is, if by "remedy" we mean a positive deterrent to police and prosecutors tempted to violate the Fourth Amendment. The appealing ring softens when we recall that in a trespass action the measure of damages is simply the extent of the injury to physical property. If the officer searches with care, he can avoid all but nominal damages—a penny, or a dollar. Are punitive damages possible? Perhaps. But a few states permit none, whatever the circumstances. In those that do, the plaintiff must show the real ill will or malice of the defendant, and surely it is not unreasonable to assume that one in honest pursuit of crime bears no malice toward the search victim. If that burden is carried, recovery may yet be defeated by the rule that there must be physical damages before punitive damages may be awarded. In addition, some states limit punitive damages to the actual expenses of litigation. . . . Others demand some arbitrary ratio between actual and punitive damages before a verdict may stand. . . . Even assuming the ill will of the officer, his reasonable grounds for belief that the home he searched harbored evidence of crime is admissible in mitigation of punitive damages. . . .

The bad reputation of the plaintiff is likewise admissible. . . . If the evidence seized was actually used at a trial, that fact has been held a complete justification of the search, and a defense against the trespass action. . . . And even if the plaintiff hurdles all these obstacles, and gains a substantial verdict, the individual officer's finances may well make the judgment useless—for the municipality, of course, is not liable without its consent. . . .

If proof of the efficacy of the federal rule were needed, there is testimony in abundance in the recruit training programs and in-service courses provided the police in states which follow the federal rule.[5] St. Louis, for example, demands extensive training in the rules of search and seizure, with emphasis upon the ease with which a case may collapse if it depends upon evidence obtained unlawfully. Current court decisions are digested and read at roll calls. The same general pattern prevails in Washington, D.C.[6] In Dallas, officers are thoroughly briefed and instructed that "the courts will follow the rules very closely and will detect any frauds."[7] In Milwaukee, a stout volume on the law of arrest and search and seizure is made the basis of extended instruction.[8] Officer preparation in the applicable rules in Jackson, Mississippi, has included the lectures of an Associate Justice of the Mississippi Supreme Court. The instructions on evidence and search and seizure given to trainees in San Antonio carefully note the rule of exclusion in Texas, and close with this statement:

> Every police officer should know the laws and the rules of evidence. Upon knowledge of these facts determines whether the . . . defendant will be convicted or acquitted. . . . When you investigate a case . . . remember throughout your investigation that only admissible evidence can be used.

5. The material which follows is gleaned from letters and other material from Commissioners of Police and Chiefs of Police in twenty-six cities. Thirty-eight large cities in the United States were selected at random, and inquiries directed concerning the instructions provided police on the rules of search and seizure. Twenty-six replies have been received to date. Those of any significance are mentioned in the text of this opinion. The sample is believed to be representative, but it cannot, of course, substitute for a thoroughgoing comparison of present-day police procedures by a completely objective observer. A study of this kind would be of inestimable value.

6. E.g., Assistant Superintendent Truscott's letter to the Washington Police Force of January 3, 1949, concerning McDonald v. United States, 335 U.S. 451.

7. Recently lectures have included two pages of discussion of the opinions in Harris v. United States, 331 U.S. 145.

8. Chief of Police John W. Polcyn notes, in a Foreword to the book, that officers were often not properly informed with respect to searches and seizures before thoroughgoing instruction was undertaken. One of their fears was that of "losing their cases in court, only because they neglected to do what they might have done with full legal sanction at the time of the arrest, or did what they had no legal right to do at such time."

But in New York City, we are informed simply that "copies of the State Penal Law and Code of Criminal Procedure" are given to officers, and that they are "kept advised" that illegally obtained evidence may be admitted in New York courts. In Baltimore, a "Digest of Laws" is distributed, and it is made clear that the statutory section excluding evidence "is limited in its application to the trial of misdemeanors. . . . It would appear . . . that . . . evidence illegally obtained may still be admissible in the trial of felonies." In Cleveland, recruits and other officers are told of the rules of search and seizure, but "instructed that it is admissible in the courts of Ohio. The Ohio Supreme Court has indicated very definitely and clearly that Ohio belongs to the 'admissionist' group of states when evidence obtained by an illegal search is presented to the court." A similar pattern emerges in Birmingham, Alabama. . . .

MR. JUSTICE RUTLEDGE, dissenting. . . .
I . . . reject any intimation that Congress could validly enact legislation permitting the introduction in federal courts of evidence seized in violation of the Fourth Amendment. I had thought that issue settled by this Court's invalidation on dual grounds, in Boyd v. United States, 116 U.S. 616, of a federal statute which in effect required the production of evidence thought probative by Government counsel—the Court there holding the statute to be "obnoxious to the prohibition of the Fourth Amendment of the Constitution, as well as of the Fifth." Id. at 632. See Adams v. New York, 192 U.S. 585, 597, 598. The view that the Fourth Amendment itself forbids the introduction of evidence illegally obtained in federal prosecutions is one of long standing and firmly established. See Olmstead v. United States, 277 U.S. 438, 462. It is too late in my judgment to question it now. . . .

NOTES AND QUESTIONS

1. Justice Frankfurter, in explaining the manner in which the Court is to determine the content of due process, asserts: "[T]he real clue to the problem . . . is not to ask where the line is once and for all to be drawn but to recognize that it is for the Court to draw it by the gradual and empiric process of 'inclusion and exclusion.' " Is it possible to engage meaningfully in this task by asking and attempting to resolve abstract questions, or must one have a sense of the factual contexts in which due process claims arise? What was it in Wolf that gave rise to the defendant's claim?[21]

21. We have not edited facts from any of the Justices' opinions. If you want the

2. What significance is there to Justice Frankfurter's statement that the *Weeks* holding was "a matter of judicial implication"? Is that not true of any judicial decision?

What is the significance of the "numbers game"? To the extent that state court decisions dealing with the exclusionary rule are relevant, which is more important—the fact that 31 out of 47 states had rejected the exclusionary rule, or the fact that following *Weeks* the ratio of states adopting the exclusionary rule changed from 1:27 to 16:47?

3. What, according to *Wolf*, is the primary purpose of the exclusionary rule? To what extent is *Wolf's* articulation of the purpose(s) of the exclusionary rule similar to or different from the articulation in *Weeks*?

MAPP v. OHIO
Appeal from the Supreme Court of Ohio
367 U.S. 643 (1961)

MR. JUSTICE CLARK delivered the opinion of the Court.

Appellant stands convicted of knowingly having had in her possession and under her control certain lewd and lascivious books, pictures, and photographs in violation of §2905.34 of Ohio's Revised Code. As officially stated in the syllabus to its opinion, the Supreme Court of Ohio found that her conviction was valid though "based primarily upon the introduction in evidence of lewd and lascivious books and pictures unlawfully seized during an unlawful search of defendant's home. . . ." 170 Ohio St. 427-428, 166 N.E.2d 387, 388.

On May 23, 1957, three Cleveland police officers arrived at appellant's residence in that city pursuant to information that "a person [was] hiding out in the home, who was wanted for questioning in connection with a recent bombing, and that there was a large amount of policy paraphernalia being hidden in the home." Miss Mapp and her daughter by a former marriage lived on the top floor of the two-family dwelling. Upon their arrival at that house, the officers knocked on the door and demanded entrance but appellant, after telephoning her attorney, refused to admit them without a search warrant. They advised their headquarters of the situation and undertook a surveillance of the house.

The officers again sought entrance some three hours later when four or more additional officers arrived on the scene. When Miss Mapp did not come to the door immediately, at least one of the several doors to the house was forcibly opened and the policemen gained admittance.

---

answer, you will have to go to the Colorado Supreme Court decision or the United States Supreme Court Record.

Meanwhile Miss Mapp's attorney arrived, but the officers, having secured their own entry, and continuing in their defiance of the law, would permit him neither to see Miss Mapp nor to enter the house. It appears that Miss Mapp was halfway down the stairs from the upper floor to the front door when the officers, in this highhanded manner, broke into the hall. She demanded to see the search warrant. A paper, claimed to be a warrant, was held up by one of the officers. She grabbed the "warrant" and placed it in her bosom. A struggle ensued in which the officers recovered the piece of paper and as a result of which they handcuffed appellant because she had been "belligerent" in resisting their official rescue of the "warrant" from her person. Running roughshod over appellant, a policeman "grabbed" her, "twisted [her] hand," and she "yelled [and] pleaded with him" because "it was hurting." Appellant, in handcuffs, was then forcibly taken upstairs to her bedroom where the officers searched a dresser, a chest of drawers, a closet and some suitcases. They also looked into a photo album and through personal papers belonging to the appellant. The search spread to the rest of the second floor including the child's bedroom, the living room, the kitchen and a dinette. The basement of the building and a trunk found therein were also searched. The obscene materials for possession of which she was ultimately convicted were discovered in the course of that widespread search.

At the trial no search warrant was produced by the prosecution, nor was the failure to produce one explained or accounted for. . . .

The State [relies on] . . . Wolf v. Colorado, 338 U.S. 25 (1949). . . . On this appeal . . . it is urged once again that we review that holding. . . .

Seventy-five years ago, in Boyd v. United States, 116 U.S. 616, 630 (1886), considering the Fourth and Fifth Amendments as running "almost into each other" on the facts before it, this Court held that the doctrines of those Amendments "apply to all invasions on the part of the government and its employees of the sanctity of a man's home and the privacies of life. . . ."

. . . [In Weeks v. United States, 232 U.S. 383 (1914),] this Court "for the first time" held that "in a federal prosecution the Fourth Amendment barred the use of evidence secured through an illegal search and seizure." Wolf v. Colorado, supra, at 28. This Court has ever since required of federal law officers a strict adherence to that command which this Court has held to be a clear, specific, and constitutionally required—even if judicially implied—deterrent safeguard without insistence upon which the Fourth Amendment would have been reduced to "a form of words." Holmes, J., Silverthorne Lumber Co. v. United States, 251 U.S. 385, 392 (1920). It meant, quite simply, that "conviction by means of unlawful seizures and enforced confessions . . . should find no sanction in the judgments of the courts . . ." Weeks v. United States, supra, at 392, and that such evidence "shall not be used at all." Silverthorne Lumber Co. v. United States, supra, at 392.

There are in the cases of this Court some passing references to the *Weeks* rule as being one of evidence. But the plain and unequivocal language of *Weeks*—and its later paraphrase in *Wolf*—to the effect that the *Weeks* rule is of constitutional origin, remains entirely undisturbed. In Byars v. United States, 273 U.S. 28 (1927), a unanimous Court declared that "the doctrine [cannot] . . . be tolerated *under our constitutional system,* that evidences of crime discovered by a federal officer in making a search without lawful warrant may be used against the victim of the unlawful search where a timely challenge has been interposed." At pp. 29-30 (emphasis added). The Court, in Olmstead v. United States, 277 U.S. 438 (1928), in unmistakable language restated the *Weeks* rule:

> The striking outcome of the *Weeks* case and those which followed it was the sweeping declaration that the Fourth Amendment, although not referring to or limiting the use of evidence in courts, really forbade its introduction if obtained by government officers through a violation of the Amendment. [At p.462.]

In McNabb v. United States, 318 U.S. 332 (1943), we note this statement:

> [A] conviction in the federal courts, the foundation of which is evidence obtained in disregard of liberties deemed fundamental by the Constitution, cannot stand. Boyd v. United States . . . Weeks v. United States. . . . And this Court has, on Constitutional grounds, set aside convictions, both in the federal and state courts, which were based upon confessions "secured by protracted and repeated questioning of ignorant and untutored persons, in whose minds the power of officers was greatly magnified" . . . or "who have been unlawfully held incommunicado without advice of friends or counsel." . . . [At pp. 339-340.]

Significantly, in *McNabb,* the Court did then pass on to formulate a rule of evidence, saying, "[i]n the view we take of the case, however, it becomes unnecessary to reach the Constitutional issue [for] . . . [t]he principles governing the admissibility of evidence in federal criminal trials have not been restricted . . . to those derived solely from the Constitution." At pp. 340-341. . . .

In 1949, 35 years after *Weeks* was announced, this Court, in Wolf v. Colorado, supra, again for the first time, discussed the effect of the Fourth Amendment upon the States through the operation of the Due Process Clause of the Fourteenth Amendment. . . . [A]fter declaring that the "security of one's privacy against arbitrary intrusion by the police" is "implicit in 'the concept of ordered liberty' and as such enforceable against the States through the Due Process Clause," . . . and announcing that it "stoutly adhere[d]" to the Weeks decision, the Court decided that the Weeks exclusionary rule would not then be imposed upon the States as "an essential ingredient of the right." 338 U.S., at 27-29. The Court's reasons for not considering essential to the right to privacy, as a curb imposed upon the States by the Due Process Clause, that which decades before had been posited as part and parcel of the Fourth Amendment's limitation upon federal encroachment of individual privacy, were bottomed on factual considerations.

While they are not basically relevant to a decision that the exclusionary rule is an essential ingredient of the Fourth Amendment as the right it embodies is vouchsafed against the States by the Due Process Clause, we will consider the current validity of the factual grounds upon which Wolf was based.

The Court in Wolf first stated that "[t]he contrariety of views of the States" on the adoption of the exclusionary rule of Weeks was "particularly impressive" (at p.29); and, in this connection, that it could not "brush aside the experience of States which deem the incidence of such conduct by the police too slight to call for a deterrent remedy . . . by overriding the [States'] relevant rules of evidence." At pp. 31-32. While in 1949, prior to the Wolf case, almost two-thirds of the States were opposed to the use of the exclusionary rule, now, despite the Wolf case, more than half of those since passing upon it, by their own legislative or judicial decision, have wholly or partly adopted or adhered to the Weeks rule. . . . Significantly, among those now following the rule is California, which, according to its highest court, was "compelled to reach that conclusion because other remedies have completely failed to secure compliance with the constitutional provisions. . . ." People v. Cahan, 44 Cal. 2d 434, 445, 282 P.2d 905, 911 (1955). In connection with this California case, we note that the second basis elaborated in Wolf in support of its failure to enforce the exclusionary doctrine against the States was that "other means of protection" have been afforded "the right to privacy." 338 U.S., at 30. The experience of California that such other remedies have been worthless and futile is buttressed by the experience of other States. The obvious futility of relegating the Fourth Amendment to the protection of other remedies has, moreover, been recognized by this Court since Wolf. See Irvine v. California, 347 U.S. 128, 137 (1954).

Likewise, time has set its face against what Wolf called the "weighty testimony" of People v. Defore, 242 N.Y. 13, 150 N.E. 585 (1926). There Justice (then Judge) Cardozo, rejecting adoption of the Weeks exclusionary rule in New York, had said that "[t]he Federal rule as it stands is either too strict or too lax." 242 N.Y., at 22, 150 N.E., at 588.

However, the force of that reasoning has been largely vitiated by later decisions of this Court. These include the recent discarding of the "silver platter" doctrine which allowed federal judicial use of evidence seized in violation of the Constitution by state agents, Elkins v. United States, [364 U.S. 206 (1960)]; the relaxation of the formerly strict requirements as to standing to challenge the use of evidence thus seized, so that now the procedure of exclusion, "ultimately referable to constitutional safeguards," is available to anyone even "legitimately on [the] premises" unlawfully searched, Jones v. United States, 362 U.S. 257, 266-267 (1960); and, finally, the formulation of a method to prevent state use of evidence unconstitutionally seized by federal agents, Rea v. United States, 350 U.S. 214 (1956). . . .

It, therefore, plainly appears that the factual considerations supporting the failure of the Wolf Court to include the Weeks exclusionary rule when it recognized the enforceability of the right to privacy against the States in 1949, while not basically relevant to the constitutional consideration, could not, in any analysis, now be deemed controlling. . . .

Some five years after Wolf, in answer to a plea made here Term after Term that we overturn its doctrine on applicability of the Weeks exclusionary rule, this Court indicated that such should not be done until the States had "adequate opportunity to adopt or reject the [Weeks] rule." Irvine v. California, supra, at 134. . . . Today we once again examine Wolf's constitutional documentation of the right to privacy free from unreasonable state intrusion, and, after its dozen years on our books, are led by it to close the only courtroom door remaining open to evidence secured by official lawlessness in flagrant abuse of that basic right, reserved to all persons as a specific guarantee against that very same unlawful conduct. We hold that all evidence obtained by searches and seizures in violation of the Constitution is, by that same authority, inadmissible in a state court.

. . . Were it otherwise, then just as without the Weeks rule the assurance against unreasonable federal searches and seizures would be "a form of words," valueless and undeserving of mention in a perpetual charter of inestimable human liberties, so too, without that rule the freedom from state invasions of privacy would be so ephemeral and so neatly severed from its conceptual nexus with the freedom from all brutish means of coercing evidence as not to merit this Court's high regard as a freedom "implicit in the concept of ordered liberty." At the time that the Court held in Wolf that the Amendment was applicable to the States through the Due Process Clause, the cases of this Court, as we have seen, had steadfastly held that as to federal officers the Fourth Amendment included the exclusion of the evidence seized in violation of its provisions.

Even *Wolf* "stoutly adhered" to that proposition. The right to privacy, when conceded operatively enforceable against the States, was not susceptible of destruction by avulsion of the sanction upon which its protection and enjoyment had always been deemed dependent under the *Boyd, Weeks* and *Silverthorne* cases. Therefore, in extending the substantive protections of due process to all constitutionally unreasonable searches—state or federal—it was logically and constitutionally necessary that the exclusion doctrine—an essential part of the right to privacy—be also insisted upon as an essential ingredient of the right newly recognized by the *Wolf* case. In short, the admission of the new constitutional right by *Wolf* could not consistently tolerate denial of its most important constitutional privilege, namely, the exclusion of the evidence which an accused had been forced to give by reason of the unlawful seizure. To hold otherwise is to grant the right but in reality to withhold its privilege and enjoyment. Only last year the Court itself recognized that the purpose of the exclusionary rule "is to deter—to compel respect for the constitutional guaranty in the only effectively available way—by removing the incentive to disregard it." Elkins v. United States, supra, at 217.

. . . This Court has not hesitated to enforce as strictly against the States as it does against the Federal Government the rights of free speech and of a free press, the rights to notice and to a fair, public trial, including, as it does, the right not to be convicted by use of a coerced confession, however logically relevant it be, and without regard to its reliability. Rogers v. Richmond, 365 U.S. 534 (1961). And nothing could be more certain than that when a coerced confession is involved, "the relevant rules of evidence" are overridden without regard to "the incidence of such conduct by the police," slight or frequent. Why should not the same rule apply to what is tantamount to coerced testimony by way of unconstitutional seizure of goods, papers, effects, documents, etc.? We find that, as to the Federal Government, the Fourth and Fifth Amendments and, as to the States, the freedom from unconscionable invasions of privacy and the freedom from convictions based upon coerced confessions do enjoy an "intimate relation" in their perpetuation of "principles of humanity and civil liberty [secured] . . . only after years of struggle," Bram v. United States, 168 U.S. 532, 543-544 (1897). . . .

Moreover, our holding that the exclusionary rule is an essential part of both the Fourth and Fourteenth Amendments is not only the logical dictate of prior cases, but it also makes very good sense. There is no war between the Constitution and common sense. Presently, a federal prosecutor may make no use of evidence illegally seized, but a State's attorney across the street may, although he supposedly is operating under the enforceable prohibitions of the same Amendment. Thus the State, by admitting evidence unlawfully seized, serves to encourage disobedience to the Federal Constitution which it is bound to uphold. Moreover, as was said in *Elkins*, "[t]he very essence of a healthy federalism depends upon the avoidance of needless conflict between state and federal courts." 364 U.S., at 221. . . . . In nonexclusionary States, federal officers, being human, were by it invited to and did, as our cases indicate, step across the street to the State's attorney with their unconstitutionally seized evidence. Prosecution on the basis of that evidence was then had in a state court in utter disregard of the enforceable Fourth Amendment. If the fruits of an unconstitutional search had been inadmissible in both state and federal courts, this inducement to evasion would have been sooner eliminated. . . .

There are those who say, as did Justice (then Judge) Cardozo, that under our constitutional exclusionary doctrine "[t]he criminal is to go free because the constable has blundered." People v. Defore, 242 N.Y., at 21, 150 N.E., at 587. In some cases this will undoubtedly be the result. But, as was said in *Elkins*, "there is another consideration—the imperative of judicial integrity." 364 U.S., at 222. The criminal goes free, if he must, but it is the law that sets him free. Nothing can destroy a government more quickly than its failure to observe its own laws, or worse, its disregard of the charter of its own existence. As Mr. Justice Brandeis, dissenting, said in Olmstead v. United States, 277 U.S. 438, 485 (1928): "Our Government is the potent, the omnipresent teacher. For good or for ill, it teaches the whole people by its example. . . . If the Government becomes a lawbreaker, it breeds contempt for law; it invites every man to become a law unto himself; it invites anarchy." Nor can it lightly be assumed that, as a practical matter, adoption of the exclusionary rule fetters law enforcement. Only last year this Court expressly considered that contention and found that "pragmatic evidence of a sort" to the contrary was not wanting. Elkins v. United States, supra, at 218. The Court noted that

> The federal courts themselves have operated under the exclusionary rule of *Weeks* for almost half a century; yet it has not been suggested either that the Federal Bureau of Investigation has thereby been rendered ineffective, or that the administration of criminal justice in the federal courts has thereby been disrupted. Moreover, the experience of the states is impressive. . . . The movement towards the rule of exclusion has been halting but seemingly inexorable. [Id., at 218-219.]

The ignoble shortcut to conviction left open to the State tends to destroy the entire system of constitutional restraints on which the liberties of the people rest. Having once recognized that the right to privacy embodied in the Fourth Amendment is enforceable against the States, and that the right to be secure against rude invasions of privacy by state officers is, therefore, constitutional in origin, we can no longer permit that right to remain an empty promise. Because it is enforceable in the same manner and to like effect as other basic rights secured by the Due Process Clause, we can no longer permit it to be revocable at the whim of any police officer who, in the name of law enforcement itself, chooses to suspend its enjoyment. Our decision, founded on reason and truth, gives to the individual no more than that which the Constitution guarantees him, to the police officer no less than that to which honest law enforcement is entitled, and, to the courts, that judicial integrity so necessary in the true administration of justice. . . . .

MR. JUSTICE BLACK, concurring.
. . . I concurred in [Wolf v. Colorado]. . . .
I am still not persuaded that the Fourth Amendment, standing alone, would be enough to bar the introduction into evidence against an accused of papers and effects seized from him in violation of its commands. For the Fourth Amendment does not itself contain any provision expressly precluding the use of such evidence, and I am extremely doubtful that such a provision could properly be inferred from nothing more than the basic command against unreasonable searches and seizures. Reflection on the problem, however, in the light of cases coming before the Court since Wolf, has led me to conclude that when the Fourth Amendment's ban against unreasonable searches and seizures is considered together with the Fifth Amendment's ban against compelled self-incrimination, a constitutional basis emerges which not only justifies but actually requires the exclusionary rule.

The close interrelationship between the Fourth and Fifth Amendments, as they apply to this problem, has long been recognized and, indeed, was expressly made the ground for this Court's holding in Boyd v. United States. . . . It was upon this ground that Mr. Justice Rutledge largely relied in his dissenting opinion in the Wolf case. And, although I rejected the argument at that time, its force has, for me at least, become compelling with the more thorough understanding of the problem brought on by recent cases. . . .

MR. JUSTICE DOUGLAS, concurring. . . .
. . . I believe that this is an appropriate case in which to put an end to the asymmetry which Wolf imported into the law. . . . It is an appropriate case because the facts it presents show—as would few other cases—the casual arrogance of those who have the untrammelled power to invade one's home and to seize one's person.
It is also an appropriate case in the narrower and more technical

sense. The issues of the illegality of the search and the admissibility of the evidence have been presented to the state court and were duly raised here in accordance with the applicable Rule of Practice.[4] The question was raised in the notice of appeal, the jurisdictional statement and in appellant's brief on the merits.[5] It is true that argument was mostly directed to another issue in the case, but that is often the fact. . . .

Memorandum of MR. JUSTICE STEWART.
Agreeing fully with Part I Of MR. JUSTICE HARLAN's dissenting opinion, I express no view as to the merits of the constitutional issue which the Court today decides. . . .

MR. JUSTICE HARLAN, whom MR. JUSTICE FRANKFURTER and MR. JUSTICE WHITTAKER join, dissenting. . . .

I

From the Court's statement of the case one would gather that the central, if not controlling, issue on this appeal is whether illegally state-seized evidence is Constitutionally admissible in a state prosecution, an issue which would of course face us with the need for re-examining *Wolf*. However, such is not the situation. For, although that question was indeed raised here and below among appellant's subordinate points, the new and pivotal issue brought to the Court by this appeal is whether . . . the *mere* knowing possession or control of obscene material . . . is consistent with the rights of free thought and expression assured against state action by the Fourteenth Amendment. That was the principal issue which was decided by the Ohio Supreme Court, which was tendered by appellant's Jurisdictional Statement, and which was briefed and argued in this Court.

In this posture of things, I think it fair to say that five members of this Court have simply "reached out" to overrule *Wolf*. With all respect for the views of the majority, and recognizing that stare decisis carries different weight in Constitutional adjudication than it does in nonconstitutional decision, I can perceive no justification for regarding this case as an appropriate occasion for re-examining *Wolf*. . . .

4. "The notice of appeal . . . shall set forth the questions presented by the appeal. . . . Only the questions set forth in the notice of appeal or fairly comprised therein will be considered by the court." Rule 10(2)(c), Rules of the Supreme Court of the United States.
5. "Did the conduct of the police in procuring the books, papers, and pictures placed in evidence by the Prosecution violate Amendment IV, Amendment V, and Amendment XIV Section I of the United States Constitution . . . ?"

II . . .

I would not impose upon the States this federal exclusionary remedy. The reasons given by the majority for now suddenly turning its back on *Wolf* seem to me notably unconvincing.

First, it is said that "the factual grounds upon which *Wolf* was based" have since changed, in that more States now follow the *Weeks* exclusionary rule than was so at the time *Wolf* was decided. While that is true, a recent survey indicates that at present one-half of the States still adhere to the common-law non-exclusionary rule, and one, Maryland, retains the rule as to felonies. . . .

. . . Problems of criminal law enforcement vary widely from State to State. One State, in considering the totality of its legal picture, may conclude that the need for embracing the *Weeks* rule is pressing because other remedies are unavailable or inadequate to secure compliance with the substantive Constitutional principle involved. Another, though equally solicitous of Constitutional rights, may choose to pursue one purpose at a time, allowing all evidence relevant to guilt to be brought into a criminal trial, and dealing with Constitutional infractions by other means. Still another may consider the exclusionary rule too rough-and-ready a remedy, in that it reaches only unconstitutional intrusions which eventuate in criminal prosecution of the victims. Further, a State after experimenting with the *Weeks* rule for a time may, because of unsatisfactory experience with it, decide to revert to a non-exclusionary rule. And so on. . . .

An approach which regards the issue as one of achieving procedural symmetry or of serving administrative convenience surely disfigures the boundaries of this Court's functions in relation to the state and federal courts. . . . Here we review state procedures whose measure is to be taken not against the specific substantive commands of the Fourth Amendment but under the flexible contours of the Due Process Clause. I do not believe that the Fourteenth Amendment empowers this Court to mould state remedies effectuating the right to freedom from "arbitrary intrusion by the police" to suit its own notions of how things should be done. . . .

A state conviction comes to us as the complete product of a sovereign judicial system. Typically a case will have been tried in a trial court, tested in some final appellate court, and will go no further. In the comparatively rare instance when a conviction is reviewed by us on due process grounds we deal then with a finished product in the creation of which we are allowed no hand, and our task, far from being one of overall supervision, is, speaking generally, restricted to a determination of whether the prosecution was Constitutionally fair. The specifics of trial procedure, which in every mature legal system will vary greatly in detail, are within the sole competence of the States. I do not see how it can be said that a trial becomes unfair simply because a State determines that evidence may be considered by the trier of fact, regardless of how it was obtained, if it is relevant to the one issue with which the trial is concerned, the guilt or innocence of the accused. Of course, a court may use its procedures as an incidental means of pursuing other ends than the correct resolution of the controversies before it. Such indeed is the Weeks rule, but if a State does not choose to use its courts in this way, I do not believe that this Court is empowered to impose this much-debated procedure on local courts, however efficacious we may consider the Weeks rule to be as a means of securing Constitutional rights.

Finally, it is said that the overruling of Wolf is supported by the established doctrine that the admission in evidence of an involuntary confession renders a state conviction Constitutionally invalid. Since such a confession may often be entirely reliable, and therefore of the greatest relevance to the issue of the trial, the argument continues, this doctrine is ample warrant in precedent that the way evidence was obtained, and not just its relevance, is Constitutionally significant to the fairness of a trial. I believe this analogy is not a true one. The "coerced confession" rule is certainly not a rule that any illegally obtained statements may not be used in evidence. I would suppose that a statement which is procured during a period of illegal detention, McNabb v. United States, 318 U.S. 332, is, as much as unlawfully seized evidence, illegally obtained, but this Court has consistently refused to reverse state convictions resting on the use of such statements. . . .

The point, then, must be that in requiring exclusion of an involuntary statement of an accused, we are concerned not with an appropriate remedy for what the police have done, but with something which is regarded as going to the heart of our concepts of fairness in judicial procedure. The operative assumption of our procedural system is that "Ours is the accusatorial as opposed to the inquisitorial system. Such has been the characteristic of Anglo-American criminal justice since it freed itself from practices borrowed by the Star Chamber from the Continent whereby the accused was interrogated in secret for hours on end." Watts v. Indiana, 338 U.S. 49, 54. See Rogers v. Richmond, 365 U.S. 534, 541. The pressures brought to bear against an accused leading to a confession, unlike an unconstitutional violation of privacy, do not, apart from the use of the confession at trial, necessarily involve independent Constitutional violations. What is crucial is that the trial defense to which an accused is entitled should not be rendered an empty formality by reason of statements wrung from him, for then "a prisoner . . . [has been] made the deluded instrument of his own conviction." 2 Hawkins,

Pleas of the Crown (8th ed., 1824), c. 46, §34. That this is a *procedural right*, and that its violation occurs at the time his improperly obtained statement is admitted at trial, is manifest. For without this right all the careful safeguards erected around the giving of testimony, whether by an accused or any other witness, would become empty formalities in a procedure where the most compelling possible evidence of guilt, a confession, would have already been obtained at the unsupervised pleasure of the police.

This, and not the disciplining of the police, as with illegally seized evidence, is surely the true basis for excluding a statement of the accused which was unconstitutionally obtained. In sum, I think the coerced confession analogy works strongly *against* what the Court does today. . . .

NOTES AND QUESTIONS

1. Why is Justice Black not content to rest the exclusionary rule on the fourth amendment? Do the *words* of the fifth amendment or the fourth and fifth amendments together point more clearly than the words of the fourth amendment alone to an exclusionary rule for evidence obtained from an illegal search? Is there any other reason why one might want to base the exclusionary rule on the combined mandate of the two amendments?

2. Justice Black's position that the fifth amendment provides essential support for the exclusionary rule was not embraced by other justices in *Mapp*, and it has not been advocated by other justices in subsequent cases. Yet his vote was essential for the reversal in *Mapp*. What, if anything, do these facts imply about the constitutional status of the exclusionary rule?

3. Justice Clark states that *Wolf* was based on "factual considerations" that are "not basically relevant" to the question whether the due process right to be free from illegal searches mandates the exclusion of unconstitutionally seized evidence. He then proceeds to discuss what he calls "the factual grounds upon which *Wolf* was based." What are these "factual grounds"? Do you agree that they were the basis for *Wolf*? Do you agree, in any event, that they are irrelevant? If they are irrelevant, as Justice Clark claims, why does he bother to discuss them?

4. Reconsider carefully *Weeks*, *Wolf*, and *Mapp* with a focus on the Court's articulations of the rationales and purposes for the exclusionary rule. How has the emphasis changed from case to case? Which of the various rationales or points made in defense or criticism of the exclusionary rule do you think are most compelling? Least compelling?

C. PROBABLE CAUSE AND THE WARRANT PROCESS

The second clause of the fourth amendment requires "probable cause" for the issuance of a warrant. The amendment, however, does not address the question when warrants are required. Rather, the first clause simply guarantees to the people the right to be free from *unreasonable* searches and seizures. Shortly, we will explore in detail the relationship between the reasonableness clause and the warrant and probable cause requirements. For present purposes, it is sufficient to note that the Supreme Court has frequently required probable cause as a condition of reasonableness in evaluating the constitutionality of warrantless searches and seizures. The rationale for reading a probable cause requirement into the reasonableness clause is as follows: (1) searches conducted pursuant to warrants are preferable to warrantless searches; (2) if warrantless searches upon less than probable cause were constitutional, there would be no incentive for the police to seek a warrant.

The preference for warrants stems from the fact that warrants typically are issued by a judge or a magistrate, who bases the decision whether to issue the warrant on information presented by the police in an affidavit. In cases in which the police do not seek a warrant, they are the sole judges of whether a search or seizure is appropriate. According to the Court, the decisions of a "neutral and detached"[22] judicial officer

> are to be preferred over the hurried action of officers and others who may happen to make arrests. Security against unlawful searches is more likely to be attained by resort to search warrants than by reliance upon the caution and sagacity of petty officers while acting under the excitement that attends the capture of persons accused of crime. . . . [United States v. Lefkowitz, 285 U.S. 452, 464 (1932).]

Whether the warrant process serves this function depends on several factors: for example, the time, ability, and inclination of the magistrate to make an independent judgment about probable cause;[23] the rigor of

---

22. Johnson v. United States, 333 U.S. 10, 14 (1946). See page 600 infra.

23. See Shadwick v. City of Tampa, 407 U.S. 345 (1972) (magistrate need not be lawyer or judge; permissible for municipal court clerks to issue arrest warrants for breaches of municipal ordinances). Should *Shadwick* be viewed as equally applicable to *search* warrants? See 2 W. LaFave, Search and Seizure: A Treatise on the Fourth Amendment §4.2c, at 158 (2d ed. 1987).

On the question whether magistrates serve as a significant screen, see generally Miller & Tiffany, Prosecutor Dominance of the Warrant Decision: A Study in Current Practices, 1964 Wash. U.L.Q. 1. See also Bloom, The Supreme Court and Its Purported Preference for Warrants, 50 Tenn. L. Rev. 231 (1983); Yackle, The Burger Court and the Fourth Amendment, 26 U. Kan. L. Rev. 375 (1978).

the probable cause standard itself; the quality of information presented to the magistrate. As you examine the materials on probable cause and the warrant process, consider how significant a protection against unreasonable searches and seizures a magistrate's judgment is likely to be. Consider also whether there are other purposes served by the warrant process.

1. The Meaning of Probable Cause

Probable cause must be based on "more than bare suspicion: Probable cause exists where 'the facts and circumstances within their [the officers'] knowledge and of which they had reasonably trustworthy information [are] sufficient in themselves to warrant a man of reasonable caution in the belief that' an offense has been or is being committed. . . ." Brinegar v. United States, 338 U.S. 160, 175-176 (1949). In the case of an arrest, the probable cause must relate to the person being arrested. In the case of a search, probable cause must exist to believe that the items being sought will be found in the place searched.

How probable is probable? Suppose that the police standing outside a hotel door smell the odor of opium being smoked. Do the police have probable cause to arrest the occupant(s) for possession of opium? See Johnson v. United States, 333 U.S. 10, 16 (1948) ("Government, in effect, concedes that the arresting officer did not have probable cause to arrest petitioner until he had entered her room and found her to be the sole occupant").

Perhaps the government conceded too much in *Johnson*. Depending on the size of the room, whether the officer heard voices, and if so how many, one might be able reasonably to conclude that all occupants in the room, if there were more than one, were in possession of the opium.[24] Such an inference will not always be reasonable, however. Consider, for example, the following possibility: A passenger in an automobile is fatally wounded by a rifle shot from a nearby building. The police immediately seal off all exits from the building and begin to search it. On the sixth floor they discover the rifle by an open window. On the first floor they find the only occupant(s) of the building. If the police discover more than one occupant, can they legally arrest each of them? Does the precise number of occupants matter? Would it matter if the passenger in the

---

24. Cf. Ulster County Court v. Allen, 442 U.S. 140 (1979) (approving instruction that from presence of defendants in car where gun was located jury may infer that each defendant was in possession of gun), commented on in Allen, Structuring Jury Decisionmaking in Criminal Cases: A Unified Constitutional Approach to Evidentiary Devices, 94 Harv. L. Rev. 321 (1980).

passing vehicle had been the President of the United States? See generally Grano, Probable Cause and Common Sense: A Reply to the Critics of Illinois v. Gates, 17 U. Mich. J.L. Reform 465, 475-506 (1984).

Situations in which the police are certain that a crime has been committed and that one of an identifiable number of suspects committed it has the virtue—or the vice—of permitting us to describe probable cause in terms of statistical probabilities. These cases, however, are relatively rare. Much more frequent is the situation in which it is impossible to assign meaningful statistical probabilities to the factors relied on to establish probable cause. How does one assess probable cause in these situations?

Consider Wong Sun v. United States, 371 U.S. 471 (1963):

> The quantum of information which constitutes probable cause—evidence which would "warrant a man of reasonable caution in the belief" that a felony has been committed . . . —must be measured by the facts of the particular case. The history of the use, and not infrequent abuse, of the power to arrest cautions that a relaxation of the fundamental requirements of probable cause would "leave law-abiding citizens at the mercy of the officers' whim or caprice." [Id. at 479.]

Is the notion of probable cause sufficiently concrete to provide the kind of protection that the Court speaks of in *Wong Sun?* If not, what is the alternative?

Consider also State v. Olsen, 315 N.W.2d 1 (Iowa 1982), in which the defendant was legally stopped by the police on Interstate 80 about 45 minutes east of Des Moines. In the course of their initial questioning of the defendant, the police discovered "several thousand dollars in cash, bundled in various denominations," and the defendant was "evasive" when questioned about the source of the money. The police then searched the trunk of the car, where they found marijuana. The legality of their search, according to the Iowa Supreme Court, depended on whether, at the time, the police had probable cause to believe that the defendant was the person described in a radio dispatch concerning a robbery that had occurred approximately four hours earlier in Des Moines. The court analyzed the question as follows:

> Olsen is a white male, in his twenties, and approximately six feet tall. This part of the radio description fit him, although the robbery subject was of a "heavy build" and Olsen weighs approximately 160 pounds. The radio description said the suspect had "bushy hair or wearing stocking cap." Olsen was described as having "long straggly hair," not bushy, but he was wearing a stocking cap. He also had a beard, while the radio dispatch was silent on whether or not the robbery suspect had one. The

suspect was said to be wearing a green parka, while Olsen was wearing a brown leather jacket, and the suspect's car was described as a yellow Oldsmobile or Chevrolet, while the car Olsen was operating was a blue Cadillac. . . .

Although it is a close question on probable cause, we believe it was established here. It would be reasonable for the officers to assume the suspect had changed cars and coats, and that the radio description merely omitted mention of the beard. . . . [In other respects the defendant matched the broadcast description; he was] admittedly traveling from Des Moines in possession of several thousand dollars in cash[;] . . . and . . . [he] said [the cash] came from a friend, whom he "didn't know." [Id. at 6.]

2. Probable Cause Based on Information from Informants and Other Third Persons

Draper v. United States, 358 U.S. 307 (1959), which figures prominently in the analysis in the next two principal cases, involved the following facts:

Marsh, a federal narcotic agent with 29 years' experience, was stationed at Denver. . . . Hereford had been engaged as a "special employee" of the Bureau of Narcotics at Denver for about six months, and from time to time gave information to Marsh regarding violations of the narcotic laws, for which Hereford was paid small sums of money. . . . Marsh had always found the information given by Hereford to be accurate and reliable. On September 3, 1956, Hereford told Marsh that James Draper (petitioner) recently had taken up abode at a stated address in Denver and "was peddling narcotics to several addicts" in that city. Four days later, on September 7, Hereford told Marsh "that Draper had gone to Chicago the day before [September 6] by train [and] that he was going to bring back three ounces of heroin [and] that he would return to Denver either on the morning of the 8th of September or the morning of the 9th of September also by train." Hereford also gave Marsh a detailed physical description of Draper and of the clothing he was wearing,[2] and said that he would be carrying "a tan zipper bag," and that he habitually "walked real fast."

On the morning of September 8, Marsh and a Denver police officer went to the Denver Union Station and kept watch over all incoming trains from Chicago, but they did not see anyone fitting the description that Hereford had given. Repeating the process on the morning of September 9, they saw a person, having the exact physical attributes and wearing the precise clothing described by Hereford, alight from an incoming Chicago

2. Hereford told Marsh that Draper was a Negro of light brown complexion, 27 years of age, 5 feet 8 inches tall, weighed about 160 pounds, and that he was wearing a light colored raincoat, brown slacks and black shoes.

train and start walking "fast" toward the exit. He was carrying a tan zipper
bag in his right hand and the left was thrust in his raincoat pocket. Marsh,
accompanied by the police officer, overtook, stopped and arrested him.
They then searched him and found the two "envelopes containing heroin"
clutched in his left hand in his raincoat pocket, and found the syringe in
the tan zipper bag. Marsh then took him (petitioner) into custody. . . .
[Id. at 309-310.]

Draper was convicted of transporting narcotics, and the court of
appeals affirmed the conviction. Before the Supreme Court Draper argued
that the police lacked probable cause to arrest him, but the Supreme
Court held otherwise.

The information given to narcotic agent Marsh by "special employee"
Hereford may have been hearsay to Marsh, but coming from one employed
for that purpose and whose information had always been found accurate
and reliable, it is clear that Marsh would have been derelict in his duties
had he not pursued it. And when, in pursuing that information, he saw
a man, having the exact physical attributes and wearing the precise clothing
and carrying the tan zipper bag that Hereford had described, alight from
one of the very trains from the very place stated by Hereford and start to
walk at a "fast" pace toward the station exit, Marsh had personally verified
every facet of the information given him by Hereford except whether
petitioner had accomplished his mission and had the three ounces of heroin
on his person or in his bag. And surely, with every other bit of Hereford's
information being thus personally verified, Marsh had "reasonable grounds"
to believe that the remaining unverified bit of Hereford's information—
that Draper would have the heroin with him—was likewise true. [Id. at
312-313.]

SPINELLI v. UNITED STATES

Certiorari to the United States Court of Appeals for the Eighth Circuit
393 U.S. 410 (1969)

MR. JUSTICE HARLAN delivered the opinion of the Court.
William Spinelli was convicted under 18 U.S.C. §1952 of traveling
to St. Louis, Missouri, from a nearby Illinois suburb with the intention
of conducting gambling activities proscribed by Missouri law. . . . At
every appropriate stage in the proceedings in the lower courts, the petitioner challenged the constitutionality of the warrant which authorized
the FBI search that uncovered the evidence necessary for his conviction. . . .
In Aguilar [v. Texas, 378 U.S. 108 (1964)], a search warrant had
issued upon an affidavit of police officers who swore only that they had

"received reliable information from a credible person and do believe" that narcotics were being illegally stored on the described premises. While recognizing that the constitutional requirement of probable cause can be satisfied by hearsay information, this Court held the affidavit inadequate for two reasons. First, the application failed to set forth any of the "underlying circumstances" necessary to enable the magistrate independently to judge of the validity of the informant's conclusion that the narcotics were where he said they were. Second, the affiant-officers did not attempt to support their claim that their informant was " 'credible' or his information 'reliable.' " The Government is, however, quite right in saying that the FBI affidavit in the present case is more ample than that in *Aguilar*. Not only does it contain a report from an anonymous informant, but it also contains a report of an independent FBI investigation which is said to corroborate the informant's tip. We are, then, required to delineate the manner in which *Aguilar's* two-pronged test should be applied in these circumstances.

In essence, the affidavit . . . contained the following allegations:

1. The FBI had kept track of Spinelli's movements on five days during the month of August 1965. On four of these occasions, Spinelli was seen crossing one of two bridges leading from Illinois into St. Louis, Missouri, between 11 A.M. and 12:15 P.M. On four of the five days, Spinelli was also seen parking his car in a lot used by residents of an apartment house at 1108 Indian Circle Drive in St. Louis, between 3:30 P.M. and 4:45 P.M. On one day, Spinelli was followed further and seen to enter a particular apartment in the building.

2. An FBI check with the telephone company revealed that this apartment contained two telephones listed under the name of Grace P. Hagen, and carrying the numbers WYdown 4-0029 and WYdown 4-0136.

3. The application stated that "William Spinelli is known to this affiant and to federal law enforcement agents and local law enforcement agents as a bookmaker, an associate of bookmakers, a gambler, and an associate of gamblers."

4. Finally, it was stated that the FBI "has been informed by a confidential reliable informant that William Spinelli is operating a handbook and accepting wagers and disseminating wagering information by means of the telephones which have been assigned the numbers WYdown 4-0029 and WYdown 4-0136."

There can be no question that the last item mentioned, detailing the informant's tip, has a fundamental place in this warrant application.

Without it, probable cause could not be established. The first two items reflect only innocent-seeming activity and data. Spinelli's travels to and from the apartment building and his entry into a particular apartment on one occasion could hardly be taken as bespeaking gambling activity; and there is surely nothing unusual about an apartment containing two separate telephones. Many a householder indulges himself in this petty luxury. Finally, the allegation that Spinelli was "known" to the affiant and to other federal and local law enforcement officers as a gambler and an associate of gamblers is but a bald and unilluminating assertion of suspicion that is entitled to no weight in appraising the magistrate's decision. . . .

So much indeed the Government does not deny. Rather, the Government claims that the informant's tip gives a suspicious color to the FBI's reports detailing Spinelli's innocent-seeming conduct and that, conversely, the FBI's surveillance corroborates the informant's tip, thereby entitling it to more weight. It is true, of course, that the magistrate is obligated to render a judgment based upon a common-sense reading of the entire affidavit. United States v. Ventresca, 380 U.S. 102, 108 (1965). We believe, however, that the "totality of circumstances" approach taken by the Court of Appeals paints with too broad a brush. Where, as here, the informer's tip is a necessary element in a finding of probable cause, its proper weight must be determined by a more precise analysis.

The informer's report must first be measured against *Aguilar's* standards so that its probative value can be assessed. If the tip is found inadequate under *Aguilar*, the other allegations which corroborate the information contained in the hearsay report should then be considered. At this stage as well, however, the standards enunciated in *Aguilar* must inform the magistrate's decision. He must ask: Can it fairly be said that the tip, even when certain parts of it have been corroborated by independent sources, is as trustworthy as a tip which would pass *Aguilar's* tests without independent corroboration? *Aguilar* is relevant at this stage of the inquiry as well because the tests it establishes were designed to implement the long-standing principle that probable cause must be determined by a "neutral and detached magistrate," and not by "the officer engaged in the often competitive enterprise of ferreting out crime." Johnson v. United States, 333 U.S. 10, 14 (1948). A magistrate cannot be said to have properly discharged his constitutional duty if he relies on an informer's tip which—even when partially corroborated—is not as reliable as one which passes *Aguilar's* requirements when standing alone.

Applying these principles to the present case, we first consider the weight to be given the informer's tip when it is considered apart from the rest of the affidavit. It is clear that a Commissioner could not credit it without abdicating his constitutional function. Though the affiant swore that his confidant was "reliable," he offered the magistrate no reason in support of this conclusion. Perhaps even more important is the fact that *Aguilar's* other test has not been satisfied. The tip does not contain a sufficient statement of the underlying circumstances from which the informer concluded that Spinelli was running a bookmaking operation. We are not told how the FBI's source received his information—it is not alleged that the informant personally observed Spinelli at work or that he had ever placed a bet with him. Moreover, if the informant came by the information indirectly, he did not explain why his sources were reliable. . . . In the absence of a statement detailing the manner in which the information was gathered, it is especially important that the tip describe the accused's criminal activity in sufficient detail that the magistrate may know that he is relying on something more substantial than a casual rumor circulating in the underworld or an accusation based merely on an individual's general reputation.

The detail provided by the informant in Draper v. United States, 358 U.S. 307 (1959), provides a suitable benchmark. While Hereford, the Government's informer in that case, did not state the way in which he had obtained his information, . . . [a] magistrate, when confronted with [the detailed information provided by Hereford], . . . could reasonably infer that the informant had gained his information in a reliable way.[5] Such an inference cannot be made in the present case. Here, the only facts supplied were that Spinelli was using two specified telephones and that these phones were being used in gambling operations. This meager report could easily have been obtained from an offhand remark heard at a neighborhood bar.

Nor do we believe that the patent doubts *Aguilar* raises as to the report's reliability are adequately resolved by a consideration of the allegations detailing the FBI's independent investigative efforts. At most, these allegations indicated that Spinelli could have used the telephones specified by the informant for some purpose. This cannot by itself be said to support both the inference that the informer was generally trustworthy and that he had made his charge against Spinelli on the basis of information obtained in a reliable way. Once again, *Draper* provides a relevant comparison. Independent police work in that case corroborated much more than one small detail that had been provided by the informant. There, the police, upon meeting the inbound Denver train on the second morning specified by informer Hereford, saw a man whose dress corresponded precisely to Hereford's detailed description. It was then

5. While *Draper* involved the question whether the police had probable cause for an arrest without a warrant, the analysis required for an answer to this question is basically similar to that demanded of a magistrate when he considers whether a search warrant should issue.

apparent that the informant had not been fabricating his report out of whole cloth; since the report was of the sort which in common experience may be recognized as having been obtained in a reliable way, it was perfectly clear that probable cause had been established.

We conclude, then, that in the present case the informant's tip—even when corroborated to the extent indicated—was not sufficient to provide the basis for a finding of probable cause. This is not to say that the tip was so insubstantial that it could not properly have counted in the magistrate's determination. Rather, it needed some further support. When we look to the other parts of the application, however, we find nothing alleged which would permit the suspicions engendered by the informant's report to ripen into a judgment that a crime was probably being committed. As we have already seen, the allegations detailing the FBI's surveillance of Spinelli and its investigation of the telephone company records contain no suggestion of criminal conduct when taken by themselves—and they are not endowed with an aura of suspicion by virtue of the informer's tip. Nor do we find that the FBI's reports take on a sinister color when read in light of common knowledge that book-making is often carried on over the telephone and from premises ostensibly used by others for perfectly normal purposes. Such an argument would carry weight in a situation in which the premises contain an unusual number of telephones or abnormal activity is observed, . . . but it does not fit this case where neither of these factors is present. All that remains to be considered is the flat statement that Spinelli was "known" to the FBI and others as a gambler. But just as a simple assertion of police suspicion is not itself a sufficient basis for a magistrate's finding of probable cause, we do not believe it may be used to give additional weight to allegations that would otherwise be insufficient.

The affidavit, then, falls short of the standards set forth in *Aguilar*, *Draper*, and our other decisions that give content to the notion of probable cause.[7] In holding as we have done, we do not retreat from the established propositions that only the probability, and not a prima facie showing, of criminal activity is the standard of probable cause, Beck v. Ohio, 379 U.S. 89, 96 (1964); that affidavits of probable cause are tested by much less rigorous standards than those governing the admissibility of evidence

---

7. In those cases in which this Court has found probable cause established, the showing made was much more substantial than the one made here. Thus, in United States v. Ventresca, 380 U.S. 102, 104 (1965), FBI agents observed repeated deliveries of loads of sugar in 60-pound bags, smelled the odor of fermenting mash, and heard " 'sounds similar to that of a motor or a pump coming from the direction of' Ventresca's house." Again, in McCray v. Illinois, 386 U.S. 300, 303-304 (1967), the informant reported that McCray " 'was selling narcotics and had narcotics on his person now in the vicinity of 47th and Calumet.' " When the police arrived at the intersection, they observed McCray engaging in various suspicious activities. 386 U.S., at 302.

at trial, McCray v. Illinois, 386 U.S. 300, 311 (1967); that in judging probable cause issuing magistrates are not to be confined by niggardly limitations or by restrictions on the use of their common sense, United States v. Ventresca, 380 U.S. 102, 108 (1965); and that their determination of probable cause should be paid great deference by reviewing courts, Jones v. United States, 362 U.S. 257, 270-271 (1960). But we cannot sustain this warrant without diluting important safeguards that assure that the judgment of a disinterested judicial officer will interpose itself between the police and the citizenry.

The judgment of the Court of Appeals is reversed and the case is remanded to that court for further proceedings consistent with this opinion.

It is so ordered.

MR. JUSTICE MARSHALL took no part in the consideration or decision of this case. . . .

MR. JUSTICE WHITE, concurring.

An investigator's affidavit that he has seen gambling equipment being moved into a house at a specified address will support the issuance of a search warrant. The oath affirms the honesty of the statement and negatives the lie or imagination. Personal observation attests to the facts asserted—that there is gambling equipment on the premises at the named address.

But if the officer simply avers, without more, that there is gambling paraphernalia on certain premises, the warrant should not issue, even though the belief of the officer is an honest one, as evidenced by his oath, and even though the magistrate knows him to be an experienced, intelligent officer who has been reliable in the past. This much was settled in Nathanson v. United States, 290 U.S. 41 (1933), where the Court held insufficient an officer's affidavit swearing he had cause to believe that there was illegal liquor on the premises for which the warrant was sought. The unsupported assertion or belief of the officer does not satisfy the requirement of probable cause. . . .

What is missing in Nathanson and like cases is a statement of the basis for the affiant's believing the facts contained in the affidavit—the good "cause" which the officer in Nathanson said he had. If an officer swears that there is gambling equipment at a certain address, the possibilities are (1) that he has seen the equipment; (2) that he has observed or perceived facts from which the presence of the equipment may reasonably be inferred; and (3) that he has obtained the information from someone else. If (1) is true, the affidavit is good. But in (2), the affidavit is insufficient unless the perceived facts are given, for it is the magistrate, not the officer, who is to judge the existence of probable cause. . . .

With respect to (3), where the officer's information is hearsay, no warrant should issue absent good cause for crediting that hearsay. Because an affidavit asserting, without more, the location of gambling equipment at a particular address does not claim personal observation of any of the facts by the officer, and because of the likelihood that the information came from an unidentified third party, affidavits of this type are unacceptable.

Neither should the warrant issue if the officer states that there is gambling equipment in a particular apartment and that his information comes from an informant, named or unnamed, since the honesty of the informant and the basis for his report are unknown. Nor would the missing elements be completely supplied by the officer's oath that the informant has often furnished reliable information in the past. This attests to the honesty of the informant, but Aguilar v. Texas, supra, requires something more—did the information come from observation, or did the informant in turn receive it from another? Absent additional facts for believing the informant's report, his assertion stands no better than the oath of the officer to the same effect. Indeed, if the affidavit of an officer, known by the magistrate to be honest and experienced, stating that gambling equipment is located in a certain building is unacceptable, it would be quixotic if a similar statement from an honest informant were found to furnish probable cause. A strong argument can be made that both should be acceptable under the Fourth Amendment, but under our cases neither is. The past reliability of the informant can no more furnish probable cause for believing his current report than can previous experience with the officer himself

If the affidavit rests on hearsay—an informant's report—what is necessary under Aguilar is one of two things: the informant must declare either (1) that he has himself seen or perceived the fact or facts asserted; or (2) that his information is hearsay, but there is good reason for believing it—perhaps one of the usual grounds for crediting hearsay information. The first presents few problems: since the report, although hearsay, purports to be first-hand observation, remaining doubt centers on the honesty of the informant, and that worry is dissipated by the officer's previous experience with the informant. The other basis for accepting the informant's report is more complicated. But if, for example, the informer's hearsay comes from one of the actors in the crime in the nature of admission against interest, the affidavit giving this information should be held sufficient.

I am inclined to agree with the majority that there are limited special circumstances in which an "honest" informant's report, if sufficiently detailed, will in effect verify itself—that is, the magistrate when confronted with such detail could reasonably infer that the informant had gained his information in a reliable way. . . . Detailed information may sometimes imply that the informant himself has observed the facts. Suppose an informant with whom an officer has had satisfactory experience states that there is gambling equipment in the living room of a specified apartment and describes in detail not only the equipment itself but also the appointments and furnishings in the apartment. Detail like this, if true at all, must rest on personal observation either of the informant or of someone else. If the latter, we know nothing of the third person's honesty or sources; he may be making a wholly false report. But it is arguable that on these facts it was the informant himself who has perceived the facts, for the information reported is not usually the subject of casual, day-to-day conversation. Because the informant is honest and it is probable that he has viewed the facts, there is probable cause for the issuance of a warrant.

So too in the special circumstances of Draper v. United States, 358 U.S. 307 (1959), the kind of information related by the informant is not generally sent ahead of a person's arrival in a city except to those who are intimately connected with making careful arrangements for meeting him. The informant, posited as honest, somehow had the reported facts, very likely from one of the actors in the plan, or as one of them himself. The majority's suggestion is that a warrant could have been obtained based only on the informer's report. I am inclined to agree, although it seems quite plain that if it may be so easily inferred from the affidavit that the informant has himself observed the facts or has them from an actor in the event, no possible harm could come from requiring a statement to that effect, thereby removing the difficult and recurring questions which arise in such situations.

Of course, Draper itself did not proceed on this basis. Instead, the Court pointed out that when the officer saw a person getting off the train at the specified time, dressed and conducting himself precisely as the informant had predicted, all but the critical fact with respect to possessing narcotics had then been verified and for that reason the officer had "reasonable grounds" to believe also that Draper was carrying narcotics. Unquestionably, verification of arrival time, dress, and gait reinforced the honesty of the informant—he had not reported a made-up story. But if what Draper stands for is that the existence of the tenth and critical fact is made sufficiently probable to justify the issuance of a warrant by verifying nine other facts coming from the same source, I have my doubts about that case.

In the first place, the proposition is not that the tenth fact may be logically inferred from the other nine or that the tenth fact is usually found in conjunction with the other nine. No one would suggest that just anyone getting off the 10:30 train dressed as Draper was, with a brisk walk and carrying a zipper bag, should be arrested for carrying narcotics. The thrust of *Draper* is not that the verified facts have independent significance with respect to proof of the tenth. The argument instead relates to the reliability of the source: because an informant is right about some things, he is more probably right about other facts, usually the critical, unverified facts.

But the Court's cases have already rejected for Fourth Amendment purposes the notion that the past reliability of an officer is sufficient reason for believing his current assertions. Nor would it suffice, I suppose, if a reliable informant states there is gambling equipment in Apartment 607 and then proceeds to describe in detail Apartment 201, a description which is verified before applying for the warrant. He was right about 201, but that hardly makes him more believable about the equipment in 607. But what if he states that there are narcotics locked in a safe in Apartment 300, which is described in detail, and the apartment manager verifies everything but the contents of the safe? I doubt that the report about the narcotics is made appreciably more believable by the verification. The informant could still have gotten his information concerning the safe from others about whom nothing is known or could have inferred the presence of narcotics from circumstances which a magistrate would find unacceptable.

The tension between *Draper* and the *Nathanson-Aguilar* line of cases is evident from the course followed by the majority opinion. First, it is held that the report from a reliable informant that Spinelli is using two telephones with specified numbers to conduct a gambling business plus Spinelli's reputation in police circles as a gambler does not add up to probable cause. This is wholly consistent with *Aguilar* and *Nathanson*: the informant did not reveal whether he had personally observed the facts or heard them from another and, if the latter, no basis for crediting the hearsay was presented. Nor were the facts, as Mr. Justice Harlan says, of such a nature that they normally would be obtainable only by the personal observation of the informant himself. The police, however, did not stop with the informant's report. Independently, they established the existence of two phones having the given numbers and located them in an apartment house which Spinelli was regularly frequenting away from his home. There remained little question but that Spinelli was using the phones, and it was a fair inference that the use was not for domestic but for business purposes. The informant had claimed the business involved gambling. Since his specific information about Spinelli using two phones with particular numbers had been verified, did not his allegation about gambling thereby become sufficiently more believable if the *Draper* principle is to be given any scope at all? I would think so, particularly since the information from the informant which was verified was not neutral, irrelevant information but was material to proving the gambling allegation: two phones with different numbers in an apartment used away from home indicates a business use in an operation, like bookmaking, where multiple phones are needed. The Draper approach would reasonably justify the issuance of a warrant in this case, particularly since the police had some awareness of Spinelli's past activities. The majority, however, while seemingly embracing *Draper*, confines that case to its own facts. Pending full-scale reconsideration of that case, on the one hand, or of the *Nathanson-Aguilar* cases on the other, I join the opinion of the Court and the judgment of reversal, especially since a vote to affirm would produce an equally divided Court.

MR. JUSTICE BLACK, dissenting. . . .
I regret to say I consider today's decision an indefensible departure from the principles of our former cases. Less than four years ago we reaffirmed these principles in United States v. Ventresca, 380 U.S. 102, 108 (1965):

> If the teachings of the Court's cases are to be followed and the constitutional policy served, affidavits for search warrants . . . must be tested and interpreted by magistrates and courts in a commonsense and realistic fashion. . . . Technical requirements of elaborate specificity once exacted under common law pleadings have no proper place in this area. . . .

Departures of this kind are responsible for considerable uneasiness in our lower courts, and I must say I am deeply troubled by the statements of Judge Gibson in the court below:

> I am, indeed, disturbed by decision after decision of our courts which place increasingly technical burdens upon law enforcement officials. I am disturbed by these decisions that appear to relentlessly chip away at the ever narrowing area of effective police operation. . . .

. . . The existence of probable cause is a factual matter that calls for the determination of a factual question. While no statistics are immediately available, questions of probable cause to issue search warrants and to make arrests are doubtless involved in many thousands of cases in state courts. All of those probable-cause state cases are now potentially reviewable by this Court. It is, of course, physically impossible for this Court to review the evidence in all or even a substantial percentage of those cases. Consequently, whether desirable or not, we must inevitably accept most of the fact findings of the state courts, particularly when, as here in a federal case, both the trial and appellate courts have decided the facts the same way. It cannot be said that the trial judge and six members of the Court of Appeals committed flagrant error in finding from evidence that the magistrate had probable cause to issue the search warrant here. It seems to me that this Court would best serve itself and the administration of justice by accepting the judgment of the two courts below. After all, they too are lawyers and judges, and much closer to the practical, everyday affairs of life than we are.

[The dissenting opinions of JUSTICE FORTAS and JUSTICE STEWART are omitted.]

NOTES AND QUESTIONS

1. One prong of the *Aguilar-Spinelli* test—the prong that asks whether the informant was "credible" or his information "reliable" meets a concern that is similar to the concern underlying the hearsay rule. Hearsay is an out-of-court statement offered to prove the truth of the matter it asserts, and several factors tend to make hearsay less trustworthy—or at least less subject to evaluation for trustworthiness than live, in-court testimony: the out-of-court statement may not have been made under oath; the factfinder is not able to observe the demeanor of the speaker; and the speaker is not subject to cross-examination about the statement. Because of these concerns, hearsay evidence is inadmissible in a trial unless it happens to fall within one of the various exceptions to the hearsay rule. These exceptions, for the most part, are based on the theory that despite the absence of oath, demeanor evidence, and cross-examination, the context within which the statement was made provides some circumstantial guarantees of trustworthiness.

In the context of evaluating an affidavit for a warrant, the officer-affiant is in a position analogous to the live witness in a trial. The magistrate can question the officer about any ambiguities in the affidavit or explore any reasons for doubting the officer's credibility. More importantly, at least in theory, the fact that the officer is under oath and the fact that the officer is a public official acting in an official capacity tend to ensure the officer's trustworthiness. By contrast, there is no particular reason to credit the assertion of an unidentified third person about the criminal activity of another. And the officer-affiant's conclusory assertion about the informant's trustworthiness does not provide the *magistrate* with any basis for evaluating the informant's credibility.

2. One of the well-established exceptions to the hearsay rule is for declarations against interest. The theory underlying the exception is that people are not likely to make false statements that are obviously against their interest and, therefore, that when a person makes such a statement,

it is likely to be trustworthy. In United States v. Harris, 403 U.S. 573 (1971), which involved a warrant to search for bootleg whiskey, the Court considered the significance of an unnamed informant's declaration against interest.

> Here the . . . affidavit recited extrajudicial statements of a declarant, who feared for his life and safety if his identity was revealed, that over the past two years he had many times and recently purchased "illicit whiskey." . . .
>
> Common sense in the important daily affairs of life would induce a prudent and disinterested observer to credit these statements. People do not lightly admit a crime and place critical evidence in the hands of the police in the form of their own admissions. Admissions of crime . . . carry their own indicia of credibility. . . . That the informant may be paid or promised a "break" does not eliminate the residual risk and opprobrium of having admitted to criminal conduct. [Id. at 583-584 (opinion of Burger, C.J., announcing judgment for Court).]

Although only three other justices joined in this portion of Chief Justice Burger's opinion, lower courts have been generally receptive to the notion that an informant's declarations against interest tend to indicate that the informant is trustworthy. Do you agree that in general declarations against interest are likely to be trustworthy? Are admissions of criminal conduct by informants likely to be more or less trustworthy than other declarations against interest?

3. One fairly common way to satisfy the "credibility" prong of the *Spinelli* test is to inform the magistrate that the informant has a "good track record," i.e., that the informant has provided the police with reliable information in the past. See, e.g., McCray v. Illinois, 386 U.S. 300 (1967).[25] When an informant's credibility is based on a track record, how specific and detailed should the track record have to be? If the current information relates to gambling, should the track record also have to relate to gambling information? Should it be sufficient to allege that the informant's information has led to numerous arrests?

4. The other prong of the *Aguilar-Spinelli* test—the "basis of knowledge" requirement—can also be analogized to standard evidentiary rules. The requirement that the affidavit provide the magistrate with "underlying circumstances" for the informant's conclusion serves a function similar to requirements that a trial witness (a) testify only from firsthand knowledge and (b) avoid offering opinions or conclusions rather than facts. The

---

25. Like *Draper*, *McCray* involved a warrantless arrest. Thus, information satisfying the two-prong test was presented for the first time at the hearing on the defendant's motion to suppress the evidence seized from him when he was arrested.

concern here is that the magistrate evaluating the affidavit or the factfinder at trial have a solid factual basis for making a decision. Even if we assume that a witness or an informant is completely honest, that individual's statement is of little value to the factfinder if it is only the reiteration of a rumor; and if it is a simple conclusion that, for example, narcotics are located in a particular place without a statement of the "underlying facts," the magistrate or factfinder has no way of knowing whether the assertion is mere rumor or whether it has a more solid basis.

5. The safest and most common way to satisfy this second prong of the *Aguilar-Spinelli* test is, as *Spinelli* suggests, to allege in the affidavit that the informant's information is based on the informant's firsthand knowledge. *Spinelli* also suggests, however, that the *basis-of-knowledge prong* may be satisfied, in the absence of an assertion of firsthand knowledge, simply by the amount of detail in the affidavit. What is the theory that justifies relying on "detail provided by the informant" as opposed to a statement of firsthand knowledge to satisfy this prong of the test?

Should the fact that an unnamed informant's account is detailed help establish the *credibility prong* of the *Spinelli* test? What, if any, theory arguably makes detail relevant to show honesty? See United States v. Harris, 403 U.S. 573, 593 (1971) (Harlan, J., dissenting).

6. Note that according to *Spinelli*, evaluation of the informant's report in terms of the two-prong test is only the first step in determining whether the information in the affidavit is sufficient to meet the probable cause standard. If the information about the informant is not sufficient to meet the two-prong test—i.e., to show that the informant is basically honest and that the informant obtained the information in a reliable manner—the test may nonetheless be satisfied by independent police investigation corroborating the informant's information. For example, corroboration of details—even innocent details—provided by a first-time informant would tend to show that the informant was generally honest. Thus such corroboration may well be an adequate substitute for "track record" evidence.[26] If the problem with the affidavit relates only to the *underlying circumstances prong*, however, what is the relevance of corroboration? Consider carefully Justice White's concurring opinion.

7. The third and final step is to evaluate all of the "good" information—including that from the informant, if the two-prong test has been satisfied—to determine whether the quantity of evidence is sufficient to establish probable cause. In the *Spinelli* affidavit, there was the additional allegation that Spinelli was known to the affiant and other law enforcement personnel as a gambler. Early in the opinion the Court

---

26. A "good liar," however, may tend to be truthful about innocent details in order to make the lie believable.

stated that such a statement was "a bald and unilluminating assertion of
suspicion that is entitled to no weight in appraising the magistrate's decision." Given the Court's conclusion about the inadequacy of the informant's information, this added bit of information probably should not
be sufficient to establish probable cause. Was the Court correct, however,
in concluding that such an assertion is entitled to "no weight"?

8. Should a defendant's background or reputation be of any significance in the initial evaluation whether the two-prong test has been
satisfied? Consider United States v. Harris, Note 2 supra. In addition to
alleging that an unnamed informant had recently observed and purchased
illegal whiskey at the defendant's premises, the affidavit alleged that the
defendant had a reputation, known to the affiant, for trafficking in illegal
whiskey.

In announcing the Court's judgment upholding the magistrate's
finding of probable cause, Chief Justice Burger, in a portion of the opinion
joined by Justices Black and Blackmun, observed:

> We cannot conclude that a policeman's knowledge of a suspect's
> reputation . . . is not a "practical consideration of everyday life" upon
> which an officer (or a magistrate) may properly rely in assessing the reli-
> ability of an informant's tip. To the extent that *Spinelli* prohibits the use
> of such probative information, it has no support in our prior cases, logic,
> or experience and we decline to apply it to preclude a magistrate from
> relying on a law enforcement officer's knowledge of a suspect's reputation.
> [403 U.S. at 583.]

Do you agree? What is the theory that arguably makes the *defendant's*
reputation relevant to the *informant's* credibility? If it is appropriate for
the magistrate to consider the defendant's reputation, should that consideration be part of the initial assessment whether the two-prong test has
been satisfied? Or should the defendant's reputation be regarded as an
independent piece of evidence to consider in determining whether the
quantum of "good" information satisfies the probable cause standard?

9. Should a defendant be entitled to learn the identity of a confidential informant and examine the informant at a suppression hearing?
In McCray v. Illinois, 386 U.S. 300 (1967), the Supreme Court held
that a defendant does not have the absolute constitutional right to this
information for the purpose of challenging the probable cause determination, and in fact requests for disclosure are rarely granted. Does the
refusal to disclose the identity of informants heighten the need for a fairly
rigorous application of the *Aguilar-Spinelli* test? Or would a rigorous
application of the test merely encourage police perjury? Indeed, is there
a danger that, regardless of how rigorously the test is applied, refusal to

require disclosure of informants' identities is a substantial incentive for the police to fabricate the existence of informants?

10. The possibility of police perjury is only one of the costs inherent in a system of investigation that relies on secret informants. Official encouragement for individuals to inform on their friends is at best somewhat unseemly; an overzealous informant may entrap the defendant;[27] the police leverage over the informant—the threat of criminal prosecution or exposure if the informant does not continue to provide information— can operate as a substantial infringement on the informant's freedom; and encouraging an individual with a criminal background to associate with other criminals in order to provide the police with information is inconsistent with the notion that we should try to rehabilitate criminals and *remove* them from a criminal environment. On the other hand, law enforcement personnel consistently maintain that a system of secret informants is absolutely critical to effective law enforcement. Because confidentiality is perceived to be critical to the effective operation of the informer system, it is virtually impossible to come to any reasoned assessment of the costs and benefits of that system. Perhaps many of the costs and benefits—whatever they are—are inevitable as long as the substantive law criminalizes activity that cannot be regulated effectively without secret informants.

11. In determining whether probable cause exists, how should courts evaluate information from a victim or a witness? A victim or witness is not likely to have a "track record" of providing reliable information, and the opportunity for meaningful corroboration may be limited.[28] Is it appropriate simply to assume that a victim or witness is honest if there is no apparent reason for a contrary conclusion?[29] Should it be sufficient

---

27. See Chapter 8 infra.

28. From the physical appearance of the victim on the scene, the police may be able to infer that a crime probably has been committed, and if the police come upon a suspect who meets the description given by the witness, the police will have corroborated that a person of that description in fact exists. Unlike the *Spinelli-Harris*-type of informant, however, the witness or victim is not likely to be able to provide verifiable information about the future activities of the suspect.

29. In Jaben v. United States, 381 U.S. 214 (1965), the Supreme Court addressed the question whether a complaint charging the defendant with income tax evasion established probable cause. The complaint included a statement that some of the information came from interviewing "third parties with whom the said taxpayer did business" and "third persons having knowledge of said taxpayer's financial condition." With respect to this part of the complaint the Court observed: "[U]nlike narcotics informants, for example, whose credibility may often be suspect, the sources of this tax evasion case are much less likely to produce false or untrustworthy information. Thus, whereas some supporting information concerning the credibility of informants in narcotics cases or other common garden varieties of crime may be required, such information is not so necessary in the context of the case before us." Id. at 224.

that the person has no interest in anonymity? What other factors might be relevant to the person's honesty?

In the case of a witness or victim, usually it will be apparent that the person is speaking from firsthand knowledge. But what about an anonymous telephone tip? Is there likely to be a basis for meeting either prong of the *Spinelli* test? Should the magistrate give any weight to such information in making a probable cause determination?

ILLINOIS v. GATES
Certiorari to the Illinois Supreme Court
462 U.S. 213 (1983)

JUSTICE REHNQUIST delivered the opinion of the Court.

Respondents Lance and Susan Gates were indicted for violation of state drug laws after police officers, executing a search warrant, discovered marijuana and other contraband in their automobile and home. Prior to trial the Gates' moved to suppress evidence seized during this search. The Illinois Supreme Court . . . affirmed the decisions of lower state courts . . . granting the motion. . . .

II

. . . Bloomingdale, Ill., is a suburb of Chicago located in DuPage County. On May 3, 1978, the Bloomingdale Police Department received by mail an anonymous handwritten letter which read as follows:

> This letter is to inform you that you have a couple in your town who strictly make their living on selling drugs. They are Sue and Lance Gates, they live on Greenway, off Bloomingdale Rd. in the condominiums. Most of their buys are done in Florida. Sue his wife drives their car to Florida, where she leaves it to be loaded up with drugs, then Lance flies down and drives it back. Sue flies back after she drops the car off in Florida. May 3 she is driving down there again and Lance will be flying down in a few days to drive it back. At the time Lance drives the car back he has the trunk loaded with over $100,000.00 in drugs. Presently they have over $100,000.00 worth of drugs in their basement.
>
> They brag about the fact that they never have to work, and make their entire living on pushers.
>
> I guarantee if you watch them carefully you will make a big catch. They are friends with some big drug dealers, who visit their house often.
>
> Lance & Susan Gates
Greenway in Condominiums

[Detective Mader learned that a person named Lance Gates resided in Bloomingdale and that "L. Gates" had a reservation to fly from Chicago to West Palm Beach, Fla., on May 5.] . . .

Mader then made arrangements with an agent of the Drug Enforcement Administration for surveillance of the May 5 Eastern Airlines flight. The agent later reported to Mader that Gates had boarded the flight, and that federal agents in Florida had observed him arrive in West Palm Beach and take a taxi to the nearby Holiday Inn. They also reported that Gates went to a room registered to one Susan Gates and that, at 7:00 A.M. the next morning, Gates and an unidentified woman left the motel in a Mercury bearing Illinois license plates and drove northbound on an interstate frequently used by travelers to the Chicago area. In addition, the DEA agent informed Mader that the license plate number on the Mercury registered to a Hornet station wagon owned by Gates. The agent also advised Mader that the driving time between West Palm Beach and Bloomingdale was approximately 22 to 24 hours.

Mader signed an affidavit setting forth the foregoing facts, and submitted it to a judge of the Circuit Court of DuPage County, together with a copy of the anonymous letter. The judge of that court thereupon issued a search warrant for the Gates' residence and for their automobile. . . .

At 5:15 A.M. on March 7th, only 36 hours after he had flown out of Chicago, Lance Gates, and his wife, returned to their home in Bloomingdale, driving the car in which they had left West Palm Beach some 22 hours earlier. The Bloomingdale police were awaiting them, searched the trunk of the Mercury, and uncovered approximately 350 pounds of marijuana. A search of the Gates' home revealed marijuana, weapons, and other contraband. . . .

In holding that the affidavit in fact did not contain sufficient additional information to sustain a determination of probable cause, the Illinois court applied a "two-pronged test," derived from our decision in Spinelli v. United States, 393 U.S. 410 (1969). . . .

The Illinois court . . . found that the test had not been satisfied. First, the "veracity" prong was not satisfied because, "there was simply no basis [for] . . . conclud[ing] that the anonymous person [who wrote the letter to the Bloomingdale Police Department] was credible." The court indicated that corroboration by police of details contained in the letter might never satisfy the "veracity" prong, and in any event, could not do so if, as in the present case, only "innocent" details are corroborated. In addition, the letter gave no indication of the basis of its writer's knowledge of the Gates' activities. The Illinois court understood Spinelli as permitting the detail contained in a tip to be used to infer that the informant had a reliable basis for his statements, but it thought that the anonymous letter failed to provide sufficient detail to permit such an inference. Thus, it concluded that no showing of probable cause had been made.

We agree with the Illinois Supreme Court that an informant's "veracity," "reliability" and "basis of knowledge" are all highly relevant in determining the value of his report. We do not agree, however, that these elements should be understood as entirely separate and independent requirements to be rigidly exacted in every case. . . . Rather, . . . they should be understood simply as closely intertwined issues that may usefully illuminate the commonsense, practical question whether there is "probable cause" to believe that contraband or evidence is located in a particular place.

III . . .

[P]robable cause is a fluid concept—turning on the assessment of probabilities in particular factual contexts—not readily, or even usefully, reduced to a neat set of legal rules. Informants' tips doubtless come in many shapes and sizes from many different types of persons. . . . Rigid legal rules are ill-suited to an area of such diversity. . . .

Moreover, the "two-pronged test" directs analysis into two largely independent channels—the informant's "veracity" or "reliability" and his "basis of knowledge." . . . There are persuasive arguments against according these two elements such independent status. Instead, they are better understood as relevant considerations in the totality of circumstances analysis that traditionally has guided probable cause determinations: a deficiency in one may be compensated for, in determining the overall reliability of a tip, by a strong showing as to the other, or by some other indicia of reliability. . . .

If, for example, a particular informant is known for the unusual reliability of his predictions of certain types of criminal activities in a locality, his failure, in a particular case, to thoroughly set forth the basis of his knowledge surely should not serve as an absolute bar to a finding of probable cause based on his tip. . . . Likewise, if an unquestionably honest citizen comes forward with a report of criminal activity—which if fabricated would subject him to criminal liability—we have found rigorous scrutiny of the basis of his knowledge unnecessary. Adams v. Williams, [407 U.S. 143 (1972)]. Conversely, even if we entertain some doubt as to an informant's motives, his explicit and detailed description of alleged wrongdoing, along with a statement that the event was observed first-hand, entitles his tip to greater weight than might otherwise be the case. Unlike a totality of circumstances analysis, which permits a balanced assessment of the relative weights of all the various indicia of reliability (and unreliability) attending an informant's tip, the "two-pronged test" has encouraged an excessively technical dissection of informants' tips,[9] with undue attention being focused on isolated issues that cannot sensibly be divorced from the other facts presented to the magistrate. . . .

We . . . have recognized that affidavits "are normally drafted by nonlawyers in the midst and haste of a criminal investigation. . . . [United States v.] Ventresca, . . . [380 U.S. 102, 108 (1965)]. Likewise, search and arrest warrants long have been issued by persons who are neither lawyers nor judges, and who certainly do not remain abreast of each judicial refinement of the nature of "probable cause." . . . [G]iven the informal, often hurried context in which it must be applied, the "built-in subtleties," Stanley v. State, 19 Md. App. 507, 313 A.2d 847, 860 (Md. App. 1974), of the "two-pronged test" are particularly unlikely to assist magistrates in determining probable cause.

Similarly, we have repeatedly said that after-the-fact scrutiny by courts of the sufficiency of an affidavit should not take the form of de novo review. A magistrate's "determination of probable cause should be paid great deference by reviewing courts." Spinelli, supra, 393 U.S., at 419. . . .

If the affidavits submitted by police officers are subjected to the type

9. Some lower court decisions, brought to our attention by the State, reflect a rigid application of such rules. In Bridger v. State, 503 S.W.2d 801 (Tex. Cr. App. 1974), the affiant had received a confession of armed robbery from one of two suspects in the robbery; in addition, the suspect had given the officer $800 in cash stolen during the robbery. The suspect also told the officer that the gun used in the robbery was hidden in the other suspect's apartment. A warrant issued on the basis of this was invalidated on the ground that the affidavit did not satisfactorily describe how the accomplice had obtained his information regarding the gun.

Likewise, in People v. Palanza, 55 Ill. App. 3d 1028, 13 Ill. Dec. 752, 371 N.E.2d 687 (Ill. App. 1978), the affidavit submitted in support of an application for a search warrant stated that an informant of proven and uncontested reliability had seen, in specifically described premises, "a quantity of a white crystalline substance which was represented to the informant by a white male occupant of the premises to be cocaine. Informant has observed cocaine on numerous occasions in the past and is thoroughly familiar with its appearance. The informant states that the white crystalline powder he observed in the above described premises appeared to him to be cocaine." The warrant issued on the basis of the affidavit was invalidated because "There is no indication as to how the informant or for that matter any other person could tell whether a white substance was cocaine and not some other substance such as sugar or salt." Id., 13 Ill. Dec., at 754, 371 N.E.2d, at 689.

Finally, in People v. Brethauer, 174 Colo. 29, 482 P.2d 369 (Colo. 1971), an informant, stated to have supplied reliable information in the past, claimed that L.S.D. and marijuana were located on certain premises. The affiant supplied police with drugs, which were tested by police and confirmed to be illegal substances. The affidavit setting forth these, and other, facts was found defective under both prongs of Spinelli.

of scrutiny some courts have deemed appropriate, police might well resort to warrantless searches, with the hope of relying on consent or some other exception to the warrant clause that might develop at the time of the search. In addition, the possession of a warrant by officers conducting an arrest or search greatly reduces the perception of unlawful or intrusive police conduct, by assuring "the individual whose property is searched or seized of the lawful authority of the executing officer, his need to search, and the limits of his power to search." United States v. Chadwick, 433 U.S. 1, 9 (1977). Reflecting this preference for the warrant process, the traditional standard for review of an issuing magistrate's probable cause determination has been that so long as the magistrate had a "substantial basis for . . . conclud[ing]" that a search would uncover evidence of wrongdoing, the Fourth Amendment requires no more. Jones v. United States, 362 U.S. 257, 271 (1960). . . . We think reaffirmation of this standard better serves the purpose of encouraging recourse to the warrant procedure and is more consistent with our traditional deference to the probable cause determinations of magistrates than is the "two-pronged test."

Finally, [t]he strictures that inevitably accompany the "two-pronged test" cannot avoid seriously impeding the task of law enforcement. . . . Ordinary citizens, like ordinary witnesses, . . . generally do not provide extensive recitations of the basis of their everyday observations. Likewise, . . . the veracity of persons supplying anonymous tips is by hypothesis largely unknown, and unknowable. As a result, anonymous tips seldom could survive a rigorous application of either of the *Spinelli* prongs. Yet, such tips, particularly when supplemented by independent police investigation, frequently contribute to the solution of otherwise "perfect crimes." While a conscientious assessment of the basis for crediting such tips is required by the Fourth Amendment, a standard that leaves virtually no place for anonymous citizen informants is not.

For all these reasons, we conclude that it is wiser to abandon the "two-pronged test" established by our decisions in *Aguilar* and *Spinelli*.[11] In its place we reaffirm the totality of the circumstances analysis that traditionally has informed probable cause determinations. . . . The task of the issuing magistrate is simply to make a practical, common-sense

---

11. . . . Whether the allegations submitted to the magistrate in *Spinelli* would, under the view we now take, have supported a finding of probable cause, we think it would not be profitable to decide. There are so many variables in the probable cause equation that one determination will seldom be a useful "precedent" for another. Suffice it to say that while we in no way abandon *Spinelli's* concern for the trustworthiness of informers and for the principle that it is the magistrate who must ultimately make a finding of probable cause, we reject the rigid categorization suggested by some of its language.

decision whether, given all the circumstances set forth in the affidavit before him, including the "veracity" and "basis of knowledge" of persons supplying hearsay information, there is a fair probability that contraband or evidence of a crime will be found in a particular place. And the duty of a reviewing court is simply to ensure that the magistrate had a "substantial basis for . . . conclud[ing]" that probable cause existed. Jones v. United States, supra, 362 U.S., at 271. . . .

Our earlier cases illustrate the limits beyond which a magistrate may not venture in issuing a warrant. A sworn statement of an affiant that "he has cause to suspect and does believe that" liquor illegally brought into the United States is located on certain premises will not do. Nathanson v. United States, 290 U.S. 41 (1933). . . . An officer's statement that "affiants have received reliable information from a credible person and believe" that heroin is stored in a home, is likewise inadequate. Aguilar v. Texas, 378 U.S. 108 (1964). As in Nathanson, this is a mere conclusory statement that gives the magistrate virtually no basis at all for making a judgment regarding probable cause. Sufficient information must be presented to the magistrate to allow that official to determine probable cause; his action cannot be a mere ratification of the bare conclusions of others. In order to ensure that such an abdication of the magistrate's duty does not occur, courts must continue to conscientiously review the sufficiency of affidavits on which warrants are issued. But when we move beyond the "bare bones" affidavits present in cases such as Nathanson and Aguilar, this area simply does not lend itself to a prescribed set of rules, like that which had developed from Spinelli. Instead, the flexible, common-sense standard articulated in Jones, Ventresca, and Brinegar better serves the purpose of the Fourth Amendment's probable cause requirement. . . .

IV

Our decisions applying the totality of circumstances analysis outlined above have consistently recognized the value of corroboration of details of an informant's tip by independent police work. . . .

Our decision in Draper v. United States, 358 U.S. 307 (1959), . . . is the classic case on the value of corroborative efforts of police officials.[12] . . .

---

12. The tip in Draper might well not have survived the rigid application of the "two-pronged test" that developed following Spinelli. The only reference to Hereford's reliability was that he had "been engaged as a 'special employee' of the Bureau of Narcotics at Denver for about six months, and from time to time gave information to [the police] for small sums of money, and that [the officer] had always found the information given

The showing of probable cause in the present case was fully as compelling as that in *Draper*. Even standing alone, the facts obtained through the independent investigation of Mader and the DEA at least suggested that the Gates were involved in drug trafficking. In addition to being a popular vacation site, Florida is well-known as a source of narcotics and other illegal drugs. . . . Lance Gates' flight to Palm Beach, his brief, overnight stay in a motel, and apparent immediate return north to Chicago in the family car, conveniently awaiting him in West Palm Beach, is as suggestive of a prearranged drug run, as it is of an ordinary vacation trip.

In addition, the magistrate could rely on the anonymous letter, which had been corroborated in major part by Mader's efforts—just as had occurred in *Draper*.[13] The Supreme Court of Illinois reasoned that *Draper* involved an informant who had given reliable information on previous occasions, while the honesty and reliability of the anonymous informant in this case were unknown to the Bloomingdale police. While this distinction might be an apt one at the time the police department received the anonymous letter, it became far less significant after Mader's independent investigative work occurred.[30] The corroboration of the letter's predictions that the Gates' car would be in Florida, that Lance Gates would fly to Florida in the next day or so, and that he would drive the car north toward Bloomingdale all indicated, albeit not with certainty, that the informant's other assertions also were true. . . . This may well not be the type of "reliability" or "veracity" necessary to satisfy some views of the veracity prong" of *Spinelli*, but we think it suffices for the practical, common-sense judgment called for in making a probable cause determination. It is enough, for purposes of assessing probable cause, that "corroboration through other sources of information reduced the chances of a reckless or prevaricating tale," thus providing "a substantial

---

by Hereford to be accurate and reliable." 358 U.S., at 309. Likewise, the tip gave no indication of how Hereford came by his information. At most, the detailed and accurate predictions in the tip indicated that, however Hereford obtained his information, it was reliable.

13. The Illinois Supreme Court thought that the verification of details contained in the anonymous letter in this case amounted only to "the corroboration of innocent activity," and that this was insufficient to support a finding of probable cause. We are inclined to agree, however, with the observation of Justice Moran in his dissenting opinion that "In this case, just as in *Draper*, seemingly innocent activity became suspicious in the light of the initial tip." And it bears noting that *all* of the corroborating detail established in *Draper*, supra, was of entirely innocent activity. . . .

This is perfectly reasonable. . . . In making a determination of probable cause the relevant inquiry is not whether particular conduct is "innocent" or "guilty," but the degree of suspicion that attaches to particular types of non-criminal acts.

30. Earlier in the opinion the Court expressed agreement with the Illinois court's conclusion that the letter, standing alone, was insufficient to establish probable cause.— Eds.

basis for crediting the hearsay." Jones v. United States, supra, 362 U.S., at 269, 271. . . .

Finally, the anonymous letter contained a range of details relating not just to easily obtained facts and conditions existing at the time of the tip, but to future actions of third parties ordinarily not easily predicted. The letter writer's accurate information as to the travel plans of each of the Gates was of a character likely obtained only from the Gates themselves, or from someone familiar with their not entirely ordinary travel plans. If the informant had access to accurate information of this type a magistrate could properly conclude that it was not unlikely that he also had access to reliable information of the Gates' alleged illegal activities.[14] Of course, the Gates' travel plans might have been learned from a talkative neighbor or travel agent; under the "two-pronged test" developed from *Spinelli*, the character of the details in the anonymous letter might well not permit a sufficiently clear inference regarding the letter writer's "basis of knowledge." But . . . probable cause does not demand the certainty we associate with formal trials. It is enough that there was a fair probability that the writer of the anonymous letter had obtained his entire story either from the Gates or someone they trusted. And corroboration of major portions of the letter's predictions provides just this probability. The judgment of the Supreme Court of Illinois therefore must be

Reversed.

JUSTICE WHITE, concurring in the judgment. . . .

. . . Although I agree that the warrant should be upheld, I reach this conclusion in accordance with the *Aguilar-Spinelli* framework.

A . . .

I agree with the Court . . . that Lance Gates' flight to Palm Beach, an area known to be a source of narcotics, the brief overnight stay in a motel, and apparent immediate return North, suggest a pattern that trained law-enforcement officers have recognized as indicative of illicit drug-dealing activity.

Even, however, had the corroboration related only to completely innocuous activities, this fact alone would not preclude the issuance of

---

14. The dissent seizes on one inaccuracy in the anonymous informant's letter—its statement that Sue Gates would fly from Florida to Illinois, when in fact she drove—and argues that the probative value of the entire tip was undermined by this allegedly "material mistake." We have never required that informants used by the police be infallible, and can see no reason to impose such a requirement in this case. Probable cause, particularly when police have obtained a warrant, simply does not require the perfection the dissent finds necessary. . . .

a valid warrant. The critical issue is not whether the activities observed by the police are innocent or suspicious. Instead, the proper focus should be on whether the actions of the suspects, whatever their nature, give rise to an inference that the informant is credible and that he obtained his information in a reliable manner.

Thus, in *Draper* . . . [t]he Court held that the police had probable cause to arrest Draper . . . even though the police had seen nothing more than the totally innocent act of a man getting off a train carrying a briefcase. As we later explained in *Spinelli*, the important point was that the corroboration showed both that the informant was credible, i.e. that he "had not been fabricating his report out of whole cloth," *Spinelli*, supra, 393 U.S., at 417, . . . and that he had an adequate basis of knowledge for his allegations, "since the report was of the sort which in common experience may be recognized as having been obtained in a reliable way." Id., at 417-418. . . . The fact that the informer was able to predict, two days in advance, the exact clothing Draper would be wearing dispelled the possibility that his tip was just based on rumor or "an off-hand remark heard at a neighborhood bar." Id., at 417. . . . Probably Draper had planned in advance to wear these specific clothes so that an accomplice could identify him. A clear inference could there-fore be drawn that the informant was either involved in the criminal scheme himself or that he otherwise had access to reliable, inside infor-mation.[22]

. . . [In the present case, after the police had corroborated the

---

22. Thus, as interpreted in *Spinelli*, the Court in *Draper* held that there was probable cause because "the kind of information related by the informant [was] not generally sent ahead of a person's arrival in a city except to those who are intimately connected with making careful arrangements for meeting him." *Spinelli*, supra, 393 U.S., at 426, . . . (White, J., concurring). As I said in *Spinelli*, the conclusion that *Draper* itself was based on this fact is far from inescapable. Prior to *Spinelli*, *Draper* was susceptible to the interpretation that it stood for the proposition that "the existence of the tenth and critical fact is made sufficiently probable to justify the issuance of a warrant by verifying nine other facts coming from the same source." *Spinelli*, supra, at 426-427, (White, J., concurring). But it now seems clear that the Court in *Spinelli* rejected this reading of *Draper*.

Justice Brennan . . . erroneously interprets my *Spinelli* concurrence as espousing the view that "corroboration of certain details in a tip may be sufficient to satisfy the veracity, but not the basis of knowledge prong of *Aguilar*." Others have made the same mistake. See, e.g., Comment, 20 Am. Crim. L. Rev. 99, 105 (1982). I did not say that corroboration could *never* satisfy the basis of knowledge prong. My concern was, and still is, that the prong might be deemed satisfied on the basis of corroboration of infor-mation that does not in any way suggest that the informant had an adequate basis of knowledge for his report. If, however, as in *Draper*, the police corroborate information from which it can be inferred that the informant's tip was grounded on inside information, this corroboration is sufficient to satisfy the basis of knowledge prong. . . .

information about the Gates' travel plans,][23] the magistrate could reasonably have inferred, as he apparently did, that the informant, who had specific knowledge of these unusual travel plans, did not make up his story and that he obtained his information in a reliable way. It is theoretically possible, as respondents insist, that the tip could have been supplied by a "vindictive travel agent" and that the Gates' activities, although unusual, might not have been unlawful. But *Aguilar* and *Spinelli*, like our other cases, do not require that certain guilt be established before a warrant may properly be issued. . . . I therefore conclude that the judgment of the Illinois Supreme Court invalidating the warrant must be reversed.

B . . .

The Court reasons . . . that the "veracity" and "basis of knowledge" tests are not independent, and that a deficiency as to one can be compensated for by a strong showing as to the other. . . . If this is so, then it must follow a fortiori that "the affidavit of an officer, known by the magistrate to be honest and experienced, stating that [contraband] is located in a certain building" must be acceptable. *Spinelli*, 393 U.S., at 424 (White, J., concurring). It would be "quixotic" if a similar statement from an honest informant, but not one from an honest officer, could furnish probable cause. Ibid. But we have repeatedly held that the unsupported assertion or belief of an officer does not satisfy the probable cause requirement. See, e.g., Whiteley v. Warden, 401 U.S. 560, 564-565, Jones v. United States, 362 U.S. 257, 269 (1960); Nathanson v. United States, 290 U.S. 41 (1933). Thus, this portion of today's holding can be read as implicitly rejecting the teachings of these prior holdings.

The Court may not intend so drastic a result. Indeed, the Court expressly reaffirms . . . the validity of cases such as *Nathanson* that have held that, no matter how reliable the affiant-officer may be, a warrant should not be issued unless the affidavit discloses supporting facts and circumstances. The Court limits these cases to situations involving affidavits containing only "bare conclusions" and holds that, if an affidavit contains anything more, it should be left to the issuing magistrate to decide, based solely on "practical[ity]" and "common-sense," whether there is a fair probability that contraband will be found in a particular place. . . .

Thus, as I read the majority opinion, it appears that the question

23. Justice Stevens is correct . . . that one of the informant's predictions proved to be inaccurate. However, I agree with the Court . . . that an informant need not be infallible.

whether the probable cause standard is to be diluted is left to the common-sense judgments of issuing magistrates. I am reluctant to approve any standard that does not expressly require, as a prerequisite to issuance of a warrant, some showing of facts from which an inference may be drawn that the informant is credible and that his information was obtained in a reliable way. The Court is correctly concerned with the fact that some lower courts have been applying Aguilar-Spinelli in an unduly rigid manner.[26] I believe, however, that with clarification of the rule of cor-roborating information, the lower courts are fully able to properly interpret Aguilar-Spinelli and avoid such unduly-rigid applications. I may be wrong; it ultimately may prove to be the case that the only profitable instruction we can provide to magistrates is to rely on common sense. But the question whether a particular anonymous tip provides the basis for issuance of a warrant will often be a difficult one, and I would at least attempt to provide more precise guidance by clarifying Aguilar-Spinelli and the relationship of those cases with Draper before totally abdicating our re-sponsibility in this area. Hence, I do not join the Court's opinion rejecting the Aguilar-Spinelli rules.

[The dissenting opinion of JUSTICE BRENNAN is omitted.]

JUSTICE STEVENS, with whom JUSTICE BRENNAN joins, dissenting.

The fact that Lance and Sue Gates made a 22-hour nonstop drive from West Palm Beach, Florida, to Bloomingdale, Illinois, only a few hours after Lance had flown to Florida provided persuasive evidence that they were engaged in illicit activity. That fact, however, was not known to the magistrate when he issued the warrant to search their home.

What the magistrate did know at that time was that the anonymous informant had not been completely accurate in his or her predictions. The informant had indicated that "Sue drives their car to Florida where she leaves it to be loaded up with drugs. . . . Sue flies back after she drops the car off in Florida." . . . (emphasis added). Yet Detective Mad-er's affidavit reported that she "left the West Palm Beach area driving the Mercury northbound." . . .

The discrepancy between the informant's predictions and the facts known to Detective Mader is significant for three reasons. First, it cast doubt on the informant's hypothesis that the Gates already had "over $100,000 worth of drugs in their basement." . . . The informant had predicted an itinerary that always kept one spouse in Bloomingdale, sug-

---

26. Bridger v. State, 503 S.W.2d 801 (Tex. Cr. App. 1974), and People v. Palanza, 55 Ill. App. 3d 1028, 13 Ill. Dec. 752, 371 N.E.2d 687 (Ill. App. 1978), which the court describes [in footnote 9] appear to me to be excellent examples of overly-technical applications of the Aguilar-Spinelli standard. The holdings in these cases could easily be disapproved without reliance on a "totality of the circumstances" analysis.

gesting that the Gates did not want to leave their home unguarded because something valuable was hidden within. That inference obviously could not be drawn when it was known that the pair was actually together over a thousand miles from home.

Second, the discrepancy made the Gates' conduct seem substantially less unusual than the informant had predicted it would be. It would have been odd if, as predicted, Sue had driven down to Florida on Wednesday, left the car, and flown right back to Illinois. But the mere facts that Sue was in West Palm Beach with the car, that she was joined by her husband at the Holiday Inn on Friday, and that the couple drove north together the next morning are neither unusual nor probative of criminal activity.

Third, the fact that the anonymous letter contained a material mistake undermines the reasonableness of relying on it as a basis for making a forcible entry into a private home.

NOTES AND QUESTIONS

1. Do you agree with Justice White that the *Spinelli* test was in fact satisfied in *Gates?* If not, does the disagreement between Justice White and the dissenters lend support to the majority's decision to do away with the test? If Justice White is correct, why should the Court be interested in repudiating the test? See Grano, Probable Cause and Common Sense: A Reply to the Critics of Illinois v. Gates, 17 U. Mich. J.L. Reform 465 (1984).

2. What precisely were the problems with the two-prong test? Did it fail to accord sufficient deference to the judgment of magistrates? Did the test unduly hinder law enforcement activities by creating too high or too difficult a burden of proof for affiants to meet? Was the test inherently too complex for application by laypersons on a day-to-day basis? To the extent that lower courts have reached undesirable results in applying the *Spinelli* test, does the fault inhere in the test itself? Or is the problem the Supreme Court's own lack of clarity about the test and perhaps the Court's attempt to reconcile unreconcilable precedents?

3. Note that Justice Rehnquist acknowledges "that an informant's 'veracity,' 'reliability,' and 'basis of knowledge' are all highly relevant in determining the value of his report." Given this acknowledgment, is *Gates* really very much of a departure from *Spinelli?* See Moylan, Illinois v. Gates: What It Did and What It Did Not Do, 20 Crim. L. Bull. 93 (1984).

Consider Massachusetts v. Upton, 466 U.S. 727 (1984) (per curiam), which arose out of the following facts:

At noon on September 11, 1980, Lt. Beland of the Yarmouth Police Department assisted in the execution of a search warrant for a motel room reserved by one Richard Kelleher at the Snug Harbor Motel in West Yarmouth. The search produced several items of identification, including credit cards, belonging to two persons whose homes had recently been burglarized. Other items taken in the burglaries, such as jewelry, silver and gold, were not found at the motel.

At 3:20 P.M. on the same day, Lt. Beland received a call from an unidentified female who told him that there was "a motor home full of stolen stuff" parked behind #5 Jefferson Ave., the home of respondent George Upton and his mother. She stated that the stolen items included jewelry, silver and gold. As set out in Lt. Beland's affidavit in support of a search warrant:

> She further stated that George Upton was going to move the motor home any time now because of the fact that Ricky Kelleher's motel room was raided and that George Upton had purchased these stolen items from Ricky Kelleher. This unidentified female stated that she had seen the stolen items but refused to identify herself because "he'll kill me," referring to George Upton. I then told this unidentified female that I knew who she was, giving her the name of Lynn Alberico, who I had met on May 16, 1980, at George Upton's repair shop off Summer St., in Yarmouthport. She was identified to me by George Upton as being his girlfriend, Lynn Alberico. The unidentified female admitted that she was the girl that I had named, stating that she was surprised that I knew who she was. She then told me that she'd broken up with George Upton and wanted to burn him. She also told me that she wouldn't give me her address or phone number but that she would contact me in the future, if need be. . . .

Following the phone call, Lt. Beland went to Upton's house to verify that a motor home was parked on the property. Then, while other officers watched the premises, Lt. Beland prepared the application for a search warrant, setting out all the information noted above in an accompanying affidavit. He also attached the police reports on the two prior burglaries, along with lists of the stolen property. . . . [Id. at 728-730.]

The Court reversed the Massachusetts Supreme Court's holding that the affidavit was insufficient to establish probable cause. In the course of its opinion, the Court emphasized that in *Gates* "[w]e did not merely refine or qualify the 'two-pronged test.' We rejected it as hypertechnical and divorced from 'the factual and practical considerations of everyday life on which reasonable and prudent men, not legal technicians, act.' Brinegar v. United States, 338 U.S. 160 (1949)." 466 U.S. at 732. The Court also reiterated its holding in *Gates* that in determining whether an affidavit establishes probable cause, a reviewing court should apply a "deferential standard of review." Rather than giving the affidavit "after-the-fact, de novo scrutiny," a reviewing court should decide "whether the evidence viewed as a whole provide[s] a 'substantial basis' for the magistrate's finding of probable cause." Id. at 734.

4. Consider both *Spinelli* and *Gates* in assessing whether probable cause to search has been established by the following affidavits:

a. State v. Brown, 96 N.M. 10, 12, 626 P.2d 1312, 1313 (Ct. App. 1981):

"Affiants are currently assigned to the Property Crimes Section [of the Albuquerque Police Department], were [sic] they maintain certain expertise in the investigation of theft related crimes. . . . In this capacity Affiants investigated a Commercial Burglary which occurred at the Alb. Tennis Complex . . . on July 26 . . . in which approximately $6,500.00 worth of various tennis equipment was stolen. On August 16, . . . Affiants were contacted by a confidential informant, who was found to be in possession of a tennis racket that had been taken in this burglary, and the confidential informant advised that he learned that this burglary had been committed by Marvin and Melvin Brown. This confidential informant wishes to remain anonymous for reasons of personal safety, however, he is deemed reliable in that he is a member in good standing in the community[,] has no arrest record in the community, is not presently under indictment nor working off any criminal charges. On August 20, . . . the burglary . . . was presented throughout the news media as the Crimestopper 'Crime of the week.' On August 21, . . . Affiants received a crimestopper tip which informed that a cheerleading squad for a football team at John Marshall Community Center . . . had been outfitted with white socks, which match 'John Newcombe' socks which were taken in the burglary. . . . The crimestopper informant further advised that these socks were supplied to the cheerleaders by Marvin and Melvin Brown. On August 22, . . . Affiants received information from another crimestopper informant . . . who advised that Marvin and Melvin Brown have been seen selling tennis equipment and have a large quantity of tennis equipment, that was stolen in the burglary of the Albuquerque Tennis Complex, in the rear bedroom of their residence which is located at 1607 Edith SE."

b. People v. Coleman, 100 Mich. App. 587, 590, 300 N.W.2d 329, 331 (1980):

[T]he affidavit was made by Deputy Sheriff Marvin Rakowski. . . . He reported that upon his arrival on the scene the complainant told him that his restaurant had just been robbed by two men and that the robber had fled across the street toward the Parkside Apartment Complex. One of the robbers fell down within 100 feet of the restaurant after the restaurant owner and one of his employees fired at the robbers. The affidavit further indicated that Officer Letts of the "K-9 Corps" and his tracking dog, Prince, arrived within 30 minutes of the robbery and were directed to the area where the robber had fallen. The robbers' tracks were in an area of ground that had no other fresh human tracks. Officer Letts and Prince in about 13 minutes tracked the footprints to the Parkside apartment at 185 Parkside Court. Prince's actions were observed by the [affiant]. . . . The police officers . . . saw two persons standing by an open window inside the apartment.

c. If you think that it is strange for a dog to be an informant, consider United States v. Sentovich, 677 F.2d 834, 835-836 (11th Cir. 1982):

The ubiquitous DEA agent Paul Markonni[31] once again sticks his nose into the drug trade. This time he is on the scent of appellant Mitchell Sentovich's drug courier activities. We now learn that among Markonni's many talents is an olfactory sense we in the past attributed only to canines. . . . Zeke,[1] Rocky,[2] Bodger and Nebuchadnezzar,[3] and the drug dogs of the southeast[4] had best beware. Markonni's sensitive proboscis may soon put them in the dog pound.

An anonymous telephone caller [reported] . . . that three males carrying seven suitcases full of marijuana would leave the Fort Myers airport at seven the next morning. The next day local police, proving they had their noses to the grindstone, . . . dogged Sentovich and two other men, Mark Diefenthaler and Randall Alander, at the airport. The men had purchased tickets for flights . . . to Montana, via Atlanta. Police located a cart with luggage to be put on the flight to Atlanta. Not having . . . . Markonni about, they had to fall back on a mere canine, Rocky, with 50-60 hours training in marijuana detection, who sniffed bags on the cart. . . . Rocky alerted strongly to two bags belonging to Diefenthaler. Police detained Diefenthaler. Alander, without being asked to do so, left the plane. . . . Sentovich, showing what a dog-eat-dog world this is, abandoned the men to their fate and flew on to Atlanta. . . .

31. As of 1981, Agent Paul Markonni had "worked for seven years with DEA airport details," during which time he "participated in more than 400 arrests of couriers carrying drugs through airports." United States v. Sanford, 658 F.2d 342, 343 (5th Cir. 1981). One such arrest eventually led to an appellate opinion beginning, "In this appeal we are once again asked to determine whether evidence taken pursuant to one of the unerring hunches of the ubiquitous Agent Paul Markonni should have been suppressed on the ground that it was taken in violation of the Fourth Amendment." United States v. Williams, 647 F.2d 588, 589 (5th Cir. 1981). As usual, the court concluded that Agent Markonni had not violated the fourth amendment. For more on Agent Markonni and the development and use of the drug courier profile, see Cloud, Search and Seizure by the Numbers: The Drug Courier Profile and Judicial Review of Investigative Formulas, 65 B.U.L. Rev. 843 (1985).—EDS.
1. See United States v. Goldstein, 635 F.2d 356 (5th Cur.), cert. denied, 452 U.S. 962 (1981).
2. See infra.
3. The Court understands that Bodger and Nebuchadnezzar are in training.
4. See United States v. Viera, 644 F.2d 509 (5th Cir.), cert. denied, 102 S. Ct. 332 (1981).

[When the plane arrived in Atlanta, Agent Paul Markonni, who had been informed of the preceding events, had the airline] locate Sentovich's bags. Markonni . . . applied his proboscis to the three bags and alerted to two of them because of the odor of marijuana.

Markonni's affidavit for a search warrant contained the above information, an allegation that he "had smelled marijuana more than 100 times over the past eleven years," and an allegation that "Sentovich was a documented drug violator and domestic drug courier." Id. at 836 & n.7.

5. If the "informant" who provides information to the arresting or searching officer is also a law enforcement officer, there is no need for a special showing that the informant is a credible, trustworthy individual. See United States v. Ventresca, 380 U.S. 102 (1965). Moreover, an officer who is relying on a radio or other communication from another officer is justified in making an arrest or a search without personal knowledge of the facts constituting probable cause. The victim of the search or seizure, however, can still challenge the initial probable cause determination. See Whiteley v. Warden, 401 U.S. 560 (1971).

3. The Warrant Process in General

a. The Oath Requirement

The fourth amendment warrant clause requires that probable cause be "supported by Oath or affirmation." Usually this requirement is satisfied by information contained in a police officer's affidavit accompanying the request for a warrant. In some instances, however, the officer may in fact have sufficient information to establish probable cause but fail to include enough of that information in the affidavit. For example, in order to preserve the anonymity of an undercover agent, the affidavit may be intentionally vague about the circumstances surrounding the agent's purchase of narcotics. In such a case, if the magistrate is not satisfied with the showing in the affidavit, supplemental oral testimony provided by the officer under oath would appear to satisfy the literal requirement of the fourth amendment. See Frazier v. Roberts, 441 F.2d 1224, 1226 (8th Cir. 1971). Some courts, however, require that all of the information be in writing. See, e.g., Orr v. State, 382 So. 2d 860, 861 (Fla. App. 1980); Thomson v. Onstad, 182 Mont. 119, 122, 594 P.2d 1137, 1139 (1979) (both relying on state constitutional provisions), Should there be a preference for a *written* sworn statement?

Some jurisdictions authorize magistrates to issue warrants on the basis of information communicated orally from a police officer via telephone or radio. The information is recorded verbatim, and if the magistrate finds that probable cause exists, the officer will sign the magistrate's name to a copy of the warrant that the officer has prepared. See, e.g., Fed. R. Crim. P. 41(c)(2). What problems, if any, do you see with the telephone warrant process? See Israel, Legislative Regulation of Searches and Seizures: The Michigan Proposals, 73 Mich. L. Rev. 221, 258-263 (1974); Note, The Cost of the Use of Unrecorded Oral Testimony to Establish Probable Cause for Search Warrants, 70 Va. L. Rev. 1603 (1984).

b. The Magistrate

The magistrate must be "neutral and detached." Johnson v. United States, 333 U.S. 10, 14 (1946). See, e.g., Connally v. Georgia, 429 U.S. 245 (1977), where a search warrant that was issued by a magistrate who received a five dollar fee for issuing a warrant but no fee for refusing to issue a warrant was declared invalid; and Coolidge v. New Hampshire, 403 U.S. 443 (1971), where a search warrant issued by the state attorney general acting, pursuant to statutory authority, as a justice of the peace was declared invalid when the attorney general had already taken over investigation of the case.

What if the attorney general in Coolidge had not taken over the investigation? Should the executive functions of the job automatically disqualify an attorney general from issuing warrants? What should the result be if the magistrate moonlights as a private security guard?

c. The Particularity Requirement

The fourth amendment requires that warrants "particularly describ[e] the place to be searched, and the persons or things to be seized."[32] The Supreme Court has said, with respect to the place to be searched, "It is enough if the description is such that the officer with a search warrant can, with reasonable effort, ascertain and identify the place intended." Steele v. United States, 267 U.S. 498, 503 (1925).

The most common type of problem that arises with description of the place to be searched is that a description that appears to be adequate on its face may turn out to be ambiguous. For example, the warrant may

---

32. The nature of the particularity requirement with respect to the interception of oral communications is considered at pages 607-608 infra.

describe the premises as a red brick single family dwelling located at 239 Elm Street. Yet, when the police arrive to execute the warrant, they may discover that 239 Elm is a duplex and that a red brick single family dwelling is located across the street or next door. If the police have no idea which dwelling to search, the particularity requirement has not been satisfied. If it is reasonably apparent which part of the description is likely to be erroneous, however, a search of the "proper" premises may be permissible. Moreover, if the police failure to discover the ambiguity prior to commencing the search is reasonable, the seizure of evidence from the "wrong" premises is not a fourth amendment violation.[33]

The particularity requirement for items sought to be seized is designed in part to ensure that citizens will not be wrongly deprived of their possessions. In addition, the requirement serves an important function in limiting the legitimate scope of searches.[34] For example, if the police are authorized to seize only television sets, they cannot rummage through desk drawers. They must restrict their search to places where television sets are likely to be found. On the other hand, if the object of the search is certain specifically described documents, it would be appropriate to search through desk drawers.

These objectives of preventing wrongful seizure of property and limiting the scope of searches tend to influence the degree of specificity required in particular cases. Thus, for example, courts are likely to require

33. See Maryland v. Garrison, 480 U.S. 79 (1987), where the police had probable cause to search the third-floor apartment of Lawrence McWebb. Without realizing that the third-floor contained *two* apartments, the police obtained a warrant to search " 'the premises known as 2036 Park Avenue third floor apartment.' " In executing the warrant the police initially entered the wrong apartment—one rented by Garrison—and seized controlled substances. In upholding Garrison's conviction, the Court, in an opinion by Justice Stevens, first considered the validity of the warrant: "The validity of the warrant must be assessed on the basis of the information that the officers disclosed, or had a duty to discover and to disclose, to the issuing magistrate. On the basis of that information, we agree with the conclusion of all three Maryland courts that the warrant, insofar as it authorized a search that turned out to be ambiguous in scope, was valid when it issued." Id. at 85-86.

The Court then turned to the execution of the warrant: "[T]he validity of the search of [Garrison's] apartment pursuant to a warrant authorizing the search of the entire third floor depends on whether the officers' failure to realize the overbreadth of the warrant was objectively understandable and reasonable." Id. at 88. After reviewing the facts, the Court concluded that the mistake was reasonable.

Justice Blackmun, in a dissenting opinion joined by Justices Brennan and Marshall, disagreed with the majority's conclusion that the mistake was reasonable. In addition, he argued that the reasonableness of an officer's mistake should not be sufficient to justify the search "with respect to one whom probable cause has not singled out and who is the victim of the officer's error." Id. at 95.

34. The particularity requirement, as Professor LaFave notes, is also closely related to the probable cause requirement. A vague, general description may indicate that the police do not have a factual basis for their suspicions. See 2 W. LaFave, Search and Seizure: A Treatise on the Fourth Amendment §4.11(a), at 336 (2d ed. 1987).

a less detailed description of narcotics than of items that people might innocently possess, and a less detailed description of stolen television sets than of business records. See generally 2 W. LaFave, Search and Seizure: A Treatise on the Fourth Amendment §4.6, at 233-260 (2d ed. 1987).

The fact that a warrant requires a particular description of items to be seized does not mean that the police are absolutely precluded from seizing other items. See pages 638-647 infra, where we consider the *plain view doctrine.*

d. Timing of Execution

Court rules or statutes in some jurisdictions require that search warrants be executed within a specified period of time. See, e.g., Fed. R. Crim. P. 41(c)(1) (10 days). The fourth amendment does not explicitly address the timing question, but the probable cause requirement carries with it an implicit time limitation: There must be probable cause to believe that the items sought are located in the place to be searched at the time of the search.[35] Depending on the mobility of the objects and what, if anything, the police know about a suspect's plans to move them, the allowable time may be even shorter than that permitted by nonconstitutional rule or statute.[36]

Although the facts supporting probable cause to search may grow "stale," a similar problem is unlikely to exist with respect to probable cause to arrest. It is conceivable, however, that subsequent investigation could raise doubts about an initial probable cause finding.

Another matter frequently regulated by rule or statute is the time of day at which warrants may be executed. Such regulation typically requires, as a condition of nighttime execution, either a showing of need to execute the warrant during the nighttime or some relatively high degree of certainty that the objects of the search will be discovered. See 2 W. LaFave, Search and Seizure: A Treatise on the Fourth Amendment §4.7(b), at 263-267 (2d ed. 1987). On the question whether the fourth

35. See United States v. Nepstead, 424 F.2d 269 (9th Cir. 1970). The Supreme Court has not addressed this precise issue. It has, however, dealt with a closely analogous point. In Sgro v. United States, 287 U.S. 206 (1932), officers obtained a warrant on July 6 to search a hotel room for intoxicating liquor but they did not execute the warrant. Three weeks later they obtained a new warrant on the basis of the same affidavit that had been presented to the magistrate on July 6. Holding the search was illegal, the Court stated that "the proof must be of facts so closely related to the time of the issue of the warrant as to justify a finding of probable cause at that time." Id. at 210.

36. See United States v. Nepstead, 424 F.2d 269, 270-271 (9th Cir. 1970) (collecting cases). But see State v. Morgan, 222 Kan. 149, 154, 563 P.2d 1056, 1060-1061 (1977).

amendment requires some limitation on nighttime searches, see pages 810-811 infra.

e. The Knock and Announce Requirement

State and federal statutes typically provide that prior to making an entry, the police should knock and announce their purpose, unless there are exigent circumstances that justify immediate entry. See, e.g., Cal. Penal Code §§843, 844; 18 U.S.C. §3109 (1988).[37] Such exigent circumstances include the officers' reasonable fear for their own safety and their reasonable belief that an announcement might result in the escape of a suspect or the destruction of evidence. What purposes are served by a knock and announcement requirement?

Although the Supreme Court has never expressly so held, it seems well accepted that the fourth amendment itself requires the police to knock and announce their purpose in the absence of exigent circumstances.[38] It is not clear, however, as a matter of constitutional law (and frequently as a matter of statutory law) precisely what the contours of the exigencies are. For example, when the asserted exigency is fear for an officer's safety, is it enough that the officer knows the occupant is armed, or must the officer have some reason for believing that the suspect will probably resist? When the asserted exigency is destruction of evidence, is it sufficient to show that the evidence being sought is easily destructible (e.g., narcotics; gambling records, which may be on flash paper), or must there be some reason in addition to the nature of the evidence for believing that it may be destroyed?

Usually the decision whether to proceed with an unannounced entry is made by the police officer at the time of entry. A few jurisdictions,

---

37. In interpreting these statutes, courts tend not to distinguish among the types of unannounced entry. See, e.g., Ker v. California, 374 U.S. 23 (1963) (for purposes of analyzing legality of entry, Court assumed entry with use of pass key was equivalent of "breaking").

38. In Ker v. California, 374 U.S. 23 (1968), the Court upheld police officers' unannounced entry into defendants' house. Justice Clark, in an opinion joined by Justices Black, White, and Stewart, relied on "the officers' belief that Ker was in possession of narcotics, which could be quickly and easily destroyed" and evidence suggesting that Ker "might well have been suspecting the police," to conclude that "in the particular circumstances of this case the officers' method of entry . . . was not unreasonable under the standards of the Fourth Amendment as applied to the States through the Fourteenth Amendment." Id. at 40-41. Justice Harlan, without reaching the fourth amendment issue, concurred in the result on the ground that the entry had not violated the more flexible " 'fundamental' fairness" mandate of the fourteenth amendment. The remaining four justices, in an opinion by Justice Brennan, disagreed with the factual conclusion that exigent circumstances were present, and thus they concluded that the entry violated the fourth amendment.

however, have statutes that authorize magistrates to issue "no-knock" warrants.[39] Do you think that such a provision is desirable?

If the premises are vacant, if the police are refused entry, or if after a reasonable time there has been no response to the announcement,[40] the police may enter by force.[41] See United States v. Gervato, 474 F.2d 40 (3d Cir. 1973).

Should it be regarded as a violation of the knock and announce requirement for a police officer to gain entry by a subterfuge? Consider, for example, the situation of a plainclothes officer with a search warrant for narcotics who comes to the door, knocks, and gains entry on the pretext of wanting to purchase marijuana or read the gas meter.

f. Dealing with People on the Premises

On some occasions the owner of the premises, or the owner's guests or other persons, will be present when the police are ready to begin a search; or they may arrive during the course of a search. In some instances probable cause may exist to search these people.[42] For example, if the police have probable cause to search a hotel room for narcotics, and if

---

39. E.g., N. Dak. Cen. Code §19-03.1-32(3) (Cum. Supp. 1989) (part of North Dakota's Uniform Controlled Substances Act):

> Any officer authorized to execute a search warrant, without notice of his authority and purpose, may break open an outer or inner door or window of a building, or any part of the building, or anything therein, if the judge or magistrate issuing the warrant has probable cause to believe that if such notice were to be given the property sought in the case *may* be easily and quickly destroyed or disposed of, or that danger to the life or limb of the officer or another *may* result, and has included in the warrant a direction that the officer executing it shall not be required to give such notice. Any officer acting under such warrant, as soon as practicable after entering the premises, shall identify himself and state the purpose of his entering the premises and his authority for doing so.

(Emphasis added.)
40. The police and the courts sometimes regard an unreasonably short time as reasonable, See 2 W. LaFave, Search and Seizure: A Treatise on the Fourth Amendment §4.8(c), at 278-279 (2d ed. 1987) (collecting cases).
41. Of course, in the case of an arrest, the police should have reason to believe that the suspect is present despite the absence of any response to the announcement. See Payton v. New York, 445 U.S. 573 (1980).
42. On other occasions the search may lead to information that establishes probable cause to arrest. For example, if the police discover narcotics and the person present resides at the premises, the police may have probable cause to believe that the resident is in possession of narcotics. Cf. Cimmino v. State, 29 A.D.2d 587, 285 N.Y.S.2d 656 (1967) (during search of tailor shop police discovered betting slips, possession of which was illegal; discovery provided probable cause to arrest defendant, who said he was in charge of establishment). They may then engage in a search of the individual pursuant to his arrest. See Chimel v. California, 395 U.S. 752 (1969).

after announcing their purpose, they enter and discover three people in the room, it is arguably reasonable to search the occupants as well as the room for narcotics.[43] Indeed, sometimes warrants specifically authorize the search of a place and any persons present.[44] On the other hand, there may be situations in which the police have no basis for believing that particular individuals possess the items sought or are in any way involved in criminal activity. Consider, for example, a case in which the police enter a neighborhood pub during business hours with a warrant to search the pub for narcotics. Assuming that the police do not have probable cause to search or arrest any particular patron, are there nonetheless circumstances under which the police should be able to detain, remove, frisk or otherwise interfere with the patrons' freedom simply because of their presence at the scene of the search? See Ybarra v. Illinois, at page 769 infra, and Michigan v. Summers, page 775 infra.

g. Reexamination of the Probable Cause Determination

Consider the situation in which a magistrate issues a warrant and a court subsequently determines that the information presented to the magistrate was not sufficient to constitute probable cause. Clearly the police should not be able to rely on new information discovered during the execution of the warrant to argue that there was probable cause. However, in a jurisdiction that permits the use of oral testimony to supplement information contained in an affidavit, should the police be permitted, following the execution of the warrant, to present to the court information that they possessed at the time they sought the warrant but that they did not include in the affidavit? Consider Whiteley v. Warden, 401 U.S. 560 (1971):

> Under the cases of this Court, an otherwise insufficient affidavit cannot be rehabilitated by testimony concerning information possessed by the affiant when he sought the warrant but not disclosed to the issuing magistrate. See Aguilar v. Texas, 378 U.S. 108, 109 n.1. A contrary rule would, of course, render the warrant requirements of the Fourth Amendment meaningless.[45] [Id. at 565 n.8.]

43. See United States v. Miller, 298 A.2d 34 (D.C. App. 1972).
44. See, e.g., Ybarra v. Illinois, 444 U.S. 85 (1979) (warrant issued for search of tavern and bartender).
45. The question whether the affidavit could have been rehabilitated was not raised by the parties. Indeed, there is no indication that potentially rehabilitating information existed. Thus, the Whiteley statement is dictum, as is a similar statement in Aguilar, on which Whiteley relied. See Aguilar, 378 U.S. at 109 n.1 (no evidence that there existed additional information not presented to magistrate). Aguilar, in turn, cited as its authority

Do you agree?

Even though the police cannot rehabilitate a deficient affidavit, a defendant may challenge a facially sufficient affidavit. In Franks v. Delaware, 438 U.S. 154 (1978), the Supreme Court held that if

> the defendant makes a substantial preliminary showing that a false statement knowingly and intentionally, or with reckless disregard for the truth, was included by the affiant in the warrant affidavit, and if the allegedly false statement is necessary to the finding of probable cause, the Fourth Amendment requires that a hearing be held at the defendant's request. In the event that at the hearing the allegation of perjury or reckless disregard is established by the defendant by a preponderance of the evidence, and, with the affidavit's false material set to one side, the affidavit's remaining content is insufficient to establish probable cause, the search warrant must be voided and the fruits of the search excluded to the same extent as if probable cause was lacking on the face of the affidavit. [Id. at 155-156.]

Is *Franks* inconsistent with the *Whiteley* dictum quoted supra? Consider the observation of Justice Rehnquist, dissenting in *Franks:* "If the function of the warrant requirement is to obtain the determination of a neutral magistrate as to whether sufficient grounds have been urged to support the issuance of a warrant, that function is fulfilled at the time the magistrate concludes that the requirement has been met." Id. at 181-182. At the very least, should the government be permitted to rehabilitate an affidavit with preexisting information following a successful *Franks* attack by the defendant?

Why should the defendant be required, as a condition of getting a hearing, to make a "substantial preliminary showing" that grounds for relief exist? What does "substantial" mean? In any event is it reasonable to expect the defendant to show initially (or to prove later) the state of mind of the affiant?

Franks makes it clear that "negligent" or "innocent" falsehoods will not invalidate a facially sufficient affidavit. With respect to "innocent" or "reasonable" mistakes, the Court's conclusion seems sound. It has never been suggested that probable cause requires certainty. Moreover, police officers who act on the basis of a reasonable belief are doing precisely what we want them to do. But why should "negligent" mistakes not count? Isn't a negligent mistake an "unreasonable" mistake? And if a police officer is acting unreasonably, how can the search and seizure meet the fourth amendment requirement of reasonableness?

"Giordenello v. United States, 357 U.S. 480, 486; 79 C.J.S. 872 (collecting cases)." Neither *Giordenello* nor the cases or discussion in CJS, however, has anything to do with the rehabilitation issue.—EDS.

Why should the false statement have to be critical to the probable cause finding? At least if the false statement was intentionally made, is not the entire affidavit suspect? Even if the truth of sufficient critical facts is not in doubt, should courts condone perjury? Cf. United States v. Karo, 468 U.S. 705 (1984) (if the affidavit for a warrant is based on both legally and illegally obtained evidence, warrant is valid if there is sufficient untainted evidence to establish probable cause).

4. The Warrant Process for Interception of Oral Communication

In Berger v. New York, 388 U.S. 41 (1967), the Supreme Court reversed the defendant's conviction, which had been obtained in part on the basis of conversations overheard as a result of electronic eavesdropping. The police had installed electronic eavesdropping devices pursuant to a warrant that complied with a New York statute authorizing warrants for electronic surveillance for up to two months upon a showing of "reasonable ground to believe that evidence of crime may thus be obtained." N.Y. Code Crim. Proc. §813a. The Court, in an opinion by Justice Clark, identified a number of constitutional deficiencies in the statute:

> First, . . . eavesdropping is authorized without requiring belief that any particular offense has been or is being committed; nor that the "property" sought, the conversations, be particularly described. The purpose of the probable-cause requirement of the Fourth Amendment, to keep the state out of constitutionally protected areas until it has reason to believe that a specific crime has been or is being committed, is thereby wholly aborted. Likewise the statute's failure to describe with particularity the conversations sought gives the officer a roving commission to "seize" any and all conversations. It is true that the statute requires the naming of "the person or persons whose communications, conversations or discussions are to be overheard or recorded. . . ." But this does no more than identify the person whose constitutionally protected area is to be invaded rather than "particularly describing" the communications, conversations, or discussions to be seized. As with general warrants this leaves too much to the discretion of the officer executing the order. Secondly, authorization of eavesdropping for a two-month period is the equivalent of a series of intrusions, searches, and seizures pursuant to a single showing of probable cause. Prompt execution is also avoided. During such a long and continuous (24 hours a day) period the conversations of any and all persons coming into the area covered by the device will be seized indiscriminately and without regard to their connection with the crime under investigation.

Moreover, the statute permits, and there were authorized here, extensions of the original two-month period—presumably for two months each—on a mere showing that such extension is "in the public interest." Apparently the original grounds on which the eavesdrop order was initially issued also form the basis of the renewal. This we believe insufficient without a showing of present probable cause for the continuance of the eavesdrop. Third, the statute places no termination date on the eavesdrop once the conversation sought is seized. This is left entirely in the discretion of the officer. Finally, the statute's procedure, necessarily because its success depends on secrecy, has no requirement for notice as do conventional warrants, nor does it overcome this defect by requiring some showing of special facts. . . . Nor does the statute provide for a return on the warrant thereby leaving full discretion in the officer as to the use of seized conversations of innocent as well as guilty parties. In short, the statute's blanket grant of permission to eavesdrop is without adequate judicial supervision or protective procedures. [Id. at 58-60.]

The year after *Berger* was decided, Congress enacted Title III of the Omnibus Crime Control and Safe Streets Act of 1968, 18 U.S.C. §§2515-2518 (1988), which permits and regulates electronic eavesdropping. The statute, inter alia, defines offenses for which investigation by electronic eavesdropping may be appropriate, has detailed provisions governing the application for a warrant (including, e.g., required statements documenting the need for electronic surveillance, the nature of conversations sought, and the names of the persons from whom conversations are sought), a requirement that an order for electronic surveillance be based on probable cause and particularly describe the conversations sought, and provisions designed to minimize the extent of the intrusion by electronic surveillance. The Supreme Court has had several occasions to interpret various Title III provisions, see, e.g., Scott v. United States, 436 U.S. 128 (1978) (compliance with minimization requirement depends on "reasonableness of the actual interception and not on whether the agents subjectively intended to minimize their interceptions;" failure to make good faith effort to minimize not necessarily violation of requirement); United States v. Chavez, 416 U.S. 562 (1974) (violation of §2518 by incorrectly identifying authorizing official as assistant attorney general rather than attorney general does not require suppression of evidence derived from interception; failure to comply with Title III requirement does not necessarily make interception "unlawful"), but the Court has not questioned the basic constitutionality of the statute.

D. EXCEPTIONS TO THE WARRANT AND PROBABLE CAUSE REQUIREMENTS

Despite the Supreme Court's frequently expressed preference for use of the warrant process, the vast majority of searches and seizures occur without warrants. Moreover, some of them are considered reasonable even though the police lack probable cause. The materials in the first part of this section consider the extent to which warrantless searches and seizures based on probable cause should be regarded as reasonable. The materials in the remaining parts of the section deal with the relationship between the concept of reasonableness embodied in the first clause of the fourth amendment and the probable cause requirement in the second clause.

1. The Relationship Between Reasonableness and the Warrant Requirement: Warrantless Searches and Seizures with Probable Cause

a. Exigent Circumstances Generally

WARDEN, MARYLAND PENITENTIARY v. HAYDEN[46]
Certiorari to the United States Court of Appeals for the Fourth Circuit
387 U.S. 294 (1967)

MR. JUSTICE BRENNAN delivered the opinion of the Court. . . .

About 8 A.M. on March 17, 1962, an armed robber entered the business premises of the Diamond Cab Company in Baltimore, Maryland. He took some $363 and ran. Two cab drivers in the vicinity, attracted by shouts of "Holdup," followed the man to 2111 Cocoa Lane. One driver notified the company dispatcher by radio that the man was a Negro about 5'8" tall, wearing a light cap and dark jacket, and that he had entered the house on Cocoa Lane. The dispatcher relayed the information to police who were proceeding to the scene of the robbery. Within minutes, police arrived at the house in a number of patrol cars. An officer knocked and announced their presence. Mrs. Hayden answered, and the officers told her they believed that a robber had entered the house, and asked to search the house. She offered no objection.

The officers spread out through the first and second floors and the

---

46. Other aspects of this case are discussed at page 451 supra.—EDS.

cellar in search of the robber. Hayden was found in an upstairs bedroom feigning sleep. He was arrested when the officers on the first floor and in the cellar reported that no other man was in the house. Meanwhile an officer was attracted to an adjoining bathroom by the noise of running water, and discovered a shotgun and a pistol in a flush tank; another officer who, according to the District Court, "was searching the cellar for a man or the money" found in a washing machine a jacket and trousers of the type the fleeing man was said to have worn. A clip of ammunition for the pistol and a cap were found under the mattress of Hayden's bed, and ammunition for the shotgun was found in a bureau drawer in Hayden's room. All these items of evidence were introduced against respondent at his trial.

. . . [N]either the entry without warrant to search for the robber, nor the search for him without warrant was invalid. Under the circumstances of this case, "the exigencies of the situation made that course imperative." McDonald v. United States, 335 U.S. 451, 456. The police were informed that an armed robbery had taken place, and that the suspect had entered 2111 Cocoa Lane less than five minutes before they reached it. They acted reasonably when they entered the house and began to search for a man of the description they had been given and for weapons which he had used in the robbery or might use against them. The Fourth Amendment does not require police officers to delay in the course of an investigation if to do so would gravely endanger their lives or the lives of others. Speed here was essential, and only a thorough search of the house for persons and weapons could have insured that Hayden was the only man present and that the police had control of all weapons which could be used against them or to effect an escape.

. . . Here, the seizures occurred prior to or immediately contemporaneous with Hayden's arrest, as part of an effort to find a suspected felon, armed, within the house into which he had run only minutes before the police arrived. The permissible scope of search must, therefore, at the least, be as broad as may reasonably be necessary to prevent the dangers that the suspect at large in the house may resist or escape.

It is argued that . . . the officer who seized the clothing was searching neither for the suspect nor for weapons when he looked into the washing machine in which he found the clothing. But even if we assume, although we do not decide, that the exigent circumstances in this case made lawful a search without warrant only for the suspect or his weapons, it cannot be said on this record that the officer who found the clothes in the washing machine was not searching for weapons. He testified that he was searching for the man or the money, but his failure to state explicitly that he was searching for weapons, in the absence of a specific question to that effect, can hardly be accorded controlling weight. He knew that the robber was armed and he did not know that some weapons had been found at the time he opened the machine. In these circumstances the inference that he was in fact also looking for weapons is fully justified. . . .

NOTES AND QUESTIONS

1. In Mincey v. Arizona, 437 U.S. 385 (1978), the defendant was convicted of murder, assault, and narcotics offenses. The killing occurred during a shootout at Mincey's apartment when police undercover agents arrived to complete a narcotics transaction. Except for making a brief sweep of the apartment to look for injured persons, the officers involved in the shootout did not search or seize anything from the apartment. Within 10 minutes of the incident, however, homicide detectives arrived and began a warrantless search of the apartment that extended over a four day period. Evidence seized during this search was admitted at Mincey's trial over his objection.

Before the Supreme Court the state maintained that there should be a "homicide scene" exception to the warrant requirement. To support this claim, the state argued, inter alia, (1) that by engaging in the shootout Mincey had forfeited any reasonable expectation of privacy in the apartment, and (2) that the initial invasion of privacy was so great that the subsequent warrantless search was constitutionally insignificant. The Court, in an opinion by Justice Stewart, responded that it had recently rejected a similar forfeiture argument,[47] and that the four day search here was not an insignificant invasion of privacy.[48] The Court went on to reaffirm the proposition that exigent circumstances could justify a warrantless search, and the Court acknowledged that exigent circumstances may frequently justify a "prompt warrantless search of . . . [a homicide scene] to see if a killer is still on the premises. . . ." Id. at 392. The

---

47. See Michigan v. Tyler, 436 U.S. 499 (1978), which dealt with the warrantless entry and search of premises damaged by fire. The state's argument, which the Court rejected, was as follows: "If the occupant of the premises set the blaze, then, in the words of petitioner's brief, his 'actions show that he had no expectation of privacy' because 'he has abandoned those premises within the meaning of the Fourth Amendment.' And if the fire had other causes, 'the occupants of the premises are treated as victims by police and fire officials.' In the petitioner's view, '[t]he likelihood that they will be aggrieved by a possible intrusion into what little remains of their privacy in badly burned premises is negligible.' " Id. at 505.

What, if anything, is wrong with the state's argument? Is the state's argument in Tyler stronger or weaker than the state's argument in Mincey?

48. The Court also noted that it had previously rejected the notion that the search of a person's residence could be regarded as an insignificant additional invasion of privacy after an arrest. See Chimel v. California, page 721 infra.

Court noted, however, that a "warrantless search must be 'strictly circumscribed by the exigencies which justify its initiation.' " Id. at 393
(quoting Terry v. Ohio, page 684 infra). Neither the particular search
here nor the general articulation by the Arizona Supreme Court of the
scope of the homicide exception was sufficiently narrow in scope, and
the breadth of the exception could not, in this Court's view, be justified
by the "vital public interest in the prompt investigation of the extremely
serious crime of murder." Ibid.

2. Is there no merit to the state's forfeiture claim in Mincey? Didn't
the defendant in White, page 512 supra, forfeit his right by choosing to
speak with a bugged informant? Is it more appropriate to apply the forfeiture concept to a person who engages in innocent rather than culpable
acts?

3. Even if Mincey's own conduct did not deprive him of the protections of the fourth amendment, what do you think of the claim that,
given the initial invasion of Mincey's rights by the entry and arrest, the
subsequent search was an insignificant additional invasion of privacy?
Would that claim be stronger if the search had not lasted as long or been
as extensive as it was?

4. Should the seriousness of the crime be a factor to consider in
determining whether there is a sufficient exigency to dispense with the
warrant requirement? Would it be possible to place rational limits on
such an exception to the warrant requirement?

Should the nonserious nature of an offense be a reason to preclude
a finding of exigency? See Welsh v. Wisconsin, page 660 infra.

5. In considering whether a particular type of circumstance is sufficiently exigent to justify an exception to the warrant requirement, is it
appropriate to consider the extent to which the warrant process in that
circumstance is likely to protect fourth amendment values? In this regard,
note that the Court in Mincey conceded, "It may well be that the circumstances described by the Arizona Supreme Court (in articulating the
scope of the homicide exception) would usually be constitutionally sufficient" to permit the issuance of a warrant for "a search of substantial
scope." 437 U.S. at 395.

6. One fairly common type of exigency is the risk that evidence
may be destroyed during the time that officers are obtaining a warrant.
In Vale v. Louisiana, 399 U.S. 30 (1970), the Louisiana Supreme Court
had relied on this ground to uphold the warrantless search of the defendant's house. The defendant had just been arrested for possessing
narcotics outside the front door, and the police had made a cursory sweep
of the house to determine whether anyone was present. Then, within
two or three minutes of the arrest and cursory sweep and before the search
which revealed narcotics in a rear bedroom, the defendant's mother and

brother returned to the house with groceries. The United States Supreme Court, in an opinion by Justice Stewart, disagreed that with the conclusion that there were sufficient exigent circumstances to justify the warrantless search:

> The Louisiana Supreme Court thought the search independently supportable because it involved narcotics, which are easily removed, hidden, or destroyed. It would be unreasonable, the Louisiana court concluded, "to require the officers under the facts of the case to first secure a search warrant before searching the premises, as time is of the essence inasmuch as the officers never know whether there is anyone on the premises to be searched who could very easily destroy the evidence." 252 La. [1056,] 1070, 215 So. 2d [811,] 816. Such a rationale could not apply to the present case, since by their own account the arresting officers satisfied themselves that no one else was in the house when they first entered the premises. But entirely apart from that point, our past decisions make clear that only in "a few specifically established and well-delineated" situations, Katz v. United States, 389 U.S. 347, 357, may a warrantless search of a dwelling withstand constitutional scrutiny, even though the authorities have probable cause to conduct it. The burden rests on the State to show the existence of such an exceptional situation. . . . And the record before us discloses none.
>
> There is no suggestion that anyone consented to the search. . . . The officers were not responding to an emergency. . . . They were not in hot pursuit of a fleeing felon. . . . The goods ultimately seized were not in the process of destruction. . . . Nor were they about to be removed from the jurisdiction. [399 U.S. at 34-35.]

The Court suggested it was significant that the evidence was "not in the process of destruction." Why is the Court seemingly so unwilling to give the police latitude to respond without a warrant to the possible destruction of evidence?

As Professor LaFave observes, lower courts "generally . . . have been inclined to state the [Vale] exception in broader terms such as a 'great likelihood that the evidence will be destroyed or removed . . . ,' that the evidence is 'threatened with imminent removal or destruction,' or that the police 'reasonably conclude that the evidence will be destroyed or removed. . . .' " 2 W. LaFave, Search and Seizure: A Treatise on the Fourth Amendment §6.5(b), at 658 (2d ed. 1987).

7. In Vale, what should the police have done? Consider Segura v. United States, 468 U.S. 796 (1984), where Chief Justice Burger, in a portion of an opinion joined only by Justice O'Connor, observed, "[A] seizure affects only possessory interests, not privacy interests. Therefore, the heightened protection we accord privacy interests is simply not im-

plicated where a *seizure* of premises, not a search, is at issue. We hold, therefore, that securing a dwelling, on the basis of probable cause, to prevent the destruction or removal of evidence while a search warrant is being sought is not itself an unreasonable seizure of either the dwelling or its contents. We reaffirm at the same time, however, that, absent exigent circumstances, a warrantless search—such as that invalidated in *Vale . . .* —is illegal." Id. at 810 (emphasis original).

b. Exigency, Privacy, and Bright Line Tests: The Search and Seizure of Automobiles and Containers

The Supreme Court, particularly in recent years, has taken a relatively broad view of the exigency created—or at least contributed to—by the inherent mobility of automobiles. Indeed, in part because of this perceived inherent exigency, courts frequently refer to the "automobile exception" to the warrant requirement.

The first Supreme Court case to deal with this type of exigency was Carroll v. United States, 267 U.S. 132 (1925), a prosecution for violation of the National Prohibition Act. After observing the defendants driving along the highway between Grand Rapids and Detroit, Michigan, federal prohibition agents stopped and searched the car without a warrant. Liquor seized during the search was used against the defendants at their trial. The Supreme Court concluded that the agents, primarily as a result of their previous investigation, had probable cause to engage in the search. With respect to the warrant requirement, the Court stated, "In cases where the securing of a warrant is reasonably practicable, it must be used. . . . In cases where seizure is impossible except without a warrant, the seizing officer acts unlawfully . . . unless he can show the court probable cause." Id. at 156.

In holding that the warrantless automobile search was lawful, the Court did not elaborate on what made obtaining a warrant not "reasonably practicable." It is clear from other parts of the opinion, however, that the inherent mobility of the automobile was not the only factor contributing to the exigency. Although the agents also had probable cause to arrest the defendants for violating the Prohibition Act, *Carroll* was not a case in which the officers had the option of initially arresting the defendants and then securing the car while a search warrant was being sought. The defendants' violation of the Prohibition Act was only a misdemeanor, see id. at 156-158, and according to the prevailing common law rule, the police could make a warrantless arrest for a misdemeanor only if they observed the crime being committed in their presence.[49]

49. The Court discussed this point in the context of rejecting the defendant's ar-

Thus, if the agents were to utilize the warrant process for the search of the automobile, one or more of them would have to have kept the automobile under surveillance and risked possibly losing track of it while a warrant was being sought.[50]

How broadly or narrowly should one read *Carroll?* See generally Moylan, The Automobile Exception: What It Is and What It Is Not— A Rationale in Search of a Clearer Label, 27 Mercer L. Rev. 987 (1976); Robb, the *Carroll* Case: The Expansion of the Automobile Exception in Warrantless Search and Seizure Cases, 15 Willamette L. Rev. 39 (1978); Wilson, The Warrantless Automobile Search: Exception Without Justification, 32 Hastings L.J. 127 (1980).

Consider Coolidge v. New Hampshire, 403 U.S. 443 (1971),[51] which supports the proposition that the inherent mobility of automobiles is not necessarily a sufficient justification for dispensing with the warrant requirement. The police, after arresting the defendant at his house and taking his wife to the home of some relatives in another town, impounded the defendant's automobile, which had been located in the driveway to his house.[52] There had been ample opportunity for the police to obtain a warrant prior to the seizure. Under these circumstances, a majority of the Court held that there was not a sufficient exigency to justify a warrantless seizure of the automobile. Id. at 462 (plurality opinion of Justice Stewart); id. at 478 (concurring opinion of Justice Harlan).

On the other hand, consider Chambers v. Maroney, the next principal case, and Cardwell v. Lewis, which is discussed in Note 3, page 621 infra.

---

gument that the right to make the warrantless seizure of the liquor should be limited by the common law rule governing warrantless arrests. According to this theory, the agents could seize the liquor only if they had a justification independent of the search to seize the defendants.

Whether the impact of the arrest rule should be regarded as critical to the *Carroll* holding on the exigency issue is unclear. On the one hand, the Court stressed the need for exigent circumstances to justify a warrantless search, and the arrest rule, which was brought to the Court's attention, in fact contributed to the exigency. On the other hand, the Court did not explicitly make this connection between the arrest rule and the exigency. Moreover, earlier in the opinion, the Court quoted at length several statutes that on their face permitted warrantless searches and seizures of vehicles without specifically mentioning exigent circumstances, and the Court stressed that there was a constitutionally significant difference between homes and vehicles.

50. Alternatively, the police could have stopped the car and detained the occupant while a warrant was being sought. But would not such a detention be the equivalent of, or at least similar to, an arrest, which the common law rule prohibited?

51. Other aspects of *Coolidge* are discussed at page 600 supra and at pages 638-646 infra.

52. Even after arresting Coolidge, removing his wife from the premises, and impounding the car, the police continued throughout the night to guard the premises. 403 U.S. at 447, 460-461.

CHAMBERS v. MARONEY
Certiorari to the United States Court of Appeals for the Third Circuit
399 U.S. 42 (1970)

MR. JUSTICE WHITE delivered the opinion of the Court.

The principal question in this case concerns the admissibility of evidence seized from an automobile, in which petitioner was riding at the time of his arrest, after the automobile was taken to a police station and was there thoroughly searched without a warrant. The Court of Appeals for the Third Circuit found no violation of petitioner's Fourth Amendment rights [and thus affirmed the district court's denial of petitioner's petition for a writ of habeas corpus]. We affirm.

During the night of May 20, 1963, a Gulf service station in North Braddock, Pennsylvania, was robbed by two men, each of whom carried and displayed a gun. The robbers took the currency from the cash register; the service station attendant, one Stephen Kovacich, was directed to place the coins in his right-hand glove, which was then taken by the robbers. Two teen-agers, who had earlier noticed a blue compact station wagon circling the block in the vicinity of the Gulf station, then saw the station wagon speed away from a parking lot close to the Gulf station. About the same time, they learned that the Gulf station had been robbed. They reported to police, who arrived immediately, that four men were in the station wagon and one was wearing a green sweater. Kovacich told the police that one of the men who robbed him was wearing a green sweater and the other was wearing a trench coat. A description of the car and the two robbers was broadcast over the police radio. Within an hour, a light blue compact station wagon answering the description and carrying four men was stopped by the police about two miles from the Gulf station. Petitioner was one of the men in the station wagon. He was wearing a green sweater and there was a trench coat in the car. The occupants were arrested and the car was driven to the police station. In the course of a thorough search of the car at the station, the police found concealed in a compartment under the dashboard two .38-caliber revolvers (one loaded with dumdum bullets), a righthand glove containing small change, and certain cards bearing the name of Raymond Havicon, the attendant at a Boron service station in McKeesport, Pennsylvania, who had been robbed at gunpoint on May 13, 1963. . . .

Petitioner was indicted for both robberies. . . . The materials taken from the station wagon were introduced into evidence, Kovacich identifying his glove and Havicon the cards taken in the May 13 robbery. . . .

. . . As the state courts correctly held, there was probable cause to arrest the occupants of the station wagon that the officers stopped; just as obviously was there probable cause to search the car for guns and stolen money.

In terms of the circumstances justifying a warrantless search, the Court has long distinguished between an automobile and a home or office. In Carroll v. United States, 267 U.S. 132 (1925), . . . the Court held that automobiles and other conveyances may be searched without a warrant in circumstances that would not justify the search without a warrant of a house or an office, provided that there is probable cause to believe that the car contains articles that the officers are entitled to seize. . . .

Neither *Carroll* . . . nor other cases in this Court require or suggest that in every conceivable circumstance the search of an auto even with probable cause may be made without the extra protection for privacy that a warrant affords. But the circumstances that furnish probable cause to search a particular auto for particular articles are most often unforeseeable; moreover, the opportunity to search is fleeting since a car is readily movable. Where this is true, as in *Carroll* and the case before us now, if an effective search is to be made at any time, either the search must be made immediately without a warrant or the car itself must be seized and held without a warrant for whatever period is necessary to obtain a warrant for the search.

. . . *Carroll* . . . holds a search warrant unnecessary where there is probable cause to search an automobile stopped on the highway; the car is movable, the occupants are alerted, and the car's contents may never be found again if a warrant must be obtained. Hence an immediate search is constitutionally permissible.

Arguably, because of the preference for a magistrate's judgment, only the immobilization of the car should be permitted until a search warrant is obtained; arguably, only the "lesser" intrusion is permissible until the magistrate authorizes the "greater." But which is the "greater" and which the "lesser" intrusion is itself a debatable question and the answer may depend on a variety of circumstances. For constitutional purposes, we see no difference between on the one hand seizing and holding a car before presenting the probable cause issue to a magistrate and on the other hand carrying out an immediate search without a warrant. Given probable cause to search, either course is reasonable under the Fourth Amendment.

On the facts before us, the blue station wagon could have been searched on the spot when it was stopped since there was probable cause to search and it was a fleeting target for a search. The probable-cause factor still obtained at the station house and so did the mobility of the car unless the Fourth Amendment permits a warrantless seizure of the car and the denial of its use to anyone until a warrant is secured. In that event there is little to choose in terms of practical consequences between an immediate search without a warrant and the car's immobilization until a warrant is obtained.[10] The same consequences may not follow where there is unforeseeable cause to search a house. Compare Vale v. Louisiana, [399 U.S. 30 (1970)]. But as *Carroll*, supra, held, for the purposes of the Fourth Amendment there is a constitutional difference between houses and cars. . . .

Affirmed.

MR. JUSTICE BLACKMUN took no part in the consideration or decision of this case.

[The concurring opinion of JUSTICE STEWART is omitted.]

MR. JUSTICE HARLAN, concurring[53] in part and dissenting in part. . . .

. . . The "general requirement that a search warrant be obtained" is basic to the Amendment's protection of privacy, and " 'the burden is on those seeking [an] exemption . . . to show the need for it.' " E.g., Chimel v. California, 395 U.S. 752, 762 (1969); Katz v. United States, 389 U.S. 347, 356-358 (1967). . . .

Fidelity to this established principle requires that, where exceptions are made to accommodate the exigencies of particular situations, those exceptions be no broader than necessitated by the circumstances presented. . . .

Where officers have probable cause to search a vehicle on a public way, a . . . limited exception to the warrant requirement is reasonable because "the vehicle can be quickly moved out of the locality or jurisdiction in which the warrant must be sought." Carroll v. United States, 267 U.S. 132, 153 (1925). Because the officers might be deprived of valuable evidence if required to obtain a warrant before effecting any search or seizure, I agree with the Court that they should be permitted to take the steps necessary to preserve evidence and to make a search possible. . . . The Court holds that those steps include making a warrantless search of the entire vehicle on the highway—a conclusion reached by the Court in *Carroll* without discussion—and indeed appears to go further and to condone the removal of the car to the police station for a

10. It was not unreasonable in this case to take the car to the station house. All occupants in the car were arrested in a dark parking lot in the middle of the night. A careful search at that point was impractical and perhaps not safe for the officers, and it would serve the owner's convenience and the safety of his car to have the vehicle and the keys together at the station house.

53. Justice Harlan concurred with the majority's conclusion that other evidence, found during a search of defendant's home, was not obtained illegally.—EDS.

warrantless search there at the convenience of the police.[7] I cannot agree that this result is consistent with our insistence in other areas that departures from the warrant requirement strictly conform to the exigency presented.

The Court concedes that the police could prevent removal of the evidence by temporarily seizing the car for the time necessary to obtain a warrant. It does not dispute that such a course would fully protect the interests of effective law enforcement; rather it states that whether temporary seizure is a "lesser" intrusion than warrantless search "is itself a debatable question and the answer may depend on a variety of circumstances." . . . I believe it clear that a warrantless search involves the greater sacrifice of Fourth Amendment values.

The Fourth Amendment proscribes, to be sure, unreasonable "seizures" as well as "searches." However, in the circumstances in which this problem is likely to occur, the lesser intrusion will almost always be the simple seizure of the car for the period—perhaps a day—necessary to enable the officers to obtain a search warrant. In the first place, as this case shows, the very facts establishing probable cause to search will often also justify arrest of the occupants of the vehicle. Since the occupants themselves are to be taken into custody, they will suffer minimal further inconvenience from the temporary immobilization of their vehicle. Even where no arrests are made, persons who wish to avoid a search—either to protect their privacy or to conceal incriminating evidence—will almost certainly prefer a brief loss of the use of the vehicle in exchange for the opportunity to have a magistrate pass upon the justification for the search. To be sure, one can conceive of instances in which the occupant, having nothing to hide and lacking concern for the privacy of the automobile, would be more deeply offended by a temporary immobilization of his vehicle than by a prompt search of it. However, such a person always remains free to consent to an immediate search, thus avoiding any delay. Where consent is not forthcoming, the occupants of the car have an interest in privacy that is protected by the Fourth Amendment even where the circumstances justify a temporary seizure. . . . The Court's endorsement of a warrantless invasion of that privacy where another course would suffice is simply inconsistent with our repeated stress on the Fourth

7. The Court disregards the fact that *Carroll*, and each of this Court's decisions upholding a warrantless vehicle search on its authority, involved a search for contraband. Brinegar v. United States, 338 U.S. 160 (1949); Scher v. United States, 305 U.S. 251 (1938); Husty v. United States, 282 U.S. 694 (1931); see United States v. Di Re, 332 U.S. 581, 584-586 (1948). Although subsequent dicta have omitted this limitation, . . . the *Carroll* decision has not until today been held to authorize a general search of a vehicle for evidence of crime, without a warrant, in every case where probable cause exists.

Amendment's mandate of " 'adherence to judicial processes.' " E.g., Katz v. United States, 389 U.S., at 357.[9]

Indeed, I believe this conclusion is implicit in the opinion of the unanimous Court in Preston v. United States, 376 U.S. 364 (1964). The Court there purported to decide whether a factual situation virtually identical to the one now before us was "such as to fall within *any* of the exceptions to the constitutional rule that a search warrant must be had before a search may be made." Id., at 367 (emphasis added). The Court concluded that no exception was available, stating that "since the men were under arrest at the police station and the car was in police custody at a garage, [there was no] danger that the car would be moved out of the locality or jurisdiction." Id., at 368. The Court's reliance on the police custody of the car as its reason for holding "that the search of the car without a warrant failed to meet the test of reasonableness under the Fourth Amendment," ibid., can only have been based on the premise that the more reasonable course was for the police to retain custody of the car for the short time necessary to obtain a warrant. . . . The Court now discards the approach taken in *Preston*, and creates a special rule for automobile searches that is seriously at odds with generally applied Fourth Amendment principles. . . .

NOTES AND QUESTIONS

1. At least in situations in which the police decide independently of any search to arrest the occupants of a car, is it not clear that the "lesser" invasion will be seizure rather than immediate search of the vehicle? In any event, why should the police have the right arbitrarily to choose which option to pursue? Would it be feasible and desirable to give the arrestee(s) the choice?

2. Even if one is willing to concede that the police had the option of engaging in an immediate warrantless search of the vehicle, why should they be able to engage in a warrantless search of the vehicle after it has been impounded? Is it sufficient to answer that the arrestee may be released or that a friend may come to claim the car before a warrant can be obtained? At least at this point, is it not clear that the lesser invasion

---

9. Circumstances might arise in which it would be impracticable to immobilize the car for the time required to obtain a warrant—for example, where a single police officer must take arrested suspects to the station, and has no way of protecting the suspects' car during his absence. In such situations it might be wholly reasonable to perform an on-the-spot search based on probable cause. However, where nothing in the situation makes impracticable the obtaining of a warrant, I cannot join the Court in shunting aside that vital Fourth Amendment safeguard.

would be to retain control over the car until a warrant could be obtained or until a search with the arrestee's consent had taken place? Compare Segura v. United States, Note 7, page 613 supra (opinion of Chief Justice Burger suggesting that *seizure* of residence is lesser invasion than search of residence) with Florida v. Meyers, 466 U.S. 380 (1984) (per curiam), and Michigan v. Thomas, 458 U.S. 259 (1982) (per curiam) (both reaffirming constitutionality of warrantless search of automobile in police custody).

3. In conjunction with *Chambers* and *Coolidge*, consider Cardwell v. Lewis, 417 U.S. 583 (1974). The police asked Lewis, a murder suspect, to come to their office for interrogation. At the time the police had a warrant for Lewis's arrest. Lewis complied with the request, and at the conclusion of the interrogation officers, without a warrant, seized Lewis's car from a public parking lot. The following day, again without a warrant, the police took paint samples from a fender of the car and compared the car tires with an imprint of a tire impression discovered at the scene of the homicide. The Supreme Court reversed the Court of Appeals' judgment that the defendant's fourth amendment rights were violated and that he, therefore, was entitled to a writ of habeas corpus. Justice Powell maintained that federal habeas corpus relief should not be available because the defendant had a fair opportunity to litigate the fourth amendment issues in state courts.[54] The other justices addressed the merits of the fourth amendment claims. In an opinion joined by the Chief Justice and Justices White and Rehnquist, Justice Blackmun first concluded that the warrantless examination of the tire and removal of paint were legal:

> An underlying factor in the *Carroll-Chambers* line of decisions has been the exigent circumstances that exist in connection with movable vehicles. . . . This is strikingly true where the automobile's owner is alerted to police intentions and, as a consequence, the motivation to remove evidence from official grasp is heightened.
>
> There is still another distinguishing factor. "The search of an automobile is far less intrusive on the rights protected by the Fourth Amendment than the search of one's person or of a building." Almeida-Sanchez v. United States, 413 U.S. 266, 279 (1973) (Powell, J., concurring). One has a lesser expectation of privacy in a motor vehicle because its function is transportation and it seldom serves as one's residence or as the repository of personal effects. A car has little capacity for escaping public scrutiny. It travels public thoroughfares where both its occupants and its contents are in plain view. . . . "What a person knowingly exposes to the public, even in his own home or office, is not a subject of Fourth Amendment

---

54. Justice Powell first articulated this view in a concurring opinion in Schneckloth v. Bustamonte, at page 829 infra. A majority of the Court adopted the position in Stone v. Powell, at page 888 infra.

protection." Katz v. United States, 389 U.S., at 351. . . . . This is not to
say that no part of the interior of an automobile has Fourth Amendment
protection; the exercise of a desire to be mobile does not, of course, waive
one's right to be free of unreasonable government intrusion. But insofar
as Fourth Amendment protection extends to a motor vehicle, it is the right
to privacy that is the touchstone of our inquiry.

In the present case, nothing from the interior of the car and no
personal effects, which the Fourth Amendment traditionally has been
deemed to protect, were searched or seized and introduced in evidence.
With the "search" limited to the examination of the tire on the wheel and
the taking of paint scrapings from the exterior of the vehicle left in the
public parking lot, we fail to comprehend what expectation of privacy was
infringed. . . . . Under circumstances such as these, where probable cause
exists, a warrantless examination of the exterior of a car is not unreasonable
under the Fourth and Fourteenth Amendments. [417 U.S. at 590-592.]

Justice Blackmun then turned to the question whether the prior
warrantless seizure of the car, for which there was admittedly probable
cause, rendered the examination illegal:

The present case differs from *Coolidge* both in the scope of the search[55]
and in the circumstances of the seizure. Since the Coolidge car was parked
on the defendant's driveway, the seizure of that automobile required an
entry upon private property. Here . . . the automobile was seized from
a public place where access was not meaningfully restricted. This is, in
fact, the ground upon which the *Coolidge* plurality opinion distinguished
Chambers, 403 U.S., at 463 n.20. . . .[56]

The fact that the car in *Chambers* was seized after being stopped on
a highway, whereas Lewis' car was seized from a public parking lot, has
little, if any, legal significance. The same arguments and considerations
of exigency, immobilization on the spot, and posting a guard obtain. In
fact, because the interrogation session ended with awareness that Lewis
had been arrested and that his car constituted incriminating evidence, the
incentive and potential for the car's removal substantially increased. There
was testimony . . . that Lewis asked one of his attorneys to see that his
wife and family got the car, and that the attorney relinquished the keys to
the police in order to avoid a physical confrontation. . . .

Respondent contends that here, unlike *Chambers*, probable cause to

55. Why should the scope of the search affect the legality of the prior seizure?
Justice Blackmun did not attempt to answer this question. Instead, he merely asserted a
"thorough and extensive search . . . of . . . the kind [in *Coolidge*] raises different and
additional considerations not present [here]." 417 U.S. at 593 n.9.—EDS.

56. The relevant portion of footnote 20 in *Coolidge* reads as follows: "[T]here is a
significant constitutional difference between stopping, seizing, and searching a car *on the
open highway*, and entering private property to seize and search an *unoccupied, parked
vehicle not then being used for any illegal purpose*." (Emphasis added.)—EDS.

search the car existed for some time prior to [the] arrest and that, therefore, there were no exigent circumstances. Assuming that probable cause previously existed, we know of no case or principle that suggests that the right to search on probable cause and the reasonableness of seizing a car under exigent circumstances are foreclosed if a warrant was not obtained at the first practicable moment."[57] Exigent circumstances with regard to vehicles are not limited to situations where probable cause is unforeseeable and arises only at the time of arrest. . . . The exigency may arise at any time, and the fact that the police might have obtained a warrant earlier does not negate the possibility of a current situation's necessitating prompt police action. [417 U.S. at 593-596.]

Justice Stewart, in an opinion joined by Justices Douglas, Brennan, and Marshall, took a different view of the exigency issue:

The facts of this case make clear beyond peradventure that the "automobile exception" is not available to uphold the warrantless seizure of the respondent's car. Well before the time that the automobile was seized, the respondent—and the keys to his car—were securely within police custody. There was thus absolutely no likelihood that the respondent could have either moved the car or meddled with it during the time necessary to obtain a search warrant. And there was no realistic possibility that anyone else was in a position to do so either. I am at a loss, therefore, to understand the plurality opinion's conclusion, . . . that there was a "potential for the car's removal" during the period immediately preceding the car's seizure. The facts of record can only support a diametrically opposite conclusion.

Finally, the plurality opinion suggests that other "exigent circumstances" might have excused the failure of the police to procure a warrant. The opinion nowhere states what these mystical exigencies might have been, and counsel for the petitioner has not been so inventive as to suggest any.[2] Since the authorities had taken care to procure an arrest warrant

57. Indeed, it may be that no case or principle requires obtaining a warrant "*at the first practicable moment.*" But if that is the only point of Justice Blackmun's assertion, is it relevant to the case at hand? Alternatively, if Justice Blackmun means to suggest that he knows of no case or principle suggesting that prior opportunity to obtain a warrant is a significant factor in evaluating the legality of a warrantless search or seizure, he has not looked very far. See Vale v. Louisiana, 399 U.S. 30 (1970); Trupiano v. United States, 334 U.S. 699 (1948), discussed in Chimel v. California, page 721 infra. For more recent cases emphasizing the significance of prior opportunity to obtain a warrant, see Payton v. New York, 445 U.S. 573 (1980); United States v. Santana, 427 U.S. 38 (1976).—Eds.

2. Even the Solicitor General, who appeared as amicus curiae urging a reversal of the Court of Appeals' judgment in this case, has candidly admitted in his brief that "no satisfactory reason appears for the failure of the law enforcement officers to have obtained a warrant—there appears on the facts of this case to have been no real likelihood that respondent would have destroyed or concealed the evidence sought during the time required to seek and procure a warrant." Brief for United States as Amicus Curiae 4-5.

even before the respondent arrived for questioning, it can scarcely be said that probable cause was not discovered until so late a point in time as to prevent the obtaining of a warrant for seizure of the automobile. And, with the automobile effectively immobilized during the period of the respondent's interrogation, the fear that evidence might be destroyed was hardly an exigency, particularly when it is remembered that no such fear prompted a seizure during all the preceding months while the respondent, though under investigation, had been in full control of the car.[3] This is, quite simply, a case where no exigent circumstances existed. [417 U.S. at 598-599.]

4. In California v. Carney, 471 U.S. 386 (1985), the Supreme Court relied on the automobile exception to uphold the warrantless search of a mobile motor home. The vehicle was a Dodge Mini Motor Home outfitted with a table, stuffed chairs, a refrigerator, cupboards, bunk beds, opaque glass, and curtains.

The fact that the vehicle was capable of functioning as a home was not sufficient, in the Court's view, to make the automobile exception inapplicable:

> Our application of the vehicle exception has never turned on the other uses to which a vehicle might be put. The exception has historically turned on the ready mobility of the vehicle, and on the presence of the vehicle in a setting that objectively indicates that the vehicle is being used for transportation.[3] These two requirements for application of the exception ensure that law enforcement officials are not unnecessarily hamstrung in their efforts to detect and prosecute criminal activity, and that the legitimate privacy interests of the public are protected. [Id. at 394.]

Would the necessity of showing some specific exigency to justify the warrantless search of a mobile motor home unduly hamstring law enforcement officers? Even if the answer is no, can *Carney* be justified on

---

3. It can hardly be argued that the questioning of the respondent by the police for the first time alerted him to their intentions. . . . Even putting to one side the question of how the respondent could have acted to destroy any evidence while he was in police custody, the fact is that he was fully aware of official suspicion during several months preceding the interrogation. He had been questioned on several occasions prior to his arrest, and he had been alerted on the day before the interrogation that the police wished to see him. Nonetheless, he voluntarily drove his car to Columbus to keep his appointment with the investigators.

3. We need not pass on the application of the vehicle exception to a motor home that is situated in a way or place that objectively indicates that it is being used as a residence. Among the factors that might be relevant in determining whether a warrant would be required in such a circumstance is its location, whether the vehicle is readily mobile or instead, for instance, elevated on blocks, whether the vehicle is licensed, whether it is connected to utilities, and whether it has convenient access to a public road.

the ground that it provides a clear, simple rule for law enforcement officers?

5. If the inherent mobility of an automobile permits the police to search it immediately without a warrant or to impound it and search it later without a warrant, should the same rules govern the search of other movable items such as suitcases? Should the answer depend on whether the movable object is located in an automobile?

Consider United States v. Chadwick, 433 U.S. 1 (1977): The police had probable cause to believe that a footlocker that had arrived at the Boston train station contained contraband. The police observed Chadwick and two companions place the footlocker in the trunk of a car. At that point, before the trunk was closed, the officers arrested the three men and took the footlocker to the Federal Building, where they searched it without a warrant. Emphasizing the inherent mobility of the footlocker, the state attempted to justify the search by analogy to the automobile exception to the warrant requirement.[58] The Supreme Court acknowledged that the warrantless seizure of the footlocker was constitutional. The Court, however, upheld the defendant's contention that the search was unconstitutional:

> [W]e have . . . sustained "warrantless searches of vehicles . . . in cases in which the possibilities of the vehicle's being removed or evidence in it destroyed were remote, if not nonexistent." Cady v. Dombrowski, 413 U.S. 433, 441-443 (1973). . . .
>
> The answer lies in the diminished expectation of privacy which surrounds the automobile. . . .
>
> The factors which diminish the privacy aspects of an automobile do not apply to respondents' footlocker. Luggage contents are not open to public view, except as a condition to a border entry or common carrier travel; nor is luggage subject to regular inspections and official scrutiny on a continuing basis. Unlike an automobile, whose primary function is transportation, luggage is intended as a repository of personal effects. In sum, a person's expectations of privacy in personal luggage are substantially greater than in an automobile. [433 U.S. at 12-13.]

In a dissenting opinion joined by then Justice Rehnquist, Justice Blackmun argued:

> Custodial arrest is such a serious deprivation that various lesser invasions of privacy may be fairly regarded as incidental. . . . [A] warrant would be routinely forthcoming in the vast majority of situations where the prop-

---

58. The government's principal argument was that "the Fourth Amendment Warrant Clause protects only interests traditionally identified with the home." 433 U.S. at 6. Not surprisingly the Supreme Court unanimously rejected this argument.

erty has been seized in conjunction with the valid arrest of a person in a public place. I therefore doubt that requiring the authorities to go through the formality of obtaining a warrant in this situation would have much practical effect in protecting Fourth Amendment values.[1] . . .

. . . Such an approach would simplify the constitutional law of criminal procedure without seriously derogating from the values protected by the Fourth Amendment's prohibition of unreasonable searches and seizures.[3] [Id. at 20, 22.]

6. Following *Chadwick* it soon became apparent that there was still much to be resolved about the propriety of warrantless searches of luggage and other movable containers, particularly when the containers were in automobiles. Some courts upheld warrantless searches of luggage found in automobiles if the relationship between the luggage and the automobile was less attenuated than it was in *Chadwick*.[59] Other courts made distinctions between "worthy" containers, for which a warrant was required, and "unworthy" containers, which could be searched without a warrant.[60]

In Arkansas v. Sanders, 442 U.S. 753 (1979), the Supreme Court again dealt with the legality of the search of a container taken from an automobile. The facts in *Sanders* were very similar to those in *Chadwick*. The police had probable cause to believe a suitcase claimed by the defendant at an airline baggage claim area contained marijuana. They observed the defendant and a companion place the suitcase in the trunk of a taxi cab and then enter the taxi. After a pursuit of several blocks, the police stopped the taxi, retrieved the suitcase from the trunk, and immediately opened it. The suitcase, which was unlocked, contained

1. A search warrant serves additional functions where an arrest takes place in a home or office. The warrant assures the occupants that the officers have legal authority to conduct the search and defines the area to be searched and the objects to be seized. . . . But a warrant would serve none of these functions where the arrest takes place in a public area and the authorities are admittedly empowered to seize the objects in question. Cf. United States v. Watson, 423 U.S. 411, 414-424 (1976) (warrant not required for arrest, based on probable cause, in public place).

3. " 'My basic premise is that Fourth Amendment doctrine, given force and effect by the exclusionary rule, is primarily intended to regulate the police in their day-to-day activities and thus ought to be expressed in terms that are readily applicable by the police in the context of the law enforcement activities in which they are necessarily engaged. A highly sophisticated set of rules, qualified by all sorts of ifs, ands, and buts and requiring the drawing of subtle nuances and hairline distinctions, may be the sort of heady stuff upon which the facile minds of lawyers and judges eagerly feed, but they may be 'literally impossible of application by the officer in the field.' " LaFave, "Case-by-Case Adjudication" versus "Standardized Procedures": The *Robinson* Dilemma, 1974 Sup. Ct. Rev. 127, 141 (footnotes omitted), quoting United States v. Robinson, 153 U.S. App. D.C. 114, 154, 471 F.2d 1082, 1122 (1972) (dissenting opinion), rev'd, 414 U.S. 218 (1973).

59. See, e.g., United States v. Milhollan, 599 F.2d 518, 525-527 (3d Cir.), cert. denied, 444 U.S. 909 (1979).

60. See Robbins v. California, 453 U.S. 420, 426 (1981) (collecting cases).

marijuana. The Court held that the search violated the fourth amendment:

> [T]he warrant requirement of the Fourth Amendment applies to personal luggage taken from an automobile to the same degree it applies to such luggage in other locations. Thus, insofar as the police are entitled to search such luggage without a warrant, their actions must be justified under some exception to the warrant requirement other than that applicable to automobiles stopped on the highway. [Id. at 766.]

In a concurring opinion, Chief Justice Burger observed:

> I . . . cannot join [the Court's] unnecessarily broad opinion, which seems to treat this case as if it involved the "automobile" exception to the warrant requirement. . . .
> This case simply does not present the question of whether a warrant is required before opening luggage when the police have probable cause to believe contraband is located *somewhere* in the vehicle, but when they do not know whether, for example, it is inside a piece of luggage in the trunk, in the glove compartment, or concealed in some part of the car's structure. I am not sure whether that would be a stronger or weaker case for requiring a warrant to search the suitcase when a warrantless search of the automobile is otherwise permissible. But it seems to me it would be better to await a case in which the question must be decided. [Id. at 766-768.]

The Supreme Court's next effort in the area, Robbins v. California, is described in the following case, which was decided only two years after *Robbins* and which overruled *Robbins*.

UNITED STATES v. ROSS
Certiorari to the United States District Court for the District of Columbia
456 U.S. 798 (1982)

JUSTICE STEVENS delivered the opinion of the Court.

. . . In this case, we consider the extent to which police officers who have legitimately stopped an automobile and who have probable cause to believe that contraband is concealed somewhere within it may conduct a probing search of compartments and containers within the vehicle whose contents are not in plain view. We hold that they may conduct a search of the vehicle that is as thorough as a magistrate could authorize in a warrant "particularly describing the place to be searched." . . .

In the evening of November 27, 1978, an informant who had previously proved to be reliable telephoned Detective Marcum of the District
of Columbia Police Department and told him that an individual known
as "Bandit" was selling narcotics kept in the trunk of a car parked at 439
Ridge Street. The informant stated that he had just observed "Bandit"
complete a sale and that "Bandit" had told him that additional narcotics
were in the trunk. The informant gave Marcum a detailed description
of "Bandit" and stated that the car was a "purplish maroon" Chevrolet
Malibu with District of Columbia license plates.

Accompanied by Detective Cassidy and Sergeant Gonzales, Marcum
immediately drove to the area and found a maroon Malibu parked in
front of 439 Ridge Street. A license check disclosed that the car was
registered to Albert Ross; a computer check on Ross revealed that he fit
the informant's description and used the alias "Bandit." In two passes
through the neighborhood the officers did not observe anyone matching
the informant's description. To avoid alerting persons on the street, they
left the area.

The officers returned five minutes later and observed the maroon
Malibu turning off Ridge Street onto Fourth Street. They pulled alongside
the Malibu, noticed that the driver matched the informant's description,
and stopped the car. Marcum and Cassidy told the driver—later identified
as Albert Ross, the respondent in this action—to get out of the vehicle.
While they searched Ross, Sergeant Gonzales discovered a bullet on the
car's front seat. He searched the interior of the car and found a pistol in
the glove compartment. Ross then was arrested and handcuffed. Detective
Cassidy took Ross' keys and opened the trunk, where he found a closed
brown paper bag. He opened the bag and discovered a number of glassine
bags containing a white powder. Cassidy replaced the bag, closed the
trunk, and drove the car to Headquarters.

At the police station Cassidy thoroughly searched the car. In addition
to the "lunch-type" brown paper bag, Cassidy found in the trunk a
zippered red leather pouch. He unzipped the pouch and discovered $3,200
in cash. The police laboratory later determined that the powder in the
paper bag was heroin. No warrant was obtained.

Ross was charged with possession of heroin with intent to distribute. . . . [The trial court denied his motion to suppress, and Ross was
convicted. The Court of Appeals upheld the warrantless search of the
trunk but held that the warrantless search of the leather pouch—but not
the search of the paper bag—was invalid. On rehearing a majority of the
entire Court of Appeals] held that the police should not have opened
either container without first obtaining a warrant. . . .

[The Court summarized its holdings in Carroll v. United States,
page 614 supra, and United States v. Chadwick, page 625 supra, and

Chief Justice Burger's concurring opinion in Arkansas v. Sanders, page 627 supra.]

Robbins v. California, 453 U.S. 420, . . . was a case in which suspicion was not directed at a specific container. In that case the Court for the first time was forced to consider whether police officers who are entitled to conduct a warrantless search of an automobile stopped on a public roadway may open a container found within the vehicle. In the early morning of January 5, 1975, police officers stopped Robbins' station wagon because he was driving erratically. Robbins got out of the car, but later returned to obtain the vehicle's registration papers. When he opened the car door, the officers smelled marijuana smoke. One of the officers searched Robbins and discovered a vial of liquid; in a search of the interior of the car the officer found marijuana. The police officers then opened the tailgate of the station wagon and raised the cover of a recessed luggage compartment. In the compartment they found two packages wrapped in green opaque plastic. The police unwrapped the packages and discovered a large amount of marijuana in each.

Robbins was charged with various drug offenses and moved to suppress the contents of the plastic packages. The California Court of Appeal [upheld the search]. . . .

This Court reversed. Writing for a plurality, Justice Stewart rejected the argument that the outward appearance of the packages precluded Robbins from having a reasonable expectation of privacy in their contents. He also squarely rejected the argument that there is a constitutional distinction between searches of luggage and searches of "less worthy" containers. Justice Stewart reasoned that all containers are equally protected by the Fourth Amendment unless their contents are in plain view. The plurality concluded that the warrantless search was impermissible because *Chadwick* and *Sanders* had established that "a closed piece of luggage found in a lawfully searched car is constitutionally protected to the same extent as are closed pieces of luggage found anywhere else." 453 U.S., at 425.

In a concurring opinion, Justice Powell, the author of the Court's opinion in *Sanders*, . . . noted that possibly "the controlling question should be the scope of the automobile exception to the warrant requirement," id., at 435. . . . The parties in *Robbins* had not pressed that argument, however, and Justice Powell concluded that institutional constraints made it inappropriate to re-examine basic doctrine without full adversary presentation. He concurred in the judgment, since it was supported—although not compelled—by the Court's opinion in *Sanders*. . . .

. . . Unlike *Chadwick* and *Sanders*, in this case police officers had probable cause to search respondent's entire vehicle. Unlike *Robbins*, in this case the parties have squarely addressed the question whether, in the course of a legitimate warrantless search of an automobile, police are entitled to open containers found within the vehicle. We now address that question. Its answer is determined by the scope of the search that is authorized by the exception to the warrant requirement set forth in *Carroll*. . . .

In *Carroll* itself, the whiskey that the prohibition agents seized was not in plain view. It was discovered only after an officer opened the rumble seat and tore open the upholstery of the lazyback. The Court did not find the scope of the search unreasonable. Having stopped Carroll and Kiro on a public road and subjected them to the indignity of a vehicle search—which the Court found to be a reasonable intrusion on their privacy because it was based on probable cause that their vehicle was transporting contraband—prohibition agents were entitled to tear open a portion of the roadster itself. The scope of the search was no greater than a magistrate could have authorized by issuing a warrant based on the probable cause that justified the search. Since such a warrant could have authorized the agents to open the rear portion of the roadster and to rip the upholstery in their search for concealed whiskey, the search was constitutionally permissible.

In Chambers v. Maroney[, 399 U.S. 42,] the police found weapons and stolen property "concealed in a compartment under the dashboard." 399 U.S., at 44. No suggestion was made that the scope of the search was impermissible. It would be illogical to assume that the outcome of *Chambers*—or the outcome of *Carroll* itself—would have been different if the police had found the secreted contraband enclosed within a secondary container and had opened that container without a warrant. If it was reasonable for prohibition agents to rip open the upholstery in *Carroll*, it certainly would have been reasonable for them to look into a burlap sack stashed inside; if it was reasonable to open the concealed compartment in *Chambers*, it would have been equally reasonable to open a paper bag crumpled within it. A contrary rule could produce absurd results inconsistent with the decision in *Carroll* itself.

In its application of *Carroll*, this Court in fact has sustained warrantless searches of containers found during a lawful search of an automobile. In Husty v. United States, 282 U.S. 694, the Court upheld a warrantless seizure of whiskey found during a search of an automobile, some of which was discovered in "whiskey bags" that could have contained other goods. In Scher v. United States, 305 U.S. 251, federal officers seized and searched packages of unstamped liquor found in the trunk of an automobile searched without a warrant. As described by a police officer who participated in the search: "I turned the handle and opened the trunk and found the trunk completely filled with packages wrapped in brown paper, and tied with twine; I think somewhere around thirty packages, each one containing six bottles." In these cases it was not contended that police officers needed a warrant to open the whiskey bags or to unwrap the brown paper packages. These decisions nevertheless "have much weight, as they show that this point neither occurred to the bar or the bench." Bank of the United States v. Deveaux, 5 Cranch 61, 88 (Marshall, C.J.). The fact that no such argument was even made illuminates the profession's understanding of the scope of the search permitted under *Carroll.* Indeed, prior to the decisions in *Chadwick* and *Sanders,* courts routinely had held that containers and packages found during a legitimate warrantless search of an automobile also could be searched without a warrant.

As we have stated, the decision in *Carroll* was based on the Court's appraisal of practical considerations viewed in the perspective of history. It is therefore significant that the practical consequences of the *Carroll* decision would be largely nullified if the permissible scope of a warrantless search of an automobile did not include containers and packages found inside the vehicle. Contraband goods rarely are strewn across the trunk or floor of a car; since by their very nature such goods must be withheld from public view, they rarely can be placed in an automobile unless they are enclosed within some form of container.[26] . . .

A lawful search of fixed premises generally extends to the entire area in which the object of the search may be found and is not limited by the possibility that separate acts of entry or opening may be required to complete the search. Thus, a warrant that authorizes an officer to search a home for illegal weapons also provides authority to open closets, chests, drawers, and containers in which the weapon might be found. A warrant to open a footlocker to search for marijuana would also authorize the opening of packages found inside. A warrant to search a vehicle would support a search of every part of the vehicle that might contain the object of the search. When a legitimate search is under way, and when its purpose and its limits have been precisely defined, nice distinctions between closets, drawers, and containers, in the case of a home, or between

26. It is noteworthy that the early legislation on which the Court relied in *Carroll* concerned the enforcement of laws imposing duties on imported merchandise. . . . Presumably such merchandise was shipped then in containers of various kinds, just as it is today. Since Congress had authorized warrantless searches of vessels and beasts for imported merchandise, it is inconceivable that it intended a customs officer to obtain a warrant for every package discovered during the search; certainly Congress intended customs officers to open shipping containers when necessary and not merely to examine the exterior of cartons or boxes in which smuggled goods might be concealed. During virtually the entire history of our country—whether contraband was transported in a horse drawn carriage, a 1921 roadster, or a modern automobile—it has been assumed that a lawful search of a vehicle would include a search of any container that might conceal the object of the search.

glove compartments, upholstered seats, trunks, and wrapped packages, in the case of a vehicle, must give way to the interest in the prompt and efficient completion of the task at hand.[28]

This rule applies equally to all containers, as indeed we believe it must. One point on which the Court was in virtually unanimous agreement in *Robbins* was that a constitutional distinction between "worthy" and "unworthy" containers would be improper. Even though such a distinction perhaps could evolve in a series of cases in which paper bags, locked trunks, lunch buckets, and orange crates were placed on one side of the line or the other,[30] the central purpose of the Fourth Amendment forecloses such a distinction. For just as the most frail cottage in the kingdom is absolutely entitled to the same guarantees of privacy as the most majestic mansion,[31] so also may a traveler who carries a toothbrush and a few articles of clothing in a paper bag or knotted scarf claim an equal right to conceal his possessions from official inspection as the sophisticated executive with the locked attache case.[61]

As Justice Stewart stated in *Robbins*, the Fourth Amendment pro-

---

28. The practical considerations that justify a warrantless search of an automobile continue to apply until the entire search of the automobile and its contents has been completed. Arguably, the entire vehicle itself (including its upholstery) could be searched without a warrant, with all wrapped articles and containers found during that search then taken to a magistrate. But prohibiting police from opening immediately a container in which the object of the search is most likely to be found and instead forcing them first to comb the entire vehicle would actually exacerbate the intrusion on privacy interests. Moreover, until the container itself was opened the police could never be certain that the contraband was not secreted in a yet undiscovered portion of the vehicle; thus in every case in which a container was found, the vehicle would need to be secured while a warrant was obtained. Such a requirement would be directly inconsistent with the rationale supporting the decisions in *Carroll* and *Chambers*. . . .

30. If the distinction is based on the proposition that the Fourth Amendment protects only those containers that objectively manifest an individual's reasonable expectation of privacy, however, the propriety of a warrantless search necessarily would turn on much more than the fabric of the container. A paper bag stapled shut and marked "private" might be found to manifest a reasonable expectation of privacy, as could a cardboard box stacked on top of two pieces of heavy luggage. The propriety of the warrantless search seemingly would turn on an objective appraisal of all the surrounding circumstances.

31. " 'The poorest man may in his cottage bid defiance to all the forces of the Crown. It may be frail; its roof may shake; the wind may blow through it; the storm may enter; the rain may enter; but the King of England cannot enter—all his forces dares not cross the threshold of the ruined tenement!' " Miller v. United States, 357 U.S. 301, 307 (quoting remarks attributed to William Pitt). . . .

61. Cf A. France, Le Lys Rouge ("The law, in its majestic equality, forbids the rich as well as the poor to sleep under bridges, to beg in the streets, and to steal bread"). But cf. Ybarra v. Illinois, 444 U.S. 85 (1980) (Burger, C.J., dissenting): "I would hold that when police execute a search warrant for narcotics in a place of known narcotics activity they may protect themselves by [frisking all persons present. The police] . . . are not required to assume that they will not be harmed by patrons of the kind of establishment shown here, something quite different from a ballroom at the Waldorf." Id. at 97.—EDS.

vides protection to the owner of every container that conceals its contents from plain view. 453 U.S., at 427 (plurality opinion). But the protection afforded by the Amendment varies in different settings. The luggage carried by a traveler entering the country may be searched at random by a customs officer. . . . A container carried at the time of arrest often may be searched without a warrant and even without any specific suspicion concerning its contents. A container that may conceal the object of a search authorized by a warrant may be opened immediately. . . .

In the same manner, an individual's expectation of privacy in a vehicle and its contents may not survive if probable cause is given to believe that the vehicle is transporting contraband. Certainly the privacy interests in a car's trunk or glove compartment may be no less than those in a movable container. An individual undoubtedly has a significant interest that the upholstery of his automobile will not be ripped or a hidden compartment within it opened. These interests must yield to the authority of a search, however, which—in light of *Carroll*—does not itself require the prior approval of a magistrate. The scope of a warrantless search based on probable cause is no narrower—and no broader—than the scope of a search authorized by a warrant supported by probable cause. Only the prior approval of the magistrate is waived; the search otherwise is as the magistrate could authorize.[32]

The scope of a warrantless search of an automobile thus is not defined by the nature of the container in which the contraband is secreted. Rather, it is defined by the object of the search and the places in which there is probable cause to believe that it may be found. Just as probable cause to believe that a stolen lawnmower may be found in a garage will not support a warrant to search an upstairs bedroom, probable cause to believe that undocumented aliens are being transported in a van will not justify a warrantless search of a suitcase. Probable cause to believe that a container placed in the trunk of a taxi contains contraband or evidence does not justify a search of the entire cab. . . .

. . . Although we have rejected some of the reasoning in *Sanders*, we adhere to our holding in that case; although we reject the precise holding in *Robbins*, there was no Court opinion supporting a single rationale for its judgment. . . .

We reaffirm the basic rule of Fourth Amendment jurisprudence stated by Justice Stewart for a unanimous Court in Mincey v. Arizona,

---

32. In choosing to search without a warrant on their own assesment of probable cause, police officers of course lose the protection that a warrant would provide to them in an action for damages brought by an individual claiming that the search was unconstitutional. Cf. Monroe v. Pape, 365 U.S. 167. Although an officer may establish that he acted in good faith in conducting the search by other evidence, a warrant issued by a magistrate normally suffices to establish it.

437 U.S. 385, 390: "The Fourth Amendment proscribes all unreasonable searches and seizures, and it is a cardinal principle that 'searches conducted outside the judicial process, without prior approval by judge or magistrate, are per se unreasonable under the Fourth Amendment—subject only to a few specifically established and well-delineated exceptions.' Katz v. United States, 389 U.S. 347, 357 (footnotes omitted)." The exception recognized in Carroll is unquestionably one that is "specifically established and well-delineated." We hold that the scope of the warrantless search authorized by that exception is no broader and no narrower than a magistrate could legitimately authorize by warrant. If probable cause justifies the search of a lawfully stopped vehicle, it justifies the search of every part of the vehicle and its contents that may conceal the object of the search.

The judgment of the Court of Appeals is reversed. The case is remanded for further proceedings consistent with this opinion.

It is so ordered.

[The concurring opinion of JUSTICE POWELL and the dissenting opinion of JUSTICE WHITE are omitted.]

JUSTICE MARSHALL, with whom JUSTICE BRENNAN joins, dissenting.[1] . . .

. . . [I]n blithely suggesting that *Carroll* "neither broadened nor limited the scope of a lawful search based on probable cause," the majority assumes what has never been the law: the scope of the automobile-mobility exception to the warrant requirement is as broad as the scope of a "lawful" probable cause search of an automobile, i.e., one authorized by a magistrate.

The majority's sleight-of-hand ignores the obvious differences between the function served by a magistrate in making a determination of probable cause and the function of the automobile exception. It is irrelevant to a magistrate's function whether the items subject to search are mobile, may be in danger of destruction, or are impractical to store, or whether an immediate search would be less intrusive than a seizure without a warrant. A magistrate's only concern is whether there is probable cause to search them. Where suspicion has focused not on a particular item but only on a vehicle, home, or office, the magistrate might reasonably authorize a search of closed containers at the location as well. But an officer on the beat who searches an automobile without a warrant is not entitled to conduct a broader search than the exigency obviating

---

1. The Court confines its holding today to automobiles stopped on the highway which police have probable cause to believe contain contraband. I do not understand the Court to address the applicability of the automobile exception rule announced today to parked cars. Cf. Coolidge v. New Hampshire, 403 U.S. 443. (1971).

the warrant justifies. After all, what justifies the warrantless search is not probable cause alone, but *probable cause coupled with the mobility of the automobile*. Because the scope of a *warrantless* search should depend on the scope of the justification for dispensing with a warrant, the entire premise of the majority's opinion fails to support its conclusion.

The majority's rule masks the startling assumption that a policeman's determination of probable cause is the functional equivalent of the determination of a neutral and detached magistrate. This assumption ignores a major premise of the warrant requirement—the importance of having a neutral and detached magistrate determine whether probable cause exists. . . .

. . . [T]he Court's argument that allowing warrantless searches of certain integral compartments of the car in *Carroll* and *Chambers*, while protecting movable containers within the car, would be "illogical" and "absurd," . . . ignores the reason why this Court has allowed warrantless searches of automobile compartments. Surely an integral compartment within a car is just as mobile, and presents the same practical problems of safekeeping, as the car itself. This cannot be said of movable containers located within the car. The fact that there may be a high expectation of privacy in both containers and compartments is irrelevant, since the privacy rationale is not, and cannot be, the justification for the warrantless search of compartments.

The Court's second argument, which focuses on the practical advantages to police of the *Carroll* doctrine, fares no better. The practical considerations which concerned the *Carroll* Court involved the difficulty of immobilizing a vehicle while a warrant must be obtained. . . . *Carroll* hardly suggested, as the Court implies, . . . that a warrantless search is justified simply because it assists police in obtaining more evidence.

. . . In a footnote, the majority suggests that "practical considerations" militate against securing containers found during an automobile search and taking them to the magistrate. . . .

[Those considerations are] unpersuasive. As this Court explained in *Sanders* and as the majority today implicitly concedes, the burden to police departments of seizing a package or personal luggage simply does not compare to the burden of seizing and safeguarding automobiles. . . . Other aspects of the Court's explanation are also implausible. The search will not always require a "combing" of the entire vehicle, since police may be looking for a particular item and may discover it promptly. If, instead, they are looking more generally for evidence of a crime, the immediate opening of the container will not protect the defendant's privacy; whether or not it contains contraband, the police will continue to search for new evidence. Finally, the defendant, not the police, should be afforded the choice whether he prefers the immediate opening of his

suitcase or other container to the delay incident to seeking a warrant. . . . The more reasonable presumption, if a presumption is to
replace the defendant's consent, is surely that the immediate search of a
closed container will be a greater invasion of the defendant's privacy
interests than a mere temporary seizure of the container.[8]

Finally, the majority's new rule is theoretically unsound and will
create anomalous and unwarranted results. . . . The Court suggests that
probable cause to search only a container does not justify a warrantless
search of an automobile in which it is placed, absent reason to believe
that the contents could be secreted elsewhere in the vehicle. This, the
majority asserts, is an indication that the new rule is carefully limited to
its justification, and is not inconsistent with *Chadwick* and *Sanders*. But
why is such a container more private, less difficult for police to seize and
store, or in any other relevant respect more properly subject to the warrant
requirement, than a container that police discover in a probable cause
search of an entire automobile?[10] This rule plainly has peculiar and
unworkable consequences: the Government "must show that the investigating officer knew enough but not too much, that he had sufficient
knowledge to establish probable cause but insufficient knowledge to know
exactly where the contraband was located." United States v. Ross, 655
F.2d 1159, 1202 (C.A.D.C. 1981) (en banc) (Wilkey, J., dissenting).

Alternatively, the majority may be suggesting that *Chadwick* and
Sanders may be explained because the connection of the container to
the vehicle was incidental in these two cases. . . . This interpretation,
however, might well be an exception that swallows up the majority's rule.
In neither *Chadwick* nor *Sanders* did the Court suggest that the delay of
the police was a pretext for taking advantage of the automobile exception.
For all that appears, the Government may have had legitimate reasons
for not searching as soon as they had probable cause. In any event, asking
police to rely on such an uncertain line in distinguishing between legitimate and illegitimate searches for containers in automobiles hardly in-

8. Seizures of automobiles can be distinguished because of the greater interest of
defendants in continuing possession of their means of transportation; in the case of
automobiles, a seizure is more likely to be a greater intrusion than an immediate search.
See Chambers v. Maroney, 399 U.S. 42, 51-52.

10. In a footnote, the Court appears to suggest a more pragmatic rationale for
distinguishing *Chadwick* and *Sanders*—that no practical problems comparable to those
engendered by a general search of a vehicle would arise if the official suspicion is confined
to a particular piece of luggage. . . . This suggestion is illogical. A general search might
disclose only a single item worth searching; conversely, pre-existing suspicion might attach
to a number of items later placed in a car. Surely the protection of the warrant requirement
cannot depend on a numerical count of the items subject to search.

dicates that the majority's approach has brought clarification to this area of the law. . . .[11]

NOTES AND QUESTIONS

1. The dissent in *Ross* suggests in footnote 1 that the Court perhaps should reach a different result in the case of containers discovered during a search of a parked car. What logical basis is there for making such a distinction? Indeed, given *Ross*, is there a logical basis for continuing to maintain that *Chadwick* and *Sanders* are still good law? Or is the point rather that, given both *Ross* and the *Chadwick/Sanders* holdings, logical consistency is impossible and that, therefore, line drawing on some other basis may be appropriate? If so, on what practical or nonlogical basis can one reconcile *Ross* with *Chadwick* and *Sanders*? See generally Gardner, Search and Seizure of Automobiles and Their Contents: Fourth Amendment Considerations in a Post-*Ross* World, 62 Neb. L. Rev. 1 (1983); Grano, Rethinking the Fourth Amendment Warrant Requirement, 19 Am. Crim. L. Rev. 603 (1982); Katz, Automobile Searches and Diminished Expectations in the Warrant Clause, 19 Am. Crim. L. Rev. 557 (1982).

2. Consider footnote 32 of the majority opinion in *Ross*. Of what relevance is this reference to the risks of civil liability when proceeding without a warrant? If there is a legitimate need for a search without a warrant, a substantial risk of liability for proceeding without a warrant would seem counterproductive. On the other hand, if the risk of possible civil liability is not a significant deterrent to warrantless searches, why does the Court bother to make the point in the first place? Incidentally, what is the risk?

3. In United States v. Johns, 469 U.S. 478 (1985), the Supreme Court in effect applied Chambers v. Maroney, page 616 supra, to *Ross*. Officers seized packages from the defendant's truck during a legal warrantless automobile search. The packages were stored in a Drug Enforcement Administration warehouse for three days and then searched without

---

11. Unless one of these alternative explanations is adopted, the Court's attempt to distinguish the holdings in *Chadwick* and *Sanders* is not only unpersuasive but appears to contradict the Court's own theory. The Court suggests that in each case, the connection of the container to the vehicle was simply coincidental, and notes that the police did not have probable cause to search the entire vehicle. But the police assuredly did have probable cause to search the vehicle *for the container*. The Court states that the scope of the permitted warrantless search is determined only by what a magistrate could authorize. . . . Once police found that container, according to the Court's own rule, they should have been entitled to search at least the container without a warrant. There was probable cause to search and the car was mobile in each case.

a warrant. The Court held that since the packages could have been searched as part of the automobile search, the delayed warrantless search was legal.

4. Justice Stevens, author of the Court's opinion in *Ross*, was part of the majority in *Johns*. Yet he dissented from the Court's application of the automobile exception to mobile motor homes in *Carney*, page 624 supra. In his *Carney* dissent, Justice Stevens argued that the majority had "accorded priority to an exception rather than the general rule, and . . . abandoned the limits on the exception imposed by prior cases." 471 U.S. at 396. Can these same criticisms fairly be made of Justice Stevens's position in *Ross?*

5. For an analysis and criticism of *Carney, Johns,* and other recent automobile exception cases, see Katz, The Automobile Exception Transformed: The Rise of a Public Place Exemption to the Warrant Requirement, 36 Case W. Res. L. Rev. 375 (1986).

c. The Plain View Doctrine

HORTON v. CALIFORNIA
Certiorari to the Court of Appeal of California
110 S. Ct. 2301 (1990)

JUSTICE STEVENS delivered the opinion of the Court.

In this case we revisit an issue that was considered, but not conclusively resolved, in Coolidge v. New Hampshire, 403 U.S. 443 (1971): Whether the warrantless seizure of evidence of crime in plain view is prohibited by the Fourth Amendment if the discovery of the evidence was not inadvertent. We conclude that even though inadvertence is a characteristic of most legitimate "plain view" seizures, it is not a necessary condition. . . .

Petitioner was convicted of the armed robbery of Erwin Wallaker, the treasurer of the San Jose Coin Club. When Wallaker returned to his home after the Club's annual show, he entered his garage and was accosted by two masked men, one armed with a machine gun and the other with an electrical shocking device, sometimes referred to as a "stun gun." The two men shocked Wallaker, bound and handcuffed him, and robbed him of jewelry and cash. . . .

Sergeant LaRault, an experienced police officer, investigated the crime and determined that there was probable cause to search petitioner's home for the proceeds of the robbery and for the weapons used by the robbers. His affidavit for a search warrant referred to police reports that described the weapons as well as the proceeds, but the warrant issued by the Magistrate only authorized a search for the proceeds, including three specifically described rings.

Pursuant to the warrant, LaRault searched petitioner's residence, but he did not find the stolen property. During the course of the search, however, he discovered the weapons in plain view and seized them. Specifically, he seized an Uzi machine gun, a .38 caliber revolver, two stun guns, a handcuff key, a San Jose Coin Club advertising brochure, and a few items of clothing identified by the victim. LaRault testified that while he was searching for the rings, he also was interested in finding other evidence connecting petitioner to the robbery. Thus, the seized evidence was not discovered "inadvertently."

The trial court refused to suppress the evidence found in petitioner's home and, after a jury trial, petitioner was found guilty and sentenced to prison. The California Court of Appeal affirmed. . . .

The criteria that generally guide "plain view" seizures were set forth in Coolidge v. New Hampshire, 403 U.S. 443 (1971). The Court held that the seizure of two automobiles parked in plain view on the defendant's driveway in the course of arresting the defendant violated the Fourth Amendment. Accordingly, particles of gun powder that had been subsequently found in vacuum sweepings from one of the cars could not be introduced in evidence against the defendant. The State endeavored to justify the seizure of the automobiles and their subsequent search at the police station, on four different grounds, including the "plain view" doctrine.[6] The scope of that doctrine as it had developed in earlier cases was fairly summarized in these three paragraphs from Justice Stewart's opinion:

> It is well established that under certain circumstances the police may seize evidence in plain view without a warrant. But it is important to keep in mind that, in the vast majority of cases, *any* evidence seized by the police will be in plain view, at least at the moment of seizure. The problem with the "plain view" doctrine has been to identify the circumstances in which plain view has legal significance rather than being simply the normal concomitant of any search, legal or illegal.
>
> An example of the applicability of the "plain view" doctrine is the situation in which the police have a warrant to search a given area for specified objects, and in the course of the search come across some other article of incriminating character. . . . Where the initial intrusion that

6. The State primarily contended that the seizures were authorized by a warrant issued by the Attorney General, but the Court held the warrant invalid because it had not been issued by "a neutral and detached magistrate." 403 U.S., at 449-453. In addition, the State relied on three exceptions from the warrant requirement: (1) search incident to arrest; (2) the automobile exception; and (3) the "plain view" doctrine. Id., at 453-473.

brings the police within plain view of such an article is supported, not by a warrant, but by one of the recognized exceptions to the warrant requirement, the seizure is also legitimate. Thus the police may inadvertently come across evidence while in "hot pursuit" of a fleeing suspect. . . . And an object that comes into view during a search incident to arrest that is appropriately limited in scope under existing law may be seized without a warrant. . . . Finally, the "plain view" doctrine has been applied where a police officer is not searching for evidence against the accused, but nonetheless inadvertently comes across an incriminating object. . . .

What the "plain view" cases have in common is that the police officer in each of them had a prior justification for an intrusion in the course of which he came inadvertently across a piece of evidence incriminating the accused. The doctrine serves to supplement the prior justification—whether it be a warrant for another object, hot pursuit, search incident to lawful arrest, or some other legitimate reason for being present unconnected with a search directed against the accused—and permits the warrantless seizure. Of course, the extension of the original justification is legitimate only where it is immediately apparent to the police that they have evidence before them; the "plain view" doctrine may not be used to extend a general exploratory search from one object to another until something incriminating at last emerges. [403 U.S at 465-466 (footnote omitted).]

Justice Stewart then described the two limitations on the doctrine that he found implicit in its rationale: First, "that plain view *alone* is never enough to justify the warrantless seizure of evidence, id., at 468; and second, "that the discovery of evidence in plain view must be inadvertent." Id., at 469.

Justice Stewart's analysis of the "plain view" doctrine did not command a majority. . . . Justice Harlan, who concurred in the Court's judgment . . . did not join the plurality's discussion of the "plain view" doctrine. . . . The decision nonetheless is a binding precedent. Before discussing the second limitation, which is implicated in this case, it is therefore necessary to explain why the first adequately supports the Court's judgment.

It is, of course, an essential predicate to any valid warrantless seizure of incriminating evidence that the officer did not violate the Fourth Amendment in arriving at the place from which the evidence could be plainly viewed. There are, moreover, two additional conditions that must be satisfied to justify the warrantless seizure. First, not only must the item be in plain view, its incriminating character must also be "immediately apparent." Id., at 466. . . . Second, not only must the officer be lawfully located in a place from which the object can be plainly seen, but he or she must also have a lawful right of access to the object itself.[7]

7. "This is simply a corollary of the familiar principle discussed above, that no

As the Solicitor General has suggested, Justice Harlan's vote in *Coolidge* may have rested on the fact that the seizure of the cars was accomplished by means of a warrantless trespass on the defendant's property. In all events, we are satisfied that the absence of inadvertence was not essential to the Court's rejection of the State's "plain view" argument in *Coolidge*. . . .

Justice Stewart concluded that the inadvertence requirement was necessary to avoid a violation of the express constitutional requirement that a valid warrant must particularly describe the things to be seized. He explained:

> The rationale of the exception to the warrant requirement, as just stated, is that a plain-view seizure will not turn an initially valid (and therefore limited) search into a "general" one, while the inconvenience of procuring a warrant to cover an inadvertent discovery is great. But where the discovery is anticipated, where the police know in advance the location of the evidence and intend to seize it, the situation is altogether different. The requirement of a warrant to seize imposes no inconvenience whatever, or at least none which is constitutionally cognizable in a legal system that regards warrantless searches as "per se unreasonable" in the absence of "exigent circumstances."
>
> If the initial intrusion is bottomed upon a warrant that fails to mention a particular object, though the police know its location and intend to seize it, then there is a violation of the express constitutional requirement of "Warrants . . . particularly describing . . . [the] things to be seized." [403 U.S., at 469-471.]

We find two flaws in this reasoning. First, evenhanded law enforcement is best achieved by the application of objective standards of conduct, rather than standards that depend upon the subjective state of mind of the officer. The fact that an officer is interested in an item of evidence and fully expects to find it in the course of a search should not invalidate its seizure if the search is confined in area and duration by the terms of a warrant or a valid exception to the warrant requirement. If the officer has knowledge approaching certainty that the item will be found, we see no reason why he or she would deliberately omit a particular description of the item to be seized from the application for a search warrant. Spec-

---

amount of probable cause can justify a warrantless search or seizure absent 'exigent circumstances.' Incontrovertible testimony of the senses that an incriminating object is on premises belonging to a criminal suspect may establish the fullest possible measure of probable cause. But even where the object is contraband, this Court has repeatedly stated and enforced the basic rule that the police may not enter and make a warrantless seizure. . . ." *Coolidge*, 403 U.S., at 468. We have since applied the same rule to the arrest of a person in his home. See Minnesota v. Olson, — U.S. — (1990); Payton v. New York, 445 U.S. 573 (1980).

ification of the additional item could only permit the officer to expand the scope of the search. On the other hand, if he or she has a valid warrant to search for one item and merely a suspicion concerning the second, whether or not it amounts to probable cause, we fail to see why that suspicion should immunize the second item from seizure if it is found during a lawful search for the first. . . .

Second, the suggestion that the inadvertence requirement is necessary to prevent the police from conducting general searches, or from converting specific warrants into general warrants, is not persuasive because that interest is already served by the requirements that no warrant issue unless it "particularly describ[es] the place to be searched and the persons or things to be seized," . . . [10] and that a warrantless search be circumscribed by the exigencies which justify its initiation. . . . If the scope of the search exceeds that permitted by the terms of a validly issued warrant or the character of the relevant exception from the warrant requirement, the subsequent seizure is unconstitutional without more. Thus, in the case of a search incident to a lawful arrest, "[i]f the police stray outside the scope of an authorized *Chimel* search they are already in violation of the Fourth Amendment, and evidence so seized will be excluded; adding a second reason for excluding evidence hardly seems worth the candle." *Coolidge*, 403 U.S., at 517. . . .

In this case, the scope of the search was not enlarged in the slightest by the omission of any reference to the weapons in the warrant. Indeed, if the three rings and other items named in the warrant had been found at the outset—or if petitioner had them in his possession and had responded to the warrant by producing them immediately—no search for weapons could have taken place. . . . Justice White's dissenting opinion in *Coolidge* is instructive:

> Police with a warrant for a rifle may search only places where rifles might be and must terminate the search once the rifle is found; the inadvertence rule will in no way reduce the number of places into which they may lawfully look. [403 U.S., at 517.]

---

10. "The Warrant Clause of the Fourth Amendment categorically prohibits the issuance of any warrant except one 'particularly describing the place to be searched and the persons or things to be seized.' The manifest purpose of this particularity requirement was to prevent general searches. By limiting the authorization to search to the specific areas and things for which there is probable cause to search, the requirement ensures that the search will be carefully tailored to its justifications, and will not take on the character of the wide-ranging exploratory searches the Framers intended to prohibit." Maryland v. Garrison, 480 U.S. 79, 84 (1987).

As we have already suggested, by hypothesis the seizure of an object in plain view does not involve an intrusion on privacy.[11] If the interest in privacy has been invaded, the violation must have occurred before the object came into plain view and there is no need for an inadvertence limitation on seizures to condemn it. The prohibition against general searches and general warrants serves primarily as a protection against unjustified intrusions on privacy. But reliance on privacy concerns that support that prohibition is misplaced when the inquiry concerns the scope of an exception that merely authorizes an officer with a lawful right of access to an item to seize it without a warrant.

In this case the items seized from petitioner's home were discovered during a lawful search authorized by a valid warrant. When they were discovered, it was immediately apparent to the officer that they constituted incriminating evidence. He had probable cause, not only to obtain a warrant to search for the stolen property, but also to believe that the weapons and handguns had been used in the crime he was investigating. The search was authorized by the warrant, the seizure was authorized by the "plain view" doctrine. The judgment is affirmed. . . .

JUSTICE BRENNAN, with whom JUSTICE MARSHALL joins, dissenting.
. . . The prohibition against unreasonable searches and the requirement that a warrant "particularly describ[e] the place to be searched" protect an interest in privacy. The prohibition against unreasonable seizures and the requirement that a warrant "particularly describ[e] . . . the . . . things to be seized" protect a possessory interest in property.[1] . . . The Fourth Amendment, by its terms, declares the privacy and possessory interests to be equally important. . . .

. . . Just as a warrantless search is per se unreasonable absent exigent circumstances, so too a seizure of personal property is "per se unreasonable within the meaning of the Fourth Amendment unless it is accomplished pursuant to a judicial warrant issued upon probable cause and particularly describing the items to be seized." United States v. Place, 462 U.S. 696, 701 (1983). . . . A decision to invade a possessory interest in property is too important to be left to the discretion of zealous officers

---

11. "Even if the item is a container, its seizure does not compromise the interest in preserving the privacy of its contents because it may only be opened pursuant to either a search warrant, see . . . United States v. Chadwick, 433 U.S. 1 (1977); . . . or one of the well-delineated exceptions to the warrant requirement. See Colorado v. Bertine, 479 U.S. 367 (1987); United States v. Ross, 456 U.S. 798 (1982).

1. As the majority recognizes, the requirement that warrants particularly describe the things to be seized also protects privacy interests by preventing general searches. . . . The scope of a search is limited to those places in which there is probable cause to believe an item particularly described in the warrant might be found. . . .

"engaged in the often competitive enterprise of ferreting out crime."
Johnson v. United States, 333 U.S. 10, 14 (1948). . . .

The plain view doctrine is an exception to the general rule that a
seizure of personal property must be authorized by a warrant. As Justice
Stewart explained in *Coolidge*, 403 U.S., at 470, we accept a warrantless
seizure when an officer is lawfully in a location and inadvertently sees
evidence of a crime because of "the inconvenience of procuring a warrant"
to seize this newly discovered piece of evidence. But "where the discovery
is anticipated, where the police know in advance the location of the
evidence and intend to seize it," the argument that procuring a warrant
would be "inconvenient" loses much, if not all of its force. Ibid. . . .

Although joined by only three other Members of the Court, Justice
Stewart's discussion of the inadvertent discovery requirement has become
widely accepted. . . . Forty-six States and the District of Columbia and
twelve United States Courts of Appeals now require plain view seizures
to be inadvertent. There has been no outcry from law enforcement officials that the inadvertent discovery requirement unduly burdens their
efforts. Given that the requirement is inescapably rooted in the plain
language of the Fourth Amendment, I cannot fathom the Court's enthusiasm for discarding this element of the plain view doctrine.

The Court posits two "flaws" in Justice Stewart's reasoning. . . .
But these flaws are illusory. First, the majority explains that it can see
no reason why an officer . . . "would deliberately omit a particular
description of the item to be seized from the application for a search
warrant." . . . But to the individual whose possessory interest has been
invaded, it matters not *why* the police officer decided to omit a particular
item from his application for a search warrant. . . . Suppression of the
evidence so seized will encourage officers to be more precise and complete
in future warrant applications.

Furthermore, there are a number of instances in which a law enforcement officer might deliberately choose to omit certain items from a
warrant application. . . . For example, the warrant application process
can often be time-consuming, especially when the police attempt to seize
a large number of items. . . . An officer might rationally find the risk
of immediately discovering the items listed in the warrant—thereby forcing him to conclude the search immediately—outweighed by the time
saved in the application process.

The majority also contends that, once an officer is lawfully in a
house and the scope of his search is adequately circumscribed by a warrant, "no additional Fourth Amendment interest is furthered by requiring
that the discovery of evidence be inadvertent." . . . The majority is
correct, but it has asked the wrong question. It is true that the inadvertent
discovery requirement furthers no privacy interests. The requirement in

no way reduces the scope of a search or the number of places into which officers may look. But it does protect possessory interests. . . . The inadvertent discovery requirement is essential if we are to take seriously the Fourth Amendment's protection of possessory interests as well as privacy interests. . . . The Court today eliminates a rule designed to further possessory interests on the ground that it fails to further privacy interests. . . .

Fortunately, this decision should have only a limited impact, for the Court is not confronted today with what lower courts have described as a "pretextual" search. See, e.g., State v. Lair, 95 Wash. 2d 706, 717-718, 630 P.2d 427, 434 (1981) (en banc) (holding pretextual searches invalid). For example, if an officer enters a house pursuant to a warrant to search for evidence of one crime when he is really interested only in seizing evidence relating to another crime, for which he does not have a warrant, his search is "pretextual" and the fruits of that search should be suppressed. See, e.g., State v. Kelsey, 592 S.W.2d 509 (Mo. App. 1979) (evidence suppressed because officers, who had ample opportunity to obtain warrant relating to murder investigation, entered the premises instead pursuant to a warrant relating to a drug investigation, and searched only the hiding place of the murder weapon, rather than conducting a "top to bottom" search for drugs). Similarly, an officer might use an exception to the generally applicable warrant requirement, such as "hot pursuit," as a pretext to enter a home to seize items he knows he will find in plain view. Such conduct would be a deliberate attempt to circumvent the constitutional requirement of a warrant "particularly describing the place to be searched, and the persons or things to be seized," and cannot be condoned.

The discovery of evidence in pretextual searches is not "inadvertent" and should be suppressed for that reason. But even state courts that have rejected the inadvertent discovery requirement have held that the Fourth Amendment prohibits pretextual searches. See State v. Bussard, 114 Idaho 781, 788, n.2, 760 P.2d 1197, 1204, n.2 (1988); State v. Kelly, 718 P.2d 385, 389, n.1 (Utah 1986). The Court's opinion today does not address pretextual searches, but I have no doubt that such searches violate the Fourth Amendment. . . .

NOTES AND QUESTIONS

1. Should inconvenience alone ever be a sufficient basis for dispensing with the warrant requirement? Although in *Coolidge* Justice Stewart emphasized inconvenience, his inadvertence requirement had the effect of ensuring that in many instances there would also be exigent

circumstances: Inadvertence ensured that there was not an opportunity to obtain a warrant prior to the discovery, and frequently there would be a risk that somebody would move or destroy the evidence after its discovery and before the police could obtain a warrant.

2. Should there be a constitutional difference between (1) the "inconvenience" that Justice Brennan acknowledges as a sufficient reason for forgoing a warrant when the discovery of an item is inadvertent and (2) the "inconvenience" that Justice Brennan offers as a reason why the police may deliberately avoid listing all items in a warrant application?

3. With respect to the role of the warrant process in protecting a person's possessory interest, consider the following: Are the police more likely to be mistaken about probable cause or whether an item is what it purports to be when they come upon the item inadvertently or when they anticipate its presence? In any event, since the police are already where they have a right to be—frequently as a result of having entered a person's home or in some other way substantially infringed on the person's privacy interest, can one justify the warrantless seizure of items found in plain view as a relatively minor additional infringement of interests protected by the fourth amendment? Cf. pages 647-650 infra (discussion of warrantless seizures of persons).

4. In both *Coolidge* and *Horton*, the Court stated that the seizable nature of the items discovered in plain view must be "immediately apparent." In Arizona v. Hicks, 480 U.S. 321 (1987),[62] the Court had interpreted this language as meaning that the police must have probable cause to seize the evidence:

> To say otherwise would be to cut the "plain view" doctrine loose from its theoretical and practical moorings. The theory of the doctrine consists of extending to nonpublic places such as the home, where searches and seizures without a warrant are presumptively unreasonable, the police's longstanding authority to make warrantless seizures in public places of such objects as weapons and contraband. . . . And the practical justification for that extension is the desirability of sparing police, whose viewing the object in the course of a lawful search is as legitimate as it would have been in a public place, the inconvenience and the risk—to themselves or to preservation of the evidence—of going to obtain a warrant. . . . Dispensing with the need for a warrant is worlds apart from permitting a lesser standard of *cause* for the seizure than a warrant would require, i.e., the standard of probable cause. No reason is apparent why an object should routinely be seizable on lesser grounds, during an unrelated search and seizure, than would have been needed to obtain a warrant for the same object if it had been known to be on the premises. [Id. at 326-327.]

62. Other aspects of *Hicks* are discussed at page 794 infra.

5. On the problem of pretext searches, see Burkoff, The Pretext Search Doctrine: Now You See It, Now You Don't, 17 U. Mich. J.L. Reform 523 (1984).

d. Arrest and Entry to Arrest

As we noted in conjunction with the discussion of Carroll v. United States, page 614 supra, the common law permitted warrantless misdemeanor arrests if the arresting officers observed the misdemeanor being committed in their presence and warrantless felony arrests if the officers had probable cause to arrest. In United States v. Watson, 423 U.S. 411 (1976), the Supreme Court for the first time addressed the question whether the fourth amendment permitted warrantless felony arrests. The police, without a warrant but with probable cause arrested Watson in a public restaurant after a reliable informant signaled that Watson was in possession of stolen credit cards. Following the arrest, the police officers obtained Watson's consent to search his car, where they found stolen credit cards. Watson claimed, inter alia, that the consent to search was invalid because it was the product of an illegal arrest. The Supreme Court, in an opinion by Justice White, held that the warrantless arrest was legal. The Court pointed out that (1) federal statutes authorize FBI agents, postal inspectors, and other federal officials to make warrantless felony arrests, (2) from 1792 on Congress had consistently authorized warrantless felony arrests, (3) the "usual" and "ancient common-law" rule permitted warrantless felony arrests based on probable cause, (4) this had been "the prevailing rule under state constitutions and statutes," and (5) the Court on various occasions had recited the rule with approval.

In a dissenting opinion Justice Marshall first argued that the Court should have decided the case on a narrower ground:

> The signal of the reliable informant that Watson was in possession of stolen credit cards gave the postal inspectors probable cause to make the arrest. . . . When law enforcement officers have probable cause to believe that an offense is taking place in their presence and that the suspect is at that moment in possession of the evidence, exigent circumstances exist. Delay could cause the escape of the suspect or the destruction of the evidence. Accordingly, Watson's warrantless arrest was valid under the recognized exigent-circumstances exception to the warrant requirement, and the Court has no occasion to consider whether a warrant would otherwise be necessary. [Id. at 434-435.]

He then argued that the common law precedent for permitting warrantless felony arrests in fact supported the defendant's claim that the fourth amendment should require an arrest warrant in the absence of exigent circumstances. Noting that crimes such as assault with intent to commit rape, murder, or robbery, abortion, bribing voters, escaping from lawful arrest, forcible entry, kidnapping, obstructing justice, and perjury were all misdemeanors at common law, Justice Marshall observed:

> Only the most serious crimes were felonies at common law, and many crimes now classified as felonies under federal or state law were treated as misdemeanors. . . . [T]he only clear lesson of history is . . . [that] the common law considered the arrest warrant far more important than today's decision leaves it. [Id. at 439-440.]

NOTES AND QUESTIONS

1. Who do you think has the better of the historical argument in *Watson?* On the one hand, as Justice Marshall points out, the changing definition of *felony* appears to support the dissent. On the other hand, the extensive statutory precedent for warrantless arrests seems to support the majority. Admittedly, the statutory precedent is not necessarily determinative of the constitutional question. But is the precedent not entitled at least to some weight? Does Justice Marshall give it any weight?

2. Justice Marshall recognizes that in some cases (including *Watson* itself), exigent circumstances will justify a warrantless arrest. Are similar exigencies likely to exist in many situations in which the police make an arrest in a public place? If so, is the administrative convenience of a flat rule that warrants are never required a sufficient justification for the *Watson* holding?

3. Consider the following passage from Justice Powell's *Watson* concurring opinion:

> Since the Fourth Amendment speaks equally to both searches and seizures, and since an arrest . . . is quintessentially a seizure, it would seem that the constitutional provision should impose the same limitations upon arrests that it does upon searches. Indeed, as an abstract matter an argument can be made that the restrictions upon arrest perhaps should be greater. A search may cause only annoyance and temporary inconvenience to the law-abiding citizen, assuming more serious dimension only when it turns up evidence of criminality. An arrest, however, is a serious personal intrusion regardless of whether the person seized is guilty or innocent. . . . Logic therefore would seem to dictate that arrests be subject to the warrant requirement at least to the same extent as searches.
>
> But logic sometimes must defer to history and experience. [423 U.S. at 428-429.]

Why?

4. Even though a warrant is not required for arrests, the probable cause determination cannot always be left solely to the police or prosecutor. One year prior to *Watson*, the Court in *Gerstein v. Pugh*, 420 U.S. 103 (1975), held that a defendant arrested without a warrant has the fourth amendment right, as a condition of continued incarceration, to a speedy probable cause determination by a judicial officer. From one perspective *Gerstein* may not seem to provide much protection to defendants. The determination must be made only for defendants who remain in custody or suffer some other "significant pretrial restraint of liberty;"[63] and it may be made ex parte, without any input from the defendant.[64] On the other hand, pre-arrest probable cause determinations that lead to the issuance of warrants are also ex parte. Moreover, an after-the-fact determination, although it will not prevent arrests on less than probable cause, is better than nothing. Indeed, *Gerstein* mandates a mechanism for judicial determination of probable cause to arrest that is not mandated for evaluating the propriety of warrantless seizures of objects.

Consider the Court's rationale for the *Gerstein* after-the-fact speedy probable cause determination:

> Once the suspect is in custody . . . the reasons that justify, dispensing with the magistrate's neutral judgment evaporate. There no longer is any danger that the suspect will escape or commit further crimes while the police submit their evidence to a magistrate. And . . . the suspect's need for a neutral determination of probable cause increases significantly. The consequences of prolonged detention may be more serious than the interference occasioned by arrest. Pretrial confinement may imperil the suspect's job, interrupt his source of income, and impair his family relationships. . . . Even pretrial release may be accompanied by burdensome conditions that effect a significant restraint of liberty. . . . When the stakes are this high, the detached judgment of a neutral magistrate is essential if the Fourth Amendment is to furnish meaningful protection from unfounded interference with liberty. [Id. at 114.]

If the stakes are really this high, was *Watson* wrongly decided? Can *Gerstein* and *Watson* be reconciled by resort to history? Consider the following:

63. 420 U.S. at 125. The Court elaborated, "There are many kinds of pretrial release and many degrees of conditional liberty. . . . We cannot define specifically those that would require a prior probable cause determination, but the key factor is significant restraint of liberty." Id. at 125 n.26.

64. If the grand jury has returned an indictment against the defendant, the grand jury's probable cause finding will suffice, and the *Gerstein* determination will not be necessary. 420 U.S. at 117 n.19.

At common law it was customary, if not obligatory, for an arrested person
to be brought before a justice of the peace shortly after arrest. . . . The
justice of the peace would "examine" the prisoner and the witnesses to
determine whether there was reason to believe the prisoner had committed
a crime. If there was, the suspect would be committed to jail or bailed
pending trial. If not, he would be discharged from custody. . . . The
initial determination of probable cause also could be reviewed by higher
courts on a writ of habeas corpus. . . . This practice furnished the model
for criminal procedure in America immediately following the adoption of
the Fourth Amendment, . . . and there are indications that the Framers
of the Bill of Rights regarded it as a model for a "reasonable" seizure. [Id.
at 114-116.]

Should the fourth amendment require a *Gerstein* probable cause
determination following the warrantless seizure of objects?

PAYTON v. NEW YORK
Appeal from the Court of Appeals of New York
445 U.S. 573 (1980)

MR. JUSTICE STEVENS delivered the opinion of the Court.

These appeals challenge the constitutionality of New York statutes
that authorize police officers to enter a private residence without a warrant
and with force, if necessary, to make a routine felony arrest. . . .

I

On January 14, 1970, after two days of intensive investigation, New York
detectives had assembled evidence sufficient to establish probable cause
to believe that Theodore Payton had murdered the manager of a gas
station two days earlier. At about 7:30 A.M, on January 15, six officers
went to Payton's apartment in the Bronx, intending to arrest him. They
had not obtained a warrant. Although light and music emanated from
the apartment, there was no response to their knock on the metal door.
They summoned emergency assistance and, about 30 minutes later, used
crowbars to break open the door and enter the apartment. No one was
there. In plain view, however, was a .30-caliber shell casing that was
seized and later admitted into evidence at Payton's murder trial.

In due course Payton surrendered to the police, was indicted for
murder, and moved to suppress the evidence taken from his apartment.
The trial judge held that the warrantless and forcible entry was authorized
by [New York law] . . . and that the evidence in plain view was properly
seized. He found that exigent circumstances justified the officers' failure

to announce their purpose before entering the apartment as required by the statute. . . .

On March 14, 1974, Obie Riddick was arrested for the commission of two armed robberies that had occurred in 1971, He had been identified by the victims in June 1973, and in January 1974 the police had learned his address. They did not obtain a warrant for his arrest. At about noon on March 14, a detective, accompanied by three other officers, knocked on the door of the Queens house where Riddick was living. When his young son opened the door, they could see Riddick sitting in bed covered by a sheet. They entered the house and placed him under arrest. Before permitting him to dress, they opened a chest of drawers two feet from the bed in search of weapons and found narcotics and related parapher- nalia. Riddick was subsequently indicted on narcotics charges. At a suppression hearing, the trial judge held that the warrantless entry into his home was authorized by [New York law] . . . and that the search of the immediate area was reasonable under Chimel v. California, [page 721 infra, as a search incident to Riddick's arrest]. . . .

The New York Court of Appeals, in a single opinion, affirmed the convictions of both Payton and Riddick. 45 N.Y.2d 300, 380 N.E.2d 224 (1978). . . .

Before addressing the narrow question presented by these appeals, we put to one side other related problems that are *not* presented today. Although it is arguable that the warrantless entry to effect Payton's arrest might have been justified by exigent circumstances, none of the New York courts relied on any such justification. The Court of Appeals ma- jority treated both Payton's and Riddick's cases as involving routine arrests in which there was ample time to obtain a warrant, and we will do the same. Accordingly, we have no occasion to consider the sort of emergency or dangerous situation, described in our cases as "exigent circumstances," that would justify a warrantless entry into a home for the purpose of either arrest or search.

Nor do these cases raise any question concerning the authority of the police, without either a search or arrest warrant, to enter a third party's home to arrest a suspect. . . . We also note that in neither case is it argued that the police lacked probable cause to believe that the suspect was at home when they entered. Finally, in both cases we are dealing with entries into homes made without the consent of any oc- cupant. . . .

II . . .

The simple language of the Amendment applies equally to seizures of persons and to seizures of property. Our analysis in this case may therefore properly commence with rules that have been well established in Fourth Amendment litigation involving tangible items. As the Court reiterated just a few years ago, the "physical entry of the home is the chief evil against which the wording of the Fourth Amendment is directed." United States v. United States District Court, 407 U.S. 297, 313. And we have long adhered to the view that the warrant procedure minimizes the danger of needless intrusions of that sort. . . .

The majority of the New York Court of Appeals, however, suggested that there is a substantial difference in the relative intrusiveness of an entry to search for property and an entry to search for a person. . . . It is true that the area that may legally be searched is broader when executing a search warrant than when executing an arrest warrant in the home. See Chimel v. California, [page 721 infra]. This difference may be more theoretical than real, however, because the police may need to check the entire premises for safety reasons, and sometimes they ignore the restrictions on searches incident to arrest.

But the critical point is that any differences in the intrusiveness of entries to search and entries to arrest are merely ones of degree rather than kind. The two intrusions share this fundamental characteristic: the breach of the entrance to an individual's home. The Fourth Amendment protects the individual's privacy in a variety of settings. In none is the zone of privacy more clearly defined than when bounded by the unambiguous physical dimensions of an individual's home—a zone that finds its roots in clear and specific constitutional terms: "The right of the people to be secure in their . . . houses . . . shall not be violated." That language unequivocally establishes the proposition that "[a]t the very core [of the Fourth Amendment] stands the right of a man to retreat into his own home and there be free from unreasonable governmental intrusion." Silverman v. United States, 365 U.S. 505, 511. In terms that apply equally to seizures of property and to seizures of persons, the Fourth Amendment has drawn a firm line at the entrance to the house. Absent exigent circumstances, that threshold may not reasonably be crossed without a warrant. . . .

IV

The parties have argued at some length about the practical consequences of a warrant requirement as a precondition to a felony arrest in the home.[55]

___

55. The State of New York argues that the warrant requirement will pressure police to seek warrants and make arrests too hurriedly, thus increasing the likelihood of arresting innocent people; that it will divert scarce resources thereby interfering with the police's

In the absence of any evidence that effective law enforcement has suffered in those States that already have such a requirement, . . . we are inclined to view such arguments with skepticism. More fundamentally, however, such arguments of policy must give way to a constitutional command that we consider to be unequivocal.

Finally, we note the State's suggestion that only a search warrant based on probable cause to believe the suspect is at home at a given time can adequately protect the privacy interests at stake, and since such a warrant requirement is manifestly impractical, there need be no warrant of any kind. We find this ingenious argument unpersuasive. It is true that an arrest warrant requirement may afford less protection than a search warrant requirement, but it will suffice to interpose the magistrate's determination of probable cause between the zealous officer and the citizen. If there is sufficient evidence of a citizen's participation in a felony to persuade a judicial officer that his arrest is justified, it is constitutionally reasonable to require him to open his doors to the officers of the law. Thus, for Fourth Amendment purposes, an arrest warrant founded on probable cause implicitly carries with it the limited authority to enter a dwelling in which the suspect lives when there is reason to believe the suspect is within.[65]

Because no arrest warrant was obtained in either of these cases, the judgments must be reversed and the cases remanded to the New York Court of Appeals for further proceedings not inconsistent with this opinion.

It is so ordered. . . .

[The concurring opinion of JUSTICE BLACKMUN and the dissenting opinion of JUSTICE REHNQUIST are omitted.]

MR. JUSTICE WHITE, with whom THE CHIEF JUSTICE and MR. JUSTICE REHNQUIST join, dissenting. . . .

. . . It is necessary in each case to assess realistically the actual extent of invasion of constitutionally protected privacy. Further, as Mr.

---

ability to do thorough investigations,—that it will penalize the police for deliberate planning; and that it will lead to more injuries. Appellants counter that careful planning is possible and that the police need not rush to get a warrant, because if an exigency arises necessitating immediate arrest in the course of an orderly investigation, arrest without a warrant is permissible; that the warrant procedure will decrease the likelihood that an innocent person will be arrested; that the inconvenience of obtaining a warrant and the potential for diversion of resources is exaggerated by the State; and that there is no basis for the assertion that the time required to obtain a warrant would create peril.

65. Cf. Dalia v. United States, 441 U.S. 238 (1979) (fourth amendment does not prohibit covert entry for purpose of installing otherwise legal electronic bugging equipment, nor does fourth amendment require that court order authorizing electronic surveillance give specific authorization for covert entry into premises described in order).— EDS.

Justice Powell observed in United States v. Watson, 423 U.S. [411], 428 [(1976)] (concurring opinion), all arrests involve serious intrusions into an individual's privacy and dignity. Yet we settled in *Watson* that the intrusiveness of a public arrest is not enough to mandate the obtaining of a warrant. The inquiry in the present case, therefore, is whether the incremental intrusiveness that results from an arrest's being made *in the dwelling* is enough to support an inflexible constitutional rule requiring warrants for such arrests whenever exigent circumstances are not present.

Today's decision ignores the carefully crafted restrictions on the common-law power of arrest entry and thereby overestimates the dangers inherent in that practice. At common law, absent exigent circumstances, entries to arrest could be made only for felony. Even in cases of felony, the officers were required to announce their presence, demand admission, and be refused entry before they were entitled to break doors. Further, it seems generally accepted that entries could be made only during daylight hours. And, in my view, the officer entering to arrest must have reasonable grounds to believe, not only that the arrestee has committed a crime, but also that the person suspected is present in the house at the time of the entry.[13]

These four restrictions on home arrest—felony, knock and announce, daytime, and stringent probable cause—constitute powerful and complementary protections for the privacy interests associated with the home. . . . [T]hese requirements, taken together, permit an individual suspected of a serious crime to surrender at the front door of his dwelling and thereby avoid most of the humiliation and indignity that the Court seems to believe necessarily accompany a house arrest entry. Such a front-door arrest, in my view, is no more intrusive on personal privacy than the public warrantless arrests which we found to pass constitutional muster in *Watson*.[14]

All of these limitations on warrantless arrest entries are satisfied on the facts of the present cases. . . .

A rule permitting warrantless arrest entries would not pose a danger that officers would use their entry power as a pretext to justify an otherwise

13. I do not necessarily disagree with the Court's discussion of the quantum of probable cause necessary to make a valid home arrest. The Court indicates that only an arrest warrant, and not a search warrant, is required. . . . To obtain the warrant, therefore, the officers need only show probable cause that a crime has been committed and that the suspect committed it. However, under today's decision, the officers apparently need an extra increment of probable cause when executing the arrest warrant, namely, grounds to believe that the suspect is within the dwelling. . . .

14. If the suspect flees or hides, of course, the intrusiveness of the entry will be somewhat greater; but the policeman's hands should not be tied merely because of the possibility that the suspect will fail to cooperate with legitimate actions by law enforcement personnel.

invalid warrantless search. A search pursuant to a warrantless arrest entry will rarely, if ever, be as complete as one under authority of a search warrant. . . . Furthermore, an arrest entry will inevitably tip off the suspects and likely result in destruction or removal of evidence not uncovered during the arrest. I therefore cannot believe that the police would take the risk of losing valuable evidence through a pretextual arrest entry rather than applying to a magistrate for a search warrant.

While exaggerating the invasion of personal privacy involved in home arrests, the Court fails to account for the danger that its rule will "severely hamper effective law enforcement," United States v. Watson, 423 U.S., at 431 (Powell, J., concurring). [Justice White here reiterated a concern expressed by Justice Powell in *Watson*, namely that a warrant obtained early may grow stale and that a delay in obtaining a warrant may preclude a finding of exigency.][66] . . .

Further, police officers will often face the difficult task of deciding whether the circumstances are sufficiently exigent to justify their entry to arrest without a warrant. This is a decision that must be made quickly in the most trying of circumstances. If the officers mistakenly decide that the circumstances are exigent, the arrest will be invalid and any evidence seized incident to the arrest or in plain view will be excluded at trial. On the other hand, if the officers mistakenly determine that exigent circumstances are lacking, they may refrain from making the arrest, thus creating the possibility that a dangerous criminal will escape into the community. The police could reduce the likelihood of escape by staking out all possible exits until the circumstances become clearly exigent or a warrant is obtained. But the costs of such a stakeout seem excessive in an era of rising crime and scarce police resources.

The uncertainty inherent in the exigent-circumstances determination burdens the judicial system as well. In the case of searches, exigent circumstances are sufficiently unusual that this Court has determined that the benefits of a warrant outweigh the burdens imposed, including the burdens on the judicial system. In contrast, arrests recurringly involve exigent circumstances, and this Court has heretofore held that a warrant can be dispensed with without undue sacrifice in Fourth Amendment values. The situation should be no different with respect to arrests in the home.

Our cases establish that the ultimate test under the Fourth Amendment is one of "reasonableness." Marshall v. Barlow's, Inc., 436 U.S. 307 315-316 (1978); Camara v. Municipal Court, 387 U.S. 523, 539 (1967).[67] I cannot join the Court in declaring unreasonable a practice

---

66. Is staleness likely to be a serious concern with *arrest* warrants?—EDS.
67. These cases are discussed at pages 666-673 infra.—EDS.

which has been thought entirely reasonable by so many for so long. It would be far preferable to adopt a clear and simple rule: after knocking and announcing their presence, police may enter the home to make a daytime arrest without a warrant when there is probable cause to believe that the person to be arrested committed a felony and is present in the house. This rule would best comport with the common-law background, with the traditional practice in the States, and with the history and policies of the Fourth Amendment. Accordingly, I respectfully dissent. . . .

NOTES AND QUESTIONS

1. In portions of the *Payton* opinions that have been deleted here, both the majority and the dissent relied extensively on and disagreed about the significance of various historical data regarding warrantless entries to arrest. Why is history relevant—particularly if, as both the majority and dissent in *Payton* came close to conceding, it is inconclusive? Consider the following passage from Amsterdam, Perspectives on the Fourth Amendment, 58 Minn. L. Rev. 349, 410-412 (1974):

Professor [Telford] Taylor observes that the preconstitutional history of the amendment was concerned exclusively with searches under general warrants and writs of assistance;[502] he infers from this history that "our constitutional fathers were not concerned about warrantless searches, but about overreaching warrants";[503] and he therefore reasons that "Justice Frankfurter, and others"—now comprising a majority of the Supreme Court—"who have viewed the fourth amendment primarily as a requirement that searches be covered by warrants, have stood the amendment on its head."[505] Professor Taylor does not conclude, of course, that warrantless searches are entirely uncovered by the amendment; his view is that they are controlled by the reasonableness requirement of the amendment's first clause;[506] and his difference from the Court is that he would allow a broader range of generally "reasonable" warrantless searches. . . .

I concur with Professor Taylor about the focus of the preconstitutional history. I concur that the framers were "concerned" about general warrants and writs, insofar as "concerned" is used to denote the specific subject that they had under consideration. I concur that the Court has stood the fourth amendment on its head, in the same wise way that the Court has stood the commerce clause on its head in order to allow a collection of states

502. [T. Taylor, Two Studies in Constitutional Interpretation 24-41 (1969).]
503. [Id.] at 41. . . .
505. [Id.] at 46-47. . . .
506. See [Id.] . . . at 98-100.

to grow into a nation. From his ultimate conclusion concerning the permissible scope of warrantless searches, I respectfully dissent.

The Court's construction of the amendment as embodying an overriding preference for search warrants is supportable, in my view, because the Court is obliged to give an internally coherent reading to the unreasonableness clause and the warrant clause as expressions of repudiation of the general warrant. In this view, the fourth amendment condemns searches conducted under general warrants and writs of assistance as "unreasonable." It also forbids unreasonable warrantless searches[, but] . . . the word "unreasonable" is hardly self-illuminating. Surely then the Court has done right to seek some part of the meaning of an "unreasonable" warrantless search by asking what the condemnation of general warrants and writs implies about the nature of "unreasonable" searches and seizures. This is not to assert that the standards of reasonableness for searches with and without warrants must be the same, but merely that warrantless searches exhibiting the same characteristics as general warrants and writs must be deemed unreasonable if there is no principled basis for distinguishing them from general warrants and writs.

The framers of the fourth amendment accepted specific warrants as reasonable: the second clause of the amendment tells us so. Therefore, the objectionable feature of general warrants and writs must be their indiscriminate character. Warrants are not to issue indiscriminately: that is the office of the probable cause requirement. Nor may indiscriminate searches be made under them: that is why particularity of description of the persons or things to be seized is demanded. The requirement of particularity of description of things is important to note, for it shows that even when there is sufficient cause to intrude upon an individual by a search, the framers decreed that it was unreasonable and should be unconstitutional to subject his premises or possessions to indiscriminate seizure.

Indiscriminate searches or seizures might be thought to be bad for either or both of two reasons. The first is that they expose people and their possessions to interferences by government when there is no good reason to do so. The concern here is against *unjustified* searches and seizures: it rests upon the principle that every citizen is entitled to security of his person and property unless and until an adequate justification for disturbing that security is shown. The second is that indiscriminate searches and seizures are conducted at the discretion of executive officials, who may act despotically and capriciously in the exercise of the power to search and seize. This latter concern runs against *arbitrary* searches and seizures: it condemns the petty tyranny of unregulated rummagers.

Although conceptually severable, these two concerns are indissolubly linked throughout the preconstitutional history of the fourth amendment in which Professor Taylor finds its "original understanding."[514] Thus, Lord

514. [Id.] at 38-44.

Camden says in Entick v. Carrington[515] that, if general warrants are sustainable, "the secret cabinets and bureaus of every subject in this kingdom will be thrown open to the search and inspection of a messenger, whenever the secretary of state shall think fit to charge, or even suspect, a person to be the author . . . of a seditious libel," and the person's house will be rifled and his secrets "taken out of his possession, before the paper for which he is charged is found to be criminal by any competent jurisdiction, and before he is convicted . . . of . . . being concerned in the paper." Thus Otis argues that the writs of assistance place "the liberty of every man in the hands of every petty officer";[516] that a man in his house, "while he is quiet, . . . is as well guarded as a prince in his castle," but that general writs "totally annihilate this privilege" because "[c]ustom house officers may enter our houses when they please— . . . bare suspicion without oath is sufficient."[517] Thus, Thatcher, in the same argument, complains that the writs are "not returnable. If the Seizures were so, before your Honors, and this Court should enquire into them you'd often find a wanton exercise of power."[518] The emphasis placed by both the judgments of Lord Camden and the arguments of the Boston advocates upon the lack of a return or inventory underscores the point that the general warrants and writs were thought abusive because they immunized the scope of executive seizure from judicial control. Under the fourth amendment, even where the initial justification for a search was determined by a magistrate, executive discretion in its execution was to be curbed by the requirement of particularity of description in the warrant of the items subject to seizure.[68]

2. The police presumably did not violate Riddick's rights merely by approaching his house, knocking on the front door, and observing him in the house when the door was opened. And Riddick presumably was at least as mobile as the automobiles in *Carroll*, page 614 supra, *Chambers*, page 616 supra, and *Cardwell*, page 621 supra. Why, then, did exigent circumstances not justify an entry to make the arrest?

Perhaps the Court simply overlooked this possible justification for the warrantless entry.[69] If not, the answer must be that the warrantless entry was illegal because the police had ample time to procure a warrant

515. 19 Howell St. Tr. 1029, 1063-64 (1765).
516. As reported in Adam's abstract, [2 L. Wroth & H. Zobel (eds.), Legal Papers of John Adams 142 (1965)].
517. Id.
518. Id. at 139.
68. For more on the relationship between the two clauses of the fourth amendment, see Wasserstrom, The Incredible Shrinking Fourth Amendment, 21 Am. Crim. L. Rev. 257 (1984). See also Harris, The Return to Common Sense: A Response to "The Incredible Shrinking Fourth Amendment," 22 Am. Crim. L. Rev. 25 (1984).—EDS.
69. Note that the Court mentioned the exigent circumstances possibility only with respect to Payton's arrest.

in advance. Cf. Vale v. Louisiana, 399 U.S. 30 (1970) (entry to search for contraband illegal because, in majority's view, police had prior opportunity to obtain warrant).

3. An arrest warrant requirement provides protection against only the unjustified or arbitrary seizure of the person. A search warrant requirement—i.e., a requirement, in the *Payton* context, that the magistrate make a finding of probable cause to believe that the person to be arrested is or will be at home at the time of the planned entry—would provide protection against the unjustified or arbitrary entry into the suspect's home. To the extent that the unreasonable entry into one's home is, as the *Payton* Court suggests, the evil with which it is concerned, why does the Court not require a *search* warrant? Is it sufficient to answer that once the police have reason to believe that the suspect is at home, the possibility that the suspect may leave before the police obtain a warrant will almost always be a sufficient exigent circumstance to justify the entry without a search warrant? An alternative, of course, would be to require the police to keep a suspect's home under surveillance long enough to learn about the suspect's routine and then present this information to the magistrate. Should we require the police, as a condition of making a home arrest, to expend resources in this manner? Would the practical result of such a requirement be more arrests in public? Would such a result be desirable?

If the Court is not going to require a search warrant to enter a suspect's premises for the purpose of arresting the suspect, why, in light of *Watson*, does the Court require an arrest warrant? Consider the following possibilities:

a. The arrest warrant requirement—like a search warrant requirement—may deter the police from making home arrests. But why would we want to discourage home arrests?

b. *Watson*'s flat rule that the police do not need an arrest warrant to make an arrest in public governs situations in which exigent circumstances (e.g., the risk of losing track of the suspect while seeking a warrant) would frequently excuse any arrest warrant requirement. By contrast, in most situations in which police make a home arrest they are likely to have had ample time to obtain an arrest warrant.

c. Although neither an entry for the limited purpose of making an arrest nor an arrest itself is alone a significant enough invasion to require invoking the warrant requirement, the risk of a mistaken seizure of a person coupled with an entry into the person's premises for the purpose of making the seizure is sufficient to require an arrest warrant. But what calculus mandates that the line be drawn at this point?

See generally Groot, Arrest in Private Dwellings, 67 Va. L. Rev. 275 (1981).

4. What should constitute a sufficient exigency to justify a warrantless entry to make an arrest? Consider Welsh v. Wisconsin, 466 U.S. 740 (1984). Shortly after the defendant had been observed driving erratically and appearing "either very inebriated or very sick," id. at 742, the police made a warrantless entry into his house and arrested him for driving while intoxicated. That offense, according to state law, was "a noncriminal violation subject to a civil forfeiture proceeding for a maximum of $200." Id. at 746. The Supreme Court, in an opinion by Justice Brennan, held that the warrantless entry violated the fourth amendment:

> It is axiomatic that "the physical entry of the home is the chief evil against which the wording of the Fourth Amendment is directed." United States v. United States District Court, 407 U.S. 297 (1972). And a principal protection against unnecessary intrusions into private dwellings is the warrant requirement imposed by the Fourth Amendment on agents of the government who seek to enter the home for purposes of search or arrest. . . . It is not surprising, therefore, that the Court has recognized, as "a 'basic principle of Fourth Amendment law[,]' that searches and seizures inside a home without a warrant are presumptively unreasonable." Payton v. New York, 445 U.S. [573, 586 (1980).] . . .
>
> We . . . hold that an important factor to be considered when determining whether any exigency exists is the gravity of the underlying offense for which the arrest is being made. Moreover, although no exigency is created simply because there is probable cause to believe that a serious crime has been committed, . . . application of the exigent-circumstances exception in the context of a home entry should rarely be sanctioned when there is probable cause to believe that only a minor offense, such as the kind at issue in this case, has been committed.
>
> Application of this principle to the facts of the present case is relatively straightforward. The petitioner was arrested in the privacy of his own bedroom for a noncriminal, traffic offense. The State attempts to justify the arrest by relying on the hot-pursuit doctrine, on the threat to public safety, and on the need to preserve evidence of the petitioner's blood-alcohol level. On the facts of this case, however, the claim of hot pursuit is unconvincing because there was no immediate or continuous pursuit of the petitioner from the scene of a crime. Moreover, because the petitioner had already arrived home, and had abandoned his car at the scene of the accident, there was little remaining threat to the public safety. Hence, the only potential emergency claimed by the State was the need to ascertain the petitioner's blood-alcohol level.
>
> Even assuming, however, that the underlying facts would support a finding of this exigent circumstance, mere similarity to other cases involving the imminent destruction of evidence is not sufficient. The State of Wisconsin has chosen to classify the first offense for driving while intoxicated as a noncriminal, civil forfeiture offense for which no imprisonment is possible. . . . This is the best indication of the state's interest

in precipitating an arrest, and is one that can be easily identified both by the courts and by officers faced with a decision to arrest. . . . Given this expression of the state's interest, a warrantless home arrest cannot be upheld simply because evidence of the petitioner's blood-alcohol level might have dissipated while the police obtained a warrant.[14] To allow a warrantless home entry on these facts would be to approve unreasonable police behavior that the principles of the Fourth Amendment will not sanction. [466 U.S. at 748-749, 753-754.]

In a dissenting opinion joined by Justice Rehnquist, Justice White observed:

A warrantless home entry to arrest is no more intrusive when the crime is "minor" than when the suspect is sought in connection with a serious felony. The variable factor, if there is one, is the governmental interest that will be served by the warrantless entry. Wisconsin's Legislature and its Supreme Court have both concluded that warrantless in-home arrests under circumstances like those present here promote valid and substantial state interests. In determining whether the challenged governmental conduct was reasonable, we are not bound by these determinations. But nothing in our previous decisions suggests that the fact that a State has defined an offense as a misdemeanor for a variety of social, cultural, and political reasons necessarily requires the conclusion that warrantless in-home arrests designed to prevent the imminent destruction or removal of evidence of that offense are always impermissible. . . .

A test under which the existence of exigent circumstances turns on the perceived gravity of the crime would significantly hamper law enforcement and burden courts with pointless litigation concerning the nature and gradation of various crimes. . . .

This problem could be lessened by creating a bright-line distinction between felonies and other crimes, but the Court—wisely in my view—does not adopt such an approach. There may have been a time when the line between misdemeanors and felonies marked off those offenses involving a sufficiently serious threat to society to justify warrantless in-home arrests under exigent circumstances. But the category of misdemeanors today includes enough serious offenses to call into question the desirability of such line drawing. [Id. at 760-761.]

5. In Minnesota v. Olson, 110 S. Ct. 1684 (1990), the Court elaborated on the exigent circumstances test for warrantless entries:

14. Nor do we mean to suggest that the prevention of drunk driving is not properly of major concern to the States. . . . Given that the classification of state crimes differs widely among the States, the penalty that may attach to any particular offense seems to provide the clearest and most consistent indication of the state's interest in arresting individuals suspected of committing that offense.

The Minnesota Supreme Court applied essentially the correct standard in determining whether exigent circumstances existed. The court observed that "a warrantless intrusion may be justified by hot pursuit of a fleeing felon, or imminent destruction of evidence, Welsh [v. Wisconsin], 466 U.S. 740 [(1984)], or the need to prevent a suspect's escape, or the risk of danger to the police or to other persons inside or outside the dwelling." 436 N.W.2d at 97. The court also apparently thought that in the absence of hot pursuit there must be at least probable cause to believe that one or more of the other factors justifying the entry were present and that in assessing the risk of danger, the gravity of the crime and likelihood that the supsect is armed should be considered. [110 S. Ct. at 1690.]

6. Steagald v. United States, 451 U.S. 204 (1981), addressed one of the issues left open by *Payton*. Federal narcotics agents, armed with an arrest warrant for Ricky Lyons, entered the home of the defendant, Steagald, and conducted a search for Lyons. Lyons was not present, but the agents discovered cocaine, which was admitted against Steagald, over his objection, during his trial on federal drug charges. In an opinion by Justice Marshall, the Court assumed that at the time of the search the agents had probable cause to believe that Lyons was present in Steagald's home. The Court, however, held that in the absence of consent or exigent circumstances—neither of which existed here—law enforcement authorities needed a *search* warrant to enter the premises of a third person in order to make an arrest.

The Court distinguished *Payton* on the following grounds: An arrest warrant "necessarily authorizes a limited invasion of . . . [the arrestee's] privacy interest when it is necessary to arrest him in his home." An arrest warrant, however, "does not authorize the police to deprive . . . [a] third person of his liberty[. Thus,] it cannot embody any derivative authority to deprive this person of his interest in the privacy of his house." Id. at 214 n.7. Furthermore, the requirement of only an arrest warrant to enter a third person's premises "would create a significant potential for abuse. Armed solely with an arrest warrant for a single person, the police could search all the homes of that individual's friends and acquaintances." Id. at 215.

With respect to the government's argument that the inherent mobility of the person subject to arrest created an exigent circumstance and that the police might lose track of the suspect while they were seeking a warrant, the Court offered several reasons for concluding the search warrant requirement would "not significantly impede effective law enforcement efforts." Id. at 221. First, the police could easily avoid the search warrant requirement by arresting the defendant in his own home or waiting until he left the home of a third person; second, the availability of telephonic search warrants, see Fed. R. Crim. P. 41(c)(1), should minimize the burden of obtaining a warrant. Finally, in cases of true exigency, such as hot pursuit, the exigency would excuse the warrant requirement.

In a dissenting opinion Justice Rehnquist argued that the *Payton* arrest warrant requirement should suffice in a *Steagald*-type situation. He argued that the majority underestimated the practical difficulties of a search warrant requirement for the police, and he pointed out that if the suspect were in fact present, there may be no invasion of the home-owner's privacy. The homeowner could simply direct the police to the suspect. He then went on to observe:

> While I cannot subscribe to the Court's decision today, I will not falsely cry "wolf" in this dissent. The decision rests on a very special set of facts, and with a change in one or more of them it is clear that no separate search warrant would be required even under the reasoning of the Court.
>
> On the one side *Payton* makes clear that an arrest warrant is all that is needed to enter the suspect's "home" to effect the arrest. 445 U.S., at 602-603. . . . If a suspect has been living in a particular dwelling for any significant period, say a few days, it can certainly be considered his "home" for Fourth Amendment purposes, even if the premises are owned by a third party and others are living there, and even if the suspect concurrently maintains a residence elsewhere as well. In such a case the police could enter the premises with only an arrest warrant. On the other side, the more fleeting a suspect's connection with the premises, such as when he is a mere visitor, the more likely that exigent circumstances will exist justifying immediate police action without departing to obtain a search warrant. The practical damage done to effective law enforcement by today's decision, without any basis in the Constitution, may well be minimal if courts carefully consider the various conjuries of facts in the actual case before them.
>
> The genuinely unfortunate aspect of today's ruling is not that fewer fugitives will be brought to book, or fewer criminals apprehended, though both of these consequences will undoubtedly occur; the greater misfortune is the increased uncertainty imposed on police officers in the field, com-mitting magistrates, and trial judges, who must confront variations and permutations of this factual situation on a day-to-day basis. They will, in their various capacities, have to weigh the time during which a suspect for whom there is an outstanding arrest warrant has been in the building, whether the dwelling is the suspect's home, how long he has lived there, whether he is likely to leave immediately, and a number of related and equally imponderable questions. Certainty and repose, as Justice Holmes said, may not be the destiny of man, but one might have hoped for a higher degree of certainty in this one narrow but important area of the law than is offered by today's decision. [451 U.S. at 230-231.]

7. Note that the Court in *Steagald* included among its list of factors that minimize the alleged practical difficulties of a warrant requirement the possibility of obtaining a warrant by telephone. Is this factor perhaps of greater significance than either the majority or dissent recognizes? For example, the majority suggests that frequently exigent circumstances may justify dispensing with the warrant requirement. If warrants are available by telephone, however, won't the situations of genuine exigency be quite few? And with respect to the dissent, won't the availability of the telephone often provide a reasonable means of alleviating uncertainties for the officer in the field?

8. In both *Payton* and *Steagald*, the nature, purpose, and scope of the initial entries were identical: The police entered private homes with probable cause to arrest; they entered for the purpose of making arrests; and thus, the scope of the searches had to be limited to areas where the suspect might be found. Given these similarities, what, if anything, justifies the imposition of a search warrant requirement only when the entry is into the premises of some third person? Is it sufficient to answer that the number of premises that can be entered without a search warrant is limited in each case? Does an individual, by permitting himself to be in a situation in which there is probable cause to believe he committed a crime, waive or forfeit some degree of legitimate privacy interest in his home? If so, why? Are there likely to be greater practical problems in administering a search warrant requirement in cases in which the police hope to find a suspect at home? Or is the critical point perhaps that there will be few cases in which *Steagald* will require the police to get a search warrant? If so, one can embrace the principle that probable cause (or an arrest warrant) is not alone sufficient to justify the entry and, at the same time, feel secure that the search warrant requirement will not be a practical impediment to effective law enforcement.

9. On some occasions the police will make a valid arrest and then permit the arrestee, while in police custody, to go briefly to a different part of the premises or perhaps, if the arrest was not made in the arrestee's home, to stop briefly at home before going to the police station. In *Washington v. Chrisman*, 455 U.S. 1 (1982), the Court held that in such a situation "it is not 'unreasonable' under the Fourth Amendment for a police officer to monitor the movements of an arrested person, as his judgment dictates following an arrest." Id. at 7. Thus, it is permissible for the officer to accompany the suspect to any part of the premises to which the officer gives the arrestee access.

As the preceding materials indicate, the Supreme Court frequently has required the existence of some type of exigent circumstance to justify dispensing with the warrant requirement for searches and seizures based on probable cause.[70] The *Coolidge/Horton* plain view doctrine, for example, can be regarded simply as a specific application of the exigent circumstances concept developed in cases like *Carroll*, *Mincey*, and *Hayden*; *Payton* and *Steagald* explicitly require either a warrant or exigent circumstances to justify an entry into a home for the purpose of making an arrest. On the other hand, various justices have relied on factors other than the exigency of the moment to support their arguments for upholding warrantless searches and seizures. We have seen, for example, resort to history, a call for rules that will be simple and easy for the police to apply, and the notion that warrants are unnecessary for minor invasions that follow legitimate major invasions of fourth amendment interests. Moreover, neither *Watson's* approval of warrantless felony arrests nor *Payton's* conclusion that an *arrest* warrant is sufficient to justify an entry into the arrestee's house can be squared with the notion that only exigent circumstances justify dispensing with search and arrest warrants. Similarly, neither the vehicle search in *Chambers* nor the container search in *Ross* can be justified on the grounds of exigency. What unifying principles, if any, are there to explain these cases? If the cases cannot be reconciled, would it be desirable to have either (1) a general standard of reasonableness for all searches and seizures or (2) a strict exigency requirement for all warrantless searches and seizures based on probable cause? See Bradley, Two Models of the Fourth Amendment, 83 Mich. L. Rev. 1468 (1985).

2. The Relationship Between Reasonableness and Probable Cause: The Sliding Scale Approach to Probable Cause

Thus far our examination of warrantless searches and seizures has dealt exclusively with situations in which the police have had probable cause to engage in the search or seizure. The focus of our inquiry has been whether such searches or seizures are reasonable despite the absence of a warrant. We now shift our focus to the relationship between the reasonableness requirement in the first clause of the fourth amendment and the *probable cause* requirement in the second clause.

In most instances, as Professor Amsterdam has observed, see page 499 supra, the fourth amendment is treated as a "monolith." For some types of investigatory and regulatory activities, however, the Supreme

---

70. In sub-sections 2 and 3 we will see that some searches and seizures are reasonable despite the absence of individualized probable cause. The exigency of the moment may also help justify the legality of some of these searches. See, e.g., Chimel v. California, page 721 infra.

Court has utilized a "balancing" or "sliding scale" approach in determining the legality of a search or seizure. Pursuant to this approach, the Court has considered whether some relatively unintrusive governmental activities can legally be engaged in without the traditional, individualized probable cause showing. The advantage of an affirmative answer to this question is that it permits the government to employ a range of flexible responses to a particular problem while, at the same time, it permits the courts to retain some regulatory supervision of the activity. The major disadvantage of the sliding scale approach, at least if it is employed on a wide scale, is, as Professor Amsterdam observed, that "it converts the fourth amendment into one immense Rorschach blot."[71] Page 500 supra.

The balancing approach to the question whether a *warrantless* search or seizure is reasonable had its origin in the context of the Supreme Court's effort to define the kind of "probable cause" that would justify issuance of a search warrant to health and building inspectors. In Frank v. Maryland, 359 U.S. 360 (1959), the Court had held that no warrant was required for these searches. Eight years later, however, the Court reconsidered its *Frank* holding.

CAMARA v. MUNICIPAL COURT OF THE CITY & COUNTY OF SAN FRANCISCO
Appeal from the District Court of Appeal of California, First Appellate District
387 U.S. 523 (1967)

MR. JUSTICE WHITE delivered the opinion of the Court.
[Appellant on several occasions refused to permit housing inspectors engaged in a routine annual inspection to enter his apartment without a warrant.] Thereafter, a complaint was filed charging him with refusing to permit a lawful inspection. . . . When his demurrer to the criminal complaint was denied, appellant filed this petition for a writ of prohibition. . . .

In Frank v. Maryland, [359 U.S. 300 (1959),] this Court upheld the conviction of one who refused to permit a warrantless inspection of

---

71. There is, of course, another disadvantage, if one disagrees with the application of the sliding scale approach to a particular problem. The nature of the disadvantage depends on the reason for objecting to the sliding scale approach. On the one hand, one might regard the sliding scale approach as permitting an undue invasion of important fourth amendment interests. On the other hand, one might maintain that even the limited regulatory requirements of the sliding scale approach impose an unnecessary burden on legitimate, desirable government activity.

private premises for the purposes of locating and abating a suspected public nuisance. . . .[4]

[T]he *Frank* opinion has generally been interpreted as carving out an additional exception to the rule that warrantless searches are unreasonable under the Fourth Amendment. . . . The District Court of Appeal so interpreted *Frank* in this case, and that ruling is the core of appellant's challenge here. We proceed to a re-examination of the factors which persuaded the *Frank* majority to adopt this construction of the Fourth Amendment's prohibition against unreasonable searches.

To the *Frank* majority, municipal fire, health, and housing inspection programs "touch at most upon the periphery of the important interests safeguarded by the Fourteenth Amendment's protection against official intrusion," 359 U.S., at 367, because the inspections are merely to determine whether physical conditions exist which do not comply with minimum standards prescribed in local regulatory ordinances. . . .

We may agree that a routine inspection of the physical condition of private property is a less hostile intrusion than the typical policeman's search for the fruits and instrumentalities of crime. . . . But we cannot agree that the Fourth Amendment interests at stake in these inspection cases are merely "peripheral." . . .

. . . [E]ven the most law-abiding citizen has a very tangible interest in limiting the circumstances under which the sanctity of his home may be broken by official authority. . . .

The *Frank* majority suggested, and appellee reasserts, two other justifications for permitting administrative health and safety inspections without a warrant. First, it is argued that . . . [t]he ordinances authorizing inspections are hedged with safeguards, and at any rate the inspector's particular decision to enter must comply with the constitutional standard of reasonableness even if he may enter without a warrant.[10] In addition, the argument proceeds, the warrant process could not function effectively in this field. The decision to inspect an entire municipal area is based upon legislative or administrative assessment of broad factors such as the area's age and condition. Unless the magistrate is to review

4. In *Frank*, the Baltimore ordinance required that the health inspector "have cause to suspect that a nuisance exists in any house, cellar or enclosure" before he could demand entry without a warrant, a requirement obviously met in *Frank* because the inspector observed extreme structural decay and a pile of rodent feces on the appellant's premises. Section 503 of the San Francisco Housing Code has no such "cause" requirement. . . .

10. The San Francisco Code requires that the inspector display proper credentials, that he inspect "at reasonable times," and that he not obtain entry by force, at least when there is no emergency. The Baltimore ordinance in *Frank* required that the inspector "have cause to suspect that a nuisance exists." Some cities notify residents in advance, by mail or posted notice, of impending area inspections. State courts upholding these inspections without warrants have imposed a general reasonableness requirement. . . .

such policy matters, he must issue a "rubber stamp" warrant which provides no protection at all to the property owner.

In our opinion, these arguments unduly discount the purposes behind the warrant machinery contemplated by the Fourth Amendment. . . .

. . . [O]nly by refusing entry and risking a criminal conviction can the occupant at present challenge the inspector's decision to search. And if the occupant possesses sufficient fortitude to take this risk, as even appellant did here, he may never learn any more about the reason for the inspection than that the law generally allows housing inspectors to gain entry. The practical effect of this system is to leave the occupant subject to the discretion of the official in the field. This is precisely the discretion to invade private property which we have consistently circumscribed by a requirement that a disinterested party warrant the need to search. . . .

The final justification suggested for warrantless administrative searches is that the public interest demands such a rule: it is vigorously argued that the health and safety of entire urban populations is dependent upon enforcement of minimum fire, housing, and sanitation standards, and that the only effective means of enforcing such codes is by routine systematized inspection of all physical structures. . . . In assessing whether the public interest demands creation of a general exception to the Fourth Amendment's warrant requirement, the question is not whether the public interest justifies the type of search in question, but whether the authority to search should be evidenced by a warrant, which in turn depends in part upon whether the burden of obtaining a warrant is likely to frustrate the government purpose behind the search. . . . It has nowhere been urged that fire, health, and housing code inspection programs could not achieve their goals within the confines of a reasonable search warrant requirement. Thus, we do not find the public need argument dispositive.

Because of the nature of the municipal programs under consideration, however, these conclusions must be the beginning, not the end, of our inquiry. . . .

The Fourth Amendment provides that, "no Warrants shall issue, but upon probable cause." Borrowing from more typical Fourth Amendment cases, appellant argues not only that code enforcement inspection programs must be circumscribed by a warrant procedure, but also that warrants should issue only when the inspector possesses probable cause to believe that a particular dwelling contains violations of the minimum standards prescribed by the code being enforced. We disagree. . . .

Unlike the search pursuant to a criminal investigation, the inspection programs at issue here are aimed at securing city-wide compliance with minimum physical standards for private property. . . . In determining whether a particular inspection is reasonable—and thus in determining whether there is probable cause to issue a warrant for the inspection—the need for the inspection must be weighed in terms of these reasonable goals of code enforcement.

There is unanimous agreement among those most familiar with this field that the only effective way to seek universal compliance with the minimum standards required by municipal codes is through routine periodic inspections of all structures. It is here that the probable cause debate is focused, for the agency's decision to conduct an area inspection is unavoidably based on its appraisal of conditions in the area as a whole, not on its knowledge of conditions in each particular building. Appellee contends that, if the probable cause standard urged by appellant is adopted, the area inspection will be eliminated as a means of seeking compliance with code standards and the reasonable goals of code enforcement will be dealt a crushing blow.

In meeting this contention, appellant argues first, that his probable cause standard would not jeopardize area inspection programs because only a minute portion of the population will refuse to consent to such inspections, and second, that individual privacy in any event should be given preference to the public interest in conducting such inspections. The first argument, even if true, is irrelevant to the question whether the area inspection is reasonable within the meaning of the Fourth Amendment. The second argument is in effect an assertion that the area inspection is an unreasonable search. Unfortunately, there can be no ready test for determining reasonableness other than by balancing the need to search against the invasion which the search entails. But we think that a number of persuasive factors combine to support the reasonableness of area code-enforcement inspections. First, such programs have a long history of judicial and public acceptance. . . . Second, the public interest demands that all dangerous conditions be prevented or abated, yet it is doubtful that any other canvassing technique would achieve acceptable results. Many such conditions—faulty wiring is an obvious example are not observable from outside the building and indeed may not be apparent to the inexpert occupant himself. Finally, because the inspections are neither personal in nature nor aimed at the discovery of evidence of crime, they involve a relatively limited invasion of the urban citizen's privacy. . . .

Having concluded that the area inspection is a "reasonable" search of private property within the meaning of the Fourth Amendment, it is obvious that "probable cause" to issue a warrant to inspect must exist if reasonable legislative or administrative standards for conducting an area inspection are satisfied with respect to a particular dwelling. Such standards, which will vary with the municipal program being enforced, may be based upon the passage of time, the nature of the building (e.g., a multi-family apartment house), or the condition of the entire area, but they will not necessarily depend upon specific knowledge of the condition of the particular dwelling. It has been suggested that so to vary the probable cause test from the standard applied in criminal cases would be to authorize a "synthetic search warrant" and thereby to lessen the overall protections of the Fourth Amendment. Frank v. Maryland, 359 U.S., at 373. But we do not agree. The warrant procedure is designed to guarantee that a decision to search private property is justified by a reasonable governmental interest. But reasonableness is still the ultimate standard. If a valid public interest justified the intrusion contemplated, then there is probable cause to issue a suitably restricted search warrant. . . . Such an approach neither endangers time-honored doctrines applicable to criminal investigations nor makes a nullity of the probable cause requirement in this area. It merely gives full recognition to the competing public and private interests here at stake and, in so doing, best fulfills the historic purpose behind the constitutional right to be free from unreasonable government invasion of privacy. . . .

Since our holding emphasizes the controlling standard of reasonableness, nothing we say today is intended to foreclose prompt inspections, even without a warrant, that the law has traditionally upheld in emergency situations. . . . On the other hand, in the case of most routine area inspections, there is no compelling urgency to inspect at a particular time or on a particular day. Moreover, most citizens allow inspections of their property without a warrant. Thus, as a practical matter and in light of the Fourth Amendment's requirement that a warrant specify the property to be searched, it seems likely that warrants should normally be sought only after entry is refused unless there has been a citizen complaint or there is other satisfactory reason for securing immediate entry. Similarly, the requirement for a warrant procedure does not suggest any change in what seems to be the prevailing local policy, in most situations, of authorizing entry, but not entry by force, to inspect. . . .

The judgment is vacated and the case is remanded for further proceedings not inconsistent with this opinion.

It is so ordered.

[The dissenting opinion of JUSTICE CLARK is omitted.]

NOTES AND QUESTIONS

1. Consider carefully the Court's three justifications for adopting a generalized probable cause standard: the history of public and judicial

acceptance of housing inspections; the public interest in code enforcement; and the limited nature of the invasion. With respect to the first factor, the judicial acceptance in fact was less than overwhelming. Indeed, there had been very few cases even addressing the issue. With respect to the "public interest," is the Court suggesting that there is a greater public interest in housing code enforcement than there is in crime detection? If not, what is the Court's point? With respect to the final factor, is the Court suggesting that the invasion is limited because the investigation is noncriminal, or because drawers and papers probably do not need to be searched? If the latter, is the point very compelling given the fact that the inspection may take the examiner into every room and closet in the house? If the former, how "noncriminal" is the process when there are criminal penalties for failing to correct violations or even for not permitting the inspection initially?

2. One potential risk of defining probable cause in terms of a balanced consideration of what is reasonable is that probable cause may itself become a kind of sliding scale concept with no particular benchmark. To date, however, this has not occurred. Indeed, in Griffin v. Wisconsin, 483 U.S. 868 (1987), which upheld the warrantless search of a probationer's residence on less than probable cause, the Court specifically refused to combine a warrant requirement with a standard of suspicion lower than traditional probable cause:

> Justice Blackmun's dissent would retain a judicial warrant requirement, though agreeing with our subsequent conclusion that reasonableness of the search does not require probable cause. This, however, is a combination that neither the text of the Constitution nor any of our prior decisions permits. While it is possible to say that Fourth Amendment reasonableness demands probable cause without a judicial warrant, the reverse runs up against the constitutional provision that "no Warrants shall issue, but upon probable cause." Amdt. 4. The Constitution prescribes, in other words, that where the matter is of such a nature as to require a judicial warrant, it is also of such a nature as to require probable cause. Although we have arguably come to permit an exception to that prescription for administrative search warrants, which may but do not necessarily have to be issued by courts, we have never done so for constitutionally mandated judicial warrants.[5] [Id. at 877-878.]

---

5. See Marshall v. Barlow's, Inc., 436 U.S. [307, 325 (1978)] ("We hold that . . . the Act is unconstitutional insofar as it purports to authorize inspections without warrant or its equivalent"). The "neutral magistrate," Camara v. [Municipal Court], 387 U.S. [523], 532 [(1967)], or "neutral officer," Marshall v. Barlow's, Inc., 436 U.S., at 323, envisioned by our administrative search cases is not necessarily the "neutral judge," . . . envisioned by the dissent.

3. What benefits are derived from imposing a warrant requirement (based on a generalized notion of probable cause) on the types of activity at issue in *Camara?* Is there a legitimate, serious concern with abuse of discretion by health and safety inspectors? If so, how will the *Camara* warrant requirement minimize the abuse? Even if the *Camara* warrant requirement may have some benefits, is it worth the administrative cost?

4. Note the Court's concern that the homeowner cannot challenge the inspection decision without risking a criminal penalty. Does *Camara* alleviate this problem? Should the homeowner have an opportunity to participate in the decision whether a warrant should issue for inspection of the homeowner's premises? If so, what procedure might be devised to permit such participation?

5. In See v. City of Seattle, 387 U.S. 541 (1967), a companion case to *Camara*, the Court extended *Camara* to the inspection of commercial property. Subsequent litigation involving the *Camara-See* doctrine has focused on the extent to which there should be exceptions to the generalized warrant requirement imposed by those cases.

Colonnade Catering Corp. v. United States, 397 U.S. 72 (1970), involved the inspection of the premises of a liquor licensee. Relying on "the long history of the regulation of the liquor industry during pre-Fourth Amendment days," id. at 75, the Supreme Court distinguished *See* and held that the warrantless inspection of the premises was legal.

In United States v. Biswell, 406 U.S. 311 (1972), the Court upheld the warrantless inspection of a licensed gun dealer's storeroom. Since selling guns did not have the long history of government regulation comparable to that in the liquor industry, *Colonnade Catering* was of only limited support for the decision. The factors deemed relevant in *Biswell* were (a) the strong public interest in regulating firearms, (b) the need for frequent and unannounced inspections in order for the regulation to be effective, and (c) the limited privacy interest of the defendant since the firearms industry was subject to pervasive (if not longstanding) regulation. Which of the factors adequately distinguishes *Biswell* from *Camara* and *See?*

6. Marshall v. Barlow's Inc., 436 U.S. 307 (1978), involved the constitutionality of a provision in the Occupational Safety and Health Act (OSHA) that permitted warrantless inspections of the work area of any employment facility within OSHA's jurisdiction. Donovan v. Dewey, 452 U.S. 594 (1981), dealt with the permissibility of warrantless inspections made pursuant to the Federal Mine Safety and Health Act. The Court held that warrantless OSHA inspections were unconstitutional, but the Court reached a contrary conclusion with respect to mine safety inspections. Among the reasons offered by the Court in *Dewey* for distinguishing the Mine Safety Act from OSHA were

(1) the pervasive regulation of the mining industry;
(2) the fact that OSHA applied to a vast number and variety of en-
    terprises, whereas the Mine Safety Act applied to one limited
    industry with a "notorious history of serious accidents and un-
    healthful working conditions";
(3) the fact that the nature and frequency of OSHA inspections de-
    pended almost entirely on the discretion of the inspectors, whereas
    the frequency and purpose of mine inspections was specified in
    the statute; and
(4) deference to the congressional finding that unannounced, war-
    rantless inspections were essential to ensure compliance with the
    Mine Safety Act.

Id. at 600-605. See generally, Rothstein, OSHA Inspections After Marshall v. Barlow's Inc., 1979 Duke L.J. 63.

7. In Michigan v. Tyler, 436 U.S. 499 (1978), and Michigan v.
Clifford, 464 U.S. 287 (1984), the Court dealt with the manner in which
the fourth amendment regulates the search of fire-damaged premises: A
warrantless entry by firefighters for the purpose of fighting a fire is reasonable because of the exigency of the moment. Michigan v. Tyler, 436
U.S. at 509. Moreover, after the fire is extinguished, officials may remain
for a reasonable time and engage in a warrantless search in order to
determine the cause and origin of the fire. Id. at 510. Unless the premises
are so badly damaged that no privacy interest in them remains, any
subsequent search must be based on consent, the existence of exigent
circumstances, or compliance with the warrant requirement. Michigan
v. Clifford, 464 U.S. at 292-293.[72] According to Clifford, the type of
warrant required depends on the purpose of the search:

> If the primary object is to determine the cause and origin of a recent fire,
> an administrative warrant will suffice.[5] To obtain such a warrant, fire
> officials need show only that a fire of undetermined origin has occurred

---

72. In Tyler the officials halted their inspection at 4:00 A.M. because of darkness,
smoke, and steam. They resumed the inspection without a warrant four hours later, at
which time they discovered evidence of arson that was admitted against the defendant.
The Court upheld the later warrantless inspection on the ground that it was a "continuation" of the initial inspection. 436 U.S. at 511, The Court, however, refused to apply
the continuing inspection concept in Clifford, where the second warrantless search occurred six hours after officials extinguished the fire and left the scene. The Court distinguished Tyler on the grounds (a) that Tyler involved a furniture store whereas Clifford
involved a home, and (b) that the owner of the premises in Clifford had taken steps to
secure the privacy of his home between the time when the fire was extinguished and the
inspectors returned. 464 U.S. at 296-297.
5. Probable cause to issue an administrative warrant exists if reasonable legislative,
administrative, or judicially prescribed standards for conducting an inspection are satisfied
with respect to a particular dwelling. . . .

on the premises, that the scope of the proposed search is reasonable and will not intrude unnecessarily on the fire victim's privacy, and that the search will be executed at a reasonable and convenient time.

If the primary object of the search is to gather evidence of criminal activity, a criminal search warrant may be obtained only on a showing of probable cause to believe that relevant evidence will be found in the place to be searched. [Id. at 294.]

8. For other Supreme Court cases dealing with the applicability of the warrant requirement to governmental activity that does not necessarily have crime detection or prevention as its primary objective, see Wyman v. James, 400 U.S. 309 (1971) (no warrant required for home inspection of welfare recipient by caseworker even though refusal to grant entry can lead to termination of assistance); G.M. Leasing Corp. v. United States, 429 U.S. 338 (1977) (warrant required for entry onto private property to seize items pursuant to levy). Cf. pages 755-769 infra (criteria for legal border searches and vehicle inspections).

NEW YORK v. BURGER
Certiorari to the Court of Appeals of New York
482 U.S. 691 (1987)

JUSTICE BLACKMUN delivered the opinion for the Court.

This case presents the question whether the warrantless search of an automobile junkyard, conducted pursuant to a statute authorizing such a search, falls within the exception to the warrant requirement for administrative inspections of pervasively regulated industries. The case also presents the question whether an otherwise proper administrative inspection is unconstitutional because the ultimate purpose of the regulatory statute pursuant to which the search is done—the deterrence of criminal behavior—is the same as that of penal laws, with the result that the inspection may disclose violations not only of the regulatory statute but also of the penal statutes.

I

Respondent Joseph Burger is the owner of a junkyard in Brooklyn, N.Y. His business consists, in part, of the dismantling of automobiles and the selling of their parts. His junkyard is an open lot with no buildings. A high metal fence surrounds it. . . . At approximately noon on November 17, 1982, Officer Joseph Vega and four other plainclothes officers, all members of the Auto Crimes Division of the New York City Police

Department, entered respondent's junkyard to conduct an inspection pursuant to N.Y. Veh. & Traf. Law §415-a5 (McKinney 1986).[1] . . . On any given day, the Division conducts from 5 to 10 inspections of vehicle dismantlers, automobile junkyards, and related businesses.[2] . . .

Upon entering the junkyard, the officers asked to see Burger's license and his "police book"—the record of the automobiles and vehicle parts in his possession. Burger replied that he had neither a license nor a police book. The officers then announced their intention to conduct a §415-a inspection. Burger did not object. . . . In accordance with their practice, the officers copied down the Vehicle Inspection Numbers (VINS) of several vehicles and parts of vehicles that were in the junkyard. After checking these numbers against a police computer, the officers determined that respondent was in possession of stolen vehicles and parts. Accordingly, Burger was arrested and charged with five counts of possession of stolen property and one count of unregistered operation as a vehicle dismantler, in violation of §415-a1.

[Burger moved to suppress the evidence found as a result of the inspection. The trial court denied motion, but the New York Court of Appeals reversed.]

II . . .

[T]he owner or operator of commercial premises in a "closely regulated" industry has a reduced expectation of privacy. . . . [W]here the privacy interests of the owner are weakened and the government interests in regulating particular businesses are concomitantly heightened, a warrantless inspection of commercial premises may well be reasonable. . . .

1. This statute reads in pertinent part:
"Records and identification. (a) . . . Every person required to be registered pursuant to this section shall maintain a record of all motor vehicles, trailers, and major component parts thereof, coming into his possession together with a record of the disposition of any such motor vehicle, trailer or part thereof and shall maintain proof of ownership for any motor vehicle, trailer or major component part thereof while in his possession. Such records shall be maintained in a manner and form prescribed by the commissioner [of the Department of Motor Vehicles]. . . . Upon request of an agent of the commissioner or of any police officer and during his regular and usual business hours, a vehicle dismantler shall produce such records and permit said agent or police officer to examine them and any vehicles or parts of vehicles which are subject to the record keeping requirements of this section and which are on the premises. . . . The failure to produce such records or to permit such inspection on the part of any person required to be registered pursuant to this section as required by this paragraph shall be a class A misdemeanor."
2. It was unclear from the record why, on that particular day, Burger's junkyard was selected for inspection. . . . The junkyards designated for inspection apparently were selected from a list of such businesses compiled by New York City police detectives.

This warrantless inspection, however, even in the context of a pervasively regulated business, will be deemed to be reasonable only so long as three criteria are met. First, there must be a "substantial" government interest that informs the regulatory scheme pursuant to which the inspection is made. . . .

Second, the warrantless inspections must be "necessary to further [the] regulatory scheme." Donovan v. Dewey, 452 U.S. [594], 600 [(1981)]. For example, in *Dewey* we recognized that forcing mine inspectors to obtain a warrant before every inspection might alert mine owners or operators to the impending inspection, thereby frustrating the purposes of the Mine Safety and Health Act—to detect and thus to deter safety and health violations. Id. at 603.

Finally, "the statute's inspection program, in terms of the certainty and regularity of its application, [must] provid[e] a constitutionally adequate substitute for a warrant." Ibid. In other words, the regulatory statute must perform the two basic functions of a warrant: it must advise the owner of the commercial premises that the search is being made pursuant to the law and has a properly defined scope, and it must limit the discretion of the inspecting officers. . . . To perform this first function, the statute must be "sufficiently comprehensive and defined that the owner of commercial property cannot help but be aware that his property will be subject to periodic inspections undertaken for specific proposes." Donovan v. Dewey, 452 U.S., at 600. In addition, in defining how a statute limits the discretion of the inspectors, we have observed that it must be "carefully limited in time, place, and scope." United States v. Biswell, 406 U.S. [311], 315 [(1972)].

III

A

Searches made pursuant to §415-a, in our view, clearly fall within this established exception to the warrant requirement for administrative inspections in "closely regulated" industries. First, the nature of the regulatory statute reveals that the operation of a junkyard, part of which is devoted to vehicle dismantling, is a "closely regulated" business in the state of New York. The provisions regulating the activity of vehicle dismantling are extensive. An operator cannot engage in this industry without first obtaining a license, which means that he must meet the registration requirements and must pay a fee. Under §415-a5(a), the operator must maintain a police book recording the acquisition and disposition of motor vehicles and vehicle parts, and make such records and inventory available for inspection by the police or any agent of the Department of Motor Vehicles. The operator also must display his registration number prominently at his place of business, on business documentation, and on vehicles and parts that pass through his business. . . . Moreover, the person engaged in this activity is subject to criminal penalties, as well as to loss of license or civil fines, for failure to comply with these provisions. . . . That other States besides New York have imposed similarly extensive regulations on automobile junkyards further supports the "closely regulated" status of this industry. . . .

. . . [A]utomobile junkyards and vehicle dismantlers have not been in existence very long and thus do not have an ancient history of government oversight. . . .

The automobile junkyard business, however, is simply a new branch of an industry that has existed, and has been closely regulated, for many years. The automobile junkyard is closely akin to the secondhand shop or the general junkyard. . . .

B

The New York regulatory scheme satisfies the three criteria necessary to make reasonable warrantless inspections pursuant to §415-a5. First, the State has a substantial interest in regulating the vehicle-dismantling and automobile junkyard industry because motor vehicle theft has increased in the State and because the problem of theft is associated with this industry. . . .

Second, regulation of the vehicle-dismantling industry reasonably serves the State's substantial interest in eradicating automobile theft. It is well established that the theft problem can be addressed effectively by controlling the receiver of, or market in, stolen property. W. LaFave & A. Scott, Criminal Law §8.10, p.765 (2d ed. 1986) ("Without [professional receivers of stolen property], theft ceases to be profitable"). . . . Automobile junkyards and vehicle dismantlers provide the major market for stolen vehicles and vehicle parts. . . .

Moreover, the warrantless administrative inspections pursuant to §415-a5 "are necessary to further [the] regulatory scheme." Donovan v. Dewey, 452 U.S., at 600. . . . Because stolen cars and parts often pass quickly through an automobile junkyard, "frequent" and "unannounced" inspections are necessary in order to detect them. . . .

Third, §415-a5 provides a "constitutionally adequate substitute for a warrant." Donovan v. Dewey, 452 U.S., at 603. The statute informs the operator of a vehicle dismantling business that inspections will be made on a regular basis. . . . Thus, the vehicle dismantler knows that the inspections to which he is subject do not constitute discretionary acts

by a government official but are conducted pursuant to statute. . . .
Section 415-a5 also sets forth the scope of the inspection and, accordingly,
places the operator on notice as to how to comply with the statute. In
addition, it notifies the operator as to who is authorized to conduct an
inspection.

Finally, the "time, place, and scope" of the inspection is limited,
United States v. Biswell, 406 U.S., at 315, to place appropriate restraints
upon the discretion of the inspecting officers. . . . The officers are
allowed to conduct an inspection only "during [the] regular and usual
business hours."[21] The inspections can be made only of vehicle-dismantling and related industries. And the permissible scope of these searches
is narrowly defined: the inspectors may examine the records, as well as
"any vehicles or parts of vehicles which are subject to the record keeping
requirements of this section and which are on the premises." Ibid.

IV

. . . The Court of Appeals . . . struck down the statute as violative of
the Fourth Amendment because, in its view, the statute had no truly
administrative purpose but was "designed simply to give the police an
expedient means of enforcing penal sanctions for possession of stolen
property." . . . The court also suggested that the identity of the inspectors—police officers—was significant in revealing the true nature of the
statutory scheme.

In arriving at this conclusion, the Court of Appeals failed to recognize that a State can address a major societal problem *both* by way of
an administrative scheme *and* through penal sanctions. Administrative
statutes and penal laws may have the same *ultimate* purpose of remedying
the social problem, but they have different subsidiary purposes and prescribe different methods of addressing the problem. An administrative
statute establishes how a particular business in a "closely regulated" industry should be operated, setting forth rules to guide an operator's conduct of the business and allowing government officials to ensure that
those rules are followed. Such a regulatory approach contrasts with that
of the penal laws, a major emphasis of which is the punishment of
individuals for specific acts of behavior. . . .

21. Respondent contends that §415-a5 is unconstitutional because it fails to limit
the number of searches that may be conducted of a particular business during any given
period. . . . While such limitations, or the absence thereof, are a factor in an analysis
of the adequacy of a particular statute, they are not determinative of the result so long
as the statute, as a whole, places adequate limits upon the discretion of the inspection
officers. . . .

This case . . . reveals that an administrative scheme may have the same ultimate purpose as penal laws, even if its regulatory goals are narrower. . . . Section 415-a, as a whole, serves the regulatory goals of seeking to ensure that vehicle dismantlers are legitimate-business persons and that stolen vehicles and vehicle parts passing through automobile junkyards can be identified. In particular, §415-a5 was designed to contribute to these goals, as explained at the time of its passage: . . .

> The various businesses which are engaged in this operation have been studied and the control and requirements on the businesses have been written in a manner which would permit the persons engaged in the business to legally operate in a manner conducive to good business practices while making it extremely difficult for a person to profitably transfer a stolen vehicle or stolen part. The general scheme is to identify every person who may legitimately be involved in the operation and to provide a record keeping system which will enable junk vehicles and parts to be traced back to the last legitimately registered or titled owner. Legitimate businessmen engaged in this field have complained with good cause that the lack of comprehensive coverage of the field has put them at a disadvantage with persons who currently are able to operate outside of statute and regulations. . . . [Letter to Stanley M. Gruss, Deputy Commissioner and Counsel, to Richard Brown, Counsel to the Governor (June 20, 1979), 1979 Bill Jacket.]

Nor do we think that this administrative scheme is unconstitutional simply because, in the course of enforcing it, an inspecting officer may discover evidence of crimes, besides violations of the scheme itself. . . .

Finally, we fail to see any constitutional significance in the fact that police officers, rather than "administrative" agents, are permitted to conduct the §415-a5 inspection. . . . [S]tate police officers, like those in New York, have numerous duties in addition to those associated with traditional police work. . . . As a practical matter, many States do not have the resources to assign the enforcement of a particular administrative scheme to a specialized agency. So long as a regulatory scheme is properly administrative, it is not rendered illegal by the fact that the inspecting officer has the power to arrest individuals for violations other than those created by the scheme itself. . . .

. . . [T]he judgment of the New York Court of Appeals is reversed and the case is remanded to that court for further proceedings not inconsistent with this opinion.

JUSTICE BRENNAN, with whom JUSTICE MARSHALL joins, and with whom JUSTICE O'CONNOR joins as to all but Part III, dissenting.

Warrantless inspections of pervasively regulated businesses are valid if necessary to further an urgent state interest, and if authorized by a statute that carefully limits their time, place, and scope. I have no objection to this general rule. . . .[2]

I

The provisions governing vehicle dismantling in New York simply are not extensive. A vehicle dismantler must register and pay a fee, display the registration in various circumstances, maintain a police book, and allow inspections. . . . Of course, the inspections themselves cannot be cited as proof of pervasive regulation justifying elimination of the warrant requirement; that would be obvious bootstrapping. Nor can registration and recordkeeping requirements be characterized as close regulation. New York City, like many states and municipalities, imposes similar, and often more stringent licensing, recordkeeping, and other regulatory requirements on a myriad of trades and businesses.[5] . . .

In sum, if New York City's administrative scheme renders the vehicle-dismantling business closely regulated, few businesses will escape such a finding. Under these circumstances, the warrant requirement is the exception not the rule, and See [v. City of Seattle, 387 U.S. 541 (1967),] has been constructively overruled.

II

. . . Section 415-a5 does not approach the level of "certainty and regularity of . . . application" necessary to provide "a constitutionally adequate substitute for a warrant." [Donovan v. Dewey, 452 U.S.], at 603.[8]

---

2. In only three industries have we invoked this exception [to the warrant requirement]. See Colonnade Catering Corp. v. United States, 397 U.S. 72 (1970) (liquor industry), United States v. Biswell, 406 U.S. 311 (1972) (firearm and ammunitions sales), Donovan v. Dewey, 452 U.S. 594 (1981) (coal mining).

5. [Citations to licensing and regulatory requirements in New York City Administrative Code for exhibitors of public amusement or sport, motion picture exhibitions, billiard and pocket billiard tables, bowling alleys, sidewalk stands and cafes, sight-seeing guides, public carts and cartmen, debt collection agencies, pawnbrokers, auctioneers, laundries, locksmiths and keymakers, sales, garages and parking lots, commercial refuse removal, public dance halls and cabarets, catering establishments, coffeehouses, sight-seeing buses and drivers, home improvement business, television, radio and audio equipment service and repairs, general vendors, and storage warehouses.—EDS.]

8. I also dispute the contention that warrantless searches are necessary to further the regulatory scheme, because of the need for unexpected and/or frequent searches. If surprise is essential (as it usually is in a criminal case), a warrant may be obtained ex parte. . . . If the state seeks to conduct frequent inspections, then the statute (or some regulatory authority) should somewhere inform the industry of that fact.

The statute does not inform the operator of a vehicle-dismantling business that inspections will be made on a regular basis; in fact, there is *no* assurance that any inspection at all will occur. There is neither an upper nor a lower limit on the number of searches that may be conducted at any given operator's establishment in any given time period. Neither the statute, nor any regulations, nor any regulatory body, provide limits or guidance on the selection of vehicle dismantlers for inspection. In fact, the State could not explain why Burger's operation was selected for inspection. . . . This is precisely what was objectionable about the inspection scheme invalidated in Marshall [v. Barlow's Inc., 436 U.S. 307 (1978)]: It failed to "provide any standards to guide inspectors either in their selection of establishments to be searched or in the exercise of their authority to search." *Dewey*, supra, at 601.

The Court also maintains that this statute effectively limits the scope of the search. We have previously found significant that "the standards with which a [business] operator is required to comply are all specifically set forth," 452 U.S., at 604, reasoning that a clear and complete definition of potential administrative violations constitutes an implied limitation on the scope of any inspection. Plainly, a statute authorizing a search which can uncover *no* administrative violations is not sufficiently limited in scope to avoid the warrant requirement. This statute fails to tailor the scope of administrative inspection to the particular concerns posed by the regulated business. I conclude that "frequency and purpose of the inspections [are left] to the unchecked discretion of Government officers." Ibid. . . .

The Court also finds significant that an operator is on notice as to who is authorized to search the premises; I do not find the statutory limitation—to "any police officer" or "agent of the commissioner"— significant. The *sole* limitation I see on a police search of the premises of a vehicle dismantler is that it must occur during business hours; otherwise it is open season. . . .

III

The fundamental defect in §415-a5 is that it authorizes searches intended solely to uncover evidence of criminal acts. . . . In the law of administrative searches, one principle emerges with unusual clarity and unanimous acceptance: the government may not use an administrative inspection scheme to search for criminal violations. See Michigan v. Clifford, 464 U.S. 287, 292 (1984) (opinion of Powell, J.) (in fire investigation, the constitutionality of a postfire inspection depends upon "whether the object of the search is to determine the cause of the fire or to gather evidence of criminal activity"); . . . Donovan v. Dewey, 452 U.S., at 598, n.6 (["warrant and probable cause requirements] pertain when commercial property is searched for contraband or evidence of crime"); Almeida-Sanchez v. United States, 413 U.S. 266, 278 (1973) (Powell, J., concurring) (traditional probable cause not required in border automobile searches because they are "undertaken primarily for administrative rather than prosecutorial purposes"). . . .

Here the State has used an administrative scheme as a pretext to search without probable cause for evidence of criminal violations. . . . This crucial point is most clearly illustrated by the fact that the police copied the serial numbers from a wheelchair and a handicapped person's walker that were found on the premises, and determined that these items had been stolen. Obviously, these objects are not vehicles or parts of vehicles, and were in no way relevant to the State's enforcement of its administrative scheme. . . .

Moreover, it is factually impossible that the search was intended to discover wrongdoing subject to administrative sanction. Burger stated that he was not registered to dismantle vehicles as required by §415-a1, and that he did not have a police book, as required by §415-a5(a). At that point he had violated every requirement of the administrative scheme. There is no administrative provision forbidding possession of stolen automobiles or automobile parts.[14] The inspection became a search for evidence of criminal acts when all possible administrative violations had been uncovered.[15]

The State contends that acceptance of this argument would allow a vehicle dismantler to thwart its administrative scheme simply by failing to register and keep records. This is false. A failure to register or keep required records violates the scheme and results in both administrative sanctions and criminal penalties. Neither is the State's further criminal investigation thwarted; the police need only obtain a warrant and then proceed to search the premises. If respondent's failure to register and maintain records amounted to probable cause, then the inspecting police officers, who worked in the Auto Crimes Division of the New York City Police Department, possessed probable cause to obtain a criminal warrant

14. Had Burger been registered as a vehicle dismantler, his registration could have been revoked for illegal possession of stolen vehicles or vehicle parts, and the examination of the vehicles and vehicle parts on his lot would have had an administrative purpose. . . .

15. In Michigan v. Clifford, 464 U.S. 287 (1984), a case involving an administrative inspection seeking the cause and origin of a fire, the Court was "unanimous in [the] opinion that after investigators have determined the cause of the fire and located the place it originated, a search of other portions of the premises may be conducted only pursuant to a warrant, issued upon probable cause that a crime has been committed." Id. at 300 (Stevens, J., concurring). . . .

authorizing a search of Burger's premises. Several of the officers might have stayed on the premises to ensure that this unlicensed dismantler did no further business, while the others obtained a warrant. . . .

The Court properly recognizes that "a State can address a major social problem *both* by way of an administrative scheme *and* through penal sanctions." . . . Administrative violations may also be crimes, and valid administrative inspections sometimes uncover evidence of crime; neither of these facts necessarily creates constitutional problems with an inspection scheme. In this case, the problem is entirely different. In no other administrative search case has this Court allowed the state to conduct an "administrative search" which violated no administrative provision and had no possible administrative consequences.[17]

The Court thus implicitly holds that if an administrative scheme has certain goals and if the search serves those goals, it may be upheld even if no concrete administrative consequences could follow from a particular search. This is a dangerous suggestion, for the goals of administrative schemes often overlap with the goals of the criminal law. Thus, on the Court's reasoning, administrative inspections would evade the requirements of the Fourth Amendment so long as they served an abstract administrative goal, such as the prevention of automobile theft. A legislature cannot abrogate constitutional protections simply by saying that the purpose of an administrative search scheme is to prevent a certain type of crime. If the Fourth Amendment is to retain meaning in the commercial context, it must be applied to searches for evidence of criminal acts even if those searches would also serve an administrative purpose, unless that administrative purpose takes the concrete form of seeking an administrative violation.

IV

The implications of the Court's opinion, if realized, will virtually eliminate Fourth Amendment protection of commercial entities in the context of administrative searches. No State may require, as a condition of doing business, a blanket submission to warrantless searches for any purpose. I respectfully dissent.

17. This case thus does not present the more difficult question whether a state could take any criminal conduct, make it an administrative violation, and then search without probable cause for violations of the newly created administrative rule. The increasing overlap of administrative and criminal violations creates an obvious temptation for the state to do so, and plainly toleration of this type of pretextual search would allow an end-run around the protections of the Fourth Amendment.

3. The Relationship Between Reasonableness and Probable Cause: The Sliding Scale Approach to the Reasonableness of Warrantless Searches and Seizures

The materials in this section examine the circumstances under which a search or seizure may be regarded as reasonable despite the absence of a traditional, individualized probable cause showing.

a. Stop and Frisk

TERRY v. OHIO
Certiorari to the Supreme Court of Ohio
392 U.S. 1 (1968)

MR. CHIEF JUSTICE WARREN delivered the opinion of the Court. . . .

Petitioner Terry was convicted of carrying a concealed weapon and sentenced to the statutorily prescribed term of one to three years in the penitentiary. Following the denial of a pretrial motion to suppress, the prosecution introduced in evidence two revolvers and a number of bullets seized from Terry and a codefendant, Richard Chilton, by Cleveland Police Detective Martin McFadden. At the hearing on the motion to suppress this evidence, Officer McFadden testified that while he was patrolling in plain clothes in downtown Cleveland at approximately 2:30 in the afternoon of October 31, 1963, his attention was attracted by two men, Chilton and Terry, standing on the corner of Huron Road and Euclid Avenue. He had never seen the two men before, and he was unable to say precisely what first drew his eye to them. However, he testified that he had been a policeman for 39 years and a detective for 35 and that he had been assigned to patrol this vicinity of downtown Cleveland for shoplifters and pickpockets for 30 years. He explained that he had developed routine habits of observation over the years and that he would "stand and watch people or walk and watch people at many intervals of the day." He added "Now, in this case when I looked over they didn't look right to me at the time."

His interest aroused, Officer McFadden took up a post of observation in the entrance to a store 300 to 400 feet away from the two men. "I get more purpose to watch them when I seen their movements," he testified. He saw one of the men leave the other one and walk southwest on Huron Road, past some stores. The man paused for a moment and looked in a store window, then walked on a short distance, turned around and walked back toward the corner, pausing once again to look in the same store window. He rejoined his companion at the corner, and the two conferred briefly. Then the second man went through the same series of motions, strolling down Huron Road, looking in the same window, walking on a short distance, turning back, peering in the store window again, and returning to confer with the first man at the corner. The two men repeated this ritual alternately between five and six times apiece—in all, roughly a dozen trips. At one point, while the two were standing together on the corner, a third man approached them and engaged them briefly in conversation. This man then left the two others and walked west on Euclid Avenue. Chilton and Terry resumed their measured pacing, peering, and conferring. After this had gone on for 10 to 12 minutes, the two men walked off together, heading west on Euclid Avenue, following the path taken earlier by the third man.

By this time Officer McFadden had become thoroughly suspicious. He testified that after observing their elaborately casual and oft-repeated reconnaissance of the store window on Huron Road, he suspected the two men of "casing a job, a stick-up," and that he considered it his duty as a police officer to investigate further. He added that he feared "they may have a gun." Thus, Officer McFadden followed Chilton and Terry and saw them stop in front of Zucker's store to talk to the same man who had conferred with them earlier on the street corner. Deciding that the situation was ripe for direct action, Officer McFadden approached the three men, identified himself as a police officer and asked for their names. At this point his knowledge was confined to what he had observed. He was not acquainted with any of the three men by name or by sight, and he had received no information concerning them from any other source. When the men "mumbled something" in response to his inquiries, Officer McFadden grabbed petitioner Terry, spun him around so that they were facing the other two, with Terry between McFadden and the others, and patted down the outside of his clothing. In the left breast pocket of Terry's overcoat Officer McFadden felt a pistol. He reached inside the overcoat pocket, but was unable to remove the gun. At this point, keeping Terry between himself and the others, the officer ordered all three men to enter Zucker's store. As they went in, he removed Terry's overcoat completely, removed a .38-caliber revolver from the pocket and ordered all three men to face the wall with their hands raised. Officer McFadden proceeded to pat down the outer clothing of Chilton and the third man, Katz. He discovered another revolver in the outer pocket of Chilton's overcoat, but no weapons were found on Katz. The officer testified that he only patted the men down to see whether they had weapons, and that he did not put his hands beneath the outer garments of either Terry or Chilton until he felt their guns. So far as appears from the record, he never placed his hands beneath Katz' outer garments. Officer McFadden seized Chilton's gun, asked the proprietor of the store to call a police wagon, and took all three men to the station, where Chilton and Terry were formally charged with carrying concealed weapons. . . .

I

. . . Unquestionably petitioner was entitled to the protection of the Fourth Amendment as he walked down the street in Cleveland. . . . The question is whether in all the circumstances of this on-the-street encounter, his right to personal security was violated by an unreasonable search and seizure.

We would be less than candid if we did not acknowledge that this question thrusts to the fore difficult and troublesome issues regarding a sensitive area of police activity—issues which have never been squarely presented to this Court. . . .

On the one hand, it is frequently argued that in dealing with the rapidly unfolding and often dangerous situations on city streets the police are in need of an escalating set of flexible responses, graduated in relation to the amount of information they possess. For this purpose it is urged that distinctions should be made between a "stop" and an "arrest" (or a "seizure" of a person), and between a "frisk" and a "search." Thus, it is argued, the police should be allowed to "stop" a person and detain him briefly for questioning upon suspicion that he may be connected with criminal activity. Upon suspicion that the person may be armed, the police should have the power to "frisk" him for weapons. If the "stop" and the "frisk" give rise to probable cause to believe that the suspect has committed a crime, then the police should be empowered to make a formal "arrest," and a full incident "search" of the person. This scheme is justified in part upon the notion that a "stop" and a "frisk" amount to a mere "minor inconvenience and petty indignity"[4] which can properly be imposed upon the citizen in the interest of effective law enforcement on the basis of a police officer's suspicion.

On the other side the argument is made that the authority of the police must be strictly circumscribed by the law of arrest and search as it has developed to date in the traditional jurisprudence of the Fourth Amendment. It is contended with some force that there is not—and cannot be—a variety of police activity which does not depend solely upon the voluntary cooperation of the citizen and yet which stops short of an arrest based upon probable cause to make such an arrest. The heart of

---

4. People v. Rivera, [14 N.Y.2d 441,] 447, 201 N.E.2d [32,] 36, 252 N.Y.S.2d [458,] 464 [(1964), cert. denied, 379 U.S. 978 (1965)].

the Fourth Amendment, the argument runs, is a severe requirement of specific justification for any intrusion upon protected personal security, coupled with a highly developed system of judicial controls to enforce upon the agents of the State the commands of the constitution. Acquiescence by the courts in the compulsion inherent in the field interrogation practices at issue here, it is urged, would constitute an abdication of judicial control over, and indeed an encouragement of substantial interference with liberty and personal security by police officers whose judgment is necessarily colored by their primary involvement in "the often competitive enterprise of ferreting out crime." Johnson v. United States, 333 U.S. 10, 14 (1948). This, it is argued, can only serve to exacerbate police-community tensions in the crowded centers of our Nation's cities.

In this context we approach the issues in this case mindful of the limitations of the judicial function in controlling the myriad daily situations in which policemen and citizens confront each other on the street. . . . Ever since its inception, the rule excluding evidence seized in violation of the Fourth Amendment has been recognized as a principal mode of discouraging lawless police conduct. . . . A ruling admitting evidence in a criminal trial, we recognize, has the necessary effect of legitimizing the conduct which produced the evidence, while an application of the exclusionary rule withholds the constitutional imprimatur.

The exclusionary rule has its limitations, however, as a tool of judicial control. It cannot properly be invoked to exclude the products of legitimate police investigative techniques on the ground that much conduct which is closely similar involves unwarranted intrusions upon constitutional protections. Moreover, in some contexts the rule is ineffective as a deterrent. . . . Encounters are initiated by the police for a wide variety of purposes, some of which are wholly unrelated to a desire to prosecute for crime.[9] Doubtless some police "field interrogation" conduct violates the Fourth Amendment. But a stern refusal by this Court to condone such activity does not necessarily render it responsive to the exclusionary rule. Regardless of how effective the rule may be where obtaining convictions is an important objective of the police, it is pow-

9. See L. Tiffany, D. McIntyre & D. Rotenberg, Detection of Crime: Stopping and Questioning, Search and Seizure, Encouragement and Entrapment 18-56 (1967). This sort of police conduct may, for example, be designed simply to help an intoxicated person find his way home, with no intention of arresting him unless he becomes obstreperous. Or the police may be seeking to mediate a domestic quarrel which threatens to erupt into violence. They may accost a woman in an area known for prostitution as part of a harassment campaign designed to drive prostitutes away without the considerable difficulty involved in prosecuting them. Or they may be conducting a dragnet search of all teenagers in a particular section of the city for weapons because they have heard rumors of an impending gang fight.

[Does the absence of "a desire to prosecute" mean that these activities should be exempt from fourth amendment regulation?—EDS.]

erless to deter invasions of constitutionally guaranteed rights where the police either have no interest in prosecuting or are willing to forgo successful prosecution in the interest of serving some other goal.

Proper adjudication of cases in which the exclusionary rule is invoked demands a constant awareness of these limitations. The wholesale harassment by certain elements of the police community, of which minority groups, particularly Negroes, frequently complain,[11] will not be stopped by the exclusion of any evidence from any criminal trial. Yet a rigid and unthinking application of the exclusionary rule, in futile protest against practices which it can never be used effectively to control, may exact a high toll in human injury and frustration of efforts to prevent crime. No judicial opinion can comprehend the protean variety of the street encounter, and we can only judge the facts of the case before us. . . .

. . . [W]e turn our attention to the quite narrow question posed by the facts before us: whether it is always unreasonable for a policeman to seize a person and subject him to a limited search for weapons unless there is probable cause for an arrest. . . .

II

. . . There is some suggestion in the use of such terms as "stop" and "frisk" that such police conduct is outside the purview of the Fourth Amendment because neither action rises to the level of a "search" or "seizure" within the meaning of the Constitution. We emphatically reject this notion. It is quite plain that the Fourth Amendment governs "seizures" of the person which do not eventuate in a trip to the station house and prosecution for crime—"arrests" in traditional terminology. It must be recognized that whenever a police officer accosts an individual and restrains his freedom to walk away, he has "seized" that person. And it

---

11. The President's Commission on Law Enforcement and Administration of Justice found that "[i]n many communities, field interrogations are a major source of friction between the police and minority groups." President's Commission on Law Enforcement and Administration of Justice, Task Force Report: The Police 183 (1967). It was reported that the friction caused by "[m]isuse of field interrogations" increases "as more police departments adopt 'aggressive patrol' in which officers are encouraged routinely to stop and question persons on the street who are unknown to them, who are suspicious, or whose purpose for being abroad is not readily evident." Id., at 184. While the frequency with which "frisking" forms a part of field interrogation practice varies tremendously with the locale, the objective of the interrogation, and the particular officer, see Tiffany, McIntyre & Rotenberg, supra, n.9, at 47-48, it cannot help but be a severely exacerbating factor in police-community tensions. This is particularly true in situations where the "stop and frisk" of youths or minority group members is "motivated by the officers' perceived need to maintain the power image of the beat officer, an aim sometimes accomplished by humiliating anyone who attempts to undermine police control of the streets." Ibid.

is nothing less than sheer torture of the English language to suggest that a careful exploration of the outer surfaces of a person's clothing all over his or her body in an attempt to find weapons is not a "search." Moreover, it is simply fantastic to urge that such a procedure performed in public by a policeman while the citizen stands helpless, perhaps facing a wall with his hands raised, is a "petty indignity."[13] It is a serious intrusion upon the sanctity of the person, which may inflict great indignity and arouse strong resentment, and it is not to be undertaken lightly.

The danger in the logic which proceeds upon distinctions between a "stop" and an "arrest," or "seizure" of the person, and between a "frisk" and a "search" is twofold. It seeks to isolate from constitutional scrutiny the initial stages of the contact between the policeman and the citizen. And by suggesting a rigid all-or-nothing model of justification and regulation under the Amendment, it obscures the utility of limitations upon the scope, as well as the initiation, of police action as a means of constitutional regulation.[15] . . .

In this case there can be no question, then, that Officer McFadden "seized" petitioner and subjected him to a "search" when he took hold of him and patted down the outer surfaces of his clothing. We must decide whether at that point it was reasonable for Officer McFadden to have interfered with petitioner's personal security as he did.[16] And in determining whether the seizure and search were "unreasonable" our inquiry is a dual one—whether the officer's action was justified at its inception, and whether it was reasonably related in scope to the circumstances which justified the interference in the first place.

13. Consider the following apt description: "[T]he officer must feel with sensitive fingers every portion of the prisoner's body. A thorough search must be made of the prisoner's arms and armpits, waistline and back, the groin and area about the testicles, and entire surface of the legs down to the feet." Priar & Martin, Searching and Disarming Criminals, 45 J. Crim. L.C. & P.S. 481 (1954).

15. . . . In our view the sounder course is to recognize that the Fourth Amendment governs all intrusions by agents of the public upon personal security, and to make the scope of the particular intrusion, in light of all the exigencies of the case, a central element in the analysis of reasonableness. Cf. Brinegar v. United States, 338 U.S. 160, 183 (1949) (Mr. Justice Jackson, dissenting). Compare Camara v. Municipal Court, 387 U.S. 523, 537 (1967). . . .

16. We thus decide nothing today concerning the constitutional propriety of an investigative "seizure" upon less than probable cause for purposes of "detention" and/or interrogation. Obviously, not all personal intercourse between policemen and citizens involves "seizures" of persons. Only when the officer, by means of physical force or show of authority, has in some way restrained the liberty of a citizen may we conclude that a "seizure" has occurred. We cannot tell with any certainty upon this record whether any such "seizure" took place here prior to Officer McFadden's initiation of physical contact for purposes of searching Terry for weapons, and we thus may assume that up to that point no intrusion upon constitutionally protected rights had occurred.

III

. . . [W]e deal here with an entire rubric of police conduct—necessarily swift action predicated upon the on-the-spot observations of the officer on the beat—which historically has not been, and as a practical matter could not be, subjected to the warrant procedure. Instead, the conduct involved in this case must be tested by the Fourth Amendment's general proscription against unreasonable searches and seizures.

Nonetheless, the notions which underlie both the warrant procedure and the requirement of probable cause remain fully relevant in this context. In order to assess the reasonableness of Officer McFadden's conduct as a general proposition, it is necessary "first to focus upon the governmental interest which allegedly justifies official intrusion upon the constitutionally protected interests of the private citizen," for there is "no ready test for determining reasonableness other than by balancing the need to search [or seize] against the invasion which the search [or seizure] entails." Camara v. Municipal Court, 387 U.S. 523, 534-535, 536-537 (1967). And in justifying the particular intrusion the police officer must be able to point to specific and articulable facts which, taken together with rational inferences from those facts, reasonably warrant that intrusion. The scheme of the Fourth Amendment becomes meaningful only when it is assured that at some point the conduct of those charged with enforcing the laws can be subjected to the more detached, neutral scrutiny of a judge who must evaluate the reasonableness of a particular search or seizure in light of the particular circumstances. And in making that assessment it is imperative that the facts be judged against an objective standard: would the facts available to the officer at the moment of the seizure or the search "warrant a man of reasonable caution in the belief" that the action taken was appropriate? . . . Anything less would invite intrusions upon constitutionally guaranteed rights based on nothing more substantial than inarticulate hunches, a result this Court has consistently refused to sanction. . . .

Applying these principles to this case, we consider first the nature and extent of the governmental interests involved. One general interest is of course that of effective crime prevention and detection; it is this interest which underlies the recognition that a police officer may in appropriate circumstances and in an appropriate manner approach a person for purposes of investigating possibly criminal behavior even though there is no probable cause to make an arrest. It was this legitimate investigative function Officer McFadden was discharging when he decided to approach petitioner and his companions. . . . It would have been poor police work indeed for an officer of 30 years' experience in the detection of thievery from stores in this same neighborhood to have failed to investigate this behavior further.

The crux of this case, however, is not the propriety of Officer McFadden's taking steps to investigate petitioner's suspicious behavior, but rather, whether there was justification for McFadden's invasion of Terry's personal security by searching him for weapons in the course of that investigation. We are now concerned with more than the governmental interest in investigating crime; in addition, there is the more immediate interest of the police officer in taking steps to assure himself that the person with whom he is dealing is not armed with a weapon that could unexpectedly and fatally be used against him. Certainly it would be unreasonable to require that police officers take unnecessary risks in the performance of their duties. American criminals have a long tradition of armed violence, and every year in this country many law enforcement officers are killed in the line of duty, and thousands more are wounded. Virtually all of these deaths and a substantial portion of the injuries are inflicted with guns and knives.

In view of these facts, we cannot blind ourselves to the need for law enforcement officers to protect themselves and other prospective victims of violence in situations where they may lack probable cause for an arrest. When an officer is justified in believing that the individual whose suspicious behavior he is investigating at close range is armed and presently dangerous to the officer or to others, it would appear to be clearly unreasonable to deny the officer the power to take necessary measures to determine whether the person is in fact carrying a weapon and to neutralize the threat of physical harm.

We must still consider, however, the nature and quality of the intrusion on individual rights which must be accepted if police officers are to be conceded the right to search for weapons in situations where probable cause to arrest for crime is lacking. Even a limited search of the outer clothing for weapons constitutes a severe, though brief intrusion upon cherished personal security, and it must surely be an annoying, frightening, and perhaps humiliating experience. Petitioner contends that such an intrusion is permissible only incident to a lawful arrest. . . . .

There are two weaknesses in this line of reasoning, however. First, it . . . recognizes no distinction in purpose, character, and extent between a search incident to an arrest and a limited search for weapons. The former, although justified in part by the acknowledged necessity to protect the arresting officer from assault with a concealed weapon, ... is also justified on other grounds, . . . and can therefore involve a relatively extensive exploration of the person. A search for weapons in the absence of probable cause to arrest, however, must, like any other search, be strictly circumscribed by the exigencies which justify its initiation. . . . Thus it must be limited to that which is necessary for the discovery of weapons which might be used to harm the officer or others nearby, and may realistically be characterized as something less than a "full" search, even though it remains a serious intrusion.

A second, and related, objection to petitioner's argument is that it assumes that the law of arrest has already worked out the balance between the particular interests involved here—the neutralization of danger to the policeman in the investigative circumstance and the sanctity of the individual. But this is not so. An arrest is a wholly different kind of intrusion upon individual freedom from a limited search for weapons, and the interests each is designed to serve are likewise quite different. An arrest is the initial stage of a criminal prosecution. It is intended to vindicate society's interest in having its laws obeyed, and it is inevitably accompanied by future interference with the individual's freedom of movement, whether or not trial or conviction ultimately follows. The protective search for weapons, on the other hand, constitutes a brief, though far from inconsiderable, intrusion upon the sanctity of the person. . . .

. . . [A] perfectly reasonable apprehension of danger may arise long before the officer is possessed of adequate information to justify taking a person into custody for the purpose of prosecuting him for a crime. Petitioner's reliance on cases which have worked out standards of reasonableness with regard to "seizures" constituting arrests and searches incident thereto is thus misplaced. It assumes that the interests sought to be vindicated and the invasions of personal security may be equated in the two cases, and thereby ignores a vital aspect of the analysis of the reasonableness of particular types of conduct under the Fourth Amendment. See Camara v. Municipal Court, supra.

Our evaluation of the proper balance that has to be struck in this type of case leads us to conclude that there must be a narrowly drawn authority to permit a reasonable search for weapons for the protection of the police officer, where he has reason to believe that he is dealing with an armed and dangerous individual, regardless of whether he has probable cause to arrest the individual for a crime. The officer need not be absolutely certain that the individual is armed; the issue is whether a reasonably prudent man in the circumstances would be warranted in the belief that his safety or that of others was in danger. . . . And in determining whether the officer acted reasonably in such circumstances, due weight must be given, not to his inchoate and unparticularized suspicion or "hunch," but to the specific reasonable inferences which he is entitled to draw from the facts in light of his experience. . . .

IV

We must now examine the conduct of Officer McFadden in this case to determine whether his search and seizure of petitioner were reasonable, both at their inception and as conducted. . . . We think on the facts and circumstances Officer McFadden detailed before the trial judge a reasonably prudent man would have been warranted in believing petitioner was armed and thus presented a threat to the officer's safety while he was investigating his suspicious behavior. The actions of Terry and Chilton were consistent with McFadden's hypothesis that these men were contemplating a daylight robbery—which, it is reasonable to assume, would be likely to involve the use of weapons—and nothing in their conduct from the time he first noticed them until the time he confronted them and identified himself as a police officer gave him sufficient reason to negate that hypothesis . . . ; and nothing in their response to his hailing them, identifying himself as a police officer, and asking their names served to dispel that reasonable belief. . . .

We need not develop at length in this case . . . the limitations which the Fourth Amendment places upon a protective seizure and search for weapons. These limitations will have to be developed in the concrete factual circumstances of individual cases. . . . Suffice it to note that such a search, unlike a search without a warrant incident to a lawful arrest, is not justified by any need to prevent the disappearance or destruction of evidence of crime. . . . The sole justification of the search in the present situation is the protection of the police officer and others nearby, and it must therefore be confined in scope to an intrusion reasonably designed to discover guns, knives, clubs, or other hidden instruments for the assault of the police officer.

The scope of the search in this case presents no serious problem in light of these standards. . . . Officer McFadden confined his search strictly to what was minimally necessary to learn whether the men were armed and to disarm them once he discovered the weapons. He did not conduct a general exploratory search for whatever evidence of criminal activity he might find.

V

We conclude that the revolver seized from Terry was properly admitted in evidence against him. . . . Each case of this sort will, of course, have to be decided on its own facts. We merely hold today that where a police officer observes unusual conduct which leads him reasonably to conclude in light of his experience that criminal activity may be afoot and that the persons with whom he is dealing may be armed and presently dangerous, where in the course of investigating this behavior he identifies himself as a policeman and makes reasonable inquiries, and where nothing in the initial stages of the encounter serves to dispel his reasonable fear for his own or others' safety, he is entitled for the protection of himself and others in the area to conduct a carefully limited search of the outer clothing of such persons in an attempt to discover weapons which might be used to assault him. Such a search is a reasonable search under the Fourth Amendment, and any weapons seized may properly be introduced in evidence against the person from whom they were taken.

Affirmed. . . .

MR. JUSTICE BLACK concurs in the judgment.

MR. JUSTICE HARLAN, concurring.

While I unreservedly agree with the Court's ultimate holding in this case, I am constrained to fill in a few gaps. . . .

. . . [I]f the frisk is justified in order to protect the officer during an encounter with a citizen, the officer must first have constitutional grounds to insist on an encounter, to make a *forcible* stop. Any person, including a policeman, is at liberty to avoid a person he considers dangerous. If and when a policeman has a right instead to disarm such a person for his own protection, he must first have a right not to avoid him but to be in his presence. That right must be more than the liberty (again, possessed by every citizen) to address questions to other persons, for ordinarily the person addressed has an equal right to ignore his interrogator and walk away; he certainly need not submit to a frisk for the questioner's protection. . . .

Where such a stop is reasonable, however, the right to frisk must be immediate and automatic if the reason for the stop is, as here, an articulable suspicion of a crime of violence. Just as a full search incident to a lawful arrest requires no additional justification, a limited frisk incident to a lawful stop must often be rapid and routine. . . .

I would affirm this conviction for what I believe to be the same reasons the Court relies on. I would, however, make explicit what I think is implicit in affirmance on the present facts. Officer McFadden's right to interrupt Terry's freedom of movement and invade his privacy arose only because circumstances warranted forcing an encounter with Terry in an effort to prevent or investigate a crime. Once that forced encounter was justified, however, the officer's right to take suitable measures for his own safety followed automatically.

Upon the foregoing premises, I join the opinion of the Court.

MR. JUSTICE WHITE, concurring. . . .

. . . I think an additional word is in order concerning the matter of interrogation during an investigative stop. There is nothing in the Constitution which prevents a policeman from addressing questions to anyone on the streets. Absent special circumstances, the person approached may not be detained or frisked but may refuse to cooperate and go on his way. However, given the proper circumstances, such as those in this case, it seems to me the person may be briefly detained against his will while pertinent questions are directed to him. Of course, the person stopped is not obliged to answer, answers may not be compelled, and refusal to answer furnishes no basis for an arrest, although it may alert the officer to the need for continued observation. . . .

MR. JUSTICE DOUGLAS, dissenting. . . .

The opinion of the Court disclaims the existence of "probable cause." . . . Had a warrant been sought, a magistrate would, therefore, have been unauthorized to issue one, for he can act only if there is a showing of "probable cause." We hold today that the police have greater authority to make a "seizure" and conduct a "search" than a judge has to authorize such action. We have said precisely the opposite over and over again.

. . . The term "probable cause" rings a bell of certainty that is not sounded by phrases such as "reasonable suspicion." Moreover, the meaning of "probable cause" is deeply imbedded in our constitutional history. . . .

The infringement on personal liberty of any "seizure" of a person can only be "reasonable" under the Fourth Amendment if we require the police to possess "probable cause" before they seize him. Only that line draws a meaningful distinction between an officer's mere inkling and the presence of facts within the officer's personal knowledge which would convince a reasonable man that the person seized has committed, is committing, or is about to commit a particular crime. . . .

To give the police greater power than a magistrate is to take a long step down the totalitarian path. Perhaps such a step is desirable to cope with modern forms of lawlessness. But if it is taken, it should be the deliberate choice of the people through a constitutional amendment. . . .

_____

The same day that it decided *Terry*, the Court decided two companion cases, Sibron v. New York and Peters v. New York, 392 U.S. 40 (1968). In *Sibron* a police officer, while patrolling his beat, observed the defendant converse with six or eight known narcotics addicts over an eight-hour period. The officer then observed Sibron conversing with three more narcotics addicts in a restaurant. The officer approached Sibron in

the restaurant and told him to come outside. Once outside, the officer
said to Sibron, " 'You know what I am after.' " Sibron then " 'mumbled
something and reached into his pocket.' " Id. at 45. The officer simultaneously thrust his own hand into the pocket, where he discovered several
glassine envelopes containing what turned out to be heroin. There was
never any suggestion that the officer feared for his own safety or that the
search was for self-protection.

The Supreme Court, after noting the state's concession that there
was not probable cause to arrest Sibron, rejected the claim that the
narcotics were discovered as the result of a reasonable "stop and frisk":

> The suspect's mere act of talking with a number of known narcotics addicts
> over an eight-hour period no more gives rise to reasonable fear of life or
> limb on the part of the police officer than it justifies an arrest for committing
> a crime. Nor did Patrolman Martin urge that when Sibron put his hand
> in his pocket, he feared that he was going for a weapon and acted in self-
> defense. His opening statement to Sibron—"You know what I am after"—
> made it abundantly clear that he sought narcotics, and his testimony at
> the hearing left no doubt that he thought there were narcotics in Sibron's
> pocket.
>
> Even assuming arguendo that there were adequate grounds to search
> Sibron for weapons, the nature and scope of the search conducted by
> Patrolman Martin were so clearly unrelated to that justification as to render
> the heroin inadmissible. The search for weapons approved in Terry con-
> sisted solely of a limited patting of the outer clothing of the suspect for
> concealed objects which might be used as instruments of assault. Only
> when he discovered such objects did the officer in Terry place his hands
> in the pockets of the men he searched. In this case, with no attempt at
> an initial limited exploration for arms, Patrolman Martin thrust his hand
> into Sibron's pocket and took from him envelopes of heroin. His testimony
> shows that he was looking for narcotics, and he found them. The search
> was not reasonably limited in scope to the accomplishment of the only
> goal which might conceivably have justified its inception—the protection
> of the officer by disarming a potentially dangerous man. [Id. at 64-65.]

In a concurring opinion Justice Harlan observed:

> In the first place, although association with known criminals may, I think,
> properly be a factor contributing to the suspiciousness of circumstances,
> it does not, entirely by itself, create suspicion adequate to support a stop.
> There must be something at least in the activities of the person being
> observed or in his surroundings that affirmatively suggests particular crim-
> inal activity, completed, current, or intended. That was the case in Terry,
> but it palpably was not the case here. . . .
>
>   Furthermore, . . . there was no reason for Officer Martin to think

that an incipient crime, or flight, or the destruction of evidence would occur if he stayed his hand; indeed, there was no more reason for him to intrude upon Sibron at the moment when he did than there had been four hours earlier, and no reason to think the situation would have changed four hours later. While no hard-and-fast rule can be drawn, I would suggest that one important factor, missing here, that should be taken into account in determining whether there are reasonable grounds for a forcible intrusion is whether there is any need for immediate action.

For these reasons I would hold that Officer Martin lacked reasonable grounds to intrude forcibly upon Sibron. In consequence, the essential premise for the right to conduct a self-protective frisk was lacking. [Id. at 73-74.]

Peters involved an apparent attempted burglary that was interrupted by an off-duty police officer. The officer was in his apartment when he heard a noise at his door. Looking through the peephole, he observed " 'two men tiptoeing out of the alcove toward the stairway.' " Id. at 48. He did not recognize either of the men as tenants.

The officer, apparently not in uniform but with his gun, went into the hallway. The two men fled. The officer caught one suspect, Peters, on the stairway, patted him down, and felt a "hard object" in the suspect's pocket. The officer testified that he did not believe the object was a gun but that it might have been a knife. He removed the object, which turned out to be an envelope containing burglar's tools.

Although the New York courts upheld the search of Peters on a stop and frisk theory, the Supreme Court held that the officer had probable cause to arrest Peters, and, therefore, that the burglar's tools were discovered in a legitimate search incident to his arrest. Justice Harlan concurred in the result but for a different reason:

I find it hard to believe that if Peters had made good his escape and there were no report of a burglary in the neighborhood, this Court would hold it proper for a prudent neutral magistrate to issue a warrant for his arrest. . . .

Although the articulable circumstances are somewhat less suspicious here than they were in *Terry*, I would affirm on the *Terry* ground that Officer Lasky had reasonable cause to make a forced stop. Unlike probable cause to arrest, reasonable grounds to stop do not depend on any degree of likelihood that a crime *has* been committed. . . . Hence although Officer Lasky had small reason to believe that a crime had been committed, his right to stop Peters can be justified if he had a reasonable suspicion that Peters was about to attempt burglary.

. . . [T]he Court's opinion in *Terry* emphasized the special qualifications of an experienced police officer. While "probable cause" to arrest or search has always depended on the existence of hard evidence that would persuade a "reasonable man," in judging on-the-street encounters it seems to me proper to take into account a police officer's trained instinctive judgment operating on a multitude of small gestures and actions impossible to reconstruct. Thus the statement by an officer that "he looked like a burglar to me" adds little to an affidavit filed with a magistrate in an effort to obtain a warrant. When the question is whether it was reasonable to take limited but forcible steps in a situation requiring immediate action, however, such a statement looms larger. A court is of course entitled to disbelieve the officer (who is subject to cross-examination), but when it believes him and when there are some articulable supporting facts, it is entitled to find action taken under fire to be reasonable. [Id. at 74-78.)

NOTES AND QUESTIONS: TERRY, SIBRON, AND PETERS

1. Note the Court's discussion in *Terry* of the relationship between the right to be free from unreasonable searches and seizures and the remedy for fourth amendment violations. The Court seems to suggest that the effectiveness of the remedy—the exclusionary rule—should have an impact on the scope of the right. Do you think the Court's reservations about the efficacy of the deterrent effect of the exclusionary rule on stop and frisk practices are well-founded? In any event, why should the supposed effectiveness or ineffectiveness of the *remedy* determine the scope of the *right?*

2. One of the concerns with stops and frisks is that the practice may be used as a pretext to search with less than probable cause individuals on whom the police would like to find incriminating evidence. The *Terry* standard is arguably so vague that a police officer—at least if the officer is willing to stretch the truth a little—should have no difficulty in proving after the fact that the requisite suspicion existed. In light of this concern and the Court's concern about the relationship between the scope of the right and the remedy, it arguably would be desirable to apply a modified exclusionary rule in stop and frisk cases: If the *Terry* standard is satisfied, weapons discovered in a legitimate stop and frisk would be admissible; All other evidence would be inadmissible in the absence of probable cause to search or arrest.[73] Would such a rule be desirable?

3. What is the nature of the test that the Court applied to uphold

---

73. The results in *Terry*, *Sibron*, and *Peters* support such a rule. In *Terry* a weapon was admitted in evidence following a valid frisk; in *Sibron* the Court arguably strained to find the frisk illegal as a means of avoiding a decision that use of the stop and frisk power can lead to the admission in evidence of narcotics; and in *Peters* the Court arguably strained to find the existence of probable cause in order to justify the admission in evidence of burglar's tools.

the stop and frisk in *Terry?* We know that the officer cannot rely solely on a subjective, intuitive feeling but that the officer must be able to articulate specific facts that make the suspicion reasonable. We also know that the degree of suspicion that will justify a stop and frisk is less than— or at least different from—that needed for probable cause. What more, if anything, can one say about the quality and quantity of proof that will satisfy the *Terry* standard?

Note that the probable cause standard, despite its familiarity, is itself vague and difficult to apply. See, e.g., the differing views about probable cause in *Peters.* Does the inherent ambiguity in the probable cause standard tend to undermine or support the position of Justice Douglas in *Terry?*

4. Why was the *Terry* standard not met in *Sibron?* Was the degree of suspicion any less there than in *Terry?* Can one seriously argue that it was unreasonable for a police officer to respond as he did when *Sibron* reached for his pocket?

Is it easier to reconcile *Terry* and *Sibron* if one focuses initially, as Justice Harlan did, on the question whether the stop in each case was legal? Given *Terry* and the inherent ambiguity of the "reasonable suspicion" standard, can one say with assurance that the officer in *Sibron* did not have reasonable suspicion to believe that Sibron was possessing narcotics? Is it sufficient to answer that regardless of the actual probabilities, we simply do not want the police to act on suspicion derived exclusively from the nature of one's associates? Or is the point rather that possession of narcotics is not sufficiently serious or dangerous enough to justify a seizure on less than probable cause?

Note that if the right to *stop* is limited to situations in which the suspect is believed to be armed and dangerous, then the right to frisk should follow automatically from the right to stop. On the other hand, if the right to stop is more extensive, then arguably there should be an independent showing of reasonable suspicion about dangerousness to justify the frisk of a stopped suspect. What should the relationship be between the right to stop and the right to frisk?

NOTES AND QUESTIONS: THE SCOPE OF THE *TERRY* DOCTRINE

1. In Dunaway v. New York, 442 U.S. 200 (1979), the Court reaffirmed that *Terry* created only a narrowly drawn exception to the warrant and probable cause requirements. The defendant, a murder suspect, was taken into custody without probable cause, and "although he was not told he was under arrest, he would have been physically restrained

if he had attempted to leave." Id. at 203. During the ensuing interrogation, the defendant made incriminating statements that were used against
him at his murder trial. Before the Supreme Court he contended that
the statements were the fruit of an illegal seizure. The Court, in an
opinion by Justice Brennan, agreed:

> Respondent State now urges the Court to apply a balancing test, rather
> than the general rule, to custodial interrogations, and to hold that "sei-
> zures" such as that in this case may be justified by mere "reasonable
> suspicion." *Terry* and its progeny clearly do not support such a result. The
> narrow intrusions involved in those cases were judged by a balancing test
> rather than by the general principle that Fourth Amendment seizures must
> be supported by the "long-prevailing standards" of probable cause, Brinegar
> v. United States, 338 U.S. [160,] 176 [(1949)], only because these intru-
> sions fell far short of the kind of intrusion associated with an arrest. . . .
>   . . . [T]he detention of petitioner was in important respects indistin-
> guishable from a traditional arrest. Petitioner was not questioned briefly
> where he was found. Instead, he was taken from a neighbor's home to a
> police car, transported to a police station, and placed in an interrogation
> room. He was never informed that he was "free to go"; indeed, he would
> have been physically restrained if he had refused to accompany the officers
> or had tried to escape their custody. The application of the Fourth Amend-
> ment's requirement of probable cause does not depend on whether an
> intrusion of this magnitude is termed an "arrest" under state law. The
> mere facts that petitioner was not told he was under arrest, was not "booked,"
> and would not have had an arrest record if the interrogation had proved
> fruitless . . . obviously do not make petitioner's seizure even roughly
> analogous to the narrowly defined intrusions involved in *Terry*, and its
> progeny. Indeed, any "exception" that could cover a seizure as intrusive
> as that in this case would threaten to swallow the general rule that Fourth
> Amendment seizures are "reasonable" only if based on probable cause.
>   The central importance of the probable-cause requirement to the
> protection of a citizen's privacy afforded by the Fourth Amendment's
> guarantees cannot be compromised in this fashion. "The requirement of
> probable cause has roots that are deep in our history." Henry v. United
> States, 361 U.S. 98, 100 (1959). Hostility to seizures based on mere
> suspicion was a prime motivation for the adoption of the Fourth Amend-
> ment, and decisions immediately after its adoption affirmed that "common
> rumor or report, suspicion, or even 'strong reason to suspect' was not
> adequate to support a warrant for arrest." Id., at 101 (footnotes omitted).
> The familiar threshold standard of probable cause for Fourth Amendment
> seizures reflects the benefit of extensive experience accommodating the
> factors relevant to the "reasonableness" requirement of the Fourth Amend-
> ment, and provides the relative simplicity and clarity necessary to the
> implementation of a workable rule. See Brinegar v. United States, supra,
> at 175-176.

In effect, respondent urges us to adopt a multifactor balancing test of "reasonable police conduct under the circumstances" to cover all seizures that do not amount to technical arrests. But the protections intended by the Framers could all too easily disappear in the consideration and balancing of the multifarious circumstances presented by different cases, especially when that balancing may be done in the first instance by police officers engaged in the "often competitive enterprise of ferreting out crime." Johnson v. United States, 333 U.S. 10, 14 (1948). A single, familiar standard is essential to guide police officers, who have only limited time and expertise to reflect on and balance the social and individual interests involved in the specific circumstances they confront. Indeed, our recognition of these dangers, and our consequent reluctance to depart from the proved protections afforded by the general rule, are reflected in the narrow limitations emphasized in the cases employing the balancing test. For all but those narrowly defined intrusions, the requisite "balancing" has been performed in centuries of precedent and is embodied in the principle that seizures are "reasonable" only if supported by probable cause. [442 U.S. at 211-214.]

2.   Compare *Dunaway* with Hayes v. Florida, 470 U.S. 811 (1985), where the defendant, without his consent and without probable cause, was taken by the police from his home to the station house where he was fingerprinted. After determining that the defendant's prints matched those discovered at the scene of a rape-burglary, the defendant was arrested. Subsequently, the fingerprints were introduced into evidence against him, and he was convicted of burglary and sexual battery. In reversing the conviction, the Supreme Court reaffirmed its holding in Davis v. Mississippi, page 883 infra, that "transportation to and investigative detention at the station house without probable cause or judicial authorization together violate the Fourth Amendment." 470 U.S. at 815. The Court suggested in dictum that detention for finger-printing in the field on the basis of articulable suspicion may be constitutional. Id. at 816. The Court also repeated the possibility, first mentioned in Davis, that "under circumscribed procedures, the Fourth Amendment might permit the judiciary to authorize the seizure of a person on less than probable cause and his removal to the police station for the purpose of fingerprinting." Id. at 817.[74]

74. In Chapter 10 we consider the inevitable discovery doctrine, see Nix v. Williams, page 1359 infra, which permits the use of illegally obtained evidence that would have been "inevitably" discovered. If articulable suspicion is all that is necessary to justify finger-printing in the field, is it perhaps likely that the inevitable discovery doctrine will frequently save convictions in cases like *Davis* and *Hayes*? In *Hayes* the state argued before the Supreme Court that the inevitable discovery doctrine should apply. The Court, however, refused to consider the issue because it had not been presented in the state courts. 470 U.S. at 814 n.1.

NOTES AND QUESTIONS: THE MEANING OF
ARTICULABLE SUSPICION

1. On several occasions, the Court has elaborated on and attempted to give content to the reasonable or articulable suspicion standard. Consider, for example, United States v. Cortez, 449 U.S. 411 (1981):

> An investigatory stop must be justified by some objective manifestation that the person stopped is, or is about to be, engaged in criminal activity.[2] . . . .
>
> Courts have used a variety of terms to capture the elusive concept of what cause is sufficient to authorize police to stop a person. Terms like "articulable reasons" and "founded suspicion" are not self-defining; they fall short of providing clear guidance dispositive of the myriad factual situations that arise. But the essence of all that has been written is that the totality of the circumstances—the whole picture—must be taken into account. Based upon that whole picture the detaining officers must have a particularized and objective basis for suspecting the particular person stopped of criminal activity. . . .
>
> The idea that an assessment of the whole picture must yield a particularized suspicion contains two elements, each of which must be present before a stop is permissible. First, the assessment must be based upon all of the circumstances. The analysis proceeds with various objective observations, information from police reports, if such are available, and consideration of the modes or patterns of operation of certain kinds of lawbreakers. From these data, a trained officer draws inferences and makes deductions—inferences and deductions that might well elude an untrained person. The process does not deal with hard certainties, but with probabilities. Long before the law of probabilities was articulated as such, practical people formulated certain common-sense conclusions about human behavior; jurors as factfinders are permitted to do the same—and so are law enforcement officers. Finally, the evidence thus collected must be seen and weighed not in terms of library analysis by scholars, but as understood by those versed in the field of law enforcement.
>
> The second element contained in the idea that an assessment of the whole picture must yield a particularized suspicion is the concept that the process just described must raise a suspicion that the particular individual being stopped is engaged in wrongdoing. Chief Justice Warren, speaking for the Court in Terry v. Ohio, [392 U.S. 1 (1968)], said that "[t]his demand for specificity in the information upon which police action is predicated is *the central teaching of this Court's Fourth Amendment jurisprudence.*" Id., at 21, n.18 (emphasis added). [449 U.S. at 417-418.]

---

2. Of course, an officer may stop and question a person if there is reasonable grounds to believe that person is wanted for past criminal conduct.

See Harper, Has the Replacement of "Probable Cause" with "Reasonable Suspicion" Resulted in the Creation of the Best of All Possible Worlds?, 22 Akron L. Rev. 13 (1988).

2. Alabama v. White, 110 S. Ct. 2412 (1990), dealt with the role of an anonymous tip in assessing whether the police had reasonable suspicion to make a stop. The case arose from the following facts:

> On April 22, 1987, at approximately 3 P.M., Corporal B. H. Davis of the Montgomery Police Department received a telephone call from an anonymous person, stating that Vanessa White would be leaving 235-C Lynwood Terrace Apartments at a particular time in a brown Plymouth station wagon with the right taillight lens broken, that she would be going to Dobey's Motel, and that she would be in possession of about an ounce of cocaine inside a brown attache case. Corporal Davis and his partner, Corporal P. A. Reynolds, proceeded to the Lynwood Terrace Apartments. The officers saw a brown Plymouth station wagon with a broken right taillight in the parking lot in front of the 235 building. The officers observed respondent leave the 235 building, carrying nothing in her hands, and enter the station wagon. They followed the vehicle as it drove the most direct route to Dobey's Motel. When the vehicle reached the Mobile Highway, on which Dobey's Motel is located, Corporal Reynolds requested a patrol unit to stop the vehicle. The vehicle was stopped at approximately 4:18 P.M., just short of Dobey's Motel. [Id. at 2414.]

Following the stop the driver gave the officers permission to look for cocaine in the car. The officers discovered a brown attache case, and on request the driver gave the officers the combination to the lock. The officers discovered marijuana in the attache case and arrested the driver. During processing at the police station, the officers found cocaine in the driver's purse. The Alabama Court of Criminal Appeals reversed the driver's convictions for possession of marijuana and possession of cocaine on the ground that the drugs were the fruits of a stop that was not based on reasonable suspicion. The United States Supreme Court, in an opinion by Justice White, disagreed:

> Illinois v. Gates, 462 U.S. 213 (1983), dealt with an anonymous tip in the probable cause context. The Court there abandoned the "two-pronged test" of Aguilar v. Texas, 378 U.S. 108 (1964), and Spinelli v. United States, 393 U.S. 410 (1969), in favor a "totality of the circumstances" approach to determining whether an informant's tip establishes probable cause. Gates made clear, however, that those factors that had been considered critical under Aguilar and Spinelli—an informant's "veracity," "reliability," "and "basis of knowledge"—remain "highly relevant in determining the value of his report." 462 U.S. at 230. These factors are also relevant in the reasonable suspicion context. . . .

. . . [A] tip such as this one, standing alone, would not " 'warrant a man of reasonable caution in the belief' that [a stop] was appropriate." Terry [v. Ohio, 392 U.S. 1,] 22 [(1968)], quoting Carroll v. United States, 267 U.S. 132, 162 (1925).

As there was in *Gates*, however, in this case there is more than the tip itself. The tip was not as detailed, and the corroboration was not as complete, as in *Gates*, but the required degree of suspicion was likewise not as high. . . .

Reasonable suspicion is a less demanding standard than probable cause not only in the sense that reasonable suspicion can be established with information that is different in quantity or content than that required to establish probable cause, but also in the sense that reasonable suspicion can arise from information that is less reliable than that required to show probable cause. . . . Thus if a tip has a relatively low degree of reliability, more information will be required to establish the requisite quantum of suspicion than would be required if the tip were more reliable. The *Gates* Court applied its totality of the circumstances approach in this manner, taking into account the facts known to the officers from personal observation, and giving the anonymous tip the weight it deserved in light of its indicia of reliability as established through independent police work. The same approach applies in the reasonable suspicion context, the only difference being the level of suspicion that must be established.

It is true that not every detail mentioned by the tipster was verified, such as the name of the woman leaving the building or the precise apartment from which she left; but the officers did corroborate that a woman left the 235 building and got into the particular vehicle that was described by the caller. . . . [I]t appears from the record before us that respondent's departure from the building was within the time frame predicted by the caller. . . . [G]iven that the four mile route driven by respondent was the most direct route possible to Dobey's Motel . . . but nevertheless involved several turns, . . . we think respondent's destination was significantly corroborated.

The Court's opinion in *Gates* gave credit to the proposition that because an informant is shown to be right about some things, he is probably right about other facts that he has alleged, including the claim that the object of the tip is engaged in criminal activity. . . . Thus, it is not unreasonable to conclude in this case that the independent corroboration by the police of significant aspects of the informer's predictions imparted some degree of reliability to the other allegations made by the caller.

We think it also important that, as in *Gates*, "the anonymous [tip] contained a range of details relating not just to easily obtained facts and conditions existing at the time of the tip, but to future actions of third parties ordinarily not easily predicted." *Gates*, 462 U.S. at 245. . . . When significant aspects of the caller's predictions were verified, there was reason to believe not only that the caller was honest but also that he was well informed, at least well enough to justify the stop.

Although it is a close case, we conclude that under the totality of the circumstances the anonymous tip, as corroborated, exhibited sufficient indicia of reliability to justify the investigatory stop of respondent's car. [110 S. Ct. at 2415-2417.]

Justice Stevens, in a dissenting opinion joined by Justices Brennan and Marshall, observed:

Millions of people leave their apartments at about the same time every day carrying an attache case and heading for a destination known to their neighbors. . . .

The record in this case does not tell us how often respondent drove from the Lynwood Terrace Apartments to Dobey's Motel; for all we know, she may have been a room clerk or telephone operator working the evening shift. . . .

. . . [U]nder the Court's holding, every citizen is subject to being seized and questioned by any officer who is prepared to testify that the warrantless stop was based on an anonymous tip predicting whatever conduct the officer just observed. Fortunately the vast majority of those in our law enforcement community would not adopt such a practice. But the Fourth Amendment was intended to protect the citizen from the overzealous and unscrupulous officer as well as from those who are conscientious and truthful. [Id. at 2417-2418.]

3. If the articulable suspicion relates to past criminal conduct, the factors that enter into the *Terry* balancing are somewhat different. The interest in crime prevention is no longer an immediate concern, and the exigency may not be as great. Indeed, in some cases the police may have a good deal of latitude in deciding when and where to approach the individual. On the other hand, there is the obvious law enforcement interest in solving past crimes. Taking these factors into account, the Supreme Court in United States v. Hensley, 469 U.S. 221 (1985), upheld the stop of an armed robbery suspect:

We need not and do not decide today whether *Terry* stops to investigate all past crimes, however serious, are permitted. It is enough to say that, if the police have a reasonable suspicion, grounded in specific and articulable facts,[75] that a person they encounter was involved in or is wanted in

---

75. The police officer who stopped Hensley did so on the basis of a "wanted flyer" that had been issued by a neighboring police department. The officer had no personal knowledge of Hensley's activities, and the flyer indicated only that Hensley was wanted for investigation. In such a situation, the Court held, it is appropriate for the stopping officer to rely on the flyer: "[E]vidence uncovered in the course of the stop is admissible if the police who *issued* the flyer or bulletin possessed a reasonable suspicion justifying the stop, . . . and if the stop that in fact occurred was not significantly more intrusive than would have been permitted by the issuing department." 469 U.S. at 231. Cf. Whitely v. Warden, 401 U.S. 560, 568 (1971) (dictum announcing same approach in probable cause context).—EDS.

connection with a completed felony, then a *Terry* stop may be made to investigate that suspicion. [Id. at 229.]

NOTES AND QUESTIONS: THE MEANING AND SCOPE OF "STOP" AND "FRISK"

1. The Court on several occasions has dealt with the question what constitutes a stop. It is now well established that the test is whether "in view of all the circumstances surrounding the incident, a reasonable person would have believed that he was not free to leave." United States v. Mendenhall, 446 U.S. 544, 554 (1980) (opinion of Justice Stewart).[76] Furthermore, in applying this standard, the Court has stated: "[P]olice questioning, by itself, is unlikely to result in a Fourth Amendment violation. While most citizens will respond to a police request, the fact that people do so, and do so without being told they are free not to respond, hardly eliminates the consensual nature of the response." Immigration & Naturalization Service v. Delgado, 466 U.S. 210, 216 (1984). See generally Butterfoss, Bright Line Seizures: The Need for Clarity in Determining When Fourth Amendment Activity Begins, 79 J. Crim. L. & Criminology 437 (1988); LaFave, "Seizure" Typology: Classifying Detentions of the Person to Resolve Warrant, Grounds, and Search Issues, 17 U. Mich. J.L. Reform 417 (1984).

2. In United States v. Sharpe, 470 U.S. 675 (1985), the Supreme Court considered the permissible length of a *Terry* stop. DEA Agent Cooke and Highway Patrol Officer Thrasher, in separate vehicles, were following the defendants, Sharpe and Savage, who were also driving separate vehicles. There was, according to the Court, articulable suspicion to believe that the defendants were engaged in marijuana trafficking.[77]

---

76. See also United States v. Mendenhall, 446 U.S. at 560 n.1 (opinion of Justice Powell); id. at 570 n.3 (opinion of Justice Blackmun). See generally Florida v. Royer, 460 U.S. 491 (1983).

77. The Court noted that the Court of Appeals had "assumed" that there was articulable suspicion to stop the vehicles and concluded that that assumption was "abundantly supported" by the following facts:

> Agent Cooke had observed the vehicles traveling in tandem for 20 miles in an area near the [North Carolina] coast known to be frequented by drug traffickers. Cooke testified that pickup trucks with camper shells were often used to transport large quantities of marihuana. . . . Savage's pickup truck appeared to be heavily loaded, and the windows of the camper were covered with a quilted bed-sheet material rather than curtains. Finally, both vehicles took evasive actions and started speeding as soon as Officer Thrasher began following them in his marked vehicle. [470 U.S. at 682.]

In a dissenting opinion Justice Brennan made a twofold attack on the Court's holding that there were reasonable grounds to stop the defendants. First, he contended that the

At Agent Cooke's radioed request that Officer Thrasher stop both vehicles, Officer Thrasher pulled alongside the lead vehicle, which was driven by Sharpe, and signaled for the driver to stop. As Sharpe pulled to the side of the road, Savage drove his pickup truck with a camper shell between Officer Thrasher and Sharpe and proceeded down the road. Agent Cooke remained with Sharpe. Officer Thrasher pursued Savage and stopped him a half mile down the highway.

Agent Cooke radioed the local police to assist him. When they arrived after about 10 minutes, he joined Officer Thrasher, who had been holding Savage. After detecting the odor of marijuana emanating from Savage's camper, Agent Cooke subjected the vehicle to a warrantless, unconsented search. The search revealed what appeared to be, and what subsequent chemical analysis proved to be, marijuana. Savage and Sharpe were arrested; the marijuana was introduced into evidence at their trial; and they were convicted of controlled substance offenses.

The time that elapsed between the initial stop of Savage and the search of his vehicle was 20 minutes.[78] If the length of this detention exceeded the permissible scope of a *Terry* seizure, the marijuana should have been excluded as the product of an illegal stop. On the other hand, if the stop were legal, the odor of marijuana detected by Agent Cooke provided probable cause for the search, and the automobile exception justified dispensing with the warrant requirement.

Chief Justice Burger, in an opinion for the Court, upheld the legality of the stop. He first distinguished *Dunaway*, Note 1 supra, on the ground that the Court there was concerned not with the length of detention but with the events that occurred during the detention—namely, "(1) the defendant was taken from a private dwelling; (2) he was transported unwillingly to the police station; and (3) he there was subjected to custodial interrogation resulting in a confession." 470 U.S. at 684 n.4. The Chief Justice continued:

> Obviously, if an investigative stop continues indefinitely, at some point it can no longer be justified as an investigative stop. But our cases impose

---

facts did not support the assertions that the defendants took evasive actions or began speeding after they saw Officer Thrasher's marked car. Id. at 705-707. Second, citing Peters v. New York, page 697 supra, Justice Brennan argued that "where police officers reasonably suspect that an individual may be engaged in criminal activity, and the individual deliberately takes flight when the officers attempt to stop and question him, the officers generally . . . have . . . probable cause to arrest." 470 U.S. at 705. Thus, if the facts were as the Court portrayed them to be, there was no need in Justice Brennan's view to address the stop issue.

78. Defendant Sharpe was detained for a longer period of time before being arrested, but as the Court noted, there was no causal connection between Sharpe's detention and the discovery of the marijuana. 470 U.S. at 683.

no rigid time limitation on *Terry* stops. While it is clear that "the brevity of the invasion of the individual's Fourth Amendment interests is an important factor in determining whether the seizure is so minimally intrusive as to be justifiable on reasonable suspicion," United States v. Place, [page 796 infra,] we have emphasized the need to consider the law enforcement purposes to be served by the stop as well as the time reasonably needed to effectuate those purposes. . . . Much as a "bright line" rule would be desirable, in evaluating whether an investigative detention is unreasonable, common sense and ordinary human experience must govern over rigid criteria. . . .

In assessing whether a detention is too long in duration to be justified as an investigative stop, we consider it appropriate to examine whether the police diligently pursued a means of investigation that was likely to confirm or dispel their suspicions quickly, during which time it was necessary to detain the defendant. . . . A court making this assessment should take care to consider whether the police are acting in a swiftly developing situation, and in such cases the court should not indulge in unrealistic second-guessing. . . . The question is not simply whether some other alternative was available, but whether the police acted unreasonably in failing to recognize and pursue it.

We readily conclude that, given the circumstances facing him, Agent Cooke pursued his investigation in a diligent and reasonable manner.[5] . . .

. . . The delay in this case was attributable almost entirely to the evasive actions of Savage, who sought to elude the police as Sharpe moved his [vehicle] to the side of the road.[6] [470 U.S. at 685-688.]

In a separate opinion Justice Marshall argued that brevity should be a threshold requirement for the legality of *Terry* stops:

Even a stop that lasts no longer than necessary to complete the investigation for which the stop was made may amount to an illegal arrest if the stop is more "minimally intrusive." The stop must first be found not unduly

---

5. It was appropriate for Officer Thrasher to hold Savage for the brief period pending Cooke's arrival. Thrasher could not be certain that he was aware of all the facts that had aroused Cooke's suspicions; and, as a highway patrolman, he lacked Cooke's training and experience in dealing with narcotics investigations. In this situation, it cannot realistically be said that Thrasher, a state patrolman called in to assist a federal agent in making a stop, acted unreasonably because he did not release Savage based solely on his own limited investigation of the situation and without the consent of Agent Cooke.

6. Even if it could be inferred that Savage was not attempting to elude the police when he drove his car *between* Thrasher's patrol car and Sharpe's Pontiac—in the process nearly hitting the patrol car—such an assumption would not alter our analysis or our conclusion. The significance of Savage's actions is that, whether innocent or purposeful, they made it necessary for Thrasher and Cooke to split up, placed Thrasher and Cooke out of contact with each other, and required Cooke to enlist the assistance of local police before he could join Thrasher and Savage.

intrusive before any balancing of the government's interest against the individual's becomes appropriate. [Id. at 690.]

He went on to suggest that normally a 20-minute stop would exceed his brevity requirement. He agreed with the majority, however, that the delay in this case was primarily attributable to the evasive actions of Savage when Sharpe pulled off to the side of the highway.[79] In such a situation, Justice Marshall concluded, a stop may legally be prolonged. Id. at 697-699.

Would Justice Marshall's brevity rule be preferable to the more general balancing approach of the majority? If Justice Marshall's approach were adopted, should evasive actions by the suspect or other circumstances justify a prolonged stop? Consider the following observation by Justice Marshall:

> Difficult questions will no doubt be presented when during the few minutes an officer learns enough to increase his suspicions but not enough to establish probable cause. But whatever the proper resolution of this problem, the very least that ought to be true of Terry's brevity requirement is that, if the initial encounter provides no greater grounds for suspicion than existed before the stop, the individual must be free to leave after the few minutes permitted for the initial encounter. Such a clear rule would provide officials with necessary and desirable certainty and would adequately protect the important liberty and privacy interests upon which Terry stops infringe. [Id. at 698.]

How much certainty will there be if there are exceptions for evasive action by or increased suspicion about a suspect?

In assessing whether a stop is unreasonably long, how should courts deal with the requirement that the police "diligently [pursue] a means of investigation that [is] likely to confirm or dispel their suspicions quickly"? Should the question be, as the majority holds, "whether the police acted unreasonably in failing to recognize or to pursue" some alternative? Consider Justice Brennan's suggestion that the government "must show at a minimum that the 'least intrusive means reasonably available' were used in carrying out the stop." Id. at 704 (Brennan, J., dissenting) (quoting Justice White's opinion in Florida v. Royer, 460 U.S. 491, 500 (1983)).

---

79. In his dissenting opinion Justice Brennan disagreed with the characterization of Savage's actions as evasive: "Neither the District Court nor the Court of Appeals ever found that Savage's actions constituted evasion or flight. . . .
. . . . Savage's actions in continuing to drive down the highway could well have been entirely consistent with those of any driver who sees the police hail someone in front of him over to the side of the road." 470 U.S. at 708.

Under either approach, how would you evaluate the conduct of Agent
Cooke and Officer Thrasher?

3. Consider Pennsylvania v. Mimms, 434 U.S. 105 (1977) (per
curiam). The defendant was lawfully stopped for a traffic violation and
ordered out of his car. As the defendant emerged from his car, the officer
noticed a bulge, which he believed might be a gun. The officer frisked
the defendant and discovered a .38 caliber revolver, which was introduced
into evidence in the defendant's trial for carrying a concealed weapon:

> The Pennsylvania court did not doubt that the officers acted reasonably
> in stopping the car. It was also willing to assume, arguendo, that the
> limited search for weapons was proper once the officer observed the bulge
> under respondent's coat. But the court nonetheless thought the search
> constitutionally infirm because the officer's order to respondent to get out
> of the car was an impermissible "seizure." This was so because the officer
> could not point to "objective observable facts to support a suspicion that
> criminal activity was afoot or that the occupants of the vehicle posed a
> threat to police safety."[2] . . .
>
> We do not agree with this conclusion. The touchstone of our analysis
> under the Fourth Amendment is always "the reasonableness in all the
> circumstances of the particular governmental invasion of a citizen's per-
> sonal security." Terry v. Ohio, 392 U.S. 1, 19 (1968). Reasonableness,
> of course, depends "on a balance between the public interest and the
> individual's right to personal security free from arbitrary interference
> by law officers." United States v. Brignoni-Ponce, 422 U.S. 873, 878
> (1975). . . .
>
> . . . [W]e look first to that side of the balance which bears the officer's
> interest in taking the action that he did. The State freely concedes the
> officer had no reason to suspect foul play from the particular driver at the
> time of the stop, there having been nothing unusual or suspicious about
> his behavior. It was apparently his practice to order all drivers out of their
> vehicles as a matter of course whenever they had been stopped for a traffic
> violation. The State argues that this practice was adopted as a precautionary
> measure to afford a degree of protection to the officer and that it may be
> justified on that ground. Establishing a face-to-face confrontation dimin-
> ishes the possibility, otherwise substantial, that the driver can make unob-
> served movements; this, in turn, reduces the likelihood that the officer
> will be the victim of an assault.[5]
>
> We think it too plain for argument that the State's proffered justifi-

2. 471 Pa., 552, 370 A.2d, at 1160.

5. The State does not, and need not, go so far as to suggest that an officer may frisk
the occupants of any car stopped for a traffic violation. Rather, it only argues that it is
permissible to order the driver out of the car. In this particular case, argues the State,
once the driver alighted, the officer had independent reason to suspect criminal activity
and present danger and it was upon this basis, and not the mere fact that respondent had
committed a traffic violation, that he conducted the search.

cation—the safety of the officer—is both legitimate and weighty. . . .

The hazard of accidental injury from passing traffic to an officer standing on the driver's side of the vehicle may also be appreciable in some situations. Rather than conversing while standing exposed to moving traffic, the officer prudently may prefer to ask the driver of the vehicle to step out of the car and off onto the shoulder of the road where the inquiry may be pursued with greater safety to both.

Against this important interest we are asked to weigh the intrusion into the driver's personal liberty occasioned not by the initial stop of the vehicle, which was admittedly justified, but by the order to get out of the car. We think this additional intrusion can only be described as de minimis. . . .[6] [434 U.S. at 107-111.]

4. If a lawfully stopped individual refuses to answer questions or otherwise cooperate with the police, should the police be permitted to prolong the stop in order to accomplish their investigatory purpose? Does your answer to the preceding question depend at least in part on whether a lawfully stopped individual has the right to refuse to cooperate with the police? Does an individual have such a right? Consider Kolender v. Lawson, 461 U.S. 352 (1983), in which the Court held unconstitutional on void for vagueness grounds a statute making it a crime for a lawfully stopped individual to refuse to provide "credible and reliable" identification and to refuse to account for his presence. In the course of her opinion for the Court Justice O'Connor observed that the disposition of the case made it unnecessary to decide "whether the individual has a legitimate expectation of privacy in his identity when he is detained lawfully under Terry." Id. at 355 n.10. Justice Brennan, in a concurring opinion, maintained that the statute, if cured of its vagueness, would violate the fourth amendment:

Merely to facilitate the general law enforcement objectives of investigating and preventing unspecified crimes, States may not authorize the arrest and criminal prosecution of an individual for failing to produce identification or further information on demand by a police officer. . . .

[Police officers] may ask their questions in a way calculated to obtain an answer. But they may not *compel* an answer, and they must allow the person to leave after a reasonably brief period of time unless the information they have acquired during the encounter has given them probable cause sufficient to justify an arrest. [Id. at 362, 366 (emphasis in original).]

6. . . . [W]e do not hold today that "whenever an officer has an occasion to speak with the driver of a vehicle, he may also order the driver out of the car." We hold only that once a motor vehicle has been lawfully detained for a traffic violation, the police officers may order the driver to get out of the vehicle without violating the Fourth Amendment's proscription of unreasonable searches and seizures.

See generally Murphy, Encounters of a Brief Kind: On Arbitrariness and Police Demands for Identification, 1986 Ariz. St. L.J. 207.

5. *Terry* and its progeny seem to establish that a search *of the person* based on articulable suspicion that the person may be armed or dangerous must at least initially be limited to a brief patdown or "frisk." To what extent should articulable suspicion that a person may be armed or dangerous justify a search of the *area* in the vicinity of the person? Consider Michigan v. Long, 463 U.S. 1032 (1983), which arose from the following facts:

> Deputies Howell and Lewis were on patrol in a rural area one evening when, shortly after midnight, they observed a car traveling erratically and at excessive speed. The officers observed the car turning down a side road, where it swerved off into a shallow ditch. The officers stopped to investigate. Long, the only occupant of the automobile, met the deputies at the rear of the car, which was protruding from the ditch onto the road. The door on the driver's side of the vehicle was left open.
>
> Deputy Howell requested Long to produce his operator's license, but he did not respond. After the request was repeated, Long produced his license. Long again failed to respond when Howell requested him to produce the vehicle registration. After another repeated request, Long, whom Howell thought "appeared to be under the influence of something," 413 Mich. 461, 469, 320 N.W.2d 866, 868 (1982), turned from the officers and began walking toward the open door of the vehicle. The officers followed Long and both observed a large hunting knife on the floorboard of the driver's side of the car. The officers then stopped Long's progress and subjected him to a *Terry* protective pat-down, which revealed no weapons.
>
> Long and Deputy Lewis then stood by the rear of the vehicle while Deputy Howell shined his flashlight into the interior of the vehicle, but did not actually enter it. The purpose of Howell's action was "to search for other weapons." Id., at 469, 320 N.W.2d, at 868. The officer noticed that something was protruding from under the armrest of the front seat. He knelt in the vehicle and lifted the armrest. He saw an open pouch on the front seat, and upon flashing his light on the pouch, determined that it contained what appeared to be marijuana. After Deputy Howell showed the pouch and its contents to Deputy Lewis, Long was arrested for possession of marijuana. [463 U.S. at 1035-1036.]

Determining that the pouch could have contained a weapon, id. at 1050-1051, the trial court denied Long's suppression motion, and Long was convicted of marijuana possession.

The Court, in an opinion by Justice O'Connor, first concluded that the stop and patdown were "clearly justified." Id. at 1050. Then, after noting that "investigative detentions involving suspects in vehicles are especially fraught with danger to police officers," id. at 1047, the Court upheld the vehicle search: "[T]he search of the passenger compartment of an automobile, limited to those areas in which a weapon may be placed or hidden, is permissible if the police . . . [have Terry-type articulable suspicion to believe] that the suspect is dangerous and . . . may gain immediate control of the weapons." Id. at 1049.[80]

In dissent, Justice Brennan argued that the police should have pursued "less intrusive, but equally effective means of ensuring their safety." Id. at 1065. He suggested that "[t]he police, for example, could have continued to detain respondent outside the car and asked him to tell them where his registration was. The police could then have retrieved the registration themselves." Id. at 1065 n.7. Justice Brennan also expressed concern over the absence of limitations on the Court's justification for the search: "An individual can lawfully possess many things that can be used as weapons. A hammer, or a baseball bat, can be used as a very effective weapon." Id. at 1061.

What do you think of Justice Brennan's concerns?

NOTES AND QUESTIONS: APPLICATION OF THE TERRY DOCTRINE

1. Michigan v. Chesternut, 486 U.S. 567 (1988), involved the question whether the pursuit of a fleeing person constituted a seizure. Police officers on a routine patrol in metropolitan Detroit observed a man approaching the defendant, Chesternut. As the officers approached in a patrol car, Chesternut turned and began to run. The patrol car followed Chesternut around a corner and drove along side him for a short distance. During this time the officers observed Chesternut discard a number of packets. One of the officers left the car to inspect the packets.

---

80. As we will see shortly, the police, as part of a search incident to an arrest, may search the area "within the immediate control" of an arrestee, Chimel v. California, page 721 infra, and when an arrestee is or has been in an automobile, this area includes the passenger compartment of the vehicle, see New York v. Belton, page 739 infra. Indeed, the Court in Long drew support from Chimel and Belton to justify the protective vehicle search. See 463 U.S. at 1049 & n.14. It is clear, however, that Long dealt with a Terry-type search, not a search incident to an arrest. Although Long's erratic driving may have given the police officers probable cause to arrest him, the state conceded that, pursuant to local practice, the police did not arrest Long for any traffic violation. As a result, the state courts and the Supreme Court did not treat Long as an arrest case. Id. at 1035 n.1. Moreover, the Court noted that under Belton the custodial arrest alone would justify the vehicle search, whereas here Terry required an individualized showing of articulable suspicion to believe that the person stopped was dangerous and could gain control of weapons in the vehicle.

They contained pills that the officer suspected were narcotics. The officers then arrested Chesternut, who by this time had ceased running. Without reaching the question whether discovery of the pills gave the officers probable cause to arrest, the magistrate dismissed the narcotics possession charges against Chesternut on the ground that the officers' pursuit of Chesternut constituted an illegal seizure. The Michigan Court of Appeals affirmed and the United States Supreme Court granted certiorari:

> The test[, first articulated in *Mendenhall*,] provides that the police can be said to have seized an individual "only if, in view of all of the circumstances surrounding the incident, a reasonable person would have believed he was not free to leave." [446 U.S. at 554.] . . .
>
> The test is necessarily imprecise because it is designed to assess the coercive effect of police conduct, taken as a whole, rather than to focus on particular details of that conduct in isolation. Moreover, what constitutes a restraint on liberty prompting a person to conclude that he is not free to "leave" will vary, not only with the particular police conduct at issue, but also with the setting in which the conduct occurs. . . .
>
> While the test is flexible enough to be applied to the whole range of police conduct in an equally broad range of settings, it calls for consistent application from one police encounter to the next, regardless of the particular individual's response to the actions of the police. The test's objective standard—looking to the reasonable man's interpretation of the conduct in question—allows the police to determine in advance whether the conduct contemplated will implicate the Fourth Amendment. . . . This "reasonable person" standard also ensures that the scope of Fourth Amendment protections does not vary with the state of mind of the particular individual being apprehended. . . .
>
> Applying the Court's test to the facts of this case, we conclude that respondent was not seized by the police before he discarded the packets containing the controlled substance. Although Officer Peltier referred to the police conduct as a "chase," . . . the characterization is not enough, standing alone, to implicate Fourth Amendment protections. Contrary to respondent's assertion that a chase necessarily communicates that detention is intended and imminent, . . . the police conduct involved here would not have communicated to the reasonable person an attempt to capture or otherwise intrude upon respondent's freedom of movement. The record does not reflect that the police activated a siren or flashers; or that they commanded respondent to halt, or displayed any weapons; or that they operated the car in an aggressive manner to block respondent's course or otherwise control the direction or speed of his movement. . . . Without more, the police conduct here—a brief acceleration to catch up with respondent, followed by a short drive along side him—was not "so intimidating" that respondent could reasonably have believed that he was not free to disregard the police presence and go about his business. . . .
>
> Because respondent was not unlawfully seized during the initial police

pursuit, we conclude that charges against him were improperly dismissed. [486 U.S. at 573-576.]

It will always be difficult to reconstruct and convey accurately all of nuances of the informal police-citizen encounters. Unless there is some reason to believe that the citizen involved in such an encounter is abnormal, is it not appropriate to give considerable weight to the citizen's reaction in assessing what a reasonable person would believe about being free to leave? If you were in Chesternut's position, would you have felt free to ignore the police?

If "consistent application from one police encounter to the next" is or should be an important objective, would it have been preferable for the Court to adopt a flat rule—either that pursuit of a fleeing individual is always a seizure or, as Justice Kennedy suggested in a concurring opinion, that there is never a seizure until the officers' conduct "achieves a restraining effect"?

2. Despite the preceding elaborations, application of the *Terry* standard has proved difficult even for the Supreme Court. In a series of cases involving airport encounters between narcotics agents and suspected drug couriers, the justices have disagreed over (a) whether the encounter constituted a "seizure," (b) if so, whether there was a reasonable basis for the seizure, and (c) if so, whether the seizure was sufficiently limited in scope. Consider how these issues should be resolved in the following cases:

a. United States v. Mendenhall, 446 U.S. 544 (1980): The defendant, Sylvia Mendenhall, was observed by two Drug Enforcement Administration agents as she disembarked from an airplane at the Detroit Metropolitan Airport. Because she appeared to fit the DEA's drug courier profile,[81] the agents "approached her . . . , identified themselves as

---

81. "The agent testified that the respondent's behavior fit the so-called 'drug courier profile'—an informally compiled abstract of characteristics thought typical of persons carrying illicit drugs. In this case the agents thought it relevant that

(1) the respondent was arriving on a flight from Los Angeles, a city believed by the agents to be the place of origin for most of the heroin brought to Detroit;
(2) the respondent was the last person to leave the plane, 'appeared to be very nervous,' and 'completely scanned the whole area where [the agents] were standing';
(3) after leaving the plane the respondent proceeded past the baggage area without claiming any luggage; and
(4) the respondent changed airlines for her flight out of Detroit."

446 U.S. at 547 n.1.
    Some commentators have severely criticized the use of the drug courier profile. See Becton, The Drug Courier Profile: "All Seems Infected That the Infected Spy, As All Looks Yellow to the Jaundic'd Eye," 65 N.C.L. Rev. 417 (1987); Cloud, Search and

federal agents, and asked to see her identification and airline ticket." Id. at 548-549. She produced a driver's license bearing her name and an airline ticket issued in the name of Annette Ford. When asked about the discrepancy in names, Mendenhall "stated that she 'just felt like using that name.' " Id. at 549. One of the agents then specifically identified himself as a narcotics agent, at which point Mendenhall " 'became quite shaken, extremely nervous. She had a hard time speaking.' " Id. Mendenhall then accompanied the agents to a DEA office in the airport where she agreed—or at least did not object—to a search of her person and her handbag. The search revealed heroin. Was Mendenhall's apparent consent the fruit of an illegal seizure?

b. Reid v. Georgia, 448 U.S. 438 (1980): The defendant was observed by DEA agents in the Atlanta airport as he got off a plane from Fort Lauderdale. The defendant and another man who was separated from the defendant by several persons were both carrying similar shoulder bags. As they proceeded through the terminal the defendant occasionally looked back at the other man, and once they were in the lobby the two men spoke briefly with each other. After they left the building, the agent approached the men, identified himself, and asked to see their tickets and some identification. The two men then agreed to accompany the agent back into the terminal. As they were entering the building, however, the defendant dropped his shoulder bag and attempted to flee. The bag turned out to contain cocaine. Was the bag discovered as the result of an illegal seizure?

c. Florida v. Royer, 460 U.S. 491 (1983):

> On January 3, 1978, Royer was observed at Miami International Airport by two plain-clothes detectives of the Dade County, Florida, Public Safety Department assigned to the County's Organized Crime Bureau, Narcotics Investigation Section. Detectives Johnson and Magdalena believed that Royer's appearance, mannerisms, luggage, and actions fit the so-called "drug courier profile." Royer, apparently unaware of the attention he had attracted, purchased a one-way ticket to New York City and checked his two suitcases, placing on each suitcase an identification tag bearing the name "Holt" and the destination, "LaGuardia." As Royer made his way to the concourse which led to the airline boarding area, the two detectives approached him, identified themselves as policemen working out of the sheriffs office, and asked if Royer had a "moment" to speak with them; Royer said "Yes."
>
> Upon request, but without oral consent, Royer produced for the detectives his airline ticket and his driver's license. The airline ticket, like

---

Seizure by the Numbers: The Drug Courier Profile and Judicial Review of Investigative Formulas, 65 B.U.L. Rev. 843 (1985). See also Note 3, page 719 infra.

the baggage identification tags, bore the name "Holt," while the driver's license carried respondent's correct name, "Royer." When the detectives asked about the discrepancy, Royer explained that a friend had made the reservation in the name of "Holt." Royer became noticeably more nervous during this conversation, whereupon the detectives informed Royer that they were in fact narcotics investigators and that they had reason to suspect him of transporting narcotics.

The detectives did not return his airline ticket and identification but asked Royer to accompany them to a room, approximately forty feet away, adjacent to the concourse. Royer said nothing in response but went with the officers as he had been asked to do. The room was later described by Detective Johnson as a "large storage closet," located in the stewardesses' lounge and containing a small desk and two chairs. Without Royer's consent or agreement, Detective Johnson, using Royer's baggage check stubs, retrieved the "Holt" luggage from the airline and brought it to the room where respondent and Detective Magdalena were waiting. Royer was asked if he would consent to a search of the suitcases. Without orally responding to this request, Royer produced a key and unlocked one of the suitcases, which the detective then opened without seeking further assent from Royer. Drugs were found in that suitcase. According to Detective Johnson, Royer stated that he did not know the combination to the lock on the second suitcase. When asked if he objected to the detective opening the second suitcase, Royer said "no, go ahead," and did not object when the detective explained that the suitcase might have to be broken open. The suitcase was pried open by the officers and more marihuana was found. Royer was then told that he was under arrest. Approximately fifteen minutes had elapsed from the time the detectives initially approached respondent until his arrest upon the discovery of the contraband. [Id. at 493-495.]

Were the drugs discovered as the result of an illegal seizure?

d. Florida v. Rodriguez, 469 U.S. 1 (1984): After reciting his narcotics training and noting that Miami was a "source city" for narcotics, Officer Charles McGee, a police officer with the Dade County Public Safety Department and the only witness at the suppression hearing, gave the following testimony.

[He] first noticed respondent Rodriguez at the National Airlines ticket counter in the Miami airport. . . . McGee's attention was drawn to respondent by the fact that he and two individuals later identified as Bianco and Ramirez behaved in an unusual manner while leaving the . . . ticket counter. . . . McGee and Detective Facchiano, who were both in plain clothes, followed respondent, Ramirez, and Blanco . . . to the airport concourse. . . . Ramirez and Blanco stood side by side on an escalator, and respondent stood directly behind them. The detectives observed Ramirez and Blanco converse with one another, although neither spoke to respondent. At the top of the escalator stairs, Blanco looked back and saw the detectives; he then spoke in a lower voice to Ramirez. Ramirez turned around and looked directly at the detectives, then turned his head back very quickly and spoke to Blanco.

As the three cohorts left the escalator single file, Blanco turned, looked directly at respondent, and said, "Let's get out of here." He then repeated in a much lower voice, "Get out of here." Respondent turned around and caught sight of the detectives. He attempted to move away, in the words of officer McGee, "His legs were pumping up and down very fast and not covering much ground, but his legs were as if the person were running in place." . . . Finding his efforts at flight unsuccessful, respondent confronted officer McGee and uttered a vulgar exclamation.

McGee then showed his badge and asked respondent if they might talk. Respondent agreed, and McGee suggested that they move approximately 15 feet to where Blanco and Ramirez were standing with Facchiano, who now also had identified himself as a police officer.

They remained in the public area of the airport. McGee asked respondent if he had some identification and an airline ticket. Respondent said that he did not, but Ramirez then handed McGee a cash ticket with three names on it—Martinez, Perez, and Rodriguez. In the ensuing discussion, [respondent and Blanco both identified themselves as Rodriguez.] Blanco later identified himself correctly. At this point, the officers informed the suspects that they were narcotics officers, and they asked for consent to search respondent's luggage. Respondent answered that he did not have the key, but Ramirez told respondent that he should let the officers look in the luggage, which prompted respondent to hand McGee the key. McGee found three bags of cocaine in the suit bag. [Id. at 3-4.]

Was the cocaine discovered as the result of an illegal seizure or search?

Consider also Immigration & Naturalization Service v. Delgado, 466 U.S. 210 (1984), which arose out of the following facts:

> In the course of enforcing the immigration laws, petitioner Immigration and Naturalization Service (INS) enters employers' worksites to determine whether any illegal aliens may be present as employees. . . .
>
> Acting pursuant to two warrants, in January and September, 1977, the INS conducted a survey of the work force at Southern California Davis Pleating Company (Davis Pleating) in search of illegal aliens. The warrants were issued on a showing of probable cause by the INS that numerous illegal aliens were employed at Davis Pleating, although neither of the search warrants identified any particular illegal aliens by name. A third factory survey was conducted with the employers' consent in October, 1977, at Mr. Pleat, another garment factory.
>
> At the beginning of the surveys several agents positioned themselves near the buildings' exits, while other agents dispersed throughout the factory to question most, but not all, employees at their work stations. The

agents displayed badges, carried walkie-talkies, and were armed, although at no point during any of the surveys was a weapon ever drawn. Moving systematically through the factory, the agents approached employees and, after identifying themselves, asked them from one to three questions relating to their citizenship. If the employee gave a credible reply that he was a United States citizen, the questioning ended, and the agent moved on to another employee. If the employee gave an unsatisfactory response or admitted that he was an alien, the employee was asked to produce his immigration papers. During the survey, employees continued with their work and were free to walk around within the factory. [Id. at 211-213.]

Delgado and several other employees who were questioned sought injunctive and declaratory relief on the ground that the surveys violated their fourth amendment rights. Was the entire work force seized? Were individuals who were questioned seized? If there was a seizure, was it reasonable?

3. In United States v. Sokolow, 109 S. Ct. 1581 (1989), DEA agents stopped the defendant at the Honolulu International Airport. After a specially trained dog was alerted to luggage the defendant was carrying, the agents seized the luggage and obtained a search warrant. The search revealed 1,063 grams of cocaine. The Supreme Court upheld the legality of the stop, which was based on the following information:

(1) [The defendant] paid $2,100 dollars for two airplane tickets from a roll of $20 bills; (2) he traveled under a name that did not match the name under which his telephone number was listed; (3) his original destination was Miami, a source city for illicit drugs; (4) he stayed in Miami for only 48 hours, even though a round-trip flight from Honolulu to Miami takes 20 hours; (5) he appeared nervous during his trip; and (6) he checked none of his luggage. [Id. at 1583.]

The Court also described defendant as "wearing a black jumpsuit and gold jewelry," both when he purchased the tickets and when he returned to Honolulu, id., but the Court did not specifically ascribe any significance to this factor.

The DEA agents had relied on a drug courier profile in deciding to stop the defendant. The Court, however, did not take this factor into account in concluding that there was a reasonable basis for stopping the defendant:

A court sitting to determine the existence of reasonable suspicion must require the agent to articulate the factors leading to that conclusion, but the fact that these factors may be set forth in a "profile" does not somehow detract from their evidentiary significance as seen by a trained agent. [Id. at 1587.]

Justice Marshall, in a dissenting opinion joined by Justice Brennan, took a different view of the significance of the drug courier profile and the assessment of reasonable suspicion:

It is highly significant that the DEA agents stopped Sokolow because he matched one of the DEA's "profiles" of a paradigmatic drug courier. In my view, a law enforcement officer's mechanistic application of a formula of personal and behavioral traits in deciding whom to detain can only dull the officer's ability and determination to make sensitive and fact-specific inferences "in light of his experience," Terry [v. Ohio, 392 U.S. 1], 27 [(1968)], particularly in ambiguous or borderline cases. . . . [As the Court of Appeals observed in this case, the] risk is enhanced by the profile's "chameleon-like way of adapting to any particular set of observations." 831 F.2d 1413, 1418 (9th Cir. 1987). Compare, e.g., United States v. Moore, 675 F.2d 802, 303 (6th Cir. 1982), cert. denied, 460 U.S. 1068 (1983) (suspect was first to deplane), with United States v. Mendenhall, 446 U.S. 544, 564 (1980) (last to deplane), with United States v. Buenaventura-Ariza, 615 F.2d 29, 31 (2d Cir. 1980) (deplaned in middle); United States v. Sullivan, 625 F.2d 9, 12 (4th Cir. 1980) (one-way ticket), with United States v. Craemer, 555 F.2d 594, 595 (6th Cir. 1977) (round-trip tickets), with United States v. McCaleb (non-stop flight), with United States v. Sokolow, 808 F.2d 1366, 1370 (9th Cir. 1987), vacated, 831 F.2d 1413 (9th Cir. 1987) (changed planes); Craemer, supra, at 595 (no luggage), with United States v. Sanford, 658 F.2d 342, 343 (5th Cir. 1981), cert. denied, 455 U.S. 991 (1982) (gym bag), with Sullivan, supra, at 12 (new suitcases); United States v. Smith, 574 F.2d 882, 883 (6th Cir. 1978) (traveling alone), with United States v. Fry, 622 F.2d 1218, 1219 (5th Cir. 1980) (traveling with companion); United States v. Andrews, 600 F.2d 563, 566 (6th Cir. 1979), cert. denied sub nom. Brooks v. United States, 444 U.S. 878 (1979) (acted nervously), with United States v. Himmelwright, 551 F.2d 991, 992 (5th Cir.), cert. denied, 434 U.S. 902 (1977) (acted too calmly). [109 S. Ct. at 1588-1589.]

In the remainder of the dissent Justice Marshall pointed out that most of the factors relied on to justify the stop were unrelated to criminal activity, and he argued that in their totality they did not constitute reasonable suspicion. In Justice Marshall's view, the facts in Sokolow were strikingly similar to the facts in Reid v. Georgia, page 716 supra, where all members of the Court except then Justice Rehnquist concluded that there was an insufficient basis for a stop.

b. Search Incident to Arrest[82]

Professor Amsterdam has observed that "for clarity and consistency, the law of the fourth amendment is not the Supreme Court's most suc-

---

82. The sections that dealt with warrantless searches and seizures based on probable

cessful product."[83] Perhaps the best—but, as we have already seen, by no means the only—illustration of the truth of Professor Amsterdam's statement is the manner in which the Court, over the years, has dealt with searches made "incident to" an arrest. Much of that background is recounted in the next principal case.

CHIMEL v. CALIFORNIA
Certiorari to the Supreme Court of California
395 U.S. 752 (1969)

MR. JUSTICE STEWART delivered the opinion of the Court.

This case raises basic questions concerning the permissible scope under the Fourth Amendment of a search incident to a lawful arrest.

The relevant facts are essentially undisputed. Late in the afternoon of September 13, 1965, three police officers arrived at the Santa Ana, California, home of the petitioner with a warrant authorizing his arrest for the burglary of a coin shop. The officers knocked on the door, identified themselves to the petitioner's wife, and asked if they might come inside. She ushered them into the house, where they waited 10 to 15 minutes until the petitioner returned home from work. When the petitioner entered the house, one of the officers handed him the arrest warrant and asked for permission to "look around." The petitioner objected, but was advised that "on the basis of the lawful arrest," the officers would nonetheless conduct a search. No search warrant had been issued.

Accompanied by the petitioner's wife, the officers then looked through the entire three-bedroom house, including the attic, the garage, and a small workshop. In some rooms the search was relatively cursory. In the master bedroom and sewing room, however, the officers directed the petitioner's wife to open drawers and "to physically move contents of the drawers from side to side so that [they] might view any items that would have come from [the] burglary." After completing the search, they seized numerous items—primarily coins, but also several medals, tokens, and a few other objects. The entire search took between 45 minutes and an hour.

---

cause, pages 609-665 supra, involved searches and seizures that one can regard as presenting variations on or specific applications of the exigent circumstances concept. See page 665 supra. The sections that deal with the relationship between reasonableness and probable cause, page 665 supra to page 828 infra, involve searches and seizures that one can regard as presenting specific applications of the Supreme Court's Terry balancing approach to reasonableness. Indeed, the analysis in the next principal case, Chimel v. California, which sets forth the constitutional standard for the scope of a search incident to arrest, draws specifically on Terry v. Ohio, page 684 supra.

83. Amsterdam, Perspectives on the Fourth Amendment, 58 Minn. L. Rev. 349, 349 (1974). See also LaFave, Search and Seizure: "The Course of True Law . . . Has Not . . . Run Smooth," 1966 U. Ill. L.F. 255.

At the petitioner's subsequent state trial on two charges of burglary, the items taken from his house were admitted into evidence against him, over his objection that they had been unconstitutionally seized. He was convicted and the judgments of conviction were affirmed. . . .

. . . [W]e proceed on the hypothesis that the California courts were correct in holding that the arrest of the petitioner was valid. . . . This brings us directly to the question whether the warrantless search of the petitioner's entire house can be constitutionally justified as incident to that arrest. The decisions of this Court bearing upon that question have been far from consistent, as even the most cursory review makes evident.

Approval of a warrantless search incident to a lawful arrest seems first to have been articulated by the Court in 1914 as dictum in Weeks v. United States, 232 U.S. 383. . . . That statement made no reference to any right to search the *place* where an arrest occurs, but was limited to a right to search the "person." Eleven years later, the case of Carroll v. United States, 267 U.S. 132, brought the following embellishment of the *Weeks* statement: "When a man is legally arrested for an offense, whatever is found upon his person *or in his control* which it is unlawful for him to have and which may be used to prove the offense may be seized and held as evidence in the prosecution." Id., at 158. (Emphasis added.) Still, that assertion too was far from a claim that the "place" where one is arrested may be searched so long as the arrest is valid. Without explanation, however, the principle emerged in expanded form a few months later in Agnello v. United States, 269 U.S. 20—although still by way of dictum:

> The right without a search warrant contemporaneously to search persons lawfully arrested while committing crime and to search the place where the arrest is made in order to find and seize things connected with the crime as its fruits or as the means by which it was committed, as well as weapons and other things to effect an escape from custody, is not to be doubted. See Carroll v. United States, 267 U.S. 132, 158; Weeks v. United States, 232 U.S. 383, 392. [269 U.S., at 30.]

And in Marron v. United States, 275 U.S. 192, two years later, the dictum of Agnello appeared to be the foundation of the Court's decision. In that case federal agents had secured a search warrant authorizing the seizure of liquor and certain articles used in its manufacture. When they arrived at the premises to be searched, they saw "that the place was used for retailing and drinking intoxicating liquors." Id., at 194. They proceeded to arrest the person in charge and to execute the warrant. In searching a closet for the items listed in the warrant they came across an incriminating ledger, concededly not covered by the warrant, which they also seized. The Court upheld the seizure of the ledger by holding that since the agents had made a lawful arrest, "[t]hey had a right without a warrant contemporaneously to search the place in order to find and seize the things used to carry on the criminal enterprise." Id., at 199.

That the *Marron* opinion did not mean all that it seemed to say became evident, however, a few years later in Go-Bart Importing Co. v. United States, 282 U.S. 344, and United States v. Lefkowitz, 285 U.S. 452. In each of those cases the opinion of the Court was written by Mr. Justice Butler, the author of the opinion in *Marron*. In *Go-Bart*, agents had searched the office of persons whom they had lawfully arrested, and had taken several papers from a desk, a safe, and other parts of the office. [In distinguishing *Marron* and holding the search illegal t]he Court noted that no crime had been committed in the agents' presence, and that although the agent in charge "had an abundance of information and time to swear out a valid [search] warrant, he failed to do so." 282 U.S., at 358. . . . This limited characterization of *Marron* was reiterated in *Lefkowitz*, a case in which the Court held unlawful a search of desk drawers and a cabinet despite the fact that the search had accompanied a lawful arrest. 285 U.S, at 465.

The limiting views expressed in *Go-Bart* and *Lefkowitz* were thrown to the winds, however, in Harris v. United States, 331 U.S. 145, decided in 1947. In that case, . . . [Harris] was arrested in the living room of his four-room apartment, and in an attempt to recover two canceled checks thought to have been used in effecting . . . [a] forgery, the officers undertook a thorough search of the entire apartment. Inside a desk drawer they found a sealed envelope marked "George Harris, personal papers." The envelope, which was then torn open, was found to contain altered Selective Service documents, and those documents were used to secure Harris' conviction for violating the Selective Training and Service Act of 1940. The Court rejected Harris' Fourth Amendment claim, sustaining the search as "incident to arrest." Id., at 151.

Only a year after *Harris*, however, the pendulum swung again. In Trupiano v. United States, 334 U.S. 699, agents raided the site of an illicit distillery, saw one of several conspirators operating the still, and arrested him, contemporaneously "seiz[ing] the illicit distillery." Id., at 702. The Court held that the arrest and others made subsequently had been valid, but that the unexplained failure of the agents to procure a search warrant—in spite of the fact that they had had more than enough time before the raid to do so—rendered the search unlawful. . . .

In 1950, two years after *Trupiano*, came United States v. Rabinowitz, 339 U.S. 56, the decision upon which California primarily relies in the case now before us. In *Rabinowitz*, federal authorities had been informed that the defendant was dealing in stamps bearing forged overprints. On the basis of that information they secured a warrant for his arrest, which they executed at his one-room business office. At the time of the arrest, the officers "searched the desk, safe, and file cabinets in the office for about an hour and a half," id., at 59, and seized 573 stamps with forged overprints. The stamps were admitted into evidence at the defendant's trial. . . . The Court held that the search in its entirety fell within the principle giving law enforcement authorities "[t]he right 'to search the place where the arrest is made in order to find and seize things connected with the crime. . . .'" Id., at 61. . . . The test, said the Court, "is not whether it is reasonable to procure a search warrant, but whether the search was reasonable." Id., at 66.

Even limited to its own facts, the *Rabinowitz* decision was, as we have seen, hardly founded on an unimpeachable line of authority. . . .

Nor is the rationale by which the State seeks here to sustain the search of the petitioner's house supported by a reasoned view of the background and purpose of the Fourth Amendment. Mr. Justice Frankfurter wisely pointed out in his *Rabinowitz* dissent that the Amendment's proscription of "unreasonable searches and seizures" must be read in light of "the history that gave rise to the words"—a history of "abuses so deeply felt by the Colonies as to be one of the potent causes of the Revolution. . . ." 339 U.S., at 69. The Amendment was in large part a reaction to the general warrants and warrantless searches that had so alienated the colonists and had helped speed the movement for independence. In the scheme of the Amendment, therefore, the requirement that "no Warrants shall issue, but upon probable cause," plays a crucial part. . . .

Only last Term in Terry v. Ohio, 392 U.S. 1, we emphasized that "the police must, whenever practicable, obtain advance judicial approval of searches and seizures through the warrant procedure," id., at 20, and that "[t]he scope of [a] search must be 'strictly tied to and justified by' the circumstances which rendered its initiation permissible." Id., at 19. . . .

A similar analysis underlies the "search incident to arrest" principle, and marks its proper extent. When an arrest is made, it is reasonable for the arresting officer to search the person arrested in order to remove any weapons that the latter might seek to use in order to resist arrest or effect his escape. Otherwise, the officer's safety might well be endangered, and the arrest itself frustrated. In addition, it is entirely reasonable for the arresting officer to search for and seize any evidence on the arrestee's person in order to prevent its concealment or destruction. And the area into which an arrestee might reach in order to grab a weapon or evidentiary items must, of course, be governed by a like rule. A gun on a table or in a drawer in front of one who is arrested can be as dangerous to the arresting officer as one concealed in the clothing of the person arrested.

There is ample justification, therefore, for a search of the arrestee's person and the area "within his immediate control"—construing that phrase to mean the area from within which he might gain possession of a weapon or destructible evidence.

There is no comparable justification, however, for routinely searching any room other than that in which an arrest occurs—or, for that matter, for searching through all the desk drawers or other closed or concealed areas in that room itself. Such searches, in the absence of well-recognized exceptions, may be made only under the authority of a search warrant. The "adherence to judicial processes" mandated by the Fourth Amendment requires no less. . . .

It is argued in the present case that it is "reasonable" to search a man's house when he is arrested in it. But that argument is founded on little more than a subjective view regarding the acceptability of certain sorts of police conduct, and not on considerations relevant to Fourth Amendment interests. Under such an unconfined analysis, Fourth Amendment protection in this area would approach the evaporation point. It is not easy to explain why, for instance, it is less subjectively "reasonable" to search a man's house when he is arrested on his front lawn— or just down the street—than it is when he happens to be in the house at the time of arrest. . . .

. . . No consideration relevant to the Fourth Amendment suggests any point of rational limitation, once the search is allowed to go beyond the area from which the person arrested might obtain weapons or evidentiary items. The only reasoned distinction is one between a search of the person arrested and the area within his reach on the one hand, and more extensive searches on the other.[12]

The petitioner correctly points out that one result of decisions such as *Rabinowitz* and *Harris* is to give law enforcement officials the oppor-

---

12. It is argued in dissent that so long as there is probable cause to search the place where an arrest occurs, a search of that place should be permitted even though no search warrant has been obtained. This position seems to be based principally on two premises: first, that once an arrest has been made, the additional invasion of privacy stemming from the accompanying search is "relatively minor"; and second, that the victim of the search may "shortly thereafter" obtain a judicial determination of whether the search was justified by probable cause. With respect to the second premise, one may initially question whether all of the States in fact provide the speedy suppression procedures the dissent assumes. More fundamentally, however, we cannot accept the view that Fourth Amendment interests are vindicated so long as "the rights of the criminal" are "protect[ed] . . . against introduction of evidence seized without probable cause." The Amendment is designed to prevent, not simply to redress, unlawful police action. In any event, we cannot join in characterizing the invasion of privacy that results from a top-to-bottom search of a man's house as "minor." And we can see no reason why, simply because some interference with an individual's privacy and freedom of movement has lawfully taken place, further intrusions should automatically be allowed despite the absence of a warrant that the Fourth Amendment would otherwise require.

tunity to engage in searches not justified by probable cause, by the simple expedient of arranging to arrest suspects at home rather than elsewhere. We do not suggest that the petitioner is necessarily correct in his assertion that such a strategy was utilized here, but the fact remains that had he been arrested earlier in the day, at his place of employment rather than at home, no search of his house could have been made without a search warrant. In any event, even apart from the possibility of such police tactics, the general point so forcefully made by Judge Learned Hand in United States v. Kirschenblatt, 16 F.2d 202, remains:

> After arresting a man in his house, to rummage at will among his papers in search of whatever will convict him, appears to us to be indistinguishable from what might be done under a general warrant; indeed, the warrant would give more protection, for presumably it must be issued by a magistrate. True, by hypothesis the power would not exist, if the supposed offender were not found on the premises, but it is small consolation to know that one's papers are safe only so long as one is not at home." Id., at 203.

Rabinowitz and *Harris* have been the subject of critical commentary for many years, and have been relied upon less and less in our own decisions. It is time, for the reasons we have stated, to hold that on their own facts, and insofar as the principles they stand for are inconsistent with those that we have endorsed today, they are no longer to be followed.

Application of sound Fourth Amendment principles to the facts of this case produces a clear result. . . . The scope of the search was . . . "unreasonable" under the Fourth and Fourteenth Amendments, and the petitioner's conviction cannot stand.

Reversed.

[The concurring opinion of JUSTICE HARLAN is omitted.]

MR. JUSTICE WHITE, with whom MR. JUSTICE BLACK joins, dissenting. . . .

[W]hen there are exigent circumstances, and probable cause, then the search may be made without a warrant, reasonably. An arrest itself may often create an emergency situation making it impracticable to obtain a warrant before embarking on a related search. Again assuming that there is probable cause to search premises at the spot where a suspect is arrested, it seems to me unreasonable to require the police to leave the scene in order to obtain a search warrant when they are already legally there to make a valid arrest, and when there must almost always be a strong possibility that confederates of the arrested man will in the meanwhile remove the items for which the police have probable cause to search. This must so often be the case that it seems to me as unreasonable to require a warrant for a search of the premises as to require a warrant for search of the person and his very immediate surroundings.

This case provides a good illustration of my point. . . . There was doubtless probable cause not only to arrest petitioner, but also to search his house. He had obliquely admitted, both to a neighbor and to the owner of the burglarized store, that he had committed the burglary. In light of this, and the fact that the neighbor had seen other admittedly stolen property in petitioner's house, there was surely probable cause on which a warrant could have issued to search the house for the stolen coins. Moreover, had the police simply arrested petitioner, taken him off to the station house, and later returned with a warrant,[5] it seems very likely that petitioner's wife, who in view of petitioner's generally garrulous nature must have known of the robbery, would have removed the coins. For the police to search the house while the evidence they had probable cause to search out and seize was still there cannot be considered unreasonable. . . .

. . . The only possible justification for the majority's rule is that in some instances arresting officers may search when they have no probable cause to do so and that such unlawful searches might be prevented if the officers first sought a warrant from a magistrate. Against the possible protection of privacy in that class of cases, in which the privacy of the house has already been invaded by entry to make the arrest—an entry for which the majority does not assert that any warrant is necessary— must be weighed the risk of destruction of evidence for which there is probable cause to search, as a result of delays in obtaining a search warrant. . . .

In considering searches incident to arrest, it must be remembered that there will be immediate opportunity to challenge the probable cause for the search in an adversary proceeding. The suspect has been apprised of the search by his very presence at the scene, and having been arrested, he will soon be brought into contact with people who can explain his rights. . . . [A warrantless] arrest demands the prompt bringing of the person arrested before a judicial officer, where the existence of probable cause is to be inquired into. Fed. Rules Crim. Proc. 5 (a) and (c). . . .

An arrested man, by definition conscious of the police interest in

5. There were three officers at the scene of the arrest, one from the city where the coin burglary had occurred, and two from the city where the arrest was made. Assuming that one policeman from each city would be needed to bring the petitioner in and obtain a search warrant, one policeman could have been left to guard the house. However, if he not only could have remained in the house against petitioner's wife's will, but followed her about to assure that no evidence was being tampered with, the invasion of her privacy would be almost as great as that accompanying an actual search. Moreover, had the wife summoned an accomplice, one officer could not have watched them both.

Paul Speer
—97 |

him, and provided almost immediately with a lawyer and a judge, is in
an excellent position to dispute the reasonableness of his arrest and contemporaneous search in a full adversary proceeding. I would uphold the
constitutionality of this search contemporaneous with an arrest since there
were probable cause both for the search and for the arrest, exigent circumstances involving the removal or destruction of evidence, and satisfactory opportunity to dispute the issues of probable cause shortly
thereafter. In this case, the search was reasonable.

NOTES AND QUESTIONS

1. Note that the police had a warrant for Chimel's arrest. In this
type of situation—when it is clear that exigent circumstances have not
made it impracticable to comply with the warrant process—what justification exists for permitting a warrantless search of the person? At the
very least, does the fact that the police apparently had an ample opportunity to obtain a search warrant undermine Justice White's contention
that a warrantless search of an arrestee's house, if based on probable
cause, should be regarded as reasonable?

2. Justice White seemed to base his position in part on the notion
that the entry to arrest, which was concededly legal, was itself a substantial
invasion of privacy and that the entry was one "for which the majority
does not assert that a warrant is necessary." Does the requirement in
Payton, page 650 supra, of an arrest warrant to enter a defendant's premises undermine Justice White's argument? Would the requirement of a
search warrant to enter undermine his argument?

3. The *Chimel* majority criticizes Justice White's argument as one
"founded on little more than a subjective view regarding the acceptability
of certain sorts of police conduct and not on considerations relevant to
Fourth Amendment interests." Is not the "acceptability of certain sorts
of police conduct" a consideration that is critically relevant to fourth
amendment interests? Is Justice White's view any more or less "subjective"
than the majority's view?

4. Should *Chimel* be regarded as creating a flat rule that permits a
full search of any arrested individual? Or, particularly in light of *Chimel's*
rejection of Justice White's flat rule, should the permissible scope of a
search incident to arrest depend on whether there is reason to believe
that the arrestee may possess or have immediate access to weapons or
evidence? Consider the next case.

UNITED STATES v. ROBINSON

Certiorari to the United States Court of Appeals for the District of
Columbia Circuit
414 U.S. 218 (1973)

MR. JUSTICE REHNQUIST delivered the opinion of the Court.

Respondent Robinson was convicted in United States District Court
for the District of Columbia of the possession and facilitation of concealment of heroin. . . . [T]he Court of Appeals en banc reversed the
judgment of conviction, holding that the heroin introduced in evidence
against respondent had been obtained as a result of a search which violated
the Fourth Amendment to the United States Constitution. . . .

On April 23, 1968, at approximately 11 P.M., Officer Richard Jenks,
a 15-year veteran of the District of Columbia Metropolitan Police Department, observed the respondent driving a 1965 Cadillac near the intersection of 8th and C Streets, N.E., in the District of Columbia. Jenks,
as a result of previous investigation following a check of respondent's
operator's permit four days earlier, determined there was reason to believe
that respondent was operating a motor vehicle after the revocation of his
operator's permit. This is an offense defined by statute in the District of
Columbia which carries a mandatory minimum jail term, a mandatory
minimum fine, or both. . . .

Jenks signaled respondent to stop the automobile, which respondent
did, and all three of the occupants emerged from the car. At that point
Jenks informed respondent that he was under arrest for "operating after
revocation and obtaining a permit by misrepresentation." It was assumed
by the Court of Appeals, and is conceded by the respondent here, that
Jenks had probable cause to arrest respondent, and that he effected a full
custody arrest.

In accordance with procedures prescribed in police department instructions,[2] Jenks then began to search respondent. He explained at a

---

2. The Government introduced testimony at the evidentiary hearing upon the original remand by the Court of Appeals as to certain standard operating procedures of the
Metropolitan Police Department. Sergeant Dennis C. Donaldson, a Metropolitan Police
Department Training Division instructor, testified that when a police officer makes "a
full custody arrest," which he defined as one where an officer "would arrest a subject
and subsequently transport him to a police facility for booking," the officer is trained to
make a full "field type search." . . .

Sergeant Donaldson testified that officers are instructed to examine the "contents of
all of the pockets" of the arrestee in the course of the field search. It was stated that these
standard operating procedures were initiated by the police department "[p]rimarily, for
[the officer's] own safety and, secondly, for the safety of the individual he has placed
under arrest and, thirdly, to search for evidence of the crime." While the officer is
instructed to make a full field search of the person of the individual he arrests, he is
instructed, and police department regulations provide, that in the case of a full-custody

subsequent hearing that he was "face-to-face" with the respondent, and "placed [his] hands on [the respondent], my right-hand to his left breast like this (demonstrating) and proceeded to pat him down thus [with the right hand]." During this patdown, Jenks felt an object in the left breast pocket of the heavy coat respondent was wearing, but testified that he "couldn't tell what it was" and also that he "couldn't actually tell the size of it." Jenks then reached into the pocket and pulled out the object, which turned out to be a "crumpled up cigarette package." Jenks testified that at this point he still did not know what was in the package: "As I felt the package I could feel objects in the package but I couldn't tell what they were. . . . I knew they weren't cigarettes."

The officer then opened the cigarette pack and found 14 gelatin capsules of white powder which he thought to be, and which later analysis proved to be, heroin. Jenks then continued his search of respondent to completion, feeling around his waist and trouser legs, and examining the remaining pockets. The heroin seized from the respondent was admitted into evidence at the trial which resulted in his conviction in the District Court.

. . . We conclude that the search conducted by Jenks in this case did not offend the limits imposed by the Fourth Amendment, and we therefore reverse the judgment of the Court of Appeals. . . .

It is well settled that a search incident to a lawful arrest is a traditional exception to the warrant requirement of the Fourth Amendment. This general exception has historically been formulated into two distinct propositions. The first is that a search may be made of the *person* of the arrestee by virtue of the lawful arrest. The second is that a search may be made of the area within the control of the arrestee.

Examination of this Court's decisions shows that these two propositions have been treated quite differently. The validity of the search of a person incident to a lawful arrest has been regarded as settled from its first enunciation, and has remained virtually unchallenged until the present case. The validity of the second proposition, while likewise conceded in principle, has been subject to differing interpretations as to the extent of the area which may be searched. . . .

---

arrest for driving after revocation, "areas beyond [the arrestee's] immediate control should not be searched because there is no probable cause to believe that the vehicle contains fruits, instrumentalities, contraband or evidence of the offense of driving after revocation." Those regulations also provide that in the case of some traffic offenses, including the crime of operating a motor vehicle after revocation of an operator's permit, the officer shall make a summary arrest of the violator and take the violator, in custody, to the station house for booking. D.C. Metropolitan Police Department General Order No. 3, series 1959 (Apr. 24, 1959).

Such operating procedures are not, of course, determinative of the constitutional issues presented by this case.

Throughout the series of cases in which the Court has addressed the second proposition relating to a search incident to a lawful arrest—the permissible area beyond the person of the arrestee which such a search may cover—no doubt has been expressed as to the unqualified authority of the arresting authority to search the person of the arrestee. . . .

. . . Since the statements in the cases speak not simply in terms of an exception to the warrant requirement, but in terms of an affirmative authority to search, they clearly imply that such searches also meet the Fourth Amendment's requirement of reasonableness. . . .

In its decision of this case, the Court of Appeals decided that even after a police officer lawfully places a suspect under arrest for the purpose of taking him into custody, he may not ordinarily proceed to fully search the prisoner. He must, instead, conduct a limited frisk of the outer clothing and remove such weapons that he may, as a result of that limited frisk, reasonably believe and ascertain that the suspect has in his possession. While recognizing that Terry v. Ohio, 392 U.S. 1 (1968), dealt with a permissible "frisk" incident to an investigative stop based on less than probable cause to arrest, the Court of Appeals felt that the principles of that case should be carried over to this probable-cause arrest for driving while one's license is revoked. Since there would be no further evidence of such a crime to be obtained in a search of the arrestee, the court held that only a search for weapons could be justified.

Terry v. Ohio, supra, did not involve an arrest for probable cause, and it made quite clear that the "protective frisk" for weapons which it approved might be conducted without probable cause. Id., at 21-22, 24-25. This Court's opinion explicitly recognized that there is a "distinction in purpose, character, and extent between a search incident to an arrest and a limited search for weapons." . . . Terry, therefore, affords no basis to carry over to a probable-cause arrest the limitations this Court placed on a stop-and-frisk search permissible without probable cause. . . .

Virtually all of the statements of this Court affirming the existence of an unqualified authority to search incident to a lawful arrest are dicta. We would not, therefore, be foreclosed by principles of stare decisis from further examination into history and practice in order to see whether the sort of qualifications imposed by the Court of Appeals in this case were in fact intended by the Framers of the Fourth Amendment or recognized in cases decided prior to Weeks. Unfortunately such authorities as exist are sparse. . . .

While these earlier authorities are sketchy, they tend to support the broad statement of the authority to search incident to arrest found in the successive decisions of this Court, rather than the restrictive one which was applied by the Court of Appeals in this case. The scarcity of case law before *Weeks* is doubtless due in part to the fact that the exclusionary rule there enunciated had been first adopted only 11 years earlier in Iowa; but it would seem to be also due in part to the fact that the issue was regarded as well settled.

The Court of Appeals in effect determined that the *only* reason supporting the authority for a *full* search incident to lawful arrest was the possibility of discovery of evidence or fruits. Concluding that there could be no evidence or fruits in the case of an offense such as that with which respondent was charged, it held that any protective search would have to be limited by the conditions laid down in *Terry* for a search upon less than probable cause to arrest. Quite apart from the fact that *Terry* clearly recognized the distinction between the two types of searches, and that a different rule governed one than governed the other, we find additional reason to disagree with the Court of Appeals.

The justification or reason for the authority to search incident to a lawful arrest rests quite as much on the need to disarm the suspect in order to take him into custody as it does on the need to preserve evidence on his person for later use at trial. . . . The standards traditionally governing a search incident to lawful arrest are not, therefore, commuted to the stricter *Terry* standards by the absence of probable fruits or further evidence of the particular crime for which the arrest is made.

Nor are we inclined, on the basis of what seems to us to be a rather speculative judgment, to qualify the breadth of the general authority to search incident to a lawful custodial arrest on an assumption that persons arrested for the offense of driving while their licenses have been revoked are less likely to possess dangerous weapons than are those arrested for other crimes.[5] It is scarcely open to doubt that the danger to an officer is far greater in the case of the extended exposure which follows the taking

5. Such an assumption appears at least questionable in light of the available statistical data concerning assaults on police officers who are in the course of making arrests. The danger to the police officer flows from the fact of the arrest, and its attendant proximity, stress, and uncertainty, and not from the grounds for arrest. One study concludes that approximately 30% of the shootings of police officers occur when an officer stops a person in an automobile. Bristow, Police Officer Shooting—A Tactical Evaluation, 54 J. Crim. L.C. & P.S. 93 (1963), cited in Adams v. Williams, 407 U.S. 143, 148 (1972). The Government in its brief notes that the Uniform Crime Reports, prepared by the Federal Bureau of Investigation, indicate that a significant percentage of murders of police officers occurs when the officers are making traffic stops. Brief for the United States 23. Those reports indicate that during January-March 1973, 35 police officers were murdered; 11 of those officers were killed while engaged in making traffic stops. Ibid.

[Does the danger flow from the fact of the *arrest*? Compare the characterization of the Bristow study in this footnote with the characterization in Adams v. Williams, 407 U.S. 143, 148 n. 3 (1972): "According to one study, approximately 30% of police shootings occurred when a police officer approached a suspect seated in an automobile." Bristow, Police Officer Shootings—A Tactical Evaluation, 54 J. Crim. L.C. & P.S. 93 (1963).— Eds.]

of a suspect into custody and transporting him to the police station than in the case of the relatively fleeting contact resulting from the typical *Terry*-type stop. This is an adequate basis for treating all custodial arrests alike for purposes of search justification.

But quite apart from these distinctions, our more fundamental disagreement with the Court of Appeals arises from its suggestion that there must be litigated in each case the issue of whether or not there was present one of the reasons supporting the authority for a search of the person incident to a lawful arrest. We do not think the long line of authorities of this Court dating back to *Weeks*, or what we can glean from the history of practice in this country and in England, requires such a case-by-case adjudication. A police officer's determination as to how and where to search the person of a suspect whom he has arrested is necessarily a quick ad hoc judgment which the Fourth Amendment does not require to be broken down in each instance into an analysis of each step in the search. The authority to search the person incident to a lawful custodial arrest, while based upon the need to disarm and to discover evidence, does not depend on what a court may later decide was the probability in a particular arrest situation that weapons or evidence would in fact be found upon the person of the suspect. A custodial arrest of a suspect based on probable cause is a reasonable intrusion under the Fourth Amendment; that intrusion being lawful, a search incident to the arrest requires no additional justification. It is the fact of the lawful arrest which establishes the authority to search, and we hold that in the case of a lawful custodial arrest a full search of the person is not only an exception to the warrant requirement of the Fourth Amendment, but is also a "reasonable" search under that Amendment.

. . . Since it is the fact of custodial arrest which gives rise to the authority to search,[6] it is of no moment that [Officer] Jenks did not indicate any subjective fear of the respondent or that he did not himself suspect that respondent was armed. Having in the course of a lawful search come upon the crumpled package of cigarettes, he was entitled to inspect it; and when his inspection revealed the heroin capsules, he was entitled to seize them as "fruits, instrumentalities, or contraband" probative of criminal conduct. . . . The judgment of the Court of Appeals holding otherwise is reversed.

[The concurring opinion of JUSTICE POWELL is omitted.]

---

6. The opinion of the Court of Appeals also discussed its understanding of the law where the police officer makes what the court characterized as "a routine traffic stop," i.e., where the officer would simply issue a notice of violation and allow the offender to proceed. Since in this case the officer did make a full-custody arrest of the violator, we do not reach the question discussed by the Court of Appeals.

MR. JUSTICE MARSHALL, with whom MR. JUSTICE DOUGLAS and MR. JUSTICE BRENNAN join, dissenting.

Certain fundamental principles have characterized this Court's Fourth Amendment jurisprudence over the years. Perhaps the most basic of these was expressed by Mr. Justice Butler, speaking for a unanimous Court in GoBart Co. v. United States, 282 U.S. 344 (1931): "There is no formula for the determination of reasonableness. Each case is to be decided on its own facts and circumstances." Id., at 357. . . .

. . . The majority's approach represents a clear and marked departure from our long tradition of case-by-case adjudication of the reasonableness of searches and seizures under the Fourth Amendment. . . .

One need not go back to Blackstone's Commentaries, Holmes' Common Law, or Pollock & Maitland in search of precedent for the approach adopted by the Court of Appeals. Indeed, given the fact that mass production of the automobile did not begin until the early decades of the present century, I find it somewhat puzzling that the majority even looks to these sources for guidance on the only question presented in this case: the permissible scope of a search of the person incident to a lawful arrest for violation of a motor vehicle regulation. The fact is that this question has been considered by several state and federal courts, the vast majority of which have held that, absent special circumstances, a police officer has no right to conduct a full search of the person incident to a lawful arrest for violation of a motor vehicle regulation. . . .

[Justice Marshall then reviewed several of these decisions.]

The majority's attempt to avoid case-by-case adjudication of Fourth Amendment issues is not only misguided as a matter of principle, but is also doomed to fail as a matter of practical application. . . . Although, in this particular case, Officer Jenks was required by police department regulations to make an in-custody arrest rather than to issue a citation, in most jurisdictions and for most traffic offenses the determination of whether to issue a citation or effect a full arrest is discretionary with the officer. There is always the possibility that a police officer, lacking probable cause to obtain a search warrant, will use a traffic arrest as a pretext to conduct a search. . . . I suggest this possibility not to impugn the integrity of our police, but merely to point out that case-by-case adjudication will always be necessary to determine whether a full arrest was effected for purely legitimate reasons or, rather, as a pretext for searching the arrestee. "An arrest may not be used as a pretext to search for evidence." United States v. Lefkowitz, 285 U.S. 452, 467 (1932). . . .

The majority states that "[a] police officer's determination as to how and where to search the person of a suspect whom he has arrested is necessarily a quick ad hoc judgment which the Fourth Amendment does not require to be broken down in each instance into an analysis of each step in the search." . . . No precedent is cited for this broad assertion—not surprisingly, since there is none. Indeed, we only recently rejected such "a rigid all-or-nothing model of justification and regulation under the Amendment, [for] it obscures the utility of limitations upon the scope, as well as the initiation, of police action as a means of constitutional regulation. This Court has held in the past that a search which is reasonable at its inception may violate the Fourth Amendment by virtue of its intolerable intensity and scope." Terry v. Ohio, 392 U.S., at 17-18. As we there concluded, "in determining whether the seizure and search were 'unreasonable' our inquiry is a dual one—whether the officer's action was justified at its inception, and whether it was reasonably related in scope to the circumstances which justified the interference in the first place." Id., at 19-20.

As I view the matter, the search in this case divides into three distinct phases: the patdown of respondent's coat pocket; the removal of the unknown object from the pocket; and the opening of the crumpled-up cigarette package. . . .

No question is raised here concerning the lawfulness of the patdown of respondent's coat pocket. . . .

With respect to the removal of the unknown object from the coat pocket, the first issue presented is whether that aspect of the search can be sustained as part of the limited frisk for weapons. . . .

In the present case, . . . Officer Jenks had no reason to believe and did not in fact believe that the object in respondent's coat pocket was a weapon. . . .

The Government does not now contend that the search of respondent's pocket can be justified by any need to find and seize evidence. . . . The only rationale for a search in this case, then, is the removal of weapons which the arrestee might use to harm the officer and attempt an escape. This rationale, of course, is identical to the rationale of the search permitted in Terry. . . . [T]he plurality of the Court of Appeals held that the removal of the package exceeded the scope of a lawful search incident to arrest of a traffic violator.

The problem with this approach, however, is that it ignores several significant differences between the context in which a search incident to arrest for a traffic violation is made, and the situation presented in Terry. . . .

The most obvious difference between the two contexts relates to whether the officer has cause to believe that the individual he is dealing with possesses weapons which might be used against him. . . . While the policeman who arrests a suspected rapist or robber may well have reason to believe he is dealing with an armed and dangerous person, certainly this does not hold true with equal force with respect to a person arrested for a motor vehicle violation of the sort involved in this case.

Nor was there any particular reason in this case to believe that respondent was dangerous. . . .

. . . [On the other hand, a]s the Court of Appeals noted, a crucial feature distinguishing the in-custody arrest from the Terry context " 'is not the greater likelihood that a person taken into custody is armed, but rather the increased likelihood of danger to the officer if in fact the person is armed.' " 153 U.S. App. D.C., at 130, 471 F.2d, at 1098, quoting People v. Superior Court of Los Angeles County, 7 Cal. 3d, at 214, 496 P.2d, at 1225 (Wright, C.J., concurring) (emphasis in original). . . . The prolonged proximity also makes it more likely that the individual will be able to extricate any small hidden weapon which might go undetected in a weapons frisk, such as a safety pin or razor blade. In addition, a suspect taken into custody may feel more threatened by the serious restraint on his liberty than a person who is simply stopped by an officer for questioning, and may therefore be more likely to resort to force.

. . . Balancing these competing considerations in order to determine what is a reasonable warrantless search in the traffic arrest context is a difficult process, one for which there may be no easy analytical guideposts. . . .

As will be explained more fully below, I do not think it necessary to solve this balancing equation in this particular case. It is important to note, however, in view of the reasoning adopted by the majority, that available empirical evidence supports the result reached by the plurality of the Court of Appeals, rather than the result reached by the Court today.

The majority relies on statistics indicating that a significant percentage of murders of police officers occurs when the officers are making traffic stops. But these statistics only confirm what we recognized in Terry—that "American criminals have a long tradition of armed violence, and every year in this country many law enforcement officers are killed in the line of duty, and thousands more are wounded." Terry v. Ohio, supra, at 23. As the very next sentence in Terry recognized, however, "[v]irtually all of these deaths and a substantial portion of the injuries are inflicted with guns and knives." Id., at 24. The statistics relied on by the Government in this case support this observation. Virtually all of the killings are caused by guns and knives, the very type of weapons which will not go undetected in a properly conducted weapons frisk.[5] It requires

5. The Uniform Crime Reports prepared by the Federal Bureau of Investigation which are relied on by the majority . . . indicate that 112 police officers were killed

more than citation to these statistics, then, to support the proposition that it is reasonable for police officers to conduct more than a *Terry*-type frisk for weapons when seeking to disarm a traffic offender who is taken into custody.

[Justice Marshall proceeded to argue that Officer Jenks' decision to open the cigarette pack violated the defendant's fourth amendment rights. This issue is considered at page 743 infra.]

NOTES AND QUESTIONS

1. Consider carefully the dual justification for searches incident to arrest: protection of the officer and discovery of evidence. With respect to the former, why should there not be a requirement of articulable suspicion to justify a search that is more extensive than an initial patdown? With respect to the latter, why should probable cause to *arrest* justify a search that is not based at least on articulable suspicion to believe that evidence may be discovered?

2. If there had been probable cause to believe that Robinson had committed a serious felony such as arson, there still might not have been reason to believe that, at the time of the arrest, he possessed any weapon or incriminating evidence. Do you think that in such a case even the dissenters would have objected to a full-scale search of the person? If not—or if, in any event, the search in *Robinson* seems more trouble-some—what is the underlying problem in *Robinson*? See generally Dwor-kin, Fact Style Adjudication and the Fourth Amendment, 48 Ind. L.J. 329 (1973); LaFave, "Case-by-Case" Adjudication Versus "Standardized Procedures": The *Robinson* Dilemma, 1974 Sup. Ct. Rev. 127.

One obvious matter for concern in a case like *Robinson* is that an arrest for a minor offense may be a pretext to permit a search. See Burkoff, The Pretext Search Doctrine: Now You See It, Now You Don't, 17 U. Mich. J.L. Reform 523 (1984).

Consider which, if any, of the following approaches to the pretext arrest problem may be desirable:

a. prohibit a full-scale search incident to arrest except upon a show-ing of at least articulable suspicion that the arrestee possesses weapons or evidence;

b. permit a full-scale search incident to all arrests but exclude any evidence discovered during the search unless the police can prove

---

nationwide in 1972. Of these, 108 were killed by firearms. Two of the remaining four were killed with knives, and the last two cases involved a bomb and an automobile.

preexisting articulable suspicion that the arrestee possessed weapons or evidence;

c. exclude evidence obtained in a search incident to an arrest if the arrestee can prove (or, alternatively, if the prosecutor cannot disprove) that the arrest was merely a pretext to allow the search;

d. prohibit custodial arrest for specified minor offenses.

3. Can *Robinson* be read as permitting a full-scale search of any person for whom probable cause to arrest exists, or must the search be predicated on the fact of a custodial arrest? Reconsider carefully the majority's reasoning in conjunction with the following hypothetical: The police with probable cause stop Defendant for a minor traffic violation. A local police regulation instructs officers in such a case to search the motorist and then to release the motorist with a citation unless the search reveals incriminating evidence. In our case the search revealed marijuana, and thus Defendant was taken into custody and charged with possession of marijuana. Should the marijuana be suppressed? See LaFave, "Seizure" Typology: Classifying Detentions of the Person to Resolve Warrant, Grounds, and Search Issues, 17 U. Mich. J.L. Reform 417, 442-448 (1984).

4. In Gustafson v. Florida, 414 U.S. 260 (1973), a companion case to *Robinson*, a police officer legally stopped the defendant, who had been driving his car back and forth across the center line of the road. On learning that the defendant did not have his driver's license with him, the officer arrested him for driving without a license. In a search incident to the arrest, the officer discovered marijuana. Arguing that the marijuana was the fruit of an illegal search the defendant attempted to distinguish *Robinson:*

> Petitioner contends that this case is different from United States v. Robinson . . . in that petitioner had experienced no previous encounters with the officer in this case, and the offense for which he was arrested was "benign or trivial in nature," carrying with it no mandatory minimum sentence as did the offense for which Robinson was arrested. Petitioner points out that here, unlike *Robinson*, there were no police regulations which required the officer to take petitioner into custody, nor were there police department policies requiring full-scale body searches upon arrest in the field. [Id. at 263.]

In rejecting the defendant's claim and upholding the legality of the search, the Supreme Court observed: "[W]e do not find these differences determinative of the constitutional issue. . . . It is sufficient that the officer had probable cause to arrest the petitioner and that he lawfully effectuated the arrest and placed the petitioner in custody." Id. at 265.

Should the existence of police regulations or policy statements ever be determinative? Might it not be desirable, for example, to uphold in close cases police conduct if, but only if, it is carried out pursuant to local regulations? See Amsterdam, Perspectives on the Fourth Amendment, 54 Minn. L. Rev. 1, 416-429 (1974).

5. The test for determining the appropriate scope of a search incident to an arrest has become a term of art. The permissible scope of a search incident to an arrest, as courts have frequently reiterated, is "the arrestee's person and the area 'within his immediate control.'" Yet despite the familiarity of the phrase and the Court's explanation that it should be construed to mean "the area from within which he might gain possession of a weapon or destructable evidence," application of the test has often led to inconsistent results. Some courts appear to attribute to arrestees the characteristics of the comic book hero, Rubberman.[84]

One recurring issue that divided courts was whether the police could rely on *Chimel* to justify the search of an automobile in which the arrestee had been located immediately prior to the arrest. The Supreme Court dealt with this question in the next principal case.

NEW YORK v. BELTON
Certiorari to the Court of Appeals of New York
453 U.S. 454 (1981)

JUSTICE STEWART delivered the opinion of the Court.

When the occupant of an automobile is subjected to a lawful custodial arrest, does the constitutionally permissible scope of a search incident to his arrest include the passenger compartment of the automobile in which he was riding? That is the question at issue in the present case. . . .

On April 9, 1978, Trooper Douglas Nicot, a New York State policeman driving an unmarked car on the New York Thruway, was passed by another automobile traveling at an excessive rate of speed. Nicot gave chase, overtook the speeding vehicle, and ordered its driver to pull it over

---

84. See, e.g., People v. Perry, 47 Ill. 2d 402, 266 N.E.2d 330 (1971). See generally Aaronson & Wallace, A Reconsideration of the Fourth Amendment's Doctrine of Search Incident to Arrest, 64 Geo. L.J. 53 (1975).

Professor LaFave has noted that decisions giving broad scope to *Chimel's* "immediate control" test were more prevalent soon after the decision. He suggests that perhaps "much of the early resistance [to *Chimel*] was attributable to a distaste for holding pre-*Chimel* searches subject to *Chimel* standards, which the Supreme Court ultimately decided was not necessary." 2 W. LaFave, Search and Seizure: A Treatise on the Fourth Amendment §6.3(c), at 627-629 (2d ed. 1987) (citing Williams v. United States, 401 U.S. 646 (1971) (*Chimel* not applied retroactively)).

to the side of the road and stop. There were four men in the car, one of whom was Roger Belton, the respondent in this case. The policeman asked to see the driver's license and automobile registration, and discovered that none of the men owned the vehicle or was related to its owner. Meanwhile, the policeman had smelled burnt marihuana and had seen on the floor of the car an envelope marked "Supergold" that he associated with marihuana. He therefore directed the men to get out of the car, and placed them under arrest for the unlawful possession of marihuana. He patted down each of the men and "split them up into four separate areas of the Thruway at this time so they would not be in physical touching area of each other." He then picked up the envelope marked "Supergold" and found that it contained marihuana. . . . He then searched the passenger compartment of the car. On the back seat he found a black leather jacket belonging to Belton. He unzipped one of the pockets of the jacket and discovered cocaine. Placing the jacket in his automobile, he drove the four arrestees to a nearby police station.

Belton was subsequently indicted for criminal possession of a controlled substance. In the trial court he moved that the cocaine the trooper had seized from the jacket pocket be suppressed. The court denied the motion. Belton then pleaded guilty to a lesser included offense, but preserved his claim that the cocaine had been seized in violation of the Fourth and Fourteenth Amendments. See Lefkowitz v. Newsome, 420 U.S. 283. The Appellate Division of the New York Supreme Court upheld the constitutionality of the search and seizure. . . .

The New York Court of Appeals reversed. . . .

. . . [A]s one commentator has pointed out, the protection of the Fourth and Fourteenth Amendments "can only be realized if the police are acting under a set of rules which, in most instances, makes it possible to reach a correct determination beforehand as to whether an invasion of privacy is justified in the interest of law enforcement." LaFave, "Case-By-Case Adjudication" versus "Standardized Procedures": The *Robinson* Dilemma, 1974 S. Ct. Rev. 127, 142. . . . In short, "[a] single familiar standard is essential to guide police officers, who have only limited time and expertise to reflect on and balance the social and individual interests involved in the specific circumstances they confront." Dunaway v. New York, 442 U.S. 200, 213-214. . . .

But no straightforward rule has emerged from the litigated cases respecting the question involved here—the question of the proper scope of a search of the interior of an automobile incident to a lawful custodial arrest of its occupants. [The Court then cited several conflicting federal and state court decisions.]

When a person cannot know how a court will apply a settled principle to a recurring factual situation, that person cannot know the scope of his constitutional protection, nor can a policeman know the scope of his authority. While the Chimel case established that a search incident to an arrest may not stray beyond the area within the immediate control of the arrestee, courts have found no workable definition of "the area within the immediate control of the arrestee" when that area arguably includes the interior of an automobile and the arrestee is its recent occupant. Our reading of the cases suggests the generalization that articles inside the relatively narrow compass of the passenger compartment of an automobile are in fact generally even if not inevitably, within "the area into which an arrestee might reach in order to grab a weapon or evidentiary ite[m]." Chimel v. California, 395 U.S. [752], 763. In order to establish the workable rule this category of cases requires, we read Chimel's definition of the limits of the area that may be searched in light of that generalization. Accordingly, we hold that when a policeman has made a lawful custodial arrest of the occupant of an automobile, he may, as a contemporaneous incident of that arrest, search the passenger compartment of that automobile.[3]

It follows from this conclusion that the police may also examine the contents of any containers found within the passenger compartment, for if the passenger compartment is within reach of the arrestee, so also will containers in it be within his reach.[4] United States v. Robinson, [414 U.S. 218 (1973)]. . . . Such a container may, of course, be searched whether it is open or closed, since the justification for the search is not that the arrestee has no privacy interest in the container, but that the lawful custodial arrest justifies the infringement of any privacy interest the arrestee may have. Thus, while the Court in Chimel held that the police could not search all the drawers in an arrestee's house simply because the police had arrested him at home, the Court noted that drawers within an arrestee's reach could be searched because of the danger their contents might pose to the police. 395 U.S., at 763.

It is true, of course, that these containers will sometimes be such that they could hold neither a weapon nor evidence of the criminal conduct for which the suspect was arrested. However, in United States v. Robinson, the Court rejected the argument that such a container— there a "crumpled up cigarette package"—located during a search of

3. Our holding today does no more than determine the meaning of Chimel's principles in this particular and problematic context. It in no way alters the fundamental principles established in the Chimel case regarding the basic scope of searches incident to lawful custodial arrests.

4. "Container" here denotes any object capable of holding another object. It thus includes closed or open glove compartments, consoles, or other receptacles located anywhere within the passenger compartment, as well as luggage, boxes, bags, clothing, and the like. Our holding encompasses only the interior of the passenger compartment of an automobile and does not encompass the trunk.

Robinson incident to his arrest could not be searched: "The authority to search the person incident to a lawful custodial arrest, while based upon the need to disarm and to discover evidence, does not depend on what a court may later decide was the probability in a particular arrest situation that weapons or evidence would in fact be found upon the person of the suspect. A custodial arrest of a suspect based on probable cause is a reasonable intrusion under the Fourth Amendment; that intrusion being lawful, a search incident to the arrest requires no additional justification." 414 U.S., at 235. . . .

    . . . [T]he judgment is reversed.

It is so ordered.

[The concurring opinions of JUSTICE REHNQUIST and JUSTICE STEVENS and the dissenting opinions of JUSTICE WHITE and JUSTICE BRENNAN are omitted.]

NOTES AND QUESTIONS

1. What is the basis for the Court's factual conclusion that "articles inside . . . the passenger compartment of an automobile are . . . generally, even if not inevitably, within 'the area into which an arrestee might reach. . . .' "? Is it not clear, at the very least, that once a police officer remove's an individual from an automobile, it is relatively easy for the officer to keep a safe distance between the individual and the automobile? Or is there still a legitimate concern that third persons might get to evidence or a weapon located in the automobile?

2. Perhaps the factual premise about what is likely to be within an arrestee's immediate control is less important to the Court than the perceived need for a "straightforward rule" governing the search of automobiles incident to an arrest. In any event, to the extent that having a straightforward rule is a legitimate concern, several questions arise.

First, why is the Court's rule more appropriate than a rule prohibiting searches of the passenger compartment following the removal of the arrestee from the compartment?

Second, and more fundamentally, was there really any need for the kind of rule announced by the Court in *Belton?* If straightforward rules are desirable and if the *Chimel* rule is inherently ambiguous, then perhaps the answer is yes. But is *Chimel* really that ambiguous? Is it not likely that the "disarray" in the case law dealing with searches of automobiles incident to an arrest is attributable to other factors? For example, some of the apparent conflict may be attributable to subtle factual differences and not to any ambiguity about the meaning, scope, or spirit of *Chimel.* Of significantly more importance may be the fact that *Belton* is the first

Supreme Court case following *Chimel* to address the question what is in an arrestee's "immediate control." Given the Court's frequent pre-*Chimel* vacillations on the appropriate scope of searches incident to arrests and the Court's failure to take the opportunity to reenforce *Chimel* in specific contexts, is it not likely that the current disarray is at least partially the result of some lower courts' understandable failure to take *Chimel* seriously rather than any inherent ambiguity in the *Chimel* test?

Finally, has the Court in fact succeeded in providing the police with a straightforward line in dealing with automobiles occupied by arrestees? Justice Brennan, in his *Belton* dissent, suggested that many unanswered questions remain. For example, how long after the arrest may the search take place? Must the arrestee be in close physical proximity to the vehicle? Does the scope of a permissible search include the luggage area of a stationwagon or hatchback car?

3. Even if the search of the interior of the automobile was legal, what is the theory that justifies the search of the jacket? The Court observed that a "lawful custodial arrest justifies the infringement of any privacy interest the arrestee may have." This justification, however, is limited by *Chimel* to things within the immediate control of the arrestee, and the officer in *Belton* could easily have kept the jacket pocket away from Belton. How can the jacket pocket in *Belton* possibly be considered within the scope of the *Chimel* rule?

Is the answer—at least after *Ross*, page 627 supra—that "containers" in automobiles are always fair game? Note that a container search upheld under *Ross* must at least be based on probable cause. No such requirement exists for a *Belton* container search.

In United States v. Robinson, page 729 supra, the Court upheld a search incident to arrest that included the examination of a crumpled cigarette package taken from the coat pocket of the arrestee while he was being searched incident to his arrest. Thus, *Robinson* provides some support for the *Belton* holding with respect to the jacket search. The majority opinion in *Robinson*, however, did not specifically discuss the legality of the examination of the cigarette package. The quotation from *Robinson* near the end of the majority opinion in *Belton* appears in *Robinson* as part of a general discussion of the propriety of searching persons who are arrested.[85]

In his *Robinson* dissent, Justice Marshall did address the container search question:

> [T]here was no justification consistent with the Fourth Amendment which would authorize his opening the package and looking inside.

85. See page 733 supra.

To begin with, after [Officer] Jenks had the cigarette package in his hands, there is no indication that he had reason to believe or did in fact believe that the package contained a weapon. More importantly, even if the crumpled-up cigarette package had in fact contained some sort of small weapon, it would have been impossible for respondent to have used it once the package was in the officer's hands. Opening the package, therefore, did not further the protective purpose of the search. . . .

It is suggested, however, that since the custodial arrest itself represents a significant intrusion into the privacy of the person, any additional intrusion by way of opening or examining effects found on the person is not worthy of constitutional protection. But such an approach was expressly rejected by the Court in *Chimel*. There it was suggested that since the police had lawfully entered petitioner's house to effect an arrest, the additional invasion of privacy stemming from an accompanying search of the entire house was inconsequential. The Court answered: "[W]e can see no reason why, simply because some interference with an individual's privacy and freedom of movement has lawfully taken place, further intrusions should automatically be allowed despite the absence of a warrant that the Fourth Amendment would otherwise require." 395 U.S., at 766-767, n.12.[7] [414 U.S. at 255.]

4. Does it follow from *Belton* and *Robinson* that if the police arrest a business executive carrying an attache case, they may search the attache case regardless of whether they have probable cause to search? If the answer to this question should be no, what is the appropriate approach to take to the question whether containers found during a search incident

7. . . . The Government argued below, as an alternative theory to justify the search in this case, that when a suspect is booked and is about to be placed in station house detention, it is reasonable to search his person to prevent the introduction of weapons or contraband into the jail facility and to inventory the personal effects found on the suspect. Since respondent's cigarette package would have been removed and opened at the station house anyway, the argument goes, the search might just as well take place in the field at the time of the arrest. This argument fails for two reasons. *First,* . . . the justification for station-house searches is not the booking process itself, but rather the fact that the suspect will be placed in jail. In the District of Columbia, petty offenses of the sort involved in the present case are bailable, and . . . the normal procedure is for offenders to be advised of the opportunity to post collateral at the station house and to avoid an inventory search unless they are unable to refuse to do so. . . .

Second, even had it become necessary to place respondent in confinement, it is still doubtful whether one could justify opening up the cigarette package and examining its contents. The purposes of preventing the introduction of weapons or contraband into the jail facility are fully served simply by removing the package from the prisoner. It is argued that the police must inventory effects found on the prisoner in order to avoid a later claim by the prisoner that jail personnel stole his property. But . . . the police can protect themselves against such claims by means involving a less extreme intrusion on privacy than would be entailed in opening up and examining the contents of all effects found on the person. As an example, the [arrestee could be given the option of depositing his belongings in a sealed envelope and signing a waiver of any claim against the police for loss]. . . .

to arrest may be searched? Even though *Ross* rejected the distinction between worthy and unworthy containers in the context of automobile searches, should the distinction be given vitality in the search incident to arrest context? Alternatively, would it be appropriate to distinguish between containers found in an arrestee's pockets (e.g., *Robinson*), which could be searched, and containers being carried by or found near the arrestee (e.g., *Belton*), which could not be searched? If distinctions of this sort do not seem satisfactory, there would appear to be only two bases for holding the search of the attache case illegal. *First,* one could reject the container search holdings of both *Belton* and *Robinson* and maintain that the police, at least in the absence of probable cause, can never search a container that is or can be easily removed from the immediate control of the arrestee. *Second,* one could define *immediate control* narrowly so as to exclude items that the arrestee can easily be prevented from reaching and then concede that "containers" found during a properly limited search of the arrestee and the area within the arrestee's control may also be searched.

Which of these various approaches do you think is preferable?

5. Even if the police do not exceed the permissible scope or intensity of a search incident to an arrest, there may be a question about the propriety of the *seizure* of items discovered in such a search. Consider, for example, State v. Elkins, 245 Or. 279, 422 P.2d 250 (1966), a case in which the police during a search incident to an arrest discovered, seized, and without a warrant subjected to laboratory analysis "an unlabeled bottle containing three kinds of capsules and pills." 245 Or. at 281; 422 P.2d at 251. Should such a *seizure* be illegal in the absence of probable cause or at least some degree of reasonable suspicion to believe that the item seized may be contraband or otherwise incriminating? Should the answer depend on whether the evidence can later be seized as part of the inventory and booking process?[86] If there is a problem with the police activity in *Elkins*, does the problem relate to the *seizure*, the subsequent warrantless inspection of the item seized, or both?

6. It is clear that a search preceding an arrest is an invalid search incident to arrest if the police must rely on items found during the search to justify the arrest. Sibron v. New York, 392 U.S. 41 (1968). On the other hand, the mere fact that a properly limited search precedes by a few moments an independently valid arrest does not render the search illegal. See Rawlings v. Kentucky, 448 U.S. 98 (1980). Problems arise, however, when the police attempt to justify as incident to an arrest a search that occurs a substantial period of time prior to or following the actual arrest. For a discussion of the propriety of a delayed search incident

---

86. Inventory searches are discussed at pages 747-755 infra.

to arrest, see Justice Marshall's concurring opinion in Illinois v. Lafayette, 462 U.S. 640, 649 (1983). See also United States v. Edwards, 415 U.S. 800 (1974).

On the question whether one can rely on a search-incident-to-arrest theory to justify a search that occurs long before the arrest, consider Cupp v. Murphy, 412 U.S. 291 (1973): The defendant, a murder suspect whom the police had probable cause to arrest, voluntarily appeared at the police station for questioning. During the course of the questioning the police, over the defendant's objection, took sample scrapings from his fingernails. The defendant was not arrested until a month later. At his trial the scrapings, which contained "traces of skin and blood cells, and fabric from the victim's nightgown," id. at 292, were admitted into evidence. The Supreme Court relied on *Chimel* to uphold the search:

> Where there is no formal arrest, as in the case before us, a person might well be less hostile to the police and less likely to take conspicuous, immediate steps to destroy incriminating evidence on his person. Since he knows he is going to be released, he might be likely instead to be concerned with diverting attention away from himself. Accordingly, we do not hold that a full *Chimel* search would have been justified in this case without a formal arrest and without a warrant. But the respondent was not subjected to such a search.
>
> At the time Murphy was being detained at the station house, he was obviously aware of the detectives' suspicions. Though he did not have the full warning of official suspicion that a formal arrest provides, Murphy was sufficiently apprised of his suspected role in the crime to motivate him to attempt to destroy what evidence he could without attracting further attention. Testimony at trial indicated that after he refused to consent to the taking of fingernail samples, he put his hands behind his back and appeared to rub them together. He then put his hands in his pockets, and a "metallic sound, such as keys or change rattling" was heard. The rationale of *Chimel*, in these circumstances, justified the police in subjecting him to the very limited search necessary to preserve the highly evanescent evidence they found under his fingernails. [Id. at 296.]

Would it have been preferable, as Justice Douglas argued in his dissent, for the police to have detained Murphy while they sought a warrant? If so would an arrest warrant have been sufficient? Note, in this regard, that while the Court agreed that there was probable cause to *arrest* Murphy, the Court did not consider whether there was probable cause to engage in the search.

How broadly or narrowly should *Cupp* be read? Consider the following passage from 2 LaFave, Search and Seizure: A Treatise on the Fourth Amendment §5.4(b), at 520 (2d ed. 1987).

At a minimum, *Cupp* should be applied so as to permit, when there are grounds upon which a formal arrest could have been made, a more extensive search for any evidence reasonably believed to be in the possession of the suspect which might be unavailable later, either because of future conduct of the suspect or by other means.

Is this too broad a reading of *Cupp?*

c. Inventory Searches

COLORADO v. BERTINE
Certiorari to the Supreme Court of Colorado
479 U.S. 367 (1987)

CHIEF JUSTICE REHNQUIST delivered the opinion of the Court.
[Following Bertine's arrest for drunk driving and prior to the arrival of a tow truck that had been summoned to take Bertine's van to an impoundment lot, a police officer searched and inventoried the contents of the van. The search included the examination of a closed backpack, which contained controlled substances. Bertine was subsequently charged with unlawful possession of drugs.]
. . . The Colorado trial court ruled that . . . the police officers had made the decisions to impound the vehicle and to conduct a thorough inventory search in good faith. Although noting that the inventory of the vehicle was performed in a "somewhat slipshod" manner, the District Court concluded that "the search of the backpack was done for the purpose of protecting the owner's property, protection of the police from subsequent claims of loss or stolen property, and the protection of the police from dangerous instrumentalities." . . . The court observed that the standard procedures for impounding vehicles mandated a "detailed inventory involving the opening of containers and the listing of [their] contents." . . . Based on these findings, the court determined that the inventory search did not violate Bertine's rights under the Fourth Amendment of the United States Constitution. . . . The court, nevertheless, granted Bertine's motion to suppress, holding that the inventory search violated the Colorado Constitution.
On the State's interlocutory appeal, the Supreme Court of Colorado affirmed. . . . In contrast to the District Court, however, the Colorado Supreme Court based its ruling on the United States Constitution. The court recognized that in South Dakota v. Opperman, 428 U.S. 364 (1976), we had held inventory searches of automobiles to be consistent with the Fourth Amendment, and that in Illinois v. Lafayette, 462 U.S.

640 (1983) we had held that the inventory search of personal effects of an arrestee at a police station was also permissible under that Amendment. The Supreme Court of Colorado felt, however, that our decisions in Arkansas v. Sanders, [page 626 supra], and United States v. Chadwick, [page 625 supra], holding searches of closed trunks and suitcases violated the Fourth Amendment, meant that *Opperman* and *Lafayette* did not govern this case.

. . . As [the Colorado Supreme Court] recognized, inventory searches are now a well-defined exception to the warrant requirement of the Fourth Amendment. . . . The policies behind the warrant requirement are not implicated in an inventory search, . . . nor is the related concept of probable cause:

> The standard of probable cause is peculiarly related to criminal investigations, not routine, noncriminal procedures. . . . The probable-cause approach is unhelpful when analysis centers upon the reasonableness of routine administrative caretaking functions, particularly when no claim is made that the protective procedures are a subterfuge for criminal investigations. [South Dakota v. Opperman, 428 U.S. at 370 n.5.]

. . . For these reasons, the Colorado Supreme Court's reliance on . . . *Sanders* . . . and . . . *Chadwick* . . . was incorrect. Both of these cases concerned searches solely for the purpose of investigating criminal conduct, with the validity of the searches therefore dependent on application of the probable-cause and warrant requirements of the Fourth Amendment.

. . . In *Opperman*, this Court assessed the reasonableness of an inventory search of the glove compartment in an abandoned automobile impounded by the police. We found that inventory procedures serve to protect an owner's property while it is in the custody of the police, to insure against claims of lost, stolen, or vandalized property, and to guard the police from danger. In light of these strong governmental interests and the diminished expectation of privacy in an automobile, we upheld the search. In reaching this decision, we observed that our cases accorded deference to police caretaking procedures designed to secure and protect vehicles and their contents within police custody. . . .[4]

In our more recent decision, *Lafayette*, a police officer conducted

---

4. The Colorado Supreme Court correctly stated that *Opperman* did not address the question whether the scope of an inventory search may extend to closed containers located in the interior of an impounded vehicle. We did note, however, that " 'when the police take custody of any sort of container [such as] an automobile . . . it is reasonable to search the container to itemize the property to be held by the police.' " 428 U.S. at 371 (quoting United States v. Gravitt, 484 F.2d 375, 378 (CA5 1973), cert. denied, 414 U.S. 1135 (1974)).

an inventory search of the contents of a shoulder bag in the possession of an individual being taken into custody. In deciding whether this search was reasonable, we recognized that the search served legitimate governmental interests similar to those identified in *Opperman*. We determined that those interests outweighed the individual's Fourth Amendment interests and upheld the search.

In the present case, as in *Opperman* and *Lafayette*, there was no showing that the police, who were following standardized procedures, acted in bad faith or for the sole purpose of investigation. In addition, the governmental interests justifying the inventory searches in *Opperman* and *Lafayette* are nearly the same as those which obtain here. In each case the police were potentially responsible for the property taken into their custody. By securing the property, the police protected the property from unauthorized interference. Knowledge of the precise nature of the property helped guard against claims of theft, vandalism, or negligence. Such knowledge also helped to avert any danger to police or others that may have been posed by the property.

The Supreme Court of Colorado opined that *Lafayette* was not controlling here because there was no danger of introducing contraband or weapons into a jail facility. Our opinion in *Lafayette*, however, did not suggest that the station-house setting of the inventory search was critical to our holding in that case. Both in the present case and in *Lafayette*, the common governmental interests described above were served by the inventory searches.

The Supreme Court of Colorado also expressed the view that the search in this case was unreasonable because Bertine's van was towed to a secure, lighted facility and because Bertine himself could have been offered the opportunity to make other arrangements for the safekeeping of his property. But the security of the storage facility does not completely eliminate the need for inventorying; the police may still wish to protect themselves or the owners of the lot against false claims of theft or dangerous instrumentalities. And while giving Bertine an opportunity to make alternative arrangements would undoubtedly have been possible, we said in *Lafayette*:

> [t]he real question is not what "could have been achieved," but whether the Fourth Amendment *requires* such steps. . . . The reasonableness of any particular governmental activity does not necessarily or invariably turn on the existence of alternative "less intrusive" means. [*Lafayette*, 462 U.S. at 647 (emphasis in original).]

isn't that exactly what we are concerned with

. . . We conclude here, as in *Lafayette*, reasonable police regulations relating to inventory procedures administered in good faith satisfy the

Fourth Amendment, even though courts might as a matter of hindsight be able to devise equally reasonable rules requiring a different procedure.[6] The Supreme Court of Colorado also thought it necessary to require that police, before inventorying a container, weigh the strength of the individual's privacy interest in the container against the possibility that the container might serve as a repository for dangerous or valuable items. We think that such a requirement is contrary to our decisions in *Opperman* and *Lafayette*, and by analogy to our decision in United States v. Ross, 456 U.S. 798 (1982):

> Even if less intrusive means existed of protecting some particular types of property, it would be unreasonable to expect police officers in the everyday course of business to make fine and subtle distinctions in deciding which containers or items may be searched and which must be sealed as a unit."
> *Lafayette*, supra, 462 U.S. at 648.
>   When a legitimate search is under way, and when its purpose and its limits have been precisely defined, nice distinctions between closets, drawers, and containers, in the case of a home, or between glove compartments, upholstered seats, trunks, and wrapped packages, in the case of a vehicle, must give way to the interest in the prompt and efficient completion of the task at hand. [United States v. Ross, supra, 456 U.S., at 821.]

We reaffirm these principles here. . . .

Bertine finally argues that the inventory search of his van was unconstitutional because departmental regulations gave the police officers discretion to choose between impounding his van and parking and locking it in a public parking place. . . . Nothing in *Opperman* or *Lafayette* prohibits the exercise of police discretion so long as that discretion is exercised according to standard criteria and on the basis of something other than suspicion of evidence of criminal activity. Here, the discretion afforded the Boulder police was exercised in light of standardized criteria, related to the feasibility and appropriateness of parking and locking a vehicle rather than impounding it.[7] There was no showing that the police

---

6. We emphasize that, in this case, the trial court found that the police department's procedures mandated the opening of closed containers and the listing of their contents. Our decisions have always adhered to the requirement that inventories be conducted according to standardized criteria. . . .

7. . . . [T]he police directive concerning the care and security of vehicles taken into policy custody . . . establishes several conditions that must be met before an officer may pursue the park and lock alternative. For example, police may not park and lock the vehicle where there is reasonable risk of damage or vandalism to the vehicle or where the approval of the arrestee cannot be obtained. . . . Not only do such conditions circumscribe the discretion of individual officers, but they also protect the vehicle and its contents and minimize claims of property loss.

chose to impound Bertine's van in order to investigate suspected criminal activity.

While both *Opperman* and *Lafayette* are distinguishable from the present case on their facts, we think that the principles enunciated in those cases govern the present one. . . .

JUSTICE BLACKMUN, with whom JUSTICE POWELL and JUSTICE O'CONNOR join, concurring.

. . . I join in the Court's opinion, but write separately to underscore the importance of having . . . inventories conducted only pursuant to standardized police procedures. The underlying rationale for allowing an inventory exception to the Fourth Amendment warrant rule is that police officers are not vested with discretion to determine the scope of the inventory search. . . . This absence of discretion ensures that inventory searches will not be used as a purposeful and general means of discovering evidence of crime. Thus, it is permissible for police officers to open closed containers in an inventory search only if they are following standard police procedures that mandate the opening of such containers in every impounded vehicle. As the Court emphasizes, the trial court in this case found that the police department's standard procedures did mandate the opening of closed containers and the listing of their contents.

JUSTICE MARSHALL, with whom JUSTICE BRENNAN joins, dissenting. . . .

The Court today . . . declar[es] that "the discretion afforded the Boulder police was exercised in light of standardized criteria, related to the feasibility and appropriateness of parking and locking a vehicle rather than impounding it." . . . This vital assertion is flatly contradicted by the record in this case. The officer who conducted the inventory, Officer Reichenbach, testified at the suppression hearing that the decision not to "park and lock" respondent's vehicle was his "own individual discretionary decision." . . . Indeed, application of these supposedly standardized "criteria" upon which the Court so heavily relies would have yielded a different result in this case. Since there was ample public parking adjacent to the intersection where respondent was stopped, consideration of "feasibility" would certainly have militated in favor of the "park and lock" option, not against it. I do not comprehend how consideration of "appropriateness" serves to channel a field officer's discretion; nonetheless, the "park and lock" option would seem particularly appropriate in this case, where respondent was stopped for a traffic offense and was not likely to be in custody for a significant length of time.

Indeed, the record indicates that *no* standardized criteria limit a Boulder police officer's discretion. According to a departmental directive, after placing a driver under arrest, an officer has three options for disposing of the vehicle. First, he can allow a third party to take custody. Second, the officer or driver (depending on the nature of the arrest) may take the car to the nearest public parking facility, lock it, and take the keys. Finally, the officer can do what was done in this case: impound the vehicle, and search and inventory its contents, including closed containers.

Under the first option, the police have no occasion to search the automobile. Under the "park and lock" option, "[c]losed containers that give no indication of containing either valuables or a weapon *may not be opened and the contents searched* (i.e., inventoried)." App. 92-93 (emphasis added). Only if the police choose the third option are they entitled to search closed containers in the vehicle. Where the vehicle is not itself evidence of a crime, as in this case, the police apparently have totally unbridled discretion as to which procedure to use. . . .

Once a Boulder police officer has made this initial completely discretionary decision to impound a vehicle, he is given little guidance as to which areas to search and what sort of items to inventory. The arresting officer, Officer Toporek, testified at the suppression hearing as to what items would be inventoried: "That would I think be very individualistic as far as what an officer may or may not go into. I think whatever arouses his suspicious [sic] as far as what may be contained in any type of article in the car." Id. at 78.

[Justice Marshall went on to maintain that, in any event, the government's interests in carrying out the search did not justify the serious invasion of the defendant's privacy interest. In part because false claims may be asserted even if there is an inventory and in part because of the " 'slipshod' " manner in which this particular inventory was carried out, Justice Marshall claimed that there was no significant interest in protecting the government from false claims. In addition, he argued that the interest in protecting the police from danger, which he regarded as "attenuated" in most automobile inventory searches, was undermined rather than promoted by the opening of closed containers: " 'No sane individual inspects for booby-traps by simply opening the container.' " "Thus," he concluded, "only the government's interest in protecting the owner's property actually justifies an inventory search of an impounded vehicle." 479 U.S. at 384 (quoting United States v. Cooper, 428 F. Supp. 652, 655 (S.D. Ohio 1977)). Justice Marshall regarded this interest as significantly weaker in this case than in *Opperman* and *Lafayette* for two reasons. First, the defendant was present and, if asked, could have made other arrangements for the protection of his property. Second, since the defendant was arrested for a traffic offense, "he was unlikely to remain in custody for more than a few hours." Id. at 385.]

NOTES AND QUESTIONS

1. In *Lafayette* the Court held "that it is not 'unreasonable' for the police, as part of the routine procedure *incident to incarcerating an arrested person*, to search any container or article in his possession, in accordance with established inventory procedures." 462 U.S. at 648 (emphasis added). An appropriate issue on remand, the Court stated, was whether the defendant was to be incarcerated after being booked for disturbing the peace. Id. at 648 n.3. Cf. footnote 4 in *Bertine* (" 'reasonable to search the container to itemize the property *to be held by the police*' ") (emphasis added).

If the police are going to incarcerate an arrestee (or hold a container), should the reasonableness of the inventory depend on likely length of the incarceration (or holding)?

2. In several respects, *Opperman*, the Court's first inventory case, is distinguishable from and easier to justify than either *Lafayette* or *Bertine*. First, it may be difficult—or at least extremely expensive—to provide for security against theft of items from an automobile located in an impoundment lot; second, as the Court has consistently held, there is a diminished privacy interest in automobiles; and finally, when the police impound an abandoned car, the owner is not present to make alternative arrangements for safekeeping of the impounded items. By contrast, it should be relatively easy for the police to provide secure storage facilities for shoulder bags, backpacks, and similar containers; there is no diminished privacy interest associated with these types of containers, at least if they are not discovered during the course of an automobile search; and the police could give an arrestee, unless seriously injured or under the influence of alcohol or drugs, some choice with respect to the inventory process. Consider, for example, a practice of permitting an arrestee to forgo an inventory in return for the arrestee's releasing the police from liability for any allegedly lost or stolen items.

Should any of these differences between *Opperman* and the situations in *Lafayette* and *Bertine* have constitutional significance?

3. *Opperman, Lafayette,* and *Bertine* all emphasize that a valid inventory search must be conducted pursuant to reasonable regulations governing inventory procedures, a requirement that the Court reiterated in Florida v. Wells, 110 S. Ct. 1632 (1990). There the Court unanimously held that the opening of a locked suitcase during an inventory search was unconstitutional because there were no standards or policies relating to the opening of containers. In dictum a majority of the Court stated that a policy giving the police some discretion whether to open containers would not necessarily be invalid:

A police officer may be allowed sufficient latitude to determine whether a particular container should or should not be opened in light of the nature of the search and the characteristics of the container itself. Thus, while policies of opening all containers or of opening no containers are unquestionably permissible, it would be equally permissible, for example, to allow the opening of closed containers whose contents officers determine they are unable to ascertain from examining the containers' exteriors. The allowance of the exercise of judgment based on concerns related to the purposes of an inventory search does not violate the Fourth Amendment. [Id. at 1635.]

4. In *Bertine*, the Colorado trial judge apparently found that the Boulder Police Department's inventory procedures complied with this requirement, and that finding was not seriously challenged in the ensuing appellate litigation. Nonetheless, as Justice Marshall pointed out, there appeared to be very little in the way of regulations or procedures to limit the discretion of the Boulder police with respect to inventory searches. The defendant's failure to focus more attention on this aspect of the case may have been in part a result of *Bertine's* somewhat unusual history: the initial holding that the search violated the state but not the federal constitution; the interlocutory appeal by the state that resulted in an affirmance on federal constitutional grounds; and the State Supreme Court's rejection of the applicability to *Bertine* of the *Opperman-Lafayette* inventory search rationale.

5. Justice Marshall's *Bertine* dissent quotes Officer Toporek as testifying that a decision about what areas to search and what items to inventory would be governed by "whatever arouses his suspicious [*sic*] as far as what may be contained in any type of article in the car." Is this an appropriate criterion for deciding whether or how thoroughly to conduct an inventory search? See Florida v. Wells, Note 3 supra; Note 6 infra.

6. The majority opinion in *Bertine* stated, "We conclude here, as in *Lafayette*, reasonable police regulations relating to inventory procedures *administered in good faith* satisfy the Fourth Amendment" (emphasis added). Presumably this reference to good faith is intended to suggest that the search must be carried out for the purpose of achieving the administrative, noninvestigative objectives that justify the inventory search in the first place.

Consider the relationship between the "reasonable regulation" requirement and the "good faith" requirement. If an officer is acting pursuant to a regulation that gives the officer no discretion with respect to whether or how thoroughly to search, the officer's subjective motive or hope of finding evidence in making the search should be irrelevant. (The officer's motive in making the seizure that led to the search, however, would not necessarily be irrelevant.) On the other hand, if the officer has discretion whether or how extensively to search, the "good faith" language in *Bertine* may be significant.

7. In some situations it may be possible to justify a search on either an inventory rationale or a search-incident-to-arrest rationale. Keep in mind though that the rationales and requirements for the two types of searches are different:

> A search incident to arrest has as its objects protection of the officer and prevention of the destruction of evidence. The search must be limited to the area within the "immediate control" [with the *Belton*, page 739 supra, gloss] of the arrestee, and [except to the extent that Cupp v. Murphy, page 746 supra, permits pre-arrest searches] the search probably must be relatively contemporaneous with the arrest.
>
> An inventory search is designed to protect the owner's property, to protect the police from dangerous instrumentalities, and to protect the police against false claims. Its object is regulatory, not investigatory. It should be carried out pursuant to regulations which limit the discretion of the searching officer; and if the officer has some discretion with respect whether or how extensively to search, it may be critical that the officer's purpose in making the search is administrative, not investigatory.

d. Border and Highway Safety Regulation

Border searches. Traditionally both Congress[87] and the courts[88] have regarded as reasonable, despite the absence of probable cause, some types of searches and seizures at an international border or its functional equivalent.[89] The routine search of a person and the person's baggage on entering the country need not be based on even reasonable suspicion. The justifications for this standardless authority to search are

1. The importance of the interest in prohibiting illegal immigration and importation of contraband,

87. The First Congress exempted border searches from the probable cause requirement. Act of July 31, 1789, ch. 5, 1 Stat. 29, 43 (1789). For a similar current statute, see 19 U.S.C. §482 (1988).

88. See, e.g., United States v. Ramsey, 431 U.S. 606 (1977); Carroll v. United States, 267 U.S. 132 (1925).

89. "For example, searches at an established station near the border, at a point marking the confluence of two or more roads that extend from the border, might be functional equivalents of border searches. For another example, a search of the passengers and cargo of an airplane arriving at a St. Louis airport after a nonstop flight from Mexico City would clearly be the functional equivalent of a border search." Almeida-Sanchez v. United States, 413 U.S. 266, 272-273 (1973).

2. The impossibility of effectively satisfying this interest if normal probable cause or perhaps even articulable suspicion standards were applicable, and

3. The assertedly (relatively) minor nature of the invasion.

With respect to this last point it has been observed that people are on notice that they may be subjected to border searches. Why is this "notice" point relevant?

The "detention of a traveler at the border beyond the scope of a routine customs search and inspection" requires *Terry*-type articulable suspicion. United States v. Montoya de Hernandez, 473 U.S. 531 (1985). As *Montoya de Hernandez* demonstrates, if the articulable suspicion exists, the infringement on the suspect's privacy may be substantial. There customs officials had articulable suspicion to believe that Montoya de Hernandez was smuggling contraband in her alimentary canal. The inspector in charge of the investigation gave her the options of returning to Colombia on the next available flight, submitting to an x-ray, or remaining in detention until she produced a monitored bowel movement. A returning flight was not available, and the suspect withdrew her consent to an x-ray after she learned that she would be handcuffed during the trip to the hospital. She remained in detention without urinating or having a bowel movement for sixteen hours, at which point customs officials for the first time sought a court order for a pregnancy test, x-ray, and rectal examination. Several hours later the order was obtained, and narcotics were discovered during the rectal examination. In holding that the length of detention was reasonable, the Supreme Court observed:

> This length of time undoubtedly exceeds any other detention we have approved under reasonable suspicion. But we have also consistently rejected hard-and-fast time limits, [United States v.] Sharpe, [page 706 supra]. . . .
>
> The rudimentary knowledge of the human body which judges possess in common with the rest of humankind tells us that alimentary canal smuggling cannot be detected in the amount of time in which other illegal activity may be investigated through brief *Terry*-type stops. . . . [W]hen [the suspect] refused [the x-ray] alternative, the customs inspectors were left with only two practical alternatives: detain her for such time as necessary to confirm their suspicions . . . or turn her loose. . . .
>
> The inspectors . . . followed this former procedure. They no doubt expected that [the suspect], having recently disembarked from a 10-hour direct flight with a full and stiff abdomen, would produce a bowel movement without extended delay. But her visible efforts to resist the call of nature, which the court below labeled "heroic," disappointed this expectation. . . . Our prior cases have refused to charge police with delays in

investigatory detention attributable to the suspect's evasive actions, see *Sharpe*, [page 706 supra], and that principle applies here. . . .

. . . [A]t the international border . . . the Fourth Amendment balance of interests leans heavily to the Government. At the border, customs officials have more than merely an investigative law enforcement role. They are also charged, along with immigration officials, with protecting this Nation from entrants who bring anything harmful into this country, whether that be communicable diseases, narcotics, or explosives. . . . In this regard, the detention of a suspected alimentary canal smuggler at the border is analogous to the detention of a suspected tuberculosis carrier at the border; both are detained until their bodily processes dispel the suspicion that they will introduce a harmful agent into this country. [473 U.S. at 543-544.]

The Court observed in a footnote that it was not presented with the question and offered no opinion on what level of suspicion, if any, would be required for nonroutine searches such as strip searches, body cavity searches, and x-rays. Id. at 541 n.4.[90]

Should a lengthy detention of the type in *Montoya de Hernandez* require the approval of a magistrate? See Mandell & Richardson, Lengthy Detentions and Invasive Searches at the Border: In Search of the Magistrate, 28 Ariz. L. Rev. 331 (1986).

Searches and seizures at fixed checkpoints. To what extent should the fourth amendment limit the authority of Border Patrol officers to engage in searches and seizures at fixed checkpoints that are not the functional equivalent of the border? The Supreme Court initially faced this question in United States v. Ortiz, 422 U.S. 891 (1975). Border Patrol officers discovered three illegal aliens in the trunk of the defendant's car, which the officers had stopped for a "routine immigration search" at the San Clemente, California, checkpoint. The checkpoint was about 65 miles north of the Mexican border, and it was on the principal highway between San Diego and Los Angeles. When the checkpoint was in operation,[91] all northbound traffic was screened. If the officer had any suspicion that a car contained illegal aliens, the officer would "stop the

90. Lower courts have required particularized showings to justify these types of searches. Thus, for example, it has been held that to engage in a strip search immigration officers need "subjective suspicion supported by objective, articulable facts that would reasonably lead an experienced, prudent customs official to suspect that a particular person . . . is concealing something on his body for the purpose of transporting it into the United States contrary to law." United States v. Guadalupe-Garza, 421 F.2d 876, 879 (9th Cir. 1970). An even higher level of suspicion may be required to justify a body cavity search. See Rivas v. United States, 368 F.2d 703, 710 (9th Cir. 1966).

91. "[B]ad weather, heavy traffic, and personnel shortages keep [the checkpoint] closed about one-third of the time." 422 U.S. at 893.

car and ask the occupants about their citizenship." Id. at 894. If the
suspicion was not abated, the officer would " 'inspect' portions of the car
in which an alien might hide. . . . [O]nly about 3% of the cars that
pass the San Clemente checkpoint are stopped for either questioning or
a search." Id. at 894, 895-896. In *Ortiz*, there was nothing in the record
to suggest "any special reason" to suspect that the car contained illegal
aliens. Id. at 892. Emphasizing the seriousness of the invasion and the
breadth of discretion exercised by the Border Patrol officers, the Supreme
Court held that the search of the trunk was unconstitutional.[92]

In contrast to *Ortiz*, which focused on the *search* of a vehicle, United
States v. Martinez-Fuerte, 428 U.S. 543 (1976), dealt with the legality
of *stops* at fixed checkpoints. Each of the defendants in *Martinez-Fuerte*
was driving an automobile that was stopped at a fixed checkpoint. On
questioning the occupants of the automobiles, Border Patrol officers learned
that the passengers were illegal aliens. The defendants argued that evidence of the aliens' status was obtained illegally because the Border Patrol
officers did not have "reasonable suspicion" to make the stops. Id. at 556.
The Supreme Court, however, held that no suspicion is required to justify
stops at fixed checkpoints. The Court emphasized that "the need to make
routine checkpoint stops is great, [and] the consequent intrusion on Fourth
Amendment rights is quite limited." Id. at 557. In dissent Justice Brennan
observed: "This defacement of Fourth Amendment protections is arrived
at by a balancing process that overwhelms the individual's protection
against unwarranted official intrusion by a governmental interest said to
justify the search and seizure. But that method is only a convenient cover
for condoning arbitrary official conduct, for the government interests
relied on or warranting intrusion here are the same as those in . . .
Ortiz." Id. at 570.

Searches and seizures by roving patrols. In addition to maintaining
fixed checkpoints, Border Patrol officers attempt to intercept importation

---

92. Consider 3 W. LaFave, Search and Seizure: A Treatise on the Fourth Amendment §10.5(i), at 762 (2d ed. 1987).

> It is useful to note that the holding in *Ortiz* appears to proscribe all warrantless
> searches without consent or probable cause at such traffic checkpoints, although
> much of the analysis was directed to the fact that the searches at this particular
> checkpoint were done on a highly selective basis at the discretion of the officers
> manning the checkpoint. The contention might be made that this risk of arbi-
> trariness would not be present if the checkpoint were operated so that *all* cars
> passing by were searched, so that *Ortiz* should not actually be read as going this
> far. However, the point seems academic, for it has not been the practice (nor,
> does it appear feasible) for agents to operate the checkpoints in this way. The Court
> in *Ortiz* noted that the volume of cars at other checkpoints was lighter and that
> consequently the officers could "routinely inspect more of them," but there is no
> suggestion in the case that a search-all-cars routine had been or could be under-
> taken.

Cf. Delaware v. Prouse, page 759 infra.

of contraband and illegal aliens by engaging in roving patrols near border crossings. In Almeida-Sanchez v. United States, 413 U.S. 266 (1973), Border Patrol officers on a roving patrol stopped and searched the defendant's car at a point 25 miles from the border. The officers did not have probable cause to search the vehicle or even to believe that it had crossed the border. The Supreme Court held that the search was illegal and, therefore, that the marijuana found during the search should have been suppressed.

In United States v. Brignoni-Ponce, 422 U.S. 873 (1975), a roving patrol stopped and briefly questioned the occupants of an automobile. During the questioning the officers learned that the passengers were illegal aliens. At his trial for transporting illegal immigrants, the driver claimed that the testimony regarding the passengers should have been suppressed because it was the fruit of an illegal stop. Noting that the "only reason" for the stop was that the "three occupants [of the vehicle] appeared to be of Mexican descent," id. at 875, the Supreme Court agreed. The Court stated, however, that such a stop, if based on reasonable, articulable suspicion, would have been proper.

Do you agree that it is appropriate to permit a stop at a fixed checkpoint without any suspicion at all and, at the same time, to require articulable suspicion for a stop by a roving patrol? Why? Consider the following case.

DELAWARE v. PROUSE
Certiorari to the Supreme Court of Delaware
440 U.S. 648 (1979)

MR. JUSTICE WHITE delivered the opinion of the Court. . . .

At 7:20 P.M. on November 30, 1976, a New Castle County, Del., patrolman in a police cruiser stopped the automobile occupied by respondent. The patrolman smelled marihuana smoke as he was walking toward the stopped vehicle, and he seized marihuana in plain view on the car floor. Respondent was subsequently indicted for illegal possession of a controlled substance. At a hearing on respondent's motion to suppress the marihuana seized as a result of the stop, the patrolman testified that prior to stopping the vehicle he had observed neither traffic or equipment violations nor any suspicious activity, and that he made the stop only in order to check the driver's license and registration. The patrolman was not acting pursuant to any standards, guidelines, or procedures pertaining to document spot checks, promulgated by either his department or the State Attorney General. Characterizing the stop as "routine," the patrolman explained, "I saw the car in the area and wasn't answering any complaints, so I decided to pull them off.". . . . The trial court granted the motion to suppress, finding the stop and detention to have been wholly capricious and therefore violative of the Fourth Amendment.

The Delaware Supreme Court affirmed. . . .

. . . We cannot assume that the physical and psychological intrusion visited upon the occupants of a vehicle by a random stop to check documents is of any less moment than that occasioned by a stop by border agents on roving patrol. Both of these stops generally entail law enforcement officers signaling a moving automobile to pull over to the side of the roadway, by means of a possibly unsettling show of authority. Both interfere with freedom of movement, are inconvenient, and consume time. Both may create substantial anxiety. For Fourth Amendment purposes, we also see insufficient resemblance between sporadic and random stops of individual vehicles making their way through city traffic and those stops occasioned by roadblocks where all vehicles are brought to a halt or to a near halt, and all are subjected to a show of the police power of the community. "At traffic checkpoints the motorist can see that other vehicles are being stopped, he can see visible signs of the officers' authority, and he is much less likely to be frightened or annoyed by the intrusion.". . . [United States v. Ortiz, 422 U.S. 891,] 894-895 [(1975)], quoted in United States v. Martinez-Fuerte, 428 U.S. [543], 558 [(1976)]. . . .

But the State of Delaware urges that even if discretionary spot checks such as occurred in this case intrude upon motorists as much as or more than do the roving patrols held impermissible in [United States v.] Brignoni-Ponce, [422 U.S. 873 (1975),] these stops are reasonable under the Fourth Amendment because the State's interest in the practice as a means of promoting public safety upon its roads more than outweighs the intrusion entailed. Although the record discloses no statistics concerning the extent of the problem of lack of highway safety, in Delaware or in the Nation as a whole, we are aware of the danger to life[14] and property posed by vehicular traffic and of the difficulties that even a cautious and an experienced driver may encounter. We agree that the States have a vital interest in ensuring that only those qualified to do so are permitted to operate motor vehicles, that these vehicles are fit for safe operation, and hence that licensing, registration, and vehicle inspection requirements are being observed. . . .

The question remains, however, whether in the service of these important ends the discretionary spot check is a sufficiently productive

14. In 1977, 47,671 persons died in motor vehicle accidents in this country. U.S. Dept. of Transportation, Highway Safety A-9 (1977).

mechanism to justify the intrusion upon Fourth Amendment interests which such stops entail. On the record before us, that question must be answered in the negative. Given the alternative mechanisms available, both those in use and those that might be adopted, we are unconvinced that the incremental contribution to highway safety of the random spot check justifies the practice under the Fourth Amendment.

The foremost method of enforcing traffic and vehicle safety regulations, it must be recalled, is acting upon observed violations. Vehicle stops for traffic violations occur countless times each day; and on these occasions, licenses and registration papers are subject to inspection and drivers without them will be ascertained. Furthermore, drivers without licenses are presumably the less safe drivers whose propensities may well exhibit themselves. Absent some empirical data to the contrary, it must be assumed that finding an unlicensed driver among those who commit traffic violations is a much more likely event than finding an unlicensed driver by choosing randomly from the entire universe of drivers. If this were not so, licensing of drivers would hardly be an effective means of promoting roadway safety. It seems common sense that the percentage of all drivers on the road who are driving without a license is very small and that the number of licensed drivers who will be stopped in order to find one unlicensed operator will be large indeed. . . . In terms of actually discovering unlicensed drivers or deterring them from driving, the spot check does not appear sufficiently productive to qualify as a reasonable law enforcement practice under the Fourth Amendment.

Much the same can be said about the safety aspects of automobiles as distinguished from drivers. Many violations of minimum vehicle-safety requirements are observable, and something can be done about them by the observing officer, directly and immediately. Furthermore, in Delaware, as elsewhere, vehicles must carry and display current license plates, which themselves evidence that the vehicle is properly registered; and, under Delaware law, to qualify for annual registration a vehicle must pass the annual safety inspection and be properly insured. . . .

The marginal contribution to roadway safety possibly resulting from a system of spot checks cannot justify subjecting every occupant of every vehicle on the roads to a seizure—limited in magnitude compared to other intrusions but nonetheless constitutionally cognizable—at the unbridled discretion of law enforcement officials. To insist neither upon an appropriate factual basis for suspicion directed at a particular automobile nor upon some other substantial and objective standard or rule to govern the exercise of discretion "would invite intrusions upon constitutionally guaranteed rights based on nothing more substantial than inarticulate hunches. . . ." Terry v. Ohio, 392 U.S. [11, 22 [(1968)]. . . . This kind of standardless and unconstrained discretion is the evil the Court has discerned when in previous cases it has insisted that the discretion of the official in the field be circumscribed, at least to some extent. . . .

Accordingly, we hold that except in those situations in which there is at least articulable and reasonable suspicion that a motorist is unlicensed or that an automobile is not registered, or that either the vehicle or an occupant is otherwise subject to seizure for violation of law, stopping an automobile and detaining the driver in order to check his driver's license and the registration of the automobile are unreasonable under the Fourth Amendment. This holding does not preclude the State of Delaware or other States from developing methods for spot checks that involve less intrusion or that do not involve the unconstrained exercise of discretion.[26] Questioning of all oncoming traffic at roadblock-type stops is one possible alternative. We hold only that persons in automobiles on public roadways may not for that reason alone have their travel and privacy interfered with at the unbridled discretion of police officers. The judgment below is affirmed.

So ordered.

MR. JUSTICE BLACKMUN, with whom MR. JUSTICE POWELL joins, concurring.

The Court . . . carefully protects from the reach of its decision other less intrusive spot checks "that do not involve the unconstrained exercise of discretion." The roadblock stop for all traffic is given as an example. I necessarily assume that the Court's reservation also includes other not purely random stops (such as every 10th car to pass a given point) that equate with, but are less intrusive than, a 100% roadblock stop. And I would not regard the present case as a precedent that throws any constitutional shadow upon the necessarily somewhat individualized and perhaps largely random examinations by game wardens in the performance of their duties. In a situation of that type, it seems to me, the Court's balancing process, and the value factors under consideration, would be quite different.

With this understanding, I join the Court's opinion and its judgment.

MR. JUSTICE REHNQUIST, dissenting.

The Court holds, in successive sentences, that absent an articulable, reasonable suspicion of unlawful conduct, a motorist may not be sub-

---

26. Nor does our holding today cast doubt on the permissibility of roadside truck weigh-stations and inspection checkpoints, at which some vehicles may be subject to further detention for safety and regulatory inspection than are others.

jected to a random license check, but that the States are free to develop "methods for spot checks that . . . do not involve the unconstrained exercise of discretion," such as "[q]uestioning . . . all oncoming traffic at roadblock-type stops. . . ." . . . Because motorists, apparently like sheep, are much less likely to be "frightened" or "annoyed" when stopped en masse, a highway patrolman needs neither probable cause nor articulable suspicion to stop *all* motorists on a particular thoroughfare, but he cannot without articulable suspicion stop *less* than all motorists. The Court thus elevates the adage "misery loves company" to a novel role in Fourth Amendment jurisprudence. The rule becomes "curiouser and curiouser" as one attempts to follow the Court's explanation for it. . . .

NOTES AND QUESTIONS

1. Recall Camara v. Municipal Court, page 666 supra, and Marshall v. Barlow's Inc., page 672 supra, both of which imposed a warrant requirement for regulatory searches. Should *Camara*-type warrants be required for routine traffic or immigration stops? Should the existence of such a warrant, even if not required in all cases, make legal a stop that would otherwise be illegal because of a lack of individualized articulable suspicion?

2. Is the state's interest in regulating hunting and fishing greater than the state's interest in highway safety? Do you agree with Justice Blackmun that after *Prouse* a game warden can stop hunters or fishermen to check for a license or to see if they have exceeded their limit even though the warden has no reason to believe such is the case?

3. Are you persuaded that the state's interest in highway safety can be significantly advanced by permitting stops for license and registration checks on less than probable cause? As a practical matter, can such stops be made after *Prouse*—except perhaps at a roadblock or pursuant to a plan to stop every tenth car? In other words, are there circumstances that are likely to give the police "articulable and reasonable suspicion," *but not probable cause* to believe, that a "motorist is unlicensed or that an automobile is unregistered"?

4. To the extent that other means of checking for licenses and registrations may be constitutional, should the critical factor be (a) that they "involve less intrusion" or (b) that they "do not involve the unconstrained exercise of discretion" or both? Consider, for example, stopping all cars at a roadblock, stopping every tenth car at a roadblock, stopping every blue car at a roadblock, or stopping every tenth car by a roving patrol. Which of these practices should be constitutional?

MICHIGAN DEPARTMENT OF
STATE POLICE v. SITZ
Certiorari to the Court of Appeals of Michigan
110 S. Ct. 2481 (1990)

CHIEF JUSTICE REHNQUIST delivered the opinion of the Court. . . .
    Petitioners . . . established a sobriety checkpoint pilot program in
early 1986. . . . [A] Sobriety Checkpoint Advisory Committee . . .
created guidelines setting forth procedures governing checkpoint operations, site selection, and publicity. . . .
    The first—and to date the only—sobriety checkpoint operated under
the program was conducted in Saginaw County. . . . During the hour-
and-fifteen-minute duration of the checkpoint's operation, 126 vehicles
passed through the checkpoint. The average delay for each vehicle was
approximately 25 seconds. Two drivers were detained for field sobriety
testing, and one of the two was arrested for driving under the influence
of alcohol. A third driver who drove through without stopping was pulled
over by an officer in an observation vehicle and arrested for driving under
the influence. . . .
    [Respondents brought this action for declaratory and injunctive re-
lief. The trial court held that the sobriety check point program violated
both the fourth amendment and the Michigan constitution. The Michigan Court of Appeals affirmed on the ground that the program violated
the fourth amendment. Both courts used a three-prong balancing test
derived from Brown v. Texas, 443 U.S. 47 (1979), in which they considered the state's interest in preventing accidents by drunk drivers, the
intrusion on individual privacy by the checkpoints, and the effectiveness
of the checkpoints in achieving their goal.]
    . . . No allegations are before us of unreasonable treatment of any
person after an actual detention. . . . We address only the initial stop
of each motorist passing through a checkpoint and the associated preliminary questioning and observation by checkpoint officers. Detention of
particular motorists for more extensive field sobriety testing may require
satisfaction of an individualized suspicion standard. . . .
    No one can seriously dispute the magnitude of the drunken driving
problem or the States' interest in eradicating it. . . . "Drunk drivers
cause an annual death toll of over 25,000 and in the same time span
cause nearly one million personal injuries and more than five billion
dollars in property damage." 4 LaFave, Search and Seizure: Treatise on
the Fourth Amendment §10.8(d), p.71 (2d ed. 1987). . . .
    Conversely, the weight bearing on the other scale—the measure of
the intrusion on motorists stopped briefly at sobriety checkpoints—is

slight. . . . [As is the case with highway checkpoints for detecting illegal aliens, see United States v. Martinez-Fuerte, 428 U.S. 543, 558 (1976),] the "objective" intrusion, measured by the duration of the seizure and the intensity of the investigation . . . [is] minimal. . . .

With respect to what it perceived to be the "subjective" intrusion on motorists, . . . the Court of Appeals found such intrusion substantial. . . . The court first affirmed the trial court's finding that the guidelines governing checkpoint operation minimize the discretion of the officers on the scene. But the court also agreed with the trial court's conclusion that the checkpoints have the potential to generate fear and surprise in motorists. . . .

. . . The "fear and surprise" to be considered are not the natural fear of one who has been drinking over the prospect of being stopped at a sobriety checkpoint, but, rather, the fear and surprise engendered in law abiding motorists by the nature of the stop. . . . Here, checkpoints are selected pursuant to the guidelines, and uniformed police officers stop every approaching vehicle. The intrusion resulting from the brief stop at the sobriety checkpoint is for constitutional purposes indistinguishable from the checkpoint stops we upheld in *Martinez-Fuerte*.

The Court of Appeals went on to consider as part of the balancing analysis the "effectiveness" of the proposed checkpoint program. Based on extensive testimony in the trial record, the court concluded that the checkpoint program failed the "effectiveness" part of the test. . . .

The actual language from Brown v. Texas, upon which the Michigan courts based their evaluation of "effectiveness," describes the balancing factor as "the degree to which the seizure advances the public interest." 443 U.S., at 51. This passage from *Brown* was not meant to transfer from politically accountable officials to the courts the decision as to which among reasonable alternative law enforcement techniques should be employed to deal with a serious public danger. Experts in police science might disagree over which of several methods of apprehending drunken drivers is preferable as an ideal. But for purposes of Fourth Amendment analysis, the choice among such reasonable alternatives remains with the governmental officials who have unique understanding of, and a responsibility for, limited public resources, including a finite number of police officers. . . .

Unlike [Delaware v.] Prouse, [page 759 supra,] this case involves neither a complete absence of empirical data nor a challenge to random highway stops. . . . [A]pproximately 1.5 percent of the drivers passing through the [Saginaw County] checkpoint were arrested for alcohol impairment. In addition, an expert witness testified at the trial that experience in other States demonstrated that, on the whole, sobriety checkpoints resulted in drunken driving arrests of around 1 percent of all motorists

stopped. . . . By way of comparison, the record from one of the consolidated cases in *Martinez-Fuerte* showed that in the associated checkpoint, illegal aliens were found in only 0.12 percent of the vehicles passing
through the checkpoint. See 428 U.S., at 554. The ratio of illegal aliens
detected to vehicles stopped (considering that on occasion two or more
illegal aliens were found in a single vehicle) was approximately 0.5 percent. . . .

In sum, the balance of the State's interest in preventing drunken
driving, the extent to which this system can reasonably be said to advance
that interest, and the degree of intrusion upon individual motorists who
are briefly stopped, weighs in favor of the state program. We therefore
hold that it is consistent with the Fourth Amendment. . . .

[The concurring opinion of JUSTICE BLACKMUN is omitted.]

JUSTICE BRENNAN, with whom JUSTICE MARSHALL joins, dissenting.
. . . In *Martinez-Fuerte*, the Court explained that suspicionless
stops were justified because "[a] requirement that stops . . . be based on
reasonable suspicion would be impractical because the flow of traffic
tends to be too heavy to allow the particularized study of a given car that
would enable it to be identified as a possible carrier of illegal aliens."
438 U.S. at 557. There has been no showing in this case that there is a
similar difficulty in detecting individuals who are driving under the influence of alcohol, nor is it intuitively obvious that such a difficulty exists.
. . . Without proof that the police cannot develop individualized suspicion that a person is driving while impaired by alcohol, I believe the
constitutional balance must be struck in favor of protecting the public
against even the "minimally intrusive" seizures involved in this case. . . .

JUSTICE STEVENS, with whom JUSTICE BRENNAN and JUSTICE MAR-
SHALL join . . . , dissenting.
. . . Because the Michigan program was patterned after an older
program in Maryland, the trial judge gave special attention to that State's
experience. Over a period of several years, Maryland operated 125 checkpoints; of the 41,000 motorists passing through those checkpoints, only
143 (0.3%) were arrested. The number of man-hours devoted to these
operations is not in the record, but it seems inconceivable that a higher
arrest rate could not have been achieved by more conventional means.
Yet, even if the 143 checkpoint arrests were assumed to involve a net
increase in the number of drunk driving arrests per year, the figure would
still be insignificant by comparison to the 71,000 such arrests made by
Michigan State Police without checkpoints in 1984 alone. . . .

Any relationship between sobriety checkpoints and an actual reduction in highway fatalities is even less substantial than the minimal impact
on arrest rates. As the Michigan Court of Appeals pointed out, "Maryland

had conducted a study comparing traffic statistics between a county using checkpoints and a control county. The results of the study showed that alcohol-related accidents in the checkpoint county decreased by ten percent, whereas the control county saw an eleven percent decrease; and while fatal accidents in the control county fell from sixteen to three, fatal accidents in the checkpoint county actually doubled from the prior year." 170 Mich. App. 433, 443, 429 N.W.2d 180, 184.

There is a critical difference between a seizure that is preceded by fair notice and one that is effected by surprise. . . . A motorist with advance notice of the location of a permanent checkpoint has an opportunity to avoid the search entirely, or at least to prepare for, and limit, the intrusion to her privacy.

No such opportunity is available in the case of a random stop or a temporary checkpoint, which both depend for their effectiveness on the element of surprise. A driver who discovers an unexpected checkpoint on a familiar local road will be startled and distressed. . . .

This element of surprise is the most obvious distinction between the sobriety checkpoints permitted by today's majority and the interior border checkpoints approved by this Court in *Martinez-Fuerte*. That distinction casts immediate doubt upon the majority's argument, for *Martinez-Fuerte* is the only case in which we have upheld suspicionless seizures of motorists. But the difference between notice and surprise is only one of the important reasons for distinguishing between permanent and mobile checkpoints. With respect to the former, there is no room for discretion in either the timing or the location of the stop—it is a permanent part of the landscape. In the latter case, however, . . . the police have extremely broad discretion in determining the exact timing and placement of the roadblock.

There is a significant difference between the kind of discretion that the officer exercises after the stop is made. A check for a driver's license, or for identification papers at an immigration checkpoint, is far more easily standardized than is a search for evidence of intoxication. A Michigan officer who questions a motorist at a sobriety checkpoint has virtually unlimited discretion to detain the driver on the basis of the slightest suspicion. A ruddy complexion, an unbuttoned shirt, bloodshot eyes or a speech impediment may suffice to prolong the detention. . . .

Finally, it is significant that many of the stops at permanent checkpoints occur during daylight hours, whereas the sobriety checkpoints are almost invariably operated at night. A seizure followed by interrogation and even a cursory search at night is surely more offensive than a daytime stop that is almost as routine as going through a toll gate. . . .

. . . On the degree to which the sobriety checkpoint seizures advance the public interest . . . the Court's position is wholly indefensible.

. . . [A]lthough the *gross* number of arrests is more than zero, there is a complete failure of proof on the question whether the wholesale seizures have produced any *net* advance in the public interest in arresting intoxicated drivers.

Indeed, the position adopted today by the Court is not one endorsed by any of the law enforcement authorities to whom the Court purports to defer. . . . The Michigan police do not rely, as the Court does, . . . on the *arrest rate* at sobriety checkpoints to justify the stops made there. Colonel Hough, the commander of the Michigan State Police and a leading proponent of the checkpoints, . . . maintained that the mere *threat* of such arrests is sufficient to deter drunk driving and so to reduce the accident rate. The Maryland police officer who testified at trial took the same position with respect to his State's program. . . . [A] law enforcement technique that reduces crime by pure deterrence without punishing anybody . . . is highly commendable. One cannot, however, prove its efficacy by counting the arrests that were made. One must instead measure the number of crimes that were avoided. Perhaps because the record is wanting, the Court simply ignores this point. . . .

NOTES AND QUESTIONS

1. Consider Brown v. Texas, 443 U.S. 47 (1979). Police officers stopped the defendant and demanded that he identify himself. When he refused, he was arrested and later convicted of violating a statute that makes it a crime for a lawfully stopped individual to refuse to identify himself. The officers had decided to stop the defendant "because the situation 'looked suspicious and we had never seen the subject in that area before.' " Id. at 49. At trial, however, they were unable "to point to any facts supporting that conclusion." Id. at 52. Nonetheless the state argued that the stop should be regarded as reasonable because of the state's interest in crime prevention. The Supreme Court disagreed: "When such a stop is not based on objective criteria, the risk of arbitrary and abusive police practices exceeds tolerable limits. See Delaware v. Prouse." Id. at 52. Thus, the Court concluded, the defendant under these circumstances could not be punished for refusing to identify himself.

Would the conviction have been sustained if all individuals in the area had been stopped and asked to identify themselves?

2. In United States v. Villamonte-Marquez, 462 U.S. 579 (1983), the Supreme Court considered what criteria should govern the authority of customs officials to "board for inspection of documents a vessel that is located in waters providing ready access to the open sea." Acting pursuant to statutory authority, customs officials in *Villamonte-Marquez* boarded defendants' vessel without probable cause or even articulable

suspicion of illegality, and while on board they discovered marihuana. The Court conceded that stopping an automobile under these circumstances would be illegal. Nonetheless, the Court held that the customs officials had not violated the fourth amendment:

> In a lineal ancestor to the statute at issue here the First Congress clearly authorized the suspicionless boarding of vessels, reflecting its view that such boardings are not contrary to the Fourth Amendment; this gives the statute before us an impressive historical pedigree. . . . The nature of waterborne commerce in waters providing ready access to the open sea is sufficiently different from the nature of vehicular traffic on highways as to make possible alternatives to the sort of "stop" made in this case less likely to accomplish the obviously essential governmental purposes involved. The system of prescribed outward markings used by States for vehicle registration is also significantly different than the system of external markings on vessels, and the extent and type of documentation required by federal law is a good deal more variable and more complex than are the state vehicle registration laws. The nature of the governmental interest in assuring compliance with documentation requirements, particularly in waters where the need to deter or apprehend smugglers is great, [is] substantial; the type of intrusion made in this case, while not minimal, is limited. [Id. at 592-593.]

e. The Seizure and Search of Persons Present at Searched Premises

YBARRA v. ILLINOIS
Appeal from the Appellate Court of Illinois, Second District
444 U.S. 85 (1979)

MR. JUSTICE STEWART delivered the opinion of the Court.

An Illinois statute authorizes law enforcement officers to detain and search any person found on premises being searched pursuant to a search warrant, to protect themselves from attack or to prevent the disposal or concealment of anything described in the warrant. The question before us is whether the application of this statute to the facts of the present case violated the Fourth and Fourteenth Amendments. . . .

On March 1, 1976, a special agent of the Illinois Bureau of Investigation [obtained a warrant to search the Aurora Tap Tavern and the bartender, Greg, for heroin and other controlled substances.] . . .

In the late afternoon of that day, seven or eight officers proceeded to the tavern. Upon entering it, the officers announced their purpose and advised all those present that they were going to conduct a "cursory search for weapons." One of the officers then proceeded to pat down each of the 9 to 13 customers present in the tavern, while the remaining officers engaged in an extensive search of the premises.

The police officer who frisked the patrons found the appellant, Ventura Ybarra, in front of the bar standing by a pinball machine. In his first patdown of Ybarra, the officer felt what he described as "a cigarette pack with objects in it." He did not remove this pack from Ybarra's pocket. Instead he moved on and proceeded to pat down other customers. After completing this process the officer returned to Ybarra and frisked him once again. This second search of Ybarra took place approximately 2 to 10 minutes after the first. The officer relocated and retrieved the cigarette pack from Ybarra's pants pocket. Inside the pack he found six tinfoil packets containing a brown powdery substance which later turned out to be heroin.

Ybarra was subsequently indicted by an Illinois grand jury for the unlawful possession of a controlled substance. He filed a pretrial motion to suppress all the contraband that had been seized from his person at the Aurora Tap Tavern. . . . The trial court denied the motion . . . and Ybarra was found guilty of the possession of heroin.

On appeal, the Illinois Appellate Court . . . affirmed Ybarra's conviction, and the Illinois Supreme Court denied his petition for leave to appeal. . . .

There is no reason to suppose that, when the search warrant was issued on March 1, 1976, the authorities had probable cause to believe that any person found on the premises of the Aurora Tap Tavern, aside from "Greg," would be violating the law. . . .

[P]robable cause to search Ybarra . . . was still absent when the police executed the warrant. Upon entering the tavern, the police did not recognize Ybarra and had no reason to believe that he had committed, was committing, or was about to commit any offense under state or federal law. Ybarra made no gestures indicative of criminal conduct, made no movements that might suggest an attempt to conceal contraband, and said nothing of a suspicious nature to the police officers. . . .

. . . [A] person's mere propinquity to others independently suspected of criminal activity does not, without more, give rise to probable cause to search that person. . . . Where the standard is probable cause, a search or seizure of a person must be supported by probable cause particularized with respect to that person[4] . . .

---

4. . . . [A] warrant to search a place cannot normally be construed to authorize a search of each individual in that place. The warrant for the Aurora Tap Tavern provided no basis for departing from this general rule. Consequently, we need not consider situations where the warrant itself authorized the search of unnamed persons in a place and

. . . We are asked to find that the first patdown search of Ybarra constituted a reasonable frisk for weapons under the doctrine of Terry v. Ohio, 392 U.S. 1. If this finding is made, it is then possible to conclude, the State argues, that the second search of Ybarra was constitutionally justified. The argument is that the patdown yielded probable cause to believe that Ybarra was carrying narcotics, and that this probable cause constitutionally supported the second search, no warrant being required in light of the exigencies of the situation coupled with the ease with which Ybarra could have disposed of the illegal substance.

We are unable to take even the first step required by this argument. The initial frisk of Ybarra was simply not supported by a reasonable belief that he was armed and presently dangerous, a belief which this Court has invariably held must form the predicate to a patdown of a person for weapons. . . . [T]he State is unable to articulate any specific fact that would have justified a police officer at the scene in even suspecting that Ybarra was armed and dangerous.

The Terry case created an exception to the requirement of probable cause, an exception whose "narrow scope" this Court "has been careful to maintain."[6] . . . Nothing in Terry can be understood to allow a generalized "cursory search for weapons" or, indeed, any search whatever for anything but weapons. . . .

What has been said largely disposes of the State's second and alternative argument in this case. Emphasizing the important governmental interest "in effectively controlling traffic in dangerous, hard drugs" and the ease with which the evidence of narcotics possession may be concealed or moved around from person to person, the State contends that the Terry "reasonable belief or suspicion" standard should be made applicable to aid the evidence-gathering function of the search warrant. More precisely, we are asked to construe the Fourth and Fourteenth Amendments to permit evidence searches of persons who, at the commencement of the search, are on "compact" premises subject to a search warrant, at least where the police have a "reasonable belief" that such persons "are connected with" drug trafficking and "may be concealing or carrying away the contraband."

Over 30 years ago, the Court rejected a similar argument in United States v. Di Re, 332 U.S. 581, 583-587. In that case, a federal investigator had been told by an informant that a transaction in counterfeit gasoline ration coupons was going to occur at a particular place. The investigator went to that location at the appointed time and saw the car of one of the

---

is supported by probable cause to believe that persons who will be in the place at the time of the search will be in possession of illegal drugs.

6. Dunaway v. New York, 442 U.S. 200, 210.

suspected parties to the illegal transaction. The investigator went over to the car and observed a man in the driver's seat, another (Di Re) in the passenger's seat, and the informant in the back. The informant told the investigator that the person in the driver's seat had given him counterfeit coupons. Thereupon, all three men were arrested and searched. Among the arguments unsuccessfully advanced by the Government to support the constitutionality of the search of Di Re was the contention that the investigator could lawfully have searched the car, since he had reasonable cause to believe that it contained contraband, and correspondingly could have searched any occupant of the car because the contraband sought was of the sort "which could easily be concealed on the person."[7] Not deciding whether or not under the Fourth Amendment the car could have been searched, the Court held that it was "not convinced that a person, by mere presence in a suspected car, loses immunities from search of his person to which he would otherwise be entitled."[8]

The *Di Re* case does not, of course, completely control the case at hand. There the Government investigator was proceeding without a search warrant, and here the police possessed a warrant authorizing the search of the Aurora Tap Tavern. Moreover, in *Di Re* the Government conceded that its officers could not search all the persons in a house being searched pursuant to a search warrant. The State makes no such concession in this case. Yet the governing principle in both cases is basically the same, and we follow that principle today. The "long-prevailing" constitutional standard of probable cause embodies " 'the best compromise that has been found for accommodating [the] often opposing interests' in 'safeguard[ing] citizens from rash and unreasonable interferences with privacy' and in 'seek[ing] to give fair leeway for enforcing the law in the community's protection.' "[10]

For these reasons, we conclude that the search of Ybarra and the seizure of what was in his pocket contravened the Fourth and Fourteenth Amendments. Accordingly, the judgment is reversed, and the case is remanded to the Appellate Court of Illinois Second District for further proceedings not inconsistent with this opinion.

It is so ordered.

MR. CHIEF JUSTICE BURGER, with whom MR. JUSTICE BLACKMUN and MR. JUSTICE REHNQUIST join, dissenting. . . .

These officers had validly obtained a warrant to search a named person and a rather small, one-room tavern for narcotics. Upon arrival,

7. 332 U.S., at 586.
8. Id., at 587.
10. Dunaway v. New York, 442 U.S., at 208, quoting Brinegar v. United States, 338 U.S. 160, 176.

they found the room occupied by 12 persons. Were they to ignore these individuals and assume that all were unarmed and uninvolved? Given the setting and the reputation of those who trade in narcotics, it does not go too far to suggest that they might pay for such an easy assumption with their lives. The law does not require that those executing a search warrant must be so foolhardy. That is precisely what Mr. Chief Justice Warren's opinion in *Terry* stands for. Indeed, the *Terry* Court recognized that a balance must be struck between the privacy interest of individuals and the safety of police officers in performing their duty. I would hold that when police execute a search warrant for narcotics in a place of known narcotics activity they may protect themselves by conducting a *Terry* search. They are not required to assume that they will not be harmed by patrons of the kind of establishment shown here, something quite different from a ballroom at the Waldorf. . . .

. . . In the "second search," the officer did no more than return to the appellant and retrieve the pack he had already discovered. That there was a delay of minutes between the search and the seizure is not dispositive in this context, where the searching officer made the on-the-spot judgment that he need not seize the suspicious package immediately. He could first reasonably make sure that none of the patrons was armed before returning to appellant. Thus I would treat the second search and its fruits just as I would had the officer taken the pack immediately upon noticing it, which plainly would have been permissible. . . .

[The dissenting opinion of JUSTICE REHNQUIST is omitted.]

NOTES AND QUESTIONS

1. Who has the better of the argument whether *Terry* justified the initial frisk? Consider Comment, 66 Iowa L. Rev. 453, 460-462 (1981):

> It is unclear whether the majority in *Ybarra* rejected the proposition that the *Terry* standard may be satisfied with respect to an individual merely by the latter's presence in a group or at a particular location. If the majority does reject that proposition, that aspect of the case conflicts with *Terry*. An underlying principle in *Terry* was that police officers should not be expected to take unnecessary risks in the performance of their duties. Consequently, they should be allowed to conduct a weapons search when they legitimately encounter persons who may pose a genuine armed threat to their safety. As long as the police officers are justified in forcing an encounter the important factor is whether the individuals are armed and dangerous, not their location or associations. Police officers may find themselves in situations in which there is a threat to their safety arising

from either the composition of a group[52] or the characteristics of a location,[53] either of which is not dispelled prior to a weapons search.

The position of the dissents in *Ybarra*, that persons can pose an armed threat to the safety to officers executing a search warrant solely because of their presence in a group or at a particular location seems to be consistent with the rationale of *Terry*. The dissenters' conclusion that the presence of Ybarra in the tavern posed a genuine armed threat to the safety of the enforcing officers cannot be supported, however. . . .

First, . . . [t]he bartender, Greg, was from all appearances a small time operator working out of a public tavern. The purchase of a small quantity of heroin from a bartender in a public tavern is less likely to be accompanied by the presence of weapons than would a major drug deal or the sale of a small quantity of heroin at night in a high crime district. The dissents in *Ybarra* cite no empirical authority to support the proposition that nonsubjects present in a public establishment during the execution of a search warrant for heroin are likely to be armed.

Second, . . . [n]othing in the Complaint for Search Warrant indicated that Greg was known to be armed, that the patrons of the tavern were frequently armed, or that the patrons had violent or hostile feelings toward any police present in the tavern in the past. Given these factors and the type of narcotics involved, a reasonably prudent policeman would not have been justified in believing that the patrons of the tavern were armed and dangerous.

That these officers did not fear for their safety is clear from their actions. After announcing their intention to execute the warrant and conduct a cursory search for weapons, only one officer conducted the weapons frisk of the patrons while the others fanned out to search the tavern. If the officers had been immediately concerned about their safety some of the remaining six or seven officers would have watched the patrons to guard against the possibility of sudden attack while Officer Johnson conducted the weapons searches.

2. If, as the *Ybarra* majority holds, probable cause is required for a search for evidence and if there is not individualized, articulable suspicion to frisk for weapons, what, if anything, can the police do to or with persons who happen to be present at the scene of a search? Could the police in *Ybarra* have ordered the patrons to leave the tavern or to get up from their tables and stand against a wall? Should the answer depend on the number of patrons or officers present? Should the authority

---

52. The classic example of a situation in which members of a group may pose a threat to the safety of the officers is when a lone officer on street patrol notices an individual who he has probable cause to arrest for a violent crime and who is accompanied by two other individuals. . . .

53. A possible example of a situation in which persons present at a particular location may pose a threat to officers would be when police encounter persons at the apartment of a known armed robber during the execution of a search warrant. . . .

to detain persons not mentioned in a warrant be greater with respect to persons who are owners of or have some other interest in the searched premises?

MICHIGAN v. SUMMERS
Certiorari to the Supreme Court of Michigan
452 U.S. 692 (1981)

JUSTICE STEVENS delivered the opinion of the Court.

As Detroit police officers were about to execute a warrant to search a house for narcotics, they encountered respondent descending the front steps. They requested his assistance in gaining entry and detained him while they searched the premises. After finding narcotics in the basement and ascertaining that respondent owned the house, the police arrested him, searched his person, and found in his coat pocket an envelope containing 8.5 grams of heroin.

Respondent was charged with possession of the heroin found on his person. He moved to suppress the heroin as the product of an illegal search in violation of the Fourth Amendment, and the trial judge granted the motion and quashed the information. That order was affirmed by . . . the Michigan Supreme Court. . . . We granted the State's petition for certiorari . . . and now reverse. . . .

The dispositive question in this case is whether the initial detention of respondent violated his constitutional right to be secure against an unreasonable seizure of his person. . . . If that detention was permissible, there is no need to reach the question whether a search warrant for premises includes the right to search persons found there, because when the police searched respondent, they had probable cause to arrest him and had done so. Our appraisal of the validity of the search of respondent's person therefore depends upon a determination whether the officers had the authority to require him to re-enter the house and to remain there while they conducted their search.[4] . . .

. . . [S]ome seizures admittedly covered by the Fourth Amendment

---

4. The "seizure" issue in this case should not be confused with the "search" issue presented in Ybarra v. Illinois, 444 U.S. 85. In *Ybarra* the police executing a search warrant for a public tavern detained and searched all of the customers who happened to be present. No question concerning the legitimacy of the detention was raised. Rather, the Court concluded that the search of Ybarra was invalid because the police had no reason to believe he had any special connection with the premises, and the police had no other basis for suspecting that he was armed or in possession of contraband. See id., at 90-93. In this case, only the detention is at issue. The police knew respondent lived in the house, and they did not search him until after they had probable cause to arrest and had done so.

constitute such limited intrusions on the personal security of those detained and are justified by such substantial law enforcement interests that they may be made on less than probable cause, so long as police have an articulable basis for suspecting criminal activity. [E.g., Terry v. Ohio, page 684 supra; United States v. Brignoni-Ponce, page 759 supra (roving border patrol agents may stop automobile and question occupants if there is articulable suspicion to believe they may be illegal aliens).] In these cases . . . the Court was applying the ultimate standard of reasonableness embodied in the Fourth Amendment. They are consistent with the general rule that every arrest, and every seizure having the essential attributes of a formal arrest, is unreasonable unless it is supported by probable cause. But they demonstrate that the exception for limited intrusions that may be justified by special law enforcement interests is not confined to the momentary, on-the-street detention accompanied by a frisk for weapons involved in *Terry*. . . . Therefore, in order to decide whether this case is controlled by the general rule, it is necessary to examine both the character of the official intrusion and its justification. . . .

Of prime importance in assessing the intrusion is the fact that the police had obtained a warrant to search respondent's house for contraband. . . . The detention of one of the residents while the premises were searched, although admittedly a significant restraint on his liberty, was surely less intrusive than the search itself. Indeed, we may safely assume that most citizens—unless they intend flight to avoid arrest— would elect to remain in order to observe the search of their possessions. Furthermore, the type of detention imposed here is not likely to be exploited by the officer or unduly prolonged in order to gain more information, because the information the officers seek normally will be obtained through the search and not through the detention. Moreover, because the detention in this case was in respondent's own residence, it could add only minimally to the public stigma associated with the search itself and would involve neither the inconvenience nor the indignity associated with a compelled visit to the police station. . . .

In assessing the justification for the detention of an occupant of premises being searched for contraband pursuant to a valid warrant, both the law enforcement interest and the nature of the "articulable facts" supporting the detention are relevant. Most obvious is the legitimate law enforcement interest in preventing flight in the event that incriminating evidence is found. Less obvious, but sometimes of greater importance, is the interest in minimizing the risk of harm to the officers. Although no special danger to the police is suggested by the evidence in this record, the execution of a warrant to search for narcotics is the kind of transaction that may give rise to sudden violence or frantic efforts to conceal or destroy evidence.[17] The risk of harm to both the police and the occupants is minimized if the officers routinely exercise unquestioned command of the situation. . . . Finally, the orderly completion of the search may be facilitated if the occupants of the premises are present. Their self-interest may induce them to open locked doors or locked containers to avoid the use of force that is not only damaging to property but may also delay the completion of the task at hand.

It is also appropriate to consider the nature of the articulable and individualized suspicion on which the police base the detention of the occupant of a home subject to a search warrant. We have already noted that the detention represents only an incremental intrusion on personal liberty when the search of a home has been authorized by a valid warrant. The existence of a search warrant, however, also provides an objective justification for the detention. A judicial officer had determined that police have probable cause to believe that someone in the home is committing a crime. Thus a neutral magistrate rather than an officer in the field has made the critical determination that the police should be given a special authorization to thrust themselves into the privacy of a home. The connection of an occupant to that home gives the police officer an easily identifiable and certain basis for determining that suspicion of criminal activity justifies a detention of that occupant.

In Payton v. New York, 445 U.S. 573, we held that police officers may not enter a private residence to make a routine felony arrest without first obtaining a warrant. In that case we rejected the suggestion that only a search warrant could adequately protect the privacy interests at stake, noting that the distinction between a search warrant and an arrest warrant was far less significant than the interposition of the magistrate's determination of probable cause between the zealous officer and the citizen. . . . That holding is relevant today. If the evidence that a citizen's residence is harboring contraband is sufficient to persuade a judicial officer that an invasion of the citizen's privacy is justified, it is constitutionally reasonable to require that citizen to remain while officers of the law execute a valid warrant to search his home.[19] Thus, for Fourth

___

17. The fact that our holding today deals with a case in which the police had a warrant does not, of course, preclude the possibility that comparable police conduct may be justified by exigent circumstances in the absence of a warrant. No such question, however, is presented by this case.

19. In refusing to approve seizures based on less than probable cause, . . . [Dunaway v. New York, page 699 supra,] declined to adopt a "multifactor balancing test of 'reasonable police conduct under the circumstances' to cover all seizures that do not amount to technical arrests." . . .

As Justice White noted in his concurrence in Dunaway, if police are to have workable rules, the balancing of the competing interests inherent in the Terry principle "must in

Amendment purposes, we hold that a warrant to search for contraband[20] founded on probable cause implicitly carries with it the limited authority to detain the occupants of the premises while a proper search is conducted.[21]

Because it was lawful to require respondent to re-enter and to remain in the house until evidence establishing probable cause to arrest him was found, his arrest and the search incident thereto were constitutionally permissible. The judgment of the Supreme Court of Michigan must therefore be reversed.

It is so ordered.

JUSTICE STEWART, with whom JUSTICE BRENNAN and JUSTICE MARSHALL join, dissenting.

The Court is correct in stating that "some seizures significantly less intrusive than an arrest have withstood scrutiny under the reasonableness standard embodied in the Fourth Amendment." . . . But to escalate this statement into some kind of a general rule is to ignore the protections that the Fourth Amendment guarantees to us all. There are only two types of seizures that need not be based on probable cause. The first, represented by the *Terry* line of cases, is a limited stop to question a person and to perform a patdown for weapons when the police have reason to believe that he is armed and dangerous. E.g., Terry v. Ohio, 392 U.S. 1, 23-24. The second is a brief stop of vehicles near our international borders to question occupants of the vehicles about their citizenship. E.g., United States v. Brignoni-Ponce, 422 U.S. 873, 881.

From these two special exceptions to the general prohibition on seizures not based on probable cause, the Court leaps to the very broad idea that courts may approve a wide variety of seizures not based on probable cause, so long as the courts find, after balancing the law enforcement purposes of the police conduct against the severity of their intrusion, that the seizure appears "reasonable."

---

large part be done on a categorical basis—not in an ad hoc, case-by-case fashion by individual police officers." 442 U.S., at 219-220. The rule we adopt today does not depend upon such an ad hoc determination, because the officer is not required to evaluate either the quantum of proof justifying detention or the extent of the intrusion to be imposed by the seizure.

20. We do not decide whether the same result would be justified if the search warrant merely authorized a search for evidence. Cf. Zurcher v. Stanford Daily, 436 U.S. 547, 560. See also id., at 581 (Stevens, J., dissenting).

21. Although special circumstances, or possibly a prolonged detention, might lead to a different conclusion in an unusual case, we are persuaded that this routine detention of residents of a house while it was being searched for contraband pursuant to a valid warrant is not such a case.

But those two lines of cases do not represent some sort of exemplary balancing test for Fourth Amendment cases. Rather, they represent two isolated exceptions to the general rule that the Fourth Amendment itself has already performed the constitutional balance between police objectives and personal privacy. . . .

The common denominator to the *Terry* cases and the border checkpoint cases is the presence of some governmental interest independent of the ordinary interest in investigating crime and apprehending suspects, an interest important enough to overcome the presumptive constitutional restraints on police conduct. . . .

Though the officer in *Terry* was engaged in investigating crime, the governmental purpose that justified the stop and patdown was not the investigation itself, but "the neutralization of danger to the policeman in the investigative circumstance." [Terry v. Ohio, 392 U.S.] at 26. . . .

In United States v. Brignoni-Ponce, supra, the Court approved a limited stop of vehicles by patrols of immigration officers near the Mexican border, but in doing so it stressed the unique governmental interest in preventing the illegal entry of aliens. . . .

It seems clear, therefore, that before a court can uphold a detention on less than probable cause on the ground that it is "reasonable" in the light of the competing interests, the government must demonstrate an important purpose beyond the normal goals of criminal investigation, or must demonstrate an extraordinary obstacle to such investigation. . . .

What the Court approves today is justified by no such special governmental interest or law enforcement need. There were only two governmental purposes supporting the detention of the respondent.[1] One was "the legitimate law enforcement interest in preventing flight in the event that incriminating evidence is found." . . . The other was that "the orderly completion of the search may be facilitated if the occupants of the premises are present." . . . Unlike the law enforcement objectives that justified the police conduct in *Terry* and the border stop cases, these objectives represented nothing more than the ordinary police interest in discovering evidence of crime and apprehending wrongdoers. . . .

Beyond the issue of the governmental interest justifying the detention, I question the Court's view that the detention here is of the limited,

---

1. As the Court acknowledges, . . . the record in this case presents no evidence whatsoever that the police feared any threat to their safety or that of others from the conduct of the respondent, or that they could reasonably have so feared. The Court says that this nevertheless was the "kind of transaction that may give rise to sudden violence. . . ." . . . But where the police cannot demonstrate, on the basis of specific and articulable facts, a reasonable belief that a person threatens physical harm to them or others, the speculation that other persons in that circumstance might pose such a threat cannot justify a search or seizure. Ybarra v. Illinois, 444 U.S. 85, 92-93.

unintrusive sort that permits the Court to engage in a "reasonableness" balancing test. . . .[3]

NOTES AND QUESTIONS

1. If, as the dissenters argue, it was impermissible to detain Summers, what could the police have done to ensure that Summers would not in some way interfere with the search? Should it be sufficient (and permissible) to give someone in Summers' position the option of leaving the premises altogether or being detained?

2. To what extent does *Summers* undermine *Ybarra*? If it is appropriate to search a person's premises and to detain the person, is it arguably appropriate to regard the frisk of the person as only a minor additional invasion of privacy? Consider also the materials on searches incident to arrest, pages 721-747 supra. The length of time that a person is detained during the search of premises may exceed the time that it takes to transport an arrestee to the police station. If a full-scale search of an arrestee is legitimate to protect the officer, why is a frisk not appropriate in the *Ybarra-Summers* context?

3. Reconsider Dunaway v. New York, page 699 supra. Is *Summers* consistent with *Dunaway*, as the majority suggests, because both *Summers* and *Dunaway* "declined to adopt a 'multifactor balancing test' "? See footnote 19 supra. Or is *Summers* inconsistent with *Dunaway* because *Summers*, unlike *Dunaway*, appears to adopt a general balancing approach to the question of reasonableness?

4. Prior to *Summers* there were a few limited, discrete types of situations in which a search or seizure would be regarded as reasonable despite the absence of individualized probable cause. Justice Stewart asserted in his *Summers* dissent there were only two contexts in which the Supreme Court had approved of *seizures* of a person on less than probable cause—*Terry* stops and stops of individuals at or near international borders. In fact, there was a third context, albeit similar in rationale to border stops: the stop of a motorist to check for driver's license and registration papers. Delaware v. Prouse, 440 U.S. 648 (1979). In addition, the Court had approved of at least four types of *searches* on less than individualized probable cause: *Camara*-type regulatory inspections, pages 666-684 supra; frisks accompanying brief stops, pages 684-720 supra;

---

3. The record does not clearly reveal the length of the search in this case. In Harris v. United States, 331 U.S. 145, a Federal Bureau of Investigation search of a one-bedroom apartment for burglar tools and a pair of checks consumed five hours. See also Stanford v. Texas, 379 U.S. 476, 477.

searches incident to arrest, pages 721-747 supra; and inventory searches, pages 747-755 supra.[93]

In *Summers* and in some subsequent cases various justices have taken the position—sometimes successfully and sometimes in dissent— that the Court should take a balancing approach to evaluating the reasonableness of a search or seizure that did not fit within one of the previously established "exceptions" to the probable cause requirement. It is not surprising that as the Court has addressed the applicability of the fourth amendment to new situations that there would be some additional exceptions to the probable cause requirement; and it is also not surprising that the justices might disagree about the propriety of using a balancing test in a particular context. That, after all, is what happened in *Camara* and *Terry*. To some extent, however, disagreement among the justices in recent years about the propriety of using a balancing test is, at least at a rhetorical level, more fundamental. Indeed, *Summers* illustrates this more fundamental difference: Does one start with the premise, as Justice Stewart did, that probable cause defines the appropriate balance except in a few narrowly defined situations? Or does one start with the premise, as Justice Stevens did, that at least if the intrusion is relatively minor, it is appropriate to evaluate the reasonableness of the activity in terms of a *Camara-Terry* type balancing test?

If one starts with Justice Stewart's premise, what criteria does one use in deciding whether there should be a new exception to the probable cause requirement? If one does not begin with Justice Stewart's premise, is it appropriate to apply a *Camara-Terry* balancing test to determine reasonableness in every situation for which there is not preexisting precedent requiring probable cause? If not, what factors other than limited nature of the intrusion may justify a search or seizure on less than probable cause? Since ultimately it would seem that responsible fourth amendment analysis would require considering both the seriousness of the invasion of privacy and the needs of law enforcement, does it matter whether one accepts or rejects Justice Stewart's premise? Consider these questions as you examine the materials in the remainder of this section.

f. Protective Sweeps and Other "Minor" Intrusions

MARYLAND v. BUIE, 110 S. Ct. 1093, 1095-1096, 1098-1101 (1990): JUSTICE WHITE delivered the opinion of the Court.

On February 3, 1986, two men committed an armed robbery of a

---

93. *Lafayette* and *Bertine* were decided after *Summers*, but *Opperman*, the Court's first inventory case, was decided prior to *Summers*.

Godfather's Pizza restaurant in Prince George's County, Maryland. One of the robbers was wearing a red running suit. . . .

On February 5, the police executed [an] arrest warrant for Buie. They first had a police department secretary telephone Buie's house to verify that he was home. The secretary spoke to a female first, then to Buie himself. Six or seven officers proceeded to Buie's house. Once inside, the officers fanned out through the first and second floors. Corporal James Rozar announced that he would "freeze" the basement so that no one could come up and surprise the officers. With his service revolver drawn, Rozar twice shouted into the basement, ordering anyone down there to come out. . . . Buie emerged from the basement. He was arrested. . . . Thereafter, Detective Joseph Frolich entered the basement "in case there was someone else" down there. . . . He noticed a red running suit lying in plain view on a stack of clothing and seized it.

The trial court denied Buie's motion to suppress the running suit. . . .

The Court of Appeals of Maryland reversed. . . .

It is not disputed that until the point of Buie's arrest the police had the right, based on the authority of the arrest warrant, to search anywhere in the house that Buie might have been found, including the basement. . . . The issue in this case is what level of justification the Fourth Amendment required before Detective Frolich could legally enter the basement to see if someone else was there. . . .

We agree with the State . . . that a warrant was not required.[1] We also hold that as an incident to the arrest the officers could, as a precautionary matter and without probable cause or reasonable suspicion, look in closets and other spaces immediately adjoining the place of arrest from which an attack could be immediately launched. Beyond that, however, we hold that there must be articulable facts which, taken together with the rational inferences from those facts, would warrant a reasonably prudent officer in believing that the area to be swept harbors an individual posing a danger to those on the arrest scene. This is no more and no less than was required in Terry [v. Ohio, page 684 supra] and [Michigan v.] Long, [page 712 supra,] and as in those cases, we think this balance is the proper one.[2]

---

1. Buie suggests that because the police could have sought a warrant to search for dangerous persons in the house, they were constitutionally required to do so. But the arrest warrant gave the police every right to enter the home to search for Buie. Once inside, the potential for danger justified a standard of less than probable cause for conducting a limited protective sweep.

2. The State's argument that no level of objective justification should be required because of "the danger that inheres in the in-home arrest for a violent crime," Brief for Petitioner 23, is rebutted by Terry v. Ohio, 392 U.S. 1 (1968), itself. . . . [D]espite the danger that inheres in on-the-street encounters and the need for police to act quickly for

We should emphasize that such a protective sweep, aimed at protecting the arresting officers, if justified by the circumstances, is nevertheless not a full search of the premises, but may extend only to a cursory inspection of those spaces where a person may be found.[3] . . .

. . . We . . . vacate the judgment below and remand this case . . . for further proceedings not inconsistent with this opinion. . . .

JUSTICE STEVENS, concurring. . . .

. . . [I]t is the state's burden to demonstrate that the officers had a reasonable basis for believing not only that someone in the basement might attack them or otherwise try to interfere with the arrest, but also that it would be safer to go down the stairs instead of simply guarding them from above until respondent had been removed from the house. The fact that respondent offered no resistance when he emerged from the basement is somewhat inconsistent with the hypothesis that the danger of an attack by a hidden confederate persisted after the arrest. Moreover, Officer Rozar testified that he was not worried about any possible danger when he arrested Buie. . . . Officer Frolich, who conducted the search, supplied no explanation for why he might have thought another person was in the basement. . . .

Indeed, were the officers concerned about safety, one would expect

---

their own safety, the Court in *Terry* did not adopt a bright-line rule authorizing frisks for weapons in all confrontational encounters. Even in high crime areas, where the possibility that any given individual is armed is significant, *Terry* requires reasonable, individualized suspicion before a frisk for weapons can be conducted. . . .

We reject the State's attempts to analogize this case to Pennsylvania v. Mimms, 434 U.S. 106 (1977) (per curiam), and Michigan v. Summers, 452 U.S. 692 (1981). The intrusion in *Mimms*—requiring the driver of a lawfully stopped vehicle to exit the car— was "de minimus," 434 U.S., at 111. *Summers* held that a search warrant for a house carries with it the authority to detain its occupants until the search is completed. The State contends that this case is the "mirror image" of *Summers* and that the arrest warrant carried with it the authority to search for persons who could interfere with the arrest. In that case, however, the search warrant implied a judicial determination that police had probable cause to believe that someone in the home was committing a crime. Here, the existence of the arrest warrant implies nothing about whether dangerous third parties will be found in the arrestee's house. Moreover, the intrusion in *Summers* was less severe and much less susceptible to exploitation than a protective sweep. A more analogous case is Ybarra v. Illinois, 444 U.S. 85 (1979), in which we held that, although armed with a warrant to search a bar and bartender, the police could not frisk the bar's patrons absent individualized, reasonable suspicion that the person to be frisked was armed and presently dangerous. . . .

3. Our reliance on the cursory nature of the search is not inconsistent with our statement in Arizona v. Hicks, 480 U.S. 321 (1987), that "[a] search is a search," id., at 325, or with our refusal in *Hicks* to sanction a standard less than probable cause on the ground that the search of the stereo was a "cursory inspection," rather than a "full-blown search," id., at 328. When the officer in *Hicks* moved the turntable to look at its serial number, he was searching for evidence plain and simple. There was no interest in officer safety or other exigency at work in that search. . . .

them to do what Officer Rozar did before the arrest: guard the basement door to prevent surprise attacks. . . .

The State may thus face a formidable task on remand. . . .

JUSTICE KENNEDY concurring.

The Court adopts the prudent course of explaining the general rule and permitting the state court to apply it in the first instance. The concurrence by Justice Stevens, however, makes the gratuitous observation that the State has a formidable task on remand. My view is quite to the contrary. Based on my present understanding of the record, I should think the officers' conduct here was in full accord with standard police safety procedure, and that the officers would have been remiss if they had not taken these precautions. This comment is necessary, lest by acquiescence the impression be left that Justice Stevens' views can be interpreted as authoritative guidance for application of our ruling to the facts of this case.

[The dissenting opinion of JUSTICE BRENNAN is omitted.]

NOTES AND QUESTIONS

1. The only requirement for a protective sweep that the *Buie* majority specifically articulates is satisfaction of the articulable suspicion standard. Is Justice Stevens's assertion that the state must prove "that it would be safer to go down the stairs instead of simply guarding them from above" implicit in the fact that the underlying rationale for the sweep is to protect the arresting officers?

Even if the state does not have to prove that it would be safer to make the protective sweep, is the state's task on remand likely to be an easy one? What facts—and we have not deleted any from the opinions— along with the rational inferences from those facts would lead a reasonably prudent officer to believe that the basement "harbors an individual posing a danger to those on the arrest scene"?

2. Consider Justice Kennedy's response to Justice Stevens. Justice Kennedy does not elaborate on his "understanding of the record," but in light of the facts that we know from the majority opinion and from Justice Stevens's opinion, Justice Stevens's assessment does not seem unreasonable. Perhaps Justice Kennedy's disagreement with Justice Stevens is based less on an assessment the extent to which the facts and inferences support a belief that there may have been a potentially dangerous third person in the basement than on the general reasonableness of the protective sweep. If so, and if Justice Kennedy's view ultimately prevails, the articulable suspicion test for protective sweeps will become

in practice less fact-specific and individualized than the articulable suspicion test for stops and frisk. If the law does or should develop in this manner, it perhaps would have been wise for the *Buie* Court to adopt the state's argument that a protective sweep is reasonable even in the absence of articulable suspicion.

3. Justice Kennedy's opinion implies that, in light of the decision to remand the case so the state court could apply the articulable suspicion test to the facts in *Buie*, it was inappropriate for Justice Stevens to offer his views on that question. Do you agree? Why is it not appropriate—indeed, desirable—for the justices to try to give content to the inherently vague articulable suspicion test by offering as much guidance as possible about how to apply it in particular situations?

4. Assume that the police, when they approached the Buie residence, knew that only Buie and his wife were present. Assume further that the police found both Mr. and Mrs. Buie in the living room. Should the police, following Buie's arrest, be permitted to make either a thorough search or a cursory sweep of the house in order to find the red running suit or other evidence?

NEW YORK v. CLASS
Certiorari to the New York Court of Appeals
475 U.S. 106 (1986)

JUSTICE O'CONNOR delivered the opinion of the Court. . . .

On the afternoon of May 11, 1981, New York City police officers Lawrence Meyer and William McNamee observed respondent Benigno Class driving above the speed limit in a car with a cracked windshield. Both driving with the cracked windshield and speeding are traffic violations under New York law. . . . Respondent followed the officers' ensuing directive to pull over. Respondent then emerged from his car and approached Officer Meyer. Officer McNamee went directly to respondent's vehicle. Respondent provided Officer Meyer with a registration certificate and proof of insurance, but stated that he had no driver's license.

Meanwhile, Officer McNamee opened the door of respondent's car to look for the VIN [Vehicle Identification Number], which is located on the left door jamb in automobiles manufactured before 1969. When the officer did not find the VIN on the door jamb, he reached into the interior of respondent's car to move some papers obscuring the area of the dashboard where the VIN is located in all post-1969 models. In doing so, Officer McNamee saw the handle of a gun protruding about one inch from underneath the driver's seat. The officer seized the gun, and respondent was promptly arrested. Respondent was also issued summonses for his traffic violations. It is undisputed that the police officers had no reason to suspect that respondent's car was stolen, that it contained contraband, or that respondent had committed an offense other than the traffic violations. Nor is it disputed that respondent committed the traffic violations with which he was charged, and that, as of the day of the arrest, he had not been issued a valid driver's license.

After the state trial court denied a motion to suppress the gun as evidence, respondent was convicted of criminal possession of a weapon in the third degree. . . . The New York Court of Appeals reversed. . . .

We granted certiorari . . . and now reverse. . . .

The VIN consists of more than a dozen digits, unique to each vehicle and required on all cars and trucks. . . .

The VIN is a significant thread in the web of regulation of the automobile. . . . The ease with which the VIN allows identification of a particular vehicle assists the various levels of government in many ways. For the Federal Government, the VIN improves the efficacy of recall campaigns, and assists researchers in determining the risks of driving various makes and models of automobiles. In combination with state insurance laws, the VIN reduces the number of those injured in accidents who go uncompensated for lack of insurance. In conjunction with the State's registration requirements and safety inspections, the VIN helps to ensure that automobile operators are driving safe vehicles. By making auto theft more difficult, the VIN safeguards not only property but life and limb. See 33 Fed. Reg. 10207 (1968) (noting that stolen vehicles are disproportionately likely to be involved in automobile accidents).

To facilitate the VIN's usefulness for these laudable governmental purposes, federal law requires that the VIN be placed in the plain view of someone *outside* the automobile. . . . In light of the important interests served by the VIN, the Federal and State Governments are amply justified in making it a part of the web of pervasive regulation that surrounds the automobile, and in requiring its placement in an area ordinarily in plain view from outside the passenger compartment. . . .

[After noting that individuals have diminished privacy interests in automobiles, that the VIN, by virtue of its location is similar to the exterior of an automobile, and that individuals have no legitimate privacy interest in the exterior of their automobiles, and after reiterating that the VIN plays an important role in the government regulation of automobiles, the Court held that automobile owners do not have a legitimate privacy interest in their VINS. The Court further held that one cannot create such an interest by covering up or hiding the VIN.] The evidence that respondent sought to have suppressed was not the VIN, however, but a gun, the handle of which the officer saw from the interior of the car while reaching for the papers that covered the VIN. While the interior of an automobile is not subject to the same expectations of privacy that exist with respect to one's home, a car's interior as a whole is nonetheless subject to Fourth Amendment protection from unreasonable intrusions by the police. . . .

If respondent had remained in the car, the police would have been justified in asking him to move the papers obscuring the VIN. New York law authorizes a demand by officers to see the VIN, . . . and even if the state law were not explicit on this point we have no difficulty in concluding that a demand to inspect the VIN, like a demand to see license and registration papers, is within the scope of police authority pursuant to a traffic violation stop. . . .

Keeping the driver of a vehicle in the car during a routine traffic stop is probably the typical police practice. . . . Nonetheless, out of a concern for the safety of the police, the Court has held that officers may, consistent with the Fourth Amendment, exercise their discretion to require a driver who commits a traffic violation to exit the vehicle even though they lack any particularized reason for believing the driver possesses a weapon. Pennsylvania v. Mimms, 434 U.S. 106, 108-111 (1977) (per curiam). . . .

. . . The pistol beneath the seat did not, of course, disappear when respondent closed the car door behind him. To have returned respondent immediately to the automobile would have placed the officers in the same situation that the holding in Mimms allows officers to avoid—permitting an individual being detained to have possible access to a dangerous weapon and the benefit of the partial concealment provided by the car's exterior. . . . In light of the danger to the officers' safety that would have been presented by returning respondent immediately to his car, we think the search to obtain the VIN was not prohibited by the Fourth Amendment.

The Fourth Amendment by its terms prohibits "unreasonable" searches and seizures. We have noted that

> there is "no ready test for determining reasonableness other than by balancing the need to search [or seize] against the invasion which the search [or seizure] entails." Camara v. Municipal Court, 387 U.S. 523, 534-535, 536-537 (1967). And in justifying the particular intrusion the police officer must be able to point to specific and articulable facts which, taken together with rational inferences from those facts, justifiably warrant that intrusion. [Terry v. Ohio, 392 U.S. 1, 21 (1968) (footnote omitted) (brackets as in Terry).]

This test generally means that searches must be conducted pursuant to a warrant backed by probable cause. . . . When a search or seizure has as its immediate object a search for a weapon, however, we have struck the balance to allow the weighty interest in the safety of the police officers to justify warrantless searches based only on a reasonable suspicion of criminal activity. See Terry v. Ohio, supra; Adams v. Williams, 407 U.S. 143 (1972). Such searches are permissible despite their substantial intrusiveness. . . .

When the officer's safety is less directly served by the detention, something more than objectively justifiable suspicion is necessary to justify the intrusion if the balance is to tip in favor of the legality of the governmental intrusion. In Pennsylvania v. Mimms, . . . 434 U.S. [106,] 107 [(1977) (per curiam)], the officers had personally observed the seized individual in the commission of a traffic offense before requesting that he exit his vehicle. In Michigan v. Summers, 452 U.S. 692, 693 (1981), the officers had obtained a warrant to search the house that the person seized was leaving when they came upon him. While the facts in Pennsylvania v. Mimms and Michigan v. Summers differ in some respects from the facts of this case, the similarities are strong enough that the balancing of governmental interests against governmental intrusion undertaken in those cases is also appropriate here. All three of the factors involved in *Mimms* and *Summers* are present in this case: the safety of the officers was served by the governmental intrusion; the intrusion was minimal; and the search stemmed from some probable cause focusing suspicion on the individual affected by the search. Indeed, here the officer's probable cause stemmed from directly observing respondent commit a violation of the law.

When we undertake the necessary balancing of "the nature and quality of the intrusion on the individual's Fourth Amendment interests against the importance of the governmental interests alleged to justify the intrusion," United States v. Place, 462 U.S. 696, 703 (1983), the conclusion that the search here was permissible follows. As we recognized in Delaware v. Prouse, 440 U.S. [648], 658 [(1979)], the governmental interest in highway safety served by obtaining the VIN is of the first order, and the particular method of obtaining the VIN here was justified by a concern for the officer's safety. The "critical" issue of the intrusiveness of the government's action, United States v. Place, supra, 462 U.S. at 722 (Blackmun, J., concurring in judgment), also here weighs in favor of allowing the search. The search was focused in its objective and no more intrusive than necessary to fulfill that objective. The search was far less intrusive than a formal arrest, which would have been permissible for a traffic offense under New York law, . . . and little more intrusive than a demand that the respondent—under the eyes of officers—move the papers himself. . . .

We note that our holding today does not authorize police officers to enter a vehicle to obtain a dashboard-mounted VIN when the VIN is visible from outside the automobile. If the VIN is in the plain view of someone outside the vehicle, there is no justification for governmental intrusion into the passenger compartment to see it.^{°°}

The judgment of the New York Court of Appeals is reversed, and the case is remanded for further proceedings not inconsistent with this opinion.

It is so ordered.

JUSTICE POWELL, with whom CHIEF JUSTICE BURGER joins, concurring.

I join in the Court's opinion but write to emphasize that, because of the unique and important governmental interests served by inspection of the Vehicle Identification Number (VIN), an officer making a lawful stop of a vehicle has the right and duty to inspect the VIN. . . .

The Court has answered correctly the question presented in this case by applying conventional Fourth Amendment analysis. I believe, however, that an officer's efforts to observe the VIN need not be subjected to the same scrutiny that courts properly apply when police have intruded into a vehicle to arrest or to search for evidence of a crime. . . .

In my view, the Fourth Amendment question may be stated simply as whether the officer's efforts to inspect the VIN were reasonable.

JUSTICE BRENNAN, with whom JUSTICE MARSHALL and JUSTICE STEVENS join, dissenting. . . .

The Court says much about the "important role played by the VIN in the pervasive governmental regulation of the automobile," and holds that respondent had no "reasonable expectation of privacy in the VIN." . . . This aspect of the Court's analysis is particularly baffling. Of course, the VIN plays a significant part in federal and state schemes for regulating automobiles. . . . However, even assuming that respondent had no reasonable expectation of privacy in the VIN, why is this relevant to the

---

^{°°}Petitioner invites us to hold that respondent's status as an unlicensed driver deprived him of any reasonable expectations of privacy in the vehicle, because the officers would have been within their discretion to have prohibited respondent from driving the car away, to have impounded the car, and to have later conducted an inventory search thereof. Cf. South Dakota v. Opperman, 428 U.S. 364 (1976) (police may conduct inventory search of car impounded for multiple parking violations); Nix v. Williams, 467 U.S. 431 (1984) (discussing the "inevitable discovery" exception to the exclusionary rule). Petitioner also argues that there can be no Fourth Amendment violation here because the police could have arrested respondent, . . . and could then have searched the passenger compartment at the time of arrest, cf. New York v. Belton, 453 U.S. 454 (1981), or arrested respondent and searched the car after impounding it pursuant to the arrest, see Cady v. Dombrowski, 413 U.S. 433 (1973). We do not, however, reach those questions here.

question we decide? Officer McNamee did not look for the VIN from outside of respondent's vehicle, but searched the car without respondent's consent in order to locate the VIN. By focusing on the object of the search—the VIN—the Court misses the issue we must decide: whether an interior search of the car to discover that object was constitutional. Regardless of whether he had a reasonable expectation of privacy in the VIN, respondent clearly retained a reasonable expectation of privacy with respect to the area searched by the police—the car's interior. As the court below noted, "[t]he fact that certain information must be kept, or that it may be of a public nature, does not automatically sanction police intrusion into private space in order to obtain it." 63 N.Y.2d 491, 495, 483 N.Y.S.2d 181, 183, 472 N.E.2d 1009, 1011 (1984); cf. id., at 496-497, 483 N.Y.S.2d, at 184-185, 472 N.E.2d, at 1012-1013 (noting that state law only requires drivers to furnish police with vehicle identification). . . .

Because vehicles are mobile and subject to pervasive government regulation, an individual's justifiable expectation of privacy in a vehicle is less than in his home. California v. Carney, [471 U.S. 386 (1985)]. This is why the Court has held that warrantless searches of cars may sometimes not violate the Fourth Amendment, but only if the searches are supported by probable cause. . . . In this case, the police clearly lacked probable cause to search for the VIN.

The Court suggests that respondent's traffic infractions provided the requisite probable cause, this on the ground that there was "probable cause focusing suspicion on the individual affected by the search." . . . This analysis makes a mockery of the Fourth Amendment. There can be no question that respondent's traffic offenses gave the police probable cause to stop the car and to demand some form of vehicle identification. Delaware v. Prouse, supra, 440 U.S. [648,] 663 [(1979)]. Too, this sort of routine traffic stop generally gives police an *opportunity* to inspect the VIN through the car windshield. But Fourth Amendment protections evaporate if this supplies the requisite probable cause to *search* for a VIN not visible from the exterior of the car. Plainly the search of the interior for the VIN was unnecessary since respondent had supplied his car registration certificate, and there is no suggestion that it was inadequate.[1] . . .

The Court supplies not an iota of reasoning to support the holding that respondent's traffic infractions gave the police probable cause to

---

1. Indeed, the facts of this case belie any suggestion that the VIN search was needed positively to identify respondent's vehicle. Officer McNamee did not wait to see respondent's vehicle registration certificate before he started to search respondent's car, and did not record the VIN he found in order to compare it to other identifying document.

search for the VIN. The Court is content simply to conclude that "the governmental interest in highway safety served by obtaining the VIN is of the first order." . . . . Although I agree that the government has a strong interest in promoting highway safety, . . . I fail to see just how the VIN search conducted here advanced that interest. Despite the Court's lengthy exposition on the variety of safety-related purposes served by the VIN, respondent's car was not searched to further any of the identified interests. If the officers intended to identify what they considered to be an "unsafe" vehicle, that could have been done without searching respondent's car. Thus, the mere fact that the state utilizes the VIN in conjunction with regulations designed to promote highway safety does not give the police a reason to *search* for such information every time a motorist violates a traffic law.[3] Absent some reason to search for the VIN, the government's admittedly strong interest in promoting highway safety cannot validate the intrusion resulting from the *search* of respondent's vehicle. . . .

The Court, relying on Pennsylvania v. Mimms . . . and Michigan v. Summers, . . . next attempts to support its holding on the ground that "in light of the danger to the officers' safety [that would be] presented by returning respondent immediately to his car [to uncover the VIN,] the search to obtain the VIN was not prohibited by the Fourth Amendment." . . . Neither cited decision supports this argument.

In *Summers*, police detained the occupant of a home being searched pursuant to a valid warrant. The Court held that this seizure was constitutional because it served several important law enforcement interests, including officer safety, and because the search warrant provided a reasonable basis for the police to determine that the occupant was engaged in criminal activity and should therefore be detained. . . . By contrast, here there was no reason for the officers to search the car to inspect the VIN. The officers knew only that respondent had committed minor traffic violations, and while this may have given them an *opportunity* to inspect the VIN, it did not provide a reason to search the interior of the car for it.

In *Mimms*, police stopped an automobile for a traffic infraction, and ordered the driver to step outside the vehicle. As the driver emerged, the officers noticed a large bulge under his jacket, and after frisking him, discovered a loaded revolver. The Court held that because such actions protected officer safety, the police could legitimately order a driver out of his car when they made a lawful traffic stop. Unlike the situation

3. By analogy, had respondent emerged from his car without his vehicle registration certificate or driver's license, I do not read the Court's opinion to hold that the police could have searched the passenger compartment in order to locate these documents, even though they also play important roles in the State's regulation of automobiles.

in Mimms, the intrusion in this case—the search of respondent's vehicle—did not directly serve officer safety. Nevertheless, the Court finds that "[t]o have returned respondent immediately to the automobile [to clear the papers on the dashboard obscuring the VIN] would have placed the officers in the same situation that the holding in Mimms allows officers to avoid." . . . Again, the Court forgets that the police, with no reason to search the interior, had no reason to return respondent to his car. Thus, the state's interest in protecting officer safety cannot validate the search.

Of course, if the officers had reasonable grounds to suspect that the traffic stop presented a threat to their safety, they would have been authorized to search respondent's vehicle for weapons. See Michigan v. Long, 463 U.S. [1032], 1051 [(1983)]. However, neither officer ever suggested that the situation posed any danger, and the court below specifically found that the facts "reveal no reason for the officer[s] . . . to act to protect [their] own safety." 63 N.Y.2d, at 496, 483 N.Y.S.2d, at 184, 472 N.E.2d, at 1012. . . .

Finally, the Court finds that "the 'critical' issue of the intrusiveness of the government's action . . . also here weighs in favor of allowing the search." . . . The Court's effort to minimize the extent of the intrusion . . . won't wash. Officer McNamee clearly searched respondent's car by opening the door and reaching into the passenger compartment to remove papers from the dashboard. Even if he did not engage in a full-scale excavation, this search exposed areas of the passenger compartment not visible from outside the vehicle. . . .

In any event, even if there had been only a limited search here that justified the Court in balancing the extent of the intrusion against the importance of the governmental interests allegedly served, this alone cannot legalize the search of respondent's car. In situations where the Court has approved of very limited intrusions on less than probable cause, the Court has always required that "the police officer . . . be able to point to specific and articulable facts which, taken together with rational inferences from those facts, reasonably warrant that intrusion." Terry v. Ohio, 392 U.S. 1, 21 (1968). . . . In this case, respondent's traffic infractions did not give the police a reason to search for the VIN, and the police offered no other justification that would reasonably warrant such an intrusion.[5] . . .

---

5. Justice Powell, in a concurring opinion joined by the Chief Justice, would find that "[w]here the VIN is not visible from outside the vehicle or voluntarily disclosed by the driver, the officer may enter the vehicle to the extent necessary to read the VIN." . . . Even were I to agree with this standard, in this case Officer McNamee searched respondent's car without ever asking him voluntarily to disclose the VIN's location.

JUSTICE WHITE, with whom JUSTICE STEVENS joins, dissenting. . . .

Had Class remained in his car and refused an officer's order (1) to turn over his registration certificate and (2) to remove the article obscuring the VIN, there would have been no more justification for entering the interior of the car and doing what was necessary to read the VIN than there would have been to enter and search for the registration certificate in the glove compartment. It may be that under our cases, Class could have been sanctioned for his refusal in such a case, but we have never held that his refusal would permit a search of the glove compartment. Even if it did, it would be different if there was no refusal at all, but just an entry to find a registration certificate. If that is the case, this one is no different in kind: there was no refusal and nothing but a non-consensual entry to search without probable cause and without emergent circumstances.

It makes no difference that the law requires the VIN to be visible from outside the car. Otherwise, a requirement that the VIN be carried in a prominent location in the trunk of the car would justify searches of that area whenever there was a stop for a traffic violation. I thus do not join the Court's opinion, which in effect holds that a search of a car for the VIN is permissible whenever there is a legal stop, whether or not the driver is even asked to consent.

Nevertheless, Class was unlicensed and the police were not constitutionally required merely to give him a citation and let his unlicensed driving continue. Arguably, one of the officers legally could have driven the car away himself and in the process noticed the gun; the car could have been towed and inspected at the station; or Class could have been arrested for driving without a license and the entire car searched. But the Court eschews these possible alternative rationales and rests its judgment on grounds that I do not accept.

NOTES AND QUESTIONS

1. Was there an alternative, perhaps preferable, ground for upholding the constitutionality of the police action in *Class?* Consider the footnote at the end of the majority opinion and the last paragraph of Justice White's dissenting opinion. See generally Maclin, *New York v. Class: A Little-Noticed Case with Disturbing Implications,* 78 J. Crim. L. & Criminology 1 (1987).

2. Is *Class* inconsistent with Ybarra v. Illinois, page 769 supra? Compare *Class* with the following case.

ARIZONA v. HICKS, 480 U.S. 321, 323-324, 335-336, 338 (1987):
JUSTICE SCALIA delivered the opinion for the Court. . . .

On April 18, 1984, a bullet was fired through the floor of respondent's apartment, striking and injuring a man in the apartment below. Police officers arrived and entered respondent's apartment to search for the shooter, for other victims, and for weapons. They found and seized three weapons, including a sawed-off rifle, and in the course of their search also discovered a stocking-cap mask.

One of the policemen, Officer Nelson, noticed two sets of expensive stereo components, which seemed out of place in the squalid and otherwise ill-appointed four-room apartment. Suspecting that they were stolen, he read and recorded their serial numbers—moving some of the components, including a Bang and Olufsen turntable, in order to do so—which he then reported by phone to his headquarters. On being advised that the turntable had been taken in an armed robbery, he seized it immediately. It was later determined that some of the other serial numbers matched those on other stereo equipment taken in the same armed robbery, and a warrant was obtained and executed to seize that equipment as well. Respondent was subsequently indicted for the robbery.

The state trial court['s granting of respondent's motion to suppress was affirmed on appeal.] . . .

Officer Nelson's moving of the equipment . . . constitute[d] a "search" separate and apart from the search for the shooter, victims, and weapons that was the lawful objective of his entry into the apartment. Merely inspecting those parts of the turntable that came into view during the latter search would not have constituted an independent search, because it would have produced no additional invasion of respondent's privacy interest. . . . But taking action, unrelated to the objectives of the authorized intrusion, which exposed to view concealed portions of the apartment or its contents, did produce a new invasion of respondent's privacy unjustified by the exigent circumstance that validated the entry. . . . It matters not that the search uncovered nothing of any great personal value to the respondent—serial numbers rather than (what might conceivably have been hidden behind or under the equipment) letters or photographs. A search is a search, even if it happens to disclose nothing but the bottom of a turntable. . . .

The . . . question is whether the search was "reasonable" under the Fourth Amendment.

. . . [I]t would be absurd to say that an object could lawfully be seized and taken from the premises, but could not be moved for closer examination. It is clear, therefore, that the search here was valid if the "plain view" doctrine would have sustained a seizure of the equipment.

There is no doubt it would have done so if Officer Nelson had probable cause to believe that the equipment was stolen. The State has conceded, however, that he had only a "reasonable suspicion," by which it means something less than probable cause. . . .

[The Court held that probable cause was required for a plain view seizure. See page 646 supra.]

We do not say, of course, that a seizure can never be justified on less than probable cause. We have held that it can—where, for example, the seizure is minimally intrusive and operational necessities render it the only practicable means of detecting certain types of crime. See, e.g., United States v. Cortez, [page 702 supra] (investigative detention of vehicle suspected to be transporting illegal aliens); United States v. Brignoni-Ponce, [page 759 supra (dictum)] (same); United States v. Place, [page 796 infra] (dictum) (seizure of suspected drug dealer's luggage at airport to permit exposure to specially trained dog). No special operational necessities are relied on here, however—but rather the mere fact that the items in question came lawfully within the officer's plain view. That alone cannot supplant the requirement of probable cause.

The same considerations preclude us from holding that, even though probable cause would have been necessary for a *seizure*, the *search* of objects in plain view that occurred here could be sustained on lesser grounds. A dwelling-place search, no less than a dwelling-place seizure, requires probable cause. . . .

Affirmed.

[The concurring opinion of JUSTICE WHITE and the dissenting opinion of JUSTICE POWELL are omitted.]

JUSTICE O'CONNOR, with whom THE CHIEF JUSTICE and JUSTICE POWELL join, dissenting. . . .

. . . I agree with the Court that even under the plain view doctrine, probable cause is required before the police seize an item, or conduct a full-blown search of evidence in plain view. . . . This is not to say, however, that even a mere inspection of a suspicious item must be supported by probable cause. . . . [I]f police officers have a reasonable, articulable suspicion that an object they come across during the course of a lawful search is evidence of crime, in my view they may make a cursory examination of the object to verify their suspicion. If the officers wish to go beyond such a cursory examination of the object, however, they must have probable cause.

. . . [T]he overwhelming majority of both state and federal courts have held that probable cause is not required for a minimal inspection of an item in plain view. . . . See, e.g., . . . United States v. Hillyard, 677 F.2d 1336, 1342 (9th Cir. 1982) (police may give suspicious documents brief perusal if they have a "reasonable suspicion"). . . .

Weighed against this minimal additional invasion of privacy are rather major gains in law enforcement. The use of identification numbers in tracing stolen property is a powerful law enforcement tool. Serial numbers are far more helpful and accurate in detecting stolen property than simple police recollection of the evidence. . . . Given the prevalence of mass produced goods in our national economy, a serial number is often the only sure method of detecting stolen property. The balance of governmental and private interests strongly supports the view accepted by a majority of courts that a standard of reasonable suspicion meets the requirements of the Fourth Amendment. . . .

NOTES AND QUESTIONS

1. In what types of situations are the police most likely to have an interest in inspecting items that they discover in plain view and that they do not have probable cause to seize? To the extent that the situation is unlikely to arise with respect to serial numbers, the "need" for cursory inspections with less than probable cause may not be as great as Justice O'Connor suggests; and to the extent that the situation is likely to arise in other contexts—e.g., the cursory inspection of documents, as in United States v. Hillyard, cited with approval by Justice O'Connor—abandoning the probable cause standard could result in more substantial invasions of privacy than Justice O'Connor acknowledges, both because there may be an inherently greater privacy interest in the items and because it may be difficult to define with any degree of precision what constitutes only a "cursory" inspection.

2. Even if articulable suspicion is not sufficient to justify the cursory inspection of plain view items generally, should it be sufficient to justify what happened in *Hicks*—moving or picking up an item to look for a serial number?

3. In what other situations should the limited or relatively minor nature of the intrusion justify a search or seizure with less than probable cause?

Consider United States v. Place, 462 U.S. 695 (1983): On the basis of prior investigation, federal narcotics officers had articulable suspicion to believe that two suitcases in the possession of Raymond Place, a deplaning passenger at LaGuardia Airport, contained narcotics. When Place refused to consent to a search, the officers took the suitcases to Kennedy Airport.[94] There, approximately 90 minutes after the initial seizure, the

---

94. The officers told Place that he was free to accompany them. He declined to do so, but he did obtain the telephone number of one of the agents. 462 U.S. at 699.

suitcases were subjected to a "sniff test" by a trained narcotics detection dog. The dog reacted positively to one suitcase. Because it was late Friday afternoon, the officers kept the luggage over the weekend. On the following Monday they obtained a search warrant for the suitcase to which the dog had reacted positively. The suitcase contained cocaine, and Place was eventually convicted of possession of cocaine with intent to distribute.

The Supreme Court, in an opinion by Justice O'Connor, reversed Place's conviction on the ground that the 90-minute retention of the suitcases without probable cause violated the fourth amendment. In dictum, the Court stated, "[W]hen an officer's observations lead him reasonably to believe that a traveler is carrying luggage that contains narcotics, the principles of *Terry* and its progeny would permit the officer to detain the luggage briefly to investigate the circumstances that aroused his suspicion, provided that the investigative detention is properly limited in scope."[95] Id. at 706.

In a concurring opinion Justice Blackmun first observed that the lengthy detention of the suitcases without probable cause was sufficient to support the Court's judgment. He then went on to address the *Terry* issue:

> I am concerned . . . with what appears to me to be an emerging tendency on the part of the Court to convert the *Terry* decision into a general statement that the Fourth Amendment requires only that any seizure be reasonable.[1] . . .
>
> Terry v. Ohio, however, teaches that in some circumstances a limited seizure that is less restrictive than a formal arrest may constitutionally occur upon mere reasonable suspicion, if "supported by a special law enforcement need for greater flexibility." Florida v. Royer, 460 U.S. [491, 514 (1983)] (dissenting opinion). . . .
>
> Because I agree with the Court that there is a significant law enforce-

---

95. The Court acknowledged that if the investigative procedure for which the luggage was seized was a search requiring probable cause, the seizure could not be justified on less than probable cause. The Court took the position, however, that exposure of luggage located in a public place to a trained canine did not constitute a "search." 462 U.S. at 706-707.

1. The Court states that the applicability of the *Terry* exception "rests on a balancing of the competing interests to determine the reasonableness of the type of seizure involved within the meaning of 'the Fourth Amendment's general proscription against unreasonable searches and seizures.'" . . . [Q]uoting *Terry*, 392 U.S., at 20. As the context of the quotation from *Terry* makes clear, however, this balancing to determine reasonableness occurs only under the exceptional circumstances that justify the *Terry* exception: "But we deal here with an entire rubric of police conduct—necessarily swift action predicated upon the on-the-spot observations of the officer on the beat—which historically has not been, and as a practical matter could not be, subjected to the warrant procedure. Instead, the conduct involved in this case must be tested by the Fourth Amendment's general proscription against unreasonable searches and seizures." 392 U.S., at 20.

ment interest in interdicting illegal drug traffic in the Nation's airports,
. . . a limited intrusion caused by a temporary seizure of luggage for
investigative purposes could fall within the *Terry* exception. The critical
threshold issue is the intrusiveness of the seizure. [462 U.S. at 721-722.]

g. Other Applications of the Sliding Scale Approach to Reasonableness

Inmates. Bell v. Wolfish, 441 U.S. 520 (1979), was a broad-ranging
class action challenging various conditions of confinement at the Metropolitan Correctional Facility, a short-term custodial facility in New
York City that housed primarily pretrial detainees. The challenged conditions of confinement included the policy of unannounced searches of
rooms in the inmate living area and the policy of subjecting all inmates
to a strip and visual body cavity search following contact with persons
from outside the institution. Assuming that the incarcerated inmates
retained some fourth amendment rights, the Court held that the searches
were reasonable. Id. at 555-560.

The Court went a step further in Hudson v. Palmer, 468 U.S. 517
(1984), where it held that a convicted inmate had *no* legitimate privacy
expectation in a jail cell. In an opinion by Chief Justice Burger the Court
stated:

> Determining whether an expectation of privacy is "legitimate" or
> "reasonably" necessarily entails a balancing of interests. The two interests
> here are the interest of society in the security of its penal institutions and
> the interest of the prisoner in privacy within his cell. The latter interest,
> of course, is already limited by the exigencies of the circumstances. . . .
> We strike the balance in favor of institutional security. [Id. at 527.]

Typically when the Supreme Court uses a balancing test, it does so
to determine whether a particular search or seizure is reasonable. In
Palmer, however, the Court employed the balancing test to determine
that the prisoner had no legitimate privacy interest in a cell, which is
the equivalent of holding that inspecting the cell is not a search or seizure.
As long as the Court's ultimate conclusion is that the governmental
activity is permissible, does it matter whether the Court uses the balancing
test to determine whether there is a legitimate expectation of privacy
rather than whether the government has unreasonably infringed upon a
legitimate privacy expectation?

Should a pretrial detainee also be regarded as having *no* legitimate
privacy expectation in a cell?

School Searches. New Jersey v. T.L.O., 469 U.S. 325 (1985), involved the search of a high school student's purse:

> [A] teacher at Piscataway High School in Middlesex County, N.J., discovered two girls smoking in a lavatory. One of the two girls was the respondent T.L.O., who at that time was a 14-year-old high school freshman. Because smoking in the lavatory was a violation of a school rule, the teacher took the two girls to the Principal's office, where they met with Assistant Vice Principal Theodore Choplick. In response to questioning by Mr. Choplick, T.L.O.'s companion admitted that she had violated the rule. T.L.O., however, denied that she had been smoking in the lavatory and claimed that she did not smoke at all.
>
> Mr. Choplick asked T.L.O. to come into his private office and demanded to see her purse. Opening the purse, he found a pack of cigarettes, which he removed from the purse and held before T.L.O. as he accused her of having lied to him. As he reached into the purse for the cigarettes, Mr. Choplick also noticed a package of cigarette rolling papers. In his experience, possession of rolling papers by high school students was closely associated with the use of marihuana. Suspecting that a closer examination of the purse might yield further evidence of drug use, Mr. Choplick proceeded to search the purse thoroughly. The search revealed a small amount of marihuana, a pipe, a number of empty plastic bags, a substantial quantity of money in one-dollar bills, an index card that appeared to be a list of students who owed T.L.O. money, and two letters that implicated T.L.O. in marihuana dealing. [Id. at 328.]

These items were subsequently introduced into evidence against T.L.O. at a delinquency proceeding.

In addressing T.L.O.'s claim that use of the evidence violated her fourth amendment rights, the Court initially rejected the state's arguments (1) that fourth amendment restrictions apply only to law enforcement personnel and (2) that the in loco parentis role of school officials exempts them from the constraints of the fourth amendment. The Court then acknowledged that students have a legitimate expectation of privacy in items of personal property they bring into the school:

> [S]choolchildren may find it necessary to carry with them a variety of legitimate, noncontraband items, and there is no reason to conclude that they have necessarily waived all rights to privacy in such items merely by bringing them onto the school grounds.[5] [Id. at 339.]

5. We do not address the question, not presented by this case, whether a schoolchild has a legitimate expectation of privacy in lockers, desks, or other school property provided for the storage of school supplies. Nor do we express any opinion on the standards (if any) governing searches of such areas by school officials or by other public authorities acting at the request of school officials. Compare Zamora v. Pomeroy, 639 F.2d 662,

Against this privacy interest, the Court concluded, one must balance the "substantial interest," id., of the school authorities in maintaining order and discipline:

> It is evident that the school requires some easing of the restrictions to which searches by public authorities are ordinarily subject. . . . [R]equiring a teacher to obtain a warrant before searching a child . . . would unduly interfere with the maintenance of the swift and informal disciplinary procedures needed in the schools. . . .
>
> The school setting also requires some modification of the level of suspicion of illicit activity needed to justify a search. . . .
>
> . . . [T]he legality of a search of a student should depend simply on the reasonableness, under all the circumstances, of the search. Determining the reasonableness of any search involves a twofold inquiry: first, one must consider "whether the . . . action was justified at its inception," Terry v. Ohio, 392 U.S. [1], 20 [(1968)]; second, one must determine whether the search as actually conducted "was reasonably related in scope to the circumstances which justified the interference in the first place," ibid. Under ordinary circumstances, a search of a student by a teacher or other school official[7] will be "justified at its inception" when there are reasonable grounds for suspecting that the search will turn up evidence that the student has violated or is violating either the law or the rules of the school.[8] Such a search will be permissible in its scope when the measures adopted are reasonably related to the objectives of the search and

---

670 (C.A. 10 1981) ("Inasmuch as the school had assumed joint control of the locker it cannot be successfully maintained that the school did not have a right to inspect it."), and People v. Overton, 24 N.Y.2d 522, 249 N.E.2d 366, 301 N.Y.S.2d 479 (1969) (school administrators have power to consent to search of a student's locker), with State v. Engerud, 94 N.J. 331, 348, 463 A.2d 934, 943 (1983) ("We are satisfied that in the context of this case the student had an expectation of privacy in the contents of his locker. . . . For the four years of high school, the school locker is a home away from home. In it the student stores the kind of personal 'effects' protected by the Fourth Amendment").

7. We here consider only searches carried out by school authorities acting alone and on their own authority. This case does not present the question of the appropriate standard for assessing the legality of searches conducted by school officials in conjunction with or at the behest of law enforcement agencies, and we express no opinion on that question. Cf. Picha v. Wielgos, 410 F. Supp. 1214, 1219-1221 (N.D. Ill. 1976) (holding probable cause standard applicable to searches involving the police).

8. We do not decide whether individualized suspicion is an essential element of the reasonableness standard we adopt for searches by school authorities. In other contexts, however, we have held that although "some quantum of individualized suspicion is usually a prerequisite to a constitutional search or seizure[,] . . . the Fourth Amendment imposes no irreducible requirement of such suspicion." United States v. Martinez-Fuerte, 428 U.S. 543, 560-561 (1976). . . . Exceptions to the requirement of individualized suspicion are generally appropriate only where the privacy interests implicated by a search are minimal and where "other safeguards" are available "to assure that the individual's reasonable expectation of privacy is not 'subject to the discretion of the official in the field.'" Delaware v. Prouse, 440 U.S. 648, 654-655 (1979) (citations omitted). . . .

not excessively intrusive in light of the age and sex of the student and the nature of the infraction.[9] [469 U.S. at 340-342.]

In a concurring opinion Justice Blackmun observed:

[T]he Court omits a crucial step in its analysis of whether a school search must be based upon probable cause. . . . [W]e have used . . . a balancing test, rather than strictly applying the Fourth Amendment's Warrant and Probable Cause Clause, only when we were confronted with "a special law enforcement need for greater flexibility." Florida v. Royer, 460 U.S. 491, 514 (1983) (Blackmun, J., dissenting). . . .

The Court's implication that the balancing test is the rule rather than the exception is troubling for me because it is unnecessary in this case. The elementary and secondary school setting presents a special need for flexibility justifying a departure from the balance struck by the Framers. [469 U.S. at 351-352.]

Does the Court's reasonableness standard require at least *Terry*-type articulable suspicion? See footnote 8 supra. Assuming that it does, did Vice Principal Choplick violate T.L.O.'s fourth amendment rights? Particularly in light of Illinois v. Gates, page 584 supra, what is it about the school setting that would justify a full-scale search based on only individualized suspicion rather than probable cause?

Work places of public employees. O'Connor v. Ortega, 480 U.S. 709 (1987), was a federal civil rights action brought by Dr. Magno Ortega, following the search of his office at the Napa State Hospital officials. The district court granted the defendants' motion for a summary judgment. The court of appeals reversed, holding that Dr. Ortega was entitled to a summary judgment. Justice O'Connor's plurality opinion announcing the judgment of the Court balanced a public employee's privacy interest against the "substantial government interests in the efficient and proper operation of the workplace." Id. at 725. According to the plurality, neither

---

9. Our reference to the nature of the infraction is not intended as [a] . . . suggestion that some rules regarding student conduct are by nature too "trivial" to justify a search based upon reasonable suspicion. . . . We are unwilling to adopt a standard under which the legality of a search is dependent upon a judge's evaluation of the relative importance of various school rules. The maintenance of discipline in the schools requires not only that students be restrained from assaulting one another, abusing drugs and alcohol, and committing other crimes, but also that students conform themselves to the standards of conduct prescribed by school authorities. . . . The promulgation of a rule forbidding specified conduct presumably reflects a judgment on the part of school officials that such conduct is destructive of school order or of a proper educational environment. Absent any suggestion that the rule violates some substantive constitutional guarantee, the courts should, as a general matter, defer to that judgment and refrain from attempting to distinguish between rules that are important to the preservation of order in the schools and rules that are not.

a warrant nor probable cause is required to justify the search of an employee's office when the search is either a noninvestigatory work-related intrusion or an investigatory search for evidence of work-related employee misfeasance:

> [These searches] should be judged by the standard of reasonableness under all the circumstances. . . . [B]oth the inception and the scope of the intrusion must be reasonable. . . .
>   . . . Because the petitioners had an "individualized suspicion of the misconduct by Dr. Ortega, we need not decide whether individualized suspicion is an essential element of the standard of reasonableness that we adopt today. [Id. at 725-726.]

Concluding that the record was inadequate to determine the purpose for the search or evaluate its reasonableness, the Court remanded the case to the district court.

Justice Scalia concurred in the Court's judgment:

> I would hold that government searches to retrieve work-related materials or to investigate violations of workplace rules—searches of the sort that are regarded as reasonable and normal in the private-employer context— do not violate the Fourth Amendment. Because the conflicting and incomplete evidence in the present case could not conceivably support summary judgment that the search did not have such a validating purpose, I agree with the plurality that the decision must be reversed and remanded. [Id. at 732.]

In a dissenting opinion joined by Justices Brennan, Marshall and Stevens, Justice Blackmun argued that the plurality here, like the majority in T.L.O., neglected the critical step of finding a special need to depart from the warrant and probable cause requirements before engaging in a balancing of interests. In contrast to his ultimate conclusion in T.L.O., however, Justice Blackmun, after characterizing the search here as "plainly exceptional and investigatory," id. at 736, maintained that there was nothing in the facts of the case to justify a departure from the warrant and probable cause requirements.

Probationers. Griffin v. Wisconsin, 483 U.S. 868 (1987), dealt with the warrantless search of a probationer's home by a probation officer. During the search the probation officer seized a gun, which was subsequently used against Griffin in his prosecution for illegally possessing a firearm. A Wisconsin Probation Department regulation permitted probation officers to engage in a warrantless search of a probationer's home when there were "reasonable grounds" to believe that contraband was present. The sole basis for the search in this case, according to the evidence developed at the suppression hearing, was that an unnamed police officer telephoned the probation officer and stated that the defendant might have had guns at his residence.[96] The State Supreme Court, held that this information gave the probationer officer "reasonable grounds" to search and that in light of a probationer's diminished expectation of privacy, a showing of reasonable grounds was sufficient to justify the search. The Supreme Court, in an opinion by Justice Scalia, found it "unnecessary to embrace a new principle of law . . . that any search of a probationer's home by a probation officer satisfies the Fourth Amendment so long as the information possessed by the probation officer satisfies a federal 'reasonable grounds' standard." Id. at 872. According to the Court:

> The search of Griffin's home satisfied the demands of the Fourth Amendment because it was carried out pursuant to a regulation that itself satisfies the Fourth Amendment's reasonableness requirement under well-established principles. . . .
> . . . [R]estrictions [placed on a probationer] are meant to assure that the probation serves as a period of genuine rehabilitation and that the community is not harmed by the probationer's being at large. . . . These same goals require and justify the exercise of supervision. . . . Recent research suggests that more intensive supervision can reduce recidivism . . . , and the importance of supervision has grown as probation has become an increasingly common sentence for those convicted of serious crimes. . . . Supervision, then, is a "special need" of the State permitting a degree of impingement upon privacy that would not be constitutional if applied to the public at large. . . .
> In determining whether the "special needs" of its probation system justify Wisconsin's search regulation, we must take that regulation as it has been interpreted by state corrections officials and state courts. As already noted, the Wisconsin Supreme Court—the ultimate authority on issues of Wisconsin law—has held that a tip from a police detective that Griffin "had" or "may have had" an illegal weapon at his home constituted the requisite "reasonable grounds." . . . Whether or not we would choose to interpret a similarly worded federal regulation in [the same] fashion, we are bound by the state court's interpretation, which is relevant to our constitutional analysis only insofar as it fixes the meaning of the regulation. We think it clear that the special needs of Wisconsin's probation system make the warrant requirement impracticable and justify replacement of the standard of probable cause by "reasonable grounds," as defined by the Wisconsin Supreme Court. [483 U.S. at 873-876.]

96. See Griffin v. Wisconsin, 483 U.S. 868, 871 (1967); State v. Griffin, 131 Wis. 2d 41, 64, 388 N.W.2d 535, 544 (1986).

The special needs that the warrant and probable cause requirements
would tend to undermine, according to the Court, included the ability
of the probation officer to respond promptly when there appeared to be
grounds to search and the deterrent effect of the supervisory arrangement.

Since the Court rested its holding on the reasonableness of the
Wisconsin regulation, as interpreted by the Wisconsin Supreme Court,
it is not clear that the probation officer's suspicion was sufficient to meet
the *Terry* fourth amendment reasonable or articulable suspicion standard.
What is it about the search of probationers' homes generally or the
Wisconsin regulation in particular that would made such a search reasonable in the absence of *Terry*-type articulable suspicion?

Drug testing. In Skinner v. Railway Labor Executives' Association,
489 U.S. 602 (1989), and National Treasury Employees Union v. Von
Raab, 489 U.S. 656 (1989), the Supreme Court, in opinions by Justice
Kennedy, upheld suspicionless drug testing programs for public employees. The *Skinner* program, promulgated by the Federal Railroad Administration (FRA) provided for mandatory blood, urine, and breath tests for
railroad employees involved in serious train accidents, incidents involving
a fatality of an employee, and other specifically defined incidents. The
Court noted that the purpose of the testing was to prevent accidents, not
to gather evidence for criminal prosecution, and that the FRA adopted
the program after documenting that alcohol and drug abuse was a significant problem in the railroad industry. The Court then continued:

> By and large, intrusions on privacy under the FRA regulations are
> limited. . . .
>
> More importantly, the expectations of privacy of covered employees
> are diminished by reason of their participation in an industry that is reg-
> ulated pervasively to ensure safety, a goal dependent, in substantial part,
> on the health and fitness of covered employees. . . .
>
> We do not suggest, of course, that the interest in bodily security
> enjoyed by those employed in a regulated industry must always be con-
> sidered minimal. Here, however, the covered employees have long been
> a principal focus of regulatory concern. . . .
>
> By contrast, the government interest in testing without a showing of
> individualized suspicion is compelling. Employees subject to the tests
> discharge duties fraught with such risk of injury to others that even a
> momentary lapse of attention can have disastrous consequences. . . .
>
> . . . [T]he FRA regulations supply an effective means of deterring
> employees engaged in safety-sensitive tasks from using controlled sub-
> stances or alcohol in the first place. . . .
>
> The testing procedures . . . also help railroads obtain invaluable
> information about the causes of major accidents and to take appropriate
> measures to safeguard the general public. . . .

. . . Investigators who arrive at the scene shortly after a major accident has occurred may find it difficult to determine which members of a train crew contributed to its occurrence. Obtaining evidence that might give rise to the suspicion that a particular employee is impaired, a difficult endeavor in the best of circumstances, is most impractical in the aftermath of a serious accident. . . .

. . . In light of the limited discretion exercised by the railroad employees under the regulations, the surpassing safety interests served by toxicological tests in this context, and the diminished expectation of privacy that attaches to information pertaining to the fitness of covered employees, we believe that it is reasonable to conduct such tests in the absence of a warrant or reasonable suspicion that any particular employee may be impaired. [489 U.S. at 624, 627-631, 634.]

Justice Marshall, in a dissenting opinion joined by Justice Brennan, maintained, inter alia, that the Court was improperly departing from the probable cause standard; that the invasions of privacy inherent in taking the blood and urine samples was substantial; that an additional privacy concern was the possibility that the tests could be used to uncover various medical disorders such as epilepsy, diabetes, or clinical depression; that prior caselaw has recognized that extensive government regulation may diminish one's privacy expectation in the *property* of an enterprise, but not in one's *person*; and that there was no substance to the majority's deterrence rationale for the FRA regulations.[97]

In *Von Raab*, a companion case to *Skinner*, the Court considered a drug testing program that made urinalysis a mandatory condition of placement or employment in three categories of United States Customs Service positions: those involving direct involvement in drug interdiction or enforcement; those requiring the employee to carry a firearm; and those which require the employee to handle classified information. After a lengthy analysis that paralleled that of *Skinner*, the Court held that mandatory drug testing for the first two categories of positions satisfied the fourth amendment reasonableness requirement. With respect to the third category the Court observed that it would be reasonable to require drug testing for those employees who handle "truly sensitive" informa-

---

97. In a concurring opinion, Justice Stevens also expressed disagreement with the deterrence rationale:

Most people—and I would think most railroad employees as well—do not go to work with the expectation that they may be involved in a major accident, particularly one causing such catastrophic results as loss of life or the release of hazardous material requiring evacuation. Moreover, even if they are conscious of the possibilities that such an accident might occur and that alcohol or drug use might be a contributing factor, if the risk of serious personal injury does not deter their use of these substances, it seems highly unlikely that the additional threat of loss of employment would have any effect on their behavior. [489 U.S. at 634.]

tion. The category, however, included, inter alia, "accountant," "animal caretaker," and "baggage clerk." The Court remanded the case for further proceedings to determine whether this category of covered positions was overly broad. Justice Marshall, in an opinion joined by Justice Brennan, dissented for the same reasons set forth in his *Skinner* dissent. Justice Scalia, in an opinion joined by Justice Stevens, also dissented:

> Until today this Court has upheld a bodily search separate from arrest and without individualized suspicion of wrongdoing only with respect to prison inmates, relying on the uniquely dangerous nature of the environment. See Bell v. Wolfish, 441 U.S. 520, 558-560 (1979). . . . I joined the Court's opinion . . . [in *Skinner*] because the demonstrated frequency of drug and alcohol use by the targeted class of employees, and the demonstrated connection between such use and grave harm, rendered the search a reasonable means of protecting society. . . .
>
> . . . While there are some absolutes in Fourth Amendment law, as soon as those have been left behind and the question comes down to whether a particular search has been "reasonable," the answer depends largely upon the social necessity that prompts the search. [See New Jersey v. T.L.O., 469 U.S. 325, 330 (1985) (documenting problem of drug usage and disorder in schools as part of justification for upholding administrative search of student's purse); United States v. Martinez-Fuerte, 428 U.S. 543, 551-552 (1976) (documenting formidable problem of interdicting illegal aliens in approving fixed checkpoint stops near Mexican border).]
>
> . . . [T]he substantive analysis of our opinion today in *Skinner* begins, "[t]he problem of alcohol use on American Railroads is as old as the industry itself," and goes on to cite statistics concerning that problem and the accidents it causes, including a 1979 study finding that "23% of the operating personnel were 'problem drinkers.'" *Skinner*, [489 U.S. at 606, 607 n.1].
>
> The Court's opinion in the present case, however, will be searched in vain for real evidence of a real problem that will be solved by urine testing of Customs Service employees. . . .
>
> . . . Perhaps concrete evidence of the severity of a problem is unnecessary when it is so well known that courts can almost take judicial notice of it; but that is surely not the case here. The Commissioner of Customs himself has stated that he "believe[s] that Customs is largely drug-free," that "[t]he extent of illegal drug use by Customs employees was not the reason for establishing the program," and that he "hope[s] and expect[s] to receive reports of very few positive findings through drug screening." . . . The test results have fulfilled those hopes and expectations. According to the Service's counsel, out of 3,600 employees tested, no more than 5 tested positive. . . .
>
> Today's decision would be wrong, but at least of more limited effect, if its approval of drug testing were confined to that category of employees assigned specifically to drug interdiction duties. Relatively few public em-

ployees fit that description. But in extending approval of drug testing to that category consisting of employees who carry firearms, the Court exposes vast numbers of public employees to this needless indignity. Logically, of course, if those who carry guns can be treated in this fashion, so can all others whose work, if performed under the influence of drugs, may endanger others—automobile drivers, operators of other potentially dangerous equipment, construction workers, school crossing guards. . . .

There is only one apparent basis that sets the testing at issue here apart from all these other situations. . . . [I]t is what the Commissioner himself offered in the concluding sentence of his memorandum to Customs Service employees announcing the program: "Implementation of the drug screening program would set an important example in our country's struggle with this most serious threat to our national health and security." . . . I think it obvious that this justification is unacceptable; that the impairment of individual liberties cannot be the means of making a point; that symbolism, even symbolism for so worthy a cause as the abolition of unlawful drugs, cannot validate an otherwise unreasonable search. [489 U.S. at 680-681, 683-687.]

What conclusions is it reasonable to draw from the *Von Raab* Court's remand with respect to employees with security clearances and from Justice Scalia's argument that there was an inadequate showing of need for the drug testing program in *Von Raab?* If there is no evidence of a need for the drug testing program in the first place, why is the majority so concerned about whether the testing program is too far-reaching? Is there simply an unexplained inconsistency between the apparent absence of any strong general need for the drug testing program and the majority's concern with the potential overbreadth of the program? Is the point that a showing of need is not very important, at least if the number or category of employees covered by a particular program is limited? Or is the significant, distinguishing feature of *Von Raab* the Customs Service's unique role in interdicting drug traffic, which arguably presents a special, symbolic need for trying to ensure that the Service is drug free? If "symbolic need" is important, is there any less of a symbolic need with respect to groups of employees who work with or act as role models for young people?

Noncriminal investigatory searches generally? Consider the following excerpt from Justice Marshall's dissent in Skinner v. Railway Labor Executives' Association, page 804 supra, which upheld the drug testing program for specified railroad employees:

The Court today takes its longest step yet toward reading the probable-cause requirement out of the Fourth Amendment. For the fourth time in as many years, a majority holds that a "special nee[d], beyond the normal need for law enforcement," makes the "requirement" of probable cause "impracticable.". . . . With the recognition of "[t]he Government's interest in regulating the conduct of railroad employees to ensure safety" as such a need, . . . the Court has now permitted "special needs" to displace constitutional text in each of the four categories of searches enumerated in the Fourth Amendment: searches of "persons," [in this case]; "houses," Griffin v. Wisconsin, 483 U.S. 868 (1987); "papers," O'Connor v. Ortega, 480 U.S. 709 (1987); and "effects," New Jersey v. T.L.O., 469 U.S. 325 (1985). . . .

Until recently, an unbroken line of cases had recognized probable cause as an indispensable prerequisite for a full-scale search, regardless whether such a search was conducted pursuant to a warrant or under one of the recognized exceptions to the warrant requirement. . . . Only where the Government action in question had a "substantially less intrusive" impact on privacy, Dunaway [v. New York, 442 U.S. 200, 210 (1979)], and thus clearly fell short of a full-scale search, did we relax the probable cause standard. . . . Even in this class of cases, we almost always required the Government to show some individualized suspicion to justify the search. The few searches which we upheld in the absence of individualized justification were routinized, fleeting, and nonintrusive encounters conducted pursuant to regulatory programs which entailed no contact with the person.[2]

In the four years since this Court in T.L.O., first began recognizing "special needs" exceptions to the Fourth Amendment, the clarity of Fourth Amendment doctrine has been badly distorted, as the Court has eclipsed the probable-cause requirement in a patchwork quilt of settings: public school principals' searches of students' belongings, T.L.O.; public employers' searches of employees' desks, O'Connor; and probation officers' searches of probationers' homes, Griffin.[3] Tellingly, each time the Court has found that "special needs" counseled ignoring the literal requirements of the Fourth Amendment for such full-scale searches in favor of a formless and unguided "reasonableness" balancing inquiry, it has concluded that the search in question satisfied that test. . . .

In widening the "special needs" exception to probable cause to authorize searches of the human body unsupported by *any* evidence of wrongdoing, the majority today completes the process begun in T.L.O. of eliminating altogether the probable-cause requirement for civil searches—

2. See, e.g., United States v. Martinez-Fuerte, 428 U.S. 543 (1976) (brief interrogative stop at permanent border checkpoint to ascertain motorist's residence status); Camara v. Municipal Court, 387 U.S. 523 (1987) (routine annual inspection by city housing department).

3. The "special needs" the Court invoked to justify abrogating the probable-cause requirement were, in New Jersey v. T.L.O., 469 U.S. 325, 341 (1985), "the substantial need of teachers and administrators for freedom to maintain order in the schools"; in O'Connor v. Ortega, 480 U.S. 709, (1987), "the efficient and proper operation of the workplace"; and in Griffin v. Wisconsin, 483 U.S. 868, 878 (1987), the need to preserve "the deterrent effect of the supervisory arrangement" of probation.

those undertaken for reasons "beyond the normal need for law enforcement." . . . In its place, the majority substitutes a manipulable balancing inquiry under which, upon the mere assertion of a "special need," even the deepest dignitary and privacy interests become vulnerable to governmental incursion. . . .

The fact is that the malleable "special needs" balancing approach can be justified only on the basis of the policy results it allows the majority to reach. The majority's concern with the railroad safety problems caused by drug and alcohol abuse is laudable; its cavalier disregard for the text of the Constitution is not. There is no drug exception to the Constitution, any more than there is a communism exception or an exception for other real or imagined sources of domestic unrest. . . . Because abandoning the explicit protections of the Fourth Amendment seriously imperils "the right to be let alone—the most comprehensive of rights and the right most valued by civilized men," Olmstead v. United States, 277 U.S. 438, 478 (1928) (Brandeis, J., dissenting), I reject the majority's "special needs" rationale as unprincipled and dangerous. [489 U.S. at 636-641.]

Is Justice Marshall correct in suggesting that the Court's recent decisions in effect create an exception from the probable cause and warrant requirement for all "civil searches—those undertaken for reasons 'beyond the normal need for law enforcement' "? Even if Justice Marshall's suggestion is not an accurate description of the current state of the law, would such an "exception"—despite Justice Marshall's antipathy for it—be desirable?

In *Place*, page 796 supra, Justice Blackmun expressed concern with what he perceived as the Court's willingness to use a balancing approach in a wide variety of situations. Is the crux of Justice Blackmun's concern in *Place* with how to define the situations in which it is appropriate to engage in a balancing of interests, or is he merely anticipating potential substantive disagreements with some other members of the Court? To put the matter somewhat differently, does Justice Blackmun's disagreement with the plurality in *Ortega*—or Justice Marshall's disagreement with the majority in *Skinner* or Justice O'Connor's disagreement with the majority in *Hicks*, page 794 supra—stem primarily from differences about the propriety of balancing interests in the first place, or do their disagreements reflect conflicting assessments of how the balance should be struck in a particular situation?

Consider the propriety of subjecting all airline passengers to magnetometer screening; visually inspecting and searching an air passenger's carry-on baggage; inspecting the attache cases of all individuals entering a courtroom; stopping and looking in the backseat and trunk of all vehicles in the hope of discovering a recent kidnap victim; or searching student lockers in a public school. What factors should determine whether it is appropriate to take the balancing approach to reasonableness? If one engages in a balancing process, what should the result be? See Mertens, The Fourth Amendment and the Control of Police Discretion, 17 U. Mich. J.L. Reform 551 (1984).

4. The Relationship Between Reasonableness and Probable Cause: Sliding the Other Way?

If in balancing the need to search against the impact of the search it is sometimes appropriate to conclude that a search is reasonable despite the absence of individualized probable cause, might there not be circumstances in which reasonableness demands *more* than the establishment of individualized probable cause and compliance with the warrant requirement? For example, should there be any special showing required in order to justify a search at night rather than during daylight hours? See Dix, Means of Executing Searches and Seizures, 67 Minn. L. Rev. 89 (1982).

In Gooding v. United States, 416 U.S. 430 (1974), the defendant sought to exclude evidence obtained during a nighttime search made pursuant to a warrant on the ground that the search had violated a District of Columbia ordinance. The ordinance required that warrants be executed only during daylight hours unless the magistrate determines that the search cannot be made in the daytime, that an immediate search is necessary to prevent removal or destruction of the property, or that the property sought is likely to be present only at night. The magistrate had not made such a determination. A majority of the Court, however, rejected the defendant's argument on the ground that a federal statute containing no similar provision rather than the District of Columbia ordinance governed the issuance and execution of the warrant. In dissent, Justice Marshall observed:

> In my view, there is no expectation of privacy more reasonable and more demanding of constitutional protection than our right to expect that we will be let alone in the privacy of our homes during the night. The idea of the police unnecessarily forcing their way into the home in the middle of the night—frequently, in narcotics cases, without knocking and announcing their purpose—rousing the residents out of their beds, and forcing them to stand by in indignity in their night clothes while the police rummage through their belongings does indeed smack of a " 'police state' lacking in the respect for . . . the right of privacy dictated by the U.S. Constitution." S. Rep. No. 91-583, p.12 (1969). . . .

This Court has consistently recognized that the intrusion upon privacy engendered by a search of a residence at night is of an order of magnitude greater than that produced by an ordinary search. Mr. Justice Harlan observed in holding a nighttime search unconstitutional in Jones v. United States, 357 U.S. 493, 498 (1958): "[I]t is difficult to imagine a more severe invasion of privacy than the nighttime intrusion into a private home." In Coolidge v. New Hampshire, 403 U.S. 443, 477 (1971), the Court again recognized that a midnight entry into a home was an "extremely serious intrusion." And our decision in Griswold v. Connecticut, 381 U.S. 479 (1965), was in large part based upon our revulsion at the thought of nighttime searches of the marital bedroom to discover evidence of illegal contraceptive use. See id., at 485-486. . . .

. . . It is by now established Fourth Amendment doctrine that increasingly severe standards of probable cause are necessary to justify increasingly intrusive searches. In Camara v. Municipal Court, 387 U.S. 523 (1967), after holding that search warrants were required to authorize administrative inspections, we held that the quantum of probable cause required for issuance of an inspection warrant must be determined in part by the reasonableness of the proposed search. As Mr. Justice White stated, "there can be no ready test for determining reasonableness other than by balancing the need to search against the invasion which the search entails." Id., at 536-537. . . . I do not regard this principle as a one-way street, to be used only to water down the requirement of probable cause when necessary to authorize governmental intrusions. In some situations—and the search of a private home during nighttime would seem to be a paradigm—this principle requires a showing of additional justification for a search over and above the ordinary showing of probable cause. [416 U.S. at 462-465.]

ZURCHER v. STANFORD DAILY

Certiorari to the United States Court of Appeals for the Ninth Circuit
436 U.S. 547 (1978)

Mr. Justice White delivered the opinion of the Court. . . .

Late in the day on Friday, April 9, 1971, officers of the Palo Alto Police Department and of the Santa Clara County Sheriff's Department responded to a call from the director of Stanford University Hospital requesting the removal of a large group of demonstrators who had seized the hospital's administrative offices and occupied them since the previous afternoon. After several futile efforts to persuade the demonstrators to leave peacefully, more drastic measures were employed. The demonstrators had barricaded the doors at both ends of a hall adjacent to the administrative offices. The police chose to force their way in at the west end of the corridor. As they did so, a group of demonstrators emerged through the doors at the east end and, armed with sticks and clubs, attacked the group of nine police officers stationed there. One officer was knocked to the floor and struck repeatedly on the head; another suffered a broken shoulder. All nine were injured. There were no police photographers at the east doors, and most bystanders and reporters were on the west side. The officers themselves were able to identify only two of their assailants, but one of them did see at least one person photographing the assault at the east doors.

On Sunday, April 11, a special edition of the Stanford Daily (Daily), a student newspaper published at Stanford University, carried articles and photographs devoted to the hospital protest and the violent clash between demonstrators and police. The photographs carried the byline of a Daily staff member and indicated that he had been at the east end of the hospital hallway where he could have photographed the assault on the nine officers. The next day, the Santa Clara County District Attorney's Office secured a warrant from the Municipal Court for an immediate search of the Daily's offices for negatives, film, and pictures showing the events and occurrences at the hospital on the evening of April 9. . . . The warrant affidavit contained no allegation or indication that members of the Daily staff were in any way involved in unlawful acts at the hospital.

The search pursuant to the warrant was conducted later that day by four police officers and took place in the presence of some members of the Daily staff. The Daily's photographic laboratories, filing cabinets, desks, and wastepaper baskets were searched. Locked drawers and rooms were not opened. The officers apparently had opportunity to read notes and correspondence during the search. . . . The search revealed only the photographs that had already been published on April 11, and no materials were removed from the Daily's office.

A month later the Daily and various members of its staff, respondents here, brought a civil action in the United States District Court for the Northern District of California seeking declaratory and injunctive relief under 42 U.S.C. §1983 against the police officers who conducted the search, the chief of police, the district attorney and one of his deputies, and the judge who had issued the warrant. The complaint alleged that the search of the Daily's office had deprived respondents under color of state law of rights secured to them by the First, Fourth, and Fourteenth Amendments of the United States Constitution.

The District Court . . . held . . . that the Fourth and Fourteenth Amendments forbade the issuance of a warrant to search for materials in possession of one not suspected of crime unless there is probable cause to believe, based on facts presented in a sworn affidavit, that a subpoena duces tecum would be impracticable. Moreover, the failure to honor a subpoena would not alone justify a warrant; it must also appear that the possessor of the objects sought would disregard a court order not to remove or destroy them. The District Court further held that where the innocent object of the search is a newspaper, First Amendment interests are also involved and that such a search is constitutionally permissible "only in the rare circumstance where there is a *clear showing* that (1) important materials will be destroyed or removed from the jurisdiction; *and* (2) a restraining order would be futile." . . . We reverse. . . .

It is an understatement to say that there is no direct authority in this or any other federal court for the District Court's sweeping revision of the Fourth Amendment. Under existing law, valid warrants may be issued to search any property, whether or not occupied by a third party, at which there is probable cause to believe that fruits, instrumentalities, or evidence of a crime will be found. . . .

. . . The Fourth Amendment has itself struck the balance between privacy and public need, and there is no occasion or justification for a court to revise the Amendment and strike a new balance by denying the search warrant in the circumstances present here and by insisting that the investigation proceed by subpoena duces tecum, whether on the theory that the latter is a less intrusive alternative or otherwise.

This is not to question that "reasonableness" is the overriding test of compliance with the Fourth Amendment or to assert that searches, however or whenever executed, may never be unreasonable if supported by a warrant issued on probable cause and properly identifying the place to be searched and the property to be seized. We do hold, however, that the courts may not, in the name of Fourth Amendment reasonableness, prohibit the States from issuing warrants to search for evidence simply because the owner or possessor of the place to be searched is not then reasonably suspected of criminal involvement. . . .

In any event, the reasons presented by the District Court and adopted by the Court of Appeals for arriving at its remarkable conclusion do not withstand analysis. *First,* . . . it is apparent that whether the third-party occupant is suspect or not, the State's interest in enforcing the criminal law and recovering the evidence remains the same; and it is the seeming innocence of the property owner that the District Court relied on to foreclose the warrant to search. But, as respondents themselves now concede, if the third party knows that contraband or other illegal materials are on his property, he is sufficiently culpable to justify the issuance of a search warrant. Similarly, if his ethical stance is the determining factor, it seems to us that whether or not he knows that the sought-after articles are secreted on his property and whether or not he knows that the articles are in fact the fruits, instrumentalities, or evidence of crime, he will be so informed when the search warrant is served, and it is doubtful that he should then be permitted to object to the search, to withhold, if it is there, the evidence of crime reasonably believed to be possessed by him or secreted on his property, and to forbid the search and insist that the officers serve him with a subpoena duces tecum.

Second, we are unpersuaded that the District Court's new rule denying search warrants against third parties and insisting on subpoenas would substantially further privacy interests without seriously undermining law enforcement efforts. . . . As the District Court understands it, denying third-party search warrants would not have substantial adverse effects on criminal investigations because the nonsuspect third party, once served with a subpoena, will preserve the evidence and ultimately lawfully respond. The difficulty with this assumption is that search warrants are often employed early in an investigation, perhaps before the identity of any likely criminal and certainly before all the perpetrators are or could be known. In any event, it is likely that the real culprits will have access to the property, and the delay involved in employing the subpoena duces tecum, offering as it does the opportunity to litigate its validity, could easily result in the disappearance of the evidence, whatever the good faith of the third party.[8] . . . .

We are also not convinced that the net gain to privacy interests by the District Court's new rule would be worth the candle.[9] In the normal course of events, search warrants are more difficult to obtain than subpoenas, since the latter do not involve the judiciary and do not require

8. It is also far from clear, even apart from the dangers of destruction and removal, whether the use of the subpoena duces tecum under circumstances where there is probable cause to believe that a crime has been committed and that the materials sought constitute evidence of its commission will result in the production of evidence with sufficient regularity to satisfy the public interest in law enforcement. Unlike the individual whose privacy is invaded by a search, the recipient of a subpoena may assert the Fifth Amendment privilege against self-incrimination in response to a summons to produce evidence or give testimony. See Maness v. Meyers, 419 U.S. 449 (1975). This privilege is not restricted to suspects. We have construed it broadly as covering any individual who might be incriminated by the evidence in connection with which the privilege is asserted. Hoffman v. United States, 341 U.S. 479 (1951). The burden of overcoming an assertion of the Fifth Amendment privilege, even if prompted by a desire not to cooperate rather than any real fear of self-incrimination, is one which prosecutors would rarely be able to meet in the early stages of an investigation despite the fact they did not regard the witness as a suspect. Even time spent litigating such matters could seriously impede criminal investigation.

9. We reject totally the reasoning of the District Court that additional protections are required to assure that the Fourth Amendment rights of third parties are not violated because of the unavailability of the exclusionary rule as a deterrent to improper searches of premises in the control of nonsuspects. . . . It is probably seldom that police during the investigatory stage when most searches occur will be so convinced that no potential defendant will have standing to exclude evidence on Fourth Amendment grounds that they will feel free to ignore constitutional restraints. In any event, it would be placing the cart before the horse to prohibit searches otherwise conforming to the Fourth Amendment because of a perception that the deterrence provided by the existing rules of standing is insufficient to discourage illegal searches. . . .

proof of probable cause. Where, in the real world, subpoenas would suffice, it can be expected that they will be employed by the rational prosecutor. On the other hand, when choice is available under local law and the prosecutor chooses to use the search warrant, it is unlikely that he has needlessly selected the more difficult course. His choice is more likely to be based on the solid belief, arrived at through experience but difficult, if not impossible, to sustain in a specific case, that the warranted search is necessary to secure and to avoid the destruction of evidence. . . .

The District Court held, and respondents assert here, that whatever may be true of third-party searches generally, where the third party is a newspaper, there are additional factors derived from the First Amendment that justify a nearly per se rule forbidding the search warrant and permitting only the subpoena duces tecum. The general submission is that searches of newspaper offices for evidence of crime reasonably believed to be on the premises will seriously threaten the ability of the press to gather, analyze, and disseminate news. This is said to be true for several reasons: *First*, searches will be physically disruptive to such an extent that timely publication will be impeded. *Second*, confidential sources of information will dry up, and the press will also lose opportunities to cover various events because of fears of the participants that press files will be readily available to the authorities. *Third*, reporters will be deterred from recording and preserving their recollections for future use if such information is subject to seizure. *Fourth*, the processing of news and its dissemination will be chilled by the prospects that searches will disclose internal editorial deliberations. *Fifth*, the press will resort to self-censorship to conceal its possession of information of potential interest to the police.

It is true that the struggle from which the Fourth Amendment emerged "is largely a history of conflict between the Crown and the press," Stanford v. Texas, 379 U.S. 476, 482 (1965), and that in issuing warrants and determining the reasonableness of a search, state and federal magistrates should be aware that "unrestricted power of search and seizure could also be an instrument for stifling liberty of expression." Marcus v. Search Warrant, 367 U.S. 717, 729 (1961). . . .

Neither the Fourth Amendment nor the cases requiring consideration of First Amendment values in issuing search warrants, however, call for imposing the regime ordered by the District Court. . . . Further, the prior cases do no more than insist that the courts apply the warrant requirements with particular exactitude when First Amendment interests would be endangered by the search. As we see it, no more than this is required where the warrant requested is for the seizure of criminal evidence reasonably believed to be on the premises occupied by a newspaper.

Properly administered, the preconditions for a warrant—probable cause, specificity with respect to the place to be searched and the things to be seized, and overall reasonableness—should afford sufficient protection against the harms that are assertedly threatened by warrants for searching newspaper offices.

There is no reason to believe, for example, that magistrates cannot guard against searches of the type, scope, and intrusiveness that would actually interfere with the timely publication of a newspaper. Nor, if the requirements of specificity and reasonableness are properly applied, po-liced, and observed, will there be any occasion or opportunity for officers to rummage at large in newspaper files or to intrude into or to deter normal editorial and publication decisions. The warrant issued in this case authorized nothing of this sort. Nor are we convinced, any more than we were in Branzburg v. Hayes, 408 U.S. 665 (1972), that confi-dential sources will disappear and that the press will suppress news because of fears of warranted searches. Whatever incremental effect there may be in this regard if search warrants, as well as subpoenas, are permissible in proper circumstances, it does not make a constitutional difference in our judgment.

The fact is that respondents and amici have pointed to only a very few instances in the entire United States since 1971 involving the issuance of warrants for searching newspaper premises. This reality hardly suggests abuse; and if abuse occurs, there will be time enough to deal with it. Furthermore, the press is not only an important, critical, and valuable asset to society, but it is not easily intimidated—nor should it be. . . .

. . . [T]he judgment of the Court of Appeals is reversed.

So ordered.

MR. JUSTICE BRENNAN took no part in the consideration or decision of these cases.

MR. JUSTICE POWELL, concurring.

. . . Even aside from the difficulties involved in deciding on a case-by-case basis whether a subpoena can serve as an adequate substitute,[1] I

---

1. For example, respondents had announced a policy of destroying any photographs that might aid prosecution of protesters. . . . While this policy probably reflected the deep feelings of the Vietnam era, and one may assume that under normal circumstances few, if any, press entities would adopt a policy so hostile to law enforcement, respondents' policy at least illustrates the possibility of such hostility. Use of a subpoena, as proposed by the dissent, would be of no utility in face of a policy of destroying evidence. And unless the policy were publicly announced, it probably would be difficult to show the impracticality of a subpoena as opposed to a search warrant. . . . While the existence of this policy was not before the magistrate at the time of the warrant's issuance, 353 F. Supp. 124, 135 n.16 (N.D.Cal. 1972), it illustrates the possible dangers of creating separate standards for the press alone.

agree with the Court that there is no constitutional basis for such a reading. . . .

MR. JUSTICE STEWART, with whom MR. JUSTICE MARSHALL joins, dissenting. . . .

It seems to me self-evident that police searches of newspaper offices burden the freedom of the press. . . . Policemen occupying a newsroom and searching it thoroughly for what may be an extended period of time[2] will inevitably interrupt its normal operations. . . .

A search warrant allows police officers to ransack the files of a newspaper, reading each and every document until they have found the one named in the warrant,[7] while a subpoena would permit the newspaper itself to produce only the specific documents requested. . . .

MR. JUSTICE STEVENS, dissenting.

The novel problem presented by this case is an outgrowth of the profound change in Fourth Amendment law that occurred in 1967, when Warden v. Hayden, 387 U.S. 294, was decided. . . .

In the pre-*Hayden* era warrants were used to search for contraband, weapons, and plunder, but not for "mere evidence." The practical effect of the rule prohibiting the issuance of warrants to search for mere evidence was to narrowly limit not only the category of objects, but also the category of persons and the character of the privacy interests that might be affected by an unannounced police search.

Just as the witnesses who participate in an investigation or a trial far outnumber the defendants, the persons who possess evidence that may help to identify an offender, or explain an aspect of a criminal transaction, far outnumber those who have custody of weapons or plunder. Countless law-abiding citizens—doctors, lawyers, merchants, customers, bystanders—may have documents in their possession that relate to an ongoing criminal investigation. The consequences of subjecting this large category of persons to unannounced police searches are extremely serious. The ex parte warrant procedure enables the prosecutor to obtain access to privileged documents that could not be examined if advance notice gave

2. One search of a radio station in Los Angeles lasted over eight hours. Note, Search and Seizure of the Media: A Statutory, Fourth Amendment and First Amendment Analysis, 28 Stan. L. Rev. 957, 957-959 (1976).

7. The Court says that "if the requirements of specificity and reasonableness are properly applied, policed, and observed" there will be no opportunity for the police to "rummage at large in newspaper files." . . . But in order to find a particular document, no matter how specifically it is identified in the warrant, the police will have to search every place where it might be—including, presumably, every file in the office—and to examine each document they find to see if it is the correct one. I thus fail to see how the Fourth Amendment would provide an effective limit to these searches.

the custodian an opportunity to object. The search for the documents described in a warrant may involve the inspection of files containing other private matter. The dramatic character of a sudden search may cause an entirely unjustified injury to the reputation of the persons searched.

Of greatest importance, however, is the question whether the offensive intrusion on the privacy of the ordinary citizen is justified by the law enforcement interest it is intended to vindicate. Possession of contraband or the proceeds or tools of crime gives rise to two inferences: that the custodian is involved in the criminal activity, and that, if given notice of an intended search, he will conceal or destroy what is being sought. The probability of criminal culpability justifies the invasion of his privacy; the need to accomplish the law enforcement purpose of the search justifies acting without advance notice and by force, if necessary. By satisfying the probable-cause standard appropriate for weapons or plunder, the police effectively demonstrate that no less intrusive method of investigation will succeed.

Mere possession of documentary evidence, however, is much less likely to demonstrate that the custodian is guilty of any wrongdoing or that he will not honor a subpoena or informal request to produce it. In the pre-*Hayden* era, evidence of that kind was routinely obtained by procedures that presumed that the custodian would respect his obligation to obey subpoenas and to cooperate in the investigation of crime. These procedures had a constitutional dimension. . . .

A showing of probable cause that was adequate to justify the issuance of a warrant to search for stolen goods in the 18th century does not automatically satisfy the new dimensions of the Fourth Amendment in the post-*Hayden* era. . . .

NOTES AND QUESTIONS

1. Consider footnote 8 of the majority opinion. Is it not clear that at the time of Boyd v. United States, page 424 supra, this point would have cut in favor of rather than against requiring a subpoena duces tecum? Which way should it cut?

2. Note that despite its holding the Court acknowledges that "reasonableness is the overriding test" and that the existence of a warrant supported by probable cause will not necessarily be sufficient to make a search reasonable.

When, if ever, might such a search be unreasonable? Reconsider the question raised in Chapter 6 about the search for and seizure of a diary. Is it possible that such a search would be inherently unreasonable— or unreasonable without some special showing of need?

Should the first amendment implications inherent in the seizure of allegedly obscene books or films alter the traditional fourth amendment balance? In A Quantity of Books v. Kansas, 378 U.S. 205 (1964), the Court held that a large-scale seizure amounting to a prior restraint had to be preceded by an adversary hearing on the question of obscenity, and in Heller v. New York, 413 U.S. 483 (1973), the Court held that other, more limited seizures must be pursuant to a warrant and that there must be an opportunity for a prompt postseizure judicial determination of obscenity. More recently, in New York v. P.J. Video, Inc., 475 U.S. 868 (1986), the Court rejected the defendant's contention that a warrant for the seizure of allegedly obscene materials must be based on a higher standard of probable cause than that required for the seizure of other items, such as drugs or contraband.

3. *Zurcher* generated legislative action at both the federal and the state level. See, the federal Privacy Protection Act of 1980, 42 U.S.C. §2000aa-2000aa-12 (1988) and the accompanying Justice Department regulations, 28 C.F.R. §§59.1, 59.4 (1984), which provide the news media with protection from searches and seizures similar to that advocated by the Stanford Daily in *Zurcher*. For a state response to *Zurcher*, see, e.g., Cal. Penal Code §1524.

TENNESSEE v. GARNER
Certiorari to the United States Court of Appeals for the Sixth Circuit
471 U.S. 1 (1985)

JUSTICE WHITE delivered the opinion of the Court.

This case requires us to determine the constitutionality of the use of deadly force to prevent the escape of an apparently unarmed suspected felon. We conclude that such force may not be used unless it is necessary to prevent the escape and the officer has probable cause to believe that the suspect poses a significant threat of death or serious physical injury to the officer or others.

I

At about 10:45 P.M. on October 3, 1974, Memphis Police Officers Elton Hymon and Leslie Wright were dispatched to answer a "prowler inside call." Upon arriving at the scene they saw a woman standing on her porch and gesturing toward the adjacent house. She told them she had heard glass breaking and that "they" or "someone" was breaking in next door. While Wright radioed the dispatcher to say that they were on the scene, Hymon went behind the house. He heard a door slam and saw someone run across the back yard. The fleeing suspect, who was appellee-respondent's decedent, Edward Garner, stopped at a 6-feet-high chain link fence at the edge of the yard. With the aid of a flashlight, Hymon was able to see Garner's face and hands. He saw no sign of a weapon, and, though not certain, was "reasonably sure" and "figured" that Garner was unarmed. . . . He thought Garner was 17 or 18 years old and about 5'5" or 5'7" tall.[2] While Garner was crouched at the base of the fence, Hymon called out "police, halt" and took a few steps toward him. Garner then began to climb over the fence. Convinced that if Garner made it over the fence he would elude capture, Hymon shot him. The bullet hit Garner in the back of the head. Garner was taken by ambulance to a hospital, where he died on the operating table. Ten dollars and a purse taken from the house were found on his body.

In using deadly force to prevent the escape, Hymon was acting under the authority of a Tennessee statute and pursuant to Police Department policy.[5]

Garner's father . . . brought this action . . . seeking damages under 42 U.S.C. §1983 for asserted violations of Garner's constitutional rights. . . . After a 3-day bench trial, the District Court entered judgment for all defendants. . . .

The Court of Appeals reversed and remanded. . . .

II . . .

A police officer may arrest a person if he has probable cause to believe that person committed a crime. E.g., United States v. Watson, [page 647 supra]. . . . Petitioners and appellant argue that if this requirement is satisfied the Fourth Amendment has nothing to say about *how* that seizure is made. This submission ignores the many cases in which this Court, by balancing the extent of the intrusion against the need for it, has examined the reasonableness of the manner in which a search or seizure is conducted. To determine the constitutionality of a seizure "[w]e must balance the nature and quality of the intrusion on the individual's Fourth Amendment interests against the importance of the governmental interests alleged to justify the intrusion." United States v. Place, 462 U.S. 696, 703 (1983). . . . Because one of the factors is the extent of the

2. In fact, Garner, an eighth-grader, was 15. He was 5'4" tall and weighed somewhere around 100 or 110 pounds. . . .

5. . . . Tennessee law forbids the use of deadly force in the arrest of a misdemeanant. See Johnson v. State, 173 Tenn. 134, 114 S.W.2d 819 (1938).

intrusion, it is plain that reasonableness depends on not only when a seizure is made, but also how it is carried out. . . .

. . . [N]otwithstanding probable cause to seize a suspect, an officer may not always do so by killing him. . . . The suspect's fundamental interest in his own life need not be elaborated upon. The use of deadly force also frustrates the interest of the individual, and of society, in judicial determination of guilt and punishment. Against these interests are ranged governmental interests in effective law enforcement.[8] It is argued that overall violence will be reduced by encouraging the peaceful submission of suspects who know that they may be shot if they flee. Effectiveness in making arrests requires the resort to deadly force, or at least the meaningful threat thereof. "Being able to arrest such individuals is a condition precedent to the state's entire system of law enforcement." Brief for Petitioners 14.

Without in any way disparaging the importance of these goals, we are not convinced that the use of deadly force is a sufficiently productive measure of accomplishing them to justify the killing of nonviolent suspects. . . . [W]hile the meaningful threat of deadly force might be thought to lead to the arrest of more live suspects by discouraging escape attempts,[9] the presently available evidence does not support this thesis.[10]

8. The dissent emphasizes that subsequent investigation cannot replace immediate apprehension. We recognize that this is so . . . ; indeed, that is the reason why there is any dispute. If subsequent arrest were assured, no one would argue that use of deadly force was justified. Thus, we proceed on the assumption that subsequent arrest is not likely. Nonetheless, it should be remembered that failure to apprehend at the scene does not necessarily mean that the suspect will never be caught. . . .

9. We note that the usual manner of deterring illegal conduct—through punishment—has been largely ignored in connection with flight from arrest. Arkansas, for example, specifically excepts flight from arrest from the offense of "obstruction of governmental operations." The commentary notes that this "reflects the basic policy judgment that, absent the use of force or violence, a mere attempt to avoid apprehension by a law enforcement officer does not give rise to an independent offense." Ark. Stat. Ann. §41-2802(3)(a)(1977) and commentary. In the few States that do outlaw flight from an arresting officer, the crime is only a misdemeanor. See, e.g., Ind. Code §35-44-3-3 (1982). Even forceful resistance, though generally a separate offense, is classified as a misdemeanor. E.g., Ill. Rev. Stat., ch. 38, §31-1 (1984); Mont. Code Ann. §45-7-301 (1984); N.H. Rev. Stat. Ann. §642:2 (Supp. 1983); Ore. Rev. Stat. §162.315 (1983).

This lenient approach does avoid the anomaly of automatically transforming every fleeing misdemeanant into a fleeing felon—subject, under the common-law rule, to apprehension by deadly force—solely by virtue of his flight. However, it is in real tension with the harsh consequences of flight in cases where deadly force is employed. For example, Tennessee does not outlaw fleeing from arrest. The Memphis City code does, §30-15, subjecting the offender to a maximum fine of $50, §1-8. Thus, Garner's attempted escape subjected him to (a) a $50 fine, and (b) being shot.

10. See Sherman, Reducing Police Gun Use, in Control in the Police Organization 98, 120-123 (M. Punch, ed. 1983); Fyfe, Observations on Police Deadly Force, 27 Crime & Delinquency 376, 378-381 (1981); W. Geller & K. Karales, Split-Second Decisions 67 (1981), App. 84 (Affidavit of William Bracey, Chief of Patrol, New York City Police Department). See generally Brief for Police Foundation et al. as Amici Curiae.

The fact is that a majority of police departments in this country have forbidden the use of deadly force against nonviolent suspects. . . . If those charged with the enforcement of the criminal law have abjured the use of deadly force in arresting nondangerous felons, there is a substantial basis for doubting that the use of such force is an essential attribute of the arrest power in all felony cases. . . . Petitioners and appellant have not persuaded us that shooting nondangerous fleeing suspects is so vital as to outweigh the suspect's interest in his own life.

The use of deadly force to prevent the escape of all felony suspects, whatever the circumstances, is constitutionally unreasonable. It is not better that all felony suspects die than that they escape. Where the suspect poses no immediate threat to the officer and no threat to others, the harm resulting from failing to apprehend him does not justify the use of deadly force to do so. It is no doubt unfortunate when a suspect who is in sight escapes, but the fact that the police arrive a little late or are a little slower afoot does not always justify killing the suspect. A police officer may not seize an unarmed, nondangerous suspect by shooting him dead. . . .

. . . Where the officer has probable cause to believe that the suspect poses a threat of serious physical harm, either to the officer or to others, it is not constitutionally unreasonable to prevent escape by using deadly force. Thus, if the suspect threatens the officer with a weapon or there is probable cause to believe that he has committed a crime involving the infliction or threatened infliction of serious physical harm, deadly force may be used if necessary to prevent escape, and if, where feasible, some warning has been given. . . .

III . . .

It is insisted that the Fourth Amendment must be construed in light of the common-law rule, which allowed the use of whatever force was necessary to effect the arrest of a fleeing felon, though not a misdemeanant. . . .

The State and city argue that because this was the prevailing rule at the time of the adoption of the Fourth Amendment and for some time thereafter, and is still in force in some States, use of deadly force against a fleeing felon must be "reasonable." It is true that this Court has often looked to the common law in evaluating the reasonableness, for Fourth Amendment purposes, of police activity. See, e.g., United States v. Watson, [page 647 supra]. . . . On the other hand, it "has not simply frozen into constitutional law those law enforcement practices that existed at the time of the Fourth Amendment's passage." Payton v. New York, . . . [page 650 supra]. Because of sweeping change in the legal and technological context, reliance on the common-law rule in this case would be a mistaken literalism that ignores the purposes of a historical inquiry. . . .

It has been pointed out many times that the common-law rule is best understood in light of the fact that it arose at a time when virtually all felonies were punishable by death. . . . Courts have also justified the common-law rule by emphasizing the relative dangerousness of felons. . . .

Neither of these justifications makes sense today. Almost all crimes formerly punishable by death no longer are or can be. . . . Many crimes classified as misdemeanors, or nonexistent, at common law are now felonies. . . . Indeed, numerous misdemeanors involve conduct more dangerous than many felonies.

There is an additional reason why the common-law rule cannot be directly translated to the present day. The common-law rule developed at a time when weapons were rudimentary. Deadly force could be inflicted almost solely in a hand-to-hand struggle during which, necessarily, the safety of the arresting officer was at risk. Handguns were not carried by police officers until the latter half of the last century. L. Kennett & J. Anderson, The Gun in America 150-151 (1975). Only then did it become possible to use deadly force from a distance as a means of apprehension. As a practical matter, the use of deadly force under the standard articulation of the common-law rule has an altogether different meaning—and harsher consequences—now than in past centuries. . . .

In evaluating the reasonableness of police procedures under the Fourth Amendment, we have also looked to prevailing rules in individual jurisdictions. [Of the 45 states in which the rule is relatively clear, 21 follow the common law, and 23 limit the right to use force to apprehend fleeing felons.] . . .

It cannot be said that there is a constant or overwhelming trend away from the common-law rule. In recent years, some States have reviewed their laws and expressly rejected abandonment of the common-law rule. Nonetheless, the long-term movement has been away from the rule that deadly force may be used against any fleeing felon, and that remains the rule in less than half the States.

This trend is more evident and impressive when viewed in light of the policies adopted by the police departments themselves. . . . Overall, only 7.5% of departmental and municipal policies explicitly permit the use of deadly force against any felon; 86.8% explicitly do not. K. Matulia, A Balance of Forces: A Report of the International Association of Chiefs of Police 161 (1982) (table). . . .

Actual departmental policies are important for an additional reason. We would hesitate to declare a police practice of long standing "unreasonable" if doing so would severely hamper effective law enforcement. But the indications are to the contrary. There has been no suggestion that crime has worsened in any way in jurisdictions that have adopted, by legislation or departmental policy, rules similar to that announced today. Amici noted that "[a]fter extensive research and consideration, [they] have concluded that laws permitting police officers to use deadly force to apprehend unarmed, nonviolent fleeing felony suspects actually do not protect citizens or law enforcement officers, do not deter crime or alleviate problems caused by crime, and do not improve the crime-fighting ability of law enforcement agencies." Brief for Police Foundation et al. as Amici Curiae 11. . . .

Nor do we agree with petitioners and appellant that the rule we have adopted requires the police to make impossible, split-second evaluations of unknowable facts. . . . We do not deny the practical difficulties of attempting to assess the suspect's dangerousness. However, similarly difficult judgments must be made by the police in equally uncertain circumstances. See, e.g., Terry v. Ohio, . . . [page 684 supra]. Nor is there any indication that in States that allow the use of deadly force only against dangerous suspects . . . the standard has been difficult to apply or has led to a rash of litigation involving inappropriate second-guessing of police officers' split-second decisions. . . .

IV

The District Court [found] . . . that Garner appeared to be unarmed, though Hymon could not be certain that was the case. . . . Restated in Fourth Amendment terms, this means Hymon had no articulable basis to think Garner was armed. . . .

. . . [T]he fact that Garner was a suspected burglar could not, without regard to the other circumstances, automatically justify the use of deadly force. Hymon did not have probable cause to believe that Garner, whom he correctly believed to be unarmed, posed any physical danger to himself or others.

The dissent argues that the shooting was justified by the fact that Officer Hymon had probable cause to believe that Garner had committed a nighttime burglary. . . . While we agree that burglary is a serious crime, we cannot agree that it is so dangerous as automatically to justify the use of deadly force. The FBI classifies burglary as a "property" rather than a "violent" crime. See Federal Bureau of Investigation, Uniform Crime Reports, Crime in the United States I (1984). Although the armed burglar would present a different situation, the fact that an unarmed suspect has broken into a dwelling at night does not automatically mean he is physically dangerous. This case demonstrates as much. . . . In fact, the available statistics demonstrate that burglaries only rarely involve physical violence. During the 10-year period from 1973-1982, only 3.8% of all burglaries involved violent crime. Bureau of Justice Statistics, Household Burglary, p. 4 (1983).[23] . . .

V

. . . We hold that the [Tennessee] statute is invalid insofar as it purported to give Hymon the authority to act as he did. . . .

The judgment of the Court of Appeals is affirmed, and the case is remanded for further proceedings consistent with this opinion. . . .

[The dissenting opinion of JUSTICE O'CONNOR, joined by CHIEF JUSTICE BURGER and JUSTICE REHNQUIST, is omitted.]

NOTES AND QUESTIONS

1. Even if the police should not have the right to use deadly force to apprehend *all* escaping suspected felons, should burglary be one of the crimes for which deadly force is prohibited? Even if the risk of personal injury from burglars is small, is it not likely that among those victims who are injured the incidence of serious injury is high? In any event, if a person who chooses to communicate by telephone in effect forfeits any privacy interest in the identity of number dialed, see Smith v. Maryland, page 540 supra, and if a person who decides to maintain a bank account in effect forfeits any privacy interest in transactions about which the bank is required to keep records, see United States v. Miller, page 540 supra, why should a person who chooses to be a fleeing burglar not forfeit the right to personal safety?

2. Justices Brennan and Marshall have frequently criticized the Court's balancing tests. See, e.g., O'Connor v. Ortega, pages 801-802

---

23. The dissent points out that three-fifths of all rapes in the home, three-fifths of all home robberies, and about a third of home assaults are committed by burglars. . . . These figures mean only that if one knows that a suspect committed a rape in the home, there is a good chance that the suspect is also a burglar. That has nothing to do with the question here, which is whether the fact that someone has committed a burglary indicates that he has committed, or might commit, a violent crime.

The dissent also points out that this 3.8% adds up to 2.8 million violent crimes over a 10-year period, as if to imply that today's holding will let loose 2.8 million violent burglars. The relevant universe is, of course, far smaller. At issue is only that tiny fraction of cases where violence has taken place and an officer who has no other means of apprehending the suspect is unaware of its occurrence.

7. The Fourth Amendment

supra. Is not the Court in *Garner*, with their approval, doing exactly what they condemned in *O'Connor*? Are they being inconsistent and solely result oriented? Or is there a principled basis for distinguishing between (1) a balancing process that may require more than probable cause and a warrant to protect fourth amendment interests and (2) a balancing process that may find adequate protection of fourth amendment interests in the absence of probable cause and a warrant?

After *Garner* would the use of excessive but nondeadly force against a minor criminal—e.g., a pickpocket—constitute a violation of the fourth amendment? See Uviller, Seizure by Gunshot: The Riddle of the Fleeing Felon, 14 N.Y.U. Rev. L. & Soc. Change 705 (1986). See also Winter, Tennessee v. Garner and the Democratic Practice of Judicial Review, 14 N.Y.U. Rev. L. & Soc. Change 679 (1986).

3. The only recent case other than *Garner* in which the Supreme Court has held that the fourth amendment demands more than probable cause plus a warrant (or an exception to the warrant requirement) is Winston v. Lee, 470 U.S. 753 (1985). Ralph Watkinson, an attempted robbery victim, shot at and believed he wounded the perpetrator of the crime. A short time later Watkinson identified Lee as his assailant. Lee was suffering from a recent gunshot wound in the area of his left chest. The state sought an order compelling removal of the bullet from Lee. After several evidentiary hearings, the trial court granted the order and the Virginia Supreme Court affirmed. The federal district court then enjoined the surgery, and the court of appeals affirmed. The United States Supreme Court, without dissent, held that permitting the surgery would violate Lee's fourth amendment rights:

> Schmerber [v. California, page 441 supra], . . . provides the appropriate framework of analysis. . . .
>
> *Schmerber* recognized that the ordinary [probable cause and warrant] requirements . . . would be the threshold requirements for conducting this kind of surgical search and seizure. . . .
>
> Beyond these standards, *Schmerber's* inquiry considered a number of other factors. . . . A crucial factor in analyzing the magnitude of the intrusion . . . is the extent to which the procedure may threaten the safety or health of the individual. . . .
>
> Another factor is the extent of intrusion upon the individual's dignitary interests in personal privacy and bodily integrity. . . .
>
> Weighed against these individual interests is the community's interest in fairly and accurately determining guilt or innocence. This interest is of course of great importance.
>
> . . . The Commonwealth plainly had probable cause. . . . In addition all parties apparently agree that respondent has had a full measure of procedural protections and has been able fully to litigate the difficult.

medical and legal questions. . . .[6] Our inquiry therefore must focus on the extent of the intrusion on respondent's privacy interests and on the State's need for the evidence.

The threats to the health or safety of respondent posed by the surgery are the subject of sharp dispute. . . .

The Court of Appeals . . . found that respondent would suffer some risks. . . .[7] One surgeon had testified that [there were] . . . ". . . risks of injury to the muscle as well as injury to the nerves, blood vessels and other tissue in the chest and pleural cavity." The court further noted that "the greater intrusion and the larger incisions increase the risks of infection." . . . One surgeon stated that [the operation] would take 15-20 minutes, while another predicted the procedure could take up to two and one-half hours. . . . The court properly took the resulting uncertainty about the medical risks into account.[8]

Both lower courts . . . believed that the proposed surgery, which for purely medical reasons required the use of a general anesthetic,[9] would be an "extensive" intrusion on respondent's personal privacy and bodily integrity. . . . [T]he Court of Appeals noted that the Commonwealth proposes to take control of respondent's body, to "drug this citizen—not yet convicted of a criminal offense—with narcotics and barbiturates into a state of unconsciousness," . . . and then to search beneath his skin for evidence of a crime. . . .

The other part of the balance concerns the Commonwealth's need [for the evidence]. . . . [Al]though we recognize the difficulty of making determinations in advance as to the strength of the case against respondent, petitioners' assertions of a compelling need for the bullet are hardly persuasive. . . . The Commonwealth has available substantial . . . evidence that respondent was the individual who accosted Watkinson. . . . No party . . . suggests that Watkinson's . . . identification of respondent . . . would be inadmissible. In addition, petitioners can no doubt prove that [respondent) was found a few blocks from Watkinson's store shortly after the incident took place. And petitioners can certainly show that the

---

6. Because the State has afforded respondent the benefit of a full adversary presentation and appellate review, we do not reach the question whether the State may compel a suspect to undergo a surgical search of this magnitude for evidence absent such special procedural protections. . . .

7. The Court of Appeals concluded, however, that "the specific physical risks from putting [respondent] under general anesthesia may . . . be considered minimal." . . . Testimony had shown that "the general risks of harm or death from general anesthesia are quite low, and that [respondent] was in the statistical group of persons with the lowest risk of injury from general anesthesia." . . .

8. One expert testified that this would be "minor" surgery. . . . The question whether the surgery is to be characterized in medical terms as "major" or "minor" is not controlling. We agree with the . . . [courts below] that "there is no reason to suppose that the definition of a medical term of art should coincide with the parameters of a constitutional standard." . . .

9. Somewhat different issues would be raised if the use of a general anesthetic became necessary because of the patient's refusal to cooperate. . . .

location of the bullet (under respondent's left collarbone) seems to correlate with Watkinson's report that the robber "jerked" to the left. . . .[10]
. . . Where the Court has found a lesser expectation of privacy, . . . the Court has held that the Fourth Amendment's protections are correspondingly less stringent. Conversely, however, the Fourth Amendment's command that searches be "reasonable" requires that when the State seeks to intrude upon an area in which our society recognizes a significantly heightened privacy interest, a more substantial justification is required to make the search "reasonable." Applying these principles, we hold that the proposed search in this case would be "unreasonable" under the Fourth Amendment.

Note that the Court refers to "petitioners' assertions of a compelling need" for the evidence. Should "compelling need" be the test that the state must meet? If so, what should the relationship be between the state's "compelling need" and the seriousness of the intrusion on fourth amendment interests? Should compelling need be a threshold requirement in every case in which the state seeks to force an individual to submit to medical procedures? If the state can show that conviction would be impossible without the evidence and virtually certain with the evidence, what level of intrusion should be permitted?

Is the "more substantial justification" that is required in *Lee* something that might also be required when the state is attempting to obtain private writings or some property of a very personal nature?

Are the Court's drug testing cases, *Skinner*, page 804 supra, and *Von Raab*, page 805 supra, compatible with *Lee?*

Compare *Lee* with Rochin v. California, 342 U.S. 165 (1952). In *Rochin* the Court relied on the due process clause to hold inadmissible morphine capsules that the police obtained by forcibly injecting an emetic into the defendant, thereby causing him to vomit up the capsules. Would it have been preferable for the *Lee* Court to rely on the due process clause rather than the fourth amendment? For an affirmative answer, see Bacigal, Dodging a Bullet, but Opening Old Wounds in Fourth Amendment Jurisprudence, 16 Seton Hall L. Rev. 597 (1986).

10. There are also some questions concerning the probative value of the bullet. . . . The evidentiary value of the bullet depends on a comparison between markings, if any, on the bullet in respondent's shoulder and markings, if any, found on a test bullet that the police could fire from Watkinson's gun. . . . [T]he bullet's markings may have been corroded in the time that the bullet has been in respondent's shoulder, thus making it useless for comparison purposes. . . . In addition, . . . [t]he record is devoid of any evidence that the police have attempted to test-fire Watkinson's gun, and there thus remains the additional possibility that a comparison of bullets is impossible because Watkinson's gun does not consistently fire bullets with the same markings. However, because the courts below made no findings on this point, we hesitate to give it significant weight in our analysis.

E. CONSENT AND PRIVATE SEARCHES

SCHNECKLOTH v. BUSTAMONTE
Certiorari to the United States Court of Appeals for the Ninth Circuit
412 U.S. 218 (1973)

MR. JUSTICE STEWART delivered the opinion of the Court. . . .

[O]ne of the specifically established exceptions to the requirements of both a warrant and probable cause is a search that is conducted pursuant to consent. . . . The constitutional question in the present case concerns the definition of "consent" in this Fourth and Fourteenth Amendment context. . . .

The respondent was brought to trial in a California court upon a charge of possessing a check with intent to defraud. He moved to suppress the introduction of certain material as evidence against him on the ground that the material had been acquired through an unconstitutional search and seizure. . . .

While on routine patrol in Sunnyvale, California, at approximately 2:40 in the morning, Police Officer James Rand stopped an automobile when he observed that one headlight and its license plate light were burned out. Six men were in the vehicle. Joe Alcala and the respondent, Robert Bustamonte, were in the front seat with Joe Gonzales, the driver. Three older men were seated in the rear. When, in response to the policeman's question, Gonzales could not produce a driver's license, Officer Rand asked if any of the other five had any evidence of identification. Only Alcala produced a license, and he explained that the car was his brother's. After the six occupants had stepped out of the car at the officer's request and after two additional policemen had arrived, Officer Rand asked Alcala if he could search the car. Alcala replied, "Sure, go ahead." Prior to the search no one was threatened with arrest and, according to Officer Rand's uncontradicted testimony, it "was all very congenial at this time." Gonzales testified that Alcala actually helped in the search of the car, by opening the trunk and glove compartment. In Gonzales' words: "[T]he police officer asked Joe [Alcala], he goes, 'Does the trunk open?' And Joe said, 'Yes.' He went to the car and got the keys and opened up the trunk." Wadded up under the left rear seat, the police officers found three checks that had previously been stolen from a car wash.

The trial judge denied the motion to suppress, and the checks in question were admitted in evidence at Bustamonte's trial. On the basis of this and other evidence he was convicted, and the California Court of Appeal for the First Appellate District affirmed the conviction. . . .

Thereafter, the respondent sought a writ of habeas corpus in a federal district court. It was denied. On appeal, the Court of Appeals for the Ninth Circuit . . . set aside the District Court's order. . . .

. . . [T]he State concedes that "[w]hen a prosecutor seeks to rely upon consent to justify the lawfulness of a search, he has the burden of proving that the consent was, in fact, freely and voluntarily given." Bumper v. North Carolina, 391 U.S. 543, 548. . . .

The precise question in this case, then, is what must the prosecution prove to demonstrate that a consent was "voluntarily" given. . . . The Court of Appeals for the Ninth Circuit concluded that it is an essential part of the State's initial burden to prove that a person knows he has a right to refuse consent. The California courts have followed the rule that voluntariness is a question of fact to be determined from the totality of all the circumstances, and that the state of a defendant's knowledge is only one factor to be taken into account in assessing the voluntariness of a consent. . . .

The most extensive judicial exposition of the meaning of "voluntariness" has been developed in those cases in which the Court has had to determine the "voluntariness" of a defendant's confession for purposes of the Fourteenth Amendment. . . .

Those cases yield no talismanic definition of "voluntariness," mechanically applicable to the host of situations where the question has arisen. "The notion of 'voluntariness,' " Mr. Justice Frankfurter once wrote, "is itself an amphibian." Culombe v. Connecticut, 367 U.S. 568, 604-605. It cannot be taken literally to mean a "knowing" choice.

> Except where a person is unconscious or drugged or otherwise lacks capacity for conscious choice, all incriminating statements—even those made under brutal treatment—are "voluntary" in the sense of representing a choice of alternatives. On the other hand, if "voluntariness" incorporates notions of "but-for" cause, the question should be whether the statement would have been made even absent inquiry or other official action. Under such a test, virtually no statement would be voluntary because very few people give incriminating statements in the absence of official action of some kind.[7]

It is thus evident that neither linguistics nor epistemology will provide a ready definition of the meaning of "voluntariness."

7. Bator & Vorenberg, Arrest, Detention, Interrogation and the Right to Counsel: Basic Problems and Possible Legislative Solutions, 66 Col. L. Rev. 62, 72-73.

Rather, "voluntariness" has reflected an accommodation of the complex of values implicated in police questioning of a suspect. . . .

. . . Is the confession the product of an essentially free and unconstrained choice by its maker? If it is, if he has willed to confess, it may be used against him. If it is not, if his will has been overborne and his capacity for self-determination critically impaired, the use of his confession offends due process. [Culombe v. Connecticut, supra, at 602.]

In determining whether a defendant's will was overborne in a particular case, the Court has assessed the totality of all the surrounding circumstances. . . .
[None of this Court's voluntary confession cases] . . . turned on the presence or absence of a single controlling criteri[on]. . . .
Similar considerations lead us to agree with the courts of California that the question whether a consent to a search was in fact "voluntary" or was the product of duress or coercion, express or implied, is a question of fact to be determined from the totality of all the circumstances. While knowledge of the right to refuse consent is one factor to be taken into account, the government need not establish such knowledge as the sine qua non of an effective consent. As with police questioning, two competing concerns must be accommodated in determining the meaning of a "voluntary" consent—the legitimate need for such searches and the equally important requirement of assuring the absence of coercion.
In situations where the police have some evidence of illicit activity, but lack probable cause to arrest or search, a search authorized by a valid consent may be the only means of obtaining important and reliable evidence. . . . And in those cases where there is probable cause to arrest or search, but where the police lack a warrant, a consent search may still be valuable. If the search is conducted and proves fruitless, that in itself may convince the police that an arrest with its possible stigma and embarrassment is unnecessary, or that a far more extensive search pursuant to a warrant is not justified. In short, a search pursuant to consent may result in considerably less inconvenience for the subject of the search, and, properly conducted, is a constitutionally permissible and wholly legitimate aspect of effective police activity.
But the Fourth and Fourteenth Amendments require that a consent not be coerced, by explicit or implicit means, by implied threat or covert force. For, no matter how subtly the coercion was applied, the resulting "consent" would be no more than a pretext for the unjustified police intrusion against which the Fourth Amendment is directed. . . .
The problem of reconciling the recognized legitimacy of consent searches with the requirement that they be free from any aspect of official

coercion cannot be resolved by any infallible touchstone. . . . In examining all the surrounding circumstances to determine if in fact the consent to search was coerced, account must be taken of subtly coercive police questions, as well as the possibly vulnerable subjective state of the person who consents. . . .

. . . [The Court of Appeals'] ruling, that the State must affirmatively prove that the subject of the search knew that he had a right to refuse consent, would, in practice, create serious doubt whether consent searches could continue to be conducted. There might be rare cases where it could be proved from the record that a person in fact affirmatively knew of his right to refuse. . . . But more commonly where there was no evidence of any coercion, explicit or implicit, the prosecution would nevertheless be unable to demonstrate that the subject of the search in fact had known of his right to refuse consent. . . .

One alternative that would go far toward proving that the subject of a search did know he had a right to refuse consent would be to advise him of that right before eliciting his consent. That, however, is a suggestion that has been almost universally repudiated by both federal and state courts, and, we think, rightly so. For it would be thoroughly impractical to impose on the normal consent search the detailed requirements of an effective warning. Consent searches are part of the standard investigatory techniques of law enforcement agencies. They normally occur on the highway, or in a person's home or office, and under informal and unstructured conditions. The circumstances that prompt the initial request to search may develop quickly or be a logical extension of investigative police questioning. The police may seek to investigate further suspicious circumstances or to follow up leads developed in questioning persons at the scene of a crime. These situations are a far cry from the structured atmosphere of a trial where, assisted by counsel if he chooses, a defendant is informed of his trial rights. . . . And, while surely a closer question, these situations are still immeasurably far removed from "custodial interrogation" where, in Miranda v. Arizona, [384 U.S. 436 (1966)], we found that the Constitution required certain now familiar warnings as a prerequisite to police interrogation. . . .

It is said, however, that a "consent" is a "waiver" of a person's rights under the Fourth and Fourteenth Amendments . . . [and] that under the doctrine of Johnson v. Zerbst, 304 U.S. 458, 464, to establish such a "waiver" the State must demonstrate "an intentional relinquishment or waiver abandonment of a known right or privilege."

But these standards were enunciated in *Johnson* in the context of the safeguards of a fair criminal trial. Our cases do not reflect an uncritical demand for a knowing and intelligent waiver in every situation where a person has failed to invoke a constitutional protection. . . .

Almost without exception, the requirement of a knowing and intelligent waiver has been applied only to those rights which the Constitution guarantees to a criminal defendant in order to preserve a fair trial. Hence, . . . the standard of a knowing and intelligent waiver has most often been applied to test the validity of a waiver of counsel, either at trial, or upon a guilty plea. And the Court has also applied the *Johnson* criteria to assess the effectiveness of a waiver of other trial rights such as the right to confrontation, to a jury trial, and to a speedy trial, and the right to be free from twice being placed in jeopardy. Guilty pleas have been carefully scrutinized to determine whether the accused knew and understood all the rights to which he would be entitled at trial, and that he had intentionally chosen to forgo them. . . .

The guarantees afforded a criminal defendant at trial also protect him at certain stages before the actual trial, and any alleged waiver must meet the strict standard of an intentional relinquishment of a "known" right. But the "trial" guarantees that have been applied to the "pretrial" stage of the criminal process are similarly designed to protect the fairness of the trial itself. [See, e.g., United States v. Wade, page 339 supra.] . . .

There is a vast difference between those rights that protect a fair criminal trial and the rights guaranteed under the Fourth Amendment. . . .

The protections of the Fourth Amendment . . . have nothing whatever to do with promoting the fair ascertainment of truth at a criminal trial. . . .

Nor can it even be said that a search, as opposed to an eventual trial, is somehow "unfair" if a person consents to a search. While the Fourth and Fourteenth Amendments limit the circumstances under which the police can conduct a search, there is nothing constitutionally suspect in a person's voluntarily allowing a search. . . . Rather, the community has a real interest in encouraging consent, for the resulting search may yield necessary evidence for the solution and prosecution of crime, evidence that may insure that a wholly innocent person is not wrongly charged with a criminal offense. . . .

. . . It would be unrealistic to expect that in the informal, unstructured context of a consent search, a policeman, upon pain of tainting the evidence obtained, could make the detailed type of examination demanded by *Johnson*. And, if for this reason a diluted form of "waiver" were found acceptable, that would itself be ample recognition of the fact that there is no universal standard that must be applied in every situation where a person forgoes a constitutional right.

Similarly, a "waiver" approach to consent searches would be thoroughly inconsistent with our decisions that have approved "third party consents." . . . . Frazier v. Cupp, 394 U.S. 731, 740, held that evidence seized from the defendant's duffel bag in a search authorized by his cousin's consent was admissible at trial. We found that the defendant had assumed the risk that his cousin, with whom he shared the bag, would allow the police to search it. . . .

Much of what has already been said disposes of the argument that the Court's decision in the *Miranda* case requires the conclusion that knowledge of a right to refuse is an indispensable element of a valid consent. The considerations that informed the Court's holding in *Miranda* are simply inapplicable in the present case. In *Miranda* the Court found that the techniques of police questioning and the nature of custodial surroundings produce an inherently coercive situation. The Court concluded that "[u]nless adequate protective devices are employed to dispel the compulsion inherent in custodial surroundings, no statement obtained from the defendant can truly be the product of his free choice." 384 U.S., at 458. And at another point the Court noted that "without proper safeguards the process of in-custody interrogation of persons suspected or accused of crime contains inherently compelling pressures which work to undermine the individual's will to resist and to compel him to speak where he would not otherwise do so freely." Id., at 467.

In this case, there is no evidence of any inherently coercive tactics— either from the nature of the police questioning or the environment in which it took place. Indeed, since consent searches will normally occur on a person's own familiar territory, the specter of incommunicado police interrogation in some remote station house is simply inapposite.[36] . . .

It is also argued that the failure to require the Government to establish knowledge as a prerequisite to a valid consent, will relegate the Fourth Amendment to the special province of "the sophisticated, the knowledgeable and the privileged." We cannot agree. The traditional definition of voluntariness we accept today has always taken into account evidence of minimal schooling, low intelligence, and the lack of any effective warnings to a person of his rights; and the voluntariness of any statement taken under those conditions has been carefully scrutinized to determine whether it was in fact voluntarily given.

Our decision today is a narrow one. We hold only that when the subject of a search is not in custody and the State attempts to justify a search on the basis of his consent, the Fourth and Fourteenth Amendments require that it demonstrate that the consent was in fact voluntarily given, and not the result of duress or coercion, express or implied. Voluntariness is a question of fact to be determined from all the circum-

---

36. . . . . [T]he present case does not require a determination of what effect custodial conditions might have on a search authorized solely by an alleged consent.

stances, and while the subject's knowledge of a right to refuse is a factor to be taken into account, the prosecution is not required to demonstrate such knowledge as a prerequisite to establishing a voluntary consent. Because the California court followed these principles in affirming the respondent's conviction, and because the Court of Appeals for the Ninth Circuit in remanding for an evidentiary hearing required more, its judgment must be reversed.

It is so ordered.

[The concurring opinions of JUSTICE BLACKMUN and JUSTICE POWELL and the dissenting opinions of JUSTICE DOUGLAS and JUSTICE BRENNAN are omitted.]

MR. JUSTICE MARSHALL, dissenting.

If consent to search means that a person has chosen to forgo his right to exclude the police from the place they seek to search, it follows that his consent cannot be considered a meaningful choice unless he knew that he could in fact exclude the police. The Court appears, however, to reject even the modest proposition that, if the subject of a search convinces the trier of fact that he did not know of his right to refuse assent to a police request for permission to search, the search must be held unconstitutional. For it says only that "knowledge of the right to refuse consent is one factor to be taken into account." . . . I find this incomprehensible. I can think of no other situation in which we would say that a person agreed to some course of action if he convinced us that he did not know that there was some other course he might have pursued. I would therefore hold, at a minimum, that the prosecution may not rely on a purported consent to search if the subject of the search did not know that he could refuse to give consent. . . .

If one accepts this view, the question then is a simple one: must the Government show that the subject knew of his rights, or must the subject show that he lacked such knowledge?

I think that any fair allocation of the burden would require that it be placed on the prosecution. On this question, the Court indulges in what might be called the "straw man" method of adjudication. The Court responds to this suggestion by overinflating the burden. And, when it is suggested that the *prosecution's* burden of proof could be easily satisfied if the police informed the subject of his rights, the Court responds by refusing to require the *police* to make a "detailed" inquiry. . . . If the Court candidly faced the real question of allocating the burden of proof, neither of these maneuvers would be available to it.

If the burden is placed on the defendant, all the subject can do is to testify that he did not know of his rights. And I doubt that many trial judges will find for the defendant simply on the basis of that testimony.

Precisely because the evidence is very hard to come by, courts have traditionally been reluctant to require a party to prove negatives such as the lack of knowledge. . . .

In contrast, there are several ways by which the subject's knowledge of his rights may be shown. The subject may affirmatively demonstrate such knowledge by his responses at the time the search took place. . . . Denials of knowledge may be disproved by establishing that the subject had, in the recent past, demonstrated his knowledge of his rights, for example, by refusing entry when it was requested by the police. The prior experience or training of the subject might in some cases support an inference that he knew of his right to exclude the police.

The burden on the prosecutor would disappear, of course, if the police, at the time they requested consent to search, also told the subject that he had a right to refuse consent and that his decision to refuse would be respected. The Court's assertions to the contrary notwithstanding, there is nothing impractical about this method of satisfying the prosecution's burden of proof. . . .

The Court contends that if an officer paused to inform the subject of his rights, the informality of the exchange would be destroyed. I doubt that a simple statement by an officer of an individual's right to refuse consent would do much to alter the informality of the exchange, except to alert the subject to a fact that he surely is entitled to know. It is not without significance that for many years the agents of the Federal Bureau of Investigation have routinely informed subjects of their right to refuse consent, when they request consent to search. . . .

The proper resolution of this case turns, I believe, on a realistic assessment of the nature of the interchange between citizens and the police, and of the practical import of allocating the burden of proof in one way rather than another. The Court seeks to escape such assessments by escalating its rhetoric to unwarranted heights, but no matter how forceful the adjectives the Court uses, it cannot avoid being judged by how well its image of these interchanges accords with reality. . . .

NOTES AND QUESTIONS

1. Regardless of whether you agree with the majority or the dissent, is it not clear that the underlying issue is the practical one of allocating the burden of proof with respect to an event that occurs outside the confines of the courtroom—and often with no witnesses other than the police officer(s) and the person allegedly consenting? How should the burden be allocated?

2. If it is appropriate, as the majority holds, to place the burden on

the government, why is it not also appropriate to hold that the burden is always or usually satisfied if, but only if, the police inform an individual of the right to refuse to consent? Why is the majority unwilling to impose this obligation to warn on the government?

3. Under the *Bustamonte* test, how significant should it be that the police officers state that they will obtain a warrant if the person refuses to consent? Should it matter whether the police in fact have (or believe that they have) probable cause? If so, which way does this factor cut? Is a threat to get a warrant likely to be said more convincingly and thus be more coercive if probable cause in fact exists? Or is it appropriate to view the honest threat to get a warrant as simply a statement of fact that will help the person make an informed decision whether to consent? Should it be significant that there is presumably less need to try to obtain a person's consent if the police suspicion is sufficiently great to constitute probable cause?

4. Should voluntariness be a question of subjective mental state, or should it be a question of objective manifestations of mental state? For example, should a defendant be permitted to try to prove that despite the appearance of a valid consent, the defendant was mentally incapable of consenting and/or that the police officers knew or should have known of this mental incapacity? (As a practical matter, there probably will be few cases that turn solely on the question whether *Bustamonte* establishes a subjective or an objective test for consent. After all, in the ordinary course of events we make decisions about people's subjective mental states by looking at their objective behavior.)

5. An issue that frequently arises in consent cases is the validity of a third party's consent. Stoner v. California, 376 U.S. 483 (1964), held that a hotel clerk could not validly consent to the search of a guest's room. United States v. Matlock, 415 U.S. 164 (1974), however, made it clear that a third person's consent to search would make a search constitutional if the third person had common authority over the premises searched.

ILLINOIS v. RODRIGUEZ, 110 S. Ct. 2793, 2796, 2799-2802 (1990):
JUSTICE SCALIA delivered the opinion of the Court.

. . . The present case presents an issue we expressly reserved in [United States v.] Matlock, [415 U.S. 164, 177 n.14 (1974)]: whether a warrantless entry is valid when based upon the consent of a third party whom the police, at the time of entry, reasonably believe to possess common authority over the premises, but who in fact does not do so. . . . The relevant facts . . . are as follows.

On July 26, 1985, police were summoned to the residence of Dorothy Jackson on South Wolcott in Chicago. They were met by Ms.

Jackson's daughter, Gail Fischer, who showed signs of a severe beating. She told the officers that she had been assaulted by respondent Edward Rodriguez earlier that day in an apartment on South California. Fischer stated that Rodriguez was then asleep in the apartment, and she consented to travel there with the police in order to unlock the door with her key so that officers could enter and arrest him. During this conversation, Fischer several times referred to the apartment on South California as "our" apartment, and said that she had clothes and furniture there. It is unclear whether she indicated that she currently lived at the apartment, or only that she used to live there. . . .

[When the officers and Fischer arrived at the apartment, she unlocked the door and gave the officers permission to enter. They arrested Rodriguez and seized narcotics, which they discovered in plain view. Rodriguez was charged with possession of narcotics with intent to deliver. The state courts held that the narcotics were not admissible against Rodriguez because Fisher, who in fact was not currently living in the apartment, did not have authority to consent to the search and because the officers' reasonable belief in her authority to consent would not be sufficient to validate the search. The Supreme Court agreed that Ms. Fischer did not have common authority over the apartment and thus had no authority to consent.]

The fundamental objective that alone validates all unconsented government searches is, of course, the seizure of persons who have committed or are about to commit crimes, or of evidence related to crimes. But "reasonableness," with respect to this necessary element, does not demand that the government be factually correct in its assessment that that is what a search will produce. Warrants need only be supported by "probable cause." . . . If a magistrate, based upon seemingly reliable but factually inaccurate information, issues a warrant for the search of a house in which the sought-after felon is not present, has never been present, and was never likely to have been present, the owner of that house suffers one of the inconveniences we all expose ourselves to as the cost of living in a safe society; he does not suffer a violation of the Fourth Amendment.

[Similarly,] . . . we have not held that "reasonableness" precludes error with respect to those factual judgments that law enforcement officials are expected to make [in executing a valid warrant. See] Maryland v. Garrison, [page 601 n.33 supra]. . . .

It would be superfluous to multiply these examples. . . . [W]hat is generally demanded of the many factual determinations that must regularly be made by agents of the government . . . is not that they always be correct, but that they always be reasonable. . . .

We see no reason to depart from this general rule with respect to facts bearing upon the authority to consent to a search. . . .

[The state courts] . . . ruled as a matter of law that a reasonable belief could not validate the entry. Since we find that ruling to be in error, we remand for consideration of that question. . . .

JUSTICE MARSHALL, with whom JUSTICE BRENNAN and JUSTICE STEVENS join, dissenting.

. . . The majority's . . . position rests on a misconception of the basis for third-party consent searches. That such searches do not give rise to claims of constitutional violations rests not on the premise that they are "reasonable" under the Fourth Amendment, . . . but on the premise that a person may voluntarily limit his expectation of privacy by allowing others to exercise authority over his possessions. Cf. Katz v. United States, 389 U.S. 347, 351 (1967) ("What a person knowingly exposes to the public, even in his home or office, is not a subject of Fourth Amendment protection."). Thus, an individual's decision to permit another "joint access [to] or control [over the property] for most purposes," United States v. Matlock, 415 U.S. 164, 171 n.7 (1974), limits that individual's reasonable expectation of privacy and to that extent limits his Fourth Amendment protections. . . . If an individual has not so limited his expectation of privacy, the police may not dispense with the safeguards established by the Fourth Amendment.

The baseline for the reasonableness of a search or seizure in the home is the presence of a warrant. . . . Indeed, "searches and seizures inside a home without a warrant are presumptively unreasonable." Payton v. New York, 445 U.S. 573, 586 (1980). Exceptions to the warrant requirement must therefore serve "compelling" law enforcement goals. Mincey v. Arizona, 437 U.S. 385, 394 (1978). Because the sole law enforcement purpose underlying third-party consent searches is avoiding the inconvenience of securing a warrant, a departure from the warrant requirement is not justified simply because an officer reasonably believes a third party has consented to a search of the defendant's home. In holding otherwise, the majority ignores our long-standing view that "the informed and deliberate determination of magistrates . . . as to what searches and seizures are permissible under the Constitution are to be preferred over the hurried action of officers and others who may happen to make arrests." United States v. Lefkowitz, 285 U.S. 452, 464 (1932).

NOTES AND QUESTIONS ON RODRIGUEZ

1. How should the reasonableness issue be resolved in *Rodriguez?*
2. Is the majority perspective or the dissent perspective on third-party consents more consistent with traditional fourth amendment jurisprudence. Consider the following response by the *Rodriguez* majority to Justice Marshall's dissent:

To describe a consented search as a non-invasion of privacy and thus a non-search is strange in the extreme. And while it must be admitted that this ingenious device can explain why consented searches are lawful, it cannot explain why seemingly consented searches are "unreasonable," which is all that the Constitution forbids. See Delaware v. Prouse, 440 U.S. 648, 653-654 (1979) ("[t]he essential purpose of the proscriptions in the Fourth Amendment is to impose a standard of 'reasonableness' upon the exercise of discretion by government officials"). The only basis for contending that the constitutional standard could not possibly have been met here is the argument that reasonableness must be judged by the facts as they were, rather than by the facts as they were known. As we have discussed . . . , that argument has long since been rejected. [110 S. Ct. at 2800 n.*.]

Is the response adequate?

NOTES AND QUESTIONS ON PRIVATE SEARCHES

1. In Burdeau v. McDowell, 256 U.S. 465 (1921), the Supreme Court confirmed that the fourth amendment was a limitation on only governmental activity. Thus, evidence obtained during a private illegal search was admissible. Of course, if the police order or instigate an illegal search by a private person, they cannot avoid the implications of the fourth amendment.[98] Generalized government encouragement, however, may not turn a private search into one subject to fourth amendment limits.[99] See generally Burkoff, Not So Private Searches and the Constitution, 66 Cornell L. Rev. 627 (1981).

2. When, if ever, should the police be held responsible for an unauthorized illegal search by an undercover informant? Should it be significant whether the informant is being paid or otherwise rewarded on the basis of the results the informant produces? How much control and supervision should the police be expected to exert over informants? To what extent is meaningful judicial inquiry into this area feasible?

3. In Marsh v. Alabama, 326 U.S. 501 (1946), the Supreme Court relied on the first and fourteenth amendments to reverse the conviction of an individual for distributing religious literature in a privately owned company town. The Court reasoned that despite the private nature of the town there was state action because the operation of the town was a "public function." Id. at 507. To what extent should the activities of private store detectives and various security guards be viewed as a "public

---

98. See, e.g., Corngold v. United States, 367 F.2d 1 (9th Cir. 1966).
99. See, e.g., Gold v. United States, 378 F.2d 588 (9th Cir. 1967).

function" and, therefore, subject to the fourth amendment? See 1 W. LaFave, Search and Seizure: A Treatise on the Fourth Amendment §1.8(d), at 198-208 (2d ed. 1987). Should the answer depend on the extent to which it is reasonable to believe that exclusion of the evidence will deter illegal searches by these private individuals?

4. On some occasions, private persons will engage in a search or seizure and then turn over the items searched or seized to the police. To what extent, if at all, should the earlier private search or seizure obviate the need for the police to obtain a warrant before they examine the items?

Consider United States v. Jacobsen, 466 U.S. 109 (1984): Employees of Federal Express, a private carrier, opened a torn package, apparently to inspect it for damage. The package was in an ordinary cardboard box wrapped in brown paper. Inside the box under some crumpled newspaper was a 10-inch long tube made of the silver tape used on basement ducts. On cutting open the tape, the employees discovered a white powdery substance inside the innermost of four plastic bags. The employees notified the Drug Enforcement Administration (DEA). They then replaced the plastic bags in the tube and put the tube and newspaper back in the box. When the DEA agents arrived, they proceeded, without a warrant, to remove the plastic bags from the tube and to subject the powdery substance to a field test. The test indicated that the substance was cocaine.

The Court, in an opinion by Justice Stevens, first observed that because of its private character, the activity of the Federal Express employees did not violate the fourth amendment. With respect to the activity of the DEA agents, the Court stated:

> The additional invasions of respondents' privacy by the government agent must be tested by the degree to which they exceeded the scope of the private search. . . .
> When the first federal agent on the scene initially saw the package, he knew it contained nothing of significance except a tube containing plastic bags and, ultimately, white powder. It is not entirely clear that the powder was visible to him before he removed the tube from the box. Even if the white powder was not itself in "plain view" because it was still enclosed in so many containers and covered with papers, there was a virtual certainty that nothing else of significance was in the package and that a manual inspection of the tube and its contents would not tell him anything more than he already had been told. Respondents do not dispute that the Government could utilize the Federal Express employees' testimony concerning the contents of the package. If that is the case, it hardly infringed respondents' privacy for the agents to reexamine the contents of the open package by brushing aside a crumpled newspaper and picking up the tube. . . .
> Similarly, the removal of the plastic bags from the tube and the agent's

visual inspection of their contents enabled the agent to learn nothing that had not previously been learned during the private search. It infringed no legitimate expectation of privacy and hence was not a "search" within the meaning of the Fourth Amendment.

While the agents' assertion of dominion and control over the package and its contents did constitute a "seizure," that seizure was not unreasonable. The fact that, prior to the field test, respondents' privacy interest in the contents of the package had been largely compromised, is highly relevant to the reasonableness of the agents' conduct in this respect. . . .

The field test at issue could disclose only one fact previously unknown to the agent—whether or not a suspicious white powder was cocaine. It could tell him nothing more, not even whether the substance was sugar or talcum powder. . . .

A chemical test that merely discloses whether or not a particular substance is cocaine does not compromise any legitimate interest in privacy. . . .

This conclusion is dictated by United States v. Place, 462 U.S.(1983), in which the Court held that subjecting luggage to a "sniff test" by a trained narcotics detection dog was not a "search." . . .

Here, as in Place, the likelihood that official conduct of the kind disclosed by the record will actually compromise any legitimate interest in privacy seems much too remote to characterize the testing as a search subject to the Fourth Amendment.

. . . Nevertheless, as Place also holds, a seizure lawful at its inception can nevertheless violate the Fourth Amendment because its manner of execution unreasonably infringes possessory interests protected by the Fourth Amendment's prohibition on "unreasonable seizures." Here, the field test did affect respondents' possessory interests protected by the Amendment, since by destroying a quantity of the powder it converted what had been only a temporary deprivation of possessory interests into a permanent one. To assess the reasonableness of this conduct, "[w]e must balance the nature and quality of the intrusion on the individual's Fourth Amendment interests against the importance of the governmental interests alleged to justify the intrusion." Id., at —.

Applying this test, we conclude that the destruction of the powder during the course of the field test was reasonable. [466 U.S. at 115, 118-125.]

What do you think of the Court's reasoning? Do you agree that what the police can do without a warrant should depend on how extensive the private search was?

Consider the facts in Walter v. United States, 447 U.S. 649 (1980): Packages of 8-millimeter film depicting homosexual activity were addressed to "Leggs, Inc.," a fictitious company. The films were mistakenly delivered by private carrier to "L'Eggs Products, Inc." After opening the packages and finding suggestive drawings and explicit descriptions of the films' contents, employees of L'Eggs notified the FBI. The FBI, without attempting to obtain a warrant or to contact either the consignor or the consignee, viewed the films. Was the warrantless viewing legal? Should the answer depend on whether the L'Eggs employees had viewed the films?[100]

F. ENFORCING THE FOURTH AMENDMENT

From its inception, the exclusionary rule has generated considerable debate and intense rhetoric.[101] Recall, for example, Justice (then Judge)

---

100. Justice Stevens announced the judgment of the Court in *Walter*. In an opinion joined by Justice Stewart, he characterized the FBI's viewing of the films as an "expansion" of the private search, 447 U.S. at 656, and he suggested that the viewing might not have been illegal if the employees of L'Eggs had viewed the films first. Id. at 657 n.9. Justice White, in a concurring opinion joined by Justice Brennan, maintained that the FBI's warrantless viewing of the films should be regarded as illegal regardless of whether the employees had viewed the film. Justice Marshall concurred in the judgment without opinion. Justice Blackmun, in a dissenting opinion joined by Chief Justice Burger, Justice Powell, and Justice Rehnquist, maintained that "by the time the FBI received the films, [the defendants] had no remaining expectation of privacy in their contents." Id. at 663.

101. The recent literature is substantial. For a sampling see, e.g., J. Herschel, Fourth Amendment Rights (1979); D. Horowitz, The Courts and Social Policy 220-254 (1977); Baier, Justice Clark, the Voice of the Past, and the Exclusionary Rule, 64 Tex. L. Rev. 415 (1985); Bradley, Present at the Creation? A Critical Guide to Weeks v. United States and Its Progeny, 30 St. Louis U.L.J. 1031 (1986); Dix, Exclusionary Rule Issues as Matters of State Law, 11 Am. J. Crim. L. 325 (1983); Goodpaster, Essay on Ending the Exclusionary Rule, 33 Hastings L.J. 1065 (1982); Halpern, Federal Habeas Corpus and the *Mapp* Exclusionary Rule After Stone v. Powell, 82 Colum. L. Rev. 1 (1982); Kamisar, Is the Exclusionary Rule an "Illogical" or "Unnatural" Interpretation of the Fourth Amendment?, 62 Judicature 66 (1978); Katz, Reflections on Search and Seizure and Illegally Seized Evidence in Canada and the United States, 3 Can.-U.S.L.J. 103 (1980); LaFave, The Fourth Amendment in an Imperfect World: On Drawing "Bright Lines" and "Good Faith," 43 U. Pitt. L. Rev. 307 (1982); Lockney, An Open Letter to the North Dakota Attorney General Concerning Search and Seizure Law and the Exclusionary Rule, 62 N.D.L. Rev. 17 (1986); Loewy, The Fourth Amendment as a Means of Protecting the Innocent, 81 Mich. L. Rev. 1229 (1983); Lushing, The Exclusionary Rule: A Disputation, 7 Cardozo L. Rev. 713 (1986); Macdougall, The Exclusionary Rule and Its Alternatives—Remedies for Constitutional Violations in Canada and the United States, 76 J. Crim. L. & Criminology 608 (1985); Morris, The Exclusionary Rule, Deterrence and Posner's Economic Analysis of Law, 57 Wash. L. Rev. 647 (1982); Posner, Excessive Sanctions for Governmental Misconduct in Criminal Cases, 57 Wash. L. Rev. 635 (1982); Posner, Rethinking the Fourth Amendment, 1981 Sup. Ct. Rev. 49; Schroeder, Deterring Fourth Amendment Violations: Alternatives to the Exclusionary Rule, 69 Geo. L.J. 1361 (1981); Stewart, The Road to Mapp v. Ohio and Beyond: The Origins, Development and Future of the Exclusionary Rule, 83 Colum. L. Rev. 1365 (1983); Symposium, 23 S. Tex. L.J. 203 (1982); Uviller, Acquisition of Evidence for Criminal Prosecution: Some Constitutional Premises and Practices in Transition, 35 Vand. L. Rev. 501 (1982); Van DeCamp & Gerry, Reforming the Exclusionary Rule: An Analysis of Two Proposed Amendments to the California Constitution, 33 Hastings

Cardozo's disparaging characterization of the rule as permitting "[t]he criminal . . . to go free because the constable had blundered." People v. Defore, 242 N.Y. 13, 21, 150 N.E. 585, 587 (1926). And recall the Supreme Court's claim in *Mapp* that

> without . . . [the exclusionary] rule the freedom from state invasions of privacy would be so ephemeral and so neatly severed from its conceptual nexus with the freedom from all brutish means of coercing evidence as not to merit this Court's high regard as a freedom "implicit in the concept of ordered liberty." [367 U.S. 643, 655 (1961).]

Modern critics of the exclusionary rule tend to focus on the high cost of permitting guilty defendants to go free and the lack of compelling evidence that the rule is an effective deterrent against illegal searches and seizures. See, e.g., Bivens v. Six Unknown Named Agents, 403 U.S. 388 (1971) (Burger, C.J., dissenting):

> Some clear demonstration of the benefits and effectiveness of the Exclusionary Rule is required to justify it in view of the high price it extracts from society—the release of countless guilty criminals. [403 U.S. at 416.]

Why should the burden of establishing the deterrent value of the exclusionary rule rest with the rule's proponents? If we took a similar approach to the role of deterrence in justifying criminal penalties, we would probably have to change radically the theory and perhaps the structure of our criminal justice system. Is it sufficient to answer that in the exclusionary rule context the proponents should carry the burden because of the rule's cost in freeing guilty defendants?

How costly is the exclusionary rule? See footnote 6 in United States v. Leon, page 892 infra. Consider the following:

AMERICAN BAR ASSOCIATION SPECIAL COMMITTEE ON CRIMINAL JUSTICE IN A FREE SOCIETY, CRIMINAL JUSTICE IN CRISIS, 12-17 (1988):

Coordination between the police and prosecutors on arrest and search issues, including legal assistance in the drafting of warrants, unheard of before the exclusionary rule, now occurs in a

---

L.J. 1109 (1982); Weisberger, Exclusionary Rule: Nine Authors in Search of a Principle, 34 Santa Clara L. Rev. 253 (1982); White, Forgotten Points in the "Exclusionary Rule" Debate, 81 Mich. L. Rev. 1273 (1983); White & Greenspan, Standing to Object to Search and Seizure, 118 U. Pa. L. Rev. 333 (1970); Wilkey, The Exclusionary Rule: Why Suppress Valid Evidence?, 62 Judicature 214 (1978).

number of cities.[16] . . . It is reasonable to conclude that police departments have made these efforts to comply with the Fourth Amendment because of the exclusionary rule.[19] . . .

What then is the "cost" of the rule? To be sure the Committee heard complaints that the body of law defining Fourth Amendment restrictions is complex, and as a result, teaching, understanding, and obeying the Fourth Amendment can be both difficult and at times, frustrating for the police departments. However, the witnesses testifying before the Committee certainly do not view the rule as an impediment to effective crime control. . . .

The conclusion that the exclusionary rule neither causes serious malfunctioning of the criminal justice system nor promotes crime is strongly supported by practically all of our . . . witnesses and by our telephone survey respondents.[102] . . .

It is especially worthy of note that the police, toward whom the deterrent force of the exclusionary rule is primarily directed, do not consider search and seizure proscriptions to be a serious obstacle. . . .

The Committee interviewed three chief prosecutors from different cities and one high ranking assistant from a large office in another city. One of these prosecutors, testifying as the designated representative of the National District Attorney's Association, noted that prosecutors identify drugs, sentencing, and various aspects of federal-state coordination as the major national issues, rather than the Fourth Amendment as currently interpreted.

Three of the four prosecutors interviewed also believe the number of cases affected by the exclusionary rule has been declining in recent years. . . .

. . . There are empirical studies conducted over the years which attempt to evaluate the costs of the rule and its impact on the criminal justice system.[30] Although there is some disagreement, the weight of this

16. [See] . . . R. Van Duizend, L. Sutton & C. Carter, The Search Warrant Process 20 (1985). . . .

19. An empirical study, conducted in Chicago in 1986, found that the exclusionary rule significantly deters police violations of Fourth Amendment rights. . . . Note, The Exclusionary Rule and Deterrence: An Empirical Study of Chicago Narcotics Officers, 54 U. Chi. L. Rev. 1016 . . . (1987). . . .

102. The survey was professionally structured and consisted of 10- to 20-minute interviews with over 800 defense lawyers, judges, prosecutors, and high ranking police administrators. Criminal Justice in Crisis, at 2.—EDS.

30. See Note, supra note 19; The Police Executive Research Forum, The Executive Summary, The Effects of United States v. Leon on Police Search Warrant Policies and Practices (1986); Nardulli, The Societal Cost of the Exclusionary Rule: An Empirical Assessment, 1983 Am. B. Found. Res. J. 585 (1983); National Institute of Justice, U.S. Dep't of Just., Criminal Justice Research Report, The Effects of the Exclusionary Rule: A Study in California (1982); U.S. General Accounting Office, Impact of the Exclusionary

authority is consistent with the committee's evidence and establishes that the cases primarily affected by the rule are drug cases. Violent crime cases rarely are lost because the rule, and the percentage of the total number of cases in the system that are lost because of the rule is relatively small. A comprehensive survey of the studies which have been conducted on how the exclusionary rule has affected the filing of cases found that the number of cases lost is small:

- Overall in jurisdictions with prosecutorial screening between 0.2% and 0.6% to 0.8% of adult felony arrests are screened out because of illegal searches.
- Adding together data on each of the stages of felony processing (police releases, prosecutor screening, and court dismissals), we find that the cumulative loss resulting from the illegal searches is in the range of 0.6% and 0.8% to 2.35% of all adult felony arrests.
- In felony arrests for offenses other than drugs or weapons possession, including violent crime arrests, the effects of the rule are lower; prosecutors screen out less than 0.3% of these felony arrests because of illegal searches, and the cumulative loss is no more than 0.3% to 0.7% of such arrests.
- Prosecutors screen out 2.4% of felony drug arrests (nowhere near the 30% claim of the National Institute of Justice), while the cumulative loss for drug arrests is probably in the range of 2.8% to 6% or 7.1%. (Weapons possession arrests may have a cumulative loss of about 3.4%, but data are very limited.)
- Very few arrests are lost by acquittals at trial following suppression of evidence.

The most striking feature of the data is the concentration of illegal searches in drug arrests (and possibly weapons possession arrests) and the extremely small effect on the arrests for other offenses, including violent crimes. [Davies, A Hard Look at What We Know (and Still Need to Learn About the "Costs" of the Exclusionary Rule: The NIJ Study and Other Studies of "Lost" Arrests, ABF J. 611, 679-680 (1983).]

Rule on Federal Criminal Prosecutions, Report by the Comptroller General of the United States (1979); Canon, Is the Exclusionary Rule in Failing Health? Some New Data and a Plea Against a Precipitatious Conclusion, 62 Ky. L.J. 681 (1974); Spiotto, The Search and Seizure Problem—Two Approaches: The Canadian Tort Remedy and the U.S. Exclusionary Rule, 1 J. Police Sci. & Ad. 36 (1973); Spiotto, Search and Seizure: An Empirical Study of the Exclusionary Rule and Its Alternatives, 2 J. Legal Stud. 243 (1973); Oaks, Studying the Exclusionary Rule in Search and Seizure, 37 U. Chi. L. Rev. 665 (1970). [See also Canon, The Exclusionary Rule: Have Critics Proven That It Doesn't Deter Police?, 62 Judicature 398 (1978); Schlessinger, The Exclusionary Rule: Have Proponents Proven That It Is a Deterrent to Police?, 62 Judicature 404 (1978).— EDS.]

Even in cases in which the exclusion of evidence results in a guilty person going free, the "cost" may not be properly attributable to the exclusionary rule. Rather in those situations in which the police would not have discovered the evidence but for the illegal search or seizure, the cost is properly attributable to the fourth amendment itself. Nonetheless,

> [t]here is an apparently widespread . . . perception that the acquittal of guilty defendants is primarily attributable to the exclusionary rule, and this perception should itself be a cause for concern. It may undermine citizens' confidence in the ability of the judicial system to deal adequately and reasonably with criminals. Moreover, to the extent that judges share the perception, the necessity of invoking the exclusionary rule may make them less willing than they otherwise would be to find that particular police conduct has violated the fourth amendment. [Kuhns, The Concept of Personal Aggrievement in Fourth Amendment Standing Cases, 65 Iowa L. Rev. 493, 510 (1980).]

See Kaplan, The Limits of the Exclusionary Rule, 26 Stan. L. Rev. 1027, 1037-1038 (1974) (fourth amendment, because "it operates only after incriminating evidence has been obtained[,] . . . flaunts before us the cost we must pay for fourth amendment guarantees. . . . Where guarantees of individual rights are actually obeyed . . . , criminals are not discovered and thus no shocking cases come to public consciousness").

In large measure because of the perceived costs of the exclusionary rule, courts have developed various doctrines to limit its applicability. The materials in the first seven subdivisions of this section consider limitations on the scope of the rule. The final subdivision considers alternatives to the exclusionary rule for enforcing fourth amendment guarantees. Before proceeding further, you should review briefly Weeks, Wolf, and Mapp, in Section B supra.

1. The Relationship Between the Right and the Remedy: Fourth Amendment "Standing"

Almost immediately after the Weeks decision, lower federal courts began to develop a limitation on the scope of the exclusionary rule, which has become known as the "standing" requirement: A criminal defendant could exclude evidence obtained from an illegal search or seizure only if the fourth amendment violation adversely affected some personal interest of the defendant. Federal Rule of Criminal Procedure 41(e) incorporated this notion by providing that a "person aggrieved" by an unlawful search and seizure could move for the return of the property or the suppression of evidence. The development of the contours of the standing requirement is described in the following excerpt.

KUHNS, THE CONCEPT OF PERSONAL AGGRIEVEMENT IN FOURTH AMENDMENT STANDING CASES
65 Iowa L. Rev. 493, 514-519, 521-524, 526-529 (1980)

A. STANDING BASED ON AN INTEREST IN THE PREMISES SEARCHED

Like the early cases defining the scope of the fourth amendment itself, the early standing[12] cases in state and lower federal courts tended to be analyzed primarily in terms of property concepts. Thus, in Olmstead v. United States[149] the Supreme Court held that electronic surveillance not accompanied by a physical trespass was not a search or seizure, and many standing cases turned on whether the defendant had a sufficient property interest in the premises searched. Individuals with an ownership or possessory interest had standing, but invitees and guests did not.

More recently, courts have focused on priva[cy] interests in defining both the scope of the fourth amendment and the content of the standing requirement. Katz v. United States,[155] which overruled *Olmstead*, held that the nontrespassory electronic surveillance of a conversation in an enclosed telephone booth "constituted a 'search and seizure.' "[156] The Court stressed that the fourth amendment "protects individual privacy

---

12. It is important to distinguish the concept of fourth amendment standing from the concept of standing associated with the "justiciability" requirement of article III of the United States Constitution. Federal judicial power can be exercised to resolve only "justiciable" controversies, and one aspect of "justiciability," commonly characterized as the standing requirement, is that litigants have a sufficient stake in the outcome of a controversy to ensure that all relevant considerations will be fully aired. See Flast v. Cohen, 392 U.S. 83, 95 (1968); Doremus v. Board of Educ., 342 U.S. 429, 432-435 (1952). See generally Scott, Standing in the Supreme Court—A Functional Analysis, 86 Harv. L. Rev. 645, 670, 675-677 (1973). A defendant's interest in excluding incriminating evidence is presumably sufficient to satisfy the justiciability requirement, regardless of whether the defendant was personally aggrieved by the allegedly illegal search or seizure. See Alderman v. United States, 394 U.S. 165, 175 (1969) ("Of course, Congress or state legislatures may extend the exclusionary rule and provide that illegally seized evidence is inadmissible against anyone for any purpose.").

149. 277 U.S. 438 (1928).
155. 389 U.S. 347 (1967).
156. Id. at 353.

against certain kinds of governmental intrusion"[157] and concluded that the absence of a physical trespass "can have no constitutional significance."[158] Similarly, in Jones v. United States[159] the Court rejected the notion that the standing of a temporary apartment guest to object to an illegal search and seizure should turn on the nature of his property interest in the premises.[160] . . .

. . . [The Court] made no attempt to elaborate on the nature of a temporary apartment guest's privacy interest that would warrant fourth amendment protection. Rather, the Court simply concluded that "[n]o just interest of the Government in the effective and rigorous enforcement of the criminal law will be hampered by recognizing that anyone legitimately on the premises where a search occurs may challenge its legality. . . ."[165]

Other cases have established that a defendant's privacy interest in premises does not depend on physical presence at the time of the search.[166] Mancusi v. DeForte,[167] which was decided after Jones, implies, however, that a defendant's mere legitimate presence or the right to be present may not always be a sufficient basis for challenging the legality of a search. DeForte, a union official, had objected to the use against him of documents discovered during the illegal search of a union office that he shared with several other officials.[168] Although the documents were not taken from an area reserved exclusively for DeForte's use, he was present at the time of the search, and there was testimony that he "spent 'a considerable amount of time' in the office." . . .[169] Assuming that DeForte would have had standing if he "had occupied a 'private' office in the union headquarters," the Court concluded that the situation was "not fundamentally changed" by the shared office arrangement.[170] The office was an area "in which there was a reasonable expectation of freedom from governmental intrusion," and DeForte "could reasonably have expected" that only other union officials or their agents and guests would

---

157. Id. at 350.
158. Id. at 353. . . .
159. 362 U.S. 257 (1960).
160. Id. at 266 ("Distinctions such as those between 'lessee,' 'licensee,' 'invitee,' and 'guest,' . . . ought not to be determinative in fashioning procedures ultimately referable to constitutional safeguards.").
165. Id. at 267. . . .
166. Bumper v. North Carolina, 391 U.S. 543, 546, 548 n.11 (1968); cf. Stoner v. California, 376 U.S. 483, 489-90 (1964) (standing cases cited to support proposition that hotel operator's consent does not justify warrantless search of absent guest's room). See also Simmons v. United States, 18 F.2d 85, 89 (8th Cir. 1927) (defendant who was not present at time of search of his home has standing).
167. 392 U.S. 364 (1968).
168. Id. at 365, 368.
169. Id. at 368-69.
170. Id. at 369.

enter the office and remove the records.[171] The Court found "strong support"[172] for its conclusion in *Jones*, but the fact that *Jones* was apparently not dispositive indicates that in at least some situations a defendant may be required to show more than legitimate presence to obtain standing. . . .

B. Standing Based on an Interest in the Items Seized

The defendant in *DeForte* had standing to object to the illegal search, and he was able to exclude the seized union documents because they constituted fruits of that search. Other defendants have been afforded standing to exclude illegally obtained evidence because of their interest in the items seized. . . .

An initial question that arises in cases in which a defendant alleges an interest in the items seized is whether that interest is sufficient to satisfy the standing requirement. The Court's approach to this issue, with one notable exception, has been similar to its approach in considering whether a defendant has a sufficient interest in premises subjected to a search. Physical presence at the time of the seizure is not a prerequisite for standing,[180] but a defendant must have a personal interest in the items seized.[181]

In addition, just as *Jones* suggested that only one with a "legitimate" interest in premises searched would have standing to object to the search,[182] there may be a legitimacy requirement in at least some cases with respect to an individual's interest in items that are seized. In Brown v. United States[183] defendants charged with transporting and conspiracy to transport stolen property unsuccessfully attempted to suppress the stolen property, which was discovered during the search of a warehouse belonging to one of the coconspirators. Before the Supreme Court, the defendants alleged as one basis for standing that each of the coconspirators had a partnership interest in the stolen property. The Court rejected the claim in part on the ground that the defendants had admittedly already "sold" the stolen

171. Id. at 368-69.
172. Id. at 370.
180. United States v. Jeffers, 342 U.S. 48, 52 (1951). But cf. Brown v. United States, 411 U.S. 223, 227, 229 (1973) (suggesting that defendant's presence on premises at time of seizure may be factor in determining whether defendant has standing).
181. For example, in *DeForte*, . . . the Court concluded that the defendant, despite the fact that he was the custodian of the seized records, was not personally aggrieved by the seizure. 392 U.S. at 367. Thus, if he had not been aggrieved by the search, he would not have been able to exclude the evidence.
182. 362 U.S. at 267.
183. 411 U.S. at 223 (1973).

goods, but it added that in any event the claimed interest in the stolen goods was "totally illegitimate."[185]

The fact that an interest in seized items is not legitimate, however, has not prevented defendants from establishing standing in other cases, and in this respect the Court's analysis of the sufficiency of a defendant's interest in items seized differs from its approach to the sufficiency of a defendant's interest in premises searched. United States v. Jeffers[187] specifically rejected the argument that the illegal nature of the defendant's possessory interest in narcotics could defeat his standing claim, and in *Jones*, despite its emphasis on the legitimate nature of the defendant's interest in the searched apartment, the Court sustained the defendant's standing claim on the independent ground that he had an interest in the narcotics that were seized. . . .

C.   STANDING TO OBJECT TO ELECTRONIC SURVEILLANCE OF CONVERSATIONS

In Alderman v. United States[221] the Court held that participants to a conversation overheard by electronic surveillance have standing to object to the use of the conversation against them. In addition, the *Alderman* Court granted standing to the owners of premises subjected to electronic surveillance regardless of whether they were participants in the overheard conversations. . . .

D.   STANDING BASED ON ONE'S STATUS AS A CODEFENDANT OR COCONSPIRATOR . . .

. . . *Alderman* specifically rejected the claim that "if evidence is inadmissible against one defendant or conspirator, because tainted by electronic surveillance illegal as to him, it is also inadmissible against his codefendant or coconspirator."[246] In reaching this conclusion the Court observed that "[t]here is no necessity to exclude evidence against one defendant in order to protect the rights of another," and it expressed its adherence to the "general rule that Fourth Amendment rights are personal rights which . . . may not be vicariously asserted."[247] The rejection of coconspirator and codefendant standing, however, did not rest solely on

185. Id. at 230 n.4.
187. 342 U.S. 48 (1951).
221. 394 U.S. 165 (1969).
246. [394 U.S.] at 171.
247. Id. at 174.

a mechanical application of the proposition that fourth amendment rights are personal. The Court considered the impact that such a holding would have on the deterrence objective of the exclusionary rule and concluded that "the additional benefits of extending the exclusionary rule to other defendants would [not] justify further encroachment upon the public interest in prosecuting those accused of crime . . . on the basis of all the evidence which exposes the truth."[248] . . .

E. STANDING BASED ON ONE'S STATUS AS THE TARGET OF A SEARCH OR SEIZURE

Prior to *Alderman*, there were indications that one's status as the target of a police investigation may satisfy the standing requirement. In several cases upholding a defendant's standing claim, the Court had observed that the search had been directed against the defendant. [For example,] *Jones* described "a 'person aggrieved by an unlawful search and seizure' [as] a victim of a search or seizure, one *against whom the search was directed.*"[252] . . .

Justice Fortas, concurring and dissenting in *Alderman*, relied on this language from *Jones* to urge that standing to object to electronic surveillance should be extended to any "person concerning whom an investigation involving . . . electronic surveillance has been conducted."[255] The Court in *Alderman*, however, granted standing only to those individuals whose premises were subjected to electronic surveillance and whose conversations were overheard. The majority opinion did not offer any reasons for this implicit rejection of the target theory of standing, but Justice Harlan addressed the issue briefly in a footnote to his separate opinion. In addition to [expressing] concern that the extension of standing to any nonparticipant in an overheard conversation would constitute an additional invasion of privacy, he argued that the administrative burden of conducting hearings to determine who were the targets of electronic surveillance would outweigh any "hypothesized marginal increase in Fourth Amendment protection."[258] . . .

---

248. Id. at 175. The Court also noted that there were severe criminal penalties for illegal electronic surveillance, see 18 U.S.C. §2511 (1976), and "[w]ithout experience showing the contrary," the Court was unwilling to assume that the criminal statute would be "cavalierly disregarded" or "not enforced against transgressors." 394 U.S. at 175 & n.8. . . .

252. 362 U.S. at 261 (emphasis added).

255. 394 U.S. at 201 (Fortas, J., concurring and dissenting).

258. 394 U.S. at 188 n.1 (Harlan, J., concurring and dissenting).

RAKAS v. ILLINOIS

Certiorari to the Appellate Court of Illinois, Third Division
439 U.S. 128 (1978)

MR. JUSTICE REHNQUIST delivered the opinion of the Court.

. . . A police officer on a routine patrol received a radio call notifying him of a robbery of a clothing store in Bourbonnais, Ill., and describing the getaway car. Shortly thereafter, the officer spotted an automobile which he thought might be the getaway car. After following the car for some time and after the arrival of assistance, he and several other officers stopped the vehicle. The occupants of the automobile, petitioners and two female companions, were ordered out of the car and, after the occupants had left the car, two officers searched the interior of the vehicle. They discovered a box of rifle shells in the glove compartment, which had been locked, and a sawed-off rifle under the front passenger seat. . . . After discovering the rifle and the shells, the officers took petitioners to the station and placed them under arrest.

Before trial petitioners moved to suppress the rifle and shells seized from the car on the ground that the search violated the Fourth and Fourteenth Amendments. They conceded that they did not own the automobile and were simply passengers; the owner of the car had been the driver of the vehicle at the time of the search. Nor did they assert that they owned the rifle or the shells seized.[1] . . . The trial court [held] that petitioners lacked standing and denied the motion to suppress the evidence. . . . In view of this holding, the court did not determine whether there was probable cause for the search and seizure. On appeal after petitioners' conviction [for armed robbery], the Appellate Court of Illinois . . . affirmed the trial court's denial of petitioners' motion to

---

1. Petitioners claim that they were never asked whether they owned the rifle or shells seized during the search and . . . argue that if the Court determines that a property interest in the items seized is an adequate ground for standing to object to their seizure, the Court should remand the case for further proceedings on the question whether petitioners owned the seized rifle or shells. . . . Petitioners do not now assert that they own the rifle or the shells.

We reject petitioners' suggestion. The proponent of a motion to suppress has the burden of establishing that his own Fourth Amendment rights were violated by the challenged search or seizure. See Simmons v. United States, 390 U.S. 377, 389-390 (1968); Jones v. United States, 362 U.S. 257, 261 (1960). The prosecutor argued that petitioners lacked standing to challenge the search because they did not own the rifle, the shells or the automobile. Petitioners did not contest the factual predicates of the prosecutor's argument and instead, simply stated that they were not required to prove ownership to object to the search. . . . The prosecutor's argument gave petitioners notice that they were to be put to their proof on any issue as to which they had the burden, and because of their failure to assert ownership, we must assume, for purposes of our review, that petitioners do not own the rifle or the shells.

suppress because it held that "without a proprietary or other similar interest in an automobile, a mere passenger therein lacks standing to challenge the legality of the search of the vehicle." . . .

II

Petitioners first urge us to relax or broaden the rule of standing enunciated in Jones v. United States, 362 U.S. 257 (1960), so that any criminal defendant at whom a search was "directed" would have standing to contest the legality of that search and object to the admission at trial of evidence obtained as a result of the search. Alternatively, petitioners argue that they have standing to object to the search under *Jones* because they were "legitimately on [the] premises" at the time of the search. . . .

A

We decline to extend the rule of standing in Fourth Amendment cases in the manner suggested by petitioners. As we stated in Alderman v. United States, 394 U.S. 165, 174 (1969), "Fourth Amendment rights are personal rights which, like some other constitutional rights, may not be vicariously asserted." . . . A person who is aggrieved by an illegal search and seizure only through the introduction of damaging evidence secured by a search of third person's premises or property has not had any of his Fourth Amendment rights infringed. . . . And since the exclusionary rule is an attempt to effectuate the guarantees of the Fourth Amendment, it is proper to permit only defendants whose Fourth Amendment rights have been violated to benefit from the rule's protections.[3] . . . There is no reason to think that a party whose rights have been infringed will not, if evidence is used against him, have ample motivation to move to suppress it. . . . Even if such a person is not a defendant in the action, he may be able to recover damages for the violation of his Fourth Amendment rights, see Monroe v. Pape, 365 U.S. 167 (1961), or seek redress under state law for invasion of privacy or trespass. . . .

Conferring standing to raise vicarious Fourth Amendment claims would necessarily mean a more widespread invocation of the exclusionary rule during criminal trials. . . . Each time the exclusionary rule is applied it exacts a substantial social cost for the vindication of Fourth

---

3. The necessity for a showing of a violation of personal rights is not obviated by recognizing the deterrent purpose of the exclusionary rule. . . . Despite the deterrent aim of the exclusionary rule, we never have held that unlawfully seized evidence is inadmissible in all proceedings or against all persons. . . .

Amendment rights. Relevant and reliable evidence is kept from the trier of fact and the search for the truth at trial is deflected. . . .

B

Had we accepted petitioners' request to allow persons other than those whose own Fourth Amendment rights were violated by a challenged search and seizure to suppress evidence obtained in the course of such police activity, it would be appropriate to retain *Jones'* use of standing in Fourth Amendment analysis. Under petitioners' target theory, a court could determine that a defendant had standing to invoke the exclusionary rule without having to inquire into the substantive question of whether the challenged search or seizure violated the Fourth Amendment rights of that particular defendant. However, having rejected petitioners' target theory and reaffirmed the principle that the "rights assured by the Fourth Amendment are personal rights, [which] . . . may be enforced by exclusion of evidence only at the instance of one whose own protection was infringed by the search and seizure," Simmons v. United States, 390 U.S. [377, 389 (1968)], . . . the question necessarily arises whether it serves any useful analytical purpose to consider this principle a matter of standing, distinct from the merits of a defendant's Fourth Amendment claim. We can think of no decided cases of this Court that would have come out differently had we concluded, as we do now, that the type of standing requirement discussed in *Jones* and reaffirmed today is more properly subsumed under substantive Fourth Amendment doctrine. Rigorous application of the principle that the rights secured by this Amendment are personal, in place of a notion of "standing," will produce no additional situations in which evidence must be excluded. The inquiry under either approach is the same. But we think the better analysis forthrightly focuses on the extent of a particular defendant's rights under the Fourth Amendment, rather than on any theoretically separate, but invariably intertwined concept of standing. . . .

Analyzed in these terms, the question is whether the challenged search and seizure violated the Fourth Amendment rights of a criminal defendant who seeks to exclude the evidence obtained during it. That inquiry in turn requires a determination of whether the disputed search and seizure has infringed an interest of the defendant which the Fourth Amendment was designed to protect. We are under no illusion that by dispensing with the rubric of standing used in *Jones* we have rendered any simpler the determination of whether the proponent of a motion to suppress is entitled to contest the legality of a search and seizure. But by frankly recognizing that this aspect of the analysis belongs more properly under the heading of substantive Fourth Amendment doctrine than under the heading of standing, we think the decision of this issue will rest on sounder logical footing.

C

Here petitioners, who were passengers occupying a car which they neither owned nor leased, seek to analogize their position to that of the defendant in Jones v. United States. In Jones, petitioner was present at the time of the search of an apartment which was owned by a friend. . . .

We do not question the conclusion in *Jones* that the defendant in that case suffered a violation of his personal Fourth Amendment rights if the search in question was unlawful. Nonetheless, we believe that the phrase "legitimately on premises" coined in *Jones* creates too broad a gauge for measurement of Fourth Amendment rights. For example, applied literally, this statement would permit a casual visitor who has never seen, or been permitted to visit, the basement of another's house to object to a search of the basement if the visitor happened to be in the kitchen of the house at the time of the search. . . .

We think that *Jones* on its facts merely stands for the unremarkable proposition that a person can have a legally sufficient interest in a place other than his own home so that the Fourth Amendment protects him from unreasonable governmental intrusion into that place. . . .

In defining the scope of that interest, we adhere to the view expressed in *Jones* and echoed in later cases that arcane distinctions developed in property and tort law between guests, licensees, invitees, and the like, ought not to control. . . .

Katz v. United States, 389 U.S. 347 (1967), provides guidance in defining the scope of the interest protected by the Fourth Amendment. . . . *Katz* held that capacity to claim the protection of the Fourth Amendment depends . . . upon whether the person who claims the protection of the Amendment has a legitimate expectation of privacy in the invaded place. 389 U.S., at 353. . . . Viewed in this manner, the holding in *Jones* can best be explained by the fact that Jones had a legitimate expectation of privacy in the premises he was using and therefore could claim the protection of the Fourth Amendment with respect to a governmental invasion of those premises, even though his "interest" in those premises might not have been a recognized property interest at common law.[12] . . .

12. Obviously, however, a "legitimate" expectation of privacy by definition means more than a subjective expectation of not being discovered. A burglar plying his trade in a summer cabin during the off season may have a thoroughly justified subjective expectation of privacy, but it is not one which the law recognizes as "legitimate." His presence, in the words of *Jones*, 362 U.S., at 267, is "wrongful"; his expectation is not

Our Brother White in dissent expresses the view that by rejecting the phrase "legitimately on [the] premises" as the appropriate measure of Fourth Amendment rights, we are abandoning a thoroughly workable, "bright line" test in favor of a less certain analysis of whether the facts of a particular case give rise to a legitimate expectation of privacy. . . . If "legitimately on premises" were the successful litmus test of Fourth Amendment rights that he assumes it is, his approach would have at least the merit of easy application, whatever it lacked in fidelity to the history and purposes of the Fourth Amendment. But a reading of lower court cases . . . reveals that this expression is not a shorthand summary for a bright-line rule which somehow encapsulates the "core" of the Fourth Amendment's protections.[13]

"one that society is prepared to recognize as 'reasonable.' " Katz v. United States, 389 U.S., at 361 (Harlan, J., concurring). And it would, of course, be merely tautological to fall back on the notion that those expectations of privacy which are legitimate depend primarily on cases deciding exclusionary-rule issues in criminal cases. Legitimation of expectations of privacy by law must have a source outside of the Fourth Amendment, either by reference to concepts of real or personal property law or to understandings that are recognized and permitted by society. One of the main rights attaching to property is the right to exclude others, see W. Blackstone, Commentaries, Book 2, ch. 1, and one who owns or lawfully possesses or controls property will in all likelihood have a legitimate expectation of privacy by virtue of this right to exclude. Expectations of privacy protected by the Fourth Amendment, of course, need not be based on a common-law interest in real or personal property, or on the invasion of such an interest. These ideas were rejected both in *Jones,* supra, and *Katz,* supra. But by focusing on legitimate expectations of privacy in Fourth Amendment jurisprudence, the Court has not altogether abandoned use of property concepts in determining the presence or absence of the privacy interests protected by that Amendment. No better demonstration of this proposition exists than the decision in Alderman v. United States, 394 U.S. 165 (1969), where the Court held that an individual's property interest in his own home was so great as to allow him to object to electronic surveillance of conversations emanating from his home, even though he himself was not a party to the conversations. On the other hand, even a property interest in premises may not be sufficient to establish a legitimate expectation of privacy with respect to particular items located on the premises or activity conducted thereon. . . .

13. An examination of lower court decisions shows that use of this purported "bright line" test has led to widely varying results. For example, compare United States v. Westerbann-Martinez, 435 F. Supp. 690 (E.D.N.Y. 1977) (defendant has standing to object to search of co-defendant's *person* at airport because defendant was lawfully present at time of search), with Sumrall v. United States, 382 F.2d 651 (C.A.10 1967), cert. denied, 389 U.S. 1055 (1968) (defendant did not have standing to object to search of codefendant's purse even though defendant present at time of search). Compare Holloway v. Wolff, 482 F.2d 110 (C.A.8 1973) (defendant has standing to object to search of bedroom in house of third person because lawfully in house at time of search even though no showing that defendant had ever been given permission to use, or had ever been in, bedroom), with Northern v. United States, 455 F.2d 427 (C.A.9 1972) (defendant lacked standing to object to search of apartment-mate's bedroom even though present in apart-ment at time of search since no showing that defendant had permission to enter or use roommate's bedroom), and United States v. Miller, 145 U.S. App. D.C. 312, 449 F.2d 974 (1971) (defendant lawfully present in third person's office has standing to object to police entry into office since lawfully present but lacks standing to object to search of drawer of third person's desk since no showing that he had permission to open or use

The dissent itself shows that the facile consistency it is striving for is illusory. The dissenters concede that "there comes a point when use of an area is shared with so many that one simply cannot reasonably expect seclusion." . . . But surely the "point" referred to is not one demarcating a line which is black on one side and white on another; it is inevitably a point which separates one shade of gray from another. . . .

. . . In abandoning "legitimately on premises" for the doctrine that we announce today, we are . . . rejecting blind adherence to a phrase which at most has superficial clarity and which conceals underneath that thin veneer all of the problems of line drawing which must be faced in any conscientious effort to apply the Fourth Amendment. . . . We would not wish to be understood as saying that legitimate presence on the premises is irrelevant to one's expectation of privacy, but it cannot be deemed controlling.

D

Judged by the foregoing analysis, petitioners' claims must fail. They asserted neither a property nor a possessory interest in the automobile, nor an interest in the property seized. And as we have previously indicated, the fact that they were "legitimately on [the] premises" in the sense that they were in the car with the permission of its owner is not determinative of whether they had a legitimate expectation of privacy in the particular areas of the automobile searched. It is unnecessary for us to decide here whether the same expectations of privacy are warranted in a car as would be justified in a dwelling place in analogous circumstances. We have on numerous occasions pointed out that cars are not to be treated identically with houses or apartments for Fourth Amendment purposes. . . . But here petitioners' claim is one which would fail even in an analogous situation in a dwelling place, since they made no showing that they had any legitimate expectation of privacy in the glove compartment or area under the seat of the car in which they were merely passengers. Like the

---

drawer). Compare United States v. Tussell, 441 F. Supp. 1092 (M.D. Pa. 1977) (lessee does not have standing because not present at time of search), with United States v. Potter, 419 F. Supp. 1151 (N.D. Ill. 1976) (lessee has standing even though not present when premises searched). Compare United States v. Fernandez, 430 F. Supp. 794 (N.D. Cal. 1976) (defendant with authorized access to apartment has standing even though not present at time of search), with United States v. Potter, supra (defendants with authorized access to premises lack standing because not present at the time of the search). Compare United States v. Delguyd, 542 F.2d 346 (C.A.6 1976) (defendant stopped by police in parking lot of apartment house which he intended to visit lacks standing to object to subsequent search of apartment since not present in apartment at time of search), with United States v. Fay, 225 F. Supp. 677 (S.D.N.Y. 1963), rev'd on other grounds, 333 F.2d 28 (C.A.2 1964) (defendant-invitee stopped in hallway of apartment building has standing to object to search of apartment he intended to visit).

trunk of an automobile, these are areas in which a passenger qua passenger simply would not normally have a legitimate expectation of privacy. . . .

Jones v. United States, 362 U.S. 257 (1960) and Katz v. United States, 389 U.S. 347 (1967), involved significantly different factual circumstances. Jones not only had permission to use the apartment of his friend, but had a key to the apartment with which he admitted himself on the day of the search and kept possessions in the apartment. Except with respect to his friend, Jones had complete dominion and control over the apartment and could exclude others from it. Likewise in *Katz*, the defendant occupied the telephone booth, shut the door behind him to exclude all others and paid the toll, which "entitled [him] to assume that the words he utter[ed] into the mouthpiece [would] not be broadcast to the world." Id., at 352. Katz and Jones could legitimately expect privacy in the areas which were the subject of the search and seizure each sought to contest. . . .

III

The Illinois courts were therefore correct in concluding that it was unnecessary to decide whether the search of the car might have violated the rights secured to someone else by the Fourth and Fourteenth Amendments to the United States Constitution. Since it did not violate any rights of these petitioners, their judgment of conviction is affirmed.

MR. JUSTICE POWELL, with whom THE CHIEF JUSTICE joins, concurring. . . .

We are concerned here with an automobile search. Nothing is better established in Fourth Amendment jurisprudence than the distinction between one's expectation of privacy in an automobile and one's expectation when in other locations. . . .

A distinction also properly may be made in some circumstances between the Fourth Amendment rights of passengers and the rights of an individual who has exclusive control of an automobile or of its locked compartments. . . . Here there were three passengers and a driver in the automobile searched. None of the passengers is said to have had control of the vehicle or the keys. It is unrealistic—as the shared experience of us all bears witness—to suggest that these passengers had any reasonable expectation that the car in which they had been riding would not be searched after they were lawfully stopped and made to get out. . . .[4]

MR. JUSTICE WHITE, with whom MR. JUSTICE BRENNAN, MR. JUSTICE MARSHALL, and MR. JUSTICE STEVENS join, dissenting.

4. The sawed-off rifle in this case was merely pushed beneath the front seat, pre-

The Court today holds that the Fourth Amendment protects property, not people, and specifically that a legitimate occupant of an automobile may not invoke the exclusionary rule and challenge a search of that vehicle unless he happens to own or have a possessory interest in it. Though professing to acknowledge that the primary purpose of the Fourth Amendment's prohibition of unreasonable searches is the protection of privacy—not property—the Court nonetheless effectively ties the application of the Fourth Amendment and the exclusionary rule in this situation to property law concepts. . . .

More importantly, the ruling today undercuts the force of the exclusionary rule in the one area in which its use is most certainly justified—the deterrence of bad-faith violations of the Fourth Amendment. . . . This decision invites police to engage in patently unreasonable searches every time an automobile contains more than one occupant. Should something be found, only the owner of the vehicle, or of the item, will have standing to seek suppression, and the evidence will presumably be usable against the other occupants.[23] After this decision, police will have little to lose by unreasonably searching vehicles occupied by more than one person.

Of course, most police officers will decline the Court's invitation and will continue to do their jobs as best they can in accord with the Fourth Amendment. But the very purpose of the Bill of Rights was to answer the justified fear that governmental agents cannot be left totally to their own devices, and the Bill of Rights is enforceable in the courts because human experience teaches that not all such officials will otherwise adhere to the stated precepts. Some policemen simply do act in

---

sumably by one of the petitioners. In that position, it could have slipped into full or partial view in the event of an accident, or indeed upon any sudden stop. As the rifle shells were in the locked glove compartment, this might have presented a closer case if it had been shown that one of the petitioners possessed the keys or if a rifle had not been found in the automobile.

The dissenting opinion suggests that the petitioners here took the same actions to preserve their privacy as did the defendant in *Katz*: Just as Katz closed the door to the telephone booth after him, petitioners closed the doors to their automobile. . . . Last Term, this Court determined in Pennsylvania v. Mimms, 434 U.S. 106 (1977), that passengers in automobiles have no Fourth Amendment right not to be ordered from their vehicle, once a proper stop is made. The dissenting opinion concedes that there is no question here of the propriety of the stopping of the automobile in which the petitioners were riding. . . . Thus, the closing of the doors of a vehicle, even if there were only one occupant, cannot have the same significance as it might in other contexts.

23. See Ingber, Procedure, Ceremony and Rhetoric: The Minimization of Ideological Conflict in Deviance Control, 56 B.U.L. Rev. 266, 304-305 (1976) (police may often be willing to risk suppression at the behest of some defendants in order to gain evidence usable against those without constitutional protection); White & Greenspan, Standing to Object to Search and Seizure, 118 U. Pa. L. Rev. 333, 349, 365 (1970) (same).

bad faith, even if for understandable ends, and some deterrent is needed. In the rush to limit the applicability of the exclusionary rule somewhere, anywhere, the Court ignores precedent, logic, and common sense to exclude the rule's operation from situations in which, paradoxically, it is justified and needed.

NOTES AND QUESTIONS

1. If the *Rakas* defendants had admitted ownership of the rifle and the shells at the suppression motion hearing, the prosecutor could not have used those statements against the defendants on the question of guilt. Simmons v. United States, 390 U.S. 377 (1968). The *Simmons* Court observed that a contrary holding would put a defendant in the position of having "either to give up what he believed . . . to be a valid Fourth Amendment claim or, in legal effect, to waive his Fifth Amendment privilege against self-incrimination." Id. at 394. The Illinois Supreme Court, however, had held that a defendant's suppression motion statements were admissible to impeach a defendant who elected to testify. People v. Sturgis, 58 Ill. 2d 211, 317 N.E.2d 545 (1974). Thus, if the *Rakas* defendants contemplated testifying in their own behalf, their admissions of ownership may have been admissible against them. For more on the impeachment use of suppression motion statements and of unconstitutionally obtained evidence generally, see Chapter 10, Section B infra.

2. In rejecting the "target" theory of standing Justice Rehnquist states, "[S]ince the exclusionary rule is an attempt to effectuate the guarantees of the Fourth Amendment . . . it is proper to permit only defendants whose Fourth Amendment rights have been violated to benefit from the rule's protections." Why should this be so? The fourth amendment speaks of the right of "the people" collectively to be free from unreasonable searches and seizures. Indeed, given the deterrence and judicial integrity rationales for the exclusionary rule, what justification is there for *any* type of "standing" requirement?

3. Why should Justice White be concerned that *Rakas* does not provide the *police* with a "bright line" rule to apply? Consider the following passage from Kuhns, The Concept of Personal Aggrievement in Fourth Amendment Standing Cases, 65 Iowa L. Rev. 493, 537 (1980):

> As Justice White . . . has urged in the past, relatively simple, easily applied rules defining the scope of permissible police behavior may be desirable. *Rakas*, however, was not dealing with whether the search itself was illegal, but only with whether the defendants could challenge its legality. This

question need not concern law enforcement officers. Indeed, in one sense uncertainty on the part of law enforcement officers about the resolution of this issue may be a virtue. The extent to which any limitation on the ability to present a fourth amendment claim undermines the deterrence objective of the exclusionary rule may be partially offset by police uncertainty as to precisely how the limitation will be applied.

4. Consider Justice Powell's statement about the "shared experience of us all." If our shared experience is that passengers can have no reasonable expectation that a legally stopped vehicle will not be searched, can an owner/driver of a vehicle with passengers reasonably entertain a different expectation? If not, it would seem to follow that a search of a vehicle—at least if it had multiple occupants—would *always* be reasonable. What is the flaw in this reasoning? Or is the conclusion correct?

5. To what extent is it appropriate to regard *Rakas* as a return to a property as opposed to privacy interest analysis? Consider carefully both the majority and dissenting characterizations of the scope of the holding. See Williamson, Fourth Amendment Standing and Expectations of Privacy: Rakas v. Illinois and New Directions for Some Old Concepts, 31 U. Fla. L. Rev. 831 (1979). See also Minnesota v. Olson, 110 S. Ct. 1684 (1990), which raised the question whether an overnight house guest had a sufficient privacy interest in the premises to exclude evidence obtained as the result of an illegal entry. Noting that the facts were similar to the facts in Jones v. United States, page 849 supra, and that the *Rakas* Court had expressed approval of the result in *Jones*, the *Olson* Court held that the guest had a legitimate privacy interest in the premises. Chief Justice Rehnquist, author of the *Rakas* opinion, appeared to have anticipated and approved of the *Olson* holding in his *Steagald* dissent. See page 663 supra. In *Olson*, however, the Chief Justice dissented without an opinion.

6. What significance is there to the decision to eliminate "standing" as an independent issue in the *Rakas* case? See Kuhns, supra Note 3, at 539-552; Gutterman, Privacy and Standing: "Wherever the Twain Shall Meet," 60 N.C.L. Rev. 1 (1981). How should emphasis on the personal nature of fourth amendment rights in *Rakas* affect the precedent for relying on a person's interest in items seized to grant standing to object to the search which led to the seizure? Consider the following case.

RAWLINGS v. KENTUCKY
Certiorari to the Supreme Court of Kentucky
448 U.S. 98 (1980)

Mr. Justice Rehnquist delivered the opinion of the Court. . . .

In the middle of the afternoon on October 18, 1976, six police officers armed with a warrant for the arrest of one Lawrence Marquess on charges of drug distribution arrived at Marquess' house in Bowling Green, Ky. In the house at the time the police arrived were one of Marquess' housemates, Dennis Saddler, and four visitors, Keith Northern, Linda Braden, Vanessa Cox, and petitioner David Rawlings. While searching unsuccessfully in the house for Marquess, several police officers smelled marihuana smoke and saw marihuana seeds on the mantel in one of the bedrooms. After conferring briefly, Officers Eddie Railey and John Bruce left to obtain a search warrant. While Railey and Bruce were gone, the other four officers detained the occupants of the house in the living room, allowing them to leave only if they consented to a body search. Northern and Braden did consent to such a search and were permitted to depart. Saddler, Cox, and petitioner remained seated in the living room.

Approximately 45 minutes later, Railey and Bruce returned with a warrant authorizing them to search the house. . . . At that time, Cox was seated on a couch with petitioner seated to her left. In the space between them was Cox's handbag.

. . . Railey . . . approached petitioner and told him to stand. Officer Don Bivens simultaneously approached Cox and ordered her to empty the contents of her purse onto a coffee table in front of the couch. Among those contents were a jar containing 1,800 tablets of LSD and a number of smaller vials containing benzphetamine, methamphetamine, methyprylan, and pentobarbital, all of which are controlled substances under Kentucky law.

Upon pouring these objects out onto the coffee table, Cox turned to petitioner and told him "to take what was his." . . . Petitioner, who was standing in response to Officer Railey's command, immediately claimed ownership of the controlled substances. . . . Railey then placed petitioner under formal arrest.

Petitioner was indicted for possession with intent to sell the various controlled substances recovered from Cox's purse. At the suppression hearing, he testified that he had flown into Bowling Green about a week before his arrest to look for a job and perhaps to attend the local university. He brought with him at that time the drugs later found in Cox's purse. Initially, petitioner stayed in the house where the arrest took place as the guest of Michael Swank, who shared the house with Marquess and Saddler. While at a party at that house, he met Cox and spent at least two nights of the next week on a couch at Cox's house.

On the morning of petitioner's arrest, Cox had dropped him off at Swank's house where he waited for her to return from class. At that time, he was carrying the drugs in a green bank bag. When Cox returned to the house to meet him, petitioner dumped the contents of the bank bag into Cox's purse. Although there is dispute over the discussion that took place, petitioner testified that he "asked her if she would carry this for me, and she said, 'yes'. . . ." . . . Petitioner then left the room to use the bathroom and, by the time he returned, discovered that the police had arrived to arrest Marquess.

The trial court denied petitioner's motion to suppress the drugs. . . . After a bench trial, petitioner was found guilty of possession with intent to sell LSD and of possession of benzphetamine, methamphetamine, methyprylan, and pentobarbital. . . .

The Supreme Court of Kentucky . . . affirmed. . . .

. . . [T]he Supreme Court of Kentucky looked to the "totality of the circumstances," including petitioner's own admission at the suppression hearing that he did not believe that Cox's purse would be free from governmental intrusion, and held that petitioner "[had] not made a sufficient showing that his legitimate or reasonable expectations of privacy were violated" by the search of the purse. 581 S.W.2d, at 530.

We believe that the record in this case supports that conclusion. Petitioner, of course, bears the burden of proving not only that the search of Cox's purse was illegal, but also that he had a legitimate expectation of privacy in that purse. See Rakas v. Illinois, . . . [439 U.S. 128,] 131, n.1 [(1978)]. . . . At the time petitioner dumped thousands of dollars worth of illegal drugs into Cox's purse, he had known her for only a few days. According to Cox's uncontested testimony, petitioner had never sought or received access to her purse prior to that sudden bailment. . . . Nor did petitioner have any right to exclude other persons from access to Cox's purse. . . .

In fact, Cox testified that Bob Stallons, a longtime acquaintance and frequent companion of Cox's, had free access to her purse and on the very morning of the arrest had rummaged through its contents in search of a hairbrush. Moreover, even assuming that petitioner's version of the bailment is correct and that Cox did consent to the transfer of possession, the precipitous nature of the transaction hardly supports a reasonable inference that petitioner took normal precautions to maintain his privacy. . . .

In addition to all the foregoing facts, the record also contains a frank admission by petitioner that he had no subjective expectation that Cox's purse would remain free from governmental intrusion. . . .

Petitioner contends nevertheless that, because he claimed ownership of the drugs in Cox's purse, he should be entitled to challenge the search regardless of his expectation of privacy. We disagree. While petitioner's ownership of the drugs is undoubtedly one fact to be considered in this case, Rakas emphatically rejected the notion that "arcane" concepts of property law ought to control the ability to claim the protections of the Fourth Amendment. . . . Had petitioner placed his drugs in plain view, he would still have owned them, but he could not claim any legitimate expectation of privacy. Prior to *Rakas*, petitioner might have been given "standing" in such a case . . . but probably would have lost his claim on the merits. After *Rakas*, the two inquiries merge into one: whether governmental officials violated any legitimate expectation of privacy held by petitioner.

In sum, we find no reason to overturn the lower court's conclusion that petitioner had no legitimate expectation of privacy in Cox's purse at the time of the search. . . .

. . . [T]he judgment of the Supreme Court of Kentucky should be, and the same hereby is affirmed.

[The concurring opinions of JUSTICE BLACKMUN and JUSTICE WHITE are omitted.]

MR. JUSTICE MARSHALL, with whom MR. JUSTICE BRENNAN joins, dissenting.

. . . [The Court's] holding cavalierly rejects the fundamental principle, unquestioned until today, that an interest in either the place searched or the property seized is sufficient to invoke the Constitution's protections against unreasonable searches and seizures.

The Court's examination of previous Fourth Amendment cases begins and ends—as it must if it is to reach its desired conclusion—with *Rakas v. Illinois*, 439 U.S. 128 (1978). Contrary to the Court's assertion, however, *Rakas* did not establish that the Fourth Amendment protects individuals against unreasonable searches and seizures only if they have a privacy interest in the place searched. . . .

No Fourth Amendment claim based on an interest in the property seized was before the Court, and, consequently, the Court did not and could not have decided whether such a claim could be maintained. In fact, the Court expressly disavowed any intention to foreclose such a claim ("This is not to say that such [casual] visitors could not contest the lawfulness of the seizure of evidence or the search if their own property were seized during the search," 439 U.S., at 142, n.11), and suggested its continuing validity ("[P]etitioners' claims must fail. They asserted neither a property nor a possessory interest in the automobile, *nor an interest in the property seized*," id., at 148 (emphasis supplied)). . . .

. . . The history of the Fourth Amendment shows that it was designed to protect property interests as well as privacy interests; in fact, until *Jones* the question whether a person's Fourth Amendment rights had been violated turned on whether he had a property interest in the place searched or the items seized. *Jones* and *Katz v. United States*, 389 U.S. 347 (1967), expanded our view of the protections afforded by the Fourth Amendment by recognizing that privacy interests are protected even if they do not arise from property rights. But that recognition was never intended to exclude interests that had historically been sheltered by the Fourth Amendment from its protection. Neither *Jones* nor *Katz* purported to provide an exclusive definition of the interests protected by the Fourth Amendment. Indeed, as *Katz* recognized: "That Amendment protects individual privacy against certain kinds of governmental intrusion, but its protections go further, and often have nothing to do with privacy at all." 389 U.S., at 350. . . .

. . . A slow and steady erosion of the ability of victims of unconstitutional searches and seizures to obtain a remedy for the invasion of their rights saps the constitutional guarantee of its life just as surely as would a substantive limitation. Because we are called on to decide whether evidence should be excluded only when a search has been "successful," it is easy to forget that the standards we announce determine what government conduct is reasonable in searches and seizures directed at persons who turn out to be innocent as well as those who are guilty. I continue to believe that ungrudging application of the Fourth Amendment is indispensable to preserving the liberties of a democratic society. Accordingly, I dissent.

NOTES AND QUESTIONS

1. Do you agree that Rawlings should be regarded as not having a protectable fourth amendment interest in Cox's purse? Regardless of your answer, to what extent do you find the Court's reasoning persuasive? How relevant is it that Rawlings had known Cox for only a few days, that Rawlings had not previously used Cox's purse, that Rawlings could not exclude others from the purse, or that Rawlings had no subjective privacy expectation with respect to the purse?

2. Frequently the owners of seized items will be the targets of searches and seizures. Thus, *Rakas's* rejection of the target theory of standing arguably would not have a significant impact on the deterrent effect of the exclusionary rule as long as owners of seized objects had standing to challenge the searches that led to the seizures. Does the combination of *Rakas* and *Rawlings* go too far in undermining the deterrent effect of the exclusionary rule? Should there be an exception to *Rakas* and *Rawlings* for situations in which the police deliberately exploit the standing rules by engaging in a clearly illegal search of a third person's property in order to obtain evidence against the defendant? See United States v. Payner, infra at 938; Burkoff, Bad Faith Searches, 57 N.Y.U.L. Rev. 70 (1982).

2. The Fruit of the Poisonous Tree Doctrine

a. The Development of the Doctrine

Frequently the relationship between unconstitutional police conduct, the *poisonous tree*, and the evidence derived from the unconstitutional conduct, the *fruit*, will be quite direct. For example, the police
may discover contraband in an arrestee's home during a search that
exceeds the legitimate scope of a search incident to the arrest; police may
discover contraband on an arrestee's person during a search that is not
based on probable cause and that is not incident to a valid arrest. In such
cases, it is clear that the arrestee may exclude the fruits of the poisonous
tree. In other cases, however, the relationship between the initial illegality
and the evidence resulting from the illegality will be less direct. For
example, assume that during a search incident to an illegal arrest of the
defendant, the police find a slip of paper with a telephone number; by
calling the number they discover a friend of the defendant who implicates
the defendant and a third person in a recent robbery; the third person
tells the police where the proceeds of the robbery are located; police find
the proceeds, on which they identify the defendant's fingerprints. In this
hypothetical there is in fact a causal relationship between the initial illegal
arrest, the poisonous tree, and the robbery proceeds, the fruit. Yet the
relationship is less direct in time and space than the relationship between
the tree and its fruit in the earlier hypotheticals. Moreover, the police
may have discovered the evidence eventually even if they had not made
the illegal arrest. In such a case, the question whether the evidence should
be admitted depends on an analysis of the relationship between the poisonous tree and its fruit, and it is in this type of case that the phrase *fruit
of the poisonous tree* is frequently employed. See generally Pitler, "The
Fruit of the Poisonous Tree" Revisited and Shepardized, 56 Calif. L.
Rev. 579 (1968).][103]

103. Although fruit of the poisonous tree problems arise most frequently in situations
in which the poisonous tree is a fourth amendment violation, the principles dealt with
here are applicable to other unconstitutional and illegal (but not unconstitutional) police
conduct. See, e.g., Nardone v. United States, 308 U.S. 338 (1939) (wiretapping in
violation of federal statute is poisonous tree); Nix v. Williams, 467 U.S. 431 (1984)
(deliberately eliciting statement in violation of defendant's sixth amendment right to
counsel is poisonous tree).
   On the question of the applicability of the fruit of the poisonous tree doctrine to
Miranda violations, see Oregon v. Elstad, page 1296 infra (evidence derived from voluntary statement obtained in violation of *Miranda* admissible; *Miranda* violation not poisonous tree for purposes of fruits analysis). Cf. Massachusetts v. White, 439 U.S. 280 (1978)
(equally divided Court affirming holding, 374 Mass. 132, 371 N.E.2d 777 (1977), that
statements obtained in violation of *Miranda* cannot be used to establish probable cause

The first Supreme Court case to utilize the phrase *fruit of the poisonous tree* was Nardone v. United States, 308 U.S. 338 (1939). Because the prosecution had introduced evidence of telephone conversations overheard as the result of an illegal wiretap, the Supreme Court had previously reversed Nardone's conviction for defrauding the Internal Revenue Service. 302 U.S. 379. At Nardone's second trial, which also resulted in a conviction, the trial court refused to permit inquiry about the possible uses to which the illegally obtained evidence had been put. Reversing Nardone's second conviction, the Court held that once the initial illegality is established, the accused must be given an opportunity "to prove that a substantial portion of the case against him was a fruit of the poisonous tree." 308 U.S. at 341. At the same time, the Court observed that establishing a connection between the initial illegality and the evidence may not always require exclusion: "as a matter of good sense, . . . such connection may have become so attenuated as to dissipate the taint." Id.

Wong Sun v. United States, 371 U.S. 471 (1963), involved the convictions of Toy and Wong Sun for transporting heroin. Federal narcotics officers illegally entered Toy's laundry and chased Toy to the living quarters in the rear of the building. Upon being questioned, Toy told the officers that Yee had been selling narcotics. The officers then went to Yee, who gave heroin to them and said he had obtained the heroin from Toy and Wong Sun. Wong Sun was subsequently arrested and released on his own recognizance. Several days later Wong Sun voluntarily returned to the police station, where he made an inculpatory statement.

After reciting the foregoing facts, the Supreme Court reaffirmed that evidence is not inadmissible " 'fruit of the poisonous tree' simply because it would not have come to light but for the illegal actions of the police." Id. at 488. According to the Court, "the more apt question . . . is 'whether, granting establishment of the primary illegality, the evidence to which instant objection is made has been come at by exploitation of that illegality or instead by means sufficiently distinguishable to be purged of the primary taint.' " Id. (quoting J. Maguire, Evidence of Guilt 221 (1959)). Applying this principle to the facts in *Wong Sun*, the Court held that both Toy's statements at the time of the arrest and the narcotics taken from Yee were inadmissible against Toy. On the other hand, Wong Sun's statement made several days after his illegal arrest was admissible against him because "the connection between the arrest and the statement had

to obtain search warrant). Compare *Elstad* with Kastigar v. United States, page 965 infra (federal immunity statute, which provides for use and derivative use immunity, is coextensive with scope of fifth amendment protection against self-incrimination).

'become so attenuated as to dissipate the taint.' " Id. at 491 (quoting *Nardone*).

Could Wong Sun successfully move to suppress the narcotics obtained from Yee?

What factors should be relevant in deciding whether the evidence has been "purged of the primary taint" or is sufficiently "attenuated" from the initial illegality? Is it more important to focus on the nature of the initial illegality or the type of evidence that the prosecution seeks to introduce?

b. Some Varieties of Fruits

In giving content to the *attenuation* or *purging the taint* concept, the Supreme Court has focused on both the nature of the underlying illegality and the type of evidence derived from the illegality. Partly for the sake of organizational convenience and partly because the Court's mode of analysis tends to vary more depending on the type of evidence involved rather than the type of initial illegality, the materials here focus on several varieties of fruits: confessions, witnesses, and identification of defendants.

BROWN v. ILLINOIS, 422 U.S. 590, 591, 600, 602-606, 610-613, 615 (1975): MR. JUSTICE BLACKMUN delivered the opinion of the Court.

. . . Petitioner was arrested without probable cause and without a warrant. He was given, in full, the warning prescribed by Miranda v. Arizona, 384 U.S. 436 (1966). Thereafter, while in custody, he made two inculpatory statements[, which were introduced into evidence over defendant's objection, at his murder trial.] . . .

The Illinois courts . . . assumed that the *Miranda* warnings, by themselves, assured that the statements . . . were of sufficient free will as to purge the primary taint of the unlawful arrest. . . .

If *Miranda* warnings, by themselves, were held to attenuate the taint of an unconstitutional arrest, regardless of how wanton and purposeful the Fourth Amendment violation, the effect of the exclusionary rule would be substantially diluted. . . . Arrests made without warrant or without probable cause, for questioning or "investigation," would be encouraged by the knowledge that evidence derived therefrom could well be made admissible at trial by the simple expedient of giving *Miranda* warnings. . . .

While we . . . reject the per se rule which the Illinois courts appear to have accepted, we also decline to adopt any alternative per se or "but for" rule. . . . The question whether a confession is the product of a free will under *Wong Sun* must be answered on the facts of each case. No single fact is dispositive. The workings of the human mind are too complex, and the possibilities of misconduct too diverse, to permit protection of the Fourth Amendment to turn on such a talismanic test. The *Miranda* warnings are an important factor, to be sure, in determining whether the confession is obtained by exploitation of an illegal arrest. But they are not the only factor to be considered. The temporal proximity of the arrest and the confession, the presence of intervening circumstances, . . . and, particularly, the purpose and flagrancy of the official misconduct are all relevant. . . . The voluntariness of the statement is a threshold requirement. . . . And the burden of showing admissibility rests, of course, on the prosecution.

. . . We conclude that the State failed to sustain the burden of showing that the evidence in question was admissible under *Wong Sun*.

Brown's first statement was separated from his illegal arrest by less than two hours, and there was no intervening event of significance whatsoever. . . . And the second statement was clearly the result and the fruit of the first.

The illegality here, moreover, had a quality of purposefulness. The impropriety of the arrest was obvious; awareness of that fact was virtually conceded by the two detectives when they repeatedly acknowledged, in their testimony, that the purpose of their action was "for investigation" or for "questioning." . . .

We emphasize that our holding is a limited one. We decide only that the Illinois courts were in error in assuming that the *Miranda* warnings, by themselves, under *Wong Sun* always purge the taint of an illegal arrest.

The judgment of the Supreme Court of Illinois is reversed and the case is remanded for further proceedings not inconsistent with this opinion.

It is so ordered.

[The concurring opinion of JUSTICE WHITE is omitted.]

MR. JUSTICE POWELL, with whom MR. JUSTICE REHNQUIST joins, concurring in part. . . .

I would require the clearest indication of attenuation in cases in which official conduct was flagrantly abusive of Fourth Amendment rights. . . .

At the opposite end of the spectrum lie "technical" violations of Fourth Amendment rights where, for example, officers in good faith arrest an individual in reliance on a warrant later invalidated or pursuant to a statute that subsequently is declared unconstitutional. Thus, with the exception of statements given in the immediate circumstances of the illegal arrest—a constraint I think is imposed by existing exclusionary-rule law—I would not require more than proof that effective *Miranda* warnings were given and that the ensuing statement was voluntary in the Fifth Amendment sense. Absent aggravating circumstances, I would consider a statement given at the station house after one has been advised of *Miranda* rights to be sufficiently removed from the immediate circumstances of the illegal arrest to justify its admission at trial.

I am not able to conclude on this record that the officers arrested petitioner solely for the purpose of questioning. . . .

. . . I therefore would remand for reconsideration. . . .

NOTES AND QUESTIONS

1. Dunaway v. New York, 442 U.S. 200 (1979), involved facts similar to *Brown*, and the Court relied on *Brown* to reverse the defendant's conviction. In a concurring opinion Justice Stevens observed:

> The flagrancy of the official misconduct is relevant, in my judgment, only insofar as it has a tendency to motivate the defendant. . . .
> I recognize that the deterrence rationale for the exclusionary rule is sometimes interpreted quite differently. Under that interpretation exclusion is applied as a substitute for punishment of the offending officer. . . . But when evidence is excluded at a criminal trial, it is the broad societal interest in effective law enforcement that suffers. The justification for the exclusion of evidence obtained by improper methods is to motivate the law enforcement profession as a whole—not the aberrant individual officer—to adopt and enforce regular procedures that will avoid the future invasion of the citizen's constitutional rights. For that reason, exclusionary rules should embody objective criteria rather than subjective considerations. [Id. at 220-221.]

Do you agree with Justice Stevens' approach to the attenuation issue?

2. Should repeatedly giving *Miranda* warnings or permitting an arrestee to visit with a friend be sufficient to purge the taint of an illegal arrest and to permit the admission of a confession? No, the Court held in Taylor v. Alabama, 457 U.S. 687 (1982), a case that the Court described as a "virtual replica" of *Brown* and *Dunaway*. See also Lanier v. South Carolina, 474 U.S. 25 (1985) (per curiam) (finding that confession is voluntary in fifth amendment sense is only threshold inquiry if issue is whether confession is fruit of illegal arrest).

3. Rawlings v. Kentucky, other aspects of which are considered at pages 862-866 supra, also involved facts similar to those in *Brown*. The defendant, following an illegal detention in the home of an acquaintance,

acknowledged that drugs discovered in the purse of a third person belonged to him. The Court rejected his claim that this statement acknowledging ownership of the drugs should have been regarded as an inadmissible fruit of the illegal detention. In an opinion by Justice Rehnquist, the Court relied on the following factors to justify its decision:

a. The defendant had been given *Miranda* warnings almost immediately before making the statement;

b. The conditions of detention in the private residence were not oppressive;

c. The statement was an apparently spontaneous reaction to the discovery of the drugs; and

d. The police activity in detaining the occupants of the house while a warrant was being obtained was not nearly as flagrant as the police activity in *Brown*.

4. On some occasions the initial illegality that leads to a confession is itself a confession. See, e.g., United States v. Bayer, 331 U.S. 532 (1947) (several months after making illegally obtained confession and after rereading illegally obtained confession, defendant made second confession; at time of second confession defendant warned that second confession could be used against him but not warned that first confession could not be used; held, second confession admissible); cf. Commonwealth v. Meehan, 377 Mass. 552, 387 N.E.2d 527 (1979) (confession following involuntary confession inadmissible).

UNITED STATES v. CECCOLINI
Certiorari to the United States Court of Appeals for the Second Circuit
435 U.S. 268 (1978)

MR. JUSTICE REHNQUIST delivered the opinion of the Court.

In December 1974, Ronald Biro, a uniformed police officer on assignment to patrol school crossings, entered respondent's place of business, the Sleepy Hollow Flower Shop, in North Tarrytown, N.Y. He went behind the customer counter and, in the words of Ichabod Crane, one of Tarrytown's more illustrious inhabitants of days gone past, "tarried," spending his short break engaged in conversation with his friend Lois Hennessey, an employee of the shop. During the course of the conversation he noticed an envelope with money sticking out of it lying on the drawer of the cash register behind the counter. Biro picked up the envelope and, upon examining its contents, discovered that it contained not only money but policy slips. He placed the envelope back on the register, and, without telling Hennessey what he had seen, asked her to whom the envelope belonged. She replied that the envelope belonged to respondent Ceccolini, and that he had instructed her to give it to someone.

The next day, Officer Biro mentioned his discovery to North Tarrytown detectives who in turn told Lance Emory, an FBI agent. . . .

. . . Four months later, Emory interviewed Hennessey at her home. . . . She then related the events which had occurred during her visit with Officer Biro.

In May 1975, respondent was summoned before a federal grand jury where he testified that he had never taken policy bets for Francis Millow at the flower shop. The next week Hennessey testified to the contrary, and shortly thereafter respondent was indicted for perjury. . . .

[The trial court, after excluding the policy slips, found the defendant guilty. The court then granted defendant's motion to suppress Ms. Hennessey's testimony and held that without her testimony there was insufficient evidence to support the finding of guilt.]

The Court of Appeals affirmed. . . .

. . . [We] reject the Government's suggestion that we adopt what would in practice amount to a per se rule that the testimony of a live witness should not be excluded at trial no matter how close and proximate the connection between it and a violation of the Fourth Amendment. We also affirm the holding of Wong Sun [v. United States, 371 U.S. 471,] 485 [(1963)], that "verbal evidence which derives so immediately from an unlawful entry and an unauthorized arrest as the officers' action in the present case is no less the 'fruit' of official illegality than the more common tangible fruits of the unwarranted intrusion." We are of the view, however, that cases decided since Wong Sun significantly qualify its further observation that "the policies underlying the exclusionary rule [do not] invite any logical distinction between physical and verbal evidence." 371 U.S., at 486. Rather, at least in a case such as this, where not only was the alleged "fruit of the poisonous tree" the testimony of a live witness, but unlike Wong Sun the witness was not a putative defendant, an examination of our cases persuades us that the Court of Appeals was simply wrong in concluding that if the road were uninterrupted, its length was immaterial. Its length, we hold, is material, as are certain other factors enumerated below to which the court gave insufficient weight.

In Stone v. Powell, 428 U.S. 465, 486 (1976), we observed that "despite the broad deterrent purpose of the exclusionary rule, it has never been interpreted to proscribe the introduction of illegally seized evidence in all proceedings or against all persons." Recognizing not only the benefits but the costs, which are often substantial, of the exclusionary rule, we have said that "application of the rule has been restricted to those areas where its remedial objectives are thought most efficaciously served," United States v. Calandra, 414 U.S. 338, 348 (1974). . . .

Evaluating the standards for application of the exclusionary rule to live-witness testimony in light of this balance, we are first impelled to conclude that the degree of free will exercised by the witness is not irrelevant in determining the extent to which the basic purpose of the exclusionary rule will be advanced by its application. . . .

The greater the willingness of the witness to freely testify, the greater the likelihood that he or she will be discovered by legal means and, concomitantly, the smaller the incentive to conduct an illegal search to discover the witness.[4] Witnesses are not like guns or documents which remain hidden from view until one turns over a sofa or opens a filing cabinet. Witnesses can, and often do, come forward and offer evidence entirely of their own volition. And evaluated properly, the degree of free will necessary to dissipate the taint will very likely be found more often in the case of live-witness testimony than other kinds of evidence. The time, place and manner of the initial questioning of the witness may be such that any statements are truly the product of detached reflection and a desire to be cooperative on the part of the witness. And the illegality which led to the discovery of the witness very often will not play any meaningful part in the witness' willingness to testify. . . .

Another factor which not only is relevant in determining the usefulness of the exclusionary rule in a particular context, but also seems to us to differentiate the testimony of all live witnesses—even putative defendants—from the exclusion of the typical documentary evidence, is that such exclusion would perpetually disable a witness from testifying about relevant and material facts, regardless of how unrelated such testimony might be to the purpose of the originally illegal search or the evidence discovered thereby. Rules which disqualify knowledgeable witnesses from testifying at trial are, in the words of Professor McCormick, "serious obstructions to the ascertainment of truth"; accordingly, "[f]or a century the course of legal evolution has been in the direction of sweeping away these obstructions." C. McCormick, Law of Evidence §71 (1954). . . .

Viewing this case in the light of the principles just discussed, we hold that the Court of Appeals erred in holding that the degree of attenuation was not sufficient to dissipate the connection between the illegality and the testimony. The evidence indicates overwhelmingly that the testimony given by the witness was an act of her own free will in no way

---

4. Of course, the analysis might be different where the search was conducted by the police for the specific purpose of discovering potential witnesses.

coerced or even induced by official authority as a result of Biro's discovery of the policy slips. Nor were the slips themselves used in questioning Hennessey. Substantial periods of time elapsed between the time of the illegal search and the initial contact with the witness, on the one hand, and between the latter and the testimony at trial on the other. While the particular knowledge to which Hennessey testified at trial can be logically traced back to Biro's discovery of the policy slips, both the identity of Hennessey and her relationship with the respondent were well known to those investigating the case. There is, in addition, not the slightest evidence to suggest that Biro entered the shop or picked up the envelope with the intent of finding tangible evidence bearing on an illicit gambling operation, much less any suggestion that he entered the shop and searched with the intent of finding a willing and knowledgeable witness to testify against respondent. Application of the exclusionary rule in this situation could not have the slightest deterrent effect on the behavior of an officer such as Biro. The cost of permanently silencing Hennessey is too great for an evenhanded system of law enforcement to bear in order to secure such a speculative and very likely negligible deterrent effect.

Obviously no mathematical weight can be assigned to any of the factors which we have discussed, but just as obviously they all point to the conclusion that the exclusionary rule should be invoked with much greater reluctance where the claim is based on a casual relationship between a constitutional violation and the discovery of a live witness than when a similar claim is advanced to support suppression of an inanimate object. The judgment of the Court of Appeals is accordingly reversed.

MR. JUSTICE BLACKMUN took no part in the consideration or decision of this case.

MR. CHIEF JUSTICE BURGER, concurring in the judgment.

I agree with the Court's ultimate conclusion that there is a fundamental difference, for purposes of the exclusionary rule, between live witness testimony and other types of evidence. I perceive this distinction to be so fundamental, however, that I would not prevent a fact finder from hearing and considering the relevant statements of any witness, except perhaps under the most remarkable of circumstances—although none such have ever been postulated that would lead me to exclude the testimony of a live witness. . . .

I would, therefore, resolve the case of a living witness on a per se basis, holding that such testimony is always admissible, provided it meets all other traditional evidentiary requirements. At very least this solution would alleviate the burden—now squarely thrust upon courts—of determining in each instance whether the witness possessed that elusive quality characterized by the term "free will."

MR. JUSTICE MARSHALL, with whom MR. JUSTICE BRENNAN joins, dissenting. . . .

. . . We long ago held that, if knowledge of evidence is gained from a source independent of police illegality, the evidence should be admitted. Silverthorne Lumber Co. v. United States, 251 U.S. 385, 392 (1920) (Holmes, J.). . . . In the instant case, however, as the Court recognizes, there is a " 'straight and uninterrupted' " road between the illegal search and the disputed testimony.

Even where the road is uninterrupted, in some cases the Government may be able to [utilize] . . . the illegally discovered evidence [by show-ing that it] . . . inevitably [would] have come to light in the normal course of a legal police investigation. [See pages 1358-1365 infra.] . . .

. . . It may be that verbal evidence is more likely to have an in-dependent source, because live witnesses can indeed come forward of their own volition, but this simply underscores the degree to which the Court's approach involves a form of judicial "double counting." The Court would apparently first determine whether the evidence stemmed from an independent source or would inevitably have been discovered; if neither of these rules was found to apply, as here, the Court would still somehow take into account the fact that, as a general proposition (but not in the particular case), witnesses sometimes do come forward of their own volition.

The Court makes a related point that "[t]he greater the willingness of the witness to freely testify . . . the smaller the incentive to conduct an illegal search to discover the witness." . . . The somewhat incredible premise of this statement is that the police in fact refrain from illegal behavior in which they would otherwise engage because they know in advance both that a witness will be willing to testify and that he or she "will be discovered by legal means." . . . This reasoning surely reverses the normal sequence of events; the instances must be very few in which a witness' willingness to testify is known before he or she is discov-ered. . . .

The only other point made by the Court is that exclusion of testimony "perpetually disable[s] a witness from testifying about relevant and ma-terial facts." The "perpetual . . . disable[ment]" of which the Court speaks, however, applies as much to physical as to verbal evidence. . . .

. . . Although . . . four months elapsed between the illegal search and the FBI's first contact with Hennessey, the . . . the time that elapsed . . . is of no more relevance than would be a similar time period between the discovery of an object during an illegal search and its later introduction into evidence at trial. In this case, moreover, there were no intervening circumstances between Hennessey's statement at the time of the search and her later testimony. . . .

UNITED STATES v. CREWS
Certiorari to the United States Court of Appeals for the Second Circuit
445 U.S. 463 (1980)

MR. JUSTICE BRENNAN delivered the opinion of the Court, except as to Part II-D.

We are called upon to decide whether in the circumstances of this case an in-court identification of the accused by the victim of a crime should be suppressed as the fruit of the defendant's unlawful arrest.

I

On the morning of January 3, 1974, a woman was accosted and robbed at gunpoint by a young man in the women's restroom on the grounds of the Washington Monument. . . .

On January 6, two other women were assaulted and robbed in a similar episode in the same restroom. . . . All three described their assailant as a young black male, 15-18 years old, approximately 5'5" to 5'8" tall, slender in build, with a very dark complexion and smooth skin.

Three days later [the respondent, who matched this general description, was] . . . taken into custody, ostensibly because he was a suspected truant. He was then transported to Park Police headquarters, where the police briefly questioned him, obtained . . . [a] photograph, telephoned his school, and released him. Respondent was never formally arrested or charged with any offense, and his detention at the station lasted no more than an hour.

On the following day, January 10, the police showed the victim of the first robbery an array of eight photographs, including one of respondent. Although she had previously viewed over 100 pictures of possible suspects without identifying any of them as her assailant, she immediately selected respondent's photograph as that of the man who had robbed her. On January 13, one of the other victims made a similar identification. Respondent was again taken into custody, and at a court-ordered lineup held on January 21, he was positively identified by the two women who had made the photographic identifications.

The grand jury returned an indictment against respondent on February 22, 1974, charging him with two counts of armed robbery, two counts of robbery, one count of attempted armed robbery, and three counts of assault with a dangerous weapon. Respondent filed a pretrial motion to suppress all identification testimony. . . . [T]he trial court found that the respondent's detention at Park Police headquarters on

January 9 constituted an arrest without probable cause. Accordingly, the court ruled that the products of that arrest—the photographic and lineup identifications—could not be introduced at trial. But the judge concluded that the victims' ability to identify respondent in court was based upon independent recollection untainted by the intervening identifications, and therefore held such testimony admissible. At trial, all three victims identified respondent as their assailant. On April 23, the jury convicted him of armed robbery of the first victim, but returned verdicts of not guilty on all other charges. . . .

On appeal, the District of Columbia Court of Appeals, sitting en banc, reversed respondent's conviction and ordered the suppression of the first robbery victim's in-court identification. 389 A. 2d 277 (1978). . . . We reverse.

II . . .

A victim's in-court identification of the accused has three distinct elements. First, the victim is present at trial to testify as to what transpired between her and the offender, and to identify the defendant as the culprit. Second, the victim possesses knowledge of and the ability to reconstruct the prior criminal occurrence and to identify the defendant from her observations of him at the time of the crime. And third, the defendant is also physically present in the courtroom, so that the victim can observe him and compare his appearance to that of the offender. In the present case, it is our conclusion that none of these three elements "has been come at by exploitation" of the violation of the defendant's Fourth Amendment rights. Wong Sun [v. United States, 371 U.S. 471,] 488 [(1963)].

A

In this case, the robbery victim's presence in the courtroom at respondent's trial was surely not the product of any police misconduct. . . . [T]his is not a case in which the witness' identity was discovered or her cooperation secured only as a result of an unlawful search or arrest of the accused. Here the victim's identity was known long before there was any official misconduct, and her presence in court is thus not traceable to any Fourth Amendment violation.

B

Nor did the illegal arrest infect the victim's ability to give accurate identification testimony. Based upon her observations at the time of the robbery, the victim constructed a mental image of her assailant. At trial, she retrieved this mnemonic representation, compared it to the figure of the defendant, and positively identified him as the robber. No part of this process was affected by respondent's illegal arrest. . . .

This is not to say that the intervening photographic and lineup identifications—both of which are conceded to be suppressible fruits of the Fourth Amendment violation—could not under some circumstances affect the reliability of the in-court identification and render it inadmissible as well. . . . But in the present case the trial court expressly found that the witness' courtroom identification rested on an independent recollection of her initial encounter with the assailant, uninfluenced by the pretrial identifications, and this determination finds ample support in the record.[18] In short, the victim's capacity to identify her assailant in court neither resulted from nor was biased by the unlawful police conduct committed long after she had developed that capacity.[19]

C

Insofar as respondent challenges his own presence at trial, he cannot claim immunity from prosecution simply because his appearance in court was precipitated by an unlawful arrest. An illegal arrest, without more, has never been viewed as a bar to subsequent prosecution, nor as a defense to a valid conviction. Gerstein v. Pugh, 420 U.S. 103, 119 (1975); Frisbee v. Collins, 342 U.S. 519 (1952); Ker v. Illinois, 119 U.S. 436 (1886). The exclusionary principle of *Wong Sun* and *Silverthorne Lumber Co.* delimits what proof the Government may offer against the accused at trial, closing the courtroom door to evidence secured by official lawlessness. Respondent is not himself a suppressible "fruit," and the illegality of his detention cannot deprive the Government of the opportunity to prove his guilt through the introduction of evidence wholly untainted by the police misconduct.

18. . . . Our reliance on the fact that the witness twice identified respondent in out-of-court confrontations is not intended to assign any independent evidentiary value to those identifications for to do so would undermine the exclusionary rule's objectives in denying the Government the benefit of any evidence wrongfully obtained. Rather, the accurate pretrial identifications assume significance only to the extent that they indicate that the witness' ability to identify respondent antedated any police misconduct, and hence that her in-court identification had an "independent source."

19. Respondent contends that the "independent source" test of United States v. Wade, [388 U.S. 218 (1967)], and Stovall v. Denno, 388 U.S. 293 (1967), although derived from an identical formulation in *Wong Sun*, see 388 U.S., at 241, seeks only to determine whether the in-court identification is sufficiently reliable to satisfy due process, and is thus inapplicable in the context of this Fourth Amendment violation. We agree that a satisfactory resolution of the reliability issue does not provide a complete answer to the considerations underlying *Wong Sun*, but note only that in the present case both concerns are met.

Inevitable Discovery Doctrine

D*

Respondent argues, however, that in one respect his corpus is itself a species of "evidence." When the victim singles out respondent and declares, "That's the man who robbed me," his physiognomy becomes something of evidentiary value, much like a photograph showing respondent at the scene of the crime. And, as with the introduction of such a photograph, he contends that the crucial inquiry for Fourth Amendment purposes is whether that evidence has become available only as a result of official misconduct. We read the Court of Appeals' opinion as essentially adopting this analysis to support its suppression order. . . .

We need not decide whether respondent's person should be considered evidence, and therefore a possible "fruit" of police misconduct. For in this case the record plainly discloses that prior to his illegal arrest, the police both knew respondent's identity and had some basis to suspect his involvement in the very crimes with which he was charged. Moreover, before they approached respondent, the police had already obtained access to the "evidence" that implicated him in the robberies, i.e., the mnemonic representations of the criminal retained by the victims and related to the police in the form of their agreement upon his description. In short, the Fourth Amendment violation in this case yielded nothing of evidentiary value that the police did not already have in their grasp.[22] Rather, respondent's unlawful arrest served merely to link together two extant ingredients in his identification. The exclusionary rule enjoins the Government from benefiting from evidence it has unlawfully obtained; it does not reach backward to taint information that was in official hands prior to any illegality.

Accordingly, this case is very different from one like Davis v. Mississippi, 394 U.S. 721 (1969), in which the defendant's identity and connection to the illicit activity were only first discovered through an illegal arrest or search. In that case, the defendant's fingerprints were ordered suppressed as the fruits of an unlawful detention. A woman had been raped in her home, and during the next 10 days, the local police rounded up scores of black youths, randomly stopping, interrogating, and fingerprinting them. Davis' prints were discovered to match a set found at the scene of the crime, and on that basis he was arrested and convicted. Had it not been for Davis' illegal detention, however, his prints would not have been obtained and he would never have become a suspect.

---

*This part is joined only by Mr. Justice Stewart and Mr. Justice Stevens.

22. Thus we are not called upon in this case to hypothesize about whether routine investigatory procedures would eventually have led the police to discover respondent's culpability. His involvement in the robberies was already suspected, and no new evidence was acquired through the violation of his Fourth Amendment rights.

Here, in contrast, the robbery investigation had already focused on respondent, and the police had independent reasonable grounds to suspect his culpability.

We find Bynum v. United States, 104 U.S. App. D.C. 368, 262 F.2d 465 (1958), cited with approval in *Davis*, supra, at 724, helpful in our analysis as well. In *Bynum*, the defendant voluntarily came down to the police station to look for his brother, who had been arrested earlier that day while driving an auto sought in connection with a robbery. After telling one of the officers that he owned the car, Bynum was arrested and fingerprinted. Those prints were later found to match a set at the scene of the robbery, and Bynum was convicted based in part on that evidence. The Court of Appeals held that the police lacked probable cause at the time of Bynum's arrest, and it ordered the prints suppressed as "something of evidentiary value which the public authorities have caused an arrested person to yield to them during illegal detention." 104 U.S. App. D.C., at 370, 262 F.2d, at 467. As this Court noted in *Davis*, however, 394 U.S., at 725-726, n.4, Bynum was subsequently reindicted for the same offense, and the Government on retrial introduced an older set of his fingerprints, taken from an FBI file, that were in no way connected with his unlawful arrest. The Court of Appeals affirmed that conviction, holding that the fingerprint identification made on the basis of information already in the FBI's possession was not tainted by the subsequent illegality and was therefore admissible. Bynum v. United States, 107 U.S. App. D.C. 109, 274 F.2d 767 (1960).

The parallels between *Bynum* and this case are apparent: The pretrial identification obtained through use of the photograph taken during respondent's illegal detention cannot be introduced; but the in-court identification is admissible, even if respondent's argument be accepted, because the police's knowledge of respondent's identity and the victim's independent recollections of him both antedated the unlawful arrest and were thus untainted by the constitutional violation. The judgment of the Court of Appeals is accordingly reversed.

MR. JUSTICE MARSHALL took no part in the consideration or decision of this case.

[The concurring opinion of JUSTICE POWELL is omitted.]

MR. JUSTICE WHITE, with whom THE CHIEF JUSTICE and MR. JUSTICE REHNQUIST join, concurring in the result.

. . . Mr. Justice Brennan's opinion reserves the question whether a defendant's face can ever be considered evidence suppressible as the "fruit" of an illegal arrest. Because I consider this question to be controlled by the rationale of Frisbie v. Collins, 342 U.S. 519 (1952), I write separately.

. . . We held in Frisbie v. Collins, supra, at 522, "that the power of a court to try a person for crime is not impaired by the fact that he had been brought within the court's jurisdiction" unlawfully. A holding that a defendant's face can be considered evidence suppressible for no reason other than that the defendant's presence in the courtroom is the fruit of an illegal arrest would be tantamount to holding that an illegal arrest effectively insulates one from conviction for any crime where an in-court identification is essential. Such a holding would be inconsistent with the underlying rationale of *Frisbie* from which we have not re-treated. . . .

Assume that a person is arrested for crime X and that answers to questions put to him without *Miranda* warnings implicate him in crime Y for which he is later tried. The victim of crime Y identifies him in the courtroom; the identification has an independent, untainted basis. I would not suppress such an identification on the grounds that the police had no reason to suspect the defendant of crime Y prior to their illegal questioning and that it is only because of that questioning that he is present in the courtroom for trial. I would reach the same result whether or not his arrest for crime X was without probable cause or reasonable suspicion.

I agree that this case is very different from Davis v. Mississippi, 394 U.S. 721 (1969), but not for the reason given in my Brother Brennan's opinion. In *Davis* we held that fingerprints obtained from a defendant during an illegal detention had to be suppressed because they were the direct product of the unlawful arrest. Here, however, the evidence ordered suppressed was eyewitness testimony of the victim which was not the product of respondent's arrest. The fact that respondent was present at trial and therefore capable of being identified by the victim is merely the inevitable result of the trial being held, which is permissible under *Frisbie*, despite respondent's unlawful arrest. Suppression would be required in the *Davis* situation, but not here, regardless of whether the respective arrests were made without any reasonable suspicion or with something just short of probable cause.

NOTES AND QUESTIONS

1. Why did the government concede that the photographic and lineup identifications were inadmissible fruits of the illegal arrest? If the defendant's face is not an inadmissible fruit at trial, what makes it an inadmissible fruit at the pretrial settings? Is the answer that prior to trial there is insufficient attenuation?

2. In Frisbie v. Collins, 342 U.S. 519 (1952), the defendant was forcibly seized in Chicago by Michigan police officers, who returned him

to Michigan where he was convicted of murder. Assuming that the action of the Michigan officers violated the Federal Kidnapping Act, the Court held that the state's right to try a defendant is "not impaired by the fact that he has been brought within the court's jurisdiction by reason of a 'forcible abduction.' " Id. at 522. In *Collins*, however, there was no claim that *evidence* was derived from the illegal abduction. By contrast, in *Crews* the defendant claimed that not merely his presence but his identification by a witness was a fruit of the illegal arrest. Should this difference have led to a different result in *Crews*?

3.   Consider Davis v. Mississippi, 394 U.S. 721 (1969), which both Justice Brennan and Justice White discuss in their opinions. Which justice provides the more convincing basis for distinguishing the finger print evidence in *Davis* from the identification testimony in *Crews*?

Consider the following observation from Justice Stewart's dissent in *Davis*:

> Fingerprints are not "evidence" in the conventional sense that weapons or stolen goods might be. Like the color of a man's eyes, his height, or his very physiognomy, the tips of his fingers are an inherent and unchanging characteristic of the man. And physical impressions of his fingertips can be exactly and endlessly reproduced. [Id. at 730.]

In Davis—or in *Crews* if the trial identification testimony had been held inadmissible—would it have been proper to rely in part on the fingerprint or identification evidence to establish probable cause to rearrest the defendant?

4.   Part II-D of Justice Brennan's opinion in *Crews* appears to adopt what has become known as the *inevitable discovery doctrine:* Evidence that would otherwise be regarded as the inadmissible fruit of the poisonous tree may nonetheless be admitted if the evidence probably or "inevitably" would have been discovered without regard to the illegality. The Supreme Court recently considered the inevitable discovery doctrine in Nix v. Williams, 467 U.S. 431 (1984), which is set forth in Chapter 10 infra.

5.   Assume that the police use unconstitutionally deadly force against a suspected fleeing burglar, Tennessee v. Garner, page 819 supra, that the suspect survives, and that the police arrest him. Immediately following the arrest, the police find contraband during a search of the suspect's clothing, obtain a confession from the suspect, obtain a blood sample from the suspect, obtain the suspect's fingerprints, and arrange for the victim of the burglary to view and identify the suspect. Will the suspect be able to suppress any of this evidence on the ground that it is the fruit of an illegal arrest? See Uviller, Seizure by Gunshot: The Riddle of the Fleeing Felon, 14 N.Y.U. Rev. L. & Soc. Change 705 (1986).

6. New York v. Harris, 110 S. Ct. 1640 (1990), raised the issue whether a confession made at the police station can be the fruit of a violation of Payton v. New York, page 650 supra, the case requiring an arrest warrant to enter a person's home to arrest that person. The four dissenting justices viewed the case as similar to Brown v. Illinois, page 869 supra, and Dunaway v. New York, page 871 supra. A majority of the Court, however, in an opinion by Justice White, relied in part on *Ceccolini* and in part on *Crews* to uphold the admissibility of the confession:

> "[W]e have declined to adopt a 'per se or "but for" rule' that would make inadmissible any evidence . . . which somehow came to light through a chain of causation that began with an illegal arrest." United States v. Ceccolini, 435 U.S. 268, 276 (1978). Rather in this context, we have stated that "[t]he penalties visited upon the Government, and in turn upon the public, because its officers have violated the law must bear some relation to the purposes which the law is to serve." Id. at 279. In light of these principles, we decline to apply the exclusionary rule in this context because the rule in *Payton* was designed to protect the physical integrity of the home; it was not intended to grant criminal suspects, like Harris, protection for statements made outside their premises where the police have probable cause to arrest the suspect for committing a crime. . . .
>
> Nothing in . . . *[Payton]* suggests that an arrest in a home without a warrant but with probable cause somehow renders unlawful continued custody of the suspect once he is removed from the house. There could be no valid claim here that Harris was immune from prosecution because his person was the fruit of an illegal arrest. United States v. Crews, 445 U.S. 463, 474 (1980). Nor is there any claim that the warrantless arrest required the police to release Harris or that Harris could not be immediately rearrested if momentarily released. Because the officers had probable cause to arrest Harris for a crime, Harris was not unlawfully in custody when he was removed to the station house, given *Miranda* warnings and allowed to talk. For Fourth Amendment purposes, the legal issue is the same as it would be had the police arrested Harris on his door step, illegally entered his home to search for evidence, and later interrogated Harris at the station house. Similarly, if the police had made a warrantless entry into Harris' home, not found him there, but arrested him on the street when he returned, a later statement made by him after proper warnings would no doubt be admissible. [110 S. Ct. at 1642-1643.]

c. The Independent Source Rule

MURRAY v. UNITED STATES, 487 U.S. 533, 537-544 (1988): JUS-TICE SCALIA delivered the opinion of the Court. . . .

[Police officers made an illegal warrantless entry into an unoccupied warehouse where they observed bales of marijuana. The officers left without disturbing the bales, and while some of the officers kept the warehouse under surveillance, others obtained a search warrant. In seeking the warrant the officers made no mention of the illegal entry and did not rely on any observations made during the entry. On obtaining the warrant, the officers searched the warehouse and seized the bales of marijuana. The defendants unsuccessfully objected to the use of the evidence against them on the grounds that the officers should have told the magistrate of the illegal entry and that the illegal entry tainted the warrant.]

Almost simultaneously with our development of the exclusionary rule . . . we . . . announced what has come to be known as the "independent source" doctrine. See Silverthorne Lumber Co. v. United States, 251 U.S. 385, 392 (1920). . . .

Our cases have used the concept of "independent source" in a more general and a more specific sense. The more general identifies *all* evidence acquired in a fashion untainted by the illegal evidence-gathering activity. Thus, where an unlawful entry has given investigators knowledge of facts x and y, but fact z has been learned by other means, fact z can be said to be admissible because derived from an "independent source." This is how we used the term in Segura v. United States, 468 U.S. 796 (1984). In that case, agents unlawfully entered the defendant's apartment and remained there until a search warrant was obtained. The admissibility of what they discovered while waiting in the apartment was not before us, . . . but we held that the evidence found for the first time during the execution of the valid and untainted search warrant was admissible because it was discovered pursuant to an "independent source." . . .

The original use of the term, however, [was] . . . with reference to that particular category of evidence acquired by an untainted search *which is identical to the evidence unlawfully acquired*—that is, in the example just given, to knowledge of facts x and y derived from an independent source:

> The essence of a provision forbidding the acquisition of evidence in a certain way is that not merely evidence so acquired shall not be used before the Court but that it shall not be used at all. Of course, this does not mean that the facts thus obtained become sacred and inaccessible. If knowledge of them is gained from an independent source they may be provided like any others. [Silverthorne Lumber, supra, at 392.]

. . .

Petitioners' asserted policy basis for excluding evidence which is initially discovered during an illegal search, but is subsequently acquired through an independent and lawful source, is that a contrary rule will remove all deterrence to, and indeed positively encourage, unlawful police searches. As petitioners see the incentives, law enforcement officers will routinely enter without a warrant to make sure that what they expect to be on the premises is in fact there. If it is not, they will have spared themselves the time and trouble of getting a warrant; if it is, they can get the warrant and use the evidence despite the unlawful entry. . . . We see the incentives differently. An officer with probable cause . . . would be foolish to enter the premises first in an unlawful manner. By doing so, he would risk suppression of all evidence on the premises, both seen and unseen, since his action would add to the normal burden of convincing a magistrate that there is probable cause the much more onerous burden of convincing a trial court that no information gained from the illegal entry affected either the law enforcement officers' decision to seek a warrant or the magistrate's decision to grant it. . . . Nor would the officer *without* sufficient probable cause . . . have any added incentive to conduct an unlawful entry, since whatever he finds cannot be used to establish probable cause. . . .[2]

The ultimate question . . . is whether the search pursuant to warrant was in fact a genuinely independent source of the information and tangible evidence at issue here. This would not have been the case if the agents' decision to seek the warrant was prompted by what they had seen during the initial entry, or if information obtained during that entry was presented to the Magistrate and affected his decision to issue the warrant. . . . The District Court found that the agents did not reveal their warrantless entry to the Magistrate, . . . and that they did not include in their application for a warrant any recitation of their observations in the warehouse. . . . It did not, however, explicitly find that the agents would have sought a warrant if they had not earlier entered the warehouse. . . .

Accordingly, we vacate the judgments and remand these cases . . . for a determination whether the warrant-authorized search of the warehouse was an independent source of the challenged evidence in the sense we have described.

2. Justice Marshall argues, in effect, that where the police cannot point to some historically verifiable fact demonstrating that the subsequent search pursuant to a warrant was wholly unaffected by the prior illegal search—e.g., that they had already sought the warrant before entering the premises—we should adopt a per se rule of inadmissibility. . . . We do not believe that such a prophylactic exception to the independent source rule is necessary. To say that a district court must be satisfied that a warrant would have been sought without the illegal entry is not to give dispositive effect to police officers' assurances on the point. Where the facts render those assurances implausible, the independent source doctrine will not apply. . . .

NOTES AND QUESTIONS

1. In conjunction with footnote 2 and the Court's discussion of incentives in *Murray*, consider the following observation from Justice Marshall's dissent:

[T]oday's decision makes the application of the independent source exception turn entirely on an evaluation of the officers' intent. It normally will be difficult for the trial court to verify, or the defendant to rebut, an assertion by officers that they always intended to obtain a warrant, regardless of the results of the illegal search. The testimony of the officers conducting the illegal search is the only direct evidence of intent, and the defendant will be relegated simply to arguing that the officers should not be believed. Under these circumstances, the litigation risk described by the Court seems hardly a risk at all; it does not significantly dampen the incentive to conduct the initial illegal search. [487 U.S. at 547-548.]

2. In Segura v. United States, 468 U.S. 796 (1984), discussed in *Murray*, the Court, in an opinion by Chief Justice Burger, purported to apply the independent source rule: "Whether the initial entry was illegal . . . is irrelevant . . . because there was an independent source for the warrant." Id. at 813-814. In *Segura*, however, when the police made their initial illegal entry into defendant's apartment, they arrested the occupants. Thus, *Segura*, unlike *Murray*, presented the possibility that, in the absence of the illegal entry *and arrest*, some of the arrestees might have removed or destroyed the subsequently seized evidence. Should this possibility make the independent source rule inapplicable? Consider the following response by Chief Justice Burger:

[The] suggestion that [the occupants] would have removed or destroyed the evidence was pure speculation. Even more important, however, we decline to extend the exclusionary rule, which already exacts an enormous price from society and our system of justice, to further "protect" criminal activity. . . .

. . . [T]here is no "constitutional right" to destroy evidence. [Id. at 816.]

For a stinging criticism of the Court's analysis in *Segura* and of the decision to grant certiorari in that case, see Dressler, A Lesson in Incaution, Overwork, and Fatigue: The Judicial Miscraftsmanship of Segura v. United States, 26 Wm. & Mary L. Rev. 375 (1985).

3. Grand Jury Testimony

In United States v. Calandra, 414 U.S. 338 (1974), the Court in an opinion by Justice Powell held that grand jury witnesses cannot refuse to answer questions on the ground that the questions are based on information derived from a fourth amendment violation. In reaching this conclusion, the Court "weigh[ed] the potential injury to the historic role and function of the grand jury against the potential benefits of the rule as applied in this context." Id. at 349. In assessing these factors the Court concluded:

> Suppression hearings would halt the orderly progress of an investigation and might necessitate extended litigation of issues only tangentially related to the grand jury's primary objective. . . .
> Any incremental deterrent effect which might be achieved by extending the rule to grand jury proceedings is uncertain at best. . . . Such an extension would deter only police investigation consciously directed toward the discovery of evidence solely for use in a grand jury investigation. The incentive to disregard the requirement of the Fourth Amendment solely to obtain an indictment from a grand jury is substantially negated by the inadmissibility of the illegally seized evidence in a subsequent criminal prosecution of the search victim. [Id. at 349, 351.]

In a dissenting opinion joined by Justices Douglas and Marshall, Justice Brennan responded:

> This downgrading of the exclusionary rule to a determination whether its application in a particular type of proceeding furthers deterrence of future police misconduct reflects a startling misconception, unless it is a purposeful rejection, of the historical objective and purpose of the rule.
> . . . [T]here is no evidence that the possible deterrent effect of the rule was given any attention by the judges chiefly responsible for its formulation. Their concern as guardians of the bill of rights was to fashion an enforcement tool to give content and meaning to the Fourth Amendment's guarantees. [Id. at 356.]

Compare Calandra with Gelbard v. United States, 408 U.S. 41 (1972) (Title III of Crime Control Act, interpreted to permit grand jury witness to refuse to answer questions based on information obtained through illegal electronic surveillance).

4. Habeas Corpus

The focus on deterrence as the primary, if not sole, objective of the exclusionary rule was also prominent in Stone v. Powell, 428 U.S. 465

(1976), where the Court, in an opinion by Justice Powell, held that "where the State has provided an opportunity for full and fair litigation of a Fourth Amendment claim, a state prisoner may not be granted federal habeas corpus relief on the ground that evidence obtained in an unconstitutional search or seizure was introduced at his trial." Id. at 494. This restriction on the availability of habeas corpus was admittedly made "in light of the nature and purpose of the Fourth Amendment exclusionary rule," id. at 481, which the Court characterized as follows:

> The exclusionary rule was a judicially created means of effectuating the rights secured by the Fourth Amendment. . . .
> Decisions prior to Mapp [v. Ohio, 367 U.S. 643 (1961),] advanced two principal reasons for application of the rule in federal trials. The Court in Elkins [v. United States, 364 U.S. 206 (1960)], for example. . . . referred to the "imperative of judicial integrity," suggesting that exclusion of illegally seized evidence prevents contamination of the judicial process. 364 U.S., at 222. But even in that context a more pragmatic ground was emphasized: "The rule is calculated to prevent, not to repair. Its purpose is to deter. . . ." Id., at 217. The Mapp majority justified the application of the rule to the States on several grounds, but relied principally upon the belief that exclusion would deter future unlawful police conduct. 367 U.S., at 658.
> Although our decisions often have alluded to the "imperative of judicial integrity," . . . they demonstrate the limited role of this justification in the determination whether to apply the rule in a particular context. Logically extended this justification would require that courts exclude unconstitutionally seized evidence despite lack of objection by the defendant. . . . It also would require abandonment of the standing limitations on who may object to the introduction of unconstitutionally seized evidence . . . and retreat from the proposition that judicial proceedings need not abate when the defendant's person is unconstitutionally seized. . . . While courts, of course, must ever be concerned with preserving the integrity of the judicial process, this concern has limited force as a justification for the exclusion of highly probative evidence. The force of this justification becomes minimal where federal habeas corpus relief is sought by a prisoner who previously has been afforded the opportunity for full and fair consideration of his search-and-seizure claim at trial and on direct review.
> The primary justification for the exclusionary rule then is the deterrence of police conduct that violates Fourth Amendment rights. Post-Mapp decisions have established that the rule is not a personal constitutional right. It is not calculated to redress the injury to the privacy of the victim of the search or seizure, for any "[r]eparation comes too late." Linkletter v. Walker, 381 U.S. 618, 637 (1965).[104] . . .

104. In Linkletter v. Walker, the Court held that Mapp would not be applied

We adhere to the view that these considerations support the implementation of the exclusionary rule at trial and its enforcement on direct appeal of state-court convictions. But the additional contribution, if any, of the consideration of search-and-seizure claims of state prisoners on collateral review is small in relation to the costs. To be sure, each case in which such claim is considered may add marginally to an awareness of the values protected by the Fourth Amendment. There is no reason to believe, however, that the overall educative effect of the exclusionary rule would be appreciably diminished if search-and-seizure claims could not be raised in federal habeas corpus review of state convictions. Nor is there reason to assume that any specific disincentive already created by the risk of exclusion of evidence at trial or the reversal of convictions on direct review would be enhanced if there were the further risk that a conviction obtained in state court and affirmed on direct review might be overturned in collateral proceedings often occurring years after the incarceration of the defendant. The view that the deterrence of Fourth Amendment violations would be furthered rests on the dubious assumption that law enforcement authorities would fear that federal habeas review might reveal flaws in a search or seizure that went undetected at trial and on appeal.[35] Even if one rationally could assume that some additional incremental deterrent effect would be present in isolated cases, the resulting advance of the legitimate goal of furthering Fourth Amendment rights would be outweighed by the acknowledged costs to other values vital to a rational system of criminal justice. [428 U.S. at 482-493.]

---

retroactively. Writing for the Court in *Linkletter*, Justice Clark, author of the *Mapp* opinion, stressed the deterrence objective of the exclusionary rule and maintained that retroactive application of *Mapp* would not further that objective.—EDS.

35. The policy arguments that respondents marshal in support of the view that federal habeas corpus review is necessary to effectuate the Fourth Amendment stem from a basic mistrust of the state courts as fair and competent forums for the adjudication of federal constitutional rights. The argument is that state courts cannot be trusted to effectuate Fourth Amendment values through fair application of the rule, and the oversight jurisdiction of this Court on certiorari is an inadequate safeguard. The principal rationale for this view emphasizes the broad difference in the respective institutional settings within which federal judges and state judges operate. Despite differences in institutional environment and the unsympathetic attitude to federal constitutional claims of some state judges in years past, we are unwilling to assume that there now exists a general lack of appropriate sensitivity to constitutional rights in the trial and appellate courts of the several States. State courts, like federal courts, have a constitutional obligation to safeguard personal liberties and to uphold federal law. Martin v. Hunter's Lessee, 1 Wheat. 304, 341-344 (1816). Moreover, the argument that federal judges are more expert in applying federal constitutional law is especially unpersuasive in the context of search-and-seizure claims, since they are dealt with on a daily basis by trial level judges in both systems. . . .

5. Good Faith[105]

UNITED STATES v. LEON

Certiorari to the United States Court of Appeals for the Ninth Circuit
468 U.S. 897 (1984)

JUSTICE WHITE delivered the opinion of the Court. . . .
[Officers of the Burbank Police Department received a tip from a
confidential informant "of unproven reliability" that two of the respondents were selling narcotics. After further investigation, Officer Cyril
Rombach, "an experienced and well-trained narcotics investigator," prepared an application for a search warrant and an affidavit that related
information from the tip and the investigation. The application was reviewed by several assistant prosecutors, and a facially valid warrant was
issued by a state superior court judge. Searches pursuant to the warrant
revealed narcotics and other evidence. The respondents were indicted for
various drug offenses. They moved] to suppress the evidence seized pursuant to the warrant. The District Court . . . granted the motions to
suppress. . . . It concluded that the affidavit was insufficient to establish
probable cause. . . . In response to a request from the Government,
the court made clear that Officer Rombach had acted in good faith. . . .
[A] divided panel of the Court of Appeals for the Ninth Circuit
affirmed. . . . The Government's petition for certiorari expressly declined to seek review of the lower courts' determinations that the search
warrant was unsupported by probable cause and presented only the question "[w]hether the Fourth Amendment exclusionary rule should be modified so as not to bar the admission of evidence seized in reasonable,
good-faith reliance on a search warrant that is subsequently held to be
defective." We granted certiorari to consider the propriety of such a
modification. . . . Although it undoubtedly is within our power to consider the question whether probable cause existed under the "totality of

105. As early as 1976, Justice White advocated a good faith exception to the ex-
clusionary rule. Stone v. Powell, 428 U.S. 465, 538-542 (1976) (dissenting opinion).
Since that time, the question whether there should be a good faith exception has generated
substantial scholarly commentary. See, e.g., Ashdown, Good Faith, the Exclusionary
Remedy, and Rule-Oriented Adjudication in the Criminal Process, 24 Wm. & Mary L.
Rev. 335 (1983); Ball, Good Faith and the Fourth Amendment: The "Reasonable"
Exception to the Exclusionary Rule, 69 J. Crim. L. 635 (1978); Jensen & Hart, The
Good Faith Restatement of the Exclusionary Rule, 73 J. Crim. L. & Criminology 916
(1982); Kamisar, Gates, "Probable Cause," "Good Faith," and Beyond, 69 Iowa L. Rev.
551 (1984); Mertens & Wasserstrom, The Good Faith Exception to the Exclusionary
Rule: Deregulating the Police and Derailing the Law, 70 Geo. L. Rev. 365 (1981);
Schlag, Assaults on the Exclusionary Rule: Good Faith Limitations and Damage Rem-
edies, 73 J. Crim. L. & Criminology 875 (1982). See also Note 5, page 906 infra.

the circumstances" test announced last Term in Illinois v. Gates, 462
U.S. 213 (1983), that question has not been briefed or argued: and it is
also within our authority, which we choose to exercise, to take the case
as it comes to us, accepting the Court of Appeals' conclusion that probable
cause was lacking under the prevailing legal standards. See This Court's
Rule 21.1(a). . . .

The Fourth Amendment contains no provision expressly precluding
the use of evidence obtained in violation of its commands, and an examination of its origin and purposes makes clear that the use of fruits of
a past unlawful search or seizure "work[s] no new Fourth Amendment
wrong." United States v. Calandra, 414 U.S. 338, 354 (1974). The wrong
condemned by the Amendment is "fully accomplished" by the unlawful
search or seizure itself, ibid., and the exclusionary rule is neither intended
nor able to "cure the invasion of the defendant's rights which he has
already suffered." Stone v. Powell, [428 U.S. 465, 540 (1976)] (White
J., dissenting). The rule thus operates as "a judicially created remedy
designed to safeguard Fourth Amendment rights generally through its
deterrent effect, rather than a personal constitutional right of the person
aggrieved." United States v. Calandra, supra, at 348.

Whether the exclusionary sanction is appropriately imposed in a
particular case, our decisions make clear, is "an issue separate from the
question whether the Fourth Amendment rights of the party seeking to
invoke the rule were violated by police conduct." Illinois v. Gates, supra,
at 223. Only the former question is currently before us, and it must be
resolved by weighing the costs and benefits of preventing the use in the
prosecution's case-in-chief of inherently trustworthy tangible evidence
obtained in reliance on a search warrant issued by a detached and neutral
magistrate that ultimately is found to be defective.

The substantial social costs exacted by the exclusionary rule for the
vindication of Fourth Amendment rights have long been a source of
concern. "Our cases have consistently recognized that unbending application of the exclusionary sanction to enforce ideals of governmental
rectitude would impede unacceptably the truth-finding functions of judge
and jury." United States v. Payner, 447 U.S. 727, 734 (1980). An objectionable collateral consequence of this interference with the criminal
justice system's truth-finding function is that some guilty defendants may
go free or receive reduced sentences as a result of favorable plea bar-
gains.[6] . . . Indiscriminate application of the exclusionary rule, there-

6. Researchers have only recently begun to study extensively the effects of the
exclusionary rule on the disposition of felony arrests. One study suggests that the rule
results in the nonprosecution or nonconviction of between 0.6% and 2.35% of individuals
arrested for felonies. Davies, A Hard Look at What We Know (and Still Need to Learn)
About the "Costs" of the Exclusionary Rule: The NIJ Study and Other Studies of "Lost"
Arrests, 1983 A.B.F. Res. J. 611, 621. The estimates are higher for particular crimes

fore, may well "generat[e] disrespect for the law and the administration of justice." [Stone v. Powell, supra], at 491. Accordingly, "[a]s with any remedial device, the application of the rule has been restricted to those areas where its remedial objectives are thought most efficaciously served." United States v. Calandra, supra, at 348. . . .

Close attention to those remedial objectives has characterized our recent decisions concerning the scope of the Fourth Amendment exclusionary rule. . . . [The Court then reviewed a number of its exclusionary rule decisions, including, inter alia, Stone v. Powell, page 888 supra, Walder v. United States, page 1333 infra, and United States v. Ceccolini, page 872 supra.]

. . . [O]ur evaluation of the costs and benefits of suppressing reliable physical evidence seized by officers reasonably relying on a warrant issued by a detached and neutral magistrate leads to the conclusion that such evidence should be admissible in the prosecution's case-in-chief. . . .

. . . To the extent that proponents of exclusion rely on its behavioral effects on judges and magistrates in these areas, their reliance is misplaced. First, the exclusionary rule is designed to deter police misconduct rather than to punish the errors of judges and magistrates. Second, there exists no evidence suggesting that judges and magistrates are inclined to ignore or subvert the Fourth Amendment or that lawlessness among these actors requires application of the extreme sanction of exclusion.[14]

Third, and most important, we discern no basis, and are offered none, for believing that exclusion of evidence seized pursuant to a warrant will have a significant deterrent effect on the issuing judge or magis-

---

the prosecution of which depends heavily on physical evidence. Thus, the cumulative loss due to nonprosecution or nonconviction of individuals arrested on felony drug charges is probably in the range of 2.8% to 7.1%. Id., at 680. Davies' analysis of California data suggests that screening by police and prosecutors results in the release because of illegal searches or seizures of as many as 1.4% of all felony arrestees, id., at 650, that 0.9% of felony arrestees are released because of illegal searches or seizures at the preliminary hearing or after trial, id., at 653, and that roughly 0.05% of all felony arrestees benefit from reversals on appeal because of illegal searches. Id., at 654. See also K. Brosi, A Cross-City Comparison of Felony Case Processing 16, 18-19 (1979); Report of the Comptroller General of the United States, Impact of the Exclusionary Rule on Federal Criminal Prosecutions 10-11, 14 (1979); F. Feeney, F. Dill & A. Weir, Arrests Without Convictions: How Often They Occur and Why 203-206 (1983); National Institute of Justice, The Effects of the Exclusionary Rule: A Study in California 1-2 (1982); Nardulli, The Societal Cost of the Exclusionary Rule: An Empirical Assessment, 1983 A.B.F. Res. J. 585, 600. The exclusionary rule also has been found to affect the plea-bargaining process. S. Schlesinger, Exclusionary Injustice: The Problem of Illegally Obtained Evidence 63 (1977). But see Davies, supra, at 668-669; Nardulli, supra, at 604-606.

Many of these researchers have concluded that the impact of the exclusionary rule is insubstantial, but the small percentages with which they deal mask a large absolute number of felons who are released because the cases against them were based in part on illegal searches or seizures. . . .

14. Although there are assertions that some magistrates become rubber stamps for the police and others may be unable effectively to screen police conduct, see, e.g., 2

trate. . . . Judges and magistrates are not adjuncts to the law enforcement team; as neutral judicial officers, they have no stake in the outcome
of particular criminal prosecutions. The threat of exclusion thus cannot
be expected significantly to deter them. Imposition of the exclusionary
sanction is not necessary meaningfully to inform judicial officers of their
errors, and we cannot conclude that admitting evidence obtained pursuant
to a warrant while at the same time declaring that the warrant was somehow defective will in any way reduce judicial officers' professional incentives to comply with the Fourth Amendment, encourage them to
repeat their mistakes, or lead to the granting of all colorable warrant
requests.[18] . . .

If exclusion of evidence obtained pursuant to a subsequently invalidated warrant is to have any deterrent effect, therefore, it must alter the
behavior of individual law enforcement officers or the policies of their
departments. One could argue that applying the exclusionary rule in
cases where the police failed to demonstrate probable cause in the warrant
application deters future inadequate presentations or "magistrate shopping" and thus promotes the ends of the Fourth Amendment. Suppressing
evidence obtained pursuant to a technically defective warrant supported
by probable cause also might encourage officers to scrutinize more closely
the form of the warrant and to point out suspected judicial errors. We
find such arguments speculative and conclude that suppression of evidence obtained pursuant to a warrant should be ordered only on a case-
by-case basis and only in those unusual cases in which exclusion will
further the purposes of the exclusionary rule.[19]

W. LaFave, Search and Seizure §4.1 (1978); Kamisar, Does (Did) (Should) the Exclusionary Rule Rest on a "Principled Basis" Rather than an "Empirical Proposition"?, 16
Creighton L. Rev. 565, 569-571 (1983); Schroeder, Deterring Fourth Amendment Vi-
olations: Alternatives to the Exclusionary Rule, 69 Geo. L.J. 1361, 1412 (1981), we are
not convinced that this is a problem of major proportions. See L. Tiffany, D. McIntyre
& D. Rotenberg, Detection of Crime 119 (1967); Israel, Criminal Procedure, the Burger
Court, and the Legacy of the Warren Court, 75 Mich. L. Rev. 1319, 1414, n. 396 (1977);
P. Johnson, New Approaches to Enforcing the Fourth Amendment 8-10 (Working Paper,
Sept. 1978), quoted in Y. Kamisar, W. LaFave & J. Israel, Modern Criminal Procedure
229-230 (5th ed. 1980); R. Van Duizend, L. Sutton & C. Carter, The Search Warrant
Process ch. 7 (Review Draft, 1983).
    18. Limiting the application of the exclusionary sanction may well increase the care
with which magistrates scrutinize warrant applications. We doubt that magistrates are
more desirous of avoiding the exclusion of evidence obtained pursuant to warrants they
have issued than of avoiding invasions of privacy.
    Federal magistrates, moreover, are subject to the direct supervision of district courts.
They may be removed for "incompetency, misconduct, neglect of duty, or physical or
mental disability." 28 U.S.C. §631(i). If a magistrate serves merely as a "rubber stamp"
for the police or is unable to exercise mature judgment, closer supervision or removal
provides a more effective remedy than the exclusionary rule.
    19. Our discussion of the deterrent effect of excluding evidence obtained in rea-
sonable reliance on a subsequently invalidated warrant assumes, of course, that the officers

We have frequently questioned whether the exclusionary rule can have any deterrent effect when the offending officers acted in the objectively reasonable belief that their conduct did not violate the Fourth Amendment. . . . [E]ven assuming that the rule effectively deters some police misconduct and provides incentives for the law enforcement profession as a whole to conduct itself in accord with the Fourth Amendment, it cannot be expected, and should not be applied, to deter objectively reasonable law enforcement activity. . . .

We conclude that the marginal or nonexistent benefits produced by suppressing evidence obtained in objectively reasonable reliance on a subsequently invalidated search warrant cannot justify the substantial costs of exclusion. We do not suggest, however, that exclusion is always inappropriate in cases where an officer has obtained a warrant and abided by its terms. . . . [An] officer's reliance on the magistrate's probable cause determination and on the technical sufficiency of the warrant he issues must be objectively reasonable,[20] . . . and it is clear that in some circumstances the officer[24] will have no reasonable grounds for believing that the warrant was properly issued.

Suppression therefore remains an appropriate remedy if the magistrate or judge in issuing a warrant was misled by information in an affidavit that the affiant knew was false or would have known was false except for his reckless disregard of the truth. Franks v. Delaware, 438 U.S. 154

---

properly executed the warrant and searched only those places and for those objects that it was reasonable to believe were covered by the warrant. . . .

20. . . . Many objections to a good-faith exception assume that the exception will turn on the subjective good faith of individual officers. "Grounding the modification in objective reasonableness, however, retains the value of the exclusionary rule as an incentive for the law enforcement profession as a whole to conduct themselves in accord with the Fourth Amendment." Illinois v. Gates, 462 U.S., at 261, n.15 (White, J., concurring in the judgment). The objective standard we adopt, moreover, requires officers to have a reasonable knowledge of what the law prohibits. . . . As Professor Jerold Israel has observed: "The key to the [exclusionary] rule's effectiveness as a deterrent lies, I believe, in the impetus it has provided to police training programs that make officers aware of the limits imposed by the fourth amendment and emphasize the need to operate within those limits. [An objective good-faith exception] . . . is not likely to result in the elimination of such programs, which are now viewed as an important aspect of police professionalism. Neither is it likely to alter the tenor of those programs; the possibility that illegally obtained evidence may be admitted in borderline cases is unlikely to encourage police instructors to pay less attention to fourth amendment limitations. Finally, [it] . . . should not encourage officers to pay less attention to what they are taught, as the requirement that the officer act in 'good faith' is inconsistent with closing one's mind to the possibility of illegality." Israel, supra note 14, at 1412-1413 (footnotes omitted).

24. References to "officer" throughout this opinion should not be read too narrowly. It is necessary to consider the objective reasonableness, not only of the officers who eventually executed a warrant, but also of the officers who originally obtained it or who provided information material to the probable-cause determination. Nothing in our opinion suggests, for example, that an officer could obtain a warrant on the basis of a "bare bones" affidavit and then rely on colleagues who are ignorant of the circumstances under which the warrant was obtained to conduct the search. . . .

(1978). The exception we recognize today will also not apply in cases where the issuing magistrate wholly abandoned his judicial role [and was not neutral and detached. See] Lo-Ji Sales, Inc. v. New York, 442 U.S. 319 (1979). . . . Nor would an officer manifest objective good faith in relying on a warrant based on an affidavit "so lacking in indicia of probable cause as to render official belief in its existence entirely unreasonable." Brown v. Illinois, 422 U.S., [590, 610-611 (1975)] (Powell, J., concurring in part). . . . Finally, depending on the circumstances of the particular case, a warrant may be so facially deficient—i.e., in failing to particularize the place to be searched or the things to be seized—that the executing officers cannot reasonably presume it to be valid. . . .

Nor are we persuaded that application of a good-faith exception to searches conducted pursuant to warrants will preclude review of the constitutionality of the search or seizure, deny needed guidance from the courts, or freeze Fourth Amendment law in its present state.[25] There is no need for courts to adopt the inflexible practice of always deciding whether the officers' conduct manifested objective good faith before turning to the question whether the Fourth Amendment has been violated. Defendants seeking suppression of the fruits of allegedly unconstitutional searches or seizures undoubtedly raise live controversies which Article III empowers federal courts to adjudicate. As cases addressing questions of good-faith immunity under 42 U.S.C. §1983, compare O'Connor v. Donaldson, 422 U.S. 563 (1975), with Procunier v. Navarette, 434 U.S. 555, 566, n.14 (1978), and cases involving the harmless-error doctrine, compare Milton v. Wainwright, 407 U.S. 371, 372 (1972), with Coleman v. Alabama, 399 U.S. 1 (1970), make clear, courts have considerable discretion in conforming their decision-making processes to the exigencies of particular cases.

If the resolution of a particular Fourth Amendment question is necessary to guide future action by law enforcement officers and magistrates, nothing will prevent reviewing courts from deciding that question before turning to the good-faith issue.[26] Indeed, it frequently will be

---

25. The argument that defendants will lose their incentive to litigate meritorious Fourth Amendment claims as a result of the good-faith exception we adopt today is unpersuasive. Although the exception might discourage presentation of insubstantial suppression motions, the magnitude of the benefit conferred on defendants by a successful motion makes it unlikely that litigation of colorable claims will be substantially diminished.

26. It has been suggested, in fact, that "the recognition of a 'penumbral zone,' within which an inadvertent mistake would not call for exclusion. . . . will make it less tempting for judges to bend fourth amendment standards to avoid releasing a possibly dangerous criminal because of a minor and unintentional miscalculation by the police." Schroeder, supra n. 14, at 1420-1421 (footnote omitted); see Ashdown, Good Faith, the Exclusionary Remedy, and Rule-Oriented Adjudication in the Criminal Process, 24 Wm. & Mary L. Rev. 335, 383-384 (1983).

difficult to determine whether the officers acted reasonably without resolving the Fourth Amendment issue. Even if the Fourth Amendment question is not one of broad import, reviewing courts could decide in particular cases that magistrates under their supervision need to be informed of their errors and so evaluate the officers' good faith only after finding a violation. In other circumstances, those courts could reject suppression motions posing no important Fourth Amendment questions by turning immediately to a consideration of the officers' good faith. We have no reason to believe that our Fourth Amendment jurisprudence would suffer by allowing reviewing courts to exercise an informed discretion in making this choice. . . .

When the principles we have enunciated today are applied to the facts of this case, it is apparent that the judgment of the Court of Appeals cannot stand. . . .

. . . Officer Rombach's application for a warrant clearly was supported by much more than a "bare bones" affidavit. The affidavit related the results of an extensive investigation and, as the opinions of the divided panel of the Court of Appeals make clear, provided evidence sufficient to create disagreement among thoughtful and competent judges as to the existence of probable cause. Under these circumstances, the officers' reliance on the magistrate's determination of probable cause was objectively reasonable, and application of the extreme sanction of exclusion is inappropriate.

Accordingly, the judgment of the Court of Appeals is reversed.

JUSTICE BLACKMUN, concurring. . . .

[T]he Court has narrowed the scope of the exclusionary rule because of an empirical judgment. . . . Because I share the view that the exclusionary rule is not a constitutionally compelled corollary of the Fourth Amendment itself. . . . I see no way to avoid making an empirical judgment of this sort, and I am satisfied that the Court has made the correct one on the information before it. . . .

What must be stressed, however, is that any empirical judgment about the effect of the exclusionary rule in a particular case necessarily is a provisional one. . . . If it should emerge from experience that, contrary to our expectations, the good faith exception to the exclusionary rule results in a material change in police compliance with the Fourth Amendment, we shall have to reconsider what we have undertaken here. The logic of a decision that rests on untested predictions about police conduct demands no less. . . .

JUSTICE BRENNAN, with whom JUSTICE MARSHALL joins, dissenting. . . .

[T]he language of deterrence and of cost/benefit analysis, if used indiscriminately, can have a narcotic effect. It creates an illusion of technical precision and ineluctability. It suggests that not only constitutional principle but also empirical data supports the majority's result. When the Court's analysis is examined carefully, however, it is clear that we have not been treated to an honest assessment of the merits of the exclusionary rule, but have instead been drawn into a curious world where the "costs" of excluding illegally obtained evidence loom to exaggerated heights and where the "benefits" of such exclusion are made to disappear with a mere wave of the hand. . . .

[The Fourth] Amendment, like other provisions of the Bill of Rights, restrains the power of the government as a whole; it does not specify only a particular agency and exempt all others. The judiciary is responsible, no less than the executive, for ensuring that constitutional rights are respected.

When that fact is kept in mind, the role of the courts and their possible involvement in the concerns of the Fourth Amendment comes into sharper focus. Because seizures are executed principally to secure evidence, and because such evidence generally has utility in our legal system only in the context of a trial supervised by a judge, it is apparent that the admission of illegally obtained evidence implicates the same constitutional concerns as the initial seizure of that evidence. Indeed, by admitting unlawfully seized evidence, the judiciary becomes a part of what is in fact a single governmental action prohibited by the terms of the Amendment. . . .

The Court evades this principle by drawing an artificial line between the constitutional rights and responsibilities that are engaged by actions of the police and those that are engaged when a defendant appears before the courts. According to the Court, the substantive protections of the Fourth Amendment are wholly exhausted at the moment when police unlawfully invade an individual's privacy and thus no substantive force remains to those protections at the time of trial when the government seeks to use evidence obtained by the police.

I submit that such a crabbed reading of the Fourth Amendment casts aside the teaching of those Justices who first formulated the exclusionary rule, and rests ultimately on an impoverished understanding of judicial responsibility in our constitutional scheme. For my part, "[t]he right of the people to be secure in their persons, houses, papers and effects, against unreasonable searches and seizures" comprises a personal right to exclude all evidence secured by means of unreasonable searches and seizures. The right to be free from the initial invasion of privacy and the right of exclusion are coordinate components of the central embracing right to be free from unreasonable searches and seizures.

Such a conception of the rights secured by the Fourth Amendment was unquestionably the original basis of what has come to be called the exclusionary rule when it was first formulated in Weeks v. United States, 232 U.S. 383 (1914). . . . A new phase in this history of the rule, however, opened with the Court's decision in Wolf v. Colorado, 338 U.S. 25 (1949). . . . Notwithstanding the force of the Weeks doctrine that the Fourth Amendment required exclusion, a state court was free to admit illegally seized evidence, according to the Court in Wolf, so long as the state had devised some other "effective" means of vindicating a defendant's Fourth Amendment rights. Id., at 31.

Twelve years later, in Mapp v. Ohio, 367 U.S. 643 (1961), the Court restored the original understanding of the Weeks case by overruling the holding of Wolf and repudiating its rationale.[7] . . .

[Over the last ten years] however, the Court . . . has gradually pressed the deterrence rationale for the rule back to center stage. . . . The various arguments advanced by the Court in this campaign have only strengthened my conviction that the deterrence theory is both misguided and unworkable. First, the Court has frequently bewailed the "cost" of excluding reliable evidence. In large part, this criticism rests upon a refusal to acknowledge the function of the Fourth Amendment itself. If nothing else, the Amendment plainly operates to disable the government from gathering information and securing evidence in certain ways. . . . Understood in this way, the Amendment directly contemplates that some reliable and incriminating evidence will be lost to the government; therefore, it is not the exclusionary rule, but the Amendment itself that has imposed this cost.

In addition, the Court's decisions over the past decade have made plain that the entire enterprise of attempting to assess the benefits and costs of the exclusionary rule in various contexts is a virtually impossible task for the judiciary to perform honestly or accurately. Although the Court's language in those cases suggests that some specific empirical basis may support its analyses, the reality is that the Court's opinions represent

---

7. Indeed, the Court in Mapp expressly noted that the "factual considerations" raised in Wolf concerning the effectiveness of alternative remedies "are not basically relevant to a decision that the exclusionary rule is an essential ingredient of the Fourth Amendment." 367 U.S., at 651. It is true that in Linkletter v. Walker, 381 U.S. 618 (1965), in holding that Mapp was not to be applied retroactively, the Court described the exclusionary rule as the "only effective deterrent to lawless police action," id., at 637, thereby suggesting that the rule rested on a deterrence rationale. But, as I have explained on another occasion, "[t]he emphasis upon deterrence in Linkletter must be understood in the light of the crucial fact that the States had justifiably relied from 1949 to 1961 upon Wolf. . . . and consequently, that application of Mapp would have required the wholesale release of innumerable convicted prisoners, few of whom could have been successfully retried. In that circumstance, Linkletter held not only that retrospective application of Mapp would not further the goal of deterrence but also that it would not further 'the administration of justice and the integrity of the judicial process.' 381 U.S., at 637." United States v. Calandra, 414 U.S. [338,] 359-360 [(1974)] (dissenting opinion).

inherently unstable compounds of intuition, hunches, and occasional pieces of partial and often inconclusive data. . . . The Court has sought to turn this uncertainty to its advantage by casting the burden of proof upon proponents of the rule. . . . "Obviously," however, "the assignment of the burden of proof on an issue where evidence does not exist and cannot be obtained is outcome determinative. [The] assignment of the burden is merely a way of announcing a predetermined conclusion."[10] . . .

Even if I were to accept the Court's general approach to the exclusionary rule, I could not agree with today's result. . . .

. . . First there is the ritual incantation of the "substantial social costs" exacted by the exclusionary rule. . . . But what evidence is there to support such a claim?

Significantly, the Court points to none, and, indeed, as the Court acknowledges, . . . recent studies have demonstrated that the "costs" of the exclusionary rule—calculated in terms of dropped prosecutions and lost convictions—are quite low. . . .

What then supports the Court's insistence that this evidence be admitted? Apparently, the Court's only answer is that even though the costs of exclusion are not very substantial, the potential deterrent effect in these circumstances is so marginal that exclusion cannot be justified. The key to the Court's conclusion in this respect is its belief that the prospective deterrent effect of the exclusionary rule operates only in those situations in which police officers, when deciding whether to go forward with some particular search, have reason to know that their planned conduct will violate the requirements of the Fourth Amendment. . . .

. . . But what the Court overlooks is that . . . the chief deterrent function of the rule is its tendency to promote institutional compliance with Fourth Amendment requirements on the part of law enforcement agencies generally.[13] . . .

10. Dworkin, Fact Style Adjudication and the Fourth Amendment: The Limits of Lawyering, 48 Ind. L.J. 329, 332-333 (1973). . . .

13. Although specific empirical data on the systemic deterrent effect of the rule is not conclusive, the testimony of those actually involved in law enforcement suggests that, at the very least, the *Mapp* decision had the effect of increasing police awareness of Fourth Amendment requirements and of prompting prosecutors and police commanders to work towards educating rank and file officers. For example, as former New York Police Commissioner Murphy explained the impact of the *Mapp* decision: "I can think of no decision in recent times in the field of law enforcement which had such a dramatic and traumatic effect. . . . I was immediately caught up in the entire program of reevaluating our procedures, which had followed the *Defore* rule, and modifying, amending, and creating new policies and new instructions for implementing *Mapp*. . . . Retraining sessions had to be held from the very top administrators down to each of the thousands of foot patrolmen." Murphy, Judicial Review of Police Methods in Law Enforcement: The Problem of Compliance by Police Departments, 44 Tex. L. Rev. 939, 941 (1966).

Further testimony about the impact of the *Mapp* decision can be found in the statement of Deputy Commissioner Reisman: "The *Mapp* case was a shock to us. We

If the overall educational effect of the exclusionary rule is considered, application of the rule to even those situations in which individual police officers have acted on the basis of a reasonable but mistaken belief that their conduct was authorized can still be expected to have a considerable long-term deterrent effect. If evidence is consistently excluded in these circumstances, police departments will surely be prompted to instruct their officers to devote greater care and attention to providing sufficient information to establish probable cause when applying for a warrant, and to review with some attention the form of the warrant that they have been issued, rather than automatically assuming that whatever document the magistrate has signed will necessarily comport with Fourth Amendment requirements. . . .

Finally, even if one were to believe, as the Court apparently does, that police are hobbled by inflexible and hypertechnical warrant procedures, today's decision cannot be justified. This is because, given the relaxed standard for assessing probable cause established just last Term in Illinois v. Gates, [page 584 supra,] . . . it is virtually inconceivable that a reviewing court, when faced with a defendant's motion to suppress, could first find that a warrant was invalid under the new *Gates* standard, but then, at the same time, find that a police officer's reliance on such an invalid warrant was nevertheless "objectively reasonable" under the test announced today. . . .

This paradox . . . perhaps explains the Court's unwillingness to remand [this case] for reconsideration in light of *Gates*, for it is quite likely that on remand the Court of Appeals would find no violation of the Fourth Amendment, thereby demonstrating that the supposed need for the good faith exception in this context is more apparent than real. Therefore, although the Court's decisions are clearly limited to the situation in which police officers reasonably rely upon an apparently valid warrant in conducting a search, I am not at all confident that the exception unleashed today will remain so confined. Indeed, the full impact of the Court's regrettable decision will not be felt until the Court attempts to

---

had to reorganize our thinking, frankly. Before this, nobody bothered to take out search warrants. Although the U.S. Constitution requires warrants in most cases, the U.S. Supreme Court had ruled that evidence obtained without a warrant—illegally, if you will—was admissible in state courts. So the feeling was, why bother? Well, once that rule was changed we knew we had better start teaching our men about it." N.Y. Times, April 28, 1965, at 50, col. 1. A former United States Attorney and now Attorney General of Maryland, Stephen Sachs, has described the impact of the rule on police practices in similar terms: "I have watched the rule deter, routinely, throughout my years as a prosecutor. . . . [P]olice prosecutor consultation is customary in all our cases when Fourth Amendment concerns arise. . . . In at least three Maryland jurisdictions, for example, prosecutors are on twenty-four hour call to field search and seizure questions presented by police officers." Sachs, The Exclusionary Rule: A Prosecutor's Defense, 1 Crim. J. Ethics 28, 30 (1982). . . .

extend this rule to situations in which the police have conducted a warrantless search solely on the basis of their own judgment about the existence of probable cause and exigent circumstances. When that question
is finally posed, I for one will not be surprised if my colleagues decide
once again that we simply cannot afford to protect Fourth Amendment
rights. . . .

    [The dissenting opinion of JUSTICE STEVENS is omitted.]

NOTES AND QUESTIONS

    1. Compare Justice Brennan's characterization of *Mapp* in his *Leon*
dissent with Justice Powell's characterization of *Mapp* in Stone v. Powell,
page 889 supra. Note also Justice Brennan's characterization of Linkletter
v. Walker in footnote 7 of his *Leon* dissent. Which interpretation of
Mapp is more sound?

    2. Prior to *Leon*, the Supreme Court had addressed the good faith
issue in only one limited context. In Michigan v. DeFillippo, 443 U.S.
31 (1979), the defendant was arrested for violating a city ordinance that
required a lawfully stopped individual to produce evidence of his identity.
During a search incident to the arrest, the police discovered drugs, and
the defendant was charged with unlawful possession. Holding that the
city ordinance was unconstitutionally vague, the Michigan Court of Appeals concluded that the arrest was illegal and, therefore, that the evidence
discovered during the search incident to the arrest was inadmissible. The
Supreme Court, in an opinion by Chief Justice Burger, reversed:

> [At the time of the arrest,] there was no controlling precedent that this
> ordinance was or was not constitutional. . . . A prudent officer . . .
> should not have been required to anticipate that a court would later hold
> the ordinance unconstitutional.
>
>   Police are charged to enforce laws until and unless they are declared
> unconstitutional. . . . Society would be ill-served if its police officers took
> it upon themselves to determine which laws are and which are not con-
> stitutionally entitled to enforcement. [Id. at 37-38.]

    3. *DeFillippo* suggested that the result might be different if the
unconstitutional statute had been one authorizing a warrantless search
rather than one defining a substantive offense. The Court addressed this
question in Illinois v. Krull, 480 U.S. 340, where the issue was the
admissibility of records seized from defendant's automobile wrecking yard
pursuant to a statute that specifically authorized the warrantless search
for and seizure of the records. Subsequent to the seizure, the state supreme
court declared the statute unconstitutional. The Supreme Court, in an
opinion by Justice Blackmun, began with the premise that the "approach

used in *Leon* is equally applicable to the present case" and that "[a]ny difference between our holding in *Leon* and our holding in the instant case, therefore, must rest on a difference between the effect of the exclusion of evidence on judicial officers and the effect of the exclusion of evidence on legislators." Id. at 349-350. The Court then analyzed the three factors that it emphasized in *Leon*—the fact that the exclusionary rule was historically designed to deter police, not judicial, misconduct; the absence of evidence suggesting that judges and magistrates are inclined to subvert the fourth amendment; and the absence of a reason to believe excluding evidence obtained pursuant to a warrant would have a deterrent impact on magistrates or judges—and concluded that with respect to these factors there was no material difference between magistrates and legislators. Since the officer who seized the records was, in the Court's view, acting on the basis of an objectively reasonable belief that his action was constitutional, the fourth amendment did not require exclusion of the evidence.

The Court explained its objective reasonableness standard in the following manner:

> The Court noted in *Leon* that the "good faith" exception to the exclusionary rule would not apply "where the issuing magistrate wholly abandoned his judicial role in the manner condemned in Lo-Ji Sales, Inc. v. New York, 442 U.S. 319 (1979)," or where the warrant was so facially deficient "that the executing officers cannot reasonably presume it to be valid." 468 U.S., at 923. Similar constraints apply to the exception to the exclusionary rule we recognize today. A statute cannot support objectively reasonable reliance if, in passing the statute, the legislature wholly abandoned its responsibility to enact constitutional laws. Nor can a law enforcement officer be said to have acted in good-faith reliance upon a statute if its provisions are such that a reasonable officer should have known that the statute was unconstitutional. Cf. Harlow v. Fitzgerald, 457 U.S. 800 (1982) ("Government officials performing discretionary functions, generally are shielded from liability for civil damages insofar as their conduct does not violate clearly established statutory or constitutional rights of which a reasonable person would have known"). [480 U.S. at 355.]

Justice O'Connor dissented in an opinion joined by Justices Brennan, Marshall, and Stevens:

> Unlike the Court, I see a powerful historical basis for the exclusion of evidence gathered pursuant to a search authorized by an unconstitutional statute. Statutes authorizing unreasonable searches were the core concern of the Framers of the Fourth Amendment. This court has repeatedly noted that reaction against the ancient Act of Parliament authorizing indiscriminate general searches by writ of assistance, 7 & 8 Wm. III, c. 22, §6 (1696), was the moving force behind the Fourth Amendment. . . .
>   . . . [T]he exclusionary rule has . . . been regularly applied to evi-

dence gathered under statutes that authorized unreasonable searches. See, e.g., Ybarra v. Illinois, [p. 769 supra] (statute authorized search and detention of persons found on premises being searched pursuant to warrant); Torres v. Puerto Rico, 442 U.S. 465 (1979) (statute authorized search of luggage of persons entering Puerto Rico); Almeida-Sanchez v. United States, [page 759 supra] (statute authorized search of automobiles without probable cause within border areas); Sibron v. New York, [page 695 supra] (statute authorized frisk absent constitutionally required suspicion that officer was in danger); Berger v. New York, [page 607 supra] (permissive eavesdropping statute). Indeed, Weeks [v. United States, 232 U.S. 383 (1914),] itself made clear that the exclusionary rule was intended to apply to evidence gathered by officers acting under "legislative . . . sanction." . . . 232 U.S. at 394. [480 U.S. at 362-363.]

Justice O'Connor maintained that the history she recited "supplies the evidence that *Leon* demanded for the proposition that the relevant state actors, here legislators, might pose a threat to the values embodied in the Fourth Amendment," and she argued that "[t]he distinction . . . between the legislative and the judicial officer is sound." Id. at 364:

The judicial role is particularized, fact-specific and nonpolitical. Judicial authorization of a particular search does not threaten the liberty of everyone, but rather authorizes a single search under particular circumstances. The legislative act, on the other hand, sweeps broadly, authorizing whole classes of searches, without any particularized showing. A judicial officer's unreasonable authorization of a search affects one person at a time; a legislature's unreasonable authorization of searches may affect thousands or millions and will almost always affect more than one. Certainly the latter poses a greater threat to liberty.

Moreover, the *Leon* court relied explicitly on the tradition of judicial independence in concluding that, until it was presented with evidence to the contrary, there was relatively little cause for concern that judicial officers might take the opportunity presented by the good-faith exception to authorize unconstitutional searches. . . . The legislature's objective in passing a law authorizing unreasonable searches, however, is explicitly to facilitate law enforcement. Fourth Amendment rights have at times proved unpopular. . . . Legislators by virtue of their political role are more often subjected to the political pressures that may threaten Fourth Amendment values than are judicial officers.

Finally, I disagree with the Court that there is "no reason to believe that applying the exclusionary rule" will deter legislation authorizing unconstitutional searches. . . . Providing legislatures a grace period during which the police may freely perform unreasonable searches in order to convict those who might have otherwise escaped creates a positive incentive to promulgate unconstitutional laws. . . . While I heartily agree with the Court that legislators ordinarily do take seriously their oaths to uphold the

Constitution and that it is proper to presume that legislative acts are constitutional, . . . it cannot be said that there is no reason to fear that a
particular legislature might yield to the temptation offered by the Court's
good faith exception.
    . . . Even conceding that the deterrent value of the exclusionary rule
in this context is arguable, I am unwilling to abandon both history and
precedent weighing in favor of suppression. [Id. at 365-366.]

Justice O'Connor then criticized the substance of the Court's good
faith test:

Officers are to be held not "to have acted in good faith reliance upon a
statute if its provisions are such that a reasonable officer should have known
that the statute was unconstitutional. Cf. Harlow v. Fitzgerald, 457 U.S.
800, 818 (1982)." . . . I think the Court errs in importing *Harlow's*
"clearly established law" test into this area, because it is not apparent how
much constitutional law the reasonable officer is expected to know. In
contrast, *Leon* simply instructs courts that police officers may rely upon a
facially valid search warrant. Each case is a fact-specific self-terminating
episode. Courts need not inquire into the officer's probable understanding
of the state of the law except in the extreme instance of a search warrant
upon which no reasonable officer would rely. Under the decision today,
however, courts are expected to determine at what point a reasonable officer
should be held to know that a statute has, under evolving legal rules,
become "clearly" unconstitutional. The process of clearly establishing constitutional rights is a long, tedious and uncertain one. Indeed, as the court
notes, . . . the unconstitutionality of the Illinois statute is not clearly
established to this day. The Court has granted certiorari on the question
of the constitutionality of a similar statutory scheme in New York v. Burger,
[479 U.S. 482] (1986).[106] Thus, some six years after the events in question
in this case, the constitutionality of statutes of this kind remains a fair
ground for litigation. Nothing justifies a grace period of such extraordinary
length for an unconstitutional legislative act.
    The difficulties in determining whether a particular statute violates
clearly established rights are substantial. See 5 K. Davis, Administrative
Law Treatise §27:24, p. 130 (2d ed. 1984) (". . . Law that can be clearly
stated in the abstract usually becomes unclear when applied to variable
and imperfectly understood facts . . ."). The need for a rule so difficult
of application outside the civil damages context is, in my view, dubious.
The Court has determined that fairness to the defendant, as well as public
policy, dictates that individual government officers ought not be subjected
to damages suits for arguably constitutional violations. . . . But suppres-

---

106. Three months after its decision in *Krull*, the Court announced its decision in
Burger. See page 674 supra.—EDS.

sion of illegally obtained evidence does not implicate this concern. [479 U.S. 366-368.]

Justice O'Connor also argued that the Court's holding "destroys all incentive on the part of individual criminal defendants to litigate the violation of their Fourth Amendment rights." Id. at 369. The majority responded to this claim by reasserting its hypothesis in *Leon* that the potential benefits of exclusion would not deter defendants from litigating claims and by noting that persons subject to a statute authorizing a warrantless search may bring an action for an injunction and declaratory judgment. Id. at 353-354. How satisfactory is this response?

4. In Massachusetts v. Sheppard, 468 U.S. 981 (1984), a companion case to *Leon*, the Court applied *Leon* to uphold the admissibility of evidence seized pursuant to a warrant that was "invalidated because of a technical error on the part of the issuing judge." Id. at 984. In *Sheppard*, the police officer presented the judge with (a) an affidavit establishing probable cause to search for clothing and other items and (b) a form warrant used in searches for controlled substances. The judge understood and approved the search proposed by the officer, and he made some changes in the form warrant before signing it. He neglected, however, to alter the portion of the form warrant that indicated what could be seized. Thus, the warrant did not in fact describe with particularity the items to be seized.

5. *Leon* and its progeny have evoked substantial commentary and criticism. See, e.g., Alschuler, "Close Enough for Government Work": The Exclusionary Rule After *Leon*, 1984 Sup. Ct. Rev. 309; Bradley, The Good Faith Exception Cases: Reasonable Exercises in Futility, 60 Ind. L.J. 287 (1985); Dripps, Living with *Leon*, 95 Yale L.J. 906 (1986); Duke, Making *Leon* Worse, 95 Yale L.J. 1405 (1986); Finer, *Gates*, *Leon*, and the Compromise of Adjudicative Fairness (Part II): Of Aggressive Majoritarianism, Wilful Deafness, and the New Exception to the Exclusionary Rule, 34 Clev. St. L. Rev. 199 (1985-1986); Finer, *Gates*, *Leon*, and the Compromise of Adjudicative Fairness (Part I): A Dialogue on Prejudicial Concurrences, 33 Clev. St. L. Rev. 707 (1984-1985); LaFave, "The Seductive Call of Expediency": United States v. Leon, Its Rationale and Ramifications, 1984 U. Ill. L. Rev. 895; Misner, Limiting *Leon*: A Mistake of Law Analogy, 77 J. Crim. L. & Criminology 507 (1986); Wasserstrom & Mertens, The Exclusionary Rule on the Scaffold, 22 Am. Crim. L. Rev. 25 (1984).

6. Illegal But Not Unconstitutional Activity

Occasionally the Supreme Court has interpreted federal statutes as requiring the exclusion of evidence obtained as a result of activity that violates the statutes. See, e.g., Gelbard v. United States, 408 U.S. 41 (1972) (exclusionary rule applicable to violations of Title III of Crime Control Act, which regulates electronic surveillance); Nardone v. United States, 302 U.S. 379 (1937) (exclusionary rule applicable to violations of §605 of Federal Communications Act of 1934 regulating wiretapping). Except in such cases of statutory interpretation, however, the Supreme Court has tended not to extend the exclusionary rule to nonconstitutional violations. See, e.g., United States v. Caceres, 440 U.S. 741 (1979) (Internal Revenue Service agent violated IRS regulations by taping, without prior authorization, conversations with taxpayer; held, tape recordings admissible in prosecution for fraud and bribery). But cf. discussion of McNabb-Mallory rule, page 1096 n.3 infra.

Do you think it would be desirable to exclude evidence obtained in violation of agency or police department regulations? Why?

7. Noncriminal Proceedings and Private Searches

In One 1958 Plymouth Sedan v. Pennsylvania, 380 U.S. 693 (1965), the Court reaffirmed the view of Boyd v. United States, page 424 supra, that forfeiture proceedings are quasi-criminal. As a result, the Court held that the exclusionary rule was applicable. Compare Plymouth Sedan with Immigration & Naturalization Service v. Lopez-Mendosa, 468 U.S. 1032 (1984) (exclusionary rule not applicable in civil deportation proceedings); United States v. Janis, 428 U.S. 433 (1976) (wagering records and cash illegally seized from taxpayer by local police; IRS levied on seized cash to satisfy assessment for wagering tax; held, fact that assessment based on illegally seized evidence does not entitle taxpayer to refund).

To what types of quasi-criminal or civil proceedings should the exclusionary rule apply? For example, should the rule apply to high school or college disciplinary proceedings, civil commitment proceedings, and juvenile delinquency adjudications?

As noted in Section E, page 840 supra, the prohibitions of the fourth amendment are limitations only on governmental action. As a result, courts generally have refused in both civil and criminal actions to exclude evidence illegally obtained by private persons. See, e.g., Barnes v. United States, 373 F.2d 517 (5th Cir. 1967) (criminal); Sackler v. Sackler, 15 N.Y.2d 40, 203 N.E.2d 481 (1964) (civil). Do you agree that evidence illegally obtained by private persons should be admissible? What about the judicial integrity rationale for the exclusionary rule?

8. Alternatives to the Exclusionary Rule

State action that results in a fourth amendment violation may entitle the victim to damages pursuant to the federal civil rights statute, 42 U.S.C. §1983 (1988).[107] See Monroe v. Pape, 365 U.S. 167 (1961) (federal remedy supplemental to state remedies; state remedies need not be sought first); Pierson v. Ray, 386 U.S. 547 (1967) (officer who acts in reasonable good faith belief that his conduct is constitutional not liable for damages);[108] cf. Bivens v. Six Unknown Named Agents, 403 U.S. 388 (1971) (despite absence of statute, similar tort remedy available for fourth amendment violation by *federal* officers). Moreover, two recent

---

107. "Every person who, under color of any statute, ordinance, regulation, custom, or usage, of any State or Territory, subjects, or causes to be subjected, any citizen of the United States or other person within the jurisdiction thereof to the deprivation of any rights, privileges, or immunities secured by the Constitution and laws, shall be liable to the party injured in an action at law, suit in equity, or other proper proceeding for relief."

108. In Malley v. Briggs, 475 U.S. 335 (1986), a federal civil rights action against a police officer, the Court rejected the defendant's argument that his decision to seek a warrant from a magistrate made his conduct inherently reasonable:

> [I]t would be incongruous to test police behavior by the "objective reasonableness" standard in a suppression hearing, see United States v. Leon [page 891 supra] while exempting police conduct in applying for an arrest or search warrant from any scrutiny whatsoever in a §1983 damages action. While we believe the exclusionary rule serves a necessary purpose, it obviously does so at a considerable cost to society as a whole, because it excludes evidence probative of guilt. On the other hand, a damage remedy for an arrest [or a search] following an objectively unreasonable request for a warrant imposes a cost directly on the officer responsible for the unreasonable request, without the side effect of hampering a criminal prosecution. Also, in the case of the §1983 action, the likelihood is obviously greater than at the suppression hearing that the remedy is benefiting the victim of police misconduct one would think most deserving of a remedy—the person who in fact has done no wrong, and has been arrested [or searched] for no reason, or a bad reason. . . .
>
> Accordingly, we hold that the same standard of objective reasonableness that we applied in the context of a suppression hearing in *Leon*, supra, defines the qualified immunity accorded an officer whose request for a warrant allegedly caused an unconstitutional arrest [or search]. Only where the warrant application is so lacking in indicia of probable cause as to render official belief in its existence unreasonable . . . will the shield of immunity be lost.
>
> . . . The . . . question . . . is whether a reasonably well-trained officer in petitioner's position would have known that his affidavit failed to establish probable cause and that he should not have applied for the warrant. [475 U.S. at 344-345.]

Cf. Daniels v. Williams, 474 U.S. 327 (1986); Davidson v. Cannon, 474 U.S. 344 (1986) (both holding that due process not implicated by negligent act of official causing unintended loss of or injury to life, liberty, or property).

decisions have increased the attractiveness of the federal civil rights action. See Monell v. New York City Dept. of Social Services, 436 U.S. 658 (1978) (although municipality not vicariously liable for acts of its employees, municipality not immune from liability for execution of its own unconstitutional policies);[109] Owen v. City of Independence, 445 U.S. 622 (1980) (municipality does not enjoy traditional tort law immunities for governmental functions and discretionary activities; municipality cannot assert good faith defense). Nonetheless, for a variety of reasons the federal civil rights action has not threatened to supplant the exclusionary rule as a significant means of vindicating fourth amendment rights. Consider, for example, the cost of maintaining the action,[110] the good faith defense for individual officers, the difficulty of establishing damages,[111] and the unsympathetic nature of many victims of illegal searches and seizures. Federal injunctive relief is also not likely to be a viable remedy for fourth amendment violations, see Rizzo v. Goode, 423 U.S. 362 (1976), and traditional state court remedies have not been an effective substitute for the exclusionary rule. See Justice Murphy's dissenting opinion in Wolf v. Colorado, pages 550-552 supra, and Justice Clark's opinion for the court in Mapp v. Ohio, pages 553-560 supra. Indeed, critics of the exclusionary rule generally concede that an effective alternative will require legislative action.

How would you structure a statute in order to make it an effective supplement to or substitution for the exclusionary rule? Consider the following:

a. S.751, 97th Cong., 1st Sess. (1981):

§2692. Tort Claims; Illegal Search and Seizure

(a) The United States shall be liable for any damages resulting from a search or seizure conducted by an investigative or law enforcement officer, acting within the scope of his office or employment, in violation of the United States Constitution.

---

109. In Pembaur v. City of Cincinnati, 475 U.S. 469 (1986), the Court elaborated on *Monell's* requirement of "official policy" as a condition of municipal liability. The Court stated that the purpose of the requirement was to distinguish between acts of employees and acts of the municipality. Thus, *Monell* does not require a generalized policy. A single act may be sufficient for municipal liability if the act is directed by the person(s) who establish municipal policy.

110. See Kentucky v. Graham, 473 U.S. 159 (1985) (42 U.S.C. §1988, which provides for awarding attorney's fees to prevailing party in §1983 actions, does not permit attorney's fees to be recovered from government entity when plaintiff sues government employees only in their personal capacities, not in their official capacities).

111. See Memphis Community School Dist. v. Stachura, 477 U.S. 299 (1986) (improper to permit compensatory damages in §1983 civil rights action on basis of jury's assessment of abstract value or importance of constitutional right violated).

(b) Any person aggrieved by such a violation may recover actual damages and such punitive damages as the court may award under subsection (c).

(c) Punitive damages may be awarded by the court, upon consideration of all of the circumstances of the case, including—

(1) The extent of the investigative or law enforcement officer's deviation from permissible conduct;

(2) The extent to which the violation was willful, reckless, or grossly negligent;

(3) The extent to which the aggrieved person's privacy was invaded;

(4) The extent of the aggrieved person's personal injury, both physical and mental;

(5) The extent of any property damage; and

(6) The effect such an award would have in preventing future violations of the United States Constitution.

(d) Notwithstanding subsections (b) and (c), the recovery of any person who is convicted of any offense for which evidence of such offense was seized in violation of the United States Constitution is limited to actual physical personal injury and to actual property damage sustained as a result of the unconstitutional search and seizure.

(e) No judgment, award, compromise, or settlement of any action brought under this section shall exceed the amount of $25,000, including actual and punitive damages. The United States shall not be liable for interest prior to judgment.

(f) Any action under this section shall be brought within the period of limitations provided in section 2401(b) of this title.

§2693. Sanctions Against Investigative or Law Enforcement Officers; Illegal Search and Seizure

An investigative or law enforcement officer who conducts a search or seizure in violation of the United States Constitution shall be subject to appropriate discipline in the discretion of the Federal agency employing such officer, if that agency determines, after notice and hearing, that the officer conducted such search or seizure lacking a good faith belief that such search or seizure was constitutional.

§2694. Judgment as a Bar

The remedy against the United States provided under this chapter shall be the exclusive civil remedy for a violation of the United States Constitution by any investigative or law enforcement officer acting within the scope of his office or employment whose act or omission gave rise to the claim.

§2695. Attorney Fees and Costs

In any action brought under this chapter, the court may award any claimant who prevails in such action reasonable attorney fees, and other litigation costs reasonably incurred. . . .

b.   Bivens v. Six Unknown Named Agents, 403 U.S. 388, 421-423 (1971) (Burger, C. J., dissenting):

The problems of both error and deliberate misconduct by law enforcement officials call for a workable remedy. Private damage actions against individual police officers concededly have not adequately met this requirement, and it would be fallacious to assume today's work of the Court in creating a remedy will really accomplish its stated objective. There is some validity to the claims that juries will not return verdicts against individual officers except in those unusual cases where the violation has been flagrant or where the error has been complete, as in the arrest of the wrong person or the search of the wrong house. There is surely serious doubt, for example, that a drug peddler caught packaging his wares will be able to arouse much sympathy in a jury on the ground that the police officer did not announce his identity and purpose fully. . . . Jurors may well refuse to penalize a police officer at the behest of a person they believe to be a "criminal" and probably will not punish an officer for honest errors of judgment. In any event an actual recovery depends on finding nonexempt assets of the police officer from which a judgment can be satisfied.

I conclude, therefore, that an entirely different remedy is necessary but it is one that in my view is as much beyond judicial power as the step the Court takes today. Congress should develop an administrative or quasi-judicial remedy against the government itself to afford compensation and restitution for persons whose Fourth Amendment rights have been violated. The venerable doctrine of respondeat superior in our tort law provides an entirely appropriate conceptual basis for this remedy. If, for example, a security guard privately employed by a department store commits an assault or other tort on a customer such as an improper search, the victim has a simple and obvious remedy—an action for money damages against the guard's employer, the department store. W. Presser, The Law of Torts §68, pp. 470-480 (3d ed. 1964).[5] Such a statutory scheme would have the added advantage of providing some remedy to the completely innocent persons who are sometimes the victims of illegal police conduct—something that the suppression doctrine, of course, can never accomplish.

A simple structure would suffice.[6] For example, Congress could enact a statute along the following lines:

---

5. Damage verdicts for such acts are often sufficient in size to provide an effective deterrent and stimulate employers to corrective action.

6. Electronic eavesdropping presents special problems. See 18 U.S.C. §§2510-2520 (1988).

(a) a waiver of sovereign immunity as to the illegal acts of law enforcement officials committed in the performance of assigned
duties;

(b) the creation of a cause of action for damages sustained by any
person aggrieved by conduct of governmental agents in violation
of the Fourth Amendment or statutes regulating official conduct;

(c) the creation of a tribunal, quasi-judicial in nature or perhaps
patterned after the United States Court of Claims, to adjudicate
all claims under the statute;

(d) a provision that this statutory remedy is in lieu of the exclusion
of evidence secured for use in criminal cases in violation of the
Fourth Amendment; and

(e) a provision directing that no evidence, otherwise admissible, shall
be excluded from any criminal proceeding because of violation
of the Fourth Amendment.

I doubt that lawyers serving on such a tribunal would be swayed either
by undue sympathy for officers or by the prejudice against "criminals" that
has sometimes moved lay jurors to deny claims. In addition to awarding
damages, the record of the police conduct that is condemned would undoubtedly become a relevant part of an officer's personnel file so that the
need for additional training or disciplinary action could be identified or
his future usefulness as a public official evaluated. Finally, appellate judicial review could be made available on much the same basis that it is
now provided as to district courts and regulatory agencies. This would
leave to the courts the ultimate responsibility for determining and articulating standards.

c. Amsterdam, Perspectives on the Fourth Amendment, 58 Minn.
L. Rev. 349, 430 (1974):

Where are the lawyers going to come from to handle these cases for
the plaintiffs? Gideon v. Wainwright and its progeny conscript them to
file suppression motions; but what on earth would possess a lawyer to file
a claim for damages before the special tribunal in an ordinary search-and-
seizure case? The prospect of a share in the substantial damages to be
expected? The chance to earn a reputation as a police-hating lawyer, so
that he can no longer count on straight testimony concerning the length
of skid marks in his personal injury cases? The gratitude of his client when
his filing of the claim causes the prosecutor to refuse a lesser-induced-
offense plea or to charge priors or to pile on "cover" charges? The opportunity to represent his client without fee in these resulting criminal
matters?

Police cases are an unadulterated investigative and litigative nightmare. Taking on the police in any tribunal involves a commitment to the
most frustrating and thankless legal work I know. And the idea that an

unrepresented, inarticulate, prosecution-vulnerable citizen can make a case against a team of professional investigators and testifiers in any tribunal beggars belief. Even in a tribunal having recognized responsibilities and some resources to conduct independent investigation, a plaintiff without assiduous counsel devoted to developing his side of the case would be utterly outmastered by the police. No, I think we shall have airings of police searches and seizures on suppression motions or nòt at all.

What should be the relationship between the exclusionary rule and some statutory remedy for fourth amendment violations? Should the exclusionary rule remain for some or all violations? If some, which ones? If one desires a statutory remedy to supplant the exclusionary rule, should the exclusionary rule be abolished prior to, simultaneously with, or following the enactment of the statutory remedy? Incidentally, does a *legislative body* have the constitutional authority to abandon or even modify the exclusionary rule?

In his *Bivens* dissent, Chief Justice Burger stated, "I do not propose . . . that we abandon the suppression doctrine until some meaningful alternative can be developed." 403 U.S. at 420. Five years later, concurring in Stone v. Powell, 428 U.S. 465 (1976), the Chief Justice expressed a different view:

> With the passage of time, it now appears that the continued existence of the rule, as presently implemented inhibits the development of rational alternatives. The reason is quite simple: Incentives for developing new procedures or remedies will remain minimal or nonexistent so long as the exclusionary rule is retained in its present form.
>
> It can no longer be assumed that other branches of government will act while judges cling to this Draconian, discredited device in its present absolutist form. Legislatures are unlikely to create statutory alternatives, or impose direct sanctions on errant police officers or on the public treasury by way of tort actions, so long as persons who commit serious crimes continue to reap the enormous and undeserved benefits of the exclusionary rule. . . . And even if legislatures were inclined to experiment with alternative remedies, they have no assurance that the judicially created rule will be abolished or even modified in response to such legislative innovations. The unhappy result, as I see it, is that alternatives will inevitably be stymied by rigid adherence on our part to the exclusionary rule. I venture to predict that overruling this judicially contrived doctrine—or limiting its scope to egregious, bad-faith conduct—would inspire a surge of activity toward providing some kind of statutory remedy for persons injured by police mistakes or misconduct. [Id. at 500-501.]

Do you agree with Chief Justice Burger's prediction?

CHAPTER 8

ENTRAPMENT, DUE PROCESS, AND THE SUPERVISORY POWER— ALTERNATIVES TO THE FOURTH AMENDMENT FOR REGULATING POLICE UNDERCOVER ACTIVITIES

On some occasions police investigatory activity will include affirmative inducements for an individual to commit a crime. For example, it will often be difficult to obtain convictions of narcotics dealers without the use of undercover agents who masquerade as drug sellers or purchasers and who attempt to gain the confidence of the suspected dealers. In the course of this undercover activity, a narcotics agent may request that the suspected dealer provide the agent with narcotics. If the plan succeeds, the suspect will have committed a crime that but for the inducement of the agent would not have been committed.

As long as we want to retain and utilize substantive criminal prohibitions that require this type of undercover investigatory activity for effective enforcement, it is essential that law enforcement personnel be permitted to engage in some types of affirmative inducing activities. At the same time, however, there are good reasons to be wary about the inducing activities of secret agents. An agent's extreme and repeated emotional appeals may induce an individual who is otherwise law-abiding and who has no particular propensity toward criminality to commit a crime. Moreover, if a secret agent commits crimes in order to win the confidence of suspected criminals, the cost of official law breaking at some point, if not always, will outweigh the benefits to law enforcement. Indeed, even noncriminal inducing activity may sometimes seem inappropriate simply because of the unseemliness of its duplicity or because of uncertainty about whether the activity will catch criminals or create criminals.

In United States v. White, page 512 supra, we learned that the use of a bugged informant to obtain statements from an individual was not a search and seizure. Should the result be different if an informant or undercover agent (1) tries to persuade an individual to commit a crime, (2) supplies the individual with instrumentalities for committing a crime, or (3) actually engages in criminal conduct?

Even if one has no fourth amendment right to expect that a person with whom one speaks is not a bugged informant, it does not necessarily follow that one should have no fourth amendment protection against the government's use of informants to induce criminal conduct. There is, however, one important respect in which the use of bugged agents and the use of inducing agents present a similar problem. Both the attempt to elicit information from an individual and the attempt to induce an individual to commit a crime are investigatory activities that are likely to have substantial benefit to the police *prior* to the development of probable cause. Imposing the warrant and individualized probable cause requirements on these types of investigatory tactics arguably would unduly restrict their use. If so, then the only fourth amendment basis for regulating the activities is the general concept of reasonableness in the first clause of the amendment. Perhaps one could define reasonableness in terms of articulable suspicion, or to obtain the benefit of the warrant requirement, one might draw on the regulatory inspection cases to devise a definition of probable cause that is suitable for the kind of undercover investigatory activity at issue. However, the types of law enforcement inducing activities and the situations in which they are used are quite varied. Moreover, it is by no means clear what the external referents should be for evaluating the propriety of inducing activity. Thus, it is understandable that courts have not considered inducing activities by secret agents as raising a fourth amendment problem.

Despite the absence of fourth amendment regulation of law enforcement inducing activities, courts have not ignored problems that arise from these investigatory practices. Rather, courts have dealt with the problems primarily through the development of the defense of entrapment—and to a lesser extent by relying on the due process clause and the courts' "supervisory powers."[1]

---

1. The entrapment defense relates exclusively to undercover police work. The due process and supervisory power doctrines apply in other contexts as well. See, e.g., Rochin v. California, n.6, page 922 infra (due process); discussion of McNabb-Mallory rule, n.3, page 1096 infra (supervisory power).

A. ENTRAPMENT

The United States Supreme Court initially recognized and applied an entrapment defense in Sorrells v. United States, 287 U.S. 435 (1932). The next occasion on which the Court addressed the defense was in Sherman v. United States, 356 U.S. 369 (1958). In both cases the Court unanimously held that the defendant had presented a viable entrapment claim, but in both the Court was divided on the meaning and scope of the defense. The facts of *Sorrells* and *Sherman* as well as the differing views on the entrapment defense are discussed in the following case.

UNITED STATES v. RUSSELL
Certiorari to the United States Court of Appeals for the Ninth Circuit
411 U.S. 423 (1973)

MR. JUSTICE REHNQUIST delivered the opinion of the Court.

Respondent Richard Russell was charged in three counts of a five-count indictment returned against him and codefendants John and Patrick Connolly. After a jury trial in the District Court, in which his sole defense was entrapment, respondent was convicted on all three counts of having unlawfully manufactured and processed methamphetamine ("speed") and of having unlawfully sold and delivered that drug. . . . On appeal, the United States Court of Appeals for the Ninth Circuit, one judge dissenting, reversed the conviction solely for the reason that an undercover agent supplied an essential chemical for manufacturing the methamphetamine which formed the basis of respondent's conviction. The court concluded that as a matter of law "a defense to a criminal charge may be founded upon an intolerable degree of governmental participation in the criminal enterprise." 459 F.2d 671, 673 (1972). We granted certiorari, . . . and now reverse that judgment.

. . . On December 7, 1969, Joe Shapiro, an undercover agent for the Federal Bureau of Narcotics and Dangerous Drugs, went to respondent's home on Whidbey Island in the State of Washington where he met with respondent and his two codefendants, John and Patrick Connolly. Shapiro's assignment was to locate a laboratory where it was believed that methamphetamine was being manufactured illicitly. He told the respondent and the Connollys that he represented an organization in the Pacific Northwest that was interested in controlling the manufacture and distribution of methamphetamine. He then made an offer to supply the defendants with the chemical phenyl-2-propanone, an essential ingredient in the manufacture of methamphetamine, in return for one-half of the drug produced. This offer was made on the condition that Agent Shapiro be shown a sample of the drug which they were making and the laboratory where it was being produced.

During the conversation, Patrick Connolly revealed that he had been making the drug since May 1969 and since then had produced three pounds of it. John Connolly gave the agent a bag containing a quantity of methamphetamine that he represented as being from "the last batch that we made." Shortly thereafter, Shapiro and Patrick Connolly left respondent's house to view the laboratory which was located in the Connolly house on Whidbey Island. At the house, Shapiro observed an empty bottle bearing the chemical label phenyl-2-propanone.

By prearrangement, Shapiro returned to the Connolly house on December 9, 1969, to supply 100 grams of propanone and observe the manufacturing process. . . . The manufacturing process having been completed the following morning, Shapiro was given one-half of the drug and respondent kept the remainder. Shapiro offered to buy, and the respondent agreed to sell, part of the remainder for $60.

About a month later, Shapiro returned to the Connolly house and met with Patrick Connolly to ask if he was still interested in their "business arrangement." Connolly replied that he was interested but that he had recently obtained two additional bottles of phenyl-2-propanone and would not be finished with them for a couple of days. He provided some additional methamphetamine to Shapiro at that time. Three days later Shapiro returned to the Connolly house with a search warrant and, among other items, seized an empty 500-gram bottle of propanone and a 100-gram bottle, not the one he had provided, that was partially filled with the chemical.

There was testimony at the trial of respondent and Patrick Connolly that phenyl-2-propanone was generally difficult to obtain. At the request of the Bureau of Narcotics and Dangerous Drugs, some chemical supply firms had voluntarily ceased selling the chemical.

At the close of the evidence, and after receiving the District Judge's standard entrapment instruction,[4] the jury found the respondent guilty on all counts charged. On appeal, the respondent conceded that the jury could have found him predisposed to commit the offenses, 459 F.2d, at 672, but argued that on the facts presented there was entrapment as a

4. The District Judge stated the governing law on entrapment as follows: "Where a person already has the willingness and the readiness to break the law, the mere fact that the government agent provides what appears to be a favorable opportunity is not entrapment." He then instructed the jury to acquit respondent if it had a "reasonable doubt whether the defendant had the previous intent or purpose to commit the offense . . . and did so only because he was induced or persuaded by some officer or agent of the government." No exception was taken by respondent to this instruction.

matter of law. The Court of Appeals agreed, although it did not find the District Court had misconstrued or misapplied the traditional standards governing the entrapment defense. Rather, the court in effect expanded the traditional notion of entrapment, which focuses on the predisposition of the defendant, to mandate dismissal of a criminal prosecution whenever the court determines that there has been "an intolerable degree of governmental participation in the criminal enterprise." In this case the court decided that the conduct of the agent in supplying a scarce ingredient essential for the manufacture of a controlled substance established that defense.

This new defense was held to rest on either of two alternative theories. One theory is based on two lower court decisions which have found entrapment, regardless of predisposition, whenever the government supplies contraband to the defendants. United States v. Bueno, 447 F.2d 903 (C.A.5 1971); United States v. Chisum, 312 F. Supp. 1307 (C.D. Cal. 1970). The second theory, a nonentrapment rationale, is based on a recent Ninth Circuit decision that reversed a conviction because a government investigator was so enmeshed in the criminal activity that the prosecution of the defendants was held to be repugnant to the American criminal justice system. Greene v. United States, 454 F.2d 783 (C.A.9 1971). The court below held that these two rationales constitute the same defense, and that only the label distinguishes them. In any event, it held that "[b]oth theories are premised on fundamental concepts of due process and evince the reluctance of the judiciary to countenance 'overzealous law enforcement.' " 459 F.2d, at 674, quoting Sherman v. United States, 356 U.S. 369, 381 (1958) (Frankfurter, J., concurring in result).

This Court first recognized and applied the entrapment defense in Sorrells v. United States, 287 U.S. 435 (1932).[5] In Sorrells, a federal prohibition agent visited the defendant while posing as a tourist and engaged him in conversation about their common war experiences. After gaining the defendant's confidence, the agent asked for some liquor, was twice refused, but upon asking a third time the defendant finally capitulated, and was subsequently prosecuted for violating the National Prohibition Act.

Mr. Chief Justice Hughes, speaking for the Court, held that as a matter of statutory construction the defense of entrapment should have

---

5. The first case to recognize and sustain a claim of entrapment by government officers as a defense was apparently Woo Wai v. United States, 223 F. 412 (C.A.9 1915).

been available to the defendant.[2] Under the theory propounded by the Chief Justice, the entrapment defense prohibits law enforcement officers from instigating a criminal act by persons "otherwise innocent in order to lure them to its commission and to punish them." 287 U.S., at 448. Thus, the thrust of the entrapment defense was held to focus on the intent or predisposition of the defendant to commit the crime. "[I]f the defendant seeks acquittal by reason of entrapment he cannot complain of an appropriate and searching inquiry into his own conduct and predisposition as bearing upon that issue." Id., at 451.

Mr. Justice Roberts concurred but was of the view "that courts must be closed to the trial of a crime instigated by the government's own agents." Id., at 459. The difference in the view of the majority and the concurring opinions is that in the former the inquiry focuses on the predisposition of the defendant, whereas in the latter the inquiry focuses on whether the government "instigated the crime."[3]

In 1958 the Court again considered the theory underlying the entrapment defense and expressly reaffirmed the view expressed by the *Sorrells* majority.[4] Sherman v. United States, supra. In *Sherman* the defendant was convicted of selling narcotics to a government informer. As in *Sorrells*, it appears that the Government agent gained the confidence of the defendant and, despite initial reluctance, the defendant finally acceded to the repeated importunings of the agent to commit the criminal

---

2. "We are unable to conclude that it was the intention of Congress in enacting this statute that its processes of detection and enforcement should be abused . . . [as they were here]. We are not forced by the letter to do violence to the spirit and purpose of the statute. . . . This view . . . obviates the objection to the exercise by the court of a dispensing power in forbidding the prosecution of one who is charged with conduct assumed to fall within the statute.

"We are unable to approve the view that the court, although treating the statute as applicable despite the entrapment, and the defendant as guilty, has authority to grant immunity, or to adopt a procedure to that end. It is the function of the court to construe that statute, not to defeat it as construed. Clemency is the function of the Executive." Sorrells v. United States, 287 U.S. 435, 448-449 (1932).—EDS.

3. Justice Roberts also criticized the majority's statutory interpretation analysis, see footnote 2 (Eds.) supra, as "strained and unwarranted." 287 U.S. at 456. For him the entrapment "doctrine rests, rather, on a fundamental rule of public policy. The protection of its own functions and the preservation of the purity of its own temple belongs only to the court." Id. at 457.—EDS.

4. Justice Rehnquist is correct in characterizing the *Sherman* majority as relying on *Sorrells*. In one sense, however, his statement that *Sherman* "expressly reaffirmed" *Sorrells* may be misleading. Chief Justice Warren, writing for the majority in *Sherman*, declined to "reassess the doctrine of entrapment according to the principles announced in . . . [Justice Robert's *Sorrells* concurrence because] to do so would be to decide the case on grounds rejected by the majority in *Sorrells and, so far as the record shows, not raised here or below by the parties before us." 356 U.S. at 376 (emphasis added).—EDS.

act. On the basis of *Sorrells,* this Court reversed the affirmance of the defendant's conviction.[5]

In affirming the theory underlying *Sorrells,* Mr. Chief Justice Warren for the Court, held that "[t]o determine whether entrapment has been established, a line must be drawn between the trap for the unwary innocent and the trap for the unwary criminal." 356 U.S., at 372. Mr. Justice Frankfurter stated in an opinion concurring in the result that he believed Mr. Justice Roberts had the better view in *Sorrells* and would have framed the question to be asked in an entrapment defense in terms of "whether the police conduct revealed in the particular case falls below standards . . . for the proper use of governmental power." Id., at 382.[7]

In the instant case, respondent asks us to reconsider the theory of the entrapment defense as it is set forth in the majority opinions in *Sorrells* and *Sherman.* His principal contention is that the defense should rest on constitutional grounds. He argues that the level of Shapiro's involvement in the manufacture of the methamphetamine was so high that a criminal prosecution for the drug's manufacture violates the fundamental prin-

---

5. Sherman v. United States, 356 U.S. 369, 371, 375 (1958):

> In late August 1951, Kalchinian, a government informer, first met petitioner at a doctor's office where apparently both were being treated to be cured of narcotics addiction. Several accidental meetings followed, either at the doctor's office or at the pharmacy where both filled their prescriptions from the doctor. From mere greetings, conversation progressed to a discussion of mutual experiences and problems, including their attempts to overcome addiction to narcotics. Finally Kalchinian asked petitioner if he knew of a good source of narcotics. He asked petitioner to supply him with a source because he was not responding to treatment. From the first, petitioner tried to avoid the issue. Not until after a number of repetitions of the request, predicated on Kalchinian's presumed suffering, did petitioner finally acquiesce. Several times thereafter he obtained a quantity of narcotics which he shared with Kalchinian. Each time petitioner told Kalchinian that the total cost of narcotics he obtained was twenty-five dollars and that Kalchinian owed him fifteen dollars. The informer thus bore the cost of his share of the narcotics plus the taxi and other expenses necessary to obtain the drug. After several such sales Kalchinian informed agents of the Bureau of Narcotics that he had another seller for them. On three occasions during November 1951, government agents observed petitioner give narcotics to Kalchinian in return for money supplied by the Government.
>
> At the trial the factual issue was whether the informer had convinced an otherwise unwilling person to commit a criminal act or whether petitioner was already predisposed to commit the act and exhibited only the natural hesitancy of one acquainted with the narcotics trade.
>
> . . . [The government's only evidence of predisposition] was petitioner's record of two past narcotics convictions. In 1942 petitioner was convicted of illegally selling narcotics; in 1946 he was convicted of illegally possessing them.

The Court concluded that this evidence was insufficient to show predisposition and held that entrapment had been established as a matter of law.—EDS.

7. Justices Douglas, Harlan, and Brennan shared the views of entrapment expressed in the Frankfurter opinion.

ciples of due process. The respondent contends that the same factors that led this Court to apply the exclusionary rule to illegal searches and seizures . . . should be considered here. But he would have the Court go further in deterring undesirable official conduct by requiring that any prosecution be barred absolutely because of the police involvement in criminal activity. The analogy is imperfect.

. . . [T]he Government's conduct here violated no independent constitutional right of the respondent. Nor did Shapiro violate any federal statute or rule or commit any crime in infiltrating the respondent's drug enterprise.

Respondent would overcome this basic weakness in his analogy to the exclusionary rule cases by having the Court adopt a rigid constitutional rule that would preclude any prosecution when it is shown that the criminal conduct would not have been possible had not an undercover agent "supplied an indispensable means to the commission of the crime that could not have been obtained otherwise, through legal or illegal channels." Even if we were to surmount the difficulties attending the notion that due process of law can be embodied in fixed rules, and those attending respondent's particular formulation, the rule he proposes would not appear to be of significant benefit to him. . . .

. . . [T]he facts in the record amply demonstrate that the propanone used in the illicit manufacture of methamphetamine not only *could* have been obtained without the intervention of Shapiro but was in fact obtained by these defendants.

While we may some day be presented with a situation in which the conduct of law enforcement agents is so outrageous that due process principles would absolutely bar the government from invoking judicial processes to obtain a conviction, cf. Rochin v. California, 342 U.S. 165 (1952),[6] the instant case is distinctly not of that breed. Shapiro's contribution of propanone to the criminal enterprise already in process was scarcely objectionable. The chemical is by itself a harmless substance and its possession is legal. . . .

The illicit manufacture of drugs is not a sporadic, isolated criminal incident, but a continuing, though illegal, business enterprise. In order

---

6. In *Rochin* police officers illegally entered the defendant's home and broke into his bedroom. The defendant seized and swallowed two capsules that had been on the nightstand. The officers initially jumped on Rochin and tried to extract the capsules. When this proved unsuccessful, Rochin was handcuffed and taken to a hospital, where a doctor "forced an emetic solution through a tube into Rochin's stomach against his will. The emetic solution produced vomiting, and the two capsules, which contained morphine, were found in the vomit." Rochin was convicted of illegal possession of morphine. Concluding that the conviction was obtained by police conduct "that shocks the conscience," the Supreme Court relied on the due process clause to reserve the conviction. 342 U.S. at 166, 169.—EDS.

to obtain convictions for illegally manufacturing drugs, the gathering of evidence of past unlawful conduct frequently proves to be an all but impossible task. Thus in drug-related offenses law enforcement personnel have turned to one of the only practicable means of detection: the infiltration of drug rings and a limited participation in their unlawful present practices. Such infiltration is a recognized and permissible means of investigation; if that be so, then the supply of some item of value that the drug ring requires must, as a general rule, also be permissible. For an agent will not be taken into the confidence of the illegal entrepreneurs unless he has something of value to offer them. . . .

Respondent also urges, as an alternative to his constitutional argument, that we broaden the nonconstitutional defense of entrapment. . . . Respondent . . . argues that the . . . views of Justices Roberts and Frankfurter, in *Sorrells* and *Sherman*, respectively, which make the essential element of the defense turn on the type and degree of governmental conduct, be adopted as the law.

We decline to overrule these cases. *Sorrells* is a precedent of long standing that has already been once reexamined in *Sherman* and implicitly there reaffirmed. Since the defense is not of a constitutional dimension, Congress may address itself to the question and adopt any substantive definition of the defense that it may find desirable.

Critics of the rule laid down in *Sorrells* and *Sherman* have suggested that its basis in the implied intent of Congress is largely fictitious, and have pointed to what they conceive to be the anomalous difference between the treatment of a defendant who is solicited by a private individual and one who is entrapped by a government agent. Questions have been likewise raised as to whether "predisposition" can be factually established with the requisite degree of certainty. Arguments such as these, while not devoid of appeal, have been twice previously made to this Court, and twice rejected by it, first in *Sorrells* and then in *Sherman*.

We believe that at least equally cogent criticism has been made of the concurring views in these cases. Commenting in *Sherman* on Mr. Justice Roberts' position in *Sorrells* that "although the defendant could claim that the Government has induced him to commit the crime, the Government could not reply by showing that the defendant's criminal conduct was due to his own readiness and not to the persuasion of government agents," Sherman v. United States, 356 U.S., at 376-377, Mr. Chief Justice Warren quoted the observation of Judge Learned Hand in an earlier stage of that proceeding: " 'Indeed, it would seem probable that, if there were no reply [to the claim of inducement], it would be impossible ever to secure convictions of any offences which consist of transactions that are carried on in secret.' United States v. Sherman, 200 F.2d 880, 882." Sherman v. United States, 356 U.S., at 377 n.7.

Nor does it seem particularly desirable for the law to grant complete immunity from prosecution to one who himself planned to commit a crime, and then committed it, simply because the government undercover agents subjected him to inducements which might have seduced a hypothetical individual who was not so predisposed. . . .

Several decisions of the United States district courts and courts of appeals have undoubtedly gone beyond this Court's opinions in *Sorrells* and *Sherman* in order to bar prosecutions because of what they thought to be, for want of a better term, "overzealous law enforcement." But the defense of entrapment enunciated in those opinions was not intended to give the federal judiciary a "chancellor's foot" veto over law enforcement practices of which it did not approve. The execution of the federal laws under our Constitution is confided primarily to the Executive Branch of the Government, subject to applicable constitutional and statutory limitations and to judicially fashioned rules to enforce those limitations. We think that the decision of the Court of Appeals in this case quite unnecessarily introduces an unmanageably subjective standard which is contrary to the holdings of this Court in *Sorrells* and *Sherman*.

Those cases establish that entrapment is a relatively limited defense. It is rooted, not in any authority of the Judicial Branch to dismiss prosecutions for what it feels to have been "overzealous law enforcement," but instead in the notion that Congress could not have intended criminal punishment for a defendant who has committed all the elements of a proscribed offense, but was induced to commit them by the Government.

Sorrells and *Sherman* both recognize "that the fact that officers or employees of the Government merely afford opportunities or facilities for the commission of the offense does not defeat the prosecution," 287 U.S., at 441; 356 U.S., at 372. Nor will the mere fact of deceit defeat a prosecution, see, e.g., Lewis v. United States, 385 U.S. 206, 208-209 (1966), for there are circumstances when the use of deceit is the only practicable law enforcement technique available. It is only when the Government's deception actually implants the criminal design in the mind of the defendant that the defense of entrapment comes into play.

Respondent's concession in the Court of Appeals that the jury finding as to predisposition was supported by the evidence is, therefore, fatal to his claim of entrapment. . . .

Reversed.

[The dissenting opinion of JUSTICE DOUGLAS is omitted.]

MR. JUSTICE STEWART, with whom MR. JUSTICE BRENNAN and MR. JUSTICE MARSHALL join, dissenting.

It is common ground that "[t]he conduct with which the defense of entrapment is concerned is the *manufacturing* of crime by law enforcement officials and their agents." Lopez v. United States, 373 U.S. 427, 434 (1963). . . . As Mr. Justice Brandeis put it, the Government "may not provoke or create a crime and then punish the criminal, its creature." Casey v. United States, 276 U.S. 413, 423 (1928) (dissenting opinion). . . .

In Sorrells v. United States, supra, and Sherman v. United States, supra, the Court took what might be called a "subjective" approach to the defense of entrapment. In that view, the defense is predicated on an unexpressed intent of Congress to exclude from its criminal statutes the prosecution and conviction of persons, "otherwise innocent," who have been lured to the commission of the prohibited act through the Government's instigation. Sorrells v. United States, supra, at 448. . . . Thus, the subjective approach focuses on the conduct and propensities of the particular defendant in each individual case. . . .

The concurring opinion of Mr. Justice Roberts . . . in the *Sorrells* case, and that of Mr. Justice Frankfurter . . . in the *Sherman* case, took a different view of the entrapment defense. In their concept, the defense is . . . grounded on . . . the belief that "the methods employed on behalf of the Government to bring about conviction cannot be countenanced." Sherman v. United States, supra, at 380. Thus, the focus of this approach is not on the propensities and predisposition of a specific defendant, but on "whether the police conduct revealed in the particular case falls below standards, to which common feelings respond, for the proper use of governmental power." Id., at 382. Phrased another way, the question is whether—regardless of the predisposition to crime of the particular defendant involved—the governmental agents have acted in such a way as is likely to instigate or create a criminal offense. Under this approach, the determination of the lawfulness of the Government's conduct must be made—as it is on all questions involving the legality of law enforcement methods—by the trial judge, not the jury.

In my view, this objective approach to entrapment . . . is the only one truly consistent with the underlying rationale of the defense.[1] . . . I find it impossible to believe that the purpose of the defense is to effectuate some unexpressed congressional intent to exclude from its criminal statutes persons who committed a prohibited act, but would not have done so except for the Government's inducements. For, as Mr. Justice Frankfurter put it, "the only legislative intention that can with any show of reason be extracted from the statute is the intention to make criminal

---

1. Both the Proposed New Federal Criminal Code (1971), Final Report of the National Commission on Reform of Federal Criminal Laws §702, and the American Law Institute's Model Penal Code §2.13 (Proposed Official Draft, 1962), adopt this objective approach.

precisely the conduct in which the defendant has engaged." Sherman v. United States, supra, at 379. . . .

Furthermore, to say that such a defendant is "otherwise innocent" or not "predisposed" to commit the crime is misleading, at best. The very fact that he has committed an act that Congress has determined to be illegal demonstrates conclusively that he is not innocent of the offense. He may not have originated the precise plan or the precise details, but he was "predisposed" in the sense that he has proved to be quite capable of committing the crime. That he was induced, provoked, or tempted to do so by government agents does not make him any more innocent or any less predisposed than he would be if he had been induced, provoked, or tempted by a private person—which, of course, would not entitle him to cry "entrapment." Since the only difference between these situations is the identity of the tempter, it follows that the significant focus must be on the conduct of the government agents, and not on the predisposition of the defendant. . . .

Moreover, a test that makes the entrapment defense depend on whether the defendant had the requisite predisposition permits the introduction into evidence of all kinds of hearsay, suspicion, and rumor—all of which would be inadmissible in any other context—in order to prove the defendant's predisposition. It allows the prosecution, in offering such proof, to rely on the defendant's bad reputation or past criminal activities, including even rumored activities of which the prosecution may have insufficient evidence to obtain an indictment, and to present the agent's suspicions as to why they chose to tempt this defendant. This sort of evidence is not only unreliable, as the hearsay rule recognizes; but it is also highly prejudicial, especially if the matter is submitted to the jury, for, despite instructions to the contrary, the jury may well consider such evidence as probative not simply of the defendant's predisposition, but of his guilt of the offense with which he stands charged.

More fundamentally, focusing on the defendant's innocence or predisposition has the direct effect of making what is permissible or impermissible police conduct depend upon the past record and propensities of the particular defendant involved. . . .

. . . And as Mr. Justice Frankfurter pointed out: "Permissible police activity does not vary according to the particular defendant concerned; surely if two suspects have been solicited at the same time in the same manner, one should not go to jail simply because he has been convicted before and is said to have a criminal disposition." Sherman v. United States, supra, at 383. . . .

This does not mean, of course, that the Government's use of undercover activity, strategy, or deception is necessarily unlawful. . . . Indeed, many crimes, especially so-called victimless crimes, could not otherwise be detected. Thus, government agents may engage in conduct that is likely, when objectively considered, to afford a person ready and willing to commit the crime an opportunity to do so. . . .

But when the agents' involvement in criminal activities goes beyond the mere offering of such an opportunity, and when their conduct is of a kind that could induce or instigate the commission of a crime by one not ready and willing to commit it, then—regardless of the character or propensities of the particular person induced—I think entrapment has occurred. For in that situation, the Government has engaged in the impermissible manufacturing of crime, and the federal courts should bar the prosecution in order to preserve the institutional integrity of the system of federal criminal justice.

. . . I would affirm the judgment of the Court of Appeals.

NOTES AND QUESTIONS

1. Note that Justice Rehnquist mentions three criticisms of the predisposition test—the artificiality of the congressional intent analysis; the apparent anomaly in the fact that the defense is not available when a private individual is the entrapper; and the difficulty in determining predisposition. He does not answer these criticisms, nor does he even acknowledge another frequently mentioned criticism of the predisposition rule—the prejudicial impact of prior crimes evidence offered to show predisposition. Instead, Justice Rehnquist limits his defense of the predisposition test to three points. *First,* he relies on the precedent of *Sorrells* and *Sherman. Second,* he quotes Learned Hand's rather puzzling statement that "if there were no reply [to the claim of inducement], it would be impossible ever to secure convictions of any offenses which consist of transactions that are carried out in secret." (Of course, if there is no response, the defendant—if believed—will be acquitted. But there is a response under the dissenters' *objective test*—namely that the police action was not improper.) Finally, Justice Rehnquist simply asserts that the predisposition test strikes a proper balance between the needs of law enforcement and the concerns with unwarranted inducements.

Perhaps Justice Rehnquist's conclusion is correct, but for several reasons it is unfortunate that he did not offer a more substantial justification for retaining the predisposition test for entrapment. As Justice Stewart pointed out in his opinion, both the Proposed New Federal Criminal Code and the Model Penal Code advocate the position of the *Russell* dissenters. Moreover, although most state courts have adopted the federal predisposition test, scholarly commentary before and after *Russell* has consistently and almost uniformly favored the *objective en-*

trapment test.[7] Finally, it is significant that in *Sherman* four justices favored the objective test and the other five refused to reconsider *Sorrells* in part because the question of reconsideration had not been briefed or even raised by the parties. Given this prior expression of support for the objective test, one would have hoped for at least a carefully reasoned consideration of the position in *Russell,* where the issue was specifically raised.

2. The federal *subjective entrapment test* purports to focus exclusively on the predisposition of the defendant, whereas the objective test advocated by the *Russell* dissenters purports to focus exclusively on the actions of the police. Neither the opinions in *Russell* nor the opinions in the Supreme Court's other entrapment cases, however, are very helpful in defining predisposition for purposes of the subjective test or improper police conduct for purposes of the objective test.

With respect to predisposition, it seems clear that the term is intended to describe some kind of quality or characteristic or propensity of the particular defendant—thus the label *subjective.* Moreover, since the existence of the test assumes that some defendants are not predisposed, we know that the notion of predisposition means something more than or different from the defendant's demonstrated disposition to commit the particular crime charged in response to the inducement offered. But what beyond these very general concepts does the Court mean by predisposition?[8]

The content of the objective test is at least as vague and unclear. Justice Stewart's statement that the entrapment defense is designed to deal with the manufacturing of crime by the government strongly implies that the underlying concern is with police conduct that may induce citizens to commit crimes. And since Justice Stewart concedes that it is appropriate for the police to use "undercover activity, strategy, or deception" in order to "afford a person ready and willing to commit the crime an opportunity to do so," it must follow that the concern is with inducing normally law-abiding citizens to commit crimes.[9] Is it all that clear,

---

7. See, e.g., Abramson & Lindeman, Entrapment and Due Process in the Federal Courts, 8 Am. J. Crim. L. 139 (1980); Donnelly, Judicial Control of Informants, Spies, Stool Pigeons, and Agents Provocateurs, 60 Yale L.J. 1091 (1951). But see Park, The Entrapment Controversy, 60 Minn L. Rev. 163 (1976).

8. It is no answer to say simply that it is for the jury to determine whether the defendant was predisposed. Regardless of who the decisionmaker is, there ideally should be some reasonably clear statement of the standard the decisionmaker is to apply.

Consider the jury instruction in footnote 4 of the· *Russell* decision. How helpful is it in giving content to the concept of entrapment?

9. See U.S. National Commission on Reform of Federal Laws, A Proposed New Federal Criminal Code §702(2) (1971):

Entrapment occurs when a law enforcement agent induces the commission of an

however, that the police activity in *Russell* would be likely to induce a normally law-abiding person to commit a crime? Indeed, would a normally law-abiding person be likely to know what to do with phenyl-2-propanone?

The preceding questions suggest two types of problems. *First,* the *Russell* dissenters may have disapproved the undercover police activity without regard to whether the activity was likely to induce a normally law-abiding person to commit a crime. If that is the case, what should the criteria or external referents be for evaluating the propriety of the police conduct? *Second,* even if one decides to evaluate police inducements solely in terms of their likely effect on normally law-abiding persons, how does one define or give content to the *normally law-abiding* person? If a defendant can ever prevail under the objective test, one must assume that the normally law-abiding person must be someone who could at least occasionally be induced to commit crimes. What characteristics or attributes should one give to this normally but not always law-abiding person? Should we give the normally law-abiding person any attributes of the particular defendant? If so, what attributes?

If the objective entrapment test is concerned solely with police conduct that may induce normally law-abiding persons to commit crimes, in what situations are the two entrapment tests likely to lead to different results?

3. Assume that we have a case in which (1) the police conduct is not sufficiently outrageous to constitute a violation of due process, (2) the conduct would be likely to induce a normally law-abiding person to commit the crime, and (3) the defendant is predisposed to commit the crime.[10] At least in the absence of unconstitutional police conduct, why should a person who is predisposed to commit a crime and who engages in the criminal act with the requisite mental state be acquitted? Indeed, is even a nonpredisposed defendant so lacking in culpability that criminal punishment is inappropriate? What is the underlying justification for the entrapment defense? Given the vagueness of both the subjective and

---

offense, using persuasion or other means likely to cause normally law-abiding persons to commit the offense. Conduct merely affording a person the opportunity to commit an offense does not constitute entrapment.

Cf. American Law Institute, Model Penal Code §2.13 (Official Draft, 1962) (police inducements improper if they "create a substantial risk that an offense will be committed by persons other than those who are ready to commit it").

10. This may simply be a description of *Russell.* The *Russell* dissenters did not challenge the majority's conclusion that there was no due process violation; the majority did not challenge the dissenters' conclusion that there was entrapment under the objective test; and the defendant conceded the predisposition point. But see Note 2 supra, suggesting that the dissenters may have thought that the police conduct constituted entrapment without regard to the effect that the conduct may have on a normally law-abiding person.

objective entrapment tests, is it likely that either test can be applied in a consistent, evenhanded manner?

4. In any particular case, procedural and evidentiary aspects of the entrapment defense may be more significant than the manner in which entrapment is defined. For example, in federal courts:

    a. entrapment is a jury issue;[11]

    b. the prosecutor may introduce otherwise inadmissible evidence of the defendant's prior crimes in order to establish predisposition;[12] and

    c. the prosecution has the burden of proving predisposition beyond a reasonable doubt.[13]

By contrast:

    a. Justice Stewart regarded the question of entrapment under the objective test as a judge issue;[14]

    b. jurisdictions following the objective test are likely not to permit the prosecutor to introduce evidence of the defendant's prior crimes for the purpose of negating an entrapment claim;[15] and

    c. the burden of persuading a factfinder that the inducements would cause a normally law-abiding person to commit the crime may rest with the defendant.[16]

These procedural and evidentiary consequences may not be necessary concomitants of the entrapment tests with which they are normally associated. There are, however, interrelationships among the issues (1) which entrapment test is better, (2) who should decide the question of entrapment, (3) whether evidence of other crimes should be admissible, and (4) which party should bear the burden of persuasion. For example, there is probably a greater need for evidence of other crimes if one adopts the subjective test. If one adopts the subjective test and severely restricts

11. See Park, note 7 supra, at 268.

12. See id. at 201-202.

13. See United States v. Russell, 411 U.S. at 428 n.4; Park, note 7 supra, at 176 n.39.

14. United States v. Russell, 411 U.S. at 447 (Stewart, J., dissenting). See Park, note 7 supra, at 268. But see State v. Mullen, 216 N.W.2d 375 (Iowa 1975) (adopting normally law-abiding person test and making entrapment a jury issue).

15. See State v. Mullen, 216 N.W.2d 375 (Iowa 1975); cf. Park, note 7 supra, at 201-204 (suggesting that sometimes such evidence may be appropriate in objective test jurisdiction).

16. See, e.g., American Law Institute, Model Penal Code §2.13(2); Park, note 12 supra, at 264-265. But see State v. Mullen, 216 N.W.2d 375 (Iowa 1975) (adopting objective test and placing burden on prosecution to disprove entrapment beyond reasonable doubt).

the use of evidence of other crimes, it may be unreasonable to place a heavy burden of persuasion on the prosecutor; if one admits evidence of other crimes, jurors may be more likely than judges to misuse the evidence.[17] It may be even harder for jurors to be objective in applying the normally law-abiding person test, since to find that the defendant was entrapped is both to condemn the police and to set free a factually guilty defendant. What is the best way to accommodate these various issues and concerns?

5. Typically defendants claiming entrapment do not challenge the prosecutor's proof of the elements of the offense. Such was not the case, however, in Mathews v. United States, 485 U.S. 58 (1988), where the defendant was charged with accepting a bribe for engaging in an official act. At trial Mathews claimed both that he lacked the requisite criminal intent to be guilty of the offense and that a government agent entrapped him. Taking the position that the entrapment defense was available only to individuals who were entrapped into committing a crime, the trial court regarded the defendant's two claims as inconsistent with each other. As a result, the trial court refused to instruct the jury on entrapment. The seventh circuit affirmed, but the Supreme Court reversed: "[E]ven if the defendant denies one or more elements of the crime, he is entitled to an entrapment instruction whenever there is sufficient evidence from which a reasonable jury could find entrapment." Id. at 62.

In the course of its opinion, the Court referred with apparent approval to (1) a federal case permitting a rape defendant to argue both that the act did not occur and that the alleged victim consented and (2) state cases permitting a homicide defendant to receive both self-defense and accident instructions. Id. at 64. The Court, however, stopped short of endorsing the general proposition that defendants are free generally to assert inconsistent positions. To what extent, in the entrapment context or in other contexts, are there sound reasons for prohibiting a criminal defendant from maintaining inconsistent positions?

B. DUE PROCESS

In discussing the inducements in *Russell* the Court observed, "[W]e may some day be presented with a situation in which the conduct of law

---

17. The rules of evidence generally are applied in a more relaxed manner in bench trials in part because we assume that judges can be more objective and dispassionate in evaluating potentially prejudicial evidence. Do you think this assumption is correct?

enforcement agents is so outrageous that due process principles would absolutely bar the government from invoking judicial processes to obtain a conviction." 411 U.S. at 431-432. *Russell* was not such a case despite the fact that the police were much more involved in the criminal activity than they were in the Court's earlier entrapment cases, *Sorrells* and *Sherman.* How much more do the police have to do before their conduct raises a serious due process issue?

Consider whether Judge Friendly's example would constitute a due process violation:

> [T]here is certainly a limit to allowing governmental involvement in crime. It would be unthinkable, for example, to permit government agents to instigate robberies and beatings merely to gather evidence to convict other members of a gang of hoodlums. Governmental "investigation" involving participation in activities that result in injury to the rights of its citizens is a course that courts should be extremely reluctant to sanction. [United States v. Archer, 486 F.2d 670, 676-677 (2d Cir. 1973).]

Even if the police conduct hypothesized by Judge Friendly would be totally improper, why should the remedy be the acquittal of a predisposed, factually guilty defendant?

The Supreme Court returned to the due process issue in Hampton v. United States, 425 U.S. 484 (1976). The defendant was convicted of selling heroin to two government agents. According to the prosecution's evidence, the defendant suggested the sale to a friend, Hutton, who happened to be a police informant and who arranged the sale. The defendant had a different version of the events:

> According to him, in response to his statement that he was short of cash, Hutton said that he had a friend who was a pharmacist who could produce a nonnarcotic counterfeit drug which would give the same reaction as heroin. Hutton proposed selling this drug to gullible acquaintances who would be led to believe they were buying heroin. Petitioner testified that they successfully duped one buyer with this fake drug and that the sales which led to the arrest were solicited by petitioner in an effort to profit further from this ploy. [Id. at 486-487.]

The trial court denied the defendant's requested jury instruction, which called for the jury to acquit him "[i]f you find that the defendant's sales of narcotics were sales of narcotics supplied to him by an informer in the employ of or acting on behalf of the government." Id. at 488. Since the defendant conceded on appeal that he was predisposed to commit the crime, the principal question before the Supreme Court was whether defendant's version of the events, if true, would constitute a due process violation. In an opinion joined only by Chief Justice Burger and Justice White, Justice Rehnquist first characterized the difference between this case and *Russell* as simply "one of degree, not of kind." He then observed:

> The remedy of the criminal defendant with respect to the acts of Government agents, which, far from being resisted, are encouraged by him, lies solely in the defense of entrapment. But, as noted, petitioner's conceded predisposition rendered this defense unavailable to him.
>
> To sustain petitioner's contention here would run directly contrary to our statement in *Russell* that the defense of entrapment is not intended "to give the federal judiciary a 'chancellor's foot' veto over law enforcement practices of which it did not approve. The execution of the federal laws under our Constitution is confided primarily to the Executive Branch of the Government, subject to applicable constitutional and statutory limitations and to judicially fashioned rules to enforce those limitations." 411 U.S., at 435.
>
> The limitations of the Due Process Clause of the Fifth Amendment come into play only when the Government activity in question violates some protected right of the *defendant*. Here, as we have noted, the police, the Government informant, and the defendant acted in concert with one another. If the result of the governmental activity is to "implant in the mind of an innocent person the disposition to commit the alleged offense and induce its commission. . ." *Sorrells* [v. United States, 287 U.S. 435], 442 [(1932)], the defendant is protected by the defense of entrapment. If the police engage in illegal activity in concert with a defendant beyond the scope of their duties the remedy lies, not in freeing the equally culpable defendant, but in prosecuting the police under the applicable provisions of state or federal law. [425 U.S. at 490.]

In a separate opinion joined by Justice Blackmun, Justice Powell agreed that the police conduct in *Hampton* was not significantly different than the police conduct in *Russell*. He objected, however, to the broad implications of the plurality opinion:

> I am not unmindful of the doctrinal and practical difficulties of delineating limits to police involvement in crime that do not focus on predisposition, as Government participation ordinarily will be fully justified in society's "war with the criminal classes." Sorrells v. United States, 287 U.S. 435, 453 (1932) (opinion of Roberts, J.). This undoubtedly is the concern that prompts the plurality to embrace an absolute rule. But we left these questions open in *Russell*, and this case is controlled completely by *Russell*. I therefore am unwilling to join the plurality in concluding that, no matter what the circumstances, neither due process principles nor our supervisory power could support a bar to conviction in any case where

the Government is able to prove predisposition.[7] [425 U.S. at 492-496 (Powell, J., concurring).]

Justice Brennan, in an opinion joined by Justices Stewart and Marshall, dissented:

Two facts significantly distinguish this case from *Russell*. First, the chemical supplied in that case was not contraband. . . . In contrast, petitioner claims that the very narcotic he is accused of selling was supplied by an agent of the Government. . . .

Second, the defendant in *Russell* "was an active participant in an illegal drug manufacturing enterprise which began before the Government agent appeared on the scene, and continued after the Government agent had left the scene." 411 U.S., at 436. . . . In contrast, the two sales for which petitioner was convicted were allegedly instigated by Government agents and completed by the Government's purchase. The beginning and end of this crime thus coincided exactly with the Government's entry into and withdrawal from the criminal activity involved in this case. . . .

. . . Where the Government's agent deliberately sets up the accused by supplying him with contraband and then bringing him to another agent as a potential purchaser, the Government's role has passed the point of toleration. . . . The Government is doing nothing less than buying contraband from itself through an intermediary and jailing the intermediary. . . . There is little, if any, law enforcement interest promoted by such conduct; plainly it is not designed to discover ongoing drug traffic. Rather, such conduct deliberately entices an individual to commit a crime. That the accused is "predisposed" cannot possibly justify the action of government officials in purposefully creating the crime. No one would suggest that the police could round up and jail all "predisposed" individuals, yet that is precisely what set-ups like the instant one are intended to accomplish. . . . Thus, this case is nothing less than an instance of "the Government . . . seeking to punish for an alleged offense which is the product of the creative activity of its own officials." Sorrells v. United States, 287 U.S., at 451.

. . . I would at a minimum hold that conviction is barred as a matter

7. I emphasize that the cases, if any, in which proof of predisposition is not dispositive will be rare. Police over-involvement in crime would have to reach a demonstrable level of outrageousness before it could bar conviction. This would be especially difficult to show with respect to contraband offenses, which are so difficult to detect in the absence of undercover Government involvement. One cannot easily exaggerate the problems confronted by law enforcement authorities in dealing effectively with an expanding narcotics traffic, . . . which is one of the major contributing causes of escalating crime in our cities. See President's Commission on Law Enforcement and Administration of Justice, The Challenge of Crime in a Free Society 221-222 (1967). Enforcement officials therefore must be allowed flexibility adequate to counter effectively such criminal activity.

of law where the subject of the criminal charge is the sale of contraband provided to the defendant by a Government agent.[4] [425 U.S. at 497-500.]

NOTES AND QUESTIONS

1. What is the significance of Justice Rehnquist's statement that the due process clause "comes into play only when the Government activity in question violates some protected right of the defendant"? What is a protected right? What was the protected right in *Rochin?*

2. If one starts with the premise that the due process clause may prohibit some types of inducing activities, what are the standards or criteria to apply in any particular case? Does the disagreement between Justice Powell and Justice Brennan vindicate Justice Rehnquist's position?

3. Justice Powell maintains that the absence of fairly clear standards for making due process judgments about police conduct should not be a reason for denying courts the opportunity to make those judgments. At the same time, he makes it clear that his notion of due process would rarely require the reversal of convictions. 425 U.S. at 495 n.7. At least one inevitable cost of Justice Powell's position is the cost of litigating due process claims that are likely to be unsuccessful. Are there benefits that outweigh this cost?

4. Subsequent to *Hampton* only a few courts have upheld defendants' claims that police inducements violated due process. One such case is United States v. Twigg, 588 F.2d 373 (3d Cir. 1978). Judge Rosenn wrote the court's opinion for a divided panel:

> These appeals are brought by Henry Neville and William Twigg from jury convictions on charges stemming from the illegal manufacture of methamphetamine hydrochloride ("speed"). . . .
> At the behest of the Drug Enforcement Agency, Kubica, a convicted felon striving to reduce the severity of his sentence, communicated with Neville and suggested the establishment of a speed laboratory. The Government gratuitously supplied about 20 percent of the glassware and the indispensable ingredient, phenyl-2-propanone. It is unclear whether the parties had the means or the money to obtain the chemical on their own. The DEA made arrangements with chemical supply houses to facilitate the purchase of the rest of the materials. Kubica, operating under the business name "Chem Kleen" supplied by the DEA, actually purchased all of the supplies with the exception of a separatory funnel. (The funnel was secured by Twigg at the direction of Kubica who was engaged in

4. For present purposes it would be sufficient to adopt this rule under our supervisory power and leave to another day whether it ought to be made applicable to the States under the Due Process Clause.

operating the laboratory.) When problems were encountered in locating an adequate production site, the Government found the solution by providing an isolated farmhouse well-suited for the location of an illegally operated laboratory. Again, there was no cost to the defendants. At all times during the production process, Kubica was completely in charge and furnished all of the laboratory expertise. Neither defendant had the know-how with which to actually manufacture methamphetamine. The assistance they provided was minimal and then at the specific direction of Kubica.

. . . The only evidence that Neville was predisposed to commit the crime was his receptivity to Kubica's proposal to engage in the venture and the testimony of Kubica that he had worked with Neville in a similar laboratory four years earlier. . . .

When Kubica, at the instance of the DEA, reestablished contact with Neville, the latter was not engaged in any illicit drug activity. . . . Fundamental fairness . . . [requires reversal of Neville's conviction. We cannot] countenance such actions by law enforcement officials and prosecution for a crime so fomented by them will be barred.[9] . . .

Twigg did not become involved in this criminal enterprise until March 1, 1977—the day the laboratory went into operation. His reason for becoming involved was to repay a debt owed to Neville. Neville introduced Twigg to Kubica, and then Twigg and Kubica went shopping for additional supplies, which Kubica purchased. There is no evidence to suggest that Twigg was aware of the ultimate purpose of these errands until informed by Kubica after returning to the farmhouse. All actions taken by Twigg from that time until his arrest were at the specific direction of Kubica, the government agent. Twigg contributed nothing in terms of expertise, money, supplies, or ideas. It also appears that Twigg would not even have shared in the proceeds from the sale of the drug. In light of these facts, we hold that Twigg's conviction is also tainted by the conduct of the DEA agents and that fundamental fairness requires its reversal. [Id. at 374, 380-382.]

C. THE SUPERVISORY POWER

On several occasions the Supreme Court has relied on a claimed inherent supervisory power over the administration of criminal justice in federal courts to reverse convictions obtained as a result of official illegality. See, e.g., McNabb v. United States, 318 U.S. 332 (1943) (police violated

---

9. We also find it baffling that the Government would urge the reduction of the jail sentence for a man who may have run as many as 50 or 100 speed laboratories in the past in exchange for the convictions of two men with no apparent criminal designs and without the expertise required to set up a single laboratory.

Rule 5 of Federal Rules of Criminal Procedure by failing to take arrestee before magistrate without unnecessary delay; supervisory power relied on to exclude confession obtained from defendant during the delay); Rea v. United States, 350 U.S. 214 (1956) (pre-*Mapp* case relying on supervisory power to prevent federal agent from providing state with evidence obtained as a result of fourth amendment violation). Because these decisions are not mandated by the due process clause or any other constitutional provision applicable to the states, the holdings are binding only on federal courts.

What constitutional or jurisprudential principle justifies the exercise of this federal "supervisory power"?[18]

Whatever the source of the supervisory power is, it may be the unarticulated basis for the objective entrapment test advocated by the dissenting justices in *Russell* and the concurring justices in *Sorrells* and *Sherman*. Entrapment was not a recognized common law defense, and the justices advocating the objective test have never suggested that it is constitutionally mandated or that it can be derived from criminal statutes on the basis of some notion of congressional intent. What, then, is there, in the absence of specific legislation, upon which to rest the objective entrapment test except the Court's supervisory power?

Regardless of which entrapment test one favors, the supervisory power arguably should be available as an independent means for dealing with particularly inappropriate police inducements. Indeed, this was the position of the *Hampton* dissenters, who suggested that reversal of the conviction could be based on the Court's supervisory power rather than the due process clause. 425 U.S. 484, 500 n.4 (1976) (Brennan, J., dissenting).

Should there be an "intermediate ground" between entrapment and due process for assessing the propriety of police investigatory activities? Justice Brennan suggested that resting *Hampton* on the supervisory power would have the benefit of leaving open the question whether state law enforcement agents should be similarly restricted in their investigatory activity. On the other hand, the problem of articulating general standards that give content to the supervisory power is just as great as the problem of articulating standards for due process. Moreover, precisely because a supervisory power holding would not have constitutional stature and would not be binding on the states, justices may be less restrained in invoking the supervisory power to vindicate their particular views of proper police conduct. Would greater judicial activism in this area be desirable?

18. See Beale, Reconsidering Supervisory Power in Criminal Cases: Constitutional and Statutory Limits on the Authority of the Federal Courts, 84 Colum. L. Rev. 1433 (1984).

Except for whatever is implicit in *Russell* and the opinions in *Hampton*, the Supreme Court has not dealt with the applicability of the supervisory power to police inducements. The Court, however, has dealt with the supervisory power in a somewhat different investigatory context:

UNITED STATES v. PAYNER

Certiorari to the United States Court of Appeals for the Sixth Circuit
447 U.S. 727 (1980)

MR. JUSTICE POWELL delivered the opinion of the Court.

The question is whether the District Court properly suppressed the fruits of an unlawful search that did not invade the respondent's Fourth Amendment rights. . . .

Respondent Jack Payner was indicted in September 1976 on a charge of falsifying his 1972 federal income tax return in violation of 18 U.S.C. §1001. The indictment alleged that respondent denied maintaining a foreign bank account at a time when he knew that he had such an account at the Castle Bank and Trust Company of Nassau, Bahama Islands. The Government's case rested heavily on a loan guarantee agreement dated April 28, 1972, in which respondent pledged the funds in his Castle Bank account as security for a $100,000 loan.

Respondent waived his right to jury trial and moved to suppress the guarantee agreement. . . . The court . . . found . . . that the Government discovered the guarantee agreement by exploiting a flagrantly illegal search that occurred on January 15, 1973. . . . [The court suppressed the evidence. As a result, there was insufficient evidence to sustain a conviction.]

The events leading up to the 1973 search are not in dispute. In 1965, the Internal Revenue Service launched an investigation into the financial activities of American citizens in the Bahamas. The project, known as "Operation Trade Winds," was headquartered in Jacksonville, Fla. Suspicion focused on the Castle Bank in 1972, when investigators learned that a suspected narcotics trafficker had an account there. Special Agent Richard Jaffe of the Jacksonville office asked Norman Casper, a private investigator and occasional informant, to learn what he could about the Castle Bank and its depositors. To that end, Casper cultivated his friendship with Castle Bank vice president Michael Wolstencroft. Casper introduced Wolstencroft to Sybol Kennedy, a private investigator and former employee. When Casper discovered that the banker intended to spend a few days in Miami in January 1973, he devised a scheme to gain access to the bank records he knew Wolstencroft would be carrying in his briefcase. Agent Jaffe approved the basic outline of the plan.

Wolstencroft arrived in Miami on January 15 and went directly to Kennedy's apartment. At about 7:30 P.M., the two left for dinner at a Key Biscayne restaurant. Shortly thereafter, Casper entered the apartment using a key supplied by Kennedy. He removed the briefcase and delivered it to Jaffe. While the agent supervised the copying of approximately 400 documents taken from the briefcase, a "lookout" observed Kennedy and Wolstencroft at dinner. The observer notified Casper when the pair left the restaurant, and the briefcase was replaced. The documents photographed that evening included papers evidencing a close working relationship between the Castle Bank and the Bank of Perrine, Fla. Subpoenas issued to the Bank of Perrine ultimately uncovered the loan guarantee agreement at issue in this case.

The District Court found that the United States, acting through Jaffe, "knowingly and willfully participated in the unlawful seizure of Michael Wolstencroft's briefcase. . . ." [434 F. Supp.] at 120. According to that court, "the Government affirmatively counsels its agents that the Fourth Amendment standing limitation permits them to purposefully conduct an unconstitutional search and seizure of one individual in order to obtain evidence against third parties. . . ." Id., at 132-133. The District Court also found that the documents seized from Wolstencroft provided the leads that ultimately led to the discovery of the critical loan guarantee agreement. Id., at 123. Although the search did not impinge upon the respondent's Fourth Amendment rights, the District Court believed that the Due Process Clause of the Fifth Amendment and the inherent supervisory power of the federal courts required it to exclude evidence tainted by the Government's "knowing and purposeful *bad faith hostility* to any person's fundamental constitutional rights." Id., at 129; see id., at 133, 134-135.

The Court of Appeals for the Sixth Circuit affirmed in a brief order endorsing the District Court's use of its supervisory power. 590 F.2d 206 (1979) (per curiam). . . .

. . . [A]s the District Court recognized, respondent lacks standing under the Fourth Amendment to suppress the documents illegally seized from Wolstencroft. . . .

We certainly can understand the District Court's commendable desire to deter deliberate intrusions into the privacy of persons who are unlikely to become defendants in a criminal prosecution. See 434 F. Supp., at 135. No court should condone the unconstitutional and possibly criminal behavior of those who planned and executed this "briefcase caper."[5] Indeed, the decisions of this Court are replete with denunciations of willfully lawless activities undertaken in the name of law enforcement. E.g., Jackson v. Denno, 378 U.S. 368, 386 (1964); see Olmstead v. United States, 277 U.S. 438, 485 (1928) (Brandeis, J., dissenting). But our cases also show that these unexceptional principles do not command the exclusion of evidence in every case of illegality. Instead, they must be weighed against the considerable harm that would flow from indiscriminate application of an exclusionary rule.

Thus, the exclusionary rule "has been restricted to those areas where its remedial objectives are most efficaciously served." United States v. Calandra, 414 U.S. 338, 348 (1974).

We conclude that the supervisory power does not authorize a federal court to suppress otherwise admissible evidence on the ground that it was seized unlawfully from a third party not before the court.[7] Our Fourth Amendment decisions have established beyond any doubt that the interest in deterring illegal searches does not justify the exclusion of tainted evidence at the instance of a party who was not the victim of the challenged practices. Rakas v. Illinois, [439 U.S. 128, 137 (1978)]; Alderman v. United States, 394 U.S. [165, 174-175 (1969)]. The values assigned to the competing interests do not change because a court has elected to analyze the question under the supervisory power instead of the Fourth Amendment. In either case, the need to deter the underlying conduct and the detrimental impact of excluding the evidence remain precisely the same. . . .

. . . [The district court's] reasoning, which the Court of Appeals affirmed, amounts to a substitution of individual judgment for the con-

---

of the House Committee on Government Operations (Operation Tradewinds, Project Haven, and Narcotics Traffickers Tax Program), 94th Cong., 1st Sess. (1975). As a result, the Commissioner of Internal Revenue "called off" Operation Trade Winds. Tr. of Oral Arg. 35. The Commissioner also adopted guidelines that require agents to instruct informants on the requirements of the law and to report known illegalities to a supervisory officer, who is in turn directed to notify appropriate state authorities. IR Manual §§9373.3(3), 9373.4 (Manual Transmittal 9-21, Dec. 27, 1977). Although these measures appear on their face to be less positive than one might expect from an agency charged with upholding the law, they do indicate disapproval of the practices found to have been implemented in this case. We cannot assume that similar lawless conduct, if brought to the attention of responsible officials, would not be dealt with appropriately. To require in addition the suppression of highly probative evidence in a trial against a third party would penalize society unnecessarily.

7. Federal courts may use their supervisory power in some circumstances to exclude evidence taken from the *defendant* by "willful disobedience of law." McNabb v. United States, 318 U.S. 332, 345 (1943); see Elkins v. United States, 364 U.S. 206, 223 (1960); Rea v. United States, 350 U.S. 214, 216-217 (1956); cf. Hampton v. United States, 425 U.S. 484, 495 (1976) (Powell, J., concurring in judgment). This Court has never held, however, that the supervisory power authorizes suppression of evidence obtained from third parties in violation of Constitution, statute, or rule. The supervisory power merely permits federal courts to supervise "the administration of criminal justice" among the parties before the bar. McNabb v. United States, supra, at 340.

trolling decisions of this Court.[9] Were we to accept this use of the supervisory power, we would confer on the judiciary discretionary power to disregard the considered limitations of the law it is charged with enforcing. We hold that the supervisory power does not extend so far.

The judgment of the Court of Appeals is reversed.

[The concurring opinion of CHIEF JUSTICE BURGER and the dissenting opinion of JUSTICE MARSHALL are omitted.]

NOTES AND QUESTIONS

1. Why is the police activity in *Payner* not a due process violation? If there is any role for the supervisory power in dealing with conduct that may fall short of due process violation, why is *Payner* not the appropriate case? Should it be sufficient to say that the fourth amendment standing rules have struck the appropriate balance with respect to illegal searches and seizures?

2. Regardless of your answer to the preceding question, is *Payner* explainable as a case in which the Court may have been primarily concerned with the possibility that the defendant's position, if accepted, could have the effect of undermining recently reaffirmed and refined fourth amendment standing principles? Or is *Payner* in effect the death knell for the supervisory power?

The *Payner* Court claimed its decision "does not limit the traditional scope of the supervisory power in any way . . . [or] render that power 'superfluous.' " 447 U.S. at 737 n.8. Even if this statement is taken at face value, do *Russell* and *Hampton* leave much room for operation of the supervisory power in dealing with police inducements?

Incidentally, what is the traditional scope of the supervisory power? Consider United States v. Hasting, 461 U.S. 499 (1983): Defendants were convicted of various counts of conspiracy, kidnapping, and transporting women across state lines for immoral purposes. In a per curiam opinion, the court of appeals concluded that the prosecutor had violated Griffin v. California, 380 U.S. 609 (1965). *Griffin* had held that a

---

9. The same difficulty attends respondent's claim to the protections of the Due Process Clause of the Fifth Amendment. The Court of Appeals expressly declined to consider the Due Process Clause. But even if we assume that the unlawful briefcase search was so outrageous as to offend fundamental " 'canons of decency and fairness,' " Rochin v. California, 342 U.S. 165, 169 (1952), quoting Malinski v. New York, 324 U.S. 401, 417 (1945) (opinion of Frankfurter, J.), the fact remains that "[t]he limitations of the Due Process Clause . . . come into play only when the Government activity in question violates some protected right of the *defendant*," Hampton v. United States. . . . [425 U.S. 484,] 490 (plurality opinion).

criminal defendant's constitutional right to remain silent includes the
right to have the prosecutor refrain from commenting on the defendant's
exercise of the right of silence. In the view of the court of appeals, the
Griffin violation required reversal of the convictions even though the
Griffin violation may have been harmless error. The Supreme Court
disagreed, and, in the course of his opinion for the Court, Chief Justice
Burger elaborated on the nature of the supervisory power:

> The opinion of the Court of Appeals does not make entirely clear its
> basis for reversing the convictions in this gruesome case. Its cursory treat-
> ment of the harmless error question and its focus on the failure generally
> of prosecutors within its jurisdiction to heed the court's prior admonitions
> about commenting on a defendant's failure to rebut the prosecution's case
> suggests that, notwithstanding the harmless nature of the error, the court
> acted in this case to discipline the prosecutor—and warn other prosecu-
> tors—for what it perceived to be continuing violations of *Griffin*. . . .
>   . . . [W]e proceed on the assumption that, without so stating, the
> court was exercising its supervisory powers to discipline the prosecutors of
> its jurisdiction. The question presented is whether, on this record, in a
> purported exercise of supervisory powers, a reviewing court may ignore the
> harmless error analysis of Chapman [v. California, 386 U.S. 18 (1967)].
> We hold that the harmless error rule of *Chapman*, . . . may not be
> avoided by an assertion of supervisory power, simply to justify a reversal
> of these criminal convictions. . . .
>   "[G]uided by considerations of justice," McNabb v. United States,
> 318 U.S. 332, 341 (1943), and in the exercise of supervisory powers,
> federal courts may, within limits, formulate procedural rules not specifi-
> cally required by the Constitution or the Congress. The purposes under-
> lying use of the supervisory powers are threefold: to implement a remedy
> for violation of recognized rights, . . . to preserve judicial integrity by
> ensuring that a conviction rests on appropriate considerations validly before
> the jury, . . . and finally, as a remedy designed to deter illegal con-
> duct. . . .
>   The goals that are implicated by supervisory powers are not, however,
> significant in the context of this case if, as the Court of Appeals plainly
> implied, the errors alleged are harmless. Supervisory power to reverse a
> conviction is not needed as a remedy when the error to which it is addressed
> is harmless since by definition, the conviction would have been obtained
> notwithstanding the asserted error. Further, in this context, the integrity
> of the process carries less weight, for it is the essence of the harmless error
> doctrine that a judgment may stand only when there is no "reasonable
> possibility that the [practice] complained of might have contributed to the
> conviction." Fahy v. Connecticut, 375 U.S. 85, 86-87 (1963). Finally,
> deterrence is an inappropriate basis for reversal where, as here, the pros-
> ecutor's remark is at most an attenuated violation of *Griffin* and where

means more narrowly tailored to deter objectionable prosecutorial conduct are available.

To the extent that the values protected by supervisory authority are at issue here, these powers are not to be exercised in a vacuum. Rather, reversals of convictions under the court's supervisory power must be approached "with some caution," [United States v.] Payner [447 U.S. 727, 734 (1980),] and with a view toward balancing the interests involved, id., at 735-736 and n.8. . . . [T]he Court of Appeals failed in this case to give appropriate—if, indeed, any—weight to these relevant interests. It did not consider the trauma the victims of these particularly heinous crimes would experience in a new trial, forcing them to relive harrowing experiences now long past, or the practical problems of retrying these sensitive issues more than four years after the events. . . . The conclusion is inescapable that the Court of Appeals focused exclusively on its concern that the prosecutors within its jurisdiction were indifferent to the frequent admonitions of the court. The court appears to have decided to deter future similar comments by the drastic step of reversal of these convictions. But the interests preserved by the doctrine of harmless error cannot be so lightly and casually ignored in order to chastise what the court viewed as prosecutorial overreaching. [461 U.S. at 504-507.]

D. POLICE INDUCEMENTS OF PUBLIC OFFICIALS

All of the Supreme Court cases considering the propriety of police inducements have dealt with illegal liquor or narcotics activity. It was in that context that the Court developed its entrapment and due process principles. Police inducements, however, are not limited to drug crimes. For example, in 1979 and 1980 the FBI conducted an elaborate sting operation known as Abscam. A number of public officials, including several congressmen, were convicted of bribery, conspiracy, and related offenses. Their challenges to the convictions on the grounds of improper police inducements were rejected.[19] For differing views on the propriety of the Abscam investigation, see ABSCAM Ethics: Moral Issues and Deception in Law Enforcement (G. Caplan ed., 1982). See also Gershman, Abscam, the Judiciary, and the Ethics of Entrapment, 91 Yale L.J. 1565 (1982).

For another example of inducements directed at public officials,

19. See, e.g., United States v. Kelly, 707 F.2d 1460 (D.C. Cir.) (per curiam), cert. denied, 464 U.S. 908 (1983); United States v. Myers, 692 F.2d 823 (2d Cir. 1982), cert. denied, 461 U.S. 961 (1983); United States v. Janotti, 673 F.2d 578 (3d Cir.) (en banc), cert. denied, 457 U.S. 1106 (1982).

consider the facts in Nigrone v. Murtagh, 46 A.D.2d 343, 362 N.Y.S.2d 513 (1974), aff'd, 36 N.Y.2d 421, 330 N.E.2d 45, 369 N.Y.S.2d 75 (1975):

> Pursuing allegedly specific information about corruption in the criminal justice system, the Special Prosecutor determined to "infiltrate" the system by setting up a simulated crime. A probationary officer from the Police Academy, using the name "Vitale," was alleged to have stolen $8,200 from a businessman, with the aid of a gun, on November 1, 1973. Both the "victim" of this "armed robbery" and the arresting officer participated in the ruse. A false felony complaint was lodged against Vitale and he was arrested, fingerprinted and placed in jail pending arraignment and the setting of bail. Bail was eventually set at $10,000 by a judge unaware of the ruse and Vitale was released. The Special Prosecutor's office also fabricated a false criminal record for Vitale, indicating that he had had two prior arrests.
>
> Thereafter, through Vitale, the Special Prosecutor sent a woman, one "Mrs. Gatti," to contact Judge Paul P. Rao, a judge of the United States Customs Court. They met on November 12, 1973 and Mrs. Gatti, apparently an old family friend of the Raos who had not seen the Judge in some 40 years, asked his help on behalf of the son of dear friends (Vitale) who was in trouble with the law. Mrs. Gatti, although allegedly unaware of the Vitale hoax, was equipped with a tape recorder. Judge Rao referred Mrs. Gatti to his son, Paul P. Rao, Jr., a practicing attorney. That same day, Mrs. Gatti saw Rao, Jr., and arranged to have him meet with Vitale, and such a meeting also took place that day. Rao, Jr., agreed to represent Vitale in his pending robbery case.
>
> On November 23, 1973 Vitale was indicted for robbery (two counts) and grand larceny (two counts) by a Kings County Grand Jury. Neither the grand jurors nor the Assistant District Attorney who presented the case knew that the whole thing was a sham and that in fact no such robbery had ever occurred. Vitale failed to appear in the Supreme Court for arraignment on the indictment and his $10,000 cash bail was declared forfeit. . . . Nevertheless, Rao, Jr., was successful in having the bail forfeiture revoked and in staving off a detailed inquiry into whether the bail money was really "the proceeds" of the "robbery." Rao, Jr., also procured a return of Vitale's $10,000 cash bail and had the bail reduced to $1,000. Again, none of the Supreme Court Justices before whom the bail matter was presented was aware that the entire case was a hoax.
>
> In March, 1974 Rao, Jr., formally withdrew as Vitale's counsel on the stated ground that Vitale was insisting that he, Rao, Jr., "fix" the case for him.
>
> In April, 1974, Judge Rao, his son Rao, Jr., and one of the latter's law partners, Salvatore Nigrone, were requested to appear before the Extraordinary Special Grand Jury. . . .
>
> The defendants waived immunity and testified. . . .

In May, 1974 Judge Rao was indicted upon two counts of perjury for denying that he had ever told Mrs. Gatti how to handle her problem in affecting a Judge's actions in a criminal case or that she should handle the bail problem by getting a lawyer who knew the Judge. Rao, Jr., was indicted upon seven counts of perjury for denying that he had ever told Vitale that he would have to get money so that he would "know how to talk" to other people (who could quash his case); for denying that he had seen a Judge, other than the Judge presiding in the case, about the Vitale matter; for denying that he had ever seen anybody in the court system to obtain assistance in the Vitale matter; for denying that he had ever discussed with Vitale or anyone else whether a "hook was in" in the Vitale case; for denying that he had helped in creating a "phony" story or defense; for testifying falsely that, at the time of his first court appearance, he had no knowledge of any of the bail money being the proceeds of the robbery; and for falsely testifying that Vitale had never told him that his parents had not furnished the bail. Nigrone was indicted upon one count of perjury for testifying falsely that he had never asked Rao, Jr., if the "hook was in" in the Vitale case. [46 A.D.2d at 344-345.]

The defendants urged that the indictments should be dismissed on the ground of prosecutorial misconduct. The court denied the defendants' motions:

> The defendants do not claim entrapment or violation of any of their personal constitutional rights. Indeed, nothing the Special Prosecutor did, no matter how offensive, could have induced or licensed them to commit perjury. Still, the defendants ask us to dismiss these indictments as the fruit of the poisonous tree or, simply, as a matter of due process. We see no reason in law or fundamental fairness to do so. [Id. at 349.]

Nonetheless, the court severely criticized the special prosecutor's tactics:

> There is no doubt whatsoever that, upon the facts here presented, the office of the special prosecutor has exceeded its proper prosecutorial function. The deception of grand jurors, Judges and Assistant District Attorneys and the filing of false official documents are absolutely intolerable. The criminal justice system operates to protect the individual from both unsubstantiated accusations of guilt and illegal or outrageous conduct by an overreaching prosecutor. . . .
> The pernicious effect of the Special Prosecutor's conduct is nowhere better exemplified than in his misuse of the Kings County Grand Jury which indicted Vitale for robbery. . . . Such a perversion of the criminal justice system by an overzealous prosecutor is illegal, outrageous and intolerable and we condemn it. If the justice system is to have any usefulness, it must be respected and believed. The necessary confidence cannot be

preserved when grand juries and Judges are duped in charades composed of lies and deceptions fabricated by the law officers of the State.

It is not an answer to say that, in searching out crime, deception is often required to bring offenders to justice. Such deception, however permissible when dealing with suspected criminals, is never justified when dealing with grand juries, trial juries, or Judges whose burden is the search for truth. Though the purpose of the Special Prosecutor may be laudable, he is not above the law and may no more resort to corruption and manipulation of the criminal justice system than the individuals he seeks to prosecute.

Governmental misuse of power breeds only apathy, contempt and more lawlessness. [Id. at 347-348.]

If the defendants had been charged with bribery, should they have been entitled to acquittals on entrapment, due process, or supervisory power grounds? Are the Supreme Court's due process and supervisory power principles, even if they are adequate for drug cases, too narrow in other contexts? Alternatively, is there *less* reason to provide an inducement defense for public officials (and particularly officers of the court)—individuals who, by virtue of their positions, have a special obligation to obey the law and not abuse their power?

CHAPTER 9

THE FIFTH AMENDMENT

A. THE SCOPE OF THE FIFTH AMENDMENT

The fifth amendment provides an evidentiary privilege that allows an individual to refuse to give testimony that may tend to incriminate that person. As with many other constitutional provisions, the relevant language—"nor shall any person . . . be compelled in any criminal case to be a witness against himself"—is somewhat cryptic. The earliest interpretation of the fifth amendment by a sitting Supreme Court Justice gave a very broad, nearly literal interpretation to the amendment. The case was the trial of Aaron Burr in 1807, and the Justice was Chief Justice Marshall. The events are related in Justice Shiras's dissenting opinion in Brown v. Walker, 161 U.S. 591 (1896):

> The first case in which there was any consideration of this constitutional provision was the proceeding in the Circuit Court of the United States for the District of Virginia, in the year 1807, wherein Aaron Burr was indicted and tried for treason, and for a misdemeanor in preparing the means of a military expedition against Mexico, a territory of the King of Spain, with whom the United States were at peace. . . .
>
> While the grand jury was considering the case, . . . one Willie was called and asked whether he had, under instructions from Aaron Burr, copied a certain paper, which was then exhibited to him. This question the witness refused to answer, lest he might thereby incriminate himself. The Chief Justice observing that, if the witness was to decide upon this, it must be on oath, interrogated the witness whether his answering the

question would criminate himself, to which he replied that it might in a certain case. Thereupon the Chief Justice withheld the point for argument. A full and able argument was had, and, after consideration, the Chief Justice expressed himself as follows:

> When a question is propounded, it belongs to the court to consider and to decide whether any direct answer to it can implicate the witness. If this be decided in the negative, then he may answer it without violating the privilege which is secured to him by law. If a direct answer to it *may* criminate himself, then he must be the sole judge what his answer would be. The court cannot participate with him in this judgment; because they cannot decide on the effect of his answer without knowing what it would be; and a disclosure of that fact to the judges would strip him of the privileges which the law allows, and which he claims. It follows, necessarily, then, from this state of things, that if the question be of such a description that an answer to it may or may not criminate the witness, according to the purport of that answer, it must rest with himself, who alone can tell what it would be, to answer the question or not. If, in such a case, he say, upon his oath, that his answer would criminate himself, the court can demand no other testimony of the fact. If the declaration be untrue, it is in conscience and in law as much a perjury as if he had declared any other untruth upon his oath; as it is one of those cases in which the rule of law must be abandoned, or the oath of the witness be received. The counsel for the United States have also laid down this rule, according to their understanding of it, but they appear to the court to have made it as much too narrow as the counsel for the witness have made it too broad. According to their statement, a witness can never refuse to answer any question, unless that answer, unconnected with other testimony, would be sufficient to convict him of a crime. This would be rendering the rule almost perfectly worthless. Many links frequently compose that chain of testimony which is necessary to convict any individual of a crime. It appears to the court to be the true sense of the rule that no witness is compellable to furnish any one of them against himself. It is certainly not only a possible, but a probable, case, that a witness, by disclosing a single fact, may complete the testimony against himself, and to every effectual purpose accuse himself as entirely as he would by stating every circumstance which would be required for his conviction. That fact of itself might be unavailing; but all other facts without it might be insufficient. While that remains concealed within his own bosom he is safe; but draw it from thence, and he is exposed to a prosecution. The rule which declares that no man is compelled to accuse himself, would most obviously be infringed by compelling a witness to disclose a fact of this description. What testimony may be possessed, or is attainable, against any individual, the court can never know. It would seem, then, that the court ought never to compel a witness to give an answer which discloses a fact that might form a necessary and essential part of a crime, which is punishable by the laws. . . . In such a case, the witness must himself judge what his answer will be; and if he say, on oath, that he cannot answer without accusing himself, he cannot be compelled to answer.

1 Burr's Trial, 244, 245 [161 U.S. at 612-615].

A literal interpretation of the amendment was unsatisfactory to the states and the federal government, however, and in the century following Burr's trial, a number of jurisdictions passed statutes providing witnesses with various types of immunity from prosecution in order to compel testimony over an otherwise legitimate invocation of the privilege. These statutes were premised on the view that a witness could hardly be seen as incriminating himself if he was given immunity from prosecution with respect to the acts testified to, or alternatively, if the state was not allowed to use the compelled testimony against the witness. When the Court first reviewed the constitutionality of one of these statues, it relied heavily on Chief Justice Marshall's opinion in the Burr trial, and on the then recent case of Boyd v. United States, 116 U.S. 616 (1886), in striking down the statute.

COUNSELMAN v. HITCHCOCK, 142 U.S. 547, 560-561, 562-564, 585-586 (1892): [The statute in question in *Counselman* provided:] . . . No pleading of a party, nor any discovery or evidence obtained from a party or witness by means of a judicial proceeding in this or any foreign country, shall be given in evidence, or in any manner used against him or his property or estate, in any court of the United States, in any criminal proceeding, or for the enforcement of any penalty or forfeiture: *Provided,* That this section shall not exempt any party or witness from prosecution and punishment for perjury committed in discovering or testifying as aforesaid. . . .

[In finding it unconstitutional, the Court first held that the fifth amendment is not limited to testimony given at the trial of a criminal case:]

It is broadly contended on the part of the appellee that a witness is not entitled to plead the privilege of silence, except in a criminal case against himself; but such is not the language of the Constitution. Its provision is that no person shall be compelled in *any* criminal case to be a witness against himself. This provision must have a broad construction in favor of the right which it was intended to secure. The matter under investigation by the grand jury in this case was a criminal matter, to inquire whether there had been a criminal violation of the Interstate Commerce Act. If Counselman had been guilty of the matters inquired of in the questions which he refused to answer, he himself was liable to criminal prosecution under the act. The case before the grand jury was, therefore, a criminal case. The reason given by Counselman for his refusal to answer the questions was that his answers might tend to criminate him, and showed that his apprehension was that, if he answered the questions truly and fully (as he was bound to do if he should answer them at all), the answers might show that he had committed a crime against the Interstate Commerce Act, for which he might be prosecuted. His answers, therefore, would be testimony against himself, and he would be compelled to give them in a criminal case.

It is impossible that the meaning of the constitutional provision can only be, that a person shall not be compelled to be a witness against himself in a criminal prosecution against himself. It would doubtless cover such cases; but it is not limited to them. The object was to insure that a person should not be compelled, when acting as a witness in any investigation, to give testimony which might tend to show that he himself had committed a crime. The privilege is limited to criminal matters, but it is as broad as the mischief against which it seeks to guard.

It is argued for the appellee that the investigation before the grand jury was not a criminal case, but was solely for the purpose of finding out whether a crime had been committed, or whether any one should be accused of an offence, there being no accuser and no parties plaintiff or defendant, and that a case could arise only when an indictment should be returned. In support of this view reference is made to article 6 of the amendments to the Constitution of the United States, which provides that in all criminal prosecutions the accused shall enjoy the right to a speedy and public trial by an impartial jury, to be confronted with the witnesses against him, to have compulsory process for witnesses, and the assistance of counsel for his defence.

But this provision distinctly means a criminal prosecution against a person who is accused and who is to be tried by a petit jury. A criminal prosecution under article 6 of the amendments, is much narrower than a "criminal case," under article 5 of the amendments. It is entirely consistent with the language of article 5, that the privilege of not being a witness against himself is to be exercised in a proceeding before a grand jury. . . .

It is an ancient principle of the law of evidence, that a witness shall not be compelled, in any proceeding, to make disclosures or to give testimony which will tend to criminate him or subject him to fines, penalties or forfeitures. . . .

The relations of Counselman to the subject of inquiry before the grand jury, as shown by the questions put to him, in connection with the provisions of the Interstate Commerce Act, entitled him to invoke the protection of the Constitution. . . .

[The Court then proceeded to determine whether the immunity provided in the statute was sufficient to protect Counselman's rights:]

It remains to consider whether §860 of the Revised Statutes removes the protection of the constitutional privilege of Counselman. That section must be construed as declaring that no evidence obtained from a witness by means of a judicial proceeding shall be given in evidence, or in any manner used against him or his property or estate, in any court of the United States, in any criminal proceeding, or for the enforcement of any penalty or forfeiture. It follows, that any evidence which might have been obtained from Counselman by means of his examination before the grand jury could not be given in evidence or used against him or his property in any court of the United States, in any criminal proceeding, or for the enforcement of any penalty or forfeiture. This, of course, protected him against the use of his testimony against him or his property in any prosecution against him or his property, in any criminal proceeding, in a court of the United States. But it had only that effect. It could not, and would not, prevent the use of his testimony to search out other testimony to be used in evidence against him or his property, in a criminal proceeding in such court. It could not prevent the obtaining and the use of witnesses and evidence which should be attributable directly to the testimony he might give under compulsion, and on which he might be convicted, when otherwise, and if he had refused to answer, he could not possibly have been convicted. . . .

We are clearly of opinion that no statute which leaves the party or witness subject to prosecution after he answers the criminating question put to him, can have the effect of supplanting the privilege conferred by the Constitution of the United States. Section 860 of the Revised Statutes does not supply a complete protection from all the perils against which the constitutional prohibition was designed to guard, and is not a full substitute for that prohibition. In view of the constitutional provision, a statutory enactment, to be valid, must afford absolute immunity against future prosecution for the offence to which the question relates. In this respect, . . . we consider that the ruling of this court in Boyd v. United States . . . supports the view we take. Section 860, moreover, affords no protection against that use of compelled testimony which consists in gaining therefrom a knowledge of the details of a crime, and of sources of information which may supply other means of convicting the witness or party. . . .

From a consideration of the language of the constitutional provision, and of all the authorities referred to, we are clearly of opinion that the appellant was entitled to refuse, as he did, to answer. The judgment of the Circuit Court must, therefore, be

Reversed, and the case remanded to that court, with a direction to discharge the appellant from custody, on the writ of habeas corpus.

When the Court next returned to the issue, however, the outcome was different, and a statute compelling testimony but granting immunity was upheld by a sharply divided court.

BROWN v. WALKER
Appeal from the Circuit Court of the United States for the Western
District of Pennsylvania
161 U.S 591 (1896)

MR. JUSTICE BROWN, after stating the case, delivered the opinion of the
court.

This case involves an alleged incompatibility between that clause of
the Fifth Amendment to the Constitution, which declares that no person
"shall be compelled in any criminal case to be a witness against himself,"
and the act of Congress of February 11, 1893, c. 83, 27 Stat. 443, which
enacts that "no person shall be excused from attending and testifying or
from producing books, papers, tariffs, contracts, agreements and documents before the Interstate Commerce Commission, or in obedience to
the subpoena of the Commission, . . . on the ground or for the reason
that the testimony or evidence, documentary or otherwise, required of
him, may tend to criminate him or subject him to a penalty or forfeiture.
But no person shall be prosecuted or subjected to any penalty or forfeiture
for or on account of any transaction, matter or thing, concerning which
he may testify, or produce evidence, documentary or otherwise, before
said Commission, or in obedience to its subpoena, or the subpoena of
either of them, or in any such case or proceeding."

The act is supposed to have been passed in view of the opinion of
this court in Counselman v. Hitchcock, 142 U.S. 547, to the effect that
section 860 of the Revised Statutes, providing that no evidence given by
a witness shall be used against him, his property or estate, in any manner,
in any court of the United States, in any criminal proceeding, did not
afford that complete protection to the witness which the amendment was
intended to guarantee. . . .

The clause of the Constitution in question is obviously susceptible
of two interpretations. If it be construed literally, as authorizing the
witness to refuse to disclose any fact which might tend to incriminate,
disgrace or expose him to unfavorable comments, then as he must necessarily to a large extent determine upon his own conscience and responsibility whether his answer to the proposed question will have that
tendency, . . . the practical result would be, that no one could be
compelled to testify to a material fact in a criminal case, unless he chose
to do so, or unless it was entirely clear that the privilege was not set up
in good faith. If, upon the other hand, the object of the provision be to
secure the witness against a criminal prosecution, which might be aided
directly or indirectly by his disclosure, then, if no such prosecution be
possible—in other words, if his testimony operate as a complete pardon

for the offence to which it relates—a statute absolutely securing to him
such immunity from prosecution would satisfy the demands of the clause
in question.

Our attention has been called to but few cases wherein this provision,
which is found with slight variation in the constitution of every State,
has been construed in connection with a statute similar to the one before
us, as the decisions have usually turned upon the validity of statutes
providing, as did section 860, that the testimony given by such witness
should never be used against him in any criminal prosecution. It can
only be said in general that the clause should be construed, as it was
doubtless designed, to effect a practical and beneficent purpose—not
necessarily to protect witnesses against every possible detriment which
might happen to them from their testimony, nor to unduly impede,
hinder or obstruct the administration of criminal justice. That the statute
should be upheld, if it can be construed in harmony with the fundamental
law, will be admitted. Instead of seeking for excuses for holding acts of
the legislative power to be void by reason of their conflict with the Constitution, or with certain supposed fundamental principles of civil liberty,
the effort should be to reconcile them if possible, and not to hold the
law invalid unless, as was observed by Mr. Chief Justice Marshall, in
Fletcher v. Peck, 6 Cranch, 87, 128, "the opposition between the Constitution and the law be such that the judge feels a clear and strong
conviction of their incompatibility with each other."

The maxim nemo tenetur seipsum accusare had its origin in a protest
against the inquisitorial and manifestly unjust methods of interrogating
accused persons, which has long obtained in the continental system, and,
until the expulsion of the Stuarts from the British throne in 1688, and
the erection of additional barriers for the protection of the people against
the exercise of arbitrary power, was not uncommon even in England.
While the admissions or confessions of the prisoner, when voluntarily
and freely made, have always ranked high in the scale of incriminating
evidence, if an accused person be asked to explain his apparent connection
with a crime under investigation, the ease with which the questions put
to him may assume an inquisitorial character, the temptation to press
the witness unduly, to browbeat him if he be timid or reluctant, to push
him into a corner, and to entrap him into fatal contradictions, which is
so painfully evident in many of the earlier state trials, notably in those
of Sir Nicholas Throckmorton, and Udal, the Puritan minister, made
the system so odious as to give rise to a demand for its total abolition.
The change in the English criminal procedure in that particular seems
to be founded upon no statute and no judicial opinion, but upon a general
and silent acquiescence of the courts in a popular demand. But, however
adopted, it has become firmly embedded in English, as well as in Amer-

ican jurisprudence. So deeply did the iniquities of the ancient system impress themselves upon the minds of the American colonists that the States, with one accord, made a denial of the right to question an accused person a part of their fundamental law, so that a maxim, which in England was a mere rule of evidence, became clothed in this country with the impregnability of a constitutional enactment.

Stringent as the general rule is, however, certain classes of cases have always been treated as not falling within the reason of the rule, and, therefore, constituting apparent exceptions. When examined, these cases will all be found to be based upon the idea that, if the testimony sought cannot possibly be used as a basis for, or in aid of, a criminal prosecution against the witness, the rule ceases to apply, its object being to protect the witness himself and no one else—much less that it shall be made use of as a pretext for securing immunity to others.

1. Thus, if the witness himself elects to waive his privilege, as he may doubtless do, since the privilege is for his protection and not for that of other parties, and discloses his criminal connections, he is not permitted to stop, but must go on and make a full disclosure. . . . So, under modern statutes permitting accused persons to take the stand in their own behalf, they may be subjected to cross-examination upon their statements. . . .

2. For the same reason if a prosecution for a crime, concerning which the witness is interrogated, is barred by the statute of limitations, he is compellable to answer. . . .

3. If the answer of the witness may have a tendency to disgrace him or bring him into disrepute, and the proposed evidence be material to the issue on trial, the great weight of authority is that he may be compelled to answer, although, if the answer can have no effect upon the case, except so far as to impair the credibility of the witness, he may fall back upon his privilege. . . . But even in the latter case, if the answer of the witness will not directly show his infamy, but only *tend* to disgrace him, he is bound to answer. . . .

  The extent to which the witness is compelled to answer such questions as do not fix upon him a criminal culpability is within the control of the legislature. . . .

4. It is almost a necessary corollary of the above propositions that, if the witness has already received a pardon, he cannot longer set up his privilege, since he stands with respect to such offence as if it had never been committed. . . .

The danger of extending the principle announced in Counselman v. Hitchcock is that the privilege may be put forward for a sentimental reason, or for a purely fanciful protection of the witness against an imaginary danger, and for the real purpose of securing immunity to some third person, who is interested in concealing the facts to which he would testify. Every good citizen is bound to aid in the enforcement of the law, and has no right to permit himself, under the pretext of shielding his own good name, to be made the tool of others, who are desirous of seeking shelter behind his privilege.

The act of Congress in question securing to witnesses immunity from prosecution is virtually an act of general amnesty, and belongs to a class of legislation which is not uncommon either in England, (2 Taylor on Evidence, §1455, where a large number of similar acts are collated,) or in this country. Although the Constitution vests in the President "power to grant reprieves and pardons for offences against the United States, except in cases of impeachment," this power has never been held to take from Congress the power to pass acts of general amnesty, and is ordinarily exercised only in cases of individuals after conviction, although, as was said by this court in Ex parte Garland, 4 Wall. 333, 380, "it extends to every offence known to the law, and may be exercised at any time after its commission, either before legal proceedings are taken, or during their pendency, or after conviction and judgment." . . .

It is entirely true that the statute does not purport, nor is it possible for any statute, to shield the witness from the personal disgrace or opprobrium attaching to the exposure of his crime; but . . . the authorities are numerous and very nearly uniform to the effect that, if the proposed testimony is material to the issue on trial, the fact that the testimony may tend to degrade the witness in public estimation does not exempt him from the duty of disclosure. A person who commits a criminal act is bound to contemplate the consequences of exposure to his good name and reputation, and ought not to call upon the courts to protect that which he has himself esteemed to be of such little value. The safety and welfare of an entire community should not be put into the scale against the reputation of a self-confessed criminal, who ought not, either in justice or in good morals, to refuse to disclose that which may be of great public utility, in order that his neighbors may think well of him. The design of the constitutional privilege is not to aid the witness in vindicating his character, but to protect him against being compelled to furnish evidence to convict him of a criminal charge. If he secure legal immunity from prosecution, the possible impairment of his good name is a penalty which it is reasonable he should be compelled to pay for the common good. If it be once conceded that the fact that his testimony may tend to bring the witness into disrepute, though not to incriminate him, does not entitle him to the privilege of silence, it necessarily follows that if it also tends to incriminate, but at the same time operates as a pardon for the offence, the fact that the disgrace remains no more entitles him to immunity in this case than in the other.

It is argued in this connection that, while the witness is granted immunity from prosecution by the Federal government, he does not obtain such immunity against prosecution in the state courts. We are unable to appreciate the force of this suggestion. It is true that the Constitution does not operate upon a witness testifying in the state courts, since we have held that the first eight amendments are limitations only upon the powers of Congress and the Federal courts, and are not applicable to the several States, except so far as the Fourteenth Amendment may have made them applicable. . . .

There is no such restriction, however, upon the applicability of Federal statutes. The Sixth Article of the Constitution declares that "This Constitution, and the Laws of the United States which shall be made in Pursuance thereof; and all Treaties made, or which shall be made, under the authority of the United States, shall be the supreme Law of the Land; and the Judges in every State shall be bound thereby, anything in the Constitution or Laws of any State to the Contrary notwithstanding." . . .

The act in question contains no suggestion that it is to be applied only to the Federal courts. It declares broadly that "no person shall be excused from attending and testifying . . . before the Interstate Commerce Commission . . . on the ground . . . that the testimony . . . required of him may tend to criminate him," etc. "But no person shall be prosecuted or subjected to any penalty or forfeiture for or on account of any transaction, matter or thing concerning which he may testify," etc. It is not that he shall not be prosecuted for or on account of any *crime* concerning which he may testify, which might possibly be urged to apply only to crimes under the Federal law and not to crimes, such as the passing of counterfeit money, etc., which are also cognizable under state laws; but the immunity extends to any *transaction, matter or thing* concerning which he may testify, which clearly indicates that the immunity is intended to be general, and to be applicable whenever and in whatever court such prosecution may be had.

But even granting that there were still a bare possibility that by his disclosure he might be subjected to the criminal laws of some other sovereignty, that, as Chief Justice Cockburn said in Queen v. Boyes, 1 B. & S. 311, in reply to the argument that the witness was not protected by his pardon against an impeachment by the House of Commons, is not a real and probable danger, with reference to the ordinary operations of the law in the ordinary courts, but "a danger of an imaginary and unsubstantial character, having reference to some extraordinary and barely possible contingency, so improbable that no reasonable man would suffer it to influence his conduct." Such dangers it was never the object of the provision to obviate.

The same answer may be made to the suggestion that the witness is imperfectly protected by reason of the fact that he may still be prosecuted and put to the annoyance and expense of pleading his immunity by way of confession and avoidance. This is a detriment which the law does not recognize. There is a possibility that any citizen, however innocent, may be subjected to a civil or criminal prosecution, and put to the expense of defending himself, but unless such prosecution be malicious, he is remediless, except so far as a recovery of costs may partially indemnify him. He may even be convicted of a crime and suffer imprisonment or other punishment before his innocence is discovered, but that gives him no claim to indemnity against the State, or even against the prosecutor if the action of the latter was taken in good faith and in a reasonable belief that he was justified in so doing.

In the case under consideration, the grand jury was engaged in investigating certain alleged violations of the Interstate Commerce Act, among which was a charge against the Allegheny Valley Railway Company of transporting coal of the Union Coal Company from intermediate points to Buffalo, at less than the established rates between the terminal points, and a further charge of discriminating in favor of such coal company by rebates, drawbacks or commissions on its coal, by which it obtained transportation at less than the tariff rates. Brown, the witness, was the auditor of the road, whose duty it was to audit the accounts of the officers, and the money paid out by them. Having audited the accounts of the freight department during the time in question, he was asked whether he knew of any such discrimination in favor of the Union Coal Company, and declined to answer upon the ground that he would thereby incriminate himself.

As he had no apparent authority to make the forbidden contracts, to receive the money earned upon such contracts, or to allow or pay any rebates, drawbacks or commissions thereon, and was concerned only in auditing accounts, and passing vouchers for money paid by others, it is difficult to see how, under any construction of section 10 of the Interstate Commerce Act, he could be said to have willfully done anything, or aided or abetted others in doing anything, or in omitting to do anything, in violation of the act—his duty being merely to see that others had done what they purported to have done, and that the vouchers rendered by them were genuine. But, however this may be, it is entirely clear that he was not the chief or even a substantial offender against the law, and that his privilege was claimed for the purpose of shielding the railway or its officers from answering a charge of having violated its provisions. To say that, notwithstanding his immunity from punishment, he would incur personal odium and disgrace from answering these questions, seems too much like an abuse of language to be worthy of serious consideration. But, even if this were true, under the authorities above cited, he would still be compelled to answer, if the facts sought to be elucidated were material to the issue.

If, as was justly observed in the opinion of the court below, witnesses standing in Brown's position were at liberty to set up an immunity from testifying, the enforcement of the Interstate Commerce law or other analogous acts, wherein it is for the interest of both parties to conceal their misdoings, would become impossible, since it is only from the mouths of those having knowledge of the inhibited contracts that the facts can be ascertained. While the constitutional provision in question is justly regarded as one of the most valuable prerogatives of the citizen, its object is fully accomplished by the statutory immunity, and we are, therefore, of opinion that the witness was compellable to answer, and that the judgment of the court below must be affirmed.

MR. JUSTICE SHIRAS, with whom concurred MR. JUSTICE GRAY and MR. JUSTICE WHITE, dissenting.

It is too obvious to require argument that, when the people of the United States, in the Fifth Amendment to the Constitution, declared that no person should be compelled in any criminal case to be a witness against himself, it was their intention, not merely that every person should have such immunity, but that his right thereto should not be divested or impaired by any act of Congress.

Did Congress, by the act of February 11, 1893, which enacted that

> no person shall be excused from attending and testifying or from producing books, papers, tariffs, contracts, agreements and documents before the Interstate Commerce Commission, or in obedience to the subpoena of the commission, on the ground or for the reason that the testimony or evidence, documentary or otherwise, required of him may tend to criminate him or subject him to a penalty or forfeiture,

seek to *compel* any person to be a witness against himself? And, if so, was such provision of that act void because incompatible with the constitutional guaranty?

That it was the intention of the act to exact compulsory disclosure by every witness of all "testimony or evidence, documentary or otherwise, required of him," regardless of the fact that such disclosure might tend to criminate him or subject him to a penalty or forfeiture, was held by the court below, and such seems to be the plain meaning of the language of the act.

That the questions put to the witness, in the present case, tended to accuse and incriminate him, was sworn to by the witness himself, and was conceded or assumed by the court below. The refusal by the witness, in the exercise of his constitutional immunity, to answer the questions put, was held by the court to be an act of contempt, and the witness was ordered to pay a fine, and to be imprisoned until he should have answered the questions.

The validity of the reasons urged in defence of the action of the court below is the matter which this court has to consider. . . .

It is . . . now contended, and that is the novel feature of the present case, that the following provision in the act of February 11, 1893, removes the constitutional difficulty: "But no person shall be prosecuted or subjected to any penalty or forfeiture for or on account of any transaction, matter or thing, concerning which he may testify, or produce evidence, documentary or otherwise, before said commission." And it is surmised that this proviso was enacted in view of a suggestion to that effect in the opinion in the *Counselman* case.

It is, indeed, true that Mr. Justice Blatchford did say that

> no statute which leaves the party or witness subject to prosecution after he answers the criminating question put to him, can have the effect of supplanting the privilege conferred by the Constitution of the United States. Section 860 of the Revised Statutes does not supply a complete protection from all the perils against which the constitutional prohibition was designed to guard, and is not a full substitute for that prohibition. In view of the constitutional provision, a statutory enactment, to be valid, must afford absolute immunity against future prosecution for the offence to which the question relates;

and it may be inferred from this language that there might be framed a legislative substitute for the constitutional privilege which would legally empower a court to compel an unwilling witness to criminate himself. But the case did not call for such expression of opinion, nor did Mr. Justice Blatchford undertake to suggest the form of such an enactment. Indeed, such a suggestion would not have comported with his previous remarks, above cited, that

> legislation cannot detract from the privilege afforded by the Constitution. It would be quite another thing if the Constitution had provided that no person shall be compelled, in any criminal case, to be a witness against himself, unless it should be provided by statute that criminating evidence extracted from a witness against his will should not be used against him.

But a mere act of Congress cannot amend the Constitution, even if it should engraft thereon such a proviso.

Is, then, the undeniable repugnancy that exists between the constitutional guaranty and the compulsory provisions of the act of February 11, 1893, overcome by the proviso relieving the witness from prosecution and from any penalty or forfeiture "for or on account of any transaction, matter or thing, concerning which he may testify or produce evidence?"

As already said, the very fact that the founders of our institutions, by making the immunity an express provision of the Constitution, disclosed an intention to protect it from legislative attack, creates a presumption against *any* act professing to dispense with the constitutional privilege. It may not be said that, by no form of enactment, can Congress supply an adequate substitute, but doubtfulness of its entire sufficiency, uncertainty of its meaning and effect, will be fatal defects.

What, then, is meant by the clause in this act that *"no person shall be prosecuted . . .* for or on account of any transaction, matter or thing, concerning which he may testify, or produce evidence, documentary or otherwise?"* How possibly can effect be given to this provision, if taken literally? If a given person is charged with a wilful violation of the Interstate Commerce Act, how can the prosecuting officers or the grand juries know whether he has been examined as a witness concerning the same matter before the commission or some court? Nor can the accused himself necessarily know what particular charge has been brought against him, until an indictment has been found. But when an indictment has been found, and the accused has been called upon to plead to it, he assuredly has been *prosecuted.* So that all that can be said is, that the witness is *not* protected, by the provision in question, from being *prosecuted,* but that he has been furnished with a good plea to the indictment, which will secure his acquittal. But is that true? Not unless the plea is sustained by competent evidence. His condition, then, is that he has been prosecuted, been compelled, presumably, to furnish bail, and put to the trouble and expense of employing counsel and furnishing the evidence to make good his plea. It is no reply to this to say that his condition, in those respects, is no worse than that of any other innocent man, who may be wrongfully charged. The latter has not been compelled, on penalty of fine and imprisonment, to disclose under oath facts which have furnished a clue to the offence with which he is charged.

Nor is it a matter of perfect assurance that a person who has compulsorily testified, before the commission, grand jury, or court, will be able, if subsequently indicted for some matter or thing concerning which he testified, to procure the evidence that will be necessary to maintain his plea. No provision is made in the law itself for the preservation of the evidence. Witnesses may die or become insane, and papers and records may be destroyed by accident or design.

Again, what is the meaning of the clause of the act that "no person so testifying shall be exempt from prosecution and punishment for perjury committed in so testifying?" The implication would seem to be that, except for such a clause, perjury could not be imputed to a witness who had been compelled to so testify. However that may be, and whether or not the clause is surplusage, it compels attention to the unfortunate situation in which the witness is placed by the provisions of this act. If he declines to testify on the ground that his answer may incriminate himself, he is fined and imprisoned. If he submits to answer, he is liable to be indicted for perjury by either or both of the parties to the controversy. His position in this respect is not that of ordinary witnesses testifying under the compulsion of a subpoena. His case is that of a person who is exempted by the Constitution from testifying at all in the matter. He is told, by the act of Congress, that he must nevertheless testify, but that he shall be protected from any prosecution, penalty or forfeiture by reason of so testifying. But he is subjected to the hazard of a charge of perjury, whether such charge be rightfully or wrongfully made. It does not do to say that other witnesses may be so charged, because if the privilege of silence, under the constitutional immunity, had not been taken away, this witness would not have testified, and could not have been subjected to a charge of perjury. . . .

Much stress was laid in the argument on the supposed importance of this provision in enabling the commission and the courts to enforce the salutary provisions of the Interstate Commerce Act. This, at the best, is a dangerous argument, and should not be listened to by a court, to the detriment of the constitutional rights of the citizen. If, indeed, experience has shown, or shall show, that one or more of the provisions of the Constitution has become unsuited to affairs as they now exist, and unduly fetters the courts in the enforcement of useful laws, the remedy must be found in the right of the nation to amend the fundamental law, and not in appeals to the courts to substitute for a constitutional guaranty the doubtful and uncertain provisions of an experimental statute.

It is certainly speaking within bounds to say that the effect of the provision in question, as a protection to the witness, is purely conjectural. No court can foresee all the results and consequences that may follow from enforcing this law in any given case. It is quite *certain* that the witness is *compelled* to testify against himself. Can any court be *certain* that a sure and sufficient substitute for the constitutional immunity has been supplied by this act; and if there be room for reasonable doubt, is not the conclusion an obvious and necessary one? . . .

A final observation, which ought not to be necessary, but which seems to be called for by the tenor of some of the arguments that have been pressed on the court, is that the constitutional privilege was intended as a shield for the innocent as well as for the guilty. A moment's thought will show that a perfectly innocent person may expose himself to accusation, and even condemnation, by being compelled to disclose facts and circumstances known only to himself, but which, when once disclosed, he may be entirely unable to explain as consistent with innocence.

But surely no apology for the Constitution, as it exists, is called for. The task of the courts is performed if the Constitution is sustained in its entirety, in its letter and spirit.

The judgment of the Circuit Court should be reversed and the cause remanded with directions to discharge the accused from custody.

MR. JUSTICE FIELD dissenting.

I am unable to concur with my associates in the affirmance of the judgment of the Circuit Court of the United States for the Western District of Pennsylvania. . . .

The Fifth Amendment of the Constitution of the United States gives absolute protection to a person called as a witness in a criminal case against the compulsory enforcement of any criminating testimony against himself. He is not only protected from any criminating testimony against himself relating to the offence under investigation, but also relating to any act which may lead to a criminal prosecution therefor.

No substitute for the protection contemplated by the amendment would be sufficient were its operation less extensive and efficient.

The constitutional amendment contemplates that the witness shall be shielded from prosecution by reason of any expressions forced from him whilst he was a witness in a criminal case. It was intended that against such attempted enforcement he might invoke, if desired, and obtain, the shield of absolute silence. No different protection from that afforded by the amendment can be substituted in place of it. The force and extent of the constitutional guarantee are in no respect to be weakened or modified, and the like consideration may be urged with reference to all the clauses and provisions of the Constitution designed for the peace and security of the citizen in the enjoyment of rights or privileges which the Constitution intended to grant and protect. No phrases or words of any provision, securing such rights or privileges to the citizen, in the Constitution are to be qualified, limited or frittered away. All are to be construed liberally that they may have the widest and most ample effect.

No compromise of phrases can be made by which one of less sweeping character and less protective force in its influences can be substituted for any of them. The citizen cannot be denied the protection of absolute silence which he may invoke, not only with reference to the offence charged, but with respect to any act of criminality which may be suggested.

The constitutional guarantee is not fully secured by simply exempting the witness from prosecution for the designated offence involved in his answer as a witness. It extends to exemption from not only prosecution for the offence under consideration but from prosecution for any offence to which the testimony produced may lead.

The witness is entitled to the shield of absolute silence respecting either. It thus exempts him from prosecution beyond the protection conferred by the act of Congress. It exempts him where the statute might subject him to self-incrimination.

The amendment also protects him from all compulsory testimony which would expose him to infamy and disgrace, though the facts disclosed might not lead to a criminal prosecution. It is contended, indeed, that it was not the object of the constitutional safeguard to protect the witness against infamy and disgrace. It is urged that its sole purpose was to protect him against incriminating testimony with reference to the offence under prosecution. But I do not agree that such limited protection was all that was secured. As stated by counsel of the appellant,

> it is entirely possible, and certainly not impossible, that the framers of the Constitution reasoned that in bestowing upon witnesses in criminal cases the privilege of silence when in danger of self-incrimination, they would at the same time save him *in all such cases* from the shame and infamy of confessing disgraceful crimes and thus preserve to him some measure of self-respect. . . .

It is true, as counsel observes, that

> both the safeguard of the Constitution and the common law rule spring alike from that sentiment of *personal self-respect, liberty, independence and dignity* which has inhabited the breasts of English speaking peoples for centuries, and to save which they have always been ready to sacrifice many governmental facilities and conveniences. In scarcely anything has that sentiment been more manifest than in the abhorrence felt at the legal compulsion upon witnesses to make concessions which must cover the witness with lasting shame and leave him degraded both in his own eyes and those of others. What can be more abhorrent . . . than to compel a man who has fought his way from obscurity to dignity and honor to reveal crimes of which he had repented and of which the world was ignorant? . . .

Every one is protected by the common law from compulsory incrimination of himself. This protection is a part of that general security which the common law affords against defamation, that is, against malicious and false imputations upon one's character, as it defends against injurious assaults upon one's person, even though the defamation is created by publication made by himself under compulsion. The defamation arising from self-incrimination may be equally injurious as if originating purely from the maliciousness of others. The reprobation of compulsory self-incrimination is an established doctrine of our civilized society. As stated by appellant's counsel, it is the "result of the long struggle between the opposing forces of the spirit of individual liberty on the one hand and the collective power of the State on the other." As such, it should be condemned with great earnestness.

The essential and inherent cruelty of compelling a man to expose his own guilt is obvious to every one, and needs no illustration. It is plain to every person who gives the subject a moment's thought.

A sense of personal degradation in being compelled to incriminate one's self must create a feeling of abhorrence in the community at its attempted enforcement.

The counsel of the appellant justly observes on this subject, as on many of the proceedings taken to escape from the enforcement of the constitutional and legal protection, established to guard a citizen from any unnecessary restraints upon his person, action or speech, that

> the proud sense of personal independence which is the basis of the most valued qualities of a free citizen is sustained and cultivated by the consciousness that there are limits which even the State cannot pass in tearing open the secrets of his bosom. The limit which the law carefully assigns to the power to make searches and seizures proceeds from the same source. . . .

The order remanding the appellant should, therefore, in my judgment, be reversed, and an order entered that he be discharged from custody and be set at liberty.

As the early constitutional cases indicate, the analytic foundation of the fifth amendment is constructed from three highly dependent variables:

1. The policies that inform the privilege,
2. The appropriate scope of the privilege in light of the relevant policies, and
3. The extent of immunity necessary to discharge the policies that inform the privilege.

As you think about the early cases and the modern conception of the fifth amendment, try to evaluate each variable separately and then in relation to the other two. The modern understanding of the fifth amendment is reflected in the next case.

KASTIGAR v. UNITED STATES

Certiorari to the United States Court of Appeals for the Ninth Circuit
406 U.S. 441 (1972)

MR. JUSTICE POWELL delivered the opinion of the Court.

This case presents the question whether the United States Government may compel testimony from an unwilling witness, who invokes the Fifth Amendment privilege against compulsory self-incrimination, by conferring on the witness immunity from use of the compelled testimony in subsequent criminal proceedings, as well as immunity from use of evidence derived from the testimony.

Petitioners were subpoenaed to appear before a United States grand jury in the Central District of California on February 4, 1971. The Government believed that petitioners were likely to assert their Fifth Amendment privilege. Prior to the scheduled appearances, the Government applied to the District Court for an order directing petitioners to answer questions and produce evidence before the grand jury under a grant of immunity conferred pursuant to 18 U.S.C. §§6002-6003. Petitioners opposed issuance of the order, contending primarily that the scope of the immunity provided by the statute was not coextensive with the scope of the privilege against self-incrimination, and therefore was not sufficient to supplant the privilege and compel their testimony. The District Court rejected this contention, and ordered petitioners to appear before the grand jury and answer its questions under the grant of immunity.

Petitioners appeared but refused to answer questions, asserting their privilege against compulsory self-incrimination. They were brought before the District Court, and each persisted in his refusal to answer the grand jury's questions, notwithstanding the grant of immunity. The court found both in contempt, and committed them to the custody of the Attorney General until either they answered the grand jury's questions or the term of the grand jury expired. The Court of Appeals for the Ninth Circuit affirmed. Stewart v. United States, 440 F.2d 954 (C.A.9 1971). This Court granted certiorari to resolve the important question whether testimony may be compelled by granting immunity from the use of compelled testimony and evidence derived therefrom ("use and derivative use" immunity), or whether it is necessary to grant immunity from prosecution for offenses to which compelled testimony relates ("transactional" immunity). . . .

I

The power of government to compel persons to testify in court or before grand juries and other governmental agencies is firmly established in Anglo-American jurisprudence.[2] The power with respect to courts was established by statute in England as early as 1562,[3] and Lord Bacon observed in 1612 that all subjects owed the King their "knowledge and discovery."[4] While it is not clear when grand juries first resorted to compulsory process to secure the attendance and testimony of witnesses, the general common-law principle that "the public has a right to every man's evidence" was considered an "indubitable certainty" that "cannot be denied" by 1742.[5] The power to compel testimony, and the corresponding duty to testify, are recognized in the Sixth Amendment requirements that an accused be confronted with the witnesses against him, and have compulsory process for obtaining witnesses in his favor. The first Congress recognized the testimonial duty in the Judiciary Act of 1789, which provided for compulsory attendance of witnesses in the federal courts.[6] . . .

But the power to compel testimony is not absolute. There are a number of exemptions from the testimonial duty, the most important of which is the Fifth Amendment privilege against compulsory self-incrimination. The privilege reflects a complex of our fundamental values and aspirations, and marks an important advance in the development of our liberty. It can be asserted in any proceeding, civil or criminal, administrative or judicial, investigatory or adjudicatory; and it protects against any disclosures that the witness reasonably believes could be used in a criminal prosecution or could lead to other evidence that might be so used. This Court has been zealous to safeguard the values that underlie the privilege.

---

2. For a concise history of testimonial compulsion prior to the adoption of our Constitution, see 8 J. Wigmore, Evidence §2190 (J. McNaughton rev. 1961). See Ullmann v. United States, 350 U.S. 422, 439 n.15 (1956); Blair v. United States, 250 U.S. 273 (1919).

3. Statute of Elizabeth, 5 Eliz. 1, c. 9, §12 (1562).

4. Countess of Shrewsbury's Case, 2 How. St. Tr. 769, 778 (1612).

5. See the parliamentary debate on the Bill to Indemnity Evidence, particularly the remarks of the Duke of Argyle and Lord Chancellor Hardwicke, reported in 12 T. Hansard, Parliamentary History of England 675, 693 (1812). See also Piemonte v. United States, 367 U.S. 556, 559 n.2 (1961); Ullmann v. United States, supra, at 439 n. 15; Brown v. Walker, 161 U.S. 591, 600 (1896).

6. 1 Stat. 73, 88-89.

Immunity statutes, which have historical roots deep in Anglo-American jurisprudence, are not incompatible with these values. Rather, they seek a rational accommodation between the imperatives of the privilege and the legitimate demands of government to compel citizens to testify. The existence of these statutes reflects the importance of testimony, and the fact that many offenses are of such a character that the only persons capable of giving useful testimony are those implicated in the crime. Indeed, their origins were in the context of such offenses, and their primary use has been to investigate such offenses. Congress included immunity statutes in many of the regulatory measures adopted in the first half of this century. Indeed, prior to the enactment of the statute under consideration in this case, there were in force over 50 federal immunity statutes.[17] In addition, every State in the Union, as well as the District of Columbia and Puerto Rico, has one or more such statutes.[18] The commentators, and this Court on several occasions, have characterized immunity statutes as essential to the effective enforcement of various criminal statutes. As Mr. Justice Frankfurter observed, speaking for the Court in Ullmann v. United States, 350 U.S. 422 (1956), such statutes have "become part of our constitutional fabric." Id., at 438.

II

Petitioners contend, first, that the Fifth Amendment's privilege against compulsory self-incrimination, which is that "[n]o person . . . shall be compelled in any criminal case to be a witness against himself," deprives Congress of power to enact laws that compel self-incrimination, even if complete immunity from prosecution is granted prior to the compulsion of the incriminatory testimony. In other words, petitioners assert that no immunity statute, however drawn, can afford a lawful basis for compelling incriminatory testimony. They ask us to reconsider and overrule Brown v. Walker, 161 U.S. 591 (1896), and Ullmann v. United States, supra, decisions that uphold the constitutionality of immunity statutes. We find no merit to this contention and reaffirm the decisions in Brown and Ullmann.

17. For a listing of these statutes, see National Commission on Reform of Federal Criminal Laws, Working Papers, 1444-1445 (1970).
18. For a listing of these statutes, see 8 Wigmore, supra, n.2, §2281, at 495 n. 11.

III

Petitioners' second contention is that the scope of immunity provided by the federal witness immunity statute, 18 U.S.C. §6002, is not coextensive with the scope of the Fifth Amendment privilege against compulsory self-incrimination, and therefore is not sufficient to supplant the privilege and compel testimony over a claim of the privilege. The statute provides that when a witness is compelled by district court order to testify over a claim of the privilege:

> the witness may not refuse to comply with the order on the basis of his privilege against self-incrimination; but no testimony or other information compelled under the order (or any information directly or indirectly derived from such testimony or other information) may be used against the witness in any criminal case, except a prosecution for perjury, giving a false statement, or otherwise failing to comply with the order.[23]

The constitutional inquiry, rooted in logic and history, as well as in the decisions of this Court, is whether the immunity granted under this statute is coextensive with the scope of the privilege. If so, petitioners' refusals to answer based on the privilege were unjustified, and the judgments of contempt were proper, for the grant of immunity has removed the dangers against which the privilege protects. Brown v. Walker, supra. If, on the other hand, the immunity granted is not as comprehensive as the protection afforded by the privilege, petitioners were justified in refusing to answer, and the judgments of contempt must be vacated.

Petitioners draw a distinction between statutes that provide transactional immunity and those that provide, as does the statute before us, immunity from use and derivative use. They contend that a statute must at a minimum grant full transactional immunity in order to be coextensive with the scope of the privilege. In support of this contention, they rely on Counselman v. Hitchcock, 142 U.S. 547 (1892), the first case in which this Court considered a constitutional challenge to an immunity statute. . . . In the course of its opinion, the Court made the following statement, on which petitioners heavily rely:

> We are clearly of opinion that no statute which leaves the party or witness subject to prosecution after he answers the criminating question put to him, can have the effect of supplanting the privilege conferred by the Constitution of the United States. [The immunity statute under consideration] does not supply a complete protection from all the perils against

23. For other provisions of the 1970 Act relative to immunity of witnesses, see 18 U.S.C. §§6001-6005.

which the constitutional prohibition was designed to guard, and is not a full substitute for that prohibition. In view of the constitutional provision, a statutory enactment, to be valid, must afford absolute immunity against future prosecution for the offence to which the question relates.

Sixteen days after the *Counselman* decision, a new immunity bill was introduced by Senator Cullom, who urged that enforcement of the Interstate Commerce Act would be impossible in the absence of an effective immunity statute. The bill, which became the Compulsory Testimony Act of 1893, was drafted specifically to meet the broad language in *Counselman* set forth above. The new Act removed the privilege against self-incrimination in hearings before the Interstate Commerce Commission and provided that: "no person shall be prosecuted or subjected to any penalty or forfeiture for or on account of any transaction, matter or thing, concerning which he may testify, or produce evidence, documentary or otherwise. . . ." Act of Feb. 11, 1893, 27 Stat. 444. This transactional immunity statute became the basic form for the numerous federal immunity statutes until 1970, when, after re-examining applicable constitutional principles and the adequacy of existing law, Congress enacted the statute here under consideration.[36] The new statute, which does not "afford [the] absolute immunity against future prosecution" referred to in *Counselman*, was drafted to meet what Congress judged to be the conceptual basis of *Counselman*, as elaborated in subsequent decisions of the Court, namely, that immunity from the use of compelled testimony and evidence derived therefrom is coextensive with the scope of the privilege.

36. The statute is a product of careful study and consideration by the National Commission on Reform of Federal Criminal Laws, as well as by Congress. The Commission recommended legislation to reform the federal immunity laws. The recommendation served as the model for this statute. In commenting on its proposal in a special report to the President, the Commission said:

> We are satisfied that our substitution of immunity from use for immunity from prosecution meets constitutional requirements for overcoming the claim of privilege. Immunity from use is the only consequence flowing from a violation of the individual's constitutional right to be protected from unreasonable searches and seizures, his constitutional right to counsel, and his constitutional right not to be coerced into confessing. The proposed immunity is thus of the same scope as that frequently, even though unintentionally, conferred as the result of constitutional violations by law enforcement officers.

Second Interim Report of the National Commission on Reform of Federal Criminal Laws, Mar. 17, 1969, Working Papers of the Commission, 1446 (1970).

The Commission's recommendation was based in large part on a comprehensive study of immunity and the relevant decisions of this Court prepared for the Commission by Prof. Robert G. Dixon, Jr., of the George Washington University Law Center, and transmitted to the President with the recommendations of the Commission. See National Commission on Reform of Federal Criminal Laws, Working Papers, 1405-1444 (1970).

The statute's explicit proscription of the use in any criminal case of "testimony or other information compelled under the order (or any information directly or indirectly derived from such testimony or other information)" is consonant with Fifth Amendment standards. We hold that such immunity from use and derivative use is coextensive with the scope of the privilege against self-incrimination, and therefore is sufficient to compel testimony over a claim of the privilege. While a grant of immunity must afford protection commensurate with that afforded by the privilege, it need not be broader. Transactional immunity, which accords full immunity from prosecution for the offense to which the compelled testimony relates, affords the witness considerably broader protection than does the Fifth Amendment privilege. The privilege has never been construed to mean that one who invokes it cannot subsequently be prosecuted. Its sole concern is to afford protection against being "forced to give testimony leading to the infliction of 'penalties affixed to . . . criminal acts.' "[38] Immunity from the use of compelled testimony, as well as evidence derived directly and indirectly therefrom, affords this protection. It prohibits the prosecutorial authorities from using the compelled testimony in *any* respect, and it therefore insures that the testimony cannot lead to the infliction of criminal penalties on the witness.

Our holding is consistent with the conceptual basis of *Counselman*. The *Counselman* statute, as construed by the Court, was plainly deficient in its failure to prohibit the use against the immunized witness of evidence derived from his compelled testimony. The Court repeatedly emphasized this deficiency, noting that the statute: "could not, and would not, prevent the use of his testimony to search out other testimony to be used in evidence against him or his property, in a criminal proceeding. . . ." 142 U.S., at 564. . . . The broad language in *Counselman* relied upon by petitioners was unnecessary to the Court's decision, and cannot be considered binding authority. . . .

In Murphy v. Waterfront Comm'n, 378 U.S. 52 (1964), the Court carefully considered immunity from use of compelled testimony and evidence derived therefrom. The *Murphy* petitioners were subpoenaed to testify at a hearing conducted by the Waterfront Commission of New York Harbor. After refusing to answer certain questions on the ground that the answers might tend to incriminate them, petitioners were granted immunity from prosecution under the laws of New Jersey and New York. They continued to refuse to testify, however, on the ground that their answers might tend to incriminate them under federal law, to which the

---

38. Ullmann v. United States, 350 U.S., at 438-439, quoting Boyd v. United States, 116 U.S., at 634. See Knapp v. Schweitzer, 357 U.S. 371, 380 (1958).

immunity did not purport to extend. They were adjudged in civil contempt, and that judgment was affirmed by the New Jersey Supreme Court.

The issue before the Court in *Murphy* was whether New Jersey and New York could compel the witnesses, whom these States had immunized from prosecution under their laws, to give testimony that might then be used to convict them of a federal crime. Since New Jersey and New York had not purported to confer immunity from federal prosecution, the Court was faced with the question what limitations the Fifth Amendment privilege imposed on the prosecutorial powers of the Federal Government, a nonimmunizing sovereign. After undertaking an examination of the policies and purposes of the privilege, the Court overturned the rule that one jurisdiction within our federal structure may compel a witness to give testimony which could be used to convict him of a crime in another jurisdiction.[42] The Court held that the privilege protects state witnesses against incrimination under federal as well as state law, and federal witnesses against incrimination under state as well as federal law. Applying this principle to the state immunity legislation before it, the Court held the constitutional rule to be that:

> [A] state witness may not be compelled to give testimony which may be incriminating under federal law unless the compelled testimony and its fruits cannot be used in any manner by federal officials in connection with a criminal prosecution against him. We conclude, moreover, that in order to implement this constitutional rule and accommodate the interests of the State and Federal Governments in investigating and prosecuting crime, the Federal Government must be prohibited from making any such use of compelled testimony and its fruits.[43]

The Court emphasized that this rule left the state witness and the Federal Government, against which the witness had immunity only from the *use* of the compelled testimony and evidence derived therefrom, "in substantially the same position as if the witness had claimed his privilege in the absence of a state grant of immunity." Ibid.

42. Reconsideration of the rule that the Fifth Amendment privilege does not protect a witness in one jurisdiction against being compelled to give testimony that could be used to convict him in another jurisdiction was made necessary by the decision in Malloy v. Hogan, 378 U.S. 1 (1964), in which the Court held the Fifth Amendment privilege applicable to the States through the Fourteenth Amendment. Murphy v. Waterfront Comm'n, 378 U.S., at 57.

43. At this point the Court added the following note: "Once a defendant demonstrates that he has testified, under a state grant of immunity, to matters related to the federal prosecution, the federal authorities have the burden of showing that their evidence is not tainted by establishing that they had an independent, legitimate source for the disputed evidence." Id., at 79 n.18. If transactional immunity had been deemed to be the "constitutional rule" there could be no federal prosecution.

It is true that in *Murphy* the Court was not presented with the precise question presented by this case, whether a jurisdiction seeking to compel testimony may do so by granting only use and derivative-use immunity, for New Jersey and New York had granted petitioners transactional immunity. The Court heretofore has not squarely confronted this question, because post-*Counselman* immunity statutes reaching the Court either have followed the pattern of the 1893 Act in providing transactional immunity, or have been found deficient for failure to prohibit the use of all evidence derived from compelled testimony. But both the reasoning of the Court in *Murphy* and the result reached compel the conclusion that use and derivative-use immunity is constitutionally sufficient to compel testimony over a claim of the privilege. Since the privilege is fully applicable and its scope is the same whether invoked in a state or in a federal jurisdiction,[47] the *Murphy* conclusion that a prohibition on use and derivative use secures a witness' Fifth Amendment privilege against infringement by the Federal Government demonstrates that immunity from use and derivative use is coextensive with the scope of the privilege. As the *Murphy* Court noted, immunity from use and derivative use "leaves the witness and the Federal Government in substantially the same position as if the witness had claimed his privilege" in the absence of a grant of immunity. The *Murphy* Court was concerned solely with the danger of incrimination under federal law, and held that immunity from use and derivative use was sufficient to displace the danger. This protection coextensive with the privilege is the degree of protection that the Constitution requires, and is all that the Constitution requires even against the jurisdiction compelling testimony by granting immunity.

IV

Although an analysis of prior decisions and the purpose of the Fifth Amendment privilege indicates that use and derivative-use immunity is coextensive with the privilege, we must consider additional arguments advanced by petitioners against the sufficiency of such immunity. We start from the premise, repeatedly affirmed by this Court, that an appropriately broad immunity grant is compatible with the Constitution.

Petitioners argue that use and derivative-use immunity will not adequately protect a witness from various possible incriminating uses of the

---

47. In Malloy v. Hogan, 378 U.S., at 10-11, the Court held that the same standards would determine the extent or scope of the privilege in state and in federal proceedings, because the same substantive guarantee of the Bill of Rights is involved. The *Murphy* Court emphasized that the scope of the privilege is the same in state and in federal proceedings. Murphy v. Waterfront Comm'n, 378 U.S., at 79.

compelled testimony: for example, the prosecutor or other law enforcement officials may obtain leads, names of witnesses, or other information not otherwise available that might result in a prosecution. It will be difficult and perhaps impossible, the argument goes, to identify, by testimony or cross-examination, the subtle ways in which the compelled testimony may disadvantage a witness, especially in the jurisdiction granting the immunity.

This argument presupposes that the statute's prohibition will prove impossible to enforce. The statute provides a sweeping proscription of any use, direct or indirect, of the compelled testimony and any information derived therefrom: "[N]o testimony or other information compelled under the order (or any information directly or indirectly derived from such testimony or other information) may be used against the witness in any criminal case." This total prohibition on use provides a comprehensive safeguard, barring the use of compelled testimony as an "investigatory lead,"[50] and also barring the use of any evidence obtained by focusing investigation on a witness as a result of his compelled disclosures.

A person accorded this immunity under 18 U.S.C. §6002, and subsequently prosecuted, is not dependent for the preservation of his rights upon the integrity and good faith of the prosecuting authorities. As stated in *Murphy*: "Once a defendant demonstrates that he has testified, under a state grant of immunity, to matters related to the federal prosecution, the federal authorities have the burden of showing that their evidence is not tainted by establishing that they had an independent, legitimate source for the disputed evidence." 378 U.S., at 79 n.18. This burden of proof, which we reaffirm as appropriate, is not limited to a negation of taint; rather, it imposes on the prosecution the affirmative duty to prove that the evidence it proposes to use is derived from a legitimate source wholly independent of the compelled testimony.

This is very substantial protection, commensurate with that resulting from invoking the privilege itself. The privilege assures that a citizen is not compelled to incriminate himself by his own testimony. It usually operates to allow a citizen to remain silent when asked a question requiring an incriminatory answer. This statute, which operates after a witness has given incriminatory testimony, affords the same protection by assuring that the compelled testimony can in no way lead to the infliction of criminal penalties. The statute, like the Fifth Amendment, grants neither pardon nor amnesty. Both the statute and the Fifth Amendment allow the government to prosecute using evidence from legitimate independent sources.

The statutory proscription is analogous to the Fifth Amendment

50. See, e.g., Albertson v. Subversive Activities Control Board, 382 U.S., at 80.

requirement in cases of coerced confessions.[52] A coerced confession, as revealing of leads as testimony given in exchange for immunity,[53] is inadmissible in a criminal trial, but it does not bar prosecution.[54] Moreover, a defendant against whom incriminating evidence has been obtained through a grant of immunity may be in a stronger position at trial than a defendant who asserts a Fifth Amendment coerced-confession claim. One raising a claim under this statute need only show that he testified under a grant of immunity in order to shift to the government the heavy burden of proving that all of the evidence it proposes to use was derived from legitimate independent sources.[55] On the other hand, a defendant raising a coerced-confession claim under the Fifth Amendment must first prevail in a voluntariness hearing before his confession and evidence derived from it become inadmissible.[56]

There can be no justification in reason or policy for holding that the Constitution requires an amnesty grant where, acting pursuant to statute and accompanying safeguards, testimony is compelled in exchange for immunity from use and derivative use when no such amnesty is required where the government, acting without colorable right, coerces a defendant into incriminating himself.

We conclude that the immunity provided by 18 U.S.C. §6002 leaves the witness and the prosecutorial authorities in substantially the same position as if the witness had claimed the Fifth Amendment privilege. The immunity therefore is coextensive with the privilege and suffices to supplant it. The judgment of the Court of Appeals for the Ninth Circuit accordingly is affirmed.

MR. JUSTICE BRENNAN and MR. JUSTICE REHNQUIST took no part in the consideration or decision of this case.

MR. JUSTICE DOUGLAS, dissenting.

The Self-Incrimination Clause says: "No person . . . shall be compelled in any criminal case to be a witness against himself." I see no answer to the proposition that he is such a witness when only "use" immunity is granted.

52. Adams v. Maryland, 347 U.S., at 181; Bram v. United States, 168 U.S. 532, 542 (1897).

53. As Mr. Justice White, concurring in *Murphy*, pointed out: "A coerced confession is as revealing of leads as testimony given in exchange for immunity and indeed is excluded in part because it is compelled incrimination in violation of the privilege. Malloy v. Hogan, [378 U.S. 1, 7-8]; Spano v. New York, 360 U.S. 315; Bram v. United States, 168 U.S. 532." 378 U.S., at 103.

54. Jackson v. Denno, 378 U.S. 368 (1964).

55. See supra, at 460; Brief for the United States 37; Cf. Chapman v. California, 386 U.S. 18 (1967).

56. Jackson v. Denno, supra.

My views on the question of the scope of immunity that is necessary to force a witness to give up his guarantee against self-incrimination contained in the Fifth Amendment are so well known, see Ullmann v. United States, 350 U.S. 422, 440 (dissenting), . . . that I need not write at length.

In Counselman v. Hitchcock, 142 U.S. 547, 586, the Court adopted the transactional immunity test: "In view of the constitutional provision, a statutory enactment, to be valid, must afford absolute immunity against future prosecution for the offense to which the question relates." Id., at 586. In Brown v. Walker, 161 U.S. 591, a case involving another federal prosecution, the immunity statute provided that the witness would be protected "on account of any transaction . . . concerning which he may testify." Id., at 594. The Court held that the immunity offered was coterminous with the privilege and that the witness could therefore be compelled to testify, a ruling that made "transactional immunity" part of the fabric of our constitutional law. . . .

This Court, however, apparently believes that *Counselman* and its progeny were overruled sub silentio in Murphy v. Waterfront Comm'n, 378 U.S. 52. *Murphy* involved state witnesses, granted transactional immunity under state law, who refused to testify for fear of subsequent federal prosecution. We held that the testimony in question could be compelled, but that the Federal Government would be barred from using any of the testimony, or its fruits, in a subsequent federal prosecution.

Murphy overruled, not *Counselman*, but Feldman v. United States, 322 U.S. 487, which had held "that one jurisdiction within our federal structure may compel a witness to give testimony which could be used to convict him of a crime in another jurisdiction." Murphy v. Waterfront Comm'n, supra, at 77. But *Counselman*, as the *Murphy* Court recognized, "said nothing about the problem of incrimination under the law of another sovereign." Id., at 72. That problem is one of federalism, as to require transactional immunity between jurisdictions might "deprive a state of the right to prosecute a violation of its criminal law on the basis of another state's grant of immunity [a result which] would be gravely in derogation of its sovereignty and obstructive of its administration of justice." United States ex rel. Catena v. Elias, 449 F.2d 40, 44 (C.A.3 1971). Moreover, as Mr. Justice Brennan has pointed out, the threat of future prosecution "substantial when a single jurisdiction both compels incriminating testimony and brings a later prosecution, may fade when the jurisdiction bringing the prosecution differs from the jurisdiction that compelled the testimony. Concern over informal and undetected exchange of information is also correspondingly less when two different jurisdictions are involved." Piccirillo v. New York, 400 U.S., at 568 (dissenting).

None of these factors apply when the threat of prosecution is from the jurisdiction seeking to compel the testimony, which is the situation we faced in *Counselman*, and which we face today. The irrelevance of *Murphy* to such a situation was made clear in Albertson v. Subversive Activities Control Board, 382 U.S. 70, in which the Court struck down an immunity statute because it failed to measure up to the standards set forth in *Counselman*. Inasmuch as no interjurisdictional problems presented themselves, *Murphy* was not even cited. That is further proof that *Murphy* was not thought significantly to undercut *Counselman*.[1] See . . . Mansfield, The Albertson Case: Conflict Between the Privilege Against Self-Incrimination and the Government's Need for Information, 1966 Sup. Ct. Rev. 103, 164.

If, as some have thought, the Bill of Rights contained only "counsels of moderation" from which courts and legislatures could deviate according to their conscience or discretion, then today's contraction of the Self-Incrimination Clause of the Fifth Amendment would be understandable. But that has not been true, starting with Chief Justice Marshall's opinion in United States v. Burr, 25 F. Cas. 38 (No. 14692e) (C.C.Va.), where he ruled that the reach of the Fifth Amendment was so broad as to make the privilege applicable when there was a mere possibility of a criminal charge being made.

The Court said in Hale v. Henkel, 201 U.S. 43, 67, that "if the criminality has already been taken away, the Amendment ceases to apply." In other words, the immunity granted is adequate if it operates as a complete pardon for the offense. Brown v. Walker, 161 U.S., at 595. That is the true measure of the Self-Incrimination Clause. As Mr. Justice

---

1. In Albertson v. Subversive Activities Control Board, 382 U.S. 70, the Court was faced with a Fifth Amendment challenge to the Communist registration provision of the Subversive Activities Control Act of 1950, 64 Stat. 987. We held that the provision violated the prospective registrant's privilege against self-incrimination, and that the registration provision was not saved by a so-called "immunity statute" (§4(f)) which prohibited the introduction into evidence in any criminal prosecution of the fact of registration under the Act. The Court's analysis of this immunity provision rested solely on *Counselman*:

> In Counselman v. Hitchcock, 142 U.S. 547, decided in 1892, the Court held "that no [immunity] statute which leaves the party or witness subject to prosecution after he answers the criminating question put to him, can have the effect of supplanting the privilege, . . ." and that such a statute is valid only if it supplies "a complete protection from all the perils against which the constitutional prohibition was designed to guard . . ." by affording "absolute immunity against future prosecution for the offence to which the question relates." Id., at 585-586. *Measured by these standards*, the immunity granted by §4(f) is not complete."

382 U.S., at 80. (Emphasis added.)

Thus, the *Albertson* Court, which could have struck the statute by employing the test approved today, went well beyond, and measured the statute solely against the more restrictive standards of *Counselman*.

Brennan has stated: "[U]se immunity literally misses half the point of the privilege, for it permits the compulsion without removing the criminality." Piccirillo v. New York, supra, at 567 (dissenting).

As Mr. Justice Brennan has also said:

> Transactional immunity . . . provides the individual with an assurance that he is not testifying about matters for which he may later be prosecuted. No question arises of tracing the use or non-use of information gleaned from the witness' compelled testimony. The sole question presented to a court is whether the subsequent prosecution is related to the substance of the compelled testimony. Both witness and government know precisely where they stand. Respect for law is furthered when the individual knows his position and is not left suspicious that a later prosecution was actually the fruit of his compelled testimony. 400 U.S., at 568-569 (dissenting).

When we allow the prosecution to offer only "use" immunity we allow it to grant far less than it has taken away. For while the precise testimony that is compelled may not be used, leads from that testimony may be pursued and used to convict the witness.[2] My view is that the framers put it beyond the power of Congress to *compel* anyone to confess his crimes. The Self-Incrimination Clause creates, as I have said before, "the federally protected right of silence," making it unconstitutional to use a law "to pry open one's lips and make him a witness against himself." Ullmann v. United States, 350 U.S., at 446 (dissenting). That is indeed one of the chief procedural guarantees in our accusatorial system. Government acts in an ignoble way when it stoops to the end which we authorize today.

I would adhere to Counselman v. Hitchcock and hold that this attempt to dilute the Self-Incrimination Clause is unconstitutional.

MR. JUSTICE MARSHALL, dissenting.

Today the Court holds that the United States may compel a witness to give incriminating testimony, and subsequently prosecute him for crimes to which that testimony relates. I cannot believe the Fifth Amendment permits that result. See Piccirillo v. New York, 400 U.S. 548, 552 (1971) (Brennan, J., dissenting from dismissal of certiorari).

2. As Mr. Justice Marshall points out, . . . it is futile to expect that a ban on use or derivative use of compelled testimony can be enforced.

It is also possible that use immunity might actually have an adverse impact on the administration of justice rather than promote law enforcement. A witness might believe, with good reason, that his "immunized" testimony will inevitably lead to a felony conviction. Under such circumstances, rather than testify and aid the investigation, the witness might decide he would be better off remaining silent even if he is jailed for contempt.

The Fifth Amendment gives a witness an absolute right to resist interrogation, if the testimony sought would tend to incriminate him. A grant of immunity may strip the witness of the right to refuse to testify, but only if it is broad enough to eliminate all possibility that the testimony will in fact operate to incriminate him. It must put him in precisely the same position, vis-a-vis the government that has compelled his testimony,* as he would have been in had he remained silent in reliance on the privilege.

The Court recognizes that an immunity statute must be tested by that standard, that the relevant inquiry is whether it "leaves the witness and the prosecutorial authorities in substantially the same position as if the witness had claimed the Fifth Amendment privilege." . . . I assume, moreover, that in theory that test would be met by a complete ban on the use of the compelled testimony, including all derivative use, however remote and indirect. But I cannot agree that a ban on use will in practice be total, if it remains open for the government to convict the witness on the basis of evidence derived from a legitimate independent source. The Court asserts that the witness is adequately protected by a rule imposing on the government a heavy burden of proof if it would establish the independent character of evidence to be used against the witness. But in light of the inevitable uncertainties of the fact-finding process, . . . a greater margin of protection is required in order to provide a reliable guarantee that the witness is in exactly the same position as if he had not testified. That margin can be provided only by immunity from prosecution for the offenses to which the testimony relates, i.e., transactional immunity.

I do not see how it can suffice merely to put the burden of proof on the government. First, contrary to the Court's assertion, the Court's rule does leave the witness "dependent for the preservation of his rights upon the integrity and good faith of the prosecuting authorities." . . . For the information relevant to the question of taint is uniquely within the knowledge of the prosecuting authorities. They alone are in a position to trace the chains of information and investigation that lead to the evidence to be used in a criminal prosecution. A witness who suspects that his compelled testimony was used to develop a lead will be hard pressed indeed to ferret out the evidence necessary to prove it. And of course it is no answer to say he need not prove it, for though the Court puts the burden of proof on the government, the government will have no difficulty in meeting its burden by mere assertion if the witness pro-

---

*This case does not, of course, involve the special considerations that come into play when the prosecuting government is different from the government that has compelled the testimony. See Murphy v. Waterfront Comm'n, 378 U.S. 52 (1964).

duces no contrary evidence. The good faith of the prosecuting authorities is thus the sole safeguard of the witness' rights. Second, even their good faith is not a sufficient safeguard. For the paths of information through the investigative bureaucracy may well be long and winding, and even a prosecutor acting in the best of faith cannot be certain that somewhere in the depths of his investigative apparatus, often including hundreds of employees, there was not some prohibited use of the compelled testimony. . . . The Court today sets out a loose net to trap tainted evidence and prevent its use against the witness, but it accepts an intolerably great risk that tainted evidence will in fact slip through that net.

In my view the Court turns reason on its head when it compares a statutory grant of immunity to the "immunity" that is inadvertently conferred by an unconstitutional interrogation. The exclusionary rule of evidence that applies in that situation has nothing whatever to do with this case. Evidence obtained through a coercive interrogation, like evidence obtained through an illegal search, is excluded at trial because the Constitution prohibits such methods of gathering evidence. The exclusionary rules provide a partial and inadequate remedy to some victims of illegal police conduct, and a similarly partial and inadequate deterrent to police officers. An immunity statute, on the other hand, is much more ambitious than any exclusionary rule. It does not merely attempt to provide a remedy for past police misconduct, which never should have occurred. An immunity statute operates in advance of the event, and it authorizes—even encourages—interrogation that would otherwise be prohibited by the Fifth Amendment. An immunity statute thus differs from an exclusionary rule of evidence in at least two critical respects.

First, because an immunity statute gives constitutional approval to the resulting interrogation, the government is under an obligation here to remove the danger of incrimination completely and absolutely, whereas in the case of the exclusionary rules it may be sufficient to shield the witness from the fruits of the illegal search or interrogation in a partial and reasonably adequate manner. For when illegal police conduct has occurred, the exclusion of evidence does not purport to purge the conduct of its unconstitutional character. The constitutional violation remains, and may provide the basis for other relief, such as a civil action for damages (see 42 U.S.C. §1983 and Bivens v. Six Agents, 403 U.S. 388 (1971)), or a criminal prosecution of the responsible officers (see 18 U.S.C. §§241-242). The Constitution does not authorize police officers to coerce confessions or to invade privacy without cause, so long as no use is made of the evidence they obtain. But this Court has held that the Constitution does authorize the government to compel a witness to give potentially incriminating testimony, so long as no incriminating use is made of the resulting evidence. Before the government puts its seal of approval on such an interrogation, it must provide an absolutely reliable guarantee that it will not use the testimony in any way at all in aid of prosecution of the witness. The only way to provide that guarantee is to give the witness immunity from prosecution for crimes to which his testimony relates.

Second, because an immunity statute operates in advance of the interrogation, there is room to require a broad grant of transactional immunity without imperiling large numbers of otherwise valid convictions. An exclusionary rule comes into play after the interrogation or search has occurred; and the decision to question or to search is often made in haste, under pressure, by an officer who is not a lawyer. If an unconstitutional interrogation or search were held to create transactional immunity, that might well be regarded as an excessively high price to pay for the "constable's blunder." An immunity statute, on the other hand, creates a framework in which the prosecuting attorney can make a calm and reasoned decision whether to compel testimony and suffer the resulting ban on prosecution, or to forgo the testimony.

For both these reasons it is clear to me that an immunity statute must be tested by a standard far more demanding than that appropriate for an exclusionary rule fashioned to deal with past constitutional violations. Measured by that standard, the statute approved today by the Court fails miserably. I respectfully dissent.

In his dissenting opinion in *Kastigar*, Justice Douglas refers to his dissenting opinion in Ullmann v. United States, 350 U.S. 422 (1956). *Ullmann* involved testimony before a grand jury, after a grant of immunity, concerning "attempts to endanger the national security by espionage and conspiracy to commit espionage." The petitioner refused to testify, notwithstanding the immunity grant, and was held in contempt. The Court reaffirmed *Brown*, page 952 supra, including the congressional power to extend immunity to state offenses. In doing so, the Court articulated its conception of the policies underlying the privilege.

ULLMANN v. UNITED STATES
Certiorari to the United States Court of Appeals for the Second Circuit
350 U.S. 422 (1956)

MR. JUSTICE FRANKFURTER delivered the opinion of the Court.

No doubt the constitutional privilege may, on occasion, save a guilty man from his just deserts. It was aimed at a more far-reaching evil—a recurrence of the Inquisition and the Star Chamber, even if not in their stark brutality. Prevention of the greater evil was deemed of more importance than occurrence of the lesser evil. Having had much experience with a tendency in human nature to abuse power, the Founders sought to close the doors against like future abuses by law-enforcing agencies. . . .

[In light of the purpose of the Fifth Amendment, the Court rejected the petitioner's attempt to distinguish *Brown:*]

Petitioner, however, attempts to distinguish Brown v. Walker. He argues that this case is different from Brown v. Walker because the impact of the disabilities imposed by federal and state authorities and the public in general—such as loss of job, expulsion from labor unions, state registration and investigation statutes, passport eligibility, and general public opprobrium—is so oppressive that the statute does not give him true immunity. This, he alleges, is significantly different from the impact of testifying on the auditor in Brown v. Walker, who could the next day resume his job with reputation unaffected. But, as this Court has often held, the immunity granted need only remove those sanctions which generate the fear justifying invocation of the privilege: "The interdiction of the Fifth Amendment operates only where a witness is asked to incriminate himself—in other words, to give testimony which may possibly expose him to a criminal charge. But if the criminality has already been taken away, the Amendment ceases to apply." Hale v. Henkel, 201 U.S. 43, 67. Here, since the Immunity Act protects a witness who is compelled to answer to the extent of his constitutional immunity, he has of course, when a particular sanction is sought to be imposed against him, the right to claim that it is criminal in nature. . . .

[The Court continued to articulate its conception of the policies underlying the fifth amendment.]

We are not dealing here with one of the vague, undefinable, admonitory provisions of the Constitution whose scope is inevitably addressed to changing circumstances. The privilege against self-incrimination is a specific provision of which it is peculiarly true that "a page of history is worth a volume of logic." New York Trust Co. v. Eisner, 256 U.S. 345, 349. For the history of the privilege establishes not only that it is not to be interpreted literally, but also that its sole concern is, as its name indicates, with the danger to a witness forced to give testimony leading to the infliction of "penalties affixed to the criminal acts. . . ." Boyd v. United States, 116 U.S. 616, 634. We leave Boyd v. United States unqualified, as it was left unqualified in Brown v. Walker. Immunity displaces the danger. Once the reason for the privilege ceases, the privilege ceases. We reaffirm Brown v. Walker, and in so doing we need not repeat the answers given by that case to the other points raised by petitioner. . . .

MR. JUSTICE DOUGLAS, joined by MR. JUSTICE BLACK, dissenting: I would reverse the judgment of conviction. I would base the reversal on Boyd v. United States, 116 U.S. 616, or, in the alternative, I would overrule the five-to-four decision of Brown v. Walker, 161 U.S. 591, and adopt the view of the minority in that case that the right of silence created by the Fifth Amendment is beyond the reach of Congress.

First, as to the *Boyd* case. There are numerous disabilities created by federal law that attach to a person who is a Communist. These disabilities include ineligibility for employment in the Federal Government and in defense facilities, disqualification for a passport, the risk of internment, the risk of loss of employment as a longshoreman—to mention only a few.[1] These disabilities imposed by federal law are forfeitures within the meaning of our cases and as much protected by the Fifth Amendment as criminal prosecution itself. But there is no indication that the Immunity Act, 68 Stat. 745, 18 U.S.C. (Supp. II) §3486, grants protection against those disabilities. The majority will not say that it does. I think, indeed, that it must be read as granting only partial, not complete, immunity for the matter disclosed under compulsion. Yet, as the Court held in Counselman v. Hitchcock, 142 U.S. 547, 586, an immunity statute to be valid must "supply a complete protection from all the perils against which the constitutional prohibition was designed to guard. . . ."

Boyd v. United States, supra, involved a proceeding to establish a forfeiture of goods alleged to have been fraudulently imported without payment of duties. The claimants resisted an order requiring the production of an invoice to be used against them in the forfeiture proceedings. The Court in an opinion by Mr. Justice Bradley sustained the defense of the Fifth Amendment. The Court said, "A witness, as well as a party, is protected by the law from being compelled to give evidence that tends to criminate him, or to subject his property to forfeiture." 116 U.S., at 638. . . . The contrary holding was deemed hostile to the spirit of our institutions:

> . . . any compulsory discovery by extorting the party's oath, or compelling the production of his private books and papers, to convict him of crime,

1. See 64 Stat. 992, 50 U.S.C. §784, as amended, 68 Stat. 777, 50 U.S.C. (Supp. II) §784 (prohibition of employment in the Federal Government and in defense facilities); 64 Stat. 993, 50 U.S.C. §785 (ineligibility for a passport); 64 Stat. 1019, 50 U.S.C. §§811-826 (the possibility of internment); 40 Stat. 220, as amended, 64 Stat. 427, 50 U.S.C. §191; 33 CFR, 1955 Cum. Supp., §§125.01, 125.29 (possibility of loss of employment as a longshoreman). And see 68 Stat. 776, 50 U.S.C. (Supp. II) §843. Moreover, under the Subversive Activities Control Act, 64 Stat. 987, 50 U.S.C. §781, discussed hereafter, it is a crime for a person who is a member of a Communist organization registered under the Act to engage in certain activity, e.g., to hold office or employment with any labor organization, to work for the Government or have employment in any defense facility, §5(a)(1), or to apply for or use a passport §6(a).

or to forfeit his property, is contrary to the principles of a free government. It is abhorrent to the instincts of an Englishman; it is abhorrent to the instincts of an American. It may suit the purposes of despotic power; but it cannot abide the pure atmosphere of political liberty and personal freedom. 116 U.S., at 631-632.

The forfeiture of property on compelled testimony is no more abhorrent than the forfeiture of rights of citizenship. Any forfeiture of rights as a result of compelled testimony is at war with the Fifth Amendment.

The Court apparently distinguishes the *Boyd* case on the ground that the forfeiture of property was a penalty affixed to a criminal act. The loss of a job and the ineligibility for a passport are also penalties affixed to a criminal act. For the case of Dennis v. United States, 341 U.S. 494, makes plain that membership in the Communist Party is a crucial link of evidence for conviction under the Smith Act, 54 Stat. 671, as amended, 62 Stat. 808, 18 U.S.C. §2385. And see Blau v. United States, 340 U.S. 159. When a man loses a job because he is a Communist, there is as much a penalty suffered as when an importer loses property because he is a tax evader. When a man loses his right to a passport because he is a Communist, there is as much a penalty suffered as when property is lost for violation of the revenue laws. If there was a penalty suffered in the *Boyd* case, there are penalties suffered here. Both are hitched to criminal acts. And the Constitution places the property rights involved in the *Boyd* case no higher than the rights of citizenship involved here.

The Court may mean that if disqualification for government employment or ineligibility for a passport is a forfeiture within the meaning of the *Boyd* case, Congress has lifted these disabilities in exchange for the witness' testimony. Congress, I think, will be surprised to hear this. There is nothing in the legislative history that would suggest that Congress was willing to pay any such price for the testimony. If the disabilities which attach under existing law are forfeitures, the Court should strike down the Act. If Congress chooses to enact a new Immunity Act broad enough to protect against all forfeitures, it is free to do so. The Court seems to commit Congress to a policy that there is no indication Congress favors.

We should apply the principle of the *Boyd* case to the present one and hold that since there is no protection in the Immunity Act against loss of rights of citizenship, the immunity granted is less than the protection afforded by the Constitution. Certainly personal freedom has at least as much constitutional dignity as property.

Second, as to Brown v. Walker. The difficulty I have with that decision and with the majority of the Court in the present case is that they add an important qualification to the Fifth Amendment. The guarantee is that no person "shall be compelled in any criminal case to be a witness against himself." The majority does not enforce that guarantee as written but qualifies it; and the qualification apparently reads, "but only if criminal conviction might result." Wisely or not, the Fifth Amendment protects against the compulsory self-accusation of crime without exception or qualification. In Counselman v. Hitchcock, supra, at 562, Mr. Justice Blatchford said, "The privilege is limited to criminal matters, but it is as broad as the mischief against which it seeks to guard."

The "mischief" to be prevented falls under at least three heads.

(1) One "mischief" is not only the risk of conviction but the risk of prosecution. . . .

The risk of prosecution is not a risk which the wise take lightly. As experienced a judge as Learned Hand once said, "I must say that, as a litigant, I should dread a lawsuit beyond almost anything else short of sickness and of death." See Frank, Courts on Trial (1949), 40. A part of the dread in a case such as this is the chain of events that may be put in motion once disclosure is made. The truth is, I think, that there is no control left, once the right of secrecy is broken. For the statute protects the accused only on account of the "transaction, matter, or thing" concerning which he is compelled to testify and bars the use as evidence of the "testimony so compelled." The forced disclosure may open up vast new vistas for the prosecutor with leads to numerous accusations not within the purview of the question and answer. What related offenses may be disclosed by leads furnished by the confession? How remote need the offense be before the immunity ceases to protect it? How much litigation will it take to determine it? What will be the reaction of the highest court when the facts of the case reach it?

It is, for example, a crime for a person who is a member of a Communist organization registered under the Subversive Activities Control Act, 64 Stat. 987, 50 U.S.C. §781, to be employed by the United States, to be employed in any defense facility, to hold office or employment with any labor organization, §5(a)(1), or to apply for a passport or to use a passport. §6(a). The crime under that Act is the application for a passport, the use of a passport, or employment by one of the named agencies, as the case may be. Are those crimes included within the "transaction, matter, or thing" protected by the Immunity Act?

The Taft-Hartley Act, 61 Stat. 146, 29 U.S.C. §159(h), requires officers of labor organizations to file non-Communist affidavits as a condition to the exercise by the National Labor Relations Board of its power to make investigations or to issue complaints. A witness before a grand jury or congressional committee is compelled under the force of the Immunity Act to testify. He testifies that he is not a member of the

Communist Party. He then files an affidavit under the Taft-Hartley Act to that effect. May he be prosecuted for filing a false affidavit?

These are real and dread uncertainties that the Immunity Act does not remove. They emphasize that one protective function of the Fifth Amendment is at once removed when the guarantee against self-incrimination is qualified in the manner it is today.

The Court leaves all those uncertainties to another day, saying that the immunity granted by Congress will extend to its constitutional limits and that those constitutional limits will be determined case by case in future litigation. That means that no one knows what the limits are. The Court will not say. Only litigation on a distant day can determine it.

The concession of the Court underlines my point. It shows that the privilege of silence is exchanged for a partial, undefined, vague immunity. It means that Congress has granted far less than it has taken away.

(2) The guarantee against self-incrimination contained in the Fifth Amendment is not only a protection against conviction and prosecution but a safeguard of conscience and human dignity and freedom of expression as well. My view is that the Framers put it beyond the power of Congress to *compel* anyone to confess his crimes. The evil to be guarded against was partly self-accusation under legal compulsion. But that was only a part of the evil. The conscience and dignity of man were also involved. So too was his right to freedom of expression guaranteed by the First Amendment. The Framers, therefore, created the federally protected right of silence and decreed that the law could not be used to pry open one's lips and make him a witness against himself.

A long history and a deep sentiment lay behind this decision. Some of those who came to these shores were Puritans who had known the hated oath ex officio used both by the Star Chamber and the High Commission. See Maguire, Attack of the Common Lawyers on the Oath Ex Officio as Administered in the Ecclesiastical Courts in England, Essays in History and Political Theory (1936), c. VII. They had known the great rebellion of Lilburn, Cartwright and others against those instruments of oppression. . . .

The literature of the Levellers, of whom Lilburn was a leader, abounds in this attitude. In 1648, there was published a Declaration in the form of a petition, item 12 of which reads:

"That all Statutes for all kinds of Oaths, whether in Corporations, Cities, or other, which insnare conscientious people, as also other Statutes, injoyning all to hear the Book of Common Prayer, be forthwith repealed and nulled, and that nothing be imposed upon the consciences of any to compel them to sin against their own consciences." Haller & Davies, The Leveller Tracts 1647-1653 (1944), 112.

In 1653, Lilburn published The Just Defence in which he wrote:

"Another fundamental right I then contended for, was, that no mans conscience ought to be racked by oaths imposed, to answer to questions concerning himself in matters criminal, or pretended to be so." Haller & Davies, id., at 454.

These are important declarations, as they throw light on the meaning of "compelled" as used in the Fifth Amendment.

The amending process that brought the Fifth Amendment into the Constitution is of little aid in our problem of interpretation. But there are indications in the debates on the Constitution that the evil to be remedied was the use of torture to exact confessions. See, e.g., Virginia Debates (2d ed. 1805), 221, 320-321; 2 Elliot's Debates (2d ed. 1876), 111. It was, indeed, the condemnation of torture to exact confessions that was written into the early law of the American Colonies. Article 45 of the Massachusetts Body of Liberties of 1641 provided in part, "No man shall be forced by Torture to confesse any Crime against himselfe nor any other. . . ." Connecticut adopted a similar provision. Laws of Connecticut Colony (1865 ed.), 65. Virginia soon followed suit: ". . . noe law can compell a man to sweare against himselfe in any matter wherein he is lyable to corporall punishment." Hening, Statutes at Large, Vol. II, 422.

The compulsion outlawed was moral compulsion as well as physical compulsion. An episode in the administration of Governor William Bradford of the Plymouth Plantation illustrates the point. He sought advice from his ministers asking, "How farr a magistrate may extracte a confession from a delinquente, to acuse him selfe of a capitall crime. . . ." The three ministers—Ralph Partrich, John Reynor, and Charles Chancy— were unanimous in concluding that the oath was against both the laws of God and the laws of man. Partrich's answer is typical: "[The magistrate] may not extracte a confession of a capitall crime from a suspected person by any violent means, whether it be by an oath imposed, or by any punishmente inflicted or threatened to be inflicted." Bradford, History of Plymouth Plantation, Mass. Hist. Soc. Coll. Ser. 4, Vol. III, 390-391. . . .

The Court, by forgetting that history, robs the Fifth Amendment of one of the great purposes it was designed to serve. To repeat, the Fifth Amendment was written in part to prevent any Congress, any court, and any prosecutor from prying open the lips of an accused to make incriminating statements against his will. The Fifth Amendment protects the conscience and the dignity of the individual, as well as his safety and security, against the compulsion of government.[3]

3. Dean Erwin N. Griswold of Harvard recently wrote:
    Where matters of a man's belief or opinions or political views are essential

(3) This right of silence, this right of the accused to stand mute serves another high purpose. Mr. Justice Field, one of the four dissenters in Brown v. Walker, stated that it is the aim of the Fifth Amendment to protect the accused from all compulsory testimony "which would expose him to infamy and disgrace," as well as that which might lead to a criminal conviction. 161 U.S., at 631. One of the most powerful opinions in the books maintaining that thesis is by Judge Peter S. Grosscup in United States v. James, 60 F. 257, involving the same Immunity Act as the one involved in Brown v. Walker. Judge Grosscup reviewed the history of the reign of intolerance that once ruled England, the contests between Church and State, and the cruelties of the old legal procedures. Judge Grosscup said concerning the aim of the Framers in drafting the Fifth Amendment (id., at 264):

> Did they originate such privilege simply to safeguard themselves against the law-inflicted penalties and forfeitures? Did they take no thought of the pains of practical outlawry? The stated penalties and forfeitures of the law might be set aside; but was there no pain in disfavor and odium among neighbors, in excommunication from church or societies that might be governed by the prevailing views, in the private liabilities that the law might authorize, or in the unfathomable disgrace, not susceptible of formulation in language, which a known violation of law brings upon the offender? Then, too, if the immunity was only against the law-inflicted pains and penalties, the government could probe the secrets of every conversation, or society, by extending compulsory pardon to one of its participants, and thus turn him into an involuntary informer. Did the framers contemplate that this privilege of silence was exchangeable always, at the will of the government, for a remission of the participant's own penalties, upon a condition of disclosure, that would bring those to whom he had plighted his faith and loyalty within the grasp of the prosecutor? I cannot think so.

Mr. Justice Field and Judge Grosscup were on strong historical ground. The Fifth Amendment was designed to protect the accused against infamy as well as against prosecution. . . . The history of infamy as a punishment was notorious. Luther had inveighed against excommunication. The Massachusetts Body of Liberties of 1641 had provided in

---

elements in the charge, it may be most difficult to get evidence from sources other than the suspected or accused person himself. Hence, the significance of the privilege over the years has perhaps been greatest in connection with resistance to prosecution for such offenses as heresy or political crimes. In these areas the privilege against self-incrimination has been a protection for freedom of thought and a hindrance to any government which might wish to prosecute for thoughts and opinions alone.

The Fifth Amendment Today, supra, 8-9.

Article 60: "No church censure shall degrad or depose any man from any Civill dignitie, office, or Authoritie he shall have in the Commonwealth." Loss of office, loss of dignity, loss of face were feudal forms of punishment. Infamy was historically considered to be punishment as effective as fine and imprisonment.

The Beccarian attitude toward infamy was a part of the background of the Fifth Amendment. The concept of infamy was explicitly written into it. We need not guess as to that. For the first Clause of the Fifth Amendment contains the concept in haec verba: "No person shall be held to answer for a capital, or otherwise *infamous* crime, unless on a presentment or indictment of a Grand Jury. . . ." (Italics added.) And the third Clause, the one we are concerned with here—"No person . . . shall be compelled in any criminal case to be a witness against himself . . ."—also reflects the revulsion of society at infamy imposed by the State. Beccaria, whose works were well known here and who was particularly well known to Jefferson, was the main voice against the use of infamy as punishment. The curse of infamy, he showed, results from public opinion. Oppression occurs when infamy is imposed on the citizen by the State. . . .

It was in this tradition that Lord Chief Justice Treby ruled in 1696 that ". . . no man is bound to answer any questions that will subject him to a penalty, or to infamy." Trial of Freind, 13 How. St. Tr. 1, 17.

There is great infamy involved in the present case, apart from the loss of rights of citizenship under federal law which I have already mentioned. The disclosure that a person is a Communist practically excommunicates him from society. School boards will not hire him. See Adler v. Board of Education, 342 U.S. 485. A lawyer risks exclusion from the bar (In re Anastaplo, 3 Ill. 2d 471, 121 N.E.2d 826); a doctor, the revocation of his license to practice (cf. Barsky v. Board of Regents, 347 U.S. 442). If an actor, he is on a black list. (See Horowitz, Loyalty Tests for Employment in the Motion Picture Industry, 6 Stan. L. Rev. 438.) And he will be able to find no employment in our society except at the lowest level, if at all. These facts make most persuasive the words of Judge Grosscup in United States v. James, supra, at 264-265, written in 1894:

> The battle for personal liberty seems to have been attained, but, in the absence of the din and clash, we cannot comprehend the meaning of all the safeguards employed. When we see the shield held before the briber, the liquor seller, the usury taker, the duelist, and the other violators of accepted law, we are moved to break or cast it aside, unmindful of the splendid purpose that first threw it forward. But, whatever its disadvantages now, it is a fixed privilege, until taken down by the same power that

extended it. It is not certain, either, that it may not yet serve some useful purpose. The oppression of crowns and principalities is unquestionably over, but the more frightful oppression of selfish, ruthless, and merciless majorities may yet constitute one of the chapters of future history. In my opinion, the privilege of silence, against a criminal accusation, guarantied by the fifth amendment, was meant to extend to all the consequences of disclosure.

It is no answer to say that a witness who exercises his Fifth Amendment right of silence and stands mute may bring himself into disrepute. If so, that is the price he pays for exercising the right of silence granted by the Fifth Amendment. The critical point is that the Constitution places the right of silence *beyond the reach of government*. The Fifth Amendment stands between the citizen and his government. When public opinion casts a person into the outer darkness, as happens today when a person is exposed as a Communist, the government brings infamy on the head of the witness when it compels disclosure. That is precisely what the Fifth Amendment prohibits.

NOTES AND QUESTIONS

1. In Murphy v. Waterfront Commission of New York Harbor, 378 U.S. 52 (1964), discussed in *Kastigar*, page 970 supra, Justice Goldberg's opinion for the Court addressed the policies then perceived to underlie the privilege:

> The privilege against self-incrimination "registers an important advance in the development of our liberty— 'one of the great landmarks in man's struggle to make himself civilized.' " Ullmann v. United States, 350 U.S. 422, 426.[4] It reflects many of our fundamental values and most noble aspirations: our unwillingness to subject those suspected of crime to the cruel trilemma of self-accusation, perjury or contempt; our preference for an accusatorial rather than an inquisitorial system of criminal justice; our fear that self-incriminating statements will be elicited by inhumane treatment and abuses; our sense of fair play which dictates "a fair state-individual balance by requiring the government to leave the individual alone until good cause is shown for disturbing him and by requiring the government in its contest with the individual to shoulder the entire load," 8 Wigmore, Evidence (McNaughton rev., 1961), 317; our respect for the inviolability of the human personality and of the right of each individual "to a private enclave where he may lead a private life," United States v. Grunewald, 233 F.2d 556, 581-582 (Frank, J., dissenting), rev'd 353 U.S. 391; our

---

4. The quotation is from Griswold, The Fifth Amendment Today (1955), 7.

distrust of self-deprecatory statements; and our realization that the privilege, while sometimes "a shelter to the guilty," is often "a protection to the innocent." Quinn v. United States, 349 U.S. 155, 162.

Compare Justice Goldberg's views with Justice Frankfurter's opinion for the Court in *Ullmann*, page 980 supra, and with Justice Powell's views as expressed in his opinion for the Court in *Kastigar*, page 965 supra. What are the implications of the different views? Consider Professor Arenella's analysis of Justice Goldberg's effort to articulate the policies of the privilege:

An examination of Justice Goldberg's fundamental values reveals three obvious points. First, some of them seem to overlap with each other (e.g., numbers two and four; or numbers one, three, and six). Second, many of these values are stated so abstractly that they can be used to justify almost any result. For example, what does it mean to speak of "our preference for an accusatorial rather than an inquisitorial system" (number two)? What criteria should a court use to determine whether state practices have upset a fair state-individual balance (number four)? Finally, this list of fundamental values suggests that the privilege against self-incrimination protects both *substantive values* (e.g., privacy, human dignity, and moral autonomy) and *accusatorial process norms* (e.g., a fair state-individual balance of advantage and adversarial determination of guilt) whose applicability may vary with the procedural context involved and whose significance may depend on the countervailing state interests at stake. Thus, when the Court confronts procedural contexts and state objectives not envisioned by the Constitution's framers, it must first identify which fifth amendment values are implicated and what state interests are at stake that might justify some impairment of these values. In other words, the Court must inevitably engage in a balancing analysis of these competing interests before it can interpret fifth amendment concepts like "compulsion" or "to be a witness against himself." [Arenella, *Schmerber* and the Privilege Against Self-Incrimination: A Reappraisal, 20 Am. Crim. L. Rev. 31, 37 (1982).]

For a recent effort to rethink the justifications for the privilege, see Stuntz, Self-Incrimination and Excuse, 88 Colum. L. Rev. 1227 (1988). For a skeptical view concerning the justifications of the fifth amendment privilege, see Dolinko, Is There a Rationale for the Privilege Against Self-Incrimination?, 33 U.C.L.A.L. Rev. 1063 (1986).

2. The Court consistently asserts that for an immunity grant to displace the privilege, it must be "co-extensive" with the privilege. What does that mean? Reconsider the dissents in *Brown*, page 958 supra, *Kastigar*, page 974 supra, and *Ullmann*, page 982 supra.

3. In Hoffman v. United States, 341 U.S. 479 (1951), the Court

articulated the standard by which the trial judge is to determine whether a witness may properly invoke the privilege:

> The privilege afforded not only extends to answers that would in themselves support a conviction under a federal criminal statute but likewise embraces those which would furnish a link in the chain of evidence needed to prosecute the claimant for a federal crime. (Patricia) Blau v. United States, 340 U.S. 159 (1950). But this protection must be confined to instances where the witness has reasonable cause to apprehend danger from a direct answer. Mason v. United States, 244 U.S. 362, 365 (1917), and cases cited. The witness is not exonerated from answering merely because he declares that in so doing he would incriminate himself—his say-so does not of itself establish the hazard of incrimination. It is for the court to say whether his silence is justified, Rogers v. United States, 340 U.S. 367 (1951), and to require him to answer if "it clearly appears to the court that he is mistaken." Temple v. Commonwealth, 75 Va. 892, 899 (1881). However, if the witness, upon interposing his claim, were required to prove the hazard in the sense in which a claim is usually required to be established in court, he would be compelled to surrender the very protection which the privilege is designed to guarantee. To sustain the privilege, it need only be evident from the implications of the question, in the setting in which it is asked, that a responsive answer to the question or an explanation of why it cannot be answered might be dangerous because injurious disclosure could result. The trial judge in appraising the claim "must be governed as much by his personal perception of the peculiarities of the case as by the facts actually in evidence." See Taft, J., in Ex parte Irvine, 74 F. 954, 960 (C.C.S.D. Ohio, 1896). [341 U.S. at 486-487.]

Justice Brown's opinion in Brown v. Walker has proved to be prescient.

Waiver. The leading case is Rogers v. United States, 340 U.S. 367 (1951). A witness must invoke the fifth amendment on being questioned, and a failure to do so is deemed a waiver. Moreover, once a witness answers a question, the witness cannot refuse to be examined further concerning the general area of the answer—"Disclosure of a fact waives the privilege as to details." Id. at 373. As to each subsequent question asked, the issue is whether the answer might subject the witness to a "real danger of further crimination," id. at 379, beyond that contained in the original answer. The *Rogers* test is not easy of application, however, since the trial judge must make very refined appraisals of the effect of any admission as well as the potential effect of any subsequent statements. The lower courts have also required subsequent disclosure where an answer to a question would result in a distortion of truth. For a discussion, see Note, Testimonial Waiver of the Privilege Against Self Incrimination, 92 Harv. L. Rev. 1752 (1979).

Prosecution barred by statute of limitations, decision "final," etc. If the statute of limitations has run, there is no risk of "incrimination," and therefore the fifth amendment is not applicable. Hale v. Henkel, 201 U.S. 43 (1906) (dicta). See also In re Folding Carton Antitrust Litigation, 609 F.2d 867 (7th Cir. 1979); Goodman v. United States, 289 F.2d 256 (4th Cir. 1961), vacated, 368 U.S. 14 (1961). Similarly, if an individual is convicted and has exhausted his appeals, the fifth amendment is satisfied. Reina v. United States, 364 U.S. 507 (1960). However, the normal rules are applicable here, so that a claim of privilege may be made if the answer to a question might subject the individual to a risk of prosecution for some other offense. United States v. Seavers, 472 F.2d 607 (6th Cir, 1973). And if a person has been convicted but not yet sentenced and still could appeal, there is authority for the proposition that the fifth amendment may still be invoked. Mills v. United States, 281 F.2d 736 (4th Cir. 1960).

A guilty plea purportedly waives the privilege. Boykin v. Alabama, 395 U.S. 238 (1969). But what of a person who pleads guilty and has yet to be sentenced? Is that analogous to someone who has been convicted but can still appeal? Note that Fed. R. Crim. P. 32(d) permits easier withdrawal of a plea before sentencing than afterwards. Consider Holloway v. Wolff, 351 F. Supp. 1033 (D. Neb. 1972), rev'd on other grounds, 482 F.2d 110 (8th Cir. 1973). In that case a defendant challenged his conviction on the ground that he was denied the right to cross-examine his co-defendants, each of whom had pled guilty, had not been sentenced, and had invoked the fifth amendment to resist answering questions. The district court found that the assertion of the privilege was justifiable.

The Supreme Court has not dealt unambiguously with the applicability of the fifth amendment to sentencing hearings. The Court has dealt with the privilege's applicability to penalty phases of capital trials, however. In Estelle v. Smith, 451 U.S. 454 (1981), the state ordered the defendant to undergo a psychiatric examination, and then it relied on the results of the examination at the penalty phase of the defendant's capital trial. Moreover, the state did not warn the defendant that he had a right to remain silent. In disposing of the state's contention that the fifth amendment was not applicable, the Court said:

> Of the several constitutional issues addressed by the District Court and the Court of Appeals, we turn first to whether the admission of Dr. Grigson's testimony at the penalty phase violated respondent's Fifth Amendment

privilege against compelled self-incrimination because respondent was not advised before the pretrial psychiatric examination that he had a right to remain silent and that any statement he made could be used against him at a sentencing proceeding. Our initial inquiry must be whether the Fifth Amendment privilege is applicable in the circumstances of this case.

(1)

The State argues that respondent was not entitled to the protection of the Fifth Amendment because Dr. Grigson's testimony was used only to determine punishment after conviction, not to establish guilt. In the State's view, "incrimination is complete once guilt has been adjudicated," and, therefore, the Fifth Amendment privilege has no relevance to the penalty phase of a capital murder trial. Brief for Petitioner 33-34. We disagree.

The Fifth Amendment, made applicable to the states through the Fourteenth Amendment, commands that "[n]o person . . . shall be compelled in any criminal case to be a witness against himself." The essence of this basic constitutional principle is "the requirement that the State which proposes to convict *and punish* an individual produce the evidence against him by the independent labor of its officers, not by the simple, cruel expedient of forcing it from his own lips." Culombe v. Connecticut, 367 U.S. 568, 581-582 (1961) (opinion announcing the judgment) (emphasis added). See also Murphy v. Waterfront Comm'n, 378 U.S. 52, 55 (1964); E. Griswold, The Fifth Amendment Today 7 (1955).

The Court has held that "the availability of the [Fifth Amendment] privilege does not turn upon the type of proceeding in which its protection is invoked, but upon the nature of the statement or admission and the exposure which it invites." In re Gault, 387 U.S. 1, 49 (1967). In this case, the ultimate penalty of death was a potential consequence of what respondent told the examining psychiatrist. Just as the Fifth Amendment prevents a criminal defendant from being made " 'the deluded instrument of his own conviction,' " Culombe v. Connecticut, supra, at 581, quoting 2 Hawkins Pleas of the Crown 595 (8th ed. 1824), it protects him as well from being made the "deluded instrument" of his own execution.

We can discern no basis to distinguish between the guilt and penalty phases of respondent's capital murder trial so far as the protection of the Fifth Amendment privilege is concerned. Given the gravity of the decision to be made at the penalty phase, the State is not relieved of the obligation to observe fundamental constitutional guarantees. . . . Any effort by the State to compel respondent to testify against his will at the sentencing hearing clearly would contravene the Fifth Amendment.[7] Yet the State's attempt to establish respondent's future dangerousness by relying on the unwarned statements he made to Dr. Grigson similarly infringes Fifth Amendment values.

7. The State conceded this at oral argument. Tr. of Oral Arg. 47, 49.

When considering the implications of Estelle v. Smith, however, bear in mind that the Supreme Court has exhibited a tendency to treat capital cases as sui generis. In Buchanan v. Kentucky, 483 U.S. 402 (1987), the Court held that Estelle v. Smith did not apply where defense counsel joined in the motion for the psychiatric examination and relied at trial on portions of the reports resulting from that examination to establish the defendant's state of mind. In that context, the government did not act inappropriately by introducing portions of the report in which the psychiatrist "set forth his general observations about the mental state of the petitioner but had not described *any* statements by petitioner dealing with the crimes with which he was charged." Id. at 423 (emphasis in original).

As *Ullmann* and *Kastigar* demonstrate, the fifth amendment is still viewed as limited to protecting against disclosures that would lead to the imposition of criminal sanctions. Indeed, a state apparently may condition employment on the grounds that employees answer questions concerning their employment and a refusal to answer can result in dismissal. However, the state must grant immunity for the answers. Gardner v. Broderick, 392 U.S. 273 (1968); Lefkowitz v. Turley, 414 U.S. 70 (1973).

The Court has also apparently maintained the other component of *Boyd* that forfeitures as a result of criminality are penalties within the fifth amendment. In United States v. United States Coin and Currency, 401 U.S. 715 (1971), the Court relied on *Boyd* for the proposition that " 'proceedings instituted for the purpose of declaring the forfeiture of a man's property by reason of offense committed by him, though they may be civil in form, are in their nature criminal' for Fifth Amendment purposes." Id. at 718. The lower courts have split, however, as to the applicability of the fifth amendment to disciplinary proceedings where a license might be revoked. In Spevack v. Klein, 385 U.S. 511 (1967), the Court held that a lawyer could not be disbarred for asserting the privilege in a disciplinary hearing, but it gave no indication as to what the outcome would have been had the state granted immunity from criminal prosecution on the basis of the answers. Some courts, analyzing disbarment as a "penalty" within the scope of the fifth amendment, have found the privilege fully applicable to such proceedings. See, e.g., Erdmann v. Stevens, 458 F.2d 1205 (2d Cir. 1972). The dominant view, though, is that the fifth amendment does not apply to disciplinary proceedings where there is no risk of subsequent criminal prosecution. See, e.g., Childs v. McCord, 420 F. Supp. 428 (D. Md. 1976).

Assuming that risk of criminal prosecution is a prerequisite of a valid fifth amendment claim, how does one determine whether a proceeding is criminal or civil in nature? This issue was addressed in United States v. Ward, 448 U.S. 242 (1980). Ward challenged the constitutionality of a statute that required any ship or facility that spilled oil into the navigable waters to report to the federal authorities. The statute also gave the reported information "use immunity" from criminal prosecution, but a different subsection allowed the imposition of a "civil" monetary fine for the act. Coincidentally, an 1899 statute made the same act a crime.

The Court rejected Ward's contention that the reporting requirements of the statute violated the fifth amendment if used to support the civil penalty.

UNITED STATES v. WARD, 448 U.S. 242, 248-256 (1980): This Court has often stated that the question whether a particular statutorily-defined penalty is civil or criminal is a matter of statutory construction. See, e.g., One Lot Emerald Cut Stones v. United States, 409 U.S. 232, 237 (1972). . . . Our inquiry in this regard has traditionally proceeded on two levels. First, we have set out to determine whether Congress, in establishing the penalizing mechanism, indicated either expressly or impliedly a preference for one label or the other. See One Lot Emerald Cut Stones v. United States, supra, at 236-237. Second, where Congress has indicated an intention to establish a civil penalty, we have inquired further whether the statutory scheme was so punitive either in purpose or effect as to negate that intention. See Flemming v. Nestor, 363 U.S. 603, 617-621 (1960). In regard to this latter inquiry, we have noted that "only the clearest proof could suffice to establish the unconstitutionality of a statute on such a ground." Id., at 617. See also One Lot Emerald Cut Stones v. United States, supra, at 237; Rex Trailer Co. v. United States, 350 U.S. 148, 154 (1956).

As for our first inquiry in the present case, we believe it quite clear that Congress intended to impose a civil penalty upon persons in Ward's position. Initially, and importantly, Congress labeled the sanction authorized in §311(b)(6) a "civil penalty," a label that takes on added significance given its juxtaposition with the criminal penalties set forth in the immediately preceding subparagraph, §311(b)(5). Thus, we have no doubt that Congress intended to allow imposition of penalties under §311(b)(6) without regard to the procedural protections and restrictions available in criminal prosecutions.

We turn then to consider whether Congress, despite its manifest intention to establish a civil, remedial mechanism, nevertheless provided for sanctions so punitive as to "transfor[m] what was clearly intended as a civil remedy into a criminal penalty." Rex Trailer Co. v. United States, supra, at 154. In making this determination, both the District Court and the Court of Appeals found it useful to refer to the seven considerations listed in Kennedy v. Mendoza-Martinez, [372 U.S. 144,] at 168-169. This list of considerations, while certainly neither exhaustive nor dispositive, has proved helpful in our own consideration of similar questions, see, e.g., Bell v. Wolfish, 441 U.S. 520, 537-538 (1979), and provides some guidance in the present case. [7]

Without setting forth here our assessment of each of the seven *Mendoza-Martinez* factors, we think only one, the fifth, aids respondent. That is a consideration of whether "the behavior to which [the penalty] applies is already a crime." 372 U.S., at 168-169. In this regard, respondent contends that §13 of the Rivers and Harbors Appropriation Act of 1899, 33 U.S.C. §407, makes criminal the precise conduct penalized in the present case. Moreover, respondent points out that at least one federal court has held that §13 of the Rivers and Harbors Appropriation Act defines a "strict liability crime," for which the Government need prove no scienter. See United States v. White Fuel Corp., 498 F.2d 619 (C.A.1 1974). According to respondent, this confirms the lower court's conclusion that this fifth factor "falls clearly in favor of a finding that [§311(b)(6)] is criminal in nature." 598 F.2d, at 1193.

While we agree that this consideration seems to point toward a finding that §311(b)(6) is criminal in nature, that indication is not as strong as it seems at first blush. We have noted on a number of occasions that "Congress may impose both a criminal and a civil sanction in respect to the same act or omission." . . . One Lot Emerald Cut Stones v. United States, supra, at 235. Moreover, in Helvering [v. Mitchell, 303 U.S. 391 (1938)] where we held a 50% penalty for tax fraud to be civil, we found it quite significant that "the Revenue Act of 1928 contains two separate and distinct provisions imposing sanctions," and that "these appear in different parts of the statute. . . ." 303 U.S., at 404. See also One Lot Emerald Cut Stones v. United States, supra, at 236-237. To the extent that we found significant the separation of civil and criminal penalties within the same statute, we believe that the placement of criminal penalties in one statute and the placement of civil penalties in another statute enacted 70 years later tends to dilute the force of the fifth *Mendoza-Martinez* criterion in this case.

In sum, we believe that the factors set forth in *Mendoza-Martinez*, while neither exhaustive nor conclusive on the issue, are in no way sufficient to render unconstitutional the congressional classification of the penalty established in §311(b)(6) as civil. Nor are we persuaded by

---

7. The standards set forth were "[w]hether the sanction involves an affirmative disability or restraint, whether it has historically been regarded as a punishment, whether it comes into play only on a finding of *scienter*, whether its operation will promote the traditional aims of punishment—retribution and deterrence, whether the behavior to which it applies is already a crime, whether an alternative purpose to which it may rationally be connected is assignable for it, and whether it appears excessive in relation to the alternative purpose assigned. . . ." 372 U.S., at 168-169 (footnotes omitted).

any of respondent's other arguments that he has offered the "clearest proof" that the penalty here in question is punitive in either purpose or effect. . . .

Our conclusion that §311(b)(6) does not trigger all the protections afforded by the Constitution to a criminal defendant does not completely dispose of this case. Respondent asserts that, even if the penalty imposed upon him was not sufficiently criminal in nature to trigger other guarantees, it was "quasi-criminal," and therefore sufficient to implicate the Fifth Amendment's protection against compulsory self-incrimination. He relies primarily in this regard upon Boyd v. United States, 116 U.S. 616 (1886), and later cases quoting its language.

In *Boyd*, [the] . . . Court found the Fifth Amendment applicable, even though the action in question was one contesting the forfeiture of certain goods. According to the Court: "We are . . . clearly of opinion that proceedings instituted for the purpose of declaring the forfeiture of a man's property by reason of offences committed by him, though they may be civil in form, are in their nature criminal." Id., at 633-634. While at this point in its opinion, the Court seemed to limit its holding to proceedings involving the forfeiture of property, shortly after the quoted passage it broadened its reasoning in a manner that might seem to apply to the present case:

> As, therefore, suits for *penalties and forfeitures* incurred by the commission of offences against the law, are of this quasi-criminal nature, we think that they are within the reason of criminal proceedings for all the purposes of the Fourth Amendment of the Constitution, and of that portion of the Fifth Amendment which declares that no person shall be compelled in any criminal case to be a witness against himself. . . . Id., at 634 (emphasis added).

Seven years later, this Court relied primarily upon *Boyd* in holding that a proceeding resulting in a "forfeit and penalty" of $1,000 for violation of an Act prohibiting the employment of aliens was sufficiently criminal to trigger the protections of the Self-Incrimination Clause of the Fifth Amendment. Lees v. United States, 150 U.S. 476 (1893). More recently, in One 1958 Plymouth Sedan v. Pennsylvania, 380 U.S. 693 (1965), and United States v. United States Coin & Currency, 401 U.S. 715 (1971), this Court applied *Boyd* to proceedings involving the forfeiture of property for alleged criminal activity. *Plymouth Sedan* dealt with the applicability of the so-called exclusionary rule to a proceeding brought by the State of Pennsylvania to secure the forfeiture of a car allegedly involved in the illegal transportation of liquor. *Coin & Currency* involved the applicability of the Fifth Amendment privilege against compulsory self-incrimination in a proceeding brought by the United States to secure forfeiture of $8,674 found in the possession of a gambler at the time of his arrest.

Read broadly, *Boyd* might control the present case. This Court has declined, however, to give full scope to the reasoning and dicta in *Boyd*, noting on at least one occasion that "[s]everal of *Boyd's* express or implicit declarations have not stood the test of time." Fisher v. United States, 425 U.S. 391, 407 (1976). In United States v. Regan, 232 U.S. 37 (1914), for example, we declined to apply *Boyd's* classification of penalties and forfeitures as criminal in a case where a defendant assessed with a $1,000 penalty for violation of the Alien Immigration Act claimed that he was entitled to have the Government prove its case beyond a reasonable doubt. *Boyd* and *Lees,* according to *Regan,* were limited in scope to the Fifth Amendment's guarantee against compulsory self-incrimination, which "is of broader scope than are the guarantees in Art. III and the Sixth Amendment governing trials and criminal prosecutions." 232 U.S., at 50. See also Helvering v. Mitchell, 303 U.S., at 400, n.3. Similarly, in Hepner v. United States, 213 U.S. 103 (1909), this Court upheld the entry of a directed verdict against the appellant under a statute similar to that examined in *Lees.* According to *Hepner,* "the *Lees* and *Boyd* cases do not modify or disturb but recognize the general rule that penalties may be recovered by civil actions, although such actions may be so far criminal in their nature that the defendant cannot be compelled to testify against himself in such actions in respect to any matters involving, or that may involve, his being guilty of a criminal offense." Id., at 112.

The question before us, then, is whether the penalty imposed in this case, although clearly not "criminal" enough to trigger the protections of the Sixth Amendment, the Double Jeopardy Clause of the Fifth Amendment, or the other procedural guarantees normally associated with criminal prosecutions, is nevertheless "so far criminal in [its] nature" as to trigger the Self-Incrimination Clause of the Fifth Amendment. Initially, we note that the penalty and proceeding considered in *Boyd* were quite different from those considered in this case. *Boyd* dealt with forfeiture of property, a penalty that had absolutely no correlation to any damages sustained by society or to the cost of enforcing the law. See also Lees v. United States, supra (fixed monetary penalty); One 1958 Plymouth Sedan v. Pennsylvania, supra (forfeiture); United States v. United States Coin & Currency, supra (forfeiture). Here the penalty is much more analogous to traditional civil damages. Moreover, the statute under scrutiny in *Boyd* listed forfeiture along with fine and imprisonment as one possible punishment for customs fraud, a fact of some significance to the *Boyd* Court. See 116 U.S., at 634. Here, as previously stated, the civil remedy and the criminal remedy are contained in separate statutes enacted

70 years apart. The proceedings in *Boyd* also posed a danger that the appellants would prejudice themselves in respect to later criminal proceedings. See Hepner v. United States, supra, at 112. Here, respondent is protected by §311(b)(5), which expressly provides that "[n]otification received pursuant to this paragraph or information obtained by the exploitation of such notification shall not be used against any such person in any criminal case, except [for] prosecution for perjury or for giving a false statement." 33 U.S.C. §1321(b)(5).

More importantly, however, we believe that in the light of what we have found to be overwhelming evidence that Congress intended to create a penalty civil in all respects and quite weak evidence of any countervailing punitive purpose or effect it would be quite anomalous to hold that §311(b)(6) created a criminal penalty for the purposes of the Self-Incrimination Clause but a civil penalty for all other purposes. We do not read *Boyd* as requiring a contrary conclusion. . . .

NOTES AND QUESTIONS

1. What does the phrase "civil penalty" mean?

2. In Allen v. Illinois, 478 U.S. 364 (1986), the Court held that the Illinois Sexually Dangerous Persons Act was civil rather than criminal in nature and thus the fifth amendment does not apply to it. The Court based its conclusion on the state's assertion of its civil nature, and the statute's "benign purpose" of providing treatment rather than punishment. As the dissent pointed out, however, the statute could only be triggered by a related criminal proceeding, could only be initiated by the state, required proof beyond reasonable doubt as well as the establishment of a criminal offense, and results in incarceration in the penal system. In Tull v. United States, 481 U.S. 421 (1987), the Court concluded that the seventh amendment required a jury trial to determine liability of a party to civil penalties and injunctive relief under the Clean Water Act, but that the judge rather than the jury could be empowered to determine the amount of the penalty. The Court found a limit on the concept of "civil penalties" in United States v. Halper, 109 S. Ct. 1892 (1989). In *Halper*, the government attempted to collect a civil penalty for acts that previously had been the foundation of a criminal conviction. The penalty greatly exceeded any reasonable approximation of reimbursement for the government's damages and costs. The Court found that such a relatively large civil penalty following a criminal conviction for the underlying event violated double jeopardy. This holding mirrors the Court's treatment of contempt issues. If a contempt order is remedial, and thus for the complainant's benefit, it is "civil." If it is punitive and

designed to vindicate the court's authority, it is "criminal," according to Hicks v. Feiock, 485 U.S. 624 (1988).

3. A criminal defendant has an absolute right not to take the stand, and it is constitutional error for the trial court or prosecutor to comment on the accused's failure to testify. Griffin v. California, 380 U.S. 609 (1965). A prosecutor may, however, comment on a defendant's failure to take the stand in response to closing arguments by defense counsel that the government had not allowed the defendant to tell his side of the story. United States v. Robinson, 485 U.S. 25 (1988). In all other cases, the person who wishes to claim the privilege may be examined, and the privilege must be interposed to the question. Moreover, an adverse inference from the refusal to testify is permitted. Baxter v. Palmigiano, 425 U.S. 308 (1976). For further discussion of the uses to which silence may be put, see Chapter 10 infra.

B. LIMITS ON THE PRIVILEGE

Immunity statutes generally contain an exception that permits the use of immunized testimony in prosecutions for perjury or for making false statements. In the next two cases, the Court dealt with the use of immunized testimony, and in doing so it provided another perspective on the scope of the fifth amendment.

NEW JERSEY v. PORTASH
Certiorari to the Superior Court of New Jersey
440 U.S. 450 (1979)

MR. JUSTICE STEWART delivered the opinion of the Court.

This case involves the scope of the privilege against compulsory self-incrimination, grounded in the Fifth Amendment and made binding against the States by the Fourteenth. The precise question is whether, despite this constitutional privilege, a prosecutor may use a person's legislatively immunized grand jury testimony to impeach his credibility as a testifying defendant in a criminal trial.

I

In the early 1970's, Joseph Portash was Mayor of Manchester Township, Executive Director of the Pinelands Environmental Council, and a member of both the Ocean County Board of Freeholders and the Manchester Municipal Utilities Authority in New Jersey. In November 1974, after a lengthy investigation, a state grand jury subpoenaed Portash. He expressed an intention to claim his privilege against compulsory self-incrimination. The prosecutors and Portash's lawyers then agreed that, if Portash testified before the grand jury, neither his statements nor any evidence derived from them could, under New Jersey law, be used in subsequent criminal proceedings (except in prosecutions for perjury or false swearing).[1] After Portash's testimony, the parties tried to come to an agreement to avoid a criminal prosecution against Portash, but no bargain was reached. In April 1975, Portash was indicted for misconduct in office and extortion by a public official.

Before trial, defense counsel sought to obtain a ruling from the trial judge that no use of the immunized grand jury testimony would be permitted. The judge refused to rule that the prosecution could not use this testimony for purposes of impeachment. After the completion of the State's case, defense counsel renewed his request for a ruling by the trial judge as to the use of the grand jury testimony. There followed an extended colloquy, and the judge finally ruled that if Portash testified and gave an answer on direct or cross-examination which was materially inconsistent with his grand jury testimony, the prosecutor could use that testimony in his cross-examination of Portash. Defense counsel then stated that, because of this ruling, he would advise his client not to take the stand. Portash did not testify, and the jury ultimately found him guilty on one of the two counts.

The New Jersey Appellate Division reversed the conviction. That court held that the Constitution requires that the immunity granted by the New Jersey statute must be at least coextensive with the privilege afforded by the Fifth and Fourteenth Amendments. To confer such protection, the court reasoned, the grant of immunity must "leave defendant and the State in the position each would have occupied had defendant's claim of privilege [before the grand jury] been honored." Use of the immunized grand jury testimony to impeach a defendant at his trial, it held, did not meet this test. Because Portash's decision not to testify was based upon the trial court's erroneous ruling to the contrary, the Appellate Division reversed the conviction and remanded the case for a new trial.

---

1. At that time a New Jersey statute provided as follows:

If any public employee testifies before any court, grand jury or the State Commission of Investigation, such testimony and the evidence derived therefrom shall not be used against such public employee in a subsequent criminal proceeding under the laws of this State; provided that no such public employee shall be exempt from prosecution or punishment for perjury committed while so testifying. New Jersey Public Employees Immunity Statute, N.J. Stat. Ann. §2A:81-17.2a2 (West 1976).

II

New Jersey presents two questions. *First*, it argues that Portash cannot properly invoke the privilege against compulsory incrimination because he did not take the witness stand and, as a result, his immunized grand jury testimony was never used against him. *Second*, it urges that the Fifth and Fourteenth Amendments do not prohibit the use of immunized grand jury testimony to impeach materially inconsistent statements made at trial.

A

The State contends that the issue presented by Portash is abstract and hypothetical because he did not, in fact, become a witness. Portash could have taken the stand, testified, objected to the prosecution's use of the immunized testimony to impeach him, and appealed any subsequent conviction. Absent that, the State would have us hold that the constitutional question was not and is not presented. This argument must be rejected. *First*, it is clear that although the trial judge was concerned about making a ruling before specific questions were asked, he did rule on the merits of the constitutional question. . . . *Second*, the New Jersey appellate court necessarily concluded that the federal constitutional question had been properly presented, because it ruled in Portash's favor on the merits.[4] . . .

Moreover, there is nothing in federal law to prohibit New Jersey from following such a procedure, or, so long as the "case or controversy" requirement of Art. III is met, to foreclose our consideration of the substantive constitutional issue now that the New Jersey courts have decided it. This is made clear by a case decided by this Court in 1972, Brooks v. Tennessee, 406 U.S. 605. There the Court held unconstitutional a Tennessee statutory requirement that a defendant in a criminal case had to be his own first witness if he was to take the stand at all. The Court held that such a requirement unconstitutionally penalized a defendant's right to remain silent, since a defendant could remain silent immediately after the close of the State's case only at the cost of never testifying in his own defense. Although Brooks had not testified, the

---

4. Lefkowitz v. Newsome, 420 U.S. 283, was another case where provisions of state law allowed federal review that may not otherwise have been available. There, New York law allowed a defendant to appeal defeat of a motion to suppress even though he later pleaded guilty. The Court held that because the State recognized such a procedure, a state prisoner who had pleaded guilty could assert his Fourth and Fourteenth Amendment claim in a federal habeas corpus proceeding, even though federal habeas corpus relief would not generally have been available to one who had pleaded guilty.

Tennessee court considered the constitutional validity of the state statute, and so did this Court. Because the rule imposed a penalty on the right to remain silent, the Court found that his constitutional rights had been infringed even though he had never taken the stand. Id., at 611 n.6.

In *Brooks* the Court held that the defendant's Fifth and Fourteenth Amendment rights had been violated because, in order to assert his Fifth Amendment right to remain silent after the prosecution's case in chief had been presented, the defendant would have had to pay a penalty. He could never testify. Here, as in *Brooks*, federal law does not insist that New Jersey was wrong in not requiring Portash to take the witness stand in order to raise his constitutional claim.[5]

B

In both Great Britain and in what later became the United States, immunity statutes, like the privilege against compulsory self-incrimination, predate the adoption of the Constitution. Kastigar v. United States, 406 U.S. 441, 445 n.13, 446 n.14. This Court first considered a constitutional challenge to an immunity statute in Counselman v. Hitchcock, 142 U.S. 547. The witness in that case had refused to testify before a federal grand jury in spite of a grant of immunity under the relevant federal statute. The Court overturned his contempt conviction. It construed the statute to permit the use of evidence *derived* from his immunized testimony. The witness was held to have validly asserted his privilege because "legislation cannot abridge a constitutional privilege, and . . . it cannot replace or supply one, at least unless it is so broad as to have the same extent in scope and effect." Id. at 585. See also Brown v. United States, 359 U.S. 41; Ullmann v. United States, 350 U.S. 422; Brown v. Walker, 161 U.S. 591. After the holding in Malloy v. Hogan, 378 U.S. 1, that the Fifth Amendment privilege against compulsory self-incrimination is also contained in the Fourteenth Amendment, this rule is necessarily applicable to state immunity statutes as well. . . .

Language in *Counselman* and its progeny was read by some to require that the witness must be immune from prosecution for the transaction his testimony concerned. Indeed, the federal statutes subsequently upheld

---

5. A similar situation existed in Wardius v. Oregon, 412 U.S. 470. The Court held in that case that state notice-of-alibi requirements could be enforced only if the State provided reciprocal discovery rights for the defendant. The defendant in that case had not given a notice of alibi. The State argued that he could not assert his constitutional claim, because he should have given his notice of alibi and then argued that the State had to grant him reciprocal discovery. The Court rejected that argument, and held that he need not give notice to raise his constitutional claim.

by the Court granted such transactional immunity. Brown v. United States, supra; Ullman v. United States, supra; Heike v. United States, 227 U.S. 131; Brown v. Walker, supra.[7] The adoption of Pub. L. 91-452 in 1970 marked a change in federal immunity legislation from the provision of transactional immunity to the provision of what is known as "use" immunity. 18 U.S.C. §§6001, 6002. This immunity, similar to that provided by the New Jersey statute in this case, protects the witness from the use of his compelled testimony and any information derived from it. In Kastigar v. United States, supra, the Court upheld that statute against a challenge that mere use immunity is not coextensive with the Fifth Amendment's privilege.

> The privilege has never been construed to mean that one who invokes it cannot subsequently be prosecuted. Its sole concern is to afford protection against being "forced to give testimony leading to the infliction of 'penalties affixed to . . . criminal acts.' " Immunity from the use of compelled testimony, as well as evidence derived directly and indirectly therefrom, affords this protection. It prohibits the prosecutorial authorities from using the compelled testimony in *any* respect, and it therefore insures that the testimony cannot lead to the infliction of criminal penalties on the witness.

Against this broad statement of the necessary constitutional scope of testimonial immunity, the State asks us to weigh Harris v. New York, 401 U.S. 222, and Oregon v. Hass, 420 U.S. 714. Those cases involved the use of statements, concededly taken in violation of Miranda v. Arizona, 384 U.S. 436, to impeach a defendant's testimony at trial. In both cases the Court weighed the incremental deterrence of police illegality against the strong policy against countenancing perjury. In the balance, use of the incriminating statements for impeachment purposes prevailed. The State asks that we apply the same reasoning to this case. It points out that the interest in preventing perjury is just as strongly involved, and that the statements made to the grand jury are at least as reliable as those made by the defendants in *Harris* and *Hass*.

But the State has overlooked a crucial distinction between those cases and this one. In *Harris* and *Hass* the Court expressly noted that the defendant made "no claim that the statements made to the police were coerced or involuntary," Harris v. New York, supra, at 224; Oregon v. Hass, supra, at 722-723. That recognition was central to the decisions in those cases.

The Fifth and the Fourteenth Amendments provide that no person "shall be *compelled* in any criminal case to be a witness against himself."

---

7. See Shapiro v. United States, 335 U.S. 1, 6 n.4, for a list of the federal statutes that provided transactional immunity.

As we reaffirmed last Term, a defendant's compelled statements, as opposed to statements taken in violation of *Miranda*, may not be put to any testimonial use whatever against him in a criminal trial. "But any criminal trial use against a defendant of his *involuntary* statement is a denial of due process of law." (Emphasis in original.) Mincey v. Arizona, 437 U.S. 385, 398.

Testimony given in response to a grant of legislative immunity is the essence of coerced testimony. In such cases there is no question whether physical or psychological pressures overrode the defendant's will; the witness is told to talk or face the government's coercive sanctions, notably, a conviction for contempt. The information given in response to a grant of immunity may well be more reliable than information beaten from a helpless defendant, but it is no less compelled. The Fifth and Fourteenth Amendments provide a privilege against *compelled* self-incrimination, not merely against unreliable self-incrimination. Balancing of interests was thought to be necessary in *Harris* and *Hass* when the attempt to deter unlawful police conduct collided with the need to prevent perjury. Here, by contrast, we deal with the constitutional privilege against compulsory self-incrimination in its most pristine form. Balancing, therefore, is not simply unnecessary. It is impermissible.

The Superior Court of New Jersey, Appellate Division, correctly ruled that a person's testimony before a grand jury under a grant of immunity cannot constitutionally be used to impeach him when he is a defendant in a later criminal trial. Accordingly, the judgment is affirmed.

It is so ordered.

[The concurring opinions of JUSTICE BRENNAN and JUSTICE MARSHALL are omitted.]

MR. JUSTICE POWELL, with whom MR. JUSTICE REHNQUIST joins, concurring. . . .

The Court has referred to two quite different interests in determining whether the Fifth Amendment permits a defendant's statements to be used against him at trial. In Harris v. New York, 401 U.S. 222 (1971), the Court emphasized the trustworthiness of a suspect's statements made to police, noting that there was no indication that the statements were "coerced or involuntary." Similarly, here there is no reason to question the veracity of the respondent's grand jury testimony. The Court today recognizes, however, that the privilege against self-incrimination protects against more than just the use of false or inaccurate statements against a criminal defendant. In addition, the Fifth Amendment, by virtue of its incorporation through the Fourteenth Amendment, prohibits a State from using compulsion to extract truthful information from a defendant, when that information is to be used later in obtaining the individual's conviction.

MR. JUSTICE BLACKMUN, with whom THE CHIEF JUSTICE joins, dissenting.

The Court in this case reaches out to decide an important constitutional question even though that question is presented in the context of an abstract dispute over a hypothetical ruling of the trial court. For me, the facts present too remote and speculative an injury to federally protected rights to support the exercise of jurisdiction by this Court. Indeed, examination of the record reveals for me that the Court decides today a question different from the one the trial court considered. This demonstrates how far afield we range when we cut loose from the requirement that only concrete disputes may be decided by this Court. Because I believe the Court is without authority to engage in this type of abstract adjudication of constitutional rights in a factual vacuum, I dissent.

Prior to trial, and again at the close of the State's evidence, respondent Portash attempted to obtain an advance evidentiary ruling from the trial court. Though the precise nature of the ruling respondent sought is a matter of dispute, it related generally to whether and to what extent the State would be permitted to use, during cross-examination of respondent and in the rebuttal phase of its own case, information supplied by respondent under the statutory grant of immunity. When respondent failed to obtain a ruling he considered satisfactory, he refrained from testifying in his own behalf. Accordingly, he did not take the stand at the trial. He was not cross-examined. He gave no answer determined by the trial court to be materially inconsistent with any prior immunized statement on a relevant issue. The State did not seek to impeach him through use of immunized testimony. And the trial court did not rule that the State could do so in response to an inconsistent answer, or that the State could otherwise make use of immunized testimony at trial. In short, because of his failure to take the stand, respondent was never incriminated through the use of the testimony he previously had supplied under the immunity grant. . . .

In these circumstances, I would hold the dispute as to the use of the immunized testimony to be too remote and speculative to enable this Court to adjudicate it. By finding sufficient controversy to exist in this case to reach the federal issue, the Court exercises jurisdiction over an abstract dispute of no concrete significance, and as a result renders an advisory opinion, informing respondent what the State would have been permitted to do or not do had respondent ever taken the stand.

UNITED STATES v. APFELBAUM
Certiorari to the United States Court of Appeals for the Third Circuit
445 U.S. 115 (1980)

MR. JUSTICE REHNQUIST delivered the opinion of the Court.

Respondent Apfelbaum invoked his privilege against compulsory self-incrimination while being questioned before a grand jury in the Eastern District of Pennsylvania. The Government then granted him immunity in accordance with 18 U.S.C. §6002, and he answered the questions propounded to him. He was then charged with and convicted of making false statements in the course of those answers.[1] The Court of Appeals reversed the conviction, however, because the District Court had admitted into evidence relevant portions of respondent's grand jury testimony that had not been alleged in the indictment to constitute the "corpus delicti" or "core" of the false-statements offense. Because proper invocation of the Fifth Amendment privilege against compulsory self-incrimination allows a witness to remain silent, but not to swear falsely, we hold that neither the statute nor the Fifth Amendment requires that the admissibility of immunized testimony be governed by any different rules than other testimony at a trial for making false statements in violation of 18 U.S.C. §1623(a) (1976 ed., Supp. II). We therefore reverse the judgment of the Court of Appeals.

I

The grand jury had been investigating alleged criminal activities in connection with an automobile dealership located in the Chestnut Hill section of Philadelphia. The investigation focused on a robbery of $175,000 in cash that occurred at the dealership on April 16, 1975, and on allegations that two officers of the dealership staged the robbery in order to repay loan-shark debts. The grand jury also heard testimony that the officers were making extortionate extensions of credit through the Chestnut Hill Lincoln-Mercury dealership.

In 1976, respondent Apfelbaum, then an administrative assistant to the District Attorney in Philadelphia, was called to testify because it was thought likely that he was an aider or abettor or an accessory after the fact to the allegedly staged robbery. When the grand jury first sought to

---

1. Title 18 U.S.C. §1623(a) (1976 ed., Supp. II) provides in pertinent part:

Whoever under oath . . . in any proceeding before . . . [a] grand jury of the United States knowingly makes any false material declaration . . . shall be fined not more than $10,000 or imprisoned not more than five years, or both.

question him about his relationship with the two dealership officials suspected of the staged robbery, he claimed his Fifth Amendment privilege against compulsory self-incrimination and refused to testify. The District Judge entered an order pursuant to 18 U.S.C. §6002 granting him immunity and compelling him to testify.[3] Respondent ultimately complied with this order to testify.

During the course of his grand jury testimony, respondent made two series of statements that served as the basis for his subsequent indictment and conviction for false swearing. The first series was made in response to questions concerning whether respondent had attempted to locate Harry Brown, one of the two dealership officials, while on a "fishing trip" in Ft. Lauderdale, Fla., during the month of December 1975. Respondent testified that he was "positive" he had not attempted to locate Brown, who was also apparently in the Ft. Lauderdale area at the time. In a second series of statements, respondent denied that he had told FBI agents that he had lent $10,000 to Brown. The grand jury later indicted respondent pursuant to 18 U.S.C. §1623(a) (1976 ed., Supp, II) for making these statements, charging that the two series of statements were false and that respondent knew they were false.

At trial, the Government introduced into evidence portions of respondent's grand jury testimony in order to put the charged statements in context and to show that respondent knew they were false. The excerpts concerned respondent's relationship with Brown, his 1976 trip to Florida to visit Brown, the discussions he had with Brown on that occasion, and his denial that he had financial dealings with the automobile dealership in Philadelphia or had cosigned a loan for Brown. Respondent objected to the use of all the immunized testimony except the portions charged in the indictment as false. The District Court overruled the objection and admitted the excerpts into evidence on the ground that they were relevant to prove that respondent had knowingly made the charged false

3. Title 18 U.S.C. §6002 provides:

Whenever a witness refuses, on the basis of his privilege against self-incrimination, to testify or provide other information in a proceeding before or ancillary to—

(1) a court or grand jury of the United States,
(2) an agency of the United States, or
(3) either House of Congress, a joint committee of the two Houses, or a committee or a subcommittee of either House,

and the person presiding over the proceeding communicates to the witness an order issued under this part, the witness may not refuse to comply with the order on the basis of his privilege against self-incrimination; but no testimony or other information compelled under the order (or any information directly or indirectly derived from such testimony or other information) may be used against the witness in any criminal case, except a prosecution for perjury, giving a false statement, or otherwise failing to comply with the order.

statements. The jury found respondent guilty on both counts of the indictment.

The Court of Appeals for the Third Circuit reversed, holding that because the immunized testimony did not constitute "the corpus delicti or core of a defendant's false swearing indictment" it could not be introduced. We granted certiorari because of the importance of the issue and because of a difference in approach to it among the Courts of Appeals.[5]

The differing views that this question has elicited from the Courts of Appeals are not surprising, because there are considered statements in one line of cases from this Court, and both statements and actual holdings in another line of cases, that as a matter of strict and literal reading cannot be wholly reconciled.[6] Though most of the decisions of the Courts of Appeals turn on the interaction between perjury and immunity statutes enacted by Congress and the privilege against compulsory self-incrimi-

5. The Seventh Circuit agrees with the Court of Appeals below that the Government may introduce into evidence so much of the witness' testimony as is essential to establish the corpus delicti of the offense of perjury. The Second and Tenth Circuits have held that false immunized testimony is admissible, but truthful immunized testimony is not, in a subsequent prosecution for perjury. The Sixth and Eighth Circuits have held that immunized testimony may be used for any purpose in such a prosecution.

6. A principal reason for this divergence in approach originates in the statement in Counselman v. Hitchcock, 142 U.S. 547, 585 (1892), that an immunity statute "cannot abridge a constitutional privilege, and that it cannot replace or supply one, at least unless it is so broad as to have the same extent in scope and effect." This language was reiterated only last Term in New Jersey v. Portash, 440 U.S. 450, 456-457 (1979).

As discussed in Part III, infra, strictly speaking even a "transactional" immunity statute, to say nothing of a "use" immunity statute, does not conform to this definition: The mere grant of immunity and consequent compulsion to testify places a witness asserting his Fifth Amendment privilege in the dilemma of having to decide whether to answer the questions truthfully or falsely, a dilemma he never would have faced had he simply been permitted to remain silent upon the invocation of his privilege. Yet properly drawn immunity statutes have long been recognized as valid in this country. . . . And it is likewise well established that one may be prosecuted for making false statements while giving immunized testimony. . . .

A source of further difficulty for the Courts of Appeals is language from our recent decisions that, if taken literally, would preclude the introduction of immunized testimony even for the purpose of establishing the "corpus delicti" or core of the perjury offense. In Kastigar v. United States, 406 U.S. 441, 453 (1972), in which we upheld the constitutionality of this immunity statute against a challenge that it did not provide protection coextensive with the Fifth Amendment, we said that it "prohibits the prosecutorial authorities from using the compelled testimony in any respect." And in New Jersey v. Portash, supra, at 459, we stated that under the Fifth and Fourteenth Amendments "a defendant's compelled statements . . . may not be put to any testimonial use whatever against him in a criminal trial. '. . . [A]ny criminal trial use against a defendant of his involuntary statement is a denial of due process of law.' " (Emphasis in original.)

Doubtless as a result of these divergent holdings and statements none of the Court of Appeals decisions referred to in footnote 5, supra, holds that false immunized testimony may not form the basis for a prosecution for perjury or false swearing, but they differ as to how much of the relevant immunized testimony other than that asserted by the Government to be false may be introduced in such a prosecution.

nation conferred by the Fifth Amendment of the United States Constitution, it is of course our first duty to decide whether the statute relied upon in this case to sustain the conviction of respondent may properly be interpreted to do so. We turn now to decision of that question.

II

Did Congress intend the federal immunity statute, 18 U.S.C. §6002, to limit the use of a witness' immunized grand jury testimony in a subsequent prosecution of the witness for false statements made at the grand jury proceeding? Respondent contends that while §6002 permits the use of a witness' false statements in a prosecution for perjury or for making false declarations, it establishes an absolute prohibition against the use of truthful immunized testimony in such prosecutions. But this contention is wholly at odds with the explicit language of the statute, and finds no support even in its legislative history.

It is a well-established principle of statutory construction that absent clear evidence of a contrary legislative intention, a statute should be interpreted according to its plain language. Here 18 U.S.C. §6002 provides that when a witness is compelled to testify over his claim of a Fifth Amendment privilege, "no testimony or other information compelled under the order (or any information directly or indirectly derived from such testimony or other information) may be used against the witness in any criminal case, *except a prosecution for perjury, giving a false statement, or otherwise failing to comply with the order.*" (Emphasis added.) The statute thus makes no distinction between truthful and untruthful statements made during the course of the immunized testimony. Rather, it creates a blanket exemption from the bar against the use of immunized testimony in cases in which the witness is subsequently prosecuted for making false statements.

The legislative history of §6002 shows that Congress intended the perjury and false-declarations exception to be interpreted as broadly as constitutionally permissible. The present statute was enacted as a part of the Organized Crime Control Act of 1970,[7] after a re-examination of the broad transactional immunity statute enacted in response to this Court's decision in Counselman v. Hitchcock. Its design was not only to bring about uniformity in the operation of immunity grants within the federal

---

7. Pub. L. 91-452, §201(a), 84 Stat. 926. The purpose of the Act was "to seek the eradication of organized crime in the United States by strengthening the legal tools in the evidence-gathering process, by establishing new penal prohibitions, and by providing enhanced sanctions and new remedies to deal with the unlawful activities of those engaged in organized crime." 84 Stat. 923.

system,[8] but also to restrict the grant of immunity to that required by the United States Constitution. Thus, the statute derives from a 1969 report of the National Commission on the Reform of the Federal Criminal Laws, which proposed a general use immunity statute under which "the immunity conferred would be confined to the scope required by the Fifth Amendment."[9] And as stated in both the Senate and House Reports on the proposed legislation: "This statutory immunity is intended to be as broad as, but no broader than, the privilege against self incrimination. . . . It is designed to reflect the use-restriction immunity concept of Murphy v. Waterfront Commission rather [than] the transaction immunity concept of Counselman v. Hitchcock.[10] In light of the language and legislative history of §6002, the conclusion is inescapable that Congress intended to permit the use of both truthful and false statements made during the course of immunized testimony if such use was not prohibited by the Fifth Amendment.

III

The limitation placed on the use of relevant evidence by the Court of Appeals may be justified, then, only if required by the Fifth Amendment. Respondent contends that his conviction was properly reversed because under the Fifth Amendment his truthful immunized statements were inadmissible at his perjury trial, and the Government never met its burden of showing that the immunized statements it introduced into evidence were not truthful. The Court of Appeals, as noted above, concluded that the Fifth Amendment prohibited the use of all immunized testimony except the "corpus delicti" or "core" of the false swearing indictment.

In reaching its conclusion, the Court of Appeals initially observed that a grant of immunity must be coextensive with the Fifth Amendment.

8. See, e.g., Measures Relating to Organized Crime, Hearings on S.30, etc., before the Subcommittee on Criminal Laws and Procedures of the Senate Committee on the Judiciary, 91st Cong., 1st Sess., 282-284 (1969) (remarks of Representative Poff and Senator McClellan). At the time the new statute was being considered, there were more than 50 separate federal immunity statues. Id., at 282.

9. Second Interim Report of the National Commission on Reform of Federal Criminal Laws, Mar. 17, 1969, reproduced in Hearings on S. 30, supra, n.8, at 292. See also id., at 15, 326; National Commission on Reform of Federal Criminal Laws, Working Papers 1405 (1970).

10. S. Rep. No. 91-617, p. 1145 (1969); H.R. Rep. No. 91-1549, p.42 (1970). Representative Poll, the bill's chief sponsor in the House, quoted Mr. Justice White's observation in Murphy v. Waterfront Comm'n, 378 U.S. 52, 107 (1964), that " '[i]mmunity must be as broad as, but not harmfully and wastefully broader than, the privilege against self-incrimination.' " 116 Cong. Rec. 35291 (1970). We express no opinion as to the possible intimation in the Reports that the Fifth Amendment would have prohibited an immunity statute any broader than §6002.

Kastigar v. United States, supra, at 449. It then reasoned that had respondent not been granted immunity, he would have been entitled under the Fifth Amendment to remain silent. And if he had remained silent, he would not have answered any questions, truthfully or falsely. There consequently would have been no testimony whatsoever to use against him. A prosecution for perjury committed at the immunized proceeding, the Court of Appeals continued, must be permitted because "as a practical matter, if immunity constituted a license to lie, the purpose of immunity would be defeated." Such a prosecution is but a "narrow exception" carved out to preserve the integrity of the truth-seeking process. But the subsequent use of statements made at the immunized proceeding, other than those alleged in the indictment to be false, is impermissible because the introduction of such statements cannot be reconciled with the privilege against self-incrimination. 584 F.2d, at 1269-1271.

A

There is more than one flaw in this reasoning. Initially, it presumes that in order for a grant of immunity to be "coextensive with the Fifth Amendment privilege," the witness must be treated as if he had remained silent. This presumption focuses on the *effect* of the assertion of the Fifth Amendment privilege, rather than on the *protection* the privilege is designed to confer. In so doing, it calls into question the constitutionality of all immunity statutes, including "transactional" immunity statutes as well as "use" immunity statutes such as §6002. Such grants of immunity would not provide a full and complete substitute for a witness' silence because, for example, they do not bar the use of the witness' statements in civil proceedings. Indeed, they fail to prevent the use of such statements for any purpose that might cause detriment to the witness other than that resulting from subsequent criminal prosecution.

This Court has never held, however, that the Fifth Amendment requires immunity statutes to preclude all uses of immunized testimony. Such a requirement would be inconsistent with the principle that the privilege does not extend to consequences of a noncriminal nature, such as threats of liability in civil suits, disgrace in the community, or the loss of employment. . . .

These cases also establish that a strict and literal reading of language in cases such as Counselman v. Hitchcock that an immunity statute "cannot abridge a constitutional privilege, and that it cannot replace or supply one, at least unless it is so broad as to have the same extent in scope and effect"—does not require the sort of "but for" analysis used by the Court of Appeals in order to enable it to survive attack as being violative of the privilege against compulsory self-incrimination. Indeed, in Brown v. Walker, this Court stated that "[t]he danger of extending the principle announced in Counselman v. Hitchcock is that the privilege may be put forward for a sentimental reason, or for a purely fanciful protection of the witness against an imaginary danger, and for the real purpose of securing immunity to some third person, who is interested in concealing the facts to which he would testify." And in Kastigar v. United States, we concluded that "[t]he broad language in *Counselman* relied upon by petitioners was unnecessary to the Court's decision, and cannot be considered binding authority." *Kastigar* also expressly declined a request by the petitioner to reconsider and overrule Brown v. Walker, supra, and Ullmann v. United States, supra, and went on to expressly reaffirm the validity of those decisions.

The reasoning of the Court of Appeals is also internally inconsistent in that logically it would not permit a prosecution for perjury or false swearing committed during the course of the immunized testimony. If a witness must be treated as if he had remained silent, the mere requirement that he answer questions, thereby subjecting himself to the possibility of being subsequently prosecuted for perjury or false swearing, places him in a position that is substantially different from that he would have been in had he been permitted to remain silent.

All of the Courts of Appeals, however, have recognized that the provision in 18 U.S.C. §6002 allowing prosecutions for perjury in answering questions following a grant of immunity does not violate the Fifth Amendment privilege against compulsory self-incrimination. And we ourselves have repeatedly held that perjury prosecutions are permissible for false answers to questions following the grant of immunity.

It is therefore analytically incorrect to equate the benefits of remaining silent as a result of invocation of the Fifth Amendment privilege with the protections conferred by the privilege—protections that may be invoked with respect to matters that pose substantial and real hazards of subjecting a witness to criminal liability at the time he asserts the privilege. For a grant of immunity to provide protection "coextensive" with that of the Fifth Amendment, it need not treat the witness as if he had remained silent. Such a conclusion, as noted above, is belied by the fact that immunity statutes and prosecutions for perjury committed during the course of immunized testimony are permissible at all.

B

The principle that the Fifth Amendment privilege against compulsory self-incrimination provides no protection for the commission of perjury has frequently been cited without any elaboration as to its underlying rationale. . . . Its doctrinal foundation, as relied on in both *Wong* and

Mandujano, is traceable to Glickstein v. United States, 222 U.S. 139, 142 (1911). *Glickstein* stated that the Fifth Amendment "does not endow the person who testifies with a license to commit perjury," ibid., and that statement has been so often repeated in our cases as to be firmly established constitutional law. But just as we have refused to read literally the broad dicta of *Counselman*, supra, we are likewise unwilling to decide this case solely upon an epigram contained in *Glickstein*, supra. Thus, even if, as the Court of Appeals said, a perjury prosecution is but a "narrow exception" to the principle that a witness should be treated as if he had remained silent, it does not follow that the Court of Appeals was correct in its view of the question before us now.

Perjury prosecutions based on immunized testimony, even if they be but a "narrow exception" to the principle that a witness should be treated as if he had remained silent after invoking the Fifth Amendment privilege, *are* permitted by our cases. And so long as they are, there is no principle or decision that limits the admissibility of evidence in a manner peculiar only to them. To so hold would not be an exercise in the balancing of competing constitutional rights, but in a comparison of apples and oranges.[11] For even if both truthful and untruthful testimony from the immunized proceeding are admissible in a subsequent perjury prosecution, the exception surely would still be properly regarded as "narrow," once it is recognized that the testimony remains inadmissible in all prosecutions for offenses committed prior to the grant of immunity that would have permitted the witness to invoke his Fifth Amendment privilege absent the grant.

While the application of the Fifth Amendment privilege to various types of claims has changed in some respects over the past three decades, the basic test reaffirmed in each case has been the same.

"The central standard for the privilege's application has been whether the claimant is confronted by substantial and 'real', and not merely trifling or imaginary, hazards of incrimination." Marchetti v. United States, 390 U.S. 39, 53 (1968).

Marchetti, which overruled earlier decisions of this Court in United States v. Kahriger, 345 U.S. 22 (1953), and Lewis v. United States, 348 U.S. 419 (1955), invalidated the federal wagering statutes at issue in *Kahriger* and *Lewis* on the ground that they contravened the petitioner's Fifth Amendment right against compulsory self-incrimination. The prac-

---

11. Thus, the Court of Appeals' position is basically a halfway house that does not withstand logical analysis. If the rule is that a witness who is granted immunity may be placed in no worse a position than if he had been permitted to remain silent, the principle that the Fifth Amendment does not protect false statements serves merely as a piece of a legal mosaic justified solely by stare decisis, rather than as part of a doctrinally consistent view of that Amendment.

tical effect of the requirements of those statutes was to compel petitioner, a professional gambler engaged in ongoing gambling activities that he had commenced and was likely to continue, to choose between openly exposing himself as acting in violation of state and federal gambling laws and risking federal prosecution for tax avoidance.[12] The Court held that petitioner was entitled to assert his Fifth Amendment privilege in these circumstances. But it also observed that "prospective acts will doubtless ordinarily involve only speculative and insubstantial risks of incrimination." 390 U.S., at 54. Thus, although *Marchetti* rejected "the rigid chronological distinction adopted in *Kahriger* and *Lewis*," id., at 53, that distinction does not aid respondent here.

In United States v. Freed, 401 U.S. 601 (1971), this Court rejected the argument that a registration requirement of the National Firearms Act violated the Fifth Amendment because the information disclosed could be used in connection with offenses that the transferee of the firearm might commit in the future. In so doing, the Court stated:

> Appellees' argument assumes the existence of a periphery of the Self-Incrimination Clause which protects a person against incrimination not only against past or present transgressions but which supplies insulation for a career of crime about to be launched. We cannot give the Self-Incrimination Clause such an expansive interpretation." Id., at 606-607. . . .

In light of these decisions, we conclude that the Fifth Amendment does not prevent the use of respondent's immunized testimony at his trial for false swearing because, at the time he was granted immunity, the privilege would not have protected him against false testimony that he later might decide to give. Respondent's assertion of his Fifth Amendment privilege arose from his claim that the questions relating to his connection with the Chestnut Hill auto dealership would tend to incriminate him. The Government consequently granted him "use" immunity under §6002, which prevents the use and derivative use of his testimony with respect to any subsequent criminal case except prosecutions for perjury and false swearing offenses, in exchange for his compelled testimony.

12. Thus, the Court observed: "Petitioner was confronted by a comprehensive system of federal and state prohibitions against wagering activities; he was required, on pain of criminal prosecution, to provide information which he might reasonably suppose would be available to prosecuting authorities, and which would surely prove a significant 'link in a chain' of evidence tending to establish his guilt." 390 U.S., at 48. And "[e]very aspect of petitioner's wagering activities," the Court continued, "subjected him to possible state or federal prosecution," and the "[i]nformation obtained as a consequence of the federal wagering tax laws is readily available to assist the efforts of state and federal authorities to enforce these penalties." Id., at 47.

The Government has kept its part of the bargain; this is a perjury prosecution and not any other kind of criminal prosecution. The Court of Appeals agreed that such a prosecution might be maintained, but as noted above severely limited the admissibility of immunized testimony to prove the Government's case. We believe that it could not be fairly said that respondent, at the time he asserted his privilege and was consequently granted immunity, was confronted with more than a "trifling or imaginary" hazard of compelled self-incrimination as a result of the possibility that he might commit perjury during the course of his immunized testimony. In United States v. Bryan, 339 U.S. 323 (1950), we held that an immunity statute that provided that "[n]o testimony given by a witness before . . . any committee of either House . . . shall be used as evidence in any criminal proceeding against him in any court, except in a prosecution for perjury committed in giving such testimony," did not bar the use at respondent's trial for willful default of the testimony given by her before a congressional committee. In so holding, we stated that "[t]here is, in our jurisprudence, no doctrine of 'anticipatory contempt.' " Id., at 341.

We hold here that in our jurisprudence there likewise is no doctrine of "anticipatory perjury." In the criminal law, both a culpable mens rea and a criminal actus reus are generally required for an offense to occur. Similarly, a future intention to commit perjury or to make false statements if granted immunity because of a claim of compulsory self-incrimination is not by itself sufficient to create a "substantial and 'real' " hazard that permits invocation of the Fifth Amendment. . . . Therefore, neither the immunity statute nor the Fifth Amendment precludes the use of respondent's immunized testimony at a subsequent prosecution for making false statements, so long as that testimony conforms to otherwise applicable rules of evidence. The exception of a perjury prosecution from the prohibition against the use of immunized testimony may be a narrow one, but it is also a complete one. The Court of Appeals having held otherwise, its judgment is accordingly reversed.

MR. JUSTICE BRENNAN, concurring in the judgment. . . .

Because I think it follows from the logic and exigencies of the perjury exception that the Government should be permitted to introduce other portions of the immunized testimony to prove elements of the offense of perjury, I concur in the judgment reversing the decision of the Court of Appeals for the Third Circuit. And because I find this ground adequate to decide the present case I see no reason to explore the terrain which the majority probes via what is in one sense dicta. More particularly, (1) I do not think that the present result compels the conclusion that there are no special constitutional constraints on the use to which immunized testimony may be put in a perjury prosecution, and (2) I am by no means persuaded that the result here would be correct were this a prosecution for false swearing occurring after the immunized testimony rather than in the course of it.

MR. JUSTICE BLACKMUN, with whom MR. JUSTICE MARSHALL joins, concurring in the judgment.

I do not join the Court's opinion. I agree, however, that the Court of Appeals too narrowly confined the use of immunized testimony in the prosecution of respondent for giving false testimony. I do not fully subscribe to the Court's holding that "neither the statute nor the Fifth Amendment requires that the admissibility of immunized testimony be governed by any different rules than other testimony at a trial for making false statements." . . . And I do not fully agree with the Court's conclusion that the practical effect of asserting the privilege against self-incrimination is an unimportant factor in determining whether a grant of immunity is coextensive with Fifth Amendment protection. . . . I therefore concur only in the judgment.

The Court's statement of its holding troubles me primarily for two reasons. *First*, it apparently makes no distinction between a prosecution for false testimony given under a grant of immunity and a prosecution for false testimony in other contexts. This case concerns the use of immunized testimony to prove that respondent made contemporaneous false statements. There is no occasion to determine whether the immunized testimony could have been used to prove perjury or false statements occurring at some other time. The Court thus states its holding in language that is broader than necessary. At the moment, I am not prepared to go so far.

Second, I am not sure I agree that the use of immunized testimony in perjury prosecutions requires no special analysis with respect to the usual rules of evidence. How the testimony is to be used may well be an important factor in determining whether the protection against self-incrimination has been honored. For example, a witness' truthful admission of prior perjury conceivably might be protected from use even though independent evidence of such a prior similar crime were admissible. Again, I would prefer to await further developments before deciding this question.

Perhaps a more fundamental reservation about the Court's opinion concerns its attempted distinction between, on the one hand, the protection afforded by the privilege against self-incrimination and, on the other, the effect of the invocation of the privilege. Since the privilege itself is *defined* in terms of the incriminating effect of truthful testimony, it does not seem irrational to weigh alternative methods for protecting this constitutional right in terms of their effect as well. As the Court demonstrates, . . . a grant of immunity may be a constitutionally adequate response to invocation of the privilege without perfectly replicating the effect of total silence, at least where a civil use of the testimony is concerned. But that observation, for me, does not obviate the relevance of a comparison between silence and immunity in determining whether the protection afforded by the latter ensures that the privilege against self-incrimination has been properly preserved. Whether as a matter of logic, history, or experience, it does not follow that an analogy is robbed of all force merely because it is not always or singly controlling in every imaginable circumstance. . . .

Nonetheless, I remain convinced that "[t]he Fifth Amendment privilege against compulsory self-incrimination provides no protection for the commission of perjury." United States v. Mandujano, 425 U.S. 564, 609 (1976) (opinion concurring in judgment). The privilege operates only to protect the witness from compulsion of *truthful* testimony of an incriminating nature. Perjury or the making of false statements under a grant of immunity thus violates a basic assumption upon which the privilege and hence the immunity depend. Preserving the integrity of the immunity "bargain," . . . by allowing the use of immunized testimony for the limited purpose of proving that the terms of immunity have been criminally breached, is an integral part of the "rational accommodation between the imperatives of the privilege and the legitimate demands of government" upon which the entire theory of immunity rests. . . . Prosecutions for perjury or making false statements differ in this respect from all other instances in which, but for the grant of immunity, the witness' testimony might be used. It is for this reason, in my view, that they have been regarded as "a 'narrow exception' to the principle that a witness should be treated as if he had remained silent after invoking the Fifth Amendment privilege." . . . Since I find this ground sufficient to dispose of the present case, I need not decide at this juncture whether I fully agree with what seem to be the broader implications of the Court's analysis and opinion.

NOTES AND QUESTIONS

1. As the Court's opinion in *Apfelbaum* suggests, the fifth amendment has generally been viewed as applicable only to prior acts; one cannot claim the privilege in anticipation of a future criminal act. Thus, prior to giving testimony, one cannot claim the privilege with respect to perjured testimony one is, or may be, about to give. This strict chronological view consistently has been reflected in the interpretation of the scope

of the privilege, the primary exception being the *Marchetti* case that is discussed in *Apfelbaum*. *Marchetti* reviewed the constitutionality of requiring those engaged in illegal wagering enterprises to register each year with the Internal Revenue Service, pay an occupational tax, post revenue stamps in their place of business, and keep certain records of their wagering activity. Moreover, principal IRS offices maintained a listing of who had paid the tax, and state officials had access to the list even in those states where the wagering activity violated state law. Claiming the privilege, Marchetti did not comply with the statutory provisions and was convicted of violating them. The Court of Appeals for the Second Circuit affirmed, relying on United States v. Kahriger, 345 U.S. 22 (1953), and Lewis v. United States, 348 U.S. 419 (1955), which constructed the chronological view of the fifth amendment relied on in *Apfelbaum*.

MARCHETTI v. UNITED STATES, 390 U.S. 39, 51-54, 55-57 (1968):
[In reversing, the Court first addressed the nature of fifth amendment protections and then their scope.]

The Court held in *Lewis* that the registration and occupational tax requirements do not infringe the constitutional privilege because they do not compel self-incrimination, but merely impose on the gambler the initial choice of whether he wishes, at the cost of his constitutional privilege, to commence wagering activities. The Court reasoned that even if the required disclosures might prove incriminating, the gambler need not register or pay the occupational tax if only he elects to cease, or never to begin, gambling. There is, the Court said, "no constitutional right to gamble." 348 U.S., at 423.

We find this reasoning no longer persuasive. The question is not whether petitioner holds a "right" to violate state law, but whether, having done so, he may be compelled to give evidence against himself. The constitutional privilege was intended to shield the guilty and imprudent as well as the innocent and foresighted; if such an inference of antecedent choice were alone enough to abrogate the privilege's protection, it would be excluded from the situations in which it has historically been guaranteed, and withheld from those who most require it. Such inferences, bottomed on what must ordinarily be a fiction, have precisely the infirmities which the Court has found in other circumstances in which implied or uninformed waivers of the privilege have been said to have occurred. See, e.g., Carnley v. Cochran, 369 U.S. 506. Compare Johnson v. Zerbst, 304 U.S. 458; and Glasser v. United States, 315 U.S. 60. To give credence to such "waivers" without the most deliberate examination of the circumstances surrounding them would ultimately license wide-spread erosion of the privilege through "ingeniously drawn legislation." Morgan, The Privilege against Self-Incrimination, 34 Minn. L.

Rev. 1, 37. We cannot agree that the constitutional privilege is meaningfully waived merely because those "inherently suspect of criminal activities" have been commanded either to cease wagering or to provide information incriminating to themselves, and have ultimately elected to do neither.

The Court held in both *Kahriger* and *Lewis* that the registration and occupational tax requirements are entirely prospective in their application, and that the constitutional privilege, since it offers protection only as to past and present acts, is accordingly unavailable. This reasoning appears to us twice deficient: first, it overlooks the hazards here of incrimination as to past or present acts; and second, it is hinged upon an excessively narrow view of the scope of the constitutional privilege.

Substantial hazards of incrimination as to past or present acts plainly may stem from the requirements to register and to pay the occupational tax. In the first place, satisfaction of those requirements increases the likelihood that any past or present gambling offenses will be discovered and successfully prosecuted. It both centers attention upon the registrant as a gambler, and compels "injurious disclosure[s]"[11] which may provide or assist in the collection of evidence admissible in a prosecution for past or present offenses. These offenses need not include actual gambling; they might involve only the custody or transportation of gambling paraphernalia, or other preparations for future gambling. Further, the acquisition of a federal gambling tax stamp, requiring as it does the declaration of a present intent to commence gambling activities, obliges even a prospective gambler to accuse himself of conspiracy to violate either state gambling prohibitions, or federal laws forbidding the use of interstate facilities for gambling purposes.

There is a second, and more fundamental, deficiency in the reasoning of *Kahriger* and *Lewis*. Its linchpin is plainly the premise that the privilege is entirely inapplicable to prospective acts; for this the Court in *Kahriger* could vouch as authority only a generalization at 8 Wigmore, Evidence §2259c (3d ed. 1940).[12] We see no warrant for so rigorous a constraint upon the constitutional privilege. History, to be sure, offers no ready illustrations of the privilege's application to prospective acts, but the occasions on which such claims might appropriately have been made must necessarily have been very infrequent. We are, in any event, bid

---

11. Hoffman v. United States, 341 U.S. 479, 487.

12. We presume that the Court referred to the following: "[T]here is no compulsory self-crimination in a rule of law which merely requires beforehand a future report on a class of future acts among which a particular one may or may not in future be criminal at the choice of the party reporting." 8 Wigmore, supra, at 349. But see Morgan, supra, at 37; and McKay, Self-Incrimination and the New Privacy, 1967 Sup. Ct. Rev. 193, 221.

to view the constitutional commands as "organic living institutions," whose significance is "vital not formal." Gompers v. United States, 233 U.S. 604, 610.

The central standard for the privilege's application has been whether the claimant is confronted by substantial and "real," and not merely trifling or imaginary, hazards of incrimination. Rogers v. United States, 340 U.S. 367, 374; Brown v. Walker, 161 U.S. 591, 600. This principle does not permit the rigid chronological distinction adopted in *Kahriger* and *Lewis*. We see no reason to suppose that the force of the constitutional prohibition is diminished merely because confession of a guilty purpose precedes the act which it is subsequently employed to evidence. Yet, if the factual situations in which the privilege may be claimed were inflexibly defined by a chronological formula, the policies which the constitutional privilege is intended to serve could easily be evaded. Moreover, although prospective acts will doubtless ordinarily involve only speculative and insubstantial risks of incrimination, this will scarcely always prove true. As we shall show, it is not true here. We conclude that it is not mere time to which the law must look, but the substantiality of the risks of incrimination.

The hazards of incrimination created by §§4411 and 4412 as to future acts are not trifling or imaginary. Prospective registrants can reasonably expect that registration and payment of the occupational tax will significantly enhance the likelihood of their prosecution for future acts, and that it will readily provide evidence which will facilitate their convictions. Indeed, they can reasonably fear that registration, and acquisition of a wagering tax stamp, may serve as decisive evidence that they have in fact subsequently violated state gambling prohibitions. Compare Ala. Code, Tit. 14, §§302(8)-(10) (1958); Ga. Code Ann. §26-6413 (Supp. 1967). Insubstantial claims of the privilege as to entirely prospective acts may certainly be asserted, but such claims are not here, and they need only be considered when a litigant has the temerity to pursue them.

We conclude that nothing in the Court's opinions in *Kahriger* and *Lewis* now suffices to preclude petitioner's assertion of the constitutional privilege as a defense to the indictments under which he was convicted. To this extent *Kahriger* and *Lewis* are overruled.

[The Court then addressed the relevance of the "required records exception" to the fifth amendment (page 438 supra).]

We must next consider the relevance in this situation of the "required records" doctrine, Shapiro v. United States, 335 U.S. 1. It is necessary first to summarize briefly the circumstances in *Shapiro*. Petitioner, a wholesaler of fruit and produce, was obliged by a regulation issued under the authority of the Emergency Price Control Act to keep and "preserve for examination" various records "of the same kind as he has customarily kept. . . ." Maximum Price Regulation 426, §14, 8 Fed. Reg. 9546, 9548-9549 (1943). He was subsequently directed by an administrative subpoena to produce certain of these records before attorneys of the Office of Price Administration. Petitioner complied, but asserted his constitutional privilege. In a prosecution for violations of the Price Control Act, petitioner urged that the records had facilitated the collection of evidence against him, and claimed immunity from prosecution under §202(g) of the Act, 56 Stat. 30. Petitioner was nonetheless convicted, and his conviction was affirmed. 159 F.2d 890.

On certiorari, this Court held both that §202(g) did not confer immunity upon petitioner, and that he could not properly claim the protection of the privilege as to records which he was required by administrative regulation to preserve. On the second question, the Court relied upon the cases which have held that a custodian of public records may not assert the privilege as to those records, and reiterated a dictum in Wilson v. United States, 221 U.S. 361, 380, suggesting that "the privilege which exists as to private papers cannot be maintained in relation to 'records required by law to be kept in order that there may be suitable information of transactions which are the appropriate subjects of governmental regulation and the enforcement of restrictions validly established.'" 335 U.S., at 33. The Court considered that "it cannot be doubted" that the records in question had "public aspects," and thus held that petitioner, as their custodian, could not properly assert the privilege as to them. Id., at 34.

We think that neither *Shapiro* nor the cases upon which it relied are applicable here. . . . Moreover, we find it unnecessary for present purposes to pursue in detail the question, left unanswered in *Shapiro*, of what "limits . . . the Government cannot constitutionally exceed in requiring the keeping of records. . . ." 335 U.S., at 32. It is enough that there are significant points of difference between the situations here and in *Shapiro* which in this instance preclude, under any formulation, an appropriate application of the "required records" doctrine.

Each of the three principal elements of the doctrine, as it is described in *Shapiro*, is absent from this situation. *First*, petitioner Marchetti was not, by the provisions now at issue, obliged to keep and preserve records "of the same kind as he has customarily kept"; he was required simply to provide information, unrelated to any records which he may have maintained, about his wagering activities. This requirement is not significantly different from a demand that he provide oral testimony. *Second*, whatever "public aspects" there were to the records at issue in *Shapiro*, there are none to the information demanded from Marchetti. The Government's anxiety to obtain information known to a private individual does not without more render that information public; if it did, no room would remain for the application of the constitutional privilege. Nor does it stamp information with a public character that the Government has formalized its demands in the attire of a statute; if this alone were sufficient, the constitutional privilege could be entirely abrogated by any Act of Congress. *Third,* the requirements at issue in *Shapiro* were imposed in "an essentially non-criminal and regulatory area of inquiry" while those here are directed to a "selective group inherently suspect of criminal activities." Cf. Albertson v. SACB, 382 U.S. 70, 79. The United States' principal interest is evidently the collection of revenue, and not the punishment of gamblers; but the characteristics of the activities about which information is sought, and the composition of the groups to which inquiries are made, readily distinguish this situation from that in *Shapiro.* There is no need to explore further the elements and limitations of *Shapiro* and the cases involving public papers; these points of difference in combination preclude any appropriate application of those cases to the present one.

---

1. Does *Marchetti* survive *Apfelbaum?* Should it survive?
2. Does *Marchetti* survive Selective Service System v. Minnesota Public Interest Research Group, 468 U.S. 841 (1984), in which the Court upheld the federal statutory scheme that denied federal financial assistance to male college students who failed to register for the draft? The relevant statutes permitted late registration, but by registering late a student would identify himself as not having obeyed the law, thus exposing himself to criminal prosecution under the Selective Service Act. Because no student had sought to register while claiming the privilege for any incriminating information, the Court found that there was no fifth amendment violation. In dissent, Justice Marshall disagreed:

> The Fifth Amendment privilege against coerced self-incrimination extends to every means of government information gathering. Lefkowitz v. Turley, 414 U.S. 70, 77 (1973); Murphy v. Waterfront Comm'n, 378 U.S. 52, 90 (1964) (White, J., concurring); Counselman v. Hitchcock, 142 U.S. 547, 562 (1892). In our regulatory state, the line between permissible conditioning of the Government's taxing and spending power and impermissible Government coercion of information that presents a real threat of self-incrimination is not easy to identify. But I am confident the line has been crossed here.
> I do not take issue with the majority's conclusion that the Title IV application process itself does not require a student to divulge incriminating information to the educational institution. The neutrality of this compliance verification system is central to the majority's acceptance of the

permissible, regulatory purpose of the statute. However, our inquiry cannot stop there. Although §12(f) does not coerce an admission of nonregistration, it does coerce registration with the Selective Service System, and hence individual reporting of self-incriminatory information directly to the Federal Government.

If appellees were to register with Selective Service now so that they could submit statements of compliance to obtain financial aid for their schooling, they would still be in violation of federal law, for, by registering late, they would not have submitted to registration "in accordance with any proclamation" issued under §3 of the Military Selective Service Act, 50 U.S.C. App. §453, §462(f)(1). Failure to comply with Selective Service registration requirements within 30 days of one's 18th birthday is a felony, punishable by imprisonment for up to five years and/or a fine of up to $10,000. 50 U.S.C. App. §462(a).

A student who registers late provides the Government with two crucial links in the chain of evidence necessary to prosecute him criminally. Cf. Marchetti v. United States, 390 U.S. 39, 48, and n.9 (1968). First, he supplies the Government with proof of two elements of a violation: his birth date and date of registration. Second, and perhaps more importantly, he calls attention to the fact that he is one of the 674,000 young men in technical violation of the Military Selective Service Act. Armed with these data, the Government need prove only that the student "knowingly" failed to register at the time prescribed by law in order to obtain a conviction. 50 U.S.C. App. §462(a). When students, such as appellees in this case, have acknowledged their awareness of their legal duty to register, the Government could prosecute the commission of a felony.

There can be little doubt that a late registration creates a "real and appreciable" hazard of incrimination and prosecution, and that the risk is not "so improbable that no reasonable man would suffer it to influence his conduct." Brown v. Walker, 161 U.S. 591, 599-600 (1896). In their brief to this Court, for example, the appellants explicitly acknowledge that, although "failure to register within [30 days of one's 18th birthday] does not disqualify the registrant for Title IV aid, it is a criminal offense punishable under 50 U.S.C. App. (& Supp. V) 462." The Government thus appears to reserve the right to use information obtained by the leverage of withholding education aid as a basis for criminal prosecution. Communications with registering men convey the same message. For example, both the "Registration Form," SSS Form 1, and the "Acknowledgement Letter," SSS Form 3A, which is mailed to men as legal proof of compliance with Selective Service registration requirements, advise registrants that the information they have provided "may be furnished to the . . . Department of Justice—for review and processing of suspected violations of the Military Selective Service Act . . . [and to the] Federal Bureau of Investigation— for location of an individual when suspected of violation of the Military Selective Service Act." Finally, recent Government actions have acknowledged the realistic potential for prosecution. For example, President Reagan declared a "grace period" in the first months of 1982, in which men could register *without* penalty. The obvious implication of this declaration is that once the grace period expires, late registrants will be prosecuted. All of these governmental actions confirm the serious risk of self-incrimination and prosecution inherent in the act of late registration.[15]

Having established that late registration is an incriminating act, the question to be asked is whether the Government has exercised its powers in a way that deprives appellees of the freedom to refrain from self-incrimination through late registration. Garrity v. New Jersey, 385 U.S. 493, 496 (1967); Malloy v. Hogan, 378 U.S. 1, 8 (1964). When the Government extracts incriminating information by the leverage of the threat of penalties, including the "threat of substantial economic sanction," Lefkowitz v. Turley, 414 U.S., at 82-83, the information is not volunteered. Thus, our cases have found coercion in statutes that extracted information through the threat of termination of state employment, Garrity v. New Jersey, supra; Uniformed Sanitation Men Assn., Inc. v. Commissioner of Sanitation, 392 U.S. 280 (1968); Gardner v. Broderick, 392 U.S. 273 (1968), through the threat of exclusion of a person from a profession, Spevack v. Klein, 385 U.S. 511 (1967), or through the threat of exclusion from participation in government contracts, Lefkowitz v. Turley, supra.

The threat of the denial of student aid is substantial economic coercion, and falls within the ambit of these cases. For students who had received federal education aid before enactment of §12(f), termination of aid is coercive because it could force these students to curtail their studies, thereby forfeiting their investment in prior education and abandoning their hopes for obtaining a degree. Five of the six appellees in these cases fall into this category. Students who have not previously received federal aid may also be coerced by §12(f). All students understand that entry into most professions and technical trades requires postsecondary education. For students who cannot otherwise afford this education, compliance with §12(f) is coerced by the threat of foreclosing future employment opportunities. All of the appellees have stated that their own career plans require them to complete a college education.

15. Appellants' contention that the threat of incrimination is speculative and that therefore the Fifth Amendment is not implicated rests entirely on the assertion that under current (but concededly not "immutable") *policy,* prosecution for late registration is unlikely. Reply Brief for Appellants 15-16; Tr. of Oral Arg. 14. Just this Term, we acknowledged that "policy choices are made by one administration, and often reevaluated by another administration." United States v. Mendoza, 464 U.S. 154, 161 (1984). Considering that the statute of limitations for Selective Service registration violations is five years from the date of compliance with the law, or, for nonregistrants, age 31, 50 U.S.C. App. §462(d), as well as the unpredictability and wide range of public and political responses to the act of noncooperation with military service over the course of our history, a nonregistrant reasonably expects immunity for his compelled disclosures, not merely references to current policy. The hard fact is that the penalty for late registration is precisely the same as the penalty for nonregistration: a possible prison term of five years and/or a possible fine of $10,000.

By withholding federal aid and the opportunity to obtain postsecondary education, §12(f) levies a substantial burden on students who have failed to register with the Selective Service System. This statutory provision coerces students into incriminating themselves by filing late registration forms. As the Court noted in Garrity v. New Jersey, supra, at 497, the "option to lose their means of livelihood or to pay the penalty of self-incrimination is the antithesis of free choice to speak out or to remain silent." I therefore completely agree with appellees that this enforcement mechanism violates the Fifth Amendment's proscription against self-incrimination as interpreted in our previous cases, and would strike the provision down on this ground alone.[16]

Moreover, I do not understand the Court today to dispute that §12(f) raises serious Fifth Amendment problems. The Court concedes that it would be incriminating for appellees to register with the Selective Service now. The Court furthermore strongly suggests that appellees could exercise their Fifth Amendment rights if they did register, cf. Garner v. United States, 424 U.S. 648 (1976), and that the Government could not compel their answers at that point without immunization.[17] The majority incorrectly assumes, however, that appellees must claim their privilege against self-incrimination before they can raise a Fifth Amendment claim in this lawsuit. What the majority fails to recognize is that it would be just as incriminating for appellees to exercise their privilege against self-incrimination when they registered as it would be to fill out the form without exercising the privilege.[18] The barrier to prosecuting Military Selective Service Act violators is not so much the Government's inability to discover a birth date or date of registration as the difficulty in identifying the 674,000 nonregistrants. The late registrant who "takes the Fifth" on SSS Form 1

---

16. Of course, the general rule that a person must affirmatively assert the Fifth Amendment privilege or be deemed to have waived it, see, e.g., United States v. Kordel, 397 U.S. 1, 7-10 (1970), is simply inapplicable in "the classic penalty situation [which excuses] the failure to assert the privilege." Minnesota v. Murphy, 465 U.S. 420, 435, and n.7 (1984); see also id., at 443-446 (Marshall, J., dissenting).

17. Appellees would have two choices: complete the registration form, or note the Fifth Amendment privilege on the incomplete form. In either case, should appellees be prosecuted, they would argue that the card could not be introduced in evidence, and that the Government has the burden of proving that it made no use whatever of the incriminating disclosures. Counselman v. Hitchcock, 142 U.S. 547, 585-586 (1982). They might also argue that, having claimed the Fifth Amendment on their registration card, they can in good faith certify to the educational institution that they have complied with the Selective Service requirement, and receive Title IV aid. A statutory grant of immunity would far better promote Congress' aims.

18. Of course, the Government can always draw an incriminating inference when a person claims a Fifth Amendment privilege. In the usual case, however, the Government has, for example, subpoenaed a witness to testify, and thus has already identified him. Whether he chooses not to appear, or appears but invokes the privilege, the Government knows of his refusal to cooperate. The appellees and other nonregistrants are not known to the Government. Therefore, invocation of the Fifth Amendment by appellees gives the Government a different quality of information.

calls attention to himself as much as, if not more than, a late registrant who marks down his birth date and date of registration.

In Marchetti v. United States, 390 U.S. 39 (1968), and the related case of Grosso v. United States, 390 U.S. 62 (1968), the Court faced a similar situation, in which complying with a federal registration requirement was the practical equivalent of confessing to a crime. In those cases, federal law required persons engaged in the business of accepting wagers to register and pay an occupational and excise tax. Compliance did not exempt the gambler from any penalties for conducting his business, which was widely prohibited under federal and state law, and the information obtained if he did comply was readily available to assist the authorities in enforcing those penalties. Petitioners failed to file the required forms because they feared that they would be prosecuted for gambling if they revealed their activities to the Federal Government; they were convicted of willful failure to do so. The Court reversed the convictions, holding that a "statutory system . . . utilized to pierce the anonymity of citizens engaged in criminal activity, is invalid." Grosso v. United States, supra, at 76 (Justice Brennan, concurring). The Court recognized that by filing an incomplete form, or explicitly invoking their Fifth Amendment privilege on the form itself, petitioners would incriminate themselves by informing the Government that they were involved in illegal gambling activities. The Court therefore ruled that petitioners could exercise their Fifth Amendment rights by making "a 'claim' by silence," Garner v. United States, supra, at 659, n.11, and refraining from filing the required forms.

The Marchetti-Grosso Court based its holding in part on the fact that the information-gathering scheme was directed at those "inherently suspect of criminal activities." Marchetti v. United States, supra, at 47. Here, it is fair to say that the Government does not expect that most registrants will be in violation of the Selective Service laws. At first blush, the required information might therefore seem less like the Marchetti-Grosso inquiries and more like income tax returns, "neutral on their face and directed at the public at large." Albertson v. Subversive Activities Control Board, 382 U.S. 70, 79 (1965). In Garner v. United States, supra, at 661, the Court noted that the great majority of persons who file income tax returns do not incriminate themselves by disclosing the information required by the Government. Because the Government has no reason to anticipate incriminating responses when requiring citizens' self-reporting of answers to neutral regulatory inquiries, our cases put the burden of asserting a Fifth Amendment privilege on the speaker, and the right to make a claim by silence is not available.

To adopt this analogy, however, is to ignore the actual case or controversy before the Court. When Congress passed §12(f), its focus was assuredly not prospective. As the majority explains, Congress forged the link between education aid and Selective Service registration in order to bring into compliance with the law the 674,000 existing nonregistrants, including the six appellees in these cases. Although as a general matter it is correct to say that registration is like an income tax return (neutral on its face and directed to the (male) population at large), §12(f)-compelled *late* registration is directed to a group inherently suspect of criminal activity, squarely presenting a *Marchetti* issue.

In my view, therefore, young men who have failed to register with Selective Service, and at whom §12(f) was substantially aimed, are entitled to the same "claim by silence" as Marchetti and Grosso. But these students are compelled to forgo that right under this statutory scheme. The defect in §12(f) is that it denies students seeking federal aid the freedom to withhold their identities from the Federal Government. If appellees assert their Fifth Amendment privilege by their silence, they are penalized for exercising a constitutional right by the withholding of education aid. If they succumb to the economic coercion either by registering, or by registering but claiming the privilege as to particular disclosures, they have incriminated themselves.

Thus, I cannot accept the majority's view that appellees' Fifth Amendment claims are not ripe for review. If the Court is suggesting that appellees must wait until they are prosecuted for late registration before adjudication of their claim, that "is, in effect, to contend that they should be denied the protection of the Fifth Amendment privilege intended to relieve claimants of the necessity of making a choice between incriminating themselves and risking serious punishments for refusing to do so." Albertson v. Subversive Activities Control Board, supra, at 76. As in *Albertson*, where a federal statute required members of the Communist Party to register, appellees are put to the choice of registering without a decision on the merits of their constitutional privilege claim, or not registering and suffering a penalty. A nonregistrant's most efficacious opportunity to exercise his privilege against self-incrimination without simultaneously compromising that privilege is to challenge §12(f) anonymously, as appellees have done in these cases.

In sum, appellees correctly state that this law coerces them into self-incrimination in the face of a substantial risk of prosecution. That risk should be cured by a statutory grant of immunity. The grant would confirm that Congress' intent in passing §12(f) was not to punish nonregistrants, but to promote compliance with the registration requirement. The Government has a substantial interest in obtaining information to assure complete and accurate Selective Service registration, but obtaining it under the compulsion of §12(f), which is "capable of forcing the self-incrimination which the Amendment forbids," Lefkowitz v. Cunningham, 431 U.S. 801, 806 (1977), is unconstitutional in the absence of immunity for the compelled disclosures. If Congress enacted §12(f) to encourage compliance with registration requirements, and not to identify and punish late registrants, the constitutional legislative purpose would be fulfilled without implicating students' Fifth Amendment privilege against self-incrimination.

3. Is 18 U.S.C. §6002 (reproduced in note 3 in *Apfelbaum*, supra) broader than the fifth amendment in certain respects, notwithstanding

the Court's argument that it is coextensive with the fifth? What if immunized testimony should prove to be relevant to a criminal prosecution for an act committed subsequent to the testimony? For example, what if a suspect, after being immunized, admits to a peculiar modus operandi that indicates that he is the only person who can commit the offense in that fashion, and after the testimony a similar crime occurs? Does the privilege forbid the use of the immunized testimony? Does §6002? Consider another scenario. Can true immunized testimony be employed to prove a subsequent perjury?

4. Reconsider *Kastigar*, page 965 supra. How can the statement in *Kastigar* that immunity prohibits use of compelled testimony in any respect, and the statement in *Portash* to the same effect, be reconciled with the result in *Apfelbaum?*

> [Indeed,] . . . if the *Kastigar* opinion is overbroad, what does that seminal decision stand for? Second, if *Portash* was decided on an overbroad premise, is the result in *Portash* correct, and if it is, why? *Portash* limited immunity to "testimonial" use of the immunized testimony, but neither defined "testimonial" nor attempted to show why impeachment is a "testimonial" use. Third, both the statement of the Court's holding and its application to the facts of *Apfelbaum* are muddled. Justice Rehnquist wrote, "we hold . . . the Fifth Amendment [does not require] that the admissibility of immunized testimony be governed by any different rules than other testimony at a trial for making false statements." The reach of this "holding" is unclear. What result follows if the immunized testimony is offered to prove perjury committed on an occasion prior to the grant of immunity? Three justices in *Apfelbaum* felt constrained to concur in result only. Fourth, if, as *Apfelbaum* reasons, immunity does not extend to perjury prosecutions because there is no privilege to commit perjury, how can *Portash* be correct when it seemingly immunizes a witness from exposure of his perjury by prohibiting impeachment based on inconsistent statements? Fifth, if *Portash* has not been overruled on its facts as well as on its broad premise, does it follow from the premise of *Apfelbaum*—the symmetry of immunity and privilege—that Portash would have had a privilege not to testify on the ground that his testimony might some day impeach him? [Lushing, Testimonial Immunity and the Privilege Against Self-Incrimination: A Study in Isomorphism, 73 J. Crim. L. & Crim. 1690, 1695 (1982).]

Moreover, does *Apfelbaum* imply that a witness cannot be given immunity with respect to present truthful testimony concerning prior perjury?

5. Is the prohibition on the use of immunized testimony a prohibition on the testimonial use only or does it forbid any use, such as using immunized testimony in planning trial strategy or preparing to rebut defenses that are likely to be advanced at trial? For a discussion, see

Humble, Nonevidentiary Use of Compelled Testimony: Beyond the Fifth Amendment, 66 Tex. L. Rev. 351 (1987).

6. Who may invoke the privilege? Reconsider *Doe* and *Braswell*, supra, Chapter 6. The Supreme Court has consistently held that the fifth amendment is a "personal right, applying only to natural individuals." United States v. White, 322 U.S. 694, 698 (1944). Thus, as in *White*, a member of an organization generally may not refuse to turn over the organization's records even if they would incriminate the holder of the records. In *White*, the Court held that an officer of a labor union could not invoke the privilege with respect to the union's records:

> This conclusion is not reached by any mechanical comparison of unions with corporations or with other entities nor by any determination of whether unions technically may be regarded as legal personalities for any or all purposes. The test, rather, is whether one can fairly say under all the circumstances that a particular type of organization has a character so impersonal in the scope of its membership and activities that it cannot be said to embody or represent the purely private or personal interests of its constituents, but rather to embody their common or group interests only. If so, the privilege cannot be invoked on behalf of the organization or its representatives in their official capacity. Labor unions—national or local, incorporated or unincorporated—clearly meet that test.

As it turns out, practically every organization "meets that test." See, e.g., Rogers v. United States, 340 U.S. 367 (1951) (communist party); McPhaul v. United States, 364 U.S. 372 (1960) (Civil Rights Congress); Hair Industry Ltd. v. United States, 340 F.2d 570 (2d Cir.), cert. denied, 381 U.S. 950 (1965) (close corporations). Indeed, in Bellis v. United States, 417 U.S. 85 (1974), the Court considered whether a partner in a small law firm may invoke his personal privilege against self-incrimination to justify his refusal to comply with a subpoena requiring production of the partnership's financial records:

> In this case, . . . we are required to explore the outer limits of the analysis of the Court in *White*. Petitioner argues that in view of the modest size of the partnership involved here, it is unrealistic to consider the firm as an entity independent of its three partners; rather, he claims, the law firm embodies little more than the personal legal practice of the individual partners. Moreover, petitioner argues that he has a substantial and direct ownership interest in the partnership records, and does not hold them in a representative capacity.[2] Despite the force of these arguments, we con-

2. Petitioner also argues that we have already decided the issue presented in this case, and held that the Fifth Amendment privilege could be claimed with respect to partnership records, in the *Boyd* case. It is true that the notice to produce involved in

clude that the lower courts properly applied the *White* rule in the circumstances of this case. While small, the partnership here did have an established institutional identity independent of its individual partners. This was not an informal association or a temporary arrangement for the undertaking of a few projects of short-lived duration. Rather, the partnership represented a formal institutional arrangement organized for the continuing conduct of the firm's legal practice. The partnership was in existence for nearly 15 years prior to its voluntary dissolution. Although it may not have had a formal constitution or bylaws to govern its internal affairs, state partnership law imposed on the firm a certain organizational structure in the absence of any contrary agreement by the partners; for example, it guaranteed to each of the partners the equal right to participate in the management and control of the firm, Pa. Stat. Ann., Tit. 59, §51(e) (1964), and prescribed that majority rule governed the conduct of the firm's business, §51(h). The firm maintained a bank account in the partnership name, had stationery using the firm name on its letterhead, and, in general, held itself out to third parties as an entity with an independent institutional identity. It employed six persons in addition to its partners, including two other attorneys who practiced law on behalf of the firm, rather than as individuals on their own behalf. It filed separate partnership returns for federal tax purposes, as required by §6031 of the Internal Revenue Code, 26 U.S.C. §6031. State law permitted the firm to be sued, Pa. Rule Civ. Proc. 2128, and to hold title to property, Pa. Stat. Ann., Tit. 59, §13(3), in the partnership name, and generally regarded the partnership as a distinct entity for numerous other purposes.

Equally important, we believe it is fair to say that petitioner is holding the subpoenaed partnership records in a representative capacity.[8] The doc-

---

Boyd was in fact issued to E. A. Boyd & Sons, a partnership. See 116 U.S. 616, 619. However, at this early stage in the development of our Fifth Amendment jurisprudence, the potential significance of this fact was not observed by either the parties or the Court. The parties treated the invoice at issue as a private business record, and the contention that it might be a partnership record held in a representative capacity, and thus not within the scope of the privilege, was not raised. The Court therefore decided the case on the premise that it involved the "compulsory production of a man's private papers." Id., at 622. It was only after *Boyd* had held that the Fifth Amendment privilege applied to the compelled production of documents that the question of the extension of this principle to the records of artificial entities arose. We do not believe that the Court in *Boyd* can be said to have decided the issue presented today. See United States v. Onassis, 125 F. Supp. 190, 208 (D.C. 1954).

In any event, the Court in *Boyd* did not inquire into the nature of the Boyd & Sons partnership or the capacity in which the invoice was acquired or held. Absent such an inquiry, we are unable to determine how our decision today would affect the result of *Boyd* on the facts of that case. . . .

8. Petitioner argues that as a partner in the firm, he has an interest in the firm's records as co-owner which entitles him to claim the privilege against self-incrimination. But such an ownership interest exists in a partnership of any size. Moreover, the same ownership interest is presented in the case of a labor union or other unincorporated association. The Court's decision in *White* clearly established that the mere existence of such an ownership interest is not in itself sufficient to establish a claim of privilege. See

uments which petitioner has been ordered to produce are merely the
financial books and records of the partnership.[9] These reflect the receipts
and disbursements of the entire firm, including income generated by and
salaries paid to the employees of the firm, and the financial transactions
of the other partners. Petitioner holds these records subject to the rights
granted to the other partners by state partnership law. Petitioner has no
direct ownership interest in the records; rather, under state law, they are
partnership property, and petitioner's interest in partnership property is a
derivative interest subject to significant limitations. See Ellis v. Ellis, 415
Pa. 412, 415-416, 203 A.2d 547, 549-550 (1964). Petitioner has no right
to use this property for other than partnership purposes without the consent
of the other partners. Pa. Stat. Ann., Tit. 59, §72(2)(a). Petitioner is of
course accountable to the partnership as a fiduciary, §54(1), and his possession of the firm's financial records is especially subject to his fiduciary
obligations to the other partners. Indeed, Pennsylvania law specifically
provides that "every partner shall at all times have access to and may
inspect and copy any of [the partnership books]." §52. To facilitate this
right of access, petitioner was required to keep these financial books and
records at the firm's principal place of business, at least during the active
life of the partnership. Ibid. The other partners in the firm were—and
still are—entitled to enforce these rights through legal action by demanding
production of the records in a suit for a formal accounting. §55.

It should be noted also that petitioner was content to leave these
records with the other members of the partnership at their principal place
of business for more than three years after he left the firm. Moreover, the
Government contends that the other partners in the firm had agreed to
turn the records over to the grand jury before discovering that petitioner
had removed them from their offices, and that they made an unavailing
demand upon petitioner to return the records. Whether or not petitioner's
present possession of these records is an unlawful infringement of the rights
of the other partners, this provides additional support for our conclusion
that it is the organizational character of the records and the representative
aspect of petitioner's present possession of them which predominates over
his belatedly discovered personal interest in them.

Petitioner relies heavily on language in the Court's opinion in White
which suggests that the "test" for determining the applicability of the Fifth
Amendment privilege in this area is whether the organization "has a character so impersonal in the scope of its membership and activities that it
cannot be said to embody or represent the purely private or personal
interests of its constituents, but rather to embody their common or group

---

also Wheeler v. United States, 226 U.S., at 489-490; Grant v. United States, 227 U.S.,
at 79-80. . . .
    9. Significantly, the District Court here excluded any client files from the scope of
its order. . . . A different case might be presented if petitioner had been ordered to
produce files containing work which he had personally performed on behalf of his clients,
even if these files might for some purposes be viewed as those of the partnership.

interests only." 322 U.S., at 701. We must admit our agreement with the Solicitor General's observation that "it is difficult to know precisely what situations the formulation in *White* was intended to include within the protection of the privilege." Brief for United States 21. The Court in *White*, after stating its test, did not really apply it, nor has any of the subsequent decisions of this Court. On its face, the test is not particularly helpful in the broad range of cases, including this one, where the organization embodies neither "purely . . . personal interests" nor "group interests only," but rather some combination of the two.

In any event, we do not believe that the Court's formulation in *White* can be reduced to a simple proposition based solely upon the size of the organization. It is well settled that no privilege can be claimed by the custodian of corporate records, regardless of how small the corporation may be. . . . Every State has now adopted laws permitting incorporation of professional associations, and increasing numbers of lawyers, doctors, and other professionals are choosing to conduct their business affairs in the corporate form rather than the more traditional partnership. Whether corporation or partnership, many of these firms will be independent entities whose financial records are held by a member of the firm in a representative capacity. In these circumstances, the applicability of the privilege should not turn on an insubstantial difference in the form of the business enterprise. See In re Grand Jury Subpoena Duces Tecum, 358 F. Supp. 661, 668 (Md. 1973).

This might be a different case if it involved a small family partnership, see United States v. Slutsky, 352 F. Supp. 1105 (S.D.N.Y. 1972); In re Subpoena Duces Tecum, 81 F. Supp., at 421, or, as the Solicitor General suggests, . . . if there were some other preexisting relationship of confidentiality among the partners. But in the circumstances of this case, petitioner's possession of the partnership's financial records in what can be fairly said to be a representative capacity compels our holding that his personal privilege against compulsory self-incrimination is inapplicable. [417 U.S. at 94-101.]

How should changing social conditions affect the interpretation of constitutional provisions like the self-incrimination clause? That is the question posed by the next four cases.

CALIFORNIA v. BYERS
Certiorari to the Supreme Court of California
402 U.S. 424 (1971)

MR. CHIEF JUSTICE BURGER announced the judgment of the Court and an opinion in which MR. JUSTICE STEWART, MR. JUSTICE WHITE, and MR. JUSTICE BLACKMUN join.

This case presents the narrow but important question of whether the constitutional privilege against compulsory self-incrimination is infringed by California's so-called "hit and run" statute which requires the driver of a motor vehicle involved in an accident to stop at the scene and give his name and address. Similar "hit and run" or "stop and report" statutes are in effect in all 50 States and the District of Columbia.

On August 22, 1966, respondent Byers was charged in a two-count criminal complaint with two misdemeanor violations of the California Vehicle Code. Count 1 charged that on August 20 Byers passed another vehicle without maintaining the "safe distance" required by §21750 (Supp. 1971). The second count charged that Byers had been involved in an accident but had failed to stop and identify himself as required by §20002(a)(1) (Supp. 1971).

This statute provides:

> The driver of any vehicle involved in an accident resulting in damage to any property including vehicles shall immediately stop the vehicle at the scene of the accident and shall then and there . . . [l]ocate and notify the owner or person in charge of such property of the name and address of the driver and owner of the vehicle involved. . . .

It is stipulated that both charges arose out of the same accident.

Byers demurred to Count 2 on the ground that it violated his privilege against compulsory self-incrimination. His position was ultimately sustained by the California Supreme Court.[2] That court held that the privilege protected a driver who "reasonably believes that compliance with the statute will result in self-incrimination." Here the court found that Byers' apprehensions were reasonable because compliance with §20002(a)(1) confronted him with "substantial hazards of self-incrimination." Nevertheless the court upheld the validity of the statute by inserting a judicially created use restriction on the disclosures that it required. The court concluded, however, that it would be "unfair" to punish Byers for his failure to comply with the statute because he could not reasonably have anticipated the judicial promulgation of the use restriction.[3] We granted certiorari to assess the validity of the California Supreme Court's premise that without a use restriction §20002(a)(1) would violate the privilege against compulsory self-incrimination. We conclude that there is no conflict between the statute and the privilege.

---

2. The illegal passing charge contained in Count 1 has never been brought to trial.

3. Presumably the California holding contemplated that persons who fail to comply with the statute in the future will be subject to prosecution and conviction since the use restriction removed the justification for a reasonable apprehension of self-incrimination. Our disposition removes the premise upon which the use restriction rested.

(1)

Whenever the Court is confronted with the question of a compelled disclosure that has an incriminating potential, the judicial scrutiny is invariably a close one. Tension between the State's demand for disclosures and the protection of the right against self-incrimination is likely to give rise to serious questions. Inevitably these must be resolved in terms of balancing the public need on the one hand, and the individual claim to constitutional protections on the other; neither interest can be treated lightly.

An organized society imposes many burdens on its constituents. It commands the filing of tax returns for income; it requires producers and distributors of consumer goods to file informational reports on the manufacturing process and the content of products, on the wages, hours, and working conditions of employees. Those who borrow money on the public market or issue securities for sale to the public must file various information reports; industries must report periodically the volume and content of pollutants discharged into our waters and atmosphere. Comparable examples are legion.[4]

In each of these situations there is some possibility of prosecution—often a very real one—for criminal offenses disclosed by or deriving from the information that the law compels a person to supply. Information revealed by these reports could well be "a link in the chain" of evidence leading to prosecution and conviction. But under our holdings the mere possibility of incrimination is insufficient to defeat the strong policies in favor of a disclosure called for by statutes like the one challenged here. . . .

Although the California Vehicle Code defines some criminal offenses, the statute is essentially regulatory, not criminal. The California Supreme Court noted that §20002(a)(1) was not intended to facilitate criminal convictions but to promote the satisfaction of civil liabilities arising from automobile accidents. In *Marchetti* the Court rested on the reality that almost everything connected with gambling is illegal under "comprehensive" state and federal statutory schemes. The Court noted that in almost every conceivable situation compliance with the statutory gambling requirements would have been incriminating. Largely because of these pervasive criminal prohibitions, gamblers were considered by the Court to be "a highly selective group inherently suspect of criminal activities."

In contrast, §20002(a)(1), like income tax laws, is directed at all persons—here all persons who drive automobiles in California. This group, numbering as it does in the millions, is so large as to render

4. See Shapiro v. United States, 335 U.S. 1 (1948).

§20002(a)(1) a statute "directed at the public at large." Albertson v. SACB, 382 U.S., at 79, construing United States v. Sullivan, 274 U.S. 259 (1927). It is difficult to consider this group as either "highly selective" or "inherently suspect of criminal activities." Driving an automobile, unlike gambling, is a lawful activity. Moreover, it is not a criminal offense under California law to be a driver "involved in an accident." An accident may be the fault of others; it may occur without any driver having been at fault. No empirical data are suggested in support of the conclusion that there is a relevant correlation between being a driver and criminal prosecution of drivers. So far as any available information instructs us, most accidents occur without creating criminal liability even if one or both of the drivers are guilty of negligence as a matter of tort law.

The disclosure of inherently illegal activity is inherently risky. Our decisions in *Albertson* and the cases following illustrate that truism. But disclosures with respect to automobile accidents simply do not entail the kind of substantial risk of self-incrimination involved in *Marchetti, Grosso,* and *Haynes*. Furthermore, the statutory purpose is noncriminal and self-reporting is indispensable to its fulfillment.

(2)

Even if we were to view the statutory reporting requirement as incriminating in the traditional sense, in our view it would be the "extravagant" extension of the privilege Justice Holmes warned against to hold that it is testimonial in the Fifth Amendment sense. Compliance with §20002(a)(1) requires two things: first, a driver involved in an accident is required to stop at the scene; second, he is required to give his name and address. The act of stopping is no more testimonial—indeed less so in some respects—than requiring a person in custody to stand or walk in a police lineup, to speak prescribed words, or to give samples of handwriting, fingerprints, or blood. United States v. Wade, 388 U.S. 218, 221-223 (1967); Schmerber v. California, 384 U.S. 757, 764 and n.8 (1966); 8 J. Wigmore, Evidence §2265, pp. 386-400 (McNaughton rev. 1961). Disclosure of name and address is an essentially neutral act. Whatever the collateral consequences of disclosing name and address, the statutory purpose is to implement the state police power to regulate use of motor vehicles.

Section 20002(a)(1) first requires that a driver involved in an accident "shall immediately stop the vehicle at the scene of the accident. . . ." It is, of course, possible that compliance with this requirement might ultimately lead to prosecution for some contemporaneous criminal violation of the motor vehicle code if one occurred, or an unrelated offense, always provided such offense could be established by independent evidence. In that sense it might furnish the authorities with what might be called "a link in the chain of evidence needed to prosecute. . . ." Hoffman v. United States, 341 U.S. 479, 486 (1951). In Schmerber v. California, supra, at 764, the Court held that "the privilege is a bar against compelling 'communications' or 'testimony,' but . . . compulsion which makes a suspect or accused the source of 'real or physical evidence' does not violate it." . . .

Stopping in compliance with §20002(a)(1) therefore does not provide the State with "evidence of a testimonial or communicative nature" within the meaning of the Constitution. Schmerber v. California, supra, at 761. It merely provides the State and private parties with the driver's identity for, among other valid state needs, the study of causes of vehicle accidents and related purposes, always subject to the driver's right to assert a Fifth Amendment privilege concerning specific inquiries.

Respondent argues that since the statutory duty to stop is imposed only on the "driver of any vehicle involved in an accident," a driver's compliance is testimonial because his action gives rise to an inference that he believes that he was the "driver of [a] vehicle involved in an accident." From this, the respondent tells us, it can be further inferred that he was indeed the operator of an "accident involved" vehicle. In Wade, however, the Court rejected the notion that such inferences are communicative or testimonial. There the respondent was placed in a lineup to be viewed by persons who had witnessed a bank robbery. At one point he was compelled to speak the words alleged to have been used by the perpetrator. Despite the inference that the respondent uttered the words in his normal undisguised voice, the Court held that the utterances were not of a "testimonial" nature in the sense of the Fifth Amendment privilege even though the speaking might well have led to identifying him as the bank robber. United States v. Wade, supra, at 222-223. Furthermore, the Court noted in Wade that no question was presented as to the admissibility in evidence at trial of anything said or done at the lineup. Id., at 223. Similarly no such problem is presented here. Of course, a suspect's normal voice characteristics, like his handwriting, blood, fingerprints, or body may prove to be the crucial link in a chain of evidentiary factors resulting in prosecution and conviction. Yet such evidence may be used against a defendant.

After having stopped, a driver involved in an accident is required by §20002(a)(1) to notify the driver of the other vehicle of his name and address. A name, linked with a motor vehicle, is no more incriminating than the tax return, linked with the disclosure of income, in United States

v. Sullivan. . . . . It identifies but does not by itself implicate anyone in criminal conduct.[6]

Although identity, when made known, may lead to inquiry that in turn leads to arrest and charge, those developments depend on different factors and independent evidence. Here the compelled disclosure of identity could have led to a charge that might not have been made had the driver fled the scene; but this is true only in the same sense that a taxpayer can be charged on the basis of the contents of a tax return or failure to file an income tax form. There is no constitutional right to refuse to file an income tax return or to flee the scene of an accident in order to avoid the possibility of legal involvement.

The judgment of the California Supreme Court is vacated and the case is remanded for further proceedings not inconsistent with this opinion.

Vacated and remanded.

MR. JUSTICE HARLAN, concurring in the judgment.

For the reasons which follow, I concur in the judgment of the Court.

I . . .

I cannot separate the requirement that the individual stop from the requirement that he identify himself for purposes of applying either the "testimonial—non-testimonial" classification of Schmerber v. California, or the "substantial danger of incrimination" test of Hoffman v. United States, 341 U.S. 479 (1951). The California Supreme Court treated these requirements, in the primary context in which the statute operates, as compelling identification of oneself as a party involved in the statutorily regulated event. If evidence of that self-identification were admitted at trial, it would certainly be "testimonial." If all that is offered at trial is the identification evidence of third-party witnesses, it still does not follow from United States v. Wade, that because the policies of the Fifth Amendment are not significantly affected by state compulsion to cooperate in the production of real evidence where the State has independently focused investigation on the defendant, these policies are similarly unaffected where the State—in pursuit of "real" evidence—demands of the defendant that he focus the investigation on himself. See generally Mansfield, The *Albertson* Case: Conflict Between the Privilege Against Self-

---

6. We are not called on to decide, but if the dictum of the *Sullivan* opinion were followed, the driver having stopped and identified himself, pursuant to the statute, could decline to make any further statement. United States v. Sullivan, supra, at 263.

Incrimination and the Government's Need for Information, 1966 Sup. Ct. Rev. 103, 121-124.

It may be said that requiring the defendant to focus attention on himself as an accident participant is not equivalent to requiring the defendant to focus attention on himself as a criminal suspect. And that proposition raises the underlying issue which we must resolve in this case: how do the various verbal formulations for assessing the legal significance of the risk of incrimination, developed by the Court primarily in the context of the criminal process . . . operate in the context of the state collection of data for purposes essentially unrelated to criminal prosecution? . . .

IV

. . . [T]he public regulation of driving behavior through a pattern of laws which includes compelled self-reporting to ensure financial responsibility for accidents and.criminal sanctions to deter dangerous driving entails genuine risks of self-incrimination from the driver's point of view. The conclusion that the Fifth Amendment extends to this regulatory scheme will impair the capacity of the State to pursue these objectives simultaneously. For compelled self-reporting is a necessary part of an effective scheme of assuring personal financial responsibility for automobile accidents. Undoubtedly, it can be argued that self-reporting is at least as necessary to an effective scheme of criminal law enforcement in this area. The fair response to that latter contention may be that the purpose of the Fifth Amendment is to compel the State to opt for the less efficient methods of an "accusatorial" system. . . . But it would not follow that the constitutional values protected by the "accusatorial" system . . . are of such overriding significance that they compel substantial sacrifices in the efficient pursuit of other governmental objectives in all situations where the pursuit of those objectives requires the disclosure of information which will undoubtedly significantly aid in criminal law enforcement.

For while this Court's Fifth Amendment precedents have instructed that the Fifth Amendment be given a construction "as broad as the mischief against which it seeks to guard," Miranda v. Arizona, 384 U.S. 436, 459-460 (1966) (quoting from Counselman v. Hitchcock, 142 U.S. 547, 562 (1892)), and while the Court in Malloy v. Hogan, 378 U.S. 1 (1964), treated the privilege as one of those fundamental rights to be "selectively incorporated" into the Fourteenth Amendment, it is also true that the Court has recognized that the "scope of the privilege [does not coincide] with the complex of values it helps to protect." Schmerber v.

California, 384 U.S., at 762. . . . In the *Schmerber* case the Court concluded that the impact of compelled disclosure of "non-testimonial" evidence on the values the privilege is designed to protect was insufficient to warrant a further restriction on the State's enforcement of its criminal laws. And the Court in *Schmerber* explicitly declined reliance on the implication of a "testimonial" limitation to be found in the language of the Fifth Amendment. 384 U.S., at 761 n.6.

The point I draw from the *Schmerber* approach to the privilege is that "[t]he Constitution contains no formulae with which we can calculate the areas within the 'full scope' to which the privilege should extend, and the Court has therefore been obliged to fashion for itself standards for the application of the privilege. In federal cases stemming from Fifth Amendment claims, the Court has chiefly derived its standards from consideration of two factors: the history and purposes of the privilege, and the character and urgency of the other public interests in-volved. . . ." Spevack v. Klein, 385 U.S. 511, 522-523 (1967) (Harlan, J., dissenting).

There are those, I suppose, who would put the "liberal construction" approach of cases like *Miranda,* and Boyd v. United States, 116 U.S. 616 (1886), side by side with the balancing approach of *Schmerber* and perceive nothing more subtle than a set of constructional antinomies to be utilized as convenient bootstraps to one result or another. But I perceive in these cases the essential tension that springs from the uncertain man-date which this provision of the Constitution gives to this Court.

This Court's cases attempting to capture the "purposes" or "policies" of the privilege demonstrate the uncertainty of that mandate. See Tehan v. Shott, 382 U.S. 406, 413-416 (1966); Murphy v. Waterfront Comm'n, 378 U.S., at 55; Miranda v. Arizona, 384 U.S., at 460; Boyd v. United States, supra. One commentator takes from these cases two basic themes: (1) the privilege is designed to secure among governmental officials the sort of respect for the integrity and worth of the individual citizen thought to flow from the commitment to an "accusatorial" as opposed to an "inquisitorial" criminal process; (2) the privilege is part of the "concern for individual privacy that has always been a fundamental tenet of the American value structure." McKay, Self-Incrimination and the New Privacy, 1967 Sup. Ct. Rev. 193, 210. Certainly, in view of the extension of the privilege to witnesses in civil lawsuits, see McCarthy v. Arndstein, 266 U.S. 34 (1924)—a context in which, in most instances, information is sought by a private party wholly for purposes of resolving a private dispute—it is unlikely that the rationale of the privilege can be limited to preservation of official respect for the individual's integrity. Though the "privacy" rubric is not without its difficulties in the Fifth Amendment area[5] it does, I think, capture an important element of the concerns of the privilege, which accounts in part for our willingness to accept its reach beyond the context of the criminal investigation or trial. The premise of the criminal sanction—and the disgrace that goes with it—is that it is more feared than the mere censure of our fellow members of society; although communal living requires us to be willing to disclose much to the government and our fellow citizens about our private affairs—and although the fear of eventually having to disclose operates as an inhibiting factor on our personal lives—it still makes sense to think of the Fifth Amendment as intended at least in part to relieve us of the very particular fear arising from the imposition of criminal sanctions.

These values are implicated by governmental compulsion to disclose information about driving behavior as part of a regulatory scheme including criminal sanctions. The privacy interest is directly implicated, while the interest in preserving a commitment to the "accusatorial" system is implicated in the more attenuated sense that an officialdom which has available to it the benefits of a self-reporting scheme may be encouraged to rely upon that scheme for all governmental purposes. But, as I have argued, it is also true that, unlike the ordinary civil lawsuit context, special governmental interests in addition to the deterrence of antisocial behavior by use of criminal sanctions are affected by extension of the privilege to this regulatory context. If the privilege is extended to the circumstances of this case, it must, I think, be potentially available in every instance where the government relies on self-reporting. And the considerable risks to efficient government of a self-executing claim of privilege will require acceptance of, at the very least, a use restriction of unspecified dimensions. Technological progress creates an ever-expanding need for governmental information about individuals. If the individual's ability in any particular case to perceive a genuine risk of self-incrimination is to be a sufficient condition for imposition of use restrictions on the government in all self-reporting contexts, then the privilege threatens the capacity of the government to respond to societal needs with a realistic mixture of criminal sanctions and other regulatory devices.[7] To the extent that our *Marchetti-Grosso* line of cases appears

5. See Friendly, The Fifth Amendment Tomorrow: The Case for Constitutional Change, 37 U. Cin. L. Rev. 671, 687-690 (1968).

7. My Brother Brennan's primary response to my view that significant interference with state regulatory goals unrelated to the deterrence of antisocial behavior through criminal sanctions may mean that there is no Fifth Amendment privilege even though from the individual's point of view there are "real" and not "imaginary" risks of self-incrimination is a citation to Mr. Justice Brandeis' distinguished dissenting opinion in Olmstead v. United States, 277 U.S. 438, 472-477 (1928). Brandeis' views were expressed in the context of a case where no such governmental interest could be said to be implicated;

to suggest that the presence of perceivable risks of incrimination in and of itself justifies imposition of a use restriction on the information gained by the Government through compelled self-reporting, I think that line of cases should be explicitly limited by this Court.

V

I would not, however, overrule that line of cases. In each of those cases,[8] the Government, relying on its taxing power, undertook to require the individual to focus attention directly on behavior which was immediately recognizable as criminal in virtually every State in the Union. Since compelled self-reporting is certainly essential to the taxing power, those cases must be taken to stand at least for the proposition that the Fifth Amendment requires some restriction on the efficiency with which government may seek to maximize both noncriminal objectives through self-reporting schemes and enforcement of criminal sanctions. If the technique of self-reporting as a means of achieving regulatory goals unrelated to deterrence of antisocial behavior through criminal sanctions is carried to an extreme, the "accusatorial" system which the Fifth Amendment is supposed to secure can be reduced to mere ritual. And the risk that such a situation will materialize is not merely a function of the willingness of an ill-disposed officialdom to exploit the protective screen of ostensible legislative purpose to bypass the procedural limitations on governmental collection of information in the criminal process. The sweep of modern governmental regulation—and the dynamic growth of techniques for gathering and using information culled from individuals by force of criminal sanctions—could of course be thought to present a significant threat to the values considered to underpin the Fifth Amendment, quite apart from any supposed illegitimate motives that might not be cognizable under ordinary canons of judicial review. As uncertain as the constitutional mandate derived from this portion of the Bill of Rights may be, it is the task of this Court continually to seek that line of accommodation which will render this provision relevant to contemporary conditions.

In other words, we must deal in degrees in this troublesome area. The question whether some sort of immunity is required as a condition

---

to sever those views from their context and transpose them ipso facto to the problem at hand is to slide softly into that "lake of generalities" from which confusion is sure to flow. . . .

    8. Marchetti v. United States, 390 U.S. 39 (1968); Grosso v. United States, 390 U.S. 62 (1968); Haynes v. United States, 390 U.S. 85 (1968); Leary v. United States, 395 U.S. 6 (1969).

of compelled self-reporting inescapably requires an evaluation of the assertedly noncriminal governmental purpose in securing the information, the necessity for self-reporting as a means of securing the information, and the nature of the disclosures required. See generally Mansfield, The *Albertson* Case: Conflict Between the Privilege Against Self-Incrimination and the Government's Need for Information, 1966 Sup. Ct. Rev. 103, 128-160.

The statutory schemes involved in *Marchetti* and related cases, see n.8, supra, focused almost exclusively on conduct which was criminal. . . .

. . . Those statutory schemes are hardly distinguishable from a governmental scheme requiring robbers to register as such for purposes of paying an occupational tax and a tax on the proceeds of their crimes. . . .

In contrast, the "hit and run" statute in the present case predicates the duty to report on the occurrence of an event which cannot, without simply distorting the normal connotations of language, be characterized as "inherently suspect"; i.e., involvement in an automobile accident with property damage. And, having initially specified the regulated event—i.e., an automobile accident involving property damage—in the broadest terms possible consistent with the regulatory scheme's concededly non-criminal purpose, the State has confined the portion of the scheme now before us, see n.1 of The Chief Justice's opinion, to the minimal level of disclosure of information consistent with the use of compelled self-reporting in the regulation of driving behavior. Since the State could—in the context of a regulatory scheme including an otherwise broad definition of the regulated event—achieve the same degree of focus on criminal conduct through detailed reporting requirements as was achieved in *Marchetti* and *Grosso* through the definition of the event triggering the reporting duties of the gambling tax scheme, the Court must take cognizance of the level of detail required in the reporting program as well as the circumstance giving rise to the duty to report; otherwise, the State, possessed as it is of increasingly sophisticated techniques of information gathering and storage, will in the zealous pursuit of its noncriminal regulatory goals, reduce the "accusatorial system" which the Fifth Amendment is intended to secure to a hollow ritual.

California's decision to compel Byers to stop after his accident and identify himself will not relieve the State of the duty to determine, entirely by virtue of its own investigation after the coerced stop, whether or not any aspect of Byers' behavior was criminal. Nor will it relieve the State of the duty to determine whether the accident which Byers was forced to admit involvement in was proximately related to the aspect of his driving behavior thought to be criminal. In short, Byers having once focused attention on himself as an accident participant, the State must still bear the burden of making the main evidentiary case against Byers as a violator of §21750 of the California Vehicle Code.[10] To characterize this burden as a merely ritualistic confirmation of the "conviction" secured through compliance with the reporting requirement in issue would be a gross distortion of reality; on the other hand, that characterization of the evidentiary burden remaining on the State and Federal Governments after compliance with the regulatory scheme involved in *Marchetti* and *Grosso* seems proper.

VI

Considering the noncriminal governmental purpose in securing the information, the necessity for self-reporting as a means of securing the information, and the nature of the disclosures involved, I cannot say that the purposes of the Fifth Amendment warrant imposition of a use restriction as a condition on the enforcement of this statute. To hold otherwise would, it seems to me, embark us on uncharted and treacherous seas. There will undoubtedly be other statutory schemes utilizing compelled self-reporting and implicating both permissible state objectives and the values of the Fifth Amendment which will render this determination more difficult to make. A determination of the status of those regulatory schemes must, of course, await a proper case.

On the premises set forth in this opinion, I concur in the judgment of the Court.

MR. JUSTICE BLACK, with whom MR. JUSTICE DOUGLAS and MR. JUSTICE BRENNAN join, dissenting. . . .

The plurality opinion labors unsuccessfully to distinguish this case from our previous holdings enforcing the Fifth Amendment guarantee against compelled self-incrimination. . . . The plurality opinion . . . appears to suggest that those previous cases are not controlling because respondent Byers would not have subjected himself to a "substantial risk of self-incrimination" by stopping after the accident and providing his name and address as required by California law. See California Vehicle Code §20002(a)(1) (Supp. 1971). This suggestion can hardly be taken

---

10. I do not minimize the aid given the State of California by virtue of the requirement to stop and identify oneself. But this minimal requirement is essential to the State's non-prosecutorial goal, and, the stop having been once coerced, virtually all information secured after the stop is likely to be tainted for purposes of exclusion under the Fifth Amendment in any subsequent prosecution.

seriously. A California driver involved in an accident causing property damage is in fact very likely to have violated one of the hundreds of state criminal statutes regulating automobiles which constitute most of two volumes of the California Code. More important, the particular facts of this case demonstrate that Byers would have subjected himself to a "substantial risk of self-incrimination," . . . had he given his name and address at the scene of the accident. He has now been charged not only with failing to give his name but also with passing without maintaining a safe distance as prohibited by California Vehicle Code §21750 (Supp. 1971). It is stipulated that the allegedly improper passing caused the accident from which Byers left without stating his name and address. In a prosecution under §21750, the State will be required to prove that Byers was the driver who passed without maintaining a safe distance. Thus, if Byers had stopped and provided his name and address as the driver involved in the accident, the State could have used that information to establish an essential element of the crime under §21750. It seems absolutely fanciful to suggest that he would not have faced a "substantial risk of self-incrimination," . . . by complying with the disclosure statute.

The plurality opinion also seeks to distinguish this case from our previous decisions on the ground that §20002(a)(1) requires disclosure in an area not "permeated with criminal statutes" and because it is not aimed at a "highly selective group inherently suspect of criminal activities." . . . Of course, these suggestions ignore the fact that *this particular respondent* would have run a serious risk of self-incrimination by complying with the disclosure statute. Furthermore, it is hardly accurate to suggest that the activity of driving an automobile in California is not "an area permeated with criminal statutes." . . . And it is unhelpful to say the statute is not aimed at an "inherently suspect" group because it applies to "all persons who drive automobiles in California." . . . The compelled disclosure is required of all persons who drive automobiles in California *who are involved in accidents causing property damage.* If this group is not "suspect" of illegal activities, it is difficult to find such a group. . . .

I also find unacceptable the alternative holding that the California statute is valid because the disclosures it requires are not "testimonial" (whatever that term may mean). . . . Even assuming that the Fifth Amendment prohibits the State only from compelling a man to produce "testimonial" evidence against himself, the California requirement here is still unconstitutional. What evidence can possibly be more "testimonial" than a man's own statement that he is a person who has just been involved in an automobile accident inflicting property damage? Neither United States v. Wade, 388 U.S. 218 (1967), nor any other case of this Court has ever held that the State may convict a man by compelling him to admit that he is guilty of conduct constituting an element of a crime. . . . Yet the plurality opinion apparently approves precisely that result.

My Brother Harlan's opinion makes it clear that today the Court "balances" the importance of a defendant's Fifth Amendment right not to be forced to help convict himself against the government's interest in forcing him to do so. As in previous decisions, this balancing inevitably results in the dilution of constitutional guarantees. . . .

MR. JUSTICE BRENNAN, with whom MR. JUSTICE DOUGLAS and MR. JUSTICE MARSHALL join, dissenting.

Although I have joined my Brother Black's opinion in this case, the importance of the issues involved and the wide range covered by the two opinions supporting the Court's judgment in this case make further comment desirable. Put briefly, one of the primary flaws of the plurality opinion is that it bears so little relationship to the case before us. Notwithstanding the fact that respondent was charged both with a violation of the California Vehicle Code which resulted in an accident, and with failing to report the accident and its surrounding circumstances as required by the statute under review, the plurality concludes, contrary to all three California courts below, that respondent was faced with no substantial hazard of self-incrimination under California law. My Brother Harlan, by contrast, recognizes the inadequacy of any such conclusion. In his view, our task is to make the Bill of Rights "relevant to contemporary conditions" by simply not applying its provisions when we think the Constitution errs. . . . In the context of the present case, this appears to mean that current technological progress enabling the Government more easily to use an individual's compelled statements against him in a criminal prosecution should be matched by frank judicial contraction of the privilege against self-incrimination lest the Government be hindered in using modern technology further to reduce individual privacy. Needless to say, neither of these approaches is consistent with the Constitution. . . .

II

The plurality opinion, unfortunately, bears little resemblance either to the facts of the case before us or to the law upon which it relies. Contrary to the plurality opinion, I do not believe that we are called upon to determine the broad and abstract question "whether the constitutional privilege against compulsory self-incrimination is infringed by California's so-called 'hit and run' statute which requires the driver of a motor vehicle involved in an accident to stop at the scene and give his name and address." . . . I believe we are called upon to decide the question presented by this case, which is whether California may punish respondent, over his claim of the privilege against self-incrimination, for failing to comply with the statutory requirement that he report his name and address, *and the fact that he was the driver of an automobile involved in this particular accident.* Despite the plurality's assurance that its "judicial scrutiny is . . . a close one," . . . I believe that in the course of explaining its own views regarding "disclosures with respect to automobile accidents" in general, . . . the plurality has lost sight of the record before us. . . . Instead of dealing with the "underlying constitutional issues in clean-cut and concrete form," Rescue Army v. Municipal Court, 331 U.S. 549, 584 (1947), the plurality seeks a broad general formula to resolve the tensions "between the State's demand for disclosures and . . . the right against self-incrimination." But only rivers of confusion can flow from a lake of generalities. . . .

Much of the plurality's confusion appears to stem from its misunderstanding of the language, embodied in several of this Court's opinions, regarding questions "directed at a highly selective group inherently suspect of criminal activities." The plurality seems to believe that membership in such a suspect group is somehow an indispensable foundation for any Fifth Amendment claim. . . . Of course, this is not so, unless the plurality is now prepared to assume that McCarthy v. Arndstein, 266 U.S. 34 (1924), Counselman v. Hitchcock, 142 U.S. 547 (1892), Garrity v. New Jersey, 385 U.S. 493 (1967), and Spevack v. Klein, 385 U.S. 511 (1967), were based, respectively, upon the unarticulated premises that bankrupts, businessmen, policemen, and lawyers are all "group[s] inherently suspect of criminal activities." Instead, in the words of the California Supreme Court, "in each case the crime-directed character of the registration requirement was . . . important only insofar as it supported the claims of the specific petitioners that they faced 'substantial hazards of self-incrimination' justifying invocation of the privilege." 458 P.2d, at 468. That this is so is evident from our emphasis in *Marchetti* that "we do not hold that these wagering tax provisions are as such constitutionally impermissible. . . . If, in different circumstances, a taxpayer is not confronted by substantial hazards of self-incrimination . . . nothing we decide today would shield him from the various penalties prescribed by the wagering tax statutes." 390 U.S., at 61. The point is that in both *Albertson* and *Marchetti*, petitioners arrived in this Court accompanied by a record showing only that they had failed to register, respectively, as Communists and as a gambler, and that, in fact, they were such. Since neither of these facts was necessarily criminal, we had to determine whether the petitioners faced "real and appreciable" or merely "imaginary and unsubstantial" hazards when they refused to register. That the petitioners belonged in each case to an inherently suspect group was relevant to that question, and that alone. By contrast, in the present case we are dealing with a record which demonstrates, as found by all three courts below, that respondent was charged by California both with illegal passing which resulted in an accident, and with failing to report himself as one of the drivers involved in that accident. It is hard to imagine a record demonstrating a more substantial hazard of self-incrimination than this. Yet the plurality somehow concludes that respondent did not face the "substantial risk of self-incrimination involved in *Marchetti*."[6] . . .

III

Similarly, I do not believe that the force of my Brother Black's reasoning may be avoided by my Brother Harlan's approach. He quite candidly admits that our prior cases compel the conclusion that respondent was entitled to rely on the privilege against self-incrimination as a defense to prosecution for failure to stop and report his involvement in an accident. . . . He would simply limit those cases because he believes that technological progress has made the privilege against self-incrimination a "threat" to "realistic" government that we can no longer afford. To the extent that this argument calls for refutation, it is adequately disposed of in Mr. Justice Brandeis' dissenting opinion in Olmstead v. United States, 277 U.S. 438, 472-477, 479 (1928). Our society is not endangered by the Fifth Amendment. "The dangers of which we must really beware are . . . that we shall fall prey to the idea that in order to preserve our free society some of the liberties of the individual must be curtailed, at least

6. Even accepting the proposition that the Fifth Amendment applies only to statutory inquiries directed at persons who can demonstrate membership in a group inherently suspect of criminal activity, I find the plurality opinion confusing in its notion of how one determines the group at which a given statute is directed. Of course, in one sense, every statute not naming the persons or organizations to whom it applies is directed at the public at large. The paradigm is a statute requiring "any person who does [or is a member of] X" to answer certain questions. The activity involved in *Sullivan* was the earning of income, in *Marchetti* was gambling, and in *Albertson* was belonging to the Communist Party. The plurality appears to agree that those statutes were, respectively, directed at income earners (very nearly the public at large), gamblers, and Communists. The statute before us directs any person who is the driver of an automobile *involved in an accident causing property damage* to answer certain questions. I would think, then, that it would be "directed at" drivers involved in accidents causing property damage. Yet the plurality states that it is "directed at . . . all persons who drive automobiles in California." Apparently four members of this Court are willing to assume that *all* California drivers at some time are involved in an automobile accident causing property damage. I would hesitate before making such an assertion.

temporarily. How wrong that kind of a program would be is surely evident from the mere statement of the proposition." J. Harlan, Live and Let Live, in The Evolution of a Judicial Philosophy 285, 288 (D. Shapiro ed. 1969).

In any event my Brother Harlan's opinion is consistent neither with the present record nor its own premises. As to the first, my Brother Harlan appears to believe that the imposition of use restrictions on the present statute would threaten the capacity of California "to respond to societal needs with a realistic mixture of criminal sanctions and other regulatory devices."[1] . . . If so, this threat passed unperceived by the California Supreme Court: that court stated that its imposition of a use restriction "will neither frustrate any apparent significant legislative purpose nor unduly hamper criminal prosecutions of drivers involved in accidents resulting in damage to the property of others." 71 Cal. 2d, at 1054, 458 P.2d, at 475. . . .

Moreover, I think my Brother Harlan's opinion falls on its own premises. For he recognizes, and apparently would follow, our cases holding that the privilege against self-incrimination may be claimed by a witness in a noncriminal proceeding who is asked to give testimony that might indicate his commission of crime. . . . He appears to believe that these cases are different from the one before us, because they involve information "sought by a private party wholly for purposes of resolving a private dispute," . . . where no "special governmental interests in addition to the deterrence of antisocial behavior by use of criminal sanctions are affected." . . . Yet this is precisely the case before us. For the only noncriminal interest that has ever been asserted to justify the California reporting statute at issue here is the State's interest in providing information "sought by a private party wholly for purposes of resolving a private dispute." Of course, state policy is exercised, in part, through the resolution of otherwise private disputes through the judicial process. But this is true of every civil case, whether it involves tort liability for

---

1. In responding to the argument that a use restriction would not interfere with legitimate state interests, Judge Harlan said:

> That is a most difficult position to maintain. By compelling Byers to stop, the State compelled Byers to focus official attention on himself in circumstances which, I agree, involved for Byers a substantial risk of self-incrimination. In this circumstance, the State, if it is to prosecute Byers after the coerced stop, will bear the burden of proving that the State could have selected Byers out from the general citizenry for prosecution even if he had not stopped. With respect to automobile drivers, that would be a heavy burden indeed. I doubt this burden could be met in most cases of this sort consistent with a good-faith judicial application of the rules relating to proof of an independent source of evidence. [402 U.S. at 444 n.4.]

—Eds.

negligent driving, the ability of private individuals to inherit from one another, Labine v. Vincent, 401 U.S. 532 (1971), or the right of private parties to dissolve a previous marriage, Boddie v. Connecticut, 401 U.S. 371 (1971) (Harlan, J.). To distinguish the ordinary "civil law suit context," . . . from the civil lawsuit context in which the present statute is involved is simply to indulge in the sort of "artificial, if not disingenuous judgments" against which my Brother Harlan's opinion otherwise warns. . . .

SOUTH DAKOTA v. NEVILLE
Certiorari to the Supreme Court of South Dakota
459 U.S. 553 (1983)

JUSTICE O'CONNOR delivered the opinion of the Court.

Schmerber v. California, 384 U.S. 757 (1966), held that a State could force a defendant to submit to a blood-alcohol test without violating the defendant's Fifth Amendment right against self-incrimination. We now address a question left open in *Schmerber*, . . . and hold that the admission into evidence of a defendant's refusal to submit to such a test likewise does not offend the right against self-incrimination.

I

Two Madison, South Dakota police officers stopped respondent's car after they saw him fail to stop at a stop sign. The officers asked respondent for his driver's license and asked him to get out of the car. As he left the car, respondent staggered and fell against the car to support himself. The officers smelled alcohol on his breath. Respondent did not have a driver's license, and informed the officers that it was revoked after a previous driving-while-intoxicated conviction. The officers asked respondent to touch his finger to his nose and to walk a straight line. When respondent failed these field sobriety tests, he was placed under arrest and read his *Miranda* rights. Respondent acknowledged that he understood his rights and agreed to talk without a lawyer present. . . . Reading from a printed card, the officers then asked respondent to submit to a blood-alcohol test and warned him that he could lose his license if he refused. Respondent refused to take the test, stating "I'm too drunk, I won't pass the test." The officers again read the request to submit to a test, and then took respondent to the police station, where they read the request to submit a third time. Respondent continued to refuse to take the test, again saying he was too drunk to pass it.

South Dakota law specifically declares that refusal to submit to a blood-alcohol test "may be admissible into evidence at the trial."[4] Nevertheless, respondent sought to suppress all evidence of his refusal to take the blood-alcohol test. The circuit court granted the suppression motion for three reasons: the South Dakota statute allowing evidence of refusal violated respondent's federal constitutional rights; the officers failed to advise respondent that the refusal could be used against him at trial; and the refusal was irrelevant to the issues before the court. The State appealed from the entire order. The South Dakota Supreme Court affirmed the suppression of the act of refusal on the grounds that §32-23-10.1, which allows the introduction of this evidence, violated the federal and state privilege against self-incrimination. The court reasoned that the refusal was a communicative act involving respondent's testimonial capacities and that the State compelled this communication by forcing respondent " 'to choose between submitting to a perhaps unpleasant examination and producing testimonial evidence against himself,' " 312 N.W.2d, at 726 (quoting State v. Andrews, 297 Minn. 260, 262, 212 N.W.2d 863, 864 (1973), cert. denied, 419 U.S. 881 (1974)).

Since other jurisdictions have found no Fifth Amendment violation from the admission of evidence of refusal to submit to blood-alcohol tests, we granted certiorari to resolve the conflict. . . .

II

The situation underlying this case—that of the drunk driver—occurs with tragic frequency on our Nation's highways. The carnage caused by drunk drivers is well documented and needs no detailed recitation here. . . .

As part of its program to deter drinkers from driving, South Dakota has enacted an "implied consent" law. S.D. Comp. Laws Ann. §32-23-10. This statute declares that any person operating a vehicle in South Dakota is deemed to have consented to a chemical test of the alcoholic content of his blood if arrested for driving while intoxicated. . . .

Schmerber . . . clearly allows a State to force a person suspected of

---

4. S.D. Comp. Laws Ann. §19-13-28.1 likewise declares that, notwithstanding the general rule in South Dakota that the claim of a privilege is not a proper subject of comment by judge or counsel, evidence of refusal to submit to a chemical analysis of blood, urine, breath or other bodily substance, "is admissible into evidence" at a trial for driving under the influence of alcohol. A person "may not claim privilege against self-incrimination with regard to admission of refusal to submit to chemical analysis." Ibid.

driving while intoxicated to submit to a blood alcohol test.[9] South Dakota, however, has declined to authorize its police officers to administer a blood-alcohol test against the suspect's will. Rather, to avoid violent confrontations, the South Dakota statute permits a suspect to refuse the test, and indeed requires police officers to inform the suspect of his right to refuse. S.D. Comp. Laws Ann. §32-23-10. This permission is not without a price, however. South Dakota law authorizes the department of public safety, after providing the person who has refused the test an opportunity for a hearing, to revoke for one year both the person's license to drive and any nonresident operating privileges he may possess. S.D. Comp. Laws Ann. §32-23-11. Such a penalty for refusing to take a blood-alcohol test is unquestionably legitimate, assuming appropriate procedural protections. See Mackey v. Montrym, 443 U.S. 1 (1979).

South Dakota further discourages the choice of refusal by allowing the refusal to be used against the defendant at trial. S.D. Comp. Laws Ann. §§32-23-10.1 and 19-13-28.1. *Schmerber* expressly reserved the question of whether evidence of refusal violated the privilege against self-incrimination. 384 U.S., at 765, n.9. The Court did indicate that general Fifth Amendment principles, rather than the particular holding of Griffin v. California, 380 U.S. 609 (1965), should control the inquiry. Ibid.[10]

Most courts applying general Fifth Amendment principles to the refusal to take a blood test have found no violation of the privilege against self-incrimination. Many courts, following the lead of Justice Traynor's opinion for the California Supreme Court in People v. Sudduth, 65 Cal. 2d 543, 55 Cal. Rptr. 393, 421 P.2d 401 (1966), cert. denied, 389 U.S. 850 (1967), have reasoned that refusal to submit is a physical act rather than a communication and for this reason is not protected by the privilege. As Justice Traynor explained more fully in the companion case of People v. Ellis, 65 Cal. 2d 529, 55 Cal. Rptr. 385, 421 P.2d 393 (1966) (refusal to display voice not testimonial), evidence of refusal to take a potentially incriminating test is similar to other circumstantial evidence of consciousness of guilt, such as escape from custody and suppression of evidence. The court below . . . rejected this view. This minority view emphasizes that the refusal is "a tacit or overt expression and communication of defendant's thoughts," State v. Neville, 312 N.W.2d, at 726,

---

9. *Schmerber* did caution that due process concerns could be involved if the police initiated physical violence while administering the test, refused to respect a reasonable request to undergo a different form of testing, or responded to resistance with inappropriate force. 384 U.S., at 760, n.4.

10. *Griffin* held that a prosecutor's or trial court's comments on a defendant's refusal to take the witness stand impermissibly burdened the defendant's Fifth Amendment right to refuse. Unlike the defendant's situation in *Griffin*, a person suspected of drunk driving has no constitutional right to refuse to take a blood-alcohol test. The specific rule of *Griffin* is thus inapplicable.

and that the Constitution "simply forbids any compulsory revealing or communication of an accused person's thoughts or mental processes, whether it is by acts, failure to act, words spoken or failure to speak." Dudley [v. State], 548 S.W.2d, at 708.

While we find considerable force in the analogies to flight and suppression of evidence suggested by Justice Traynor, we decline to rest our decision on this ground. As we recognized in *Schmerber*, the distinction between real or physical evidence, on the one hand, and communications or testimony, on the other, is not readily drawn in many cases. 384 U.S., at 764.[12] The situations arising from a refusal present a difficult gradation from a person who indicates refusal by complete inaction, to one who nods his head negatively, to one who states "I refuse to take the test," to the respondent here, who stated "I'm too drunk, I won't pass the test." Since no impermissible coercion is involved when the suspect refuses to submit to take the test, regardless of the form of refusal, we prefer to rest our decision on this ground, and draw possible distinctions when necessary for decision in other circumstances.[13] . . .

Here, the state did not directly compel respondent to refuse the test, for it gave him the choice of submitting to the test or refusing. Of course, the fact the government gives a defendant or suspect a "choice" does not always resolve the compulsion inquiry. The classic Fifth Amendment violation—telling a defendant at trial to testify—does not, under an extreme view, compel the defendant to incriminate himself. He could submit to self accusation, or testify falsely (risking perjury) or decline to testify (risking contempt). But the Court has long recognized that the Fifth Amendment prevents the state from forcing the choice of this "cruel trilemma" on the defendant. . . . Similarly, *Schmerber* cautioned that the Fifth Amendment may bar the use of testimony obtained when the

---

12. The Court in *Schmerber* pointed to the lie detector test as an example of evidence that is difficult to characterize as testimonial or real. Even though the test may seek to obtain physical evidence, we reasoned that to compel a person to submit to such testing "is to evoke the spirit and history of the Fifth Amendment." 384 U.S., at 764. See also People v. Ellis, 65 Cal. 2d, at 537, and n.9, 55 Cal. Rptr., at 389, and n.9, 421 P.2d, at 397, and n.9 (analyzing lie detector tests as within the Fifth Amendment privilege). A second example of seemingly physical evidence that nevertheless invokes Fifth Amendment protection was presented in Estelle v. Smith, 451 U.S. 454 (1981). There, we held that the Fifth Amendment privilege protected compelled disclosures during a court-ordered psychiatric examination. We specifically rejected the claim that the psychiatrist was observing the patient's communications simply to infer facts of his mind, rather than to examine the truth of the patient's statements.

13. Many courts have found no self-incrimination problem on the ground of no coercion, or on the analytically related ground that the state, if it can compel submission to the test, can qualify the right to refuse the test. See, e.g., Welch v. District Court, 594 F.2d 903 (C.A.2 1979); State v. Meints, 189 Neb. 264, 202 N.W.2d 202 (1972); State v. Gardner, 52 Or. App. 663, 629 P.2d 412 (1981); State v. Brean, 136 Vt. 147, 385 A.2d 1085 (1978).

proffered alternative was to submit to a test so painful, dangerous, or severe, or so violative of religious beliefs, that almost inevitably a person would prefer "confession." *Schmerber*, 384 U.S., at 765, n.9.[14] . . .

In contrast to these prohibited choices, the values behind the Fifth Amendment are not hindered when the state offers a suspect the choice of submitting to the blood-alcohol test or having his refusal used against him. The simple blood-alcohol test is so safe, painless, and commonplace . . . that respondent concedes, as he must, that the state could legitimately compel the suspect, against his will, to accede to the test. Given, then, that the offer of taking a blood-alcohol test is clearly legitimate, the action becomes no *less* legitimate when the State offers a second option of refusing the test, with the attendant penalties for making that choice. Nor is this a case where the State has subtly coerced respondent into choosing the option it had no right to compel, rather than offering a true choice. To the contrary, the State wants respondent to choose to take the test, for the inference of intoxication arising from a positive blood-alcohol test is far stronger than that arising from a refusal to take the test.

We recognize, of course, that the choice to submit or refuse to take a blood-alcohol test will not be an easy or pleasant one for a suspect to make. But the criminal process often requires suspects and defendants to make difficult choices. . . . We hold, therefore, that a refusal to take a blood-alcohol test, after a police officer has lawfully requested it, is not an act coerced by the officer, and thus is not protected by the privilege against self-incrimination.

III

[The Court proceeded to determine that the failure of the police to warn the defendant that the test results, or the refusal to take the test, could be used at trial against the defendant did not amount to a violation of Due Process. For more on this general issue, see Section C, infra.]

IV

The judgment of the South Dakota Supreme Court is reversed, and the case is remanded for further proceedings not inconsistent with this opinion.

14. Nothing in the record suggests that respondent made or could sustain such a claim in this case.

It is so ordered.

[JUSTICE STEVENS and JUSTICE MARSHALL dissented on the grounds that the South Dakota Supreme Court rested its decision on an adequate state ground.]

DOE v. UNITED STATES

Certiorari to the United States Court of Appeals for the Fifth Circuit
487 U.S. 201 (1988)

JUSTICE BLACKMUN delivered the opinion of the Court.

This case presents the question whether a court order compelling a target of a grand jury investigation to authorize foreign banks to disclose records of his accounts, without identifying those documents or acknowledging their existence, violates the target's Fifth Amendment privilege against self-incrimination.

I

Petitioner, named here as John Doe, is the target of a federal grand jury investigation into possible federal offenses arising from suspected fraudulent manipulation of oil cargoes and receipt of unreported income. Doe appeared before the grand jury pursuant to a subpoena that directed him to produce records of transactions in accounts at three named banks in the Cayman Islands and Bermuda. Doe produced some bank records and testified that no additional records responsive to the subpoena were in his possession or control. When questioned about the existence or location of additional records, Doe invoked the Fifth Amendment privilege against self-incrimination.

The United States branches of the three foreign banks also were served with subpoenas commanding them to produce records of accounts over which Doe had signatory authority. Citing their governments' bank-secrecy laws, which prohibit the disclosure of account records without the customer's consent,[1] the banks refused to comply. The Government

---

1. It is a criminal offense for a Cayman bank to divulge any confidential information with respect to a customer's account unless the customer has consented to the disclosure.

Apparently, Bermuda common law has been interpreted as imposing an implied contract of confidentiality between a Bermuda bank and its customers, pursuant to which "no Bermuda bank may release information in its possession concerning its customers' affairs unless (1) it is ordered to do so by a court of competent jurisdiction in Bermuda, or (2) it receives a specific written direction from its customer requesting the bank to release such information." Letter dated August 1, 1984, from Richard A. Bradspies, Vice President–Operations, of the Bank of Bermuda International Ltd., to David Geneson, Esq., Fraud Section, Criminal Division, U.S. Dept. of Justice. The Government has not yet sought contempt sanctions against the banks.

then filed a motion with the United States District Court for the Southern District of Texas that the court order Doe to sign 12 forms consenting to disclosure of any bank records respectively relating to 12 foreign bank accounts over which the Government knew or suspected that Doe had control. The forms indicated the account numbers and described the documents that the Government wished the banks to produce.

The District Court denied the motion, reasoning that by signing the consent forms, Doe would necessarily be admitting the existence of the accounts. The District Court believed, moreover, that if the banks delivered records pursuant to the consent forms, those forms would constitute "an admission that [Doe] exercised signatory authority over such accounts." The court speculated that the Government in a subsequent proceeding then could argue that Doe must have guilty knowledge of the contents of the accounts. Thus, in the court's view, compelling Doe to sign the forms was compelling him "to perform a testimonial act that would entail admission of knowledge of the contents of potentially incriminating documents," and such compulsion was prohibited by the Fifth Amendment. The District Court also noted that Doe had not been indicted, and that his signing of the forms might provide the Government with the incriminating link necessary to obtain an indictment, the kind of "fishing expedition" that the Fifth Amendment was designed to prevent.

The Government sought reconsideration. Along with its motion, it submitted to the court a revised proposed consent directive that was substantially the same as that approved by the Eleventh Circuit in United States v. Ghidoni, 732 F.2d 814. The form purported to apply to any and all accounts over which Doe had a right of withdrawal, without acknowledging the existence of any such account. The District Court denied this motion also, reasoning that compelling execution of the consent directive might lead to the uncovering and linking of Doe to accounts that the grand jury did not know were in existence. The court concluded that execution of the proposed form would "admit signatory authority over the speculative accounts [and] would implicitly authenticate any records of the speculative accounts provided by the banks pursuant to the consent."

The Court of Appeals for the Fifth Circuit reversed. We granted certiorari to resolve a conflict among the Courts of Appeals as to whether the compelled execution of a consent form directing the disclosure of foreign bank records is inconsistent with the Fifth Amendment. We conclude that a court order compelling the execution of such a directive as is at issue here does not implicate the Amendment.

II

It is undisputed that the contents of the foreign bank records sought by the Government are not privileged under the Fifth Amendment. See *Braswell, Doe,* and *Fisher.* There also is no question that the foreign banks cannot invoke the Fifth Amendment in declining to produce the documents; the privilege does not extend to such artificial entities. Similarly, petitioner asserts no Fifth Amendment right to prevent the banks from disclosing the account records, for the Constitution "necessarily does not proscribe incriminating statements elicited from another." *Couch v. United States,* 409 U.S. 322, 328 (1973). Petitioner's sole claim is that his execution of the consent forms directing the banks to release records as to which the banks believe he has the right of withdrawal has independent testimonial significance that will incriminate him, and that the Fifth Amendment prohibits governmental compulsion of that act.

The Self-Incrimination Clause of the Fifth Amendment reads: "No person . . . shall be compelled in any criminal case to be a witness against himself." This Court has explained that "the privilege protects a person only against being incriminated by his own compelled testimonial communications." *Fisher v. United States,* 425 U.S., at 409. The execution of the consent directive at issue in this case obviously would be compelled, and we may assume that its execution would have an incriminating effect.[5] The question on which this case turns is whether the act of executing the form is a "testimonial communication." The parties disagree about both the meaning of "testimonial" and whether the consent directive fits the proposed definitions.

A

Petitioner contends that a compelled statement is testimonial if the Government could use the content of the speech or writing, as opposed to its physical characteristics, to further a criminal investigation of the witness. The second half of petitioner's "testimonial" test is that the statement must be incriminating, which is, of course, already a separate requirement for invoking the privilege. Thus, Doe contends, in essence, that every written and oral statement significant for its content is nec-

---

5. As noted above, the District Court concluded that the consent directive was incriminating in that it would furnish the Government with a link in the chain of evidence leading to Doe's indictment. Because we ultimately find no testimonial significance in either the contents of the directive or Doe's execution of it, we need not, and do not, address the incrimination element of the privilege.

essarily testimonial for purposes of the Fifth Amendment.[6] Under this view, the consent directive is testimonial because it is a declarative statement of consent made by Doe to the foreign banks, a statement that the Government will use to persuade the banks to produce potentially incriminating account records that would otherwise be unavailable to the grand jury.

The Government, on the other hand, suggests that a compelled statement is not testimonial for purposes of the privilege, unless it implicitly or explicitly relates a factual assertion or otherwise conveys information to the Government. It argues that, under this view, the consent directive is not testimonial because neither the directive itself nor Doe's execution of the form discloses or communicates facts or information. Petitioner disagrees.

The Government's view of the privilege . . . is derived largely from this Court's decisions in *Fisher* and *Doe*. The issue presented in those cases was whether the act of producing subpoenaed documents, not itself the making of a statement, might nonetheless have some protected testimonial aspects. The Court concluded that the act of production could constitute protected testimonial communication because it might entail implicit statements of fact: by producing documents in compliance with a subpoena, the witness would admit that the papers existed, were in his possession or control, and were authentic.

We reject petitioner's argument that this test does not control the determination as to when the privilege applies to oral or written statements. While the Court in *Fisher* and *Doe* did not purport to announce a universal test for determining the scope of the privilege, it also did not purport to establish a more narrow boundary applicable to acts alone. To the contrary, the Court applied basic Fifth Amendment principles. An examination of the Court's application of these principles in other cases indicates the Court's recognition that, in order to be testimonial, an accused's communication must itself, explicitly or implicitly, relate a factual assertion or disclose information.[9] Only then is a person compelled to be a "witness" against himself.

6. Petitioner's blanket assertion that a statement is testimonial for Fifth Amendment purposes if its content can be used to obtain evidence confuses the requirement that the compelled communication be "testimonial" with the separate requirement that the communication be "incriminating." If a compelled statement is "not testimonial and for that reason not protected by the privilege, it cannot become so because it will lead to incriminating evidence." In re Grand Jury Subpoena, 826 F.2d, at 1172, n.2 (concurring opinion). . . .

9. We do not disagree with the dissent that "[t]he expression of the contents of an individual's mind" is testimonial communication for purposes or the Fifth Amendment. We simply disagree with the dissent's conclusion that the execution of the consent directive at issue here forced petitioner to express the contents of his mind. In our view, such

This understanding is perhaps most clearly revealed in those cases in which the Court has held that certain acts, though incriminating, are not within the privilege. Thus, a suspect may be compelled to furnish a blood sample, *Schmerber;* to provide a handwriting exemplar, *Gilbert,* or a voice exemplar, United States v. Dionisio, 410 U.S. 1, 7 (1973); to stand in a lineup, *Wade;* and to wear particular clothing, Holt v. United States, 218 U.S. 245, 252-253 (1910). These decisions are grounded on the proposition that "the privilege protects an accused only from being compelled to testify against himself, or otherwise provide the State with evidence of a testimonial or communicative nature." *Schmerber,* 384 U.S., at 761. The Court accordingly held that the privilege was not implicated in each of those cases, because the suspect was not required "to disclose any knowledge he might have," or "to speak his guilt," *Wade,* 388 U.S., at 222-223. It is the "extortion of information from the accused," Couch v. United States, 409 U.S., at 328, the attempt to force him "to disclose the contents of his own mind," Curcio v. United States, 354 U.S. 118, 128 (1957), that implicates the Self-Incrimination Clause.[10]

It is consistent with the history of and the policies underlying the Self-Incrimination Clause to hold that the privilege may be asserted only to resist compelled explicit or implicit disclosures of incriminating information. . . . These policies are served when the privilege is asserted to spare the accused from having to reveal, directly or indirectly, his knowledge of facts relating him to the offense or from having to share his thoughts and beliefs with the Government.[11]

---

compulsion is more like [in the words of the dissent] "be[ing] forced to surrender a key to a strong box containing incriminating documents," than it is like "be[ing] compelled to reveal the combination to [petitioner's] wall safe."

10. Petitioner's reliance on a statement in this Court's decision in *Schmerber* for the proposition that all verbal statements sought for their content are testimonial is misplaced. In *Schmerber,* the Court stated that the privilege extends to "an accused's communications, whatever form they might take," but it did so in the context of clarifying that the privilege may apply not only to verbal communications, as was once thought, but also to physical communications. Contrary to petitioner's urging, the *Schmerber* line of cases does not draw a distinction between unprotected evidence sought for its physical characteristics and protected evidence sought for its content. Rather, the Court distinguished between the suspect's being compelled himself to serve as evidence and the suspect's being compelled to disclose or communicate information or facts that might serve as or lead to incriminating evidence. . . . In order to be privileged, it is not enough that the compelled communication is sought for its content. The content itself must have testimonial significance.

11. Petitioner argues that at least some of these policies would be undermined unless the Government is required to obtain evidence against an accused from sources other than his compelled statements, whether or not the statements make a factual assertion or convey information. Petitioner accordingly maintains that the policy of striking an appropriate balance between the power of the Government and the sovereignty of the individual precludes the Government from compelling an individual to utter or write words that lead to incriminating evidence. Even if some of the policies underlying the

We are not persuaded by petitioner's arguments that our articulation of the privilege fundamentally alters the power of the Government to compel an accused to assist in his prosecution. There are very few instances in which a verbal statement, either oral or written, will not convey information or assert facts. The vast majority of verbal statements thus will be testimonial and, to that extent at least, will fall within the privilege. Furthermore, it should be remembered that there are many restrictions on the Government's prosecutorial practices in addition to the Self-Incrimination Clause. Indeed, there are other protections against governmental efforts to compel an unwilling suspect to cooperate in an investigation, including efforts to obtain information from him. We are confident that these provisions, together with the Self-Incrimination Clause, will continue to prevent abusive investigative techniques.[13]

B

The difficult question whether a compelled communication is testimonial for purposes of applying the Fifth Amendment often depends on the facts and circumstances of the particular case. This case is no exception. We turn, then, to consider whether Doe's execution of the consent directive at issue here would have testimonial significance. We agree with the Court of Appeals that it would not, because neither the form, nor its execution, communicates any factual assertions, implicit or explicit, or conveys any information to the Government.

The consent directive itself is not "testimonial." It is carefully drafted not to make reference to a specific account, but only to speak in the

---

privilege might support petitioner's interpretation of the privilege, "it is clear that the scope of the privilege does not coincide with the complex of values it helps to protect. Despite the impact upon the inviolability of the human personality, and upon our belief in an adversary system of criminal justice in which the Government must produce the evidence against an accused through its own independent labors, the prosecution is allowed to obtain and use . . . evidence which although compelled is generally speaking not 'testimonial,' Schmerber v. California, 384 U.S. 757, 761." Grosso v. United States, 390 U.S. 62, 72-73 (1968) (Brennan, J., concurring). If the societal interests in privacy, fairness, and restraint of governmental power are not unconstitutionally offended by compelling the accused to have his body serve as evidence that leads to the development of highly incriminating testimony, as Schmerber and its progeny make clear, it is difficult to understand how compelling a suspect to make a nonfactual statement that facilitates the production of evidence by someone else offends the privilege.

13. For example, the Fourth Amendment generally prevents the Government from compelling a suspect to consent to a search of his home, cf. Schneckloth v. Bustamonte, 412 U.S. 218, 248-249 (1973); the attorney-client privilege prevents the Government from compelling a suspect to direct his attorney to disclose confidential communications, see generally Upjohn Co. v. United States, 449 U.S. 383, 389 (1981); and the Due Process Clause imposes limitations on the Government's ability to coerce individuals into participating in criminal prosecutions, see generally Rochin v. California, 342 U.S. 165, 174 (1952).

hypothetical. Thus, the form does not acknowledge that an account in a foreign financial institution is in existence or that it is controlled by petitioner. Nor does the form indicate whether documents or any other information relating to petitioner are present at the foreign bank, assuming that such an account does exist. The form does not even identify the relevant bank. Although the executed form allows the Government access to a potential source of evidence, the directive itself does not point the Government toward hidden accounts or otherwise provide information that will assist the prosecution in uncovering evidence. The Government must locate that evidence " 'by the independent labor of its officers,' " Estelle v. Smith, 451 U.S. 454, 462 (1981), quoting Culombe v. Connecticut, 367 U.S. 568, 582 (1961) (opinion announcing the judgment). As in *Fisher*, the Government is not relying upon the " 'truthtelling' " of Doe's directive to show the existence of, or his control over, foreign bank account records.

Given the consent directive's phraseology, petitioner's compelled act of executing the form has no testimonial significance either. By signing the form, Doe makes no statement, explicit or implicit, regarding the existence of a foreign bank account or his control over any such account. Nor would his execution of the form admit the authenticity of any records produced by the bank. Not only does the directive express no view on the issue, but because petitioner did not prepare the document, any statement by Doe to the effect that it is authentic would not establish that the records are genuine. Authentication evidence would have to be provided by bank officials.

Finally, we cannot agree with petitioner's contention that his execution of the directive admits or asserts Doe's consent. The form does not state that Doe "consents" to the release of bank records. Instead, it states that the directive "shall be construed as consent" with respect to Cayman Islands and Bermuda bank-secrecy laws. Because the directive explicitly indicates that it was signed pursuant to a court order, Doe's compelled execution of the form sheds no light on his actual intent or state of mind. The form does "direct" the bank to disclose account information and release any records that "may" exist and for which Doe "may" be a relevant principal. But directing the recipient of a communication to do something is not an assertion of fact or, at least in this context, a disclosure of information. In its testimonial significance, the execution of such a directive is analogous to the production of a handwriting sample or voice exemplar: it is a nontestimonial act. In neither case is the suspect's action compelled to obtain "any knowledge he might have." *Wade*, 388 U.S. at 222.[15]

15. Petitioner apparently maintains that the performance of every compelled act

We read the directive as equivalent to a statement by Doe that, although he expresses no opinion about the existence of, or his control over, any such account, he is authorizing the bank to disclose information relating to accounts over which, in the bank's opinion, Doe can exercise the right of withdrawal. When forwarded to the bank along with a subpoena, the executed directive, if effective under local law,[16] will simply make it possible for the recipient bank to comply with the Government's request to produce such records. As a result, if the Government obtains bank records after Doe signs the directive, the only factual statement made by anyone will be the *bank's* implicit declaration, by its act of production in response to the subpoena, that *it* believes the accounts to be petitioner's. The fact that the bank's customer has directed the disclosure of his records "would say nothing about the correctness of the bank's representations." Brief for United States 21-22. Indeed, the Second and Eleventh Circuits have concluded that consent directives virtually identical to the one here are inadmissible as an admission by the signator

---

carries with it an implied assertion that the act has been performed by the person who was compelled, and therefore the performance of the act is subject to the privilege. In *Wade, Gilbert,* and *Dionisio,* the Court implicitly rejected this argument. It could be said in those cases that the suspect, by providing his handwriting or voice exemplar, implicitly "acknowledged" that the writing or voice sample was his. But as the holdings make clear, this kind of simple acknowledgement—that the suspect in fact performed the compelled act—is not "sufficiently testimonial for purposes of the privilege." *Fisher,* 425 U.S., at 411. Similarly, the acknowledgement that Doe directed the bank to disclose any records the bank thinks are Doe's—an acknowledgement implicit in Doe's placing his signature on the consent directive—is not sufficiently testimonial for purposes of the privilege.

The dissent apparently disagrees with us on this point, although the basis for its disagreement is unclear. Surely, the fact that the executed form creates "a new piece of evidence that may be used against petitioner" is not relevant to whether the execution has testimonial significance, for the same could be said about the voice and writing exemplars the Court found were not testimonial in nature. Similarly irrelevant to the issue presented here is the dissent's invocation of the First Circuit's hypothetical of how the Government might use the directive to link petitioner to whatever documents the banks produce. That hypothetical . . . goes only to showing that the directive may be *incriminating,* an issue not presented in this case. It has no bearing on whether the compelled execution of the directive is *testimonial.*

16. The Government of the Cayman Islands maintains that a compelled consent, such as the one at issue in this case, is not sufficient to authorize the release of confidential financial records protected by Cayman law. The Grand Court of the Cayman Islands has held expressly that a consent directive signed pursuant to an order of a United States court and at the risk of contempt sanctions, could not constitute "consent" under the Cayman confidentiality law. See In re ABC Ltd., 1984 C.I.L.R. 130 (1984). Respondent observes that the cited decision has not been appealed and argues accordingly that Cayman law on the point has not been definitely settled.

The effectiveness of the directive under foreign law has no bearing on the constitutional issue in this case. Nevertheless, we are not unaware of the international comity questions implicated by the Government's attempts to overcome protections afforded by the laws of another nation. We are not called upon to address those questions here.

of either control or existence. In re Grand Jury Subpoena, 826 F.2d, at 1171; Ghidoni, 732 F.2d, at 818, and n.9.

III

Because the consent directive is not testimonial in nature, we conclude that the District Court's order compelling petitioner to sign the directive does not violate his Fifth Amendment privilege against self-incrimination. Accordingly, the judgment of the Court of Appeals is affirmed.

JUSTICE STEVENS, dissenting.

A defendant can be compelled to produce material evidence that is incriminating. Fingerprints, blood samples, voice exemplars, handwriting specimens or other items of physical evidence may be extracted from a defendant against his will. But can he be compelled to use his mind to assist the prosecution in convicting him of a crime? I think not. He may in some cases be forced to surrender a key to a strong box containing incriminating documents, but I do not believe he can be compelled to reveal the combination to his wall safe—by word or deed.

The document the Government seeks to extract from John Doe purports to order third parties to take action that will lead to the discovery of incriminating evidence. The directive itself may not betray any knowledge petitioner may have about the circumstances of the offenses being investigated by the Grand Jury, but it nevertheless purports to evidence a reasoned decision by Doe to authorize action by others. The forced execution of this document differs from the forced production of physical evidence just as human beings differ from other animals.[1]

---

1. The forced production of physical evidence, which we have condoned involves no intrusion upon the contents of the mind of the accused. See *Schmerber*, 384 U.S., at 765 (forced blood test permissible because it does not involve "even a shadow of testimonial compulsion upon or enforced communication by the accused"). The forced execution of a document that purports to convey the signer's authority, however, does invade the dignity of the human mind; it purports to communicate a deliberate command. The intrusion on the dignity of the individual is not diminished by the fact that the document does not reflect the true state of the signer's mind. Indeed, that the assertions petitioner is forced to utter by executing the document are false causes an even greater violation of human dignity. For the same reason a person cannot be forced to sign a document purporting to authorize the entry of judgment against himself, cf. Brady v. United States, 397 U.S. 742, 748 (1970), I do not believe he can be forced to sign a document purporting to authorize the disclosure of incriminating evidence. In both cases the accused is being compelled "to be a witness against himself"; indeed, here he is being compelled to bear false witness against himself.

The expression of the contents of an individual's mind falls squarely within the protection of the Fifth Amendment. Justice Holmes' observation that "the prohibition of compelling a man in a criminal court to be witness against himself is a prohibition

If John Doe can be compelled to use his mind to assist the Government in developing its case, I think he will be forced "to be a witness against himself." The fundamental purpose of the Fifth Amendment was to mark the line between the kind of inquisition conducted by the Star Chamber and what we proudly describe as our accusatorial system of justice. It reflects "our respect for the inviability of the human personality," Murphy v. Waterfront Comm'n of New York Harbor, 378 U.S. 52, 55 (1964). "[I]t is an explicit right of a natural person, protecting the realm of human thought and expression." Braswell v. United States, (KENNEDY, J., dissenting). In my opinion that protection gives John Doe the right to refuse to sign the directive authorizing access to the records of any bank account that he may control.[2] Accordingly, I respectfully dissent.

---

of the use of physical or moral compulsion to extort communications from him," Holt v. United States, 218 U.S., at 252-253, manifests a recognition that virtually any communication reveals the contents of the mind of the speaker. Thus the Fifth Amendment privilege is fulfilled only when the person is guaranteed the right " 'to remain silent unless he chooses to speak in the unfettered exercise of his own will.' " Miranda v. Arizona, 384 U.S. 436, 460 (1966) (quoting Malloy v. Hogan, 378 U.S. 1, 8 (1964)). The deviation from this principle can only lead to mischievous abuse of the dignity of the Fifth Amendment commands the Government afford its citizens. The instant case is illustrative. In allowing the Government to compel petitioner to execute the directive, the Court permits the Government to compel petitioner to speak against his will in answer to the question "Do you consent to the release of these documents." Beyond this affront, however, the Government is being permitted also to demand that the answer be "Yes."

2. The Fifth Amendment provides that no person "shall be compelled in any criminal case to be a *witness* against himself." A witness is one who "gives evidence in a cause." T. Cunningham, 2 New and Complete Law Dictionary (2nd ed. 1771). The Court carefully scrutinizes the particular directive at issue here to determine whether its "form" or "execution" "communicates any factual assertions, implicit or explicit, or conveys any information to the Government." But the Court's opinion errs in focusing only on whether the directive reveals historical facts, ignoring that the execution of the directive *creates new* facts and a new piece of evidence that may be used against petitioner. The Court determines that the document's form has no testimonial significance because it does not reveal the identity of any particular banks or acknowledge the existence of any particular foreign accounts. This much is true. But the document does reveal exactly what it purports to reveal, which is that petitioner "directs," the release of any documents that conform to the description contained in the statement. Thus, by executing the document, petitioner admits a state of mind, a present tense desire. That the directive asserts that it was executed "pursuant to" court order does not save petitioner from this compelled admission. Only the most sophisticated bank officer could be expected to understand the phase "pursuant to that certain order," to mean "executed involuntarily under pain of contempt." But even if the directive expressly revealed its involuntary character, it would still communicate the direction that incriminating documents be produced.

By executing the document, petitioner creates evidence that has independent significance. The Court's opinion does not foreclose the possibility that the Government will attempt to introduce the directive itself to create a link between petitioner and whatever documents the Government is able to secure through use of the directive. This danger was fully described in an example employed by the First Circuit in its analysis of a document, which, like the one at issue here, did not assert the existence of any particular

BALTIMORE CITY DEPARTMENT OF SOCIAL SERVICES v. BOUKNIGHT

Certiorari to Maryland Court of Appeals
—U.S.—, 110 S. Ct. 900 (1990)

JUSTICE O'CONNOR delivered the opinion of the Court.

In this action, we must decide whether a mother, the custodian of a child pursuant to a court order, may invoke the Fifth Amendment privilege against self-incrimination to resist an order of the Juvenile Court to produce the child. We hold that she may not.

I

Petitioner Maurice M. is an abused child. When he was three months old, he was hospitalized with a fractured left femur, and examination revealed several partially healed bone fractures and other indications of severe physical abuse. In the hospital, respondent Bouknight, Maurice's mother, was observed shaking Maurice, dropping him in his crib despite his spica cast, and otherwise handling him in a manner inconsistent with

---

bank records or accounts:

> Suppose that at trial the government were to introduce bank records produced in response to a subpoena that had been accompanied by the consent form and that it was not apparent from the face of the records or otherwise how [defendant] was linked to them. Suppose also that the government then introduced the subpoena and consent form, and a government witness testified that the bank records were received in response to the subpoena and consent form. . . . Would not the evidence linking [defendant] to the records be his own testimonial admission of consent? In re Grand Jury Proceedings (Ranauro), 814 F.2d 791, 793 (1987).

The example reveals that the compelled execution causes the creation of evidence that did not exist before and which through the Government's artifice may become part of the prosecution's case against petitioner. The example also demonstrates that the "testimonial" significance of the directive can only be appreciated if the document is considered in its completed form from the perspective of an individual who knows no more about the circumstances of its creation than is revealed on its face. The fact that the document was produced under compulsion, which the Court relies on in asserting that the directive "sheds no light on [petitioner's] actual intent or state of mind," is not relevant to consideration of the document's testimonial significance.

A critical issue at any trial at which the Government seeks to introduce bank records produced by a compulsory directive would be proof that the documents pertain to accounts within the control of the defendant. The directive relates the testimonial fact that the defendant ordered the production of those documents which relate to any account he has at a bank or trust company or over which he has signatory authority. Perhaps this testimony alone does not prove the fact of control, but it is certainly probative of that fact. The defendant can no longer testify without contradiction from the face of the directive that he never authorized the production of records relating to his accounts. The directive that he was compelled to create testifies against him.

his recovery and continued health. Hospital personnel notified Baltimore City Department of Social Services (BCDSS) of suspected child abuse. In February 1987, BCDSS secured a court order removing Maurice from Bouknight's control and placing him in shelter care. Several months later, the shelter care order was inexplicably modified to return Maurice to Bouknight's custody temporarily. Following a hearing held shortly thereafter, the Juvenile Court declared Maurice to be a "child in need of assistance," thus asserting jurisdiction over Maurice and placing him under BCDSS's continuing oversight. BCDSS agreed that Bouknight could continue as custodian of the child, but only pursuant to extensive conditions set forth in a court-approved protective supervision order. The order required Bouknight to "cooperate with BCDSS," "continue in therapy," participate in parental aid and training programs, and "refrain from physically punishing [Maurice]." The order's terms were "all subject to the further Order of the Court." Bouknight's attorney signed the order, and Bouknight in a separate form set forth her agreement to each term.

Eight months later, fearing for Maurice's safety, BCDSS returned to Juvenile Court. BCDSS caseworkers related that Bouknight would not cooperate with them and had in nearly every respect violated the terms of the protective order. BCDSS states that Maurice's father had recently died in a shooting incident and that Bouknight, in light of the results of a psychological examination and her history of drug use, could not provide adequate care for the child. On April 20, 1988, the Court granted BCDSS's petition to remove Maurice from Bouknight's control for placement in foster care. BCDSS officials also petitioned for judicial relief from Bouknight's failure to produce Maurice or reveal where he could be found. The petition recounted that on two recent visits by BCDSS officials to Bouknight's home, she had refused to reveal the location of the child or had indicated that the child was with an aunt whom she would not identify. The petition further asserted that inquiries of Bouknight's known relatives had revealed that none of them had recently seen Maurice and that BCDSS had prompted the police to issue a missing persons report and referred the case for investigation by the police homicide division. Also on April 20, the Juvenile Court, upon a hearing on the petition, cited Bouknight for violating the protective custody order and for failing to appear at the hearing. Bouknight had indicated to her attorney that she would appear with the child, but also expressed fear that if she appeared the State would "snatch the child." The court issued an order to show cause why Bouknight should not be held in civil contempt for failure to produce the child. Expressing concern that Maurice was endangered or perhaps dead, the court issued a bench warrant for Bouknight's appearance.

Maurice was not produced at subsequent hearings. At a hearing one week later, Bouknight claimed that Maurice was with a relative in Dallas. Investigation revealed that the relative had not seen Maurice. The next day, following another hearing at which Bouknight again declined to produce Maurice, the Juvenile Court found Bouknight in contempt for failure to produce the child as ordered. There was and has been no indication that she was unable to comply with the order. The court directed that Bouknight be imprisoned until she "purge[d] herself of contempt by either producing [Maurice] before the court or revealing to the court his exact whereabouts."

The Juvenile Court rejected Bouknight's subsequent claim that the contempt order violated the Fifth Amendment's guarantee against self-incrimination. The court stated that the production of Maurice would purge the contempt and that "[t]he contempt is issued not because she refuse[d] to testify in any proceeding . . . [but] because she had failed to abide by the Order of this Court mainly [for] the production of Maurice M." While that decision was being appealed, Bouknight was convicted of theft and sentenced to 18 months' imprisonment in separate proceedings. The Court of Appeals of Maryland vacated the Juvenile Court's judgment upholding the contempt order. The Court of Appeals found that the contempt order unconstitutionally compelled Bouknight to admit through the act of production "a measure of continuing control and dominion over Maurice's person" in circumstances in which "Bouknight has a reasonable apprehension that she will be prosecuted." We granted certiorari, and we now reverse.

II

The Fifth Amendment provides that "No person . . . shall be compelled in any criminal case to be a witness against himself." The Fifth Amendment's protection "applies only when the accused is compelled to make a testimonial communication that is incriminating." Fisher v. United States, 425 U.S. 391, 408 (1976). The courts below concluded that Bouknight could comply with the order through the unadorned act of producing the child, and we thus address that aspect of the order. When the government demands that an item be produced, "the only thing compelled is the act of producing the [item]." Fisher, supra, at 410 n.11. The Fifth Amendment's protection may nonetheless be implicated because the act of complying with the government's demand testifies to the existence, possession, or authenticity of the things produced. But a person may not claim the Amendment's protection based upon the incrimination that may result from the contents or nature of the thing demanded. Bouknight therefore cannot claim the privilege based upon anything that examination of Maurice might reveal, nor can she assert the privilege upon the theory that compliance would assert that the child produced is in fact Maurice (a fact the State could readily establish, rendering any testimony regarding existence of authenticity insufficiently incriminating). Rather, Bouknight claims the benefit of the privilege because the act of production would amount to testimony regarding her control over and possession of Maurice. Although the State could readily introduce evidence of Bouknight's continuing control over the child—e.g., the custody order, testimony of relatives, and Bouknight's own statements to Maryland officials before invoking the privilege—her implicit communication of control over Maurice at the moment of production might aid the State in prosecuting Bouknight.

The possibility that a production order will compel testimonial assertions that may prove incriminating does not, in all contexts, justify invoking the privilege to resist production. Even assuming that this limited testimonial assertion is sufficiently incriminating and "sufficiently testimonial for purposes of the privilege," *Fisher*, supra, at 411, Bouknight may not invoke the privilege to resist the production order because she has assumed custodial duties related to production and because production is required as part of a noncriminal regulatory regime.

The Court has on several occasions recognized that the Fifth Amendment privilege may not be invoked to resist compliance with a regulatory regime constructed to effect the State's public purposes unrelated to the enforcement of its criminal laws. In Shapiro v. United States, 335 U.S. 1 (1948), the Court considered an application of the Emergency Price Control Act and a regulation issued thereunder which required licensed businesses to maintain records and make them available for inspection by administrators. The Court indicated that no Fifth Amendment protection attached to production of the "required records," which the "defendant was required to keep, not for his private uses, but for the benefit of the public, and for public inspection.' " Id., at 17-18 (quoting Wilson v. United States, 221 U.S. 361, 381 (1911)). The Court's discussion of the constitutional implications of the scheme focused upon the relation between the Government's regulatory objectives and the Government's interest in gaining access to the records in Shapiro's possession:

> It may be assumed at the outset that there are limits which the Government cannot constitutionally exceed in requiring the keeping of records which may be inspected by an administrative agency and may be used in prosecuting statutory violations committed by the recordkeeper himself. But no serious misgiving that those bounds have been overstepped would appear to be evoked when there is a sufficient relation between the activity sought to be regulated and the public concern so that the Government can con-

stitutionally regulate or forbid the basic activity concerned, and can constitutionally require the keeping of particular records, subject to inspection
by the Administrator. 335 U.S., at 32.

The Court has since refined those limits to the government's authority
to gain access to items or information vested with this public character.
The Court has noted that "the requirements at issue in *Shapiro* were
imposed in "an essentially non-criminal and regulatory area of inquiry,"
and that *Shapiro's* reach is limited where requirements "are directed to
a 'selective group inherently suspect of criminal activities,' " Marchetti
v. United States, 390 U.S. 39, 57 (1968) (quoting Albertson v. Subversive
Activities Control Board, 382 U.S. 70, 79 (1965)). . . .

California v. Byers confirms that the ability to invoke the privilege
may be greatly diminished when invocation would interfere with the
effective operation of a generally applicable, civil regulatory requirement.
In *Byers*, the Court upheld enforcement of California's statutory requirement that drivers of cars involved in accidents stop and provide their
names and addresses. A plurality found the risk of incrimination too
insubstantial to implicate the Fifth Amendment and noted that the statute
"was not intended to facilitate criminal convictions but to promote the
satisfaction of civil liabilities." . . . . Justice Harlan, the author of *Marchetti* [and] *Grosso*, concurred in the judgment. He distinguished those
. . . cases as considering statutory schemes that "focused almost exclusively on conduct which was criminal." While acknowledging that in
particular cases the California statute would compel incriminating testimony, he concluded that the noncriminal purpose and the general
applicability of the reporting requirement demanded compliance even in
such cases.

When a person assumes control over items that are the legitimate
object of the government's non-criminal regulatory powers, the ability to
invoke the privilege is reduced. In Wilson v. United States, supra, the
Court surveyed a range of cases involving the custody of public documents
and records required by law to be kept because they related to "the
appropriate subjects of governmental regulation and the enforcement of
restrictions validly established." Id., at 380. The principle the Court drew
from these cases is:

[W]here, by virtue of their character and the rules of law applicable to
them, the books and papers are held subject to examination by the demanding authority, the custodian has no privilege to refuse production
although their contents tend to criminate him. In assuming their custody
he has accepted the incident obligation to permit inspection. Id., at 382.

In *Shapiro*, the Court interpreted this principle as extending well beyond the corporate context, and emphasized that Shapiro had assumed and retained control over documents in which the government had a direct and particular regulatory interest. Indeed, it was in part Shapiro's custody over items having this public nature that allowed the Court in *Marchetti* [and] *Grosso* to distinguish the measures considered in those cases from the regulatory requirement at issue in *Shapiro*.

These principles readily apply to this case. Once Maurice was adjudicated a child in need of assistance, his care and safety became the particular object of the State's regulatory interests. . . . Maryland first placed Maurice in shelter care, authorized placement in foster care, and then entrusted responsibility for Maurice's care to Bouknight. By accepting care of Maurice subject to the custodial order's conditions (including requirements that she cooperate with BCDSS, follow a prescribed training regime, and be subject to further court orders), Bouknight submitted to the routine operation of the regulatory system and agreed to hold Maurice in a manner consonant with the State's regulatory interests and subject to inspection by BCDSS. In assuming the obligations attending custody, Bouknight "has accepted the incident obligation to permit inspection." *Wilson*, 221 U.S., at 382. The State imposes and enforces that obligation as part of a broadly directed, noncriminal regulatory regime governing children cared for pursuant to custodial orders.

Persons who care for children pursuant to a custody order, and who may be subject to a request for access to the child, are hardly a "selective group inherently suspect of criminal activities." The Juvenile Court may place a child within its jurisdiction with social service officials or "under supervision in his own home or in the custody or under the guardianship of a relative or other fit person, upon terms the court deems appropriate." Md. Cts. & Jud. Proc. Code Ann. §3-820(c)(1)(i) (Supp. 1989). Children may be placed, for example, in foster care, in homes of relatives, or in the care of state officials. Even when the court allows a parent to retain control of a child within the court's jurisdiction, that parent is not one singled out for criminal conduct, but rather has been deemed to be, without the State's assistance, simply "unable or unwilling to give proper care and attention to the child and his problems." Md. Cts. & Jud. Proc. Code Ann. §3-801(e) (Supp. 1989).

Similarly, BCDSS's efforts to gain access to children, as well as judicial efforts to the same effect, do not "focu[s] almost exclusively on conduct which was criminal." *Byers*, 402 U.S., at 454 (Harlan, J., concurring in judgment). Many orders will arise in circumstances entirely devoid of criminal conduct. Even when criminal conduct may exist, the court may properly request production and return of the child, and enforce that request through exercise of the contempt power, for reasons related entirely to the child's well-being and through measures unrelated to criminal law enforcement or investigation. This case provides an illustration: concern for the child's safety underlay the efforts to gain access to and then compel production of Maurice. Finally, production in the vast majority of cases will embody no incriminating testimony, even if in particular cases the act of production may incriminate the custodian through an assertion of possession, the existence, or the identity of the child. These orders to produce children cannot be characterized as efforts to gain some testimonial component of the act of production. The government demands production of the very public charge entrusted to a custodian, and makes the demand for compelling reasons unrelated to criminal law enforcement and as part of a broadly applied regulatory regime. In these circumstances, Bouknight cannot invoke the privilege to resist the order to produce Maurice.

We are not called upon to define the precise limitations that may exist upon the State's ability to use the testimonial aspects of Bouknight's act of production in subsequent criminal proceedings. But we note that imposition of such limitations is not foreclosed. The same custodial role that limited the ability to resist the production order may give rise to corresponding limitations upon the direct and indirect use of that testimony. See *Braswell*, 487 U.S., at 118, and n.11. The State's regulatory requirement in the usual case may neither compel incriminating testimony nor aid a criminal prosecution, but the Fifth Amendment protections are not thereby necessarily unavailable to the person who complies with the regulatory requirement after invoking the privilege and subsequently faces prosecution. See *Marchetti*, 390 U.S., at 58-59 (the "attractive and apparently practical" course of subsequent use restriction not appropriate where a significant element of the regulatory requirement is to aid law enforcement). In a broad range of contexts, the Fifth Amendment limits prosecutors' ability to use testimony that has been compelled. . . .

III

The judgment of the Court of Appeals of Maryland is reversed and the cases remanded to that court for further proceedings not inconsistent with this opinion.

JUSTICE MARSHALL, with whom JUSTICE BRENNAN joins, dissenting.

Although the Court assumes that respondent's act of producing her child would be testimonial and could be incriminating, it nonetheless concludes that she cannot invoke her privilege against self-incrimination and refuse to reveal her son's current location. Neither of the reasons the Court articulates to support its refusal to permit respondent to invoke her constitutional privilege justifies its decision. I therefore dissent.

I

The Court correctly assumes that Bouknight's production of her son to the Maryland court would be testimonial because it would amount to an admission of Bouknight's physical control over her son. The Court also assumes that Bouknight's act of production would be self-incriminating. I would not hesitate to hold explicitly that Bouknight's admission of possession or control presents a "real and appreciable" threat of self-incrimination. Marchetti v. United States, 390 U.S. 39, 48 (1968). Bouknight's ability to produce the child would conclusively establish her actual and present physical control over him, and thus might "prove a significant 'link in a chain' of evidence tending to establish [her] guilt."

Indeed, the stakes for Bouknight are much greater than the Court suggests. Not only could she face criminal abuse and neglect charges for her alleged mistreatment of Maurice, but she could also be charged with causing his death. The State acknowledges that it suspects that Maurice is dead, and the police are investigating his case as a possible homicide. In these circumstances, the potentially incriminating aspects to Bouknight's act of production are undoubtedly significant.

II

Notwithstanding the real threat of self-incrimination, the Court holds that "Bouknight may not invoke the privilege to resist the production order because she has assumed custodial duties related to production and because production is required as part of a noncriminal regulatory regime." In characterizing Bouknight as Maurice's "custodian," and in describing the relevant Maryland juvenile statutes as part of a noncriminal regulatory regime, the Court relies on two distinct lines of Fifth Amendment precedent, neither of which applies to this case.

A

The Court's first line of reasoning turns on its view that Bouknight has agreed to exercise on behalf of the State certain custodial obligations with respect to her son, obligations that the Court analogizes to those of a custodian of the records of a collective entity. This characterization is baffling, both because it is contrary to the facts of this case and because this Court has never relied on such a characterization to override the privilege against self-incrimination except in the context of a claim of privilege by an agent of a collective entity.[1]

Jacqueline Bouknight is Maurice's mother; she is not, and in fact could not be, his "custodian" whose rights and duties are determined solely by the Maryland juvenile protection law. Although Bouknight surrendered physical custody of her child during the pendency of the proceedings to determine whether Maurice was a "child in need of assistance" (CINA) within the meaning of the Maryland Code, Maurice's placement in shelter care was only temporary and did not extinguish her legal right to custody of her son. When the CINA proceedings were settled, Bouknight regained physical custody of Maurice and entered into an agreement with the Baltimore City Department of Social Services (BCDSS). In that agreement, which was approved by the juvenile court, Bouknight promised, among other things, to "cooperate with BCDSS," but she retained legal custody of Maurice.

A finding that a child is in need of assistance does not by itself divest a parent of legal or physical custody, nor does it transform such custody to something conferred by the State. Thus, the parent of a CINA continues to exercise custody because she is the child's parent, not because the State has delegated that responsibility to her. Although the State has obligations "[t]o provide for the care, protection, and wholesome mental and physical development of children" who are in need of assistance, Md. Cts. & Jud. Proc. Code Ann. §3-802(a)(1) (1984), these duties do not eliminate or override a parent's continuing legal obligations similarly to provide for her child.

In light of the statutory structure governing a parent's relationship to a CINA, Bouknight is not acting as a custodian in the traditional sense of that word because she is not acting on behalf of the State. In reality,

---

1. The Court claims that the principle espoused in the collective entity cases was "extend[ed] well beyond the corporate context" in Shapiro v. United States, 335 U.S. 1 (1948). Shapiro, however, did not rest on the existence of an agency relationship between a collective entity and the custodian of its records. Instead, the petitioner was denied the Fifth Amendment privilege because the records sought were kept as part of a generalized regulatory system that required all businesses, unincorporated as well as incorporated, to retain records of certain transactions. See 335 U.S., at 22-23, 27, 33. Shapiro turned on the Court's view "that the privilege which exists as to private papers cannot be maintained in relation to 'records required by law to be kept in order that there may be suitable information of transactions which are the appropriate subjects of governmental regulation and the enforcement of restrictions validly established.' " Id., at 33 (quoting Davis v. United States, 328 U.S. 582, 589-590 (1946)). Thus, Shapiro is properly analyzed with the cases concerning testimony required as a part of a noncriminal regulatory regime, rather than with the cases concerning testimony compelled from custodians of collective entities' records.

she continues to exercise her parental duties, constrained by an agreement between her and the State. That agreement, which includes a stipulation that Maurice was a CINA, allows the State, in certain circumstances, to intercede in Bouknight's relationship with her child. It does not, however, confer custodial rights and obligations on Bouknight in the same way corporate law creates the custodial status of a corporate agent.

Moreover, the rationale for denying a corporate custodian Fifth Amendment protection for acts done in her representative capacity does not apply to this case. The rule for a custodian of corporate records rests on the well-established principle that a collective entity, unlike a natural person, has no Fifth Amendment privilege against self-incrimination. Because an artificial entity can act only through its agents, a custodian of such an entity's documents may not invoke her personal privilege to resist producing documents that may incriminate the entity, even if the documents may also incriminate the custodian. Wilson v. United States, 221 U.S. 361, 384-385 (1911). As we explained in *White:*

> [I]ndividuals, when acting as representatives of a collective group, cannot be said to be exercising their personal rights and duties nor to be entitled to their purely personal privileges. Rather they assume the rights, duties and privileges of the artificial entity or association of which they are agents or officers and they are bound by its obligations. . . . And the official records and documents of the organization that are held by them *in a representative rather than in a personal capacity* cannot be the subject of the personal privilege against self-incrimination, even though production of the papers might tend to incriminate them personally. 322 U.S., at 699.

Jacqueline Bouknight is not the agent for an artificial entity that possesses no Fifth Amendment privilege. Her role as Maurice's parent is very different from the role of a corporate custodian who is merely the instrumentality through whom the corporation acts. I am unwilling to extend the collective entity doctrine into a context where it denies individuals, acting in their personal rather than representative capacities, their constitutional privilege against self-incrimination.

B

The Court's decision rests as well on cases holding that "the ability to invoke the privilege may be greatly diminished when invocation would interfere with the effective operation of a generally applicable, civil regulatory requirement." The cases the Court cites have two common features: they concern civil regulatory systems not primarily intended to facilitate criminal investigations, and they target the general public. See

California v. Byers, 402 U.S. 424, 430-431 (1971) (determining that a "hit and run" statute that required a driver involved in an accident to stop and give certain information was primarily civil). In contrast, regulatory regimes that are directed at a " 'selective group inherently suspect of criminal activities,' " *Marchetti*, 390 U.S. at 57 (quoting Albertson v. Subversive Activities Control Board, 382 U.S. 70, 79 (1965)), do not result in a similar diminution of the Fifth Amendment privilege.

1

Applying the first feature to this case, the Court describes Maryland's juvenile protection scheme as "a broadly directed, noncriminal regulatory regime governing children cared for pursuant to custodial orders." The Court concludes that Bouknight cannot resist an order necessary for the functioning of that system. The Court's characterization of Maryland's system is dubious and highlights the flaws inherent in the Court's formulation of the appropriate Fifth Amendment inquiry. Virtually any civil regulatory scheme could be characterized as essentially non-criminal by looking narrowly or, as in this case, solely to the avowed non-criminal purpose of the regulations. If one focuses instead on the practical effects, the same scheme could be seen as facilitating criminal investigation. The fact that the Court holds Maryland's juvenile statute to be essentially noncriminal, notwithstanding the overlapping purposes underlying that statute and Maryland's criminal child abuse statutes, proves that the Court's test will never be used to find a relationship between the civil scheme and law enforcement goals significant enough to implicate the Fifth Amendment.

The regulations embodied in the juvenile welfare statute are intimately related to the enforcement of state criminal statutes prohibiting child abuse. State criminal decisions suggest that information supporting criminal convictions is often obtained through civil proceedings and the subsequent protective oversight by BCDSS. In this respect, Maryland's juvenile protection system resembles the revenue system at issue in *Marchetti*, which required persons engaged in the business of accepting wagers to provide certain information about their activities to the Federal Government. Focusing on the effects of the regulatory scheme, the Court held that this revenue system was not the sort of neutral civil regulatory scheme that could trump the Fifth Amendment privilege. Even though the Government's "principal interest [was] evidently the collection of revenue," 390 U.S., at 57, the information sought would increase the "likelihood that any past or present gambling offenses [would] be discovered and successfully prosecuted," id., at 52.

In contrast to *Marchetti*, the Court here disregards the practical implications of the civil scheme and holds that the juvenile protection system does not " 'focu[s] almost exclusively on conduct which was criminal.' " (quoting *Byers, supra,* at 454 (Harlan, J., concurring in judgment)). I cannot agree with this approach. The State's goal of protecting children from abusive environments through its juvenile welfare system cannot be separated from criminal provisions that serve the same goal. When the conduct at which a civil statute aims—here, child abuse and neglect—is frequently the same conduct subject to criminal sanction, it strikes me as deeply problematic to dismiss the Fifth Amendment concerns by characterizing the civil scheme as "unrelated to criminal law enforcement investigation." A civil scheme that *inevitably* intersects with criminal sanctions may not be used to coerce, on pain of contempt, a potential criminal defendant to furnish evidence crucial to the success of her own prosecution.

I would apply a different analysis, one that is more faithful to the concerns underlying the Fifth Amendment. This approach would target the respondent's particular claim of privilege, the precise nature of the testimony sought, and the likelihood of self-incrimination caused by this respondent's compliance. "To sustain the privilege, it need only be evident from the implications of the question, in the setting in which it is asked, that a responsive answer to the question or an explanation of why it cannot be answered might be dangerous because injurious disclosure could result." Hoffman v. United States, 341 U.S. 479, 486-487 (1951). This analysis unambiguously indicates that Bouknight's Fifth Amendment privilege must be respected to protect her from the serious risk of self-incrimination.

An individualized inquiry is preferable to the Court's analysis because it allows the privilege to turn on the concrete facts of a particular case, rather than on abstract characterizations concerning the nature of a regulatory scheme. Moreover, this particularized analysis would not undermine any appropriate goals of civil regulatory schemes that may intersect with criminal prohibitions. Instead, the ability of a State to provide immunity from criminal prosecution permits it to gather information necessary for civil regulation, while also preserving the integrity of the privilege against self-incrimination. The fact that the State throws a wide net in seeking information does not mean that it can demand from the few persons whose Fifth Amendment rights are implicated that they participate in their own criminal prosecutions. Rather, when the State demands testimony from its citizens, it should do so with an explicit grant of immunity.

2

The Court's approach includes a second element; it holds that a civil regulatory scheme cannot override Fifth Amendment protection unless it is targeted at the general public. Such an analysis would not be necessary under the particularized approach I advocate. Even under the Court's test, however, Bouknight's right against self-incrimination should not be diminished because Maryland's juvenile welfare scheme clearly is *not* generally applicable. A child is considered in need of assistance because "[h]e is mentally handicapped or is not receiving ordinary and proper care and attention, and . . . [h]is parents . . . are unable or unwilling to give proper care and attention to the child and his problems." The juvenile court has jurisdiction only over children who are alleged to be in need of assistance, not over all children in the State. It thus has power to compel testimony only from those parents whose children are alleged to be CINAs. In other words, the regulatory scheme that the Court describes as "broadly directed," is actually narrowly targeted at parents who through abuse or neglect deny their children the minimal reasonable level of care and attention. Not all such abuse or neglect rises to the level of criminal child abuse, but parents of children who have been so seriously neglected or abused as to warrant allegations that the children are in need of state assistance are clearly "a selective group inherently suspect of criminal activities."

III

In the end, neither line of precedents relied on by the Court justifies riding roughshod over Bouknight's constitutional privilege against self-incrimination. The Court cannot accurately characterize her as a "custodian" in the same sense as the Court has used that word in the past. Nor is she the State's "agent," whom the State may require to act on its behalf. Moreover, the regulatory scheme at issue here is closely intertwined with the criminal regime prohibiting child abuse and applies only to parents whose abuse or neglect is serious enough to warrant state intervention.

Although I am disturbed by the Court's willingness to apply inapposite precedent to deny Bouknight her constitutional right against self-incrimination, especially in light of the serious allegations of homicide that accompany this civil proceeding, I take some comfort in the Court's recognition that the State may be prohibited from using any testimony given by Bouknight in subsequent criminal proceedings.[2] Because I am

2. I note, with both exasperation and skepticism about the bona fide nature of the State's intentions, that the State may be able to grant Bouknight use immunity under a recently enacted immunity statute, even though it has thus far failed to do so. See 1989 Md. Laws, Ch. 288 (amending §9-123). Although the statute applies only to testimony "in a criminal prosecution or a proceeding before a grand jury of the State," Md. Cts.

not content to deny Bouknight the constitutional protection required by the Fifth Amendment now in the hope that she will not be convicted later on the basis of her own testimony, I dissent.

NOTES AND QUESTIONS

1. Justice Harlan provided the fifth vote in *Byers*, but what, exactly, is his point? Is it that a conventional (traditional) understanding of the self-incrimination clause unmistakably indicates that Byers's rights were violated, but that the conventional understanding is no longer adequate? Has this view matured into a definite holding in *Bouknight?* If so, there is a problem—how is one to judge the "adequacy" of traditional understandings of constitutional language? If the demands of the state justify modifying the contours of the self-incrimination clause in the context of vehicular and child custody law, why not in other contexts as well? Is it obvious, for example, that the demands of the modern state are greater here than in, say, the regulation of the banking industry, or for that matter in the regulation of interpersonal conflicts through the criminal law? Alternatively, do these questions misperceive the essence of these cases? Is *Byers* perhaps just a slight extension of the "required records" doctrine, and *Bouknight* an application of the *Fisher* doctrine?

2. Note that in *Neville* Justice O'Connor did not rely on *Schmerber*. Should she have done so? Could she have done so? Consider Arenella, *Schmerber* and the Privilege Against Self-Incrimination: A Reappraisal, 20 Am. Crim. L. Rev. 31, 42-45 (1982), which was written in anticipation of *Neville*.

> It is necessary to provide a clear definition of what constitutes a "communicative act," before turning to the question of whether Neville's refusal to comply with a police request should be considered a testimonial or communicative act under *Schmerber*. For sound analytical reasons, Justice Brennan attempted to separate the question of what types of evidence were covered by the privilege from the question of what types of government activity constituted testimonial compulsion proscribed by the privilege. Separating the concepts of testimony and testimonial compulsion is useful for two different reasons. *First*, if the state only extracts nontestimonial evidence from the accused such as the blood test in *Schmerber*, one need

---

& Jud. Proc. Code Ann. §9-123(b)(1) (Supp. 1989), the State represented to this Court that "[a]s a matter of law, [granting limited use immunity for the testimonial aspects of Bouknight's compliance with the production order] would now be possible," Tr. of Oral Arg. 10. If such a grant of immunity has been possible since July 1989 and the State has refused to invoke it so that it can litigate Bouknight's claim of privilege, I have difficulty believing that the State is sincere in its protestations of concern for Maurice's well-being.

not worry about testimonial compulsion because the threshold requirement of testimonial evidence is missing. . . .

Second, by separating the two concepts, one recognizes that an individual's conduct may qualify as a testimonial act and still not be protected by the privilege if the conduct was not the product of fifth amendment compulsion. . . . Justice Brennan's examples of communicative conduct qualifying as testimonial acts focused on situations where (1) the actor's conduct reflected his subjective intent to communicate his thoughts to another and (2) the state could make testimonial use of those intentionally communicated thoughts to help prove the individual's guilt at trial. This assertive conduct test for defining communicative acts is useful because it draws an important distinction between conduct reflecting the *actor's intent* to communicate and conduct that may convey something about the actor's state of mind to *the observer of the conduct* even though the actor *did not intend* to communicate anything. Since almost all conduct may convey something about the actor's state of mind to the objective observer, an assertive conduct test *usually* provides a more suitable benchmark for defining the types of communicative conduct covered by the privilege.

An assertive conduct test helps explain, for example, why evidence of flight, escape from custody, or destruction of evidence should not be considered testimonial acts for purposes of the fifth amendment privilege. Such guilty conduct evidence has probative value because it may communicate to the observer of such conduct or the factfinder at trial the actor's consciousness of guilt at the time of the conduct. However, such an elastic definition of a testimonial act qualifying as testimonial evidence would obliterate any meaningful distinction between testimonial acts and guilty conduct evidence. Justice Brennan's assertive conduct test permits us to distinguish between communicative acts and guilty conduct evidence. Flight does not qualify as a testimonial act under Brennan's test because the actor does not intend to communicate his consciousness of guilt to the objective observer and the factfinder at trial does not draw any inferences concerning the defendant's state of mind from any *intended* communication he makes.

However, *Schmerber's* apparent distinction between assertive conduct and real or physical evidence does not offer a completely satisfying formulation of the types of evidence the privilege should protect. Consider Justice Brennan's compelled lie detector example in *Schmerber*. As Justice Brennan conceded, one could easily characterize the lie detector's measurement of the defendant's involuntary physiological responses as real or physical evidence not protected by the privilege. Regardless of what the accused *intends* to communicate, no testimonial use need be made of his *intended* communications. His actual mental answer will be inferred from his involuntary physiological responses. Yet, Justice Brennan concluded that "to compel a person to submit to testing in which an effort will be made to determine his guilt or innocence on the basis of physiological responses, whether willed or not, is to evoke the spirit and history of the

Fifth Amendment." The compelled polygraph test problem demonstrates
the futility of trying to separate one's definition of what constitutes testimony for fifth amendment purposes from one's view of the core values
that are impaired by permitting testimonial compulsion. If the privilege's
primary objective is to prevent the state from intruding upon the individual's mental privacy, then the individual's intent to communicate his
thoughts, beliefs, and feelings to another should not be a dispositive factor
where the state has developed investigatory techniques that force the individual to reveal involuntarily the contents of his mind. Relying exclusively on an assertive conduct definition of testimonial acts would simply
encourage the state to develop more sophisticated mind-probing techniques
to circumvent the privilege's protections.

Therefore, I propose the following two-part definition of communicative conduct to describe the types of evidence falling within the privilege's
protection. An individual's conduct should be considered testimonial when
(1) it reflects the actor's *subjective* intent to communicate his thoughts to
another, and the state proposes to make testimonial use of these thoughts,
or (2) the state forces the accused to disclose *involuntarily* his private
thoughts, feelings, and beliefs about the crime charged and then proposes
to make testimonial use of these extracted thoughts.

A polygraph test's measurements of the individual's involuntary physiological responses to the operator's questions would constitute communicative conduct under this test for two reasons. *First*, the state would have
compelled the accused to communicate involuntarily his own thoughts
and feelings about the crime. *Second*, the test results—whether the accused
was lying or not as measured by his involuntary physiological responses—
would make testimonial use of these communicated, private, mental answers. In a religious society, the oath ex officio effectively used moral
compulsion to extract a confession from the defendant's own lips. In a
secular society that takes its science seriously, the polygraph test effectively
uses scientific compulsion to extract a confession from the private recesses
of the defendant's mind. In both cases, the state's action forces the accused
to condemn himself in a manner violating the individual's mental privacy.[70]

70. Professor Gerstein rejects mental privacy as the core substantive value protected
by the privilege because of the "incoherence between the focus on privacy and the Fifth
Amendment's obvious preoccupation with self-incrimination." Gerstein, The Demise
of *Boyd*: Self-Incrimination and Private Papers in the Burger Court, 27 U.C.L.A.L. Rev.
343, 388 (1979). According to Gerstein, it makes little sense to speak of mental privacy
as the core value when it is only protected where a threat of self-incrimination exists. Id.
at 386-89. Gerstein's perceived "incoherency" disappears, however, once one recognizes
that the privilege only protects against invasions of mental privacy that impair accusatorial
process values. See supra note 58. Instead of recognizing that the privilege protects both
substantive and procedural values, Gerstein argues that the privilege can best be understood as vindicating the core value of moral autonomy. Gerstein, supra, at 345-56. His
definition of a testimonial act reflects this emphasis. Gerstein has suggested that: "[w]hat
makes an act testimonial is the fact-finder's reliance upon the actor's moral responsibility
for truth-telling in making use of it as evidence. This, in turn, must imply the existence

How does *Doe* come out under Professor Arenella's test?

3. Justice O'Connor's opinion in *Neville* made much more of the nature of the police-citizen interaction than it did of the results of that interaction. Why? Professor Westen has argued that the fifth amendment should be understood as permitting the states to require that citizens respond in specified ways to an improper state compulsion to provide incriminating material and that failure to do so can result in the forfeiture of fifth amendment protections. See Westen & Mandell, To Talk, to Balk, or to Lie: The Emerging Fifth Amendment Doctrine of the "Pre-referred Response," 19 Crim. L. Rev. 521 (1982).

4. Does, or should, a defendant have the right to have defense witnesses granted immunity in order to secure their testimony? See Note, The Sixth Amendment Right to Have Use Immunity Granted to Defense Witnesses, 91 Harv. L. Rev. 1266 (1978). At least one circuit has so held, see Government of Virgin Islands v. Smith, 615 F.2d 964 (3d Cir. 1980), but the trend seems to the contrary. See United States v. D'Apice, 664 F.2d 75 (5th Cir. 1981), specifically rejecting *Smith*. Does it matter whether the witness is relying on the fifth amendment or an evidentiary privilege? Interestingly enough, most courts say that it does matter and will order witnesses to testify over the invocation of evidentiary privilege. For a fascinating exchange on this issue in particular, see Hill, Testimonial Privilege and Fair Trial, 80 Colum. L. Rev. 1173 (1980), and Westen, Reflections on Alfred Hill's "Testimonial Privilege and Fair Trial," 14 U. Mich. J.L. Ref. 371 (1981).

5. Fifth amendment problems can arise in myriad ways.

a. Questions relevant to a civil case may ask for information that may be self-incriminating. For a thorough discussion of the implications of the fifth amendment for civil litigation, see Heidt, The Conjurer's Circle—The Fifth Amendment Privilege in Civil Cases, 91 Yale L.J. 1062 (1982). For a discussion of ways to minimize this type of problem, see Note, Toward a Rational Treatment of Plaintiffs Who Invoke the Privilege Against Self-Incrimination During Discovery, 66 Iowa L. Rev. 575 (1981).

b. In United States v. Peister, 631 F.2d 658 (10th Cir. 1980), the defendant claimed that he had impermissibly been forced to choose between his sixth amendment right to counsel and his fifth amendment right to silence. Peister, who was being prosecuted for supplying fraud-

---

of an opportunity to be truthful or not." Id. at 346 n.17. Since an effective and reliable lie detector test deprives the individual of any opportunity to deceive the questioner, its results might be admissible under Gerstein's test. Gerstein's definition of a testimonial act places too much emphasis on the substantive value of moral autonomy at the expense of disregarding the individual's right to limit access to his private thought processes and the accusatorial process norm of preserving a fair state-individual balance of advantage.

ulent data on his withholding form, was informed that counsel would be provided for him if he was indigent. To qualify, however, he would have to file a financial affidavit. Peister asked for immunity for the information provided in the affidavit, claiming the answers would incriminate him on matters involved in that prosecution. The trial court did not grant immunity and said that no constitutional rights are violated when a defendant has to choose between the right to counsel and the privilege against self-incrimination.

On appeal the circuit court held that there was no constitutional violation. It reasoned that the defendant has the burden of showing the need for appointed counsel and that speculative fifth amendment claims do not reduce that burden. Moreover, because filing the affidavit is a pretrial proceeding, any incriminating information provided by the defendant would be given use immunity pursuant to Simmons v. United States, 390 U.S. 377 (1968). The Court noted that at least three other circuits also apply the *Simmons* use immunity when the right to counsel is involved.

c. United States v. Jeffers, 621 F.2d 221 (5th Cir. 1980), was a prosecution for failure to comply with the tax provisions that had been amended after *Marchetti* and *Grosso*. Jeffers challenged the statutes, claiming that forced compliance with them would violate the fifth amendment privilege because incriminating information could become public if Jeffers ever were in a proceeding to enforce the tax and because close cooperation between the IRS and the Dallas police department could possibly make him subject to prosecution. The court noted that the laws said the disclosures were to be kept confidential, that Congress intended the disclosures to be kept confidential, and that there were no facts to support the idea that the disclosures were being used to prosecute gambling. In light of this, it concluded that the risk of prosecution was too speculative to support a fifth amendment claim and that the tax laws as amended provide the taxpayer with protection as broad in scope and effect as the fifth amendment.

d. In United States v. Stirling, 571 F.2d 708 (2d Cir.), cert. denied, 439 U.S. 824 (1978), defendants had been convicted of, among other things, violating SEC regulations by failing to disclose material facts about certain stock transactions. The defendants claimed that the fifth amendment should have protected them from prosecution for that failure because disclosure would have left them open to prosecution under the Taft-Hartley Act. The court first cited California v. Byers, 402 U.S. 424 (1971), for the proposition that an essentially regulatory statute, where

1. Self-reporting is essential to fulfill its objectives,
2. The burden of reporting is not placed on a highly selective group inherently suspect of criminal activities,

3. The general activity is lawful, and
4. The possibility of incrimination is not substantial,

does not violate the fifth amendment. The court found that all conditions were met and affirmed the conviction.

e. In Walker v. Butterworth, 599 F.2d 1074 (1st Cir. 1979), the court reversed a Massachusetts murder conviction. The defendant was relying on an insanity defense, but the trial court followed traditional Massachusetts practice in homicide cases and made the defendant exercise his preemptory challenges personally. He announced each challenge after consulting with his lawyer (who had objected to the process). In the closing argument the prosecutor alluded to the exercises of the challenge as indicative of the defendant's sanity. Instead of giving a specific cautionary instruction, as requested by defense counsel, the judge informed the jury that Walker was required to exercise the challenges and that counsel's arguments are not to be considered evidence.

The Massachusetts Supreme Judicial Court affirmed the conviction, stating that the challenges may have been probative of competency at the time of trial but had little, if any, relation to the issue of sanity at the time of the offense. The federal district court, on habeas, reasoned that the exercise was analogous to physical actions that possessed little or no communicative content.

The court of appeals held that the practice and the comment combined violated the fifth amendment. It said the critical question was whether the forced utterances had communicative content. Although not typical testimony, the court stated they were still communicative because the words were used to transmit information. This communication revealed Walker's mental process. It transmitted the message that he could act rationally and sanely, communicate with his lawyer, and make important trial decisions. (The possibility that his message was wrong was more reason to find the fifth amendment violated, because it was intended to prevent unreliable testimony. Id. at 1082 n.9.) In addition, the jurors did not use the words as identifying characteristics or physical properties. And any doubts of the communicative nature were resolved by the prosecutor's comments. Because the forced utterances were communicative and directly relevant to the sole issue at trial, the central values of the privilege would be threatened by allowing the conviction to stand. Id. at 1082, 1083.

f. In re Layden, 446 F. Supp. 53 (N.D. Ill. 1978), held that making a defendant give a convoluted writing sample against his will (to compare with a sample already determined to be disguised) is compulsion that violates the fifth amendment. Compelling the writing would make the defendant show an unnatural (for him) characteristic and would be "acting-out" within the meaning of Gilbert v. California, 388 U.S. 263,

266 (1967). The court also held it would violate the fourth amendment (citing *Schmerber*) and violate fundamental fairness.

g. In Davis v. Israel, 453 F. Supp. 1316 (E.D. Wisc. 1978), aff'd, 601 F.2d 594 (7th Cir. 1979), several police officers came to Davis's apartment the morning after a murder. He was arrested, read his rights, and because he was just wearing underwear, was told to put on the clothes he wore the night before. Blood that matched that of the victim was found on the pants and was admitted into evidence over Davis's objection that it violated his fifth amendment privilege. The trial judge denied the objection on the ground that no oral testimonial utterances were involved.

The federal district court reversed, reasoning that although clothing per se is physical evidence and not testimonial, the act of putting on certain clothing and thereby identifying it for the police was testimonial. It found no difference between stating that he wore the clothes and admitting the fact by putting them on in response to an order to do so.

h. The significance of the risk of foreign prosecution for application of the privilege has not been resolved by the Supreme Court, and the circuit courts are not entirely in agreement. See, e.g., In re Grand Jury Subpoena of Flanagan, 691 F.2d 116 (2d Cir. 1982); In re Grand Jury Proceeding Nigro v. United States, 705 F.2d 1224 (10th Cir. 1982); In re Campbell, 628 F.2d 1260 (9th Cir. 1980).

6. Should the fifth amendment privilege ever apply where the witness will not be exposed to an increased risk of incrimination? What if a witness is called to testify before a legislative committee and the relevant statute of limitations has run? Should the possible public disgrace be sufficient grounds for invoking the privilege? What if the reason the committee subpoenaed the person's appearance was precisely to subject the person to public humiliation? For a discussion of these problems, and much more, see Mansfield, The *Albertson* Case: Conflict Between the Privilege Against Self-Incrimination and the Government's Need for Information, 1966 S. Ct. Rev. 103.

C. POLICE INTERROGATION

1. Police Interrogation and the Miranda Revolution

Since earliest recorded times, officialdom has interrogated individuals suspected of or charged with criminality. In more barbaric times, the questioning was often accompanied by physical abuse or torture, and a confession resulting from such methods, no matter the extent of the physical coercions applied to the suspect, could form part of the basis of a conviction. Nonetheless, the factual accuracy of statements made under extreme duress is obviously problematic where the only means of halting an interrogation is to assent to the views of the interrogator. Thus, there developed the view that a person ought not to face coercive interrogation designed to yield self-incriminating responses.

The opposition to coercive interrogation gained support from the opposition to the practices of the High Commission and the Court of Star Chamber in England, in particular the use of the oath ex officio, which required those called before the court to swear to answer truthfully all questions, on pain of perjury, without being informed of the subject matter of the inquiry and prior to any official allegation of criminality. The resistance to the practices of the High Commission and the Star Chamber, while initially resting on the common law principle that a person could not be compelled to answer questions under oath to charges that had not been formally made, came to rest on the moral ground that it was unfair for the state to attempt to coerce an individual to contribute to his or her own conviction. These interrelated concerns about trustworthiness, the developing view of the requirements of fairness, and the demands for privacy and autonomy, discussed in Section A and Chapter 6 supra, together seem to have formed the basis of the fifth amendment.[1]

Nonetheless, the applicability of the fifth amendment to pretrial interrogation was not generally accepted at an early date in this country. Notwithstanding the periodic recognition of the abuses of pretrial interrogation similar to those that gave rise in part to the fifth amendment,[2] the early treatment of confessions in this country excluded confessions only if they were untrustworthy, see, e.g., Hopt v. Utah, 110 U.S. 574 (1884), although one important determinant of trustworthiness was the nature of the interrogation process that led to the incriminating statements. In 1897, however, the Supreme Court, in a remarkable opinion, appeared to bring pretrial interrogation within the scope of the fifth amendment in a fashion that unified the Court's treatment of the various issues underlying the fourth and fifth amendments. Not surprisingly, Boyd v. United States played a significant role:

---

1. For a complete discussion of these developments, see L. Levy, The Origins of the Fifth Amendment (1968). The constitutional debates over the fifth amendment are peculiarly unenlightening, thus the word "seem" in the text.

2. See, e.g., National Commission on Law Observance and Enforcement, Report on Lawlessness in Law Enforcement (1931) (often referred to as the Wickersham Commission).

BRAM v. UNITED STATES

Error to the Circuit Court of the United States for the
District of Massachusetts
168 U.S. 532 (1897)

MR. JUSTICE WHITE delivered the opinion of the court.

This writ of error is prosecuted to a verdict and sentence thereon, by which the plaintiff was found guilty of murder, and condemned to suffer death. The homicide was committed on board the American ship Herbert Fuller while on the high seas bound from Boston to a port in South America. The accused was the first officer of the ship, and the deceased, of whose murder he was convicted, was the master of the vessel. . . .

The bill of exceptions further states that when the ship arrived at Halifax [to which it changed course after the events in question] the accused and Brown [another suspect] were held in custody by the chief of police at that place, and that whilst in such custody the accused was taken from prison to the office of a detective and there questioned under circumstances to be hereafter stated. Subsequently to this occurrence at Halifax, all the officers, the crew and the passenger were examined before the American consul and gave their statements, which were reduced to writing and sworn to. They were thereafter, at the request of the American consul, sent to Boston, where the accused was indicted for the murder of Nash, the captain, of Mrs. Nash, and the second mate Blomberg. The trial and the conviction, now under review, related to the first of these charges. . . .

We first examine the error relied on which seems to us deserving of the most serious consideration. During the trial, a detective by whom the accused was questioned whilst at Halifax was placed upon the stand as a witness for the prosecution for the purpose of testifying to the conversation had between himself and the accused at Halifax, at the time and place already stated. . . .

The contention is that the foregoing conversation, between the detective and the accused, was competent only as a confession by him made; that it was offered as such, and that it was erroneously admitted, as it was not shown to have been voluntary. . . .

In criminal trials, in the courts of the United States, wherever a question arises whether a confession is incompetent because not voluntary, the issue is controlled by that portion of the Fifth Amendment to the Constitution of the United States, commanding that no person "shall be compelled in any criminal case to be a witness against himself." The legal principle by which the admissibility of the confession of an accused person is to be determined is expressed in the textbooks.

In 3 Russell on Crimes, (6th ed.) 478, it is stated as follows:

> But a confession, in order to be admissible, must be free and voluntary: that is, must not be extracted by any sort of threats or violence, nor obtained by any direct or implied promises, however slight, nor by the exertion of any improper influence. . . . A confession can never be received in evidence where the prisoner has been influenced by any threat or promise; for the law cannot measure the force of the influence used, or decide upon its effect upon the mind of the prisoner, and therefore excludes the declaration if any degree of influence has been exerted.

And this summary of the law is in harmony with the doctrine as expressed by other writers, although the form in which they couch its statement may be different.

These writers but express the result of a multitude of American and English cases, which will be found collected by the authors and editors either in the text or in notes, especially in the ninth edition of Taylor, second volume, tenth chapter, and the American notes, following page 588, where a very full reference is made to decided cases. The statement of the rule is also in entire accord with the decisions of this court on the subject.

A brief consideration of the reasons which gave rise to the adoption of the Fifth Amendment, of the wrongs which it was intended to prevent and of the safeguards which it was its purpose unalterably to secure, will make it clear that the generic language of the Amendment was but a crystallization of the doctrine as to confessions, well settled when the Amendment was adopted, and since expressed in the text writers and expounded by the adjudications, and hence that the statements on the subject by the text writers and adjudications but formulate the conceptions and commands of the Amendment itself. In Boyd v. United States, 116 U.S. 616, attention was called to the intimate relation existing between the provision of the Fifth Amendment securing one accused against being compelled to testify against himself, and those of the Fourth Amendment protecting against unreasonable searches and seizures; and it was in that case demonstrated that both of these Amendments contemplated perpetuating, in their full efficacy, by means of a constitutional provision, principles of humanity and civil liberty, which had been secured in the mother country only after years of struggle, so as to implant them in our institutions in the fullness of their integrity, free from the possibilities of future legislative change. In commenting on the same subject, in Brown v. Walker, 161 U.S. 591, 596, the court, speaking through Mr. Justice Brown, said:

. . . While the admissions or confessions of the prisoner, when voluntarily and freely made, have always ranked high in the scale of incriminating evidence, if an accused person be asked to explain his apparent connection with a crime under investigation, the ease with which the questions put to him may assume an inquisitorial character, the temptation to press the witness unduly, to browbeat him if he be timid or reluctant, to push him into a corner, and to entrap him into fatal contradictions, which is so painfully evident in many of the earlier state trials, notably in those of Sir Nicholas Throckmorton and Udal, the Puritan minister, made the system so odious as to give rise to a demand for its total abolition. The change in the English criminal procedure in that particular seems to be founded upon no statute and no judicial opinion, but upon a general and silent acquiescence of the courts in a popular demand. But, however adopted, it has become firmly embedded in English, as well as in American jurisprudence. So deeply did the iniquities of the ancient system impress themselves upon the minds of the American colonists that the States, with one accord, made a denial of the right to question an accused person a part of their fundamental law, so that a maxim, which in England was a mere rule of evidence, became clothed in this country with the impregnability of a constitutional enactment.

There can be no doubt that long prior to our independence the doctrine that one accused of crime could not be compelled to testify against himself had reached its full development in the common law, was there considered as resting on the law of nature, and was embedded in that system as one of its great and distinguishing attributes.

[The Court reviewed the English precedents.]

Looking at the doctrine as thus established, it would seem plainly to be deducible that as the principle from which, under the law of nature, it was held that one accused could not be compelled to testify against himself, was in its essence comprehensive enough to exclude all manifestations of compulsion, whether arising from torture or from moral causes, the rule formulating the principle with logical accuracy, came to be so stated as to embrace all cases of compulsion which were covered by the doctrine. As the facts by which compulsion might manifest itself, whether physical or moral, would be necessarily ever different, the measure by which the involuntary nature of the confession was to be ascertained was stated in the rule, not by the changing causes, but by their resultant effect upon the mind, that is, hope or fear, so that, however diverse might be the facts, the test of whether the confession was voluntary would be uniform, that is, would be ascertained by the condition of mind which the causes ordinarily operated to create. The well settled nature of the rule in England at the time of the adoption of the Constitution and of the Fifth Amendment, and the intimate knowledge had by the framers of the principles of civil liberty which had become a part of the common law, aptly explain the conciseness of the language of that Amendment. And the accuracy with which the doctrine as to confessions as now formulated embodies the rule existing at common law and embedded in the Fifth Amendment was noticed by this court in Wilson v. United States, . . . where, after referring to the criteria of hope and fear, speaking through Mr. Chief Justice Fuller, it was said: "In short, the true test of admissibility is that the confession is made freely, voluntarily and without compulsion or inducement of any sort." 162 U.S. 613, 623.

In approaching the adjudicated cases for the purpose of endeavoring to deduce from them what quantum of proof, in a case presented, is adequate to create, by the operation of hope or fear, an involuntary condition of the mind, the difficulty encountered is, that all the decided cases necessarily rest upon the state of facts which existed in the particular case, and, therefore, furnish no certain criterion, since the conclusion that a given state of fact was adequate to have produced an involuntary confession does not establish that the same result has been created by a different although somewhat similar condition of fact. Indeed, the embarrassment which comes from the varying state of fact, considered in the decided cases, has given rise to the statement that there was no general rule of law by which the admissibility of a confession could be determined, but that the courts had left the rule to be evolved from the facts of each particular case. . . . And, again, it has been said that so great was the perplexity resulting from an attempt to reconcile the authorities that it was manifest that not only must each case solely depend upon its own facts, but that even the legal rule to be applied was involved in obscurity and confusion. . . .

The first of these statements but expresses the thought that whether a confession was voluntary was primarily one of fact, and therefore every case must depend upon its own proof. The second is obviously a misconception, for, however great may be the divergence between the facts decided in previous cases and those presented in any given case, no doubt or obscurity can arise as to the rule itself, since it is found in the text of the Constitution. Much of the confusion which has resulted from the effort to deduce from the adjudged cases what would be a sufficient quantum of proof to show that a confession was or was not voluntary, has arisen from a misconception of the subject to which the proof must address itself. The rule is not that in order to render a statement admissible the proof must be adequate to establish that the particular communications contained in a statement were voluntarily made, but it must be sufficient to establish that the making of the statement was voluntary; that is to say, that from the causes, which the law treats as legally sufficient to engender in the mind of the accused hope or fear in respect to the crime charged, the accused was not involuntarily impelled to make a statement, when but for the improper influences he would have remained silent. . . .

Whilst . . . there is no question that a police officer having a prisoner in custody is a person in authority within the rule in England, and therefore that any inducement by him offered, calculated to operate upon the mind of the prisoner, would render a confession as a consequence thereof inadmissible, there seems to be doubt in England whether the doctrine does not extend further, and hold that the mere fact of the interrogation of a prisoner by a police officer would per se render the confession inadmissible, because of the inducement resulting from the very nature of the authority exercised by the police officer, assimilating him in this regard to a committing or examining magistrate. . . . Whatever be the rule in this regard in England, however, it is certain that where a confession is elicited by the questions of a policeman, the fact of its having been so obtained, it is conceded, may be an important element in determining whether the answers of the prisoner were voluntary. The attempt on the part of a police officer to obtain a confession by interrogating has been often reproved by the English courts as unfair to the prisoner and as approaching dangerously near to a violation of the rule protecting an accused from being compelled to testify against himself. . . .

From this review it clearly appears that the rule as to confessions, by an accused . . . is in England to-day what it was prior to and at the adoption of the Fifth Amendment, and that whilst all the decided cases necessarily rest upon the state of facts which the cases considered, nevertheless the decisions as a whole afford a safe guide by which to ascertain whether in this case the confession was voluntary, since the facts here presented are strikingly like those considered in many of the English cases.

We come then to the American authorities. In this court the general rule that the confession must be free and voluntary, that is, not produced by inducements engendering either hope or fear, is settled by the authorities referred to at the outset. The facts in the particular cases decided in this court, and which have been referred to, manifested so clearly that the confessions were voluntary, that no useful purpose can be subserved by analyzing them. In this court also it has been settled that the mere fact that the confession is made to a police officer, while the accused was under arrest in or out of prison, or was drawn out by his questions, does not necessarily render the confession involuntary, but, as one of the circumstances, such imprisonment or interrogation may be taken into account in determining whether or not the statements of the prisoner were voluntary. Hopt v. Utah, 110 U.S. 174; Sparf v. United States, 156 U.S. 51, 55. And this last rule thus by this court established is also the doctrine upheld by the state decisions. . . .

We come, then, to a consideration of the circumstances surrounding, and the facts established to exist, in reference to the confession, in order to determine whether it was shown to have been voluntarily made. Before analyzing the statement of the police detective as to what took place between himself and the accused it is necessary to recall the exact *Facts* situation. The crime had been committed on the high seas. Brown, immediately after the homicide, had been arrested by the crew in consequence of suspicion aroused against him, and had been by them placed in irons. As the vessel came in sight of land, and was approaching Halifax, the suspicions of the crew having been also directed to Bram, he was arrested by them and placed in irons. On reaching port, these two suspected persons were delivered to the custody of the police authorities of Halifax and were there held in confinement awaiting the action of the United States consul, which was to determine whether the suspicions which had caused the arrest justified the sending of one or both of the prisoners into the United States for formal charge and trial. Before this examination had taken place the police detective caused Bram to be brought from jail to his private office, and when there alone with the detective *he was stripped of his clothing*, and either whilst the detective was in the act of so stripping him, or after he was denuded, the conversation offered as a confession took place. The detective repeats what he said to the prisoner, whom he had thus stripped, as follows:

> When Mr. Bram came into my office I said to him: "Bram, we are trying to unravel this horrible mystery." I said: "Your position is rather an awkward one. I have had Brown in this office, and he made a statement that he saw you do the murder." He said: "He could not have seen me. Where was he?" I said: "He states he was at the wheel." "Well," he said, "he could not see me from there."

The fact, then, is, that the language of the accused, which was offered in evidence as a confession, was made use of by him as a reply to the statement of the detective that Bram's co-suspect had charged him with the crime, and, although the answer was in the form of a denial, it was doubtless offered as a confession because of an implication of guilt which it was conceived the words of the denial might be considered to mean. But the situation of the accused, and the nature of the communication made to him by the detective, necessarily overthrows any possible implication that his reply to the detective could have been the result of a purely voluntary mental action; that is to say, when all the surrounding circumstances are considered in their true relations, not only is the claim that the statement was voluntary overthrown, but the impression is irresistibly produced that it must necessarily have been the result of either hope or fear, or both, operating on the mind.

It cannot be doubted that, placed in the position in which the accused was when the statement was made to him that the other suspected person had charged him with crime, the result was to produce upon his mind the fear that if he remained silent it would be considered an admission of guilt, and therefore render certain his being committed for trial as the guilty person, and it cannot be conceived that the converse impression would not also have naturally arisen, that by denying there was hope of removing the suspicion from himself. If this must have been the state of mind of one situated as was the prisoner when the confession was made, how in reason can it be said that the answer which he gave and which was required by the situation was wholly voluntary and in no manner influenced by the force of hope or fear? To so conclude would be to deny the necessary relation of cause and effect. Indeed, the implication of guilt resulting from silence has been considered by some state courts of last resort, in decided cases, to which we have already made reference, as so cogent that they have held that where a person is accused of guilt, under circumstances which call upon him to make denial, the fact of his silence is competent evidence as tending to establish guilt. Whilst it must not be considered that by referring to these authorities we approve them, it is yet manifest that if learned judges have deduced the conclusion that silence is so weighty as to create an inference of guilt, it cannot, with justice, be said that the mind of one who is held in custody under suspicion of having committed a crime, would not be impelled to say something, when informed by one in authority that a co-suspect had declared that he had seen the person to whom the officer was addressing himself, commit the offence, when otherwise he might have remained silent but for fear of the consequences which might ensue; that is to say, he would be impelled to speak either for fear that his failure to make answer would be considered against him, or of hope that if he did reply he would be benefited thereby. And these self-evident deductions are greatly strengthened by considering the place where the statements were made and the conduct of the detective towards the accused. Bram had been brought from confinement to the office of the detective, and there, when alone with him, in a foreign land, while he was in the act of being stripped or had been stripped of his clothing, was interrogated by the officer, who was thus, while putting the questions and receiving answers thereto, exercising complete authority and control over the person he was interrogating. Although these facts may not, when isolated each from the other, be sufficient to warrant the inference that an influence compelling a statement had been exerted, yet when taken as a whole, in conjunction with the nature of the communication made, they give room to the strongest inference that the statements of Bram were not made by one who in law could be considered a free agent. To communicate to a person suspected of the commission of crime the fact that his co-suspect has stated that he has seen him commit the offence, to make this statement to him under circumstances which call imperatively for an admission or denial and to accompany the communication with conduct which necessarily perturbs the mind and engenders confusion of thought, and then to use the denial made by the person so situated as a confession, because of the form in which the denial is made, is not only to compel the reply but to produce the confusion of words supposed to be found in it, and then use statements thus brought into being for the conviction of the accused. A plainer violation as well of the letter as of the spirit and purpose of the constitutional immunity could scarcely be conceived of.

Moreover, aside from the natural result arising from the situation of the accused and the communication made to him by the detective, the conversation conveyed an express intimation rendering the confession involuntary within the rule laid down by the authorities. What further was said by the detective? "Now, look here, Bram, I am satisfied that you killed the captain from all I have heard from Mr. Brown. But, 'I said', some of us here think you could not have done all that crime alone. If you had an accomplice, you should say so, and not have the blame of this horrible crime on your own shoulders." But how could the weight of the whole crime be removed from the shoulders of the prisoner as a consequence of his speaking, unless benefit as to the crime and its punishment was to arise from his speaking? Conceding that, closely analyzed, the hope of benefit which the conversation suggested was that of the removal from the conscience of the prisoner of the merely moral weight resulting from concealment, and therefore would not be an inducement, we are to consider the import of the conversation, not from a mere abstract point of view, but by the light of the impression that it was calculated to produce on the mind of the accused, situated as he was at the time the conversation took place. Thus viewed, the weight to be removed by speaking naturally imported a suggestion of some benefit as to the crime and its punishment as arising from making a statement.

This is greatly fortified by a consideration of the words which preceded this language—that is, that Brown had declared he had witnessed the homicide, and that the detective had said he believed the prisoner was guilty and had an accomplice. It, in substance, therefore, called upon the prisoner to disclose his accomplice, and might well have been understood as holding out an encouragement that by so doing he might at least obtain a mitigation of the punishment for the crime which otherwise would assuredly follow. As said in the passage from Russell on Crimes already quoted, "the law cannot measure the force of the influence used or decide upon its effect upon the mind of the prisoner, and, therefore, excludes the declaration if any degree of influence has been exerted." In the case before us we find that an influence was exerted, and as any doubt as to whether the confession was voluntary must be determined in favor of the accused, we cannot escape the conclusion that error was committed by the trial court in admitting the confession under the circumstances disclosed by the record. . . .

The judgment is reversed and the cause remanded with directions to set aside the verdict and to order a new trial.

MR. JUSTICE BREWER, with whom concurred MR. CHIEF JUSTICE FULLER, and MR. JUSTICE BROWN [dissented on the ground that the confession was voluntary but not on the Court's holding concerning the fifth amendment's applicability].

The *Bram* decision proved to be remarkably prescient in its anticipation of the contours of the argument over the proper role of police interrogation that would mature half a century later. However, the case proved, just as remarkably, to have little immediate impact for two reasons. *First*, it was not until 1964 that the Supreme Court ruled that the fifth amendment privilege was applicable to the states. Malloy v. Hogan, 378 U.S. 1 (1964). Thus, *Bram* was limited to federal cases. *Second*, although *Bram* invoked the fifth amendment, without dissent on this point, the standard actually employed was the voluntariness standard of the common law. Later federal cases, including Supreme Court cases, tested confessions by the voluntariness standard without development or elaboration of the fifth amendment aspect of *Bram*. Nonetheless, *Bram* was never expressly repudiated, and the Court periodically referred to the case with approval. See, e.g., Burdeau v. McDowell, 256 U.S. 465 (1921).

The Supreme Court applied the spirit of *Bram*, even though not its letter, to the states in Brown v. Mississippi, 297 U.S. 278 (1936), where the Court held that the use of an involuntary coerced confession—in *Brown* the suspects were beaten until they confessed—violates fourteenth amendment due process. *Brown* was followed by a host of decisions attempting to articulate what the Court in *Bram* believed to defy articulation, the "standard" to be applied to test the question of voluntariness.

In the pursuit of this effort, two trends emerged. The first was the effort of the Court to protect the basic thrust of the confession rule by forbidding the use of statements coerced from individuals. Unfortunately, there is no easy way, in fact there may be *no* way, to make that determination, especially as interrogation changed from the type of physical brutality exhibited in *Brown* to psychological brutality found in cases like Payne v. Arkansas, 356 U.S. 560 (1958) (person with fifth-grade education told that a mob would be waiting for him unless he confessed). Indeed, the standard may be incoherent in its reliance on the distinction between a statement made "in the exercise of free will" and one that is "involuntary." Such a distinction presents all the problems associated with the free will–determinism debate. Presumably anyone who confesses does so for a reason, and it is not clear why some "reasons" should be labeled as "exercises of free will" but others not. Why, for example, should the confession be excluded in *Payne* in part because Payne had only a fifth-grade education, but admitted in a case such as Crooker v. California, 357 U.S. 433 (1958), in part because Crooker had gone through a year of law school? A similarly curious application of the notion of "voluntariness" occurred in Stein v. New York, 346 U.S. 156 (1953), in which a confession was admitted in part because the accused was a veteran criminal, a factor that if it has any effect suggests lack of voluntariness. In short, the factors focused on by the Court in this line of decisions may be legitimate criteria in determining the admissibility of confessions, but their relationship to any coherent notion of voluntariness is far from obvious.

Perhaps in response to these philosophical and practical problems, the Court took another tack and began to concentrate on the nature of the police practices involved instead of the impact of those procedures on the suspect presently before the Court. See, e.g., Ashcraft v. Tennessee, 322 U.S. 143 (1944), and Allen, The Supreme Court, Federalism, and State Systems of Criminal Justice, 8 De Paul L. Rev. 213, 235 (1959). See also Watts v. Indiana, 338 U.S. 49 (1949). Two developments conspired to make this approach less than satisfactory, however. First, it is nearly as factually bound as the pure voluntariness approach; inappropriate police practices have obvious referents in that behavior which is likely to make an innocent person confess through giving an "involuntary" statement. More importantly, the Court came to mistrust the fact-finding process of the state courts; and if the state courts could not be counted on to do a conscientious job of applying constitutional mandates, a factually bound test would not do. A court not wishing to apply the test could simply manipulate its factual findings to reach whatever result it desired. See Amsterdam, The Supreme Court and the Rights of Suspects in Criminal Cases, 45 N.Y.U.L. Rev. 785 (1970); Stone, The *Miranda* Doctrine in the Burger Court, 1977 Sup. Ct. Rev. 92.

As a result of the Court's increasing dissatisfaction with the voluntariness approach, apparent distrust of state fact-finding procedures, the practical inability of the Court to act as an effective court of error over the state criminal process, and the fact that the implications of habeas corpus had not yet been fully recognized, the Court began to search for alternatives to the voluntariness test, and it found one in the right to counsel as is indicated in the next case.[3]

MASSIAH v. UNITED STATES
Certiorari to the United States Court of Appeals for the Second Circuit
377 U.S. 201 (1964)

MR. JUSTICE STEWART delivered the opinion of the Court.

The petitioner was indicted for violating the federal narcotics laws. He retained a lawyer, pleaded not guilty, and was released on bail. While he was free on bail a federal agent succeeded by surreptitious means in listening to incriminating statements made by him. Evidence of these statements was introduced against the petitioner at his trial over his objection. He was convicted, and the Court of Appeals affirmed. We granted certiorari to consider whether, under the circumstances here presented, the prosecution's use at the trial of evidence of the petitioner's own incriminating statements deprived him of any right secured to him under the Federal Constitution. . . .

The petitioner, a merchant seaman, was in 1958 a member of the crew of the S.S. Santa Maria. In April of that year federal customs officials in New York received information that he was going to transport a quantity of narcotics aboard that ship from South America to the United States. As a result of this and other information, the agents searched the Santa Maria upon its arrival in New York and found in the afterpeak of the vessel five packages containing about three and a half pounds of cocaine. They also learned of circumstances, not here relevant, tending to connect the petitioner with the cocaine. He was arrested, promptly arraigned, and subsequently indicted for possession of narcotics aboard a United States vessel. In July a superseding indictment was returned, charging the petitioner and a man named Colson with the same substantive offense, and in separate counts charging the petitioner, Colson, and others with having conspired to possess narcotics aboard a United States vessel, and to import, conceal, and facilitate the sale of narcotics. The petitioner, who had

---

3. The Court toyed with another alternative in two federal cases, McNabb v. United States, 318 U.S. 332 (1943), and Mallory v. United States, 354 U.S. 449 (1957). Together, the cases structured what has come to be known as the McNabb-Mallory Rule that excludes confessions obtained in violation of Fed. R. Crim. P. 5(a)'s requirement that an arrested person be taken without unnecessary delay to the nearest community officer. The Court invoked its supervisory power over the federal courts as the basis for the rule, and it never applied the rule to the states through the fourteenth amendment.

retained a lawyer, pleaded not guilty and was released on bail, along with Colson.

A few days later, and quite without the petitioner's knowledge, Colson decided to cooperate with the government agents in their continuing investigation of the narcotics activities in which the petitioner, Colson, and others had allegedly been engaged. Colson permitted an agent named Murphy to install a Schmidt radio transmitter under the front seat of Colson's automobile, by means of which Murphy, equipped with an appropriate receiving device, could overhear from some distance away conversations carried on in Colson's car.

On the evening of November 19, 1959, Colson and the petitioner held a lengthy conversation while sitting in Colson's automobile, parked on a New York street. By prearrangement with Colson, and totally unbeknown to the petitioner, the agent Murphy sat in a car parked out of sight down the street and listened over the radio to the entire conversation. The petitioner made several incriminating statements during the course of this conversation. At the petitioner's trial these incriminating statements were brought before the jury through Murphy's testimony, despite the insistent objection of defense counsel. The jury convicted the petitioner of several related narcotics offenses, and the convictions were affirmed by the Court of Appeals.

The petitioner argues that it was an error of constitutional dimensions to permit the agent Murphy at the trial to testify to the petitioner's incriminating statements which Murphy had overheard under the circumstances disclosed by this record. This argument is based upon two distinct and independent grounds. First, we are told that Murphy's use of the radio equipment violated the petitioner's rights under the Fourth Amendment, and, consequently, that all evidence which Murphy thereby obtained was, under the rule Weeks v. United States, 232 U.S. 383, inadmissible against the petitioner at the trial. Secondly, it is said that the petitioner's Fifth and Sixth Amendment rights were violated by the use in evidence against him of incriminating statements which government agents had deliberately elicited from him after he had been indicted and in the absence of his retained counsel. Because of the way we dispose of the case, we do not reach the Fourth Amendment issue.

In Spano v. New York, 360 U.S. 315, this Court reversed a state criminal conviction because a confession had been wrongly admitted into evidence against the defendant at his trial. In that case the defendant had already been indicted for first-degree murder at the time he confessed. The Court held that the defendant's conviction could not stand under the Fourteenth Amendment. While the Court's opinion relied upon the totality of the circumstances under which the confession had been obtained, four concurring justices pointed out that the Constitution required reversal of the conviction upon the sole and specific ground that the confession had been deliberately elicited by the police after the defendant had been indicted, and therefore at a time when he was clearly entitled to a lawyer's help. It was pointed out that under our system of justice the most elemental concepts of due process of law contemplate that an indictment be followed by a trial, "in an orderly courtroom, presided over by a judge, open to the public, and protected by all the procedural safeguards of the law." 360 U.S., at 327 (Stewart, J., concurring). It was said that a Constitution which guarantees a defendant the aid of counsel at such a trial could surely vouchsafe no less to an indicted defendant under interrogation by the police in a completely extrajudicial proceeding. Anything less, it was said, might deny a defendant "effective representation by counsel at the only stage when legal aid and advice would help him." 360 U.S., at 326 (Douglas, J., concurring). . . .

This view no more than reflects a constitutional principle established as long ago as Powell v. Alabama, 287 U.S. 45, where the Court noted that ". . . during perhaps the most critical period of the proceedings . . . that is to say, from the time of their arraignment until the beginning of their trial, when consultation, thoroughgoing investigation and preparation [are] vitally important, the defendants . . . [are] as much entitled to such aid [of counsel] during that period as at the trial itself." Id., at 57. And since the *Spano* decision the same basic constitutional principle has been broadly reaffirmed by this Court. Hamilton v. Alabama, 368 U.S. 52; White v. Maryland, 373 U.S. 59. See Gideon v. Wainwright, 372 U.S. 335.

Here we deal not with a state court conviction, but with a federal case, where the specific guarantee of the Sixth Amendment directly applies. Johnson v. Zerbst, 304 U.S. 458. We hold that the petitioner was denied the basic protections of that guarantee when there was used against him at his trial evidence of his own incriminating words, which federal agents had deliberately elicited from him after he had been indicted and in the absence of his counsel. It is true that in the *Spano* case the defendant was interrogated in a police station, while here the damaging testimony was elicited from the defendant without his knowledge while he was free on bail. But, as Judge Hays pointed out in his dissent in the Court of Appeals, "if such a rule is to have any efficacy it must apply to indirect and surreptitious interrogations as well as those conducted in the jailhouse. In this case, Messiah was more seriously imposed upon . . . because he did not even know that he was under interrogation by a government agent." 307 F.2d, at 72-73.

The Solicitor General, in his brief and oral argument, has strenuously contended that the federal law enforcement agents had the right, if not indeed the duty, to continue their investigation of the petitioner and his alleged criminal associates even though the petitioner had been indicted. He points out that the Government was continuing its investigation in order to uncover not only the source of narcotics found on the S.S. Santa Maria, but also their intended buyer. He says that the quantity of narcotics involved was such as to suggest that the petitioner was part of a large and well-organized ring, and indeed that the continuing investigation confirmed this suspicion, since it resulted in criminal charges against many defendants. Under these circumstances the Solicitor General concludes that the government agents were completely "justified in making use of Colson's cooperation by having Colson continue his normal associations and by surveilling them."

We may accept and, at least for present purposes, completely approve all that this argument implies, Fourth Amendment problems to one side. We do not question that in this case, as in many cases, it was entirely proper to continue an investigation of the suspected criminal activities of the defendant and his alleged confederates, even though the defendant had already been indicted. All that we hold is that the defendant's own incriminating statements, obtained by federal agents under the circumstances here disclosed, could not constitutionally be used by the prosecution as evidence against *him* at his trial.

Reversed.

MR. JUSTICE WHITE, with whom MR. JUSTICE CLARK and MR. JUSTICE HARLAN join, dissenting. . . .

It is . . . a rather portentous occasion when a constitutional rule is established barring the use of evidence which is relevant, reliable and highly probative of the issue which the trial court has before it—whether the accused committed the act with which he is charged. Without the evidence, the quest for truth may be seriously impeded and in many cases the trial court, although aware of proof showing defendant's guilt, must nevertheless release him because the crucial evidence is deemed inadmissible. This result is entirely justified in some circumstances because exclusion serves other policies of overriding importance, as where evidence seized in an illegal search is excluded, not because of the quality of the proof, but to secure meaningful enforcement of the Fourth Amendment. Weeks v. United States, 232 U.S. 383; Mapp v. Ohio, 367 U.S. 643. But this only emphasizes that the soundest of reasons is necessary to warrant the exclusion of evidence otherwise admissible and the creation of another area of privileged testimony. With all due deference, I am not at all convinced that the additional barriers to the pursuit of truth which the Court today erects rest on anything like the solid foundations which decisions of this gravity should require.

The importance of the matter should not be underestimated, for today's rule promises to have wide application well beyond the facts of this case. The reason given for the result here—the admissions were obtained in the absence of counsel—would seem equally pertinent to statements obtained at any time after the right to counsel attaches, whether there has been an indictment or not; to admissions made prior to arraignment, at least where the defendant has counsel or asks for it; to the fruits of admissions improperly obtained under the new rule; to criminal proceedings in state courts; and to defendants long since convicted upon evidence including such admissions. The new rule will immediately do service in a great many cases.

Whatever the content or scope of the rule may prove to be, I am unable to see how this case presents an unconstitutional interference with Massiah's right to counsel. Massiah was not prevented from consulting with counsel as often as he wished. No meetings with counsel were disturbed or spied upon. Preparation for trial was in no way obstructed. It is only a sterile syllogism—an unsound one, besides—to say that because Massiah had a right to counsel's aid before and during the trial, his out-of-court conversations and admissions must be excluded if obtained without counsel's consent or presence. The right to counsel has never meant as much before, . . . and its extension in this case requires some further explanation, so far unarticulated by the Court.

Since the new rule would exclude all admissions made to the police, no matter how voluntary and reliable, the requirement of counsel's presence or approval would seem to rest upon the probability that counsel would foreclose any admissions at all. This is nothing more than a thinly disguised constitutional policy of minimizing or entirely prohibiting the use in evidence of voluntary out-of-court admissions and confessions made by the accused. Carried as far as blind logic may compel some to go, the notion that statements from the mouth of the defendant should not be used in evidence would have a severe and unfortunate impact upon the great bulk of criminal cases.

Viewed in this light, the Court's newly fashioned exclusionary principle goes far beyond the constitutional privilege against self-incrimination, which neither requires nor suggests the barring of voluntary pretrial admissions. The Fifth Amendment states that no person "shall be compelled in any criminal case to be a witness against himself. . . ." The defendant may thus not be compelled to testify at his trial, but he may if he wishes. Likewise he may not be compelled or coerced into saying anything before trial; but until today he could if he wished to, and if he did, it could be used against him. Whether as a matter of self-incrimination or of due process, the proscription is against compulsion—coerced incrimination. Under the prior law, announced in countless cases in this Court, the defendant's pretrial statements were admissible evidence if

C. Police Interrogation

[handwritten marginalia: would this case have involved coercion?]

[handwritten marginalia: afterall, every Δ runs the risk a 1101 cop will turn on him]

voluntarily made; inadmissible if not the product of his free will. Hardly any constitutional area has been more carefully patrolled by this Court, and until now the Court has expressly rejected the argument that admissions are to be deemed involuntary if made outside the presence of counsel.* . . .

The Court presents no facts, no objective evidence, no reasons to warrant scrapping the voluntary-involuntary test for admissibility in this area. Without such evidence I would retain it in its present form. . . .

Applying the new exclusionary rule is peculiarly inappropriate in this case. At the time of the conversation in question, petitioner was not in custody but free on bail. He was not questioned in what anyone could call an atmosphere of official coercion. What he said was said to his partner in crime who had also been indicted. There was no suggestion or any possibility of coercion. What petitioner did not know was that Colson had decided to report the conversation to the police. Had there been no prior arrangements between Colson and the police, had Colson simply gone to the police after the conversation had occurred, his testimony relating Massiah's statements would be readily admissible at the trial, as would a recording which he might have made of the conversation. In such event, it would simply be said that Massiah risked talking to a friend who decided to disclose what he knew of Massiah's criminal activities. But if, as occurred here, Colson had been cooperating with the police prior to his meeting with Massiah, both his evidence and the recorded conversation are somehow transformed into inadmissible evidence despite the fact that the hazard to Massiah remains precisely the same—the defection of a confederate in crime.

Reporting criminal behavior is expected or even demanded of the ordinary citizen. Friends may be subpoenaed to testify about friends, relatives about relatives and partners about partners. I therefore question the soundness of insulating Massiah from the apostasy of his partner in crime and of furnishing constitutional sanctions for the strict secrecy and discipline of criminal organizations. Neither the ordinary citizen nor the confessed criminal should be discouraged from reporting what he knows to the authorities and from lending his aid to secure evidence of crime. Certainly after this case the Colsons will be few and far between; and the

---

*Today's rule picks up where the Fifth Amendment ends and bars wholly voluntary admissions. I would assume, although one cannot be sure, that the new rule would not have a similar supplemental role in connection with the Fourth Amendment. While the Fifth Amendment bars only compelled incrimination, the Fourth Amendment bars only unreasonable searches. It could be argued, fruitlessly I would hope, that if the police must stay away from the defendant they must also stay away from his house once the right to counsel has attached and that a court must exclude the products of a reasonable search made pursuant to a properly issued warrant but without the consent or presence of the accused's counsel.

Massiahs can breathe much more easily, secure in the knowledge that the Constitution furnishes an important measure of protection against faithless compatriots and guarantees sporting treatment for sporting peddlers of narcotics.

Meanwhile, of course, the public will again be the loser and law enforcement will be presented with another serious dilemma. The general issue lurking in the background of the Court's opinion is the legitimacy of penetrating or obtaining confederates in criminal organizations. For the law enforcement agency, the answer for the time being can only be in the form of a prediction about the future application of today's new constitutional doctrine. More narrowly, and posed by the precise situation involved here, the question is this: when the police have arrested and released on bail one member of a criminal ring and another member, a confederate, is cooperating with the police, can the confederate be allowed to continue his association with the ring or must he somehow be withdrawn to avoid challenge to trial evidence on the ground that it was acquired after rather than before the arrest, after rather than before the indictment?

Defendants who are out on bail have been known to continue their illicit operations. See Rogers v. United States, 325 F.2d 485 (C.A. 10th Cir.). That an attorney is advising them should not constitutionally immunize their statements made in furtherance of these operations and relevant to the question of their guilt at the pending prosecution. In this very case there is evidence that after indictment defendant Aiken tried to persuade Agent Murphy to go into the narcotics business with him. Under today's decision, Murphy may neither testify as to the content of this conversation nor seize for introduction in evidence any narcotics whose location Aiken may have made known.

Undoubtedly, the evidence excluded in this case would not have been available but for the conduct of Colson in cooperation with Agent Murphy, but is it this kind of conduct which should be forbidden to those charged with law enforcement? It is one thing to establish safeguards against procedures fraught with the potentiality of coercion and to outlaw "easy but self-defeating ways in which brutality is substituted for brains as an instrument of crime detection." McNabb v. United States, 318 U.S. 332, 344. But here there was no substitution of brutality for brains, no inherent danger of police coercion justifying the prophylactic effect of another exclusionary rule. Massiah was not being interrogated in a police station, was not surrounded by numerous officers or questioned in relays, and was not forbidden access to others. Law enforcement may have the elements of a contest about it, but it is not a game. McGuire v. United States, 273 U.S. 95, 99. Massiah and those like him receive ample protection from the long line of precedents in this Court holding that confessions may not be introduced unless they are voluntary. In making these determinations the courts must consider the absence of counsel as one of several factors by which voluntariness is to be judged. . . . This is a wiser rule than the automatic rule announced by the Court, which requires courts and juries to disregard voluntary admissions which they might well find to be the best possible evidence in discharging their responsibility for ascertaining truth.

The meaning of *Massiah* was not altogether clear, however. For example, did it matter whether the defendant had been indicted? Arraigned? Obtained counsel? The Court returned to these matters a year later in Escobedo v. Illinois. In *Escobedo*, the defendant had been arrested but not charged and had invoked his right to counsel (presuming he had one), his lawyer was present at the stationhouse but not allowed to see his client, and the defendant was subject to interrogation during which incriminating statements were made. Over a sharp dissent, the Court in a schizoid opinion, marked by an uneasy relationship between sweeping assertion and narrow holding, held that the defendant's constitutional rights had been violated. The curious progression of the opinion can be seen in the following excerpt:

ESCOBEDO v. ILLINOIS, 378 U.S. 478, 488-491 (1964): It is argued that if the right to counsel is afforded prior to indictment, the number of confessions obtained by the police will diminish significantly, because most confessions are obtained during the period between arrest and indictment,[10] and "any lawyer worth his salt will tell the suspect in no uncertain terms to make no statement to police under any circumstances." Watts v. Indiana, 338 U.S. 49, 59 (Jackson, J., concurring in part and dissenting in part). This argument, of course, cuts two ways. The fact that many confessions are obtained during this period points up its critical nature as a "stage when legal aid and advice" are surely needed. . . . The right to counsel would indeed be hollow if it began at a period when few confessions were obtained. There is necessarily a direct relationship between the importance of a stage to the police in their quest for a confession and the criticalness of that stage to the accused in his need for legal advice. Our Constitution, unlike some others, strikes the balance in favor of the right of the accused to be advised by his lawyer of his privilege against self-incrimination. . . .
We have learned the lesson of history, ancient and modern, that a

10. See Barrett, Police Practices and the Law—From Arrest to Release or Charge, 50 Cal. L. Rev. 11, 43 (1962).

system of criminal law enforcement which comes to depend on the "confession" will, in the long run, be less reliable and more subject to abuses than a system which depends on extrinsic evidence independently secured through skillful investigation. As Dean Wigmore so wisely said:

> [A]*ny system of administration which permits the prosecution to trust habitually to compulsory self-disclosure as a source of proof must itself suffer morally thereby.* The inclination develops to rely mainly upon such evidence, and to be satisfied with an incomplete investigation of the other sources. The exercise of the power to extract answers begets a forgetfulness of the just limitations of that power. The simple and peaceful process of questioning breeds a readiness to resort to bullying and to physical force and torture. If there is a right to an answer, there soon seems to be a right to the expected answer,—that is, to a confession of guilt. Thus the legitimate use grows into the unjust abuse; ultimately, the innocent are jeopardized by the encroachments of a bad system. Such seems to have been the course of experience in those legal systems where the privilege was not recognized." 8 Wigmore, Evidence (3d ed. 1940), 309. (Emphasis in original.)

This Court also has recognized that "history amply shows that confessions have often been extorted to save law enforcement officials the trouble and effort of obtaining valid and independent evidence. . . ." Haynes v. Washington, 373 U.S. 503, 519.

We have also learned the companion lesson of history that no system of criminal justice can, or should, survive if it comes to depend for its continued effectiveness on the citizens' abdication through unawareness of their constitutional rights. No system worth preserving should have to *fear* that if an accused is permitted to consult with a lawyer, he will become aware of, and exercise, these rights.[13] If the exercise of consti-

---

13. Cf. Report of Attorney General's Committee on Poverty and the Administration of Federal Criminal Justice (1963), 10-11:

> The survival of our system of criminal justice and the values which it advances depends upon a constant, searching, and creative questioning of official decisions and assertions of authority at all stages of the process. . . . Persons [denied access to counsel] are incapable of providing the challenges that are indispensable to satisfactory operation of the system. The loss to the interests of accused individuals, occasioned by these failures, are great and apparent. It is also clear that a situation in which persons are required to contest a serious accusation but are denied access to the tools of contest is offensive to fairness and equity. Beyond these considerations, however, is the fact that [this situation is] detrimental to the proper functioning of the system of justice and that the loss in vitality of the adversary system, thereby occasioned, significantly endangers the basic interests of a free community.

tutional rights will thwart the effectiveness of a system of law enforcement then there is something very wrong with that system.[14]

We hold, therefore, that where, as here, the investigation is no longer a general inquiry into an unsolved crime but has begun to focus on a particular suspect, the suspect has been taken into police custody, the police carry out a process of interrogations that lends itself to eliciting incriminating statements, the suspect has requested and been denied an opportunity to consult with his lawyer, and the police have not effectively warned him of his absolute constitutional right to remain silent, the accused has been denied "the Assistance of Counsel" in violation of the Sixth Amendment to the Constitution as "made obligatory upon the States by the Fourteenth Amendment," Gideon v. Wainwright, 372 U.S., at 342, and that no statement elicited by the police during the interrogation may be used against him at a criminal trial. . . .

Was *Escobedo* a simple application of *Massiah?* Was it a harbinger of the complete elimination of confessions, or at least of police interrogation as then conceived? Or was it an example of a Court realizing that it was breaking new ground but not altogether sure of the way to proceed or of the implications of its actions? Some of these questions were answered two years later in the *Miranda* case.

MIRANDA v. ARIZONA
Certiorari to the Supreme Court of Arizona
384 U.S. 436 (1966)

MR. CHIEF JUSTICE WARREN delivered the opinion of the Court.

The cases before us raise questions which go to the roots of our concepts of American criminal jurisprudence: the restraints society must observe consistent with the Federal Constitution in prosecuting individuals for crime. More specifically, we deal with the admissibility of statements obtained from an individual who is subjected to custodial police interrogation and the necessity for procedures which assure that the individual is accorded his privilege under the Fifth Amendment to the Constitution not to be compelled to incriminate himself.

We dealt with certain phases of this problem recently in Escobedo v. Illinois, 378 U.S. 478 (1964). . . .

---

14. The accused may, of course, intelligently and knowingly waive his privilege against self-incrimination and his right to counsel either at a pretrial stage or at the trial. See Johnson v. Zerbst, 304 U.S. 458. But no knowing and intelligent waiver of any constitutional right can be said to have occurred under the circumstances of this case.

. . . We have undertaken a thorough re-examination of the *Escobedo* decision and the principles it announced, and we reaffirm it. That case was but an explication of basic rights that are enshrined in our Constitution—that "No person . . . shall be compelled in any criminal case to be a witness against himself," and that "the accused shall . . . have the Assistance of Counsel"—rights which were put in jeopardy in that case through official overbearing. These precious rights were fixed in our Constitution only after centuries of persecution and struggle. And in the words of Chief Justice Marshall, they were secured "for ages to come, and . . . designed to approach immortality as nearly as human institutions can approach it," Cohens v. Virginia, 6 Wheat. 264, 387 (1821). . . .

Our holding will be spelled out with some specificity in the pages which follow but briefly stated it is this: the prosecution may not use statements, whether exculpatory or inculpatory, stemming from custodial interrogation of the defendant unless it demonstrates the use of procedural safeguards effective to secure the privilege against self-incrimination. By custodial interrogation, we mean questioning initiated by law enforcement officers after a person has been taken into custody or otherwise deprived of his freedom of action in any significant way.[4] As for the procedural safeguards to be employed, unless other fully effective means are devised to inform accused persons of their right of silence and to assure a continuous opportunity to exercise it, the following measures are required. Prior to any questioning, the person must be warned that he has a right to remain silent, that any statement he does make may be used as evidence against him, and that he has a right to the presence of an attorney, either retained or appointed. The defendant may waive effectuation of these rights, provided the waiver is made voluntarily, knowingly and intelligently. If, however, he indicates in any manner and at any stage of the process that he wishes to consult with an attorney before speaking there can be no questioning. Likewise, if the individual is alone and indicates in any manner that he does not wish to be interrogated, the police may not question him. The mere fact that he may have answered some questions or volunteered some statements on his own does not deprive him of the right to refrain from answering any further inquiries until he has consulted with an attorney and thereafter consents to be questioned.

---

4. This is what we meant in *Escobedo* when we spoke of an investigation which had focused on an accused.

I

The constitutional issue we decide in each of these cases is the admissibility of statements obtained from a defendant questioned while in custody or otherwise deprived of his freedom of action in any significant way. In each, the defendant was questioned by police officers, detectives, or a prosecuting attorney in a room in which he was cut off from the outside world. In none of these cases was the defendant given a full and effective warning of his rights at the outset of the interrogation process. In all the cases, the questioning elicited oral admissions, and in three of them, signed statements as well which were admitted at their trials. They all thus share salient features—incommunicado interrogation of individuals in a police-dominated atmosphere, resulting in self-incriminating statements without full warnings of constitutional rights.

An understanding of the nature and setting of this in-custody interrogation is essential to our decisions today. The difficulty in depicting what transpires at such interrogations stems from the fact that in this country they have largely taken place incommunicado. From extensive factual studies undertaken in the early 1930's, including the famous Wickersham Report to Congress by a Presidential Commission, it is clear that police violence and the "third degree" flourished at that time.[5] In a series of cases decided by this Court long after these studies, the police resorted to physical brutality—beating, hanging, whipping—and to sustained and protracted questioning incommunicado in order to extort confessions. The Commission on Civil Rights in 1961 found much evidence to indicate that "some policemen still resort to physical force to obtain confessions," 1961 Comm'n on Civil Rights Rep., Justice, pt. 5, 17. The use of physical brutality and violence is not, unfortunately, relegated to the past or to any part of the country. Only recently in Kings County, New York, the police brutally beat, kicked and placed lighted cigarette butts on the back of a potential witness under interrogation for the purpose of securing a statement incriminating a third party. People v. Portelli, 15 N.Y.2d 235, 205 N.E.2d 857, 257 N.Y.S.2d 931 (1965).[7]

---

5. See, for example, IV National Commission on Law Observance and Enforcement, Report on Lawlessness in Law Enforcement (1931) [Wickersham Report]. . . .

7. In addition, see People v. Wakat, 415 Ill. 610, 114 N.E.2d 706 (1953); Wakat v. Harlib, 253 F.2d 59 (C.A. 7th Cir. 1958) (defendant suffering from broken bones, multiple bruises and injuries sufficiently serious to require eight months' medical treatment after being manhandled by five policemen); Kier v. State, 213 Md. 556, 132 A.2d 494 (1957) (police doctor told accused, who was strapped to a chair completely nude, that he proposed to take hair and skin scrapings from anything that looked like blood or sperm from various parts of his body); Bruner v. People, 113 Colo. 194, 156 P.2d 111 (1945) (defendant held in custody over two months, deprived of food for 15 hours, forced to submit to a lie detector test when he wanted to go to the toilet); People v. Matlock,

The examples given above are undoubtedly the exception now, but they are sufficiently widespread to be the object of concern. Unless a proper limitation upon custodial interrogation is achieved—such as these decisions will advance—there can be no assurance that practices of this nature will be eradicated in the foreseeable future. . . .

Again we stress that the modern practice of in-custody interrogation is psychologically rather than physically oriented. As we have stated before, "Since Chambers v. Florida, 309 U.S. 227, this Court has recognized that coercion can be mental as well as physical, and that the blood of the accused is not the only hallmark of an unconstitutional inquisition." Blackburn v. Alabama, 361 U.S. 199, 206 (1960). Interrogation still takes place in privacy. Privacy results in secrecy and this in turn results in a gap in our knowledge as to what in fact goes on in the interrogation rooms. A valuable source of information about present police practices, however, may be found in various police manuals and texts which document procedures employed with success in the past, and which recommend various other effective tactics.[8] These texts are used by law enforcement agencies themselves as guides. It should be noted that these texts professedly present the most enlightened and effective means presently used to obtain statements through custodial interrogation. By considering these texts and other data, it is possible to describe procedures observed and noted around the country.

The officers are told by the manuals that the "principal psychological factor contributing to a successful interrogation is *privacy*—being alone with the person under interrogation."[10] The efficacy of this tactic has been explained as follows:

> If at all practicable, the interrogation should take place in the investigator's office or at least in a room of his own choice. The subject should be deprived of every psychological advantage. In his own home he may be confident, indignant, or recalcitrant. He is more keenly aware of his rights

---

51 Cal. 2d 682, 336 P.2d 505 (1959) (defendant questioned incessantly over an evening's time, made to lie on cold board and to answer questions whenever it appeared he was getting sleepy). Other cases are documented in American Civil Liberties Union, Illinois Division, Secret Detention by the Chicago Police (1959); Potts, The Preliminary Examination and "The Third Degree," 2 Baylor L. Rev. 131 (1950); Sterling, Police Interrogation and the Psychology of Confession, 14 J. Pub. L. 25 (1965).

8. The manuals quoted in the text following are the most recent and representative of the texts currently available. Material of the same nature appears in Kidd, Police Interrogation (1940); Mulbar, Interrogation (1951); Dienstein, Technics for the Crime Investigator 97-115 (1952). Studies concerning the observed practices of the police appear in LaFave, Arrest: The Decision to Take a Suspect into Custody 244-437, 490-521 (1965); LaFave, Detention for Investigation by the Police: An Analysis of Current Practices, 1962 Wash. U.L.Q. 331; Barrett, Police Practices and the Law—From Arrest to Release or Charge, 50 Calif. L. Rev. 11 (1962); Sterling, supra, n.7, at 47-65.

10. Inbau & Reid, Criminal Interrogation and Confessions (1962), at 1.

and more reluctant to tell of his indiscretions or criminal behavior within the walls of his home. Moreover his family and other friends are nearby, their presence lending moral support. In his own office, the investigator possesses all the advantages. The atmosphere suggests the invincibility of the forces of the law.[11]

To highlight the isolation and unfamiliar surroundings, the manuals instruct the police to display an air of confidence in the suspect's guilt and from outward appearance to maintain only an interest in confirming certain details. The guilt of the subject is to be posited as a fact. The interrogator should direct his comments toward the reasons why the subject committed the act, rather than court failure by asking the subject whether he did it. Like other men, perhaps the subject has had a bad family life, had an unhappy childhood, had too much to drink, had an unrequited desire for women. The officers are instructed to minimize the moral seriousness of the offense,[12] to cast blame on the victim or on society.[13] These tactics are designed to put the subject in a psychological state where his story is but an elaboration of what the police purport to know already—that he is guilty. Explanations to the contrary are dismissed and discouraged.

The texts thus stress that the major qualities an interrogator should possess are patience and perseverance. One writer describes the efficacy of these characteristics in this manner:

In the preceding paragraphs emphasis has been placed on kindness and stratagems. The investigator will, however, encounter many situations where the sheer weight of his personality will be the deciding factor. Where emotional appeals and tricks are employed to no avail, he must rely on an oppressive atmosphere of dogged persistence. He must interrogate steadily and without relent, leaving the subject no prospect of surcease. He must dominate his subject and overwhelm him with his inexorable will to obtain the truth. He should interrogate for a spell of several hours pausing only for the subject's necessities in acknowledgment of the need to avoid a charge of duress that can be technically substantiated. In a serious case, the interrogation may continue for days, with the required intervals for food and sleep, but with no respite from the atmosphere of domination. It is possible in this way to induce the subject to talk without resorting to

11. O'Hara, [Fundamentals of Criminal Investigation (1956),] at 99.
12. Inbau & Reid, supra, at 34-43, 87. For example, in Leyra v. Denno, 347 U.S. 556 (1954), the interrogator-psychiatrist told the accused, "We do sometimes things that are not right, but in a fit of temper or anger we sometimes do things we aren't really responsible for," id., at 562, and again, "We know that morally you were just in anger. Morally, you are not to be condemned," id., at 582.
13. Inbau & Reid, supra, at 43-55.

duress or coercion. The method should be used only when the guilt of the subject appears highly probable.[14]

The manuals suggest that the suspect be offered legal excuses for his actions in order to obtain an initial admission of guilt. Where there is a suspected revenge-killing, for example, the interrogator may say:

> Joe, you probably didn't go out looking for this fellow with the purpose of shooting him. My guess is, however, that you expected something from him and that's why you carried a gun—for your own protection. You knew him for what he was, no good. Then when you met him he probably started using foul, abusive language and he gave some indication that he was about to pull a gun on you, and that's when you had to act to save your own life. That's about it, isn't it Joe?[15]

Having then obtained the admission of shooting, the interrogator is advised to refer to circumstantial evidence which negates the self-defense explanation. This should enable him to secure the entire story. One text notes that "Even if he fails to do so, the inconsistency between the subject's original denial of the shooting and his present admission of at least doing the shooting will serve to deprive him of a self-defense 'out' at the time of trial."[16]

When the techniques described above prove unavailing, the texts recommend they be alternated with a show of some hostility. One ploy often used has been termed the "friendly-unfriendly" or the "Mutt and Jeff" act:

> . . . In this technique, two agents are employed. Mutt, the relentless investigator, who knows the subject is guilty and is not going to waste any time. He's sent a dozen men away for this crime and he's going to send the subject away for the full term. Jeff, on the other hand, is obviously a kindhearted man. He has a family himself. He has a brother who was involved in a little scrape like this. He disapproves of Mutt and his tactics and will arrange to get him off the case if the subject will cooperate. He can't hold Mutt off for very long. The subject would be wise to make a quick decision. The technique is applied by having both investigators present while Mutt acts out his role. Jeff may stand by quietly and demur

14. O'Hara, supra, at 112.
15. Inbau & Reid, supra, at 40.
16. Ibid.

at some of Mutt's tactics. When Jeff makes his plea for cooperation, Mutt is not present in the room.[17]

The interrogators sometimes are instructed to induce a confession out of trickery. The technique here is quite effective in crimes which require identification or which run in series. In the identification situation, the interrogator may take a break in his questioning to place the subject among a group of men in a line-up. "The witness or complainant (previously coached, if necessary) studies the line-up and confidently points out the subject as the guilty party."[18] Then the questioning resumes "as though there were now no doubt about the guilt of the subject." A variation on this technique is called the "reverse line-up":

> The accused is placed in a line-up, but this time he is identified by several fictitious witnesses or victims who associated him with different offenses. It is expected that the subject will become desperate and confess to the offense under investigation in order to escape from the false accusations.[19]

The manuals also contain instructions for police on how to handle the individual who refuses to discuss the matter entirely, or who asks for an attorney or relatives. The examiner is to concede him the right to remain silent. "This usually has a very undermining effect. First of all, he is disappointed in his expectation of an unfavorable reaction on the part of the interrogator. Secondly, a concession of this right to remain silent impresses the subject with the apparent fairness of his interrogator."[20] After this psychological conditioning, however, the officer is told to point out the incriminating significance of the suspect's refusal to talk:

> Joe, you have a right to remain silent. That's your privilege and I'm the last person in the world who'll try to take it away from you. If that's the way you want to leave this, O.K. But let me ask you this. Suppose you were in my shoes and I were in yours and you called me in to ask me about this and I told you, "I don't want to answer any of your questions." You'd think I had something to hide, and you'd probably be right in

17. O'Hara, supra, at 104, Inbau & Reid, supra, at 58-59. See Spano v. New York, 360 U.S. 315 (1959). A variant on the technique of creating hostility is one of engendering fear. This is perhaps best described by the prosecuting attorney in Malinski v. New York, 324 U.S. 401, 407 (1945): "Why this talk about being undressed? Of course, they had a right to undress him to look for bullet scars, and keep the clothes off him. That was quite proper police procedure. That is some more psychology—let him sit around with a blanket on him, humiliate him there for a while; let him sit in the corner, let him think he is going to get a shellacking."

18. O'Hara, supra, at 105-106.

19. Id., at 106.

20. Inbau & Reid, supra, at 111.

thinking that. That's exactly what I'll have to think about you, and so will everybody else. So let's sit here and talk this whole thing over.[21]

Few will persist in their initial refusal to talk, it is said, if this monologue is employed correctly.

In the event that the subject wishes to speak to a relative or an attorney, the following advice is tendered:

> [T]he interrogator should respond by suggesting that the subject first tell the truth to the interrogator himself rather than get anyone else involved in the matter. If the request is for an attorney, the interrogator may suggest that the subject save himself or his family the expense of any such professional service, particularly if he is innocent of the offense under investigation. The interrogator may also add, "Joe, I'm only looking for the truth, and if you're telling the truth, that's it. You can handle this by yourself."[22]

From these representative samples of interrogation techniques, the setting prescribed by the manuals and observed in practice becomes clear. In essence, it is this: To be alone with the subject is essential to prevent distraction and to deprive him of any outside support. The aura of confidence in his guilt undermines his will to resist. He merely confirms the preconceived story the police seek to have him describe. Patience and persistence, at times relentless questioning, are employed. To obtain a confession, the interrogator must "patiently maneuver himself or his quarry into a position from which the desired objective may be attained."[23] When normal procedures fail to produce the needed result, the police may resort to deceptive stratagems such as giving false legal advice. It is important to keep the subject off balance, for example, by trading on his insecurity about himself or his surroundings. The police then persuade, trick, or cajole him out of exercising his constitutional rights.

Even without employing brutality, the "third degree" or the specific stratagems described above, the very fact of custodial interrogation exacts a heavy toll on individual liberty and trades on the weakness of individuals.[24] This fact may be illustrated simply by referring to three confes-

21. Ibid.
22. Inbau & Reid, supra, at 112.
23. Inbau & Reid, Lie Detection and Criminal Interrogation 185 (3d ed. 1953).
24. Interrogation procedures may even give rise to a false confession. The most recent conspicuous example occurred in New York, in 1964, when a Negro of limited intelligence confessed to two brutal murders and a rape which he had not committed. When this was discovered, the prosecutor was reported as saying: "Call it what you want—brainwashing, hypnosis, fright. They made him give an untrue confession. The only thing I don't believe is that Whitmore was beaten." N.Y. Times, Jan. 28, 1965, p.1, col. 5. In two other instances, similar events had occurred. N.Y. Times, Oct. 20, 1964, p.22, col. 1; N.Y. Times, Aug. 25, 1965, p.1, col. 1. In general, see Borchard, Convicting the Innocent (1932); Frank & Frank, Not Guilty (1957).

sion cases decided by this Court in the Term immediately preceding our
Escobedo decision. In Townsend v. Sain, 372 U.S. 293 (1963), the
defendant was a 19-year-old heroin addict, described as a "near mental
defective," id., at 307-310. The defendant in Lynumn v. Illinois, 372
U.S. 528 (1963), was a woman who confessed to the arresting officer
after being importuned to "cooperate" in order to prevent her children
from being taken by relief authorities. This Court as in those cases reversed
the conviction of a defendant in Haynes v. Washington, 373 U.S. 503
(1963), whose persistent request during his interrogation was to phone
his wife or attorney.[25] In other settings, these individuals might have
exercised their constitutional rights. In the incommunicado police-dominated atmosphere, they succumbed.

In the cases before us today, given this background, we concern
ourselves primarily with this interrogation atmosphere and the evils it
can bring. In No. 759, Miranda v. Arizona, the police arrested the
defendant and took him to a special interrogation room where they secured a confession. In No. 760, Vignera v. New York, the defendant
made oral admissions to the police after interrogation in the afternoon,
and then signed an inculpatory statement upon being questioned by an
assistant district attorney later the same evening. In No. 761, Westover
v. United States, the defendant was handed over to the Federal Bureau
of Investigation by local authorities after they had detained and interrogated him for a lengthy period, both at night and the following morning.
After some two hours of questioning, the federal officers had obtained
signed statements from the defendant. Lastly, in No. 584, California v.
Stewart, the local police held the defendant five days in the station and
interrogated him on nine separate occasions before they secured his inculpatory statement.

In these cases, we might not find the defendant's statements to have
been involuntary in traditional terms. Our concern for adequate safeguards to protect precious Fifth Amendment rights is, of course, not
lessened in the slightest. In each of the cases, the defendant was thrust
into an unfamiliar atmosphere and run through menacing police interrogation procedures. The potentiality for compulsion is forcefully apparent, for example, in *Miranda*, where the indigent Mexican defendant
was a seriously disturbed individual with pronounced sexual fantasies,

---

25. In the fourth confession case decided by the Court in the 1962 Term, Fay v.
Noia, 372 U.S. 391 (1963), our disposition made it unnecessary to delve at length into
the facts. The facts of the defendant's case there, however, paralleled those of his codefendants, whose confessions were found to have resulted from continuous and coercive
interrogation for 27 hours, with denial of requests for friends or attorney. See United
States v. Murphy, 222 F.2d 698 (C.A. 2d Cir. 1955) (Frank, J.); People v. Bonino, 1
N.Y.2d 752, 135 N.E.2d 51 (1956).

and in *Stewart,* in which the defendant was an indigent Los Angeles Negro who had dropped out of school in the sixth grade. To be sure, the records do not evince overt physical coercion or patent psychological ploys. The fact remains that in none of these cases did the officers undertake to afford appropriate safeguards at the outset of the interrogation to insure that the statements were truly the product of free choice.

It is obvious that such an interrogation environment is created for no purpose other than to subjugate the individual to the will of his examiner. This atmosphere carries its own badge of intimidation. To be sure, this is not physical intimidation, but it is equally destructive of human dignity.[26] The current practice of incommunicado interrogation is at odds with one of our Nation's most cherished principles—that the individual may not be compelled to incriminate himself. Unless adequate protective devices are employed to dispel the compulsion inherent in custodial surroundings, no statement obtained from the defendant can truly be the product of his free choice.

From the foregoing, we can readily perceive an intimate connection between the privilege against self-incrimination and police custodial questioning. It is fitting to turn to history and precedent underlying the Self-Incrimination Clause to determine its applicability in this situation.

II . . .

The question in these cases is whether the privilege is fully applicable during a period of custodial interrogation. In this Court, the privilege has consistently been accorded a liberal construction. . . . We are satisfied that all the principles embodied in the privilege apply to informal compulsion exerted by law-enforcement officers during in-custody questioning. An individual swept from familiar surroundings into police custody, surrounded by antagonistic forces, and subjected to the techniques

26. The absurdity of denying that a confession obtained under these circumstances is compelled is aptly portrayed by an example in Professor Sutherland's recent article, Crime and Confession, 79 Harv. L. Rev. 21, 37 (1965):

> Suppose a well-to-do testatrix says she intends to will her property to Elizabeth. John and James want her to bequeath it to them instead. They capture the testatrix, put her in a carefully designed room, out of touch with everyone but themselves and their convenient "witness," keep her secluded there for hours while they make insistent demands, weary her with contradictions of her assertions that she wants to leave her money to Elizabeth, and finally induce her to execute the will in their favor. Assume that John and James are deeply and correctly convinced that Elizabeth is unworthy and will make base use of the property if she gets her hands on it, whereas John and James have the noblest and most righteous intentions. Would any judge of probate accept the will so procured as the "voluntary" act of the testatrix?

of persuasion described above cannot be otherwise than under compulsion to speak. As a practical matter, the compulsion to speak in the isolated setting of the police station may well be greater than in courts or other official investigations, where there are often impartial observers to guard against intimidation or trickery.

This question, in fact, could have been taken as settled in federal courts almost 70 years ago, when, in Bram v. United States, 168 U.S. 532, 542 (1897), this Court held:

> In criminal trials, in the courts of the United States, wherever a question arises whether a confession is incompetent because not voluntary, the issue is controlled by that portion of the Fifth Amendment . . . commanding that no person "shall be compelled in any criminal case to be a witness against himself." . . .

In addition to the expansive historical development of the privilege and the sound policies which have nurtured its evolution, judicial precedent thus clearly establishes its application to incommunicado interrogation. [See also Escobedo v. Illinois.[35]] . . .

III

Today, then, there can be no doubt that the Fifth Amendment privilege is available outside of criminal court proceedings and serves to protect persons in all settings in which their freedom of action is curtailed in any significant way from being compelled to incriminate themselves. We have concluded that without proper safeguards the process of in-custody interrogation of persons suspected or accused of crime contains inherently compelling pressures which work to undermine the individual's will to resist and to compel him to speak where he would not otherwise do so freely. In order to combat these pressures and to permit a full opportunity to exercise the privilege against self-incrimination, the accused must be adequately and effectively apprised of his rights and the exercise of those rights must be fully honored.

It is impossible for us to foresee the potential alternatives for protecting the privilege which might be devised by Congress or the States in the exercise of their creative rule-making capacities. Therefore we

---

35. The police [in Escobedo] also prevented the attorney from consulting with his client. Independent of any other constitutional proscription, this action constitutes a violation of the Sixth Amendment right to the assistance of counsel and excludes any statement obtained in its wake. See People v. Donovan, 13 N.Y.2d 148, 193 N.E.2d 628, 243 N.Y.S.2d 841 (1963) (Fuld, J.).

cannot say that the Constitution necessarily requires adherence to any particular solution for the inherent compulsions of the interrogation process as it is presently conducted. Our decision in no way creates a constitutional straitjacket which will handicap sound efforts at reform, nor is it intended to have this effect. We encourage Congress and the States to continue their laudable search for increasingly effective ways of protecting the rights of the individual while promoting efficient enforcement of our criminal laws. However, unless we are shown other procedures which are at least as effective in apprising accused persons of their right of silence and in assuring a continuous opportunity to exercise it, the following safeguards must be observed.

At the outset, if a person in custody is to be subjected to interrogation, he must first be informed in clear and unequivocal terms that he has the right to remain silent. For those unaware of the privilege, the warning is needed simply to make them aware of it—the threshold requirement for an intelligent decision as to its exercise. More important, such a warning is an absolute prerequisite in overcoming the inherent pressures of the interrogation atmosphere. It is not just the subnormal or woefully ignorant who succumb to an interrogator's imprecations, whether implied or expressly stated, that the interrogation will continue until a confession is obtained or that silence in the face of accusation is itself damning and will bode ill when presented to a jury. Further, the warning will show the individual that his interrogators are prepared to recognize his privilege should he choose to exercise it.

The Fifth Amendment privilege is so fundamental to our system of constitutional rule and the expedient of giving an adequate warning as to the availability of the privilege so simple, we will not pause to inquire in individual cases whether the defendant was aware of his rights without a warning being given. Assessments of the knowledge the defendant possessed, based on information as to his age, education, intelligence, or prior contact with authorities, can never be more than speculation; a warning is a clearcut fact. More important, whatever the background of the person interrogated, a warning at the time of the interrogation is indispensable to overcome its pressures and to insure that the individual knows he is free to exercise the privilege at that point in time.

The warning of the right to remain silent must be accompanied by the explanation that anything said can and will be used against the individual in court. This warning is needed in order to make him aware not only of the privilege, but also of the consequences of forgoing it. It is only through an awareness of these consequences that there can be any assurance of real understanding and intelligent exercise of the privilege. Moreover, this warning may serve to make the individual more acutely aware that he is faced with a phase of the adversary system—that he is not in the presence of persons acting solely in his interest.

The circumstances surrounding in-custody interrogation can operate very quickly to overbear the will of one merely made aware of his privilege by his interrogators. Therefore, the right to have counsel present at the interrogation is indispensable to the protection of the Fifth Amendment privilege under the system we delineate today. Our aim is to assure that the individual's right to choose between silence and speech remains unfettered throughout the interrogation process. A once-stated warning, delivered by those who will conduct the interrogation, cannot itself suffice to that end among those who most require knowledge of their rights. A mere warning given by the interrogators is not alone sufficient to accomplish that end. Prosecutors themselves claim that the admonishment of the right to remain silent without more "will benefit only the recidivist and the professional." Brief for the National District Attorneys Association as amicus curiae, p. 14. Even preliminary advice given to the accused by his own attorney can be swiftly overcome by the secret interrogation process. . . . Thus, the need for counsel to protect the Fifth Amendment privilege comprehends not merely a right to consult with counsel prior to questioning, but also to have counsel present during any questioning if the defendant so desires.

The presence of counsel at the interrogation may serve several significant subsidiary functions as well. If the accused decides to talk to his interrogators, the assistance of counsel can mitigate the dangers of untrustworthiness. With a lawyer present the likelihood that the police will practice coercion is reduced, and if coercion is nevertheless exercised the lawyer can testify to it in court. The presence of a lawyer can also help to guarantee that the accused gives a fully accurate statement to the police and that the statement is rightly reported by the prosecution at trial. . . .

An individual need not make a pre-interrogation request for a lawyer. While such request affirmatively secures his right to have one, his failure to ask for a lawyer does not constitute a waiver. No effective waiver of the right to counsel during interrogation can be recognized unless specifically made after the warnings we here delineate have been given. The accused who does not know his rights and therefore does not make a request may be the person who most needs counsel. . . .

Accordingly we hold that an individual held for interrogation must be clearly informed that he has the right to consult with a lawyer and to have the lawyer with him during interrogation under the system for protecting the privilege we delineate today. As with the warnings of the right to remain silent and that anything stated can be used in evidence against him, this warning is an absolute prerequisite to interrogation. No amount of circumstantial evidence that the person may have been aware of this right will suffice to stand in its stead. Only through such a warning is there ascertainable assurance that the accused was aware of this right.

If an individual indicates that he wishes the assistance of counsel before any interrogation occurs, the authorities cannot rationally ignore or deny his request on the basis that the individual does not have or cannot afford a retained attorney. The financial ability of the individual has no relationship to the scope of the rights involved here. The privilege against self-incrimination secured by the Constitution applies to all individuals. The need for counsel in order to protect the privilege exists for the indigent as well as the affluent. In fact, were we to limit these constitutional rights to those who can retain an attorney, our decisions today would be of little significance. The cases before us as well as the vast majority of confession cases with which we have dealt in the past involve those unable to retain counsel. While authorities are not required to relieve the accused of his poverty, they have the obligation not to take advantage of indigence in the administration of justice. Denial of counsel to the indigent at the time of interrogation while allowing an attorney to those who can afford one would be no more supportable by reason or logic than the similar situation at trial and on appeal struck down in Gideon v. Wainwright, 372 U.S. 335 (1963), and Douglas v. California, 372 U.S. 353 (1963).

In order fully to apprise a person interrogated of the extent of his rights under this system then, it is necessary to warn him not only that he has the right to consult with an attorney, but also that if he is indigent a lawyer will be appointed to represent him. Without this additional warning, the admonition of the right to consult with counsel would often be understood as meaning only that he can consult with a lawyer if he has one or has the funds to obtain one. The warning of a right to counsel would be hollow if not couched in terms that would convey to the indigent—the person most often subjected to interrogation—the knowledge that he too has a right to have counsel present. As with the warnings of the right to remain silent and of the general right to counsel, only by effective and express explanation to the indigent of this right can there be assurance that he was truly in a position to exercise it.

Once warnings have been given, the subsequent procedure is clear. If the individual indicates in any manner, at any time prior to or during questioning, that he wishes to remain silent, the interrogation must cease. At this point he has shown that he intends to exercise his Fifth Amendment privilege; any statement taken after the person invokes his privilege cannot be other than the product of compulsion, subtle or otherwise. Without the right to cut off questioning, the setting of in-custody interrogation operates on the individual to overcome free choice in producing a statement after the privilege has been once invoked. If the individual states that he wants an attorney, the interrogation must cease until an attorney is present. At that time, the individual must have an opportunity to confer with the attorney and to have him present during any subsequent questioning. If the individual cannot obtain an attorney and he indicates that he wants one before speaking to police, they must respect his decision to remain silent. This does not mean, as some have suggested, that each police station must have a "station house lawyer" present at all times to advise prisoners. It does mean, however, that if police propose to interrogate a person they must make known to him that he is entitled to a lawyer and that if he cannot afford one, a lawyer will be provided for him prior to any interrogation. If authorities conclude that they will not provide counsel during a reasonable period of time in which investigation in the field is carried out, they may refrain from doing so without violating the person's Fifth Amendment privilege so long as they do not question him during that time.

If the interrogation continues without the presence of an attorney and a statement is taken, a heavy burden rests on the government to demonstrate that the defendant knowingly and intelligently waived his privilege against self-incrimination and his right to retained or appointed counsel. Escobedo v. Illinois, 378 U.S. 478, 490, n.14. This Court has always set high standards of proof for the waiver of constitutional rights, Johnson v. Zerbst, 304 U.S. 458 (1938), and we re-assert these standards as applied to in-custody interrogation. Since the State is responsible for establishing the isolated circumstances under which the interrogation takes place and has the only means of making available corroborated evidence of warnings given during incommunicado interrogation, the burden is rightly on its shoulders.

An express statement that the individual is willing to make a statement and does not want an attorney followed closely by a statement could constitute a waiver. But a valid waiver will not be presumed simply from the silence of the accused after warnings are given or simply from the fact that a confession was in fact eventually obtained. . . . Moreover, where in-custody interrogation is involved, there is no room for the contention that the privilege is waived if the individual answers some questions or gives some information on his own prior to invoking his right to remain silent when interrogated.[45]

45. Although this Court held in Rogers v. United States, 340 U.S. 367 (1951), over strong dissent, that a witness before a grand jury may not in certain circumstances decide to answer some questions and then refuse to answer others, that decision has no application to the interrogation situation we deal with today. No legislative or judicial fact-finding authority is involved here, nor is there a possibility that the individual might make self-serving statements of which he could make use at trial while refusing to answer incriminating statements.

Whatever the testimony of the authorities as to waiver of rights by an accused, the fact of lengthy interrogation or incommunicado incarceration before a statement is made is strong evidence that the accused did not validly waive his rights. In these circumstances the fact that the individual eventually made a statement is consistent with the conclusion that the compelling influence of the interrogation finally forced him to do so. It is inconsistent with any notion of a voluntary relinquishment of the privilege. Moreover, any evidence that the accused was threatened, tricked, or cajoled into a waiver will, of course, show that the defendant did not voluntarily waive his privilege. The requirement of warnings and waiver of rights is a fundamental with respect to the Fifth Amendment privilege and not simply a preliminary ritual to existing methods of interrogation.

The warnings required and the waiver necessary in accordance with our opinion today are, in the absence of a fully effective equivalent, prerequisites to the admissibility of any statement made by a defendant. No distinction can be drawn between statements which are direct confessions and statements which amount to "admissions" of part or all of an offense. The privilege against self-incrimination protects the individual from being compelled to incriminate himself in any manner; it does not distinguish degrees of incrimination. Similarly, for precisely the same reason, no distinction may be drawn between inculpatory statements and statements alleged to be merely "exculpatory." If a statement made were in fact truly exculpatory it would, of course, never be used by the prosecution. In fact, statements merely intended to be exculpatory by the defendant are often used to impeach his testimony at trial or to demonstrate untruths in the statement given under interrogation and thus to prove guilt by implication. These statements are incriminating in any meaningful sense of the word and may not be used without the full warnings and effective waiver required for any other statement. In *Escobedo* itself, the defendant fully intended his accusation of another as the slayer to be exculpatory as to himself.

The principles announced today deal with the protection which must be given to the privilege against self-incrimination when the individual is first subjected to police interrogation while in custody at the station or otherwise deprived of his freedom of action in any significant way. It is at this point that our adversary system of criminal proceedings commences, distinguishing itself at the outset from the inquisitorial system recognized in some countries. Under the system of warnings we delineate today or under any other system which may be devised and found effective, the safeguards to be erected about the privilege must come into play at this point.

Our decision is not intended to hamper the traditional function of police officers in investigating crime. . . . When an individual is in custody on probable cause, the police may, of course, seek out evidence in the field to be used at trial against him. Such investigation may include inquiry of persons not under restraint. General on-the-scene questioning as to facts surrounding a crime or other general questioning of citizens in the fact-finding process is not affected by our holding. It is an act of responsible citizenship for individuals to give whatever information they may have to aid in law enforcement. In such situations the compelling atmosphere inherent in the process of in-custody interrogation is not necessarily present.

In dealing with statements obtained through interrogation, we do not purport to find all confessions inadmissible. Confessions remain a proper element in law enforcement. Any statement given freely and voluntarily without any compelling influences is, of course, admissible in evidence. The fundamental import of the privilege while an individual is in custody is not whether he is allowed to talk to the police without the benefit of warnings and counsel, but whether he can be interrogated. There is no requirement that police stop a person who enters a police station and states that he wishes to confess to a crime, or a person who calls the police to offer a confession or any other statement he desires to make. Volunteered statements of any kind are not barred by the Fifth Amendment and their admissibility is not affected by our holding to-day. . . .

IV

A recurrent argument made in these cases is that society's need for interrogation outweighs the privilege. This argument is not unfamiliar to this Court. . . . The whole thrust of our foregoing discussion demonstrates that the Constitution has prescribed the rights of the individual when confronted with the power of government when it provided in the Fifth Amendment that an individual cannot be compelled to be a witness against himself. That right cannot be abridged. . . .

In announcing these principles, we are not unmindful of the burdens which law enforcement officials must bear, often under trying circumstances. We also fully recognize the obligation of all citizens to aid in enforcing the criminal laws. This Court, while protecting individual rights, has always given ample latitude to law enforcement agencies in the legitimate exercise of their duties. The limits we have placed on the interrogation process should not constitute an undue interference with a proper system of law enforcement. As we have noted, our decision does not in any way preclude police from carrying out their traditional investigatory functions. Although confessions may play an important role in some convictions, the cases before us present graphic examples of the overstatement of the "need" for confessions. In each case authorities conducted interrogations ranging up to five days in duration despite the presence, through standard investigating practices, of considerable evidence against each defendant.[51] . . .

It is also urged that an unfettered right to detention for interrogation should be allowed because it will often redound to the benefit of the person questioned. When police inquiry determines that there is no reason to believe that the person has committed any crime, it is said, he will be released without need for further formal procedures. The person who has committed no offense, however, will be better able to clear himself after warnings with counsel present than without. It can be assumed that in such circumstances a lawyer would advise his client to talk freely to police in order to clear himself.

Custodial interrogation, by contrast, does not necessarily afford the innocent an opportunity to clear themselves. A serious consequence of the present practice of the interrogation alleged to be beneficial for the innocent is that many arrests "for investigation" subject large numbers of innocent persons to detention and interrogation. In one of the cases before us, No. 584, California v. Stewart, police held four persons, who were in the defendant's house at the time of the arrest, in jail for five days until defendant confessed. At that time they were finally released. Police stated that there was "no evidence to connect them with any crime." Available statistics on the extent of this practice where it is condoned indicate that these four are far from alone in being subjected to arrest, prolonged detention, and interrogation without the requisite probable cause.[53]

Over the years the Federal Bureau of Investigation has compiled an exemplary record of effective law enforcement while advising any suspect or arrested person, at the outset of an interview, that he is not required

51. Miranda, Vignera, and Westover were identified by eyewitnesses. Marked bills from the bank robbed were found in Westover's car. Articles stolen from the victim as well as from several other robbery victims were found in Stewart's home at the outset of the investigation.

53. See, e.g., Report and Recommendations of the [District of Columbia] Commissioners' Committee on Police Arrests for Investigation (1962); American Civil Liberties Union, Secret Detention by the Chicago Police (1959). An extreme example of this practice occurred in the District of Columbia in 1958. Seeking three "stocky" young Negroes who had robbed a restaurant, police rounded up 90 persons of that general description. Sixty-three were held overnight before being released for lack of evidence. A man not among the 90 arrested was ultimately charged with the crime. Washington Daily News, January 21, 1958, p.5, col. 1; Hearings before a Subcommittee of the Senate Judiciary Committee on H.R. 11477, S. 2970, S. 3325, and S. 3355, 85th Cong., 2d Sess. (July 1958), pp. 40, 78.

to make a statement, that any statement may be used against him in court, that the individual may obtain the services of an attorney of his own choice and, more recently, that he has a right to free counsel if he is unable to pay. . . .

The practice of the FBI can readily be emulated by state and local enforcement agencies. The argument that the FBI deals with different crimes than are dealt with by state authorities does not mitigate the significance of the FBI experience.

The experience in some other countries also suggests that the danger to law enforcement in curbs on interrogation is overplayed. The English procedure since 1912 under the Judges' Rules is significant. As recently strengthened, the Rules require that a cautionary warning be given an accused by a police officer as soon as he has evidence that affords reasonable grounds for suspicion; they also require that any statement made be given by the accused without questioning by police. The right of the individual to consult with an attorney during this period is expressly recognized.

The safeguards present under Scottish law may be even greater than in England. Scottish judicial decisions bar use in evidence of most confessions obtained through police interrogation. In India, confessions made to police not in the presence of a magistrate have been excluded by rule of evidence since 1872, at a time when it operated under British law. Identical provisions appear in the Evidence Ordinance of Ceylon, enacted in 1895. Similarly, in our country the Uniform Code of Military Justice has long provided that no suspect may be interrogated without first being warned of his right not to make a statement and that any statement he makes may be used against him. Denial of the right to consult counsel during interrogation has also been proscribed by military tribunals. There appears to have been no marked detrimental effect on criminal law enforcement in these jurisdictions as a result of these rules. Conditions of law enforcement in our country are sufficiently similar to permit reference to this experience as assurance that lawlessness will not result from warning an individual of his rights or allowing him to exercise them. Moreover, it is consistent with our legal system that we give at least as much protection to these rights as is given in the jurisdictions described. We deal in our country with rights grounded in a specific requirement of the Fifth Amendment of the Constitution, whereas other jurisdictions arrived at their conclusions on the basis of principles of justice not so specifically defined.

It is also urged upon us that we withhold decision on this issue until state legislative bodies and advisory groups have had an opportunity to deal with these problems by rule making. We have already pointed out that the Constitution does not require any specific code of procedures for protecting the privilege against self-incrimination during custodial interrogation. Congress and the States are free to develop their own safeguards for the privilege, so long as they are fully as effective as those described above in informing accused persons of their right of silence and in affording a continuous opportunity to exercise it. In any event, however, the issues presented are of constitutional dimensions and must be determined by the courts. The admissibility of a statement in the face of a claim that it was obtained in violation of the defendant's constitutional rights is an issue the resolution of which has long since been undertaken by this Court. See Hopt v. Utah, 110 U.S. 574 (1884). Judicial solutions to problems of constitutional dimension have evolved decade by decade. As courts have been presented with the need to enforce constitutional rights, they have found means of doing so. That was our responsibility when *Escobedo* was before us and it is our responsibility today. Where rights secured by the Constitution are involved, there can be no rule making or legislation which would abrogate them.

V

Because of the nature of the problem and because of its recurrent significance in numerous cases, we have to this point discussed the relationship of the Fifth Amendment privilege to police interrogation without specific concentration on the facts of the cases before us. We turn now to these facts to consider the application to these cases of the constitutional principles discussed above. In each instance, we have concluded that statements were obtained from the defendant under circumstances that did not meet constitutional standards for protection of the privilege.

NO. 759. MIRANDA v. ARIZONA

On March 13, 1963, petitioner, Ernesto Miranda, was arrested at his home and taken in custody to a Phoenix police station. He was there identified by the complaining witness. The police then took him to "Interrogation Room No. 2" of the detective bureau. There he was questioned by two police officers. The officers admitted at trial that Miranda was not advised that he had a right to have an attorney present. Two hours later, the officers emerged from the interrogation room with a written confession signed by Miranda. At the top of the statement was a typed paragraph stating that the confession was made voluntarily, without threats or promises of immunity and "with full knowledge of my legal rights, understanding any statement I make may be used against me."[67]

At his trial before a jury, the written confession was admitted into evidence over the objection of defense counsel, and the officers testified to the prior oral confession made by Miranda during the interrogation. Miranda was found guilty of kidnapping and rape. . . .

We reverse. From the testimony of the officers and by the admission of respondent, it is clear that Miranda was not in any way apprised of his right to consult with an attorney and to have one present during the interrogation, nor was his right not to be compelled to incriminate himself effectively protected in any other manner. Without these warnings the statements were inadmissible. The mere fact that he signed a statement which contained a typed-in clause stating that he had "full knowledge" of his "legal rights" does not approach the knowing and intelligent waiver required to relinquish constitutional rights.

NO. 760. VIGNERA v. NEW YORK

Petitioner, Michael Vignera, was picked up by New York police on October 14, 1960, in connection with the robbery three days earlier of a Brooklyn dress shop. They took him to the 17th Detective Squad headquarters in Manhattan. Sometime thereafter he was taken to the 66th Detective Squad. There a detective questioned Vignera with respect to the robbery. Vignera orally admitted the robbery to the detective. The detective was asked on cross-examination at trial by defense counsel whether Vignera was warned of his right to counsel before being interrogated. The prosecution objected to the question and the trial judge sustained the objection. Thus, the defense was precluded from making any showing that warnings had not been given. While at the 66th Detective Squad, Vignera was identified by the store owner and a saleslady as the man who robbed the dress shop. At about 3 P.M. he was formally arrested. The police then transported him to still another station, the 70th Precinct in Brooklyn, "for detention." At 11 P.M. Vignera was questioned by an assistant district attorney in the presence of a hearing reporter who transcribed the questions and Vignera's answers. This verbatim account of these proceedings contains no statement of any warnings given by the assistant district attorney. At Vignera's trial on a charge of first degree robbery, the detective testified as to the oral confession. The transcription of the statement taken was also introduced in evidence. . . .

---

67. One of the officers testified that he read this paragraph to Miranda. Apparently, however, he did not do so until after Miranda had confessed orally.

Vignera was found guilty of first degree robbery.

We reverse. The foregoing indicates that Vignera was not warned of any of his rights before the questioning by the detective and by the assistant district attorney. No other steps were taken to protect these rights. Thus he was not effectively apprised of his Fifth Amendment privilege or of his right to have counsel present and his statements are inadmissible.

NO. 761. WESTOVER v. UNITED STATES

At approximately 9:45 P.M. on March 20, 1963, petitioner, Carl Calvin Westover, was arrested by local police in Kansas City as a suspect in two Kansas City robberies. A report was also received from the FBI that he was wanted on a felony charge in California. The local authorities took him to a police station and placed him in a line-up on the local charges, and at about 11:45 P.M. he was booked. Kansas City police interrogated Westover on the night of his arrest. He denied any knowledge of criminal activities. The next day local officers interrogated him again throughout the morning. Shortly before noon they informed the FBI that they were through interrogating Westover and that the FBI could proceed to interrogate him. There is nothing in the record to indicate that Westover was ever given any warning as to his rights by local police. At noon, three special agents of the FBI continued the interrogation in a private interview room of the Kansas City Police Department, this time with respect to the robbery of a savings and loan association and a bank in Sacramento, California. After two or two and one-half hours, Westover signed separate confessions to each of these two robberies which had been prepared by one of the agents during the interrogation. At trial one of the agents testified, and a paragraph on each of the statements states, that the agents advised Westover that he did not have to make a statement, that any statement he made could be used against him, and that he had the right to see an attorney.

Westover was tried by a jury in federal court and convicted of the California robberies. His statements were introduced at trial. He was sentenced to 15 years' imprisonment on each count, the sentences to run consecutively. On appeal, the conviction was affirmed by the Court of Appeals for the Ninth Circuit. 342 F.2d 684.

We reverse. On the facts of this case we cannot find that Westover knowingly and intelligently waived his right to remain silent and his right to consult with counsel prior to the time he made the statement.[69] At

---

69. The failure of defense counsel to object to the introduction of the confession at trial, noted by the Court of Appeals and emphasized by the Solicitor General, does not preclude our consideration of the issue. Since the trial was held prior to our decision

the time the FBI agents began questioning Westover, he had been in custody for over 14 hours and had been interrogated at length during that period. The FBI interrogation began immediately upon the conclusion of the interrogation by Kansas City police and was conducted in local police headquarters. Although the two law enforcement authorities are legally distinct and the crimes for which they interrogated Westover were different, the impact on him was that of a continuous period of questioning. There is no evidence of any warning given prior to the FBI interrogation nor is there any evidence of an articulated waiver of rights after the FBI commenced its interrogation. The record simply shows that the defendant did in fact confess a short time after being turned over to the FBI following interrogation by local police. Despite the fact that the FBI agents gave warnings at the outset of their interview, from Westover's point of view the warnings came at the end of the interrogation process. In these circumstances an intelligent waiver of constitutional rights cannot be assumed.

We do not suggest that law enforcement authorities are precluded from questioning any individual who has been held for a period of time by other authorities and interrogated by them without appropriate warnings. A different case would be presented if an accused were taken into custody by the second authority, removed both in time and place from his original surroundings, and then adequately advised of his rights and given an opportunity to exercise them. But here the FBI interrogation was conducted immediately following the state interrogation in the same police station—in the same compelling surroundings. Thus, in obtaining a confession from Westover the federal authorities were the beneficiaries of the pressure applied by the local in-custody interrogation. In these circumstances the giving of warnings alone was not sufficient to protect the privilege.

NO. 584. CALIFORNIA v. STEWART

In the course of investigating a series of purse-snatch robberies in which one of the victims had died of injuries inflicted by her assailant, respondent, Roy Allen Stewart, was pointed out to Los Angeles police as the endorser of dividend checks taken in one of the robberies. At about 7:15 P.M., January 31, 1963, police officers went to Stewart's house and arrested him. One of the officers asked Stewart if they could search the house, to which he replied, "Go ahead." The search turned up various

---

in *Escobedo* and, of course, prior to our decision today making the objection available, the failure to object at trial does not constitute a waiver of the claim. See, e.g., United States ex rel. Angelet v. Fay, 333 F.2d 12, 16 (C.A. 2d Cir. 1964), aff'd, 381 U.S. 654 (1965). Cf. Ziffrin, Inc. v. United States, 318 U.S. 73, 78 (1943).

items taken from the five robbery victims. At the time of Stewart's arrest, police also arrested Stewart's wife and three other persons who were visiting him. These four were jailed along with Stewart and were interrogated. Stewart was taken to the University Station of the Los Angeles Police Department where he was placed in a cell. During the next five days, police interrogated Stewart on nine different occasions. Except during the first interrogation session, when he was confronted with an accusing witness, Stewart was isolated with his interrogators.

During the ninth interrogation session, Stewart admitted that he had robbed the deceased and stated that he had not meant to hurt her. Police then brought Stewart before a magistrate for the first time. Since there was no evidence to connect them with any crime, the police then released the other four persons arrested with him.

Nothing in the record specifically indicates whether Stewart was or was not advised of his right to remain silent or his right to counsel. In a number of instances, however, the interrogating officers were asked to recount everything that was said during the interrogations. None indicated that Stewart was ever advised of his rights.

Stewart was charged with kidnapping to commit robbery, rape, and murder. At his trial, transcripts of the first interrogation and the confession at the last interrogation were introduced in evidence. The jury found Stewart guilty of robbery and first degree murder and fixed the penalty as death. On appeal, the Supreme Court of California reversed. 62 Cal. 2d 571, 400 P.2d 97, 43 Cal. Rptr. 201. It held that under this Court's decision in *Escobedo*, Stewart should have been advised of his right to remain silent and of his right to counsel and that it would not presume in the face of a silent record that the police advised Stewart of his rights.

We affirm. In dealing with custodial interrogation, we will not presume that a defendant has been effectively apprised of his rights and that his privilege against self-incrimination has been adequately safeguarded on a record that does not show that any warnings have been given or that any effective alternative has been employed. Nor can a knowing and intelligent waiver of these rights be assumed on a silent record. Furthermore, Stewart's steadfast denial of the alleged offenses through eight of the nine interrogations over a period of five days is subject to no other construction than that he was compelled by persistent interrogation to forgo his Fifth Amendment privilege.

It is so ordered.

MR. JUSTICE CLARK, dissenting in Nos. 759, 760, and 761, and concurring in the result in No. 584.

It is with regret that I find it necessary to write in these cases. However, I am unable to join the majority because its opinion goes too far on too little, while my dissenting brethren do not go quite far enough. Nor can I join in the Court's criticism of the present practices of police and investigatory agencies as to custodial interrogation. The materials it refers to as "police manuals" are, as I read them, merely writings in this field by professors and some police officers. Not one is shown by the record here to be the official manual of any police department, much less in universal use in crime detection. Moreover, the examples of police brutality mentioned by the Court are rare exceptions to the thousands of cases that appear every year in the law reports. The police agencies—all the way from municipal and state forces to the federal bureaus—are responsible for law enforcement and public safety in this country. I am proud of their efforts, which in my view are not fairly characterized by the Court's opinion.

I

The ipse dixit of the majority has no support in our cases. Indeed, the Court admits that "we might not find the defendents' statements [here] to have been involuntary in traditional terms." . . . In short, the Court has added more to the requirements that the accused is entitled to consult with his lawyer and that he must be given the traditional warning that he may remain silent and that anything that he says may be used against him. Escobedo v. Illinois, 378 U.S. 478, 490-491 (1964). Now, the Court fashions a constitutional rule that the police may engage in no custodial interrogation without additionally advising the accused that he has a right under the Fifth Amendment to the presence of counsel during interrogation and that, if he is without funds, counsel will be furnished him. When at any point during an interrogation the accused seeks affirmatively or impliedly to invoke his rights to silence or counsel, interrogation must be forgone or postponed. The Court further holds that failure to follow the new procedures requires inexorably the exclusion of any statement by the accused, as well as the fruits thereof. Such a strict constitutional specific inserted at the nerve center of crime detection may well kill the patient.[3] Since there is at this time a paucity of information

---

3. The Court points to England, Scotland, Ceylon and India as having equally rigid rules. As my Brother Harlan points out, . . . the Court is mistaken in this regard, for it overlooks counterbalancing prosecutorial advantages. Moreover, the requirements of the Federal Bureau of investigation do not appear . . . to be as strict as those imposed today in at least two respects:

> (1) The offer of counsel is articulated only as "a right to counsel"; nothing is said about a right to have counsel present at the custodial interrogation. (See also the examples cited by the Solicitor General, Westover v. United

and an almost total lack of empirical knowledge on the practical operation of requirements truly comparable to those announced by the majority, I would be more restrained lest we go too far too fast.

II . . .

The rule prior to today—as Mr. Justice Goldberg, the author of the Court's opinion in *Escobedo*, stated it in Haynes v. Washington—depended upon "a totality of circumstances evidencing an involuntary . . . admission of guilt." 373 U.S., at 514. And he concluded:

> Of course, detection and solution of crime is, at best, a difficult and arduous task requiring determination and persistence on the part of all responsible officers charged with the duty of law enforcement. And, certainly, we do not mean to suggest that all interrogation of witnesses and suspects is impermissible. Such questioning is undoubtedly an essential tool in effective law enforcement. The line between proper and permissible police conduct and techniques and methods offensive to due process is, at best, a difficult one to draw, particularly in cases such as this where it is necessary to make fine judgments as to the effect of psychologically coercive pressures and inducements on the mind and will of an accused. . . . We are here impelled to the conclusion, from all of the facts presented, that the bounds of due process have been exceeded.

III

I would continue to follow that rule. Under the "totality of circumstances" rule of which my Brother Goldberg spoke in *Haynes*, I would consider

---

States, 342 F.2d 684, 685 (1965) ("right to consult counsel"); Jackson v. United States, 337 F.2d 136, 138 (1964) (accused "entitled to an attorney").) Indeed, the practice is that whenever the suspect "decides that he wishes to consult with counsel before making a statement, the interview is terminated at that point. . . . When counsel appears in person, he is permitted to confer with his client in private." This clearly indicates that the FBI does not warn that counsel may be present during custodial interrogation.

(2) The Solicitor General's letter states: "[T]hose who have been arrested for an offense under FBI jurisdiction, or whose arrest is contemplated following the interview, [are advised] of a right to free counsel *if* they are unable to pay, and the availability of such counsel from the Judge." So phrased, this warning does not indicate that the agent will secure counsel. Rather, the statement may well be interpreted by the suspect to mean that the burden is placed upon himself and that he may have counsel appointed only when brought before the judge or at trial—but not at custodial interrogation. As I view the FBI practice, it is not as broad as the one laid down today by the Court.

in each case whether the police officer prior to custodial interrogation added the warning that the suspect might have counsel present at the interrogation and, further, that a court would appoint one at his request if he was too poor to employ counsel. In the absence of warnings, the burden would be on the State to prove that counsel was knowingly and intelligently waived or that in the totality of the circumstances, including the failure to give the necessary warnings, the confession was clearly voluntary.

Rather than employing the arbitrary Fifth Amendment rule[4] which the Court lays down I would follow the more pliable dictates of the Due Process Clauses of the Fifth and Fourteenth Amendments which we are accustomed to administering and which we know from our cases are effective instruments in protecting persons in police custody. In this way we would not be acting in the dark nor in one full sweep changing the traditional rules of custodial interrogation which this Court has for so long recognized as a justifiable and proper tool in balancing individual rights against the rights of society. It will be soon enough to go further when we are able to appraise with somewhat better accuracy the effect of such a holding. . . .

MR. JUSTICE HARLAN, whom MR. JUSTICE STEWART and MR. JUSTICE WHITE join, dissenting.

I believe the decision of the Court represents poor constitutional law and entails harmful consequences for the country at large. How serious these consequences may prove to be only time can tell. But the basic flaws in the Court's justification seem to me readily apparent now once all sides of the problem are considered.

I. INTRODUCTION . . .

While the fine points of [the Court's holding] are far less clear than the Court admits, the tenor is quite apparent. The new rules are not designed to guard against police brutality or other unmistakably banned forms of coercion. Those who use third-degree tactics and deny them in court are equally able and destined to lie as skillfully about warnings and waivers. Rather, the thrust of the new rules is to negate all pressures, to reinforce the nervous or ignorant suspect, and ultimately to discourage any confes-

---

4. In my view there is "no significant support" in our cases for the holding of the Court today that the Fifth Amendment privilege, in effect, forbids custodial interrogation. For a discussion of this point see the dissenting opinion of my Brother White. . . .

sion at all. The aim in short is toward "voluntariness" in a utopian sense, or to view it from a different angle, voluntariness with a vengeance.

To incorporate this notion into the Constitution requires a strained reading of history and precedent and a disregard of the very pragmatic concerns that alone may on occasion justify such strains. I believe that reasoned examination will show that the Due Process Clauses provide an adequate tool for coping with confessions and that, even if the Fifth Amendment privilege against self-incrimination be invoked, its precedents taken as a whole do not sustain the present rules. Viewed as a choice based on pure policy, these new rules prove to be a highly debatable, if not one-sided, appraisal of the competing interests, imposed over widespread objection, at the very time when judicial restraint is most called for by the circumstances.

II. CONSTITUTIONAL PREMISES

It is most fitting to begin an inquiry into the constitutional precedents by surveying the limits on confessions the Court has evolved under the Due Process Clause of the Fourteenth Amendment. This is so because these cases show that there exists a workable and effective means of dealing with confessions in a judicial manner; because the cases are the baseline from which the Court now departs and so serve to measure the actual as opposed to the professed distance it travels; and because examination of them helps reveal how the Court has coasted into its present position.

The earliest confession cases in this Court emerged from federal prosecutions and were settled on a nonconstitutional basis, the Court adopting the common-law rule that the absence of inducements, promises, and threats made a confession voluntary and admissible. Hopt v. Utah, 110 U.S. 574; Pierce v. United States, 160 U.S. 355. While a later case said the Fifth Amendment privilege controlled admissibility, this proposition was not itself developed in subsequent decisions.[2] The Court did, however, heighten the test of admissibility in federal trials to one of voluntariness "in fact," Wan v. United States, 266 U.S. 1, 14,

---

2. The case was Bram v. United States, 168 U.S. 532. . . . Its historical premises were afterwards disproved by Wigmore, who concluded "that no assertions could be more unfounded." 3 Wigmore, Evidence §823, at 250, n.5 (3d ed. 1940). The Court in United States v. Carignan, 342 U.S. 36, 41, declined to choose between Bram and Wigmore, and Stein v. New York, 346 U.S. 156, 191, n.35, cast further doubt on Bram. There are, however, several Court opinions which assume in dicta the relevance of the Fifth Amendment privilege to confessions. Burdeau v. McDowell, 256 U.S. 465, 475; see Shotwell Mfg. Co. v. United States, 371 U.S. 341, 347. On Bram and the federal confession cases generally, see Developments in the Law—Confessions, 79 Harv. L. Rev. 935, 959-961 (1966).

. . . and then by and large left federal judges to apply the same standards the Court began to derive in a string of state court cases.

This new line of decisions, testing admissibility by the Due Process Clause, began in 1936 with Brown v. Mississippi, 297 U.S. 278, and must now embrace somewhat more than 30 full opinions of the Court. While the voluntariness rubric was repeated in many instances, . . . the Court never pinned it down to a single meaning but on the contrary infused it with a number of different values. To travel quickly over the main themes, there was an initial emphasis on reliability, e.g., Ward v. Texas, 316 U.S. 547, supplemented by concern over the legality and fairness of the police practices, e.g., Ashcraft v. Tennessee, 322 U.S. 143, in an "accusatorial" system of law enforcement, Watts v. Indiana, 338 U.S. 49, 54, and eventually by close attention to the individual's state of mind and capacity for effective choice, e.g., Gallegos v. Colorado, 370 U.S. 49. The outcome was a continuing re-evaluation on the facts of each case of *how much* pressure on the suspect was permissible. . . .

There are several relevant lessons to be drawn from this constitutional history. The first is that with over 25 years of precedent the Court has developed an elaborate, sophisticated, and sensitive approach to admissibility of confessions. It is "judicial" in its treatment of one case at a time, . . . flexible in its ability to respond to the endless mutations of fact presented, and ever more familiar to the lower courts. Of course, strict certainty is not obtained in this developing process, but this is often so with constitutional principles, and disagreement is usually confined to that borderland of close cases where it matters least.

The second point is that in practice and from time to time in principle, the Court has given ample recognition to society's interest in suspect questioning as an instrument of law enforcement. Cases countenancing quite significant pressures can be cited without difficulty,[5] and the lower courts may often have been yet more tolerant. Of course the limitations imposed today were rejected by necessary implication in case after case, the right to warnings having been explicitly rebuffed in this Court many years ago. Powers v. United States, 223 U.S. 303; Wilson v. United States, 162 U.S. 613. As recently as Haynes v. Washington, 373 U.S. 503, 515, the Court openly acknowledged that questioning of witnesses and suspects "is undoubtedly an essential tool in effective law enforcement." Accord, Crooker v. California, 357 U.S. 433, 441.

Finally, the cases disclose that the language in many of the opinions overstates the actual course of decision. It has been said, for example,

---

5. . . . One not too distant example is Stroble v. California, 343 U.S. 181, in which the suspect was kicked and threatened after his arrest, questioned a little later for two hours, and isolated from a lawyer trying to see him; the resulting confession was held admissible.

that an admissible confession must be made by the suspect "in the unfettered exercise of his own will," Malloy v. Hogan, 378 U.S. 1, 8, and
that "a prisoner is not 'to be made the deluded instrument of his own
conviction,' " Culombe v. Connecticut, 367 U.S. 568, 581 (Frankfurter,
J., announcing the Court's judgment and an opinion). Though often
repeated, such principles are rarely observed in full measure. Even the
word "voluntary" may be deemed somewhat misleading, especially when
one considers many of the confessions that have been brought under its
umbrella. . . . The tendency to overstate may be laid in part to the
flagrant facts often before the Court; but in any event one must recognize
how it has tempered attitudes and lent some color of authority to the
approach now taken by the Court.

I turn now to the Court's asserted reliance on the Fifth Amendment,
an approach which I frankly regard as a trompe l'oeil. The Court's opinion
in my view reveals no adequate basis for extending the Fifth Amendment's
privilege against self-incrimination to the police station. Far more important, it fails to show that the Court's new rules are well supported, let
alone compelled, by Fifth Amendment precedents. Instead, the new rules
actually derive from quotation and analogy drawn from precedents under
the Sixth Amendment, which should properly have no bearing on police
interrogation.

The Court's opening contention, that the Fifth Amendment governs
police station confessions, is perhaps not an impermissible extension of
the law but it has little to commend itself in the present circumstances.
Historically, the privilege against self-incrimination did not bear at all
on the use of extra-legal confessions, for which distinct standards evolved;
indeed, "the *history* of the two principles is wide apart, differing by one
hundred years in origin, and derived through separate lines of precedents. . . ." 8 Wigmore, Evidence §2266, at 401 (McNaughton rev.
1961). Practice under the two doctrines has also differed in a number of
important respects.[6] Even those who would readily enlarge the privilege
must concede some linguistic difficulties since the Fifth Amendment in
terms proscribes only compelling any person "in any criminal case to be
a witness against himself." Cf. Kamisar, Equal Justice in the Gatehouses
and Mansions of American Criminal Procedure, in Criminal Justice in
Our Time 1, 25-26 (1965).

Though weighty, I do not say these points and similar ones are

---

6. Among the examples given in 8 Wigmore, Evidence §2266, at 401 (McNaughton
rev. 1961), are these: the privilege applies to any witness, civil or criminal, but the
confession rule protects only criminal defendants; the privilege deals only with compulsion, while the confession rule may exclude statements obtained by trick or promise; and
where the privilege has been nullified—as by the English Bankruptcy Act—the confession
rule may still operate.

conclusive, for, as the Court reiterates, the privilege embodies basic principles always capable of expansion. Certainly the privilege does represent a protective concern for the accused and an emphasis upon accusatorial rather than inquisitorial values in law enforcement, although this is similarly true of other limitations such as the grand jury requirement and the reasonable doubt standard. Accusatorial values, however, have openly been absorbed into the due process standard governing confessions; this indeed is why at present "the kinship of the two rules [governing confessions and self-incrimination] is too apparent for denial." Mc-Cormick, Evidence 155 (1954). Since extension of the general principle has already occurred, to insist that the privilege applies as such serves only to carry over inapposite historical details and engaging rhetoric and to obscure the policy choices to be made in regulating confessions.

Having decided that the Fifth Amendment privilege does apply in the police station, the Court reveals that the privilege imposes more exacting restrictions than does the Fourteenth Amendment's voluntariness test. It then emerges . . . that the Fifth Amendment requires for an admissible confession that it be given by one distinctly aware of his right not to speak and shielded from "the compelling atmosphere" of interrogation. . . . From these key premises, the Court finally develops the safeguards of warning, counsel, and so forth. I do not believe these premises are sustained by precedents under the Fifth Amendment.

The more important premise is that pressure on the suspect must be eliminated though it be only the subtle influence of the atmosphere and surroundings. The Fifth Amendment, however, has never been thought to forbid *all* pressure to incriminate one's self in the situations covered by it. On the contrary, it has been held that failure to incriminate one's self can result in denial of removal of one's case from state to federal court, Maryland v. Soper, 270 U.S. 9; in refusal of a military commission, Orloff v. Willoughby, 345 U.S. 83; in denial of a discharge in bankruptcy, Kaufman v. Hurwitz, 176 F.2d 210; and in numerous other adverse consequences. See 8 Wigmore, Evidence §2272, at 441-444, n.18 (McNaughton rev. 1961); Maguire, Evidence of Guilt §2.062 (1959). This is not to say that short of jail or torture any sanction is permissible in any case; policy and history alike may impose sharp limits. See, e.g., Griffin v. California, 380 U.S. 609. However, the Court's unspoken assumption that *any* pressure violates the privilege is not supported by the precedents and it has failed to show why the Fifth Amendment prohibits that relatively mild pressure the Due Process Clause permits.

The Court appears similarly wrong in thinking that precise knowledge of one's rights is a settled prerequisite under the Fifth Amendment to the loss of its protections. . . . No Fifth Amendment precedent is cited for the Court's contrary view. There might of course be reasons apart from the Fifth Amendment precedent for requiring warning or any other safeguard on questioning but that is a different matter entirely. . . .

A closing word must be said about the Assistance of Counsel Clause of the Sixth Amendment, which is never expressly relied on by the Court but whose judicial precedents turn out to be linchpins of the confession rules announced today. To support its requirements of a knowing and intelligent waiver, the Court cites Johnson v. Zerbst, 304 U.S. 458, . . . appointment of counsel for the indigent suspect is tied to Gideon v. Wainwright, 372 U.S. 335, and Douglas v. California, 372 U.S. 353, . . . the silent-record doctrine is borrowed from Carnley v. Cochran, 369 U.S. 506, . . . as is the right to an express offer of counsel. . . . All these cases imparting glosses to the Sixth Amendment concerned counsel at trial or on appeal. While the Court finds no pertinent difference between judicial proceedings and police interrogation, I believe the differences are so vast as to disqualify wholly the Sixth Amendment precedents as suitable analogies in the present cases.[10]

The only attempt in this Court to carry the right to counsel into the station house occurred in *Escobedo*, the Court repeating several times that that stage was no less "critical" than trial itself. See 378 U.S., 485-488. This is hardly persuasive when we consider that a grand jury inquiry, the filing of a certiorari petition, and certainly the purchase of narcotics by an undercover agent from a prospective defendant may all be equally "critical" yet provision of counsel and advice on that score have never been thought compelled by the Constitution in such cases. The sound reason why this right is so freely extended for a criminal trial is the severe injustice risked by confronting an untrained defendant with a range of technical points of law, evidence, and tactics familiar to the prosecutor but not to himself. This danger shrinks markedly in the police station where indeed the lawyer in fulfilling his professional responsibilities of necessity may become an obstacle to truthfinding. See infra, n.12. The Court's summary citation of the Sixth Amendment cases here seems to me best described as "the domino method of constitutional adjudication . . . wherein every explanatory statement in a previous opinion is made the basis for extension to a wholly different situation." Friendly, supra, n.10, at 950.

10. Since the Court conspicuously does not assert that the Sixth Amendment itself warrants its new police-interrogation rules, there is no reason now to draw out the extremely powerful historical and precedential evidence that the Amendment will bear no such meaning. See generally Friendly, The Bill of Rights as a Code of Criminal Procedure, 53 Calif. L. Rev. 929, 943-948 (1965).

III. POLICY CONSIDERATIONS

Examined as an expression of public policy, the Court's new regime proves so dubious that there can be no due compensation for its weakness in constitutional law. The foregoing discussion has shown, I think, how mistaken is the Court in implying that the Constitution has struck the balance in favor of the approach the Court takes. . . . Rather, precedent reveals that the Fourteenth Amendment in practice has been construed to strike a different balance, that the Fifth Amendment gives the Court little solid support in this context, and that the Sixth Amendment should have no bearing at all. Legal history has been stretched before to satisfy deep needs of society. In this instance, however, the Court has not and cannot make the powerful showing that its new rules are plainly desirable in the context of our society, something which is surely demanded before those rules are engrafted onto the Constitution and imposed on every State and county in the land.

Without at all subscribing to the generally black picture of police conduct painted by the Court, I think it must be frankly recognized at the outset that police questioning allowable under due process precedents may inherently entail some pressure on the suspect and may seek advantage in his ignorance or weaknesses. The atmosphere and questioning techniques, proper and fair though they be, can in themselves exert a tug on the suspect to confess, and in this light "[t]o speak of any confessions of crime made after arrest as being 'voluntary' or 'uncoerced' is somewhat inaccurate, although traditional. A confession is wholly and incontestably voluntary only if a guilty person gives himself up to the law and becomes his own accuser." Ashcraft v. Tennessee, 322 U.S. 143, 161 (Jackson, J., dissenting). Until today, the role of the Constitution has been only to sift out *undue* pressure, not to assure spontaneous confessions.

The Court's new rules aim to offset these minor pressures and disadvantages intrinsic to any kind of police interrogation. The rules do not serve due process interests in preventing blatant coercion since, as I noted earlier, they do nothing to contain the policeman who is prepared to lie from the start. The rules work for reliability in confessions almost only in the Pickwickian sense that they can prevent some from being given at all.[12] In short, the benefit of this new regime is simply to lessen or wipe

---

12. The Court's version of a lawyer "mitigat[ing] the dangers of untrustworthiness" . . . by witnessing coercion and assisting accuracy in the confession is largely a fancy; for if counsel arrives, there is rarely going to be a police station confession. Watts v. Indiana, 338 U.S. 49, 59 (separate opinion of Jackson, J.): "[A]ny lawyer worth his salt will tell the suspect in no uncertain terms to make no statement to police under any circumstances." See Enker & Elsen, Counsel for the Suspect, 49 Minn. L. Rev. 47, 66-68 (1964).

out the inherent compulsion and inequalities to which the Court devotes some nine pages of description. . . .

What the Court largely ignores is that its rules impair, if they will not eventually serve wholly to frustrate, an instrument of law enforcement that has long and quite reasonably been thought worth the price paid for it. There can be little doubt that the Court's new code would markedly decrease the number of confessions. To warn the suspect that he may remain silent and remind him that his confession may be used in court are minor obstructions. To require also an express waiver by the suspect and an end to questioning whenever he demurs must heavily handicap questioning. And to suggest or provide counsel for the suspect simply invites the end of the interrogation. . . .

While passing over the costs and risks of its experiment, the Court portrays the evils of normal police questioning in terms which I think are exaggerated. Albeit stringently confined by the due process standards interrogation is no doubt often inconvenient and unpleasant for the suspect. However, it is no less so for a man to be arrested and jailed, to have his house searched, or to stand trial in court, yet all this may properly happen to the most innocent given probable cause, a warrant, or an indictment. Society has always paid a stiff price for law and order, and peaceful interrogation is not one of the dark moments of the law.

This brief statement of the competing considerations seems to me ample proof that the Court's preference is highly debatable at best and therefore not to be read into the Constitution. However, it may make the analysis more graphic to consider the actual facts of one of the four cases reversed by the Court. Miranda v. Arizona serves best, being neither the hardest nor easiest of the four under the Court's standards.

On March 3, 1963, an 18-year-old girl was kidnapped and forcibly raped near Phoenix, Arizona. Ten days later, on the morning of March 13, petitioner Miranda was arrested and taken to the police station. At this time Miranda was 23 years old, indigent, and educated to the extent of completing half the ninth grade. He had "an emotional illness" of the schizophrenic type, according to the doctor who eventually examined him; the doctor's report also stated that Miranda was "alert and oriented as to time, place, and person," intelligent within normal limits, competent to stand trial, and sane within the legal definition. At the police station, the victim picked Miranda out of a lineup, and two officers then took him into a separate room to interrogate him, starting about 11:30 A.M. Though at first denying his guilt, within a short time Miranda gave a detailed oral confession and then wrote out in his own hand and signed a brief statement admitting and describing the crime. All this was accomplished in two hours or less without any force, threats or promises and—I will assume this though the record is uncertain, ...—without any effective warnings at all.

Miranda's oral and written confessions are now held inadmissible under the Court's new rules. One is entitled to feel astonished that the Constitution can be read to produce this result. These confessions were obtained during brief, daytime questioning conducted by two officers and unmarked by any of the traditional indicia of coercion. They assured a conviction for a brutal and unsettling crime, for which the police had and quite possibly could obtain little evidence other than the victim's identifications, evidence which is frequently unreliable. There was, in sum, a legitimate purpose, no perceptible unfairness, and certainly little risk of injustice in the interrogation. Yet the resulting confessions, and the responsible course of police practice they represent, are to be sacrificed to the Court's own finespun conception of fairness which I seriously doubt is shared by many thinking citizens in this country. . . .

. . . No state in the country has urged this Court to impose the newly announced rules, nor has any State chosen to go nearly so far on its own.

The Court in closing its general discussion invokes the practice in federal and foreign jurisdictions as lending weight to its new curbs on confessions for all the States. A brief resume will suffice to show that none of these jurisdictions has struck so one-sided a balance as the Court does today. Heaviest reliance is placed on the FBI practice. Differing circumstances may make this comparison quite untrustworthy, but in any event the FBI falls sensibly short of the Court's formalistic rules. For example, there is no indication that FBI agents must obtain an affirmative "waiver" before they pursue their questioning. Nor is it clear that one invoking his right to silence may not be prevailed upon to change his mind. And the warning as to appointed counsel apparently indicates only that one will be assigned by the judge when the suspect appears before him; the thrust of the Court's rules is to induce the suspect to obtain appointed counsel before continuing the interview. . . . Apparently American military practice, briefly mentioned by the Court, has these same limits and is still less favorable to the suspect than the FBI warning, making no mention of appointed counsel. . . .

The law of the foreign countries described by the Court also reflects a more moderate conception of the rights of the accused as against those of society when other data are considered. Concededly, the English experience is most relevant. In that country, a caution as to silence but not counsel has long been mandated by the "Judges' Rules," which also place other somewhat imprecise limits on police cross-examination of suspects. However, in the court's discretion confessions can be and apparently quite frequently are admitted in evidence despite disregard of the Judges' Rules, so long as they are found voluntary under the common-law test. Moreover, the check that exists on the use of pretrial statements is counterbalanced by the evident admissibility of fruits of an illegal confession and by the judge's often-used authority to comment adversely on the defendant's failure to testify.

India, Ceylon and Scotland are the other examples chosen by the Court. In India and Ceylon the general ban on police-adduced confessions cited by the Court is subject to a major exception: if evidence is uncovered by police questioning, it is fully admissible at trial along with the confession itself, so far as it relates to the evidence and is not blatantly coerced. . . . Scotland's limits on interrogation do measure up to the Court's; however, restrained comment at trial on the defendant's failure to take the stand is allowed the judge, and in many other respects Scotch law redresses the prosecutor's disadvantage in ways not permitted in this country. The Court ends its survey by imputing added strength to our privilege against self-incrimination since, by contrast to other countries, it is embodied in a written Constitution. Considering the liberties the Court has today taken with constitutional history and precedent, few will find this emphasis persuasive. . . .

MR. JUSTICE WHITE, with whom MR. JUSTICE HARLAN and MR. JUSTICE STEWART join, dissenting.

I

The proposition that the privilege against self-incrimination forbids in-custody interrogation without the warnings specified in the majority opinion and without a clear waiver of counsel has no significant support in the history of the privilege or in the language of the Fifth Amendment. As for the English authorities and the common-law history, the privilege, firmly established in the second half of the seventeenth century, was never applied except to prohibit compelled judicial interrogations. The rule excluding coerced confessions matured about 100 years later, "[b]ut there is nothing in the reports to suggest that the theory has its roots in the privilege against self-incrimination. And so far as the cases reveal, the privilege, as such, seems to have been given effect only in judicial proceedings, including the preliminary examinations by authorized magistrates." Morgan, The Privilege Against Self-Incrimination, 34 Minn. L. Rev. 1, 18 (1949).

Our own constitutional provision provides that no person "shall be compelled in any criminal case to be a witness against himself." These words, when "[c]onsidered in the light to be shed by grammar and the dictionary . . . appear to signify simply that nobody shall be compelled to give oral testimony against himself in a criminal proceeding under way in which he is defendant." Corwin, The Supreme Court's Construction of the Self-Incrimination Clause, 29 Mich. L. Rev. 1, 2. And there is very little in the surrounding circumstances of the adoption of the Fifth Amendment or in the provisions of the then existing state constitutions or in state practice which would give the constitutional provision any broader meaning. Mayers, The Federal Witness' Privilege Against Self-Incrimination: Constitutional or Common-Law? 4 American Journal of Legal History 107 (1960). Such a construction, however, was considerably narrower than the privilege at common law, and when eventually faced with the issues, the Court extended the constitutional privilege to the compulsory production of books and papers, to the ordinary witness before the grand jury and to witnesses generally. Boyd v. United States, 116 U.S. 616, and Counselman v. Hitchcock, 142 U.S. 547. Both rules had solid support in common-law history, if not in the history of our own constitutional provision.

A few years later the Fifth Amendment privilege was similarly extended to encompass the then well-established rule against coerced confessions:

> In criminal trials, in the courts of the United States, wherever a question arises whether a confession is incompetent because not voluntary, the issue is controlled by that portion of the Fifth Amendment to the Constitution of the United States, commanding that no person "shall be compelled in any criminal case to be a witness against himself." [Bram v. United States, 168 U.S. 532, 542.]

Bram, however, itself rejected the proposition which the Court now espouses. The question in *Bram* was whether a confession, obtained during custodial interrogation, had been compelled, and if such interrogation was to be deemed inherently vulnerable the Court's inquiry could have ended there. After examining the English and American authorities, however, the Court declared that:

> In this court also it has been settled that the mere fact that the confession is made to a police officer, while the accused was under arrest in or out of prison, or was drawn out by his questions, does not necessarily render the confession involuntary, but, as one of the circumstances, such imprisonment or interrogation may be taken into account in determining whether or not the statements of the prisoner were voluntary. [168 U.S., at 558.]

In this respect the Court was wholly consistent with prior and subsequent pronouncements in this Court. . . .

Only a tiny minority of our judges who have dealt with the question, including today's majority, have considered in-custody interrogation, without more, to be a violation of the Fifth Amendment. And this Court, as every member knows, has left standing literally thousands of criminal convictions that rested at least in part on confessions taken in the course of interrogation by the police after arrest.

II

That the Court's holding today is neither compelled nor even strongly suggested by the language of the Fifth Amendment, is at odds with American and English legal history, and involves a departure from a long line of precedent does not prove either that the Court has exceeded its powers or that the Court is wrong or unwise in its present reinterpretation of the Fifth Amendment. It does, however, underscore the obvious— that the Court has not discovered or found the law in making today's decision, nor has it derived it from some irrefutable sources; what it has done is to make new law and new public policy in much the same way that is has in the course of interpreting other great clauses of the Constitution. This is what the Court historically has done. Indeed, it is what it must do and will continue to do until and unless there is some fundamental change in the constitutional distribution of governmental powers.

But if the Court is here and now to announce new and fundamental policy to govern certain aspects of our affairs, it is wholly legitimate to examine the mode of this or any other constitutional decision in this Court and to inquire into the advisability of its end product in terms of the long-range interest of the country. At the very least the Court's text and reasoning should withstand analysis and be a fair exposition of the constitutional provision which its opinion interprets. Decisions like these cannot rest alone on syllogism, metaphysics, or some ill-defined notions of natural justice, although each will perhaps play its part. In proceeding to such constructions as it now announces, the Court should also duly consider all the factors and interests bearing upon the cases, at least insofar as the relevant materials are available; and if the necessary considerations are not treated in the record or obtainable from some other reliable source, the Court should not proceed to formulate fundamental policies based on speculation alone.

III

First, we may inquire what are the textural and factual bases of this new fundamental rule. To reach the result announced on the grounds it does, the Court must stay within the confines of the Fifth Amendment, which forbids self-incrimination only if *compelled*. Hence the core of the Court's opinion is that because of the "compulsion inherent in custodial surroundings, no statement obtained from [a] defendant [in custody] can truly be the product of his free choice," . . . absent the use of adequate protective devices as described by the Court. However, the Court does not point to any sudden inrush of new knowledge requiring the rejection of 70 years' experience. Nor does it assert that its novel conclusion reflects a changing consensus among state courts, see Mapp v. Ohio, 367 U.S. 643, or that a succession of cases had steadily eroded the old rule and proved it unworkable, see Gideon v. Wainwright, 372 U.S. 335. Rather than asserting new knowledge, the Court concedes that it cannot truly know what occurs during custodial questioning, because of the innate secrecy of such proceedings. It extrapolates a picture of what it conceives to be the norm from police investigatorial manuals, published in 1959 and 1962 or earlier, without any attempt to allow for adjustments in police practices that may have occurred in the wake of more recent decisions of state appellate tribunals or this Court. But even if the relentless application of the described procedures could lead to involuntary confessions, it most assuredly does not follow that each and every case will disclose this kind of interrogation or this kind of consequence.[2] Insofar as appears from the Court's opinion, it has not examined a single transcript of any police interrogation, let alone the interrogation that took place in any one of these cases which it decides today. Judged by any of the standards for empirical investigation utilized in the social sciences the factual basis for the Court's premise is patently inadequate.

Although in the Court's view in-custody interrogation is inherently coercive, the Court says that the spontaneous product of the coercion of arrest and detention is still to be deemed voluntary. An accused, arrested on probable cause, may blurt out a confession which will be admissible

---

2. In fact, the type of sustained interrogation described by the Court appears to be the exception rather than the rule. A survey of 399 cases in one city found that in almost half of the cases the interrogation lasted less than 30 minutes. Barrett, Police Practices and the Law—From Arrest to Release or Charge, 50 Calif. L. Rev. 11, 41-45 (1962). Questioning tends to be confused and sporadic and is usually concentrated on confrontations with witnesses or new items of evidence, as these are obtained by officers conducting the investigation. See generally LaFave, Arrest: The Decision to Take a Suspect into Custody 386 (1965); ALI, A Model Code of Pre-Arraignment Procedure, Commentary §5.01, at 170, n.4 (Tent. Draft No. 1, 1966).

despite the fact that he is alone and in custody, without any showing that he had any notion of his right to remain silent or of the consequences of his admission. Yet, under the Court's rule, if the police ask him a single question such as "Do you have anything to say?" or "Did you kill your wife?" his response, if there is one, has somehow been compelled, even if the accused has been clearly warned of his right to remain silent. Common sense informs us to the contrary. While one may say that the response was "involuntary" in the sense the question provoked or was the occasion for the response and thus the defendant was induced to speak out when he might have remained silent if not arrested and not questioned, it is patently unsound to say the response is compelled.

Today's result would not follow even if it were agreed that to some extent custodial interrogation is inherently coercive. . . . The test has been whether the totality of circumstances deprived the defendant of a "free choice to admit, to deny, or to refuse to answer," Lisenba v. California, 314 U.S. 219, 241, and whether physical or psychological coercion was of such a degree that "the defendant's will was overborne at the time he confessed," Haynes v. Washington, 373 U.S. 503, 513; Lynumn v. Illinois, 372 U.S. 528, 534. The duration and nature of incommunicado custody, the presence or absence of advice concerning the defendant's constitutional rights, and the granting or refusal of requests to communicate with lawyers, relatives or friends have all been rightly regarded as important data bearing on the basic inquiry. . . . But it has never been suggested, until today, that such questioning was so coercive and accused persons so lacking in hardihood that the very first response to the very first question following the commencement of custody must be conclusively presumed to be the product of an overborne will.

If the rule announced today were truly based on a conclusion that all confessions resulting from custodial interrogation are coerced, then it would simply have no rational foundation. . . . Even if one were to postulate that the Court's concern is not that all confessions induced by police interrogation are coerced but rather that some such confessions are coerced and present judicial procedures are believed to be inadequate to identify the confessions that are coerced and those that are not, it would still not be essential to impose the rule that the Court has now fashioned. Transcripts or observers could be required, specific time limits, tailored to fit the cause, could be imposed, or other devices could be utilized to reduce the chances that otherwise indiscernible coercion will produce an inadmissible confession.

On the other hand, even if one assumed that there was an adequate factual basis for the conclusion that all confessions obtained during in-custody interrogation are the product of compulsion, the rule propounded by the Court would still be irrational, for, apparently, it is only if the accused is also warned of his right to counsel and waives both that right and the right against self-incrimination that the inherent compulsiveness of interrogation disappears. But if the defendant may not answer without a warning a question such as "Where were you last night?" without having his answer be a compelled one, how can the Court ever accept his negative answer to the question of whether he wants to consult his retained counsel or counsel whom the court will appoint? And why if counsel is present and the accused nevertheless confesses, or counsel tells the accused to tell the truth, and that is what the accused does, is the situation any less coercive insofar as the accused is concerned? The Court apparently realizes its dilemma of foreclosing questioning without the necessary warnings but at the same time permitting the accused, sitting in the same chair in front of the same policemen, to waive his right to consult an attorney. It expects, however, that the accused will not often waive the right; and if it is claimed that he has, the State faces a severe, if not impossible burden of proof.

All of this makes very little sense in terms of the compulsion which the Fifth Amendment proscribes. That amendment deals with compelling the accused himself. It is his free will that is involved. Confessions and incriminating admissions, as such, are not forbidden evidence; only those which are compelled are banned. I doubt that the court observes these distinctions today. By considering any answers to any interrogation to be compelled regardless of the content and course of examination and by escalating the requirements to prove waiver, the Court not only prevents the use of compelled confessions but for all practical purposes forbids interrogation except in the presence of counsel. That is, instead of confining itself to protection of the right against compelled self-incrimination the Court has created a limited Fifth Amendment right to counsel—or, as the Court expresses it, a "need for counsel to protect the Fifth Amendment privilege. . . ." The focus then is not on the will of the accused but on the will of counsel and how much influence he can have on the accused. Obviously there is no warrant in the Fifth Amendment for thus installing counsel as the arbiter of the privilege.

In sum, for all the Court's expounding on the menacing atmosphere of police interrogation procedures, it has failed to supply any foundation for the conclusions it draws or the measures it adopts.

IV . . .

The obvious underpinning of the Court's decision is a deep-seated distrust of all confessions. As the Court declares that the accused may not be interrogated without counsel present, absent a waiver of the right to counsel, and as the Court all but admonishes the lawyer to advise the accused to remain silent, the result adds up to a judicial judgment that evidence from the accused should not be used against him in any way, whether compelled or not. This is the not so subtle overtone of the opinion—that it is inherently wrong for the police to gather evidence from the accused himself. And this is precisely the nub of this dissent. I see nothing wrong or immoral, and certainly nothing unconstitutional, in the police's asking a suspect whom they have reasonable cause to arrest whether or not he killed his wife or in confronting him with the evidence on which the arrest was based, at least where he has been plainly advised that he may remain completely silent. . . . Until today, "the admissions or confessions of the prisoner, when voluntarily and freely made, have always ranked high in the scale of incriminating evidence." Brown v. Walker, 161 U.S. 591, 596; see also Hopt v. Utah, 110 U.S. 574, 584-585. Particularly when corroborated, as where the police have confirmed the accused's disclosure of the hiding place of implements or fruits of the crime, such confessions have the highest reliability and significantly contribute to the certitude with which we may believe the accused is guilty. Moreover, it is by no means certain that the process of confessing is injurious to the accused. To the contrary it may provide psychological relief and enhance the prospects for rehabilitation.

This is not to say that the value of respect for the inviolability of the accused's individual personality should be accorded no weight or that all confessions should be indiscriminately admitted. This Court has long read the Constitution to proscribe compelled confessions, a salutary rule from which there should be no retreat. But I see no sound basis, factual or otherwise, and the Court gives none, for concluding that the present rule against the receipt of coerced confessions is inadequate for the task of sorting out inadmissible evidence and must be replaced by the per se rule which is now imposed. Even if the new concept can be said to have advantages of some sort over the present law, they are far outweighed by its likely undesirable impact on other very relevant and important interests.

The most basic function of any government is to provide for the security of the individual and of his property. Lanzetta v. New Jersey, 306 U.S. 451, 455. These ends of society are served by the criminal laws which for the most part are aimed at the prevention of crime. Without the reasonably effective performance of the task of preventing private violence and retaliation, it is idle to talk about human dignity and civilized values. . . .

The rule announced today will measurably weaken the ability of the criminal law to perform these tasks. It is a deliberate calculus to prevent interrogations, to reduce the incidence of confessions and pleas of guilty and to increase the number of trials. Criminal trials, no matter how efficient the police are, are not sure bets for the prosecution, nor should they be if the evidence is not forthcoming. Under the present law, the prosecution fails to prove its case in about 30% of the criminal cases actually tried in the federal courts. . . . . But it is something else again to remove from the ordinary criminal case all those confessions which heretofore have been held to be free and voluntary acts of the accused and to thus establish a new constitutional barrier to the ascertainment of truth by the judicial process. There is, in my view, every reason to believe that a good many criminal defendants who otherwise would have been convicted on what this Court has previously thought to be the most satisfactory kind of evidence will now, under this new version of the Fifth Amendment, either not be tried at all or will be acquitted if the State's evidence, minus the confession, is put to the test of litigation.

I have no desire whatsoever to share the responsibility for any such impact on the present criminal process.

In some unknown number of cases the Court's rule will return a killer, a rapist or other criminal to the streets and to the environment which produced him to repeat his crime whenever it pleases him. As a consequence, there will not be a gain, but a loss, in human dignity. The real concern is not the unfortunate consequences of this new decision on the criminal law as an abstract, disembodied series of authoritative proscriptions, but the impact on those who rely on the public authority for protection and who without it can only engage in violent self-help with guns, knives and the help of their neighbors similarly inclined. There is, of course, a saving factor: the next victims are uncertain, unnamed and unrepresented in this case.

Nor can this decision do other than have a corrosive effect on the criminal law as an effective device to prevent crime. A major component in its effectiveness in this regard is its swift and sure enforcement. The easier it is to get away with rape and murder, the less the deterrent effect on those who are inclined to attempt it. This is still good common sense. If it were not, we should posthaste liquidate the whole law enforcement establishment as a useless, misguided effort to control human conduct.

And what about the accused who has confessed or would confess in response to simple, noncoercive questioning and whose guilt could not otherwise be proved? Is it so clear that release is the best thing for him in every case? Has it so unquestionably been resolved that in each and every case it would be better for him not to confess and to return to his environment with no attempt whatsoever to help him? I think not. It may well be that in many cases it will be no less than a callous disregard for his own welfare as well as for the interests of his next victim. . . .

Much of the trouble with the Court's new rule is that it will operate indiscriminately in all criminal cases, regardless of the severity of the crime or the circumstances involved. It applies to every defendant, whether the professional criminal or one committing a crime of momentary passion who is not part and parcel of organized crime. It will slow down the investigation and the apprehension of confederates in those cases where time is of the essence, . . . and some of those involving organized crime. In the latter context the lawyer who arrives may also be the lawyer for the defendant's colleagues and can be relied upon to insure that no breach of the organization's security takes place even though the accused may feel that the best thing he can do is to cooperate.

At the same time, the Court's per se approach may not be justified on the ground that it provides a "bright line" permitting the authorities to judge in advance whether interrogation may safely be pursued without jeopardizing the admissibility of any information obtained as a consequence. Nor can it be claimed that judicial time and effort, assuming that is a relevant consideration, will be conserved because of the ease of application of the new rule. Today's decision leaves open such questions as whether the accused was in custody, whether his statements were spontaneous or the product of interrogation, whether the accused has effectively waived his rights, and whether nontestimonial evidence introduced at trial is the fruit of statements made during a prohibited interrogation, all of which are certain to prove productive of uncertainty during investigation and litigation during prosecution. For all these reasons, if further restrictions on police interrogation are desirable at this time, a more flexible approach makes much more sense than the Court's constitutional straitjacket which forecloses more discriminating treatment by legislative or rule-making pronouncements.

Applying the traditional standards to the cases before the Court, I would hold these confessions voluntary. . . .

NOTES AND QUESTIONS

1. Compare *Bram* and *Miranda*. Which, in your view is "better" and why? Which is more realistic? Which better relates the remedy provided to the wrong done? Which provides more serious protections for the accused? In this regard, consider the contemporary role of plea bargaining in which the accused and the State negotiate a plea where the accused "trades" his procedural protections for sentencing or charging concessions by the State. The normal outcome is a plea of guilty that is generally tantamount to a legally binding confession. The Supreme Court has legitimized this practice, Brady v. United States, 397 U.S. 742 (1970), but how would it have fared under *Bram?* How *should* it fare today?

2. The Court in *Miranda* relies heavily on various interrogation manuals that the Court apparently thought were of great relevance to the cases before it. Review the facts in the four cases before the Court. Were any of the "abuses" of the interrogation process that the Court used the manuals to document present in these cases? If not, what is the relevance of the manuals? One answer, as previously suggested, may be that the Court did not trust the "facts" as found by the state courts in this type of case generally. Indeed, one reason for the broad, prophylactic rule approach of *Miranda* could be precisely a distrust of the state factfinding process, a problem exacerbated by the open-texturedness of the voluntariness standard. For discussions of this, see Amsterdam, The Supreme Court and the Rights of Suspects in Criminal Cases, 45 N.Y.U. L. Rev. 785 (1970); Stone, The *Miranda* Doctrine in the Burger Court, 1977 Sup. Ct. Rev. 99, 102.

3. The Court suggests that the standards it is imposing on the states is not that burdensome as is proven by the fact that the FBI and other countries—in particular England—have labored successfully under similar restrictions for years. But how cogent are the Court's analogies? How do you think the normal business of the FBI compares to that of the police? What other differences, or similarities, are there between the police and the FBI?

Reconsider the Court's description of the English practice. Unfortunately, it appears to be either in error or misleading. Consider the following excerpt from the Royal Commission on Criminal Procedure, The Investigation and Prosecution of Criminal Offenses in England and Wales: The Law and Procedure (1981).

> 68. It has always been an essential part of the criminal justice system that there was some official body or person to inquire into offenses. At one time it was the jury; by 1700 the function had passed to the justices of the peace, and by the early part of the nineteenth century the de facto power was in the hands of the police. This inquiry involved questioning people who might have knowledge of the offence, one or more of whom might well turn out to be a suspect. The questioning of suspects by the police included those who had been arrested and were being kept in custody. Although a person cannot be arrested merely for the purpose of questioning, the police may question someone who has been lawfully arrested and is in police custody. This power has never been statutorily stated, though judicial guidance has been given in decided cases and in the Judges' Rules and Administrative Directions to the Police. . . .
>
> 70. The present Rules (which are prefaced by an important note stating certain principles not affected by the Rules) were issued to the police in 1964 following a review of the earlier Rules by the judges. Appended to them is a set of Administrative Directions to the Police, drawn up by

the Home Office and approved by the judges. . . . . The general effect of the Rules may be summarized as follows. A police officer may question a suspect whether in custody or not (Rule I). He need not caution the suspect unless and until he has enough evidence to suspect that he has committed an offence (Rule II). In Rule II the word "evidence" means information of a nature that would be admissible as evidence in court. . . . The suspect is not required to answer questions put to him by the police. As Lord Parker, C.J. said in Rice v. Connolly,[2] ". . . the whole basis of the common law is the right of the individual to refuse to answer questions put to him by persons in authority. . . ." Accordingly, the caution should have a number of effects. In addition to advising him of his "right of silence" it informs the suspect that he may be in peril of prosecution; and it tends to help in showing the voluntariness of any statement subsequently made. But the Rules place no limit on the questions which may be put to a suspect before charge. And neither the Rules nor any common law principle require that if the suspect indicates that he wishes to remain silent no more questions may be asked. Further, evidence of the questions posed and the fact that the suspect did not answer, or gave an evasive answer, is admissible (see paragraph 81).

71. As soon as a police officer has enough evidence to charge the suspect (that is, enough to establish a prima facie case)[3] he should cause him to be charged without delay and thereafter may not question him about the offence charged (paragraph (d) of the Introduction to the Judges' Rules and Rule III). When a person is charged, or informed that he may be prosecuted, he is again cautioned. The caution is similar to that quoted in paragraph 69 except that the suspect is told that anything he says will (as distinct from may) be taken down in writing (Rule III(a)). . . .

81. Evidence may be given of questions put to the accused by a police officer and the accused's response thereto. The response (in addition to a straightforward answer) may be a statement to the effect "I am not prepared to comment" or it may be silence, that is, no answer at all. Where the accused exercises his right of silence in this way, it is not the law that no adverse inference may be drawn. It is clearly the law that the mere exercise of the right of silence is not *of itself* evidence of guilt; but it is equally clearly the law that the fact of the exercise of the right is admissible evidence and forms a part of the whole of the case, and it becomes part of the fact which the jury or magistrates have to consider. [Id. at 24-26, 30.]

Moreover, breach of the Rules does not necessarily result in exclusion of any inculpating statements obtained. Statements are excluded only if found to be involuntary. Id. at 26-27. Indeed, the Royal Commission has recommended that the limited exclusionary rule be maintained. For

2. [1966] 2 Q.B. 414.
3. This is a higher standard than enough information to found a reasonable suspicion, see Lord Devlin in Hussein v. Chong Fook Kam (1970) A.C. 942.

a discussion, see Inman, The Admissibility of Confessions, 1981 Crim. L. Rev. 469.

For an exhaustive comparison of the English and American approaches to police interrogation, see Van Kessel, The Suspect as a Source of Testimonial Evidence: A Comparison of the English and American Approaches, 38 Hast. L.J. 1 (1986).

4. Does suppressing a confession obtained in violation of the dictates of the majority opinion in *Miranda* adequately accommodate the competing considerations, or does the Court focus too much on the plight of the accused and not enough on the demands of law enforcement? Consider Justice Jackson's separate opinion in Watts v. Indiana. In *Watts*, and two companion cases, the Court concluded that certain statements were involuntarily given, and thus violative of the fifth amendment. Justice Jackson concurred in one case but dissented in the other two:

WATTS v. INDIANA, 338 U.S. 49, 57-62 (1949): These three cases, from widely separated states, present essentially the same problem. Its recurrence suggests that it has roots in some condition fundamental and general to our criminal system.

In each case police were confronted with one or more brutal murders which the authorities were under the highest duty to solve. Each of these murders was unwitnessed, and the only positive knowledge on which a solution could be based was possessed by the killer. In each there was reasonable ground to *suspect* an individual but not enough legal evidence to *charge* him with guilt. In each the police attempted to meet the situation by taking the suspect into custody and interrogating him. This extended over varying periods. In each, confessions were made and received in evidence at the trial. Checked with external evidence, they are inherently believable, and were not shaken as to truth by anything that occurred at the trial. Each confessor was convicted by a jury and state courts affirmed. This Court sets all three convictions aside.

The seriousness of the Court's judgment is that no one suggests that any course held promise of solution of these murders other than to take the suspect into custody for questioning. The alternative was to close the books on the crime and forget it, with the suspect at large. This is a grave choice for a society in which two-thirds of the murders already are closed out as insoluble. . . .

Others would strike down these confessions because of conditions which they say make them "involuntary." In this, on only a printed record, they pit their judgment against that of the trial judge and the jury. Both, with the great advantage of hearing and seeing the confessor and also the officers whose conduct and bearing toward him is in question, have found that the confessions were voluntary. In addition, the majority overrule in each case one or more state appellate courts, which have the same limited opportunity to know the truth that we do.

Amid much that is irrelevant or trivial, one serious situation seems to me to stand out in these cases. The suspect neither had nor was advised of his right to get counsel. This presents a real dilemma in a free society. To subject one without counsel to questioning which may and is intended to convict him, is a real peril to individual freedom. To bring in a lawyer means a real peril to solution of the crime, because, under our adversary system, he deems that his sole duty is to protect his client—guilty or innocent—and that in such a capacity he owes no duty whatever to help society solve its crime problem. Under this conception of criminal procedure, any lawyer worth his salt will tell the suspect in no uncertain terms to make no statement to police under any circumstances.

If the State may arrest on suspicion and interrogate without counsel, there is no denying the fact that it largely negates the benefits of the constitutional guaranty of the right to assistance of counsel. Any lawyer who has ever been called into a case after his client has "told all" and turned any evidence he has over to the Government, knows how helpless he is to protect his client against the facts thus disclosed.

I suppose the view one takes will turn on what one thinks should be the right of an accused person against the State. Is it his right to have the judgment on the facts? Or is it his right to have a judgment based on only such evidence as he cannot conceal from the authorities, who cannot compel him to testify in court and also cannot question him before? Our system comes close to the latter by any interpretation, for the defendant is shielded by such safeguards as no system of law except the Anglo-American concedes to him.

Of course, no confession that has been obtained by any form of physical violence to the person is reliable and hence no conviction should rest upon one obtained in that manner. Such treatment not only breaks the will to conceal or lie, but may even break the will to stand by the truth. Nor is it questioned that the same result can sometimes be achieved by threats, promises, or inducements, which torture the mind but put no scar on the body. If the opinion of Mr. Justice Frankfurter in the *Watts* case were based solely on the State's admissions as to the treatment of *Watts*, I should not disagree. But if ultimate quest in a criminal trial is the truth and if the circumstances indicate no violence or threats of it, should society be deprived of the suspect's help in solving a crime merely because he was confined and questioned when uncounseled?

We must not overlook that, in these as in some previous cases, once a confession is obtained it supplies ways of verifying its trustworthiness. In these cases before us the verification is sufficient to leave me in no doubt that the admissions of guilt were genuine and truthful. Such corroboration consists in one case of finding a weapon where the accused has said he hid it, and in others that conditions which could only have been known to one who was implicated correspond with his story. It is possible, but it is rare, that a confession, if repudiated on the trial, standing alone will convict unless there is external proof of its verity.

In all such cases, along with other conditions criticized, the continuity and duration of the questioning is invoked and it is called an "inquiry," "inquest" or "inquisition," depending mainly on the emotional state of the writer. But as in some of the cases here, if interrogation is permissible at all, there are sound reasons for prolonging it—which the opinions here ignore. The suspect at first perhaps makes an effort to exculpate himself by alibis or other statements. These are verified, found false, and he is then confronted with his falsehood. Sometimes (though such cases do not reach us) verification proves them true or credible and the suspect is released. Sometimes, as here, more than one crime is involved. The duration of an interrogation may well depend on the temperament, shrewdness and cunning of the accused and the competence of the examiner. But, assuming a right to examine at all, the right must include what is made reasonably necessary by the facts of the particular case.

If the right of interrogation be admitted, then it seems to me that we must leave it to trial judges and juries and state appellate courts to decide individual cases, unless they show some want of proper standards of decision. I find nothing to indicate that any of the courts below in these cases did not have a correct understanding of the Fourteenth Amendment, unless this Court thinks it means absolute prohibition of interrogation while in custody before arraignment.

I suppose no one would doubt that our Constitution and Bill of Rights, grounded in revolt against the arbitrary measures of George III and in the philosophy of the French Revolution, represent the maximum restrictions upon the power of organized society over the individual that are compatible with the maintenance of organized society itself. They were so intended and should be so interpreted. It cannot be denied that, even if construed as these provisions traditionally have been, they contain an aggregate of restrictions which seriously limit the power of society to solve such crimes as confront us in these cases. Those restrictions we should not for that reason cast aside, but that is good reason for indulging in no unnecessary expansion of them.

I doubt very much if they require us to hold that the State may not take into custody and question one suspected reasonably of an unwitnessed murder. If it does, the people of this country must discipline themselves to seeing their police stand by helplessly while those suspected of murder prowl about unmolested. Is it a necessary price to pay for the fairness which we know as "due process of law"? And if not a necessary one, should it be demanded by this Court? I do not know the ultimate answer to these questions; but, for the present, I should not increase the handicap on society.

---

5. Is there a middle ground between the dictates of *Miranda* and the awkwardness of the voluntariness test to judge the admissibility of confessions obtained through pre-trial interrogation? Note that in *Miranda* the Court said that equally effective procedures to ensure the fifth amendment's protections could supplement the Court's requirements. Yet before "equally effective" procedures can be provided, one must know the answer to the question "equally effective" as to what? Consider once again the fact that the answer to that question cannot be to protect the unfettered exercise of the suspect's "free will." Every time a person provides incriminating statements, there is a reason for giving the statement acting on the "will." To be sure, some distinctions can be made. There are, for example, a number of reasons we do not countenance the use of serious physical abuse to induce statements, but does it follow from that proposition that no incentive to speak should be brought to bear on the suspect by the state? If you think it does not follow, again you must construct what does. In that regard, consider the following short excerpt from a remarkable article written over half a century ago by Professor Kauper. Bear in mind that Professor Kauper was writing prior to the "procedural revolution" and also that his focus was a means to eliminate brutal police practices. Nonetheless, consider whether his proposal has any relevance to contemporary society.

KAUPER, JUDICIAL EXAMINATION OF THE ACCUSED—A REMEDY FOR THE THIRD DEGREE, 30 MICH. L. REV. 1224, 1239-1241 (1932): The remedy proposed consists of two essentials:

(1) That the accused be promptly produced before a magistrate for interrogation; and,
(2) That the interrogation be supported by the threat that refusal to answer questions of the magistrate will be used against the accused at the trial.

It is submitted that the two features of the proposed plan must be linked together. The magistrate must have power to interrogate the prisoner. The present system which allows the accused an opportunity to make a statement but denies the magistrate power to ask questions is not effective for the purpose of securing information. And the power to interrogate must be supported by some compulsion to answer questions; otherwise it will be rendered impotent. Neither is the compulsion afforded by the right to comment on *failure to testify at the trial* sufficient. The comment must be upon the prisoner's *refusal to answer questions at the interrogation*. It is true that some writers have asserted that the problem of the police third degree would be solved if the judge and prosecutor were given the right to comment on the prisoner's failure to testify at his trial. But analysis of that proposition makes the conclusion appear to be a non sequitur. The possibility that at the trial an inference of guilt may be drawn from the accused's silence is hardly equivalent in the eyes of the police to a confession or other valuable information obtained shortly after arrest. In other words, making criminal procedure at the trial more effective against the accused does not satisfy police motives that demand interrogation immediately upon arrest. . . .

The plan proposed of requiring prompt interrogation by a magistrate supported by the threat of comment on failure to answer carries considerable promise. The plan necessarily involves prompt production of the accused before a magistrate. This is a sine qua non in the mitigation of third degree abuses, for so long as prisoners are in the control of officers there is a temptation to resort to third degree practices.

The plan provides an *immediate* opportunity for questioning the accused while the pursuit is still hot and the clues are yet fresh. By warning the accused that the whole record of the interrogation will go to the trial court, so that his silence in refusing to answer questions or make explanations will be used with telling effect against him before the jury, a strong psychic pressure will induce him to break his silence. Nor should it be forgotten that the larger number of those who are arrested are willing to speak and answer questions.[82] Even the fact of a false statement made by a prisoner after arrest in order to cover his guilt can be used against him at the trial often with as much effectiveness as a truthful incriminating statement. Questioned immediately upon arrest, the accused does not have time to work out a coherent fabricated story or defense alibi. From the viewpoint of police psychology it appears that inauguration of a scheme of magisterial interrogation will greatly weaken the police motive for private interrogation since that motive will find vicarious expression in a substituted device. Viewing the problem his-

---

82. "In Washtenaw County, Michigan, of the 312 judgments of the county court in criminal cases in one year, 305 were on pleas of guilty. The prosecuting attorney's explanation of his success in obtaining so many confessions of guilt was his practice of himself interviewing every person arrested on a felony charge immediately after the arrest while he was still excited and before he had opportunity to consult with a lawyer. In that way, the prosecutor said, he got the truth. None of the confessions were repudiated in court nor did any of the 305 defendants make allegations of mistreatment. If all be as it appears, that prompt interrogation produced justice." 30 Mich. L. Rev. 54 at 59 (1931).

torically, Dean Pound ascribes the extra-legal development of the "unhappy system of police examination" in the United States to the sloughing off by justices of the peace of their police powers, including examination of the accused, thereby leaving "a gap which in practice had to be filled outside of the law."[83] The proposed plan would fill the gap which resulted from the differentiation in function between magistrate and police with the effect of forcing the police to adopt the system of extra-legal interrogation. It would vest the power of interrogation in officers who are better qualified to exercise the power of interrogation fairly and effectively. . . .

2. The Scope of Miranda

a. What Is "Interrogation"?

RHODE ISLAND v. INNIS
Certiorari to the Rhode Island Supreme Court
446 U.S. 291 (1980)   dissented   MIRANDA
in

MR. JUSTICE STEWART delivered the opinion of the Court. . . .

I

On the night of January 12, 1975, John Mulvaney, a Providence, R.I., taxicab driver, disappeared after being dispatched to pick up a customer. His body was discovered four days later buried in a shallow grave in Coventry, R.I. He had died from a shotgun blast aimed at the back of his head.

On January 17, 1975, shortly after midnight, the Providence police received a telephone call from Gerald Aubin, also a taxicab driver, who reported that he had just been robbed by a man wielding a sawed-off shotgun. Aubin further reported that he had dropped off his assailant near Rhode Island College in a section of Providence known as Mount Pleasant. While at the Providence police station waiting to give a statement, Aubin noticed a picture of his assailant on a bulletin board. Aubin so informed one of the police officers present. The officer prepared a photo array, and again Aubin identified a picture of the same person.

83. Criminal Justice in America 88 (1930). See also Wickersham Comm. Rep. No. 8, pp. 9, 10 (1930).

That person was the respondent. Shortly thereafter, the Providence police began a search of the Mount Pleasant area.

At approximately 4:30 A.M. on the same date, Patrolman Lovell, while cruising the streets of Mount Pleasant in a patrol car, spotted the respondent standing in the street facing him. When Patrolman Lovell stopped his car, the respondent walked towards it. Patrolman Lovell then arrested the respondent, who was unarmed, and advised him of his so-called *Miranda* rights. While the two men waited in the patrol car for other police officers to arrive, Patrolman Lovell did not converse with the respondent other than to respond to the latter's request for a cigarette.

Within minutes, Sergeant Sears arrived at the scene of the arrest, and he also gave the respondent the *Miranda* warnings. Immediately thereafter, Captain Leyden and other police officers arrived. Captain Leyden advised the respondent of his *Miranda* rights. The respondent stated that he understood those rights and wanted to speak with a lawyer. Captain Leyden then directed that the respondent be placed in a "caged wagon," a four-door police car with a wire screen mesh between the front and rear seats, and be driven to the central police station. Three officers, Patrolmen Gleckman, Williams, and McKenna, were assigned to accompany the respondent to the central station. They placed the respondent in the vehicle and shut the doors. Captain Leyden then instructed the officers not to question the respondent or intimidate or coerce him in any way. The three officers then entered the vehicle, and it departed.

While en route to the central station, Patrolman Gleckman initiated a conversation with Patrolman McKenna concerning the missing shotgun.[1] As Patrolman Gleckman later testified:

> A. At this point, I was talking back and forth with Patrolman McKenna stating that I frequent this area while on patrol and [that because a school for handicapped children is located nearby,] there's a lot of handicapped children running around in this area, and God forbid one of them might find a weapon with shells and they might hurt themselves.

Patrolman McKenna apparently shared his fellow officer's concern:

> A. I more or less concurred with him [Gleckman] that it was a safety factor and that we should, you know, continue to search for the weapon and try to find it.

While Patrolman Williams said nothing, he overheard the conversation between the two officers:

---

1. Although there was conflicting testimony about the exact seating arrangements, it is clear that everyone in the vehicle heard the conversation.

A. He [Gleckman] said it would be too bad if the little—I believe he said a girl—would pick up the gun, maybe kill herself.

The respondent then interrupted the conversation, stating that the officers should turn the car around so he could show them where the gun was located. At this point, Patrolman McKenna radioed back to Captain Leyden that they were returning to the scene of the arrest, and that the respondent would inform them of the location of the gun. At the time the respondent indicated that the officers should turn back, they had traveled no more than a mile, a trip encompassing only a few minutes.

The police vehicle then returned to the scene of the arrest where a search for the shotgun was in progress. There, Captain Leyden again advised the respondent of his *Miranda* rights. The respondent replied that he understood those rights but that he "wanted to get the gun out of the way because of the kids in the area in the school." The respondent then led the police to a nearby field, where he pointed out the shotgun under some rocks by the side of the road. . . .

We granted certiorari to address for the first time the meaning of "interrogation" under Miranda v. Arizona.

II . . .

A

The starting point for defining "interrogation" in this context is, of course, the Court's *Miranda* opinion. There the Court observed that "[b]y custodial interrogation, we mean *questioning* initiated by law enforcement officers after a person has been taken into custody or otherwise deprived of his freedom of action in any significant way." Id., at 444 (emphasis added). This passage and other references throughout the opinion to "questioning" might suggest that the *Miranda* rules were to apply only to those police interrogation practices that involve express questioning of a defendant while in custody.

We do not, however, construe the *Miranda* opinion so narrowly. The concern of the Court in *Miranda* was that the "interrogation environment" created by the interplay of interrogation and custody would "subjugate the individual to the will of his examiner" and thereby undermine the privilege against compulsory self-incrimination. Id., at 457-458. The police practices that evoked this concern included several that did not involve express questioning. For example, one of the practices discussed in *Miranda* was the use of lineups in which a coached witness would pick the defendant as the perpetrator. This was designed to establish that the defendant was in fact guilty as a predicate for further interrogation. Id., at 453. A variation on this theme discussed in *Miranda* was the so-called "reverse line-up" in which a defendant would be identified by coached witnesses as the perpetrator of a fictitious crime, with the object of inducing him to confess to the actual crime of which he was suspected in order to escape the false prosecution. Ibid. The Court in *Miranda* also included in its survey of interrogation practices the use of psycho- logical ploys, such as to "posi[t]" "the guilt of the subject," to "minimize the moral seriousness of the offense," and "to cast blame on the victim or on society." Id., at 450. It is clear that these techniques of persuasion, no less than express questioning, were thought, in a custodial setting,·to amount to interrogation.[3]

This is not to say, however, that all statements obtained by the police after a person has been taken into custody are to be considered the product of interrogation. As the Court in *Miranda* noted:

> Confessions remain a proper element in law enforcement. Any statement given freely and voluntarily without any compelling influences is, of course, admissible in evidence. *The fundamental import of the privilege while an individual is in custody is not whether he is allowed to talk to the police without the benefit of warnings and counsel, but whether he can be inter- rogated.* . . . Volunteered statements of any kind are not barred by the Fifth Amendment and their admissibility is not affected by our holding today.

It is clear therefore that the special procedural safeguards outlined in *Miranda* are required not where a suspect is simply taken into custody, but rather where a suspect in custody is subjected to interrogation. "In- terrogation," as conceptualized in the *Miranda* opinion, must reflect a measure of compulsion above and beyond that inherent in custody itself.[4]

3. To limit the ambit of *Miranda* to express questioning would "place a premium on the ingenuity of the police to devise methods of indirect interrogation, rather than to implement the plain mandate of *Miranda*." Commonwealth v. Hamilton, 445 Pa. 292, 297, 285 A.2d 172, 175.
4. There is language in the opinion of the Rhode Island Supreme Court in this case suggesting that the definition of "interrogation" under *Miranda* is informed by this Court's decision in Brewer v. Williams [which is reproduced at page 1243 infra]. This suggestion is erroneous. Our decision in *Brewer* rested solely on the Sixth and Fourteenth Amendment right to counsel. That right, as we held in Massiah v. United States, 377 U.S. 201, 206, prohibits law enforcement officers from "deliberately elicit[ing]" incrim- inating information from a defendant in the absence of counsel after a formal charge against the defendant has been filed. Custody in such a case is not controlling; indeed, the petitioner in *Massiah* was not in custody. By contrast, the right to counsel at issue in the present case is based not on the Sixth and Fourteenth Amendments, but rather on the Fifth and Fourteenth Amendments as interpreted in the *Miranda* opinion. The definitions of "interrogation" under the Fifth and Sixth Amendments, if indeed the term

We conclude that the *Miranda* safeguards come into play whenever a person in custody is subjected to either express questioning or its functional equivalent. That is to say, the term "interrogation" under *Miranda* refers not only to express questioning, but also to any words or actions on the part of the police (other than those normally attendant to arrest and custody) that the police should know are reasonably likely to elicit an incriminating response from the suspect.[6] The latter portion of this definition focuses primarily upon the perceptions of the suspect, rather than the intent of the police. This focus reflects the fact that the *Miranda* safeguards were designed to vest a suspect in custody with an added measure of protection against coercive police practices, without regard to objective proof of the underlying intent of the police. A practice that the police should know is reasonably likely to evoke an incriminating response from a suspect thus amounts to interrogation.[7] But, since the police surely cannot be held accountable for the unforeseeable results of their words or actions, the definition of interrogation can extend only to words or actions on the part of police officers that they *should have known* were reasonably likely to elicit an incriminating response.[8]

B

Turning to the facts of the present case, we conclude that the respondent was not "interrogated" within the meaning of *Miranda*. It is undisputed that the first prong of the definition of "interrogation" was not satisfied, for the conversation between Patrolmen Gleckman and McKenna included no express questioning of the respondent. Rather, that conversation was, at least in form, nothing more than a dialogue between the two officers to which no response from the respondent was invited.

"interrogation" is even apt in the Sixth Amendment context, are not necessarily interchangeable, since the policies underlying the two constitutional protections are quite distinct. See Kamisar, Brewer v. Williams, *Massiah*, and *Miranda*: What is "Interrogation"? When Does it Matter?, 67 Geo. L.J. 1, 41-55 (1978).

6. One of the dissenting opinions seems totally to misapprehend this definition in suggesting that it "will almost certainly exclude every statement [of the police] that is not punctuated with a question mark." . . .

7. This is not to say that the intent of the police is irrelevant, for it may well have a bearing on whether the police should have known that their words or actions were reasonably likely to evoke an incriminating response. In particular, where a police practice is designed to elicit an incriminating response from the accused, it is unlikely that the practice will not also be one which the police should have known was reasonably likely to have that effect.

8. Any knowledge the police may have had concerning the unusual susceptibility of a defendant to a particular form of persuasion might be an important factor in determining whether the police should have known that their words or actions were reasonably likely to elicit an incriminating response from the suspect.

Moreover, it cannot be fairly concluded that the respondent was subjected to the "functional equivalent" of questioning. It cannot be said, in short, that Patrolmen Gleckman and McKenna should have known that their conversation was reasonably likely to elicit an incriminating response from the respondent. There is nothing in the record to suggest that the officers were aware that the respondent was peculiarly susceptible to an appeal to his conscience concerning the safety of handicapped children. Nor is there anything in the record to suggest that the police knew that the respondent was unusually disoriented or upset at the time of his arrest.[9]

The case thus boils down to whether, in the context of a brief conversation, the officers should have known that the respondent would suddenly be moved to make a self-incriminating response. Given the fact that the entire conversation appears to have consisted of no more than a few offhand remarks, we cannot say that the officers should have known that it was reasonably likely that Innis would so respond. This is not a case where the police carried on a lengthy harangue in the presence of the suspect. Nor does the record support the respondent's contention that, under the circumstances, the officers' comments were particularly "evocative." It is our view, therefore, that the respondent was not subjected by the police to words or actions that the police should have known were reasonably likely to elicit an incriminating response from him.

The Rhode Island Supreme Court erred, in short, in equating "subtle compulsion" with interrogation. That the officers' comments struck a responsive chord is readily apparent. Thus, it may be said, as the Rhode Island Supreme Court did say, that the respondent was subjected to "subtle compulsion." But that is not the end of the inquiry. It must also be established that a suspect's incriminating response was the product of words or actions on the part of the police that they should have known were reasonably likely to elicit an incriminating response.[10] This was not established in the present case.

For the reasons stated, the judgment of the Supreme Court of Rhode

9. The record in no way suggests that the officers' remarks were *designed* to elicit a response. See n.7, supra. It is significant that the trial judge, after hearing the officers' testimony, concluded that it was "entirely understandable that [the officers] would voice their concern [for the safety of the handicapped children] to each other."

10. By way of example, if the police had done no more than to drive past the site of the concealed weapon while taking the most direct route to the police station, and if the respondent, upon noticing for the first time the proximity of the school for handicapped children, had blurted out that he would show the officers where the gun was located, it could not seriously be argued that this "subtle compulsion" would have constituted "interrogation" within the meaning of the *Miranda* opinion.

Island is vacated, and the case is remanded to that court for further proceedings not inconsistent with this opinion.

It is so ordered. . . .

JUSTICE STEVENS, dissenting.

As the Court recognizes, Miranda v. Arizona makes it clear that, once respondent requested an attorney, he had an absolute right to have any type of interrogation cease until an attorney was present. As it also recognizes, *Miranda* requires that the term "interrogation" be broadly construed to include "either express questioning or its functional equivalent." . . . In my view any statement that would normally be understood by the average listener as calling for a response is the functional equivalent of a direct question, whether or not it is punctuated by a question mark. The Court, however, takes a much narrower view. It holds that police conduct is not the "functional equivalent" of direct questioning unless the police should have known that what they were saying or doing was likely to elicit an incriminating response from the suspect. This holding represents a plain departure from the principles set forth in *Miranda*.

In *Miranda* the Court required the now-familiar warnings to be given to suspects prior to custodial interrogation in order to dispel the atmosphere of coercion that necessarily accompanies such interrogations. In order to perform that function effectively, the warnings must be viewed by both the police and the suspect as a correct and binding statement of their respective rights. Thus, if, after being told that he has a right to have an attorney present during interrogation, a suspect chooses to cut off questioning until counsel can be obtained, his choice must be "scrupulously honored" by the police. See Michigan v. Mosley, 423 U.S. 96, 104; id., at 110, n.2 (White, J., concurring in result). At the least this must mean that the police are prohibited from making deliberate attempts to elicit statements from the suspect.[7] Yet the Court is unwilling to characterize all such attempts as "interrogation," noting only that "where a police practice is designed to elicit an incriminating response from the accused, it is unlikely that the practice will not also be one which

---

7. In Brewer v. Williams, 430 U.S. 387, 398-399, the Court applied the "deliberately elicited" standard in determining that statements were extracted from Williams in violation of his Sixth Amendment right to counsel. Although this case involves Fifth Amendment rights and the *Miranda* rules designed to safeguard those rights, respondent's invocation of his right to counsel makes the two cases indistinguishable. In both cases the police had an unqualified obligation to refrain from trying to elicit a response from the suspect in the absence of his attorney. See Kamisar, Brewer v. Williams, *Massiah*, and *Miranda*: What Is "Interrogation"? When Does It Matter?, Geo. L.J. 1, 73 (1978).

the police should have known was reasonably likely to have that effect."[8] . . .

From the suspect's point of view, the effectiveness of the warnings depends on whether it appears that the police are scrupulously honoring his rights. Apparent attempts to elicit information from a suspect after he has invoked his right to cut off questioning necessarily demean that right and tend to reinstate the imbalance between police and suspect that the *Miranda* warnings are designed to correct.[9] Thus, if the rationale for requiring those warnings in the first place is to be respected, any police conduct or statements that would appear to a reasonable person in the suspect's position to call for a response must be considered "interrogation."[10]

In short, in order to give full protection to a suspect's right to be free from any interrogation at all, the definition of "interrogation" must include any police statement or conduct that has the same purpose or effect as a direct question. Statements that appear to call for a response from the suspect, as well as those that are designed to do so, should be considered interrogation. By prohibiting only those relatively few statements or actions that a police officer should know are likely to elicit an incriminating response, the Court today accords a suspect considerably less protection. Indeed, since I suppose most suspects are unlikely to incriminate themselves even when questioned directly, this new definition will almost certainly exclude every statement that is not punctuated with a question mark from the concept of "interrogation."

The difference between the approach required by a faithful adherence to *Miranda* and the stinted test applied by the Court today can be illustrated by comparing three different ways in which Officer Gleckman could have communicated his fears about the possible dangers posed by the shotgun to handicapped children. He could have:

8. This factual assumption is extremely dubious. I would assume that police often interrogate suspects without any reason to believe that their efforts are likely to be successful in the hope that a statement will nevertheless be forthcoming.

9. See White, Police Trickery in Inducing Confessions, 127 U. Pa. L. Rev. 581, 609-611 (1979). As Mr. Justice White pointed out in his opinion concurring in the result in Michigan v. Mosley, 423 U.S. 96, when a suspect invokes his right to an attorney, he is expressing "his own view that he is not competent to deal with the authorities without legal advice." Id., at 110, n.2. Under these circumstances, continued interrogation is likely to produce the same type of coercive atmosphere that the *Miranda* warnings are supposed to dispel.

10. I would use an objective standard both to avoid the difficulties of proof inherent in a subjective standard and to give police adequate guidance in their dealings with suspects who have requested counsel.

(1) directly asked Innis:
Will you please tell me where the shotgun is so we can protect handicapped schoolchildren from danger?
(2) announced to the other officers in the wagon:
If the man sitting in the back seat with me should decide to tell us where the gun is, we can protect handicapped children from danger.

or

(3) stated to the other officers:
It would be too bad if a little handicapped girl would pick up the gun that this man left in the area and maybe kill herself.

In my opinion, all three of these statements should be considered interrogation because all three appear to be designed to elicit a response from anyone who in fact knew where the gun was located.[12] Under the Court's test, on the other hand, the form of the statements would be critical. The third statement would not be interrogation because in the Court's view there was no reason for Officer Gleckman to believe that Innis was susceptible to this type of an implied appeal, . . . therefore, the statement would not be reasonably likely to elicit an incriminating response. Assuming that this is true, . . . then it seems to me that the first two statements, which would be just as unlikely to elicit such a response, should also not be considered interrogation. But, because the first statement is clearly an express question, it *would* be considered interrogation under the Court's test. The second statement, although just as clearly a deliberate appeal to Innis to reveal the location of the gun, would presumably not be interrogation because (a) it was not in form a direct question and (b) it does not fit within the "reasonably likely to elicit an incriminating response" category that applies to indirect interrogation.

As this example illustrates, the Court's test creates an incentive for police to ignore a suspect's invocation of his rights in order to make continued attempts to extract information from him. If a suspect does not appear to be susceptible to a particular type of psychological pressure, the police are apparently free to exert that pressure on him despite his request for counsel, so long as they are careful not to punctuate their

12. See White, Rhode Island v. Innis: The Significance of a Suspect's Assertion of His Right to Counsel, 17 Am. Crim. L. Rev. 53, 68 (1979), where the author proposes the same test and applies it to the facts of this case, stating: "Under the proposed objective standard, the result is obvious. Since the conversation indicates a strong desire to know the location of the shotgun, any person with knowledge of the weapon's location would be likely to believe that the officers wanted him to disclose its location. Thus, a reasonable person in Innis's position would believe that the officers were seeking to solicit precisely the type of response that was given."

statements with question marks. And if, contrary to all reasonable expectations, the suspect makes an incriminating statement, that statement can be used against him at trial. The Court thus turns *Miranda's* unequivocal rule against any interrogation at all into a trap in which unwary suspects may be caught by police deception. . . .

CHIEF JUSTICE BURGER's and JUSTICE WHITE's concurring opinions are omitted, as is JUSTICE MARSHALL's dissent, in which JUSTICE BRENNAN joined.

NOTES AND QUESTIONS

1. Would *Innis* have come out differently if the Officer's remarks had been directed at Innis? If they had been directed at him in the form of a question? If so, what is the point of imposing a "reasonable likelihood of success" limitation on what actually occurred? Is it because possibly the *Miranda* rules already go too far, and an arbitrary limitation is better than extending them further still?

2. Suppose an individual is arrested for murder and invokes his *Miranda* rights. Suppose further that his wife is also being interrogated and insists on seeing her husband. The police attempt to dissuade her from talking with her husband, but she insists. The police accede to her demand but inform the couple that a police officer will be present during the meeting and their conversation will be tape-recorded. During the meeting of husband and wife, a conversation occurs that is subsequently admitted at the husband's trial to demonstrate that he was not insane at the time of the alleged event. Assuming that the police knew that there was a substantial risk that incriminating statements would be made, does the husband have a legitimate claim that his fifth amendment rights have been violated?

No, according to the Court in a 5 to 4 decision in Arizona v. Mauro, 481 U.S. 421 (1987). Although the police knew that there was a substantial likelihood that incriminating material would be obtained, the police attempted to discourage the wife from seeing her husband. Thus, this was not a "psychological ploy that properly could be treated as the functional equivalent of interrogation," a conclusion bolstered in the Court's view by the fact that there was "no evidence that the officers sent Mrs. Mauro in to see her husband for the purpose of eliciting incriminating statements."

What do you think of the wisdom of incorporating the subjective state of mind of the police into the definition of "interrogation"? How could a suspect's will possibly be overborne merely because the police consciously constructed a ruse analogous to the facts of *Mauro*, but not overborne in the actual case? From Mauro's point of view, what is the significance of whether the police (1) had no idea what would occur during the meeting; (2) hoped an incriminating conversation would occur; (3) intended for it to occur; (4) urged the wife to bring about such a conversation? If these four possibilities cannot be distinguished in terms of their effect on Mauro, should they all be allowed or all disallowed? *Innis* suggests the first two are acceptable and the last two are violations of *Miranda*. Is the problem in *Innis* or in *Miranda*?

Do the police interrogate someone within the meaning of *Miranda* when they put him through field sobriety tests or ask him questions to facilitate booking him for driving while intoxicated? Consider the next case, which involves an interaction between the meaning of "testimonial" for purposes of the fifth amendment and "interrogation" for the purposes of *Miranda*:

PENNSYLVANIA v. MUNIZ
Certiorari to the Superior Court of Pennsylvania
—U.S.—, 110 S. Ct. 2638 (1990)

JUSTICE BRENNAN delivered the opinion of the court with respect to Parts I, II, III-A, III-B, and IV.

We must decide in this case whether various incriminating utterances of a drunk-driving suspect, made while performing a series of sobriety tests, constitute testimonial responses to custodial interrogation for purposes of the Self-Incrimination Clause of the Fifth Amendment.

I

During the early morning hours of November 30, 1986, a patrol officer spotted respondent Inocencio Muniz and a passenger parked in a car on the shoulder of a highway. When the officer inquired whether Muniz needed assistance, Muniz replied that he had stopped the car so he could urinate. The officer smelled alcohol on Muniz' breath and observed that Muniz' eyes were glazed and bloodshot and his face was flushed. The officer then directed Muniz to remain parked until his condition improved, and Muniz gave assurances that he would do so. But as the officer returned to his vehicle, Muniz drove off. After the officer pursued Muniz down the highway and pulled him over, the officer asked Muniz to perform three standard field sobriety tests: a "horizontal gaze nystagmus" test, a "walk and turn" test, and a "one leg stand" test.[1] Muniz performed these tests poorly, and he informed the officer that he had failed the tests because he had been drinking.

The patrol officer arrested Muniz and transported him to the West Shore facility of the Cumberland County Central Booking Center. Following its routine practice for receiving persons suspected of driving while intoxicated, the Booking Center videotaped the ensuing proceedings. Muniz was informed that his actions and voice were being recorded, but he was not at this time (nor had he been previously) advised of his rights under Miranda v. Arizona. Officer Hosterman first asked Muniz his name, address, height, weight, eye color, date of birth, and current age. he responded to each of these questions, stumbling over his address and age. The officer then asked Muniz, "Do you know what the date was of your sixth birthday?" After Muniz offered an inaudible reply, the officer repeated, "When you turned six years old, do you remember what the date was?" Muniz responded, "No, I don't."

Officer Hosterman next requested Muniz to perform each of the three sobriety tests that Muniz had been asked to perform earlier during the initial roadside stop. The videotape reveals that his eyes jerked noticeably during the gaze test, that he did not walk a very straight line, and that he could not balance himself on one leg for more than several seconds. During the latter two tests, he did not complete the requested verbal counts from one to nine and from one to thirty. Moreover, while performing these tests, Muniz "attempted to explain his difficulties in performing the various tasks, and often requested further clarification of the tasks he was to perform."

Finally, Officer Deyo asked Muniz to submit to a breathalyzer test designed to measure the alcohol content of his expelled breath. Officer Deyo read to Muniz the Commonwealth's Implied Consent Law, and explained that under the law his refusal to take the test would result in automatic suspension of his drivers' license for one year. Muniz asked a number of questions about the law, commenting in the process about his state of inebriation. Muniz ultimately refused to take the breath test.

---

1. The "horizontal gaze nystagmus" test measures the extent to which a person's eyes jerk as they follow an object moving from one side of the person's field of vision to the other. The test is premised on the understanding that, whereas everyone's eyes exhibit some jerking while turning to the side, when the subject is intoxicated "the onset of the jerking occurs after fewer degrees of turning, and the jerking at more extreme angles becomes more distinct." 1 R. Erwin et al., Defense of Drunk Driving Cases §8A.99, pp. 8A-43, 8A-45 (1989). The "walk and turn" test requires the subject to walk heel-to-toe along a straight line for nine paces, pivot, and then walk back heel-to-toe along the line for another nine paces. The subject is required to count each pace aloud from one to nine. The "one leg stand" test requires the subject to stand on one leg with the other leg extended in the air for 30 seconds, while counting aloud from one to thirty.

At this point, Muniz was for the first time advised of his *Miranda* rights. Muniz then signed a statement waiving his rights and admitted in response to further questioning that he had been driving while intoxicated.

Both the video and audio portions of the videotape were admitted into evidence at Muniz' bench trial, along with the arresting officer's testimony that Muniz failed the roadside sobriety tests and made incriminating remarks at that time. Muniz was convicted of driving under the influence of alcohol. . . . On appeal, the Superior Court of Pennsylvania reversed . . . [and] we granted certiorari.

II

. . . This case implicates both the "testimonial" and "compulsion" components of the privilege against self-incrimination in the context of pretrial questioning. Because Muniz was not advised of his *Miranda* rights until after the videotaped proceedings at the Booking Center were completed, any verbal statements that were both testimonial in nature and elicited during custodial interrogation should have been suppressed. We focus first on Muniz' responses to the initial information questions, then on his questions and utterances while performing the physical dexterity and balancing tests, and finally on his questions and utterances surrounding the breathalyzer test.

III

In the initial phase of the record proceedings, Officer Hosterman asked Muniz his name, address, height, weight, eye color, date of birth, current age, and the date of his sixth birthday. Both the delivery and content of Muniz' answers were incriminating. As the state court found, "Muniz' videotaped responses . . . certainly led the finder of fact to infer that his confusion and failure to speak clearly indicated a state of drunkenness that prohibited him from safely operating his vehicle." The Commonwealth argues, however, that admission of Muniz' answers to these questions does not contravene Fifth Amendment principles because Muniz' statement regarding his sixth birthday was not "testimonial" and his answers to the prior questions were not elicited by custodial interrogation. We consider these arguments in turn.

A

We agree with the Commonwealth's contention that Muniz' answers are not rendered inadmissible by *Miranda* merely because the slurred nature of his speech was incriminating. The physical inability to articulate words in a clear manner due to "the lack of muscular coordination of his tongue and mouth," Brief for Petitioner 16, is not itself a testimonial component of Muniz' responses to Officer Hosterman's introductory questions. In Schmerber v. California, we drew a distinction between "testimonial" and "real or physical evidence" for purposes of the privilege against self-incrimination. We noted that in Holt v. United States, 218 U.S. 245, 252-253 (1910), Justice Holmes had written for the Court that " '[t]he prohibition of compelling a man in a criminal court to be witness against himself is a prohibition of the use of physical or moral compulsion to extort communications from him, not an exclusion of his body as evidence when it may be material.' " 384 U.S., at 763. We also acknowledged that "both federal and state courts have usually held that it offers no protection against compulsion to submit to fingerprinting, photographing, or measurements, to write or speak for identification, to appear in court, to stand, to assume a stance, to walk, or to make a particular gesture." Id., at 764. Embracing this view of the privilege's contours, we held that "the privilege is a bar against compelling 'communications' or 'testimony,' but that compulsion which makes a suspect or accused the source of 'real or physical evidence' does not violate it." . . .

Under Schmerber and its progeny, we agree with the Commonwealth that any slurring of speech and other evidence of lack of muscular coordination revealed by Muniz' responses to Officer Hosterman's direct questions constitute nontestimonial components of those responses. Requiring a suspect to reveal the physical manner in which he articulates words, like requiring him to reveal the physical properties of the sound produced by his voice, does not, without more, compel him to provide a "testimonial" response for purposes of the privilege.

B

This does not end our inquiry, for Muniz' answer to the sixth birthday question was incriminating, not just because of his delivery, but also because of his answer's content; the trier of fact could infer from Muniz' answer (that he did not know the proper date) that his mental state was confused. The Commonwealth and United States as amicus curiae argue that this incriminating inference does not trigger the protections of the Fifth Amendment privilege because the inference concerns "the physiological functioning of [Muniz'] brain," Brief for Petitioner 21, which is asserted to be every bit as "real or physical" as the physiological makeup of his blood and the timbre of his voice.

But this characterization addresses the wrong question; that the "fact" to be inferred might be said to concern the physical status of Muniz' brain merely describes the way in which the inference is incriminating. The correct question for present purposes is whether the incriminating inference of mental confusion is drawn from a testimonial act or from physical evidence. In *Schmerber*, for example, we held that the police could compel a suspect to provide a blood sample in order to determine the physical makeup of his blood and thereby draw an inference about whether he was intoxicated. This compulsion was outside of the Fifth Amendment's protection, not simply because the evidence concerned the suspect's physical body, but rather because the evidence was obtained in a manner that did not entail any testimonial act on the part of the suspect: "[n]ot even a shadow of testimonial compulsion upon or enforced communication by the accused was involved either in the extraction or in the chemical analysis." 384 U.S., at 765. In contrast, had the police instead asked the suspect directly whether his blood contained a high concentration of alcohol, his affirmative response would have been testimonial even though it would have been used to draw the same inference concerning his physiology. See ibid. ("[T]he blood test evidence . . . was neither [suspect's] testimony nor evidence relating to some communicative act"). In this case, the question is not whether a suspect's "impaired mental faculties" can fairly be characterized as an aspect of his physiology, but rather whether Muniz' response to the sixth birthday question that gave rise to the inference of such an impairment was testimonial in nature.

We recently explained in Doe v. United States, 487 U.S. 201 (1988), that "in order to be testimonial, an accused's communication must itself, explicitly or implicitly, relate a factual assertion or disclose information." . . . After canvassing the purposes of the privilege recognized in prior cases, we concluded that "[t]hese policies are served when the privilege is asserted to spare the accused from having to reveal, directly or indirectly, his knowledge of facts relating him to the offense or from having to share his thoughts and beliefs with the Government."[9] . . .

We need not explore the outer boundaries of what is "testimonial" today, for our decision flows from the concept's core meaning. Because the privilege was designed primarily to prevent "a recurrence of the Inquisition and the Star Chamber, even if not in their stark brutality," Ullmann v. United States, 350 U.S. 422, 428 (1956), it is evident that a suspect is "compelled . . . to be a witness against himself" at least whenever he must face the modern-day analog of the historic trilemma—

---

9. This definition applies to both verbal and nonverbal conduct; nonverbal conduct contains a testimonial component whenever the conduct reflects the actor's communication of his thoughts to another. . . .

either during a criminal trial where a sworn witness faces the identical three choices, or during custodial interrogation where, as we explained in *Miranda*, the choices are analogous and hence raise similar concerns. Whatever else it may include, therefore, the definition of "testimonial" evidence articulated in *Doe* must encompass all responses to questions that, if asked of a sworn suspect during a criminal trial, could place the suspect in the "cruel trilemma." This conclusion is consistent with our recognition in *Doe* that "[t]he vast majority of verbal statements thus will be testimonial" because "[t]here are very few instances in which a verbal statement, either oral or written, will not convey information or assert facts." 487 U.S., at 213. Whenever a suspect is asked for a response requiring him to communicate an express or implied assertion of fact or belief, the suspect confronts the "trilemma" of truth, falsity, or silence and hence the response (whether based on truth or falsity) contains a testimonial component. . . .

[Therefore], the sixth birthday question in this case required a testimonial response. When Officer Hosterman asked Muniz if he knew the date of his sixth birthday and Muniz, for whatever reason, could not remember or calculate that date, he was confronted with the trilemma. By hypothesis, the inherently coercive environment created by the custodial interrogation precluded the option of remaining silent. Muniz was left with the choice of incriminating himself by admitting that he did not then know the date of his sixth birthday, or answering untruthfully by reporting a date that he did not then believe to be accurate (an incorrect guess would be incriminating as well as untruthful). The content of his truthful answer supported an inference that his mental faculties were impaired, because his assertion (he did not know the date of his sixth birthday) was different from the assertion (he knew the date was [correct date]) that the trier of fact might reasonably have expected a lucid person to provide. Hence, the incriminating inference of impaired mental faculties stemmed, not just from the fact that Muniz slurred his response, but also from a testimonial aspect of that response.[13]

13. The Commonwealth's protest that it had no investigatory interest in the actual date of Muniz's sixth birthday is inapposite. The critical point is that the Commonwealth had an investigatory interest in Muniz's assertion of belief that was communicated by his answer to the question. Putting it another way, the Commonwealth may not have cared about the correct answer, but it cared about Muniz's answer. The incriminating inference stems from the then-existing contents of Muniz's mind as evidenced by his assertion of his knowledge at that time.

This distinction is reflected in Estelle v. Smith, 451 U.S. 454 (1981), where we held that a defendant's answers to questions during a psychiatric examination were testimonial in nature. The psychiatrist asked a series of questions, some focusing on the defendant's account of the crime. After analyzing both the "statements [the defendant] made, and remarks he omitted," id., at 464, the psychiatrist made a prognosis as to the defendant's "future dangerousness" and testified to this effect at his capital sentencing

The state court held that the sixth birthday question constituted an unwarned interrogation for purposes of the privilege against self-incrimination, and that Muniz' answer was incriminating. The Commonwealth does not question either conclusion. Therefore, because we conclude that Muniz' response to the sixth birthday question was testimonial, the response should have been suppressed.

c

The Commonwealth argues that the seven questions asked by Officer Hosterman just prior to the sixth birthday question—regarding Muniz' name, address, height, weight, eye color, date of birth, and current age—did not constitute custodial interrogation as we have defined the term in *Miranda* and subsequent cases. In *Miranda*, the Court referred to "interrogation" as actual "questioning initiated by law enforcement officers." We have since clarified that definition, finding that the "goals of the *Miranda* safeguards could be effectuated if those safeguards extended not only to express questioning, but also to 'its functional equivalent.'" Arizona v. Mauro, 481 U.S. 520, 526 (1987). In Rhode Island v. Innis, the Court defined the phrase "functional equivalent" of express questioning to include "any words or actions on the part of the police (other than those normally attendant to arrest and custody) that the police should know are reasonably likely to elicit an incriminating response from the suspect. The latter portion of this definition focuses primarily upon the perceptions of the suspect, rather than the intent of the police." Id., at 301. However, "[a]ny knowledge the police may have had concerning the unusual susceptibility of a defendant to a particular form of persuasion might be an important factor in determining" what the police reasonably should have known. *Innis*, supra, at 302, n.8. Thus, custodial interrogation for purposes of *Miranda* includes both express questioning, and also words or actions that, given the officer's knowledge of any special susceptibilities of the suspect, the officer knows or reasonably should know are likely to "have . . . the force of a question on the accused,"

---

hearing. The psychiatrist had no investigative interest in whether the defendant's account of the crime and other disclosures were either accurate or complete as a historical matter; rather, he relied on the remarks—both those made and omitted—to infer that the defendant would likely pose a threat to society in the future because of his state of mind. We nevertheless explained that the "Fifth Amendment privilege . . . is directly involved here because the State used as evidence against [the defendant] the substance of his disclosures during the pretrial psychiatric examination." Id., at 464-465 (emphasis added). The psychiatrist may have presumed the defendant's remarks to be truthful for purposes of drawing his inferences as to the defendant's state of mind, but that is true in Muniz' case as well: the incriminating inference of mental confusion is based on the premise that Muniz was responding truthfully to Officer Hosterman's question when he stated that he did not then know the date of his sixth birthday.

Harryman v. Estelle, 616 F.2d 870, 874 (CA5 1980), and therefore be reasonably likely to elicit an incriminating response.

We disagree with the Commonwealth's contention that Officer Hosterman's first seven questions regarding Muniz' name, address, height, weight, eye color, date of birth, and current age do not qualify as custodial interrogation as we defined the term in *Innis*, merely because the questions were not intended to elicit information for investigatory purposes. As explained above, the *Innis* test focuses primarily upon the perspective of the suspect. We agree with amicus United States, however, that Muniz' answers to these first seven questions are nonetheless admissible because the questions fall within a "routine booking question" exception which exempts from *Miranda*'s coverage questions to secure the "biographical data necessary to complete booking or pretrial services." Brief for the United States as Amicus Curiae 12. The state court found that the first seven questions were "requested for record-keeping purposes only," and therefore the questions appear reasonably related to the police's administrative concerns.[14] In this context, therefore, the first seven questions asked at the Booking Center fall outside the protections of *Miranda* and the answers thereto need not be suppressed.

IV

During the second phase of the videotaped proceedings, Officer Hosterman asked Muniz to perform the same three sobriety tests that he had earlier performed at roadside prior to his arrest: the "horizontal gaze nystagmus" test, the "walk and turn" test, and the "one leg stand" test. While Muniz was attempting to comprehend Officer Hosterman's instructions and then perform the requested sobriety tests, Muniz made several audible and incriminating statements. Muniz argued to the state court that both the videotaped performance of the physical tests themselves and the audiorecorded verbal statements were introduced in violation of *Miranda*.

The court refused to suppress the videotaped evidence of Muniz' paltry performance on the physical sobriety tests, reasoning that "[r]equiring a driver to perform physical [sobriety] tests . . . does not violate the privilege against self-incrimination because the evidence procured is of a physical nature rather than testimonial." With respect to Muniz' verbal

14. As amicus United States explains, "[r]ecognizing a 'booking exception' to *Miranda* does not mean, of course, that any question asked during the booking process falls within that exception. Without obtaining a waiver of the suspect's *Miranda* rights, the police may not ask questions, even during booking, that are designed to elicit incriminatory admissions." Brief for United States as Amicus Curiae 13.

statements, however, the court concluded that "none of Muniz' utterances were spontaneous, voluntary verbalizations, and because they were "elicited before Muniz received his *Miranda* warnings, they should have been excluded as evidence."

We disagree. Officer Hosterman's dialogue with Muniz concerning the physical sobriety tests consisted primarily of carefully scripted instructions as to how the tests were to be performed. These instructions were not likely to be perceived as calling for any verbal response and therefore were not "words or actions" constituting custodial interrogation, with two narrow exceptions not relevant here.[17] The dialogue also contained limited and carefully worded inquiries as to whether Muniz understood those instructions, but these focused inquiries were necessarily "attendant to" the police procedure held by the court to be legitimate. Hence, Muniz' incriminating utterances during this phase of the videotaped proceedings were "voluntary" in the sense that they were not elicited in response to custodial interrogation. See South Dakota v. Neville, 459 U.S. 553, 564, n.15 (1983) (drawing analogy to "police request to submit to fingerprinting or photography" and holding that police inquiry whether suspect would submit to blood-alcohol test was not "interrogation within the meaning of *Miranda*").

Similarly, we conclude that *Miranda* does not require suppression of the statements Muniz made when asked to submit to a breathalyzer examination. Officer Deyo read Muniz a prepared script explaining how the test worked, the nature of Pennsylvania's Implied Consent Law, and the legal consequences that would ensue should he refuse. Officer Deyo then asked Muniz whether he understood the nature of the test and the law and whether he would like to submit to the test. Muniz asked Officer Deyo several questions concerning the legal consequences of refusal, which Deyo answered directly, and Muniz then commented upon his state of inebriation. After offering to take the test only after waiting a couple of hours or drinking some water, Muniz ultimately refused.

We believe that Muniz' statements were not prompted by an interrogation within the meaning of *Miranda*, and therefore the absence of

17. The two exceptions consist of Officer Hosterman's requests that Muniz count aloud from one to nine while performing the "walk-the-line" test and that he count aloud from one to thirty while balancing during the "one leg stand" test. Muniz's counting at the officer's request qualifies as a response to custodial interrogation. However, as Muniz counted accurately (in Spanish) for the duration of his performance on the "one leg stand" test (though he did not complete it), his verbal response to this instruction was not incriminating except to the extent that it exhibited a tendency to slur words, which we have already explained is a nontestimonial component of his response. Muniz did not count during the "walk and turn" test, and he does not argue that his failure to do so has any independent incriminating significance. We therefore need not decide today whether Muniz' counting (or not) itself was "testimonial" within the meaning of the privilege.

Miranda warnings does not require suppression of these statements at trial. As did Officer Hosterman when administering the three physical sobriety tests, Officer Deyo carefully limited her role to providing Muniz with relevant information about the breathalyzer test and the implied consent law. She questioned Muniz only as to whether he understood her instructions and wished to submit to the test. These limited and focused inquiries were necessarily "attendant to" the legitimate police procedure, see *Neville,* and were not likely to be perceived as calling for any incriminating response.

V

We agree with the state court's conclusion that *Miranda* requires suppression of Muniz' response to the question regarding the date of his sixth birthday, but we do not agree that the entire audio portion of the videotape must be suppressed. Accordingly, the court's judgment reversing Muniz' conviction is vacated, and the case is remanded for further proceedings not inconsistent with this opinion.

CHIEF JUSTICE REHNQUIST, with whom JUSTICE WHITE, JUSTICE BLACKMUN and JUSTICE STEVENS join, concurring in part, concurring in the result in part, and dissenting in part.

I join Parts I, II, III-A, and IV of the Court's opinion. In addition, although I agree with the conclusion in Part III-C that the seven "booking" questions should not be suppressed, I do so for a reason different from that of Justice Brennan. I dissent from the Court's conclusion that Muniz' response to the "sixth birthday question" should have been suppressed.

The Court holds that the sixth birthday question Muniz was asked required a testimonial response, and that its admission at trial therefore violated Muniz' privilege against compulsory self-incrimination. The Court says that

> [w]hen Officer Hosterman asked Muniz if he knew the date of his sixth birthday and Muniz, for whatever reason, could not remember or calculate that date, he was confronted with the trilemma [i.e., the "trilemma" of "truth, falsity, or silence."] . . . Muniz was left with the choice of in-criminating himself by admitting that he did not then know that date of his sixth birthday, or answering untruthfully by reporting a date that he did not then believe to be accurate (an incorrect guess would be incrim-inating as well as untruthful).

As an assumption about human behavior, this statement is wrong. Muniz would no more have felt compelled to fabricate a false date than one who cannot read the letters on an eye-chart feels compelled to fabricate false letters; nor does a wrong guess call into question a speaker's veracity. The Court's statement is also a flawed predicate on which to base its conclusion that Muniz' answer to this question was "testimonial" for purposes of the Fifth Amendment.

The need for the use of the human voice does not automatically make an answer testimonial, any more than does the fact that a question calls for the exhibition of one's handwriting in written characters. . . .

The sixth birthday question here was an effort on the part of the police to check how well Muniz was able to do a simple mathematical exercise. Indeed, had the question related only to the date of his birth, it presumably would have come under the "booking exception" to Miranda v. Arizona to which the Court refers elsewhere in its opinion. The Court holds in this very case that Muniz may be required to perform a "horizontal gaze nystagmus" test, the "walk and turn" test, and the "one leg stand" test, all of which are designed to test a suspect's physical coordination. If the police may require Muniz to use his body in order to demonstrate the level of his physical coordination, there is no reason why they should not be able to require him to speak or write in order to determine his mental coordination. That was all that was sought here. Since it was permissible for the police to extract and examine a sample of Schmerber's blood to determine how much that part of his system had been affected by alcohol, I see no reason why they may not examine the functioning of Muniz' mental processes for the same purpose.

Surely if it were relevant, a suspect might be asked to take an eye examination in the course of which he might have to admit that he could not read the letters on the third line of the chart. At worst, he might utter a mistaken guess. Muniz likewise might have attempted to guess the correct response to the sixth birth question instead of attempting to calculate the date or answer "I don't know." But the potential for giving a bad guess does not subject the suspect to the truth-falsity-silence predicament that renders a response testimonial and, therefore, within the scope of Fifth Amendment privilege.

For substantially the same reasons, Muniz' responses to the videotaped "booking" questions were not testimonial and do not warrant application of the privilege. Thus, it is unnecessary to determine whether the questions fall within the "routine booking question" exception to *Miranda* Justice Brennan recognizes. . . .

JUSTICE MARSHALL, concurring in part and dissenting in part.

I concur in Part III-B of the Court's opinion that the "sixth birthday question" required a testimonial response from respondent Muniz. For the reasons discussed below that question constituted custodial interro-

gation. Because the police did not apprise Muniz of his *Miranda* rights
before asking the question, his response should have been suppressed.

I disagree, however, with the plurality's recognition in Part III-C of
a "routine booking question" exception to *Miranda*. Moreover, even
were such an exception warranted, it should not extend to booking questions that the police should know are reasonably likely to elicit incriminating responses. Because the police in this case should have known
that the seven booking questions were reasonably likely to elicit incriminating responses and because those questions were not preceded by
Miranda warnings, Muniz' testimonial responses should have been suppressed.

I dissent from the Court's holding in Part IV that Muniz' testimonial
statements in connection with the three sobriety tests and the breathalyzer
test were not the products of custodial interrogation. The police should
have known that the circumstances in which they confronted Muniz,
combined with the detailed instructions and questions concerning the
tests and the State's Implied Consent Law, were reasonably likely to elicit
an incriminating response, and therefore constituted the "functional
equivalent" of express questioning. Muniz' statements to the police in
connection with these tests thus should have been suppressed because
he was not first given the *Miranda* warnings.

Finally, the officer's directions to Muniz to count aloud during two
of the sobriety tests sought testimonial responses, and Muniz' responses
were incriminating. Because Muniz was not informed of his *Miranda*
rights prior to the tests, those responses also should have been suppressed.

I

A

The plurality would create yet another exception to Miranda v.
Arizona; the "routine booking question" exception. See also Illinois v.
Perkins, 495 U.S.(1990) (creating exception to *Miranda* for custodial
interrogation by an undercover police officer posing as the suspect's fellow
prison inmate) [reproduced at page 1196 infra]. Such exceptions undermine *Miranda's* fundamental principle that the doctrine should be clear
so that it can be easily applied by both police and court. The plurality's
position, were it adopted by a majority of the Court, would necessitate
difficult, time-consuming litigation over whether particular questions asked
during booking are "routine," whether they are necessary to secure biographical information, whether the information is itself necessary for
recordkeeping purposes, and whether the questions are—despite their

routine nature—designed to elicit incriminating testimony. The far better course would be to maintain the clarity of the doctrine by requiring police to preface all direct questioning of a suspect with *Miranda* warnings if they want his responses to be admissible at trial.

B

The plurality nonetheless asserts that *Miranda* does not apply to express questioning designed to secure "biographical data necessary to complete booking or pretrial services," so long as the questioning is not "designed to elicit incriminatory admissions." Even if a routine booking question exception to *Miranda* were warranted, that exception should not extend to any booking question that the police should know is reasonably likely to elicit an incriminating response, regardless of whether the question is "designed" to elicit an incriminating response. Although the police's intent to obtain an incriminating response is relevant to this inquiry, the key components of the analysis are the nature of the questioning, the attending circumstances, and the perceptions of the suspect. Accordingly, *Miranda* warnings are required before the police may engage in any questioning reasonably likely to elicit an incriminating response.

Here, the police should have known that the seven booking questions—regarding Muniz' name, address, height, weight, eye color, date of birth, and age—were reasonably likely to elicit incriminating responses from a suspect whom the police believed to be intoxicated. Indeed, as the Court acknowledges, Muniz did in fact "stumbl[e] over his address and age"; more specifically, he was unable to give his address without looking at his license and initially told police the wrong age. Moreover, the very fact that, after a suspect has been arrested for driving under the influence, the Pennsylvania police regularly videotape the subsequent questioning strongly implies a purpose to the interrogation other than "recordkeeping." The seven questions in this case, then, do not fall within the routine booking question exception even under the majority's standard.

C

Although the plurality does not address this issue, the booking questions sought "testimonial" responses for the same reason the sixth birthday question did: because the content of the answers would indicate Muniz' state of mind. The booking questions, like the sixth birthday question, required Muniz to (1) answer correctly, indicating lucidity, (2) answer incorrectly, implying that his mental faculties were impaired, or (3) state that he did not know the answer, also indicating impairment. Muniz' initial incorrect response to the question about his age and his inability to give his address without looking at his license, like his inability to answer the sixth birthday question, in fact gave rise to the incriminating inference that his mental faculties were impaired. Accordingly, because the police did not inform Muniz of his *Miranda* rights before asking the booking questions, his responses should have been suppressed.

II

A

The Court finds in Part IV of its opinion that *Miranda* is inapplicable to Muniz' statements made in connection with the three sobriety tests and the breathalyzer examination because those statements (which were undoubtedly testimonial) were not the products of "custodial interrogation." In my view, however, the circumstances of this case—in particular, Muniz' apparent intoxication—rendered the officers' words and actions the "functional equivalent" of express questioning because the police should have known that their conduct was "reasonably likely to evoke an incriminating response." *Innis*, supra, at 301. As the Court recounts, Officer Hosterman instructed Muniz how to perform the sobriety test, inquired whether Muniz understood the instructions, and then directed Muniz to perform the tests. Officer Deyo later explained the breathalyzer examination and the nature of the State's Implied Consent Law, and asked several times if Muniz understood the Law and wanted to take the examination. Although these words and actions might not prompt most sober persons to volunteer incriminating statements, Officers Hosterman and Deyo had good reason to believe—from the arresting officer's observations, from Muniz' failure of the three roadside sobriety tests, and from their own observations—that Muniz was intoxicated. The officers thus should have known that Muniz was reasonably likely to have trouble understanding their instructions and their explanation of the Implied Consent Law, and that he was reasonably likely to indicate, in response to their questions, that he did not understand the tests or the Law. Moreover, because Muniz made several incriminating statements regarding his intoxication during and after the roadside tests, the police should have known that the same tests at the Booking Center were reasonably likely to prompt similar incriminating statements.

The Court today, however, completely ignores Muniz' condition and focuses solely on the nature of the officers' words and actions. As the Court held in *Innis*, however, the focus in the "functional equivalent" inquiry is on "the perceptions of the suspect," not on the officers' conduct viewed in isolation. 446 U.S., at 301. Moreover, the *Innis* Court emphasized that the officers' knowledge of any "unusual susceptibility" of a suspect to a particular means of eliciting information is relevant to the question whether they should have known that they conduct was reasonably likely to elicit an incriminating response. Muniz' apparent intoxication, then, and the police's knowledge of his statements during and after the roadside tests compel the conclusion that the police should have known that their words and actions were reasonably likely to elicit an incriminating response.[2] Muniz' statements were thus the product of custodial interrogation and should have been suppressed because Muniz was not first given the *Miranda* warnings.

B

The Court concedes that Officer Hosterman's directions that Muniz count aloud to 9 while performing the "walk-the-line" test and to 30 while performing the "one-leg-stand" test constituted custodial interrogation. Also indisputable is the testimonial nature of the responses sought by those directions; the content of Muniz' counting, just like his answers to the sixth birthday and the booking questions, would provide the basis for an inference regarding his state of mind. The Court finds the admission at trial of Muniz' responses permissible, however, because they were not incriminating "except to the extent [they] exhibited a tendency to slur words, which [the Court already found to be] nontestimonial [evidence]." The Court's conclusion is wrong for two reasons. First, as a factual matter, Muniz' responses were incriminating for a reason other than his apparent slurring. Muniz did not count at all during the walk-the-line test, supporting the inference that he was unable to do so.[3] And, contrary to the

2. An additional factor strongly suggests that the police expected Muniz to make incriminating statements. Pursuant to their routine in such cases, the police allotted 20 minutes for the three sobriety tests and for "observation." Because Muniz finished the tests in approximately 6 minutes, the police required him to wait another 14 minutes before they asked him to submit to the breathalyzer examination. Given the absence of any apparent technical or administrative reason for the delay and the stated purpose of "observing" Muniz, the delay appears to have been designed in part to give Muniz the opportunity to make incriminating statements.

3. The Commonwealth could not use Muniz' failure to count against him regardless of whether his silence during the walk-the-line test was itself testimonial in those circumstances. A defendant's silence in response to police questioning is not admissible at trial even if the silence is not, in the particular circumstances, a form of communicative conduct. Miranda v. Arizona, 384 U.S 436, 468, n.37 ("[I]t is impermissible to penalize an individual for exercising his Fifth Amendment privilege when he is under police custodial interrogation. The prosecution may not, therefore, use at trial the fact that he stood mute or claimed his privilege in the face of accusation"). Cf. Griffin v. California, 380 U.S. 609, 615 (1965) ("[T]he Fifth Amendment . . . forbids either comment by the prosecution on the accused's silence or instructions by the court that such silence is evidence of guilt").

Court's assertion, during the one-leg-stand test, Muniz incorrectly counted in Spanish from one to six, skipping the number two. Even if Muniz had not skipped "two," his failure to complete the count was incriminating in itself.

Second, and more importantly, Muniz' responses would have been "incriminating" for purposes of *Miranda* even if he had fully and accurately counted aloud during the two tests. As the Court stated in *Innis*, "[b]y 'incriminating response' we refer to any response—whether inculpatory or exculpatory—that the prosecution may seek to introduce at trial." 446 U.S., at 301, n.5. See also *Miranda*, 384 U.S., at 476-477 ("The privilege against self-incrimination protects the individual from being compelled to incriminate himself in any manner; it does not distinguish degrees of incrimination. Similarly, for precisely the same reason, no distinction may be drawn between inculpatory statements and statements alleged to be merely 'exculpatory' "). Thus, any response by Muniz that the prosecution sought to use against him was incriminating under *Miranda*. That the majority thinks Muniz' responses were incriminating only because of his slurring is therefore irrelevant. Because Muniz did not receive the *Miranda* warnings, then, his responses should have been suppressed. *but given how drunk he was, could any waiver of MIRANDA be knowing and intelligent?*

III

All of Muniz' responses during the videotaped session were prompted by questions that sought testimonial answers during the course of custodial interrogation. Because the police did not read Muniz the *Miranda* warnings before he gave those responses, the responses should have been suppressed. I would therefore affirm the judgment of the state court.

b. What Is "Custody"?

Miranda has consistently been interpreted to be applicable only to custodial interrogation, but custody has been given a functional definition. For example, in Orozco v. Texas, 394 U.S. 324 (1969), the Court applied *Miranda* to the questioning of a suspect in his bedroom at 4:00 A.M. by four police. The Court also applied *Miranda* to the testimony of a psychiatrist at the penalty stage of a capital case based on his psychiatric examination of the defendant where the defendant was not given the *Miranda* warnings prior to the examination. Estelle v. Smith, 451 U.S. 454 (1981). In contrast, the Court found no violation of *Miranda* in Oregon v. Mathiason, 429 U.S. 492 (1977), and California v. Beheler,

463 U.S. 1121 (1983), where the defendants voluntarily went to the stationhouses, were not under arrest, and confessed during a noncustodial interrogation. Nor has it been applied to grand jury witnesses, United States v. Mandujano, 425 U.S. 564 (1976). Nor is *Miranda* applicable when an investigation has focused on a suspect, but the suspect is not in custody. Beckwith v. United States, 425 U.S. 341 (1976).

The lower courts have been in disagreement over the test for custody, however. Should it be an objective standard virtually synonymous with arrest, or should it have a subjective referent in what *this* suspect thought? The Supreme Court resolved the issue in Berkemer v. McCarty 468 U.S. 420 (1984), by holding that custody is to be determined by reference to whether a reasonable person in defendant's position would have believed himself to be deprived of his freedom in a significant manner by the police. The Court also made clear that custodial interrogation triggers *Miranda* no matter how minor the offense the police are investigating or with which the suspect is ultimately charged. However, the Court also held that an ordinary traffic stop is "comparatively nonthreatening" and therefore does not constitute custody for *Miranda* purposes.

Is a meeting between a person on probation and his probation officer equally "comparatively nonthreatening" so that it should not count as custody for purposes of *Miranda?* Consider:

MINNESOTA v. MURPHY
Certiorari to the Supreme Court of Minnesota
465 U.S. 420 (1984)

JUSTICE WHITE delivered the opinion of the Court.

In this case, respondent Murphy, who was on probation, made incriminating admissions during a meeting with his probation officer. The issue before us is whether the Fifth and Fourteenth Amendments prohibit the introduction into evidence of the admissions in Murphy's subsequent criminal prosecution.

I

In 1974, Marshall Murphy was twice questioned by Minneapolis Police concerning the rape and murder of a teenage girl. No charges were then brought. In 1980, in connection with a prosecution for criminal sexual conduct arising out of an unrelated incident, Murphy pleaded guilty to a reduced charge of false imprisonment. He was sentenced to a prison term of 16 months, which was suspended, and three years' probation.

(handwritten margin note: definition of custody)

The terms of Murphy's probation required, among other things, that he participate in a treatment program for sexual offenders at Alpha House, report to his probation officer as directed, and be truthful with the probation officer "in all matters." Failure to comply with these conditions, Murphy was informed, could result in his return to the sentencing court for a probation revocation hearing.

Murphy met with his probation officer at her office approximately once a month, and his probation continued without incident until July 1981, when the officer learned that he had abandoned the treatment program. The probation officer then wrote to Murphy and informed him that failure to set up a meeting would "result in an immediate request for a warrant." . . . At a meeting in late July, the officer agreed not to seek revocation of probation for nonparticipation in the treatment program since Murphy was employed and doing well in other areas.

In September 1981, an Alpha House counselor informed the probation officer that, during the course of treatment, Murphy had admitted to a rape and murder in 1974. After discussions with her superior, the officer determined that the police should have this information. She then wrote to Murphy and asked him to contact her to discuss a treatment plan for the remainder of his probationary period. Although she did not contact the police before the meeting, the probation officer knew in advance that she would report any incriminating statements.

Upon receipt of the letter, Murphy arranged to meet with his probation officer in her office on September 28, 1981. The officer opened the meeting by telling Murphy about the information she had received from the Alpha House counselor and expressing her belief that this information evinced his continued need for treatment. Murphy became angry about what he considered to be a breach of his confidences and stated that he "felt like calling a lawyer."[3] The probation officer replied that Murphy would have to deal with that problem outside the office for the moment, their primary concern was the relationship between the crimes that Murphy had admitted to the Alpha House counselor and the incident that led to his conviction for false imprisonment.

During the course of the meeting, Murphy denied the false im-

---

3. The trial court concluded that Murphy's statement did not constitute an invocation of the privilege against self-incrimination: "[W]hatever his real intent may have been, we are persuaded by the probation officer's testimony that he did not express [the] desire [to talk to an attorney] in any other context other than a civil suit for the breach of confidentiality." . . . The Minnesota Supreme Court did not reach this question, and, although we see no reason to question the trial court's factual finding, our analysis of the case makes further consideration unnecessary. Although a request for a lawyer during custodial interrogation is sufficient to invoke the privilege against self-incrimination, . . . Murphy was not in custody . . . and he had no federal right to have an attorney present at the meeting. . . .

prisonment charge, admitted that he had committed the rape and murder, and attempted to persuade the probation officer that further treatment was unnecessary because several extenuating circumstances explained the prior crimes. At the conclusion of the meeting, the officer told Murphy that she had a duty to relay the information to the authorities and encouraged him to turn himself in. Murphy then left the office. Two days later, Murphy called his probation officer and told her that he had been advised by counsel not to surrender himself to the police. The officer then procured the issuance of an arrest and detention order from the judge who had sentenced Murphy on the false imprisonment charge. On October 29, 1981, a State grand jury returned an indictment charging Murphy with first-degree murder.

Murphy sought to suppress testimony concerning his confession on the ground that it was obtained in violation of the Fifth and Fourteenth Amendments. The trial court found that he was not "in custody" at the time of the statement and that the confession was neither compelled nor involuntary despite the absence of warnings similar to those required by Miranda v. Arizona. The Minnesota Supreme Court reversed on federal constitutional grounds. Although recognizing that the Fifth Amendment privilege generally is not self-executing, it concluded that, notwithstanding the lack of custody in the usual sense, Murphy's failure to claim the privilege when he was questioned was not fatal to his claim "[b]ecause of the compulsory nature of the meeting, because [Murphy] was under court order to respond truthfully to his agent's questions, and because the agent had substantial reason to believe that [Murphy's] answers were likely to be incriminating." In the court's view, "the agent should have warned [Murphy] of his privilege against self-incrimination before she questioned him and . . . her failure to do so, when she had already decided to report his answers to the police, bars use of [Murphy's] confession at this trial."

We granted certiorari to resolve a conflict among state and federal courts concerning whether a statement made by a probationer to his probation officer without prior warnings is admissible in a subsequent criminal proceeding. We now reverse.

II

The Fifth Amendment, in relevant part, provides that no person "shall be compelled in any criminal case to be a witness against himself." It has long been held that this prohibition not only permits a person to refuse to testify against himself at a criminal trial in which he is a defendant, but also "privileges him not to answer official questions put to him in any other proceeding, civil or criminal, formal or informal, where the answers might incriminate him in future criminal proceedings." Lefkowitz v. Turley, 414 U.S. 70, 77 (1973). In all such proceedings,

> a witness protected by the privilege may rightfully refuse to answer unless and until he is protected at least against the use of his compelled answers and evidence derived therefrom in any subsequent criminal case in which he is a defendant. . . . Absent such protection, if he is nevertheless compelled to answer, his answers are inadmissible against him in a later criminal prosecution." [Id., at 78.]

A defendant does not lose this protection by reason of his conviction of a crime; notwithstanding that a defendant is imprisoned or on probation at the time he makes incriminating statements, if those statements are compelled they are inadmissible in a subsequent trial for a crime other than that for which he has been convicted. See Baxter v. Palmigiano, 425 U.S. 308, 316 (1976). The issue in this case is whether the Fifth Amendment right that Murphy enjoyed was violated by the admission into evidence at his trial for another crime of the prior statements made by him to his probation officer.

A

We note first that the general obligation to appear and answer questions truthfully did not in itself convert Murphy's otherwise voluntary statements into compelled ones. In that respect, Murphy was in no better position than the ordinary witness at a trial or before a grand jury who is subpoenaed, sworn to tell the truth, and obligated to answer on the pain of contempt, unless he invokes the privilege and shows that he faces a realistic threat of self-incrimination. The answers of such a witness to questions put to him are not compelled within the meaning of the Fifth Amendment unless the witness is required to answer over his valid claim of the privilege. . . .

Although we have sometimes suggested in dicta that the usual rule might give way in situations where the government has "substantial reason to believe that the requested disclosures are likely to be incriminating," Roberts v. United States, 445 U.S. 552, 559 (1980), we have never adopted the view that a witness must "put the Government on notice by formally availing himself of the privilege" only when he alone "is reasonably aware of the incriminating tendency of the questions." Id., at 562, n.* (Brennan, J., concurring). . . .

If a witness—even one under a general compulsion to testify—answers a question that both he and the government should reasonably expect to incriminate him, the Court need ask only whether the particular disclosure was "compelled" within the meaning of the Fifth Amendment. . . .

B. . .

1

A well-known exception to the general rule addresses the problem of confessions obtained from suspects in police custody. . . .

The Minnesota Supreme Court recognized that Murphy was not "in custody" when he made his incriminating admissions. He was, to be sure, subject to a number of restrictive conditions governing various aspects of his life, and he would be regarded as "in custody" for purposes of federal habeas corpus. . . . But custody in that context has been defined broadly to effectuate the purposes of the writ, . . . and custody for *Miranda* purposes has been more narrowly circumscribed. . . . Under the narrower standard appropriate in the *Miranda* context, it is clear that Murphy was not "in custody" for purposes of receiving *Miranda* protection since there was no " 'formal arrest or restraint on freedom of movement' of the degree associated with a formal arrest." California v. Beheler, 463 U.S. 1121, 1125 (1983) (per curiam) (quoting Oregon v. Mathiason, 429 U.S., at 495).

Notwithstanding the inapplicability of *Miranda*, the Minnesota Supreme Court held that the probation officer's failure to inform Murphy of the Fifth Amendment privilege barred use of his confession at trial. Four factors have been advanced in support of this conclusion, but we find them, alone or in combination, insufficient to excuse Murphy's failure to claim the privilege in a timely manner.

First, the probation officer could compel Murphy's attendance and truthful answers. The Minnesota Supreme Court failed to explain how this transformed a routine interview into an inherently coercive setting. In our view, this factor subjected Murphy to less intimidating pressure than is imposed on grand jury witnesses, who are sworn to tell the truth and placed in a setting conducive to truthtelling. Although warnings in both contexts might serve to dissipate "any possible coercion or unfairness resulting from a witness' misimpression that he must answer truthfully even questions with incriminating aspects," United States v. Washington, 431 U.S., at 188, we have never held that they must be given to grand jury witnesses, and we decline to require them here since the totality of the circumstances is not such as to overbear a probationer's free will. . . .

Second, the probation officer consciously sought incriminating evidence. We have already explained that this factor does not give rise to a self-executing privilege. . . . and we pause here only to emphasize that police officers questioning persons suspected of crimes often consciously seek incriminating statements. The mere fact that an investigation has focused on a suspect does not trigger the need for *Miranda* warnings in noncustodial settings, Beckwith v. United States, 425 U.S. 341 (1976), and the probation officer's knowledge and intent have no bearing on the outcome of this case.

Third, Murphy did not expect questions about prior criminal conduct and could not seek counsel before attending the meeting. But the nature of probation is such that probationers should expect to be questioned on a wide range of topics relating to their past criminality. Moreover, the probation officer's letter, which suggested a need to discuss treatment from which Murphy had already been excused, would have led a reasonable probationer to conclude that new information had come to her attention. In any event, Murphy's situation was in this regard indistinguishable from that facing suspects who are questioned in noncustodial settings and grand jury witnesses who are unaware of the scope of an investigation or that they are considered potential defendants. . . .

Fourth, there were no observers to guard against abuse or trickery. Again, this often will be true when a suspect is subjected to noncustodial interrogation, where no warnings are required. Murphy does not allege that the probation officer was not legitimately concerned with the need for further treatment, and we cannot conclude that her actions would have led a reasonable probationer to believe that his statements to her would remain confidential. A probationer cannot pretend ignorance of the fact that his probation officer "is a peace officer, and as such is allied, to a greater or lesser extent, with his fellow peace officers." Fare v. Michael C., 442 U.S. 707, 720 (1979). . . . Absent some express or implied promise to the contrary, he may also be charged with knowledge that "the probation officer is duty bound to report wrongdoing by the [probationer] when it comes to his attention, even if by communication from the [probationer] himself." Fare v. Michael C., 442 U.S., at 720. The fact that Murphy apparently expressed no surprise on being informed that his statements would be made available to the police, moreover, strongly suggests that he was not misled by any expectation that his statements would remain confidential. . . .

Even a cursory comparison of custodial interrogation and probation interviews reveals the inaptness of the Minnesota Supreme Court's analogy to *Miranda*. Custodial arrest is said to convey to the suspect a message that he has no choice but to submit to the officers' will and to confess. It is unlikely that a probation interview, arranged by appointment at a mutually convenient time, would give rise to a similar impression. Moreover, custodial arrest thrusts an individual into "an unfamiliar atmosphere" or "an interrogation environment . . . created for no purpose other than to subjugate the individual to the will of his examiner." Many of the psychological ploys discussed in *Miranda* capitalize on the suspect's unfamiliarity with the officers and the environment. Murphy's regular meetings with his probation officer should have served to familiarize him with her and her office and to insulate him from psychological intimidation that might overbear his desire to claim the privilege. Finally, the coercion inherent in custodial interrogation derives in large measure from an interrogator's insinuations that the interrogation will continue until a confession is obtained. Id., at 468. Since Murphy was not physically restrained and could have left the office, any compulsion he might have felt from the possibility that terminating the meeting would have led to revocation of probation was not comparable to the pressure on a suspect who is painfully aware that he literally cannot escape a persistent custodial interrogator.

We conclude, therefore, that Murphy cannot claim the benefit of the first exception to the general rule that the Fifth Amendment privilege is not self-executing.

2

The general rule that the privilege must be claimed when self-incrimination is threatened has also been deemed inapplicable in cases where the assertion of the privilege is penalized so as to "foreclos[e] a free choice to remain silent, and . . . compe[l] . . . incriminating testimony." Garnet v. United States, 424 U.S., at 661. Because revocation of his probation was threatened if he was untruthful with his probation officer, Murphy argues that he was compelled to make incriminating disclosures instead of claiming the privilege. Although this contention is not without force, we find it unpersuasive on close examination.

In each of the so-called "penalty" cases, the state not only compelled an individual to appear and testify, but also sought to induce him to forgo the Fifth Amendment privilege by threatening to impose economic or other sanctions "capable of forcing the self-incrimination which the Amendment forbids." Lefkowitz v. Cunningham, 431 U.S. 801, 806 (1977). In most of the cases, the attempt to override the witnesses' privilege proved unsuccessful, and the Court ruled that the state could not constitutionally make good on its prior threat. . . . These cases make clear that "a State may not impose substantial penalties because a witness elects to exercise his Fifth Amendment right not to give incriminating testimony against himself." Lefkowitz v. Cunningham, . . . 431 U.S., at 805. Occasionally, however, an individual succumbed to the pressure placed upon him, failed to assert the privilege, and disclosed incriminating information, which the state later sought to use against him in a criminal prosecution. Garrity v. New Jersey, 385 U.S. 493 (1967), was such a case, and the Court held that an individual threatened with discharge from employment for exercising the privilege had not waived it by responding to questions rather than standing on his right to remain silent. Id., at 498-499.

The threat of punishment for reliance on the privilege distinguishes cases of this sort from the ordinary case in which a witness is merely required to appear and give testimony. A state may require a probationer to appear and discuss matters that affect his probationary status; such a requirement, without more, does not give rise to a self-executing privilege. The result may be different if the questions put to the probationer, however relevant to his probationary status, call for answers that would incriminate him in a pending or later criminal prosecution. There is thus a substantial basis in our cases for concluding that if the state, either expressly or by implication, asserts that invocation of the privilege would lead to revocation of probation, it would have created the classic penalty situation, the failure to assert the privilege would be excused, and the probationer's answers would be deemed compelled and inadmissible in a criminal prosecution.

Even so we must inquire whether Murphy's probation conditions merely required him to appear and give testimony about matters relevant to his probationary status or whether they went farther and required him to choose between making incriminating statements and jeopardizing his conditional liberty by remaining silent. Because we conclude that Minnesota did not attempt to take the extra, impermissible step, we hold that Murphy's Fifth Amendment privilege was not self-executing.

As we have already indicated, Murphy was informed that he was required to be truthful with his probation officer in all matters and that failure to do so could result in revocation of probation. The opinion of the Minnesota Supreme Court made clear that this was indeed the case, but its conclusion that the probation officer's failure to give Murphy adequate warnings barred the use of his incriminating statements in the criminal trial did not rest on the ground that a refusal to furnish incriminating information would have justified revocation of probation. Although the court recognized that imposing a penalty for a valid exercise of the Fifth Amendment privilege could impermissibly foreclose a free choice to remain silent, it did not purport to find that Minnesota's probation revocation statute had such an effect. The court relied instead on the fact that Murphy was under legal compulsion to attend the meeting and to answer truthfully the questions of a probation officer who anticipated incriminating answers. Such compulsion, however, is indistinguishable from that felt by any witness who is required to appear and give testimony, and, as we have already made clear, it is insufficient to excuse Murphy's failure to exercise the privilege in a timely manner. . . .

Whether we employ a subjective or an objective test, there is no reasonable basis for concluding that Minnesota attempted to attach an impermissible penalty to the exercise of the privilege against self-incrimination. There is no direct evidence that Murphy confessed because he feared that his probation would be revoked if he remained silent. Unlike the police officers in Garrity v. New Jersey, 385 U.S. 493 (1967), Murphy was not expressly informed during the crucial meeting with his probation officer that an assertion of the privilege would result in the imposition of a penalty. And the fact that Murphy apparently felt no compunction about adamantly denying the false imprisonment charge on which he had been convicted before admitting to the rape and murder strongly suggests that the "threat" of revocation did not overwhelm his resistance.

If Murphy did harbor a belief that his probation might be revoked for exercising the Fifth Amendment privilege, that belief would not have been reasonable. Our decisions have made clear that the State could not constitutionally carry out a threat to revoke probation for the legitimate exercise of the Fifth Amendment privilege. It is not surprising, then, that neither the State court nor any State officer has suggested otherwise. Indeed, in its brief in this Court, the State submits that it would not, and legally could not, revoke probation for refusing to answer questions calling for information that would incriminate in separate criminal proceedings. . . .

Accordingly, we cannot conclude that Murphy was deterred from claiming the privilege by a reasonably perceived threat of revocation.

3

A third exception to the general requirement of a timely assertion of the Fifth Amendment privilege, closely related to the penalty exception, has been developed in the context of the federal occupational and excise taxes on gamblers. In recognition of the pervasive criminal regulation of gambling activities and the fact that claiming the privilege in lieu of filing a return would tend to incriminate, the Court has held that the privilege may be exercised by failing to file. . . .

[M]aking a claim of privilege when the disclosures were requested, i.e., when the returns were due, would have identified the claimant as a gambler. The Court therefore forgave the usual requirement that the claim of

privilege be presented for evaluation in favor of a 'claim' by silence. . . .
If a particular gambler would not have incriminated himself by filing the
tax returns, the privilege would not justify a failure to file. [Garner v.
United States, 424 U.S., at 658-659, n. 11.]

But, while a taxpayer who claims the privilege instead of filing gambling
tax returns necessarily identifies himself as a gambler, a probationer confronted with incriminating questions ordinarily will have no problem
effectively claiming the privilege at the time disclosures are requested.
There exists, therefore, no reason to forgive the requirement that the
claim be presented for evaluation in a timely manner.[8]

III

We conclude, in summary, that since Murphy revealed incriminating
information instead of timely asserting his Fifth Amendment privilege,
his disclosures were not compelled incriminations. Because he had not
been compelled to incriminate himself, Murphy could not successfully
invoke the privilege to prevent the information he volunteered to his
probation officer from being used against him in a criminal prosecution.
The judgment of the Minnesota Supreme Court is reversed.

JUSTICE MARSHALL, joined by JUSTICE STEVENS and in all but Part
II-A by JUSTICE BRENNAN, dissenting. . . .

8. Nothing in Mackey v. United States, 401 U.S. 667 (1971), requires a different
conclusion. In that case, which arose before the Court recognized a privilege not to file
gambling tax returns, the taxpayer filed a return that was introduced as evidence in a
criminal prosecution for income tax evasion. A majority of the Court considered the
disclosures to have been compelled incriminations, id., at 672 (plurality opinion); id.,
at 704-705 (Brennan, J., concurring in the judgment); id., at 713 (Douglas, J., dissenting),
but the taxpayer was not immunized against their use because Marchetti and Grosso were
not given retroactive effect. Id., at 674-675 (plurality opinion); id., at 700-701 (Harlan,
J., concurring in the judgment). Even assuming that the taxpayer's disclosures would
have been excluded if we had applied Marchetti and Grosso retroactively, "[i]t does not
follow necessarily that a taxpayer would be immunized against use of disclosures made
on gambling tax returns when the Fifth Amendment would have justified a failure to
file at all." Garner v. United States, 424 U.S. 648, 659, n. 13 (1976). In other words, a
taxpayer making incriminating disclosures on a return filed after Marchetti and Grosso
could not necessarily prevent the use of those disclosures in a criminal prosecution because
he had been afforded an effective way to assert the privilege. Murphy's situation, we
believe, is analogous to that of the post-Marchetti taxpayer: Since he could have asserted
the privilege effectively but failed to do so, his disclosures cannot be viewed as compelled
incriminations.

I

As the majority acknowledges, if an officer of a state asks a person a question under circumstances that deprive him of a " 'free choice to admit, to deny, or to refuse to answer,' " and he answers the question without attempting to assert his privilege against self-incrimination, his response will be deemed to have been "compelled" and will be inadmissible as evidence against him. . . . Our cases make clear that the state will be found to have deprived the person of such a "free choice" if it threatens him with a substantial sanction if he refuses to respond. Lefkowitz v. Turley, 414 U.S., at 82-83. Two rules flow from the foregoing principle: If the state presents a person with the "Hobson's choice" of incriminating himself or suffering a penalty, and he nevertheless refuses to respond, the state cannot constitutionally make good on its threat to penalize him. . . . Conversely, if the threatened person decides to talk instead of asserting his privilege, the state cannot use his admissions against him in a subsequent criminal prosecution. Garrity v. New Jersey, 385 U.S. 493, 500 (1967).

It might appear that these two rules would defeat one another. A person presented with what appears to be a Hobson's choice could be charged with the knowledge that, under this Court's precedents, he may choose either option with impunity. His awareness that the state can use neither his silence nor his confessions against him would seem to eliminate the "compulsion" supposedly inherent in the situation. More specifically, it might be argued that, because it is now settled that a person cannot be penalized for asserting his Fifth-Amendment privilege, if he decides to talk rather than assert his constitutional right to remain silent, his statements should be deemed voluntary.

This Court has consistently refused to allow the two rules to undercut each other in this way. Our refusal derives from two considerations. First, many—probably most—of the persons threatened with sanctions if they refuse to answer official questions lack sufficient knowledge of this Court's decisions to be aware that the state's threat is idle. Second, the state's *attempt* to coerce self-incriminating statements by promising to penalize silence is itself constitutionally offensive, and the mere possibility that the state profited from the attempt is sufficient to forbid it to make use of the admissions it elicited. See Gardner v. Broderick, 392 U.S., at 279.

For similar reasons, when a person who has been threatened with a penalty makes self-incriminating statements, we have declined to inquire whether his decision to speak was the proximate result of the threat. In most cases it would be difficult for the person to prove that, but for the threat, he would have held his peace and that no other intervening causes (such as pangs of conscience) induced him to confess. The state, having exerted pressures repugnant to the Constitution, should not be allowed to profit from the uncertainty whether those pressures had their intended effect. Sensitivity to the foregoing concerns is reflected in our decision in Garrity v. New Jersey, supra. The petitioners in that case had never argued that their confessions were in fact induced by the state's warning that they might be fired if they refused to answer, and the lower courts had not so found. Nevertheless, the Court concluded that the petitioners' statements "were infected by the coercion inherent in this scheme of questioning and cannot be sustained as voluntary." 385 U.S., at 497-498 (footnote omitted).

In sum, the majority errs when it suggests that, to claim the benefit of the Fifth Amendment, a person who made self-incriminating statements after being threatened with a penalty if he remained silent must show that his apprehension that the state would carry out its promise was objectively "reasonable." . . . Our decisions make clear that the threat alone is sufficient to render all subsequent testimony "compelled." . . . Likewise, the majority errs when it implies that a defendant has a duty to prove that the state's threat, and not some other motivation, prompted his confession. . . . Under our precedents, the defendant need only prove that the state presented him with a constitutionally impermissible choice and that he thereupon incriminated himself. . . .

When the foregoing principles are applied to this case, it becomes clear that Murphy's confession to the 1974 murder must be deemed to have been "compelled." . . .

In short, the State of Minnesota presented Murphy with a set of official instructions that a reasonable man would have interpreted to require him, upon pain of the revocation of his probation, to answer truthfully all questions asked by his probation officer. Probation revocation surely constitutes a "substantial sanction." Under our precedents, therefore, by threatening Murphy with that sanction if he refused to answer, Minnesota deprived itself of constitutional authority to use Murphy's subsequent answers in a criminal prosecution against him. . . .

II

Even if Minnesota had not impaired Murphy's freedom to respond or to refuse to respond to incriminating questions regarding the 1974 murder, I would hold his confession inadmissible because, in view of the circumstances under which he was interrogated, the State had a duty to prove that Murphy waived his privilege against self-incrimination, and it has not made such a showing.

A

It is now settled that, in most contexts, the privilege against self-incrimination is not self-executing. . . .

The explanation for our seemingly callous willingness to countenance forfeitures of Fifth Amendment rights must be sought in a combination of three factors. *First* and most importantly, we presume that most people are aware that they need not answer an official question when a truthful answer might expose them to criminal prosecution. "At this point in our history virtually every schoolboy is familiar with the concept, if not the language," of the constitutional ban on compelled self-incrimination. Michigan v. Tucker, 417 U.S. 433, 439 (1974). We thus take for granted that, in most instances, when a person discloses damaging information in response to an official inquiry, he has made an intelligent decision to waive his Fifth Amendment rights.

Second, in the vast majority of situations in which an officer of the state asks a citizen a question, the officer has no reason to know that a truthful response would reveal that the citizen has committed a crime. Under such circumstances, one of the central principles underlying the Fifth Amendment—that governments should not "deliberately seek[] to avoid the burdens of independent investigation by compelling self-incriminating disclosures"—has little relevance. Garner v. United States, 424 U.S., at 655-656. Thus, in the ordinary case, few constitutional values are threatened when the government fails to preface an inquiry with an explicit reminder that a response is not required if it might expose the respondent to prosecution.

Third, a general requirement that government officials preface all questions with such reminders would be highly burdensome. Our concern with the protection of constitutional rights should not blind us to the fact that, in general, governments have the right to everyone's testimony. E.g., Branzburg v. Hayes, 408 U.S. 665, 688 (1972). A rule requiring officials, before asking citizens for information, to tell them that they need not reveal incriminating evidence would unduly impede the capacity of government to gather the data it needs to function effectively. . . .

It should be apparent that these considerations do not apply with equal force in all contexts. Until today, the Court has been sensitive to variations in their relevance and strength. Accordingly, we have adhered to the general principle that a defendant forfeits his privilege if he fails to assert it before making incriminating statements only in situations implicating several of the factors that support the principle. More specifically, we have applied the principle only in cases in which at least two of the following statements have been true:

(a) At the time the damaging disclosures were made, the defendant's constitutional right not to make them was clearly established.

(b) The defendant was given sufficient warning that he would be asked potentially incriminating questions to be able to secure legal advice and to reflect upon how he would respond.

(c) The environment in which the questions were asked did not impair the defendant's ability intelligently to exercise his rights.

(d) The questioner had no reason to assume that truthful responses would be self-incriminating. . . .

B

If we remain sensitive to the concerns implicit in the foregoing pattern of cases, we should insist that the State, in the instant case, demonstrate that Murphy intelligently waived his right to remain silent. None of the four conditions that favor application of the principle that a defendant forfeits his privilege if he fails to claim it before confessing can be found in the circumstances under which Murphy was interrogated. *First*, the existence and scope of Murphy's constitutional right to refuse to testify were at best unclear when he appeared in the probation officer's office. It is undisputed that the conditions of Murphy's probation imposed on him a duty to answer all questions presented by his probation officer except those implicating his Fifth Amendment rights. What exactly those rights were was far from apparent. The majority opinion in this case constitutes the first authoritative analysis of the privilege against self-incrimination available to a probationer. . . .

Second, contrary to the suggestion of the majority, . . . Murphy was given no warning that he would be asked potentially incriminating questions. The letter in which Murphy's probation officer instructed him to make an appointment informed him that the purpose of the meeting was "[t]o further discuss a treatment plan for the remainder of [his] probation." . . .

Third, the environment in which the questioning occurred impaired Murphy's ability to recognize and claim his constitutional rights. It is true, as the majority points out, that the discussion between a probation officer and a probationer is likely to be less coercive and intimidating than a discussion between a police officer and a suspect in custody. . . . But it is precisely in that fact that the danger lies. In contrast to the inherently adversarial relationship between a suspect and a policeman, the relationship between a probationer and the officer to whom he reports is likely to incorporate elements of confidentiality, even friendship. Indeed, many probation officers deliberately cultivate such bonds with their charges. The point should not be overstated; undoubtedly, few probationers are entirely blind to the fact that their probation officers are "peace officer[s], . . . allied, to a greater or lesser extent, with [their] fellow peace officers." Fare v. Michael C., 442 U.S. 707, 720 (1979). On the other hand, many probationers develop "relationship[s] of trust and confidence" with their officers. Id., at 722. Through abuse of that trust, a probation officer can elicit admissions from a probationer that the probationer would be unlikely to make to a hostile police interrogator.

Finally, it is indisputable that the probation officer had reason to know that truthful responses to her questions would expose Murphy to criminal liability. This case does not arise out of a spontaneous confession to a routine question innocently asked by a government official. Rather, it originates in precisely the sort of situation the Fifth Amendment was designed to prevent—in which a government, instead of establishing a defendant's guilt through independent investigation, seeks to induce him, against his will, to convict himself out of his own mouth.

In sum, none of the factors that, in most contexts, justify application of the principle that a defendant loses his Fifth Amendment privilege unless he claims it in a timely fashion are present in this case. Accordingly, the State should be obliged to demonstrate that Murphy knew of his constitutional rights and freely waived them. Because the State has made no such showing, I would hold his confession inadmissible.

c. Police Trickery: Implications for the Meaning of "Interrogation" and "Custody"

Some commentators have argued that the fifth amendment should be interpreted to forbid what is called "trickery." See, e.g., White, Police Trickery in Inducing Confessions, 127 U. Pa. L. Rev 581 (1979). The objected to practices come in two forms. The first is "tricking" a suspect to waive the *Miranda* rights, which is discussed at pages 1208-1224 infra. The second form involves "tricking" a suspect to make voluntary, incriminating statements in such a manner as to avoid *Miranda*'s dictates. The Court considered this latter problem in Illinois v. Perkins.

ILLINOIS v. PERKINS
Certiorari to the Appellate Court of Illinois
—U.S.—, 110 S. Ct. 2394 (1990)

JUSTICE KENNEDY delivered the opinion of the Court.

An undercover government agent was placed in the cell of respondent Perkins, who was incarcerated on charges unrelated to the subject of the agent's investigation. Respondent made statements that implicated him in the crime that the agent sought to solve. Respondent claims that the statements should be inadmissible because he had not been given

Miranda warnings by the agent. We hold that the statements are admissible. *Miranda* warnings are not required when the suspect is unaware that he is speaking to a law enforcement officer and gives a voluntary statement.   *but what @ 6th counsel rts*

I

In November 1984, Richard Stephenson was murdered in a suburb of East St. Louis, Illinois. The murder remained unsolved until March 1986, when one Donald Charlton told police that he had learned about a homicide from a fellow inmate at the Graham Correctional Facility, where Charlton had been serving a sentence for burglary. The fellow inmate was Lloyd Perkins, who is the respondent here. Charlton told police that, while at Graham, he had befriended respondent, who told him in detail about a murder that respondent had committed in East St. Louis. On hearing Charlton's account, the police recognized details of the Stephenson murder that were not well known, and so they treated Charlton's story as a credible one.

By the time the police heard Charlton's account, respondent had been released from Graham, but police traced him to a jail in Montgomery County, Illinois, where he was being held pending trial on a charge of aggravated battery, unrelated to the Stephenson murder. The police wanted to investigate further respondent's connection to the Stephenson murder, but feared that the use of an eavesdropping device would prove impracticable and unsafe. They decided instead to place an undercover agent in the cellblock with respondent and Charlton. The plan was for Charlton and undercover agent John Parisi to pose as escapees from a work release program who had been arrested in the course of a burglary. Parisi and Charlton were instructed to engage respondent in casual conversation and report anything he said about the Stephenson murder.

Parisi, using the alias "Vito Bianco," and Charlton, both clothed in jail garb, were placed in the cellblock with respondent at the Montgomery County jail. The cellblock consisted of 12 separate cells that opened onto a common room. Respondent greeted Charlton who, after a brief conversation with respondent, introduced Parisi by his alias. Parisi told respondent that he "wasn't going to do any more time," and suggested that the three of them escape. Respondent replied that the Montgomery County jail was "rinky-dink" and that they could "break out." The trio met in respondent's cell later that evening, after the other inmates were asleep, to refine their plan. Respondent said that his girlfriend could smuggle in a pistol. Charlton said "Hey, I'm not a murderer, I'm a

burglar. That's your guys' profession." After telling Charlton that he
would be responsible for any murder that occurred, Parisi asked respondent if he had ever "done" anybody. Respondent said that he had, and
proceeded to describe at length the events of the Stephenson murder.
Parisi and respondent then engaged in some casual conversation before
respondent went to sleep. Parisi did not give respondent *Miranda* warnings before the conversations.

Respondent was charged with the Stephenson murder. Before trial,
he moved to suppress the statements made to Parisi in the jail. The trial
court granted the motion to suppress, and the State appealed. The Appellate Court of Illinois affirmed, holding that Miranda v. Arizona prohibits all undercover contacts with incarcerated suspects which are
reasonably likely to elicit an incriminating response.

We granted certiorari to decide whether an undercover law enforcement officer must give *Miranda* warnings to an incarcerated suspect
before asking him questions that may elicit an incriminating response.
We now reverse.

II

In Miranda v. Arizona, the Court held that the Fifth Amendment privilege against self-incrimination prohibits admitting statements given by a
suspect during "custodial interrogation" without a prior warning. Custodial interrogation means "questioning initiated by law enforcement
officers after a person has been taken into custody. . . ." The warning
mandated by *Miranda* was meant to preserve the privilege during "incommunicado interrogation of individuals in a police-dominated atmosphere." That atmosphere is said to generate "inherently compelling
pressures which work to undermine the individual's will to resist and to
compel him to speak where he would not otherwise do so freely." "Fidelity
to the doctrine announced in *Miranda* requires that it be enforced strictly,
but only in those types of situations in which the concerns that powered
the decision are implicated." Berkemer v. McCarty, 468 U.S. 420, 437
(1984).

Conversations between suspects and undercover agents do not implicate the concerns underlying *Miranda*. The essential ingredients of a
"police-dominated atmosphere" and compulsion are not present when
an incarcerated person speaks freely to someone that he believes to be a
fellow inmate. Coercion is determined from the perspective of the suspect.
When a suspect considers himself in the company of cellmates and not
officers, the coercive atmosphere is lacking. There is no empirical basis
for the assumption that a suspect speaking to those whom he assumes

are not officers will feel compelled to speak by the fear of reprisal for remaining silent or in the hope of more lenient treatment should be confess.

It is the premise of *Miranda* that the danger of coercion results from the interaction of custody and official interrogation. We reject the argument that *Miranda* warnings are required whenever a suspect is in custody in a technical sense and converses with someone who happens to be a government agent. Questioning by captors, who appear to control the suspect's fate, may create mutually reinforcing pressures that the Court has assumed will weaken the suspect's will, but where a suspect does not know that he is conversing with a government agent, these pressures do not exist. The State Court here mistakenly assumed that because the suspect was in custody, no undercover questioning could take place. When the suspect has no reason to think that the listeners have official power over him, it should not be assumed that his words are motivated by the reaction he expects from his listeners. "[W]hen the agent carries neither badge nor gun and wears not 'police blue,' but the same prison gray" as the suspect, there is no "interplay between police interrogation and police custody." Kamisar, Brewer v. Williams, *Massiah* and *Miranda*: What Is "Interrogation"? When Does It Matter?, 67 Geo. L.J. 1, 67, 63 (1978).

Miranda forbids coercion, not mere strategic deception by taking advantage of a suspect's misplaced trust in one he supposes to be a fellow prisoner. As we recognized in *Miranda*, "[c]onfessions remain a proper element in law enforcement. Any statement given freely and voluntarily without any compelling influences is, of course, admissible in evidence." 384 U.S., at 478. Ploys to mislead a suspect or lull him into a false sense of security that do not rise to the level of compulsion or coercion to speak are not within *Miranda's* concerns.

Miranda was not meant to protect suspects from boasting about their criminal activities in front of persons whom they believe to be their cellmates. This case is illustrative. Respondent had no reason to feel that undercover agent Parisi had any legal authority to force him to answer questions or that Parisi could affect respondent's future treatment. Respondent viewed the cellmate-agent as an equal and showed no hint of being intimidated by the atmosphere of the jail. In recounting the details of the Stephenson murder, respondent was motivated solely by the desire to impress his fellow inmates. He spoke at his own peril.

The tactic employed here to elicit a voluntary confession from a suspect does not violate the Self-Incrimination Clause. We held in Hoffa v. United States, 385 U.S. 293 (1966), that placing an undercover agent near a suspect in order to gather incriminating information was permissible under the Fifth Amendment. In *Hoffa*, while petitioner Hoffa was on trial, he met often with one Partin, who, unbeknownst to Hoffa, was cooperating with law enforcement officials. Partin reported to officials that Hoffa had divulged his attempts to bribe jury members. We approved using Hoffa's statements at his subsequent trial for jury tampering, on the rationale that "no claim ha[d] been or could [have been] made that [Hoffa's] incriminating statements were the product of any sort of coercion, legal or factual." Id., at 304. In addition, we found that the fact that Partin had fooled Hoffa into thinking that Partin was a sympathetic colleague did not affect the voluntariness of the statement. Cf. Oregon v. Mathiason, 429 U.S., at 495-496 (officer's falsely telling suspect that suspect's fingerprints had been found at crime scene did not render interview "custodial" under *Miranda*). The only difference between this case and *Hoffa* is that the suspect here was incarcerated, but detention, whether or not for the crime in question, does not warrant a presumption that the use of an undercover agent to speak with an incarcerated suspect makes any confession thus obtained involuntary.

Our decision in Mathis v. United States, 391 U.S. 1 (1968), is distinguishable. In *Mathis*, an inmate in a state prison was interviewed by an Internal Revenue Service agent about possible tax violations. No *Miranda* warning was given before questioning. The Court held that the suspect's incriminating statements were not admissible at his subsequent trial on tax fraud charges. The suspect in *Mathis* was aware that the agent was a government official, investigating the possibility on non-compliance with the tax laws. The case before us now is different. Where the suspect does not know that he is speaking to a government agent there is no reason to assume the possibility that the suspect might feel coerced. (The bare fact of custody may not in every instance require a warning even when the suspect is aware that he is speaking to an official, but we do not have occasion to explore that issue here.)

This Court's Sixth Amendment decisions [such as] Massiah v. United States, also do not avail respondent. We held in those cases that the government may not use an undercover agent to circumvent the Sixth Amendment right to counsel once a suspect has been charged with the crime. After charges have been filed, the Sixth Amendment prevents the government from interfering with the accused's right to counsel. In the instant case no charges had been filed on the subject of the interrogation, and our Sixth Amendment precedents are not applicable.

Respondent can seek no help from his argument that a bright-line rule for the application of *Miranda* is desirable. Law enforcement officers will have little difficulty putting into practice our holding that undercover agents need not give *Miranda* warnings to incarcerated suspects. The use of undercover agents is a recognized law enforcement technique, often employed in the prison context to detect violence against correctional officials or inmates, as well as for the purposes served here. The interests protected by *Miranda* are not implicated in these cases, and the warnings are not required to safeguard the constitutional rights of inmates who make voluntary statements to undercover agents.

We hold that an undercover law enforcement officer posing as a fellow inmate need not give *Miranda* warnings to an incarcerated suspect before asking questions that may elicit an incriminating response. The statements at issue in this case were voluntary, and there is no federal obstacle to their admissibility at trial. We now reverse and remand for proceedings not inconsistent with our opinion.

JUSTICE BRENNAN, concurring in the judgment.

The Court holds that Miranda v. Arizona does not require suppression of a statement made by an incarcerated suspect to an undercover agent. Although I do not subscribe to the majority's characterization of *Miranda* in its entirety, I do agree that when a suspect does not know that his questioner is a police agent, such questioning does not amount to "interrogation" in an "inherently coercive" environment so as to require application of *Miranda*. Since the only issue raised at this stage of the litigation is the applicability of *Miranda*,* I concur in the judgment of the Court.

This is not to say that I believe the Constitution condones the method by which the police extracted the confession in this case. To the contrary, the deception and manipulation practiced on respondent raise a substantial claim that the confession was obtained in violation of the Due Process Clause. As we recently stated in Miller v. Fenton, 474 U.S. 104, 109-110 (1985):

> This Court has long held that certain interrogation techniques, either in isolation or as applied to the unique characteristics of a particular suspect,

*As the case comes to us, it involves only the question whether *Miranda* applies to the questioning of an incarcerated suspect by an undercover agent. Nothing in the Court's opinion suggests that, had respondent previously invoked his Fifth Amendment right to counsel or right to silence, his statements would be admissible. If respondent had invoked either right, the inquiry would focus on whether he subsequently waived the particular right. See Edwards v. Arizona, 451 U.S. 477 (1981); Michigan v. Mosley, 423 U.S. 96, 104 (1975). As the Court made clear in Moran v. Burbine, 475 U.S. 412, 421 (1986), the waiver of *Miranda* rights "must [be] voluntary in the sense that it [must be] the product of a free and deliberate choice rather than intimidation, coercion or deception." (Emphasis added). Since respondent was in custody on an unrelated charge when he was questioned, he may be able to challenge the admission of these statements if he previously had invoked his *Miranda* rights with respect to that charge. See Arizona v. Roberson, 486 U.S. 675 (1988); Mosley, supra, at 104. Similarly, if respondent had been formally charged on the unrelated charge and had invoked his Sixth Amendment right to counsel, he may have a Sixth Amendment challenge to the admissibility of these statements. See Michigan v. Jackson, 475 U.S. 625, 629-636 (1986). Cf. Roberson, supra, at 683-685. [These matters are discussed at page 1269 infra.—EDS.].

are so offensive to a civilized system of justice that they must be condemned
under the Due Process Clause of the Fourteenth Amendment. . . . Although these decisions framed the legal inquiry in a variety of different
ways, usually through the "convenient shorthand" of asking whether the
confession was "involuntary," Blackburn v. Alabama, 361 U.S. 199, 207
(1960), the Court's analysis has consistently been animated by the view
that "ours is an accusatorial and not an inquisitorial system," Rogers v.
Richmond, 365 U.S. 534, 541 (1961), and that, accordingly, tactics for
eliciting inculpatory statements must fall within the broad constitutional
boundaries imposed by the Fourteenth Amendment's guarantee of fundamental fairness.

That the right is derived from the Due Process Clause "is significant
because it reflects the Court's consistently held view that the admissibility
of a confession turns as much on whether the techniques for extracting
the statements, as applied to this suspect, are compatible with a system
that presumes innocence and assures that a conviction will not be secured
by inquisitorial means as on whether the defendant's will was in fact
overborne." Miller, supra, at 116. See Spano v. New York, 360 U.S.
315, 320-321 (1959) ("The abhorrence of society to the use of involuntary
confessions does not turn alone on their inherent untrustworthiness. It
also turns on the deep-rooted feeling that the police must obey the law
while enforcing the law; that in the end life and liberty can be as much
endangered from illegal methods used to convict those thought to be
criminals as from the actual criminals themselves").

The method used to elicit the confession in this case deserves close
scrutiny. The police devised a ruse to lure respondent into incriminating
himself when he was in jail on an unrelated charge. A police agent,
posing as a fellow inmate and proposing a sham escape plot, tricked
respondent into confessing that he had once committed a murder, as a
way of proving that he would be willing to do so again should the need
arise during the escape. The testimony of the undercover officer and a
police informant at the suppression hearing reveal the deliberate manner
in which the two elicited incriminating statements from respondent. We
have recognized that "the mere fact of custody imposes pressures on the
accused; confinement may bring into play subtle influences that will
make him particularly susceptible to the ploys of undercover Government
agents." United States v. Henry, 447 U.S. 264, 274 (1980). As Justice
Marshall points out [in dissent], the pressures of custody make a suspect
more likely to confide in others and to engage in "jailhouse bravado."
The State is in a unique position to exploit this vulnerability because it
has virtually complete control over the suspect's environment. Thus, the
State can ensure that a suspect is barraged with questions from an un-

dercover agent until the suspect confesses. The testimony in this case suggests the State did just that.

The deliberate use of deception and manipulation by the police appears to be incompatible "with a system that presumes innocence and assures that a conviction will not be secured by inquisitorial means," Miller, supra, at 116, and raises serious concerns that respondent's will was overborne. It is open to the lower court on remand to determine whether, under the totality of the circumstances, respondent's confession was elicited in a manner that violated the Due Process Clause. That the confession was not elicited through means of physical torture, or overt psychological pressure, does not end the inquiry. "[A]s law enforcement officers become more responsible, and the methods used to extract confessions more sophisticated, [a court's] duty to enforce federal constitutional protections does not cease. It only becomes more difficult because of the more delicate judgments to be made." Spano, supra, at 321.

JUSTICE MARSHALL, dissenting.

This Court clearly and simply stated its holding in Miranda v. Arizona: "[T]he prosecution may not use statements, whether exculpatory or inculpatory, stemming from custodial interrogation of the defendant unless it demonstrates the use of procedural safeguards effective to secure the privilege against self-incrimination." The conditions that require the police to apprise a defendant of his constitutional rights—custodial interrogation conducted by an agent of the police—were present in this case. Because Lloyd Perkins received no Miranda warnings before he was subjected to custodial interrogation, his confession was not admissible.

The Court reaches the contrary conclusion by fashioning an exception to the Miranda rule that applies whenever "an undercover law enforcement officer posing as a fellow inmate . . . ask[s] questions that may elicit an incriminating response" from an incarcerated suspect. This exception is inconsistent with the rationale supporting Miranda and allows police officers intentionally to take advantage of suspects unaware of their constitutional rights. I therefore dissent.

The Court does not dispute that the police officer here conducted a custodial interrogation of a criminal suspect. Perkins was incarcerated in county jail during the questioning at issue here; under these circumstances, he was in custody as that term is defined in Miranda. The Solicitor General argues that Perkins was not in custody for purpose of Miranda because he was familiar with the custodial environment as a result of being in jail for two days and previously spending time in prison. Perkins' familiarity with confinement, however, does not transform his incarceration into some sort of noncustodial arrangement. Cf. Orozco

v. Texas, 394 U.S. 324 (1969) (holding that suspect who had been arrested in his home and then questioned in his bedroom was in custody, notwithstanding his familiarity with the surroundings).

While Perkins was confined, an undercover police officer, with the help of a police informant, questioned him about a serious crime. Although the Court does not dispute that Perkins was interrogated, it downplays the nature of the 35-minute questioning by disingenuously referring to it as a "conversatio[n]." The officer's narration of the "conversation" at Perkins' trial, however, reveals that it clearly was an interrogation.

> [Agent:] You ever do anyone?
> [Perkins:] Yeah, once in East St. Louis, in a rich white neighborhood.
> Informant: I didn't know they had any rich white neighborhoods in East St. Louis.
> Perkins: It wasn't in East St. Louis, it was by a race track in Fairview Heights. . . .
> [Agent]: You did a guy in Fairview Heights?
> Perkins: Yeah in a rich white section where most of the houses look the same.
> [Informant]: If all the houses look the same, how did you know you had the right house?
> Perkins: Me and two guys cased the house for about a week. I knew exactly which house, the second house on the left from the corner.
> [Agent]: How long ago did this happen?
> Perkins: Approximately about two years ago. I got paid $5,000 for that job.
> [Agent]: How did it go down?
> Perkins: I walked up to . . . this guy['s] house with a sawed-off under my trench coat.
> [Agent]: What type gun[?]
> Perkins: A .12 gauge Remmington [sic] Automatic Model 1100 sawed-off.

The police officer continued the inquiry, asking a series of questions designed to elicit specific information about the victim, the crime scene, the weapon, Perkins' motive, and his actions during and after the shooting. This interaction was not a "conversation"; Perkins, the officer, and the informant were not equal participants in a free-ranging discussion, with each man offering his views on different topics. Rather, it was an interrogation: Perkins was subjected to express questioning likely to evoke an incriminating response.

Because Perkins was interrogated by police while he was in custody, *Miranda* required that the officer inform him of his rights. In rejecting that conclusion, the Court finds that "conversations" between undercover agents and suspects are devoid of the coercion inherent in stationhouse interrogations conducted by law enforcement officials who openly represent the State. *Miranda* was not, however, concerned solely with police coercion. It dealt with any police tactics that may operate to compel a suspect in custody to make incriminating statements without full awareness of his constitutional rights. See *Miranda*, supra, at 468 (referring to "inherent pressures of the interrogation atmosphere"); Estelle v. Smith, 451 U.S. 454, 467 (1981) ("The purpose of [the *Miranda*] admonitions is to combat what the Court saw as 'inherently compelling pressures' at work on the person and to provide him with an awareness of the Fifth Amendment privilege and the consequences of forgoing it") (quoting *Miranda*, 384 U.S., at 467). Thus, when a law enforcement agent structures a custodial interrogation so that a suspect feels compelled to reveal incriminating information, he must inform the suspect of his constitutional rights and give him an opportunity to decide whether or not to talk.

The compulsion proscribed by *Miranda* includes deception by the police. See *Miranda*, supra, at 453 (indicting police tactics "to induce a confession out of trickery," such as using fictitious witnesses or false accusations); Berkemer v. McCarty, 468 U.S. 420, 433 (1984) ("The purposes of the safeguards prescribed by *Miranda* are to ensure that the police do not coerce or trick captive suspects into confessing"). Cf. Moran v. Burbine, 475 U.S. 412, 421 (1986) ("[T]he relinquishment of the right [protected by the *Miranda* warnings] must have been voluntary in the sense that it was the product of a free and deliberate choice rather than intimidation, coercion, or deception"). Although the Court did not find trickery by itself sufficient to constitute compulsion in Hoffa v. United States, the defendant in that case was not in custody. Perkins, however, was interrogated while incarcerated. As the Court has acknowledged in the Sixth Amendment context: "[T]he mere fact of custody imposes pressures on the accused; confinement may bring into play subtle influences that will make him particularly susceptible to the ploys of undercover Government agents." United States v. Henry, 447 U.S. 264, 274 (1980). . . .

Custody works to the State's advantage in obtaining incriminating information. The psychological pressures inherent in confinement increase the suspect's anxiety, making him likely to seek relief by talking with others. . . . The inmate is thus more susceptible to efforts by undercover agents to elicit information from him. Similarly, where the suspect is incarcerated, the constant threat of physical danger peculiar to the prison environment may make him demonstrate his toughness to other inmates by recounting or inventing past violent acts. "Because the suspect's ability to select people with whom he can confide is completely within their control, the police have a unique opportunity to exploit the suspect's vulnerability. In short, the police can insure that if the pressures of confinement lead the suspect to confide in anyone, it will be a police agent." White, Police Trickery in Inducing Confessions, 127 U. Pa. L. Rev. 581, 605 (1979). In this case, the police deceptively took advantage of Perkins' psychological vulnerability by including him in a sham escape plot, a situation in which he would feel compelled to demonstrate his willingness to shoot a prison guard by revealing his past involvement in a murder. . . .

Thus, the pressures unique to custody allow the police to use deceptive interrogation tactics to compel a suspect to make an incriminating statement. The compulsion is not eliminated by the suspect's ignorance of his interrogator's true identity. The Court therefore need not inquire past the bare facts of custody and interrogation to determine whether *Miranda* warnings are required.

The Court's adoption of an exception to the *Miranda* doctrine is incompatible with the principle, consistently applied by this Court, that the doctrine should remain simple and clear. . . . We explained the benefits of a bright-line rule in Fare v. Michael C., 442 U.S. 707 (1979): "*Miranda*'s holding has the virtue of informing police and prosecutors with specificity as to what they may do in conducting custodial interrogation, and of informing courts under what circumstances statements obtained during such interrogation are not admissible." Id., at 718.

The Court's holding today complicates a previously clear and straightforward doctrine. The Court opines that "[l]aw enforcement officers will have little difficulty putting into practice our holding that undercover agents need not give *Miranda* warnings to incarcerated suspects." Perhaps this prediction is true with respect to fact patterns virtually identical to the one before the Court today. But the outer boundaries of the exception created by the Court are by no means clear. Would *Miranda* be violated, for instance, if an undercover police officer beat a confession out of a suspect, but the suspect thought the officer was another prisoner who wanted the information for his own purposes?

Even if *Miranda*, as interpreted by the Court, would not permit such obviously compelled confessions, the ramifications of today's opinion are still disturbing. The exception carved out of the *Miranda* doctrine today may well result in a proliferation of departmental policies to encourage police officers to conduct interrogations of confined suspects through undercover agents, thereby circumventing the need to administer *Miranda* warnings. Indeed, if *Miranda* now requires a police officer to issue warnings only in those situations in which the suspect might feel compelled "to speak by the fear of reprisal for remaining silent or in the hope of more lenient treatment should he confess," presumably it allows custodial interrogation by an undercover officer posing as a member of the clergy or a suspect's defense attorney. Although such abhorrent tricks would play on a suspect's need to confide in a trusted adviser, neither would cause the suspect to "think that the listeners have official power over him." The Court's adoption of the "undercover agent" exception to the *Miranda* rule thus is necessarily also the adoption of a substantial loophole in our jurisprudence protecting suspects' Fifth Amendment rights.

   I dissent.

d. Adequacy of the Warnings Given

The Supreme Court has not given talismanic effect to the precise language in which the required warnings were first articulated. In California v. Prysock, 453 U.S. 355 (1981), the Court upheld a conviction where the warnings given the defendant did not expressly state that an attorney would be made available prior to interrogation, and in Duckworth v. Eagan, 109 S. Ct. 2875 (1989), the Court held that the following statement of rights satisfied *Miranda*:

> Before we ask you any questions, you must understand your rights. You have the right to remain silent. Anything you say can be used against you in court. You have a right to talk to a lawyer for advice before we ask you any questions, and to have him with you during questioning. You have this right to the advice and the presence of a lawyer even if you cannot afford to hire one. We have no way of giving you a lawyer, but one will be appointed for you, if you wish, if and when you go to court. If you wish to answer questions now without a lawyer present, you have the right to stop answering questions at any time. You also have the right to stop answering at any time until you've talked to a lawyer.

The majority concluded that the "if and when" language merely accurately described Indiana procedure, and anticipated a suspect's natural question concerning when counsel might be appointed. The Court also reiterated the language of *Miranda* to the effect that states are not required to have station house lawyers present at all times. The dissent argued that a suspect might construe the warnings as providing a right to counsel before questioning only to those who can afford to pay for it. In the dissent's view, "It poses no great burden on law enforcement officers to eradicate confusion stemming from the 'if and when' caveat." Does it impose any great burden on suspects who do not understand what they are told to inquire about the matter? And of course there is no evidence that Eagan did not understand. What, then, would justify reversing his conviction? Is it that the "compelling atmosphere of the jailhouse" will be presumed to make suspects incompetent in virtually every sense? Does carrying *Miranda* to such metaphysical heights obscure its real message?

e. Waiver

The *Miranda* opinion indicated that the state would have to meet a heavy burden to demonstrate waiver, but that dicta has never been developed. Indeed, in North Carolina v. Butler, 441 U.S. 369 (1979), the Court held that the *Miranda* rights did not have to be "specifically" waived by an express oral or written waiver. It is enough that "waiver can be clearly inferred from the actions and words of the person interrogated." In Colorado v. Connelly, 479 U.S. 157 (1986), the Court held that the state need only prove waiver by a preponderance of the evidence. The opinion, including the waiver aspect, is reproduced at page 1313 infra.

Is it sensible to allow waiver of one's rights under *Miranda*? If the primary concern is with coerced incriminating statements, why is there not a similar concern with "coerced" waivers? Indeed, from one perspective is this the crucial failing of *Miranda*? What alternatives might there be to allowing fairly unfettered waivers and at what cost could they be implemented? Can we restrict a person's "right" to waive these rights in any event? Compare this issue to Faretta v. California, page 283 supra. Does it, or should it, matter whether the suspect is already represented by counsel? In New York it does. The New York Court of Appeals has rendered a series of decisions that do not permit the police to approach the suspect after the police are aware that the suspect is represented by counsel. See, e.g., People v. Arthur, 22 N.Y.2d 325, 292 N.Y.S.2d 663, 239 N.E.2d 537 (1968); People v. Rogers, 48 N.Y.2d 167, 422 N.Y.S.2d 18, 397 N.E.2d 709 (1979).

Should oral waivers be permitted? Indeed, should the entire interrogation process be observed by a disinterested third party or taped in some fashion? In this regard, consider Stephan v. State, 711 P.2d 1156 (Alaska 1985), where the Alaska Supreme Court held that the failure to tape record an interrogation occurring in a place of detention violates the state constitution.

The Supreme Court has recently returned to the issue of waiver. In Colorado v. Spring, 479 U.S. 564 (1987), the Court held a *Miranda* waiver valid even though the defendant was not apprised of every alleged crime with respect to which the police intended to interrogate him. Even if the police deliberately failed to inform Spring that they intended to interrogate him about another crime, the Court "has never held that mere silence by law enforcement officials as to the subject matter of an interrogation is 'trickery' sufficient to invalidate a suspect's waiver of *Miranda* rights, and we expressly decline so to hold today. Once *Miranda* warnings are given, it is difficult to see how official silence could cause a suspect to misunderstand the nature of his constitutional right . . . to refuse to answer any question which might incriminate him. . . . Here, the additional information could affect only the wisdom of a . . . waiver, not its essential voluntary and knowing nature." The dissent, by contrast, again accused the majority of letting the state "take unfair advantage of the suspect's psychological state, as the unexpected questions cause the compulsive pressures [of custodial interrogation] suddenly to reappear."

What if the police inform a suspect of the scope of the investigation but fail to mention that a lawyer is trying to contact the suspect? That was the question in the following case.

MORAN v. BURBINE
Certiorari to The United States Court of Appeals for the First Circuit
475 U.S. 412 (1986)

JUSTICE O'CONNOR delivered the opinion of the Court.

After being informed of his rights pursuant to Miranda v. Arizona, and after executing a series of written waivers, respondent confessed to the murder of a young woman. At no point during the course of the interrogation, which occurred prior to arraignment, did he request an attorney. While he was in police custody, his sister attempted to retain a lawyer to represent him. The attorney telephoned the police station and received assurances that respondent would not be questioned further until the next day. In fact, the interrogation session that yielded the inculpatory statements began later that evening. The question presented is whether either the conduct of the police or respondent's ignorance of the attorney's efforts to reach him taints the validity of the waivers and therefore requires exclusion of the confessions.

I

On the morning of March 3, 1977, Mary Jo Hickey was found unconscious in a factory parking lot in Providence, Rhode Island. Suffering from injuries to her skull apparently inflicted by a metal pipe found at the scene, she was rushed to a nearby hospital. Three weeks later she died from her wounds.

Several months after her death, the Cranston, Rhode Island, police arrested respondent and two others in connection with a local burglary.

Shortly before the arrest, Detective Ferranti of the Cranston police force had learned from a confidential informant that the man responsible for Ms. Hickey's death lived at a certain address and went by the name of "Butch." Upon discovering that respondent lived at that address and was known by that name, Detective Ferranti informed respondent of his *Miranda* rights. When respondent refused to execute a written waiver, Detective Ferranti spoke separately with the two other suspects arrested on the breaking and entering charge and obtained statements further implicating respondent in Ms. Hickey's murder. At approximately 6 P.M., Detective Ferranti telephoned the police in Providence to convey the information he had uncovered. An hour later, three officers from that department arrived at the Cranston headquarters for the purpose of questioning respondent about the murder.

That same evening, at about 7:45 P.M., respondent's sister telephoned the Public Defender's Office to obtain legal assistance for her brother. Her sole concern was the breaking and entering charge, as she was unaware that respondent was then under suspicion for murder. She asked for Richard Casparian who had been scheduled to meet with respondent earlier that afternoon to discuss another charge unrelated to either the break-in or the murder. As soon as the conversation ended, the attorney who took the call attempted to reach Mr. Casparian. When those efforts were unsuccessful, she telephoned Allegra Munson, another Assistant Public Defender, and told her about respondent's arrest and his sister's subsequent request that the office represent him.

At 8:15 P.M., Ms. Munson telephoned the Cranston police station and asked that her call be transferred to the detective division. In the words of the Supreme Court of Rhode Island . . . the conversation proceeded as follows:

> A male voice responded with the word "Detectives." Ms. Munson identified herself and asked if Brian Burbine was being held; the person responded affirmatively. Ms. Munson explained to the person that Burbine was represented by attorney Casparian who was not available; she further stated that she would act as Burbine's legal counsel in the event that the police intended to place him in a lineup or question him. The unidentified person told Ms. Munson that the police would not be questioning Burbine or putting him in a lineup and that they were through with him for the night. Ms. Munson was not informed that the Providence Police were at the Cranston police station or that Burbine was a suspect in Mary's murder.

At all relevant times, respondent was unaware of his sister's efforts to retain counsel and of the fact and contents of Ms. Munson's telephone conversation.

Less than an hour later, the police brought respondent to an interrogation room and conducted the first of a series of interviews concerning the murder. Prior to each session, respondent was informed of his *Miranda* rights, and on three separate occasions he signed a written form acknowledging that he understood his right to the presence of an attorney and explicitly indicating that he "[did] not want an attorney called or appointed for [him]" before he gave a statement. Uncontradicted evidence at the suppression hearing indicated that at least twice during the course of the evening, respondent was left in a room where he had access to a telephone, which he apparently declined to use. Eventually, respondent signed three written statements fully admitting to the murder.

Prior to trial, respondent moved to suppress the statements. The court denied the motion, finding that respondent had received the *Miranda* warnings and had "knowingly, intelligently, and voluntarily waived his privilege against self-incrimination [and] his right to counsel." . . . The jury found respondent guilty of murder in the first degree, and he appealed to the Supreme Court of Rhode Island. A divided court rejected his contention that the Fifth and Fourteenth Amendments to the Constitution required the suppression of the inculpatory statements and affirmed the conviction. . . . After unsuccessfully petitioning the United States District Court for the District of Rhode Island for a writ of habeas corpus, respondent appealed to the Court of Appeals for the First Circuit. That court reversed.

We granted certiorari to decide whether a prearraignment confession preceded by an otherwise valid waiver must be suppressed either because the police misinformed an inquiring attorney about their plans concerning the suspect or because they failed to inform the suspect of the attorney's efforts to reach him. We now reverse.

II

. . . Respondent does not dispute that the Providence police followed [the *Miranda*] procedures with precision. . . . Nor does respondent contest the Rhode Island courts' determination that he at no point requested the presence of a lawyer. He contends instead that the confessions must be suppressed because the police's failure to inform him of the attorney's telephone call deprived him of information essential to his ability to knowingly waive his Fifth Amendment rights. In the alternative, he suggests that to fully protect the Fifth Amendment values served by *Miranda*, we should extend that decision to condemn the conduct of the Providence police. We address each contention in turn.

A

standards for Waiver

Echoing the standard first articulated in Johnson v. Zerbst, 304 U.S. 458, 464 (1938), *Miranda* holds that "[t]he defendant may waive effectuation" of the rights conveyed in the warnings "provided the waiver is made voluntarily, knowingly and intelligently." The inquiry has two distinct dimensions. First, the relinquishment of the right must have been voluntary in the sense that it was the product of a free and deliberate choice rather than intimidation, coercion, or deception. Second, the waiver must have been made with a full awareness of both the nature of the right being abandoned and the consequences of the decision to abandon it. Only if the "totality of the circumstances surrounding the interrogation" reveals both an uncoerced choice and the requisite level of comprehension may a court properly conclude that the *Miranda* rights have been waived.

Under this standard, we have no doubt that respondent validly waived his right to remain silent and to the presence of counsel. The voluntariness of the waiver is not at issue. As the Court of Appeals correctly acknowledged, the record is devoid of any suggestion that police resorted to physical or psychological pressure to elicit the statements. Indeed it appears that it was respondent, and not the police, who spontaneously initiated the conversation that led to the first and most damaging confession. Nor is there any question about respondent's comprehension of the full panoply of rights set out in the *Miranda* warnings and of the potential consequences of a decision to relinquish them. Nonetheless, the Court of Appeals believed that the "[d]eliberate or reckless" conduct of the police, in particular their failure to inform respondent of the telephone call, fatally undermined the validity of the otherwise proper waiver. We find this conclusion untenable as a matter of both logic and precedent.

Events occurring outside of the presence of the suspect and entirely unknown to him surely can have no bearing on the capacity to comprehend and knowingly relinquish a constitutional right. Under the analysis of the Court of Appeals, the same defendant, armed with the same information and confronted with precisely the same police conduct, would have knowingly waived his *Miranda* rights had a lawyer not telephoned the police station to inquire about his status. Nothing in any of our waiver decisions or in our understanding of the essential components of a valid waiver requires so incongruous a result. No doubt the additional information would have been useful to respondent; perhaps even it might have affected his decision to confess. But we have never read the Constitution to require that the police supply a suspect with a flow of information to help him calibrate his self-interest in deciding whether to speak or stand by his rights. Once it is determined that a suspect's decision not to rely on his rights was uncoerced, that he at all times knew he could stand mute and request a lawyer, and that he was aware of the State's intention to use his statements to secure a conviction, the analysis is complete and the waiver is valid as a matter of law. The Court of Appeals' conclusion to the contrary was in error.

Nor do we believe that the level of the police's culpability in failing to inform respondent of the telephone call has any bearing on the validity of the waivers. In light of the state-court findings that there was no "conspiracy or collusion" on the part of the police, we have serious doubts about whether the Court of Appeals was free to conclude that their conduct constituted "deliberate or reckless irresponsibility." 753 F.2d, at 185. But whether intentional or inadvertent, the state of mind of the police is irrelevant to the question of the intelligence and voluntariness of respondent's election to abandon his rights. Although highly inappropriate, even deliberate deception of an attorney could not possibly affect a suspect's decision to waive his *Miranda* rights unless he were at least aware of the incident. Compare Escobedo v. Illinois (excluding confession where police incorrectly told the suspect that his lawyer " 'didn't want to see' him"). Nor was the failure to inform respondent of the telephone call the kind of "trick[ery]" that can vitiate the validity of a waiver. Miranda, 384 U.S., at 476. Granting that the "deliberate or reckless" withholding of information is objectionable as a matter of ethics, such conduct is only relevant to the constitutional validity of a waiver if it deprives a defendant of knowledge essential to his ability to understand the nature of his rights and the consequences of abandoning them. Because respondent's voluntary decision to speak was made with full awareness and comprehension of all the information *Miranda* requires the police to convey, the waivers were valid.

B

At oral argument respondent acknowledged that a constitutional rule requiring the police to inform a suspect of an attorney's efforts to reach him would represent a significant extension of our precedents. He contends, however, that the conduct of the Providence police was so inimical to the Fifth Amendment values *Miranda* seeks to protect that we should read that decision to condemn their behavior. Regardless of any issue of waiver, he urges, the Fifth Amendment requires the reversal of a conviction if the police are less than forthright in their dealings with an attorney or if they fail to tell a suspect of a lawyer's unilateral efforts to contact him. Because the proposed modification ignores the underlying purposes of the *Miranda* rules and because we think that the decision as written strikes the proper balance between society's legitimate law enforcement interests and the protection of the defendant's Fifth Amendment rights, we decline the invitation to further extend *Miranda*'s reach.

At the outset, while we share respondent's distaste for the deliberate misleading of an officer of the court, reading *Miranda* to forbid police deception of an attorney would cut [the decision] completely loose from its own explicitly stated rationale. As is now well established, "[t]he . . . *Miranda* warnings are 'not themselves rights protected by the Constitution but [are] instead measures to insure that the [suspect's] right against compulsory self-incrimination [is] protected.' " Their objective is not to mold police conduct for its own sake. Nothing in the Constitution vests in us the authority to mandate a code of behavior for state officials wholly unconnected to any federal right or privilege. The purpose of the *Miranda* warnings instead is to dissipate the compulsion inherent in custodial interrogation and, in so doing, guard against abridgment of the suspect's Fifth Amendment rights. Clearly, a rule that focuses on how the police treat an attorney—conduct that has no relevance at all to the degree of compulsion experienced by the defendant during interrogation—would ignore both *Miranda*'s mission and its only source of legitimacy. . . . [The Court also expressed concerns about adding unnecessary complexity to the *Miranda* rules.]

Moreover, problems of clarity to one side, reading *Miranda* to require the police in each instance to inform a suspect of an attorney's efforts to reach him would work a substantial and, we think, inappropriate shift in the subtle balance struck in that decision. Custodial interrogations implicate two competing concerns. On the one hand, the need for police questioning as a tool for effective enforcement of criminal laws cannot be doubted. Admissions of guilt are more than merely "desirable"; they are essential to society's compelling interest in finding, convicting, and punishing those who violate the law. On the other hand, the Court has recognized that the interrogation process is "inherently coercive" and that, as a consequence, there exists a substantial risk that the police will inadvertently traverse the fine line between legitimate efforts to elicit admissions and constitutionally impermissible compulsion. *Miranda* attempted to reconcile these opposing concerns by giving the defendant the power to exert some control over the course of the interrogation. Declining to adopt the more extreme position that the actual presence of a lawyer was necessary to dispel the coercion inherent in custodial interrogation, the Court found that the suspect's Fifth Amendment rights could be adequately protected by less intrusive means. Police questioning, often an essential part of the investigatory process, could continue in its traditional form, the Court held, but only if the suspect clearly understood that, at any time, he could bring the proceeding to a halt or, short of that, call in an attorney to give advice and monitor the conduct of his interrogators.

The position urged by respondent would upset this carefully drawn approach in a manner that is both unnecessary for the protection of the Fifth Amendent privilege and injurious to legitimate law enforcement. Because, as *Miranda* holds, full comprehension of the rights to remain silent and request an attorney are sufficient to dispel whatever coercion is inherent in the interrogation process, a rule requiring the police to inform the suspect of an attorney's efforts to contact him would contribute to the protection of the Fifth Amendment privilege only incidentally, if at all. This minimal benefit, however, would come at a substantial cost to society's legitimate and substantial interest in securing admissions of guilt. Indeed, the very premise of the Court of Appeals was not that awareness of Ms. Munson's phone call would have dissipated the coercion of the interrogation room, but that it might have convinced respondent not to speak at all. Because neither the letter nor purposes of *Miranda* require this additional handicap on otherwise permissible investigatory efforts, we are unwilling to expand the *Miranda* rules to require the police to keep the suspect abreast of the status of his legal representation.

III

[The Court rejected the argument that the sixth amendment applies in these circumstances.]

IV

Finally, respondent contends that the conduct of the police was so offensive as to deprive him of the fundamental fairness guaranteed by the Due Process Clause of the Fourteenth Amendment. Focusing primarily on the impropriety of conveying false information to an attorney, he invites us to declare that such behavior should be condemned as violative of canons fundamental to the "traditions and conscience of our people." We do not question that on facts more egregious than those presented here police deception might rise to a level of a due process violation. Accordingly, Justice Stevens' apocalyptic suggestion that we have approved any and all forms of police misconduct is demonstrably incorrect.[4]

---

4. Among its other failings, the dissent declines to follow Oregon v. Elstad [repro-

We hold only that, on these facts, the challenged conduct falls short of the kind of misbehavior that so shocks the sensibilities of civilized society as to warrant a federal intrusion into the criminal processes of the States.

We hold therefore that the Court of Appeals erred in finding that the Federal Constitution required the exclusion of the three inculpatory statements. Accordingly, we reverse and remand for proceedings consistent with this opinion.

JUSTICE STEVENS, with whom JUSTICE BRENNAN and JUSTICE MARSHALL join, dissenting.

This case poses fundamental questions about our system of justice. As this Court has long recognized, and reaffirmed only weeks ago, "ours is an accusatorial and not an inquisitorial system." Miller v. Fenton, 474 U.S. 104, 110 (1985). The Court's opinion today represents a startling departure from that basic insight.

The Court concludes that the police may deceive an attorney by giving her false information about whether her client will be questioned, and that the police may deceive a suspect by failing to inform him of his attorney's communications and efforts to represent him. For the majority, this conclusion, though "distaste[ful]," is not even debatable. The deception of the attorney is irrelevant because the attorney has no right to information, accuracy, honesty, or fairness in the police response to her questions about her client. The deception of the client is acceptable,

---

duced at page 1296 infra] a decision that categorically forecloses Justice Stevens' major premise—that Miranda requires the police to inform a suspect of any and all information that would be useful to a decision whether to remain silent or speak with the police. The dissent also launches a novel "agency" theory of the Fifth Amendment under which any perceived deception of a lawyer is automatically treated as deception of his or her client. This argument entirely disregards the elemental and established proposition that the privilege against compulsory self-incrimination is, by hypothesis, a personal one that can only be invoked by the individual whose testimony is being compelled.

Most importantly, the dissent's misreading of Miranda itself is breath-taking in its scope. For example, it reads Miranda as creating an undifferentiated right to the presence of an attorney that is triggered automatically by the initiation of the interrogation itself. Yet, as both Miranda and subsequent decisions construing Miranda make clear beyond refute, the interrogation must cease until an attorney is present only if the individual states that he wants an attorney. The dissent condemns us for embracing "incommunicado questioning . . . as a societal goal of the highest order that justifies police deception of the shabbiest kind." We, of course, do nothing of the kind. As any reading of Miranda reveals, the decision, rather than proceeding from the premise that the rights and needs of the defendant are paramount to all others, embodies a carefully crafted balance designed to fully protect both the defendant's and society's interests. The dissent may not share our view that the Fifth Amendment rights of the defendant are amply protected by application of Miranda as written. But the dissent is "simply wrong," in suggesting that exclusion of Burbine's three confessions follows perfunctorily from Miranda's mandate.

Quite understandably, the dissent is outraged by the very idea of police deception of a lawyer. Significantly less understandable is its willingness to misconstrue this Court's constitutional holdings in order to implement its subjective notions of sound policy.

because, although the information would affect the client's assertion of his rights, the client's actions in ignorance of the availability of his attorney are voluntary, knowing, and intelligent; additionally, society's interest in apprehending, prosecuting, and punishing criminals outweighs the suspect's interest in information regarding his attorney's efforts to communicate with him. Finally, even mendacious police interference in the communications between a suspect and his lawyer does not violate any notion of fundamental fairness because it does not shock the conscience of the majority. . . .

II

Well-settled principles of law lead inexorably to the conclusion that the failure to inform Burbine of the call from his attorney makes the subsequent waiver of his constitutional rights invalid. Analysis should begin with an acknowledgment that the burden of proving the validity of a waiver of constitutional rights is always on the government. When such a waiver occurs in a custodial setting, that burden is an especially heavy one because custodial interrogation is inherently coercive, because disinterested witnesses are seldom available to describe what actually happened, and because history has taught us that the danger of overreaching during incommunicado interrogation is so real.

In applying this heavy presumption against the validity of waivers, this Court has sometimes relied on a case-by-case totality of the circumstances analysis. We have found, however, that some custodial interrogation situations require strict presumptions against the validity of a waiver. [For example] *Miranda* established that a waiver is not valid in the absence of certain warnings. . . . Like the failure to give warnings . . . , police deception of a suspect through omission of information regarding attorney communications greatly exacerbates the inherent problems of incommunicado interrogation and requires a clear principle to safeguard the presumption against the waiver of constitutional rights. [Accordingly,] the police deception should render a subsequent waiver invalid.

Indeed, as *Miranda* itself makes clear, proof that the required warnings have been given is a necessary, but by no means sufficient, condition for establishing a valid waiver. As the Court plainly stated in *Miranda*, "any evidence that the accused was threatened, tricked, or cajoled into a waiver will, of course, show that the defendant did not voluntarily waive his privilege. The requirement of warnings and waiver of rights is a fundamental with respect to the Fifth Amendment privilege and not simply a preliminary ritual to existing methods of interrogation." 384 U.S., at 476.

In this case it would be perfectly clear that Burbine's waiver was invalid if, for example, Detective Ferranti had "threatened, tricked, or cajoled" Burbine in their private pre-confession meeting—perhaps by misdescribing the statements obtained from DiOrio and Sparks—even though, under the Court's truncated analysis of the issue, Burbine fully understood his rights. For *Miranda* clearly condemns threats or trickery that cause a suspect to make an unwise waiver of his rights even though he fully understands those rights. In my opinion there can be no constitutional distinction—as the Court appears too draw—between a deceptive misstatement and the concealment by the police of the critical fact that an attorney retained by the accused or his family has offered assistance, either by telephone or in person.

Thus, the Court's truncated analysis, which relies in part on a distinction between deception accomplished by means of an omission of a critically important fact and deception by means of a misleading statement, is simply untenable. If, as the Court asserts, "the analysis is at an end" as soon as the suspect is provided with enough information to have the capacity to understand and exercise his rights, I see no reason why the police should not be permitted to make the same kind of misstatements to the suspect that they are apparently allowed to make to his lawyer. *Miranda*, however, clearly establishes that both kinds of deception vitiate the suspect's waiver of his right to counsel. . . .[42]

In short, settled principles about construing waivers of constitutional rights and about the need for strict presumptions in custodial interrogations, as well as a plain reading of the *Miranda* opinion itself, overwhelmingly support the conclusion reached by almost every state court that has considered the matter—a suspect's waiver of his right to counsel is invalid if police refuse to inform the suspect of his counsel's communications.

III

The Court makes the alternative argument that requiring police to inform a suspect of his attorney's communications to and about him is not

---

42. . . . The majority mischaracterizes this dissent by stating that its "major premise" is that "*Miranda* requires the police to inform a suspect of any and all information that would be useful to a decision whether to remain silent or speak with the police." The majority's response ignores the fact that the police action here is not simply a failure to provide "useful" information; rather, it is affirmative police interference in a communication between an attorney and a suspect. Moreover, the "information" intercepted by the police bears directly on the right to counsel that police are asking the suspect to waive. The "information" at issue is thus far different from information about "the nature and quality of the evidence," Oregon v. Elstad, or about a grand jury witness' possible target status, United States v. Washington, 431 U.S. 181, 188-189 (1977).

required because it would upset the careful "balance" of *Miranda*. Despite its earlier notion that the attorney's call is an "outside event" that has "no bearing" on a knowing and intelligent waiver, the majority does acknowledge that information of attorney Munson's call "would have been useful to respondent" and "might have affected his decision to confess." Thus, a rule requiring the police to inform a suspect of an attorney's call would have two predictable effects. It would serve "*Miranda*'s goal of dispelling the compulsion inherent in custodial interrogation," and it would disserve the goal of custodial interrogation because it would result in fewer confessions. By a process of balancing these two concerns, the Court finds the benefit to the individual outweighed by the "substantial cost to society's legitimate and substantial interest in securing admissions of guilt."

The Court's balancing approach is profoundly misguided. The cost of suppressing evidence of guilt will always make the value of a procedural safeguard appear "minimal," "marginal," or "incremental." Indeed, the value of any trial at all seems like a "procedural technicality" when balanced against the interest in administering prompt justice to a murderer or a rapist caught redhanded. The individual interest in procedural safeguards that minimize the risk of error is easily discounted when the fact of guilt appears certain beyond doubt.

What is the cost of requiring the police to inform a suspect of his attorney's call? It would decrease the likelihood that custodial interrogation will enable the police to obtain a confession. This is certainly a real cost, but it is the same cost that this Court has repeatedly found necessary to preserve the character of our free society and our rejection of an inquisitorial system. . . .

Just as the "cost" does not justify taking a suspect into custody or interrogating him without giving him warnings simply because police desire to question him, so too the "cost" does not justify permitting police to withhold from a suspect knowledge of an attorney's communication, even though that communication would have an unquestionable effect on the suspect's exercise of his rights. The "cost" that concerns the Court amounts to nothing more than an acknowledgment that the law enforcement interest in obtaining convictions suffers whenever a suspect exercises the rights that are afforded by our system of criminal justice. In other words, it is the fear that an individual may exercise his rights that tips the scales of justice for the Court today. The principle that ours is an accusatorial, not an inquisitorial, system, however, has repeatedly led the Court to reject that fear as a valid reason for inhibiting the invocation of rights.

If the Court's cost-benefit analysis were sound, it would justify a repudiation of the right to a warning about counsel itself. There is only a difference in degree between a presumption that advice about the immediate availability of a lawyer would not affect the voluntariness of a decision to confess, and a presumption that every citizen knows that he has a right to remain silent and therefore no warnings of any kind are needed. In either case, the withholding of information serves precisely the same law enforcement interests. And in both cases, the cost can be described as nothing more than an incremental increase in the risk that an individual will make an unintelligent waiver of his rights.

In cases like *Escobedo* [and] *Miranda,* the Court has viewed the balance from a much broader perspective. In these cases—indeed, whenever the distinction between an inquisitorial and an accusatorial system of justice is implicated—the law enforcement interest served by incommunicado interrogation has been weighed against the interest in individual liberty that is threatened by such practices. The balance has never been struck by an evaluation of empirical data of the kind submitted to legislative decisionmakers—indeed, the Court relies on no such data today. Rather, the Court has evaluated the quality of the conflicting rights and interests. In the past, that kind of balancing process has led to the conclusion that the police have no right to compel an individual to respond to custodial interrogation, and that the interest in liberty that is threatened by incommunicado interrogation is so precious that special procedures must be followed to protect it. The Court's contrary conclusion today can only be explained by its failure to appreciate the value of the liberty that an accusatorial system seeks to protect. . . .

V

At the time attorney Munson made her call to the Cranston police station, she was acting as Burbine's attorney. Under ordinary principles of agency law the deliberate deception of Munson was tantamount to deliberate deception of her client. If an attorney makes a mistake in the course of her representation of her client, the client must accept the consequences of that mistake. It is equally clear that when an attorney makes an inquiry on behalf of her client, the client is entitled to a truthful answer. Surely the client must have the same remedy for a false representation to his lawyer that he would have if he were acting pro se and had propounded the question himself. The majority brushes aside the police deception involved in the misinformation of attorney Munson. It is irrelevant to the Fifth Amendment analysis, concludes the majority, because that right is personal.

In my view, as a matter of law, the police deception of Munson was tantamount to deception of Burbine himself. It constituted a violation of

Burbine's right to have an attorney present during the questioning that began shortly thereafter. The existence of that right is undisputed. Whether the source of that right is the Sixth Amendment, the Fifth Amendment, or a combination of the two is of no special importance, for I do not understand the Court to deny the existence of the right.

The pertinent question is whether police deception of the attorney is utterly irrelevant to that right. In my judgment, it blinks at reality to suggest that misinformation which prevented the presence of an attorney has no bearing on the protection and effectuation of the right to counsel in custodial interrogation. The majority parses the role of attorney and suspect so narrowly that the deception of the attorney is of no constitutional significance. In other contexts, however, the Court does not hesitate to recognize an identity between the interest of attorney and accused.[52] The character of the attorney-client relationship requires rejection of the Court's notion that the attorney is some entirely distinct, completely severable entity and that deception of the attorney is irrelevant to the right of counsel in custodial interrogation.

The possible reach of the Court's opinion is stunning. For the majority seems to suggest that police may deny counsel all access to a client who is being held. At least since Escobedo v. Illinois, it has been widely accepted that police may not simply deny attorneys access to their clients who are in custody. This view has survived the recasting of *Escobedo* from a Sixth Amendment to a Fifth Amendment case that the majority finds so critically important. That this prevailing view is shared by the police can be seen in the state-court opinions detailing various forms of police deception of attorneys. For, if there were no obligation to give attorneys access, there would be no need to take elaborate steps to avoid access, such as shuttling the suspect to a different location, or taking the lawyer to different locations; police could simply refuse to allow the attorneys to see the suspects. But the law enforcement profession has apparently believed, quite rightly in my view, that denying lawyers access to their clients is impermissible. The Court today seems to assume that this view was error—that, from the federal constitutional perspective, the lawyer's access is, as a question from the Court put it in oral argument, merely "a matter of prosecutorial grace." Certainly, nothing in the Court's Fifth and Sixth Amendment analysis acknowledges that there is any

---

52. See, e.g., Strickland v. Washington, 466 U.S. 668, 690 (1984) (when client challenges effectiveness of assistance, "counsel is strongly presumed to have rendered adequate assistance and made all significant decisions in the exercise of reasonable professional judgment"); Wainwright v. Sykes, 433 U.S. 72, 91, n.14 (1977) ("[D]ecisions of counsel relating to trial strategy, even when made without the consultation of the defendant, would bar direct federal review of claims thereby forgone, except where 'the circumstances are exceptional' ").

federal constitutional bar to an absolute denial of lawyer access to a suspect who is in police custody.

In sharp contrast to the majority, I firmly believe that the right to counsel at custodial interrogation is infringed by police treatment of an attorney that prevents or impedes the attorney's representation of the suspect at that interrogation.

VI

The Court devotes precisely five sentences to its conclusion that the police interference in the attorney's representation of Burbine did not violate the Due Process Clause. In the majority's view, the due process analysis is a simple "shock the conscience" test. Finding its conscience troubled, but not shocked, the majority rejects the due process challenge.

In a variety of circumstances, however, the Court has given a more thoughtful consideration to the requirements of due process. For instance, we have concluded that use of a suspect's post-*Miranda* warnings silence against him violates the due process requirement of fundamental fairness because such use breaches an implicit promise that "silence will carry no penalty."[58] Similarly, we have concluded that "the suppression by the prosecution of evidence favorable to an accused upon request violates due process where the evidence is material either to guilt or to punishment."[59] We have also concluded that vindictive prosecution violates due process;[60] so too does vindictive sentencing.[61] Indeed, we have emphasized that analysis of the "voluntariness" of a confession is frequently a "convenient shorthand" for reviewing objectionable police methods under the rubric of the due process requirement of fundamental fairness. What emerges from these cases is not the majority's simple "shock the conscience" test, but the principle that due process requires fairness, integrity, and honor in the operation of the criminal justice system, and in its treatment of the citizen's cardinal constitutional protections.

In my judgment, police interference in the attorney-client relationship is the type of governmental misconduct on a matter of central importance to the administration of justice that the Due Process Clause prohibits. Just as the police cannot impliedly promise a suspect that his silence will not be used against him and then proceed to break that promise, so too police cannot tell a suspect's attorney that they will not

58. See Wainwright v. Greenfield, 474 U.S., at 295; Doyle v. Ohio, 426 U.S., at 618.
59. Brady v. Maryland, 373 U.S. 83, 87 (1963).
60. Blackledge v. Perry, 417 U.S. 21 (1974).
61. North Carolina v. Pearce, 395 U.S. 711 (1969).

question the suspect and then proceed to question him. Just as the government cannot conceal from a suspect material and exculpatory evidence, so too the government cannot conceal from a suspect the material fact of his attorney's communication.

Police interference with communications between an attorney and his client violates the due process requirement of fundamental fairness. Burbine's attorney was given completely false information about the lack of questioning; moreover, she was not told that her client would be questioned regarding a murder charge about which she was unaware. Burbine, in turn, was not told that his attorney had phoned and that she had been informed that he would not be questioned. Quite simply, the Rhode Island police effectively drove a wedge between an attorney and a suspect through misinformation and omissions.

The majority does not "question that on facts more egregious than those presented here police deception might rise to a level of a due process violation." In my view, the police deception disclosed by this record plainly does rise to that level.

VII

This case turns on a proper appraisal of the role of the lawyer in our society. If a lawyer is seen as a nettlesome obstacle to the pursuit of wrongdoers—as in an inquisitorial society—then the Court's decision today makes a good deal of sense. If a lawyer is seen as an aid to the understanding and protection of constitutional rights—as in an accusatorial society—then today's decision makes no sense at all.

Like the conduct of the police in the Cranston station on the evening of June 29, 1977, the Court's opinion today serves the goal of insuring that the perpetrator of a vile crime is punished. Like the police on that June night as well, however, the Court has trampled on well-established legal principles and flouted the spirit of our accusatorial system of justice.

NOTES AND QUESTIONS

1. If "whether intentional or inadvertent, the state of mind of the police is irrelevant to the question of the intelligence and voluntariness of respondent's election to abandon his rights," why is the "state of mind of the police" relevant to whether interrogation occurs, as it is at least indirectly in *Innis?*

2. How does *Moran* differ from *Escobedo?* Would the case have come out differently if the lawyer had been at the station house? If Burbine

had asked if "anybody" had tried to contact him? If his lawyer had done so? Would it make any difference whether the police were truthful or dishonest in responding to such questions?

3. Does *Moran* apply or reject the implications of *Miranda*? Professor Stuntz has suggested that *Moran* represents a shift in the Court's concern from protecting well-informed choices to protecting voluntary ones. Stuntz, Self-Incrimination and Excuse, 88 Colum. L. Rev. 1227 (1988).

f. The Implications of Invoking the Right to Remain Silent or of Counsel

In Michigan v. Mosley, Mosley was arrested in connection with certain robberies, was briefly interrogated, and then invoked his right to remain silent, at which point the interrogation ceased. Some time later, a different police officer interrogated Mosley about a homicide. The second officer advised Mosley of his rights, obtained a waiver, and secured incriminating information. In finding Mosley's rights not to have been violated, the Court stated the following.

MICHIGAN v. MOSLEY, 423 U.S. 96, 101-107 (1975): [*Miranda*] . . . could be literally read to mean that a person who has invoked his "right to silence" can never again be subjected to custodial interrogation by any police officer at any time or place on any subject. Another possible construction of the passage would characterize "any statement taken after the person invokes his privilege" as "the product of compulsion" and would therefore mandate its exclusion from evidence, even if it were volunteered by the person in custody without any further interrogation whatever. Or the passage could be interpreted to require only the immediate cessation of questioning and to permit a resumption of interrogation after a momentary respite.

It is evident that any of these possible literal interpretations would lead to absurd and unintended results. To permit the continuation of custodial interrogation after a momentary cessation would clearly frustrate the purposes of *Miranda* by allowing repeated rounds of questioning to undermine the will of the person being questioned. At the other extreme, a blanket prohibition against the taking of voluntary statements or a permanent immunity from further interrogation, regardless of the circumstances, would transform the *Miranda* safeguards into wholly irrational obstacles to legitimate police investigative activity, and deprive suspects of an opportunity to make informed and intelligent assessments of their interests. Clearly, therefore, . . . the *Miranda* opinion can [not] sensibly be read to create a per se proscription of indefinite duration upon any further questioning by any police officer on any subject, once the person in custody has indicated a desire to remain silent.

A reasonable and faithful interpretation of the *Miranda* opinion must rest on the intention of the Court in that case to adopt "fully effective means . . . to notify the person of his right of silence and to assure that the exercise of the right will be scrupulously honored. . . ." 384 U.S., at 479. The critical safeguard identified in the passage at issue is a person's "right to cut off questioning." Id., at 474. Through the exercise of his option to terminate questioning he can control the time at which questioning occurs, the subjects discussed and the duration of the interrogation. The requirement that law enforcement authorities must respect a person's exercise of that option counteracts the coercive pressures of the custodial setting. We therefore conclude that the admissibility of statements obtained after the person in custody has decided to remain silent depends under *Miranda* on whether his "right to cut off questioning" was "scrupulously honored."

A review of the circumstances leading to Mosley's confession reveals that his "right to cut off questioning" was fully respected in this case. Before his initial interrogation, Mosley was carefully advised that he was under no obligation to answer any questions and could remain silent if he wished. He orally acknowledged that he understood the *Miranda* warnings and then signed a printed notification of rights form. When Mosley stated that he did not want to discuss the robberies, Detective Cowie immediately ceased the interrogation and did not try either to resume the questioning or in any way to persuade Mosley to reconsider his position. After an interval of more than two hours, Mosley was questioned by another police officer at another location about unrelated holdup murder. He was given full and complete *Miranda* warnings at the outset of the second interrogation. He was thus reminded again that he could remain silent and could consult with a lawyer, and was carefully given a full and fair opportunity to exercise these options. The subsequent questioning did not undercut Mosley's previous decision not to answer Detective Cowie's inquiries. Detective Hill did not resume the interrogation about the White Tower Restaurant robbery or inquire about the Blue Goose Bar robbery, but instead focused exclusively on the Leroy Williams homicide, a crime different in nature and in time and place of occurrence from the robberies for which Mosley had been arrested and interrogated by Detective Cowie. Although it is not clear from the record how much Detective Hill knew about the earlier interrogation, his questioning of Mosley about an unrelated homicide was quite consistent with a reasonable interpretation of Mosley's earlier refusal to answer any questions about the robberies.

This is not a case, therefore, where the police failed to honor a decision of a person in custody to cut-off questioning, either by refusing to discontinue the interrogation upon request or by persisting in repeated efforts to wear down his resistance and make him change his mind. In contrast to such practices, the police here immediately ceased the interrogation, resumed questioning only after the passage of a significant period of time and the provision of a fresh set of warnings, and restricted the second interrogation to a crime that had not been a subject of the earlier interrogation.

The Michigan Court of Appeals viewed this case as factually similar to Westover v. United States, 384 U.S. 436, a companion case to *Miranda*. But the controlling facts of the two cases are strikingly different.

In *Westover*, the petitioner was arrested by the Kansas City police at 9:45 P.M. and taken to the police station. Without giving any advisory warnings of any kind to Westover, the police questioned him that night and throughout the next morning about various local robberies. At noon, three FBI agents took over, gave advisory warnings to Westover, and proceeded to question him about two California bank robberies. After two hours of questioning, the petitioner confessed to the California crimes. The Court held that the confession obtained by the FBI was inadmissible because the interrogation leading to the petitioner's statement followed on the heels of prolonged questioning that was commenced and continued by the Kansas City police without preliminary warnings to Westover of any kind. The Court found that "the federal authorities were the beneficiaries of the pressure applied by the local in-custody interrogation" and that the belated warnings given by the federal officers were "not sufficient to protect" Westover because from his point of view "the warnings came at the end of the interrogation process." 384 U.S., at 496-497.

Here, by contrast, the police gave full "Miranda warnings" to Mosley at the very outset of each interrogation, subjected him to only a brief period of initial questioning, and suspended questioning entirely for a significant period before beginning the interrogation that led to his incriminating statement. The cardinal fact of *Westover*—the failure of the police officers to give any warnings whatever to the person in their custody before embarking on an intense and prolonged interrogation of him— was simply not present in this case. The Michigan Court of Appeals was mistaken, therefore, in believing that Detective Hill's questioning of Mosley was "not permitted" by the *Westover* decision. 51 Mich. 105, 108, 214 N.W.2d 564, 566.

Are you convinced by the Court's treatment of *Westover*? Compare *Mosley* and *Westover* to the next case.

[handwritten annotations in top margin: "MIRANDA 5th Amend. rt. to counsel violated when interrogate — cops D other for — for which one invoked MIRANDA"]

EDWARDS v. ARIZONA, 451 U.S. 477, 478-487 (1981): On January 19, 1976, a sworn complaint was filed against Edwards in Arizona state court charging him with robbery, burglary, and first-degree murder. An arrest warrant was issued pursuant to the complaint, and Edwards was arrested at his home later that same day. At the police station, he was informed of his rights as required by Miranda v. Arizona, 384 U.S. 436 (1966). Petitioner stated that he understood his rights, and was willing to submit to questioning. After being told that another suspect already in custody had implicated him in the crime, Edwards denied involvement and gave a taped statement presenting an alibi defense. He then sought to "make a deal." The interrogating officer told him that he wanted a statement, but that he did not have the authority to negotiate a deal. The officer provided Edwards with the number of a county attorney. Petitioner made the call, but hung up after a few moments. Edwards then said, "I want an attorney before making a deal." At that point, questioning ceased and Edwards was taken to county jail.

At 9:15 the next morning, two detectives, colleagues of the officer who had interrogated Edwards the previous night, came to the jail and asked to see Edwards. When the detention officer informed Edwards that the detectives wished to speak with him, he replied that he did not want to talk to anyone. The guard told him that "he had" to talk and then took him to meet with the detectives. The officers identified themselves, stated they wanted to talk to him and informed him of his *Miranda* rights. Edwards was willing to talk, but he first wanted to hear the taped statement of the alleged accomplice who had implicated him. After listening to the tape for several minutes, petitioner said that he would make a statement so long as it was not tape recorded. The detectives informed him that the recording was irrelevant since they could testify in court concerning whatever he said. Edwards replied "I'll tell you anything you want to know, but I don't want it on tape." He thereupon implicated himself in the crime. . . .

Miranda . . . declared that an accused has a Fifth and Fourteenth Amendment right to have counsel present during custodial interrogation. Here, the critical facts as found by the Arizona Supreme Court are that Edwards asserted his right to counsel and his right to remain silent on January 19, but that the police, without furnishing him counsel, returned the next morning to confront him and as a result of the meeting secured incriminating oral admissions. Contrary to the holdings of the state courts, Edwards insists that having exercised his right on the 19th to have counsel present during interrogation, he did not validly waive that right on the 20th. For the following reasons, we agree.

First, the Arizona Supreme Court applied an erroneous standard for determining waiver where the accused has specifically invoked his right to counsel. It is reasonably clear under our cases that waivers of counsel must not only be voluntary, but constitute a knowing and intelligent relinquishment or abandonment of a known right or privilege, a matter which depends in each case "upon the particular facts and circumstances surrounding that case, including the background, experience and conduct of the accused." Johnson v. Zerbst, 304 U.S. 458, 464 (1938). . . .

Considering the proceedings in the state courts in the light of this standard, we note that in denying petitioner's motion to suppress, the trial court found the admission to have been "voluntary" . . . without separately focusing on whether Edwards had knowingly and intelligently relinquished his right to counsel. The Arizona Supreme Court, in a section of its opinion entitled "Voluntariness of Waiver," stated that in Arizona, confessions are prima facie involuntary and that the State had the burden of showing by a preponderance of the evidence that the confession was freely and voluntarily made. The court stated that the issue of voluntariness should be determined based on the totality of the circumstances as it related to whether an accused's action was "knowing and intelligent and whether his will was overborne." Once the trial court determines that "the confession is voluntary, the finding will not be upset on appeal absent clear and manifest error." . . . The court then upheld the trial court's finding that the "waiver and confession were voluntarily and knowingly made." . . .

In referring to the necessity to find Edwards' confession knowing and intelligent, the State Supreme Court cited Schneckloth v. Bustamonte, 412 U.S. 218, 226 (1973). Yet, it is clear that *Schneckloth* does not control the issue presented in this case. The issue in *Schneckloth* was under what conditions an individual could be found to have consented to a search and thereby waived his Fourth Amendment rights. The Court declined to impose the "intentional relinquishment or abandonment of a known right or privilege" standard and required only that the consent be voluntary under the totality of the circumstances. The Court specifically noted that the right to counsel was a prime example of those rights requiring the special protection of the knowing and intelligent waiver standard, id., at 241, but held that "[t]he considerations that informed the Court's holding in *Miranda* are simply inapplicable in the present case." 412 U.S., at 246. *Schneckloth* itself thus emphasized that the voluntariness of a consent or an admission on the one hand, and a knowing and intelligent waiver on the other, are discrete inquiries. Here, however sound the conclusion of the state courts as to the voluntariness of Edwards' admission may be, neither the trial court nor the Arizona Supreme Court undertook to focus on whether Edwards understood his right to counsel and intelligently and knowingly relinquished it. It is thus apparent that the decision below misunderstood the requirement for finding a valid waiver of the right to counsel, once invoked.

Second, although we have held that after initially being advised of his *Miranda* rights, the accused may himself validly waive his rights and respond to interrogation, see North Carolina v. Butler, 441 U.S., at 372-376, the Court has strongly indicated that additional safeguards are necessary when the accused asks for counsel; and we now hold that when an accused has invoked his right to have counsel present during custodial interrogation, a valid waiver of that right cannot be established by showing only that he responded to further police-initiated custodial interrogation even if he has been advised of his rights. We further hold that an accused, such as Edwards, having expressed his desire to deal with the police only through counsel, is not subject to further interrogation by the authorities until counsel has been made available to him, unless the accused himself initiates further communication, exchanges or conversations with the police.

Miranda itself indicated that the assertion of the right to counsel was a significant event and that once exercised by the accused, "interrogation must cease until an attorney is present." 384 U.S., at 474. Our later cases have not abandoned that view. In Michigan v. Mosley, 423 U.S. 96 (1975), the Court noted that *Miranda* had distinguished between the procedural safeguards triggered by a request to remain silent and a request for an attorney and had required that interrogation cease until an attorney was present only if the individual stated that he wanted counsel. In Fare v. Michael C., 442 U.S., at 719, the Court referred to *Miranda's* "rigid rule that an accused's request for an attorney is per se an invocation of his Fifth Amendment rights, requiring that all interrogation cease." And just last Term, in a case where a suspect in custody had invoked his *Miranda* right to counsel, the Court again referred to the "undisputed right" under *Miranda* to remain silent and to be free of interrogation "until he had consulted with a lawyer." Rhode Island v. Innis, 446 U.S. 291, 298 (1980). We reconfirm these views and to lend them substance, emphasize that it is inconsistent with *Miranda* and its progeny for the authorities, at their instance, to reinterrogate an accused in custody if he has clearly asserted his right to counsel.

In concluding that the fruits of the interrogation initiated by the police on January 20 could not be used against Edwards, we do not hold or imply that Edwards was powerless to countermand his election or that the authorities could in no event use any incriminating statements made by Edwards prior to his having access to counsel. Had Edwards initiated the meeting on January 20, nothing in the Fifth and Fourteenth Amendments would prohibit the police from merely listening to his voluntary, volunteered statements and using them against him at the trial. The Fifth Amendment right identified in *Miranda* is the right to have counsel present at any custodial interrogation. Absent such interrogation, there would have been no infringement of the right that Edwards invoked and there would be no occasion to determine whether there had been a valid waiver. Rhode Island v. Innis, supra, makes this sufficiently clear. 446 U.S., at 298, n.2.[9]

But this is not what the facts of this case show. Here, the officers conducting the interrogation on the evening of January 19, ceased interrogation when Edwards requested counsel as he had been advised he had the right to do. The Arizona Supreme Court was of the opinion that this was a sufficient invocation of his *Miranda* rights, and we are in accord. It is also clear that without making counsel available to Edwards, the police returned to him the next day. This was not at his suggestion or request. Indeed, Edwards informed the detention officer that he did not want to talk to anyone. At the meeting, the detectives told Edwards that they wanted to talk to him and again advised him of his *Miranda* rights. Edwards stated that he would talk, but what prompted this action does not appear. He listened at his own request to part of the taped statement made by one of his alleged accomplices and then made an incriminating statement, which was used against him at his trial. We think it is clear that Edwards was subjected to custodial interrogation on January 20 within the meaning of Rhode Island v. Innis, supra, and that this occurred at the instance of the authorities. His statement made without having had access to counsel, did not amount to a valid waiver and hence was inadmissible.

Accordingly, the holding of the Arizona Supreme Court that Edwards had waived his right to counsel was infirm and the judgment of that court is reversed.

So ordered. . . .

Can *Mosley* and *Edwards* be reconciled? What is the nature of the "right" being protected by these cases, or does it matter? In that regard, consider Michigan v. Tucker, 417 U.S. 433 (1974), where the Court asserted that the *Miranda* "procedural safeguards were not themselves

---

9. If, as frequently would occur in the course of a meeting initiated by the accused, the conversation is not wholly one-sided, it is likely that the officers will say or do something that clearly would be "interrogation." In that event, the question would be whether a valid waiver of the right to counsel and the right to silence had occurred, that is, whether the purported waiver was knowing and intelligent and found to be so under the totality of the circumstances, including the necessary fact that the accused, not the police, reopened the dialogue with the authorities. . . .

rights protected by the Constitution but were instead measures to insure that the right against compulsory self-incrimination was protected." If that is true, why did the Court rely on Johnson v. Zerbst in *Edwards?*

Edwards has generated difficulties, and the Court has gone back to it a number of times already. The Court first rendered a per curiam opinion:

WYRICK v. FIELDS, 459 U.S. 42, 43-49 (1982): Per Curiam. In this case, the United States Court of Appeals for the Eighth Circuit, over a dissent by Judge Ross, directed that respondent Edward Fields' petition for a writ of habeas corpus be granted; it did so on the ground that Fields had been convicted with evidence obtained in violation of his Fifth Amendment right to have counsel present at an interrogation. We have concluded that the Court of Appeals' majority misconstrued this Court's recent decision in Edwards v. Arizona, and imposed a new and unjustified limit on police questioning of a suspect who voluntarily, knowingly, and intelligently waives his right to have counsel present. . . .

Respondent, a soldier then stationed at Fort Leonard Wood, Mo., was charged with raping an 81 year old woman on September 21, 1974. After his arrest on September 25, Fields was released on his own recognizance. He retained private defense counsel. After discussing the matter with his counsel and with a military attorney provided him by the Army, Fields requested a polygraph examination. This request was granted and the examination was conducted on December 4 by an agent of the Army's Criminal Investigation Division (CID) at the Fort.

Prior to undergoing the polygraph examination, Fields was given a written consent document, which he signed, informing him of his rights, as required by Miranda v. Arizona, 384 U.S. 436 (1966), and of his rights under the Uniform Code of Military Justice and the Eighth Amendment. In addition, the CID agent read to Fields the following detailed statement:

> Before I ask you any questions, you must understand your rights. You do not have to answer my questions or say anything. Anything you say or do can be used against you in a criminal trial. You have a right to talk to a lawyer before questioning or have a lawyer present with you during the questioning. This lawyer can be a civilian lawyer of your own choice, or a military lawyer, detailed for you at no expense to you. Also, you may ask for a military lawyer of your choice by name and he will be detailed for you if superiors determine he's reasonably available. *If you are now going to discuss the offense under investigation, which is rape, with or without a lawyer present, you have a right to stop answering questions at any time or speak to a lawyer before answering further, even if you sign a waiver certificate.* Do you want a lawyer at this time? [See State v. Fields, 538 S.W.2d 348, 350 n.1 (Mo. App. 1976) (emphasis added).]

Fields answered: "No." . . . [Fields was subsequently convicted, but the conviction was reversed by the Eight Circuit Court of Appeals.]

When the suspect has initiated [a] dialogue, *Edwards* makes clear that the right to have a lawyer present can be waived:

> If, as frequently would occur in the course of a meeting initiated by the accused, the conversation is not wholly one-sided, it is likely that the officers will say or do something that clearly would be 'interrogation.' In that event, the question would be whether a valid waiver of the right to counsel and the right to silence had occurred, that is, whether the purported waiver was knowing and intelligent and found to be so under the totality of the circumstances, including the necessary fact that the accused, not the police, reopened the dialogue with the authorities. [451 U.S., at 486, n.9.]

Citing this language, the Eighth Circuit acknowledged—as it had to—that "[t]here is no question that Fields waived his right to have counsel present while the [polygraph] examination itself was being conducted." Yet that court found that the State had failed to satisfy its burden of proving that "Fields knowingly and intelligently waived his right to have counsel present at the post-test interrogation." The court suggested that had the CID agent merely "paus[ed] to remind the defendant" of his rights, thus providing "*meaningfully timed Miranda* warnings" (emphasis in original), there would have been no violation. . . .

In reaching this result, the Court of Appeals did not examine the "totality of the circumstances," as *Edwards* requires. Fields did not merely initiate a "meeting." By requesting a polygraph examination, he initiated interrogation. That is, Fields waived not only his right to be free of contact with the authorities in the absence of an attorney, but also his right to be free of interrogation about the crime of which he was suspected. Fields validly waived his right to have counsel present at "post-test" questioning, unless the circumstances changed so seriously that his answers no longer were voluntary, or unless he no longer was making a "knowing and intelligent relinquishment or abandonment" of his rights.

The Court of Appeals relied on two facts indicating the need for a new set of warnings: the polygraph examination had been discontinued, and Fields was asked if he could explain the test's unfavorable results. To require new warnings because of these two facts is unreasonable. Disconnecting the polygraph equipment effectuated no significant change in the character of the interrogation. The CID agent could have informed Fields during the examination that his answers indicated deceit; asking Fields, after the equipment was disconnected, why the answers were bothering him was not any more coercive. The Court of Appeals stated that there was no indication that Fields or his lawyer anticipated that Fields would be asked questions after the examination. But it would have been unreasonable for Fields and his attorneys to assume that Fields would not be informed of the polygraph readings and asked to explain any unfavorable result. Moreover, Fields had been informed that he could stop the questioning at any time, and could request at any time that his lawyer join him. Merely disconnecting the polygraph equipment could not remove this knowledge from Fields' mind.

The only plausible explanation for the court's holding is that, encouraged by what it regarded as a *per se* rule established in *Edwards*, it fashioned another rule of its own: that, notwithstanding a voluntary, knowing, and intelligent waiver of the right to have counsel present at a polygraph examination, and notwithstanding clear evidence that the suspect understood that right and was aware of his power to stop questioning at any time or to speak to an attorney at any time, the police again must advise the suspect of his rights before questioning him at the same interrogation about the results of the polygraph. The court indicated that this rule was needed because it thought that the use of polygraph "results" in questioning, although it does not necessarily render a response involuntary, is inherently coercive. But Courts of Appeals, including a different panel of the Eighth Circuit itself, and state courts, have rejected such a rule. The Eighth Circuit's rule certainly finds no support in *Edwards*, which emphasizes that the totality of the circumstances, including the fact that the suspect initiated the questioning, is controlling. Nor is the rule logical; the questions put to Fields after the examination would not have caused him to forget the rights of which he had been advised and which he had understood moments before. The rule is simply an unjustifiable restriction on reasonable police questioning. . . .

[JUSTICE STEVENS's concurring opinion and JUSTICE MARSHALL's dissenting opinion are omitted.]

The Court soon returned again to the implications of *Edwards*:

OREGON v. BRADSHAW
Certiorari to the Oregon Court of Appeals
462 U.S. 1039 (1983)

JUSTICE REHNQUIST announced the judgment of the Court and delivered an opinion in which THE CHIEF JUSTICE, JUSTICE WHITE, and JUSTICE O'CONNOR joined.

After a bench trial in an Oregon trial court, respondent James Edward Bradshaw was convicted of the offenses of first degree manslaughter, driving while under the influence of intoxicants, and driving while his license was revoked. The Oregon Court of Appeals reversed his conviction, holding that an inquiry he made of a police officer at the time he was in custody did not "initiate" a conversation with the officer, and that therefore statements by the respondent growing out of that conversation should have been excluded from evidence under Edwards v. Arizona. . . . .

In September, 1980, Oregon police were investigating the death of one Lowell Reynolds in Tillamook County. Reynolds' body had been found in a wrecked pickup truck, in which he appeared to have been a passenger at the time the vehicle left the roadway, struck a tree and an embankment, and finally came to rest on its side in a shallow creek. Reynolds had died from traumatic injury, coupled with asphyxia by drowning. During the investigation of Reynolds' death, respondent was asked to accompany a police officer to the Rockaway Police Station for questioning.

Once at the station, respondent was advised of his rights as required by Miranda v. Arizona, 384 U.S. 436 (1966). Respondent then repeated to the police his earlier account of the events of the evening of Reynolds' death, admitting that he had provided Reynolds and others with liquor for a party at Reynolds' house, but denying involvement in the traffic accident that apparently killed Reynolds. Respondent suggested that Reynolds might have met with foul play at the hands of the assailant whom respondent alleged had struck him at the party.

At this point, respondent was placed under arrest for furnishing liquor to Reynolds, a minor, and again advised of his *Miranda* rights. A police officer then told respondent the officer's theory of how the traffic accident that killed Reynolds occurred; a theory which placed respondent behind the wheel of the vehicle. Respondent again denied his involvement, and said "I do want an attorney before it goes very much further." . . . The officer immediately terminated the conversation.

Sometime later respondent was transferred from the Rockaway Police Station to the Tillamook County jail, a distance of some ten or fifteen miles. Either just before, or during, his trip from Rockaway to Tillamook, respondent inquired of a police officer, "Well, what is going to happen to me now?" The officer answered by saying "You do not have to talk to me. You have requested an attorney and I don't want you talking to me unless you so desire because anything you say—because—since you have requested an attorney, you know, it has to be at your own free will." App. 16. . . . Respondent said he understood. There followed a discussion between respondent and the officer concerning where respondent was being taken and the offense with which he would be charged. The officer suggested that respondent might help himself by taking a polygraph examination. Respondent agreed to take such an examination, saying that he was willing to do whatever he could to clear up the matter.

The next day, following another reading to respondent of his *Miranda* rights, and respondent's signing a written waiver of those rights, the polygraph was administered. At its conclusion, the examiner told respondent that he did not believe respondent was telling the truth. Respondent then recanted his earlier story, admitting that he had been at the wheel of the vehicle in which Reynolds was killed, that he had consumed a considerable amount of alcohol, and that he had passed out at the wheel before the vehicle left the roadway and came to rest in the creek.

Respondent was charged with first degree manslaughter, driving while under the influence of intoxicants, and driving while his license was revoked. His motion to suppress the statements described above was denied, and he was found guilty after a bench trial. The Oregon Court of Appeals, relying on our decision in Edwards v. Arizona, reversed, concluding that the statements had been obtained in violation of respondent's Fifth Amendment rights. We now conclude that the Oregon Court of Appeals misapplied our decision in *Edwards*.

In *Edwards* the defendant had voluntarily submitted to questioning but later stated that he wished an attorney before the discussions continued. The following day detectives accosted the defendant in the county jail, and when he refused to speak with them he was told that "he had" to talk. We held that subsequent incriminating statements made without his attorney present violated the rights secured to the defendant by the Fifth and Fourteenth Amendments to the United States Constitution. . . .

Respondent's question in the present case, "Well, what is going to happen to me now?," admittedly was asked prior to respondent being "subject[ed] to further interrogation by the authorities." Id., at 484. The Oregon Court of Appeals stated that it did not "construe defendant's question about what was going to happen to him to have been a waiver of his right to counsel, invoked only minutes before. . . ." The Court of Appeals, after quoting relevant language from *Edwards*, concluded that "under the reasoning enunciated in *Edwards*, defendant did not make a valid waiver of his Fifth Amendment rights, and his statements were inadmissible." . . .

We think the Oregon Court of Appeals misapprehended the test laid down in *Edwards*. We did not there hold that the "initiation" of a conversation by a defendant such as respondent would amount to a waiver of a previously invoked right to counsel; we held that after the right to counsel had been asserted by an accused, further interrogation of the accused should not take place "unless the accused himself initiates further communication, exchanges, or conversations with the police." This was in effect a prophylactic rule, designed to protect an accused in police custody from being badgered by police officers in the manner in which the defendant in *Edwards* was. We recently restated the requirement in *Wyrick v. Fields* to be that before a suspect in custody can be subjected to further interrogation after he requests an attorney there must be a showing that the "suspect himself initiates dialogue with the authorities."

But even if a conversation taking place after the accused has "expressed his desire to deal with the police only through counsel," is initiated by the accused, where reinterrogation follows, the burden remains upon the prosecution to show that subsequent events indicated a waiver of the Fifth Amendment right to have counsel present during the interrogation. . . .

Thus, the Oregon Court of Appeals was wrong in thinking that an "initiation" of a conversation or discussion by an accused not only satisfied the *Edwards* rule, but ex proprio vigore sufficed to show a waiver of the previously asserted right to counsel. The inquiries are separate, and clarity of application is not gained by melding them together.

There can be no doubt in this case that in asking, "Well, what is going to happen to me now?," respondent "initiated" further conversation in the ordinary dictionary sense of that word. While we doubt that it would be desirable to build a superstructure of legal refinements around the word "initiate" in this context, there are undoubtedly situations where a bare inquiry by either a defendant or by a police officer should not be held to "initiate" any conversation or dialogue. There are some inquiries, such as a request for a drink of water or a request to use a telephone that are so routine that they cannot be fairly said to represent a desire on the part of an accused to open up a more generalized discussion relating directly or indirectly to the investigation. Such inquiries or statements, by either an accused or a police officer, relating to routine incidents of the custodial relationship, will not generally "initiate" a conversation in the sense in which that word was used in *Edwards*.

Although ambiguous, the respondent's question in this case as to what was going to happen to him evinced a willingness and a desire for a generalized discussion about the investigation; it was not merely a necessary inquiry arising out of the incidents of the custodial relationship. It could reasonably have been interpreted by the officer as relating generally to the investigation. That the police officer so understood it is apparent from the fact that he immediately reminded the accused that "you do not have to talk to me," and only after the accused told him that he "understood" did they have a generalized conversation. On these facts we believe that there was not a violation of the *Edwards* rule.

Since there was no violation of the *Edwards* rule in this case, the next inquiry was "whether a valid waiver of the right to counsel and the right to silence had occurred, that is, whether the purported waiver was knowing and intelligent and found to be so under the totality of the circumstances, including the necessary fact that the accused, not the police, reopened the dialogue with the authorities." As we have said many times before, this determination depends "upon the particular facts and circumstances surrounding the case, including the background, experience, and conduct of the accused." North Carolina v. Butler, 441 U.S. 369, 374-375 (1979).

The state trial court made this inquiry and, in the words of the Oregon Court of Appeals, "found that the police made no threats, promises or inducements to talk, that defendant was properly advised of his rights and understood them and that within a short time after requesting an attorney he changed his mind without any impropriety on the part of the police. The court held that the statements made to the polygraph examiner were voluntary and the result of a knowing waiver of his right to remain silent." 54 Or. App., at 952, 636 P.2d, at 1012.

We have no reason to dispute these conclusions, based as they are upon the trial court's first-hand observation of the witnesses to the events involved. The judgment of the Oregon Court of Appeals is therefore reversed, and the cause remanded for further proceedings.

It is so ordered.

[JUSTICE POWELL's concurring opinion is omitted.]

JUSTICE MARSHALL, with whom JUSTICE BRENNAN, JUSTICE BLACK-MUN, and JUSTICE STEVENS join, dissenting.

Because in my view the plurality has misapplied Edwards v. Arizona, 451 U.S. 477 (1981), I respectfully dissent.

I . . .

The Oregon Court of Appeals properly applied *Edwards*.[1] When this Court in *Edwards* spoke of "initiat[ing] further communication" with the

---

1. In rebuking the Oregon Court of Appeals for failing to distinguish between the initiation of a conversation and a valid waiver of the right to counsel, . . . the plurality is attacking a straw man. Because it concluded that respondent had not initiated any conversation, the Oregon Court never even undertook the distinct inquiry into the existence of a knowing and intelligent waiver. *Edwards* makes clear that, in the absence of "initiation" by an accused, there can be no valid waiver regardless of whatever else the accused may say or do. 451 U.S., at 484. Having concluded that respondent did not initiate further conversation, the Oregon Court thus stated that there was no valid waiver in this case. This conclusion is entirely consistent with *Edwards*. Indeed, the Oregon

police and "reopen[ing] the dialogue with the authorities," it obviously had in mind communication or dialogue *about the subject matter of the criminal investigation*. The rule announced in *Edwards* was designed to ensure that any interrogation subsequent to an invocation of the right to counsel be at the instance of the accused, not the authorities. Thus, a question or statement which does not invite further interrogation before an attorney is present cannot qualify as "initiation" under *Edwards*. To hold otherwise would drastically undermine the safeguards that *Miranda* and *Edwards* carefully erected around the right to counsel in the custodial setting.

The safeguards identified in *Edwards* hardly pose an insurmountable obstacle to an accused who truly wishes to waive his rights after invoking his right to counsel. A waiver can be established, however, only when the accused himself reopens the dialogue about the subject matter of the criminal investigation.[2] . . .

II

I agree with the plurality that, in order to constitute "initiation" under *Edwards*, an accused's inquiry must demonstrate a desire to discuss the subject matter of the criminal investigation. . . . I am baffled, however, at the plurality's application of that standard to the facts of this case. The plurality asserts that respondent's question, "What is going to happen to me now?," evinced both "a willingness and a desire for a generalized discussion about the investigation." . . . If respondent's question had been posed by Jean-Paul Sartre before a class of philosophy students, it might well have evinced a desire for a "generalized" discussion. But under the circumstances of this case, it is plain that respondent's only "desire" was to find out where the police were going to take him. As the Oregon

---

Court's decision contains lengthy quotations from *Edwards*. Unless we are to assume that the State Court did not read the very portions of *Edwards* that it quotes, the plurality's attack is completely unjustified.

2. In his opinion concurring in the judgment, Justice Powell suggests that there is confusion as to whether *Edwards* announced a per se rule. . . . In my view, *Edwards* unambiguously established such a rule. See 451 U.S., at 484-486 and n.9. In any event, no confusion on this point can remain after today's decision for eight Justices manifestly agree that *Edwards* did create a per se rule. The plurality explicitly refers to the "prophylactic rule" of *Edwards*. . . . The rule is simply stated: unless the accused himself initiates further communication with the police, a valid waiver of the right to counsel cannot be established. If an accused has himself initiated further communication with the police, it is still necessary to establish as a separate matter the existence of a knowing and intelligent waiver under Johnson v. Zerbst, 304 U.S. 458, 464 (1938). The only dispute between the plurality and the dissent in this case concerns the meaning of "initiation" for purposes of *Edwards'* per se rule.

Court of Appeals stated, respondent's query came only minutes after his invocation of the right to counsel and was simply "a normal reaction to being taken from the police station and placed in a police car, obviously for transport to some destination." 54 Or. App., at 949, 636 P.2d, at 1013.[3] On these facts, I fail to see how respondent's question can be considered "initiation" of a conversation about the subject matter of the criminal investigation.

To hold that respondent's question in this case opened a dialogue with the authorities flies in the face of the basic purpose of the *Miranda* safeguards. When someone in custody asks, "What is going to happen to me now?," he is surely responding to his custodial surroundings. The very essence of custody is the loss of control over one's freedom of movement. The authorities exercise virtually unfettered control over the accused. To allow the authorities to recommence an interrogation based on such a question is to permit them to capitalize on the custodial setting. Yet *Miranda's* procedural protections were adopted precisely in order "to dispel the compulsion inherent in custodial surrounding." 384 U.S., at 458.

Accordingly, I dissent.

NOTES AND QUESTIONS

1. The Court issued another per curiam opinion concerning the implications of *Edwards* in Smith v. Illinois, 469 U.S. 91 (1984). Over a sharp dissent, it held that the following facts and "interrogation" violated *Edwards:*

> Shortly after his arrest, 18-year-old Steven Smith was taken to an interrogation room at the Logan County Safety Complex for questioning by two police detectives. The session began as follows:
>
> Q. Steve, I want to talk with you in reference to the armed robbery that took place at McDonald's restaurant on the morning of the 19th. Are you familiar with this?

3. The plurality seems to place some reliance on the police officer's reaction to respondent's question. The officer described his response as follows. "I says, 'You do not have to talk to me. You have requested an attorney and I don't want you talking to me unless you so desire because anything you say—because—since you have requested an attorney, you know, it has to be at your own free will.' I says, 'I can't prevent you from talking, but you understand where your place—you know, where your standing is here?' and he agreed. He says 'I understand.' "

As the officer's testimony indicates, respondent's statement was at best ambiguous. In any event, as the Oregon Court of Appeals noted, the officer clearly took advantage of respondent's inquiry to commence once again his questioning—a practice squarely at odds with *Edwards*. See 54 Or. App., at 953, 636 P.2d, at 1013.

A. Yeah. My cousin Greg was.
Q. Okay. But before I do that I must advise you of your rights. Okay? You have a right to remain silent. You do not have to talk to me unless you want to do so. Do you understand that?
A. Uh. She told me to get my lawyer. She said you guys would railroad me.
Q. Do you understand that as I gave it to you, Steve?
A. Yeah.
Q. If you do want to talk to me I must advise you that whatever you say can and will be used against you in court. Do you understand that?
A. Yeah.
Q. You have a right to consult with a lawyer and to have a lawyer present with you when you're being questioned. Do you understand that?
A. *Uh, yeah, Id like to do that.*
Q. Okay.

Instead of terminating the questioning at this point, the interrogating officers proceeded to finish reading Smith his *Miranda* rights and then pressed him again to answer their questions:

Q. . . . If you want a lawyer and you're unable to pay for one a lawyer will be appointed to represent you free of cost, do you understand that?
A. Okay.
Q. Do you wish to talk to me at this time without a lawyer being present?
A. *Yeah and no, uh, I don't know what's what really.*
Q. *Well. You either have to talk to me this time without a lawyer being present and if you do agree to talk with me without a lawyer being present you can stop at any time you want to.*
Q. All right. I'll talk to you then.

Smith then told the detectives that he knew in advance about the planned robbery, but contended that he had not been a participant. After considerable probing by the detectives, Smith confessed that "I committed it," but he then returned to his earlier story that he had only known about the planned crime. Upon further questioning, Smith again insisted that "I wanta get a lawyer." This time the detectives honored the request and terminated the interrogation.

In a curious linguistic exercise, the Court held "only that, under the logical force of settled precedent, an accused's *postrequest* [for counsel] responses to further interrogation may not be used to cast retrospective doubt on the clarity of the initial request itself. Such subsequent statements are relevant only to the distinct question of waiver." Id. at 495. As the dissent pointed out, it is not clear why informing a suspect of the remainder of his rights amounts to "interrogation," nor is it clear why subsequent events that may shed light on prior ones should be ignored in attempting to determine the exact nature of those prior events.

2. For another linguistic exercise, see Connecticut v. Barrett, 479

U.S. 523 (1987). In *Barrett*, the defendant agreed to talk to the police, but he refused to make a written statement without counsel present. According to the Court, this did not amount to a generalized assertion of counsel sufficient to invoke the implications of *Edwards*. Whether you agree with this decision or not, contemplate the nature of the decision-making process involved in the *Edwards* line of cases. Are the distinctions beginning to become too fine to be convincing, or is there no escape from such an approach in a precedential system of adjudication? Last term, the Court applied *Edwards* to a situation where a defendant was interrogated for a different crime after requesting counsel. Arizona v. Roberson, 486 U.S. 675 (1988). *Mosley* was distinguished on the ground that it involved an invocation of the right to remain silent, not the right to counsel.

3. In Minnick v. Mississippi, — U.S. — (1990), the court considered whether *Edwards* is satisfied when a suspect is allowed to consult with counsel and is subsequently interrogated. The court held that this violates *Edwards*:

> In our view, a fair reading of *Edwards* and subsequent cases demonstrates that we have interpreted the rule to bar police-initiated interrogation unless the accused has counsel with him at the time of questioning. Whatever the ambiguities of our earlier cases on this point, we now hold that when counsel is requested, interrogation must cease, and officials may not reinitiate interrogation without counsel present, whether or not the accused has consulted with his attorney.
>
> We consider our ruling to be an appropriate and necessary application of the *Edwards* rule. A single consultation with an attorney does not remove the suspect from persistent attempts by officials to persuade him to waive his rights, or from the coercive pressures that accompany custody and that may increase as custody is prolonged. The case before us well-illustrates the pressures, and abuses, that may be concomitants of custody. Petitioner testified that though he resisted, he was required to submit to both the F.B.I. and the Denham interviews. In the latter instance, the compulsion to submit to interrogation followed petitioner's unequivocal request during the F.B.I. interview that questioning cease until counsel was present. The case illustrates also that consultation is not always effective in instructing the suspect of his rights. One plausible interpretation of the record is that petitioner thought he could keep his admissions out of evidence by refusing to sign a formal waiver of rights. If the authorities had complied with Minnick's request to have counsel present during interrogation, the attorney could have corrected Minnick's misunderstanding or indeed counseled him that he need not make a statement at all. We decline to remove protection from police-initiated questioning based on isolated consultation with counsel who is absent when the interrogation resumes.

Justice Scalia, joined by Chief Justice Rehnquist, dissented:

> Today's extension of the *Edwards* prohibition is the latest stage of prophylaxis built upon prophylaxis, producing a veritable fairyland castle of imagined Constitutional restrictions upon law enforcement. This newest tower, according to the court, is needed to avoid inconsistency with the purpose of *Edwards'* prophylactic rule, which was needed to protect *Miranda's* prophylactic right to have counsel present, which was needed to protect the right against *compelled self-incrimination* found (at last!) in the Constitution.
>
> It seems obvious to me that, even in *Edwards* itself but surely in today's decision, we have gone far beyond any genuine concern about suspects who do not *know* their right to remain silent, or who have been *coerced* to abandon it. Both holdings are explicable, in my view, only as an effort to protect suspects against what is regarded as their own folly. The sharp-witted criminal would know better than to confess; why should the dull-witted suffer for his lack of mental endowment? Providing him with an attorney at every stage where he might be induced or persuaded (though not coerced) to incriminate himself will even the odds. Apart from the fact that this protective enterprise is beyond our authority under the Fifth Amendment or any other provision of the Constitution, it is unwise. The procedural protections of the Constitution protect the guilty as well as the innocent. But it is not their objective to set the guilty free. That some clever criminals may employ those protections to their advantage is poor reason to allow criminals who have not done so to escape justice.
>
> Thus, even if I were to concede that an honest confession is a foolish mistake, I would welcome rather than reject it; a rule that foolish mistakes do not count would leave most offenders not only unconvicted but undetected. More fundamentally, however, it is wrong, and subtly corrosive of our criminal justice system, to regard an honest confession as a "mistake." While every person is entitled to stand silent, it is more virtuous for the wrongdoer to admit his offense and accept the punishment he deserves. . . . To design our laws on premises contrary to these is to abandon belief in either personal responsibility or the moral claim of just government to obedience. Today's decision is misguided, it seems to me, in so readily exchanging, for marginal, *super-Zerbst* protection against genuinely compelled testimony, investigators' ability to urge, or even ask, a person in custody to do what is right.

4. What suffices to invoke *Miranda* in the first place? In Fare v. Michael C., 442 U.S. 707 (1979), a juvenile was interrogated about a murder. After being given his rights, he asked "Can I have my probation officer here?" The police officer said that he was not going to call the probation officer and "If you want to talk to us without an attorney present, you can. If you don't want to, you don't have to." The juvenile agreed to talk and made incriminating statements. The Court found the

statements admissible, on the grounds that *Miranda* had not adequately been invoked and that attorneys play a unique role in the criminal justice system.

g. The Right to Counsel Revisited

What is the relationship between *Massiah*, *Escobedo*, and *Miranda*? Does each subsequent case supplant the previous one? There is good reason to believe that is true of *Escobedo* and *Miranda*, see note 4 to *Miranda*, page 1106 supra. But what of *Massiah*? Was that just the first contemporary attempt to handle the problem of interrogation, or did it rest on independent values? Consider the next case.

BREWER v. WILLIAMS
Certiorari to the Eighth Circuit Court of Appeals
430 U.S. 387 (1977)

MR. JUSTICE STEWART delivered the opinion of the Court.

An Iowa trial jury found the respondent, Robert Williams, guilty of murder. The judgment of conviction was affirmed in the Iowa Supreme Court by a closely divided vote. In a subsequent habeas corpus proceeding a Federal District Court ruled that under the United States Constitution Williams is entitled to a new trial, and a divided Court of Appeals for the Eighth Circuit agreed. The question before us is whether the District Court and the Court of Appeals were wrong.

I

On the afternoon of December 24, 1968, a 10-year-old girl named Pamela Powers went with her family to the YMCA in Des Moines, Iowa, to watch a wrestling tournament in which her brother was participating. When she failed to return from a trip to the washroom, a search for her began. The search was unsuccessful.

Robert Williams, who had recently escaped from a mental hospital, was a resident of the YMCA. Soon after the girl's disappearance Williams was seen in the YMCA lobby carrying some clothing and a large bundle wrapped in a blanket. He obtained help from a 14-year-old boy in opening the street door of the YMCA and the door to his automobile parked outside. When Williams placed the bundle in the front seat of his car the boy "saw two legs in it and they were skinny and white." Before anyone could see what was in the bundle Williams drove away. His abandoned car was found the following day in Davenport, Iowa, roughly 160 miles east of Des Moines. A warrant was then issued in Des Moines for his arrest on a charge of abduction.

On the morning of December 26, a Des Moines lawyer named Henry McKnight went to the Des Moines police station and informed the officers present that he had just received a long-distance call from Williams, and that he had advised Williams to turn himself in to the Davenport police. Williams did surrender that morning to the police in Davenport, and they booked him on the charge specified in the arrest warrant and gave him the warnings required by Miranda v. Arizona. 384 U.S. 436. The Davenport police then telephoned their counterparts in Des Moines to inform them that Williams had surrendered. McKnight, the lawyer, was still at the Des Moines police headquarters, and Williams conversed with McKnight on the telephone. In the presence of the Des Moines chief of police and a police detective named Leaming, McKnight advised Williams that Des Moines police officers would be driving to Davenport to pick him up, that the officers would not interrogate him or mistreat him, and that Williams was not to talk to the officers about Pamela Powers until after consulting with McKnight upon his return to Des Moines. As a result of these conversations, it was agreed between McKnight and the Des Moines police officials that Detective Leaming and a fellow officer would drive to Davenport to pick up Williams, that they would bring him directly back to Des Moines, and that they would not question him during the trip.

In the meantime Williams was arraigned before a judge in Davenport on the outstanding arrest warrant. The judge advised him of his *Miranda* rights and committed him to jail. Before leaving the courtroom, Williams conferred with a lawyer named Kelly, who advised him not to make any statements until consulting with McKnight back in Des Moines.

Detective Leaming and his fellow officer arrived in Davenport about noon to pick up Williams and return him to Des Moines. Soon after their arrival they met with Williams and Kelly, who, they understood, was acting as Williams' lawyer. Detective Leaming repeated the *Miranda* warnings, and told Williams: "[W]e both know that you're being represented here by Mr. Kelly and you're being represented by Mr. McKnight in Des Moines, and . . . I want you to remember this because we'll be visiting between here and Des Moines." Williams then conferred again with Kelly alone, and after this conference Kelly reiterated to Detective Leaming that Williams was not to be questioned about the disappearance of Pamela Powers until after he had consulted with McKnight back in Des Moines. When Leaming expressed some reservations, Kelly firmly stated that the agreement with McKnight was to be carried out—that there was to be no interrogation of Williams during the automobile journey to Des Moines. Kelly was denied permission to ride in the police car back to Des Moines with Williams and two officers.

The two detectives, with Williams in their charge, then set out on the 160-mile drive. At no time during the trip did Williams express a willingness to be interrogated in the absence of an attorney. Instead, he stated several times that "[w]hen I get to Des Moines and see Mr. McKnight, I am going to tell you the whole story." Detective Leaming knew that Williams was a former mental patient, and knew also that he was deeply religious.

The detective and his prisoner soon embarked on a wide-ranging conversation covering a variety of topics, including the subject of religion. Then, not long after leaving Davenport and reaching the interstate highway, Detective Leaming delivered what has been referred to in the briefs and oral arguments as the "Christian burial speech." Addressing Williams as "Reverend," the detective said:

> I want to give you something to think about while we're traveling down the road. . . . Number one, I want you to observe the weather conditions, it's raining, it's sleeting, it's freezing, driving is very treacherous, visibility is poor, it's going to be dark early this evening. They are predicting several inches of snow for tonight, and I feel that you yourself are the only person that knows where this little girl's body is, that you yourself have only been there once, and if you get a snow on top of it you yourself may be unable to find it. And, since we will be going right past the area on the way into Des Moines, I feel that we could stop and locate the body, that the parents of this little girl should be entitled to a Christian burial for the little girl who was snatched away from them on Christmas [E]ve and murdered. And I feel we should stop and locate it on the way in rather than waiting until morning and trying to come back out after a snow storm and possibly not being able to find it at all.

Williams asked Detective Leaming why he thought their route to Des Moines would be taking them past the girl's body, and Leaming responded that he knew the body was in the area of Mitchellville—a town they would be passing on the way to Des Moines.[1] Leaming then stated: "I do not want you to answer me. I don't want to discuss it any further. Just think about it as we're riding down the road."

As the car approached Grinnell, a town approximately 100 miles west of Davenport, Williams asked whether the police had found the victim's shoes. When Detective Leaming replied that he was unsure, Williams directed the officers to a service station where he said he had

---

1. The fact of the matter, of course, was that Detective Leaming possessed no such knowledge.

left the shoes; a search for them proved unsuccessful. As they continued towards Des Moines, Williams asked whether the police had found the blanket, and directed the officers to a rest area where he said he had disposed of the blanket. Nothing was found. The car continued towards Des Moines, and as it approached Mitchellville, Williams said that he would show the officers where the body was. He then directed the police to the body of Pamela Powers.

Williams was indicted for first-degree murder. Before trial, his counsel moved to suppress all evidence relating to or resulting from any statements Williams had made during the automobile ride from Davenport to Des Moines. After an evidentiary hearing the trial judge denied the motion. He found that "an agreement was made between defense counsel and the police officials to the effect that the Defendant was not to be questioned on the return trip to Des Moines," and that the evidence in question had been elicited from Williams during "a critical stage in the proceedings requiring the presence of counsel on his request." The judge ruled, however, that Williams had "waived his right to have an attorney present during the giving of such information."[2]

The evidence in question was introduced over counsel's continuing objection at the subsequent trial. The jury found Williams guilty of murder, and the judgment of conviction was affirmed by the Iowa Supreme Court, a bare majority of whose members agreed with the trial court that Williams had "waived his right to the presence of his counsel" on the automobile ride from Davenport to Des Moines. State v. Williams, 182 N.W.2d 396, 402. The four dissenting justices expressed the view that "when counsel and police have agreed defendant is not to be questioned until counsel is present and defendant has been advised not to talk and repeatedly has stated he will tell the whole story after he talks with counsel, the state should be required to make a stronger showing of intentional voluntary waiver than was made here." Id., at 408.

Williams then petitioned for a writ of habeas corpus in the United States District Court for the Southern District of Iowa. Counsel for the State and for Williams stipulated that "the case would be submitted on the record of facts and proceedings in the trial court, without taking of further testimony." The District Court made findings of fact as summarized above, and concluded as a matter of law that the evidence in question had been wrongly admitted at Williams' trial. This conclusion was based on three alternative and independent grounds: (1) that Williams had been denied his constitutional right to the assistance of counsel; (2) that he had been denied the constitutional protections defined by this Court's decisions in Escobedo v. Illinois, 378 U.S. 478, and Miranda v. Arizona, 384 U.S. 436; and (3) that in any event, his self-incriminatory statements on the automobile trip from Davenport to Des Moines had

2. The opinion of the trial court denying Williams' motion to suppress is unreported.

been involuntarily made. Further, the District Court ruled that there had been no waiver by Williams of the constitutional protections in question. 375 F. Supp. 170.

The Court of Appeals for the Eighth Circuit, with one judge dissenting, affirmed this judgment, 509 F.2d 227, and denied a petition for rehearing en banc. We granted certiorari to consider the constitutional issues presented. . . .

II . . .

B

As stated above, the District Court based its judgment in this case on three independent grounds. The Court of Appeals appears to have affirmed the judgment on two of those grounds.[5] We have concluded that only one of them need be considered here.

Specifically, there is no need to review in this case the doctrine of Miranda v. Arizona, a doctrine designed to secure the constitutional privilege against compulsory self-incrimination, Michigan v. Tucker, 417 U.S. 433, 438-439. It is equally unnecessary to evaluate the ruling of the District Court that Williams' self-incriminating statements were, indeed, involuntarily made. Cf. Spano v. New York, 360 U.S. 315. For it is clear that the judgment before us must in any event be affirmed upon the ground that Williams was deprived of a different constitutional right—the right to the assistance of counsel. . . .

There can be no doubt in the present case that judicial proceedings had been initiated against Williams before the start of the automobile ride from Davenport to Des Moines. A warrant had been issued for his arrest, he had been arraigned on that warrant before a judge in a Davenport courtroom, and he had been committed by the court to confinement in jail. The State does not contend otherwise.

There can be no serious doubt, either, that Detective Leaming deliberately and designedly set out to elicit information from Williams just as surely as—and perhaps more effectively than—if he had formally interrogated him. Detective Leaming was fully aware before departing for Des Moines that Williams was being represented in Davenport by Kelly and in Des Moines by McKnight. Yet he purposely sought during Williams' isolation from his lawyers to obtain as much incriminating information as possible. Indeed, Detective Leaming conceded as much when he testified at Williams' trial:

5. The Court of Appeals did not address the District Court's ruling that Williams' statements had been made involuntarily.

> Q: In fact, Captain, whether he was a mental patient or not, you were trying to get all the information you could before he got to his lawyer, weren't you?
> A: I was sure hoping to find out where that little girl was, yes sir. . . .
> Q: Well, I'll put it this way: You was [sic] hoping to get all the information you could before Williams got back to McKnight, weren't you?
> A: Yes, sir.[6]

The state courts clearly proceeded upon the hypothesis that Detective Leaming's "Christian burial speech" had been tantamount to interrogation. Both courts recognized that Williams had been entitled to the assistance of counsel at the time he made the incriminating statements. Yet no such constitutional protection would have come into play if there had been no interrogation.

The circumstances of this case are thus constitutionally indistinguishable from those presented in Massiah v. United States, supra. . . .

That the incriminating statements were elicited surreptitiously in the Massiah case, and otherwise here, is constitutionally irrelevant. . . . Rather, the clear rule of Massiah is that once adversary proceedings have commenced against an individual, he has a right to legal representation when the government interrogates him.[8] It thus requires no wooden or technical application of the Massiah doctrine to conclude that Williams was entitled to the assistance of counsel guaranteed to him by the Sixth and Fourteenth Amendments.

III

The Iowa courts recognized that Williams had been denied the consti-

6. Counsel for petitioner, in the course of oral argument in this Court, acknowledged that the "Christian burial speech" was tantamount to interrogation:

> Q: But isn't the point, really, Mr. Attorney General, what you indicated earlier, and that is that the officer wanted to elicit information from Williams—
> A: Yes, sir.
> Q: —by whatever techniques he used, I would suppose a lawyer would consider that he were pursuing interrogation.
> A: It is, but it was very brief. [Tr. of Oral Arg. 17.]

8. The only other significant factual difference between the present case and Massiah is that here the police had agreed that they would not interrogate Williams in the absence of his counsel. This circumstance plainly provides petitioner with no argument for distinguishing away the protection afforded by Massiah.

It is argued that this agreement may not have been an enforceable one. But we do not deal here with notions of offer, acceptance, consideration, or other concepts of the law of contracts. We deal with constitutional law. And every court that has looked at this case has found an "agreement" in the sense of a commitment made by the Des Moines police officers that Williams would not be questioned about Pamela Powers in the absence of his counsel.

tutional right to the assistance of counsel. They held, however, that he had waived that right during the course of the automobile trip from Davenport to Des Moines. . . .

In its lengthy opinion affirming this determination, the Iowa Supreme Court applied "the totality-of-circumstances test for a showing of waiver of constitutionally-protected rights in the absence of an express waiver," and concluded that

> evidence of the time element involved on the trip, the general circumstances of it, and the absence of any request or expressed desire for the aid of counsel before or at the time of giving information, were sufficient to sustain a conclusion that defendant did waive his constitutional rights as alleged. [182 N.W.2d, at 401, 402.]

In the federal habeas corpus proceeding the District Court, believing that the issue of waiver was not one of fact but of federal law, held that the Iowa courts had "applied the wrong constitutional standards" in ruling that Williams had waived the protections that were his under the Constitution. 375 F. Supp., at 182. The court held "that it is the government which bears a heavy burden . . . but that is the burden which explicitly was placed on [Williams] by the state courts." Ibid. (emphasis in original). . . .

The Court of Appeals approved the reasoning of the District Court. . . .

The District Court and the Court of Appeals were correct in the view that the question of waiver was not a question of historical fact, but one which, in the words of Mr. Justice Frankfurter, requires "application of constitutional principles to the facts as found. . . ." Brown v. Allen, 344 U.S. 443, 507 (separate opinion). . . .

The District Court and the Court of Appeals were also correct in their understanding of the proper standard to be applied in determining the question of waiver as a matter of federal constitutional law—that it was incumbent upon the State to prove "an intentional relinquishment or abandonment of a known right or privilege." Johnson v. Zerbst, 304 U.S., at 464. . . .

We conclude . . . that the Court of Appeals was correct in holding that, judged by these standards, the record in this case falls far short of sustaining petitioner's burden. It is true that Williams had been informed of and appeared to understand his right to counsel. But waiver requires not merely comprehension but relinquishment, and Williams' consistent reliance upon the advice of counsel in dealing with the authorities refutes any suggestion that he waived that right. He consulted McKnight by long-distance telephone before turning himself in. He spoke with McKnight by telephone again shortly after being booked. After he was arraigned,

Williams sought out and obtained legal advice from Kelly. Williams again consulted with Kelly after Detective Leaming and his fellow officer arrived in Davenport. Throughout, Williams was advised not to make any statements before seeing McKnight in Des Moines, and was assured that the police had agreed not to question him. His statements while in the car that he would tell the whole story after seeing McKnight in Des Moines were the clearest expressions by Williams himself that he desired the presence of an attorney before any interrogation took place. But even before making these statements, Williams had effectively asserted his right to counsel by having secured attorneys at both ends of the automobile trip, both of whom, acting as his agents, had made clear to the police that no interrogation was to occur during the journey. Williams knew of that agreement and, particularly in view of his consistent reliance on counsel, there is no basis for concluding that he disavowed it.

Despite Williams' express and implicit assertions of his right to counsel, Detective Leaming proceeded to elicit incriminating statements from Williams. Leaming did not preface this effort by telling Williams that he had a right to the presence of a lawyer, and made no effort at all to ascertain whether Williams wished to relinquish that right. The circumstances of record in this case thus provide no reasonable basis for finding that Williams waived his right to the assistance of counsel.

The Court of Appeals did not hold, nor do we, that under the circumstances of this case Williams *could not*, without notice to counsel, have waived his rights under the Sixth and Fourteenth Amendments. It only held, as do we, that he did not.

IV

The crime of which Williams was convicted was senseless and brutal, calling for swift and energetic action by the police to apprehend the perpetrator and gather evidence with which he could be convicted. No mission of law enforcement officials is more important. Yet "[d]isinterested zeal for the public good does not assure either wisdom or right in the methods it pursues." Haley v. Ohio, 332 U.S. 596, 605 (Frankfurter, J., concurring in judgment). Although we do not lightly affirm the issuance of a writ of habeas corpus in this case, so clear a violation of the Sixth and Fourteenth Amendments as here occurred cannot be condoned. The pressures on state executive and judicial officers charged with the administration of the criminal law are great, especially when the crime is murder and the victim a small child. But it is precisely the predictability of those pressures that makes imperative a resolute loyalty to the guarantees that the Constitution extends to us all.

The judgment of the Court of Appeals is affirmed.[12]
It is so ordered.

MR. JUSTICE MARSHALL, concurring.

I concur wholeheartedly in my Brother Stewart's opinion for the Court, but add these words in light of the dissenting opinions filed today. The dissenters have, I believe, lost sight of the fundamental constitutional backbone of our criminal law. They seem to think that Detective Leaming's actions were perfectly proper, indeed laudable, examples of "good police work." In my view, good police work is something far different from catching the criminal at any price. It is equally important that the police, as guardians of the law, fulfill their responsibility to obey its commands scrupulously. For "in the end life and liberty can be as much endangered from illegal methods used to convict those thought to be criminals as from the actual criminals themselves." Spano v. New York, 360 U.S. 315, 320-321 (1959).

In this case, there can be no doubt that Detective Leaming consciously and knowingly set out to violate Williams' Sixth Amendment right to counsel and his Fifth Amendment privilege against self-incrimination, as Leaming himself understood those rights. Leaming knew that Williams had been advised by two lawyers not to make any statements to police until he conferred in Des Moines with his attorney there, Mr. McKnight. Leaming surely understood, because he had overheard McKnight tell Williams as much, that the location of the body would be revealed to police. Undoubtedly Leaming realized the way in which that information would be conveyed to the police: McKnight would learn it from his client and then he would lead police to the body. Williams would thereby be protected by the attorney-client privilege from incriminating himself by directly demonstrating his knowledge of the body's location, and the unfortunate Powers child could be given a "Christian burial."

Of course, this scenario would accomplish all that Leaming sought

12. The District Court stated that its decision "does not touch upon the issue of what evidence, if any, beyond the incriminating statements themselves must be excluded as 'fruit of the poisonous tree.' " 375 F. Supp. 170, 185. We, too, have no occasion to address this issue, and in the present posture of the case there is no basis for the view of our dissenting Brethren . . . that any attempt to retry the respondent would probably be futile. While neither William's incriminating statements themselves nor any testimony describing his having led the police to the victim's body can constitutionally be admitted into evidence, evidence of where the body was found and of its condition might well be admissible on the theory that the body would have been discovered in any event, even had incriminating statements not been elicited from Williams. Cf. Killough v. United States, 119 U.S. App. D.C. 10, 336 F.2d 929. In the event that a retrial is instituted, it will be for the state courts in the first instance to determine whether particular items of evidence may be admitted.

from his investigation except that it would not produce incriminating statements or actions from Williams. Accordingly, Leaming undertook his charade to pry such evidence from Williams. After invoking the no-passengers rule to prevent attorney Kelly from accompanying the prisoner, Leaming had Williams at his mercy: during the three- or four-hour trip he could do anything he wished to elicit a confession. The detective demonstrated once again "that the efficiency of the rack and the thumb-screw can be matched, given the proper subject, by more sophisticated modes of 'persuasion.' " Blackburn v. Alabama, 361 U.S. 199, 206 (1960).

Leaming knowingly isolated Williams from the protection of his lawyers and during that period he intentionally "persuaded" him to give incriminating evidence. It is this intentional police misconduct—not good police practice—that the Court rightly condemns. The heinous nature of the crime is no excuse, as the dissenters would have it, for condoning knowing and intentional police transgression of the consti-tutional rights of a defendant. If Williams is to go free—and given the ingenuity of Iowa prosecutors on retrial or in a civil commitment pro-ceeding, I doubt very much that there is any chance a dangerous criminal will be loosed on the streets, the bloodcurdling cries of the dissents notwithstanding—it will hardly be because he deserves it. It will be because Detective Leaming, knowing full well that he risked reversal of Williams' conviction, intentionally denied Williams the right of *every* American under the Sixth Amendment to have the protective shield of a lawyer between himself and the awesome power of the State. . . .

[MR. JUSTICE POWELL's and MR. JUSTICE STEVENS's concurring opinions are omitted.]

MR. CHIEF JUSTICE BURGER, dissenting.

The result in this case ought to be intolerable in any society which purports to call itself an organized society. It continues the Court—by the narrowest margin—on the much-criticized course of punishing the public for the mistakes and misdeeds of law enforcement officers, instead of punishing the officer directly, if in fact he is guilty of wrongdoing. It mechanically and blindly keeps reliable evidence from juries whether the claimed constitutional violation involves gross police misconduct or hon-est human error.

Williams is guilty of the savage murder of a small child; no member of the Court contends he is not. While in custody, and after no fewer than *five* warnings of his rights to silence and to counsel, he led police to the concealed body of his victim. The Court concedes Williams was not threatened or coerced and that he spoke and acted voluntarily and with full awareness of his constitutional rights. In the face of all this, the Court now holds that because Williams was prompted by the detective's statement—not interrogation but a statement—the jury must not be told how the police found the body.

Today's holding fulfills Judge (later Mr. Justice) Cardozo's grim prophecy that someday some court might carry the exclusionary rule to the absurd extent that its operative effect would exclude evidence relating to the body of a murder victim because of the means by which it was found.[1] In so ruling the Court regresses to playing a grisly game of "hide and seek," once more exalting the sporting theory of criminal justice which has been experiencing a decline in our jurisprudence. With Justices White, Blackmun, and Rehnquist, I categorically reject the remarkable notion that the police in this case were guilty of unconstitutional misconduct, or any conduct justifying the bizarre result reached by the Court. Apart from a brief comment on the merits, however, I wish to focus on the irrationality of applying the increasingly discredited exclusionary rule to this case.

(1) THE COURT CONCEDES WILLIAMS' DISCLOSURES WERE VOLUNTARY

Under well-settled precedents which the Court freely acknowledges, it is very clear that Williams had made a valid waiver of his Fifth Amendment right to silence and his Sixth Amendment right to counsel when he led police to the child's body. Indeed, even under the Court's analysis I do not understand how a contrary conclusion is possible.

The Court purports to apply as the appropriate constitutional waiver standard the familiar "intentional relinquishment or abandonment of a known right or privilege" test of Johnson v. Zerbst, 304 U.S. 458, 464 (1938). . . . The Court assumes, without deciding, that Williams conduct and statements were voluntary. It concedes, as it must, . . . that Williams had been informed of and fully understood his constitutional rights and the consequences of their waiver. Then, having either assumed or found every element necessary to make out a valid waiver under its own test, the Court reaches the astonishing conclusion that no valid waiver has been demonstrated.

This remarkable result is compounded by the Court's failure to define

---

1. "The criminal is to go free because the constable has blundered. . . . A room is searched against the law, and the body of a murdered man is found. . . . The privacy of the home has been infringed, and the murderer goes free." People v. Defore, 242 N.Y. 13, 21, 23-24, 150 N.E. 585, 587, 588 (1926)

The Court protests, . . . that its holding excludes only "Williams' incriminating statements themselves [as well as] any testimony describing his having led the police to the victim's body," thus hinting that successful retrial of this palpably guilty felon is realistically possible. Even if this were all, and the corpus delicti could be used to establish the fact and manner of the victim's death, the Court's holding clearly bars all efforts to let the jury know how the police found the body. But the Court's further—and re-what evidentiary showing the State failed to make. Only recently, in Schneckloth v. Bustamonte, 412 U.S. 218, 238, n.25 (1973), the Court analyzed the distinction between a voluntary act and the waiver of a right; there Mr. Justice Stewart stated for the Court:

> [T]he question whether a person has acted "voluntarily" is quite distinct from the question whether he has "waived" a trial right. The former question, as we made clear in Brady v. United States, 397 U.S. [742,] 749, can be answered only by examining all the relevant circumstances to determine if he has been coerced. The latter question turns on the extent of his knowledge.

Similarly, in McMann v. Richardson, 397 U.S. 759, 766 (1970), we said that since a guilty plea constituted a waiver of a host of constitutional rights, "It must be an intelligent act 'done with sufficient awareness of the relevant circumstances and likely consequences.' " If the Court today applied these standards with fidelity to the *Schneckloth* and *McMann* holdings it could not reach the result now announced.

The evidence is uncontradicted that Williams had abundant knowledge of his right to have counsel present and of his right to silence. Since the Court does not question his mental competence, it boggles the mind to suggest that Williams could not understand that leading police to the child's body would have other than the most serious consequences. All of the elements necessary to make out a valid waiver are shown by the record and acknowledged by the Court; we thus are left to guess how the Court reached its holding.

One plausible but unarticulated basis for the result reached is that once a suspect has asserted his right not to talk without the presence of an attorney, it becomes legally impossible for him to waive that right until he has seen an attorney. But constitutional rights are *personal*, and an otherwise valid waiver should not be brushed aside by judges simply because an attorney was not present. The Court's holding operates to "imprison a man in his privileges," Adams v. United States ex rel. McCann, 317 U.S. 269, 280 (1942); it conclusively presumes a suspect is legally incompetent to change his mind and tell the truth until an attorney is present. It denigrates an individual to a non-person whose free will has become hostage to a lawyer so that until the lawyer consents,

---

markable—statement that "evidence of where the body was found and of its condition" could be admitted *only* "on the theory that the body would have been discovered in any event" makes clear that the Court is determined to keep the truth from the jurors pledged to find the truth. If all use of the corpus delicti is to be barred by the Court as "fruit of the poisonous tree" under Wong Sun v. United States, 371 U.S. 471 (1963), except on the unlikely theory suggested by the Court, the Court renders the prospects of doing justice in this case exceedingly remote.

the suspect is deprived of any legal right or power to decide for himself that he wishes to make a disclosure. It denies that the rights to counsel and silence are personal, nondelegable, and subject to a waiver only by that individual.[2] The opinions in support of the Court's judgment do not enlighten us as to why police conduct—whether good or bad—should operate to suspend Williams' right to change his mind and "tell all" at once rather than waiting until he reached Des Moines.[3]

In his concurring opinion Mr. Justice Powell suggests that the result in this case turns on whether Detective Leaming's remarks constituted "interrogation," as he views them, or whether they were "statements" intended to prick the conscience of the accused. I find it most remarkable that a murder case should turn on judicial interpretation that a statement becomes a question simply because it is followed by an incriminating disclosure from the suspect. The Court seems to be saying that since Williams said he would "tell the whole story" at Des Moines, the police should have been content and waited; of course, that would have been the wiser course, especially in light of the nuances of constitutional jurisprudence applied by the Court, but a murder case ought not turn on such tenuous strands.

In any case, the Court assures us, this is not at all what it intends, and that a valid waiver was *possible* in these circumstances, but was not quite made. Here, of course, Williams did not confess to the murder in so many words; it was his conduct in guiding police to the body, not his words, which incriminated him. And the record is replete with evidence that Williams knew precisely what he was doing when he guided police to the body. The human urge to confess wrongdoing is, of course, normal in all save hardened, professional criminals, as psychiatrists and analysts have demonstrated. T. Reik, The Compulsion to Confess (1972).

(2) THE EXCLUSIONARY RULE SHOULD NOT BE APPLIED TO NON-EGREGIOUS POLICE CONDUCT

Even if there was no waiver, and assuming a technical violation occurred, the Court errs gravely in mechanically applying the exclusionary rule

---

2. Such a paternalistic rule is particularly anomalous in the Sixth Amendment context, where this Court has only recently discovered an independent constitutional right of self-representation, allowing an accused the absolute right to proceed without a lawyer at trial, once he is aware of the consequences. Faretta v. California, 422 U.S. 806 (1975).

3. Paradoxically, in light of the result reached, the Court acknowledges that Williams repeatedly stated: "When I get to Des Moines and see Mr. McKnight, I am going to tell you the whole story." Read in context in it is plain that Williams was saying he intended to confess. The Court then goes on to hold, in effect, that Williams could not change his mind until he reached Des Moines.

without considering whether that Draconian judicial doctrine should be invoked in these circumstances, or indeed whether any of its conceivable goals will be furthered by its application here.

The obvious flaws of the exclusionary rule as a judicial remedy are familiar. . . . Today's holding interrupts what has been a more rational perception of the constitutional and social utility of excluding reliable evidence from the truth-seeking process. In its Fourth Amendment context, we have now recognized that the exclusionary rule is in no sense a *personal* constitutional right, but a judicially conceived remedial device designed to safeguard and effectuate guaranteed legal rights generally. . . . We have repeatedly emphasized that deterrence of unconstitutional or otherwise unlawful police conduct is the only valid justification for excluding reliable and probative evidence from the criminal factfinding process. . . .

Accordingly, unlawfully obtained evidence is not automatically excluded from the factfinding process in all circumstances. In a variety of contexts we inquire whether application of the rule will promote its objectives sufficiently to justify the enormous cost it imposes on society. . . .

This is, of course, the familiar balancing process applicable to cases in which important competing interests are at stake. It is a recognition, albeit belated, that "the policies behind the exclusionary rule are not absolute," Stone v. Powell, [428 U.S.] at 488. It acknowledges that so serious an infringement of the crucial truth-seeking function of a criminal prosecution should be allowed only when imperative to safeguard constitutional rights. An important factor in this amalgam is whether the violation at issue may properly be classed as "egregious." . . . The Court understandably does not try to characterize the police actions here as "egregious."

Against this background, it is striking that the Court fails even to consider whether the benefits secured by application of the exclusionary rule in this case outweigh its obvious social costs. Perhaps the failure is due to the fact that this case arises not under the Fourth Amendment, but under Miranda v. Arizona, 384 U.S. 436 (1966), and the Sixth Amendment right to counsel. The Court apparently perceives the function of the exclusionary rule to be so different in these varying contexts that it must be mechanically and uncritically applied in all cases arising outside the Fourth Amendment.[5]

---

5. Indeed, if this were a Fourth Amendment case our course would be clear; only last Term, in Stone v. Powell, we held that application of the exclusionary rule in federal habeas corpus has such a minimal deterrent effect on law enforcement officials that habeas relief should not be granted on the ground that unconstitutionally seized evidence was introduced at trial. Since the quantum of deterrence provided by federal habeas does

But this is demonstrably not the case where police conduct collides with *Miranda's* procedural safeguards rather than with the Fifth Amendment privilege against compulsory self-incrimination. Involuntary and coerced admissions are suppressed because of the inherent unreliability of a confession wrung from an unwilling suspect by threats, brutality, or other coercion. . . . We can all agree on " '[t]he abhorrence of society to the use of involuntary confessions,' " Linkletter v. Walker, [381 U.S.] at 638, and the need to preserve the integrity of the human personality and individual free will. . . .

But use of Williams' disclosures and their fruits carries no risk whatever of unreliability, for the body was found where he said it would be found. Moreover, since the Court makes no issue of voluntariness, no dangers are posed to individual dignity or free will. *Miranda's* safeguards are premised on presumed unreliability long associated with confessions extorted by brutality or threats; they are not personal constitutional rights, but are simply judicially created prophylactic measures. Michigan v. Tucker, 417 U.S. 433 (1974). . . .

Thus, in cases where incriminating disclosures are voluntarily made without coercion, and hence not violative of the Fifth Amendment, but are obtained in violation of one of the *Miranda* prophylaxes, suppression is no longer automatic. Rather, we weigh the deterrent effect on unlawful police conduct, together with the normative Fifth Amendment justifications for suppression, against "the strong interest under any system of justice of making available to the trier of fact all concededly relevant and trustworthy evidence which either party seeks to adduce. . . . We also 'must consider society's interest in the effective prosecution of criminals. . . .' " Michigan v. Tucker, supra, at 450.[6] This individualized consideration or balancing process with respect to the exclusionary sanction is possible in this case, as in others, because Williams' incriminating disclosures are not infected with any element of compulsion the Fifth Amendment forbids; nor, as noted earlier, does this evidence pose any danger of unreliability to the factfinding process. In short, there is no reason to exclude this evidence.

Similarly, the exclusionary rule is not uniformly implicated in the Sixth Amendment, particularly its pretrial aspects. We have held that "the core purpose of the counsel guarantee was to assure 'Assistance' at trial, when the accused was confronted with both the intricacies of the law and the advocacy of the public prosecutor." United States v. Ash,

---

not vary with the constitutional provision at issue, it appears that the Court sees fundamental, though unarticulated, differences in the exclusionary sanction when it is applied in other contexts.

6. Statements obtained in violation of *Miranda* have long been used for impeachment purposes. Oregon v. Hass, 420 U.S. 714 (1975); Harris v. New York, 401 U.S. 222 (1971). See also Walder v. United States, 347 U.S. 62 (1954).

413 U.S. 300, 309 (1973). Thus, the right to counsel is fundamentally a "trial" right necessitated by the legal complexities of a criminal prosecution and the need to offset, to the trier of fact, the power of the State as prosecutor. See Schneckloth v. Bustamonte, supra, at 241. It is now thought that modern law enforcement involves pretrial confrontations at which the defendant's fate might effectively be sealed before the right of counsel could attach. In order to make meaningful the defendant's opportunity to a fair trial and to assistance of counsel at that trial—the core purposes of the counsel guarantee—the Court formulated a per se rule guaranteeing counsel at what it has characterized as "critical" pretrial proceedings where substantial rights might be endangered. . . .

As we have seen in the Fifth Amendment setting, violations of prophylactic rules designed to safeguard other constitutional guarantees and deter impermissible police conduct need not call for the automatic suppression of evidence without regard to the purposes served by exclusion; nor do Fourth Amendment violations merit uncritical suppression of evidence. In other situations we decline to suppress eyewitness identifications which are the products of unnecessarily suggestive lineups or photo displays unless there is a "very substantial likelihood of irreparable misidentification." Simmons v. United States, 390 U.S. 377, 384 (1968). Recognizing that "[i]t is the likelihood of misidentification which violates a defendant's right to due process," Neil v. Biggers, 409 U.S. 188, 198 (1972), we exclude evidence only when essential to safeguard the integrity of the truth-seeking process. The test, in short, is the reliability of the evidence.

So, too, in the Sixth Amendment sphere failure to have counsel in a pretrial setting should not lead to the "knee-jerk" suppression of relevant and reliable evidence. Just as even uncounseled "critical" pretrial confrontations may often be conducted fairly and not in derogation of Sixth Amendment values, Stovall v. Denno, 388 U.S. 293, 298-299 (1967), evidence obtained in such proceedings should be suppressed only when its use would imperil the core values the Amendment was written to protect. Having extended Sixth Amendment concepts originally thought to relate to the trial itself to earlier periods when a criminal investigation is focused on a suspect, application of the drastic bar of exclusion should be approached with caution.

In any event, the fundamental purpose of the Sixth Amendment is to safeguard the fairness of the trial and the integrity of the factfinding process.[7] In this case, where the evidence of how the child's body was

---

7. Indeed, we determine whether pretrial proceedings are "critical" by asking whether counsel is there needed to protect the fairness of the trial. See United States v. Ash, 413 U.S. 300, 322 (1973) (Stewart, J., concurring); Schneckloth v. Bustamonte, 412 U.S. 218, 239 (1973). It is also clear that the danger of actual error was the moving force

found is of unquestioned reliability, and since the Court accepts Williams' disclosures as voluntary and uncoerced, there is no issue either of fairness or evidentiary reliability to justify suppression of truth. It appears suppression is mandated here for no other reason than the Court's general impression that it may have a beneficial effect on future police conduct; indeed, the Court fails to say even that much in defense of its holding.

Thus, whether considered under *Miranda* or the Sixth Amendment, there is no more reason to exclude the evidence in this case than there was in Stone v. Powell;[8] that holding was premised on the utter reliability of evidence sought to be suppressed, the irrelevancy of the constitutional claim to the criminal defendant's factual guilt or innocence, and the minimal deterrent effect of habeas corpus on police misconduct. . . . Relevant factors in this case are thus indistinguishable from those in *Stone,* and from those in other Fourth Amendment cases suggesting a balancing approach toward utilization of the exclusionary sanction. Rather than adopting a formalistic analysis varying with the constitutional provision invoked,[9] we should apply the exclusionary rule on the basis of its benefits and costs, at least in those cases where the police conduct at issue is far from being outrageous or egregious. . . .

MR. JUSTICE WHITE, with whom MR. JUSTICE BLACKMUN and MR. JUSTICE REHNQUIST join, dissenting.

The respondent in this case killed a 10-year-old child. The majority sets aside his conviction, holding that certain statements of unquestioned reliability were unconstitutionally obtained from him, and under the circumstances probably makes it impossible to retry him. Because there is nothing in the Constitution or in our previous cases which requires the Court's action, I dissent. . . .

---

behind the counsel guarantee in such cases as United States v. Wade, 388 U.S. 218 (1967) (post-indictment lineups).

8. This is a far cry from Massiah v. United States, 377 U.S. 201 (1964). Massiah's statements had no independent indicia of reliability as do respondent's. Moreover, Massiah was unaware that he was being interrogated by ruse and had not been advised of his right to counsel.

Here, as Mr. Justice Blackmun has noted, there was no interrogation of Williams in the sense that term was used in *Massiah,* Escobedo v. Illinois, 378 U.S. 478 (1964), or *Miranda.* That the detective's statement appealed to Williams' conscience is not a sufficient reason to equate it to a police station grilling. It could well be that merely driving on the road and passing the intersection where he had turned off to bury the body might have produced the same result without any suggestive comments.

9. Clearly there will be many cases where evidence obtained in violation of right-to-counsel rules is inadmissible, either for reasons related to the normative purposes of the Sixth Amendment or to the deterrence of unlawful police conduct. But this is, on the Court's facts, not such a case, and it hardly furthers reasoned analysis to lump it into an undifferentiated conceptual category for reasons which do not apply to it.

II

The strictest test of waiver which might be applied to this case is that set forth in Johnson v. Zerbst, 304 U.S. 458, 464 (1938), and quoted by the majority. . . . In order to show that a right has been waived under this test, the State must prove "an intentional relinquishment or abandonment of a known right or privilege." The majority creates no new rule preventing an accused who has retained a lawyer from waiving his right to the lawyer's presence during questioning. The majority simply finds that no waiver was *proved* in this case. I disagree. That respondent knew of his right not to say anything to the officers without advice and presence of counsel is established on this record to a moral certainty. He was advised of the right by three officials of the State—telling at least one that he understood the right—and by two lawyers.[4] Finally, he further demonstrated his knowledge of the right by informing the police that he would tell them the story in the presence of McKnight when they arrived in Des Moines. The issue in this case, then, is whether respondent relinquished that right intentionally.

Respondent relinquished his right not to talk to the police about his crime when the car approached the place where he had hidden the victim's clothes. Men usually intend to do what they do, and there is nothing in the record to support the proposition that respondent's decision to talk was anything but an exercise of his own free will. Apparently, without any prodding from the officers, respondent—who had earlier said that he would tell the whole story when he arrived in Des Moines—spontaneously changed his mind about the timing of his disclosures when the car approached the places where he had hidden the evidence. However, even if his statements were influenced by Detective Leaming's above-quoted statement, respondent's decision to talk in the absence of counsel can hardly be viewed as the product of an overborne will. The statement by Leaming was not coercive; it was accompanied by a request that respondent not respond to it; and it was delivered hours before respondent decided to make any statement. Respondent's waiver was thus knowing and intentional.

The majority's contrary conclusion seems to rest on the fact that respondent "asserted" his right to counsel by retaining and consulting with one lawyer and by consulting with another. How this supports the conclusion that respondent's later relinquishment of his right not to talk in the absence of counsel was unintentional is a mystery. The fact that respondent consulted with counsel on the question whether he should talk to the police in counsel's absence makes his later decision to talk in

---

4. Moreover, he in fact received advice of counsel on at least two occasions on the question whether he should talk to the police on the trip to Des Moines.

counsel's absence *better* informed and, if anything, more intelligent.

The majority recognizes that even after this "assertion" of his right to counsel, it would have found that respondent waived his right not to talk in counsel's absence if his waiver had been express—i.e., if the officers had asked him in the car whether he would be willing to answer questions in counsel's absence and if he had answered "yes." . . . But waiver is not a formalistic concept. Waiver is shown whenever the facts establish that an accused knew of a right and intended to relinquish it. Such waiver, even if not express, was plainly shown here. The only other conceivable basis for the majority's holding is the implicit suggestion . . . that the right involved in Massiah v. United States, 377 U.S. 201 (1964), as distinguished from the right involved in Miranda v. Arizona, 384 U.S. 436 (1966), is a right not to be *asked* any questions in counsel's absence rather than a right not to *answer* any questions in counsel's absence, and that the right not to be *asked* questions must be waived *before* the questions are asked. Such wafer-thin distinctions cannot determine whether a guilty murderer should go free. The only conceivable purpose for the presence of counsel during questioning is to protect an accused from making incriminating *answers*. Questions, unanswered, have no significance at all. Absent coercion[6]—no matter how the right involved is defined—an accused is amply protected by a rule requiring waiver before or simultaneously with the giving by him of an answer or the making by him of a statement.

III

The consequence of the majority's decision is, as the majority recognizes, extremely serious. A mentally disturbed killer whose guilt is not in question may be released. Why? Apparently the answer is that the majority believes that the law enforcement officers acted in a way which involves

---

6. There is a rigid prophylactic rule set forth in Miranda v. Arizona that once an arrestee requests presence of counsel at questioning, *questioning* must cease. The rule depends on an indication by the *accused* that he will be unable to handle the decision whether or not to answer questions without advice of counsel, see Michigan v. Mosley, 423 U.S. 96, 110 n.2 (1975) (White, J., concurring), and is inapplicable to this case for two reasons. First, at no time did *respondent* indicate a desire not to be asked questions outside the presence of his counsel—notwithstanding the fact that he was told that he and the officers would be "visiting in the car." The majority concludes, although studiously avoiding reliance on *Miranda*, that respondent *asserted* his right to counsel. This he did in some respects, but he never, himself, asserted a right not to be questioned in the absence of counsel. Second, as is noted in the dissenting opinion of Mr. Justice Blackmun, respondent was not questioned. The rigid prophylactic rule—as the majority implicitly recognizes—is designed solely to prevent involuntary waivers of the right against self-incrimination and is not to be applied to a statement by a law enforcement officer accompanied by a request by the officer that the accused make no response followed by more than an hour of silence and an apparently spontaneous statement on a subject—

some risk of injury to society and that such conduct should be deterred. However, the officers' conduct did not, and was not likely to, jeopardize the fairness of respondent's trial or in any way risk the conviction of an innocent man—the risk against which the Sixth Amendment guarantee of assistance of counsel is designed to protect. . . . The police did nothing "wrong," let alone anything "unconstitutional." To anyone not lost in the intricacies of the prophylactic rules of Miranda v. Arizona, the result in this case seems utterly senseless; and for the reasons stated in Part II, supra, even applying those rules as well as the rule of Massiah v. United States, supra, the statements made by respondent were properly admitted. In light of these considerations, the majority's protest that the result in this case is justified by a "clear violation" of the Sixth and Fourteenth Amendments has a distressing hollow ring. I respectfully dissent.

MR. JUSTICE BLACKMUN, with whom MR. JUSTICE WHITE and MR. JUSTICE REHNQUIST join, dissenting. . . .

What the Court chooses to do here, and with which I disagree, is to hold that respondent Williams' situation was in the mold of Massiah v. United States, 377 U.S. 201 (1964), that is, that it was dominated by a denial to Williams of his Sixth Amendment right to counsel after criminal proceedings had been instituted against him. The Court rules that the Sixth Amendment was violated because Detective Leaming "purposely sought during Williams' isolation from his lawyers to obtain as much incriminating information as possible." I cannot regard that as unconstitutional per se.

First, the police did not deliberately seek to isolate Williams from his lawyers so as to deprive him of the assistance of counsel. Cf. Escobedo v. Illinois, 378 U.S. 478 (1964). The isolation in this case was a necessary incident of transporting Williams to the county where the crime was committed.[1]

Second, Leaming's purpose was not solely to obtain incriminating evidence. The victim had been missing for only two days, and the police could not be certain that she was dead. Leaming, of course, and in accord with his duty, was "hoping to find out where that little girl was," . . . but such motivation does not equate with an intention to evade the Sixth

---

the victim's shoes—not broached in the "speech." Under such circumstances there is not even a small risk that the waiver will be involuntary.

1. Neither attorney McKnight nor attorney Kelly objected to Williams' being returned to Des Moines, although each sought assurance that he would not be interrogated. That "the entire setting was conducive to . . . psychological coercion," Powell, J., concurring, . . . was more attributable to Williams' flight from Des Moines than to any machinations of the police. Surely the police are not to be blamed for the facts that the murder was committed on Christmas Eve and that the weather was ominous.

Amendment.[2] Moreover, the Court seems to me to place an undue emphasis . . . and aspersion on what it and the lower courts have chosen to call the "Christian burial speech," and on Williams' "deeply religious" convictions.

Third, not every attempt to elicit information should be regarded as "tantamount to interrogation," I am not persuaded that Leaming's observations and comments, made as the police car traversed the snowy and slippery miles between Davenport and Des Moines that winter afternoon, were an interrogation, direct or subtle, of Williams. Contrary to this Court's statement, . . . the Iowa Supreme Court appears to me to have thought and held otherwise, State v. Williams, 182 N.W.2d 396, 403-405 (1970), and I agree. Williams, after all, was counseled by lawyers, and warned by the arraigning judge in Davenport and by the police, and yet it was he who started the travel conversations and brought up the subject of the criminal investigation. Without further reviewing the circumstances of the trip, I would say it is clear there was no interrogation. In this respect, I am in full accord with Judge Webster in his vigorous dissent, 509 F.2d 227, 234-237, and with the views implicitly indicated by Chief Judge Gibson and Judge Stephenson, who joined him in voting for rehearing en banc.

In summary, it seems to me that the Court is holding that *Massiah* is violated whenever police engage in any conduct, in the absence of counsel, with the subjective desire to obtain information from a suspect after arraignment. Such a rule is far too broad. Persons in custody frequently volunteer statements in response to stimuli other than interrogation. . . . When there is no interrogation, such statements should be admissible as long as they are truly voluntary.[3] . . .

NOTES AND QUESTIONS

1. Brewer v. Williams, as well as virtually the entire law of confessions, is thoroughly reviewed in two exhaustive articles by Professor Kamisar. Forward: Brewer v. Williams—A Hard Look at a Discomfiting Record, 66 Geo. L.J. 209 (1977); Brewer v. Williams, *Massiah*, and *Miranda*: What Is "Interrogation"? When Does It Matter?, 67 Geo. L.J. 1 (1978).

2. Indeed, Williams already had promised Leaming that he would tell "the whole story" when he reached Des Moines. . . .

3. With all deference to the Court, I do not agree that *Massiah* regarded it as "constitutionally irrelevant" that the statements in that case were surreptitiously obtained. . . . The *Massiah* opinion quoted with approval the dissenting Circuit Judge's statement that "Massiah was more seriously imposed upon . . . because he did not even know that he was under interrogation by a government agent." 377 U.S., at 206.

2. *Williams* was retried on remand. The body was admitted at trial on the theory that it would have been inevitably discovered, and the Supreme Court ultimately approved of its admission. Nix v. Williams, 467 U.S. 431 (1984). *Nix* is considered in Chapter 10.

3. Although *Massiah* and *Miranda* apparently are premised on differing policies, the concerns of the cases possess striking similarities. Both are designed to elaborate upon the conditions under which the state may elicit information from a person suspected of criminality. Still, the conditions precedent for the application of each case do differ. The adversarial process must be initiated before the sixth amendment rights discussed in *Massiah* come into play, and custody is not directly relevant to the analysis. The fifth amendment rights discussed in *Miranda*, by contrast, are relevant only at the point of custodial interrogation and the initiation of formal proceedings is irrelevant.

The significance of these distinctions was demonstrated by United States v. Henry, 447 U.S. 264. In *Henry*, an informant was planted in a cell with Henry, who had previously been indicted. The informant apparently initiated conversations with Henry, who made incriminating comments later used against him. The Court held that this violated Henry's sixth amendment rights. Once formal proceedings have begun, the government may not "deliberately elicit" information from a suspect without first obtaining a waiver of rights. *Henry* was important for two reasons. First, it revived *Massiah*, indicating that *Massiah* had avoided *Escobedo*'s fate. Second, it suggested that merely planting an informant, even if the informant remained passive and did not initiate any conversations, would violate the sixth amendment: by "intentionally creating a situation likely to induce Henry to make incriminating statements without the assistance of counsel, the government violated the sixth amendment right to counsel." The broad implications of this language did not long survive, however.

KUHLMANN v. WILSON, 477 U.S. 436 (1986): POWELL, J., delivered the opinion of the Court.

. . . In the early morning of July 4, 1970, respondent and two confederates robbed the Star Taxicab Garage in the Bronx, New York, and fatally shot the night dispatcher. Shortly before, employees of the garage had observed respondent, a former employee there, on the premises conversing with two other men. They also witnessed respondent fleeing after the robbery, carrying loose money in his arms. After eluding the police for four days, respondent turned himself in. Respondent admitted that he had been present when the crimes took place, claimed that he had witnessed the robbery, gave the police a description of the robbers, but denied knowing them. Respondent also denied any involvement in the robbery or murder, claiming that he had fled because he was afraid of being blamed for the crimes.

After his arraignment, respondent was confined in the Bronx House of Detention, where he was placed in a cell with a prisoner named Benny Lee. Unknown to respondent, Lee had agreed to act as a police informant. Respondent made incriminating statements that Lee reported to the police. Prior to trial, respondent moved to suppress the statements on the ground that they were obtained in violation of his right to counsel. The trial court held an evidentiary hearing on the suppression motion, which revealed that the statements were made under the following circumstances.

Before respondent arrived in the jail, Lee had entered into an arrangement with Detective Cullen, according to which Lee agreed to listen to respondent's conversations and report his remarks to Cullen. Since the police had positive evidence of respondent's participation, the purpose of placing Lee in the cell was to determine the identities of respondent's confederates. Cullen instructed Lee not to ask respondent any questions, but simply to "keep his ears open" for the names of the other perpetrators. Respondent first spoke to Lee about the crimes after he looked out the cellblock window at the Star Taxicab Garage, where the crimes had occurred. Respondent said, "someone's messing with me," and began talking to Lee about the robbery, narrating the same story that he had given the police at the time of his arrest. Lee advised respondent that this explanation "didn't sound too good," but respondent did not alter his story.

Over the next few days, however, respondent changed details of his original account. Respondent then received a visit from his brother, who mentioned that members of his family were upset because they believed that respondent had murdered the dispatcher. After the visit, respondent again described the crimes to Lee. Respondent now admitted that he and two other men, whom he never identified, had planned and carried out the robbery, and had murdered the dispatcher. Lee informed Cullen of respondent's statements and furnished Cullen with notes that he had written surreptitiously while sharing the cell with respondent.

After hearing the testimony of Cullen and Lee, the trial court found that Cullen had instructed Lee "to ask no questions of [respondent] about the crime but merely to listen as to what [respondent] might say in his presence." The court determined that Lee obeyed these instructions, that he "at no time asked any questions with respect to the crime," and that he "only listened to [respondent] and made notes regarding what [respondent] had to say." The trial court also found that respondent's statements to Lee were "spontaneous" and "unsolicited." Under state precedent, a defendant's volunteered statements to a police agent were admissible in evidence because the police were not required to prevent talkative defendants from making incriminating statements. The trial court accordingly denied the suppression motion.

The jury convicted respondent of common-law murder and felonious possession of a weapon. . . . Respondent filed a petition for federal habeas corpus relief. Respondent argued, among other things, that his statements to Lee were obtained pursuant to police investigative methods that violated his constitutional rights. . . . The District Court for the Southern District of New York denied the writ. . . . The record demonstrated "no interrogation whatsoever" by Lee and "only spontaneous statements" from respondent. In the District Court's view, these "fact[s] preclude[d] any Sixth Amendment violation.". . .

A . . . panel of the Court of Appeals reversed. The court . . . reasoned that the circumstances under which respondent made his incriminating statements to Lee were indistinguishable from the facts of *Henry*. . . . We now reverse.

IV

. . . We conclude that [the Court of Appeals] erred in holding that respondent was entitled to relief under United States v. Henry. As the District Court observed, *Henry* left open the question whether the Sixth Amendment forbids admission in evidence of an accused's statements to a jailhouse informant who was "placed in close proximity but [made] no effort to stimulate conversations about the crime charged." Our review of the line of cases beginning with Massiah v. United States shows that this question must, as the District Court properly decided, be answered negatively.

A

. . . In United States v. Henry, the Court applied the *Massiah* test to incriminating statements made to a jailhouse informant. The Court of Appeals in that case found a violation of *Massiah* because the informant had engaged the defendant in conversations and "had developed a relationship of trust and confidence with [the defendant] such that [the defendant] revealed incriminating information." This Court affirmed, holding that the Court of Appeals reasonably concluded that the Government informant "deliberately used his position to secure incriminating information from [the defendant] when counsel was not present." Although the informant had not questioned the defendant, the informant had "stimulated" conversations with the defendant in order to "elicit" incriminating information. The Court emphasized that those facts, like the facts of *Massiah*, amounted to " 'indirect and surreptitious interrogatio[n]' " of the defendant.

. . . [T]he primary concern of the *Massiah* line of decisions is secret interrogation by investigatory techniques that are the equivalent of direct police interrogation. Since "the Sixth Amendment is not violated whenever—by luck or happenstance—the State obtains incriminating statements from the accused after the right to counsel has attached," a defendant does not make out a violation of that right simply by showing that an informant, either through prior arrangement or voluntarily, reported his incriminating statements to the police. Rather, the defendant must demonstrate that the police and their informant took some action, beyond merely listening, that was designed deliberately to elicit incriminating remarks. . . .

CHIEF JUSTICE BURGER's concurrence is omitted.

JUSTICE BRENNAN, with whom JUSTICE MARSHALL joins, dissenting.

. . . The Sixth Amendment guarantees an accused, at least after the initiation of formal charges, the right to rely on counsel as the "medium" between himself and the State. Accordingly, the Sixth Amendment "imposes on the State an affirmative obligation to respect and preserve the accused's choice to seek [the assistance of counsel]," and therefore "[t]he determination whether particular action by state agents violates the accused's right to . . . counsel must be made in light of this obligation." To be sure, the Sixth Amendment is not violated whenever, "by luck or happenstance," the State obtains incriminating statements from the accused after the right to counsel has attached. It is violated, however, when "the State obtains incriminating statements by knowingly circumventing the accused's right to have counsel present in a confrontation between the accused and a state agent." As we explained in *Henry*, where the accused has not waived his right to counsel, the government knowingly circumvents the defendant's right to counsel where it "deliberately elicit[s]" inculpatory admissions, that is, "intentionally creat[es] a situation likely to induce [the accused] to make incriminating statements without the assistance of counsel."

In *Henry*, we found that the Federal Government had "deliberately elicited" incriminating statements from Henry based on the following circumstances. The jailhouse informant, Nichols, had apparently followed instructions to obtain information without directly questioning Henry and without initiating conversations concerning the charges pending against Henry. We rejected the Government's argument that because Henry initiated the discussion of his crime, no Sixth Amendment violation had occurred. We pointed out that under Massiah v. United States it is irrelevant whether the informant asks pointed questions about the crime or "merely engage[s] in general conversation about it." Nichols, we noted, "was not a passive listener; . . . he had 'some conversations with Mr. Henry' while he was in jail and Henry's incriminatory statements were 'the product of this conversation.' "

In deciding that Nichols' role in these conversations amounted to deliberate elicitation, we also found three other factors important. First, Nichols was to be paid for any information he produced and thus had an incentive to extract inculpatory admissions from Henry. Second, Henry was not aware that Nichols was acting as an informant. "Conversation stimulated in such circumstances," we observed, "may elicit information that an accused would not intentionally reveal to persons known to be Government agents." Third, Henry was in custody at the time he spoke with Nichols. This last fact is significant, we stated, because "custody imposes pressures on the accused [and] confinement may bring into play subtle influences that will make him particularly susceptible to the ploys of undercover Government agents." We concluded that by "intentionally creating a situation likely to induce Henry to make incriminating statements without the assistance of counsel, the Government violated Henry's Sixth Amendment right to counsel."

In the instant case, as in *Henry*, the accused was incarcerated and therefore was "susceptible to the ploys of undercover Government agents." Like Nichols, Lee was a secret informant, usually received consideration for the services he rendered the police, and therefore had an incentive to produce the information which he knew the police hoped to obtain. Just as Nichols had done, Lee obeyed instructions not to question respondent and to report to the police any statements made by the respondent in Lee's presence about the crime in question. And, like Nichols, Lee encouraged respondent to talk about his crime by conversing with him on the subject over the course of several days and by telling respondent that his exculpatory story would not convince anyone without more work. However, unlike the situation in *Henry*, a disturbing visit from respondent's brother, rather than a conversation with the informant, seems to have been the immediate catalyst for respondent's confession to Lee. While it might appear from this sequence of events that Lee's comment regarding respondent's story and his general willingness to converse with respondent about the crime were not the immediate causes of respondent's admission, I think that the deliberate-elicitation standard requires consideration of the entire course of government behavior.

The State intentionally created a situation in which it was forseeable that respondent would make incriminating statements without the assistance of counsel—it assigned respondent to a cell overlooking the scene of the crime and designated a secret informant to be respondent's cellmate.

The informant, while avoiding direct questions, nonetheless developed a relationship of cellmate camaraderie with respondent and encouraged him to talk about his crime. While the coup de grace was delivered by respondent's brother, the groundwork for respondent's confession was laid by the State. Clearly the State's actions had a sufficient nexus with respondent's admission of guilt to constitute deliberate elicitation within the meaning of *Henry*. I would affirm the judgment of the Court of Appeals.

[JUSTICE STEVENS's dissenting opinion is omitted.]

see Gilberts p 50

4. Why the differences between *Innis* on the one hand and *Henry* and *Kuhlman* on the other? For a discussion, see White, Interrogation Without Questions: Rhode Island v. Innis and United States v. Henry, 78 Mich. L. Rev. 1209 (1980).

5. Should it matter if the state takes advantage, postindictment, of a co-defendant's offer to assist the state's investigation? In other words, does "deliberate elicitation" extend to obtaining information as a result of a meeting between co-defendants that was initiated by the noncooperating defendant? In addition, does it matter whether the reason prompting the state authorities to accept the co-defendant's offer of assistance was the ongoing investigation of other crimes for which no indictments had yet been returned? In Maine v. Moulton, 474 U.S. 159 (1985), the Court held that *Massiah* controls in such a case but that any information obtained may be used in the prosecution of those offenses for which an indictment had not been returned at the time the incriminating statements were made. What values are served by excluding such statements from the trial of the offense for which the defendant had previously been indicted? Compare *Moultan* to Arizona v. Roberson, 486 U.S. 675 (1988), in which the Court held that *Edwards* was violated where the police interrogate a suspect with respect to one crime if the suspect has already invoked his *Miranda* right to counsel with respect to some other crime. Why is it that the invocation of the *Miranda* right to counsel of a person in custody protects a suspect from any further state efforts to elicit information, but initiation of the sixth amendment right to counsel is limited to the particular charge with respect to which formal proceedings have begun?

5th is broader than 6th

Perhaps the answer is that the fifth amendment and sixth amendment are concerned with different matters, even if their concerns overlap in the confession area. If distinctions are going to be drawn, is there a value in respecting them? Does the majority opinion in the following case impress you more with its creativity or lack of discipline?

MICHIGAN v. JACKSON
Certiorari to the Supreme Court of Michigan
475 U.S. 625 (1986)

JUSTICE STEVENS delivered the opinion of the Court.

In Edwards v. Arizona, we held that an accused person in custody who has "expressed his desire to deal with the police only through counsel, is not subject to further interrogation by the authorities until counsel has been made available to him, unless the accused himself initiates further communication, exchanges, or conversations with the police." In Solem v. Stumes, we reiterated that "Edwards established a bright-line rule to safeguard preexisting rights"[;] "once a suspect has invoked the right to counsel, any subsequent conversation must be initiated by him."

The question presented by these two cases is whether the same rule applies to a defendant who has been formally charged with a crime and who has requested appointment of counsel at his arraignment. In both cases, the Michigan Supreme Court held that postarraignment confessions were improperly obtained—and the Sixth Amendment violated—because the defendants had "requested counsel during their arraignments, but were not afforded an opportunity to consult with counsel before the police initiated further interrogations." We agree with that holding. . . .

II

The question is not whether respondents had a right to counsel at their postarraignment, custodial interrogations. The existence of that right is clear. It has two sources. The Fifth Amendment protection against compelled self-incrimination provides the right to counsel at custodial interrogations. The Sixth Amendment guarantee of the assistance of counsel also provides the right to counsel at postarraignment interrogations. The arraignment signals "the initiation of adversary judicial proceedings" and thus the attachment of the Sixth Amendment; thereafter, government efforts to elicit information from the accused, including interrogation, represent "critical stages" at which the Sixth Amendment applies. The question in these cases is whether respondents validly waived their right to counsel at the postarraignment custodial interrogations.

In Edwards, the request for counsel was made to the police during custodial interrogation, and the basis for the Court's holding was the Fifth Amendment privilege against compelled self-incrimination. The Court noted the relevance of various Sixth Amendment precedents, but found it unnecessary to rely on the possible applicability of the Sixth Amendment. In these cases, the request for counsel was made to a judge during arraignment, and the basis for the Michigan Supreme Court opinion was the Sixth Amendment's guarantee of the assistance of counsel. The State argues that the *Edwards* rule should not apply to these circumstances because there are legal differences in the basis for the claims; because there are factual differences in the contexts of the claims; and because respondents signed valid waivers of their right to counsel at the post-arraignment custodial interrogations. We consider these contentions in turn.

The State contends that differences in the legal principles underlying the Fifth and Sixth Amendments compel the conclusion that the *Edwards* rule should not apply to a Sixth Amendment claim. *Edwards* flows from the Fifth Amendment's right to counsel at custodial interrogations, the State argues; its relevance to the Sixth Amendment's provision of the assistance of counsel is far less clear, and thus the *Edwards* principle for assessing waivers is unnecessary and inappropriate.

In our opinion, however, the reasons for prohibiting the interrogation of an uncounseled prisoner who has asked for the help of a lawyer are even stronger after he has been formally charged with an offense than before. The State's argument misapprehends the nature of the pretrial protections afforded by the Sixth Amendment. In United States v. Gouveia, we explained the significance of the formal accusation, and the corresponding attachment of the Sixth Amendment right to counsel:

> [G]iven the plain language of the Amendment and its purpose of protecting the unaided layman at critical confrontations with his adversary, our conclusion that the right to counsel attaches at the initiation of adversary judicial criminal proceedings "is far from a mere formalism." Kirby v. Illinois, 460 U.S., at 689. It is only at that time "that the government has committed itself to prosecute, and only then that the adverse positions of government and defendant have solidified. It is then that a defendant finds himself faced with the prosecutorial forces of organized society, and immersed in the intricacies of substantive and procedural criminal law." [467 U.S., at 189.]

As a result, the "Sixth Amendment guarantees the accused, at least after the initiation of formal charges, the right to rely on counsel as a 'medium' between him and the State." Maine v. Moulton, 474 U.S., at 176. Thus, the Sixth Amendment right to counsel at a postarraignment interrogation requires at least as much protection as the Fifth Amendment right to counsel at any custodial interrogation.

Indeed, after a formal accusation has been made—and a person who had previously been just a "suspect" has become an "accused" within the meaning of the Sixth Amendment—the constitutional right to the assistance of counsel is of such importance that the police may no longer employ techniques for eliciting information from an uncounseled defendant that might have been entirely proper at an earlier stage of their investigation. Thus, the surreptitious employment of a cellmate may violate the defendant's Sixth Amendment right to counsel even though the same methods of investigation might have been permissible before arraignment or indictment. Far from undermining the *Edwards* rule, the difference between the legal basis for the rule applied in *Edwards* and the Sixth Amendment claim asserted in these cases actually provides additional support for the application of the rule in these circumstances.

The State also relies on the factual differences between a request for counsel during custodial interrogation and a request for counsel at an arraignment. The State maintains that respondents may not have actually intended their request for counsel to encompass representation during any further questioning by the police. This argument, however, must be considered against the backdrop of our standard for assessing waivers of constitutional rights. Almost a half century ago, in Johnson v. Zerbst, a case involving an alleged waiver of a defendant's Sixth Amendment right to counsel, the Court explained that we should "indulge every reasonable presumption against waiver of fundamental constitutional rights." For that reason, it is the State that has the burden of establishing a valid waiver. Doubts must be resolved in favor of protecting the constitutional claim. This settled approach to questions of waiver requires us to give a broad, rather than a narrow, interpretation to a defendant's request for counsel—we presume that the defendant requests the lawyer's services at every critical stage of the prosecution.[6] We thus reject the State's suggestion that respondents' requests for the appointment of counsel should be construed to apply only to representation in formal legal proceedings.[7]

---

6. In construing respondents' request for counsel, we do not, of course, suggest that the right to counsel turns on such a request. See Brewer v. Williams, 430 U.S., at 404 ("the right to counsel does not depend upon a request by the defendant"); Carnley v. Cochran, 369 U.S. 506, 513 (1962) ("it is settled that where the assistance of counsel is a constitutional requisite, the right to be furnished counsel does not depend on a request"). Rather, we construe the defendant's request for counsel as an extremely important fact in considering the validity of a subsequent waiver in response to police-initiated interrogation.

7. We also agree with the comments of the Michigan Supreme Court about the nature of an accused's request for counsel:

> Although judges and lawyers may understand and appreciate the subtle distinctions between the Fifth and Sixth Amendment rights to counsel, the average person does not. When an accused requests an attorney, either before a police officer or a magistrate, he does not know which constitutional right he is invoking; he therefore should not be expected to articulate exactly why or for what purposes he is seeking counsel. It makes little sense to afford relief from further interrogation

The State points to another factual difference: the police may not know of the defendant's request for attorney at the arraignment. That claimed distinction is similarly unavailing. In the cases at bar, in which the officers in charge of the investigations of respondents were present at the arraignments, the argument is particularly unconvincing. More generally, however, Sixth Amendment principles require that we impute the State's knowledge from one state actor to another. For the Sixth Amendment concerns the confrontation between the State and the individual. One set of state actors (the police) may not claim ignorance of defendants' unequivocal request for counsel to another state actor (the court).

The State also argues that, because of these factual differences, the application of *Edwards* in a Sixth Amendment context will generate confusion. However, we have frequently emphasized that one of the characteristics of *Edwards* is its clear, "bright line" quality. We do not agree that applying the rule when the accused requests counsel at an arraignment, rather than in the police station, somehow diminishes that clarity. To the extent that there may have been any doubts about interpreting a request for counsel at an arraignment, or about the police responsibility to know of and respond to such a request, our opinion today resolves them.

Finally, the State maintains that each of the respondents made a valid waiver of his Sixth Amendment rights by signing a postarraignment confession after again being advised of his constitutional rights. In *Edwards*, however, we rejected the notion that, after a suspect's request for counsel, advice of rights and acquiescence in police-initiated questioning could establish a valid waiver. We find no warrant for a different view under a Sixth Amendment analysis. Indeed, our rejection of the comparable argument in *Edwards* was based, in part, on our review of earlier Sixth Amendment cases. Just as written waivers are insufficient to justify police-initiated interrogations after the request for counsel in a Fifth Amendment analysis, so too they are insufficient to justify police-initiated interrogations after the request for counsel in a Sixth Amendment analysis.

III

Edwards is grounded in the understanding that "the assertion of the right to counsel [is] a significant event," and that "additional safeguards are

---

to a defendant who asks a police officer for an attorney, but permit further interrogation to a defendant who makes an identical request to a judge. The simple fact that defendant has requested an attorney indicates that he does not believe that he is sufficiently capable of dealing with his adversaries singlehandedly. 421 Mich., at 63-64, 365 N.W.2d, at 67.

necessary when the accused asks for counsel." We conclude that the assertion is no less significant, and the need for additional safeguards no less clear, when the request for counsel is made at an arraignment and when the basis for the claim is the Sixth Amendment. We thus hold that, if police initiate interrogation after a defendant's assertion, at an arraignment or similar proceeding, of his right to counsel, any waiver of the defendant's right to counsel for that police-initiated interrogation is invalid.

Although the *Edwards* decision itself rested on the Fifth Amendment and concerned a request for counsel made during custodial interrogation, the Michigan Supreme Court correctly perceived that the reasoning of that case applies with even greater force to these cases. The judgments are accordingly affirmed.

It is so ordered.

Justice Rehnquist, with whom Justice Powell and Justice O'Connor join, dissenting.

The Court's decision today rests on the following deceptively simple line of reasoning: Edwards v. Arizona created a bright-line rule to protect a defendant's Fifth Amendment rights; Sixth Amendment rights are even more important than Fifth Amendment rights; therefore, we must also apply the *Edwards* rule to the Sixth Amendment. The Court prefers this neat syllogism to an effort to discuss or answer the only relevant question: Does the *Edwards* rule make sense in the context of the Sixth Amendment? I think it does not, and I therefore dissent from the Court's unjustified extension of the *Edwards* rule to the Sixth Amendment.

My disagreement with the Court stems from our differing understandings of *Edwards*. In *Edwards*, this Court held that once a defendant has invoked his right under Miranda v. Arizona to have counsel present during custodial interrogation, "a valid waiver of that right cannot be established by showing only that he responded to further police-initiated custodial interrogation even if he has been advised of his rights." 451 U.S., at 484. This "prophylactic rule" was deemed necessary to prevent the police from effectively "overriding a defendant's assertion of his *Miranda* rights by "badgering" him into waiving those rights. In short, as we explained in later cases "*Edwards* did not confer a substantive constitutional right that had not existed before; it 'created a protective umbrella serving to enhance a constitutional guarantee.' " Solem v. Stumes, 465 U.S. at 644 n.4.

What the Court today either forgets or chooses to ignore is that the "constitutional guarantee" referred to in Solem v. Stumes is the Fifth Amendment's prohibition on compelled self-incrimination. This prohibition, of course, is also the constitutional underpinning for the set of prophylactic rules announced in *Miranda* itself.[2] *Edwards*, like *Miranda*, imposes on the police a bright-line standard of conduct intended to help ensure that confessions obtained through custodial interrogation will not be "coerced" or "involuntary." Seen in this proper light, *Edwards* provides nothing more than a second layer of protection, in addition to those rights conferred by *Miranda*, for a defendant who might otherwise be compelled by the police to incriminate himself in violation of the Fifth Amendment.

The dispositive question in the instant case, and the question the Court should address in its opinion, is whether the same kind of prophylactic rule is needed to protect a defendant's right to counsel under the Sixth Amendment. The answer to this question, it seems to me, is clearly "no." The Court does not even suggest that the police commonly deny defendants their Sixth Amendment right to counsel. Nor, I suspect, would such a claim likely be borne out by empirical evidence. Thus, the justification for the prophylactic rules this Court created in *Miranda* and *Edwards*, namely, the perceived widespread problem that the police were violating, and would probably continue to violate, the Fifth Amendment rights of defendants during the course of custodial interrogations, is conspicuously absent in the Sixth Amendment context. To put it simply, the prophylactic rule set forth in *Edwards* makes no sense at all except when linked to the Fifth Amendment's prohibition against compelled self-incrimination.

Not only does the Court today cut the *Edwards* rule loose from its analytical moorings, it does so in a manner that graphically reveals the illogic of the Court's position. The Court phrases the question presented in this case as whether the *Edwards* rule applies "to a defendant who has been formally charged with a crime *and who has requested appointment of counsel at his arraignment*" (emphasis added). And the Court ultimately limits its holding to those situations where the police "initiate interrogation *after a defendant's assertion, at an arraignment or similar proceeding, of his right to counsel*" (emphasis added).

In other words, the Court most assuredly does *not* hold that the *Edwards* per se rule prohibiting all police-initiated interrogations applies from the moment the defendant's Sixth Amendment right to counsel attaches, with or without a request for counsel by the defendant. Such a holding would represent, after all, a shockingly dramatic restructuring

---

2. The Court suggests, in dictum, that the Fifth Amendment also provides defendants with a "right to counsel." But our cases make clear that the Fifth Amendment itself provides no such "right." See Moran v. Burbine, 475 U.S., at 423, n.1, Oregon v. Elstad, 470 U.S., at 304-305. Instead, *Miranda* confers upon a defendant a "right to counsel," *but only when such counsel is requested during custodial interrogations*. Even under *Miranda*, the "right to counsel" exists solely as a means of protecting the defendant's Fifth Amendment right not to be compelled to incriminate himself.

of the balance this Court has traditionally struck between the rights of the defendant and those of the larger society. Applying the *Edwards* rule to situations in which a defendant has not made an explicit request for counsel would also render completely nugatory the extensive discussion of "waiver" in such prior Sixth Amendment cases as Brewer v. Williams.[4]

This leaves the Court, however, in an analytical straitjacket. The problem with the limitation the Court places on the Sixth Amendment version of the *Edwards* rule is that, unlike a defendant's "right to counsel" under *Miranda*, which does not arise until affirmatively invoked by the defendant during custodial interrogation, a defendant's Sixth Amendment right to counsel does not depend at all on whether the defendant has requested counsel. The Court acknowledges as much in footnote six of its opinion, where it stresses that "we do not, of course, suggest that the right to counsel turns on . . . a request [for counsel]."

The Court provides no satisfactory explanation for its decision to extend the *Edwards* rule to the Sixth Amendment, yet limit that rule to those defendants foresighted enough, or just plain lucky enough, to have made an explicit request for counsel which we have always understood to be completely unnecessary for Sixth Amendment purposes. The Court attempts to justify its emphasis on the otherwise legally insignificant request for counsel by stating that "we construe the defendant's request for counsel as an extremely important fact in considering the validity of a subsequent waiver in response to police-initiated interrogation." This statement sounds reasonable, but it is flatly inconsistent with the remainder of the Court's opinion, in which the Court holds that there can be no waiver of the Sixth Amendment right to counsel after a request for counsel has been made. It is obvious that, for the Court, the defendant's request for counsel is not merely an "extremely important fact"; rather, it is the *only* fact that counts.

4. See also Moran v. Burbine, 475 U.S., at 428. ("It is clear, of course, that, *absent a valid waiver*, the defendant has the right to the presence of an attorney during any interrogation occurring after the first formal charging proceeding, the point at which the Sixth Amendment right to counsel initially attaches").

Several of our Sixth Amendment cases have indeed erected virtually per se barriers against certain kinds of police conduct. See, e.g., Maine v. Moulton, 474 U.S. 159 (1985); United States v. Henry, 447 U.S. 264 (1980); Massiah v. United States, 377 U.S. 201 (1964). These cases, however, all share one fundamental characteristic that separates them from the instant case; in each case, the nature of the police conduct was such that it would have been impossible to find a valid waiver of the defendant's Sixth Amendment right to counsel. See Maine v. Moulton, supra, at 176-174 (undisclosed electronic surveillance of conversations with a third party); United States v. Henry, supra, 447 U.S., at 265, 273 (use of undisclosed police informant); Massiah v. United States, supra, 377 U.S., at 202 (undisclosed electronic surveillance). Here, on the other hand, the conduct of the police was totally open and above-board, and could not be said to prevent the defendant from executing a valid Sixth Amendment waiver under the standards set forth in Johnson v. Zerbst, 304 U.S. 458 (1938).

The truth is that there is no satisfactory explanation for the position the Court adopts in this case. The glaring inconsistencies in the Court's opinion arise precisely because the Court lacks a coherent, analytically sound basis for its decision. The prophylactic rule of *Edwards*, designed from its inception to protect a defendant's right under the Fifth Amendment not to be compelled to incriminate himself, simply does not meaningfully apply to the Sixth Amendment. I would hold that *Edwards* has no application outside the context of the Fifth Amendment, and would therefore reverse the judgment of the court below.

———————————

makes 6th like 5th (EDWARDS)

Continuing the development first started in Michigan v. Jackson of *warning cops* ignoring the differences between the fifth and sixth amendment "right to *from reopening interrogation* counsel," the Court in Patterson v. Illinois, 478 U.S. 285 (1988), held *once it to* that *Miranda* warnings sufficed to warn an indicted suspect of his sixth *counsel is* amendment right to counsel and that a waiver following such warnings *asserted* was a knowing and intelligent waiver of the sixth amendment right to counsel as well. The Court noted that it rejected the suggestion that the sixth amendment right to counsel is somehow "superior" to fifth amendment rights. In a somewhat curious passage, however, the Court stated that such a waiver would not be valid in the sixth amendment context, although it would in the fifth amendment context, if a suspect is not informed that his lawyer was trying to reach him. The Court cited Moran v. Burbine, 475 U.S. 424 (1986), in support of its view, although the proposition is not easily extracted from that case.

h. A Return to Voluntariness?

The central conundrum of *Miranda*, which makes it such an elusive case, is that one cannot appraise its remedial aspects without first resolving what it is to be remedied. Is the concern protecting "fair trials," inhibiting "coercion" of suspects, facilitating "knowledgeable" choices by suspects, protecting "privacy," "human dignity," a combination of some of these values, or something else altogether? These questions have evoked myriad answers. See, e.g., Friendly, The Fifth Amendment Tomorrow: The Case for Constitutional Change, 37 U. Cinn. L. Rev. 671 (1968); Schrock, Welsh, & Collins, Interrogational Rights: Reflections on Miranda v. Arizona, 52 S. Calif. L. Rev. 1 (1978).

Moreover, once one crystallizes the substantive concerns, argument then begins over the relationship of any particular remedy to those concerns. Indeed, in some ways *Miranda* reflects an ongoing cycle of efforts to balance the need to interrogate suspects with a desire to minimize

abusive state practices. Not surprisingly, we are beginning to see revivals
of interest in testing confessions by a modified "voluntariness" standard,
the most important of these works being Grano, Voluntariness, Free
Will, and the Law of Confessions, 65 Va. L. Rev. 859 (1979). As Professor
Grano summarizes his own argument:

> The primary thesis of this article is that the law of confessions should revert
> to a new due process voluntariness test, one that preserves a certain degree
> of mental freedom, protects against fundamentally unfair influence, and
> prevents interrogation practices that create a risk of untrustworthy confes-
> sions. The fifth amendment in the confession context merely duplicates
> the mental freedom component of the due process voluntariness analysis,
> and the sixth amendment right to counsel is inapplicable to interrogation
> occurring prior to the commencement of formal adversary judicial pro-
> ceedings. By introduction, this section provides a synopsis of the reason-
> ing—fully delineated in the remainder of this article—behind these
> conclusions.
>
> To avoid question-begging assumptions, a re-examination of the
> confession riddle must start with basic premises. An exploration of the free
> will/determinism debate and its relevance to the choice between a confes-
> sion law based on psychological evaluations of overborne wills and one
> based on considerations of policy and morality yields the conclusion that,
> as in the substantive criminal law, a concern for mental freedom must
> play a role in the law of confessions. This conclusion, however, requires
> acceptance of neither the free will postulate, which assumes a contra-
> causal freedom of choice,[34] nor the notion that an individual's confession
> is involuntary when "his will has been overborne." Instead, the mental
> freedom inquiry requires us to make normative judgments about various
> degrees of impairment of mental freedom.
>
> Even without statements about overborne wills, confession law and
> voluntariness doctrines in general seem wedded to the language of caus-
> ation. Empirical pursuits of "the" cause or the most "significant" cause
> of any given confession, however, are utterly meaningless. Rather, causal
> identification requires an exercise of discretion that depends on our purpose
> in asking the causal question. Again, therefore, the voluntariness inquiry
> ultimately requires a normative judgment about impairment of mental
> freedom.
>
> Unfortunately, there are no categorical answers to the voluntariness
> question at a purely normative level, because reasonable people can be
> expected to disagree about how much impairment of mental freedom is

34. Contra-causal freedom of choice is not determined by antecedent conditions or
events. When one billiard ball strikes another, the direction and velocity of the struck
ball can be ascertained with the proper equations and enough information about the
antecedent physical conditions. The free will postulate, however, states that people are
free at any given moment to choose among competing options; such choice is not dictated
by an antecedent cause. . . .

legitimate. Fortunately, however, the law of confessions requires a constitutional rather than a purely normative answer to the line-drawing question. The distinction is vital because much that is morally or pragmatically desirable may not be constitutionally mandated and thus must depend on the political process for implementation. Identification of the correct constitutional line for the voluntariness determination requires a brief excursion into the sources of due process interpretation. Judicially developed due process principles are on strongest ground when they are rooted in history and tradition, but a case—by no means conclusive—nevertheless can be made for taking into account contemporary morality. Due process principles derived from contemporary morality, however, are legitimate, if at all, only when a broadly-based community consensus has developed.

In applying these due process principles to the mental freedom question, the constitutional line should be drawn by reference to an objective standard. The mental freedom component of the due process voluntariness doctrine should render inadmissible any confession produced by interrogation pressures that a person of reasonable firmness, with some of the defendant's characteristics, could not resist. This standard is workable and provides as much protection for mental freedom as can be warranted by constitutional imposition. Although similarities most certainly exist, this proposed objective standard has marked advantages over the Supreme Court's "overborne will" approach.

Concerns other than mental freedom also have played a role in due process confession law. One such concern, expressed in the concept of fairness, is that the police not take undue advantage of, or unduly influence, a defendant. The notion of fairness simpliciter, however, cannot define the constitutional standard. Accordingly, many of the fairness concerns reflected in the Supreme Court's confession cases are not of constitutional stature. Nevertheless, a core notion of fundamental fairness, rooted in tradition and embedded in the national conscience, does play a limited role in confession law.

Concerns about the trustworthiness of confessions and the offensiveness of police practices often are associated with the due process voluntariness doctrine. Neither a focus on trustworthiness qua trustworthiness nor a focus on police practices qua police practices, however, can be justified on a constitutional level. Rather, these two concerns are necessarily intertwined. Indeed, once the mental freedom and undue influence concerns are taken into account, only the danger of false confessions can justify further constitutional examination of police interrogation procedures.

Aside from reflecting the above concerns, the due process voluntariness doctrine sometimes is described as protecting the essential attributes of our adversary system. This concern requires consideration of specific provisions of the Bill of Rights: the privilege against compulsory self-incrimination and the right to counsel. With respect to the fifth amendment protection against compulsory self-incrimination, the Court arguably erred as a matter of constitutional history in applying this protection to the police station. Given the Court's position, however, pursuit of this argument, exhaustively presented by others, would be unproductive. The current choice is between applying the fifth amendment to the police station with the same rigor as in the judicial context or applying it as an expression of voluntariness. Since the first alternative virtually would eliminate police interrogation, it should not be surprising that courts basically have chosen the second. Given this choice, fifth amendment voluntariness, at least in the context of confession law, requires the same normative and policy choices as due process voluntariness.

In considering the applicability of the sixth amendment right to counsel to the confession context, we should face squarely the constitutional policy questions underlying the issue rather than tying the counsel issue, as the *Miranda* Court did, to abstract notions of "inherent compulsion." Such a consideration reveals that a sufficient case has not been made for constitutionally applying a counsel requirement to police interrogation that occurs prior to the formal institution of adversary judicial proceedings.

In appraising Professor Grano's suggestion, do not neglect the problems that led the Court from the pre-*Miranda* voluntariness standard to its present position. These include, among others, the intractable factual questions posed by any voluntariness standard, the difficulty that standard poses for judicial review of police practices, and a concern for protecting the ignorant and the weak. For an excellent summary of these general problems, and a brief appraisal of Grano's suggestion, see Schulhofer, Confessions and the Court, 79 Mich. L. Rev. 865 (1981). For further appraisals of *Miranda*, see the exhaustive treatment in Y. Kamisar, W. LaFave & J. Israel, Modern Criminal Procedure 543-558 (7th. ed. 1989), the primary message of which is that *Miranda* remains a highly controversial decision.

Regardless of the wisdom of Professor Grano's argument that confession law should recur to questions of voluntariness, voluntariness is an important consideration for another reason. There are many situations where *Miranda* is not applicable: noncustodial interrogations, judging the admissibility of statements used to impeach, questioning by individuals who are not state agents and by the police after a waiver of the *Miranda* rights. For discussions, see White, Police Trickery in Inducing Confessions, 127 U. Pa. L. Rev. 581 (1979), which should be compared to Inbau & Reid, Criminal Interrogation and Confessions (2d ed. 1967); Dix, Mistake, Ignorance, Expectation of Benefit, and the Modern Law of Confessions, 1975 Wash. U.L.Q. 275. For example, the Court has permitted statements obtained in violation of *Miranda* (but not of the voluntariness test) to be used to impeach defendants who take the stand in their own behalf. For a discussion see Chapter 10 infra, and consider how this can be reconciled with *Portash*, page 1000 supra. On the other side of this particular coin, the Court has also made clear that defendants must be allowed to present evidence concerning the events surrounding any statements for both substantive and impeachment purposes. Crane v. Kentucky, 476 U.S. 683 (1986).

For years, indeed for decades, there have been predictions that *Miranda* would be overruled. These predictions have so far not come true, but a number of its decisions suggest that the Court may now be engaged in reconsidering the scope of the *Miranda* rules and of the fifth amendment. In addition to the cases previously presented, consider the implications of the next three cases for the meaning of the fifth amendment.

NEW YORK v. QUARLES

Certiorari to the Court of Appeals of New York
467 U.S. 649 (1984)

JUSTICE REHNQUIST delivered the opinion of the Court.

Respondent Benjamin Quarles was charged in the New York trial court with criminal possession of a weapon. The trial court suppressed the gun in question, and a statement made by respondent, because the statement was obtained by police before they read respondent his "*Miranda* rights." That ruling was affirmed on appeal through the New York Court of Appeals. We granted certiorari, and we now reverse. We conclude that under the circumstances involved in this case, overriding considerations of public safety justify the officer's failure to provide *Miranda* warnings before he asked questions devoted to locating the abandoned weapon.

On September 11, 1980, at approximately 12:30 A.M., Officer Frank Kraft and Officer Sal Scarring were on road patrol in Queens, New York, when a young woman approached their car. She told them that she had just been raped by a black male, approximately six feet tall, who was wearing a black jacket with the name "Big Ben" printed in yellow letters on the back. She told the officers that the man had just entered an A&P supermarket located nearby and that the man was carrying a gun.

The officers drove the woman to the supermarket, and Officer Kraft entered the store while Officer Scarring radioed for assistance. Officer Kraft quickly spotted respondent, who matched the description given by the woman, approaching a check-out counter. Apparently upon seeing the officer, respondent turned and ran toward the rear of the store, and Officer Kraft pursued him with a drawn gun. When respondent turned the corner at the end of an aisle, Officer Kraft lost sight of him for several seconds, and upon regaining sight of respondent, ordered him to stop and put his hands over his head.

Although more than three other officers had arrived on the scene by that time, Officer Kraft was the first to reach respondent. He frisked him and discovered that he was wearing a shoulder holster which was then empty. After handcuffing him, Office Kraft asked him where the gun was. Respondent nodded in the direction of some empty cartons and responded, "the gun is over there." Officer Kraft thereafter retrieved a loaded .38 caliber revolver from one of the cartons, formally placed respondent under arrest, and read him his *Miranda* rights from a printed card. Respondent indicated that he would be willing to answer questions without an attorney present. Officer Kraft then asked respondent if he owned the gun and where he had purchased it. Respondent answered that he did own it and that he had purchased it in Miami, Florida.

In the subsequent prosecution of respondent for criminal possession of a weapon,[2] the judge excluded the statement, "the gun is over there," and the gun because the officer had not given respondent the warnings required by our decision in Miranda v. Arizona, before asking him where the gun was located. The judge excluded the other statements about respondent's ownership of the gun and the place of purchase, as evidence tainted by the prior *Miranda* violation. The Appellate Division of the Supreme Court of New York affirmed without opinion. . . .

The Court of Appeals granted leave to appeal and affirmed by a 4-3 vote. . . . It concluded that respondent was in "custody" within the meaning of *Miranda* during all questioning and rejected the state's argument that the exigencies of the situation justified Officer Kraft's failure to read respondent his *Miranda* rights until after he had located the gun. The court declined to recognize an exigency exception to the usual requirements of *Miranda* because it found no indication from Officer Kraft's testimony at the suppression hearing that his subjective motivation in asking the question was to protect his own safety or the safety of the public. . . . For the reasons which follow, we believe that this case presents a situation where concern for public safety must be paramount to adherence to the literal language of the prophylactic rules enunciated in *Miranda*.[3] . . .

---

2. The state originally charged respondent with rape, but the record provides no information as to why the state failed to pursue that charge.

3. We have long recognized an exigent circumstances exception to the warrant requirement in the Fourth Amendment context. See, e.g., Michigan v. Tyler, 436 U.S. 499, 509 (1978); Warden v. Hayden, 387 U.S. 294, 298-300 (1967); Johnson v. United States, 333 U.S. 10, 14-15 (1948). We have found the warrant requirement of the Fourth Amendment inapplicable in cases where the " 'exigencies of the situation' make the needs

In this case we have before us no claim that respondent's statements were actually compelled by police conduct which overcame his will to resist. . . . Thus the only issue before us is whether Officer Kraft was justified in failing to make available to respondent the procedural safeguards associated with the privilege against compulsory self-incrimination since *Miranda*.[5]

The New York Court of Appeals was undoubtedly correct in deciding that the facts of this case come within the ambit of the *Miranda* decision as we have subsequently interpreted it. We agree that respondent was in police custody. . . . Quarles was surrounded by at least four police officers and was handcuffed when the questioning at issue took place. As the New York Court of Appeals observed, there was nothing to suggest that any of the officers were any longer concerned for their own physical safety. . . .

We hold that on these facts there is a "public safety" exception to the requirement that *Miranda* warnings be given before a suspect's answers may be admitted into evidence, and that the availability of that exception does not depend upon the motivation of the individual officers involved. In a kaleidoscopic situation such as the one confronting these officers, where spontaneity rather than adherence to a police manual is necessarily the order of the day, the application of the exception which we recognize today should not be made to depend on post hoc findings at a suppression hearing concerning the subjective motivation of the arresting officer.[6] Undoubtedly most police officers, if placed in Officer

[handwritten margin notes: could this exception work in INN's? (shotgun hidden near handicap school) Orozco v. Texas, statement seems to say no - maybe]

---

of law enforcement so compelling that the warrantless search is objectively reasonable under the Fourth Amendment." Mincey v. Arizona, 437 U.S. 385, 394 (1978), quoting McDonald v. United States, 335 U.S. 451, 456 (1948). Although "the Fifth Amendment's strictures, unlike the Fourth's, are not removed by showing reasonableness," Fisher v. United States, 425 U.S. 391, 400 (1976), we conclude today that there are limited circumstances where the judicially imposed strictures of *Miranda* are inapplicable.

5. The dissent curiously takes us to task for "endors[ing] the introduction of coerced self-incriminating statements in criminal prosecutions," and for "sanctioning sub silentio criminal prosecutions based on compelled self-incriminating statements." . . . Of course our decision today does nothing of the kind. As the *Miranda* Court itself recognized, the failure to provide *Miranda* warnings in and of itself does not render a confession involuntary, . . . and respondent is certainly free on remand to argue that his statement was coerced under traditional due process standards. Today we merely reject the only argument that respondent has raised to support the exclusion of his statement, that the statement must be *presumed* compelled because of Officer Kraft's failure to read him his *Miranda* warnings.

6. Similar approaches have been rejected in other contexts. See Rhode Island v. Innis, supra, at 301 (officer's subjective intent to incriminate not determinative of whether "interrogation" occurred); United States v. Mendenhall, 446 U.S. 544, 554 and n.6 (1980) (opinion of Stewart, J.) (officer's subjective intent to detain not determinative of whether a "seizure" occurred within the meaning of the Fourth Amendment); United States v. Robinson, 414 U.S. 218, 236 and n.7 (1973) (officer's subjective fear not determinative of necessity for "search incident to arrest" exception to the Fourth Amendment warrant requirement).

Kraft's position, would act out of a host of different, instinctive, and largely unverifiable motives—their own safety, the safety of others, and perhaps as well the desire to obtain incriminating evidence from the suspect.

Whatever the motivation of individual officers in such a situation, we do not believe that the doctrinal underpinnings of *Miranda* require that it be applied in all its rigor to a situation in which police officers ask questions reasonably prompted by a concern for the public safety. The *Miranda* decision was based in large part on this Court's view that the warnings which it required police to give to suspects in custody would reduce the likelihood that the suspects would fall victim to constitutionally impermissible practices of police interrogation in the presumptively coercive environment of the station house. : . . . The dissenters warned that the requirement of *Miranda* warnings would have the effect of decreasing the number of suspects who respond to police questioning. . . . The *Miranda* majority, however, apparently felt that whatever the cost to society in terms of fewer convictions of guilty suspects, that cost would simply have to be borne in the interest of enlarged protection for the Fifth Amendment privilege.

The police in this case, in the very act of apprehending a suspect, were confronted with the immediate necessity of ascertaining the whereabouts of a gun which they had every reason to believe the suspect had just removed from his empty holster and discarded in the supermarket. So long as the gun was concealed somewhere in the supermarket, with its actual whereabouts unknown, it obviously posed more than one danger to the public safety: an accomplice might make use of it, a customer or employee might later come upon it.

In such a situation, if the police are required to recite the familiar *Miranda* warnings before asking the whereabouts of the gun, suspects in Quarles' position might well be deterred from responding. Procedural safeguards which deter a suspect from responding were deemed acceptable in *Miranda* in order to protect the Fifth Amendment privilege; when the primary social cost of those added protections is the possibility of fewer convictions, the *Miranda* majority was willing to bear that cost. Here, had *Miranda* warnings deterred Quarles from responding to Officer Kraft's question about the whereabouts of the gun, the cost would have been something more than merely the failure to obtain evidence useful in convicting Quarles. Officer Kraft needed an answer to his question not simply to make his case against Quarles but to insure that further danger to the public did not result from the concealment of the gun in a public area.

We conclude that the need for answers to questions in a situation posing a threat to the public safety outweighs the need for the prophylactic rule protecting the Fifth Amendment's privilege against self-incrimination. We decline to place officers such as Officer Kraft in the untenable position of having to consider, often in a matter of seconds, whether it best serves society for them to ask the necessary questions without the *Miranda* warnings and render whatever probative evidence they uncover inadmissible, or for them to give the warnings in order to preserve the admissibility of evidence they might uncover but possibly damage or destroy their ability to obtain that evidence and neutralize the volatile situation confronting them.[7]

In recognizing a narrow exception to the *Miranda* rule in this case, we acknowledge that to some degree we lessen the desirable clarity of that rule. At least in part in order to preserve its clarity, we have over the years refused to sanction attempts to expand our *Miranda* holding. See, e.g., Minnesota v. Murphy (refusal to extend *Miranda* requirements to interviews with probation officers); Fare v. Michael C. (refusal to equate request to see a probation officer with request to see a lawyer for *Miranda* purposes); Beckwith v. United States (refusal to extend *Miranda* requirements to questioning in non-custodial circumstances). As we have in other contexts, we recognize here the importance of a workable rule "to guide police officers, who have only limited time and expertise to reflect on and balance the social and individual interests involved in the specific circumstances they confront." But as we have pointed out, we believe that the exception which we recognize today lessens the necessity of that on-the-scene balancing process. The exception will not be difficult for police officers to apply because in each case it will be circumscribed by the exigency which justifies it. We think police officers can and will distinguish almost instinctively between questions necessary to secure their own safety or the safety of the public and questions designed solely to elicit testimonial evidence from a suspect.

The facts of this case clearly demonstrate that distinction and an officer's ability to recognize it. Officer Kraft asked only the question necessary to locate the missing gun before advising respondent of his rights. It was only after securing the loaded revolver and giving the warnings that he continued with investigatory questions about the ownership and place of purchase of the gun. The exception which we recognize today, far from complicating the thought processes and the on-the-scene

7. The dissent argues that a public safety exception to *Miranda* is unnecessary because in every case an officer can simply ask the necessary questions to protect himself or the public, and then the prosecution can decline to introduce any incriminating responses at a subsequent trial. . . . But absent actual coercion by the officer, there is no constitutional imperative requiring the exclusion of the evidence that results from police inquiry of this kind; and we do not believe that the doctrinal underpinnings of *Miranda* require us to exclude the evidence, thus penalizing officers for asking the very questions which are the most crucial to their efforts to protect themselves and the public.

judgments of police officers, will simply free them to follow their legitimate instincts when confronting situations presenting a danger to the public safety.[8]

We hold that the Court of Appeals in this case erred in excluding the statement, "the gun is over there," and the gun because of the officer's failure to read respondent his *Miranda* rights before attempting to locate the weapon. Accordingly we hold that it also erred in excluding the subsequent statements as illegal fruits of a *Miranda* violation.[9] We therefore reverse and remand for further proceedings not inconsistent with this opinion.

It is so ordered.

JUSTICE O'CONNOR, concurring in part in the judgment and dissenting in part.

In Miranda v. Arizona, . . . the Court held unconstitutional, because inherently compelled, the admission of statements derived from in-custody questioning not preceded by an explanation of the privilege against self-incrimination and the consequences of foregoing it. Today, the Court concludes that overriding considerations of public safety justify the admission of evidence—oral statements and a gun—secured without the benefit of such warnings. . . . In so holding, the Court acknowledges that it is departing from prior precedent, . . . and that it is "lessen[ing] the desirable clarity of [the *Miranda*] rule." Were the Court writing from a clean slate, I could agree with its holding. But *Miranda* is now the law and, in my view, the Court has not provided sufficient justification for departing from it or for blurring its now clear strictures. Accordingly, I would require suppression of the initial statement taken from respondent in this case. On the other hand, nothing in *Miranda*

8. Although it involves police questions in part relating to the whereabouts of a gun, Orozco v. Texas, supra, is in no sense inconsistent with our disposition of this case. In Orozco four hours after a murder had been committed at a restaurant, four police officers entered the defendant's boardinghouse and awakened the defendant, who was sleeping in his bedroom. Without giving him *Miranda* warnings, they began vigorously to interrogate him about whether he had been present at the scene of the shooting and whether he owned a gun. The defendant eventually admitted that he had been present at the scene and directed the officers to a washing machine in the backroom of the boardinghouse where he had hidden the gun. We held that all the statements should have been suppressed. In *Orozco*, however, the questions about the gun were clearly investigatory; they did not in any way relate to an objectively reasonable need to protect the police or the public from any immediate danger associated with the weapon. In short there was no exigency requiring immediate action by the officers beyond the normal need expeditiously to solve a serious crime. . . .

9. Because we hold that there is no violation of *Miranda* in this case, we have no occasion to reach arguments made by the state and the United States as amicus curiae that the gun is admissible either because it is nontestimonial or because the police would inevitably have discovered it absent their questioning.

or the privilege itself requires exclusion of nontestimonial evidence derived from informal custodial interrogation, and I therefore agree with the Court that admission of the gun in evidence is proper. . . . Since the time *Miranda* was decided, the Court has repeatedly refused to bend the literal terms of that decision. To be sure, the Court has been sensitive to the substantial burden the *Miranda* rules place on local law enforcement efforts, and consequently has refused to extend the decision or to increase its strictures on law enforcement agencies in almost any way. . . . Similarly, where statements taken in violation of the *Miranda* principles have not been used to prove the prosecution's case at trial, the Court has allowed evidence derived from those statements to be admitted. But wherever an accused has been taken into "custody" and subjected to "interrogation" without warnings, the Court has consistently prohibited the use of his responses for prosecutorial purposes at trial. . . . As a consequence, the "meaning of *Miranda* has become reasonably clear and law enforcement practices have adjusted to its strictures."

In my view, a "public safety" exception unnecessarily blurs the edges of the clear line heretofore established and makes *Miranda's* requirements more difficult to understand. In some cases, police will benefit because a reviewing court will find that an exigency excused their failure to administer the required warnings. But in other cases, police will suffer because, though they thought an exigency excused their noncompliance, a reviewing court will view the "objective" circumstances differently and require exclusion of admissions thereby obtained. The end result will be a finespun new doctrine on public safety exigencies incident to custodial interrogation, complete with the hair-splitting distinctions that currently plague our Fourth Amendment jurisprudence. . . .

The justification the Court provides for upsetting the equilibrium that has finally been achieved—that police cannot and should not balance considerations of public safety against the individual's interest in avoiding compulsory testimonial self-incrimination—really misses the critical question to be decided. . . . *Miranda* has never been read to prohibit the police from asking questions to secure the public safety. Rather, the critical question *Miranda* addresses is who shall bear the cost of securing the public safety when such questions are asked and answered: the defendant or the State. *Miranda*, for better or worse, found the resolution of that question implicit in the prohibition against compulsory self-incrimination and placed the burden on the State. When police ask custodial questions without administering the required warnings, *Miranda* quite clearly requires that the answers received be presumed compelled and that they be excluded from evidence at trial. . . .

The Court concedes, as it must, both that respondent was in "custody" and subject to "interrogation" and that his statement "the gun is

over there" was compelled within the meaning of our precedent. . . .
In my view, since there is nothing about an exigency that makes custodial
interrogation any less compelling, a principled application of *Miranda*
requires that respondent's statement be suppressed.

II

The court below assumed, without discussion, that the privilege against
self-incrimination required that the gun derived from respondent's statement also be suppressed, whether or not the State could independently
link it to him. That conclusion was, in my view, incorrect.

A

. . . Only the introduction of a defendant's own *testimony* is proscribed by the Fifth Amendment's mandate that no person "shall be
compelled in any criminal case to be a witness against himself." U.S.
Const., Amend. 5. That mandate does not protect an accused from being
compelled to surrender *nontestimonial* evidence against himself. . . .

B

The gun respondent was compelled to supply is clearly evidence of
the "real or physical" sort. What makes the question of its admissibility
difficult is the fact that, in asking respondent to produce the gun, the
police also "compelled" him, in the *Miranda* sense, to create an incriminating testimonial response. In other words, the case is problematic
because police compelled respondent not only to provide the gun but
also to admit that he knew where it was and that it was his.
   It is settled that *Miranda* did not itself determine whether physical
evidence obtained in this manner would be admissible. But the Court
in *Schmerber*, with *Miranda* fresh on its mind, did address the issue. . . .
Schmerber resolved the dilemma by allowing admission of the nontestimonial, but not the testimonial, products of the State's compulsion. . . .
   To be sure, admission of nontestimonial evidence secured through
informal custodial interrogation will reduce the incentives to enforce the
Miranda code. But that fact simply begs the question of *how much*
enforcement is appropriate. There are some situations, as the Court's
struggle to accommodate a "public safety" exception demonstrates, in
which the societal cost of administering the *Miranda* warnings is very

high indeed.[3] The *Miranda* decision quite practically does not express any societal interest in having those warnings administered for their own sake. Rather, the warnings and waiver are only required to ensure that "testimony" used against the accused at trial is voluntarily given. Therefore, if the testimonial aspects of the accused's custodial communications are suppressed, the failure to administer the *Miranda* warnings should cease to be of concern. . . . The harm caused by failure to administer *Miranda* warnings relates only to admission of testimonial self-incriminations, and the suppression of such incriminations should by itself produce the optimal enforcement of the *Miranda* rule.

C

There are, of course, decisions of this Court which suggest that the privilege against self-incrimination requires suppression of not only compelled statements but also of all evidence derived therefrom. See, e.g., Kastigar v. United States. In each of these cases, however, the Court was responding to the dilemma that confronts persons asserting their Fifth Amendment privilege to a court or other tribunal vested with the contempt power. In each instance, the tribunal can require witnesses to appear without any showing of probable cause to believe they have committed an offense or that they have relevant information to convey, and require the witnesses to testify even if they have formally and expressly asserted a privilege of silence. Individuals in this situation are faced with "the cruel trilemma of self-accusation, perjury, or contempt." If the witness' invocation of the privilege at trial is not to be defeated by the State's refusal to let him remain silent at an earlier proceeding, the witness has to be protected "against the use of his compelled answers and evidence derived therefrom in any subsequent criminal case. . . . " Lefkowitz v. Turley, 414 U.S. 70, 78 (1973).

By contrast, suspects subject to informal custodial police interrogation of the type involved in this case are not in the same position as witnesses required to appear before a court, grand jury, or other such formal tribunal. Where independent evidence leads police to a suspect, and probable cause justifies his arrest, the suspect cannot seriously urge that the police have somehow unfairly infringed on his right "to a private enclave where he may lead a private life." Murphy v. Waterfront Comm'n, supra, at 55. Moreover, when a suspect interjects not the privilege itself but a post hoc complaint that the police failed to administer *Miranda*

3. The most obvious example, first suggested by Judge Henry Friendly, involves interrogation directed to the discovery and termination of an ongoing criminal activity such as kidnapping or extortion. See Friendly, The Bill of Rights as a Code of Criminal Procedure, 53 Calif. L. Rev. 929, 949 (1965).

warnings, he invokes only an irrebuttable presumption that the interrogation was coercive. He does not show that a privilege was raised and that the police actually or overtly coerced him to provide testimony and other evidence to be used against him at trial. . . . He could have remained silent and the interrogator could not have punished him for refusing to speak. Indeed, the accused is in the unique position of seeking the protection of the privilege without having timely asserted it. . . . The person in police custody surely may sense that he is in "trouble," but he is in no position to protest that he faced the Hobson's choice of self-accusation, perjury, or contempt. He therefore has a much less sympathetic case for obtaining the benefit of a broad suppression ruling. . . .

Indeed, whatever case can be made for suppression evaporates when the statements themselves are not admitted, given the rationale of the *Schmerber* line of cases. Certainly interrogation which provides leads to other evidence does not offend the values underlying the Fifth Amendment privilege any more than the compulsory taking of blood samples, fingerprints, or voice exemplars, all of which may be compelled in an "attempt to discover evidence that might be used to prosecute [a defendant] for a criminal offense." Use of a suspect's answers "merely to find other evidence establishing his connection with the crime [simply] differs only by a shade from the permitted use for that purpose of his body or his blood." H. Friendly, Benchmarks 280 (1967). The values underlying the privilege may justify exclusion of an unwarned person's out-of-court statements, as perhaps they may justify exclusion of statements and derivative evidence compelled under the threat of contempt. But when the only evidence to be admitted is derivative evidence such as a gun— derived not from actual compulsion but from a statement taken in the absence of *Miranda* warnings—those values simply cannot require suppression, at least no more so than they would for other such nontestimonial evidence.[4]

---

4. In suggesting that Wong Sun v. United States, 371 U.S. 471 (1963), requires exclusion of the gun, . . . Justice Marshall fails to acknowledge this Court's holding in Michigan v. Tucker. In *Tucker*, the Court very clearly held that *Wong Sun* is inapplicable in cases involving mere departures from *Miranda*. *Wong Sun* and its "fruit of the poisonous tree" analysis lead to exclusion of derivative evidence only where the underlying police misconduct infringes a "core" constitutional right. Failure to administer *Miranda* warnings violates only a nonconstitutional prophylactic. . . .

Nix v. Williams [discussed at page 1359 infra] is not to the contrary. In *Nix*, the Court held that evidence which inevitably would have been discovered need not be excluded at trial because of independent police misconduct. The Court in *Nix* discusses *Wong Sun* and its "fruit of the poisonous tree" analysis only to show that, even assuming a "core" violation of the Fourth, Fifth, or Sixth Amendment, evidence with a separate causal link need not be excluded at trial. Thus, *Nix* concludes that only "where 'the subsequent trial [cannot] cure a[n otherwise] one-sided confrontation between prosecuting authorities and the uncounseled defendant,' " should derivative evidence be excluded.

JUSTICE MARSHALL, with whom JUSTICE BRENNAN and JUSTICE STEVENS join, dissenting.

I

. . . The majority's entire analysis rests on the factual assumption that the public was at risk during Quarles' interrogation. This assumption is completely in conflict with the facts as found by New York's highest court. Before the interrogation began, Quarles had been "reduced to a condition of physical powerlessness." Contrary to the majority's speculations, . . . Quarles was not believed to have, nor did he in fact have, an accomplice to come to his rescue. When the questioning began, the arresting officers were sufficiently confident of their safety to put away their guns. As Officer Kraft acknowledged at the suppression hearing, "the situation was under control." Based on Officer Kraft's own testimony, the New York Court of Appeals found: "Nothing suggests that any of the officers was by that time concerned for his own physical safety." The Court of Appeals also determined that there was no evidence that the interrogation was prompted by the arresting officers' concern for the public's safety. . . .

The majority attempts to slip away from these unambiguous findings of New York's highest court by proposing that danger be measured by objective facts rather than the subjective intentions of arresting officers. . . . Though clever, this ploy was anticipated by the New York Court of Appeals: "[T]here is no evidence in the record before us that there were exigent circumstances posing a risk to the public safety. . . ."

The New York court's conclusion that neither Quarles nor his missing gun posed a threat to the public's safety is amply supported by the evidence presented at the suppression hearing. Again contrary to the majority's intimations, . . . no customers or employees were wandering about the store in danger of coming across Quarles' discarded weapon. Although the supermarket was open to the public, Quarles' arrest took place during the middle of the night when the store was apparently deserted except for the clerks at the checkout counter. The police could easily have cordoned off the store and searched for the missing gun. Had they done so, they would have found the gun forthwith. The police were well aware that Quarles had discarded his weapon somewhere near the scene of the arrest. As the State acknowledged before the New York Court of Appeals: "After Officer Kraft had handcuffed and frisked the defendant in the supermarket, *he knew with a high degree of certainty that the defendant's gun was within the immediate vicinity of the encounter.* He undoubtedly would have searched for it in the carton a few feet away without the defendant having looked in that direction and saying that it was there."

III

Though unfortunate, the difficulty of administering the "public-safety" exception is not the most profound flaw in the majority's decision. The majority has lost sight of the fact that Miranda v. Arizona and our earlier custodial-interrogation cases all implemented a constitutional privilege against self-incrimination. The rules established in these cases were designed to protect criminal defendants against prosecutions based on coerced self-incriminating statements. The majority today turns its back on these constitutional considerations, and invites the government to prosecute through the use of what necessarily are coerced statements.

A

The majority's error stems from a serious misunderstanding of Miranda v. Arizona and of the Fifth Amendment upon which that decision was based. The majority implies that *Miranda* consisted of no more than a judicial balancing act in which the benefits of "enlarged protection for the Fifth Amendment privilege" were weighed against "the cost to society in terms of fewer convictions of guilty suspects." . . . Supposedly because the scales tipped in favor of the privilege against self-incrimination, the *Miranda* Court erected a prophylactic barrier around statements made during custodial interrogations. The majority now proposes to return to the scales of social utility to calculate whether *Miranda's* prophylactic rule remains cost-effective when threats to public's safety are added to the balance. . . .

When *Miranda* reached this Court, it was undisputed that both the States and the Federal Government were constitutionally prohibited from prosecuting defendants with confessions coerced during custodial interrogations. As a theoretical matter, the law was clear. In practice, however, the courts found it exceedingly difficult to determine whether a given confession had been coerced. Difficulties of proof and subtleties of interrogation technique made it impossible in most cases for the judiciary to decide with confidence whether the defendant had voluntarily confessed his guilt or whether his testimony had been unconstitutionally compelled. Courts around the country were spending countless hours reviewing the facts of individual custodial interrogations. . . .

Miranda dealt with these practical problems. After a detailed examination of police practices and a review of its previous decisions in the area, the Court in *Miranda* determined that custodial interrogations are inherently coercive. The Court therefore created a constitutional presumption that statements made during custodial interrogations are compelled in violation of the Fifth Amendment and are thus inadmissible in criminal prosecutions. As a result of the Court's decision in *Miranda*, a statement made during a custodial interrogation may be introduced as proof of a defendant's guilt only if the prosecution demonstrates that the defendant knowingly and intelligently waived his constitutional rights before making the statement. The now-familiar *Miranda* warnings offer law-enforcement authorities a clear, easily administered device for ensuring that criminal suspects understand their constitutional rights well enough to waive them and to engage in consensual custodial interrogation.

In fashioning its "public-safety" exception to *Miranda*, the majority makes no attempt to deal with the constitutional presumption established by that case. The majority does not argue that police questioning about issues of public safety is any less coercive than custodial interrogations into other matters. The majority's only contention is that police officers could more easily protect the public if *Miranda* did not apply to custodial interrogations concerning the public's safety.[7] But *Miranda* was not a decision about public safety; it was a decision about coerced confessions. Without establishing that interrogations concerning the public's safety are less likely to be coercive than other interrogations, the majority cannot endorse the "public-safety" exception and remain faithful to the logic of Miranda v. Arizona.

B

The majority's avoidance of the issue of coercion may not have been inadvertent. It would strain credulity to contend that Officer Kraft's ques-

---

7. The majority elsewhere attempts to disguise its decision as an effort to cut back on the overbreadth of *Miranda's* prophylactic standard. . . . The disguise is transparent. Although *Miranda* was overbroad in that its application excludes some statements made during custodial interrogations that are not in fact coercive, the majority is not dealing with a class of cases affected by *Miranda's* overbreadth. The majority is exempting from *Miranda's* prophylactic rule incriminating statements that were elicited to safeguard the public's safety. As is discussed below, the majority supports the "public safety" exception because "public-safety" interrogations can be coercive. In this respect, the Court's decision differs greatly from Michigan v. Tucker, in which the Court sanctioned the admission of the fruits of a *Miranda* violation, but only because the violation was technical and the interrogation itself noncoercive.

tioning of respondent Quarles was not coercive.[8] In the middle of the night and in the back of an empty supermarket, Quarles was surrounded by four armed police officers. His hands were handcuffed behind his back. The first words out of the mouth of the arresting officer were: "Where is the gun?" In the majority's phrase, the situation was "kaleidoscopic." . . . Police and suspect were acting on instinct. Officer Kraft's abrupt and pointed question pressured Quarles in precisely the way that the *Miranda* Court feared the custodial interrogations would coerce self-incriminating testimony.

That the application of the "public-safety" exception in this case entailed coercion is no happenstance. The majority's ratio decidendi is that interrogating suspects about matters of public safety *will* be coercive. In its cost-benefit analysis the Court's strongest argument in favor of a public-safety exception to *Miranda* is that the police would be better able to protect the public's safety if they were not always required to give suspects their *Miranda* warnings. The crux of this argument is that, by deliberately withholding *Miranda* warnings, the police can get information out of suspects who would refuse to respond to police questioning were they advised of their constitutional rights. The "public-safety" exception is efficacious precisely because it permits police officers to coerce criminal defendants into making involuntary statements.

Indeed, in the efficacy of the "public-safety" exception lies a fundamental and constitutional defect. Until today, this Court could truthfully state that the Fifth Amendment is given "broad scope" "where there has been genuine compulsion of testimony." Coerced confessions were simply inadmissible in criminal prosecutions. The "public-safety" exception departs from this principle by expressly inviting police officers to coerce defendants into making incriminating statements, and then permitting prosecutors to introduce those statements at trial. Though the majority's opinion is cloaked in the beguiling language of utilitarianism, the Court has sanctioned sub silentio criminal prosecutions based on compelled self-incriminating statements. I find this result in direct conflict with the Fifth Amendment's dictate that "No person . . . shall be compelled in any criminal case to be a witness against himself."

The irony of the majority's decision is that the public's safety can be perfectly well protected without abridging the Fifth Amendment. If a bomb is about to explode or the public is otherwise imminently imperiled,

---

8. The majority's reliance on respondent's failure to claim that his testimony was compelled by police conduct can only be disingenuous. Before today's opinion, respondent had no need to claim actual compulsion. Heretofore, it was sufficient to demonstrate that the police had conducted nonconsensual custodial interrogation. But now that the law has changed, it is only fair to examine the facts of the case to determine whether coercion probably was involved.

the police are free to interrogate suspects without advising them of their constitutional rights. Such unconsented questioning may take place not only when police officers act on instinct but also when higher faculties lead them to believe that advising a suspect of his constitutional rights might decrease the likelihood that the suspect would reveal life-saving information. If trickery is necessary to protect the public, then the police may trick a suspect into confessing. While the Fourteenth Amendment sets limits on such behavior, nothing in the Fifth Amendment or our decision in Miranda v. Arizona proscribes this sort of emergency questioning. All the Fifth Amendment forbids is the introduction of coerced statements at trial. . . .

To a limited degree, the majority is correct that there is a cost associated with the Fifth Amendment's ban on introducing coerced self-incriminating statements at trial. Without a "public-safety" exception, there would be occasions when a defendant incriminated himself by revealing a threat to the public, and the State was unable to prosecute because the defendant retracted his statement after consulting with counsel and the police cannot find independent proof of guilt. Such occasions would not, however, be common. The prosecution does not always lose the use of incriminating information revealed in these situations. After consulting with counsel, a suspect may well volunteer to repeat his statement in hopes of gaining a favorable plea bargain or more lenient sentence. The majority thus overstates its case when it suggests that a police officer must necessarily choose between public safety and admissibility.

But however frequently or infrequently such cases arise, their regularity is irrelevant. The Fifth Amendment prohibits compelled self-incrimination.[10] As the Court has explained on numerous occasions, this prohibition is the mainstay of our adversarial system of criminal justice. Not only does it protect us against the inherent unreliability of compelled testimony, but it also ensures that criminal investigations will be conducted with integrity and that the judiciary will avoid the taint of official lawlessness. . . . The policies underlying the Fifth Amendment's privilege against self-incrimination are not diminished simply because testimony is compelled to protect the public's safety. The majority should not be permitted to elude the Amendment's absolute prohibition simply by calculating special costs that arise when the public's safety is at issue. Indeed, were constitutional adjudication always conducted in such an ad

10. In this sense, the Fifth Amendment differs fundamentally from the Fourth Amendment, which only prohibits unreasonable searches and seizures. See Fisher v. United States, 425 U.S. 391, 400 (1976). Accordingly, the various exceptions to the Fourth Amendment permitting warrantless searches under various circumstances should have no analogy in the Fifth Amendment context. Curiously, the majority accepts this point, . . . but persists in limiting the protections of the Fifth Amendment.

hoc manner, the Bill of Rights would be a most unreliable protector of
individual liberties. . . .

The Court appears to have settled whether the *Miranda* warnings
are merely prophylactic rules or constitutionally required. Reaffirming
the holding of Michigan v. Tucker, 417 U.S. 433 (1974), and portions
of *Quarles* not reproduced here, the Court in Oregon v. Elstad, 470 U.S.
298 (1985), held that a prior unwarned but voluntary statement given in
violation of *Miranda* does not automatically result in the suppression of
a subsequent statement given after the *Miranda* rights have been waived.
The Court's opinion raises a number of questions, however.

OREGON v. ELSTAD
Certiorari to the Supreme Court of Oregon
470 U. 298 (1985)

JUSTICE O'CONNOR delivered the opinion of the Court.
    This case requires us to decide whether an initial failure of law
enforcement officers to administer the warnings required by Miranda v.
Arizona, without more, "taints" subsequent admissions made after a
suspect has been fully advised of and has waived his *Miranda* rights.
Respondent, Michael James Elstad, was convicted of burglary by an
Oregon trial court. The Oregon Court of Appeals reversed, holding that
respondent's signed confession, although voluntary, was rendered inadmissible by a prior remark made in response to questioning without benefit
of *Miranda* warnings. We granted certiorari, and we now reverse.

I

In December, 1981, the home of Mr. and Mrs. Gilbert Gross, in the
town of Salem, Polk County, Ore., was burglarized. Missing were art
objects and furnishings valued at $150,000. A witness to the burglary
contacted the Polk County Sheriff's office, implicating respondent Michael Elstad, an 18-year-old neighbor and friend of the Grosses' teenage
son. Thereupon, Officers Burke and McAllister went to the home of
respondent Elstad, with a warrant for his arrest. Elstad's mother answered
the door. She led the officers to her son's room where he lay on his bed,
clad in shorts and listening to his stereo. The officers asked him to get
dressed and to accompany them into the living room. Officer McAllister
asked respondent's mother to step into the kitchen, where he explained

that they had a warrant for her son's arrest for the burglary of a neighbor's residence. Officer Burke remained with Elstad in the living room. He later testified:

> I sat down with Mr. Elstad and I asked him if he was aware of why Detective McAllister and myself were there to talk with him. He stated no, he had no idea why we were there. I then asked him if he knew a person by the name of Gross, and he said yes, he did, and also added that he heard that there was a robbery at the Gross house. And at that point I told Mr. Elstad that I felt he was involved in that, and he looked at me and stated, "Yes, I was there."

The officers then escorted Elstad to the back of the patrol car. As they were about to leave for the Polk County Sheriff's office, Elstad's father arrived home and came to the rear of the patrol car. The officers advised him that his son was a suspect in the burglary. Officer Burke testified that Mr. Elstad became quite agitated, opened the rear door of the car and admonished his son: "I told you that you were going to get into trouble. You wouldn't listen to me. You never learn."

Elstad was transported to the Sheriff's headquarters and approximately one hour later, Officers Burke and McAllister joined him in McAllister's office. McAllister then advised respondent for the first time of his *Miranda* rights, reading from a standard card. Respondent indicated he understood his rights, and, having these rights in mind, wished to speak with the officers. Elstad gave a full statement, explaining that he had known that the Gross family was out of town and had been paid to lead several acquaintances to the Gross residence and show them how to gain entry through a defective sliding glass door. The statement was typed, reviewed by respondent, read back to him for correction, initialed and signed by Elstad and both officers. As an afterthought, Elstad added and initialed the sentence, "After leaving the house Robby & I went back to [the] van & Robby handed me a small bag of grass." Respondent concedes that the officers made no threats or promises either at his residence or at the Sheriff's office.

Respondent was charged with first-degree burglary. He was represented at trial by retained counsel, Elstad waived his right to a jury and his case was tried by a Circuit Court judge. Respondent moved at once to suppress his oral statement and signed confession. He contended that the statement he made in response to questioning at his house "let the cat out of the bag," citing United States v. Bayer, 331 U.S. 532 (1947), and tainted the subsequent confession as "fruit of the poisonous tree," citing Wong Sun v. United States, 371 U.S. 471 (1963). The judge ruled that the statement, "I was there," had to be excluded because the defendant had not been advised of his *Miranda* rights. The written confession taken after Elstad's arrival at the Sheriffs office, however, was admitted in evidence. . . .

Elstad was found guilty of burglary in the first degree. He received a 5-year sentence and was ordered to pay $18,000 in restitution.

Following his conviction, respondent appealed to the Oregon Court of Appeals, relying on *Wong Sun* and *Bayer*. . . . The Court of Appeals reversed respondent's conviction, identifying the crucial constitutional inquiry as "whether there was a sufficient break in the stream of events between [the] inadmissible statement and the written confession to insulate the latter statement from the effect of what went before.". . .

This Court granted certiorari to consider the question whether the Self-Incrimination Clause of the Fifth Amendment requires the suppression of a confession, made after proper *Miranda* warnings and a valid waiver of rights, solely because the police had obtained an earlier voluntary but unwarned admission from the defendant.

II

The arguments advanced in favor of suppression of respondent's written confession rely heavily on metaphor. One metaphor, familiar from the Fourth Amendment context, would require that respondent's confession, regardless of its integrity, voluntariness, and probative value, be suppressed as the "tainted fruit of the poisonous tree" of the *Miranda* violation. A second metaphor questions whether a confession can be truly voluntary once the "cat is out of the bag." Taken out of context, each of these metaphors can be misleading, They should not be used to obscure fundamental differences between the role of the Fourth Amendment exclusionary rule and the function of *Miranda* in guarding against the prosecutorial use of compelled statements as prohibited by the Fifth Amendment. The Oregon court assumed and respondent here contends that a failure to administer *Miranda* warnings necessarily breeds the same consequences as police infringement of a constitutional right, so that evidence uncovered following an unwarned statement must be suppressed as "fruit of the poisonous tree." We believe this view misconstrues the nature of the protections afforded by *Miranda* warnings and therefore misreads the consequences of police failure to supply them.

A

. . . Respondent's contention that his confession was tainted by the earlier failure of the police to provide *Miranda* warnings and must be excluded as "fruit of the poisonous tree" assumes the existence of a constitutional violation. This figure of speech is drawn from Wong Sun v. United States, in which the Court held that evidence and witnesses discovered as a result of a search in violation of the Fourth Amendment must be excluded from evidence. The Wong Sun doctrine applies as well when the fruit of the Fourth Amendment violation is a confession. . . .

But as we explained in Quarles and Tucker, a procedural Miranda violation differs in significant respects from violations of the Fourth Amendment, which have traditionally mandated a broad application of the "fruits" doctrine. The purpose of the Fourth Amendment exclusionary rule is to deter unreasonable searches, no matter how probative their fruits. . . . Where a Fourth Amendment violation "taints" the confession, a finding of voluntariness for the purposes of the Fifth Amendment is merely a threshold requirement in determining whether the confession may be admitted in evidence. Beyond this, the prosecution must show a sufficient break in events to undermine the inference that the confession was caused by the Fourth Amendment violation.

The Miranda exclusionary rule, however, serves the Fifth Amendment and sweeps more broadly than the Fifth Amendment itself. It may be triggered even in the absence of a Fifth Amendment violation.[1] The Fifth Amendment prohibits use by the prosecution in its case in chief only of compelled testimony. Failure to administer Miranda warnings creates a presumption of compulsion. Consequently, unwarned statements that are otherwise voluntary within the meaning of the Fifth Amendment must nevertheless be excluded from evidence under Miranda. Thus, in the individual case, Miranda's preventive medicine provides a remedy even to the defendant who has suffered no identifiable constitutional harm.

But the Miranda presumption, though irrebuttable for purposes of the prosecution's case in chief, does not require that the statements and their fruits be discarded as inherently tainted. Despite the fact that patently voluntary statements taken in violation of Miranda must be excluded from the prosecution's case, the presumption of coercion does not bar their use for impeachment purposes on cross-examination. . . .

In Michigan v. Tucker, the Court was asked to extend the Wong

---

1. Justice Stevens expresses puzzlement at our statement that a simple failure to administer Miranda warnings is not in itself a violation of the Fifth Amendment. Yet the Court so held in New York v. Quarles, and Michigan v. Tucker. The Miranda Court itself recognized this point when it disclaimed any intent to create a "constitutional straight-jacket" and invited Congress and the States to suggest "potential alternatives for protecting the privilege." A Miranda violation does constitute coercion but rather affords a bright-line, legal presumption of coercion, requiring suppression of all unwarned statements. It has never been remotely suggested that any statement taken from Mr. Elstad without benefit of Miranda warnings would be admissible.

Sun fruits doctrine to suppress the testimony of a witness for the prosecution whose identity was discovered as the result of a statement taken from the accused without benefit of full *Miranda* warnings. As in respondent's case, the breach of the *Miranda* procedures in *Tucker* involved no actual compulsion. The Court concluded that the unwarned questioning "did not abridge respondent's constitutional privilege . . . but departed only from the prophylactic standards later laid down by this Court in *Miranda* to safeguard that privilege." Since there was no actual infringement of the suspect's constitutional rights, the case was not controlled by the doctrine expressed in *Wong Sun* that fruits of a constitutional violation must be suppressed. In deciding "how sweeping the judicially imposed consequences" of a failure to administer *Miranda* warnings should be, the *Tucker* Court noted that neither the general goal of deterring improper police conduct nor the Fifth Amendment goal of assuring trustworthy evidence would be served by suppression of the witness' testimony. The unwarned confession must, of course, be suppressed, but the Court ruled that introduction of the third-party witness' testimony did not violate Tucker's Fifth Amendment rights.

We believe that this reasoning applies with equal force when the alleged "fruit" of a noncoercive *Miranda* violation is neither a witness nor an article of evidence but the accused's own voluntary testimony. As in *Tucker*, the absence of any coercion or improper tactics undercuts the twin rationales—trustworthiness and deterrence—for a broader rule. Once warned, the suspect is free to exercise his own volition in deciding whether or not to make a statement to the authorities. The Court has often noted that " 'a living witness is not to be mechanically equated with the proffer of inanimate evidentiary objects illegally seized. . . . [T]he living witness is an individual human personality whose attributes of will, perception, memory and *volition* interact to determine what testimony he will give.' " United States v. Ceccolini, 435 U.S. 268, 277 (1978).

Because *Miranda* warnings may inhibit persons from giving information, this Court has determined that they need be administered only after the person is taken into "custody" or his freedom has otherwise been significantly restrained. Unfortunately, the task of defining "custody" is a slippery one, and "policemen investigating serious crimes [cannot realistically be expected to] make no errors whatsoever." Michigan v. Tucker, 417 U.S., at 446. If errors are made by law enforcement officers in administering the prophylactic *Miranda* procedures, they should not breed the same irremediable consequences as police infringement of the Fifth Amendment itself. It is an unwarranted extension of *Miranda* to hold that a simple failure to administer the warnings, unaccompanied by any actual coercion or other circumstances calculated to undermine the suspect's ability to exercise his free will so taints the investigatory process that a subsequent voluntary and informed waiver is ineffective for some indeterminate period. Though *Miranda* requires that the unwarned admission must be suppressed, the admissibility of any subsequent statement should turn in these circumstances solely on whether it is knowingly and voluntarily made.

B

The Oregon court, however, believed that the unwarned remark compromised the voluntariness of respondent's later confession. It was the court's view that the prior *answer* and not the unwarned questioning impaired respondent's ability to give a valid waiver and that only lapse of time and change of place could dissipate what it termed the "coercive impact" of the inadmissible statement. When a prior statement is actually coerced, the time that passes between confessions, the change in place of interrogations, and the change in identity of the interrogators all bear on whether that coercion has carried over into the second confession. The failure of police to administer *Miranda* warnings does not mean that the statements received have actually been coerced, but only that courts will presume the privilege against compulsory self-incrimination has not been intelligently exercised. In these circumstances, a careful and thorough administration of *Miranda* warnings serves to cure the condition that rendered the unwarned statement inadmissible. The warning conveys the relevant information and thereafter the suspect's choice whether to exercise his privilege to remain silent should ordinarily be viewed as an "act of free will."

The Oregon court nevertheless identified a subtle form of lingering compulsion, the psychological impact of the suspect's conviction that he has let the cat out of the bag and, in so doing, has sealed his own fate. But endowing the psychological effects of *voluntary* unwarned admissions with constitutional implications would, practically speaking, disable the police from obtaining the suspect's informed cooperation even when the official coercion proscribed by the Fifth Amendment played no part in either his warned or unwarned confessions. As the Court remarked in *Bayer*:

> [A]fter an accused has once let the cat out of the bag by confessing, no matter what the inducement, he is never thereafter free of the psychological and practical disadvantages of having confessed. He can never get the cat back in the bag. The secret is out for good. In such a sense, a later confession may always be looked upon as fruit of the first. But this Court has never gone so far as to hold that making a confession under circumstances which preclude its use, perpetually disables the confessor from

making a usable one after those conditions have been removed. [331 U.S., at 540-541.]

Even in such extreme cases as Lyons v. Oklahoma, 322 U.S. 596 (1944), in which police forced a full confession from the accused through unconscionable methods of interrogation, the Court has assumed that the coercive effect of the confession could, with time, be dissipated.

This Court has never held that the psychological impact of voluntary disclosure of a guilty secret qualifies as state compulsion or compromises the voluntariness of a subsequent informed waiver. The Oregon court, by adopting this expansive view of Fifth Amendment compulsion, effectively immunizes a suspect who responds to pre-*Miranda* warning questions from the consequences of his subsequent informed waiver of the privilege of remaining silent. This immunity comes at a high cost to legitimate law enforcement activity, while adding little desirable protection to the individual's interest in not being *compelled* to testify against himself. When neither the initial nor the subsequent admission is coerced, little justification exists for permitting the highly probative evidence of a voluntary confession to be irretrievably lost to the factfinder.

There is a vast difference between the direct consequences flowing from coercion of a confession by physical violence or other deliberate means calculated to break the suspect's will and the uncertain consequences of disclosure of a "guilty secret" freely given in response to an unwarned but noncoercive question, as in this case. Justice Brennan's contention that it is impossible to perceive any causal distinction between this case and one involving a confession that is coerced by torture is wholly unpersuasive.[3] Certainly, in respondent's case, the causal con-

---

3. Most of the 50 cases cited by Justice Brennan in his discussion of consecutive confessions concern an initial unwarned statement obtained through overtly or inherently coercive methods which raise serious Fifth Amendment and Due Process concerns. Without describing each case cited, the following are representative of the situations Justice Brennan views as analogous to this case: e.g., Darwin v. Connecticut, 391 U.S. 346 (1968) (suspect interrogated for 48 hours incommunicado while officers denied access to counsel); Beecher v. Alabama, 389 U.S. 35, 36 (1967) (officer fired rifle next to suspect's ear and said "If you don't tell the truth I am going to kill you"); Clewis v. Texas, 386 U.S. 707 (1967) (suspect was arrested without probable cause, interrogated for 9 days with little food or sleep, and gave 3 unwarned "confessions" each of which he immediately retracted); Reck v. Pate, 367 U.S. 433, 439-440, n.3 (1961) (mentally retarded youth interrogated incommunicado for a week "during which time he was frequently ill, fainted several times, vomited blood on the floor of the police station and was twice taken to the hospital on a stretcher"). . . .

Justice Brennan cannot seriously mean to equate such situations with the case at bar. Likewise inapposite are the cases the dissent cites concerning suspects whose invocation of their rights to remain silent and to have counsel present were flatly ignored while police subjected them to continued interrogation. Finally, many of the decisions Justice Brennan claims to require that the "taint" be "dissipated" simply recite the stock

nection between any psychological disadvantage created by his admission and his ultimate decision to cooperate is speculative and attenuated at best. It is difficult to tell with certainty what motivates a suspect to speak. A suspect's confession may be traced to factors as disparate as "a prearrest event such as a visit with a minister," Dunaway v. New York, 442 U.S., at 220 (Stevens, J., concurring), or an intervening event such as the exchange of words respondent had with his father. We must conclude that, absent deliberately coercive or improper tactics in obtaining the initial statement, the mere fact that a suspect has made an unwarned admission does not warrant a presumption of compulsion. A subsequent administration of *Miranda* warnings to a suspect who has given a voluntary but unwarned statement ordinarily should suffice to remove the conditions that precluded admission of the earlier statement. In such circumstances, the finder of fact may reasonably conclude that the suspect made a rational and intelligent choice whether to waive or invoke his rights.

III

. . . Respondent has argued that he was unable to give a fully *informed* waiver of his rights because he was unaware that his prior statement could not be used against him. Respondent suggests that Deputy McAllister, to cure this deficiency, should have added an additional warning to those given him at the Sheriff's office. Such a requirement is neither practicable nor constitutionally necessary. In many cases, a breach of *Miranda* procedures may not be identified as such until long after full *Miranda* warnings are administered and a valid confession obtained. The standard *Miranda* warnings explicitly inform the suspect of his right to consult a lawyer before speaking. Police officers are ill equipped to pinch-hit for counsel, construing the murky and difficult questions of when "custody" begins or whether a given unwarned statement will ultimately be held admissible.

This Court has never embraced the theory that a defendant's ignorance of the full consequences of his decisions vitiates their voluntariness. See California v. Beheler, 463 U.S., at 1125-1126, n.3; McMann v. Richardson, 397 U.S. 759, 769 (1970). If the prosecution has actually violated the defendant's Fifth Amendment rights by introducing an inadmissible confession at trial, compelling the defendant to testify in re-

---

"cat" and "tree" metaphors but go on to find the second confession voluntary without identifying any break in the stream of events beyond the simple administration of a careful and thorough warning. . . .

buttal, the rule announced in Harrison v. United States precludes use of that testimony on retrial. 392 U.S. 219 (1968). "Having 'released the spring' by using the petitioner's unlawfully obtained confessions against him, the Government must show that its illegal action did not induce his testimony." Id., at 224-225. But the Court has refused to find that a defendant who confesses, after being falsely told that his codefendant has turned state's evidence, does so involuntarily. Frazier v. Cupp, 394 U.S. 731, 739 (1969). The Court has also rejected the argument that a defendant's ignorance that a prior coerced confession could not be admitted in evidence compromised the voluntariness of his guilty plea. McMann v. Richardson, 397 U.S., at 769. Likewise, in California v. Beheler, supra, the Court declined to accept defendant's contention that, because he was unaware of the potential adverse consequences of statements he made to the police, his participation in the interview was involuntary. Thus we have not held that the sine qua non for a knowing and voluntary waiver of the right to remain silent is a full and complete appreciation of all of the consequences flowing from the nature and the quality of the evidence in the case.

. . . The judgment of the Court of Appeals of Oregon is reversed, and the case is remanded for further proceedings not inconsistent with this opinion.

It is so ordered.

JUSTICE BRENNAN, with whom JUSTICE MARSHALL joins, dissenting.
The Self-Incrimination Clause of the Fifth Amendment guarantees every individual that, if taken into official custody, he shall be informed of important constitutional rights and be given the opportunity knowingly and voluntarily to waive those rights before being interrogated about suspected wrongdoing. Miranda v. Arizona, 384 U.S. 436 (1966). This guarantee embodies our society's conviction that "no system of criminal justice can, or should, survive if it comes to depend for its continued effectiveness on the citizens abdication through unawareness of their constitutional rights." Escobedo v. Illinois, 378 U.S. 478, 490 (1964).

Even while purporting to reaffirm these constitutional guarantees, the Court has engaged of late in a studied campaign to strip the *Miranda* decision piecemeal and to undermine the rights *Miranda* sought to secure. Today's decision not only extends this effort a further step, but delivers a potentially crippling blow to *Miranda* and the ability of courts to safeguard the rights of persons accused of crime. For at least with respect to successive confessions, the Court today appears to strip remedies for *Miranda* violations of the "fruit of the poisonous tree" doctrine prohibiting the use of evidence presumptively derived from official illegality.

. . . The Court's decision says much about the way the Court currently goes about implementing its agenda. In imposing its new rule, for example, the Court mischaracterizes our precedents, obfuscates the central issues, and altogether ignores the practical realities of custodial interrogation that have led nearly every lower court to reject its simplistic reasoning. Moreover, the Court adopts startling and unprecedented methods of construing constitutional guarantees. . . .

Today's decision, in short, threatens disastrous consequences far beyond the outcome in this case. . . .

I

The threshold question is this: What effect should an admission or confession of guilt obtained in violation of an accused's *Miranda* rights be presumed to have upon the voluntariness of subsequent confessions that are preceded by *Miranda* warnings? . . .

If this Court's reversal of the judgment below reflected mere disagreement with the Oregon court's application of the "cat out of the bag" presumption to the particular facts of this case, the outcome, while clearly erroneous, would be of little lasting consequence. But the Court rejects the "cat out of the bag" presumption *entirely* and instead adopts a new rule presuming that "ordinarily" there is *no* causal connection between a confession extracted in violation of *Miranda* and a subsequent confession preceded by the usual *Miranda* warnings. The Court suggests that it is merely following settled lower-court practice in adopting this rule and that the analysis followed by the Oregon Court of Appeals was aberrant. This is simply not so. Most federal courts have rejected the Court's approach and instead held that (1) there is a rebuttable presumption that a confession obtained in violation of *Miranda* taints subsequent confessions, and (2) the taint cannot be dissipated solely by giving *Miranda* warnings. Moreover, those few federal courts that have suggested approaches similar to the Court's have subsequently qualified their positions. Even more significant is the case among state courts. Although a handful have adopted the Court's approach, the overwhelming majority of state courts that have considered the issue have concluded that subsequent confessions are presumptively tainted by a first confession taken in violation of *Miranda* and that *Miranda* warnings alone cannot dissipate the taint.[6]

6. . . . The Court scrambles to distinguish some of the cases cited in this footnote and in notes 3 and 4 supra [citations omitted], arguing that "[t]he dissent cannot seriously mean to equate" these precedents with the case at hand. To the contrary. Although many of these cases unquestionably raised traditional due process questions on their individual facts, that is not the ground on which they were decided. Instead, courts in every one

The Court today sweeps aside this common-sense approach as "speculative" reasoning, adopting instead a rule that "the psychological impact of *voluntary* disclosure of a guilty secret" neither "qualifies as state compulsion" nor "compromises the voluntariness" of subsequent confessions. So long as a suspect receives the usual *Miranda* warning before further interrogation, the Court reasons, the fact that he "is free to exercise his own volition in deciding whether or not to make" further confessions "ordinarily" is a sufficient "cure" and serves to break any causal connection between the illegal confession and subsequent statements.

The Court's marble-palace psychoanalysis is tidy, but it flies in the face of our own precedents, demonstrates a startling unawareness of the realities of police interrogation, and is completely out of tune with the experience of state and federal courts over the last 20 years. Perhaps the Court has grasped some psychological truth that has eluded persons far more experienced in these matters; if so, the Court owes an explanation of how so many could have been so wrong for so many years.

A

(1)

. . . One of the factors that can vitiate the voluntariness of a subsequent confession is the hopeless feeling of an accused that he has nothing to lose by repeating his confession, even where the circumstances that rendered his first confession illegal have been removed. . . .

The Court today decries the "irremediable consequences" of this reasoning, but it has always been clear that even after "let[ting] the cat out of the bag" the accused is not "perpetually disable[d]" from giving an admissible subsequent confession. Rather, we have held that subsequent confessions in such circumstances may be admitted if the prosecution demonstrates that, "[c]onsidering the 'totality of the circumstances,' " there was a " 'break in the stream of events . . . sufficient to insulate' " the subsequent confession from the damning impact of the first. Darwin v. Connecticut, 391 U.S. 346, 349 (1968) (citations omitted). Although we have thus rejected a per se rule forbidding the introduction of subsequent statements in these circumstances, we have emphasized that the psychological impact of admissions and confessions of criminal guilt nevertheless can have a decisive impact in undermining the voluntariness of a suspect's responses to continued police interrogation and must be accounted for in determining their admissibility. . . .

---

of the cited cases explicitly or implicitly recognized the applicability of traditional derivative-evidence analysis in evaluating the consequences of *Miranda* violations.

(2)

Our precedents did not develop in a vacuum. They reflect an understanding of the realities of police interrogation and the everyday experience of lower courts. Expert interrogators, far from dismissing a first admission or confession as creating merely a "speculative and attenuated" disadvantage for a suspect, understand that such revelations frequently lead directly to a full confession. Standard interrogation manuals advise that "[t]he securing of the first admission is the biggest stumbling block. . . ." A. Aubry & R. Caputo, Criminal Interrogation 290 (3d ed. 1980). If this first admission can be obtained, "there is every reason to expect that the first admission will lead to others, and eventually to the full confession." . . .

I would have thought that the Court, instead of dismissing the "cat out of the bag" presumption out of hand, would have accounted for these practical realities. . . . Expert interrogators and experienced lower court judges will be startled, to say the least, to learn that the connection between multiple confessions is "speculative" and that a subsequent rendition of *Miranda* warnings "ordinarily" enables the accused in these circumstances to exercise his "free will" and to make "a rational and intelligent choice whether to waive or invoke his rights." . . .

B

The correct approach, administered for almost 20 years by most courts with no untoward results, is to presume that an admission or confession obtained in violation of *Miranda* taints a subsequent confession unless the prosecution can show that the taint is so attenuated as to justify admission of the subsequent confession.[14] Although the Court

---

14. The Court cites three cases in support of its assertion that an illegally obtained "guilty secret" does not "ordinarily" compromise the voluntariness of a subsequent confession preceded by the usual *Miranda* warnings. These cases are all inapposite. The Court in McMann v. Richardson, 397 U.S. 759 (1970), held that a defendant's guilty plea may not be attacked on federal collateral review on the ground that it was induced by the mistaken assumption that an illegal confession might have been admitted at trial and have led to conviction. Id., at 770. The Court emphasized that this bar applies only when the defendant pleads in "open court" and the decision not to challenge the confession is based on "the good-faith evaluations of a reasonably competent attorney."Id., at 770, 773. Thus the defendant's decision to reiterate the confession is insulated in these circumstances by the assistance of counsel *and* review by a court—factors wholly absent in the confession context at hand. The Court in *McMann* noted that collateral review is available where the defendant "was incompetently advised by his attorney," id., at 772, and in light of this qualification I cannot see how that case is at all analogous to *uncounseled* decisions to repeat a proximate confession.

Similarly, in Frazier v. Cupp, 394 U.S. 731 (1969), the Court held that police misrepresentations concerning an accomplice, while "relevant" to the admissibility of the

warns against the "irremediable consequences" of this presumption, it is obvious that a subsequent confession, just like any other evidence that follows upon illegal police action, does not become "sacred and inaccessible." As with any other evidence, the inquiry is whether the subsequent confession " 'has been come at by exploitation of [the] illegality or instead by means sufficiently distinguishable to be purged of the primary taint.' "

Until today the Court has recognized that the dissipation inquiry requires the prosecution to demonstrate that the official illegality did not taint the challenged confession, and we have rejected the simplistic view that abstract notions of "free will" are alone sufficient to dissipate the challenged taint. . . . Instead, we have instructed courts to consider carefully such factors as the strength of the causal connection between the illegal action and the challenged evidence, their proximity in time and place, the presence of intervening factors, and the "purpose and flagrancy of the official misconduct."

The Court today shatters this sensitive inquiry and decides instead that, since individuals possess " 'will, perception, memory and volition,' " a suspect's "exercise [of] his own volition in deciding whether or not to make a [subsequent] statement to the authorities" must "ordinarily" be viewed as sufficient to dissipate the coercive influence of a prior confession obtained in violation of *Miranda*. But "[w]ill, perception, memory and volition are only relevant as they provide meaningful alternatives in the causal chain, not as mystical qualities which in themselves invoke the doctrine of attenuation." Hirtle, Inadmissible Confessions and Their Fruits: A Comment on *Harrison v. United States*, 60 J. Crim. L., C., & P.S. 58, 62 (1969). Thus we have *always* rejected, until today, the notion that "individual will" alone presumptively serves to insulate a person's actions from the taint of earlier official illegality. . . .

Nor have we ever allowed *Miranda* warnings alone to serve talismanically to purge the taint of prior illegalities. In Brown v. Illinois, for example, we emphasized that "*Miranda* warnings, *alone* and per se,

---

defendant's confession, did not vitiate the voluntariness of the confession under the totality of the circumstances of that case. Id., at 739. The defendant there, however, had received warnings which were proper at the time. And under the Fifth Amendment, there of course are significant distinctions between the use of third-party statements in obtaining a confession and the use of the accused's own previously compelled illegal admissions.

Finally, the petitioner in California v. Beheler, 463 U.S. 1121 (1983) (per curiam), was not in custody at all when he spoke with the police, and the Court rejected his contention that "his lack of awareness [of the consequences of what he said] transformed the situation into a custodial one." Id., at 1125, n.3. The Court emphasized that a person is in "custody" for purposes of the Fifth Amendment only if "there is a 'formal arrest or restraint on freedom of movement' of the degree associated with a formal arrest," id., at 1125 (citation omitted). Michael Elstad obviously was in custody at the time he was questioned.

cannot always make [a confession] sufficiently a product of free will to break . . . the causal connection between [an illegal arrest] and the confession."[15] The reason we rejected this rule is manifest: "[t]he *Miranda* warnings in no way inform a person of his Fourth Amendment rights, including his right to be released from unlawful custody following an arrest made without a warrant or without probable cause." Brown v. Illinois, supra, 422 U.S., at 601, n.6.

This logic applies with even greater force to the Fifth Amendment problem of successive confessions. Where an accused believes that it is futile to resist because the authorities already have elicited an admission of guilt, the mere rendition of *Miranda* warnings does not convey the information most critical at that point to ensuring his informed and voluntary decision to speak again: that the earlier confession may not be admissible and thus that he need not speak out of any feeling that he already has sealed his fate. The Court therefore is flatly wrong in arguing, as it does repeatedly, that the mere provision of *Miranda* warnings prior to subsequent interrogation supplies the accused with "the relevant information" and ensures that a subsequent confession "ordinarily" will be the product of "a rational and intelligent choice" and "an act of free will."

The Court's new approach is therefore completely at odds with established dissipation analysis. . .

III

The Court's decision today vividly reflects its impatience with the constitutional rights that the authorities attack as standing in the way of combatting crime. But the States that adopted the Bill of Rights struck that balance and it is not for this Court to balance the Bill of Rights away on a cost/benefit scale "where the 'costs' of excluding illegally obtained evidence loom to exaggerated heights and where the 'benefits' of such exclusion are made to disappear with a mere wave of the hand." United States v. Leon, 468 U.S., at 929 (Brennan, J., dissenting). It is precisely in that vein, however, that the Court emphasizes that the subsequent confession in this case was "voluntary," and "highly probative evidence," that application of the derivative-evidence presumption would cause the confession to be "irretrievably lost," and that such a result would come at an impermissibly "high cost to legitimate law enforcement activity."

15. Under a contrary rule, we emphasized, "[a]ny incentive to avoid Fourth Amendment violations would be eviscerated by making the warnings, in effect, a 'cure-all,' and the constitutional guarantee against unlawful searches and seizures could be said to be reduced to 'a form of words.' " 422 U.S., at 602-603.

Failure of government to obey the law cannot ever constitute "legitimate law enforcement activity." In any event, application of the derivative-evidence presumption does not "irretrievably" lead to suppression. If a subsequent confession is truly independent of earlier, illegally obtained confessions, nothing prevents its full use to secure the accused's conviction. If the subsequent confession *did* result from the earlier illegalities, however, there is nothing "voluntary" about it. And even if a tainted subsequent confession is "highly probative," we have never until today permitted probity to override the fact that the confession was "the product of constitutionally impermissible methods in [its] inducement." Rogers v. Richmond, 365 U.S. 534, 541 (1961). In such circumstances, the Fifth Amendment makes clear that the prosecutor has *no* entitlement to use the confession in attempting to obtain the accused's conviction.

The lesson of today's decision is that, at least for now, what the Court decrees are "legitimate" violations by authorities of the rights embodied in *Miranda* shall "ordinarily" go undeterred. It is but the latest of the escalating number of decisions that are making this tribunal increasingly irrelevant in the protection of individual rights, and that are requiring other tribunals to shoulder the burden. "There is hope, however, that in time this or some later Court will restore these precious freedoms to their rightful place as a primary protection for our citizens against over-reaching officialdom." United States v. Leon, 468 U.S., at 960 (Brennan, J., dissenting).

I dissent.

JUSTICE STEVENS, dissenting.

The Court concludes its opinion with a carefully phrased statement of its holding: "We hold today that a suspect who has once responded to unwarned yet uncoercive questioning is not thereby disabled from waiving his rights and confessing after he has been given the requisite *Miranda* warnings." I find nothing objectionable in such a holding. Moreover, because the Court expressly endorses the "bright line rule of *Miranda*," which conclusively presumes that incriminating statements obtained from a suspect in custody without administering the required warnings are the product of compulsion, and because the Court places so much emphasis on the special facts of this case, I am persuaded that the Court intends its holding to apply only to a narrow category of cases in which the initial questioning of the suspect was made in a totally uncoercive setting and in which the first confession obviously had no influence on the second. I nevertheless dissent because even such a narrowly confined exception is inconsistent with the Court's prior cases, because the attempt to identify its boundaries in future cases will breed confusion and uncertainty in the administration of criminal justice, and because it denigrates the importance of one of the core constitutional rights that protects every American citizen from the kind of tyranny that has flourished in other societies.

I

The desire to achieve a just result in this particular case has produced an opinion that is somewhat opaque and internally inconsistent. If I read it correctly, its conclusion rests on two untenable premises: (1) that the respondent's first confession was not the product of coercion; and (2) that no constitutional right was violated when respondent was questioned in a tranquil, domestic setting.

Even before the decision in Miranda v. Arizona, it had been recognized that police interrogation of a suspect who has been taken into custody is presumptively coercive. That presumption had its greatest force when the questioning occurred in a police station, when it was prolonged, and when there was evidence that the prisoner had suffered physical injury. To rebut the presumption, the prosecutor had the burden of proving the absence of any actual coercion. Because police officers are generally more credible witnesses than prisoners and because it is always difficult for triers of fact to disregard evidence of guilt when addressing a procedural question, more often than not the presumption of coercion afforded only slight protection to the accused.

The decision in Miranda v. Arizona clarified the law in three important respects. First, it provided the prosecutor with a simple method of overcoming the presumption of coercion. If the police interrogation is preceded by the warning specified in that opinion, the usual presumption does not attach. Second, it provided an important protection to the accused by making the presumption of coercion irrebuttable if the prescribed warnings are not given. Third, the decision made it clear that a self-incriminatory statement made in response to custodial interrogation was always to be considered "compelled" within the meaning of the Fifth Amendment to the Federal Constitution if the interrogation had not been preceded by appropriate warnings. Thus the irrebuttable presumption of coercion that applies to such a self-incriminatory statement, like a finding of actual coercion, renders the resulting confession inadmissible as a matter of federal constitutional law.

In my opinion, the Court's attempt to fashion a distinction between actual coercion "by physical violence or other deliberate means calculated to break the suspect's will," and irrebuttably presumed coercion cannot succeed. The presumption is only legitimate if it is assumed that there is always a coercive aspect to custodial interrogation that is not preceded by adequate advice of the constitutional right to remain silent. Although

I would not support it, I could understand a rule that refused to apply the presumption unless the interrogation took place in an especially coercive setting—perhaps only in the police station itself—but if the presumption arises whenever the accused has been taken into custody or his freedom has been restrained in any significant way, it will surely be futile to try to develop subcategories of custodial interrogation. Indeed, a major purpose of treating the presumption of coercion as irrebuttable is to avoid the kind of fact-bound inquiry that today's decision will surely engender.

As I read the Court's opinion, it expressly accepts the proposition that routine *Miranda* warnings will not be sufficient to overcome the presumption of coercion and thereby make a second confession admissible when an earlier confession is tainted by coercion "by physical violence or other deliberate means calculated to break the suspect's will." Even in such a case, however, it is not necessary to assume that the earlier confession will always "effectively immunize" a later voluntary confession. But surely the fact that an earlier confession was obtained by unlawful methods should add force to the presumption of coercion that attaches to subsequent custodial interrogation and should require the prosecutor to shoulder a heavier burden of rebuttal than in a routine case. Simple logic, as well as the interest in not providing an affirmative incentive to police misconduct, requires that result. I see no reason why the violation of a rule that is as well recognized and easily administered as the duty to give *Miranda* warnings should not also impose an additional burden on the prosecutor. If we are faithful to the holding in *Miranda* itself, when we are considering the admissibility of evidence in the prosecutor's case-in-chief, we should not try to fashion a distinction between police misconduct that warrants a finding of actual coercion and police misconduct that establishes an irrebuttable presumption of coercion.

II

For me, the most disturbing aspect of the Court's opinion is its somewhat opaque characterization of the police misconduct in this case. The Court appears ambivalent on the question whether there was any constitutional violation. This ambivalence is either disingenuous or completely lawless. This Court's power to require state courts to exclude probative self-incriminatory statements rests entirely on the premise that the use of such evidence violates the Federal Constitution. The same constitutional analysis applies whether the custodial interrogation is actually coercive or irrebuttably presumed to be coercive. If the Court does not accept that premise, it must regard the holding in the *Miranda* case itself, as well as all of the Federal jurisprudence that has evolved from that decision, as nothing more than an illegitimate exercise of raw judicial power. If the Court accepts the proposition that respondent's self incriminatory statement was inadmissible, it must also acknowledge that the Federal Constitution protected him from custodial police interrogation without first being advised of his right to remain silent.

The source of respondent's constitutional protection is the Fifth Amendment's privilege against compelled self-incrimination that is secured against state invasion by the Due Process Clause of the Fourteenth Amendment. Like many other provisions of the Bill of Rights, that provision is merely a procedural safeguard. It is, however, the specific provision that protects all citizens from the kind of custodial interrogation that was once employed by the Star Chamber, by "the Germans of the 1930's and early 1940's"[18] and by some of our own police departments only a few decades ago. Custodial interrogation that violates that provision of the Bill of Rights is a classic example of a violation of a constitutional right.

I respectfully dissent.

Finally, consider the implications of the following case for the meaning of "voluntariness."

COLORADO v. CONNELLY
Certiorari to the Supreme Court of Colorado
479 U.S. 157 (1987)

CHIEF JUSTICE REHNQUIST, delivered the opinion of the Court.

In this case, the Supreme Court of Colorado held that the United States Constitution requires a court to suppress a confession when the mental state of the defendant, at the time he made the confession, interfered with his "rational intellect" and his "free will." Because this decision seemed to conflict with prior holdings of this Court, we granted certiorari. We conclude that the admissibility of this kind of statement is governed by state rules of evidence, rather than by our previous decisions regarding coerced confessions and *Miranda* waivers. We therefore reverse.

---

18. See Burger, Who Will Watch the Watchman?, 14 Am. U.L. Rev. 1, 14 (1964).

I

On August 18, 1983, Officer Patrick Anderson of the Denver Police Department was in uniform, working in an off-duty capacity in downtown Denver. Respondent Francis Connelly approached Officer Anderson and, without any prompting, stated that he had murdered someone and wanted to talk about it. Anderson immediately advised respondent that he had the right to remain silent, that anything he said could be used against him in court and that he had the right to an attorney prior to any police questioning. Respondent stated that he understood these rights but he still wanted to talk about the murder. Understandably bewildered by this confession, Officer Anderson asked respondent several questions. Connelly denied that he had been drinking, denied that he had been taking any drugs, and stated that, in the past, he had been a patient in several mental hospitals. Officer Anderson again told Connelly that he was under no obligation to say anything. Connelly replied that it was "all right," and that he would talk to Officer Anderson because his conscience had been bothering him. To Officer Anderson, respondent appeared to understand fully the nature of his acts.

Shortly thereafter, Homicide Detective Stephen Antuna arrived. Respondent was again advised of his rights, and Detective Antuna asked him "what he had on his mind." Respondent answered that he had come all the way from Boston to confess to the murder of Mary Ann Junta, a young girl whom he had killed in Denver sometime during November 1982. Respondent was taken to police headquarters, and a search of police records revealed that the body of an unidentified female had been found in April 1983. Respondent openly detailed his story to Detective Antuna and Sergeant Thomas Haney, and readily agreed to take the officers to the scene of the killing. Under Connelly's sole direction, the two officers and respondent proceeded in a police vehicle to the location of the crime. Respondent pointed out the exact location of the murder. Throughout this episode, Detective Antuna perceived no indication whatsoever that respondent was suffering from any kind of mental illness.

Respondent was held overnight. During an interview with the public defender's office the following morning, he became visibly disoriented. He began giving confused answers to questions, and for the first time, stated that "voices" had told him to come to Denver and that he had followed the directions of these voices in confessing. Respondent was sent to a state hospital for evaluation. He was initially found incompetent to assist in his own defense. By March 1984, however, the doctors evaluating respondent determined that he was competent to proceed to trial.

At a preliminary hearing, respondent moved to suppress all of his statements. Doctor Jeffrey Metzner, a psychiatrist employed by the state hospital, testified that respondent was suffering from chronic schizophrenia and was in a psychotic state at least as of August 17, 1983, the day before he confessed. Metzner's interviews with respondent revealed that respondent was following the "voice of God." This voice instructed respondent to withdraw money from the bank, to buy an airplane ticket, and to fly from Boston to Denver. When respondent arrived from Boston, God's voice became stronger and told respondent either to confess to the killing or to commit suicide. Reluctantly following the command of the voices, respondent approached Officer Anderson and confessed.

Dr. Metzner testified that, in his expert opinion, respondent was experiencing "command hallucinations." This condition interfered with respondent's "volitional abilities; that is, his ability to make free and rational choices." Dr. Metzner further testified that Connelly's illness did not significantly impair his cognitive abilities. Thus, respondent understood the rights he had when Officer Anderson and Detective Antuna advised him that he need not speak. Dr. Metzner admitted that the "voices" could in reality be Connelly's interpretation of his own guilt, but explained that in his opinion, Connelly's psychosis motivated his confession.

On the basis of this evidence the Colorado trial court decided that respondent's statements must be suppressed because they were "involuntary." Relying on our decisions in Townsend v. Sain, 372 U.S. 293 (1963), and Culombe v. Connecticut, 367 U.S. 568 (1961), the court ruled that a confession is admissible only if it is a product of the defendant's rational intellect and "free will." Although the court found that the police had done nothing wrong or coercive in securing respondent's confession, Connelly's illness destroyed his volition and compelled him to confess. The trial court also found that Connelly's mental state vitiated his attempted waiver of the right to counsel and the privilege against compulsory self-incrimination. Accordingly, respondent's initial statements and his custodial confession were suppressed.

The Colorado Supreme Court affirmed.

II

The Due Process Clause of the Fourteenth Amendment provides that no State shall "deprive any person of life, liberty, or property, without due process of law." Just last Term, in Miller v. Fenton, we held that by virtue of the Due Process Clause "certain interrogation techniques, either in isolation or as applied to the unique characteristics of a particular suspect, are so offensive to a civilized system of justice that they must be condemned."

Indeed, coercive government misconduct was the catalyst for this Court's seminal confession case, Brown v. Mississippi. In that case, police officers extracted confessions from the accused through brutal torture. The Court had little difficulty concluding that even though the Fifth Amendment did not at that time apply to the States, the actions of the police were "revolting to the sense of justice." The Court has retained this due process focus, even after holding, in Malloy v. Hogan, that the Fifth Amendment privilege against compulsory self-incrimination applies to the States. See Miller v. Fenton, 474 U.S., at 109-110.

Thus the cases considered by this Court over the 50 years since Brown v. Mississippi have focused upon the crucial element of police overreaching.[1] While each confession case has turned on its own set of factors justifying the conclusion that police conduct was oppressive, all have contained a substantial element of coercive police conduct. Absent police conduct causally related to the confession, there is simply no basis for concluding that any state actor has deprived a criminal defendant of due process of law.[2] Respondent correctly notes that as interrogators have turned to more subtle forms of psychological persuasion, courts have found the mental condition of the defendant a more significant factor in the "voluntariness" calculus. But this fact does not justify a conclusion that a defendant's mental condition, by itself and apart from its relation to official coercion, should ever dispose of the inquiry into constitutional "voluntariness."

Respondent relies on Blackburn v. Alabama, 361 U.S. 199 (1960), and Townsend v. Sain, 372 U.S. 293 (1963), for the proposition that the "deficient mental condition of the defendants in those cases was sufficient to render their confessions involuntary." But respondent's reading of Blackburn and Townsend ignores the integral element of police

---

1. E.g., Mincey v. Arizona, 437 U.S. 385 (1978) (defendant subjected to four-hour interrogation while incapacitated and sedated in intensive-care unit); Greenwald v. Wisconsin, 390 U.S. 519 (1968) (defendant, on medication, interrogated for over eighteen hours without food or sleep); Beecher v. Alabama, 389 U.S. 35 (1967) (police officers held gun to the head of wounded confessant to extract confession); Davis v. North Carolina, 384 U.S. 737 (1966) (sixteen days of incommunicado interrogation in closed cell without windows, limited food, and coercive tactics); Reck v. Pate, 367 U.S. 433 (1961) (defendant held for four days with inadequate food and medical attention until confession obtained); Culombe v. Connecticut, 367 U.S. 568 (1961) (defendant held for five days of repeated questioning during which police employed coercive tactics); Payne v. Arkansas, 356 U.S. 560 (1958) (defendant held incommunicado for three days with little food; confession obtained when officers informed defendant that Chief of Police was preparing to admit lynch mob into jail); Ashcraft v. Tennessee, 322 U.S. 143 (1944) (defendant questioned by relays of officers for thirty-six hours without an opportunity to sleep).

2. Even where there is causal connection between police misconduct and a defendant's confession, it does not automatically follow that there has been a violation of the Due Process Clause. See, e.g., Frazier v. Cupp, 394 U.S. 731, 739 (1969).

over-reaching present in both cases. In *Blackburn*, the Court found that the petitioner was probably insane at the time of his confession and the police learned during the interrogation that Blackburn had a history of mental problems. The police exploited this weakness with coercive tactics: "the eight- to nine-hour sustained interrogation in a tiny room which was upon occasion literally filled with police officers; the absence of Blackburn's friends, relatives, or legal counsel; [and] the composition of the confession by the Deputy Sheriff rather than by Blackburn." These tactics supported a finding that the confession was involuntary. Indeed, the Court specifically condemned police activity that "wrings a confession out of an accused against his will." *Townsend* presented a similar instance of police wrongdoing. In that case, a police physician had given Townsend a drug with truth-serum properties. The subsequent confession, obtained by officers who knew that Townsend had been given drugs, was held involuntary. These two cases demonstrate that while mental condition is surely relevant to an individual's susceptibility to police coercion, mere examination of the confessant's state of mind can never conclude the due process inquiry.

Our "involuntary confession" jurisprudence is entirely consistent with the settled law requiring some sort of "state action" to support a claim of violation of the Due Process Clause of the Fourteenth Amendment. The Colorado trial court, of course, found that the police committed no wrongful acts, and that finding has been neither challenged by the respondent nor disturbed by the Supreme Court of Colorado. The latter court, however, concluded that sufficient state action was present by virtue of the admission of the confession into evidence in a court of the State.

The difficulty with the approach of the Supreme Court of Colorado is that it fails to recognize the essential link between coercive activity of the State, on the one hand, and a resulting confession by a defendant, on the other. The flaw in respondent's constitutional argument is that it would expand our previous line of "voluntariness" cases into a far-ranging requirement that courts must divine a defendant's motivation for speaking or acting as he did even though there be no claim that governmental conduct coerced his decision.

The most outrageous behavior by a private party seeking to secure evidence against a defendant does not make that evidence inadmissible under the Due Process Clause. We have also observed that "[j]urists and scholars have recognized that the exclusionary rule imposes a substantial cost on the societal interest in law enforcement by its proscription of what concededly is relevant evidence." United States v. Janis, 428 U.S. 433, 448-449 (1976). Moreover, suppressing respondent's statements would serve absolutely no purpose in enforcing constitutional guarantees. The

Conservative slant

purpose of excluding evidence seized in violation of the Constitution is to substantially deter future violations of the Constitution. Only if we were to establish a brand new constitutional right—the right of a criminal defendant to confess to his crime only when totally rational and properly motivated—could respondent's present claim be sustained.

We have previously cautioned against expanding "currently applicable exclusionary rules by erecting additional barriers to placing truthful and probative evidence before state juries. . . ." Lego v. Twomey, 404 U.S. 477, 488-489 (1972). We abide by that counsel now. "[T]he central purpose of a criminal trial is to decide the factual question of the defendant's guilt or innocence," Delaware v. Van Arsdall, 475 U.S., at 681 (1986), and while we have previously held that exclusion of evidence may be necessary to protect constitutional guarantees, both the necessity for the collateral inquiry and the exclusion of evidence deflect a criminal trial from its basic purpose. Respondent would now have us require sweeping inquiries into the state of mind of a criminal defendant who has confessed, inquiries quite divorced from any coercion brought to bear on the defendant by the State. We think the Constitution rightly leaves this sort of inquiry to be resolved by state laws governing the admission of evidence and erects no standard of its own in this area. A statement rendered by one in the condition of respondent might be proved to be quite unreliable, but this is a matter to be governed by the evidentiary laws of the forum, see, e.g., Fed. Rule Evid. 601, and not by the Due Process Clause of the Fourteenth Amendment. "The aim of the requirement of due process is not to exclude presumptively false evidence, but to prevent fundamental unfairness in the use of evidence whether true or false." Lisenba v. California, 314 U.S. 219, 236 (1941).

We hold that coercive police activity is a necessary predicate to the finding that a confession is not "voluntary" within the meaning of the Due Process Clause of the Fourteenth Amendment. We also conclude that the taking of respondent's statements, and their admission into evidence, constitute no violation of that Clause.

III

A

The Supreme Court of Colorado went on to affirm the trial court's ruling that respondent's later statements made while in custody should be suppressed because respondent had not waived his right to consult an attorney and his right to remain silent. That court held that the State must bear its burden of proving waiver of these *Miranda* rights by "clear and convincing evidence." Although we have stated in passing that the State bears a "heavy" burden in proving waiver, we have never held that the "clear and convincing evidence" standard is the appropriate one.

In Lego v. Twomey this Court upheld a procedure in which the State established the voluntariness of a confession by no more than a preponderance of the evidence. We upheld it for two reasons. First, the voluntariness determination has nothing to do with the reliability of jury verdicts; rather, it is designed to determine the presence of police coercion. Thus, voluntariness is irrelevant to the presence or absence of the elements of a crime, which must be proved beyond a reasonable doubt. Second, we rejected Lego's assertion that a high burden of proof was required to serve the values protected by the exclusionary rule. We surveyed the various reasons for excluding evidence, including a violation of the requirements of Miranda v. Arizona, and we stated that "[i]n each instance and without regard to its probative value, evidence is kept from the trier of guilt or innocence for reasons wholly apart from enhancing the reliability of verdicts." Lego v. Twomey, 404 U.S., at 488. Moreover, we rejected the argument that "the importance of the values served by exclusionary rules is itself sufficient demonstration that the Constitution also requires admissibility to be proved beyond a reasonable doubt." Indeed, the Court found that "no substantial evidence has accumulated that federal rights have suffered from determining admissibility by a preponderance of the evidence."

We now reaffirm our holding in *Lego*: Whenever the State bears the burden of proof in a motion to suppress a statement that the defendant claims was obtained in violation of our *Miranda* doctrine, the State need prove waiver only by a preponderance of the evidence. If, as we held in Lego v. Twomey, the voluntariness of a confession need be established only by a preponderance of the evidence, then a waiver of the auxiliary protections established in *Miranda* should require no higher burden of proof. "[E]xclusionary rules are very much aimed at deterring lawless conduct by police and prosecution and it is very doubtful that escalating the prosecution's burden of proof in . . . suppression hearings would be sufficiently productive in this respect to outweigh the public interest in placing probative evidence before juries for the purpose of arriving at truthful decisions about guilt or innocence." Lego v. Twomey, 404 U.S. at 489.

B

We also think that the Supreme Court of Colorado was mistaken in its analysis of the question of whether respondent had waived his

Miranda rights in this case.[3] Of course, a waiver must at a minimum be "voluntary" to be effective against an accused. The Supreme Court of Colorado in addressing this question relied on the testimony of the court-appointed psychiatrist to the effect that respondent was not capable of making a "free decision with respect to his constitutional right of silence . . . and his constitutional right to confer with a lawyer before talking to the police."

We think that the Supreme Court of Colorado erred in importing into this area of constitutional law notions of "free will" that have no place there. There is obviously no reason to require more in the way of a "voluntariness" inquiry in the *Miranda* waiver context than in the Fourteenth Amendment confession context. The sole concern of the Fifth Amendment, on which *Miranda* was based, is governmental coercion. Indeed, the Fifth Amendment privilege is not concerned "with moral and psychological pressures to confess emanating from sources other than official coercion." Oregon v. Elstad, 470 U.S. 298, 305 (1985). The voluntariness of a waiver of this privilege has always depended on the absence of police overreaching, not on "free choice" in any broader sense of the word.

Respondent urges this Court to adopt his "free will" rationale, and to find an attempted waiver invalid whenever the defendant feels compelled to waive his rights by reason of any compulsion, even if the compulsion does not flow from the police. But such a treatment of the waiver issue would cut this Court's holding in *Miranda* completely loose from its own explicitly stated rationale. *Miranda* protects defendants against government coercion leading them to surrender rights protected by the Fifth Amendment; it goes no further than that. Respondent's perception of coercion flowing from the "voice of God," however important or significant such a perception may be in other disciplines, is a matter to which the United States Constitution does not speak.

IV

The judgment of the Supreme Court of Colorado is accordingly reversed, and the cause remanded for further proceedings not inconsistent with this opinion.[4]

---

3. Petitioner conceded at oral argument that when Officer Anderson handcuffed respondent, the custody requirement of *Miranda* was satisfied. For purposes of our decision we accept that concession, and we similarly assume that the police officers "interrogated" respondent within the meaning of *Miranda*.

4. It is possible to read the opinion of the Supreme Court of Colorado as finding respondent's *Miranda* waiver invalid on other grounds. Even if that is the case, however,

JUSTICE STEVENS, concurring in the judgment in part and dissenting in part.

Respondent made incriminatory statements both before and after he was handcuffed and taken into custody. The only question presented by the Colorado district attorney in his certiorari petition concerned the admissibility of respondent's precustodial statements. I agree with the State of Colorado that the United States Constitution does not require suppression of those statements, but in reaching that conclusion, unlike the Court, I am perfectly willing to accept the state trial court's finding that the statements were involuntary.

The state trial court found that, in view of the "overwhelming evidence presented by the Defense," the prosecution did not meet its burden of demonstrating that respondent's initial statements to Officer Anderson were voluntary. Nevertheless, in my opinion, the use of these involuntary precustodial statements does not violate the Fifth Amendment because they were not the product of state compulsion. Although they may well be so unreliable that they could not support a conviction, at this stage of the proceeding I could not say that they have no probative force whatever. The fact that the statements were involuntary—just as the product of Lady Macbeth's nightmare was involuntary[2]—does not mean that their use for whatever evidentiary value they may have is fundamentally unfair or a denial of due process.

The postcustodial statements raise an entirely distinct question. When the officer whom respondent approached elected to handcuff him and to take him into custody, the police assumed a fundamentally different relationship with him. Prior to that moment, the police had no duty to give respondent *Miranda* warnings and had every right to continue their exploratory conversation with him. Once the custodial relationship was established, however, the questioning assumed a presumptively coercive character. In my opinion the questioning could not thereafter go forward in the absence of a valid waiver of respondent's constitutional rights unless he was provided with counsel. Since it is undisputed that respondent was not then competent to stand trial, I would also conclude that he was not competent to waive his constitutional right to remain silent.

The Court seems to believe that a waiver can be voluntary even if it is not the product of an exercise of the defendant's "free will." The

we nonetheless reverse the judgment in its entirety because of our belief that the Supreme Court of Colorado's analysis was influenced by its mistaken view of "voluntariness" in the constitutional sense. Reconsideration of other issues, not inconsistent with our opinion, is of course open to the Supreme Court of Colorado on remand.

2. "What, will these hands ne'er be clean? . . .

"Here's the smell of the blood still: all the perfumes of Arabia will not sweeten this little hand." W. Shakespeare, Macbeth, Act V, scene 1, lines 41, 47. Lady Macbeth's "eyes are open," "but their sense is shut." Id., at line 23.

Court's position is not only incomprehensible to me; it is also foreclosed by the Court's recent pronouncement in Moran v. Burbine that "the relinquishment of the right must have been voluntary in the sense that it was the product of a free and deliberate choice. . . ."[5] Because respondent's waiver was not voluntary in that sense, his custodial interrogation was presumptively coercive. The Colorado Supreme Court was unquestionably correct in concluding that his post-custodial incriminatory statements were inadmissible. . . .

JUSTICE BRENNAN, with whom JUSTICE MARSHALL joins, dissenting.

Today the Court denies Mr. Connelly his fundamental right to make a vital choice with a sane mind, involving a determination that could allow the State to deprive him of liberty or even life. This holding is unprecedented: "Surely in the present stage of our civilization a most basic sense of justice is affronted by the spectacle of incarcerating a human being upon the basis of a statement he made while insane. . . ." Blackburn v. Alabama, 361 U.S. 199, 207 (1960). Because I believe that the use of a mentally ill person's involuntary confession is antithetical to the notion of fundamental fairness embodied in the Due Process Clause, I dissent. . . .

II

The absence of police wrongdoing should not, by itself, determine the voluntariness of a confession by a mentally ill person. The requirement that a confession be voluntary reflects a recognition of the importance of free will and of reliability in determining the admissibility of a confession, and thus demands an inquiry into the totality of the circumstances surrounding the confession.

A

Today's decision restricts the application of the term "involuntary" to those confessions obtained by police coercion. Confessions by mentally ill individuals or by persons coerced by parties other than police officers are now considered "voluntary." The Court's failure to recognize all forms of involuntariness or coercion as antithetical to due process reflects a

5. The Court relies on the further statement in Moran v. Burbine that the waiver must result from "free and deliberate choice rather than intimidation, coercion, or deception. . . ." Obviously this dichotomy does not exhaust the possibilities; the mere absence of police misconduct does not establish that the suspect has made a free and deliberate choice when the suspect is not competent to stand trial.

refusal to acknowledge free will as a value of constitutional consequence. But due process derives much of its meaning from a conception of fundamental fairness that emphasizes the right to make vital choices voluntarily. . . .

This Court's assertion that we would be required "to establish a brand new constitutional right" to recognize the respondent's claim ignores 200 years of constitutional jurisprudence.[1] As we stated in Culombe v. Connecticut:

> The ultimate test remains that which has been the only clearly established test in Anglo-American courts for two hundred years: the test of voluntariness. Is the confession the product of an essentially free and unconstrained choice by its maker? . . . The line of distinction is that at which governing self-direction is lost *and compulsion, of whatever nature or however infused,* propels or helps to propel the confession.

A true commitment to fundamental fairness requires that the inquiry be "not whether the conduct of state officers in obtaining the confession is shocking, but whether the confession was 'free and voluntary.' . . ." Malloy v. Hogan, 378 U.S. at 7.

We have never confined our focus to police coercion, because the value of freedom of will has demanded a broader inquiry. The confession cases decided by this Court over the 50 years since Brown v. Mississippi have focused upon both police overreaching and free will. While it is true that police overreaching has been an element of every confession case to date, it is also true that in every case the Court has made clear that ensuring that a confession is a product of free will is an independent concern.[2] The fact that involuntary confessions have always been ex-

---

1. Cf. Bram v. United States, 168 U.S. 532, 547-548 (1897) (reviewing the "rule [of law] in England at the time of the adoption of the Constitution and of the Fifth Amendment" and citing Hawkins' Pleas of the Crown (6th ed. 1787): "[a] confession, therefore, whether made upon an official examination or *in discourse with private persons,* which is obtained from a defendant, either by the flattery of hope, or by the impressions of fear, however slightly the emotions may be implanted, . . . is not admissible evidence; for the law will not suffer a prisoner to be made the deluded instrument of his own conviction") (emphasis added).

2. E.g., Mincey v. Arizona, 437 U.S. 385, 398 (1978) ("It is hard to imagine a situation less conductive to the exercise of 'a rational intellect and a free will' than Mincey's"); Greenwald v. Wisconsin, 390 U.S. 519, 521 (1968) ("Considering the totality of these circumstances, we do not think it credible that petitioner's statements were the product of his free and rational choice"); Beecher v. Alabama, 389 U.S. 35, 37 (1967) ("Still in a 'kind of slumber' from his last morphine injection, feverish, and in intense pain, the petitioner signed the written confessions thus prepared for him"); Davis v. North Carolina, 384 U.S. 737, 742 (1966) ("His level of intelligence is such that it prompted the comment by the court below, even while deciding against him on his claim of involuntariness, that there is a moral question whether a person of Davis' mentality

cluded in part because of police overreaching, signifies only that this is a case of first impression. Until today, we have never upheld the admission of a confession that does not reflect the exercise of free will.

The Court cites Townsend v. Sain, and *Blackburn* in support of its view that police wrongdoing should be the central focus of inquiry. In *Townsend*, we overturned a murder conviction because the defendant's conviction was determined to be involuntary. The defendant suffered from stomach pains induced by heroin withdrawal. The police properly contacted a physician who administered medications alleviating the withdrawal symptoms. The defendant then confessed. Although the physician denied that he purposely administered "truth serum," there was an indication that the medications could have had such a side effect upon a narcotic addict.

The *Townsend* Court examined "many relevant circumstances": "Among these are [the defendant's] lack of counsel at the time, his drug addiction, the fact that he was a 'near mental defective,' and his youth and inexperience." According to today's Court, the police wrong-doing in *Townsend* was that the police physician had allegedly given the defendant a drug with truth-serum properties, and that the confession was obtained by officers who knew that the defendant had been given drugs. But in fact, "the police . . . did not know what [medications] the doctor had given [the defendant]." And the *Townsend* Court expressly states that police wrongdoing was not an essential factor:

> It is not significant that the drug may have been administered and the questions asked by persons unfamiliar with hyoscine's properties as a "truth serum," if these properties exist. Any questioning by police officers which *in fact* produces a confession which is not the product of a free intellect renders that confession inadmissible. The Court has usually so stated the test.

Furthermore, in prescient refutation of this Court's "police wrong-doing" theory, the *Townsend* Court analyzed *Blackburn*, the other case relied upon by this Court to "demonstrate" that police wrongdoing was

---

should be executed"); Reck v. Pate, 367 U.S. 433, 440 (1961) ("If [a defendant's will was overborne], the confession cannot be deemed 'the product of a rational intellect and a free will' "); Culombe v. Connecticut, 367 U.S. 568, 583 (1961) ("[A]n extra-judicial confession, if it was to be offered in evidence against a man, must be the product of his own free choice"); Payne v. Arkansas, 356 U.S. 560, 567 (1958) (footnotes omitted) ("It seems obvious from the *totality* of this course of conduct, and particularly the culminating threat of mob violence, that the confession was coerced and did not constitute an 'expression of free choice' "); Ashcraft v. Tennessee, 322 U.S. 143, 147 (1944) ("He was induced by the fear of violence at the hands of a mob and by fear of the officers").

a more important factor than the defendant's state of mind. The Court in *Townsend* stated:

> [I]n Blackburn v. Alabama, we held *irrelevant* the absence of evidence of improper purpose on the part of the questioning officers. There the evidence indicated that the interrogating officers thought the defendant sane when he confessed, but we judged the confession inadmissible because the probability was that the defendant was *in fact* insane at the time. [372 U.S., at 309 (emphasis added).]

Thus the *Townsend* Court interpreted *Blackburn* as a case involving a confession by a mentally ill defendant in which the police harbored no improper purpose.[3]

The only "flaw" which the Court detects in this argument is that it would require courts to "divine a defendant's motivation for speaking or acting as he did even though there be no claim that governmental conduct coerced his decision." Such a criticism, however, ignores the fact that we have traditionally examined the totality of the circumstances, including the motivation and competence of the defendant, in determining whether a confession is voluntary. Even today's Court admits that "as interrogators have turned to more subtle forms of psychological persuasion, courts have found the mental condition of the defendant a more significant factor in the 'voluntariness' calculus." The Court's holding that involuntary confessions are only those procured through police misconduct is thus inconsistent with the Court's historical insistence that only confessions reflecting an exercise of free will be admitted into evidence.

---

3. Even if police knowledge of the defendant's insanity is required to exclude an involuntary confession, the record supports a finding of police knowledge in this case. The Court accepts the trial court's finding of no police wrongdoing since, in the trial judge's view, none of the police officers knew that Mr. Connelly was insane. After plenary review of the record, I conclude that this finding is clearly erroneous.

When the defendant confessed to Officer Anderson, the officer's first thought was that Mr. Connelly was a "crackpot." Today's Court describes Officer Anderson as "[u]nderstandably bewildered." After giving *Miranda* warnings, the officer questioned the defendant about whether he used drugs or alcohol. He also asked Mr. Connelly if he had been treated for any mental disorders, and the defendant responded that he had been treated in five different mental hospitals. While this Court concludes that "Detective Antuna perceived no indication whatsoever that respondent was suffering from any kind of mental illness," the record indicates that Officer Anderson informed the detective about the defendant's five hospitalizations in mental institutions. Thus, even under this Court's test requiring police wrongdoing, the record indicates that the officers here had sufficient knowledge about the defendant's mental incapacity to render the confession "involuntary."

B

Since the Court redefines voluntary confessions to include confessions by mentally ill individuals, the reliability of these confessions becomes a central concern. A concern for reliability is inherent in our criminal justice system, which relies upon accusatorial rather than inquisitorial practices. While an inquisitorial system prefers obtaining confessions from criminal defendants, an accusatorial system must place its faith in determinations of "guilt by evidence independently and freely secured." Rogers v. Richmond, 365 U.S. 534, 541 (1961). . . .

Because the admission of a confession so strongly tips the balance against the defendant in the adversarial process, we must be especially careful about a confession's reliability. We have to date not required a finding of reliability for involuntary confessions only because *all* such confessions have been excluded upon a finding of involuntariness, regardless of reliability. See Jackson v. Denno, 378 U.S. 368, 383-386 (1964).[4] The Court's adoption today of a restrictive definition of an "involuntary" confession will require heightened scrutiny of a confession's reliability.

The instant case starkly highlights the danger of admitting a confession by a person with a severe mental illness. The trial court made no findings concerning the reliability of Mr. Connelly's involuntary confession, since it believed that the confession was excludable on the basis of involuntariness. However, the overwhelming evidence in the record points to the unreliability of Mr. Connelly's delusional mind. Mr. Connelly was found incompetent to stand trial because he was unable to relate accurate information, and the court-appointed psychiatrist indicated that Mr. Connelly was actively hallucinating and exhibited delusional thinking at the time of his confession. The Court, in fact, concedes that "[a] statement rendered by one in the condition of respondent might be proved to be quite unreliable. . . ."

Moreover, the record is barren of any corroboration of the mentally ill defendant's confession. No physical evidence links the defendant to the alleged crime. Police did not identify the alleged victim's body as the woman named by the defendant. Mr. Connelly identified the alleged scene of the crime, but it has not been verified that the unidentified body was found there or that a crime actually occurred there. There is not a shred of competent evidence in this record linking the defendant to the charged homicide. There is only Mr. Connelly's confession.

Minimum standards of due process should require that the trial court

---

4. Prior to establishing this rule excluding all involuntary confessions, we held the view that the Fifth Amendment, at bottom, served as "a guarantee against conviction on inherently untrustworthy evidence." Stein v. New York, 346 U.S. 156, 192 (1953).

find substantial indicia of reliability, on the basis of evidence extrinsic to the confession itself, before admitting the confession of a mentally ill person into evidence. I would require the trial court to make such a finding on remand. To hold otherwise allows the State to imprison and possibly to execute a mentally ill defendant based solely upon an inherently unreliable confession.

III

This Court inappropriately reaches out to address two *Miranda* issues not raised by the prosecutor in his petition for certiorari: (1) the burden of proof upon the government in establishing the voluntariness of *Miranda* rights, and (2) the effect of mental illness on the waiver of those rights in the absence of police misconduct. I emphatically dissent from the Court's holding that the government need prove waiver by only a preponderance of the evidence, and from its conclusion that a waiver is automatically voluntary in the absence of police coercion.

A

. . . The Court bases its [burden of proof] holding on Lego v. Twomey.[6] . . .

I adhere to my *Lego* dissent. The constitutional ideal that involuntary confessions should never be admitted against the defendant in criminal cases deserves protection by the highest standard of proof—proof beyond a reasonable doubt. The lower standard of proof results "in the admission of more involuntary confessions than would be admitted were the prosecution required to meet a higher standard." "Compelled self-incrimination is so alien to the American sense of justice that I see no way that such a view could ever be justified." . . .

The ultimate irony is that, even accepting the preponderance of the evidence as the correct standard, the prosecution still failed to meet this burden of proof. The Colorado Supreme Court found that Dr. Metzner, the court-appointed psychiatrist and the only expert to testify, "clearly established" that Mr. Connelly "was incapable" of making a "free decision" respecting his *Miranda* rights. Thus the prosecution failed—even by the modest standard imposed today—to prove that Mr. Connelly voluntarily waived his *Miranda* rights.

6. Contrary to this Court's assertion, nowhere does the *Lego* Court state that "the voluntariness determination . . . is designed to determine the presence of police coercion." The *Lego* court did not distinguish coercion by police from coercion exerted from other sources.

B

The Court imports its voluntariness analysis, which makes police coercion a requirement for a finding of involuntariness, into its evaluation of the waiver of *Miranda* rights. My reasoning in Part II applies a fortiori to involuntary confessions made in custody involving the waiver of constitutional rights. I will not repeat here what I said there.

I turn then to the second requirement, apart from the voluntariness requirement, that the State must satisfy to establish a waiver of *Miranda* rights. Besides being voluntary, the waiver must be knowing and intelligent. We recently noted [in Moran v. Burbine] that "the waiver must have been made with a full awareness both of the nature of the right being abandoned and the consequences of the decision to abandon it." The two requirements are independent: "Only if the 'totality of the circumstances surrounding the interrogation' reveal *both* an uncoerced choice *and* the requisite level of comprehension may a court properly conclude that the *Miranda* rights have been waived."

Since the Colorado Supreme Court found that Mr. Connelly was "clearly" unable to make an "intelligent" decision, clearly its judgment should be affirmed. The Court reverses the entire judgment, however, without explaining how a "mistaken view of voluntariness" could "taint" this independent justification for suppressing the custodial confession, but leaving the Supreme Court of Colorado free on remand to reconsider other issues, not inconsistent with the Court's opinion. Such would include, in my view, whether the requirement of a knowing and intelligent waiver was satisfied. Moreover, on the remand, today's holding does not, of course, preclude a contrary resolution of this case based upon the State's separate interpretation of its own constitution.

Has Justice Brennan conflated "purpose" and "knowledge" with "causation"? Should they be conflated?

One last note on *Miranda* and voluntariness. In Miller v. Fenton, 474 U.S. 104 (1985), the Court concluded that the "voluntariness" of a confession is not a "fact" to be presumed correctly decided by state courts under 28 U.S.C. §2254(d). Rather, federal courts are "independently" to decide the issue. The majority opinion also suggested that lying by police officers to an individual who may be suffering from serious mental problems may be sufficient for a conclusion that any statements made by the defendant were not given "voluntarily." To be sure, this was only suggested and not decided, but in any event this point ought to be compared to the implications of *Connelly*.

CHAPTER 10

ADMINISTRATION OF THE EXCLUSIONARY RULES

A. THE RULING ON ADMISSIBILITY— THE SUPPRESSION PROCESS

In most jurisdictions a defendant must make a motion to suppress illegally obtained evidence prior to trial. See, e.g., Fed. R. Crim. P. 12(b). Failure to make such a pretrial motion will result in a forfeiture of the claim unless the defendant can show good cause for the failure. See, e.g., Fed. R. Crim. P. 12(f). Cause would exist, for example, if the defendant was not aware that the prosecutor possessed the evidence in question.

Some jurisdictions require that the motion to suppress be in writing; others permit oral as well as written motions. Depending on the jurisdiction, the defendant will need to state with varying degrees of particularity the factual basis and legal grounds for the suppression motion.

In some jurisdictions both parties must submit affidavits setting forth the relevant facts, and sometimes affidavits are submitted in the absence of such a requirement. If there is no material dispute concerning the facts, the judge will be able to rule on the motion without an evidentiary hearing. If there are no affidavits or if the facts are in dispute, there will be a hearing on the motion to suppress. The hearing frequently will take place at least several weeks prior to the trial. On some occasions, however, the hearing may take place immediately before or during the trial. This might occur, for example, if the same individuals were to be witnesses at both the suppression hearing and the trial.

If the subject of the suppression motion is the voluntariness of a

1329

confession, the defendant has the constitutional right to have the voluntariness decision made by the trial judge outside the presence of the jury. Jackson v. Denno, 378 U.S. 368 (1964). The defendant, however, does not have a constitutional right to have all admissibility decisions made outside the presence of the jury. See Watkins v. Sowders, 449 U.S. 341 (1981) (defendant challenged in-court identification on ground that it was product of impermissibly suggestive pretrial identification; hearing and rejecting challenge in presence of jury not a denial of due process). Nonetheless, the preferred practice, as even *Watkins* acknowledged, is to hold admissibility hearings outside the presence of the jury. Cf. Fed. R. Evid. 104(c) ("Hearings on the admissibility of confessions shall in all cases be conducted out of the hearing of the jury. Hearings on other preliminary matters shall be so conducted when the interests of justice require or, when an accused is a witness and so requests"); Fed. R. Evid. 103(c) ("In jury cases, proceedings shall be conducted, to the extent practicable, so as to prevent inadmissible evidence from being suggested to the jury by any means").

If the defendant chooses to testify at the suppression hearing, this choice will not be regarded as a waiver or forfeiture of the defendant's right against self-incrimination at trial. Moreover, at least with respect to fourth amendment claims, the prosecutor cannot use a defendant's suppression motion testimony at trial to establish any of the elements of the offense. See Simmons v. United States, 390 U.S. 377 (1968). A defendant's suppression motion statements, however, may be admissible for impeachment if the defendant testifies. See Note 7, page 1340 infra.

Although practices vary, the suppression motion hearing is likely to be fairly formal and elaborate—although not quite as much so as the trial itself. An indication of the formality surrounding suppression motions is the body of law that has developed regarding standards and burdens of proof. For example, with respect to fourth amendment claims, most jurisdictions allocate the burden of proof differently depending on whether the search or seizure was made pursuant to a warrant: A defendant must initially produce evidence and ultimately persuade the factfinder of the illegality of a search made pursuant to a warrant; the prosecutor bears both the production burden and the persuasion burden with respect to warrantless searches and seizures. See, e.g., United States v. Impson, 482 F.2d 197 (5th Cir. 1973).[1] The burden of proving that a defendant validly consented to a search rests with the prosecutor. See Schneckloth v. Bustamonte, page 829 supra. Similarly, the prosecutor must prove

---

1. Some jurisdictions distinguish between the production and the persuasion burdens, and some place both burdens on either the prosecutor or the defendant without regard to whether the search is made pursuant to a warrant. See 3 W. LaFave, Search and Seizure: A Treatise on the Fourth Amendment §11.2(b), pp. 217-233 (2d ed. 1978).

the validity of a *Miranda* waiver, see Miranda v. Arizona, page 1105 supra, or a waiver of a defendant's right to counsel at a lineup. See United States v. Wade, page 339 supra. The burden of proving the voluntariness of a confession probably rests with the prosecutor. See Lego v. Twomey, 404 U.S. 477 (1972).

For most issues on which the prosecution has the burden of persuasion, the standard of proof is a preponderance of the evidence. In Lego v. Twomey, supra, the Supreme Court rejected the defendant's constitutional claim that the prosecutor should be required to prove the voluntariness of a confession beyond a reasonable doubt and held that a preponderance standard was sufficient.[2] Given the importance that the Court traditionally has attached to the question of voluntariness, see, e.g., page 1350 infra (involuntary confession never harmless error), it seems likely that a higher standard of proof seldom would be constitutionally mandated for other suppression motion issues. See, e.g., Colorado v. Connelly, 479 U.S. 157 (1986) (prosecutor must prove *Miranda* waiver by preponderance of the evidence). But cf. United States v. Wade, page 339 supra (if pretrial identification obtained in violation of defendant's right to counsel, prosecution must establish independent source for in-court identification by clear and convincing evidence), discussed in Nix v. Williams, page 1360 n.5 infra. Courts could, however, impose higher nonconstitutional standards of proof.

Is the standard of proof or the allocation of the burden of proof likely to have a significant impact on the outcome of suppression motions or the planning of litigation strategy generally? See A. Amsterdam, B. Segal & M. Miller, Trial Manual for the Defense of Criminal Cases §252 (3d ed. 1974). To the extent that the standard of proof and its allocation are important, what factors should inform decisions about these matters? See Saltzburg, Standards of Proof and Preliminary Questions of Fact, 27 Stan. L. Rev. 271 (1975).

2. Prior to *Lego*, the Court in Jackson v. Denno, 378 U.S. 368 (1964), held that a defendant has the constitutional right to a clearcut determination of voluntariness by the trial judge. Thus, *Jackson* disapproved the practice that had existed in some jurisdictions of admitting into evidence an allegedly involuntary confession with instructions for the jury to make the voluntariness determination and to disregard the statement if they found it to be involuntary.

Lego involved two issues: The standard of proof and the question whether, in the event the judge determines that the confession is voluntary, the defendant is entitled to have the jury reevaluate the voluntariness determination. *Lego* held that the defendant has no such constitutional right. Some states, however, continue to follow the practice of giving the defendant a second chance on the voluntariness question. Do you think such a practice is desirable?

Even though the defendant has no constitutional right to have the jury reevaluate the judge's determination that a confession is voluntary, the defendant does have the right to introduce evidence of the atmosphere surrounding the confession in order to attack its veracity. Crane v. Kentucky, 476 U.S. 683 (1986).

There are two principal ways in which suppression motion hearings tend to be less elaborate and less formal than trials:

First, there may be some restrictions on the defendant's opportunity to confront and cross-examine witnesses at the suppression hearing. For example, concern with maintaining the confidentiality of government informants and with preventing the defendant from turning the suppression hearing into a general discovery device may lead to restrictions on cross-examination or to the inspection of some evidence by the judge in camera. See, e.g., United States v. Bell, 464 F.2d 667 (2d Cir. 1972) (defendant—but not defense counsel—properly excluded during presentation of evidence of secret highjacker detection profile).

Second, the rules of evidence may not be applied with as much rigor, if at all, during the suppression hearing. In United States v. Matlock, 415 U.S. 164 (1974), the Supreme Court observed that "the rules of evidence normally applicable in criminal trials do not operate with full force at a hearing before the judge to determine the admissibility of evidence." See Fed. R. Evid. 104(a) (rules of evidence not applicable to determination of preliminary facts regarding admissibility of evidence). In some courts, however, the practice is to adhere fairly closely to the rules of evidence.

If a defendant does not prevail at the suppression hearing, it will be necessary in a few jurisdictions to renew the objection at trial in order to preserve the suppression issue for appeal. In addition, a defendant, even if not required to do so, may renew the suppression request at trial in the hope of getting a favorable ruling from the trial judge, who may not have presided at the suppression hearing. As a practical matter, however, the suppression hearing determination—regardless of who wins—is likely to be binding at trial. Although many jurisdictions grant the trial judge discretion to reconsider the suppression motion decision, such reconsideration is unlikely unless the party seeking reconsideration produces new—and perhaps substantial—evidence. See generally 3 W. LaFave, supra, at §11.2(f), pp. 255-261.

Except for whatever opportunities may exist for renewal of the suppression motion at trial or for direct appeal or state postconviction relief, the decision of the judge at the suppression hearing is likely to be conclusive. In Stone v. Powell, 428 U.S. 465 (1976), the Supreme Court held that federal courts would not entertain a habeas corpus petition alleging a fourth amendment violation if the petitioner had had a full and fair opportunity to litigate the fourth amendment issue in the state courts. Subsequently in Allen v. McCurry, 449 U.S. 90 (1980), a criminal defendant, after losing a suppression motion, filed a §1983 civil rights action alleging a violation of his fourth amendment rights. He argued that because of Stone v. Powell, his §1983 action was the only means available to vindicate a federal right in a federal forum and, therefore, that he should not be precluded from relitigating the fourth amendment issue. The Supreme Court disagreed and held that the un-availability of federal habeas corpus relief did not render "the doctrine of collateral estoppel inapplicable to his §1983 suit." 449 U.S. at 105.[3] At the same time, the Court reiterated the traditional requirement that a person cannot be collaterally estopped from relitigating an issue without initially having had a full and fair opportunity to litigate the issue. Given the relaxation of evidentiary rules and occasional restrictions on cross-examination at suppression hearings, under what circumstances should it be appropriate to regard an individual—for collateral estoppel pur-poses—as having had a full and fair opportunity to litigate a fourth amendment issue? Should the substance of the "full and fair opportunity" requirement be the same for collateral estoppel purposes as for deter-mining whether an individual can pursue a fourth amendment claim on federal habeas corpus?

B. IMPEACHMENT WITH UNCONSTITUTIONALLY OBTAINED EVIDENCE

WALDER v. UNITED STATES
Certiorari to the United States Court of Appeals for the Eighth Circuit
347 U.S. 62 (1954)

MR. JUSTICE FRANKFURTER delivered the opinion of the Court.

In May 1950, petitioner was indicted . . . for purchasing and pos-sessing one grain of heroin. Claiming that the heroin capsule had been obtained through an unlawful search and seizure, petitioner moved to suppress it. The motion was granted, and shortly thereafter, on the Gov-ernment's motion, the case against petitioner was dismissed.

In January of 1952, petitioner was again indicted, this time for four other illicit transactions in narcotics. The Government's case consisted principally of the testimony of two drug addicts who claimed to have procured the illicit stuff from petitioner under the direction of federal

---

3. Cf. Haring v. Prosise, 462 U.S. 306 (1983) (§1983 plaintiff who pled guilty in state court without challenging allegedly illegal search would not be precluded by state from litigating fourth amendment issue in subsequent suit and no independent federal interest bars litigation of the federal claim; district court erred in granting summary judgment to §1983 defendant on ground that prior guilty plea barred §1983 claim).

agents. The only witness for the defense was the defendant himself, petitioner here. He denied any narcotics dealings with the two Government informers and attributed the testimony against him to personal hostility.

Early on his direct examination petitioner testified as follows:

> Q: Now, first, Mr. Walder, before we go further in your testimony, I want to you [sic] tell the Court and jury whether, not referring to these informers in this case, but whether you have ever sold any narcotics to anyone.
>
> A: I have never sold any narcotics to anyone in my life.
>
> Q: Have you ever had any narcotics in your possession, other than what may have been given to you by a physician for an ailment?
>
> A: No.
>
> Q: Now, I will ask you one more thing. Have you ever handed or given any narcotics to anyone as a gift or in any other manner without the receipt of any money or any other compensation?
>
> A: I have not.
>
> Q: Have you ever even acted as, say, have you acted as a conduit for the purpose of handling what you knew to be a narcotic from one person to another?
>
> A: No, sir.

On cross-examination, in response to a question by Government counsel making reference to this direct testimony, petitioner reiterated his assertion that he had never purchased, sold or possessed any narcotics. Over the defendant's objection, the Government then questioned him about the heroin capsule unlawfully seized from his home in his presence back in February 1950. The defendant stoutly denied that any narcotics were taken from him at that time.[1] The Government then put on the stand one of the officers who had participated in the unlawful search and seizure and also the chemist who had analyzed the heroin capsule there seized. The trial judge admitted this evidence, but carefully charged the jury that it was not to be used to determine whether the defendant had committed the crimes here charged, but solely for the purpose of impeaching the defendant's credibility. The defendant was convicted, and the Court of Appeals for the Eighth Circuit affirmed. . . . The . . . sole issue here, is whether the defendant's assertion on direct examination that he had never possessed any narcotics opened the door, solely for the purpose of attacking the defendant's credibility, to evidence of the heroin unlawfully seized in connection with the earlier proceeding. . . .

---

1. This denial squarely contradicted the affidavit filed by the defendant in the earlier proceeding, in connection with his motion under Rule 41(e) to suppress the evidence unlawfully seized.

The Government cannot violate the Fourth Amendment . . . and use the fruits of such unlawful conduct to secure a conviction. . . . Nor can the Government make indirect use of such evidence for its case, . . . or support a conviction on evidence obtained through leads from the unlawfully obtained evidence. . . . All these methods are outlawed, and convictions obtained by means of them are invalidated, because they encourage the kind of society that is obnoxious to free men.

It is one thing to say that the Government cannot make an affirmative use of evidence unlawfully obtained. It is quite another to say that the defendant can turn the illegal method by which evidence in the Government's possession was obtained to his own advantage, and provide himself with a shield against contradiction of his untruths. Such an extension of the [exclusionary rule] would be a perversion of the Fourth Amendment.

Take the present situation. Of his own accord, the defendant went beyond a mere denial of complicity in the crimes of which he was charged and made the sweeping claim that he had never dealt in or possessed any narcotics. Of course, the Constitution guarantees a defendant the fullest opportunity to meet the accusation against him. He must be free to deny all the elements of the case against him without thereby giving leave to the Government to introduce by way of rebuttal evidence illegally secured by it, and therefore not available for its case in chief. Beyond that, however, there is hardly justification for letting the defendant affirmatively resort to perjurious testimony in reliance on the Government's disability to challenge his credibility.[3]

The situation here involved is to be sharply contrasted with that presented by Agnello v. United States, 269 U.S. 20. There the Government, after having failed in its efforts to introduce the tainted evidence in its case in chief, tried to smuggle it in on cross-examination by asking the accused the broad question "Did you ever see narcotics before?"[4] After eliciting the expected denial, it sought to introduce evidence of narcotics located in the defendant's home by means of an unlawful search and seizure, in order to discredit the defendant. In holding that the Government could no more work in this evidence on cross-examination

---

3. Cf. Michelson v. United States, 335 U.S. 469, 479: "The price a defendant must pay for attempting to prove his good name is to throw open the entire subject which the law has kept closed for his benefit and to make himself vulnerable where the law otherwise shields him."

The underlying rationale of the Michelson case also disposes of the evidentiary question raised by petitioner, to wit, "whether defendant's actual guilt under a former indictment which was dismissed may be proved by extrinsic evidence introduced to impeach him in a prosecution for a subsequent offense."

4. Transcript of Record, p.476, Agnello v. United States, 269 U.S. 20.

than it could in its case in chief, the Court foreshadowed, perhaps unwittingly, the result we reach today:

> And the contention that the evidence of the search and seizure was ad-
> missible in rebuttal is without merit. In his direct examination, Agnello
> was not asked and did not testify concerning the can of cocaine. In cross-
> examination, in answer to a question permitted over his objection, he said
> he had never seen it. He did nothing to waive his constitutional protection
> or to justify cross-examination in respect of the evidence claimed to have
> been obtained by the search. . . . [269 U.S., at 35.]

The judgment is affirmed.

MR. JUSTICE BLACK and MR. JUSTICE DOUGLAS dissent.

HARRIS v. NEW YORK

Certiorari to the Court of Appeals of New York
401 U.S. 222 (1971)

MR. CHIEF JUSTICE BURGER delivered the opinion of the Court.

We granted the writ in this case to consider petitioner's claim that
a statement made by him to police under circumstances rendering it
inadmissible to establish the prosecution's case in chief under Miranda
v. Arizona, 384 U.S. 436 (1966), may not be used to impeach his
credibility.

The State of New York charged petitioner in a two-count indictment
with twice selling heroin to an undercover police officer. At a subsequent
jury trial the officer was the State's chief witness, and he testified as to
details of the two sales. A second officer verified collateral details of the
sales, and a third offered testimony about the chemical analysis of the
heroin.

Petitioner took the stand in his own defense. He admitted knowing
the undercover police officer but denied a sale on January 4, 1966. He
admitted making a sale of contents of a glassine bag to the officer on
January 6 but claimed it was baking powder and part of a scheme to
defraud the purchaser.

On cross-examination petitioner was asked seriatim whether he had
made specified statements to the police immediately following his arrest
on January 7—statements that partially contradicted petitioner's direct
testimony at trial. In response to the cross-examination, petitioner testified
that he could not remember virtually any of the questions or answers
recited by the prosecutor. At the request of petitioner's counsel the written
statement from which the prosecutor had read questions and answers in

his impeaching process was placed in the record for possible use on appeal; the statement was not shown to the jury.

The trial judge instructed the jury that the statements attributed to petitioner by the prosecution could be considered only in passing on petitioner's credibility and not as evidence of guilt. In closing summations both counsel argued the substance of the impeaching statements. The jury then found petitioner guilty on the second count of the indictment. . . .

At trial the prosecution made no effort in its case in chief to use the statements allegedly made by petitioner, conceding that they were inadmissible under Miranda v. Arizona, 384 U.S. 436 (1966). . . . Petitioner makes no claim that the statements made to the police were coerced or involuntary.

Some comments in the *Miranda* opinion can indeed be read as indicating a bar to use of an uncounseled statement for any purpose, but discussion of that issue was not at all necessary to the Court's holding and cannot be regarded as controlling. . . .

In Walder v. United States, 347 U.S. 62 (1954), the Court permitted physical evidence, inadmissible in the case in chief, to be used for impeachment purposes.

> It is one thing to say that the Government cannot make an affirmative use of evidence unlawfully obtained. It is quite another to say that the defendant can turn the illegal method by which evidence in the Government's possession was obtained to his own advantage, and provide himself with a shield against contradiction of his untruths. Such an extension of the *Weeks* doctrine would be a perversion of the Fourth Amendment.
>
> [T]here is hardly justification for letting the defendant affirmatively resort to perjurious testimony in reliance on the Government's disability to challenge his credibility. [347 U.S., at 65.]

It is true that Walder was impeached as to collateral matters included in his direct examination, whereas petitioner here was impeached as to testimony bearing more directly on the crimes charged. We are not persuaded that there is a difference in principle that warrants a result different from that reached by the Court in *Walder*. Petitioner's testimony in his own behalf concerning the events of January 7 contrasted sharply with what he told the police shortly after his arrest. The impeachment process here undoubtedly provided valuable aid to the jury in assessing petitioner's credibility, and the benefits of this process should not be lost, in our view, because of the speculative possibility that impermissible police conduct will be encouraged thereby. Assuming that the exclusionary rule has a deterrent effect on proscribed police conduct, sufficient deterrence flows when the evidence in question is made unavailable to the prosecution in its case in chief.

Every criminal defendant is privileged to testify in his own defense, or to refuse to do so. But that privilege cannot be construed to include the right to commit perjury. . . . Having voluntarily taken the stand, petitioner was under an obligation to speak truthfully and accurately, and the prosecution here did no more than utilize the traditional truth-testing devices of the adversary process. . . .

The shield provided by *Miranda* cannot be perverted into a license to use perjury by way of a defense, free from the risk of confrontation with prior inconsistent utterances. We hold, therefore, that petitioner's credibility was appropriately impeached by use of his earlier conflicting statements.

Affirmed.

[JUSTICE BLACK dissented without an opinion. The dissenting opinion of JUSTICE BRENNAN, joined by JUSTICES DOUGLAS and MARSHALL, is omitted.]

NOTES AND QUESTIONS

1. In both *Walder* and *Harris*, what precisely is the theoretical or logical difference between using the evidence only to impeach the defendant's credibility and using the evidence to establish the substantive elements of an offense? Is the jury, even with detailed limiting instructions, likely to be able to grasp the difference? Did the Court in *Harris* grasp the difference?

The illegally obtained "impeaching" evidence in *Harris* was a prior inconsistent statement, and according to the rules of evidence such a prior statement is not admissible for its truth. Rather, the impeachment comes from the fact of inconsistency without regard to the truth of either the prior statement or the in-court testimony. Note, however, that the *Harris* Court justified the admissibility of the prior statement primarily on the ground that a defendant should not be permitted to subvert *Miranda* into a license to commit perjury. This justification appears to rest on the premise that Harris's in-court testimony was false, which in turn necessarily implies that the prior inconsistent statement was true. If it is the truth of the prior statement about the defendant's involvement in the charged crime that's important, is it meaningful to speak of the prior statement as being used only to impeach the defendant's credibility? In any event, once the *Walder/Harris* criteria for admissibility are satisfied, what, if any, purpose is served by taking the position that the factfinder can consider the evidence only for its impeachment value?

2. The illegally obtained impeachment evidence in *Walder* dealt with a transaction that was wholly separate from the crime for which the defendant was being tried. By contrast, the statements obtained from Harris in violation of *Miranda* concerned the very crimes with which Harris was charged. The *Harris* Court, however, did not believe that this difference was significant. Would the *Walder* Court have agreed? Consider carefully the quotation from *Walder* in *Harris*, and compare that quotation, which was edited by the *Harris* Court, with the unedited penultimate paragraph of *Walder*.

Why, in the words of *Walder*, should a defendant "be free to deny [even falsely] all the elements of the case against him without thereby giving leave to the government to introduce by way of rebuttal evidence illegally secured by it, and therefore not available for its case in chief"? Even if a defendant should be free to deny all elements of a charge by pleading not guilty and thereby putting the government to its proof, does it follow that a defendant should be equally free to offer false exculpatory evidence in a trial?

3. Do you agree with the *Harris* Court that the deterrent value of *Miranda* will be adequately served by making statements taken in violation of *Miranda* unavailable to the prosecution only in its case-in-chief? Given *Harris*, what incentive exists for the police to comply with *Miranda*? Even if there remains some incentive initially to give proper *Miranda* warnings and to obtain a valid waiver, is there any incentive to honor the request of a defendant who attempts to invoke *Miranda* in order to stop police interrogation? See Oregon v. Hass, 420 U.S. 714 (1975) (after properly warned defendant requested counsel, police, in violation of *Miranda*, continued to question defendant; statements made by defendant during illegal questioning admissible to impeach defendant's trial testimony). Can the collateral matter limitation in *Walder* be justified as a viable means of preserving the deterrent value of the exclusionary rule?

4. Note that the Court in *Harris* asserted that there was no claim that the statements obtained from the defendant were coerced or involuntary.[4] In Mincey v. Arizona, 437 U.S. 385 (1978), the Court observed that "*any* criminal trial use against a defendant of his *involuntary* statement is a denial of due process" (emphasis in original). Why should an involuntary statement, at least if there is no reason to question its reliability, be treated differently from a voluntary statement obtained in violation of *Miranda*? Is an involuntary statement inherently unreliable?

---

4. This assertion may not be accurate. For a stinging criticism of both the Court's characterization of the record in *Harris* and the Court's analysis, see Dershowitz & Ely, Harris v. New York: Some Anxious Observations on the Candor and Logic of the Emerging Nixon Majority, 80 Yale L.J. 1198 (1971).

Is the nature of police conduct that leads to an involuntariness finding inevitably more outrageous and unacceptable than police conduct that violates *Miranda?*

5. Reconsider New Jersey v. Portash, page 1000 supra, in which the Supreme Court held that a defendant's grand jury testimony given after a grant of immunity could not be used to impeach the defendant at his trial for extortion and misconduct in office. The Court distinguished *Harris* and *Hass* on the ground that in those cases the defendants did not claim that their statements were coerced or involuntary. By contrast, according to the *Portash* Court, "Testimony given in response to a grant of legislative immunity is the essence of coerced testimony. . . . Here . . . we deal with the constitutional privilege against compulsory self-incrimination in its most pristine form." 440 U.S. at 459.

How can one reconcile *Harris* and *Portash?*

6. Should statements obtained in violation of a defendant's sixth amendment right to counsel be admissible to impeach the defendant's credibility? Should the answer depend on the nature of the sixth amendment violation? See Michigan v. Harvey, 110 S. Ct. 1176 (1990), where the Court upheld the admissibility for impeachment purposes of a statement obtained in violation of Michigan v. Jackson, page 1270 supra. After discussing *Harris*, the *Harvey* Court observed:

> There is no reason for a different result in a *Jackson* case, *where the prophylactic rule is designed to ensure voluntary, knowing, and intelligent waivers* of the Sixth Amendment right to counsel rather than the Fifth Amendment privilege against self-incrimination or "right to counsel." . . . We have never prevented use by the prosecution of relevant voluntary statements by a defendant, *particularly when the violations alleged by a defendant relate only to procedural safeguards that are"not themselves rights protected by the Constitution,"* [Michigan v.] Tucker, [417 U.S. 433,] 444 [(1974)], but are instead measures designed to ensure that constitutional rights are protected. [110 S. Ct. at 1081 (emphasis added).]

7. In Simmons v. United States, 390 U.S. 377 (1968), the defendant, in order to establish fourth amendment standing, admitted during a suppression hearing that certain seized items belonged to him. The Supreme Court held that the defendant's suppression motion statements could not be used by the prosecutor as evidence of the defendant's guilt. Could a defendant's suppression motion statements be admitted for impeachment purposes? Are statements made at a suppression hearing more like statements made to a grand jury after a grant of immunity or more like statements made to the police? Is it as probable in the suppression hearing context as the Court thought it was in *Harris* that the earlier

statement is true and the trial testimony false? Is the argument for admissibility stronger in the suppression hearing context then in *Harris* simply because there is no direct violation of the fifth amendment? See People v. Sturgis, 58 Ill. 2d 211, 317 N.E.2d 545 (1974) (defendant's suppression motions statements admissible to impeach his trial testimony).

8.   In Doyle v. Ohio, 426 U.S. 610 (1976), two defendants charged with sale of marijuana testified at trial that they had been framed by the government informant who had allegedly made the purchase. On cross-examination each defendant was questioned about why he didn't give his exculpatory story to the police at the time of arrest. Before the Supreme Court the state attempted to justify this line of questioning on the theory that the defendants' postarrest silence was inconsistent with their trial testimony and, thus, admissible to impeach their credibility. The Supreme Court disagreed and held that the impeachment use of the defendants' postarrest silence following *Miranda* warnings violated their right to due process:

> Silence in the wake of these warnings may be nothing more than an arrestee's exercise of these *Miranda* rights. Thus, every post-arrest silence is insolubly ambiguous because of what the State is required to advise the person arrested. . . . Moreover, while it is true that the *Miranda* warnings contain no express assurance that silence will carry no penalty, such assurance is implicit to any person who receives the warnings. In such circumstances, it would be fundamentally unfair . . . to allow the arrested person's silence to be used to impeach an explanation subsequently offered at trial. [Id. at 617-618.]

The Court recently reaffirmed *Doyle* and stressed the unfairness of using a defendant's post-*Miranda*-warning silence against him. Wainwright v. Greenfield, 474 U.S. 284 (1986) (arrest and *Miranda* warnings within several hours of charged crime, sexual assault; improper to use postwarning silence to rebut defendant's defense of insanity; dictum that it would be permissible to use evidence of defendant's rational discourse). In other cases, however, the Court has tended to interpret and apply *Doyle* narrowly rather than expansively. Thus, in Jenkins v. Anderson, 447 U.S. 231 (1980), where a murder defendant testified at trial that the killing was in self-defense, the Court found no constitutional barrier to questions on cross-examination about why the defendant had remained silent and not reported the matter to the police during the two weeks between the killing and the time that he turned himself in to the authorities. According to the Court, "In this case, no governmental action induced petitioner to remain silent before arrest. The failure to speak occurred before the petitioner was taken into custody and given *Miranda* warnings. Consequently, the fundamental unfairness present in *Doyle* is not present in this case." Id. at 240. In a dissenting opinion Justice Marshall, joined by Justice Brennan, maintained:

> [T]he mere fact of prearrest silence is so unlikely to be probative of the falsity of the defendant's trial testimony that its use for impeachment purposes is contrary to . . . Due Process. . . .
>
> In order for petitioner to offer his explanation of self-defense, he would necessarily have had to admit that it was he who fatally stabbed the victim, thereby supplying against himself the strongest possible proof of an essential element of criminal homicide. It is hard to imagine a purer case of self-incrimination. Since we cannot assume that in the absence of official warnings individuals are ignorant of or oblivious to their constitutional rights, we must recognize that petitioner may have acted in reliance on the constitutional guarantee. In fact, petitioner had most likely been in-formed previously of his privilege against self-incrimination, since he had two prior felony convictions. . . . One who has at least twice before been given the *Miranda* warnings, which carry the implied promise that silence will not be penalized by use for impeachment purposes, . . . may well remember the rights of which he has been informed, and believe that the promise is still in force. Accordingly, the inference that petitioner's conduct was inconsistent with his exculpatory trial testimony is precluded. [Id. at 246-247.[5]]

If, as the dissent maintains, a defendant's prearrest silence is so inherently ambiguous, what harm is there in letting the jury hear about the silence? Will it not be easy for defense counsel to point out the ambiguity to the jury?

If, as *Jenkins* suggests, the key to *Doyle* is the *Miranda* warning about the defendant's right to silence, would it be constitutionally per-missible and desirable to modify *Miranda* by including in the warning a statement that postwarning silence could be used for impeachment purposes?

For other cases interpreting *Doyle* narrowly, see Greer v. Miller, 483 U.S. 756 (1987) (essence of *Doyle* violation is *use* of post-*Miranda*-warning silence; where objection to prosecutor's single question about

---

5. With Justices Marshall and Brennan dissenting, the Court also rejected the argument that use of the defendant's prearrest silence would induce persons to talk and thereby impermissibly burden the fifth amendment right to remain silent. The Court did not specifically address another point raised by the dissenters, namely that permitting impeachment with prearrest silences would impermissibly burden a defendant's right to testify at trial. For a criticism of the Court's fifth amendment analysis, see Saltzburg, Forward: The Flow and Ebb of Constitutional Criminal Procedure iii the Warren and Burger Courts, 69 Geo. L.J. 151, 204-205 (1980).

postwarning silence was sustained and jury was twice warned to ignore question, no *Doyle* violation took place); Fletcher v. Weir, 455 U.S. 603 (1982) (per curiam) (impeachment with postarrest silence permissible where record does not indicate that *Miranda* warnings had been given to defendant); Anderson v. Charles, 447 U.S. 404 (1980) (per curiam) (*Doyle* not violated by defendant's cross-examination that included not only questions about prior inconsistent statement to police but also questions about why defendant did not initially tell police what he testified to at trial; cross-examination viewed in its totality was legitimate effort to elicit explanation for inconsistency). See also South Dakota v. Neville, 459 U.S. 553 (1983) (evidence of refusal to take blood-alcohol test admissible to show defendant guilty of drunk driving; warning given to defendant at time of refusal to take test contained no reference to possible evidentiary use of refusal and thus did not constitute implicit promise to forego use of evidence. See Poulin, Evidentiary Use of Silence and the Constitutional Privilege Against Self-Incrimination, 52 Geo. Wash. L. Rev. 191 (1984).

9. In all of the preceding cases in which the prosecutor was permitted to use a defendant's prior statement or silence for impeachment, the apparent inconsistency existed between the prior statement or silence and the defendant's *direct* examination testimony. Should it make any difference whether the apparent inconsistency comes to light on cross-examination rather than direct examination? Consider the following case.

UNITED STATES v. HAVENS

Certiorari to the United States Court of Appeals for the Fifth Circuit
446 U.S. 620 (1980)

MR. JUSTICE WHITE delivered the opinion of the Court.

The petition for certiorari filed by the United States in this criminal case presented a single question: whether evidence suppressed as the fruit of an unlawful search and seizure may nevertheless be used to impeach a defendant's false trial testimony, given in response to proper cross-examination, where the evidence does not squarely contradict the defendant's testimony on direct examination. . . .

Respondent was convicted of importing, conspiring to import, and intentionally possessing a controlled substance, cocaine. According to the evidence at his trial, Havens and John McLeroth, both attorneys from Ft. Wayne, Ind., boarded a flight from Lima, Peru, to Miami, Fla. In Miami, a customs officer searched McLeroth and found cocaine sewed into makeshift pockets in a T-shirt he was wearing under his outer clothing. McLeroth implicated respondent, who had previously cleared customs and who was then arrested. His luggage was seized and searched without a warrant. The officers found no drugs but seized a T-shirt from which pieces had been cut that matched the pieces that had been sewn to McLeroth's T-shirt. The T-shirt and other evidence seized in the course of the search were suppressed on motion prior to trial.

Both men were charged in a three-count indictment, but McLeroth pleaded guilty to one count and testified against Havens. Among other things, he asserted that Havens had supplied him with the altered T-shirt and had sewed the makeshift pockets shut. Havens took the stand in his own defense and denied involvement in smuggling cocaine. His direct testimony included the following:

> Q: And you heard Mr. McLeroth testify earlier as to something to the effect that this material was taped or draped around his body and so on, you heard that testimony?
> A: Yes, I did.
> Q: Did you ever engage in that kind of activity with Mr. McLeroth and Augusto or Mr. McLeroth and anyone else on that fourth visit to Lima, Peru?
> A: I did not. [App. 34.]

On cross-examination, Havens testified as follows:

> Q: Now, on direct examination, sir, you testified that on the fourth trip you had absolutely nothing to do with the wrapping of any bandages or tee shirts or anything involving Mr. McLeroth; it that correct?
> A: I don't—I said I had nothing to do with any wrapping or bandages or anything, yes. I had nothing to do with anything with McLeroth in connection with this cocaine matter. . . .
> Q: And your testimony is that you had nothing to do with the sewing of the cotton swatches to make pockets on that tee shirt?
> A: Absolutely not. . . .
> Q: On that day, sir, did you have in your luggage a Size 38-40 medium man's tee shirt with swatches of clothing missing from the tail of that tee shirt?
> A: Not to my knowledge. . . .
> Q: Mr. Havens, I'm going to hand you what is Government's Exhibit 9 for identification and ask you if this tee shirt was in your luggage on October 2nd, 1975 [sic]?
> A: Not to my knowledge. No. [Id., at 46.]

Respondent Havens also denied having told a Government agent that the T-shirts found in his luggage belonged to McLeroth.

On rebuttal, a Government agent testified that Exhibit 9 had been found in respondent's suitcase and that Havens claimed the T-shirts found in his bag, including Exhibit 9, belonged to McLeroth. Over objection, the T-shirt was then admitted into evidence, the jury being instructed that the rebuttal evidence should be considered only for impeaching Havens' credibility.

The Court of Appeals reversed, relying on Agnello v. United States, 269 U.S. 20 (1925), and Walder v. United States, 347 U.S. 62 (1954). . . .

These cases were understood by the Court of Appeals to hold that tainted evidence, inadmissible when offered as part of the Government's main case, may not be used as rebuttal evidence to impeach a defendant's credibility unless the evidence is offered to contradict a particular statement made by a defendant during his direct examination; a statement made for the first time on cross-examination may not be so impeached. This approach required the exclusion of the T-shirt taken from Haven's luggage because, as the Court of Appeals read the record, Havens was asked nothing on his direct testimony about the incriminating T-shirt or about the contents of his luggage; the testimony about the T-shirt, which the Government desired to impeach first appeared on cross-examination, not on direct.

. . . In our view . . . a flat rule permitting only statements on direct examination to be impeached misapprehends the underlying rationale of *Walder*. . . . Furthermore, in *Walder*, the Court said that in *Agnello*, the Government had "smuggled in" the impeaching opportunity in the course of cross-examination. . . . The implication of *Walder* is that *Agnello* was a case of cross-examination having too tenuous a connection with any subject opened upon direct examination to permit impeachment by tainted evidence.

In reversing the District Court in the case before us, the Court of Appeals did not stop to consider how closely the cross-examination about the T-shirt and the luggage was connected with matters gone into in direct examination. If these questions would have been suggested to a reasonably competent cross-examiner by Havens' direct testimony, they were not "smuggled in"; and forbidding the Government to impeach the answers to these questions by using contrary and reliable evidence in its possession fails to take account of our cases, particularly Harris [v. New York, page 1336 supra,] and [Oregon v.] Hass[, page 1339 supra]. In both cases, the Court stressed the importance of arriving at the truth in criminal trials, as well as the defendant's obligation to speak the truth in response to proper questions. . . . Both cases also held that the deterrent function of the rules excluding unconstitutionally obtained evidence is sufficiently served by denying its use to the government on its direct case. . . .

Neither *Harris* nor *Hass* involved the impeachment of assertedly false testimony first given on cross-examination, but the reasoning of those cases controls this one. There is no gainsaying that arriving at the truth is a fundamental goal of our legal system. . . . We have repeatedly insisted that when defendants testify, they must testify truthfully or suffer the consequences. . . . It is essential, therefore, to the proper functioning of the adversary system that when a defendant takes the stand, the government be permitted proper and effective cross-examination in an attempt to elicit the truth. The defendant's obligation to testify truthfully is fully binding on him when he is cross-examined. His privilege against self-incrimination does not shield him from proper questioning. . . . He would unquestionably be subject to a perjury prosecution if he knowingly lies on cross-examination. . . . In terms of impeaching a defendant's seemingly false statements with his prior inconsistent utterances or with other reliable evidence available to the government, we see no difference of constitutional magnitude between the defendant's statements on direct examination and his answers to questions put to him on cross-examination that are plainly within the scope of the defendant's direct examination. Without this opportunity, the normal function of cross-examination would be severely impeded.

We also think that the policies of the exclusionary rule no more bar impeachment here than they did in *Walder, Harris,* and *Hass.* In those cases, the ends of the exclusionary rules were thought adequately implemented by denying the government the use of the challenged evidence to make out its case in chief. The incremental furthering of those ends by forbidding impeachment of the defendant who testifies was deemed insufficient to permit or require that false testimony go unchallenged, with the resulting impairment of the integrity of the factfinding goals of the criminal trial. We reaffirm this assessment of the competing interests, and hold that a defendant's statements made in response to proper cross-examination reasonably suggested by the defendant's direct examination are subject to otherwise proper impeachment by the government, albeit by evidence that has been illegally obtained and that is inadmissible on the government's direct case, or otherwise, as substantive evidence of guilt.

. . . [W]e do not understand the District Court to have indicated that the Government's question, the answer to which is sought to be impeached, need not be proper cross-examination in the first instance. The Court of Appeals did not suggest that either the cross-examination or the impeachment of Havens would have been improper absent the use of illegally seized evidence, and we cannot accept respondent's suggestions that because of the illegal search and seizure, the Government's questions about the T-shirt were improper cross-examination. McLeroth testified that Havens had assisted him in preparing the T-shirt for smuggling. Havens, in his direct testimony, acknowledged McLeroth's prior testimony that the cocaine "was taped or draped around his body and so on" but denied that he had "ever engage[d] in that kind of activity with Mr. McLeroth. . . ." This testimony could easily be understood as a denial of any connection with McLeroth's T-shirt and as a contradiction of McLeroth's testimony. Quite reasonably, it seems to us, the Government on cross-examination called attention to his answers on direct and then asked whether he had anything to do with sewing the cotton swatches on McLeroth's T-shirt. This was cross-examination growing out of Havens' direct testimony; and, as we hold above, the ensuing impeachment did not violate Havens' constitutional rights.

We reverse the judgment of the Court of Appeals and remand the case to that court for further proceedings consistent with this opinion. So ordered.

MR. JUSTICE BRENNAN, joined by MR. JUSTICE MARSHALL and joined in Part I by MR. JUSTICE STEWART and MR. JUSTICE STEVENS, dissenting.

I

The question before us is not of first impression. The identical issue was confronted in Agnello v. United States, 269 U.S. 20 (1925), which determined—contrary to the instant decision—that it was constitutionally impermissible to admit evidence obtained in violation of the Fourth Amendment to rebut a defendant's response to a matter first raised during the Government's cross-examination. . . .

. . . The cross-examination about Agnello's previous connection with cocaine was reasonably related to his direct testimony that he lacked knowledge that the commodity he was transporting was cocaine. 269 U.S., at 29-30. For "[t]he possession by Frank Agnello of the can of cocaine which was seized tended to show guilty knowledge and criminal intent on his part. . . ." Id., at 35. Thus, the constitutional flaw found in *Agnello* was that the introduction of the tainted evidence had been prompted by statements of the accused first elicited upon cross-examination. And the case was so read in Walder v. United States. That decision specifically stated that a defendant "must be free to deny all the elements of the case against him without thereby giving leave to the Government to introduce by way of rebuttal evidence illegally secured by it, and therefore not available for its case in chief." 347 U.S., at 65. Since as a matter of the law of evidence it would be perfectly permissible to cross-examine a defendant as to his denial of complicity in the crime, the quoted passage in *Walder* must be understood to impose a further condition before the prosecutor may refer to tainted evidence—that is, some particular direct testimony by the accused that relies upon "the Government's disability to challenge his credibility." Ibid.

In fact, the Court's current interpretation of *Agnello* and *Walder* simply trivializes those decisions by transforming their Fourth Amendment holdings into nothing more than a constitutional reflection of the common-law evidentiary rule of relevance.

. . . To be sure, the Court requires that cross-examination be "proper"; however, traditional evidentiary principles accord parties fairly considerable latitude in cross-examining opposing witnesses. See C. McCormick, Law of Evidence §§21-24 (2d ed. 1972). In practical terms, therefore, today's holding allows even the moderately talented prosecutor to "work in . . . evidence on cross-examination [as it would] in its case in chief. . . ." Walder v. United States, 347 U.S., at 66. To avoid this consequence, a defendant will be compelled to forgo testifying on his own behalf.

"[T]he Constitution guarantees a defendant the fullest opportunity to meet the accusation against him." Id., at 65. . . . Regrettably, surrender of that guarantee is the price the Court imposes for the defendant to claim his right not to be convicted on the basis of evidence obtained in violation of the Constitution.[2] I cannot agree that one constitutional privilege must be purchased at the expense of another.

II

The foregoing demonstration of its break with precedent provides a sufficient ground to condemn the present ruling—unleashing, as it does, a hitherto relatively confined exception to the exclusionary rule. But I have a more fundamental difference with the Court's holding here, which culminates the approach taken in Harris v. New York and Oregon v. Hass. For this sequence of decisions undercuts the constitutional canon that convictions cannot be procured by governmental lawbreaking. . . .

Of course, '[t]here is no gainsaying that arriving at the truth is a fundamental goal of our legal system." . . . But it is also undeniable that promotion of that objective must be consonant with other ends, in

---

2. Although evidence of prior inconsistent utterances or behavior may ostensibly be offered merely to attack a defendant's credibility by contradicting his trial testimony, such evidence can also serve to buttress the affirmative elements of the prosecution's case. Thus, almost anytime an accused takes the stand, the prosecution will have an opportunity to enhance its case in chief. And it is unrealistic to assume that limiting instructions will afford the defendant significant protection. Cf. Bruton v. United States, 391 U.S. 123 (1968).

particular those enshrined in our Constitution. . . . . [W]hat is important
is that the Constitution does not countenance police misbehavior, even
in the pursuit of truth. The processes of our judicial system may not be
fueled by the illegalities of government authorities. . . .

Nevertheless, the Court has undertaken to strike a "balance" between
the "policies" it finds in the Bill of Rights and the "competing interes[t]"
in accurate trial determinations. . . . This balancing effort is completely
freewheeling. Far from applying criteria intrinsic to the Fourth and Fifth
Amendments, the Court resolves succeeding cases simply by declaring
that so much exclusion is enough to deter police misconduct. . . . That
hardly conforms to the disciplined analytical method described as "legal
reasoning," through which judges endeavor to formulate or derive principles of decision that can be applied consistently and predictably.

Ultimately, I fear, this ad hoc approach to the exclusionary rule
obscures the difference between judicial decisionmaking and legislative
or administrative policymaking. More disturbingly, by treating Fourth
and Fifth Amendment privileges as mere incentive schemes, the Court
denigrates their unique status as *constitutional* protections. Yet efficacy
of the Bill of Rights as the bulwark of our national liberty depends precisely
upon public appreciation of the special character of constitutional prescriptions. The Court is charged with the responsibility to enforce constitutional guarantees; decisions such as today's patently disregard that
obligation.

Accordingly, I dissent.

NOTES AND QUESTIONS

1. Justice Brennan criticizes the majority's balancing of interests as
"freewheeling," inconsistent with "disciplined analytical method," and
"ad hoc." Regardless of whether you agree with the result in *Havens*, do
you believe that this criticism is legitimate? Is not the balancing of competing interests essential to sound constitutional decisionmaking? How
free is Justice Brennan's opinion from the criticisms he makes of the
majority opinion? Is *Havens* a significant departure from the Court's
earlier cases? See Spector & Foster, Swords, Shields, and the Quest for
Truth in the Trial Process: The Road From Constitutional Standards to
Evidentiary Havens, 33 Okla. L. Rev. 520 (1980).

2. If there is a problem with *Havens*, what precisely is it? Undermining of the exclusionary rule? Placing too great a burden on the defendant's right to testify at trial? See Bradley, *Havens, Jenkins, Salvucci,*
and the Defendant's "Right" to Testify, 18 Am. Crim. L. Rev. 419 (1981).
What would you propose doing to clarify or limit *Havens*?

3. All of the preceding cases involved efforts by the prosecutor to introduce unconstitutionally obtained evidence to impeach the credibility of a criminal defendant. In James v. Illinois, 110 S. Ct. 648 (1990), the Court refused to extend the impeachment exception to the exclusionary rule to the use of illegally obtained evidence to impeach the credibility of other defense witnesses. What justification is there for this limitation on the impeachment exception to the exclusionary rule?

C. HARMLESS CONSTITUTIONAL ERROR

The Supreme Court has consistently held that some constitutional violations require reversal of a conviction without regard to whether the error might be considered harmless. See Mincey v. Arizona, 437 U.S. 38 (1978) (reaffirming rule of automatic reversal for admission of involuntary or coerced confession); Gideon v. Wainwright, 372 U.S. 335 (1963) (right to counsel at trial); Tumey v. Ohio, 273 U.S. 510 (1927) (right to impartial judge).[6] See also Chapman v. California, 386 U.S. 18 (1967). For other constitutional violations, however, the Court has taken the position that reversal is appropriate only if the error is not harmless. See, e.g., Harrington v. California, page 1352 infra. The present harmless constitutional error standard—or at least one version of it—was first articulated in Fahy v. Connecticut, 375 U.S. 85 (1963), a case involving the admission of evidence obtained in violation of the fourth amendment. The Supreme Court found it unnecessary to decide whether a harmless error rule should apply to the admission of the evidence in Fahy because in its view the admission of the evidence was clearly prejudicial. In the course of explaining why the evidence was prejudicial, the Court characterized the harmless error standard in the following manner:

> We are not concerned . . . with whether there was sufficient evidence on which the petitioner could have been convicted without the evidence complained of. The question is whether there is a reasonable possibility that the evidence complained of might have contributed to the conviction. [Id. at 86-87.]

---

6. In Young v. United States ex rel. Vuitton et Fils S.A., 481 U.S. 787 (1987), the Supreme Court, relying on its supervisory power, held that it was error to appoint as a prosecutor in a criminal contempt proceeding counsel for an interested party in the underlying civil suit. The Court went on to hold that the error required automatic reversal.

In Chapman v. California, 386 U.S. 18 (1967), a case involving the prosecutor's violation of the defendant's fifth amendment right against self-incrimination by commenting on the defendant's failure to testify,[7] the Supreme Court asserted for the first time that some constitutional errors could be harmless. The Court held that the question of the appropriate harmless constitutional error standard was a federal question,[8] and then elaborated on the standard suggested previously in *Fahy*:

> All 50 States have harmless-error statutes or rules, and the United States long ago through its Congress established for its courts the rule that judgments shall not be reversed for "errors or defects which do not affect the substantial rights of the parties." 28 U.S.C. §2111. None of these rules on its face distinguishes between federal constitutional errors and errors of state law or federal statutes and rules. All of these rules, state or federal, serve a very useful purpose insofar as they block setting aside convictions for small errors or defects that have little, if any, likelihood of having changed the result of the trial. We conclude that there may be some constitutional errors which in the setting of a particular case are so unimportant and insignificant that they may, consistent with the Federal Constitution, be deemed harmless, not requiring the automatic reversal of the conviction. . . .
>
> In fashioning a harmless-constitutional-error rule, we must recognize that harmless-error rules can work very unfair and mischievous results when, for example, highly important and persuasive evidence, or argument, though legally forbidden, finds its way into a trial in which the question of guilt or innocence is a close one. What harmless-error rules all aim at is a rule that will save the good in harmless-error practices while avoiding the bad, so far as possible.
>
> The federal rule emphasizes "substantial rights" as do most others. The California constitutional rule emphasizes "a miscarriage of justice," but the California courts have neutralized this to some extent by emphasis, and perhaps overemphasis, upon the court's view of "overwhelming evidence." We prefer the approach of this Court in deciding what was harmless error in our recent case of Fahy v. Connecticut, 375 U.S. 85. There we said: "The question is whether there is a reasonable possibility that the

---

7. In Griffin v. California, 380 U.S. 609 (1965), the Court held that prosecutorial comment about a criminal defendant's failure to testify violates the defendant's fifth and fourteenth amendment right against self-incrimination.

8. In a dissenting opinion Justice Harlan maintained that the *validity* of a state harmless error rule was a federal question, but he did not believe there was a single mandated federal standard. 386 U.S. at 50. Rather, he would hold that "a state appellate court's reasonable application of a constitutionally proper state harmless-error rule to sustain a state conviction constitutes an independent and adequate state ground of judgment." Id., at 46. His review of the California cases led him to the conclusion that the state rule, although described in somewhat different language, was similar, if not identical, to the *Fahy* rule. Furthermore, he maintained that the state court's conclusion that the error was harmless was reasonable.

evidence complained of might have contributed to the conviction." Id., at 86-87. . . . An error in admitting plainly relevant evidence which possibly influenced the jury adversely to a litigant cannot, under *Fahy*, be conceived of as harmless. Certainly error, constitutional error, in illegally admitting highly prejudicial evidence or comments, casts on someone other than the person prejudiced by it a burden to show that it was harmless. It is for that reason that the original common-law harmless-error rule put the burden on the beneficiary of the error either to prove that there was no injury or to suffer a reversal of his erroneously obtained judgment. There is little, if any, difference between our statement in Fahy v. Connecticut about "whether there is a reasonable possibility that the evidence complained of might have contributed to the conviction" and requiring the beneficiary of a constitutional error to prove beyond a reasonable doubt that the error complained of did not contribute to the verdict obtained. We, therefore, do no more than adhere to the meaning of our *Fahy* case when we hold, as we now do, that before a federal constitutional error can be held harmless, the court must be able to declare a belief that it was harmless beyond a reasonable doubt. While appellate courts do not ordinarily have the original task of applying such a test, it is a familiar standard to all courts, and we believe its adoption will provide a more workable standard, although achieving the same result as that aimed at in our *Fahy* case. [386 U.S. at 22-24.]

The Court then examined the prosecutor's comments about the defendant's failure to testify and concluded that the error was not harmless. Id. at 25-26.

HARRINGTON v. CALIFORNIA

Certiorari to the Court of Appeals of California, Second Appellate District
395 U.S. 250 (1969)

MR. JUSTICE DOUGLAS delivered the opinion of the Court. . . .
The question whether the alleged error in the present case was "harmless" under the rule of *Chapman* arose in a state trial for attempted robbery and first-degree murder. Four men were tried together—Harrington, a Caucasian, and Bosby, Rhone, and Cooper, Negroes—over an objection by Harrington that his trial should be severed. Each of his three codefendants confessed and their confessions were introduced at the trial with limiting instructions that the jury was to consider each confession only against the confessor. Rhone took the stand and Harrington's counsel cross-examined him. The other two did not take the stand.[1]

1. All four were found to have participated in an attempted robbery in the course

In Bruton v. United States, 391 U.S. 123, a confession of a codefendant who did not take the stand was used against Bruton in a federal prosecution. We held that Bruton had been denied his rights under the Confrontation Clause of the Sixth Amendment. Since the Confrontation Clause is applicable as well in state trials by reason of the Due Process Clause of the Fourteenth Amendment (Pointer v. Texas, 380 U.S. 400), the rule of *Bruton* applies here. . . .

Petitioner made statements which fell short of a confession but which placed him at the scene of the crime. He admitted that Bosby was the trigger man; that he fled with the other three; and that after the murder he dyed his hair black and shaved off his moustache. Several eyewitnesses placed petitioner at the scene of the crime. But two of them had previously told the police that four Negroes committed the crime. Rhone's confession, however, placed Harrington inside the store with a gun at the time of the attempted robbery and murder.

Cooper's confession did not refer to Harrington by name. He referred to the fourth man as "the white boy" or "this white guy." And he described him by age, height, and weight.

Bosby's confession likewise did not mention Harrington by name but referred to him as a blond-headed fellow or "the white guy" or "the Patty."

Both Cooper and Bosby said in their confessions that they did not see "the white guy" with a gun, which is at variance with the testimony of the prosecution witnesses.

Petitioner argues that it is irrelevant that he was not named in Cooper's and Bosby's confessions, that reference to "the white guy" made it as clear as pointing and shouting that the person referred to was the white man in the dock with the three Negroes. We make the same assumption. But we conclude that on these special facts the lack of opportunity to cross-examine Cooper and Bosby constituted harmless error under the rule of *Chapman*.

Rhone, whom Harrington's counsel cross-examined, placed him in the store with a gun at the time of the murder. Harrington himself agreed he was there. Others testified he had a gun and was an active participant. Cooper and Bosby did not put a gun in his hands when he denied it. They did place him at the scene of the crime. But others, including Harrington himself, did the same. Their evidence, supplied through their confessions, was of course cumulative. But apart from them the case against Harrington was so overwhelming that we conclude that this violation of *Bruton* was harmless beyond a reasonable doubt, unless we

---

of which a store employee was killed. Each was found guilty of felony murder and sentenced to life imprisonment.

adopt the minority view in *Chapman* . . . that a departure from constitutional procedures should result in an automatic reversal, regardless of the weight of the evidence.

It is argued that we must reverse if we can imagine a single juror whose mind might have been made up because of Cooper's and Bosby's confessions and who otherwise would have remained in doubt and unconvinced. We of course do not know the jurors who sat. Our judgment must be based on our own reading of the record and on what seems to us to have been the probable impact of the two confessions on the minds of an average jury. We admonished in *Chapman* . . . against giving too much emphasis to "overwhelming evidence" of guilt, stating that constitutional errors affecting the substantial rights of the aggrieved party could not be considered to be harmless. By that test we cannot impute reversible weight to the two confessions.

We do not depart from *Chapman*; nor do we dilute it by inference. We reaffirm it. We do not suggest that, if evidence bearing on all the ingredients of the crime is tendered, the use of cumulative evidence, though tainted, is harmless error. Our decision is based on the evidence in this record. The case against Harrington was not woven from circumstantial evidence. It is so overwhelming that unless we say that no violation of *Bruton* can constitute harmless error, we must leave this state conviction undisturbed.

Affirmed.

MR. JUSTICE BRENNAN, With whom THE CHIEF JUSTICE and MR. JUSTICE MARSHALL join, dissenting.

The Court today overrules Chapman v. California, 386 U.S. 18 (1967), the very case it purports to apply. Far more fundamentally, it severely undermines many of the Court's most significant decisions in the area of criminal procedure.

In *Chapman*, we recognized that "harmless-error rules can work very unfair and mischievous results" unless they are narrowly circumscribed. Id., at 22. We emphasized that "[a]n error in admitting plainly relevant evidence which possibly influenced the jury adversely to a litigant cannot . . . be conceived of as harmless." Id., at 23-24. Thus, placing the burden of proof on the beneficiary of the error, we held that "before a federal constitutional error can be held harmless, the court must be able to declare a belief that it was harmless beyond a reasonable doubt." Id., at 24. And, we left no doubt that for an error to be "harmless" it must have made *no* contribution to a criminal conviction. Id., at 26.

Chapman, then, meant no compromise with the proposition that a conviction cannot constitutionally be based to any extent on constitutional error. The Court today by shifting the inquiry from whether the constitutional error contributed to the conviction to whether the untainted evidence provided "overwhelming" support for the conviction puts aside the firm resolve of *Chapman* and makes that compromise. As a result, the deterrent effect of such cases as Mapp v. Ohio, 367 U.S. 643 (1961); Griffin v. California, 380 U.S. 609 (1965); Miranda v. Arizona, 384 U.S. 436 (1966); United States v. Wade, 388 U.S. 218 (1967); and Bruton v. United States, 391 U.S. 123 (1968), on the actions of both police and prosecutors, not to speak of trial courts, will be significantly undermined.

The Court holds that constitutional error in the trial of a criminal offense may be held harmless if there is "overwhelming" untainted evidence to support the conviction. This approach, however, was expressly rejected in *Chapman*, . . . and with good reason. For, where the inquiry concerns the extent of accumulation of untainted evidence rather than the impact of tainted evidence on the jury's decision, convictions resulting from constitutional error may be insulated from attack. By its nature, the issue of substantiality of evidence admits of only the most limited kind of appellate review. Thus, the Court's rule will often effectively leave the vindication of constitutional rights solely in the hands of trial judges. If, instead, the task of appellate courts is to appraise the impact of tainted evidence on a jury's decision, as *Chapman* required, these courts will be better able to protect against deprivations of constitutional rights of criminal defendants. The focus of appellate inquiry should be on the character and quality of the tainted evidence as it relates to the untainted evidence and not just on the amount of untainted evidence.

The instant case illustrates well the difference in application between the approach adopted by the Court today and the approach set down in *Chapman*. At issue is the evidence going to Harrington's participation in the crime of attempted robbery, not the evidence going to his presence at the scene of the crime. Without the admittedly unconstitutional evidence against Harrington provided by the confessions of codefendants Bosby and Cooper, the prosecutor's proof of Harrington's participation in the crime consisted of the testimony of two victims of the attempted robbery and of codefendant Rhone. The testimony of the victims was weakened by the fact that they had earlier told the police that all the participants in the attempted robbery were Negroes. Rhone's testimony against Harrington was self-serving in certain aspects. At the time of his arrest, Rhone was found in possession of a gun. On the stand, he explained that he was given the gun by Harrington after the attempted robbery, and that Harrington had carried the gun during the commission of the robbery. Thus, although there was more than ample evidence to establish Harrington's participation in the attempted robbery, a jury might still have concluded that the case was not proved beyond a reasonable doubt. The confessions of the other two codefendants implicating Harrington in the crime were less self-serving and might well have tipped the balance in the jurors' minds in favor of conviction. Certainly, the State has not carried its burden of demonstrating beyond a reasonable doubt that these two confessions did not contribute to Harrington's conviction.

There should be no need to remind this Court that the appellate role in applying standards of sufficiency or substantiality of evidence is extremely limited. To apply such standards as threshold requirements to the raising of constitutional challenges to criminal convictions is to shield from attack errors of a most fundamental nature and thus to deprive many defendants of basic constitutional rights. I respectfully dissent.

NOTES AND QUESTIONS

1. Does *Harrington* change the focus of the harmless error question from the possible impact of the unconstitutional evidence to the sufficiency of the other evidence? Does even Justice Brennan depart from *Chapman* by suggesting that "the focus . . . should be on the character and quality of the tainted evidence *as it relates* to the untainted evidence" (emphasis added)? Or can both the majority and dissenting opinions be read simply as requiring, as a necessary part of the reasonable doubt analysis, an evaluation whether the tainted evidence is purely cumulative? See Field, Assessing the Harmlessness of Federal Constitutional Error— A Process in Need of a Rationale, 125 U. Pa. L. Rev. 15 (1976).

2. What should be the appropriate harmless constitutional error standard be? Or should all constitutional error be regarded as harmful? Would appellate courts be less willing to give content to constitutional provisions that protect criminal defendants if there were no harmless error doctrine? Alternatively, is the inevitable effect of the doctrine the dilution of constitutional rights? For criticisms of the harmless error concept, see Goldberg, Harmless Error: Constitutional Sneak Thief, 71 J. Crim. L. & Criminology 421 (1980); Saltzburg, The Harm of Harmless Error, 59 Va. L. Rev. 988 (1973); Stacy & Dayton, Rethinking Harmless Constitutional Error, 88 Colum. L. Rev. 79 (1988).

3. In addition to the fifth amendment self-incrimination violation in *Chapman* and the sixth amendment confrontation violation in *Harrington*,[9] the Supreme Court has applied or indicated that it would apply

---

9. In Davis v. Alaska, 415 U.S. 308 (1974), where the confrontation clause violation consisted of the curtailment of the defendant's cross-examination for bias of a critical state witness, the Court seemed to suggest that the constitutional violation required automatic reversal. In Delaware v. VanArsdale, 475 U.S. 673 (1986), however, the Court rejected this interpretation of *Davis*, and reaffirmed *Harrington's* general holding that confrontation clause violations are subject to harmless error analysis.

the harmless error doctrine to fourth amendment violations, [10] violations of a defendant's right to counsel at pretrial identifications [11] and preliminary hearings, [12] the admission of a psychiatric report obtained in violation of a defendant's Estelle v. Smith, page 992 supra, right to counsel, [13] violations of a defendant's sixth amendment *Massiah-Williams-Henry* rights, [14] and jury instructions that violate a defendant's right to have guilt proven beyond a reasonable doubt by stating that a homicide is presumed to be malicious, [15] On the other hand, as noted at page 1350 supra, the Court has been unwilling to apply the harmless constitutional error doctrine to the admission of involuntary confessions, the denial of a defendant's right to counsel at trial, [16] and the denial of the defendant's constitutional right to an impartial judge. What principled basis is there for distinguishing between those constitutional violations that lead to automatic reversal and those constitutional violations that are subjected to a harmless error analysis? Are some types of error so likely to be prejudicial that it is simply not worth the effort of engaging in the harmless error inquiry? If so, which ones?

4. Should the fact that a particular constitutional violation is especially shocking or outrageous be a reason to forgo application of the harmless error doctrine? Consider United States v. Hasting, 461 U.S. 499 (1983), which, like *Chapman*, involved an alleged violation of the Griffin v. California prohibition against prosecutorial comment on a defendant's failure to testify. Apparently because of what the Supreme Court referred to as a "history of tension" between the Seventh Circuit and federal prosecutors over what the Seventh Circuit regarded as repeated *Griffin* violations, the Court of Appeals in a brief per curiam opinion reversed the convictions of Hasting and his co-defendants without considering whether the *Griffin* violation was harmless. Recognizing that the Court of Appeals "acted in this case to discipline the prosecutor—and warn other prosecutors," the Supreme Court characterized the reversal as based on the judiciary's supervisory power over federal criminal justice. The Court then held that it is impermissible to rely on the supervisory power in order to avoid the harmless error analysis required by *Chapman*.

In a concurring and dissenting opinion Justice Brennan pointed out that the Court of Appeals had not specifically relied on the supervisory power for its decision. Since it was unclear why the lower court has

10. See Chambers v. Maroney, 399 U.S. 42 (1970).
11. See United States v. Wade, 388 U.S. 218 (1967).
12. See Coleman v. Alabama, 399 U.S. 1 (1970).
13. Satterwhite v. Texas, 486 U.S. 249 (1988).
14. See Milton v. Wainwright, 407 U.S. 371 (1972).
15. See Rose v. Clark, 106 S. Ct. 3101 (1986).
16. But cf. Rushen v. Spain, 464 U.S. 114 (1983) (per curiam) (unrecorded ex parte communication between trial judge and juror can be harmless error).

ignored the harmless error analysis, he was prepared to remand the case. He was unwilling, and thought it unnecessary, to adopt a broad general rule precluding reliance on the supervisory power to avoid the harmless error analysis.

    Under what circumstances, if any, should a harmless but outrageous constitutional violation lead to reversal of a conviction?

D. INEVITABLE DISCOVERY

A rule that is most commonly associated with the fourth amendment exclusionary rule and the fruit of the poisonous tree concept is the inevitable discovery rule: Evidence that would otherwise be regarded as the inadmissible fruit of the poisonous tree may nonetheless be admitted if the evidence probably or "inevitably" would have been discovered by legal means. The rule is considered here because of its similarity in purpose to the harmless error rule[17] and because the Supreme Court first fully addressed the issue in the context of the *sixth* amendment. The case, Nix v. Williams, 467 U.S. 431 (1984), is a sequel to Brewer v. Williams, which is set forth in Chapter 9, page 1243 supra. Williams, you will recall, led police officers to the body of the victim, Pamela Powers, after Detective Leaming made what has become known as the Christian Burial Speech. In *Brewer*, the Court held that Detective Leaming had elicited statements about the location of the body in violation of Williams' right to counsel. When Williams was retried, his statements were excluded, but the trial court, heeding the suggestion of the Supreme Court in *Brewer*,[18] admitted evidence relating to the discovery and condition of the body on the ground that the body would have been inevitably discovered. The Iowa Supreme Court affirmed.[19] The federal district court denied Williams' petition for a writ of habeas corpus,[20] but the eighth circuit reversed.[21] The Supreme Court granted certiorari.[22]

    17. See Nix v. Williams, 467 U.S. 431, 444 n.5 (1984), set forth at page 1359 infra.
    18. 430 U.S. 387, 406 n.12 (1977): "[E]vidence of where the body was found and of its condition might well be admissible on the theory that the body would have been discovered in any event. . . . In the event that retrial is instituted, it will be for the state courts in the first instance to determine whether particular items of evidence may be admitted."
    19. 285 N.W.2d 248 (Iowa 1979).
    20. 528 F. Supp. 664 (S.D. Iowa 1981).
    21. 700 F.2d 1175 (8th Cir. 1983).
    22. 461 U.S. 956 (1983).

NIX v. WILLIAMS
Certiorari to the United States Court of Appeals for the Eighth Circuit
467 U.S. 431 (1984)

CHIEF JUSTICE BURGER delivered the opinion of the Court. . . .

The Court of Appeals for the Eighth Circuit . . . assumed, without deciding, that there is an inevitable discovery exception to the Exclusionary Rule and that the Iowa Supreme Court correctly stated that exception to require proof that the police did not act in bad faith and that the evidence would have been discovered absent any constitutional violation. In reversing the District Court's denial of habeas relief, the Court of Appeals stated:

> We hold that the State has not met the first requirement. It is therefore unnecessary to decide whether the state courts' finding that the body would have been discovered anyway is fairly supported by the record. It is also unnecessary to decide whether the State must prove the two elements of the exception by clear and convincing evidence, as defendant argues, or by a preponderance of the evidence, as the state courts held. [700 F.2d 1164, 1169 (8th Cir. 1983).] . . .

The doctrine requiring courts to suppress evidence as the tainted "fruit" of unlawful governmental conduct had its genesis in Silverthorne Lumber Co. v. United States, 251 U.S. 385 (1920). . . . The holding of *Silverthorne* was carefully limited, however, for the Court emphasized that such information does not automatically become "sacred and inaccessible." Id., at 392. "If knowledge of [such facts] is gained from an *independent source*, they may be proved like any others. . . ." Ibid. (emphasis added).

. . . The independent source doctrine allows admission of evidence that has been discovered by means wholly independent of any constitutional violation. That doctrine, although closely related to the inevitable discovery doctrine, does not apply here; Williams' statements to Leaming indeed led police to the child's body, but that is not the whole story. The independent source doctrine teaches us that the interest of society in deterring unlawful police conduct and the public interest in having juries receive all probative evidence of a crime are properly balanced by putting the police in the same, not a *worse*, position than they would have been in if no police error or misconduct had occurred.[4] . . . When the chal-

4. The ultimate or inevitable discovery exception to the Exclusionary Rule is closely related in purpose to the harmless-error rule of Chapman v. California, 386 U.S. 18, 22 (1967). The harmless-constitutional-error rule "serve[s] a very useful purpose insofar as [it] block[s] setting aside convictions for small errors or defects that have little, if any,

lenged evidence has an independent source, exclusion of such evidence would put the police in a worse position than they would have been in absent any error or violation. There is a functional similarity between these two doctrines in that exclusion of evidence that would inevitably have been discovered would also put the government in a worse position, because the police would have obtained that evidence if no misconduct had taken place. Thus, while the independent source exception would not justify admission of evidence in this case, its rationale is wholly consistent with and justifies our adoption of the ultimate or inevitable discovery exception to the Exclusionary Rule.

It is clear that the cases implementing the Exclusionary Rule "begin with the premise that the challenged evidence is *in some sense* the product of illegal governmental activity." United States v. Crews, 445 U.S. 463, 471 (1980) (emphasis added). Of course, this does not end the inquiry. If the prosecution can establish by a preponderance of the evidence that the information ultimately or inevitably would have been discovered by lawful means—here the volunteers' search—then the deterrence rationale has so little basis that the evidence should be received.[5] Anything less would reject logic, experience, and common sense.

The requirement that the prosecution must prove the absence of bad faith, imposed here by the Court of Appeals, would place courts in the position of withholding from juries relevant and undoubted truth that would have been available to police absent any unlawful police activity.

likelihood of having changed the result of the trial." The purpose of the inevitable discovery rule is to block setting aside convictions that would have been obtained without police misconduct.

5. As to the quantum of proof, we have already established some relevant guidelines. In United States v. Mattock, 415 U.S. 164, 178 n.14 (1974) (emphasis added), we stated that "the controlling burden of proof at suppression hearings should impose *no greater burden* than proof by a preponderance of the evidence." In Lego v. Twomey, 404 U.S. 477, 488 (1972), we observed "from our experience [that] no substantial evidence has accumulated that federal rights have suffered from determining admissibility by a pre-ponderance of the evidence" and held that the prosecution must prove by a preponderance of the evidence that a confession sought to be used at trial was voluntary. We are unwilling to impose added burdens on the already difficult task of proving guilt in criminal cases by enlarging the barrier to placing evidence of unquestioned truth before juries.

Williams argues that the preponderance of the evidence standard used by the Iowa courts is inconsistent with United States v. Wade, 388 U.S. 218 (1967). In requiring clear and convincing evidence of an independent source for an in-court identification, the Court gave weight to the effect an uncounseled pretrial identification has in "crys-talliz[ing] the witnesses' identification of the defendant for the future reference." Id. at 240. The Court noted as well that possible unfairness at the lineup "may be the sole means of attack upon the unequivocal courtroom identification," ibid., and recognized the difficulty of determining whether an in-court identification was based on independent recollection unaided by the lineup identification, id., at 240-241. By contrast, inevitable discovery involves no speculative elements but focuses on demonstrated historical facts capable of ready verification or impeachment and does not require a departure from the usual burden of proof at suppression hearings.

Of course, that view would put the police in a *worse* position than they would have been in if no unlawful conduct had transpired. And, of equal importance, it wholly fails to take into account the enormous societal cost of excluding truth in the search for truth in the administration of justice. Nothing in this Court's prior holdings supports any such formalistic, pointless, and punitive approach.

The Court of Appeals concluded, without analysis, that if an absence of bad faith requirement were not imposed, "the temptation to risk deliberate violations of the Sixth Amendment would be too great, and the deterrent effect of the Exclusionary Rule reduced too far." 700 F.2d, at 1169, n.5. We reject that view. A police officer who is faced with the opportunity to obtain evidence illegally will rarely, if ever, be in a position to calculate whether the evidence sought would inevitably be discovered. . . . On the other hand, when an officer is aware that the evidence will inevitably be discovered, he will try to avoid engaging in any questionable practice. In that situation, there will be little to gain from taking any dubious "shortcuts" to obtain the evidence. Significant disincentives to obtaining evidence illegally—including the possibility of departmental discipline and civil liability—also lessen the likelihood that the ultimate or inevitable discovery exception will promote police misconduct. See Bivens v. Six Unknown Federal Narcotics Agents, 403 U.S. 388, 397 (1971). In these circumstances, the societal costs of the Exclusionary Rule far outweigh any possible benefits to deterrence that a good-faith requirement might produce.

Williams contends that because he did not waive his right to the assistance of counsel, the Court may not balance competing values in deciding whether the challenged evidence was properly admitted. He argues that, unlike the Exclusionary Rule in the Fourth Amendment context, the essential purpose of which is to deter police misconduct, the Sixth Amendment Exclusionary Rule is designed to protect the right to a fair trial and the integrity of the factfinding process. Williams contends that, when those interests are at stake, the societal costs of excluding evidence obtained from responses presumed involuntary are irrelevant in determining whether such evidence should be excluded. We disagree.

Exclusion of physical evidence that would inevitably have been discovered adds nothing to either the integrity or fairness of a criminal trial. The Sixth Amendment right to counsel protects against unfairness by preserving the adversary process in which the reliability of proffered evidence may be tested in cross-examination. . . . Here, however, Detective Leaming's conduct did nothing to impugn the reliability of the evidence in question—the body of the child and its condition as it was found, articles of clothing found on the body, and the autopsy. . . .

Nor would suppression ensure fairness on the theory that it tends to safeguard the adversary system of justice. To assure the fairness of trial proceedings, this Court has held that assistance of counsel must be available at pretrial confrontations where "the subsequent trial [cannot] cure a[n otherwise] one-sided confrontation between prosecuting authorities and the uncounseled defendant." United States v. Ash, [413 U.S. 300, 315 (1973)]. Fairness can be assured by placing the State and the accused in the same positions they would have been in had the impermissible conduct not taken place. However, if the government can prove that the evidence would have been obtained inevitably and, therefore, would have been admitted regardless of any overreaching by the police, there is no rational basis to keep that evidence from the jury in order to ensure the fairness of the trial proceedings. In that situation, the State has gained no advantage at trial and the defendant has suffered no prejudice. Indeed, suppression of the evidence would operate to undermine the adversary system by putting the State in a *worse* position than it would have occupied without any police misconduct. . . .

The Court of Appeals did not find it necessary to consider whether the record fairly supported the finding that the volunteer search party would ultimately or inevitably have discovered the victim's body. However, three courts independently reviewing the evidence have found that the body of the child inevitably would have been found by the searchers. Williams challenges these findings, asserting that the record contains only the "post hoc rationalization" that the search effort would have proceeded two and one-half miles into Polk County where Williams had led police to the body.

When that challenge was made at the suppression hearing preceding Williams' second trial, the prosecution offered the testimony of Agent Ruxlow of the Iowa Bureau of Criminal Investigation. Ruxlow had organized and directed some 200 volunteers who were searching for the child's body. Tr. of Hearings on Motion to Suppress in State v. Williams, No. CR 55805, p. 34 (May 31, 1977). The searchers were instructed "to check all the roads, the ditches, any culverts. . . . If they came upon any abandoned farm buildings, they were instructed to go onto the property and search those abandoned farm buildings or any other places where a small child could be secreted." Id., at 35. Ruxlow testified that he marked off highway maps of Poweshiek and Jasper Counties in grid fashion, divided the volunteers into teams of four to six persons, and assigned each team to search specific grid areas. Id. at 34. Ruxlow also testified that, if the search had not been suspended because of Willams' promised cooperation, it would have continued into Polk County, using the same grid system. Id., at 36, 39-40. Although he had previously marked off into grids only the highway maps of Poweshiek and Jasper Counties, Ruxlow had obtained a map of Polk County, which he said he would have marked off in the same manner had it been necessary for the search to continue. Id., at 39.

The search had commenced at approximately 10 A.M. and moved westward through Poweshiek County into Jasper County. At approximately 3 P.M., after Williams had volunteered to cooperate with the police, Officer Leaming, who was in the police car with Williams, sent word to Ruxlow and the other Special Agent directing the search to meet him at the Grinnell truck stop and the search was suspended at that time. Id., at 51-52. Ruxlow also stated that he was "under the impression that there was a possibility" that Williams would lead them to the child's body at that time. Id., at 61. The search was not resumed once it was learned that Williams had led the police to the body, id., at 57, which was found two and one-half miles from where the search had stopped in what would have been the easternmost grid to be searched in Polk County, id., at 39. There was testimony that it would have taken an additional three to five hours to discover the body if the search had continued, id., at 41; the body was found near a culvert, one of the kinds of places the teams had been specifically directed to search.

On this record it is clear that the search parties were approaching the actual location of the body and we are satisfied, along with three courts earlier, that the volunteer search teams would have resumed the search had Williams not earlier led the police to the body and the body inevitably would have been found. . . .

The judgment of the Court of Appeals is reversed, and the case is remanded for further proceedings consistent with this opinion.[7]

[The concurring opinions of JUSTICE WHITE and JUSTICE STEVENS and the dissenting opinion of JUSTICE BRENNAN are omitted.]

NOTES AND QUESTIONS

1. Prior to Nix, every federal circuit court and many state courts had adopted some version of the inevitable discovery rule. See Nix, 467 U.S. at 440 n.2; State v. Williams, 285 N.W.2d 248, 256 (Iowa 1979) (both collecting cases). Commentators, however, have been divided on the desirability of the rule. See id. at 258 (collecting authorities). See also Wasserstrom & Mertens, The Exclusionary Rule on the Scaffold, 22 Am. Crim. L. Rev. 25 (1984).

7. In view of our holding that the challenged evidence was admissible under the inevitable discovery exception to the Exclusionary Rule, we find it unnecessary to decide whether Stone v. Powell, 428 U.S. 465 (1976), should be extended to bar federal habeas corpus review of Williams' Sixth Amendment claim and we express no view on that issue.

2. What is the relationship between the notion of inevitability and the preponderance of evidence standard approved by the Court in *Nix*? Preponderance is commonly understood to mean "more likely than not" or slightly more than 50 percent. If this standard applies to the ultimate conclusion of inevitability, the judge must be convinced only that it is slightly more likely than not that the evidence would have been discovered. Alternatively, the term *inevitable* may imply some much higher degree of probability, and the preponderance standard may apply only to the historical facts upon which the inevitability conclusion is based. Thus, for example, the judge, in order to admit the illegally obtained evidence, may have to conclude that there is a high probability (e.g., 80 percent or 95 percent or whatever percentage is deemed to constitute inevitability) that, given fact X, the evidence would have been discovered and that there is a slightly more than 50 percent probability that fact X existed. How inevitable is inevitable under this latter approach?[23]

3. Note that in justifying application of the preponderance standard, the Court in *Nix* observed, "[I]nevitable discovery involves no speculative elements but focuses on demonstrated historical facts capable of ready verification or impeachment." 467 U.S. 444 n.5. Even if the relevant historical facts are not in dispute, however, the conclusion that these facts would have led to the discovery of the evidence in the absence of illegal conduct is necessarily speculative. Does this speculative aspect of the inevitable discovery determination suggest that it would have been appropriate for the Court to require a higher standard of proof for the historical facts? What practical impact do you think a higher standard of proof would have?

4. Do you agree with the Court in *Nix* that there is no need to adopt a good faith limitation to the inevitable discovery rule? If there were such a requirement, how should it have been applied in *Nix*? Compare the following characterizations of Detective Leaming's conduct:

> The majority refers to the "societal costs" of excluding probative evidence. In my view, the more relevant cost is that imposed on society by police officers who decide to take procedural shortcuts instead of complying with the law. What is the consequence of the shortcut that Detective Leaming took when he decided to question Williams in this case and not

23. If there are two or more *independent* historical facts that must be established to support the inevitability conclusion, and if each fact must be proved by only a preponderance of the evidence, the probability of the existence of the factual basis for the inevitability conclusion may be *less* than 50 percent. E.g., 70 percent probability that X existed times 60 percent probability that Y existed equals 42 percent probability that X and Y existed together. Cf. In re Winship, 397 U.S. 358, 364 (1970) (due process requires "proof beyond a reasonable doubt of *every fact* necessary to constitute the crime . . . charged") (emphasis added).

to wait an hour or so until he arrived in Des Moines? The answer is years and years of unnecessary but costly litigation. Instead of having a 1969 conviction affirmed in routine fashion, the case is still alive 15 years later. Thanks to Detective Leaming, the State of Iowa has expended vast sums of money and countless hours of professional labor in his defense. That expenditure surely provides an adequate deterrent to similar violations; the responsibility for that expenditure lies not with the Constitution, but rather with the constable. [Nix v. Williams, 104 S. Ct. at 2516-2517 (Stevens, J., concurring.)]

. . . Brewer v. Williams was a 5-4 decision and . . . four members of the Court, including myself, were of the view that Officer Leaming had done nothing wrong at all, let alone anything unconstitutional. . . . It is thus an unjustified reflection on Officer Leaming to say that he "decided to dispense with the requirements of the law," or that he decided "to take procedural shortcuts instead of complying with the law," . . . He was no doubt acting as many competent police officers would have acted under similar circumstances and in light of the then-existing law. That five Justices later thought he was mistaken does not call for making him out to be a villain or for a lecture on deliberate police misconduct and its resulting costs to society. [Id. at 450-451 (White, J., concurring.)]

APPENDICES

APPENDIX A

UNITED STATES CONSTITUTION
(Selected Provisions)

ARTICLE I

Section 9. . . .

The Privilege of the Writ of Habeas Corpus shall not be suspended, unless when in Cases of Rebellion or Invasion the public Safety may require it.

No Bill of Attainder or ex post facto Law shall be passed. . . .

ARTICLE III

Section 1. The judicial Power of the United States, shall be vested in one supreme Court, and in such inferior Courts as the Congress may from time to time ordain and establish. . . .

Section 2. The judicial Power shall extend to all Cases, in Law and Equity, arising under this Constitution, the Laws of the United States, and Treaties made, or which shall be made, under their Authority;—to all Cases affecting Ambassadors, other public Ministers and Consuls;— to all Cases of admiralty and maritime Jurisdiction;—to Controversies to which the United States shall be a Party;—to Controversies between two or more States;—between a State and Citizens of another State;—between Citizens of different States;—between Citizens of the same State claiming Lands under Grants of different States, and between a State, or the Citizens thereof, and foreign States, Citizens or Subjects.

In all Cases affecting Ambassadors, other public Ministers and Consuls, and those in which a State shall be Party, the supreme Court shall

1369

have original Jurisdiction. In all the other Cases before mentioned, the supreme Court shall have appellate Jurisdiction, both as to Law and Fact, with such Exceptions, and under such Regulations as the Congress shall make.

The Trial of all Crimes, except in Cases of Impeachment, shall be by Jury; and such Trial shall be held in the State where the said Crimes shall have been committed; but when not committed within any State, the Trial shall be at such Place or Places as the Congress may by Law have directed.

ARTICLE IV

Section 2.   The Citizens of each State shall be entitled to all Privileges and Immunities of Citizens in the several States.

A Person charged in any State with Treason, Felony, or other Crime, who shall flee from Justice, and be found in another State, shall on Demand of the executive Authority of the State from which he fled, be delivered up, to be removed to the State having jurisdiction of the Crime. . . .

ARTICLE VI

. . . This Constitution, and the laws of the United States which shall be made in Pursuance thereof; and all Treaties made, or which shall be made, under the Authority of the United States, shall be the supreme Law of the Land; and the judges in every State shall be bound thereby, any Thing in the Constitution or Laws of any State to the Contrary notwithstanding. . . .

AMENDMENT I

Congress shall make no law respecting an establishment of religion, or prohibiting the free exercise thereof; or abridging the freedom of speech, or of the press; or the right of the people peaceably to assemble, and to petition the Government for a redress of grievances.

AMENDMENT II

A well regulated militia, being necessary to the security of a free State, the right of the people to keep and bear arms, shall not be infringed.

Amendment III

No Soldier shall, in time of peace be quartered in any house, without the consent of the owner, nor in time of war, but in a manner to be prescribed by law.

Amendment IV

The right of the people to be secure in their persons, houses, papers, and effects, against unreasonable searches and seizures, shall not be violated, and no warrants shall issue, but upon probable cause, supported by oath or affirmation, and particularly describing the place to be searched, and the persons or things to be seized.

Amendment V

No person shall be held to answer for a capital, or otherwise infamous crime, unless on a presentment or indictment of a Grand Jury, except in cases arising in the land or naval forces, or in the militia, when in actual service in time of war or public danger; nor shall any person be subject for the same offence to be twice put in jeopardy of life or limb; nor shall be compelled in any criminal case to be a witness against himself, nor be deprived of life, liberty, or property, without due process of law; nor shall private property be taken for public use, without just compensation.

Amendment VI

In all criminal prosecutions, the accused shall enjoy the right to a speedy and public trial, by an impartial jury of the State and district wherein the crime shall have been committed, which district shall have been previously ascertained by law, and to be informed of the nature and cause of the accusation; to be confronted with the witnesses against him; to have compulsory process for obtaining witnesses in his favor, and to have the assistance of counsel for his defence.

Amendment VII

In Suits at common law, where the value in controversy shall exceed twenty dollars, the right of trial by jury shall be preserved, and no fact tried by a jury, shall be otherwise reexamined in any Court of the United States, than according to the rules of the common law.

AMENDMENT VIII

Excessive bail shall not be required, nor excessive fines imposed, nor cruel and unusual punishments inflicted.

AMENDMENT IX

The enumeration in the Constitution, of certain rights, shall not be construed to deny or disparage others retained by the people.

AMENDMENT X

The powers not delegated to the United States by the Constitution, nor prohibited by it to the States, are reserved to the States respectively, or to the people.

AMENDMENT XIII

Section 1.   Neither slavery nor involuntary servitude, except as a punishment for crime whereof the party shall have been duly convicted, shall exist within the United States, or any place subject to their jurisdiction.

Section 2.   Congress shall have power to enforce this article by appropriate legislation.

AMENDMENT XIV

Section 1.   All persons born or naturalized in the United States, and subject to the jurisdiction thereof, are citizens of the United States and of the State wherein they reside. No State shall make or enforce any law which shall abridge the privileges or immunities of citizens of the United States; nor shall any State deprive any person of life, liberty, or property, without due process of law; nor deny to any person within its jurisdiction the equal protection of the laws. . . .

Section 5.   The Congress shall have power to enforce, by appropriate legislation, the provisions of this article.

APPENDIX B

FEDERAL RULES OF CRIMINAL PROCEDURE FOR THE UNITED STATES DISTRICT COURTS
(Selected Provisions)

As Amended, Effective December 1, 1989

RULE 3. THE COMPLAINT

The complaint is a written statement of the essential facts constituting the offense charged. It shall be made upon oath before a magistrate.

RULE 4. ARREST WARRANT OR SUMMONS UPON COMPLAINT

(a) Issuance. If it appears from the complaint, or from an affidavit or affidavits filed with the complaint, that there is probable cause to believe that an offense has been committed and that the defendant has committed it, a warrant for the arrest of the defendant shall issue to any officer authorized by law to execute it. Upon the request of the attorney for the government a summons instead of a warrant shall issue. More than one warrant or summons may issue on the same complaint. If a defendant fails to appear in response to the summons, a warrant shall issue.

 (b) Probable Cause. The finding of probable cause may be based upon hearsay evidence in whole or in part.

 (c) Form.

  (1) Warrant. The warrant shall be signed by the magistrate and shall contain the name of the defendant or, if the defendant's name is unknown, any name or description by which the defendant can be identified with reasonable certainty. It shall describe the offense charged in the complaint. It shall command that the defendant be arrested and brought before the nearest available magistrate.

(2) **Summons.** The summons shall be in the same form as the warrant except that it shall summon the defendant to appear before a magistrate at a stated time and place.

(d) **Execution or Service; and Return.**

(1) **By Whom.** The warrant shall be executed by a marshal or by some other officer authorized by law. The summons may be served by any person authorized to serve a summons in a civil action.

(2) **Territorial Limits.** The warrant may be executed or the summons may be served at any place within the jurisdiction of the United States.

(3) **Manner.** The warrant shall be executed by the arrest of the defendant. The officer need not have the warrant at the time of the arrest but upon request shall show the warrant to the defendant as soon as possible. If the officer does not have the warrant at the time of the arrest, the officer shall then inform the defendant of the offense charged and of the fact that a warrant has been issued. The summons shall be served upon a defendant by delivering a copy to the defendant personally, or by leaving it at the defendant's dwelling house or usual place of abode with some person of suitable age and discretion then residing therein and by mailing a copy of the summons to the defendant's last known address.

(4) **Return.** The officer executing a warrant shall make return thereof to the magistrate or other officer before whom the defendant is brought pursuant to Rule 5. At the request of the attorney for the government any unexecuted warrant shall be returned to and cancelled by the magistrate by whom it was issued. On or before the return day the person to whom a summons was delivered for service shall make return thereof to the magistrate before whom the summons is returnable. At the request of the attorney for the government made at any time while the complaint is pending, a warrant returned unexecuted and not cancelled or a summons returned unserved or a duplicate thereof may be delivered by the magistrate to the marshal or other authorized person for execution or service.

RULE 5. INITIAL APPEARANCE BEFORE THE MAGISTRATE

(a) **In General.** An officer making an arrest under a warrant issued upon a complaint or any person making an arrest without a warrant shall take the arrested person without unnecessary delay before the nearest available federal magistrate or, in the event that a federal magistrate is not reasonably available, before a state or local judicial officer authorized by 18 U.S.C. §3041. If a person arrested without a warrant is brought before a magistrate, a complaint shall be filed forthwith which shall comply with the requirements of Rule 4(a) with respect to the showing of probable cause. When a person, arrested with or without a warrant or given a summons, appears initially before the magistrate, the magistrate shall proceed in accordance with the applicable subdivisions of this rule.

(b) **Misdemeanors.** If the charge against the defendant is a misdemeanor triable by a United States magistrate under 18 U.S.C. §3401, the United States magistrate shall proceed in accordance with the Rules of Procedure for the Trial of Misdemeanors before United States Magistrates.

(c) **Offenses Not Triable by the United States Magistrate.** If the charge against the defendant is not triable by the United States magistrate, the defendant shall not be called upon to plead. The magistrate shall inform the defendant of the complaint against the defendant and of any affidavit filed therewith, of the defendant's right to retain counsel or to request the assignment of counsel if the defendant is unable to obtain counsel, and of the general circumstances under which the defendant may secure pretrial release. The magistrate shall inform the defendant that the defendant is not required to make a statement and that any statement made by the defendant may be used against the defendant. The magistrate shall also inform the defendant of the right to a preliminary examination. The magistrate shall allow the defendant reasonable time and opportunity to consult counsel and shall detain or conditionally release the defendant to bail as provided by statute or in these rules.

A defendant is entitled to a preliminary examination, unless waived, when charged with any offense, other than a petty offense, which is to be tried by a judge of the district court. If the defendant waives preliminary examination, the magistrate shall forthwith hold the defendant to answer in the district court. If the defendant does not waive the preliminary examination, the magistrate shall schedule a preliminary examination. Such examination shall be held within a reasonable time but in any event not later than 10 days following the initial appearance if the defendant is in custody and no later than 20 days if the defendant is not in custody, provided, however, that the preliminary examination shall not be held if the defendant is indicted or if an information against the defendant is filed in district court before the date set for the preliminary examination. With the consent of the defendant and upon a showing of good cause, taking into account the public interest in the prompt disposition of criminal cases, time limits specified in this subdivision may be extended one or more times by a federal magistrate. In the absence of such consent by the defendant, time limits may be extended by a judge of the United

States only upon a showing that extraordinary circumstances exist and that delay is indispensable to the interests of justice.

Rule 7. The Indictment and the Information

(a) Use of Indictment or Information.   An offense which may be punished by death shall be prosecuted by indictment. An offense which may be punished by imprisonment for a term exceeding one year or at hard labor shall be prosecuted by indictment or, if indictment is waived, it may be prosecuted by information. Any other offense may be prosecuted by indictment or by information. An information may be filed without leave of court.

(b) Waiver of Indictment.   An offense which may be punished by imprisonment for a term exceeding one year or at hard labor may be prosecuted by information if the defendant, after having been advised of the nature of the charge and of the rights of the defendant, waives in open court prosecution by indictment.

(c) Nature and Contents.

(1) In General.   The indictment or the information shall be a plain, concise and definite written statement of the essential facts constituting the offense charged. It shall be signed by the attorney for the government. It need not contain a formal commencement, a formal conclusion or any other matter not necessary to such statement. Allegations made in one count may be incorporated by reference in another count. It may be alleged in a single count that the means by which the defendant committed the offense are unknown or that the defendant committed it by one or more specified means. The indictment or information shall state for each count the official or customary citation of the statute, rule, regulation or other provision of law which the defendant is alleged therein to have violated. . . .

Rule 9. Warrant or Summons Upon Indictment or Information

(a) Issuance.   Upon the request of the attorney for the government the court shall issue a warrant for each defendant named in an information supported by a showing of probable cause under oath as is required by Rule 4(a), or in an indictment. Upon the request of the attorney for the government a summons instead of a warrant shall issue. If no request is made, the court may issue either a warrant or a summons in its discretion. More than one warrant or summons may issue for the same defendant.

The clerk shall deliver the warrant or summons to the marshal or other person authorized by law to execute or serve it. If a defendant fails to appear in response to the summons, a warrant shall issue. When a defendant arrested with a warrant or given a summons appears initially before a magistrate, the magistrate shall proceed in accordance with the applicable subdivisions of Rule 5.

(b) **Form.**

(1) **Warrant.**   The form of the warrant shall be as provided in Rule 4(c)(1) except that it shall be signed by the clerk, it shall describe the offense charged in the indictment or information and it shall command that the defendant be arrested and brought before the nearest available magistrate. The amount of bail may be fixed by the court and endorsed on the warrant.

(2) **Summons.**   The summons shall be in the same form as the warrant except that it shall summon the defendant to appear before a magistrate at a stated time and place.

(c) **Execution or Service; and Return.**

(1) **Execution or Service.**   The warrant shall be executed or the summons served as provided in Rule 4(d)(1), (2) and (3). A summons to a corporation shall be served by delivering a copy to an officer or to a managing or general agent or to any other agent authorized by appointment or by law to receive service or process and, if the agent is one authorized by statute to receive service and the statute so requires, by also mailing a copy to the corporation's last known address within the district or at its principal place of business elsewhere in the United States. The officer executing the warrant shall bring the arrested person without unnecessary delay before the nearest available federal magistrate or, in the event that a federal magistrate is not reasonably available, before a state or local judicial officer authorized by 18 U.S.C. §3041.

(2) **Return.**   The officer executing a warrant shall make return thereof to the magistrate or other officer before whom the defendant is brought. At the request of the attorney for the government any unexecuted warrant shall be returned and cancelled. On or before the return day the person to whom a summons was delivered for service shall make return thereof. At the request of the attorney for the government made at any time while the indictment or information is pending, a warrant returned unexecuted and not cancelled or a summons returned unserved or a duplicate thereof may be delivered by the clerk to the marshal or other authorized person for execution or service.

Rule 10. Arraignment

Arraignment shall be conducted in open court and shall consist of reading the indictment or information to the defendant or stating to the defendant the substance of the charge and calling on the defendant to plead thereto. The defendant shall be given a copy of the indictment or information before being called upon to plead.

Rule 11. Pleas

(a) Alternatives.

 (1) In general. A defendant may plead not guilty, guilty, or nolo contendere. If a defendant refuses to plead or if a defendant corporation fails to appear, the court shall enter a plea of not guilty.

 (2) Conditional pleas. With the approval of the court and the consent of the government, a defendant may enter a conditional plea of guilty or nolo contendere, reserving in writing the right, on appeal from the judgment, to review of the adverse determination of any specified pretrial motion. A defendant who prevails on appeal shall be allowed to withdraw the plea.

 (b) Nolo Contendere. A defendant may plead nolo contendere only with the consent of the court. Such a plea shall be accepted by the court only after due consideration of the views of the parties and the interest of the public in the effective administration of justice.

 (c) Advice to Defendant. Before accepting a plea of guilty or nolo contendere, the court must address the defendant personally in open court and inform the defendant of, and determine that the defendant understands, the following:

 (1) the nature of the charge to which the plea is offered, the mandatory minimum penalty provided by law, if any, and the maximum possible penalty provided by law, including the effect of any special parole or supervised release term, the fact that the court is required to consider any applicable sentencing guidelines but may depart from those guidelines under some circumstances, and, when applicable, that the court may also order the defendant to make restitution to any victim of the offense; and

 (2) if the defendant is not represented by an attorney, that the defendant has the right to be represented by an attorney at every stage of the proceeding and, if necessary, one will be appointed to represent the defendant; and

 (3) that the defendant has the right to plead not guilty or to persist in that plea if it has already been made, the right to be tried by a jury

and at that trial the right to the assistance of counsel, the right to confront and cross-examine witnesses, and the right against compelled self-incrimination; and

(4) that if a plea of guilty or nolo contendere is accepted by the court there will not be a further trial of any kind, so that by pleading guilty or nolo contendere the defendant waives the right to a trial; and

(5) if the court intends to question the defendant under oath, on the record, and in the presence of counsel about the offense to which the defendant has pleaded, that the defendant's answers may later be used against the defendant in a prosecution for perjury or false statement.

(d) **Insuring That the Plea Is Voluntary.** The court shall not accept a plea of guilty or nolo contendere without first, by addressing the defendant personally in open court, determining that the plea is voluntary and not the result of force or threats or of promises apart from a plea agreement. The court shall also inquire as to whether the defendant's willingness to plead guilty or nolo contendere results from prior discussions between the attorney for the government and the defendant or the defendant's attorney.

(e) **Plea Agreement Procedure.**

(1) **In General.** The attorney for the government and the attorney for the defendant or the defendant when acting pro se may engage in discussions with a view toward reaching an agreement that, upon the entering of a plea of guilty or nolo contendere to a charged offense or to a lesser or related offense, the attorney for the government will do any of the following:

(A) move for dismissal of other charges; or

(B) make a recommendation, or agree not to oppose the defendant's request, for a particular sentence, with the understanding that such recommendation or request shall not be binding upon the court; or

(C) agree that a specific sentence is the appropriate disposition of the case.

The court shall not participate in any such discussions.

(2) **Notice of Such Agreement.** If a plea agreement has been reached by the parties, the court shall, on the record, require the disclosure of the agreement in open court or, on a showing of good cause, in camera, at the time the plea is offered. If the agreement is the type specified in subdivision (e)(1)(A) or (C), the court may accept or reject the agreement, or may defer its decision as to the acceptance or rejection until there has been an opportunity to consider the presentence report. If the agreement is of the type specified in subdivision (e)(1)(B), the court shall advise the defendant that if the court does not

accept the recommendation or request the defendant nevertheless has no right to withdraw the plea.

(3) Acceptance of a Plea Agreement. If the court accepts the plea agreement, the court shall inform the defendant that it will embody in the judgment and sentence the disposition provided for in the plea agreement.

(4) Rejection of a Plea Agreement. If the court rejects the plea agreement, the court shall, on the record, inform the parties of this fact, advise the defendant personally in open court or, on a showing of good cause, in camera, that the court is not bound by the plea agreement, afford the defendant the opportunity to then withdraw the plea, and advise the defendant that if the defendant persists in a guilty plea or plea of nolo contendere the disposition of the case may be less favorable to the defendant than that contemplated by the plea agreement.

(5) Time of Plea Agreement Procedure. Except for good cause shown, notification to the court of the existence of a plea agreement shall be given at the arraignment or at such other time, prior to trial, as may be fixed by the court.

(6) Inadmissibility of Pleas, Plea Discussions, and Related Statements. Except as otherwise provided in this paragraph, evidence of the following is not, in any civil or criminal proceeding, admissible against the defendant who made the plea or was a participant in the plea discussions:

(A) a plea of guilty which was later withdrawn;

(B) a plea of nolo contendere;

(C) any statement made in the course of any proceedings under this rule regarding either of the foregoing pleas; or

(D) any statement made in the course of plea discussions with an attorney for the government which do not result in a plea of guilty or which result in a plea of guilty later withdrawn.

However, such a statement is admissible (i) in any proceeding wherein another statement made in the course of the same plea or plea discussions has been introduced and the statement ought in fairness be considered contemporaneously with it, or (ii) in a criminal proceeding for perjury or false statement if the statement was made by the defendant under oath, on the record, and in the presence of counsel.

(f) Determining Accuracy of Plea. Notwithstanding the acceptance of a plea of guilty, the court should not enter a judgment upon such plea without making such inquiry as shall satisfy it that there is a factual basis for the plea.

(g) Record of Proceedings. A verbatim record of the proceedings at which the defendant enters a plea shall be made and, if there is a plea of guilty or nolo contendere, the record shall include, without limitation, the court's advice to the defendant, the inquiry into the voluntariness of the plea including any plea agreement, and the inquiry into the accuracy of a guilty plea.

(h) **Harmless Error.**   Any variance from the procedures required by this rule which does not affect substantial rights shall be disregarded.

RULE 12.   PLEADINGS AND MOTIONS BEFORE TRIAL; DEFENSES AND OBJECTIONS

(a) **Pleadings and Motions.**   Pleadings in criminal proceedings shall be the indictment and the information, and the pleas of not guilty, guilty and nolo contendere. All other pleas, and demurrers and motions to quash are abolished, and defenses and objections raised before trial which heretofore could have been raised by one or more of them shall be raised only by motion to dismiss or to grant appropriate relief, as provided in these rules.

(b) **Pretrial Motions.**   Any defense, objection, or request which is capable of determination without the trial of the general issue may be raised before trial by motion. Motions may be written or oral at the discretion of the judge. The following must be raised prior to trial: . . .

(3) Motions to suppress evidence . . .

(c) **Motion Date.**   Unless otherwise provided by local rule, the court may, at the time of the arraignment or as soon thereafter as practicable, set a time for the making of pretrial motions or requests and, if required, a later date of hearing.

(d) **Notice by the Government of the Intention to Use Evidence.**

(1) **At the Discretion of the Government.**   At the arraignment or as soon thereafter as is practicable, the government may give notice to the defendant of its intention to use specified evidence at trial in order to afford the defendant an opportunity to raise objections to such evidence prior to trial under subdivision (b)(3) of this rule.

(2) **At the Request of the Defendant.**   At the arraignment or as soon thereafter as is practicable the defendant may, in order to afford an opportunity to move to suppress evidence under subdivision (b)(3) of this rule, request notice of the government's intention to use (in its evidence in chief at trial) any evidence which the defendant may be entitled to discover under Rule 16 subject to any relevant limitations prescribed in Rule 16. . . .

Rule 23. Trial by Jury or by the Court

(a) Trial by Jury.   Cases required to be tried by jury shall be so tried unless the defendant waives a jury trial in writing with the approval of the court and the consent of the government.

   (b) Jury of Less than Twelve.   Juries shall be of 12 but at any time before verdict the parties may stipulate in writing with the approval of the court that the jury shall consist of any number less than 12 or that a valid verdict may be returned by a jury of less than 12 should the court find it necessary to excuse one or more jurors for any just cause after trial commences. Even absent such stipulation, if the court finds it necessary to excuse a juror for just cause after the jury has retired to consider its verdict, in the discretion of the court a valid verdict may be returned by the remaining 11 jurors. . . . .

Rule 31. Verdict

(a) Return.   The verdict shall be unanimous. It shall be returned by the jury to the judge in open court. . . . .

Rule 41. Search and Seizure

(a) Authority to Issue Warrant.   A search warrant authorized by this rule may be issued by a federal magistrate or a judge of a state court of record within the district wherein the property or person sought is located, upon request of a federal law enforcement officer or an attorney for the government.

   (b) Property or Persons Which May Be Seized With a Warrant. A warrant may be issued under this rule to search for and seize any (1) property that constitutes evidence of the commission of a criminal offense; or (2) contraband, the fruits of crime, or things otherwise criminally possessed; or (3) property designed or intended for use or which is or has been used as the means of committing a criminal offense; or (4) person for whose arrest there is probable cause, or who is unlawfully restrained.

   (c) Issuance and Contents.

   (1) Warrant Upon Affidavit.   A warrant other than a warrant upon oral testimony under paragraph (2) of this subdivision shall issue only on an affidavit or affidavits sworn to before the federal magistrate or state judge and establishing the grounds for issuing the warrant. If the federal magistrate or state judge is satisfied that grounds for the application exist or that there is probable cause to believe that they exist, the magistrate or state judge shall issue a warrant identifying the property or person to be seized and naming or describing the person or place to be searched. The finding of probable cause may be based upon hearsay evidence in whole or in part. Before ruling on a request for a warrant the federal magistrate or state judge may require the affiant to appear personally and may examine under oath the affiant and any witnesses the affiant may produce, provided that such proceeding shall be taken down by a court reporter or recording equipment and made part of the affidavit. The warrant shall be directed to a civil officer of the United States authorized to enforce or assist in enforcing any law thereof or to a person so authorized by the President of the United States. It shall command the officer to search, within a specified period of time not to exceed 10 days, the person or place named for the property or person specified. The warrant shall be served in the daytime, unless the issuing authority, by appropriate provision in the warrant, and for reasonable cause shown, authorizes its execution at times other than daytime. It shall designate a federal magistrate to whom it shall be returned.

(2) **Warrant Upon Oral Testimony.**

(A) **General Rule.** If the circumstances make it reasonable to dispense with a written affidavit, a Federal magistrate may issue a warrant based upon sworn oral testimony communicated by telephone or other appropriate means.

(B) **Application.** The person who is requesting the warrant shall prepare a document to be known as a duplicate original warrant and shall read such duplicate original warrant, verbatim, to the Federal magistrate. The Federal magistrate shall enter, verbatim, what is so read to such magistrate on a document to be known as the original warrant. The Federal magistrate may direct that the warrant be modified.

(C) **Issuance.** If the Federal magistrate is satisfied that the circumstances are such as to make it reasonable to dispense with a written affidavit and that grounds for the application exist or that there is probable cause to believe that they exist, the Federal magistrate shall order the issuance of a warrant by directing the person requesting the warrant to sign the Federal magistrate's name on the duplicate original warrant. The Federal magistrate shall immediately sign the original warrant and enter on the face of the original warrant the exact time when the warrant was ordered to be issued. The finding of probable cause for a warrant upon oral testimony may be based on the same kind of evidence as is sufficient for a warrant upon affidavit.

(D) **Recording and Certification of Testimony.** When a caller informs the Federal magistrate that the purpose of the call is to request a warrant, the Federal magistrate shall immediately place under oath each person whose testimony forms a basis of the application and each person applying for that warrant. If a voice recording device is available, the Federal magistrate shall record by means of such device all of the call after the caller informs the Federal magistrate that the purpose of the call is to request a warrant. Otherwise a stenographic or longhand verbatim record shall be made. If a voice recording device is used or a stenographic record made, the Federal magistrate shall have the record transcribed, shall certify the accuracy of the transcription, and shall file a copy of the original record and the transcription with the court. If a longhand verbatim record is made, the Federal magistrate shall file a signed copy with the court.

(E) **Contents.**   The contents of a warrant upon oral testimony shall be the same as the contents of a warrant upon affidavit.

(F) **Additional Rule for Execution.**   The person who executes the warrant shall enter the exact time of execution on the face of the duplicate original warrant.

(G) **Motion to Suppress Precluded.**   Absent a finding of bad faith, evidence obtained pursuant to a warrant issued under this paragraph is not subject to a motion to suppress on the ground that the circumstances were not such as to make it reasonable to dispense with a written affidavit.

(d) **Execution and Return with Inventory.**   The officer taking property under the warrant shall give to the person from whom or from whose premises the property was taken a copy of the warrant and a receipt for the property taken or shall leave the copy and receipt at the place from which the property was taken. The return shall be made promptly and shall be accompanied by a written inventory of any property taken. The inventory shall be made in the presence of the applicant for the warrant and the person from whose possession or premises the property was taken, if they are present, or in the presence of at least one credible person other than the applicant for the warrant or the person from whose possession or premises the property was taken, and shall be verified by the officer. The federal magistrate shall upon request deliver a copy of the inventory to the person from whom or from whose premises the property was taken and to the applicant for the warrant.

(e) **Motion for Return of Property.**   A person aggrieved by an unlawful search and seizure or by the deprivation of property may move the district court for the district in which the property was seized for the return of the property on the ground that such person is entitled to lawful possession of the property. The court shall receive evidence on any issue of fact necessary to the decision of the motion. If the motion is granted, the property shall be returned to the movant, although reasonable conditions may be imposed to protect access and use of the property in subsequent proceedings. If a motion for return of property is made or comes on for hearing in the district of trial after an indictment or information is filed, it shall be treated also as a motion to suppress under Rule 12.

(f) **Motion to Suppress.** A motion to suppress evidence may be made in the court of the district of trial as provided in Rule 12.

(g) **Return of Papers to Clerk.** The federal magistrate before whom the warrant is returned shall attach to the warrant a copy of the return, inventory and all other papers in connection therewith and shall file them with the clerk of the district court for the district in which the property was seized.

(h) **Scope and Definition.** This rule does not modify any act, inconsistent with it, regulating search, seizure and the issuance and execution of search warrants in circumstances for which special provision is made. The term "property" is used in this rule to include documents, books, papers and any other tangible objects. The term "daytime" is used in this rule to mean the hours from 6:00 A.M. to 10:00 P.M. according to local time. The phrase "federal law enforcement officer" is used in this rule to mean any government agent, other than an attorney for the government as defined in Rule 54(c), who is engaged in the enforcement of the criminal laws and is within any category of officers authorized by the Attorney General to request the issuance of a search warrant.

RULE 44. RIGHT TO AND ASSIGNMENT OF COUNSEL

(a) **Right to Assigned Counsel.** Every defendant who is unable to obtain counsel shall be entitled to have counsel assigned to represent the defendant at every stage of the proceedings from initial appearance before the federal magistrate or the court through appeal, unless the defendant waives such appointment.

(b) **Assignment Procedure.** The procedures for implementing the right set out in subdivision (a) shall be those provided by law and by local rules of court established pursuant thereto.

(c) **Joint Representation.** Whenever two or more defendants have been jointly charged pursuant to Rule 8(b) or have been joined for trial pursuant to Rule 13, and are represented by the same retained or assigned counsel or by retained or assigned counsel who are associated in the practice of law, the court shall promptly inquire with respect to such joint representation and shall personally advise each defendant of the

right to the effective assistance of counsel, including separate representation. Unless it appears that there is good cause to believe no conflict
of interest is likely to arise, the court shall take such measures as may be
appropriate to protect each defendant's right to counsel.

RULE 52. HARMLESS ERROR AND PLAIN ERROR

(a) **Harmless Error.**   Any error, defect, irregularity or variance which
does not affect substantial rights shall be disregarded.
    (b) **Plain Error.**   Plain errors or defects affecting substantial rights
may be noticed although they were not brought to the attention of the
court.

TABLE OF CASES

1387

TABLE OF AUTHORITIES

Amsterdam, Perspectives on the Fourth Amendment, 58 Minn. L. Rev. 349 (1974), 499, 510, 519, 656, 721

Amsterdam, The Supreme Court and the Rights of Suspects in Criminal Cases, 45 N.Y.U.L. Rev. 785 (1970), 1095, 1149

Amsterdam, A., B. Segal & M. Miller, Trial Manual for the Defense of Criminal Cases (3d ed. 1974), 1331

Arenella, Rethinking the Functions of Criminal Procedure: The Warren and Burger Courts' Competing Ideologies, 72 Geo. L.J. 185 (1983), 24

Arenella, Schmerber and the Privilege Against Self-Incrimination: A Reappraisal, 20 Am. Crim. L. Rev. 31 (1982), 990, 1078

Ashdown, Good Faith, the Exclusionary Remedy, and Rule-Oriented Adjudication in the Criminal Process, 24 Wm. & Mary L. Rev. 335 (1983), 891

Bacigali, Dodging a Bullet, but Opening Old Wounds in Fourth Amendment Jurisprudence, 16 Seton Hall L. Rev. 597 (1986), 828

Baier, Justice Clark, the Voice of the Past, and the Exclusionary Rule, 64 Tex. L. Rev. 415 (1985), 843

Ball, Good Faith and the Fourth Amendment: The "Reasonable" Exception to the Exclusionary Rule, 69 J. Crim. L. 635 (1978), 891

Bazelon, The Defective Assistance of Counsel, 42 U. Cin. L. Rev. 1 (1973), 210

Bazelon, The Realities of Gideon and Argersinger, 64 Geo. L.J. 811 (1976), 210, 244

Beale, Reconsidering Supervisory Power in Criminal Cases: Constitutional and Statutory Limits on the Authority of the Federal Courts, 84 Colum. L. Rev. 1433 (1984), 937

Becton, The Drug Courier Profile: "All Seems Infected That the Infected Spy, As All Looks Yellow to the Jaundic'd Eye," 65 N.C.L. Rev. 417 (1987), 715

Bloom, The Supreme Court and Its Purported Preference for Warrants, Tenn. L. Rev. 231 (1983), 565

Bradley, The Good Faith Exception Cases: Reasonable Exercises in Futility, 60 Ind. L.J. 287 (1985), 906

Bradley, Havens, Jenkins, Salvucci, and the Defendant's "Right" to Testify, 18 Am. Crim. L. Rev. 419 (1981), 1349

Bradley, Present at the Creation?, A Critical Guide to Weeks v. United States and Its Progeny, 30 St. Louis U.L.J. 1031 (1986), 843

Bradley, Two Models of the Fourth Amendment, 83 Mich. L. Rev. 1468 (1985), 665

Brennan, State Courts and the Protection of Individual Rights, 90 Harv. L. Rev. 489 (1977), 98

Bristow, Police Officer Shootings—A Tactical Evaluation, 54 J. Crim. L. Criminology & Police Sci. 93 (1963), 732

Burger, The Special Skills of Advocacy: Are Specialized Training and Certifi-

Hill, Testimonial Privilege and Fair Trial, 80 Colum. L. Rev. 1173 (1980), 1081

Holmes, O., The Common Law (1881), 423

Horowitz, D., The Courts and Social Policy (1977), 843

Howard, State Courts and Constitutional Rights in the Day of the Burger Court, 62 Va. L. Rev. 873 (1976), 98

Humble, Nonevidentiary Use of Compelled Testimony: Beyond the Fifth Amendment, 66 Tex. L. Rev. 351 (1987), 1030

Inbau & Reid, Criminal Interrogation and Confessions (2d ed. 1967), 1280

Inman, The Admissibility of Confessions, 1981 Crim. L. Rev. 469, 1151

Israel, Criminal Procedure, the Burger Court, and the Legacy of the Warren Court, 75 Mich. L. Rev. 1319 (1977), 65

Israel, Gideon v. Wainwright: The "Art" of Overruling, 1963 Sup. Ct. Rev. 211, 137

Israel, Legislative Regulation of Searches and Seizures: The Michigan Proposals, 73 Mich. L. Rev. 221 (1974), 600

Jackson, B., Law and Disorder: Criminal Justice in America, 48

Jensen & Hart, The Good Faith Restatement of the Exclusionary Rule, 73 J. Crim. L. & Criminology 916 (1982), 891

Johnson, Cross-Racial Identification Errors in Criminal Cases, 69 Cornell L. Rev. 934 (1984), 339

Jonakait, Reliable Identification: Could the Supreme Court Tell in Manson v. Brathwaite?, 52 U. Colo. L. Rev. 511 (1981), 390, 411

Kadish, The Advocate and the Expert-Counsel in the Peno-Correctional Process, 45 Minn. L. Rev. 803 (1961), 157

Kamisar, Betts v. Brady Twenty Years Later: The Right to Counsel and Due Process Values, 61 Mich. L. Rev. 219 (1962), 127

Kamisar, Brewer v. Williams, Messiah, and Miranda: What Is "Interrogation?" When Does It Matter?, 67 Geo. L.J. 1 (1978), 1263

Kamisar, Forward: Brewer v. Williams—A Hard Look at a Discomfiting Record, 66 Geo. L.J. 209 (1977), 1263

Kamisar, Gates, "Probable Cause," "Good Faith," and Beyond, 69 Iowa L. Rev. 551 (1984), 891

Kamisar, Is the Exclusionary Rule an "Illogical" or "Unnatural" Interpretation of the Fourth Amendment?, 62 Judicature 66 (1978), 843

Kamisar, The Right to Counsel and the Fourteenth Amendment: A Dialogue on "The Most Pervasive Right" of an Accused, 30 U. Chi. L. Rev. 1 (1962), 136

Kamisar, Y., W. LaFave & J. Israel, Modern Criminal Procedure (7th ed. 1989), 1280

Kaplan, The Limits of the Exclusionary Rule, 26 Stan. L. Rev. 1027 (1974), 847

Scott, Standing in the Supreme Court—A Functional Analysis, 86 Harv. L. Rev. 645 (1973), 848

Skolnick, J., & D. Bayley, Community Policing Issues and Practices (1988), 31

Spector & Foster, Swords, Shields, and the Quest for Truth in the Trial Process: The Road from Constitutional Standards to Evidentiary Havens, 33 Okla. L. Rev. 520 (1980), 1349

Stacy & Dayton, Rethinking Harmless Constitutional Error, 88 Colum. L. Rev. 79 (1988), 1356

Standards of Proof and Preliminary Questions of Fact, 27 Stan. L. Rev. 271 (1975), 1331, 1356

Stewart, The Road to Mapp v. Ohio and Beyond: The Origins, Development and Future of the Exclusionary Rule, 83 Colum. L. Rev. 1365 (1983), 843

Stone, The *Miranda* Doctrine in the Burger Court, 1977 Sup. Ct. Rev. 92, 1095, 1149

Stuntz, Self-Incrimination and Excuse, 88 Colum. L. Rev. 1227 (1988), 1224

Suni, Subpoenas to Criminal Defense Lawyers: A Proposal for Limits, 65 Or. L. Rev. 215 (1986), 267

The Supreme Court, 1980 Term: Indigents' Rights to State Funding in Civil Actions, 95 Harv. L. Rev. 132 (1981), 207

Symposium, Limitations on the Effectiveness of Criminal Defense Counsel, 136 U. Pa. L. Rev. 1779 (1988), 267

Symposium, 23 S. Tex. L.J. 203 (1982), 843

Tague, An Indigent's Right to the Attorney of His Choice, 27 Stan. L. Rev. 73 (1974), 311

Tague, Multiple Representation and Conflicts of Interest in Criminal Cases, 67 Geo. L.J. 1075 (1979), 272, 281

Uviller, Acquisition of Evidence for Criminal Prosecution: Some Constitutional Premises and Practices in Transition, 35 Vand. L. Rev. 501 (1982), 843

Uviller, Seizure by Gunshot: The Riddle of the Fleeing Felon, 14 N.Y.U. Rev. L. & Soc. Change 705 (1986), 826, 883

Van DeCamp & Gerry, Reforming the Exclusionary Rule: An Analysis of Two Proposed Amendments to the California Constitution, 33 Hastings L.J. 1109 (1982), 843

Van Kessel, The Suspect as Source of Testimonial Evidence: A Comparison of the English and American Approaches, 38 Hastings L.J. 1 (1986), 1151

Waltz, Inadequacy of Trial Defense Representation as a Ground for Post Conviction Relief in Criminal Cases, 59 Nw. U.L. Rev. 289 (1964), 209

Wasserstrom, The Incredible Shrinking Fourth Amendment, 21 Am. Crim. L. Rev. 257 (1984), 658

Wasserstrom & Mertens, The Exclusionary Rule on the Scaffold, 22 Am. Crim. L. Rev. 25 (1984), 906, 1363

Weisberger, Exclusionary Rule: Nine Authors in Search of a Principle, 34 Santa Clara L. Rev. 253 (1982), 844

Weisburg, Forward: Criminal Procedure Doctrine: Some Versions of the Skeptical, 76 J. Crim. L. & Criminology 832 (1985), 65

Westen, On "Confusing Ideas": Reply, 91 Yale L.J. 1153 (1982), 190

Westen, The Empty Idea of Equality, 95 Harv. L. Rev. 537 (1982), 183

Westen, The Meaning of Equality in Law, Science, Math, and Morals: A Reply, 81 Mich. L. Rev. 604 (1983), 190

Westen, Reflections on Alfred Hills "Testimonial Privilege and Fair Trial," 14 Mich. J.L. Ref. 371 (1981), 1081

Westen, To Lure the Tarantula from Its Hole: A Response, 83 Colum. L. Rev. 1186 (1983), 190

Westen & Mandell, To Talk, To Balk, or To Lie: The Emerging Fifth Amendment Doctrine of the "Preferred Response," 19 Am. Crim. L. Rev. 521 (1982), 1081

White, Forgotten Points in the "Exclusionary Rule" Debate, 81 Mich. L. Rev. 1273 (1983), 844

White, Interrogation Without Questions: Rhode Island v. Innis and United States v. Henry, 78 Mich. L. Rev. 1209 (1980), 1269

White, Police Trickery in Inducing Confessions, 127 U. Pa. L. Rev. 581 (1979), 1196, 1280

White & Greenspan, Standing to Object to Search and Seizure, 118 U. Pa. L. Rev. 333 (1970), 844

Whitebread, The Burger Court's Counter-Revolution in Criminal Procedure: The Recent Criminal Decisions of the United States Supreme Court, 24 Washburn L.J. 471 (1987), 65

Wice, P., Chaos in the Courthouse: The Inner Workings of the Urban Criminal Courts, 46

Wilkes, First Things Last: Amendomania and State Bills of Rights, 54 Miss. L.J. 223 (1984), 98

Wilkes, The New Federalism in Criminal Procedure: State Court Evasion of the Burger Court, 62 Ky. L.J. 421 (1974), 98

Wilkey, The Exclusionary Rule: Why Suppress Valid Evidence?, 62 Judicature 214 (1978), 844

Williamson, Fourth Amendment Standing and Expectations of Privacy: Rakas v. Illinois and New Directions for Some Old Concepts, 31 U. Fla. L. Rev. 831 (1979), 862

Wilson, J., Varieties of Police Behavior (1973), 33

Wilson, The Warrantless Automobile Search: Exception Without Justification, 32 Hastings L.J. 127 (1980), 615

Winter, Tennessee v. Garner and the Democratic Practice of Judicial Review, 14 N.Y.U. Rev. L. & Soc. Change 679 (1986), 826

INDEX